A EUROPE OF RIGHTS

A Europe of Rights

*The Impact of the ECHR
on National Legal Systems*

Edited by
HELEN KELLER and ALEC STONE SWEET

OXFORD
UNIVERSITY PRESS

This book has been printed digitally and produced in a standard specification in order to ensure its continuing availability

OXFORD
UNIVERSITY PRESS

Great Clarendon Street, Oxford OX2 6DP
United Kingdom

Oxford University Press is a department of the University of Oxford.
It furthers the University's objective of excellence in research, scholarship,
and education by publishing worldwide. Oxford is a registered trade mark of
Oxford University Press in the UK and in certain other countries

British Library Cataloguing in Publication Data
Data available

Library of Congress Cataloging in Publication Data
Data available

ISBN 978-0-19-953526-2

Printed and bound by CPI Group (UK) Ltd, Croydon, CR0 4YY

Contents

III. ASSESSMENT

APPENDIX

Acknowledgments

This book could not have been published without the active participation of our "team of experts", those judges, human rights lawyers, government agents and academics who generously shared their time and expertise with us. At the European level, heartfelt thanks are due: to Dr. ANDREW DRZEMCZEWSKI, Head, Secretariat of the Committee on Legal Affairs and Human Rights, Council of Europe; to FREDRIK SUNDBERG, European Expert, Deputy to the Head of Department for the execution of judgments of the European Court of Human Rights, Directorate of Monitoring, Council of Europe; and to Mrs. NINA VAJIC, Judge, European Court of Human Rights (ECtHR). At the national level, we are grateful to the following experts: for *Germany and France* to JENS MEYER-LADEWIG, former Agent for Germany before the ECtHR, Germany, to Dr. HANS-JÖRG BEHRENS, Second Government Agent for Germany before the ECtHR and to ROGER ERRERA, former Judge of the Cour de Cassation, France, and Conseiller d'Etat Honoraire, Visiting Professor, Central European University, Budapest; for *Ireland and the United Kingdom* to LIA O'HEGARTY, Commissioner, Irish Human Rights Commission, Ireland and to ERIK METCALFE, Human Rights Policy Director, Justice, United Kindgom; *for Sweden and Norway* to Dr. KARIN ÅHMAN, Lecturer, Uppsala University, Sweden and to NJAL HOSTMAELINGEN, Research Fellow, PhD Candidate, Norwegian Centre for Human Rights, Norway; *for the Netherlands and Belgium* to TOM BARKHUYSEN, Professor of Constitutional and Administrative Law, Leiden University, The Netherlands, to MARTIN KUIJER, Senior Legal Adviser Human Rights, Netherlands Ministry of Justice, Professor of Human Rights Law, Free University, Amsterdam, to TIES PRAKKEN, former Professor of Criminal Law, University of Maastricht, and defence lawyer in Amsterdam, to JAN FERMON, Lawyer at the Brussels Bar, Belgium, specialising in Belgian, European and international criminal law and to PAUL LEMMENS, Extraordinary Professor, Catholic University Leuven, Belgium; for *Austria and Switzerland* to Dr. INGRID SIESS-SCHERZ, Head of Division for International Affairs and General Administrative Affairs at the Austrian Federal Chancellery, Constitutional Service, to Dr. ILSE FREIWIRTH, Head of Division, Registry of ECtHR, to MMag. ANDREAS TH. MÜLLER, Research Associate at the Department of European Law and Public International Law at the Leopold-Franzens University in Innsbruck, Austria, to Dr. iur. HEINZ AEMISEGGER, Judge of the Swiss Federal Supreme Court, to ADRIAN SCHEIDEGGER, Second Government Agent for Switzerland, Ministry of Justice, and to LUDWIG A. MINELLI, Attorney, Zurich; for *Spain and Italy* to PEDRO CRUZ VILLALÓN, Universidad Autónoma de Madrid, to ANTONIO BULTRINI, Associate Professor of International Law and Human Rights, Florence University, to ANGEL AROZAMENA LASO, Magistrate, technical committee, Supreme Court, Spain, to MANUEL CAMPOS SANCHEZ BORDONA, Judge of the Supreme Court, Spain, to MICHELE DE SALVIA, Professor of Human rights at Catholic University of Milan, to BRUNO NASCIMBENE, Professor of International and European Union Law at the University Statale of Milan, to PIETRO PUSTORINO, Associate Professor of international organisations, Siena University, Faculty of Political Sciences, and of International Protection of human rights, LUISS Guido Carli Univerisity, Faculty of Law, Rome and to SIVIA MIRATE, lecturer in administrative law at the University of Turin; for *Greece and Turkey* to Dr. CHRISTIAN RUMPF, attorney and lecturer at the University of Bamberg and the Yeditepe University in Istanbul, to FATOS ARACI, Deputy Registrar of the Fourth Section, ECtHR, to Dr. KEMAL BASLAR, Associate Professor of International Law, Baskent University Law Faculty, Ankara and to JULIA ILIOPOULOS-STRANGAS, Professor of Constitutional Law, University of Athens, Faculty of Law; for *Poland and Slovakia* to EWA ŁĘTOWSKA, Judge, Polish Constitutional Court, to ŁUKASZ BOJARSKI, Access to Justice Project Coordinator, Helsinki Foundation for Human Rights, Warsaw, to RYSZARDA STASIAK, the President of the Płońsk District Court, Poland, to EWA BOŃKOWSKA-KONCA, Judge of the Plock Regional Court, Poland, to MILAN BLAŠKO, Head of Division, Registry of the ECtHR, to MICHAL KUČERA, Registry of the ECtHR, to VANDA DURBAKOVÀ, Lawyer, Center for Civil and Human Rights, Slovakia, to ADRIANA LAMAČKOVÀ, legal consultant with Pro Choice Slovakia, Bratislava and to MARICA PIROSIKOVÀ, Agent of the Slovak Republic before the ECtHR; for *Russia and Ukraine* to SERHIY HOLOVATY, Member of the European Commission for Democracy through Law (Venice Commission), Chairman of the Sub-Committee of the Verkhovna Rada (Parliament) of Ukraine on Implementation of the Judgements of the ECtHR, President of the Ukrainian Legal Foundation, to Dr. ALEXEI TROCHEV, Research Associate, Institute of Intergovernmental Relations School of Policy Studies, Queen's University, Kingston, Canada, and to ANTON BURKOV, PhD candidate in law, University of Cambridge, United Kingdom.

Over the past three years, the Group met in workshops held at the Universities of Lucerne and Zurich, and at a conference sponsored by the Columbia Law School, New York. These meetings proved to be invaluable. For support of these meetings and of the Project, we deeply appreciate the generous support provided by: The University of Lucerne; the Federal Department of Foreign Affairs, Directorate of International Law, Switzerland; the Swiss National Science Foundation; the Ebnet-Foundation; the Swiss Academy of Human and Social Sciences; the Zurich University Association; the Hermann und Marianne Straniak-Foundation; and the F.F. Randolph Jr. Speakers Fund, Columbia Law School.

We also benefited enormously from the research and editing assistance of an extraordinary group of young scholars: MARKUS LANTER, DANIELA KÜHNE, MAGDALENA FOROWICZ, ANDREAS FISCHER and DAVID SUTER (all assistants from the Law School of the University of Zurich). Finally, the manuscript benefited greatly from the work of MORGAN MCCURDY (editing assistant) and MICHAEL ANDERAU (InDesign expert).

Contributors

Samantha Besson, Professor of Public International Law and European Law, University of Fribourg, Switzerland.

Mercedes Candela Soriano, Assistant Professor of European and International Public Law, University of Tilburg, The Netherlands.

Ibrahim Özden Kaboğlu, Professor of Constitutional Law, University of Marmara, Istanbul, and former President of the National Advisory Board on Human Rights, Turkey.

Helen Keller, Professor of Public Law, International Law and European Law, University of Zurich, Switzerland.

Stylianos-Ioannis G. Koutnatzis, Ph.D. Candidate, Freie Universität Berlin, Germany; Alexander S. Onassis Foundation Scholar, and Attorney at Law, Athens, Greece.

Elisabeth Lambert Abdelgawad, Junior Researcher, Institute of Comparative Law (University of Paris 1 Panthéon-Sorbonne, National Centre for scientific research), France.

Magda Krzyżanowska-Mierzewska, Lawyer at the Registry of the European Court of Human Rights, France.

Angelika Nußberger, Professor of Public Law, International Law and Eastern European Law and Director of the Institute for Eastern European Law of the University of Cologne, Germany.

Alec Stone Sweet, Leitner Professor of Law, Politics, and International Studies, Yale Law School, United States.

Daniela Thurnherr, Assistant Professor of Public Law, University of Basel, Switzerland.

Ola Wiklund, Associate Professor, University of Stockholm and Lawyer, Stockholm, Sweden.

Anne Weber, Clemens Heller Scholar (Clemens Heller Program, Fondation Maison des Sciences de l'Homme / Fritz Thyssen Stiftung), Max Planck Institute for Comparative Public Law and International Law, Heidelberg, Germany.

Erika de Wet, Professor of International Constitutional Law, University of Amsterdam, The Netherlands; Extraordinary Professor, Northwest University (Potchefstroom campus), South Africa.

Note on Style and Citations

This book covers the ECHR and eighteen different national legal systems. There exists wide variance in scientific traditions and citation styles. While we did not seek to eliminate these differences, we have sought to make them comprehensible to both interested foreign readers and national specialists.

The European Commission on Human Rights and the European Court of Human Rights have changed its citation practices several times since the 1960s. We based our citation of the Court's case law on the current guidelines. All the judgements and decisions are available on the Court's site (http://cmiskp.echr.coe.int), although not all cases are reported in printed form. The remark "not reported" indicates that a given decision or judgment has not been published in the official publication series (Reports of Judgments and Decisions). Judgements issued after 1 January 2005 will be referred to as "not yet reported", unless they have already been published in the official publication series.

The material for the research project is comprehensive through December 2006, and the statistics reported in the annex cover periods from accession to 31 December 2006. Vital developments that took place in 2007 are addressed in the reports.

Table of Cases

I. EUROPEAN COMMISSION OF HUMAN RIGHTS[1]

---

[1] The Decisions and Reports of the Commission were published until 1 November 1999 (Article 5(3) of the Protocol no. 11 to the ECHR (entered into force on 1 November 1998)).

Abbreviations:
EHRR = European Human Rights Reports; DR = Decisions and Reports; YB = Yearbook of the European Convention of Human Rights.

II. EUROPEAN COURT OF HUMAN RIGHTS

PART I

INTRODUCTION

1

The Reception of the ECHR
in National Legal Orders

Alec Stone Sweet and Helen Keller

The European Convention on Human Rights[1] is the most effective human rights regime in the world. The Convention (ECHR), which entered into force in 1953, established a basic catalogue of rights binding on the signatories, and new institutions charged with monitoring and enforcing compliance. Distinctive at its conception, the ECHR has since evolved into an intricate legal system. The High Contracting Parties have steadily upgraded the regime's scope and capacities, in successive treaty revisions. They have added new rights, enhanced the powers of the European Court of Human Rights (ECtHR), and strengthened the links between individual applicants and the regime. For its part, the Strasbourg Court has built a sophisticated jurisprudence, whose progressive tenor and expansive reach has helped to propel the system forward. Today, the Court is an important, autonomous source of authority on the nature and content of fundamental rights in Europe. In addition to providing justice in individual cases, it works to identify and to consolidate universal standards of rights protection, in the face of wide national diversity and a steady stream of seemingly intractable problems.

This book focuses on the impact of the Court and the Convention on the domestic legal systems of the regime's members, a topic that has been understudied, given its increasing importance. Two previously published pieces of research inspired and guided this project. The book entitled "The European Court and the National Courts: Legal Change in its Social, Political, and Economic Context",[2] published in 1998, presented a series of single-country reports and comparative analyses of how the national courts reacted to, and ultimately, accommodated the European Court of Justice's doctrine of the supremacy of European Community law. One premise of that earlier volume, which we share, is that national judges are important actors in their own right in the process through which European

---

[1] Convention for the Protection of Human Rights and Fundamental Freedoms, 213 U.N.T.S. 222, signed on 4 November 1950, entered into force on 3 September 1953. The Convention has now been ratified by 47 countries (31 December 2007).
[2] Slaughter, Stone Sweet and Weiler (1998).

law becomes effective in national legal orders. This volume's scope is somewhat wider, in that the reports examine the role of all national officials, not only judges, in facilitating or resisting the influence of the Convention. The basic template for the research was established by Helen Keller's pilot study entitled "Reception of the European Convention for the Protection of Human Rights and Fundamental Freedoms in Poland and Switzerland",[3] an agenda we extended for this project.[4]

A first point of departure was the view that the Court is today institutionally well-positioned to exercise such influence. The Court has final jurisdiction over disputes concerning the content of the Convention, the compliance with the Convention of the High Contracting Parties, and the scope of its own jurisdiction (*Kompetenz-Kompetenz*); it has a burgeoning caseload in the form of individual applications; and it has produced a case law that defines what States owe to their own citizens under the Convention. A second point of departure was the observation that the regime's influence on national officials and their decision making varies widely across States and across time. Indeed, as our research shows, the Court's impact has been broad and pervasive in some States, and weak in others. Moreover, in those States that have been heavily influenced by the Convention, impact has been registered through quite different processes. How national officials use Convention norms, and the extent to which they resist or adapt to the Court's case law, has also changed across time, sometimes radically. Our major objective, then, was to describe and analyse this variance, as systematically as possible, and to take some initial steps toward explaining it.

This volume reports our results. Each of the nine substantive chapters examines comparatively what we will call "the reception of the ECHR" in two States. By reception, we mean how – that is, through what mechanisms – national officials confront, make use of, and resist or give agency to Convention rights.[5] The book is fundamentally a work of comparative law, albeit with a twist. The project focuses empirical attention on the capacity of an international regime, and its transnational court, to shape law and politics at the domestic level. It thus addresses some of the same basic questions asked by students of the Europeanization of law and politics, of multi-level governance, and of the constitutionalization of treaty-based legal systems. The project also has a normative dimension, namely, to identify how the effectiveness of Convention rights in national legal orders has been, and can be, enhanced over time. We chart how the status of the Convention in domestic law and politics has changed over time, and examine, from a comparative perspective, the regime's overall effectiveness.

---

[3] Keller (2005).
[4] See *infra* Section B.1.
[5] For an extensive discussion of reception, see *infra* Section B.1.

A. The Convention and its Court

1. Origins and Evolution

In 1950, the new Council of Europe[6] completed its first major venture: the drafting of the ECHR. The Convention was negotiated in the immediate aftermath of a cataclysmic war, against the background of economic, social, and political reconstruction, the results of which were then far from certain. This context heavily conditioned the "original intent"[7] of the fourteen States that would sign the Treaty, understood as the aims and purposes that the Council of Europe expected the ECHR to serve. Most important, States considered the Convention to be one instrument, among others, to prevent future European wars, bolster liberal democracy, oppose Communism, and express a common European identity, through their joint commitment to rights.

From today's vantage point, it is obvious that the underlying nature and purposes of the Convention system have changed. The broader environment in which the regime is embedded has undergone deep systemic transformation. In the 50's and 70's, West European States successively embraced a new constitutionalism,[8] entrenching constitutional rights and their protection; NATO and the EU succeeded in providing security and market and political integration; the EU was gradually constitutionalised, through the consolidation, in national legal systems, of the European Court of Justice's doctrines of direct effect and supremacy; the Cold War ended and the Soviet bloc disintegrated. In the post-1990 period, the territorial scope of European commitments to rights-based constitutionalism, to the EU and NATO, and to the Convention further widened and deepened. Since 1990, membership in the ECHR has increased by 24 States, covering a territory of roughly 450 million people. Today, the Convention's territorial scope is truly pan-European, covering 47 States and more than 800 million people.

Over this same period, the ECHR experienced its own "evolutionary, sometimes revolutionary changes".[9] To take the most telling example, the founding signatories of the Convention were deeply divided on the question of establishing an autonomous legal system with supranational authority to monitor and enforce compliance. In 1950, they agreed to disagree. After voting seven to four against creating a Court with compulsory jurisdiction, they made acceptance of the Court's authority voluntary, through an optional Protocol. When objections were levied against proposals to allow individual applications, States made the individual petition optional as well. Additionally, they placed an administrative

---

[6] The Council of Europe was established by the Treaty of London, which was signed on 5 May 1949 by Belgium, Denmark, France, Ireland, Italy, Luxembourg, the Netherlands, Norway, Sweden and the United Kingdom. For an overview of the Council of Europe and a survey of its main functions, see Winkler (2006).

[7] See Nichol (2005); Moravcsik (2000); Simpson (2001).

[8] Shapiro and Stone Sweet (1994); Stone Sweet (2000).

[9] Shelton (2003), 100.

body, the European Commission of Human Rights (which began operation in 1954), between applicants and the Court (which began operating only in 1959). Until it was abolished in 1998, it was the Commission's task to process applications, whether interstate or individual. Petitions reached the Court only after the Commission had completed its work, and only under certain conditions. Today, the High Contracting Parties are "locked-in"[10] to a transnational system of rights protection that is managed and supervised by a supranational Court. State acceptance of the individual application and the compulsory jurisdiction of the Court is mandatory.

The High Contracting Parties have been complicit in the expansion of the legal system's autonomy and supranational character. The process has not taken place without the knowledge and consent of the Parties, or against their will. On the contrary, the ECHR and its Court have had remarkable success in socialising the regime's members into the logics of collective, transnational rights protection, and in enlisting participation in the Convention's expansionary dynamics.

These dynamics are easily observed. Although the ECHR was originally considered to have established minimum, and largely minimal, standards for basic human rights, the Strasbourg Court has interpreted Convention rights in a progressive manner. According to the Court, the ECHR is not static but a living instrument,[11] and its contents must be read to secure effective rights protection for individuals, as European society evolves.[12] Alongside this teleology of purpose and effectiveness, the Court has developed an overarching comparative methodology, one result of which is to ensure a creative lawmaking role for itself. In defining the content and scope of Convention rights, for example, the Court will typically survey the state of law and practice in the States, and sometimes beyond. Where it finds an emerging consensus on a new, higher standard of rights protection among States, it may move to consolidate this consensus, as a point of Convention law binding upon all members.

Formally, the Court's role is restricted to determining whether a State has infringed upon Convention rights in any specific case. The Court regularly invokes the principle of subsidiarity and its doctrinal corollary, the margin of appreciation (the discretion to define the scope of Convention rights in the first instance) afforded national authorities. And it regularly reminds States that it does not possess the *de jure* power to revise the Convention on its own. Increasingly, however, the Court appears to consider that an important oracular, rights-creating, function inheres in its jurisdiction. Today, the Court is the unrivalled master of

---

[10] Ibid., 101.

[11] *Tyrer v. United Kingdom* (appl. no. 5856/72), Judgement (Chamber), 25 April 1978, Series A, Vol. 36, para. 31; *Loizidou v. Turkey (Preliminary objections)* (appl. no. 15318/89), Judgement (Grand Chamber), 23 March 1995, Series A, Vol. 310, para. 71.

[12] The Court requires national authorities to interpret Convention rights so as to make them effective for individuals, in fact. See *Soering v. United Kingdom* (appl. no. 14038/88), Judgement (Plenary), 7 July 1989, Series A, Vol. 161.

the Convention, a posture it uses to construct European fundamental rights in a prospective and progressive way.

Although the Court routinely identifies and develops what appear to be, from the perspective of at least some States, new rights and remedies, States have not mounted a campaign to roll back their commitments, or to curb the Court. On the contrary, they have added new rights to the Convention catalogue, using a series of optional protocols (each of which has gained adherents over time). States have also introduced major organizational and procedural changes, the most important of which came through Protocol no. 11. That Protocol, which entered into force in 1998, abolished the Commission of Human Rights, and centralised administrative authority to process claims in a new Court and its staff, the Registry. Under Protocol no. 11, individuals may petition the Court after exhausting domestic remedies. Within national legal orders, most States have clarified and enhanced the nature and status of the Convention through the incorporation of the Convention into domestic law. In most cases, incorporation means that individuals may plead Convention rights before national judges, who can directly enforce them.

As a result of these and other developments, scholars and judges now engage a lively debate about the regime's constitutionalization, and its possible constitutional futures.[13] In Greer's view, for example, the Court "is already 'the Constitutional Court for Europe', in the sense that it is the final authoritative judicial tribunal in the only pan-European constitutional system there is".[14] This debate is an important indicator of the regime's transformation. It is undeniable that, in the 21st century, the Convention and the Court perform functions that are comparable to those performed by national constitutions and national constitutional courts in Europe, a point to which we will return[15]. Further, the Court itself has come to see its role in constitutional terms. In a 1995 decision, the Court called the ECHR "a constitutional document" of European public law.[16] And, in 2000, the President of the Court, Luzius Wildhaber, writing in a personal capacity but echoing prevailing sentiments on the Court, argued strongly in favour of enhancing its constitutional role and authority.[17]

We take no position here on how best to characterize the nature of the regime. For our purposes, the constitutionalization debate is of interest in that it focuses attention on the structural relationship, as it has evolved, between the Convention and national legal orders.[18] Structural questions once dismissed as

---

[13] Alkema (2000); Flauss (1999). See also Greer (2006), discussing the constitutionalisation of the ECHR and the constitutional justice dispensed by the European Court of Human Rights.

[14] Greer (2006), 173.

[15] See *infra* Section B.2.

[16] *Loizidou v. Turkey* (*supra* note 11), para. 75.

[17] Wildhaber (2000).

[18] The debate is also data, indicating that something important is happening. At the very least, how these debates are settled will determine how the regime evolves in the future.

largely academic are now being urgently debated by judges and politicians. Is the primary role of the Convention system to provide individual or constitutional justice? To what extent does, or should, the Court's rights jurisprudence bind national judges, including those sitting on supreme or constitutional courts? What *erga omnes* status, if any, should important rulings of the Court be given? Can the principle of subsidiarity be reconciled with the Court's preferred interpretive strategy, that of a forward-looking, living instrument approach?[19] In the context of enlargement, can the Court maintain consistent standards of rights protection, or is the emergence of a two-track Europe inevitable? The contributions to this volume respond in various ways to these and other questions, from the perspective of national legal systems.

2. Determinants of Impact

We designed this project on the presumption that the Court is well positioned to exert influence on national legal systems, a presumption that deserves a defence. Other things equal, no judicial body anywhere will accrete influence over its broader legal and political environment in the absence of three conditions: (1) the institutional competence to determine the law in an authoritative manner; (2) a regular caseload; and (3) a minimally robust conception of precedent. In the ECHR context, too, these three factors are necessary conditions for strengthening, over time, the Convention's effectiveness in national legal orders. They are not sufficient conditions, since the Court cannot, on its own, give agency to its jurisprudence in domestic legal orders. National officials – legislators, executives, and judges – have made choices about how to respond to the evolution of Convention norms. For the Convention to make a difference domestically, officials must take decisions that will strengthen its effectiveness. We will turn now to each of these conditions.

a. Jurisdiction

Since the entry into force of Protocol no. 11, at least, the Court has possessed all of the formal power required for it to acquire and exert dominance over the evolution of the Convention system. Indeed, the jurisdictional basis of its power compares favourably to that of the European Court of Justice, and exceeds that of most national constitutional courts.[20]

As presently constituted, the ECHR is characterized by structural judicial supremacy. Consider the situation in light of contemporary delegation theory. In the jargon of that theory, "principals", those in power at the *ex ante* constitutive

---

[19] Nichol (2005). Nichol argues for the more expansive, evolutionary approach and against minimalism, while showing that the debate between minimalists and activists (those who desire a progressive construction or rights), has gone unabated since 1950.

[20] In comparison to rights under the ECHR, it is usually easier for a national constitution to be revised by those seeking to overturn a constitutional court decision, although there are exceptions to this rule (as when rights provisions are made immune from revision).

moment, delegate power to "agents", in order to help them manage their responsibilities, *ex post*. A "trusteeship" situation is created when the principals (in this case, the High Contracting Parties) transfer significant "political property rights" to a new organ, the *trustee* (in this case, the Court), in order to help them govern themselves collectively.[21] A trustee, then, possesses legal authority to govern the principals in light of priorities – legal commitments – to which the latter has agreed. By definition, a trustee court possesses final authority to determine the scope and content of the law, and the principals have reduced means of overruling judicial determinations that they may find objectionable. A paradigmatic example of such a trustee, the Strasbourg Court exercises extensive "fiduciary" authority over the Convention. Under Article 46 ECHR, the High Contracting Parties, acting collectively as the Committee of Ministers of the Council of Europe, "supervise [the] execution" of the Court's final judgements.[22] In this account, structural judicial supremacy is legitimized by the fact that States designed the system for their own express purposes, and they help to make it effective on a continuous basis.

The core of the Convention is a catalogue of rights, as supplemented by the various optional protocols.[23] Under Article 1 ECHR, the High Contracting Par-

---

[21] For a discussion of judicial trusteeship, see Stone Sweet (2002), building on the contributions of Majone (2001) and Moe (1990).

[22] For an overview of the Council of Europe's system of supervision and enforcement of the Court's judgements, see Polakiewicz (2001).

[23] Articles 2–14 comprise the substantive core of the Convention, beginning with the right to life (Article 2), the right to be free from torture, and inhuman and degrading treatment (Article 3), and the right not to be held in slavery or servitude (Article 4). Basic procedural guarantees are established in the form of rights to personal liberty and security (Article 5), a fair trial (Article 6), and no punishment without law (Article 7). Articles 8–12 provide for: the right to respect of one's privacy and family life, and to marry; and the freedom of thought, conscience, religion, expression, assembly, and association. Article 13 states that "everyone whose [Convention] rights and freedoms are violated shall have an effective remedy"; and Article 14 proclaims that "the enjoyment" of Convention rights "shall be secured without discrimination on any ground", including race, sex, language, social origin, and religion, among other categories. Optional protocols have added: rights to property, education, and free elections (Protocol no. 1); freedom of movement and the rights of nationals not to be expelled from their own State, and of aliens not to be expelled collectively (Protocol no. 4). Protocol no. 6 abolishes the death penalty except in times of war, and Protocol no. 13 outlaws the death penalty in all circumstances. Protocol no. 7 enhances certain due process requirements, including rights to appeal and compensation for wrongful punishment. Finally, Protocol no. 12 (2002) establishes a general prohibition on discrimination "by any public authority on any ground", while permitting affirmative action policies. With the exception of provisions on torture, inhuman, and degrading treatment (Article 3), and on slavery and servitude (Article 4), which may be considered absolute, other rights are explicitly "qualified" in various ways. Articles 8–11, for example, are qualified by a necessity clause. States may only "interfere" with the exercise of these rights when "necessary in a democratic society" and "in the interests of" some specified public interest. States purposes mentioned include "national security", "public safety", "the economic well-being of the country," "the prevention of disorder or crime", "the protection of health or morals", and "the protection of the rights and freedoms of others". Even in times of war and other public emergency, States may not derogate from Articles 2, 3, 4(1) and 7 ECHR (*e contrario* Article 15(2) ECHR). Under Article 18, states may not impose restrictions on rights "for any purpose other than those for which [restrictions] have been prescribed".

ties are legally required "to secure to everyone within their jurisdiction the rights and freedoms" this catalogue contains. The Court's duty is to ensure that States meet this obligation, and its authority to do so is largely insulated from the latter's control. Article 32 ECHR grants the Court exclusive, final jurisdiction over "all matters concerning the interpretation and application of the Convention", and gives the Court the competence to determine the limits of its own jurisdiction. Under Article 46 ECHR, the Parties "undertake to abide by the final judgement of the Court in any case to which they are parties". The High Contracting Parties, as principals, could overturn an objectionable interpretation of the Court, but only by revising Convention norms. In practice, the prospect is a virtual impossibility, given the decision-rule governing the regime's revision: unanimity of all of its members.

In addition to direct grants of authority, States can be said to have indirectly conferred additional powers on the Court, as the system has evolved. Convention norms, like modern rights provisions generally, are relatively open-ended and incomplete. Few rights are expressed in absolute terms; most rights are qualified in terms of public interest goals that States may legitimately pursue. As research on the *travaux préparatoires* shows,[24] the founding States were never able to settle differences concerning the nature and content of the rights they enshrined. They disagreed, for example, about whether the Convention expressed minimum common denominator conceptions of basic rights and nothing more, or established a legal foundation for a more expansive evolution of rights. This disagreement necessarily conditioned attitudes toward establishing a court. In 1950, the founding States were not prepared to establish a judicial mechanism for settling these disagreements. It is difficult to imagine the Convention today without its Court, but only because States have chosen, over time, to strengthen their commitment to adjudication. In doing so, States have transferred authority to complete or construct Convention rights, rendering them more determinate over time for all members, despite national diversity.[25]

Given structural judicial supremacy, it is not surprising that the Court dominates the process through which Convention rights are given concrete expression. Inspired by German constitutional doctrine, for example, the Court embraced proportionality as a basic balancing approach to rights adjudication. Proportionality is an analytical framework that is particularly well suited to managing the

---

[24]   See Nichol (2005).

[25]   As with most constitutions and treaty-based regimes, the ECHR can be analyzed as an "incomplete contract". And, like any complex instruments of governance designed to last indefinitely, if not forever, the Convention is a "relational contract". Rights provisions are expressed in general terms. Generalities and vagueness may facilitate agreement at the bargaining stage. But vagueness, by definition, is legal uncertainty, and legal uncertainty threatens to undermine the reason for contracting in the first place. The establishment of the Court can be seen as an institutional response to the incomplete contract, that is, to the problems of uncertainty and enforcement. Adjudication then functions to clarify the meaning of the constitution over time, and to adapt it to changing circumstances. Milgrom and Roberts (1992), 127–33.

litigation of qualified rights. Through it, the Court resolves conflicts between a pleaded right, on the one hand, and the public interests that may justify its limitation, by public authority, on the other. Despite its advantages, proportionality review is one of the most intrusive forms of judicial supervision known: it requires courts to stand in judgement of the policy choices of State officials. In the "necessity" stage of the analysis, courts deploy a "least-restrictive means" test, censuring government if its preferred policies infringe more on a right than is necessary to achieve an otherwise legitimate public purpose. For many rights, including those enumerated in Articles 8–11 and 14 of the Convention, individuals today possess a right to proportionality analysis under the "effective remedy" requirement of Article 13. This development is momentous, considering that proportionality analysis was native only to the legal systems of Germany and Switzerland.[26] It has diffused, through Europeanization, under the tutelage of the Court.

There are important signs that the nature of the Court's jurisdiction is currently undergoing an important expansion. As formally constituted, the ECHR is geared toward the rendering of individual justice. The Court is activated by applications from individuals, and its decisions have, technically, only *inter partes* effects (Article 46 ECHR). Further, if the Court finds a State to be in violation of a Convention right, it may, under Article 41, award damages to the injured party. With enlargement and the advent of Protocol no. 11, the system has become flooded with dozens, often hundreds, of virtually identical complaints generated by a systemic defect in a national legal order. In this situation, how to control the docket, and how to mete out justice, are problems that necessarily overlap. In 2004, the Committee of Ministers of the Council of Europe invited the Court, in the ordinary course of its work, to identify the source of systemic failure, to suggest systemic solutions to the problems identified, and to recommend appropriate remedies for the class of individuals who have been injured by such failures.[27] In response, the Court has begun issuing what it calls pilot judgements,[28] whose underlying purpose is to make Convention rights effective for victims of systemic dysfunction, in effect, as a class of plaintiffs. When it does so, it acts managerially, proposing law of a general and prospective quality for a State whose existing arrangements are defective.

---

[26] In the 80s, Turkish courts also used an approach akin to proportionality when it adjudicated certain fundamental rights, although it did not do so consistently. See in this volume Kaboğlu and Koutnatzis, Section F.2.b.

[27] The Council of Europe, Committee of Ministers, Resolution (Res(2004)3) on Judgements Revealing an Underlying Systemic Problem, 12 May 2004. The Council of Europe, Committee of Ministers, Resolution (Res(2004)6) on the Improvement of Domestic Remedies, 12 May 2004.

[28] E.g., *Broniowski v. Poland* (appl. no. 31443/96), Judgement (Grand Chamber), 22 June 2004, Reports 2004-V, 1. See Krzyżanowska-Mierzewska, this volume, Section G.1.

b. Activity

In order to exert influence on national legal orders, the Court must have a caseload. In this book, we focus on the individual application, because it constitutes the primary means through which the regime generates the kinds of outcomes in which we are concerned. Individual rights claims make up, almost entirely,[29] the Court's docket. Each petition contains a detailed record of the domestic law and procedures that, allegedly, have failed to protect the applicant. Petitions thus provide a window into the internal workings of the national legal order. It is through this window that the Court will observe and review national law and practice in light of Convention requirements.

This system is a victim of its own success. Not only does the Court receive a steady stream of cases, the rising tide of applications now threatens to overwhelm the Court. A brief survey of annual rates of activity in this area is revealing.[30] The European Commission of Human Rights received 49 individual applications in the decade of the 60's, 163 in the 70's, and 455 in the 80's. With the enlargement and entry into force of Protocol no. 11, the numbers have exploded. In 1998, the Registry of the Court received 18,200 individual applications, a figure that has increased every year thereafter, to 50,500 in 2006. Although some 98% of all applications will be determined to be inadmissible for one reason or another, the Court is nonetheless overloaded.[31] Today there are nearly 100,000 applications, in the post-admissibility phase, pending before the organs of the Court. The delay between application and a decision on the merits, has now reached more than five years (though only 5% of applications judged admissible will reach the merits stage). The annual rate of judgements on the merits rendered by the Court shows a similar pattern. Through 1982, the Court had rendered, in its history, only 61 such rulings pursuant to applications by individuals. It issued 72 such rulings in 1995; 695 in 2000; 1,105 in 2005; and 1,560 in 2006.

Sheer numbers tell only part of the story, and nothing about the nature of the claims and of the domestic contexts that generate the applications. Simplifying a complex set of issues, we can distinguish between quite different situations, or types of general problems, that the Court now regularly confronts. In a first situation, the Court seeks to enhance standards of rights protection, on the margins, in States that otherwise have a relatively good record of compliance with the Convention. The Court identifies gaps in rights protection and encourages States to adjust their law to fill those gaps. In this mode of operation, the Court may also develop new rights for discreet communities (e.g., of transsexuals) or for

---

[29] Through 2003, there were only twenty interstate applications, although some of these have resulted in important Court judgements.

[30] The source for these data is the annual *Survey of Activities* published by the ECtHR on its website: http://www.echr.coe.int/ECHR/EN/Header/Reports+and+Statistics/Reports/Annual+surveys+of+activity/ (most recently checked 31 January 2008).

[31] The Court itself, in its *Survey of Activities 2006*, ibid., p. 3 states: "This enormous caseload has raised concerns over the continuing effectiveness of the Convention system."

specific situations (e.g., religious teaching in the schools). In post-Protocol no. 11 Europe, the Court will never want for such opportunities. Where Convention standards for rights protection are higher than those in domestic legal orders, the Court can expect to be activated – systematically – by individuals seeking to change domestic law. And the more the Court undertakes to interpret the Convention in a progressive, expansive, and open-ended way, the more likely it is that rights protection in one or several States will routinely fall below Convention standards, creating pressure for national adaptation. In this situation, the Court arguably plays the role of a European Constitutional Court.

The Court faces a second, qualitatively different, type of problem when it encounters systemic failures to protect rights. Across Europe, many States find it virtually impossible to meet Convention standards, under Article 6(1) ECHR, for ensuring that judicial proceedings are initiated and completed in a reasonable time. In this area, floods of clone applications from certain countries, such as Italy, have become chronic.[32] With enlargement into East and into the Balkans, the Court now confronts a third kind of problem: massive State failures to provide even minimal protection of the most basic rights, including the prohibition of torture and inhuman and degrading treatment laid down by Article 3 ECHR. In some States, institutional capacities to protect rights are simply under-developed; in others, including Georgia, Russia, Turkey, and the Ukraine, political officials and judges fail to uphold even the most basic principles of rule of law. At present, the majority of judgements[33] concern serious problems of either systemic or massive failure to protect Convention rights. In this situation, the Court arguably plays the role of a High Court of Appeal, or Court of Cassation.

Given these challenges, it is difficult to see how the Convention regime can prosper, if the Court sees its role primarily as providing individual justice. Indeed, as discussed, the Court has had little choice but to explore other options, such as the pilot judgements, in which it takes on the mantle of judicial lawmaker for States, in the context of a specific problem. To the extent that it does, of course, the Court positions itself to exercise relatively direct impact on domestic legal systems.

c. Jurisprudence

If, arguably, the ECHR has evolved certain constitutional features, the regime remains a creature of international law. Most important, unlike national constitutional or supreme courts, the Strasbourg Court does not possess the authority to invalidate national legal norms judged to be incompatible with the Convention. The absence of such authority constitutes a serious disadvantage to the extent

---

[32] See also in this volume Candela Soriano, Section C.2.b.

[33] In 2006, 964 of the 1,560 rulings (63%) of the Court concerned just six states: Italy, Poland, Russia, Slovenia, Turkey, and the Ukraine. Data reported in European Court of Human Rights, *Survey of Activities 2006* (*supra* note 30).

that the regime is expected not only to render retrospective justice in individual cases, but also to construct Convention rights and to ensure their general effectiveness across Europe, prospectively. The Court can count on the Council of Europe's support of a robust doctrine of *pacta sunt servanda* (under Article 46 ECHR), and for the development of innovative approaches to systemic failures, such as pilot judgements. Such support, along with the good will and good faith of most States, should not be underestimated. The Court would fail at its mission without them. Nonetheless, the ECHR is an autonomous legal regime. The Court does not preside over a hierarchically constituted judicial system in which it exercises appellate review, or cassation powers, when it comes to decisions of national courts. Put differently, the Court's command and control capacities are weak, at best. They are primarily reduced to the ordering of compensatory damages to be paid in just satisfaction to successful applicants.

In consequence, the Court performs its most important governance functions through the building of a precedent-based case law.[34] Through precedent, the Court seeks to structure the argumentation of applicants and defendant States, to ground its rulings, and to persuade States to comply with findings of violation. The Court also relies heavily on precedent-based rationales to develop Convention rights, and to manage a complex environment, prospectively. The Court does so in the name of "legal certainty and the orderly development of [its] case law".[35] Convention rights, like the rights provisions of national constitutions, have been judicially constructed, and precedent both enables and constrains the Court's creativity. The Court will abandon a line of case law in order to correct an earlier error, or "to ensure that the interpretation of the Convention reflects societal change and remains in line with present day conditions".[36]

This mode of governance – through precedent – raises an empirical issue that is at the heart of our concerns. Convention rights will only have impact beyond any individual case to the extent that national officials take into account the Court's jurisprudence in their own decision making. Incorporating the Convention directly into national legal orders, as directly enforceable law, may induce, or may legally require, national officials to do so. But incorporating the Convention in this way is not obligatory. National officials, including judges, will always possess some measure of discretion as to how to make use of the Court's case law. They may decide to ignore the Court's interpretation of the Convention, even when on point, and even where Convention rights have been domesticated through incorporation. Thus, the development of a coherent jurisprudence is a third necessary condition, but not sufficient in itself, for the ECHR to exert influence on national legal orders.

---

[34] See Shelton (2003), 127.
[35] *Cossey v. United Kingdom* (appl. no. 10843/84), Judgement (Plenary), 27 September 1990, Series A, Vol. 184, para. 35.
[36] Ibid.

In summary, the Court possesses all of the formal power required for it to acquire dominance over the evolution of the Convention regime; today, its *de facto* dominance over the regime is fully secure. On the input side, we can expect that most important violations of Convention rights will be referred to Strasbourg, by one or more applicants. On the output side, the Court has produced a dense and elaborate case law that provides an authoritative construction of Convention rights and, thus, guidance to national officials who mean to apply the Convention on their own. If and how national officials actually do so is the major preoccupation of this book.

B. Nature and Scope of the Project

1. *Methodological Considerations*

The goal of this volume is to assess, cross-nationally and across time, the impact of the Convention on national legal orders. Each chapter pairs two relatively like cases for comparative analysis, and the book as a whole should be read comparatively, across relatively unlike cases. Our coverage is wide, comprising countries in Western Europe (Ireland/the UK; France/Germany; Austria/Switzerland; Belgium/the Netherlands); Central and Eastern Europe (Poland/Slovakia; Russia/ Ukraine); Southern Europe (Greece/Turkey, Spain/Italy); and Scandinavia (Sweden/Norway). For each report, authors responded to the same research questions, collecting and analysing the same types of data. In addition, external experts – including judges on the Strasbourg Court, national judges, and senior litigators and academics – were integrated into the project from the beginning.[37] They attended our workshops, consulted with reporters in the course of their research, and commented on drafts of the reports.

For purely pragmatic reasons (space and resource limitations) this book does not cover all the Member States of the Council of Europe. Nonetheless, we chose a representative sample of States that vary on dimensions thought to be pertinent. States vary in terms of their length of time in the regime, region, difference in legal tradition, domestic experience with rights protection, and so on. We therefore selected a mix of older and newer members, of States belonging to different families of legal systems, and of systems that had and did not have strong national experience with rights protection. We also considered the importance of national systems as sources of applications to the Court. A considerable amount of case law stems from Central and Eastern Europe, so it was crucial to have State Parties of this region represented (Poland, Slovakia, Russia, and Ukraine); the same can be said of Southern Europe (Greece, Italy, and Turkey). At the same time, we also needed to include States that generate relatively few applications, not least, in order to evaluate the extent to which lower numbers of applications might be

---

[37] See the Acknowledgements, this volume.

due to how these States have incorporated the ECHR into domestic law, and developed effective mechanisms of coordination. In any event, we chose to pair countries represented in this volume for reasons both theoretical and practical. The focus on States that are alike in certain ways helps us to control for certain common factors, while focusing more attention on contrasts that make a difference to the overall reception process. In fact, this type of design can eliminate some *prima facie* similarities between countries as important factors impinging on reception (see, for example, the chapter on Ireland and the United Kingdom[38]). While there is no denying that comparing two legal systems always poses methodological challenges, this volume shows that the advantages of comparison far outweigh the disadvantages, if we are to gain a better understanding of the impact of the ECHR on national legal systems.

Comparative case studies are typically designed with specific purposes in mind. Since ours is no exception, it is important to be clear about what this project is, and is not, about. It bears emphasis up-front that this type of research is constrained in three important ways. First, well-specified, causal theory on the impact of the ECHR on its members does not exist. Thus, we could not design the project to test a specific set of hypotheses, or to adjudicate among contending theories. Second, extant empirical knowledge on the topic is sparse, and even the best research is rarely comparative.[39] This project involves comparison at two levels: each of the nine chapters compares reception in two countries; and the book compares across eighteen State Parties to the ECHR. We chose a comparative approach to the national reports in order to maintain the advantages of in-depth, empirical case studies, while avoiding well-known problems associated with generalising the findings of a single case. The authors of the national reports themselves engage in comparison as a mode of explanation. Further, the reports raise important issues that would not have come to light in the absence of comparison. In the concluding chapter of the volume, we evaluate reception across all of our cases, in light of the data collected and the preliminary comparisons undertaken by the national reporters. Third, research of this kind can be fiercely difficult. Our approach is not limited to consulting published legal materials, but requires original research into matters outside the formal law. Indeed, each of the reports presents data that had never been collected before.

We recognize that for many of our readers, the most important contribution of this book may well be the presentation of basic data on the status and effectiveness of the ECHR in the various States under consideration. We nonetheless designed the research to move beyond basic description. We hope to offer useful insights on the dynamics of reception, and on the effectiveness of the ECHR, insights that can only be obtained through relatively systematic data collection and comparative analysis. Each chapter provides a comparative analysis of similarities

---

[38] See in this volume Besson, Section IV.
[39] Blackburn and Polakiewicz (2001) is an excellent exception.

and differences found in two cases, and the concluding chapter of this volume is devoted to a broad summary of findings across all cases.

Although we did not set up our project to test a set of pre-existing hypotheses in any formal, scientific sense, we nonetheless defined our research problem in ways that would maximize prospects for building more general theory. Our empirical focus is on the reception of the ECHR regime within national legal orders. By "national legal order", we include the domains of the legislature, the executive, and the judiciary. It is through the decision-making of national officials that the Convention is given domestic agency. By national officials, we mean all agents of public authority – including judges, legislators, and administrators – who are authorised to take decisions that are capable of affecting the status of the ECHR within the national legal order. Reception may entail decisions that serve to enhance the effectiveness of the ECHR, as when officials adjust the law to comply with the judgements of the Strasbourg Court. Reception may also involve resistance to the Convention, as when officials seek to limit its domestic reach and scope. To understand the extent to which the ECHR and national legal systems are coordinated over time, one must pay attention to both kinds of reaction.

This project therefore conceptualizes reception broadly, as a process that is not reducible to compliance with the ECHR in a strict legal sense. Our empirical focus is on how the Convention and the Court's case law impact upon the decision making of domestic officials, primarily legislators, administrators, and judges. If and how national officials institutionalize specific mechanisms for the ongoing coordination of national law with the ECHR, as the latter evolves, is of particular interest. First, officials may develop preventive procedures for assessing future compliance problems, whether related to ratification or with day-to-day lawmaking after accession. Second, the Court's judgements themselves may push officials to develop new practices that will impinge on reception: to comply with concrete rulings and to monitor future compliance; to translate and disseminate judgements; to implement pertinent recommendations of the Council of Europe; to amend laws and practices. Further, specific Court's rulings may attract the interest of the media, and of scholars or other elites, which, in turn, may shape how officials react. Third, some mechanisms of reception operate at a more general level: on legal scholarship and education; on media coverage and public awareness, and on how police officers, judges, members of parliament, and other officials are trained. As discussed in the next section, our research project is designed to assess reception on each of these three dimensions.

Stated in the language of the social sciences, our dependent variable (the phenomenon to be explained) is the effectiveness of the ECHR within national legal systems. Effectiveness varies both across legal systems, and diachronically within any single State. The ECHR can be said to be effective to the extent that national officials give agency or enforce Convention rights, within national legal orders, through their decisions. The Court's evolving jurisprudence comprises the main independent variable (the external catalyst of change in the national legal systems). Over time, the Court has progressively constructed Convention rights in ways that pressure national officials to adapt, or coordinate, the national legal systems with the ECHR. The various mechanisms of reception and coordination that the chapters describe constitute intermediate variables (determinates of how the independent variable acts upon the dependent variable), in that these processes condition if, how, and to what extent Convention rights influence national legal orders.

As a matter of comparative method, the book presents a series of structured-focused comparisons,[40] in which authors evaluate the parallel experiences of two countries with reference to data collected on the same research questions. The method of structured-focused comparison is commonly used to organize research on topics that are under-developed, both empirically and theoretically. We employ the method for classic purposes, namely, to develop (a) appropriate concepts, (b) a theoretical lexicon for analysing reception, and (c) empirical measures of effectiveness. Each is a preliminary stage in the derivation of candidate hypotheses to explain variance in the reception process. Single case studies are sometimes employed to perform some of these same tasks. Nonetheless, comparing two – relatively like – cases, as we do in each chapter, provides a stronger basis on which to build a more general comparative and theoretical framework.[41] Moreover, as discussed in the concluding chapter, the scope of our research enables us to compare across unlike cases, as we move from report to report.

We also proceeded in light of specific candidate propositions, which entailed collecting basic information on the various factors that we thought, *a priori*, might condition the reception process. Each of the chapters, for example, assesses the influence of national constitutional law, separation of powers doctrines, and the organization of the judiciary. The reports also evaluate various mechanisms for coordinating national legal orders with the ECHR, not all of which may operate effectively in any given national system. In their research, reporters searched for these and other mechanisms, and were asked to trace their origins and consequences. Thus, the project began with some basic *ex ante* hypotheses on the table. We did not assume, however, that any of the hypotheses would be validated through empirical scrutiny. On the contrary, we had good reason to expect[42] that the reception process would be the product of a complex mixture of the factors and social logics. The reports evaluate these propositions for each paired comparison, and we revisit our findings as a whole in the concluding chapter.

---

[40] The classic statement of the method is George (1979). For an updated and extended discussion, see George and Bennett (2005).

[41] For a discussion of the aims of different research designs, see Eckstein (1975) and Lijphart (1971).

[42] See Keller (2005). The model for the template that follows was derived from this paper by participants in the project.

2. Empirical Questions

For each chapter, reporters respond to the same empirical questions. They present data collected on the same variables and indicators of effectiveness; they identify the processes and mechanisms of reception that have developed; and they assess the importance of these mechanisms over time, in two national cases. Taken together, the reports chart cross-national variance in the impact of the ECHR on national legal systems, and they provide materials for generating hypotheses that might explain this variance.[43]

a. Historical Context: Accession and Ratification

The chapters provide basic accession information for two States, reporting on the procedures through which they signed and ratified the Convention and the various protocols. Over time, States have acceded to the regime more smoothly, reflecting the growing political legitimacy of the Convention and its Court. In the 50's, the leaders of most States assumed that ratifying the Convention would not require any meaningful adjustment on their part, in that they considered that the level of national rights protection was more than adequate. Yet they were more reticent to accept the right of individual application and the compulsory jurisdiction of the Court, and they took, on average, longer to ratify the Treaty instruments. Of the original signatories, five (Belgium, France, Italy, the Netherlands, and Turkey) took more than three years to move to ratification. France decided to ratify the ECHR only in the 1970s, more than 20 years after it signed the ECHR; and Greece ratified the Convention twice, in 1953 and for a second time in 1974 (the military regime had renounced membership in 1969). After the entry into force of the Convention, no State that signed the ECHR took more than three years to ratify it. By the 80's, every new signatory was well aware that ECHR membership would require substantial adjustment, but the benefits of membership by then far outweighed the inconveniences. Today, membership in the ECHR confers a kind of certificate of approval on States.[44] The reports also consider national debates on ratification, on lodging reservations, and on the degree to which these decisions reflected concern for how much change in domestic law would be required by membership in the regime. The more a State fully accepts its obligations under the Convention, of course, the more it will be exposed to the influence of the Convention.

---

[43] Of course, one cannot both test hypotheses against the data used to construct the hypotheses. One could, however, test such hypotheses in research on cases of reception that fall outside of our study. See the concluding chapter for further discussion of this point, Section A.

[44] Thus, in the 90's, membership became obligatory for states who wished to join the European Union.

b. Status of the ECHR in National Law: Formal (Doctrinal) Elements

Certain factors – especially constitutional structure – will help to determine how the ECHR enters into and subsequently affects the national legal system. Of fundamental importance is the question of whether Convention rights possess viable supra-legislative status in the national legal order that judges may directly enforce. A first set of issues concerns national constitutions deal with the law of international treaties. Every chapter explores the extent to which the national constitution contemplates monist, as opposed to dualist, solutions to conflicts between treaty law and national law, including statutes. A State that adopts a more monist posture to the ECHR – including the abandonment of the *lex posteriori derogat legi priori* principle – will be much more capable of building stable mechanisms for coordinating the ECHR with the national legal order than a State that maintains a strong dualist posture. A functionally equivalent situation can be created through the legislative incorporation of the ECHR into the national legal system, if the incorporation statute provides for the direct effect of Convention rights and their supra-legislative status. Thus, each report considers if, how, and with what effect on the national legal order the ECHR has been incorporated, and each assesses the extent to which incorporation changes outcomes. As discussed in the concluding chapter,[45] some States that are formally dualist (Belgium) or that have traditionally denied the direct applicability of treaty law in the domestic legal system (Austria) have nonetheless conferred on Convention rights constitutional or quasi-constitutional status, with truly transformative effects.

A second set of issues concerns separation of powers doctrines (or other explicit provisions of public law) that permit or prohibit the judicial review of legislative and executive acts with reference to higher norms. It could be supposed that the more experience national judges have with judicial review and rights adjudication, the easier it will be for the Convention to gain traction in the national legal order. Informed by research on the reception of the EU's doctrines of supremacy, we also considered that the opposite might be true. In States without secure systems of rights and review, the ECHR might fill the void, substituting for constitutional rights, especially if monist doctrines or incorporation confers on Convention rights primacy over legislation. We find as much in monist Netherlands, and in dualist UK, after incorporation. In States that have well-established systems of constitutional justice, such as Germany and Ireland, litigators are far more likely to plead domestic constitutional law, rather than the Convention, before national judges. National judges, especially those sitting on constitutional courts, will have a weaker interest in developing Convention rights; they may even be jealous of their positions, and resist recognizing the primacy of Convention rights when they come into tension with constitutional rights.

A third set of issues concern how the State is organized. Among other factors, the reports examine the influence of federalism, the relationship between

---

[45] See Keller and Stone Sweet, this volume, Section A.3.b.

parliaments and executives, and the organization of the judiciary. Of particular importance is the question of how many high (or supreme) courts exist. In some countries, one supreme court, of general jurisdiction, sits at the apex of a unified judiciary (e.g., Ireland, the Netherlands, Norway). In others, the legal system is itself divided into functionally differentiated sub-systems, each of which has its own high court (e.g., France, Germany). In the former case, the Supreme Court may be asked to clarify the law given divergent interpretations percolating up from below, or asked to ratify new interpretations of national law in light of the ECHR. In the latter case, different supreme courts may take varying doctrinal positions on the status of the ECHR, and these differences may or may not be subject to harmonisation.

With respect to rights protection, Europe today is characterized by a complex pluralism[46] in which various sources of law and multiple courts interact to produce outcomes. In those countries in which constitutional courts hold a privileged position, it is usually the interactions between constitutional judges and the ECHR that are crucial, although the positions of the European Court of Justice may also weigh heavily. In other countries, Belgium being a good example, the high ordinary courts may use the Convention in ways to assert their own authority over rights, undermining the presumptive monopoly of the constitutional judge. In virtually every country, the Convention has enhanced judicial authority *vis-à-vis* the legislative and executive branches. Most of the reports therefore explore these complex judicial politics in some detail, as we do in the concluding chapter.

c. Overview of the Activity of the Court

For each State covered, authors present basic information on the formal interactions between the Strasbourg Court and the national legal order, including data on the following activity: the annual number of applications filed against each State; the annual number of judgements on the merits since national accession; the Article(s) of the ECHR concerned for each application and judgement; and the decision of the Court on these applications (violation or non-violation of Convention rights). A State that generates relatively more applications and more findings of violation is a State placed under relatively more pressure to adapt to the ECHR. National officials may resist adaptation, of course. After all, it may be that relatively higher levels of censure by the ECHR are artefacts of past failures to adapt on the part of national officials.

The data, which are comprehensive through 2006, provide a dynamic, multi-dimensional view of the Court's direct interactions with national legal orders. They also show wide cross-national variation, and raise questions in and of themselves. Why do some countries generate more application than others? Why does the same country generate more applications in some domains than others? The

---

[46] Krisch (2008).

data reveal these and other puzzles, many of which we are not in the position to resolve. Nonetheless, in their analyses, reporters depict and seek to explain variation across their cases, and we discuss these matters further in the concluding chapter.

d. The European Court's Case Law

In this Section, authors focus on the impact of the Strasbourg Court's rulings on applications originating from the legal systems on which they report. The extent of the Court's influence can be assessed most directly following a finding of violation on the part of the Court. Such rulings challenge national officials to take decisions that will render national law compatible with the Convention. The chapters identify the most important ECHR findings of violation for each State covered, and then trace how national officials in fact responded to these rulings. The Court's rulings on admissibility, on national law finding no violation, on applications originating in other members, might also influence the decision-making of national officials, to the extent that the Court has given guidance as to how the right must be interpreted and applied in national legal orders. The question then would be whether national officials take these clarifications on board in making their own decisions.

e. Mechanisms of Coordination

One of the most important and difficult tasks facing the authors of the reports was the analysis of the various mechanisms of coordination that have emerged in national legal orders over time. Reception takes place through those procedures that enable national officials to adapt national law to the evolving dictates of ECHR law. These procedures may be legislative, administrative, or judicial; they may be *ad hoc* or fully entrenched; and they may be more or less successful at rendering Convention rights more effective. The chapters trace the development of these mechanisms and evaluate how they operate, in light of the project's over-arching concern for the effectiveness of the ECHR in national legal orders.

As discussed, one basis on which stable mechanisms of coordination may emerge and institutionalize is through conferring on the ECHR both direct effect and primacy in any conflict with statute and infra-legislative norms. Some States have done so through adopting a strong monist posture; others have incorporated the Convention through special statutes that are recognized as having supra-legislative status. In doing so, States open the door to the development of practices (mechanisms) designed to promote the effectiveness of the ECHR in the national legal orders. Judges may assert a new, or more robust, authority to review the Conventionality of legislative and administrative acts; and executives and legislators may evolve new procedures for scrutinizing, *ex ante* and in-house, the compatibility of new law with Convention rights.

Many States have, in fact, evolved such mechanisms, altering, sometimes profoundly, how parliamentary governance operates in Europe. In States where the dogmas of legislative sovereignty had previously gone unchallenged, the development of stable, effective mechanisms of coordination will, inevitably, subvert traditional separation of powers arrangements and expectations.[47] In countries that possess a catalogue of national constitutional rights and a supreme or constitutional court, it has generally been left to the constitutional judge to determine the status of Convention rights. In most countries, supreme and constitutional courts have found ways, over time, to enhance the effectiveness of Convention rights in the national legal order while maintaining the centrality of their own positions, even in the face of dualism. We will discuss these points at length in the concluding chapter, with reference to the book's findings.

Mechanisms of coordination are typically embedded in larger governmental processes that take account of important public interests and priorities beyond protecting Convention rights. A national judge who is placed under a duty to interpret a statute in light of Convention rights may still be bound by that statute, which is itself a product of legislative authority. A national judge who controls the proportionality of a national statute reviews how the legislature has already balanced the ECHR and the public good. The legislative committee charged with evaluating the Conventionality of a parliamentary bill submitted by the Government is made up of Members of Parliament who have agendas beyond protecting rights. We could go on. The broader point is that mechanisms do not organize coordination in any mechanical or linear way. National officials have choices to make, and these are conditioned by a complex structure of incentives, many of which do not flow from the national legal order's relationship to the ECHR.

Generally, national officials will not work to enhance the effectiveness of the ECHR in national legal orders if they do not see it in their interest to do so. One of the more ambitious goals of this volume is to chart, over time, changes in the interests of national officials. In some States, hostility and resistance to the Court have been replaced by a cooperative attitude (e.g., France). In other States (e.g., the Scandinavian countries), we find judges and politicians starting to take notice of the regime that they all but ignored over many decades. In some situations, it may be that the incentives in place are basically negative: in the face of a rising number of negative rulings by the Court, national officials develop mechanisms of coordination to help them insulate the national legal order from censure in Strasbourg. In other situations, judges and politicians may invoke and give agency to Convention rights for their own purposes. Judges may wish to expand their capacity to control elected politicians; a governing party may wish to enshrine rights that will constrain other parties when the latter come to power; officials may be responding to an increasing societal demand for enhanced

---

[47] As discussed in the concluding chapter of this volume, the reception of the European Court of Justice's doctrines of supremacy and direct effect have had effects in the same direction, see Keller and Stone Sweet, this volume, Section A.3.b.

rights protection. In any case, reception provokes dynamics of change and some of these changes will alter the strategic setting of national officials which will, in turn, alter the choices they make.

f. Remedies and Proportionality

The effectiveness of national remedies for violations of Convention rights is itself a direct indicator of the effectiveness of the ECHR in national legal orders. The reports examine the evolution of national systems of remedies, as they have evolved with reference to the ECHR. The Convention does not stipulate remedial requirements beyond the terms of Article 13 ECHR, which requires States to provide victims of a violation of their rights with an effective remedy before a national authority. Nonetheless, in its case law on Article 13 ECHR, now dense and sophisticated, the Court has steadily raised standards. Today, Article 13 covers virtually every aspect of how national legal systems are organized and function. Applicants routinely invoke Article 13, leading the Court to review how national systems of justice operate at a deep structural level. When the Court finds violations of Article 13, it exerts heavy pressure on the State to reform its institutions and established practices, or risk ongoing exposure to ECHR censure. As the reports vividly show, the Court goes far beyond the rendering of individual justice in this area. Indeed, many of its decisions concern how the national legal order must be reformed structurally, and such reforms are often constitutionally significant.

The impact of Article 13 on national legal orders has also been registered on judicial doctrines and, in particular, on standards of judicial review. As discussed above, the Court adopted proportionality balancing as a standard approach for managing conflicts between Convention rights and the government's interest in pursuing collective goods that may qualify those rights. Proportionality analysis, however, was not native to most States. In a series of cases involving the UK, the ECHR gradually adopted the view that Article 13 required judges to engage in proportionality review of government acts that infringe upon certain core Convention rights, Articles 8–11 and 14, in particular. In doing so, the ECHR destroyed the viability of the traditional reasonableness tests long employed by UK judges and others. As the Court noted in *Peck v. United Kingdom*,[48] under that test, individuals would have to show that UK authorities had acted "irrationally in the sense that they had taken leave of their senses or had acted in a manner in which no reasonable authority could have acted"[49] in order to have their claims reviewed. The ECHR's position, in contrast, is that, once a *prima facie* case for a violation of Convention rights has been established, judges must move to necessity analysis, which involves applying a least-restrictive means test.

---

[48] *Peck v. United Kingdom* (appl. no. 44647/98), Judgement (Fourth Section), 28 January 2003, Reports 2003-I, 123.

[49] Ibid., para. 105, quoting the High Court ruling rejecting Peck's appeal.

Stated in American parlance, the adaptation requires a shift from a rational basis to a strict scrutiny standard, although proportionality analysis also leaves room for deference to the States under the margin of appreciation doctrine.[50]

Under the Court's supervision, proportionality – today a transnational, constitutional principle in Europe – is in the process of diffusing to every national legal order in Europe. The reports examine this process and assess its impact on rights protection at the national level.

g. Knowledge and Practice

To this point we have focused on relatively direct and formal measures of impact, such as the institutionalisation of judicial and legislative mechanisms of reception, and the reform of national law after a finding of violation by the Court. To measure the more sociological influence of the Convention, at the level of cognition, practice, and social reproduction, for example, it is necessary to go beyond a focus on formal procedures and law. The chapters report if, how, and the extent to which three types of practices – lawyering, teaching, and scholarship – have changed as a result of the reception of the ECHR in national legal orders. Each of these practices may track and measure impact.[51] Changes in these practices may also reinforce reception, or accelerate it. The more lawyers, teachers and students, and doctrinal authorities consider and reference the ECHR, the more they may help to institutionalize mechanisms of coordination, for example. Indeed, it may even be useful to consider their activities, under certain conditions, to be supplementary mechanisms of coordination. Changes in knowledge and practice may alter the mix of costs and benefits that national officials consider when deciding how to make reception-relevant decisions. Each chapter thus reports on how the ECtHR's ruling are disseminated domestically, and on the extent to which layering, teaching, and scholarship have changed over time.

C. A Europe of Rights

The ECHR has evolved into a sophisticated legal system whose Court can be expected to exercise substantial influence on the national legal systems of its members. In the 21st Century, Europe is a Europe of rights. The Convention system constitutes an authoritative, dynamic, and transnational source of law. At the same time, most High Contracting Parties have incorporated the ECHR, thereby domesticating it in important ways. We therefore proceeded on the view that the Convention's legal system, post-Protocol No. 11, ought to be conceptualized

---

[50] For a general overview of the doctrine of margin of appreciation in the ECHR, see Arai-Takahasi (2002). The inconsistencies in how the ECHR deploys the doctrine of margin of appreciation have come under a great deal of criticism, see Letsas (2006) and Bruach (2005).

[51] This list is not exhaustive, indeed, there are many other indirect measures that can and should be the focus of research.

broadly (rather than in more narrow, formalistic terms) to include the reception of the ECHR, by national officials, at the domestic level. As the reports that follow this introduction show, one cannot understand how the Convention system actually functions without paying close attention to how that system interacts with, and impacts upon, national law. In the concluding chapter of this volume, we will return to these themes in light of this volume's most important findings.

Bibliography[52]

Alkema, E. A., 'The European Convention as a Constitution and its Court as a Constitutional Court', in Mahoney, P., Matscher, F., Petzold, H., and Wildhaber, L. (eds.) *Protecting Human Rights: The European Perspective* (Cologne, 2000), 41.

Arai-Takahasi, Y., *The Margin of Appreciation Doctrine and the Principle of Proportionality in the Jurisprudence of the European Court* (Antwerp, Oxford, New York, 2002).

Blackburn, R. and Polakiewicz, J. (eds.), *Fundamental Rights in Europe: The European Convention on Human Rights and Its Member States, 1950–2000* (Oxford, 2001).

Bruach, J.A., 'The Margin of Appreciation and the Jurisprudence of the European Court of Human Rights: Threat to the Rule of Law', *Columbia Journal of European Law* 11 (2005), 113.

Eckstein, H., 'Case Studies and Theory in Political Science', in Greenstein, F. and Polsby, N. (eds.), *Handbook of Political Science*, Volume 7, 79 (Reading, Mass., 1975).

Flauss, J. F. 'La Cour Européenne des droits de l'homme est-elle une cour constitutionnelle?', 36 *Revue française de droit international* 36 (1999), 711.

George, A., 'Case Studies and Theory Development: The Method of Structured, Focused Comparison', in P. Lauren, P. (ed.), *Diplomacy: New Approaches in History, Theory, and Policy* (New York, 1979).

George, A. and Bennet, A., *Case Studies and Theory Development in the Social Sciences* (Cambridge, 2005).

Greer, S., *The European Convention on Human Rights* (Cambridge, 2006).

Keller, H., 'Reception of the European Convention for the Protection of Human Rights and Fundamental Freedoms (ECHR) in Poland and Switzerland', *Zeitschift für ausländisches und öffentliches Recht und Völkerrecht* 65 (2005), 283.

Krisch, N. 'The Open Architecture of European Human Rights Law', forthcoming in *Modern Law Review* 71 (2008), 183.

Letsas, G., 'Two Concepts of the Margin of Appreciation', *Oxford Journal of Legal Studies* 26 (2006), 705.

Lijphart, A., 'Comparative Politics and the Comparative Method', *The American Political Science Review* 65 (1971), 682.

Majone, G., 'Two Logics of Delegation: Agency and Fiduciary Relations in EU Governance', *European Union Politics* 2 (2001), 103.

Milgrom, P. and Roberts, J., *Economics, Organization and Management* (Englewood Cliffs, NJ, 1992), 127.

Moe, T., 'Political Institutions: The Neglected Side of the Story', *Journal of Law, Economics, and Organization* 6/1 (1990), 213.

Moravcsik, A., 'The Origins of Human Rights Regimes: Democratic Delegation in Post-War Europe', *International Organization* 54 (2000), 217.

Nichol, D., 'Original Intent and the European Convention on Human Rights', *Public Law* (2005), 152.

---

[52] See also the bibliography to the concluding chapter.

Polakiewicz, J., 'The Execution of Judgments of the European Court of Human Rights', in Blackburn R. and Polakiewicz, J. (eds.), *Fundamental Rights in Europe: The European Convention on Human Rights and Its Member States, 1950–2000* (Oxford, 2001), 55.

Shapiro, M. and Stone Sweet, A., 'The New Constitutional Politics of Europe', *Comparative Political Studies* 26 (1994), 397.

Shelton, D., 'The Boundaries of Human Rights Jurisdiction in Europe', *Duke Journal of Comparative and International Law* 13 (2003), 95.

Simpson, A. W. B., *Human Rights and the End of Empire: Britain and the Genesis of the European Convention* (Oxford: Oxford University Press, 2001).

Slaughter, A.-M., Stone Sweet, A. and Weiler, J. (eds.), The European Court and the National Courts: Legal Change in its Social, Political, and Economic Context (Oxford, 1998).

Stone Sweet, A., Governing with Judges: Constitutional Politics in Western Europe (Oxford, 2000).

—, 'Constitutional Courts and Parliamentary Democracy', *Western European Politics* 25 (2002), 77.

Wildhaber, L., 'A Constitutional Future for the European Court of Human Rights?', *Human Rights Law Journal* 23 (2000), 161.

Winkler, G., *The Council of Europe* (Vienna, 2006).

PART II
NATIONAL REPORTS

2

The Reception Process in Ireland and the United Kingdom

Samantha Besson*

I. Introduction[1]

Although they were among the first countries to ratify the European Convention on Human Rights (ECHR), in 1953, the United Kingdom (UK) and Ireland were the last of these to integrate it into their domestic legal orders. With the

* Many thanks are due to Nicholas Bamforth, Nick Barber, Eimear Brown, Cathryn Costello and Marianna Patané for helpful comments on earlier versions of this report and/or useful indications and discussions in the course of my research. I am especially endebted to Alec Stone Sweet for having helped me drastically shorten the considerably longer version of this report which will be published separately. I owe special thanks to Marynelle Debétaz for her valuable editorial and research assistance with finalizing the report. Last but not least, I would like to thank Joanna Bourke-Martignoni, Céline Briguet, Lorna Loup, Stéphanie Murenzi and Verena Seiler for their research assistance at various stages of preparation of the present report between 2005 and 2007.

[1] Abbreviations: AC = Appeal Cases; All ER = All England Law Reports; ATCSA = Anti-terrorism, Crime and Security Act 2001; BVerfGE = Entscheidungen des Bundesverfassungsgerichts (decisions of the German Federal Constitutional Court); CA = Criminal Appeal; CAR= Criminal Appeal Reports; CCA= Court of Criminal Appeal; CD = Collection of Decisions of the European Commission of Human Rights 1960–1999; Ch. = Law Reports Chancery Division; Charter = EU Charter of Fundamental Rights; Cm. = Command Papers (1986–…); DPP = Director of Public Prosecutions; ECR = European Court of Justice Reports; ECHR Act = European Convention on Human Rights Act 2003; EHRR = European Human Rights Reports; EHRR CD = European Human Rights Reports, Commission Decisions; EMLR = Entertainment and Media Law Reports; EWCA = England and Wales Court of Appeal; EWCA Civ = England and Wales Court of Appeal Civil Division; EWCA Crim = England and Wales Court of Appeal Criminal Division; EWHC = England and Wales High Court; EWHC (Admin) = England and Wales High Court (Administrative Court); EWHC (Ch) = England and Wales High Court (Chancery Division); EWHC (QB) = England and Wales High Court (Queen's Bench Division); EWHC (Comm) = England and Wales High Court (Commercial Division); EWHC (Admlty) = England and Wales High Court (Admiralty); EWHC (Fam) = England and Wales High Court (Family Division); EWHC (Pat) = England and Wales High Court (Patents Court); EWHC (TCC) = England and Wales High Court (Technology & Construction Court); HC = House of Commons; HL = House of Lords; HRA = Human Rights Act 1998; ICCPR = International Covenant On Civil and Political Rights (UN); ICR = Industrial Cases Reports; IEHC = High Court of Ireland Decisions; IESC = Supreme Court of Ireland Decisions; ILR = Irish Law Reports; ILRM = Irish Law Reports Monthly; IR = Irish Reports; JCHR = Joint Committee on Human Rights; JJ. = Judges/Justices; SC = Scots Session Cases; SCR = Supreme Court Reports (Canada); UKHL = United Kingdom House of Lords; UKHRR = United

entry into force of the UK Human Rights Act (HRA) in 2000, and of the Irish ECHR Act in 2003, both countries incorporated the Convention, making it an immediate source of individual rights against national authorities and, in cases of violation, a source of remedies before national courts. In doing so, both countries opened their legal orders to the complete reception of the Convention, at least in a passive way, and they are now positioned to play a more active role in the development of the European constitutional order through judicial dialogue. This chapter examines the reception of the ECHR both before and after incorporation.

The UK and Ireland are relatively 'like cases', sharing important geographical, cultural, and linguistic similarities. Most important for our purposes, both countries are dualist, parliamentary democracies with similar approaches to international law. International legal norms are only valid in domestic law, and judicially enforceable by national courts, after incorporation through Parliamentary Statute. Both States joined the EU in 1973, and both had to adapt to the immediate validity, primacy, and direct effect of EU law. From the perspective of internal law, both have a long experience in judge-made, common law.

Despite these similarities, the Convention's role in, and impact on, the respective legal systems have been quite different. One crucial factor accounts for most of this difference: the prior existence of rights review. Ireland has a written, entrenched Constitution with a detailed Bill of Rights and strong judicial review of legislation, whereas the UK has no codified Constitution, no Bill of Rights, and the doctrine of Parliamentary supremacy prohibits judicial review of statutes. In Ireland, the Catholic religion traditionally undergirded an expansive approach to unenumerated rights whose source is natural law. In the UK, one observes a more positivist approach, and hostility to constitutional rights *per se*. Though the common law in the UK is judge-made law, its capacity to develop in a rights-enhancing direction is constrained by statutory sovereignty (statute trumps conflicting common law). As we will see, this combination of structural factors – codified constitution/rights/judicial review – plays a central role at virtually every stage of the analysis presented here.

The application of the ECHR is based on the principle of national jurisdiction, which remains largely territorial (Article 1 ECHR) although jurisdiction is interpreted broadly by the ECtHR.[2] Ireland is a unitary jurisdiction; thus, the

---

Kingdom Human Rights Reports; UKPC = United Kingdom Privy Council; V = violation; WLR = Weekly Law Reports.

[2] See e.g. *Ilaşcu and Others v. Moldova and Russia* (appl. no. 48787/99), Judgement (Grand Chamber), 8 July 2004, Reports 2004-VII, 179 et seq.; [2005] 40 EHRR 46. See, however, for the limited interpretation of the UK House of Lords, *R (on the application of Hilal Abdul-Razzaq Ali Al-Jedda) v. Government for Defence* [2006] EWCA Civ 327; *R (on the application of Mazin Mumaa Galteh Al-Skeini & others) v. Secretary of State for Defence* [2005] EWCA Civ 1609, upheld by the House of Lords in *Al-Skeini and others (Respondents) v. Secretary of State for Defence (Appellant)* and *Al-Skeini and others (Appellants) v. Secretary of State for Defence (Respondent) (Consolidated Appeals)* [2007] UKHL 26.

territorial scope of Convention rights in Ireland is its whole territory.[3] The UK situation is more complicated, for two reasons. A first complexity concerns the application of the ECHR in overseas territories. On 23 October 1953, the UK extended the effect of the Convention, but not Protocol no. 1, to 42 colonies and dependencies. Since 1965, most British colonies have been granted independence, although the Convention still influences law in some of these countries.[4] A second complexity concerns the UK itself. The UK has four constituent parts, with three legal systems (for England and Wales, Scotland, and Northern Ireland). Recent devolution has entailed new legislative assemblies in Scotland, Wales, and Northern Ireland and different incorporation regimes of the Convention.[5] This chapter will focus only on the reception of the ECHR in England and Wales.

Although the chapter will discuss the pre-incorporation status and role of the ECHR in each country, its focus is on reception of the ECHR post-incorporation, being six years for the UK, and three for Ireland. Although there have been a few cases of declarations of incompatibility under the HRA since 2000,[6] there has only been one so far in Ireland, and the ECHR Act has only been applied sporadically by Irish courts since 2003. Thus, it is obviously too soon to offer an authoritative evaluation of the influence of the Convention on the UK and Irish legal orders, particularly for Ireland.[7]

II. Overview of the National Constitutional Orders

A. United Kingdom

The UK does not have a written, entrenched Constitution. It does, however, possess a constitution in the material sense: a system of laws, customs, and principles which sets out the nature, function and limits of the constitutive elements of the State. There are no entrenched fundamental rights. The formal statements

---

[3] Of course, the 1921 partition in the Republic of Ireland and Northern Ireland has been a source not only of political struggle, but also of legal difficulties. Differences in the legal regimes applicable to these two parts of the island of Ireland have regularly led to comparisons and hence to cases being brought to Strasbourg when similar situations were not treated in similar ways. See e.g. pertaining to the discrimination of homosexuals, *Norris v. Attorney General* [1984] IR 36 to be compared to *Dudgeon v. the United Kingdom* (appl. no. 7525/76), Judgement (Plenary), 22 October 1981, Series A, Vol. 45; [1982] 4 EHRR 149.

[4] See Blackburn (2001), 943–944.

[5] Ibid., 955–956; Reed and Murdoch (2001). See also Department for Constitutional Affairs, *Review of the Implementation of the Human Rights Act*, July 2006, 36, http://www.dca.gov.uk/peoples-rights/human-rights/pdf/full_review.pdf (Unless indicated otherwise, all websites in this report were checked on 31 December 2006).

[6] See tables published by the Department for Constitutional Affairs, http://www.dca.gov.uk/peoples-rights/human-rights/pdf/decl-incompat-tabl.pdf.

[7] See for Ireland, O'Connell et al. (2006); and for the United Kingdom, Klug and Starmer (2005); and Department for Constitutional Affairs, *Review of the Implementation of the Human Rights Act*, July 2006, http://www.dca.gov.uk/peoples-rights/human-rights/pdf/full_review.pdf.

of rights worth mentioning in English legal history, such as the Magna Carta of 1215, were designed to limit the arbitrary rule of the monarch. The 1688 Bill of Rights, to take another example, codified a settlement that resulted in the establishment of constitutional monarchy. One also finds important legal principles, such as the writ of *habeas corpus*. For the rest, the English common law is held to guarantee all fundamental rights and freedoms of the individual, although statutory provisions trump conflicting common law.[8]

The Parliamentary system is a British invention. The legislative branch comprises the House of Commons, which is made up of elected Members of Parliament, and the House of Lords, today composed of appointed and hereditary peers.[9] The Lords' veto is only suspensive nowadays. The legislative agenda of Parliament is directed by the Government, which is, in turn, led by the Prime Minister. The Executive – Government Ministries headed by Members of Parliament who are collectively responsible to the Commons – directs the Civil Service and other parts of the administration.

A Parliament Statute is sovereign in the legal order. Statutory sovereignty means that judges may not invalidate or refuse to apply a Parliamentary Act, and no sitting Parliament can bind a future Parliament through statute. Thus any Parliament may repeal any existing statute. Further, under the doctrine of implied repeal, judges must resolve inconsistency between an earlier and a later statute in favour of the latter. The doctrine of implied repeal is relaxed with respect to the HRA 1998.[10] The HRA binds the Judiciary and the Executive, but it also has been construed by judges as requiring express Parliamentary intention to repeal its provisions in the case of any later, inconsistent statute.[11] The only other exception to the rule of implied repeal is that provided by the European Communities Act 1972, under which judges disapply statutes that are incompatible with EU law.

The House of Lords – the Appellate Committee of Law Lords – is the highest appeal jurisdiction in almost all cases in England and Wales. The Law Lords may also sit on the Judicial Committee of the Privy Council, which is the court that hears appeals from beyond England and Wales, including appeals from Scotland and Northern Ireland or the Caribbean. HRA challenges to the devolved assemblies' legislation are heard by the Privy Council. Until 2006, the Lord Chancellor was the most senior judge on the Appellate Committee of the House of Lords, and he also sat in Government, as Minister of Justice. The European Court of Human Rights' (ECtHR) decision in *McGonnell v. UK* (2000)[12] made this over-

---

[8] See e.g. *Attorney General v. Guardian Newspapers (Spycatcher)* [1987] 1 WLR 1248 (CA). See also Blackburn (1999), *Bill of Rights,* 169–173.
[9] See White Paper, *The House of Lords: Reform* (Cm. 7027, February 2007): http://www.official-documents.gov.uk/document/cm70/7027/7027.pdf.
[10] For a detailed discussion, see Bamforth (2004).
[11] See *infra* Section III. B.
[12] *McGonnell v. the United Kingdom* (appl. no. 28488/95), Judgement (Third Section), 8 Februa-

lap in functions untenable. The Constitutional Reform Act 2000 removed these incompatibilities, and also created the Supreme Court of the UK in lieu of the House of Lords.[13] The Supreme Court will take over the judicial functions of the Law Lords in the House of Lords in 2009.

The High Court, the Court of Appeal and the House of Lords (including the Supreme Court) supervise the acts of the Executive.[14] They have the power to declare executive decisions and acts unlawful.

Although it does not have any constitutional status, one other public institution deserves mention upfront. The 1998 Belfast ('Good Friday') Agreement between Ireland and the United Kingdom committed the parties to establishing a Human Rights Commission whose remit would be to supervise the enforcement of human rights obligations.[15] The UK initially created a Commission whose competence was limited to the territory of Northern Ireland. In October 2003, the Government announced its intention to establish a single Commission for Equality and Human Rights for the whole of the United Kingdom (except Northern Ireland), and the new Commission became operational in October 2007.[16] Its remit is to promote human rights, but also to bring together disparate bodies which currently have responsibilities in the field of equality, thus making it unlikely it will have the same impact as the Irish Human Rights Commission. According to the Equality Act 2006, the Commission should advise employers and service providers on good practice and the promotion of equality and good relations; conduct inquiries and carry out investigations; provide advice and information on rights and equality laws; campaign on issues affecting the diverse groups in society that can suffer discrimination; make arrangements for conciliation to assist with disputes; assist individuals who believe they have been the victim of unlawful discrimination; and provide grants.

B. Ireland

The Irish Constitution (1937) is entrenched and cannot be easily revised.[17] It contains both written and unenumerated rights, which overlap most of the ECHR's rights provisions. The National Parliament (*Oireachtas*) consists of the President and two Houses: the House of Representatives (*Dáil Éireann*) and the

---

ry 2000, Reports 2000-II, 107 et seq.; [2000] 30 EHRR 289. See Cornes (2000). See *infra* Section III. D.

[13] See e.g. Le Sueur (2004).

[14] Please note that the report will focus on higher courts only and on their majority decisions, unless decisions by lower courts and dissenting judgements present a specific interest in a concrete case.

[15] See e.g. O'Connell (2001), 470.

[16] See http://www.cehr.org.uk.

[17] This is somewhat counterbalanced by the frequency of constitutional referenda in Ireland, often to undo jurisprudential developments. See Costello (2005).

Senate (*Seanad Éireann*). As in the UK, the work of the Parliament is directed by the Government, which is, in turn, led by the Prime Minister (*Taoiseach*). The Executive consists of Government Ministries which are collectively responsible to the House of Representatives and direct the Civil Service and other parts of the administration.

The Judiciary is a key actor of the Irish human rights scene thanks to its prolific and activist jurisprudence on fundamental rights.[18] The Constitution states that it is the highest law of the land, and it grants the Supreme Court authority to interpret its provisions, and to strike down legislative and executive acts when these are found to be unconstitutional. Outside the United States, the Irish Supreme Court is said to have the longest and most extensive experience of judicial review in the English-speaking world.[19]

After the 1998 Belfast Agreement, Ireland adopted the Human Rights Commission Act 2000. The Act confers wide-ranging powers on the Commission to promote and protect human rights, including: monitoring rights protection, examining draft legislation and reporting on its human rights implications; consulting with national or international human rights bodies; making recommendations on measures to strengthen, protect and uphold human rights in the State; promoting understanding and awareness of the importance of human rights in the State; conducting inquiries; appearing before the superior courts as *amicus curiae* in proceedings which concern human rights; instituting legal proceedings; providing legal assistance in certain circumstances; and establishing and participating in the Joint Committee with the Northern Ireland Human Rights Commission.

III. Reception of the ECHR

A. Historical Context: Accession, Ratification and Incorporation

1. United Kingdom

a. Drafting the Convention
Prior to the HRA, it was assumed that Parliament and judges, through the common law, guaranteed the fundamental rights and freedoms of the individual. The distrust of entrenched human rights catalogues was present on 4 November 1950, when the UK signed the ECHR, but international protection of human rights was seen by the British Foreign Office as part of a larger effort to promote a stable Europe.[20] Given the UK's dualism, it was easier for the UK to sign and

---

[18] See e.g. Costello (2005) on the relationship between judicial activism and constitutional referenda in Ireland and on the legitimation of the former in the absence of the latter.

[19] See e.g. Hogan (2004), 14–15.

[20] See e.g. Marson (1993); Robertson and Merrills (1993).

ratify the ECHR, than for monist countries, in which the ECHR might be given immediate validity in domestic law.

The UK helped to create the Council of Europe and to negotiate the ECHR, although it was opposed to an international court with the authority to adjudicate human rights matters.[21] In the end, States reached a compromise to confer compulsory interstate jurisdiction on the Court, but to make the individual right of petition optional. The UK valued precision over vagueness, and it was a British representative who drafted the Articles 2 to 17 ECHR, easing adoption by the UK.[22] A compromise was also reached according to which an express declaration by Contracting States was necessary before the Convention could extend to overseas territories. Finally, sensitive rights, such as theright to education, the rights relative to property or democratic rights, were guaranteed in a (first) separate and optional Protocol to the ECHR in 1952. As a result, despite initial scepticism, the UK became one of the first States to sign the Convention.

b. Ratifying the Convention

Since treaties can be ratified in the UK without legislative approval, the Government swiftly ratified the ECHR on 8 March 1951, and it came into force on 3 September 1953. In the first interstate case (*Greece v. UK*)[23] brought under the Convention, the UK found itself the defendant, which helped to discourage the British Government from signing the optional Protocol to confer jurisdiction on the ECtHR in cases brought by individuals. In addition, the UK perceived such jurisdiction as a threat to legislative and administrative autonomy in its colonies and dependencies. After most decolonization was completed, the UK recognized the right of individual petition to the ECtHR on 13 January 1966, recognition which entered into force on 14 July 1966.[24]

All optional Protocols to the Convention, with the exception of Protocols nos 4, 7, and 12, have now been ratified by the UK. Protocol no. 1, dealing with those rights to property, education and free election which had been made optional by the UK in 1950, entered into force on 18 May 1954. Protocol no. 6 came into force on 1 June 1999 and Protocol no. 13 on 1 February 2004. Protocol no. 14, which has not entered into force yet, was signed on 13 July 2004 and ratified shortly thereafter on 28 January 2005. Protocol no. 6 was signed and ratified as a consequence of debates about the Human Rights Act in 1998 and the inclusion of the prohibition of the death penalty for criminal offences in the Act. The death penalty was largely abolished in 1965 and completely in 1998, whereupon the UK signed and ratified Protocol no. 6 in 1999.

---

[21] See on the international and British politics surrounding the adoption of the Convention, Simpson (2001); Blackburn (2001), 936–938.

[22] See Hoffman and Rowe (2003), 27.

[23] *Greece v. the United Kingdom* (appl. no. 176/56), Report (Plenary), Commission, 2 June 1956, Report of 26 September 1958.

[24] See Lester (1998), *UK Acceptance*.

There are several reasons for non-ratification of Protocols nos 4, 7, and 12. Not all of the rights contained in Protocols no. 4 (freedom of movement for State's nationals within and between countries, prohibition of expulsion of people from their own country, prohibition of the collective exclusion of aliens) and 7 (right of appeal in criminal cases, *ne bis in idem*, procedural safeguards in case of expulsion of non-nationals) are consistent with existing British law. Whereas there is a right of appeal in criminal cases and a right not to be punished twice for the same offence, other rights under Protocol no. 7 are not fully secured. An example is the definition of those to be treated as "lawful residents" under British law and its compatibility with Article 1(1) of Protocol no. 7. This is also the case with provisions in family law concerning the requirement of equality between spouses under Article 5 of Protocol no. 7.[25] As to Protocol no. 4 (signed on 16 September 1963), immigration laws in general would need to be harmonized with the rights under that Protocol. The British Government has chosen, however, not to ratify these Protocols until inconsistencies have been removed.[26] The UK has not yet signed Protocol no. 12, given the difference in approaches to the concept of discrimination and burden of proof, although developments in EU law may be eroding these differences.[27]

Regarding reservations, the only reservation lodged by the UK to date is with respect to Article 2 of Protocol no. 1, valid from 18 May 1954, according to which "the principle affirmed in the second sentence of Article 2 is accepted by the UK only so far as it is compatible with the provision of efficient instruction and training, and the avoidance of unreasonable public expenditure". The same reservation was also made later on in 1988 and 2001 with respect to different overseas territories where education legislation allows for further exceptions to Article 2. As to derogations, the UK currently has none, although it has registered some in the past. Thus, it made a derogation under Article 15 ECHR to Article 5(3) ECHR on 23 December 1988 and 23 March 1989 (withdrawn on 19 February 2001 with respect to the UK, and on 5 May 2006 pertaining to all other dependencies of the UK). The UK registered another derogation on 18 December 2001 to Article 5(1)(f) ECHR in relation to powers to detain suspected terrorists or illegal immigrants pending deportation under the Anti-terrorism, Crime and Security Act 2001 (ATCSA), which was withdrawn on 16 March 2005 following a House of Lords decision.[28] Finally, the UK made numerous declarations regarding the 23 October 1953 extension of the territorial scope of application of the ECHR to 42 overseas territories and dependencies, though decolonization has reduced their importance.

---

[25] See e.g. Blackburn (2001), 940–941.

[26] Home Office, White Paper, *Rights Brought Home: The Human Rights Bill* (Cm. 3782, October 1997). See Mr O'Brien, Home Office Minister, HC, vol. 312, col. 1006.

[27] See on the convergence between the ECtHR and the ECJ's conceptions of equality and discrimination, Martin (2006).

[28] See *A. and Others v. Secretary of State for the Home Department* [2004] UKHL 56.

Table 1: United Kingdom[29]

Protocol	Signature	Ratification	Entry into force	Declarations/ Reservations
Protocol no. 1	20 March 1952	3 Nov. 1952	18 May 1954	6 declarations and reservations concerning Articles 2, 4
Protocol no. 2	6 May 1963	6 May 1963	21 Sept. 1970	–
Protocol no. 3	6 May 1963	6 May 1963	21 Sept. 1970	–
Protocol no. 4	16 Sept. 1963	–	–	–
Protocol no. 5	10 Feb. 1966	24 Oct. 1967	20 Dec. 1971	–
Protocol no. 6	27 Jan. 1999	20 May 1999	1 June 1999	1 declaration
Protocol no. 7	–	–	–	–
Protocol no. 8	19 March 1985	21 April 1986	1 Nov. 1990	–
Protocol no. 9	–	–	–	–
Protocol no. 10	25 March 1992	9 March 1993	–	1 declaration
Protocol no. 11	11 May 1994	9 Dec. 1994	1 Nov. 1998	1 declaration
Protocol no. 12	–	–	–	–
Protocol no. 13	3 May 2002	10 Oct. 2003	1 Feb. 2004	4 declarations concerning Article 4
Protocol no. 14	13 July 2004	28 Jan. 2005	–	1 declaration

c. Applying the Convention Indirectly

Prior to the HRA 1998, the ECHR possessed the status of an international convention without immediate validity in domestic law. Legal subjects in the UK, who felt their rights had been infringed, could bring a legal action in respect of such a breach before the ECtHR only. Incorporation was not envisaged during the first 30 years that followed accession, and only cursory references to the ECHR were made in Parliament in the early years of the ECHR.[30]

Although the UK has a classic dualist approach to international law, entry into the EU weakened dualist orthodoxies. When the UK became a member of the EU on 1 January 1973, the doctrines of the supremacy and direct effect of EU law were gradually recognized as having been incorporated into national law through the European Communities Act 1972. The supremacy of EU law, further, applies even to conflicting Parliamentary statutes passed later in time; the doctrine of implied repeal, otherwise a core precept of legislative sovereignty in

---

[29] Source: http://conventions.coe.int/Treaty/Commun/ChercheMembres.asp?CM=3&CL=ENG.
[30] The Attorney General told the House of Commons on 20 November 1950: "(...) it is not contemplated that any legislation will be necessary in order to give effect to the terms of this Convention."

the UK, is not applied in conflicts between EC law and later UK statutes.[31] The increasingly central place given to human rights and especially Convention rights in EU law, and the stringency of judicial remedies before the ECJ by comparison to the ECtHR,[32] have been important, indirect factors in the reception of the ECHR in British law.[33] During the pre-incorporation period (1973–2000), EU fundamental rights, in effect, pre-empted the field, while ensuring a minimal reception of the ECHR in British law. This has been the case, for instance, in the fields of anti-discrimination law, and especially the prohibition of indirect discrimination[34] or the protection of pregnancy at work,[35] as well as rights of free movement.[36] As EU law established itself in national law, appellate judges and legal academics began, with increasing vigour, to worry about the inconsistency of the UK's position on the ECHR.[37] Lord Slynn, a former UK judge at the European Court of Justice, stated his views in the House of Lords in 1992 as follows:

"Every time the European Court recognises a principle set out in the Convention as being part of Community law, it must be enforced in the UK courts in relation to Community law matters, but not in domestic law. So the Convention becomes in part a part of our law through the back door because we have to apply the Convention in respect of Community law matters as a part of Community law."[38]

d. Incorporating the Convention: The Human Rights Act

In the 80's, as the UK began to lose cases before the ECtHR, pressure for incorporation began to build, not least, as British judges came to realise that English common law was not a sufficient means to protect Convention rights.[39] If the choice came down to incorporation versus the drafting a Bill of Rights, the former seemed quicker, less complicated, and less politically controversial.[40] The decisive moment came when the Labour Party entered into Government on 1 May 1997, under the leadership of Tony Blair, who promised renewed attention

---

[31] In this sense, the difference between monism and dualism may matter in the ECHR's reception process much more than it did in the EU (see e.g. Craig (1998)).

[32] See e.g. Alston (1999).

[33] See e.g. *Matthews v. the United Kingdom* (appl. no. 24833/94), Judgement (Grand Chamber), 18 February 1999, Reports 1999-I, 251 et seq.; [1999] 28 EHRR 361 and case C-36/02, *Omega Spielhallen- und Automatenaufstellungs-GmbH v. Oberbürgermeisterin der Bundesstadt Bonn*, [2004] ECR I-9609.

[34] See e.g. case C-96/80, *J.P. Jenkins v. Kingsgate (Clothing Productions) Ltd* [1981] ECR 911.

[35] See e.g. case C-32/93, *Carole Louise Webb v. EMO Air Cargo (UK) Ltd* [1994] ECR I-3567.

[36] See e.g. case C-60/00, *Mary Carpenter v. Secretary of State for the Home Department* [2002] ECR I-6279; case C-370/90, *The Queen v. Immigration Appeal Tribunal and Surinder Singh, ex parte Secretary of State for Home Department* [1992] ECR I-4265.

[37] See e.g. Blackburn (1997), 25–29.

[38] House of Lords Debates, 26 November 1992, col. 1095 et seq.

[39] See e.g. *Malone v. Metropolitan Police Commissioner* [1979] Ch. 344, 379–380.

[40] See Report of the House of Lords Select Committee on a Bill of Rights, HL Paper 176 Session 1977–1978.

to human rights, both domestically[41] and in British foreign policy.[42] In its White Paper, *Rights Brought Home* (October 1997),[43] it emphasized that the UK had been the progenitor of human rights in Europe, and that "bringing rights home" would submit British authorities to legal standards that were, in the end, British, not foreign.

In its case for incorporation,[44] the Government argued that in the absence of a domestic remedy in case of infringement of the ECHR, individuals would go to Strasbourg, raising costs to everyone involved. Requiring judges to interpret national law in conformity with the Convention would reduce the number of cases brought to and sanctioned in Strasbourg, and the political embarrassment thus generated.[45] Further, the more the UK Judiciary actively adjudicated Convention rights, the more the UK would build influence on the ECtHR's jurisprudence, thereby reducing discrepancies between national and supra-national methods and findings.

The Human Rights Bill was the subject of wide-ranging and lengthy debates in the House of Commons and the House of Lords during the 1997–98 Parliamentary session,[46] before being adopted on 9 November 1998. Due to the important amount of official preparation of an administrative and educational nature internal to the Civil Service, the Act only entered into force on 2 October 2000. There is no special procedure provided for in the HRA regarding the means by which it may be amended in the future, although it is not entrenched. Even if repealing of the Act is sometimes called for by the popular press and certain politicians, there is a broad consensus that repeal is not feasible, since it would probably lead to denouncing the ECHR *per se*, thus raising difficulties for the UK's membership of the Council of Europe and the European Union, but also a return to the problems pre-incorporation already mentioned. One may even venture that the level of incorporation of the Convention and the kind of human rights judicial review developed by British courts since 2000 have already become part of the common law and would stay so despite the repeal of the Act. A more commonly considered alternative to complete *dis*incorporation might be to adopt a British Bill of Rights on the basis of the HRA.[47]

---

[41] See e.g. Straw (2000).

[42] See e.g. Robin Cook, Opening Statement by the Foreign Secretary, Press Conference on the Foreign and Commonwealth Office Mission Statement, 12 May 1997. See also: http://hrpd.fco.gov.uk.

[43] Home Office, White Paper, *Rights Brought Home: The Human Rights Bill* (Cm. 3782, October 1997).

[44] See e.g. Hoffman and Rowe (2003), 29. See also Finlay (1999); Steyn (2000).

[45] See Blackburn (2001), 958–959.

[46] See on these debates, Blackburn (1999), *Bill of Rights*.

[47] See Department for Constitutional Affairs, *Review of the Implementation of the Human Rights Act*, July 2006, 37–39, http://www.dca.gov.uk/peoples-rights/human-rights/pdf/full_review.pdf. See also the discussion paper by Justice, *A Bill of Rights for Britain?* (London, 2007), http://www.justice.org.uk/images/pdfs/A%20Bill%20of%20Rights%20for%20Britain.pdf.

The HRA incorporates – albeit indirectly[48] – the ECHR and the case law of the ECtHR into the domestic law of the UK. According to its long title, it "gives further effect" to the rights and freedoms guaranteed by the Convention. It requires the courts and other public authorities to apply the ECHR directly within the British legal system; and it empowers individuals to plead the ECHR against public authorities in the courts. Fifty years after its ratification by the UK, the Convention entered British domestic law in 2000.

According to Section 1 para. 1 HRA, the rights brought into British law are those provided for by Articles 2 to 12 and 14 ECHR, together with the rights comprised in the optional Protocols ratified by the UK (Protocols nos 1, 6, and 13). The Act also incorporates Articles 16 to 18 ECHR. Curiously, Articles 1 and 13 are omitted, allegedly because the Act itself is meant to secure the rights of the Convention under Article 1 ECHR, on the one hand, and because incorporating Article 13 would duplicate Section 8 of the Act (which gives the courts authority to provide a remedy), on the other.[49]

Under Section 1 para. 4 HRA, rights can be added to the Act by a statutory instrument, after the UK signs and/or ratifies a new Protocol to the Convention. In the former case, this amendment is conditional on the entry into force of the Protocol itself (Section 1 para. 6 HRA). Thus, when Protocol no. 14 enters into force, a statutory amendment of the HRA will be required to incorporate it into British law. According to Section 1 para. 2 HRA, reservations and derogations to the rights under the Convention and its Protocols extend to the rights incorporated in the Act. The only reservation in force at the current time is a reservation to Article 2 of Protocol no. 1. If a derogation is amended or replaced, it ceases to be a designated derogation under Section 1 para. 2 HRA and a new order is required to designate the new or amended derogation. According to Section 16 HRA, all derogations expire after five years, but may be extended expressly for another five years. Section 17 HRA provides that derogations must be kept under review by the appropriate Minister.

Incorporation proceeds in four main steps. First (Section 6), it is unlawful for a public authority, including courts, to act in a way which is incompatible with a Convention right. Second (Section 8), the courts are authorized to provide remedies for breaches of Convention rights. Third (Section 2), all public authorities must take account of the decisions of the ECtHR in their decisions on Convention rights. As a consequence, judges must interpret all Parliamentary statutes, whenever possible, to be compatible with the Convention (Section 3). Last (Section 4), when this is not possible, a declaration of incompatibility may

---

[48] For that reason, some authors do not regard the HRA as an incorporating act *stricto sensu*, but merely as an act that gives effect to an international convention in British law. See e.g. Clayton and Tomlinson (2006). See *infra* Section III. B.

[49] See e.g. the Lord Chancellor (House of Lords Debates, 18 November 1997, vol. 583, col. 475) and the Home Secretary, Jack Straw (House of Commons Debates, 20 May 1998, vol. 312, col. 981).

be issued by higher courts and addressed to the Parliament, although the latter is not bound by such a finding.

2. Ireland

a. Drafting the Convention

Because Irish courts always had to enforce the Irish Bill of Rights, there was no domestic pressure for the development of a European human rights catalogue and court. Ireland was among the creators of the Council of Europe, however, and one of its first members and, in that context, the Government took the view that supporting the adoption of the ECHR would benefit the country for foreign policy reasons. Unofficial motivations also included anti-British or anti-partition sentiment,[50] a view seemingly confirmed later by the 1978 *Ireland v. UK* case, the only interstate procedure ever launched by Ireland.[51]

b. Ratifying the Convention

The ECHR was signed by the Irish Minister for External Affairs on 4 November 1950, upon adoption by the Council of Europe. Under Article 29(1) and (2) of the Irish Constitution, the power to ratify a treaty rests in most cases solely with the Executive. The Executive thus ratified the ECHR on 25 February 1953, and it entered into force on 3 September 1953.

Ratification of the Convention was relatively unqualified. Ireland ratified all optional clauses right from the beginning in 1953. Along with Sweden, Ireland was the first Contracting State to accept the right of individual petition to the ECtHR, in February 1953 (entry into force on 5 June 1955), and it was involved in the first individual petition ever considered by the ECtHR, in 1961 (*Lawless v. Ireland No. 3,* 1961[52]). All optional Protocols to the Convention, with the exception of Protocol no. 12, have now been ratified in Ireland. Protocol no. 1 entered into force on 18 May 1954, Protocol no. 4 on 29 October 1968, Protocol no. 6 on 1 July 1994, Protocol no. 7 on 1 November 2001 and Protocol no. 13 on 1 July 2003. Protocol no. 14, which has not yet entered into force, was signed on 13 May 2004 and ratified on 10 October 2004. Although Ireland signed Protocol no. 12 on 4 November 2000, it chose not to ratify it. The most important reason given for non-ratification is the fear that Conventional protection might lead to constitutional conflicts in Ireland, given that equality and non-discrimination are protected by Article 40 para. 1 of the Irish Constitution. It would appear that

---

[50] See O'Connell (2001), 423–424; Blake (2002).

[51] *Ireland v. the United Kingdom* (appl. no. 5310/71), Judgement (Plenary), 18 January 1978, Series A, Vol. 25; [1979–1980] 2 EHRR 25.

[52] *Lawless v. Ireland (No. 3)* (appl. no. 332/57), Judgement (Chamber), 1 July 1961, Series A, Vol. 3; [1979–1980] 1 EHRR 15. See also Doolan (2001).

Irish case law in this area takes a different approach to that taken by Protocol no. 12 on positive duties and the allocation of the burden of proof.[53]

Ireland's only reservation, dated 25 February 1953, pertains to Article 6 and free legal aid. According to the Government, Ireland will "not interpret Article 6(3)(c) ECHR as requiring the provision of free legal assistance to any wider extent than is now provided in Ireland." In 1976–1977, the Irish Government chose to derogate from some of the provisions in the Convention due to security emergencies, but these derogations were withdrawn on 20 October 1977. Ireland has made only three declarations to date: to Article 2 of Protocol no. 1 on 18 May 1954, Article 3 of Protocol no. 4 on 29 October 1968 and Protocol no. 8 on 1 January 1990.

Table 2: Ireland[54]

Protocol	Signature	Ratification	Entry into force	Declarations/ Reservations
Protocol no. 1	20 March 1952	25 Feb. 1953	18 May 1954	1 declaration concerning Article 2
Protocol no. 2	6 May 1963	12 Sept. 1963	21 Sept. 1970	–
Protocol no. 3	6 May 1963	12 Sept. 1963	21 Sept. 1970	–
Protocol no. 4	16 Sept. 1963	29 Oct. 1968	29 Oct. 1968	1 declaration concerning Article 3
Protocol no. 5	18 Feb. 1966	18 Feb. 1966	20 Dec. 1971	–
Protocol no. 6	24 June 1994	24 June 1994	1 July 1994	–
Protocol no. 7	11 Dec. 1984	3 Aug. 2001	1 Nov. 2001	–
Protocol no. 8	20 March 1985	21 March 1988	1 Jan. 1990	1 declaration
Protocol no. 9	24 June 1994	24 June 1994	1 Oct. 1994	–
Protocol no. 10	24 June 1994	24 June 1994	–	–
Protocol no. 11	11 May 1994	16 Dec. 1996	1 Nov. 1998	–
Protocol no. 12	4 Nov. 2000	–	–	–
Protocol no. 13	3 May 2002	3 May 2002	1 July 2003	–
Protocol no. 14	13 May 2004	10 Nov. 2004	–	–

c. Applying the Convention Indirectly

The ECHR did not form part of domestic law until the Parliament adopted the ECHR Act in 2003, according to Article 29 para. 6 of the Constitution (through which an international agreement can be made part of Irish law by statute).[55]

[53] See Mullan (2004), 234–241.
[54] Source: http://conventions.coe.int/Treaty/Commun/ChercheMembres.asp?CM=3&CL=ENG.
[55] See O'Connell (2004), *Critical Perspective,* 2.

Whether due to the strong constitutional rights tradition in Ireland, fear of a *de facto* levelling-down of human rights protection,[56] or the very low number of cases brought against Ireland in Strasbourg, Irish authorities did not seriously debate incorporation before the end of the 90's.[57] Not surprisingly, the Convention attracted very little attention in the years following its entry into force.

Ireland became a member of the EU on 1 January 1973, and like the UK, inherited the *acquis* of supremacy and direct effect of EU law in the absence of formal incorporation. This transfer of a measure of legal sovereignty to the European Court of Justice required a constitutional amendment on 8 June 1972. Prior to incorporation (1973–2003), EU fundamental rights ensured a minimal reception of the Convention in Irish law,[58] particularly in the context of free movement rights and anti-discrimination guarantees.[59] The reception of Convention rights *via* EU law proceeded with difficulty in Ireland.[60] Conflicts between EU fundamental rights and Irish constitutional rights have given rise to the famous dilemma between revolt (against the primacy of EU law) and revolution (in the Irish constitutional order).[61] One example of this dilemma arose in the *SPUC v. Grogan* case, where the European Court of Justice ruled that the ban on publicity in Ireland, for abortion services in the UK, violated the basic freedom of services under EU law.[62] In reaction, Ireland negotiated a Protocol to the Maastricht Treaty in 1992 stating that the right to life under the Irish Constitution remained untouched by EU law. A similar case brought before the ECtHR led to a judgement under Article 10 ECHR's (freedom of expression) the same year, forcing Ireland to soften its ban on information services on abortion outside Ireland.[63] Neither of these judgements has put an end to issues related to abortion information, given the traditional influence of the Catholic tradition and the right to life (of the unborn) found in the Irish Constitution.

d. Incorporating the Convention: The ECHR Act

Following the 1998 Belfast Agreement, it was the UK's incorporation of the Convention in the HRA 1998, that led Ireland to consider incorporation, and

---

[56] See e.g. Hogan (2004), 16, by reference to the Supreme Court's decision in *Re Article 26 and the Illegal Immigrants (Trafficking) Bill* [2000] 2 IR 360. For another confirmation, see e.g. *Lobe & Osayande v. Minister for Justice, Equality and Law Reform* [2003] IESC 1.

[57] O'Connell (2001), 468.

[58] See e.g. Costello and Browne (2004).

[59] See e.g. case C-138/02, *Brian Francis Collins v. Secretary of State for Work and Pensions* [2004] ECR I-02703 and case C-191/03, *North Western Health Board v. Margaret McKenna* [2005] ECR I-7631.

[60] See e.g. Costello (2002) on case C-63/93, *Duff and Others v. Minister for Agriculture and Food and Attorney General* [1996] ECR I-569.

[61] See e.g. Phelan (1992) and (1997).

[62] Case C-159/90, *SPUC v. Grogan* [1991] ECR I-4685.

[63] *Open Door and Dublin Well Woman v. Ireland* (appl. nos 14234/88; 14235/88), Judgement (Plenary), 29 October 1992, Series A, Vol. 246-A; [1993] 15 EHRR 244.

the HRA served as a model.[64] On 30 June 2003, the Parliament adopted the ECHR Act, following debates that were surprisingly uncontroversial.[65] The Bill was defended as a neutral template for sensitive cross-border dealings with Northern Ireland that one could otherwise attain only through a constitutional settlement.[66] Upon entry into force on 31 December 2003, Ireland became the last dualist country to incorporate the ECHR, after the UK in 1998 and Norway in 1999. In contrast to the UK, no period of general education, official training and judicial reorganization was planned before the Act's entry into force.[67] It was assumed that Irish human rights traditions were strong enough, and judges knowledgeable enough, to apply the Act straight away. As in the UK, the ECHR Act is not an entrenched statute, but it is unlikely to be overruled.[68]

The ECHR Act 2003 requires public authorities to apply Convention rights directly within the Irish legal system and empowers people to bring domestic legal proceedings against public authorities for breach of their Convention rights. According to Section 1 para. 1 ECHR Act, the Convention rights brought into Irish law are those provided for by Articles 2 to 14 ECHR, together with the rights comprised in the Protocols ratified by Ireland, i.e. Protocols nos 1, 4, 6, 7, and 13. The Act also incorporates Articles 16 to 18 ECHR. In contrast to the HRA, Article 13 ECHR is incorporated into Irish law. As a result, the Act provides for effective remedy in case of infringement of the ECHR, under Irish law.

In contrast to the HRA, litigants may not plead the Convention, under the ECHR Act, against Parliament or the courts, while the equivalent Irish constitutional rights can be invoked against all authorities including the Irish Parliament. A further contrast is that the ECHR Act does not specify the conditions under which rights can be added to the Act through additional Protocols and statute. One presumes that additions will be conditional on the entry into force of the Protocol itself. Thus, when Protocol no. 14 enters into force, a statutory amendment of the ECHR Act will be required to incorporate it into Irish law. Nor is there a Section of the ECHR Act comparable to Section 1 para. 2 HRA. One presumes that Irish reservations and derogations to the rights under the Convention and its Protocols will extend to the rights incorporated in the Act.

Incorporation proceeds in five main steps. First, Section 3 para. 1 ECHR Act provides that every "organ of the State" must perform its functions in a Convention-compliant manner. Second (in case of breach of Section 3 para. 1), Section 3 para. 2 ECHR Act provides that a person who has suffered a loss,

---

[64] See on previous models: Report of the Constitution Review Group (Pn 2632, Stationery Office, Dublin 1996) and Hogan (2004), 17 on the Review Group's proposal.

[65] See O'Connell (2004), *Critical Perspective*, 3. See also Hogan (2004), 18–21 on these debates.

[66] See Hogan (1999); Hogan (2004), 15; O'Connell et al. (2006), 12. See also Submission of the Human Rights Commission to the Joint Oireachtas Committee on Justice, Equality, Defence and Women's Rights (2001).

[67] See *infra* Section III. B.

[68] See *infra* Section III. G.

injury or damage may, if no other remedy in damages is available, institute proceedings in respect of the loss in either the Circuit Court or the High Court.
Third (Section 4), judicial notice shall be taken of the Convention provisions
and of any of the case law of the European Court of Human Rights. Fourth,
Section 2 para. 1 ECHR Act requires that the courts interpret and apply, in so far
as it is possible, statutory provisions or rules of law in a Convention-compatible
manner. Fifth, where a Convention-compatible interpretation is not available,
Section 5 para. 1 ECHR Act provides that the High Court or Supreme Court
may declare that the statutory provision or rule of law is incompatible with the
State's obligations under the Convention. Such a declaration of incompatibility
does not affect the validity, continuing operation or enforcement of the relevant
legal provision (Section 5 para. 2).

3. Comparison and Conclusion

Ireland and the UK incorporated the ECHR into their national legal orders in
similar ways; indeed, the 1998 HRA provided the model for the 2003 ECHR
Act. Yet, significant underlying differences remain.[69] Most importantly, incorporation works differently in the UK and in Ireland: the HRA takes on the function
of a catalogue of rights, while the ECHR Act in general simply supplements what
is arguably the most advanced system of judicial protection of constitutional
rights in Europe. This difference helps to explain much of the rest of the variance.
In the UK, the indirect incorporation of Convention rights through EU law,
in the absence of competing constitutional norms, proceeded more smoothly
than in Ireland, where constitutional resistance proved stronger. In the UK, the
ECtHR's numerous adverse judgements against it weighed in favour of incorporation, whereas in Ireland, it was not the absence of judicially-enforceable rights
at issue, but the peace process in Northern Ireland. Whereas the UK allegedly
brought rights home by internalising the Convention, Ireland externalized rights
politics, accepting incorporation of the ECHR as the price for peace in Northern
Ireland.[70] Finally, although the HRA provided the template for the ECHR Act,
the courts and the legislature are excluded from liability under the latter.

B. Status of the ECHR in National Law

1. United Kingdom

a. Pre-Incorporation Validity and Rank
In the UK, treaties can be ratified without legislative approval, but they acquire
the status of judicially-enforceable law only by means of an act of Parliament.

---

[69] In addition to differences listed, the UK has registered many derogations under Article 15
ECHR, whereas Ireland only has filed one, and a minor one at that.
[70] See for a similar critique, O'Connell (2004), *Critical Perspective*, 5.

Prior to incorporation, the ECHR remained an international convention without immediate validity in domestic law,[71] and its status was, at best, a distant standard of interpretation for judges, whose rank in the legal order did not matter as a result. Its impact on British law in the early years was quite limited. At times, lawyers would quote the ECtHR's case law in their submissions, and judges would apply principles analogous to those in the European Court's judgements, but they did so usually to state the conformity of British law with the Convention.[72] Courts that invoked the ECtHR's case law did so just as they did for comparative law more generally, as they might cite a ruling of the US Supreme Court, for example.

The Convention's impact began to increase in the late 80's.[73] Before 1988, for example, the Convention was rarely mentioned in domestic judgements, between nil and fifteen times per year. After 1988, their number exploded. In the 70's, such references were short and passing; by 1990, they became more detailed and systematic in cases where judges worked to interpret uncertain or ambiguous UK norms in conformity with the Convention.

Thus, even before incorporation, judges gained experience using the ECHR as an interpretive aid.[74] The first reported case of this kind was *R v. Miah* in 1973 in which the court interpreted the Immigration Act 1971 in conformity with Article 7 ECHR and the prohibition of retrospective penal sanctions.[75] Judicial use of the Convention to clarify ambiguities in the common law was initially more contested, however, since it implied a more active lawmaking posture.[76] Gradually, however, Convention-compliant interpretation was extended to common law as well, culminating in the *Derbyshire* case.[77] The Convention was also invoked to assist in the exercise of judicial discretion, most famously so in the *Spycatcher* case where the Convention was referred to at all judicial levels in the litigation of the case.[78] From the 90's onwards, reference to the ECHR became a regular component of virtually all judgements pertaining to human rights.

The legitimacy of Convention-compliant judicial interpretation rested on

---

[71] By immediate validity, the present report means validity *qua* national legal norm in the national legal order without transposition into national law. Immediate validity usually also means direct applicability to all authorities, although we will see this should sometimes be nuanced. Direct applicability should be carefully distinguished from direct effect which pertains to the justiciability of the norm and more generally its direct invocability by individuals.

[72] See e.g. *Zoernsch v. Waldock*, [1964] 1 WLR 675; *Broome v. Cassell & Co* [1972] AC 1027. See more generally on judicial references to the Convention before 2000, Hunt (1997); Bratza (1991); Blackburn (2001), 950 et seq.

[73] See e.g. Jacobs and Roberts (1987).

[74] See e.g. *R. v. Secretary of State for the Home Department ex parte Phansopkar* [1976] 1 QB 606; *Home Secretary, ex parte Brind* [1991] 1 AC 696.

[75] *R v. Miah*, [1974] 1 WLR 683.

[76] See *Malone v. Metropolitan Police Commissioner* (*supra* note 39), 379.

[77] See e.g. *Derbyshire County Council v. Times Newspapers*, [1992] 1 QB 770, 812–813, Court of Appeal; [1993] AC 534, House of Lords.

[78] See e.g. *Attorney General v. Guardian Newspapers (Spycatcher)* [1987] 1 WLR 1287, 1296.

identifying some uncertainty or ambiguity in the law to be applied, since the judge would be eschewing the normal, literal approach to, say, statutory interpretation. According to Lord Scarman in *Phansokpar* and to Lord Bridge in *Brind*, however, there was by then a clear duty vested on public authorities administering the law and of courts interpreting and applying the law to have regard to the Convention.[79] While it was a duty to have regard to the Convention, this did not entail a duty to fully apply the latter. As a result, Convention-compliant interpretation was never extended to the exercise of discretionary powers conferred upon public bodies. The reverse would have involved imputing to Parliament "an intention to import the Convention into domestic law through the back door when it has quite clearly refrained from doing so by the front door", by granting discretionary powers.[80]

References to the ECtHR's case law were rarer. If the British dualist approach to the ECHR prevented courts from considering its provisions as binding, the ECtHR's case law was deemed as even less relevant, especially with respect to decisions involving other countries (although there are important exceptions[81]).

Although the ECHR's rank was never really in question before incorporation, judges applied a presumption of compatibility with the ECHR.[82] What this meant was that certain aspects of British law were presumed to be in conformity with the Convention and hence were to be interpreted in conformity with it.[83] The Parliament could not indeed be presumed to have intended violating Convention rights. Of course, if the intention of the Parliament to legislate in contradiction to the Convention was clearly stated, such an interpretation was not possible by respect for Parliamentary sovereignty. Moreover, when a Convention-compliant interpretation was simply not possible without breaching the statute, two cases could arise. First, if the incompatible legislation was primary, it simply remained valid. Second, if it was subordinate legislation that could not be interpreted in conformity with the Convention, it could be quashed and declared invalid.

b. Post-Incorporation Validity and Rank

After incorporation, the Convention gained immediate validity in the British legal order. With the HRA 1998, the ECHR has become the source of statutory rights, and the ECtHR's case law pertaining to them directly binds public

---

[79] See *R. v. Secretary of State for the Home Department ex parte Phansopkar* (*supra* note 74). See also *Home Secretary, ex parte Brind* (*supra* note 74); [1991] All ER 720, 722–723.

[80] *Home Secretary, ex parte Brind* (*supra* note 74), 718.

[81] See e.g. *Malone v. Metropolitan Police Commissioner* (*supra* note 39), 379, by reference to *Klass and Others v. Germany* (appl. no. 5029/71), Judgement (Plenary), 6 September 1978, Series A, Vol. 28; [1979–1980] 2 EHRR 214. See also *United Kingdom Association of Professional Engineers v. Advisory, Conciliation and Arbitration Service* (HL) [1980] 2 WLR 254; *Attorney General v. Guardian Newspapers Ltd (No. 2)* [1988] 3 All ER 545 (Ch.).

[82] Blackburn (2001), 950.

[83] See *Home Secretary, ex parte Brind* (*supra* note 74); [1991] All ER 720, 722–723. See also more recently, Lord Hoffmann in *R. v. Home Secretary, ex parte Simms* [2000] 2 AC 115, 131.

authorities, and must be considered in national courts, alone or alongside other sources of law. Two key features characterize the new status and validity of the Convention in British law: the direct applicability of Convention rights to the acts and decisions of "public authorities" including courts; and the indirect applicability of Convention rights to the acts of Parliament. The balance between the eminently interpretive approach to unconventional statutes and the identification of a few cases of Convention-related invalidity explains why one may also refer to the model of incorporation used in the HRA as a semi-direct incorporation.

The meaning of "public authority" (Section 6 paras 3 and 5 HRA) is contested.[84] The HRA defines courts and tribunals as public authorities, which means that they must apply Convention rights directly when reaching their decisions, and that they can be held accountable if they fail to do so. As a result, convention rights are today used regularly to interpret both legislation and the common law.[85] Under Section 2 para. 1 HRA, while British courts must take into account the European Court's case law, they are not strictly speaking bound by it. For reasons pertaining to Parliamentary sovereignty, both Houses of Parliament and persons exercising Parliamentary functions are expressly excluded from the notion of "public authorities" (Section 6 para. 3 HRA). As a result, Members of Parliament cannot be held accountable for infringing Convention rights in legislation. Nor can a public authority that implements legislation incompatible with the Convention be said to have acted unlawfully, so long as it could not have acted differently without breaching the statute (Section 6 para. 2 HRA). The only way a judge may prevent or remedy a legislative breach of the Convention is to interpret a statute in conformity with the Convention.

Prior to incorporation, the ECHR's rank in domestic law was never really in question.[86] Since incorporation, the issue has become more pressing. In a nutshell, the incorporation model used in the HRA is sub-constitutional: the Act is not entrenched, and it does not confer upon Convention rights any degree of constitutional priority over earlier or subsequent domestic legislation. That said, subsequent legislation can only resist a Convention-compliant interpretation if the Parliament's intention was clear and express; even then, a court might issue a declaration of incompatibility, thus placing political pressure on the Parliament to amend the law. As a result, some consider that the HRA has some supra-legislative elements. To emphasize the paradox, the HRA is sometimes referred to as a constitutional statute.[87]

[84] See *infra* Section III. F.
[85] See e.g. in the field of privacy: *Campbell v. Mirror Group Newspapers* [2004] 2 WLR 1232.
[86] The issue of "rank" has traditionally only been addressed as one of "status" in British law; there is indeed strictly speaking no supra-legislative category in British law. All there is is primary and secondary legislation, and the common law. The often used concept of "constitutional statute" is recent; the House of Lords refers to statutes "of constitutional importance", whose construction must be generous and whose repeal may only be done explicitly. In order to ensure consistency with the other reports in the volume, however, the concept of "rank" will be used in what follows.
[87] See Black-Branch (2002); Elliot (2002).

Two complementary mechanisms capture this mix of sub-constitutional/supra-legislative rank of Convention rights in British law: the courts' duty to interpret legislation in conformity with the Convention and, when the former is not possible, their duty to declare legislation incompatible with the Convention.

The most far-reaching principle in the whole Act is Section 3 HRA, which instructs the courts to read and give effect to legislation in a Convention-compatible way. The rule – when there is more than one interpretation possible, the one that complies most with the Convention should be chosen – replaces the traditional common law practice of ascertaining the true meaning of the statute, or establishing the intention of the Parliament.[88] According to Section 3 para. 2(a) HRA, the duty of Convention-compliant interpretation applies to all past and present Acts of Parliament. There is one exception to this rule: cases where the Parliament has expressly declared its intention to infringe the Convention and hence where Convention-compliant interpretation is not possible without breaching the statute.

When a Convention-compliant interpretation is not possible, the HRA distinguishes between primary and subordinate legislation. Judges may declare subordinate legislation invalid, if it cannot be interpreted in conformity with the ECHR, unless the source of its incompatibility is primary legislation (Section 3 paras 2(b) and (c) HRA *a contrario*).[89] But Section 3 does not affect the validity of incompatible primary legislation (Section 3 paras 2(b) and (c)), a concession to Parliamentary sovereignty.[90] Where a Convention-compliant interpretation of incompatible primary legislation is not possible, Section 4 HRA enables higher courts to make a declaration of incompatibility.[91] For England and Wales, the following courts have power to make such a declaration: the High Court, Court of Appeal, House of Lords, Judicial Committee of the Privy Council, and the Courts-Martial Appeal Court. Where a lesser court or tribunal is faced with such an issue, it must apply the incompatible legislation and the matter will only be addressed again on appeal. The declaration of incompatibility is not *erga omnes*. It merely invites and requires the Parliament to rectify the situation by passing the appropriate repealing legislation.[92] Although there is no remedy for a Parliamentary breach of the ECHR, decisions of incompatibility have political weight

---

[88] See e.g. Marshall (1996) and (1999); Lester (1998), *Interpreting Statutes*; Steyn (1998); Kavanagh (2004), *Anderson; Interpretation and Legislation*, (2005) and (2006).

[89] See Hoffman and Rowe (2003), 60.

[90] See e.g. *R. v. Lyons* [2002] WLR 1562, 1580, 1584, 1595. This was confirmed later on by the European Court in *Lyons and Others v. the United Kingdom* (appl. no. 15227/03), Decision (Fourth Section), 8 July 2003, Reports 2003-IX, 405 et seq.; [2003] 37 EHRR CD 183.

[91] The first declaration ever made was issued in *R v. Secretary of State for the Environment, ex parte Alconbury* [2001] 2 All ER 929.

[92] See e.g. *Wilson v. First County Trust Limited* [2001] 3 WLR 42. See also the follow-up of other cases like *R. (Anderson) v. Secretary of State for the Home Department* [2002] UKHL 46 [2003] 1 AC 837 (right to life of convicted murderers) or *Bellinger v. Bellinger* [2003] UKHL 21, [2003] 2 AC 467 (rights of post-operative transsexuals).

and are, therefore, "likely to prompt government and Parliament to respond".[93] The HRA foresees the introduction of amending legislation by the competent Minister or the Crown,[94] including under a fast-track procedure (Section 10 and Schedule 2 HRA).[95]

2. Ireland

a. Pre-Incorporation Validity and Rank

The Irish Constitution is strongly dualist: Article 29 para. 6 states that an international agreement can only be made part of Irish law through legislative incorporation. Prior to the ECHR Act in 2003, the Convention was binding *on* Ireland, but not *in* it.[96] The ECHR had no strict validity in Irish Law. As in the UK, it mostly operated as a standard of interpretation. As a result, the ECHR's rank in the legal order was not a matter of interest either.

The Irish Parliament hardly ever invoked the Convention when passing a law, and judges did not entertain Convention-specific challenges to legislative, executive or judicial measures. Courts might take note of Convention rights and of the ECtHR's case law, but they were not required to. Although the first reference to the Convention occurred in the Supreme Court decision in *Re O Laighléis* in 1960,[97] judicial references were sporadic until the 80's. It is only after the 80's that High Court judges[98] began invoking the Convention to bolster their reasoning in relation to a matter of Irish law.[99] The Supreme Court took pains not to do so, even when the case at bar presented similar facts to a case decided by the ECtHR.[100] Where the Supreme Court did invoke the Convention, it was only to make explicit something which was already implicit in the Irish Constitution.[101]

Of course, judges were expected to presume that Irish law conformed with

[93] Lord Chancellor Lord Irvine, House of Lords Debates, 3 November 1997, vol. 582, col. 1231. This was confirmed by the European Court in *Burden and Burden v. the United Kingdom* (appl. no. 13378/05), Judgement (Fourth Section), 12 December 2006, referred to the Grand Chamber (not yet reported); [2007] 44 EHRR 51.

[94] The first use of the remedial order procedure took place in 2002 in *R. (H.) v. Mental Health Tribunal North and East London Region* [2002] QB 1 (CA).

[95] See *infra* Section III. E.

[96] See Kilkelly (2004), *Introduction*, lvi; Symmons (2005).

[97] *Re O Laighleis* [1960] IR 93.

[98] See e.g. *O'Leary v. Attorney General* [1993] 1 IR 102; *Heaney v. Ireland* [1994] 2 ILRM 420. Compare with *O'Leary v. Attorney General* [1995] 1 IR 254, 259; *Heaney v. Ireland* [1996] 1 IR 580. See, however, the dissenting judgements of McGuinness and Fennelly, JJ., in *L & O v. Minister of Justice, Equality and Law Reform* [2003] 1 IR.

[99] See O'Connell et al. (2006), 11; O'Connell (2001), 427; Flynn (1994); Whyte (1982).

[100] See e.g. *Finucane v. McMahon*, [1990] IR 165, to be compared to *Soering v. the United Kingdom* (appl. no. 14038/88), Judgement (Plenary), 7 July 1989, Series A, Vol. 161; [1989] 11 EHRR 439. See also *Norris v. Attorney General* (*supra* note 3) to be compared to *Dudgeon v. the United Kingdom* (*supra* note 3)

[101] See e.g. *The Irish Times and Others v. His Honour Judge Anthony G. Murphy and Others*, [1982] 2 ILRM 161, 192–193.

the Convention, and to interpret it in conformity with the ECHR.[102] This presumption applied to statutes adopted after 1953, provided there was no contrary intention on the part of the Legislature (it could not be used *contra legem*). Such cases were rare, not least since the presumption was not easily applicable in the context of constitutional rights.[103] The Irish Supreme Court never mentioned the possibility of interpreting Irish law in conformity with the Convention, as long as there was a concurrent constitutionality challenge.[104]

b. Post-Incorporation Validity and Rank

As in the UK, the ECHR Act 2003 incorporates Convention rights into Irish law in an indirect (interpretive) way. The 2003 ECHR Act distinguishes between the direct applicability of the Convention to the acts and decisions of some State organs, with the important exception of courts, and the indirect applicability to the acts of the Irish Parliament.

According to Section 3 ECHR Act, courts do not belong to the listed "organs of the State" and are not therefore directly bound by Convention rights. They are not placed under a duty to apply the Convention directly, a substantial limitation in a legal system based on judicial law-making and which knows of far-reaching constitutional constructions of legislation in court.[105] Though this exclusion may protect judges from suit for breach of statutory duty, they are still subject to applications before the ECtHR, and before the European Court of Justice in EU matters.[106] Although courts must take notice of the relevant case law of the ECtHR, they are not strictly speaking bound by the European Court's case law.[107]

Because the Parliament is excluded from the list of "organs of the State" under Section 3 of the Act, remedies cannot be sought directly in cases where legislation is not Convention-compliant. Judges can only interpret legislation in compliance with the Convention under Section 2 of the Act to give it effect in cases at bar. Where a compliant interpretation is not possible, Section 5 para. 1 ECHR Act provides that the High Court or Supreme Court may, where no other legal remedy is adequate or available, declare that the statutory provision is Convention-incompatible.

Since 2003, the ECHR possesses sub-constitutional rank in Irish law. The Convention preempts neither the supremacy of the Irish Constitution nor the primacy of Parliament with respect to the Convention. The transplantation of

---

[102] See e.g. *The State (DPP) v. Walsh and Conneely* [1981] IR 412, 440. See also *Desmond v. Glackin* [1992] ILRM 490, 513.

[103] See e.g. *O'Domhnaill v. Merrick* [1984] IR 151, 159, 166.

[104] See e.g. *Norris v. Attorney General* (*supra* note 3), 66.

[105] O'Connell (2004), *Critical Perspective*, 7.

[106] See e.g. *Doran v. Ireland* (appl. no. 50389/99), Judgement (Third Section), 31 July 2003, Reports 2003-X, 1 et seq. (extracts); [2006] 42 EHRR 13. In EU law, see e.g. case C-224/01, *Gerhard Köbler v. Republik Österreich* [2003] ECR I-10239.

[107] See *infra* Section III. F.

the British sub-constitutional mode of incorporation into Ireland appears somewhat incoherent, however, in that it does not match the Irish pre-existing human
rights tradition and its judicial review mechanisms.[108] In fact, the Irish mode
of incorporation is even more moderate than that of the UK, in that judges
may not base the direct invalidation of (subordinate) legislation on Convention
rights, but may only interpret the former in favour of the latter, and, when this is
not possible, declare the statute incompatible. This is surprising given that Irish
courts have long experience with rights review and corresponding invalidation of
statute law. Further, the remedies foreseen in case of breach of the ECHR Act are
residual, available to higher courts only, and apply only to a more limited list of
public authorities. This conservative approach may surprise, given the objective
of the ECHR Act to give "further effect" to the Convention in Irish law.

According to Section 2 para. 1 ECHR Act, there is a rebuttable presumption
of compatibility of legislation, a kind of 'double construction rule', on the model
of what already applies to the control of constitutionality of statutes in Ireland.
This rule, which trumps other doctrines of interpretation, requires that courts,
when faced with a choice between two constructions of a statute, one constitutional and the other unconstitutional, choose the constitutional construction.[109]
Applied to the ECHR, interpretations of legislation which are in conformity
with the Convention must be chosen. Contrary to the HRA, Section 2 ECHR
Act does not distinguish between subordinate and primary legislation, or between prior and ulterior primary legislation. When a Convention-compliant
interpretation is not possible, the validity of the incompatible legislation remains
untouched, whether it is subordinate or primary and whether the incompatibility
of an ulterior legislative act is intentional or not. This feature of the ECHR Act
has been heavily criticized for "placing the courts in a position where they can
identify a breach of human rights and not be in a position to give an effective
remedy."[110] In the absence of remedy, courts are led to construct statutes in the
most artificial way or else to declare them unconstitutional,[111] in order to make
sure they do not leave the claimant without relief or remedy.[112] The Irish Human

---

[108] See O'Connell (2004), *Critical Perspective*.

[109] Kelly (2003), 884. See *Re National Irish Bank* [1999] 1 IR 145; *Doyle v. An Taoiseach* [1986]
ILRM 693.

[110] Irish Human Rights Commission, Submission to the Joint Oireachtas Committee on Justice,
Equality, Defence and Women's Rights (2002), 4.

[111] Interestingly, two recent appeals to the Supreme Court are about to test its willingness to
use the Convention when the Constitution does not provide a clear answer: *M.R. v. T.R. & Others*
[2006] IEHC 359 (frozen embryos) and *Zappone and Gilligan v. Revenue Commissioners* [2006]
IEHC 404 (gay marriage).

[112] See Hogan (2004), 30–31, 21–22, 34: "The Constitution and its declaration of constitutional
invalidity mechanism is, so to speak, like a vintage car (which has been constantly overhauled and
renovated) with a powerful engine and automatic gears. By comparison, the United Kingdoms'
Human Rights Act model – with its declaration of incompatibility which ultimately depends on
Parliament – resembles a new car with complicated manual gears, albeit one in respect of which
the new owners – who never had a car before and who had spent much of the previous generation

Rights Commission argues in this respect that the whole procedure is of "questionable constitutional validity".[113]

A declaration of incompatibility – issued against a statutory provision or other rule of law – does not affect the validity, continuing operation, or enforcement of the relevant legal provision (Section 5 para. 2(a) ECHR Act). In contrast to Section 4 HRA, however, the remedy provided is purely residual, since it only applies to cases "where no other legal remedy is adequate or available". Once a court makes a declaration of incompatibility, the Human Rights Commission is notified. The declaration must then be placed before each House of Parliament within 21 days. In contrast to the HRA regime, the Parliament is not required to indicate what remedial action (if any) is to be taken, no fast-track procedures for remedies are provided for, and there is no obligation to pay compensation.[114]

3. Comparison and Conclusion

Although both countries chose more or less the same mode of incorporation, the validity of Convention rights varies extensively in practice, given pre-existing differences in constitutional rights culture. In the UK, incorporation filled a gap of huge importance in the British legal order, and the HRA grants British courts review powers they did not possess before.[115] Public authorities directly bound by the HRA include courts. And, even though they exclude Parliament, the possibility to invalidate subordinate legislation when it is incompatible with the Convention is worth emphasising. In Ireland, by contrast, the incorporation of the Convention looks much less dramatic, even beside the point, in comparison to the force of, and remedies available under, the Constitution. Litigants may plead Convention rights against some public authorities but not against Parliament or the courts, while the equivalent Irish constitutional rights can be invoked against all authorities including the Irish Parliament. Further, given that the Judiciary has continuously expanded the scope and content of constitutional rights, it would seem that Convention rights have been given a residual, almost superfluous status, at least in some areas. Thus, while dualism implies the choice to incorporate or not to incorporate, the importance of incorporation will depend heavily on a state's domestic tradition of rights protection.

With respect to the Convention's rank in national law, the 1998 HRA and

---

protesting that they did not need one – are extremely proud. To continue the metaphor, Ireland, in order to keep up appearances, has now also acquired the same type of car with manual gears and is presently contemplating – having grown up with the automatic models – which of the two models we would prefer to drive and whether, indeed, they can both be safely driven in harmony at the same time. […] All of this means that, in the end, we will find that we are still driving the 1937 vintage model, albeit that its power and capacity have been boosted by spare parts borrowed from the 1998 and 2003 models."

[113] Irish Human Rights Commission, Submission to the Joint Oireachtas Committee on Justice, Equality, Defence and Women's Rights (2002), 4.

[114] See *infra* Section III. F.

[115] See Lord Hope of Craighead, *R v. DPP ex parte Kebilene* [2000] 2 AC 326, 375.

the 2003 ECHR Act follow the same statutory sovereignty model, conferring on Convention rights sub-constitutional rank. This similarity, too, is less important than the fact that both countries have very different approaches to rights and judicial review of legislation. In the UK, where there are no entrenched constitutional rights and the Parliament is supreme, the HRA is gradually becoming a kind of constitutional statute. It has nuanced the implied repeal principle, which was already weakened by developments in EU law. In Ireland, due, somewhat ironically, to the existence of an entrenched Constitution and strong judicial review of legislation, the Convention has had less impact on the legal order. One can state that Convention rights occupy a *de jure* sub-constitutional but nonetheless *de facto* supra-legislative rank in the UK. In Ireland, the ECHR has only an (indirect) legislative rank. Time will tell how effective the Convention will actually be in either country, but there currently appear to be more obstinate structural obstacles to enhancing the ECHR's effectiveness in Ireland, compared to the UK.

C. The European Court's Case Law

1. *United Kingdom*

a. General Overview

This section focuses on cases brought by individual petition to the ECtHR.[116] The ECtHR rendered its first adverse judgement against the UK on 21 February 1975, in the case *Golder v. UK*.[117] In total, 11,994 applications have been registered against the UK before the Court and the Committee of Ministers through 31 December 2006. 255 of these cases were decided by the Court on the merits,[118] and the others were struck out of the list for various reasons. From 1953 to 1999, the number of cases decided on the merits increased slowly but steadily (see table), from between nil and three each year during the 1975–85 period, to a high of seven per year in the 80's, a high of twelve per year in the 90's, and a high of 34 per year in the 2000's. In 53 years of membership in the Convention system, fully half of the judgements of the ECtHR pertaining to the UK were rendered between 2000 and 2006. The number of decisions rendered since 2000 averages 22 *per annum*, due undoubtedly to the growing awareness of the Convention in the UK, post-incorporation. Numbers have decreased during the last three years (between fifteen and twenty per year since 2004). This decline

---

[116] Besides individual applications, one should mention numerous interstate applications brought against the United Kingdom, including the first one ever in 1956 (*Greece v. the United Kingdom* (*supra* note 23)) or the case brought against the United Kingdom by Ireland in 1978 (*Ireland v. the United Kingdom* (*supra* note 51)).

[117] *Golder v. the United Kingdom* (appl. no. 4451/70), Judgement (Plenary), 21 February 1975, Series A, Vol. 18; [1979–80] 1 EHRR 524.

[118] Scope precludes listing them all here. See, however, tables in appendix.

is likely due to a better incorporation of conventional concerns in domestic decisions and to the increasing effectiveness of Convention rights and case law in the legal order more generally.[119]

Of the 255 judgements that have gone against the UK (see tables), the majority (148 rulings) pertain to Article 6(1) or (3) ECHR, followed, notably, by 75 judgements relative to Article 8 ECHR and 56 to Article 13 ECHR. 198 of these rulings resulted in a judgement in condemnation, leading either to the payment of compensation or to legislative change. In a predictable way, most decisions of non-violation occurred after the increase of cases brought against the UK in Strasbourg after 2000.

A statistical assessment of all cases brought before the ECtHR and decided on the merits, shows that the UK has one of the highest totals among the Council of Europe's original Member States. This high number of cases overall may be explained in several ways. First, the fact that the UK did not incorporate the Convention into British law before 2000 may have led to an initial spike in cases. Second, the lack of entrenched rights and the weakness of rights-based remedies in the UK might have made going to Strasbourg attractive. Third, the UK has experienced serious anti-terrorism difficulties (first in Northern Ireland and then in the rest of the UK as well[120]) and complex immigration problems (due to its former and present overseas territories), and these have provoked a steady flow of cases over decades. Finally, the associative and support network in the field of human rights has grown in the UK, arguably without comparison in Europe; voluntary human rights associations, non-governmental organizations and *pro bono* work in the legal profession are particularly well-organized and common in the UK.[121] These groups have always supported individual litigation in British courts and before the European Court, helping to push up the UK's numbers.

b. Selected Examples

The subjects addressed in the UK cases before the European Court are diverse. They range from telephone-tapping, closed-shop trade union practices, discretionary life sentences, official birching of juvenile offenders, corporal in schools, over-restrictive injunctions on freedom of expression, punishment for non-disclosure of journalistic sources of information, parents' rights of access to children, access to child-care records, prisoners' right of access to a lawyer, oppressive use of incriminatory self-statement at trial, inhumane treatment of terrorist suspects, homosexuality in Northern Ireland, status of frozen embryos, discriminatory im-

---

[119] See e.g. Gearty (2004).

[120] On the difference, see Gearty (2006), 104–105.

[121] One may mention civil liberties pressure groups, like *Liberty* (the National Council for Civil Liberties), *Amnesty* or *Justice*. For other organizations, see the British Human Rights Institute's website: http://www.bihr.org/. See also *infra* Section III. G.

migration rules and inhumane extradition procedures.[122] Interestingly, landmark decisions were released by the ECtHR in British cases and have had an impact on the development of a European constitutional order. This has been the case of British applications concerning the rights of persons compulsorily detained in psychiatric institutions,[123] but also of cases pertaining to euthanasia,[124] torture and extradition.[125] The present report concentrates on cases that have had the most impact on British law, namely those based on Articles 3, 6, 8, and 10 ECHR.

aa. The treatment of terrorist suspects. Anti-terrorism legislation and measures have given rise to numerous complaints against the UK since the 70's, first with respect to Northern Ireland and recently with respect to post-9/11 anti-terrorism measures. The first case against the UK on this issue was brought in 1971 by Ireland,[126] which complained *inter alia* of interrogation techniques introduced in Northern Ireland. The Court declared these techniques to be inhumane and contrary to Article 3 ECHR. In 1988, the Court decided in *Brogan and Others v. UK*[127] that the UK had violated Article 5(3) ECHR by holding terrorist suspects between four and six days under the Prevention of Terrorism Act 1983, without bringing them before a judge. Following this case, the UK lodged a derogation under Article 15(1) ECHR. Its lawfulness was confirmed by the Court in *Brannigan and McBride v. UK* in 1993.[128] The derogation was finally withdrawn in 2001. In 1995 *McCann, Farrell and Savage v. UK* case, the Court decided that the UK had violated Article 2 ECHR by allowing the shooting of three terrorist suspects in Gibraltar by UK SAS soldiers.[129] The ECtHR rendered further rulings relative to security forces' violence in Northern Ireland and in particular

---

[122] For detailed accounts of the European case law pertaining to the UK until 2000, see Blackburn (2001), 971–991; Dickson (1997), chapters 3, 4, 5 and 7; Gearty (1997), 84–100; Farran (1996); Bradley (1991), 185–214; Hampson (1990), 121.

[123] See e.g. *H.L. v. the United Kingdom* (appl. no. 45508/99), Judgement (Fourth Section), 5 October 2004, Reports 2004-IX, 191 et seq.; [2005] 40 EHRR 32; *Johnson v. the United Kingdom* (appl. no. 22520/93), Judgement (Chamber), 24 October 1997, Reports 1997-VII, 2391 et seq.; [1999] 27 EHRR 296.

[124] See e.g. *Pretty v. the United Kingdom* (appl. no. 2346/02), Judgement (Fourth Section), 29 April 2002, Reports 2002-III, 155 et seq.; [2002] 35 EHRR 1.

[125] See e.g. *Chahal v. the United Kingdom* (appl. no. 22414/93), Judgement (Grand Chamber), 15 November 1996, Reports 1996-V, 1831 et seq.; [1997] 23 EHRR 413.

[126] *Ireland v. the United Kingdom* (*supra* note 51).

[127] *Brogan, Coyle, McFaden and Tracey v. the United Kingdom* (appl. nos 11209/84; 11234/84; 11266/84; 11386/85), Judgement (Plenary), 29 November 1988, Series A, Vol. 145-B; [1989] 11 EHRR 117.

[128] *Brannigan and McBride v. the United Kingdom* (appl. nos 14553/89; 14553/89), Judgement (Plenary), 26 May 1993, Series A, Vol. 258-B; [1994] 17 EHRR 539.

[129] *McCann, Farrell and Savage v. the United Kingdom* (appl. no. 18984/91), Judgement (Grand Chamber), 27 September 1995, Series A, Vol. 324; [1996] 21 EHRR 97.

McKerr v. UK in 2001[130] and *Finucane v. UK* in 2003.[131] New cases pertaining to Articles 2 and 3 ECHR are likely to arise in the next few years with respect to anti-terrorist measures adopted in the UK since 2005.

bb. The protection of freedom of the press. Another set of landmark decisions of the European Court on UK complaints concerns actions brought by newspapers to protect their freedom of expression. In *Sunday Times v. UK* (1979), the Court decided that, although some limitation on press freedom was necessary to protect the independence and the working of the courts, a number of competing factors had to be taken into account, such as the right to impart but also to receive information of public importance and the level of likelihood of serious prejudice to the trial.[132] In another famous ruling, *Spycatcher* (1991), the Court decided that an injunction against publication violates Article 10 ECHR when the book that is the object of the injunction has already been published elsewhere.[133]

cc. The treatment of homosexuals and transsexuals. In *Dudgeon v. UK* (1981), the Court decided that the UK had violated Article 8 ECHR for failing to repeal a Northern Ireland law imposing criminal sanctions upon homosexual activities between consenting male adults. In a long judgement, the European Court argued that most Member States of the Council of Europe did not treat homosexuality as a criminal offence and held that interference with the applicant's right to private life could not be justified on the ground of what was necessary in a democratic society, pressing social need or injury to moral standards.[134] A more recent 1999 case concerned the armed forces. In *Lustig Prean and Beckett v. UK*, the Court held that the discharge of four applicants from the armed forces on the ground of their homosexuality violated Article 8 ECHR.[135] The Court determined that there was a lack of concrete evidence to substantiate the alleged damage to morale and operational effectiveness in cases where homosexuals were admitted to the armed forces. Transsexuals in the UK also benefited from the European Court's interpretation of Article 8 ECHR. After a series of cases brought against the UK pertaining to the rights of transsexuals where no violation was

---

[130] *McKerr v. the United Kingdom* (appl. no. 28883/95), Judgement (Third Section), 4 May 2001, Reports 2001-III, 475 et seq.; [2002] 34 EHRR 20.

[131] *Finucane v. the United Kingdom* (appl. no. 29178/95), Judgement (Fourth Section), 1 July 2003, Reports 2003-VIII, 1 et seq.; [2003] 37 EHRR 29.

[132] *Sunday Times v. the United Kingdom* (appl. no. 6538/74), Judgement (Plenary), 26 April 1979, Series A, Vol. 30; [1979–1980] 2 EHRR 245.

[133] *The Observer and The Guardian v. the United Kingdom* (appl. no. 13585/88), Judgement (Plenary), 26 November 1991, Series A, Vol. 216; [1992] 14 EHRR 153.

[134] *Dudgeon v. the United Kingdom* (*supra* note 3).

[135] *Lustig-Prean and Beckett v. the United Kingdom* (appl. nos 31417/96; 32377/96), Judgement (Third Section), 27 September 1999 (not reported); [2000] 29 EHRR 548.

found,[136] the European Court rendered two judgements in 2002 (*Christine Goodwin v. UK* and *I. v. UK*), in which it held that the Government's failure to alter the birth certificates of transsexual people or to allow them to marry in their new gender role was a breach of Articles 8 and 12 ECHR.[137] The *Christine Goodwin v. UK* judgement was recently confirmed in 2006 in *Grant v. UK*.[138]

dd. The organization of the State. In *McGonnell v. UK* (2000), the European Court decided that the UK had violated the claimant's right to a fair hearing by an independent and impartial tribunal under Article 6 ECHR on the ground that the presiding judge of the Royal Court of Guernsey, the Bailiff, had also been the presiding officer in the Guernsey Parliament, which enacted the legislation restricting the claimant's land use.[139] The case was very controversial, given similar overlaps existing between Parliamentary and judicial functions in the House of Lords, but also between the executive, Parliamentary and judicial functions of the Lord Chancellor.

ee. The protection of parents' and children's rights. In the case *P., C. and S. v. UK* (2002), the ECtHR ruled that the absence of legal representation for the applicant in the care and adoption proceedings of her own children breached Article 6(1) and Article 8 ECHR, and that the removal of the applicant's child immediately after birth could not be justified under Article 8(2) ECHR, and, therefore, breached the Convention.[140] In another case *E. and Others v. UK* (2002), the Court held in relation to two applicants who, as children, had been subjected to severe physical and sexual abuse in their home, that local authority social services should have known of the abuse, since the mother's partner had a past history of sexual abuse against children in the family. The Court decided that social services had taken insufficient steps to investigate or prevent the abuse, in breach of their positive duty to protect from inhuman or degrading treatment under Article 3 ECHR.[141]

---

[136] See e.g. *Rees v. the United Kingdom* (appl. no. 9532/81), Judgement (Plenary), 17 October 1986, Series A, Vol. 106; [1987] 9 EHRR 56; *Cossey v. the United Kingdom* (appl. no. 10843/84), Judgement (Plenary), 27 September 1990, Series A, Vol. 184; [1991] 13 EHRR 622; *Sheffield and Horsham v. the United Kingdom* (appl. nos 22985/93; 23390/94), Judgement (Grand Chamber), 30 July 1998, Reports 1998-V, 2011 et seq.; [1999] 27 EHRR 163.

[137] *Christine Goodwin v. the United Kingdom* (appl. no. 28957/95), Judgement (Grand Chamber), 11 July 2002, Reports 2002-VI, 1 et seq.; [2002] 35 EHRR 18; *I. v. the United Kingdom* (appl. no. 25680/94), Judgement (Grand Chamber), 11 July 2002 (not reported); [2003] 36 EHRR 53.

[138] *Grant v. the United Kingdom* (appl. no. 32570/03), Judgement (Fourth Section), 23 May 2006 (not yet reported); [2007] 44 EHRR 1.

[139] See e.g. *McGonnell v. the United Kingdom* (*supra* note 12). See Cornes (2000).

[140] *P., C. and S. v. the United Kingdom* (appl. no. 56547/00), Judgement (Second Section), 16 July 2002, Reports 2002-VI, 197 et seq.; [2002] 35 EHRR 31.

[141] *E. and Others v. the United Kingdom* (appl. no. 33218/96), Judgement (Second Section), 26 November 2002 (not reported); [2003] 36 EHRR 31.

ff. Protection against self-incrimination and the right to silence. In *Allan v. UK* (2002), the Court examined the case of an applicant placed under surveillance whilst held on remand on charges of murder, subject to electronic surveillance in his cell and in the visiting area of the prison, and placed in a cell with a police informant who was instructed to press him for information. The Court ruled that the UK violated Article 6 ECHR and the right to silence and to freedom from self-incrimination in allowing the use of the transcripts of the surveillance, as well as the use of evidence from the police informer in trial.[142] This case followed the 1996 decision in *John Murray v. UK* on the inferences drawn from the silence of the accused.[143]

2. Ireland

a. General Overview

With Sweden, Ireland was among the first Contracting States to accept the right of individual petition to the ECtHR. In total, 524 applications have been registered against Ireland before the Court and the Committee of Ministers through 31 December 2006, of which eighteen were decided on the merits – the others were struck off the list for different reasons. As the tables show, there have never been more than three ECtHR judgements rendered per year. In 53 years of membership in the Convention system, three-fifths of the judgements of the ECtHR pertaining to Ireland were rendered between 2000 and 2005. This increase of cases in recent years can be explained by the growing awareness of the Convention since the entry into force of the ECHR Act in Ireland in 2003. There have been no judgements on the merits against Ireland since December 2005.

Half of the eigtheen ECtHR judgements concerning Ireland pertain to Article 6(1) ECHR, closely followed by six judgements relative to Article 8 ECHR. While eighteen cases is a relatively low number, thirteen of these applications were successful and resulted in a judgement in violation, leading either to the payment of compensation or to legislative change. Overall, the numbers place Ireland among the countries with the lowest total of cases filed and of adverse judgements. One might explain this exemplary record primarily by reference to the lively and strong human rights tradition in Ireland.[144] This explanation may also account, however, for the sense of jurisprudential self-sufficiency evidenced in some of the case law discussed in the previous sections.[145] One might even speculate that the lack of interest in going to Strasbourg is also partly due to the

---

[142] *Allan v. the United Kingdom* (appl. no. 48539/99), Judgement (Fourth Section), 5 November 2002, Reports 2002-IX, 420 et seq.; [2003] 36 EHRR 12.

[143] *John Murray v. the United Kingdom* (appl. no. 18731/91), Judgement (Grand Chamber), 8 February 1996, Reports 1996-I, 30 et seq.; [1996] 22 EHRR 29.

[144] See Hogan (2004), 14.

[145] See *supra* Section III. A.

relatively weaker remedies available under the ECHR Act, as well as the prospect of lengthy and costly proceedings under the ECHR.[146]

b. Selected Examples

Although the number of Irish cases before the ECtHR is relatively limited in comparison to the UK, the areas of law and society concerned reflect important crises in Ireland. Given the high degree of protection granted to fundamental rights by the Irish Constitution, the areas in which an additional conventional protection is needed, one would suppose, are those areas in which the Irish society is traditionally more conservative than the European common denominator, or where political divisions make decisions difficult. One may think, for instance, of cases pertaining to the compulsory acquisition of land by the Land Commission (until it was abolished in 1980), homosexuality, abortion, artificial reproduction and emergency or anti-terrorism measures. In those areas, political divisions are often too important to allow an easy judicial resolution of the issue and recourse to a supra-national jurisdiction is welcome.[147] Thus, the report will concentrate on the cases which concern four of the most problematic provisions for Irish law: Articles 6, 8, and 13 ECHR and Article 1 of Protocol no. 1.[148]

aa. The protection of private life. In *Johnston v. Ireland* (1978), the applicants argued that the unequal treatment of children born out of wedlock in Irish law was discriminatory, and the ECtHR agreed that the unequal treatment of the child of unmarried parents by comparison with that of the child of validly married parents constituted a violation of Article 8 ECHR.[149] In the 1988 *Norris v. Ireland* case,[150] the Court followed its judgement in *Dudgeon v. UK*[151] and argued that the criminalization of homosexual acts between men in Irish nineteenth-century legislation violated Article 8 ECHR. According to the Court, public shock or disturbance at the commission of private homosexual acts did not in itself warrant their criminalization. In *Keegan v. Ireland* (1994), the Court decided that Irish law permitting the adoption of a child without the consent of its natural father

---

[146] See Kilkelly (2004), *Introduction*, lvi; O'Connell (2001), 468.

[147] See e.g. the two recent appeals to the Supreme Court that are about to test its willingness to use the Convention when the Constitution does not provide a clear answer: *M.R. v. T.R. & Others*, [2006] IEHC 359 (frozen embryos) and *Zappone and Gilligan v. Revenue Commissioners*, [2006] IEHC 404 (gay marriage).

[148] For a presentation of all Irish cases judged on the merits, see O'Connell et al. (2006), chapter 1.

[149] *Johnston and Others v. Ireland* (appl. no. 9697/82), Judgement (Plenary), 18 December 1986, Series A, Vol. 112; [1987] 9 EHRR 203.

[150] *Norris v. Ireland* (appl. no. 10581/83), Judgement (Plenary), 26 October 1988, Series A, Vol. 142; [1991] 13 EHRR 186.

[151] *Dudgeon v. the United Kingdom* (*supra* note 3)

violated Articles 8 and 6 ECHR, as it interfered with the latter's right to respect for family life and denied his access to a hearing respectively.[152]

bb. Access to courts. In *Airey v. Ireland (No. 1)*, the applicant complained that due to the prohibitive cost of civil litigation and the absence of a scheme of legal aid in Ireland, she was effectively denied access to the courts for the purposes of seeking a judicial separation from her husband contrary to Article 6(1) ECHR. According to the Court (1979), Article 6(1) ECHR granted a positive right of access to a judge, and a correlative right not to be faced with prohibitive legal costs in doing so. Moreover, Article 8 ECHR entailed a positive duty for States to ensure respect of private and family life, and Mrs Airey's inability to avail herself of the remedy of judicial separation infringed that right.[153] In *Quinn v. Ireland* and *Heaney and McGuiness v. Ireland* (2000), three applicants were arrested and charged under Section 52 of the Offences Against the State Act 1939 by the Special Criminal Court on mere suspicion of serious terrorist offence, which the ECtHR judged violated the right to a fair trial under Article 6(1) ECHR and the presumption of innocence under Article 6(2) ECHR.[154] In two cases decided in 2004, *O'Reilly and Others v. Ireland* and *McMullen v. Ireland*, the Court found that Ireland was in breach of Articles 6(1) and 13 ECHR because of unreasonable delays arising in two sets of domestic proceedings for which there was no domestic remedy.[155] In *Barry v. Ireland* (2005), the Court held that criminal proceedings which lasted ten years and four months were excessive and failed to satisfy the reasonable time requirement under Articles 6(1) and 13 ECHR.[156]

cc. The protection of property. In the 1991 case *Pine Valley Developments and Others v. Ireland*, the Court decided that there had been discriminatory treatment contrary to Article 14 ECHR combined with Article 1 of Protocol no. 1. The second and third applicants had indeed been treated unequally in the overturning of planning permissions for development property.[157]

---

[152] *Keegan v. Ireland* (appl. no. 16969/90), Judgement (Chamber), 26 May 1994, Series A, Vol. 290; [1994] 18 EHRR 342.

[153] *Airey v. Ireland (No. 1)* (appl. no. 6289/73), Judgement (Chamber), 9 October 1979, Series A, Vol. 32; [1979–1980] 2 EHRR 305.

[154] *Quinn v. Ireland* (appl. no. 36887/97), Judgement (Fourth Section), 21 December 2000 (not reported); and *Heaney and McGuinness v. Ireland* (appl. no. 34720/97), Judgement (Fourth Section), 21 December 2000, Reports 2000-XII, 419 et seq.; [2001] 33 EHRR 12.

[155] *O'Reilly and Others v. Ireland* (appl. no. 54725/00), Judgement (Third Section), 29 July 2004 (not reported); [2005] 40 EHRR 40; and *McMullen v. Ireland* (appl. no. 42297/98), Judgement (Third Section), 29 July 2004 (not reported).

[156] *Barry v. Ireland* (appl. no. 18273/04), Judgement (Third Section), 15 December 2005 (not yet reported).

[157] *Pine Valley Developments Ltd and Others v. Ireland (No. 1)* (appl. no. 12742/87), Judgement (Chamber), 29 November 1991, Series A, Vol. 222; [1992] 14 EHRR 319.

dd. The protection of freedom of information. In 1992, the Court decided in *Open Door and Dublin Well Woman v. Ireland* that the restriction from imparting information to pregnant women concerning abortion facilities outside Ireland was a violation of the freedom of information guaranteed in Article 10 ECHR.[158] Although these last two cases seem relatively isolated, they are the tip of an iceberg in Ireland, where a commentator once stated that "Ireland's sometimes hysterical obsession with abortion is matched only by its historical obsession with land".[159]

3. Comparison and Conclusion

While the UK is among the original Contracting States to the Convention with the highest total of cases brought against it, Ireland is among the countries with the lowest total. Several factors may account for this divergence, the most important of which – again – is probably the difference between the countries' respective human rights traditions. Articles 6 and 8 ECHR have been the basis of most of the adverse judgements in both countries. The legal systems share a common historical origin, and the courts are embedded in a common cultural take on the protection of privacy and family life.[160] The conflict over Northern Ireland has also generated cases, with important consequences for detention regimes and anti-terrorist measures on both sides.

D. The European Court's Case Law's Effects in National Law

The previous section presented basic data on the ECtHR's activities with respect to Ireland and the UK. This section assesses their impact on national law in both countries. Of course, the ECtHR's rulings also impact on national legal orders in less visible ways, as when adverse judgements generate new orientations to domestic law principles,[161] changes in the criteria governing officials' conduct at international level,[162] or new cultural outlooks and attitudes on the part of officials and administrators *vis-à-vis* the Convention and the European Court.

1. United Kingdom

Primary responsibility for compliance with the Court's judgements rests with the Foreign Secretary. Upon reception of a judgement, a designated legal agent in the

[158] *Open Door and Dublin Well Woman v. Ireland* (*supra* note 63).

[159] O'Connell (2001), 444.

[160] Compare *Norris v. Attorney General* (*supra* note 3) to *Dudgeon v. the United Kingdom* (*supra* note 3)

[161] See e.g. *Osman v. the United Kingdom* (appl. no. 23452/94), Judgement (Grand Chamber), 28 October 1998, Reports 1998-VIII, 3124 et seq.; [2000] 29 EHRR 245 in the field of English tort law. See, however, *Z. and Others v. the United Kingdom* (appl. no. 29392/95), Judgement (Grand Chamber), 10 May 2001, Reports 2001-V, 1 et seq.; [2002] 34 EHRR 3.

[162] See e.g. *Soering v. the United Kingdom* (*supra* note 100). See also (esp. dissenting opinions) *Al-Adsani v. the United Kingdom* (appl. no. 35763/97), Judgement (Grand Chamber), 21 November 2001, Reports 2001-XI, 79 et seq.; [2002] 34 EHRR 11.

Foreign Office communicates it to the relevant department(s) of State concerned, along with a statement of proposed remedy. The following sections will provide examples of remedial action taken in response to being held in violation of the Convention, both by the British Legislature and the Judiciary.

a. Pre-Incorporation Impact

Overall, during the pre-incorporation period, the UK met most of its obligations to amend its laws so as to bring them into conformity with the Court's rulings, though the Thatcher Government lodged a derogation under Article 15 ECHR following one adverse ruling.[163] That point made, the UK has typically sought to limit adaptation of national law as much as possible. Following the adverse judgement of the Court in *Abdulaziz, Cabales and Balkandali v. UK* (1985),[164] for example, the UK suppressed the discrimination of married women under immigration rules. Rather than raise women's positions to that of men, the new regulations levelled down the position of men, so as to prevent wives from joining resident husbands. Nonetheless, the impact of the Court's judgements against the UK prior to the HRA was profound, giving the UK a body of human rights law, and corresponding principles which it would not otherwise have had.[165] In addition, the scope of judicial authority was gradually enhanced, whereas the scope of Parliamentary sovereignty was eroded.[166]

aa. The treatment of terrorist suspects. Before its condemnation in *Ireland v. UK* (1978),[167] the UK Prime Minister had given its solemn undertaking in 1972 that the techniques of interrogation complained of would be abandoned. The European Court decided to adjudicate the application further in order to elucidate the question of principle in any case. Following the ruling in *Brogan and Others v. UK* (1988),[168] the UK Government insisted that the special arrest and detention powers under the Prevention of Terrorism Act 1983 were necessary to combat terrorism connected to Northern Ireland. It then lodged a derogation under Article 15(1) ECHR, which was only withdrawn in 2001, replacing it with a derogation (of 18 December 2001) to Article 5(1) ECHR in relation to powers to detain suspected terrorists or illegal immigrants pending deportation under

---

[163] *Brogan, Coyle, McFaden and Tracey v. the United Kingdom* (appl. nos 11209/84; 11234/84; 11266/84; 11386/85), Judgement (Plenary), 29 November 1988, Series A, Vol. 145-B; [1989] 11 EHRR 117.

[164] *Abdulaziz, Cabales and Balkandali v. the United Kingdom* (appl. nos 9214/80; 9473/81; 9474/81), Judgement (Plenary), 28 May 1985, Series A, Vol. 94; [1985] 7 EHRR 471.

[165] See e.g. Gearty (2006), 66–67 by reference to *R. (Limbuela) v. Secretary of State for the Home Department* [2005] UKHL 66.

[166] An example often given is that of *Lustig-Prean and Beckett v. the United Kingdom* (*supra* note 135); *Christine Goodwin v. the United Kingdom* (*supra* note 137); or *Evans v. the United Kingdom* (appl. no. 6339/05), Judgement (Grand Chamber), 10 April 2007 (not yet.reported).

[167] *Ireland v. the United Kingdom* (*supra* note 51).

[168] *Brogan, Coyle, McFaden and Tracey v. the United Kingdom* (*supra* note 163).

ATCSA. Following a 2004 decision of the House of Lords on its conventionality, this latter derogation was withdrawn on 16 March 2005.[169] Looking ahead, it is obvious that this area remains a fertile field, not only for litigation and intra-judicial interaction, but also for Governmental decision-making on compliance. New derogations might be taken soon, given that the measures under the Prevention of Terrorism Act 2005 (which replaced detention without trial under ATCSA with a regime of "control orders"), and under the Terrorism Act 2006, are likely to be judged Convention-incompatible.[170]

bb. The protection of freedom of the press. Following *Sunday Times v. UK* (1979),[171] the UK established the Contempt of Court Act 1981, which aligned domestic law with the principles expressed in the decision. Following the *Spycatcher* case,[172] British judges have referred systematically to the Court's reasoning in processing applications for injunctions against the press.

cc. The treatment of homosexuals. Following *Dudgeon v. UK* (1981),[173] the Government passed the Homosexual Offences (Northern Ireland) Order 1982, which decriminalized homosexual acts conducted in private between consenting male adults. In response to *Lustig-Prean and Beckett v. UK* (1999)[174] and *Smith and Grady v. UK* (1999),[175] the Government introduced The Armed Forces Code of Social Conduct Policy Statement on 12 January 2000 lifting the ban on gays serving in the military.

b. Post-incorporation Impact
The HRA 1998 creates various obligations to monitor and take into account the decisions of the European Court in domestic law, and to provide new domestic remedies in case of violation of Convention rights. These obligations supplement the UK Government's international duties under Article 46 ECHR. Section 10 HRA creates a new legislative process in order to enact fast-track remedial orders to respond to human rights violations in primary legislation. These violations may be identified by a declaration of incompatibility of the High Court or appellate bodies, but also by a judgement in violation of the ECtHR. This fast-track procedure following an adverse judgement of the Court has not been used very often since 2000, however.

At present, a large number of past ECtHR judgements have not yet been fully

---

[169] See *A. and Others v. Secretary of State for the Home Department* (*supra* note 28).
[170] See e.g. *Secretary of State for the Home Department v. E* [2007] EWHC 233(Admin).
[171] *Sunday Times v. the United Kingdom* (*supra* note 132).
[172] *The Observer and The Guardian v. the United Kingdom* (*supra* note 133).
[173] *Dudgeon v. the United Kingdom* (*supra* note 3)
[174] *Lustig-Prean and Beckett v. the United Kingdom* (*supra* note 135).
[175] *Smith and Grady v. the United Kingdom* (appl. nos 33985/96; 33986/96), Judgement (Third Section), 27 September 1999, Reports 1999-VI, 45 et seq.; [2000] 29 EHRR 493.

implemented, due to delays in the adoption of remedial legislation. Among those mentioned by the Committee on Legal Affairs and the Human Rights' Rapporteur after his 8 March 2006 visit to the UK,[176] one finds the pre-HRA pending reforms: to prohibit the physical punishment of children following *A. v. UK* (1998);[177] to introduce adequate safeguards during detention in mental hospitals following *Stanley Johnson v. UK* (1997);[178] and to ensure that no negative conclusion could be drawn from the accused person's silence during interrogation without legal council following *John Murray v. UK* (1996).[179] With respect to other measures still pending, the UK has been slow to deal with the consequences of several judgements relative to security forces' violence in Northern Ireland, in particular *Finucane v. UK* (2003)[180] or *McKerr v. UK* (2001).[181] The controversy surrounding the Inquiries Act 2005 is also not likely to be set at rest by the single inquiry in the *Finucane* case.[182] The Report criticizes the traditional British way of addressing general problems through adopting *ad hoc* practical measures, i.e. by preventing repetition of the Government action which violated the Convention, without at the same time initiating a formal change in legislation or other policy instrument.

aa. The treatment of transsexuals. Following *Christine Goodwin v. UK* (2002)[183] and *I. v. UK* (2002),[184] the Government immediately committed itself to carrying forward the Court's judgements. It was only after the entry into force of the Gender Recognition Act 2004, however, that transsexuals' rights were fully recognized. Nonetheless, the British Government's slow reception of the *Christine Goodwin* judgement was actually censured again by the Court as a renewed breach of Article 8 ECHR in *Grant v. UK* (2006).[185]

bb. The organization of the State. Since the European Court's decision in *McGonnell v. UK* (2000),[186] the overlap between executive, judicial and Parliamentary functions mentioned above was no longer tenable. As a result, the Constitutional Reform Act 2005 removed the Parliamentary and judicial functions of the Lord

---

[176] See http://assembly.coe.int/Mainf.asp?link=/Documents/WorkingDocs/Doc06/EDOC11020.htm#2.

[177] *A. v. the United Kingdom* (appl. no. 25599/94), Judgement (Chamber), 23 September 1998, Reports 1998-VI, 2692 et seq.; [1999] 27 EHRR 611.

[178] *Johnson v. the United Kingdom* (*supra* note 123).

[179] *John Murray v. the United Kingdom* (*supra* note 143).

[180] *Finucane v. the United Kingdom* (*supra* note 131).

[181] *McKerr v. the United Kingdom* (*supra* note 130).

[182] See e.g. Amnesty International (2006).

[183] *Christine Goodwin v. the United Kingdom* (*supra* note 137).

[184] *I. v. the United Kingdom* (appl. no. 25680/94), Judgement (Grand Chamber), 11 July 2002 (not reported); [2003] 36 EHRR 53.

[185] *Grant v. the United Kingdom* (*supra* note 138).

[186] *McGonnell v. the United Kingdom* (*supra* note 12).

Chancellor (as opposed to his role in the administration of the court system), and a Supreme Court will replace the House of Lords in 2009.

cc. The protection of parents' and children's rights. The case *P., C., and S. v. UK* (2002)[187] raised general issues of good practice for social service authorities regarding the circumstances in which children are taken into care. For the courts, it raised issues of how to ensure the provision of legal representation in child care cases, at all stages of the proceedings, and to adjourn proceedings where necessary. In its judgement, the Court demanded broad dissemination of the principles to the Judiciary, and a revision of guidelines applying to local authority social services. In his response, the Lord Chancellor stated that his department were carefully considering the implications of the judgement, together with the senior Judiciary, and that the judgement would be taken into account with respect to implementation of the Adoption and Children Act 2002.

dd. Protection against self-incrimination and the right to silence. Following *Allan v. UK* (2002–03),[188] the Home Office noted that the Association of Chief Police Officers with appropriate Home Office input was preparing a Police and Criminal Evidence Act 1984 Sections 76 and 78 guide designed to ensure police compliance with Article 6 ECHR. Whilst this is welcome, *Allan v. UK* identifies a deeper problem not only with police practice, but also with judicial application of Sections 76 and 78. Consideration should, therefore, be given to legislation to ensure that Sections 76 and 78 are fully in compliance with Article 6 ECHR. This is a very topical issue as the use of suspect evidence, including evidence obtained through torture, has spread since 2001, and even more since 2005 under the Prevention of Terrorism Act 2005. In a December 2005 decision, the House of Lords unanimously confirmed that such evidence is inadmissible.[189] What it also ruled, however, was that such evidence should only be excluded if it is considered by judges that it is more likely than not that the evidence was obtained by torture – a condition difficult to satisfy in ordinary circumstances, and left therefore to judicial appreciation.

Under Section 2 HRA, British courts are required to take into account the ECtHR's case law not only in cases pertaining to the United Kingdom, but in all cases pertaining to the rights incorporated into British law by the Act. As a consequence, British courts and Government authorities are expected to take a closer and more general interest in the Court's decisions in other Contracting States, although they are not, strictly speaking, binding on British courts under the HRA.[190]

---

[187] *P., C. and S. v. the United Kingdom* (*supra* note 140).
[188] *Allan v. the United Kingdom* (*supra* note 142).
[189] *A. and Others v. Secretary of State for the Home Department* [2005] UKHL 71.
[190] See *infra* Section III. E.

Even with respect to the European Court's case law involving the United Kingdom, British courts often dissent and decide the next case differently if they think that there are good reasons to do so.[191] In such a case, the European Court is of course free to follow the newest British decision rather than its previous decision.[192] This situation may create difficult issues pertaining to judicial hierarchy in the UK. Imagine that the British Court of Appeal decides a case in a certain way, while the European Court decides differently later on. Should a lower court seized on a similar issue subsequently respect the Court of Appeal decision or that of the European Court? It would seem that the lower court should decide as it deems most correct; since it is not strictly speaking bound by the European Court's case law, but deciding without regard to the ECtHR's case law risks another adverse judgement from Strasbourg.[193] To save time and expense, it is argued, the Court of Appeal should be free to take this step itself.[194] Reaffirming strongly the principle of *stare decisis*, the House of Lords decided otherwise, however, in a recent case argued by reference to the possibilities offered by the fast-track procedure under Section 10 HRA.[195]

An interesting issue in this respect is whether it is open to British courts to give Convention rights a more expansive interpretation than the one adopted by the European Court. Given that the Convention is meant as a minimal standard, as confirmed by Article 53 ECHR, national courts have the latitude to go further than the European Court in protecting them. The view expressed in decisions, however, is that British courts cannot adopt an interpretation of the Convention which gives a broader effect to a right than is indicated by existing jurisprudence of the European Court.[196] A recent example of this strict interpretation of Convention rights according to the European Court's case law may be found in the challenge raised against Section 23 of the ATCSA before the House of Lords.[197]

---

[191] See e.g. *Z. and Others v. the United Kingdom* (*supra* note 161) confirming the British Courts' decision (*Barrett v. Enfield LBC*, [2001] 2 AC 550) that had been intentionally decided against the European Court's decision in *Osman v. the United Kingdom* (*supra* note 161). See on this judicial dialogue, Department for Constitutional Affairs, Review of the Implementation of the Human Rights Act, July 2006, http://www.dca.gov.uk/peoples-rights/human-rights/pdf/full_review.pdf.

[192] See e.g. *R. v. Lyons* [2002] (*supra* note 90). This was confirmed later on by the European Court in *Lyons and Others v. the United Kingdom* (*supra* note 90). See also *Cooper v. the United Kingdom* (appl. no. 48843/99), Judgement (Grand Chamber), 16 December 2003, Reports 2003-XII, 145 et seq.; [2004] 39 EHRR 8, following *R. v. Boyd and Others* [2002] UKHL 31, that was decided against *Findlay v. the United Kingdom* (appl. no. 22107/93), Judgement (Chamber), 25 February 1997, Reports 1997-I, 263 et seq.; [1997] 24 EHRR 221. See Anderson (2004).

[193] See Hoffman and Rowe (2003), 53.

[194] See Rodger of Earlsferry (2005).

[195] See *Price v. Leeds CC* [2006] UKHL 10.

[196] See e.g. *R. v. Secretary of State for the Home Department ex parte Uttley* [2004] UKHL 38. See also *R. v. Special Adjudicator ex parte Ullah (FC)*, [2004] UKHL 26.

[197] See *Lord Hoffman in A. and Others v. Secretary of State for the Home Department* (*supra* note 28).

2. Ireland

The following sections will provide examples of remedial action taken in response to adverse judgements by the ECtHR, both by the Irish Legislature and the Judiciary.[198] Interestingly, some Irish cases have been significant in the evolution of the European constitutional order in general.[199]

a. Pre-incorporation Impact

Before the ECHR Act 2003, Ireland typically fulfilled its duties under Article 46 ECHR. One of the major exceptions pertained to *abortion*. Given the sensitivity of the issue in Ireland, many questions remained unresolved. Different constitutional mechanisms at Irish constitutional level and at EU level have only aggravated the situation.[200]

aa. Protection of private life. Following the *Johnston v. Ireland* (1986) case,[201] the Minister of Justice introduced the Status of Children Act 1987 abolishing the legal status of illegitimacy of children born out of wedlock, thereby remedying the violation of Article 8 ECHR. Following the *Norris v. Ireland* case (1988),[202] the Irish Government failed to respond until, under direct Council of Europe pressure, it decriminalized homosexual activity by adopting the Criminal Law Sexual Offences Act in 1993. The breach of Article 8 ECHR identified in *Keegan v. Ireland* (1994)[203] was remedied by the Adoption Act 1998 which provides for consultation of the natural father in the adoption process.

bb. Access to courts. In response to the 1979 *Airey v. Ireland* judgement,[204] the Irish Government introduced a non-statutory scheme of civil legal aid and advice in 1980. As the latter did not fully remedy the breach of Article 6(1) ECHR found by the Court, the scheme was revised and given a statutory basis in the Civil Legal Aid Act 1995. Following *Quinn v. Ireland* and *Heaney and McGuiness v. Ireland* (2001),[205] Ireland still needs to revise Section 52 of the Offences Against the State Act 1939 to prevent further violations of Article 6 ECHR by the Special Criminal Court.

---

[198] For further information, see e.g. Egan (2004) (refugee law); Kilkelly (2004), *Child and Family* (child and family law); Bacik (2004) (criminal law); Austin and McClean (2004) (detention); Mullan (2004) (discrimination law); Dillon-Malone (2004) (privacy and media law); Kenna (2004), *Property* (property, housing and environment).

[199] See e.g. *Lawless v. Ireland (No. 3)* (*supra* note 52); *Airey v. Ireland (No. 1)* (*supra* note 153); and *Bosphorus Hava Yollari Turizm Ve Ticaret Anonim Sirketi v. Ireland* (appl. no. 45036/98), Judgement (Grand Chamber), 30 June 2005, Reports 2005-VI, 107; [2006] 42 EHRR 1.

[200] See *supra* Section III. A.

[201] *Johnston and Others v. Ireland* (*supra* note 149).

[202] *Norris v. Ireland* (*supra* note 150).

[203] *Keegan v. Ireland* (*supra* note 152).

[204] *Airey v. Ireland (No. 1)* (*supra* note 153).

[205] *Quinn v. Ireland* (appl. no. 36887/97) (*supra* note 154).

cc. Protection of freedom of information. In response to the judgement in violation of Article 10 ECHR in the *Open Door and Dublin Well Woman v. Ireland*
(1992) case,[206] the Irish Constitution was amended to allow the imparting of information on abortion services lawfully available in other jurisdictions. Remaining legislative limitations are, however, still in place and in particular penalties
for providing information and advice about abortion. The fact that the Supreme
Court has upheld this legislation creates difficulties, since it cannot be challenged
constitutionally before an Irish court as long as it remains in force.[207]

b. Post-incorporation Impact
The ECHR Act 2003 creates new remedies in case of violation of Convention
rights, and mechanisms of coordination between the ECHR and the Irish legal
order. This framework supplements the Irish Government's international duties
under Article 46 ECHR. In contrast to Section 10 HRA, however, there are no
direct legislative requirements under Section 3 ECHR Act to remedy a breach of
the Convention following an adverse judgement of the European Court.[208]

The Irish Government has been faced with one major difficulty in the implementation of ECtHR's adverse judgements in Irish law: that of the length
of criminal proceedings. Following the *Doran v. Ireland* (2003),[209] *O'Reilly and
Others v. Ireland* (2004),[210] *McMullen v. Ireland* (2004),[211] and *Barry v. Ireland*
(2005)[212] decisions, the Irish Government has suggested that new violations of
the Convention could be avoided in future by informing the authorities concerned of the requirements of the Convention. Even if the deeper structural
problem remains in this type of cases, overall the impact of the European Court's
judgements post-incorporation has been rather positive.

Under Section 4 ECHR Act, Irish courts are required to take into account
the ECtHR's case law not only in cases in which Ireland is a defendant, but
in all cases concerning the rights incorporated into Irish law by the Act. Since
Irish courts did not respect the European Court's decisions pertaining to other
countries too closely before incorporation, one may fear that, in the absence of
a domestic duty to do so under the ECHR Act, convergence with the European
Court's case law may not occur.[213]

---

[206] *Open Door and Dublin Well Woman v. Ireland (supra* note 63).
[207] See, however, the decision of inadmissibility in *D. v. Ireland* (appl. no. 26499/02), Admissibility Decision (Fourth Section), 28 June 2006 (not reported); [2006] 43 EHRR SE16.
[208] See Hogan (2004), 27.
[209] *Doran v. Ireland (supra* note 106).
[210] *O'Reilly and Others v. Ireland (supra* note 155).
[211] *McMullen v. Ireland (supra* note 155).
[212] *Barry v. Ireland (supra* note 156).
[213] See *infra* Section III. E.

3. Comparison and Conclusion

Remedial actions have always been very good in Ireland and remain good, though difficult structural issues have arisen in recent years. In the UK, remedial action was minimalist before incorporation, and the Government has dragged its feet on security issues since 2001. Nonetheless, the UK possesses more effective remedial mechanisms following adverse judgements (e.g. the fast-track procedure) than does Ireland.[214]

As to the ECHR's impact on judicial authorities, both the Irish and the British courts have demonstrated a fierce sense of independence *vis-à-vis* the European Court's case law. Judges do not accept that they are bound by previous decisions of that Court, and neither act of incorporation requires them to apply the ECtHR's reasoning in cases at bar. Where the countries' courts differ is with respect to giving a higher protection to Convention rights than does the ECtHR. UK judges consider Convention rights as both minimal and maximal standards, while Irish judges consider the Convention to state minimal standards for rights protection, in comparison to the higher standards offered under their Constitution. As the new powers and practices associated with HRA are being consolidated, one can expect that UK judges will gradually become more assertive.

E. Mechanisms of Coordination

1. United Kingdom

a. Preventive Compliance

Before incorporation in 2000, the Convention played no formal part in the proceedings of the British Parliament or the Executive, and there existed no Parliamentary committee on human rights until the 90's.[215] The HRA introduced a system of preventive compliance.[216]

To start with, the HRA has established formal procedures of pre-legislative scrutiny of legislation. Section 19 HRA requires the Minister introducing a Bill in Parliament to state whether it is compatible with the Convention, or to decline to do so, but to indicate that the Government nevertheless wishes to proceed.[217] The Government chose the latter course with the ATCSA, which contained a number of provisions deemed potentially incompatible with the Convention. A derogation under Article 15 ECHR was made and Parliament adopted the Act. The fact that the Government asserts the compatibility of a Bill before Parliament

---

[214] See *infra* Section III. E.
[215] See e.g. Kinley (1993); Ryle (1994).
[216] See e.g. Blackburn (2001), 992 et seq.; Blackburn (1998); Justice (1999).
[217] See also The Human Rights Act 1998 Guidance for Departments (Home Office, 2nd ed., 2000).

does not guarantee that the statement is correct: the Bill, once passed, may be deemed incompatible by a court.[218]

Both Houses of Parliament are also responsible to scrutinize legislative initiatives. Scrutiny typically takes place in various Parliamentary Committees. The most important of these is the Joint Committee on Human Rights, which is composed of twelve members (six from each House) who consider matters relating to human rights, and to the HRA in particular. The Commission for Equality and Human Rights also plays a role in pre-legislative scrutiny of Bills, and may suggest amendments when necessary to put British law in line with the Convention.

With incorporation, mechanisms of preventive compliance of Executive decision-making have also appeared. It is now a mandatory legal requirement for Ministries to examine and draw up a written report on the human rights implications of all legislation that is being prepared. As just discussed, the Government must also include a statement of Convention compatibility with each Bill introduced into Parliament. The Executive's commitment to preventive compliance has clearly weakened since September 2001, however, which has affected the taking and reinforcement of anti-terrorism measures.[219] The Commission for Equality and Human Rights also has certain functions in the context of executive preventive compliance. It is able to initiate enquiries, which might be concluded by an unlawful act notice in cases where a violation of the Convention is identified. If that notice is not acted upon, the Commission may seek an agreement with those responsible for the violation.

As discussed above, the HRA requires the courts to apply the Convention, and to pay close attention to the ECtHR's case law. In fact, UK judges have been quite attentive to both, if only to avoid a referral to Strasbourg.[220] Typically, judges are careful in the formulation of their reasoning, deliberately explaining their rulings in terms that can be readily understood by the European Court. Incorporation has thus influenced how appeal judgements are framed. Dissenting judgements are encouraged, so as to provide the European Court with a record of serious deliberation and detailed reasoning.[221] Still, judges do not go further in protecting Convention rights than the European Court has in its case law, so one can characterize preventive judicial compliance as relatively minimalist.

b. *Ex Post* Compliance

Prior to the HRA, the UK routinely met its obligations in response to adverse judgements of the European Court, including amending its laws so as to bring them into conformity with the Court's ruling. Since incorporation, *ex post* leg-

---

[218] See *A. and Others v. Secretary of State for the Home Department* (*supra* note 28).
[219] See e.g. Amnesty International (2006) about the debate over the Inquiries Act 2005.
[220] See e.g. the dissent of Lord Steyn in *Roberts v. Parole Board* [2005] UKHL 45.
[221] See Rodger of Earlsferry (2005).

islative compliance includes various mechanisms for post-legislative monitoring of legislation, as well as fast-track remedial orders to respond to rights violations in primary legislation. The Joint Human Rights Committee also presents regular progress reports on the implementation of ECtHR's judgements before the House of Lords, a new practice that should improve *ex post* compliance.[222]

As mentioned, the HRA creates a process to enact fast-track remedial orders in response to human rights violations in primary legislation. Once an authorized court issues a declaration of incompatibility, the Executive is to consider whether there exist compelling reasons to amend the censured law, and "may by order make such amendments to the legislation as he considers necessary to remove the incompatibility" (Section 10 para. 2 HRA).[223] Adverse ECtHR's judgements may also lead to fast-track remedial legislative revision, on the same basis. Remedial orders, that are affirmative statutory instruments, are subject to a simplified procedure: a single stage of approval in each House as opposed to the three readings and committee stages applicable to a normal Bill. Despite this simplified procedure, these orders are authorized to change primary legislation in major respects. To prevent abuses, proposed remedial orders should be scrutinized by the Joint Select Committee on Human Rights. Of course, the making of a remedial order does not deprive the Parliament of the opportunity to consider the matter because the order is still subject to being approved by Parliament before it can become law (schedule 2 para. 2 HRA). The only exception to this is where the matter is considered urgent (Schedule 2 para. 2(b) HRA); in such cases, the order has to be approved by Parliament within 120 days, or else the order will cease to have effect (Schedule 2 para. 4(4) HRA). A recent report of the Law Commission explores ways to make these post-legislative mechanisms more systematic.[224]

With respect to the Judiciary, the situation has also changed dramatically with incorporation. Before 2000, British judges did not always refer or consider adverse judgements of ECtHR in later cases pertaining to the same issue, even when they went against the UK. With the HRA (Section 2 HRA), British courts must, when interpreting and applying Convention provisions, take due account of the principles laid down in the ECtHR's decisions and judgements, whether or not they concern the UK. Nonetheless, the courts are not strictly speaking bound by the European Court's case law, and they often distance themselves from it and justify their position.[225]

As to the impact of an ECtHR's decision condemning the United Kingdom on the very judicial proceedings that were deemed contrary to the Convention,

---

[222] See e.g. Joint Committee on Human Rights, *Implementation of Strasbourg Judgements: First Progress Report*, 8 March 2006, http://www.publications.parliament.uk/pa/jt200506/jtselect/jtrights/133/133.pdf.

[223] See e.g. *R. v. Mental Health Review Tribunal* [2001] 3 WLR 512.

[224] See The Law Commission, *Post-Legislative Scrutiny*, Report October 2006, http://www.lawcom.gov.uk/docs/lc302.pdf.

[225] See *supra* Section III. D.

the regime has not changed drastically since incorporation.[226] The conviction or ruling remains valid and cannot be set aside. Some have suggested establishing Review Commissions, on the model of the Criminal Case Review Commission, that would have the power to refer cases on which an adverse judgement has been made to the relevant appeal court for reconsideration as a brand new appeal. Based on the German Federal Constitutional Court's decision in *Görgülü*,[227] one may argue, however, that ordinary civil proceedings provide more opportunity to take account of a ECtHR's decision later on and this without a Review Commission.[228]

2. Ireland

a. Preventive Compliance

Before the ECHR Act 2003, the Executive rarely invoked the Convention as a reason for introducing a piece of legislation or amending existing legislation, such as when a case was brought against Ireland in an area, but also when a relevant case had been brought before the ECtHR. The Parliamentary Draftsman's Office had the task of ensuring compatibility with the Convention's provisions,[229] but in Parliamentary proceedings, concern for compatibility was not strict or systematic; after all, the ECHR was not part of Irish law.

Incorporation has done little to change things. The ECHR Act does not create a complete system of Parliamentary scrutiny of legislation for compatibility with Convention rights on the model of the British HRA.[230] In practice, the Irish Human Rights Commission actually performs the most important monitoring role for concerned legislators. Since 2003, the Commission has a statutory duty to review proposed legislation with reference to international human rights obligations, and its activities in this respect have proven to be a vital resource for Parliamentarians. It appears from transcripts of the proceedings of certain Parliamentary Committees that the views of the Commission enjoy significant credibility. The same influence cannot be said to exist on the Executive at the pre-Parliamentary stage, although ministers can refer proposals to the Commission at this stage, and the Minister for Justice has frequently done so.

Before 2003, preventive compliance on the part of Irish judges was also rare.[231]

---

[226] Compare *R. v. Lyons* [2003] 1 AC 976 (where facts took place before the HRA came into force) with *In re McKerr*, [2004] 1 WLR 807.

[227] Bundesverfassungsgericht, 14 October 2004, *Görgülü*, BVerfGE, 2 BvR 1481/04.

[228] See e.g. Rodger of Earlsferry (2005).

[229] See e.g. O'Connell (2001), 436–438; Flynn (1994); Donelan (1992).

[230] See O'Connell (2004), *Critical Perspective*, 5.

[231] See *supra* Section III. B. Empirical research on the work of the courts is rare in Ireland. Since incorporation, however, all cases in which a declaration of incompatibility under the ECHR Act is sought are being notified to the Irish Human Rights Commission, thus making it possible to monitor this dimension of judicial compliance. See also the Irish Law Society's 2006 report on the cases decided since incorporation: http://www.lawsociety.ie/documents/committees/hr/ECHR/DecidedCases.pdf.

Since incorporation, Irish courts have become more attentive to the ECHR and the European Court's case law, mostly in order to avoid an appeal to Strasbourg. Courts now take a relatively strict approach to the ECtHR's rulings.[232] It would seem that the authority, in the Irish legal order, of the latter's case law has been reinforced rather than diminished by the indirect model of incorporation chosen in Ireland. Overall, however, the ECHR Act itself has not provoked decisive changes in the Judiciary's approach to rights.[233] Instead, Irish judges exhibit a tendency to subsume Convention rights and arguments under domestic constitutional remedies themselves,[234] even when constitutional and conventional guarantees are not entirely congruent.[235] As a result, only one Section 5 declaration of incompatibility has been granted by Irish courts so far.[236]

b. *Ex Post* Compliance

Prior to 2003, Ireland proved diligent in meeting its obligation to amend its laws so as to bring them into conformity with adverse rulings of the ECtHR, although decisions in the area of abortion are a major exception. In contrast to the UK HRA, the ECHR Act did not establish formal procedures for monitoring legislative activity after an adverse decision. As discussed, under Section 5 para. 3 ECHR Act, the High Court and other appellate bodies may detect violations of the Convention and declare Irish law Convention incompatible, at which point the Human Rights Commission is automatically notified. Parliament must deal with the declaration within 21 days, but there is no obligation for the Government or the Parliament to indicate what remedial action (if any) is to be taken. Moreover, fast-track procedures are not available. In any case, no court has yet issued a declaration of incompatibility following an adverse judgement by the ECtHR.

The ECtHR's decisions had no measurable impact on the Judiciary prior to incorporation. The ECHR Act does change the legal situation, but only in ways that have already been discussed, namely, that the courts must, when interpreting and applying Convention provisions, take due account of the principles laid down in the ECtHR's decisions and judgements, without being bound by them.[237] As to the impact of an ECtHR's decision condemning Ireland on the very judicial proceedings that are deemed as contrary to the Convention in a specific decision,

---

[232] See *Hogan (2006)*, Declaration of Incompatibility.

[233] See O'Connell et al. (2006), 29; Hogan (2006), *Declaration of Incompatibility*; Hogan (2006), *Ireland*.

[234] See e.g. Hardiman J. in *J.F. v. DPP* [2005] 2 IR 174. See also *T.H. v. DPP & His Honour Judge Peter Smithwick* [2004] IEHC 76. See *supra* Section III. B.

[235] See e.g. *Gashi & Others v. Minister for Justice, Equality and Law Reform & Others* [2004] IEHC 394; *Margine v. Minister for Justice, Equality and Law Reform & Others* [2004] IEHC 127.

[236] See O'Connell et al. (2006), chapter 3 by reference to the 54 superior court judgements rendered since incorporation in which the ECHR is mentioned.

[237] See e.g. *Spartariu v. Minister of Justice, Equality and Law Reform* [2005] IEHC 104.

the regime has remained the same prior and post-incorporation.[238] The conviction or ruling remains valid and cannot be set aside. There is no obligation under Irish law to re-open the conviction or provide a fresh trial and hence to do other than change the law with prospective effect.[239]

3. Comparison and Conclusion

Pre-incorporation compliance mechanisms, whether preventive or *ex post*, and whether executive, legislative or judicial, were much the same in both countries. With incorporation, the UK now possesses a better organized and more efficient system of monitoring and responding to compliance problems than does Ireland. In the latter country, pre-existing constitutional mechanisms, unknown in the UK, have either blocked the introduction of monitoring and control mechanisms, or subsumed them into mechanisms of constitutional compliance.

Compliance must be assessed in the long term, however, and against the background of rights protection as a whole. The fact is that Ireland created its Human Rights Commission long before the UK, and has had a better overall record of rights protection as well, at least as measured by ECtHR rulings. It may be that the Irish tendency to integrate conventional and constitutional compliance might in the long run guarantee better protection of Convention rights than in the UK.

F. Remedies and Proportionality Tests

1. *United Kingdom*

a. Remedies
Before the HRA 1998, UK courts could provide no remedies in case of infringement of the ECHR, a situation the HRA reverses. According to Section 7 para. 1 HRA, anyone claiming that a public authority has acted or will act in a way incompatible with Convention rights, and hence unlawfully under Section 6 para. 1, can initiate proceedings against that authority (Section 7 para. 1(a) HRA) on the basis of Convention rights (Section 7 para. 1(b) HRA). The *locus standi* (Section 7(3) HRA) is the same in judicial review proceedings: the claimant must have been a "victim of [an] unlawful act".

Under Section 7 para. 7 HRA, a person is a victim only if they are a victim for the purposes of Article 34 ECHR and under the ECtHR's interpretation of that Article, which includes any person, non-governmental organization or group of individuals who claim that their Convention rights have been infringed by a public authority. A Governmental body cannot, therefore, be regarded as a

---

[238] See e.g. *E. v. E.* [1982] ILRM 497 in relation to *Airey v. Ireland (No. 1)* (*supra* note 153). See also most recently *W O'R v. EH* [1996] 2 IR 248 in relation to *Keegan v. Ireland* (*supra* note 152).
[239] See Hogan (2004), 27.

victim under Article 34 ECHR. The congruence between the Convention and the Act is enhanced by the incorporation of the ECtHR's case law on the notion of victim; legal proceedings are generally confined to those who are personally in need of protection by the court whether actually, potentially or indirectly.[240] Section 7 para. 7 HRA excludes the *actio popularis* of one or more citizens whose grievance is simply that domestic law might contravene the Convention, and excludes other groups or bodies, even though they are able to challenge acts and decisions of Government and public bodies by ordinary common law judicial review actions.[241] Under ordinary common law, the test is one of sufficient interest, which is much broader than that of "victim" under Article 34 ECHR. The victim requirement of the HRA has been heavily contested,[242] not least since it creates a dichotomy within the UK judicial review system. A way out might be to have recourse to an alternative (Section 7 para. 1(b) HRA), in which a party might seek initial *locus standi* on the basis of a common law right, but in subsequent proceedings argue that this common law right overlaps a Convention right.[243]

According to Section 6 para. 1 HRA, "it is unlawful for a public authority to act in a way which is incompatible with a Convention right." As discussed, the notion of "public authority" is controversial. The guiding test is a functional one: liability attaches to those bodies which, at the time in which the Convention rights of the litigant are prejudiced, are carrying out business or are in the act of performing a function of a public nature (as confirmed by Section 6 paras 3 and 5 HRA).[244] The test then is material and not formal.[245] Other bodies for whose actions the UK Government is answerable before the European Court[246] include all those whose functions are public, and in particular executive agencies, local Government, the police, immigration officers, and prisons. Mixed private/public bodies are included only when they exercise a public function, but the latter

---

[240] See *Klass and Others v. Germany* (appl. no. 5029/71), Judgement (Plenary), 6 September 1978, Series A, Vol. 28, § 33;[1979–1980] 2 EHRR 214; *Tauira and Others v. France* (appl. no. 28204/95), Decision (Plenary), Commission, 4 December 1995, Decisions and Reports 83-B, 112, 130.

[241] Rules of the Supreme Court, order 53; Supreme Court Act 1981, Section 31 (3).

[242] See e.g. Blackburn (2001), 966–68; Loveland (1999), 121.

[243] See Loveland (1999), 122.

[244] See generally Joint Committee on Human Rights, *The Meaning of Public Authority under the Human Rights Act: Seventh Report*, 3 March 2004, http://www.publications.parliament.uk/pa/jt200304/jtselect/jtrights/39/39.pdf. See also the most recent report by the Joint Committee on Human Rights, *The Meaning of Public Authority under the Human Rights Act: Ninth Report*, 28 March 2007, http://www.publications.parliament.uk/pa/jt200607/jtselect/jtrights/77/77.pdf.

[245] Home Secretary Jack Straw, House of Commons Debates, 17 June 1998, vol. 314, col. 433.

[246] Home Secretary Jack Straw, House of Commons Debates, 17 June 1998, vol. 314, col. 406–408, 432–433.

has been interpreted narrowly.[247] Thus, a railway company or a water company exercises a public function when it supplies its services and their safety, but not when it is conducting commercial transactions.[248]

A controversial issue is that of the horizontal effect of the HRA and in particular the possibility to bring proceedings against another private party or group of individuals. Prior to the HRA, British law had no tradition of horizontal effect. The HRA (Section 6 para. 5) expressly excludes the direct horizontal effect of the Act.[249] However, it may still be possible to require judges to interpret the applicable law in conformity with the Convention (Section 3 HRA),[250] bestowing indirect horizontal effect on ECHR. Moreover, one may also argue that securing indirect effect is a judicial obligation, since courts *qua* public authorities are under a positive duty (Section 6 HRA) to interpret all legal norms in conformity with the Convention.[251] The courts now make extensive use of this duty, and one can affirm that the ECHR is vested with indirect horizontal effect in the UK legal order.[252]

ECHR rights may be invoked in one's own legal action (Section 7 para. 1(a) HRA), as well as in any other existing legal proceedings (Section 7 para. 1(b) HRA), such as in criminal or civil proceedings. According to Section 7 para. 6 HRA, "legal proceedings" applies to a criminal prosecution as well as an appeal of a court or tribunal decision, criminal or civil. The procedure for bringing a civil claim under the Act is generally the same as for any other civil claim, although certain specific provisions may be found in the rules applying to civil and family cases. The main provisions are the following. First, only High Court Judges, Circuit Judges or County Courts Recorders can entertain claims under the HRA.

---

[247] See the most recent report by the Joint Committee on Human Rights, *The Meaning of Public Authority under the Human Rights Act: Ninth Report*, 28 March 2007, http://www.publications.parliament.uk/pa/jt200607/jtselect/jtrights/77/77.pdf. See also the House of Lords' decision in *YL (FC) v. Birmingham City Council and others*, [2007] UKHL 27, confirming the *Leonard Cheshire* decision (*R (Heather) v. Leonard Cheshire Foundation*, [2002] EWCA Civ 366, [2002] 2 All ER 936).

[248] Lord Chancellor Lord Irvine, House of Lords Debates, 24 November 1997, vol. 583, col. 796. See e.g. *Poplar Housing Association Ltd v. Donoghue*, [2001] 3 WLR 183; *R (Heather) v. Leonard Cheshire Foundation* [2002] EWCA Civ 366 [2002] 2 All ER 936; *Aston Cantlow Parish Church Council v. Wallbank* [2001] 3 All ER 393.

[249] See *R. (Johnson & Others) v. Secretary of State for Constitutional Affairs & Another* [2007] EWCA Civ 26. See e.g. Joint Committee on Human Rights, *The Meaning of Public Authority under the Human Rights Act*: Ninth Report, 28 March 2007, http://www.publications.parliament.uk/pa/jt200607/jtselect/jtrights/77/77.pdf.

[250] See e.g. Hunt (1998); Wade (1998); Leigh (1999); Philippson (1999); Raphael (1999); Beatson et al. (2000); Wade (2000); Bamforth (2001); Brinktrine (2001); Hunt (2001); Young (2002), *Horizontality*; McDougall (2003); Du Plessis and Ford (2004). See e.g. *X v. Y* [2004] ICR 1634.

[251] See Lester and Pannick (2004), 31. See also Lord Chancellor Lord Irvine, House of Lords Debates, 24 November 1997, vol. 583, col. 783: the courts "have the duty of acting compatibly with the Convention not only in cases involving other public authorities, but also in developing the common law in deciding cases between individuals".

[252] See e.g. *Douglas v. Hello!* [2001] 2 WLR 992, 1027 and *Venables and Thompson News Group Newspapers* [2001] 2 WLR 1038.

Claims under the Act that challenge what other judges have done are to be tried only in the High Court. Second, plaintiffs (Section 4 para. 5 HRA) may only ask the High Court, Court of Appeal, House of Lords and Privy Council to issue declarations of incompatibility. Third, litigants must give proper notice that they will be pleading the HRA in a claim or an appeal, not least, to allow the Government to make representations in defence.

According to the HRA (Section 7 para. 5), proceedings should normally be brought within one year of the act being challenged (a longer period under equity). This limitation is subject to any shorter period applicable to the particular court proceedings being pursued, for example, judicial review applications where there is a three-month limitation period.[253] Under the ECtHR's case law, States enjoy a certain margin of appreciation under Article 6 ECHR's right to a fair trial with respect to the limitation periods,[254] though this limitation period does not apply to claims that are not directly made under the Act (Section 7 para. 1(b) HRA).

Claims may only be made with respect to facts taking place after the HRA came into force on 2 October 2000, as confirmed in the case of *In Re McKerr*. In this case, the House of Lords rejected the application for judicial review to compel the Secretary of State for Northern Ireland to hold an investigation into the death of the applicant's son under Article 2 ECHR and this despite the ECtHR's decision in *McKerr v. UK*.[255] The only limited exception to the non-retroactivity of the HRA (Section 22 para. 4) occurs when pending appeal proceedings began before that date, provided the claim is brought to defend an appeal in respect of a trial before 2 October 2000 and not to bring that appeal.[256] Thus, the Act can be used as a shield to prevent public authorities from instigating proceedings against an individual in relation to public action that took place prior to 2000, but not as a sword to attack a public authority.[257]

Under the HRA (Section 8), the Court that finds an act of a public authority unlawful may grant appropriate relief or remedy, or, under certain circumstances, damages, as it considers "just and appropriate". Judges possess broad discretion over choice of remedy, including ordering damages, granting an injunction to prevent a threatening or ongoing breach, invalidating a decision or legislation,[258] and making a declaration of incompatibility. The principles applicable to damages and injunctions are similar. Injunctions are generally ordered when damages would not be an adequate remedy. Courts have general discretion as to costs,[259]

---

[253] Rules of the Supreme Court, order 53; Supreme Court Act 1981, Section 31.

[254] See e.g. *Stubbings and Others v. the United Kingdom* (appl. nos 22083/93; 22095/93), Judgement (Chamber), 22 October 1996, Reports 1996-IV, 1487 et seq.; [1997] 23 EHRR 213.

[255] Compare *In Re McKerr*, [2004] 1 WLR with *McKerr v. the United Kingdom* (*supra* note 130). See Gordon (2005).

[256] See *R. v. Lambert* [2001] 3 WLR 206. Contra: *R. v. DPP ex parte Kebilene* [2000] 2 AC 326.

[257] O'Connell et al. (2006), 25–26.

[258] See e.g. *R. (Mahmood) v. Secretary of State for the Home Department* [2001] 1 WLR 840.

[259] Supreme Court Act 1981, Section 51(3) and Prosecution of Offences Act 1985, Sections 16 and 17.

though damages may be awarded only under the conditions specified (Section 8 paras 1, 3 and 4 HRA), by a court that possesses the power to award damages in civil proceedings (Section 8 para. 2 HRA).[260]

Compensation awarded must be "just and appropriate" which, according to the ECtHR, is to be defined on a case-by-case basis. The fact that a court has found a violation of the Convention may be deemed a sufficient remedy, without the provision of further damages. But compensation may also be "necessary to award just satisfaction" to the persons whose rights have been infringed, bearing in mind other available remedies. Finally, the courts must respect the principles applied by the ECtHR (under Article 41 ECHR), in order to reduce the temptation of plaintiffs going to Strasbourg.[261] The basic principle is that the injured party should be restored to the position they would have been in had the breach not taken place. When the act being complained of is a judicial decision, the procedure is that of appeal (Section 9 para. 1 HRA). Adequate remedy in those cases will be judicial review, including quashing a criminal conviction, except (Section 9 paras 3 and 4 HRA) in cases of wrongful detention in contravention of Article 5(5) ECHR, wherein compensation may be ordered.

An infringement of a right may be justifiable, but the burden of proof lies with State authorities. In the absence of legitimate justification, claimants bear the burden to prove their losses for purposes of compensation, and to show that losses suffered were caused by the infringement of the rights alleged. The ECtHR traditionally takes a strict approach to causation, and often skips monetary awards because it is not satisfied that the losses in question were caused by the infringement alleged. In fact, these principles are not very distant from those that apply to the remedies available from British courts in case of common law violations.[262]

The declaration of incompatibility is not regarded by the European Court as an effective domestic remedy under Article 35 ECHR; the fact that it is non-binding on the parties has been regarded as decisive by the Court.[263] For the ECtHR, to borrow the famous expression by Geoffrey Marshall, "a declaration of incompatibility is not a legal remedy, but a species of booby prize."[264] Empirically,

---

[260] See Hoffman and Rowe (2003), 71–73.

[261] Lord Chancellor, House of Lords Debates, 3 November 1997, vol. 582, col. 1232: "our aim is that people should receive damages equivalent to what they would have obtained had they taken their case to Strasbourg."

[262] On the difference between damages awarded in common law and those under the HRA, see *Anufrijeva v. Southwark London Borough Council* [2003] EWCA Civ 1406, 2204 QB 1124. See also The Law Commission and the Scottish Law Commission, *Damages under the Human Rights Act 1998*, Report October 2000, http://www.lawcom.gov.uk/docs/lc266.pdf.

[263] See e.g. *Hobbs, Richard, Walsh and Green v. the United Kingdom* (appl. nos 63684/00, 63475/00, 63484/00; 63468/00), Judgement (Fourth Section), 14 November 2006 (not yet reported); [2007] 44 EHRR 54; *Walker v. the United Kingdom* (appl. no. 37212/02), Judgement (Fourth Section), 22 August 2006 (not yet reported).

[264] Marshall (1999), 382.

one finds that decisions on incompatibility are strongly subject-dependent.[265] Deferral to the legislative branch tends to depend on whether the issue at stake is one of legislative policy or not, one that balances interests or not, one of expertise or not, etc.[266] In a series of controversial cases, of which *R. v. A.* and *Ghaidan* are good examples, the House of Lords has stressed that, while there is a limit to what can be done through Convention-compliant interpretation, judicial power is far-reaching.[267] As a result, judges are not always required to identify an ambiguity or absurdity in order to rely on the rule of construction of Section 3 HRA, although such interpretive freedom "does not entitle judges to act as legislators". Because drawing a line between legislating and interpreting is difficult or impossible,[268] outcomes are relatively unpredictable.[269] In any event, judges have no reason to consider that a declaration of incompatibility will automatically result in a comprehensive law reform, as confirmed by the *Anderson* case,[270] and often assume that such a declaration would fail to remedy the injustice in the case at hand.[271]

b. Proportionality Test

The ECtHR has gradually developed the criteria for justification of an interference to a right, whether that interference is foreseen expressly as in Articles 8 to 11(2) ECHR or not. These criteria are (i) legality, (ii) proportionality and (iii) the protection of a public interest or others' rights. A fourth element that is now added by the case law is the inviolability of a fundamental right's inner core.[272] Proportionality analysis comprises several elements, the most important of which is a least restrictive means test.[273] One obvious effect of the Court's reliance on proportionality review has been to require national officials to employ proportionality reasoning in their own decisions when assessing justifications of restrictions to the Convention. Proportionality review – especially the 'least-restrictive means' prong – is a highly intrusive form of judicial scrutiny of State action. One outcome of the reception of the ECHR has been the reception of proportionality, despite separation of powers doctrines that express hostility to judicial review.

---

[265] Compare *Bellinger v. Bellinger* [2003] 2 AC 467 or *International Transport Roth v. Secretary of State for the Home Department*, [2003] QB 728 with *R. v. A.* [2001] 3 All ER 1 or *Ghaidan v. Godin Mendoza* [2004] 2 AC 557.

[266] See the list of criteria in *International Transport Roth v. Secretary of State for the Home Department* [2002] 3 WLR 344.

[267] See *R. v. A.* [2001] 3 All ER 1 and *Ghaidan v. Godin Mendoza* [2004] 3 WLR 113. Contra: *R (Anderson) v. Secretary of State for the Home Department* [2003] 1 AC 837.

[268] See *Poplar Housing Association Ltd v. Donoghue* [2001] 3 WLR 183.

[269] See e.g. Kavanagh (2004), *Interpretation and Legislation*; Lester (2004); Rose and Weir (2003); Nicol (2004), *Statutory Interpretation*; Gearty (2002), *Reconciling*.

[270] See e.g. *R (Anderson) v. Secretary of State for the Home Department* (*supra* note 92). See Nicol (2004), *Statutory Interpretation*.

[271] See Jowell (2003).

[272] See e.g. *Jäggi v. Switzerland* (appl. no. 58757/00), Judgement (Third Section), 13 July 2006 (not yet reported).

[273] See e.g. *Vogt v. Germany* (appl. no. 17851/91), Judgement (Grand Chamber), 26 September 1995, Series A, Vol. 323; [1996] 21 EHRR 205.

The incorporation of the ECtHR's case law into British law made proportionality an all but required procedure for the scrutiny of executive action when Convention rights are relied upon. Before 2000, that scrutiny was ensured through the *Wednesbury* unreasonableness test: if a decision was lawful and within the bounds of a reasonable decision, it could not be challenged further.[274] Conflicts of rights were usually solved by balancing, or by priority rules, since statutory rights traditionally take priority over English common law rights. Questions pertaining to the absolute inner core of fundamental rights or to absolute rights *tout court* hardly ever arose. EU law had already contributed to acclimating public law to proportionality,[275] but only in limited areas. Since incorporation, judicial scrutiny of Government has sharpened and some would call it "anxious scrutiny".[276] British courts are now required to consider cases concerning human rights with a more substantive approach, including through proportionality analysis.[277] To quote Lord Steyn in the *Daly* case, in which the differences between the *Wednesbury* test and proportionality were described:

"The intensity of review is somewhat greater under the proportionality approach. [The] doctrine of proportionality may require the reviewing Court to assess the balance which the decision maker has struck [... and] attention to be directed to the relative weight accorded to interests and considerations."[278]

The European Court grants national officials a certain measure of autonomy, under the margin of appreciation doctrine. It is important to emphasize, however, that the margin of appreciation has no preventive application when a case is decided by a national court; national courts cannot anticipate the cases in which the European Court will recognize their margin of appreciation. Of course, there are times when national judges feel obliged to defer to the judgement of the Parliament or Government, for democratic reasons,[279] and where, as a consequence, the European Court might subsequently respect the national margin of appreciation. In any case, allowing a margin of appreciation does not suppress the European Court's overall supervision, and in particular over the requirement of proportionality between the infringement of the right and its justification.[280]

What might be feared is a national tendency to revert to prior tests in case of difficulties, as these tests are still used in various nuances in other areas of scrutiny of executive action and the presence of Convention rights does not al-

---

[274] See Jowell and Lester (1988) on the similarities and differences between the two principles.

[275] See e.g. De Burca (1993).

[276] See e.g. Lord Chancellor's Department's Study Guide 2002, pt 2.5.

[277] See e.g. De Burca (1998); Feldman (1999), *Proportionality*. See e.g. *Campbell v. Mirror Group Newspapers* [2004] UKHL 22.

[278] *R. (Daly) v. Secretary of State for the Home Department* [2001] 2 AC 532.

[279] See e.g. *R. v. DPP ex parte Kebilene* (*supra* note 256), 375.

[280] See e.g. *Handyside v. the United Kingdom* (appl. no. 5493/72), Judgement (Plenary), 7 December 1976, Series A, Vol. 24 and, more recently, *Evans v. the United Kingdom* (appl. no. 6339/05), Judgement (Grand Chamber), 10 April 2007 (not reported), § 77.

ways suffice to trigger the application of the proportionality test.[281] The European Court reemphasized the shortcomings of the *Wednesbury* test in a few decisions against the United Kingdom just before and after incorporation.[282] The debate surrounding the weighing of rights against national security interests in the UK and the British Government's intervention in the pending *Ramzy v. the Netherlands* case[283] is a case in point as it is clearly motivated by the Government's wish to see the European Court reverse its decisions in *Chahal v. UK*.[284] Moreover, proportionality tests may not always be used in conformity with the standards set by the European Court, as recent decisions of the House of Lords attest.[285]

2. Ireland

a. Remedies

Before incorporation, no remedies were afforded by Irish courts in case of infringement of Convention rights, though the courts guaranteed extensive remedies in case of infringement of the corresponding constitutional rights. The remedies available range in the latter cases from injunctions and declarations of invalidity to damages. The traditional declaration of constitutional invalidity in Irish law has an *erga omnes* effect; it is often said that such a finding amounts to a "judicial death certificate".[286] Further, the discretion of judges pertaining to the award of damages and their extent is broad, and the *locus standi* of potential victims has always been quite generous.

The ECHR Act enables individuals under the Irish jurisdiction to bring legal proceedings directly against public authorities on the ground that their Convention rights have been infringed. Under Section 3 para. 2 of the Act, a person who has "suffered injury, loss or damage" as a result of a contravention of Section 3 para. 1 of the Act may, if no other remedy in damages is available, institute proceedings to recover damages in respect of the contravention in the High Court or the Circuit Court. The main condition is that the victim has "suffered

---

[281] See e.g. Bondy (2003). See *R. (ProLife Alliance) v. British Broadcasting Corporation*, [2003] UKHL 23 [2003] 2 WLR 1403.

[282] See e.g. *H.L. v. the United Kingdom* (appl. no. 45508/99), Judgement (Fourth Section), 5 October 2004, Reports 2004-IX, 191 et seq.; [2005] 40 EHRR 32, arising from *Re L* [1999] 1 AC 458 (HL), [1998] 2 WLR 764 (CA); *Lustig-Prean and Beckett v. the United Kingdom* (*supra* note 135); *Smith and Grady v. the United Kingdom* (*supra* note 175). See, after that, Home Office Circular 32/2001, http://www.homeoffice.gov.uk/documents/cons-2001-communications-data/accessing-communications-da1.pdf?view=Binary, pt 4.4.

[283] Registry of the European Court of Human Rights, Press Release, Application no. 25424/05 lodged with the Court *Ramzy v. the Netherlands*, 20 October 2005.

[284] *Chahal v. the United Kingdom* (*supra* note 125). See, however, the ECtHR's most recent case in *Salah v. the Netherlands* (appl. no. 8196/02), Judgement (Third Section), 8 March 2007 (not yet reported) confirming *Chahal v. the United Kingdom*.

[285] See e.g. *Huang (FC) v. Secretary of State for the Home Department*, [2007] UKHL 11, paras 12–13. See also decisions in the context of the Prevention of Terrorism Act 2005, Section 10.

[286] See *Murphy v. Attorney General* [1982] IR 241 at 307. See also *Dunne Stores (Ireland) Co Ltd v. Ryan* [2002] 2 IR 60; *Cox v. Ireland* [1992] 2 IR 503.

injury, loss or damage" as a result of the Convention's violation. In contrast to the HRA, the ECHR Act does not expressly foresee that a person is a victim under the ECHR Act only if she can be a victim under Article 34 ECHR. The need for congruence between the Convention and the Act is confirmed, however, by the incorporation of the ECtHR's case law under Section 4 ECHR Act. Accordingly, there can be no *actio popularis* on the part of one or more citizens whose grievance is simply that domestic law might contravene the Convention. The issue is a sensitive one in Ireland, since the *locus standi* under constitutional law is more liberal than under Article 34 ECHR. It is often suggested, therefore, claimants seek *locus standi* on the basis of a constitutional right in an Irish law proceeding, then in subsequent proceedings argue that the constitutional right mirrors the protection offered by the Convention.

The ECHR Act (Section 3 para. 1) implies that a claim may be brought against every organ of the State that has not performed its functions in a manner compatible with the State's obligations under the Convention. As discussed, the notion of "organ of the State" is controversial. Any body established by law or through which any of the legislative, executive or judicial powers of the State are exercised is included, thus excluding the courts and Parliament. But, in contrast to the HRA, the definition is not founded on public functions, but on the formal delegation of public powers, which has the effect of excluding private or semi-public bodies, even when they exercise public functions. Thus, privately owned hospitals or residences, schools or other regulatory bodies can never be directly bound by Convention rights.

The direct horizontal effect of Convention rights is excluded; this is not surprising since Irish constitutional rights have no direct horizontal effect either. Since courts are precluded from the definition of the public bodies of Section 3 ECHR Act , they cannot be said to have a positive duty to apply the Convention to whatever legal material they are asked to apply. In contrast to what applies under the HRA, this prevents, therefore, courts from giving Convention rights an indirect horizontal effect through a construction of private law norms. This is quite limitative in a legal system based on judicial law-making.[287] This is even more surprising, as Irish courts often grant an indirect horizontal effect to constitutional rights through the constitutional interpretation of the common law, for instance.[288]

Infringements of the ECHR cannot give rise to criminal liability, but only to a civil claim for tortuous act (Section 3 para. 4 ECHR Act). The procedure for bringing a civil claim mirrors that of any other civil action, though ECHR claims can only be heard by judges of the High Court and Circuit Court. Further, under Section 5 para. 1 ECHR Act, only the High Court and the Supreme Court may grant a declaration of incompatibility (in any proceedings). Judges must give

---

[287] O'Connell (2004), *Critical Perspective*, 7.
[288] See e.g. Binchy (2002), 4.

proper notice to the Attorney General and the Human Rights Commission when a declaration of incompatibility under the Act is under consideration (Section 6 of the Act). Finally, proceedings to recover damages and to obtain declarations of incompatibility may only be granted when there is no other available and adequate remedy (Sections 3 para. 2 and 5 para. 1 ECHR Act). It may seem unreasonable and unduly burdensome to force an applicant to exhaust all normal remedies, such as judicial review, tort or constitutional action, before instituting Section 3 proceedings. However, the sub-constitutional status of the ECHR Act suggests the subsidiarity of remedies, compared to constitutional remedies. Section 3 remedies seem, therefore, to retain a residual quality at the most, and this makes for a suboptimal alternative to traditional remedies.[289]

According to Section 3 para. 5(a) ECHR Act, proceedings should normally be brought within one year of the act complained of. Under Section 3 para. 5(b), a longer period may be allowed where the court or tribunal considers it appropriate in the interest of justice. By comparison to the time limit applicable to other constitutional remedies under Irish law, this limitation seems anomalously short.[290] Litigation may pertain to facts taking place only after the Act came into force on 31 December 2003. In its decision in the *Dublin County Council* case, the court held that the ECHR Act has no retrospective effect and could not be used to judge a District Court hearing that had taken place before 31 December 2003.[291]

In case of breach of Section 3 para. 1 ECHR Act, Section 3 para. 2 provides that a person who has suffered a loss, injury or damage may, if no other remedy in damages is available, institute proceedings to recover damages in respect of the loss in either the Circuit Court or the High Court. Damages appear to be the most commonly sought remedy under Section 3, often together with a declaration of incompatibility under Section 5.[292] Note that the first ever declaration of incompatibility was granted by the High Court in the *Foy* case on 19 October 2007 in the case of a transsexual woman where, although (and probably because) Irish law was not unconstitutional, the fact that a post-operative transgendered woman was not entitled to an altered birth certificate under Irish law was regarded as clearly incompatible with the Convention, thus calling upon the Parliament to act.[293]

---

[289] Kilkelly (2004), *Introduction*, lviii; O'Connell et al. (2006), 32.

[290] See O'Connell (2004), *Critical Perspective*.

[291] *Dublin County Council v. Fennell*, [2005] 1 IR 604.

[292] See O'Connell et al. (2006), 77–79.

[293] See the High Court judgement of 19 October, 2007 *Lydia Foy v. Ireland*, [2007] IEHC. This case actually has a long running history. Back in 2002 in the High Court, McKechnie J. declined relief but, making reference to the ECHR he strongly urged the Oireachtas to legislate in the area (*Foy v. An t-Ard Chláraitheoir & Ors.* (High Court, 9 July 2002) [2002] IEHC 116). By the time the case went to the Supreme Court on appeal, the ECHR Act had been passed and the Supreme Court allowed amendment of the pleadings to include this point, as a result of which the case was sent back to the High Court for decision in November 2005. Meanwhile also the ECHR had made major

In contrast to the HRA, higher courts have no discretion as to what would constitute an appropriate relief or remedy; they are limited to granting *damages*, though they may award such damages as they consider appropriate. Following the ECtHR, this notion is to be defined on a case-by-case basis, but the injured party should be restored to the position they would have been in if the breach had not taken place. According to Section 3 para. 3 ECHR Act, the damages recoverable in the Circuit Court should not exceed the amount prescribed as the limit of that court's jurisdiction in tort. Unlike UK courts, higher courts in Ireland can neither grant an injunction to prevent a threatening or ongoing breach nor declare the invalidity of a decision, rule of law, or statute. The exclusion of remedies of an injunctive nature marginalizes the Convention as a human rights litigation instrument in Irish law.

The absence of declaration of invalidity also weakens the effectiveness of remedies provided. As mentioned, this gap may lead judges into constructing artificial interpretations of statutes to bring them in conformity with the Convention.[294] To be sure, higher courts may declare legislation incompatible (Section 5 ECHR Act), but this places "courts in a position where they can identify a breach of human rights and not be in a position to give an effective remedy."[295] If the same legislation was deemed asunconstitutional, it could be declared invalid *erga omnes* by Irish courts rather than merely incompatible. Although there is no obligation to pay compensation where an incompatibility has been established, the declaration of incompatibility entitles the parties to the proceedings to apply to the Attorney General for compensation in respect of an injury, loss or damage suffered as a result of the incompatibility concerned. The Government may then make an *ex gratia* payment of compensation to that party; its amount is related, under the Act, to the typically low amounts awarded by the European Court under Article 41 ECHR.

Overall, the ECHR Act's approach to remedies is difficult to square with Article 13 ECHR. In fact, future claimants are likely to go to Strasbourg and argue that they were not obliged to exhaust remedies under the ECHR Act.[296] Providing domestic remedies under the ECHR Act would have ensured that Convention infringements, and potential conflicts between the Irish Constitution and the ECHR, would be addressed by Irish courts, rather than set aside until the claimant goes to Strasbourg. There is a clear need for a radical expansion of the rem-

---

rulings in the area (see Goodwin case, *supra* note 137), just two days after the original High Court case. On 19 October, McKechnie J. declared that Irish law was incompatible with the ECHR. He did not however circulate an approved copy of the judgement, and invited the parties back at a later stage to make submissions on the precise form of order which he should make.

[294] Hogan (2004), 30–31. On proposals for reform of the interpretive model, see Hogan (2004); Binchy (2002); and O'Connell (2004), *Critical Perspective*.

[295] Irish Human Rights Commission, Submission to the Joint Oireachtas Committee on Justice, Equality, Defence and Women's Rights (2002), 4.

[296] See O'Connell (2004), *Critical Perspective*, 5; O'Connell et al. (2006), 119.

edies provided for under the 2003 ECHR Act. In the absence of revision, many hope that conventional control by the Judiciary can gradually be assimilated into Irish traditional constitutional review.[297] Indeed, there is hope that conventional guarantees will be *de facto* subsumed in Irish constitutional law, leading to declarations of conventional invalidity, rather than to conventional reconstructions of statutes or, worse, declarations of conventional incompatibility.[298]

As it stands, the Supreme Court may have the last word on the issue, when it decides an appeal to a High Court's ruling in *Carmody* – holding that the issue of ECHR compatibility must always be considered prior to constitutionality.[299] In a more recent case, however, the issue of constitutional compatibility was dealt with first, while the question of compatibility with the ECHR was put aside given that certiorari had already been granted on constitutional grounds.[300] The argument for this *sequencing* of constitutional and conventional issues is allegedly supported by the residual character of Section 5 ECHR Act's declaration of incompatibility and by the sub-constitutional nature of the mode of incorporation chosen. The Supreme Court will have to choose, but it might also suggest a middle path whereby conventional and constitutional issues are considered together.[301] In constitutional cases, the courts already go through an interpretive exercise at the outset, to assess whether the law can be read in a constitutional manner and in accordance with the presumption of constitutionality. Matters may prove complex if the ECHR is not taken into account at all at this early stage and is stored up for a second reading of the statute.

b. Proportionality Test

In the context of Irish judicial review, proportionality has been used as a principle of scrutiny well before incorporation in 2003. Traditionally, most cases of scrutiny went through the reasonableness and equity test, but in the 90's the courts began to use methods more akin to proportionality, albeit not always expressly recognized as such.[302]

The first express statement by an Irish court of the principle of proportionality dates back to 1994 in *Heaney v. Ireland*,[303] where the Supreme Court judges borrowed its formulation from a Canadian case. Three years later, in *Rock v. Ireland*,[304] a judge noted that the principle of proportionality was a well established tenet of Irish constitutional Law. Of course, the principle has also been

---

[297] O'Connell (2004), *Critical Perspective*, 11.

[298] Hogan (2004), 34.

[299] *Carmody v. Minister for Justice, Equality and Law Reform* [2005] 2 ILRM 1.

[300] See *Law Society v. Competition Authority* [2005] IEHC 455. See also Hogan (2006), *Declaration of Incompatibility*.

[301] See O'Connell et al. (2006), 32–33.

[302] See e.g. Hogan and Whyte (2003), 389–390. See already *Cox v. Ireland*, [1992] 2 LR 503 and *Re Article 26 and the Matrimonial Home Bill 1993* [1994] 1 IR 305.

[303] *Heaney v. Ireland* [1994] 3 IR 593.

[304] *Rock v. Ireland* [1997] 3 IR 484.

progressively reinforced by developments in EU law and their impact on Irish law.[305] As a result, the ECtHR's proportionality test was applied without difficulties to restrictions of Convention rights post-incorporation.

3. Comparison and Conclusion

While both countries differed greatly before incorporation – no specific human rights remedies in British law and full-blown constitutional remedies in Ireland – incorporation has led to more convergence, at least *prima facie*. Sections 7 and 8 HRA provided the basis for the drafting of Sections 3 and 5 ECHR Act. The usual concerns may be reiterated, however, pertaining, on the one hand, to the incompatibility between the chosen remedies under the ECHR Act and constitutional remedies under Irish law and, on the other, to the watering-down in the ECHR Act of many of the remedies provided for in the HRA. In sum, incorporation has brought the least effective new human rights remedies into the legal order where there were the most constitutional remedies, i.e. Ireland, and the strongest new remedies in the country which had the least, i.e. the UK.

Under the ECHR Act, remedies are residual, while HRA remedies are central. While the HRA does allow for broad discretion of judges who can choose between injunctions, declarations of invalidity, judicial review and damages, the ECHR Act restricts remedies to damages. Since declarations of incompatibility are not regarded by the European Court as an effective remedy in the sense of Article 13 ECHR, the only solution for Irish judges who insist on applying the ECHR through ECHR Act procedures is Convention-compliant interpretation, which may entail stretching statutory meaning to respect Convention rights. While some authors call for a revision of the ECHR Act in this respect, others argue that the ECHR will be more effective if subsumed under constitutional review by Irish judges, thus progressively extending the benefit of constitutional remedies to Convention rights as it has taken place in other Contracting States.

Finally, judges in both countries have adapted to the requirement of deploying proportionality tests. Diffusion to Ireland has been less problematic, since Irish courts had imported proportionality into constitutional law in 1994. Surprisingly, given the traditional opposition to strong judicial review of public acts in the UK, British judges seemed to have fully adopted the ECHR's proportionality requirement. Recently, however, the British Government has developed hostility towards it, at least in the context of national security measures against terrorism adopted since 2001.

---

[305] See e.g. Fennelly (1998).

G. Knowledge and Practice

In the UK and Ireland, the ECtHR's decisions are usually available in their English translation, shortly after judgement and simultaneously on-line on the HUDOC website.[306] Rulings are also reported in the *European Human Rights Reports*, published by Sweet and Maxwell. The system of informing practitioners and the public about national remedial measures, following an adverse judgement by the European Court, could be improved.[307]

National officials are not the only users and sources of information about the ECHR. This section also examines the important role played by private actors – human rights litigators, law teachers, doctrinal authorities and the media – in the reception process, including the dissemination of knowledge about the Convention.

1. United Kingdom

a. Public Education

The first source of dissemination of the European Court's judgements is the Executive itself. The entry into force of the HRA 1998 was postponed until 2000, in part, to train public officials for new responsibilities. From 1998 onwards, the Government has organized measures aimed at educating a broader public. Today, information and documents are regularly published by the Department for Constitutional Affairs, which has its own separate human rights website.[308]

Six years after incorporation, however, British residents, including non-specialist lawyers, are not very aware of the European Court, and even less of its judgements. Beyond the activities of Government and the courts, the impact of the ECHR has been less important than expected, post-incorporation. Britons do not identify with the HRA in a way that is comparable, say, to the way Germans identify with the rights provisions of their Basic Law. Since the UK has governed itself successfully without entrenched rights for centuries, it may be that the public will never identify with the HRA in that way without its own Bill of Rights,[309] or only over many years.

---

[306] See http://www.echr.coe.int/ECHR/EN/Header/Case-Law/HUDOC/HUDOC+database/.

[307] See in the United Kingdom, Joint Committee on Human Rights, *Implementation of Strasbourg Judgements: First Progress Report*, 8 March 2006, http://www.publications.parliament.uk/pa/jt200506/jtselect/jtrights/133/133.pdf, para. 7.

[308] http://www.dca.gov.uk/peoples-rights/human-rights.

[309] On this proposal, see e.g. Lester (2004). See also the discussion paper by Justice, *A Bill of Rights for Britain?* (London, 2007), http://www.justice.org.uk/images/pdfs/A%20Bill%20of%20Rights%20for%20Britain.pdf. See also on the potential content of that Bill, Department for Constitutional Affairs, Review of the Implementation of the Human Rights Act, July 2006, http://www.dca.gov.uk/peoples-rights/human-rights/pdf/full_review.pdf.

b. Judiciary

Judges have been key actors in the reception process. They frame national decisions so as to prevent adverse judgements by the European Court and generally contribute to the judicial dialogue that is the mark of a successful reception. Judges have also contributed to the diffusion of knowledge pertaining not only to the Convention, but to the European Court's judgements. There has been no shortage of conferences and publications involving British judges since 1998, and these have provoked and sustained interest in the HRA and dialogue about its implications.

Judges were carefully prepared to face the expected rise in litigation following incorporation. They received new training and the senior, appellate Judiciary was reorganized to ensure that experienced judges would be in place to deal with cases in which primary legislation would be subject to rights review. At the same time, the UK has made efforts to recruit future judges from a wider social and educational background.[310]

c. Lawyering

Incorporation generated reorganization of certain chambers, as barristers positioned themselves to more specialist work in the human rights field.[311] Some lawyers now work to defend victims' rights against public authorities, while others are engaged by the Government as junior counsels to defend against claims.

Incorporation of the Convention has also strengthened existing human rights protection groups and other non-governmental organizations,[312] sparked the creation of new groups and associations, and encouraged *pro bono* work among practitioners. Some groups have been extremely active not only in the information process since 1998, but also in the training (conferences and seminars) and the defence of victims of rights violations. The growth in the UK's associational and support network in the field of human rights would seem to be without comparison in Europe. Due to the limited scope of Section 7 HRA, these organi-

[310] See Report of the Home Affairs Committee on Judicial Appointments Procedures, HC Paper 52 Session 1995–1996.

[311] See e.g. Doughty Street Chambers (http://www.doughtystreet.co.uk/human_rights/), Matrix Chambers (http://www.matrixlaw.co.uk/AreasOfPractice_HumanRightsLaw.aspx) or Blackstone Chambers (http://www.blackstonechambers.com).

[312] One may mention civil liberties pressure groups, like *Liberty* (the National Council for Civil Liberties) (http://www.liberty-human-rights.org.uk/ and http://www.yourrights.org.uk), *AIRE* (Advice on Individual Rights in Europe), *Legal Action Group* (http://www.lag.org.uk/), *Charter 88* (http://www.charter88.org.uk/), the *1990 Trust* (http://www.blink.org.uk/), *Interrights* (http://www.interights.org/) or *Justice (British Section of the International Commission of Jurists)* (http://www.justice.org.uk/), but also *Amnesty* (http://www.amnesty.org.uk/) and *Human Rights Watch* (http://www.hrw.org/europe/uk.php). See also the *Northern Ireland Human Rights Consortium* (http://www.billofrightsni.org/), the *British Irish Human Rights Watch* (http://www.birw.org/), *Human Rights Lawyers Association* (http://www.hrla.co.uk/) and *Human Rights First* (http://www.humanrightsfirst.org). For other organizations, see the *British Human Rights Institute*'s website: http://www.bihr.org/.

zations have no *locus standi* under the HRA, although they may participate in common law proceedings pertaining to Convention rights violations. Even under HRA proceedings, they help litigants organize and frame their submissions, and they may represent claimants. They also regularly brief British courts and intervene as third party in pending proceedings,[313] and they provide information to the press.

d. Teaching

In addition to training future practitioners, law faculties produce and disseminate knowledge of the ECHR in obvious ways. At Oxford, to take one example, the ECHR, pre-incorporation, constituted part of the undergraduate Public International Law curriculum. There existed no specific human rights course, even within the International Law module. The reading lists in English Constitutional/Administrative Law mentioned human rights, but did not emphasize the ECHR. Most undergraduates might hear about human rights in domestic law through reading EU law, although those courses were not always compulsory. At the graduate level, Oxford offered a Comparative Human Rights class focusing on rights protection in the UK, Ireland, Canada, the United States, South Africa, India, Israel and sometimes countries like France and Germany.[314] Since 2000, much has changed. The Oxford undergraduate curriculum in English Constitutional/Administrative Law now entails an entire section on the Human Rights Act, and a new graduate class on International Human Rights was added. There are as yet no courses dedicated exclusively to the ECHR, although a new on-line Master's Degree in International Human Rights Law was launched in 2007.[315]

The situation was slightly better elsewhere in the UK, where some Bachelor and Master programmes offered human rights classes since the 90's, some even earlier.[316] Still, most law programmes developed specialist courses on the ECHR and international human rights after incorporation.[317] Recent years have seen an acceleration in the creation or strengthening of academy-based Human Rights Institutes and Centres all around the UK.[318]

---

[313] See e.g. Gearty (2006), 90–91; Hannett (2003); Smith (2004).

[314] See e.g. Gearty (2006), 94–95 on the New Zealand Bill of Rights *qua* model for the HRA 1998 and in particular relative to convention-compatible interpretation. See also Justice, *A Bill of Rights for Britain?* (London, 2007), http://www.justice.org.uk/images/pdfs/A%20Bill%20of%20Rights%20for%20Britain.pdf.

[315] See http://www.conted.ox.ac.uk/courses/international/mastersdegreeininternationalhuman rightslaw.asp#coursecontent.

[316] Note that given the two-years earlier incorporation of the Convention in Scotland through the Scotland Act 1998, Scottish Universities, and the University of Glasgow in particular, were the first to create courses in human rights in the United Kingdom.

[317] See e.g. Essex (http://www2.essex.ac.uk/law/postgraduates/prospectus/llm_ihr_prospective. html), Nottingham (http://www.nottingham.ac.uk/law/hrlc/courses/), London School of Economics (http://www.lse.ac.uk/Depts/human-rights/Teaching/msc_human_rights.htm) and Queen's University Belfast (http://www.law.qub.ac.uk/prospective/pg/crosscj.html).

[318] See e.g. Human Rights Centre at Essex (http://www2.essex.ac.uk/human_rights_centre/),

e. Scholarship

In the period just before and after the adoption of the HRA, academic discussions about incorporation were extremely lively. As an academic domain of inquiry, the field of human rights barely existed in domestic law as late as fifteen years ago. It has since exploded into prominence, as scholars produced a rising "torrent"[319] of books, new specialist journals,[320] and took to organizing practitioners' seminars and academic conferences on human rights.

Recently, human rights scholarship has been mainstreamed; one now finds in generalist legal journals and periodicals articles and even special sections on human rights and the Convention. Such is the case, for example, of the Oxford Journal of Legal Studies and the Modern Law Review, but also of specialized journals like Public Law. Since 2003, the scene has somewhat calmed. The field of human rights is now being institutionalized as a domain of scholarship among others in the UK, just as it has long been in other European states.

f. Media

Media coverage of ECtHR's judgements is irregular. The press usually covers cases pertaining to the UK, albeit with a critical eye and often inaccurately. Cases that relate to issues of interest to the man on the Clapham omnibus are usually more often reported than others. The *Lustig Prean and Beckett v. UK* case,[321] for example, was reported in virtually every serious outlet, including The Guardian, The Times, The Independent, The Daily Mail and The Daily Telegraph. Cases involving other European countries are typically not reported, unless they concern issues which might be of relevance to the UK at a later stage. One should, however, mention *The Times Law Reports*, which are an important vector for the dissemination of Convention law to the British general public.

2. Ireland

a. Public Education

In contrast to the UK, Ireland did not develop a structured programme of training in rights protection, for those working as "organ[s] of the State" under Section 3 ECHR Act. Nor did it organize an education scheme for the broader public. It was simply assumed that the Act could not bring much new in terms of protection to victims of human rights violations, given existing constitutional

---

Nottingham Human Rights Law Centre (http://www.nottingham.ac.uk/law/hrlc/), London School of Economics Centre for the Study of Human Rights (http://www.lse.ac.uk/Depts/human-rights/) and at Queen's University Belfast (http://www.law.qub.ac.uk/humanrts/). See also the British-Irish Human Rights Centres Network (http://www.law.qub.ac.uk/humanrts/network/index.htm) and the Transitional Justice Institute (http://www.transitionaljustice.ulster.ac.uk/index.html).

[319] Blackburn (2001), 961.

[320] See e.g. the *Human Rights Law Review* first published in 2001 and the *European Human Rights Law Review* first published in 1995.

[321] *Lustig-Prean and Beckett v. the United Kingdom* (*supra* note 135).

protections. Most of the education and information dissemination functions were left to the Irish Human Rights Commission and to the Irish Law Society, whose websites are well-organized and informative.[322]

b. Judiciary

The Irish Judiciary received no additional training either before or after incorporation in 2003,[323] nor was it regarded as necessary to reorganize the Judiciary and its staff to prevent a rise in ECHR litigation. It comes as no surprise then that Irish judges have never taken an active part in the dissemination of information about the Convention and its case law. Moreover, it has never been a practice for Irish judges to publish on Irish constitutional law, and incorporation did not change the situation with respect to the ECHR.[324]

c. Lawyering

No important changes occurred among barristers after the 2003 incorporation.[325] Lawyers simply included practice associated with the ECHR into their constitutional law practice. That said, incorporation does seem to have opened up some new areas of interest, including children's rights *qua* human rights.[326]

The Irish Bar Council and (especially) the Irish Law Society did much to provide information about the Convention and the impact of incorporation on Irish law in 2003 and 2004. The Society organized seminars and publications addressed to barristers, especially in the Law Society Gazette and the Bar Review.[327] The Bar itself also organized supplementary training.

It seems that the incorporation of the Convention has neither strengthened existing human rights protection groups and other non-governmental organizations, nor triggered the creation of new groups and associations in the field and *pro bono* work among practitioners.[328] The human rights community has always been very lively and independent in Ireland, an independence regarded as the price of an effective protection of human rights and democracy.[329] The Irish Council for

---

[322] See http://www.lawsociety.ie and http://www.ihrc.ie.

[323] Note, however, that the British NGO *Justice* organized training seminars based on the British experience shortly before incorporation in Ireland for the Attorney General's office and the State Prosecutor's office. See also the Judicial Studies Institute, http://www.jsijournal.ie/index.htm.

[324] See, however, O'Donnell (2007).

[325] See the Irish Bar Council website, http://www.lawlibrary.ie.

[326] See e.g. Kilkelly (2004), *Child and Family*.

[327] See the Irish Law Society website, http://www.lawsociety.ie.

[328] See e.g. *International Human Rights Network* (http://www.ihrnetwork.org) or the *Irish Section of the International Commission of Jurists* (http://www.icj.org/world_pays.php3?id_mot=274&lang=en). See also *Amnesty International Ireland* (http://www.amnesty.ie/), *Human Rights Watch Ireland* (http://hrw.org/doc?t=europe&c=irelan) or *Front Line: the International Foundation for the Defenders of Human Rights* (http://www.frontlinedefenders.org/).

[329] With respect to the key role played by these groups, one should mention Mary Robinson's *pro bono* work which allowed cases such as *Airey v. Ireland (No. 1)* (*supra* note 153) or *Norris v. Ireland* (*supra* note 150) 186 to be brought to Strasbourg.

Civil Liberties, for example, was founded in 1976 and quickly became a leading independent non-governmental organization working to defend and promote human rights and civil liberties in Ireland.[330] Due to the limited scope of Section 3(2) ECHR Act, these organizations have no *locus standi* under the ECHR Act, but they may, as discussed, bring Convention claims to bear through constitutional law proceedings. Although rights groups often help litigants pursue their claims, a notable difference with the British associative scene is the little funding available to Irish associations to react to human rights violations.

d. Teaching

Among the seven universities in Ireland, the National University of Ireland in Galway shelters one of the most important centres for human rights studies, the Irish Centre for Human Rights.[331] It was also the first university to create a Chair in human rights law, and it offers an LLM in International Human Rights Law as well. Another important centre, albeit not an Irish one strictly speaking, is the University of Ulster Human Rights and Equality Centre,[332] which organizes an LLM in Human Rights and Equality Law. One should also mention the Irish Centre for European Law based in Trinity College, Dublin and founded by Mary Robinson in 1988, whose remit includes European human rights law.[333]

The other universities do not offer specialized graduate courses in human rights as such, but human rights have always had an important place in Irish law school curricula. This applies both at undergraduate and graduate level, where the teaching of Constitutional Law, EU law and Public International Law has long encompassed chapters on Fundamental Rights including the Convention. There usually also offer specialist classes on Human Rights Law.[334]

Traditional administrative and constitutional law textbooks have long included an important section on constitutional rights and the Convention, and they now entail a section on the ECHR Act. The standard textbook in the field, J.M. Kelly's *Fundamental Rights in Irish Law and Constitution*, made regular references to the Convention as long ago as 1967. As one may see in the report's bibliography, however, editors did not organize many re-editions of the main textbooks, to adapt them to the ECHR Act, and no specific textbooks on human rights in Ireland have been published since incorporation.

e. Scholarship

In Ireland, too, the move to incorporate the Convention generated a great deal of academic discussion. After a flurry of conferences and publications in 2003 and 2004, interest receded. Scholars publish in generalist journals like the Irish

---

[330] See http://www.iccl.ie.
[331] See http://www.nuigalway.ie/human_rights/.
[332] See http://www.ulster.ac.uk/hrec/.
[333] See http://www.icel.ie/.
[334] See e.g. Trinity College Dublin (http://www.tcd.ie/Law/Courses.html).

Journal of European Law or the Dublin University Law Journal, or in specialist journals like the Irish Criminal Law Journal. But the greatest number of articles appears in the Law Society Gazette or the Bar Review, demonstrating the close links existing between practitioners and academia in Ireland generally, specifically on human rights issues.

The only new journal pertaining to human rights specifically is the *Irish Human Rights Law Review*, first published in 2006.[335] A unique feature of the journal is its *Annual Review of Human Rights Law* which summarizes all domestic and international human rights developments of relevance to Ireland, including a survey of cases taken against Ireland before international courts and committees, and analysis of leading cases under the ECHR Act 2003. Human rights scholarship is diverse in Ireland, and often highly politicized, not least when comparing British and Irish incorporation.[336]

f. Media
The Irish press has always covered news about adjudicating constitutional and fundamental rights, including news from Strasbourg. As early as the late 50's, for instance, the *Lawless v. Ireland No. 3* case attracted a lot of media attention.[337] Incorporation did not change much in this respect, not least, since the number of cases brought to Strasbourg has not increased dramatically. Generally speaking, and contrary to the attitude of the British (tabloid) press, 'international' standards are well regarded by the Irish media.

3. Comparison and Conclusion
While incorporation heavily impacted the law world in the UK, in Ireland judges, lawyers, scholars, and activists continued with business as usual. As we have seen, again and again, Ireland's pre-existing, domestic system of rights protection, one that enjoys huge support, meant that incorporation did not appear to be a great innovation, whereas in the UK incorporation comprises, in fact, a profound transformation of traditional practices. There is a second, international explanation. In Ireland, international human rights standards have always enjoyed wide support, whereas for the UK public, press, and political and legal elites, such standards can be regarded with scepticism.

IV. Concluding Comments

Although one cannot generalize from two cases, this chapter does tell us something about the reception of the ECHR in dualist States, at least in the negative.

---

[335] See http://www.claruspress.ie/ihlr.html.
[336] See e.g. Hogan (2004); O'Connell (2004), *Critical Perspective*.
[337] See e.g. Doolan (2001), 231.

In the absence of incorporation, both cases show, the Convention's effectiveness in dualist national legal orders may be virtually inexistent. Nearly 50 after signing the ECHR, both countries incorporated it, using roughly the same model. One might have assumed that the mode of incorporation into a dualist legal order would largely determine outcomes. In Ireland and the UK, however, the impact of acts of incorporation has been heavily mediated by pre-existing constitutional structure and practice.

In Ireland, a vibrant tradition of Constitutional rights and creative judicial review possesses far more standing and legitimacy than does the ECHR and the ECtHR. In the UK, given its own constitutional tradition of unrivalled legislative sovereignty, a corollary of which is the prohibition of judicial review of statute, the HRA is far more capable of disturbing the order of things. Indeed, one observes the HRA taking on the features of a quasi-constitutional statute, grounding new practices of rights protection that one commonly observes in legal systems in which rights review is more firmly established. These new practices may, in fact, pave the way to the gradual constitutionalization of an entrenched HRA. In Ireland, given the immense prestige and authority of the Constitution, the mode of incorporation chosen appears so weak that it may operate as little more than a 'legal irritant' for judges and others now required to make use of it.

In both countries, the evolution of EU law has played a significant role in the reception of the ECHR. The Luxembourg Court's doctrines of supremacy and direct effect, premised on a sophisticated monism, required painful adjustment in dualist countries like Ireland and the UK. As a source of enforceable Convention rights during the pre-incorporation period, EU law was actually more important to Irish and UK judges than the ECHR itself. Further, the European Court of Justice developed proportionality tests in various areas of EU law, which it required national judges to use as well. These developments prefigured aspects of the reception process of the ECHR in the UK and Ireland post-incorporation, giving that process a smoother quality than it might have had otherwise.

The comparison of our two cases also shows that late incorporation in dualist countries does not necessarily make for bad reception. Much depends on the rank given to the Convention, compared with other sources of law, and on the various powers given to public authorities, including courts, to tailor remedies for violation of rights guaranteed by the ECHR. If done right, dualist countries may have an advantage in incorporating through legislation, compared with the monist technique of enabling immediate validity and reception through adjudication. In addition to the benefits of enhanced political legitimacy, statutory incorporation can resolve, *ex ante*, many of the basic – but often difficult – questions of validity, applicability, and rank, rather than leaving such problems to judges to deal with on an *ad hoc* but continuous basis.

In the UK, it may be that late incorporation also served to empower the Judiciary more easily, whereas a frontal assault on Parliamentary sovereignty in the 50's was unimaginable; even in 2000, it would surely have failed. Through use, the HRA has enhanced judicial authority in relation to legislative and executive authority, an outcome that deserves emphasis, given separation of powers dogmas still in place. In Ireland, under different separation of powers arrangements, judges, who were already as powerful as judges anywhere in the world, are actually sheltered from the remedial reach of the ECHR Act. In the UK, statutory incorporation is transforming the reception process, giving it a more constructive, positive dynamic. British judges are now positioned to engage in a more serious dialogue of give-and-take with the ECtHR. The Irish Judiciary seems less interested in the ECHR, for the very reasons stated throughout this chapter.

For the analyst, late incorporation should be taken as a source of anxiety, in that future developments may quickly outpace one's conclusions. Comparing the status and effectiveness of the Convention over six years in one country, and over three years in another, is hazardous at best. In the case of Ireland, it is far too soon to measure the impact of incorporation on the legislative, executive and judicial machinery.

Finally, the United Kingdom and Ireland have been mutually regarding when it comes to human rights policy and protection mechanisms, due largely to their troubled joint history, and their conflict in Northern Ireland. This conflict has produced a dynamic of reaction and counter-reaction, mimicry, and endless comparison of each other's rights records. There is an irony to this dynamic. Over many decades, neither country thought that it needed to adapt its domestic legal system to the ECHR. Yet, in the end, dealing with their conflict has facilitated, at times even driven, the incorporation and reception of the ECHR into their respective legal orders.

Recapitulative comparative table

		United Kingdom	Ireland
National constitutional orders in general	Decentralization	Yes (devolution in Scotland, Northern Ireland and Wales)	No
	Religion (majority)	Anglican (NB: Northern Ireland)	Catholic
	Codified constitution	No	Yes
	Judicial review of legislation	No	Yes
	Entrenched human rights	No	Yes
	Natural rights	No	Yes
	Human rights remedies	No	Yes
	Relation to international law	Dualist	Dualist
	EU membership	Yes since 1973	Yes since 1973
Historical context: accession, ratification and incorporation	ECHR signatories	Yes since 1953	Yes since 1953
	Individual right of petition	Yes since 1966	Yes since 1953
	ECHR incorporated	Yes since 2000	Yes since 2003
	ECHR rights incorporated	- All rights except Articles 1 and 13 - All Protocols except Protocols nos 4, 7 and 12	- All rights except Article 1 - All Protocols except Protocol no. 12
	Reservations and derogations	- Only one reservation to Article 2 P1 - No more derogations under Article 15 ECHR, but had many	- Only one reservation to Article 6 ECHR - No more derogations under Article 15 ECHR, but had few
Status and rank of the ECHR in national law	Type of ECHR incorporation	- Sub-constitutional, but supra-legislative (rank) - Semi-direct (effect)	- Sub-constitutional and legislative (rank) - Indirect or interpretive (effect)

		United Kingdom	Ireland
Remedies in national law	Horizontal effect of ECHR	Yes (indirect only, positive duties of courts)	Yes (indirect only, no positive duties of courts)
	Courts as ECHR duty-bearers	Yes	No
	Remedies for ECHR infringement	- Specific remedies besides damages and declaration of incompatibility	- No specific remedies besides damages and declaration of incompatibility
		- No need to exhaust alternative remedies	- Need to exhaust alternative remedies
	Proportionality test	Yes, thanks to EU law and ECHR	Yes, expressly since 1994 (Canadian law and EU law)
Overview of the ECtHR's case law	Adverse judgements of the ECtHR	One of the highest numbers among original Contracting States in Europe, with a rise after incorporation (1/2 cases) and until three years after incorporation	One of the lowest numbers in Europe, with a rise after incorporation (3/5 cases) and until three years after incorporation
	Articles most violated	- Article 6(1) ECHR	- Article 6(1) ECHR
		- Article 8 ECHR	- Article 8 ECHR
Impact of the ECtHR's case law	Legislative remedial action	Average to negligent, both before and after incorporation (NB: fast-track remedial orders)	Good, both before and after incorporation (no fast-track remedial orders)
	Judicial remedial action in the case	No re-opening of the case (NB: JCHR's report)	No re-opening of the case
	Judicial remedial action in later cases	- No duty to follow case law pertaining to the UK or other countries	- No duty to follow case law pertaining to IRL or other countries
		- ECtHR's case law as maximal standard	- ECtHR's case law as minimal standard

		United Kingdom	Ireland
Mechanisms of coordination	Preventive legislative compliance	Yes (JCHR, pre-legislative scrutiny)	No (no pre-legislative scrutiny)
	Ex post legislative compliance	Yes (JCHR, fast-track remedial procedure)	No (no fast-track procedure)
	Human Rights Commission	Yes, in Northern Ireland since 1998 and in the United Kingdom since 2007 (Commission for Equality and Human Rights)	Yes, since 2000
Knowledge and practice of the ECHR	Human rights community (NGOs)	Yes (mostly since the 90's)	Yes (traditional)
	Media attitude & coverage	Hostile (euro-scepticism)	Favourable (peace-process)

Bibliography

Alston, P., *The EU and Human Rights* (Oxford, 1999).

Amnesty International, 'United Kingdom. Human Rights: A Broken Promise', *Amnesty International Online Documentation Archive* (23 February 2006) [http://web.amnesty.org/library/Index/ENGEUR450042006].

Amos, M., *Human Rights Law* (Oxford, 2006).

Anderson, D., 'The Law Lords and the European Courts', in Le Sueur, A. (ed.), *Building the UK's New Supreme Court, National and Comparative Perspectives* (Oxford, 2004), 199.

Austin, A. and McClean, E., 'Detention', in Kilkelly, U. (ed.), *ECHR and Irish Law* (Bristol, 2004), 181.

Bacik, I., 'Criminal Law', in Kilkelly, U. (ed.), *ECHR and Irish Law* (Bristol, 2004), 151.

Bamforth, N., 'Understanding the Impact and Status of the Human Rights Act 1998 within English Law', Global Law Working Paper 10/04 [http://www.nyulawglobal.org/workingpapers/documents/GLWP1004Bamforth_000.pdf].

—, 'The True Horizontal Effect of the Human Rights Act 1998', *Law Quarterly Review* 117 (2001), 34.

Beatson, J., et al., 'Horizontality: A Footnote', *Law Quarterly Review* 116 (2000), 385.

Binchy, W., 'The Bill, the Advantages and Disadvantages of the Approach Taken, and Possible Alternatives', paper delivered at Law Society of Ireland Conference on The Incorporation of the European Convention on Human Rights into Irish Law (Dublin, October, 2002).

Black-Branch, J., 'Parliamentary Supremacy or Political Expediency?: The Constitutional Position of the Human Rights Act under British Law', *Statute Law Review* 23 (2002), 59.

Blackburn, R., 'The United Kingdom', in Blackburn, R. and Polakiewicz, J. (eds.), *Fundamental Rights in Europe, The ECHR and its Member States, 1950–2000* (Oxford, 2001), 935.

—, 'A Parliamentary Committee on Human Rights', in Blackburn, R. and Plant, R. (eds.), *Constitutional Reform: the Labour Government's Constitutional Reform Agenda* (London, 1999).

—, *Towards a Constitutional Bill of Rights for the United Kingdom* (London, 1999).

—, 'A Human Rights Committee for the UK Parliament: The Options', *European Human Rights Law Review* 3 (1998), 534.

—, 'A Bill of Rights for the 21st Century', in Blackburn, R., and Busuttil, J. (eds.), *Human Rights for the 21st Century* (London, 1997), 25.

Blake, N., 'Importing Proportionality : Clarification or Confusion ?', *European Human Rights Law Review* 7 (2002), 19.

Blake, T., 'The National Archives: New Perspectives on Ireland's Approach to the International Protection of Human Rights', *Irish Law Times* 10 (1992), 44.

Bondy, V., 'The Impact of the Human Rights Act on Judicial Review: An Empirical Research Study', *Judicial Review* 8:3 (2003), 31.

Bradley, A., 'The UK before the Strasbourg Court 1975–1990', in Finnie, W., Himsworth, C. and Walker, N. (eds.), *Edinburgh Essays in Public Law* (Edinburgh, 1991), 185.

Bratza, N., 'The Treatment and Interpretation of the European Convention on Human Rights by the English Courts', in Gardner, J. (ed.), *Aspects of Incorporation of the European Convention on Human Rights into Domestic Law* (London, 1991), 65.

Brinktrine, R., 'The Horizontal Effect of Human Rights in German Constitutional Law : The British Debate on Horizontality and the possible role model of the German Doctrine of 'Mittelbare Drittwirkung der Grundrechte", *European Human Rights Law Review* 6 (2001), 421.

Clayton, R., Tomlinson, H., *The Law of Human Rights* (Oxford, 2006).

Cornes, R., 'McGonnell v. United Kingdom, The Lord Chancellor and the Law Lords', *Public Law* (2000), 166.

Costello, C., 'Ireland's Nice Referenda', *European Constitutional Law Review* (2005), 357.

—, 'European Community Judicial Review', in Keville, C. and Lucey, M. C. (eds.), *EU Law in Ireland* (Dublin, 2002), 17.

Costello, C. and Browne, E., 'ECHR and the European Union', in Kilkelly, U. (ed.), *ECHR and Irish Law* (Bristol, 2004), 35.

Craig, P., 'Report on the United Kingdom', in Slaughter, A.-M., Stone Sweet, A., and Weiler, J. (eds.), *The European Courts and National Courts – Doctrine and Jurisprudence* (Oxford, 1998), 196.

De Burca, G., 'Wednesbury Unreasonableness and Proportionality', in Andenas, M. (ed.), *English Public Law and the Common Law of Europe* (London, 1998).

—, 'The Influence of European Legal Concepts on UK Law: Proportionality and Wednesbury Unreasonableness', *European Public Law* 3 (1993), 561.

Dickson, B., *Human Rights and the European Convention: The Effects of the Convention on the United Kingdom and Ireland* (London, 1997).

Dillon-Malone, P., 'Privacy and Media Law', in Kilkelly, U. (ed.), *ECHR and Irish Law* (Bristol, 2004), 243.

Doolan, B., *Lawless v Ireland 1957–1961: A study of the first case to come before the European Court of Human Rights* (Aldershot, 2001).

Du Plessis, M. and Ford, J., 'Developing the Common Law Progressively – Horizontality, the Human Rights Act and the South African Experience', *European Human Rights Law Review* 9 (2004), 286.

Egan, S., 'Refugee Law', in Kilkelly, U. (ed.), *ECHR and Irish Law* (Bristol, 2004), 81.

Elliot, M., 'Parliamentary Sovereignty and the New Constitutional Order: Legislative Freedom, Political Reality and Convention', *Legal Studies* 22 (2002), 340.

Farran, S., *The UK Before the European Court of Human Rights: Case Law and Commentary* (London, 1996).

Feldman, D., 'Proportionality and the Human Rights Act 1998', in Ellis, E. (ed.), *The Principle of Proportionality in the Laws of Europe* (Oxford, 1999), 117.

Fennelly, N., 'Legal interpretation – towards freedom of movement of principles', in Andenas, M. (ed.), *English Public Law and the Common Law of Europe* (London, 1998).

Finlay, A., 'The Human Rights Act: The Lord Chancellor's Department's Preparations for Implementation', *European Human Rights Law Review* 4 (1999), 512.

Flynn, L., 'The Significance of the European Convention on Human Rights in the Irish Legal Order', *Irish Journal of European Law* 3 (1994), 4.

Gearty, C., *Can Human Rights Survive?* (Cambridge, 2006).

—, *Principles of Human Rights Adjudication* (Oxford, 2004).

—, 'Reconciling Parliamentary Democracy and Human Rights', *Law Quarterly Review* 118 (2002), 248.

—, 'The United Kingdom', in Gearty, C. (ed.), *European Civil Liberties and the European Convention on Human Rights* (The Hague, 1997), 53.

Gordon, A., 'Human Rights in Northern Ireland after McKerr', *European Public Law* 11 (2005), 5.

Hampson, F., 'The UK Before the European Court of Human Rights', *Yearbook of European Law* (1990), 121.

Hannett, S., 'Third Party Interventions: In the Public Interest?', *Public Law* (2003), 128.

Hoffman, D. and Rowe, J., *Human Rights in the UK, An Introduction to the Human Rights Act 1998* (London, 2003).

Hogan, G., 'The Value of Declarations of Incompatibility and the Rule of Avoidance', *Dublin University Law Journal* 28 (2006), 408.

—, 'Ireland: The European Convention on Human Rights Act 2003', *European Public Law* 12 (2006), 331.

—, 'Incorporation of the ECHR: Some Issues of Methodology and Process', in Kilkelly, U. (ed.), *ECHR and Irish Law* (Bristol, 2004), 13.

—, 'The Belfast Agreement and the Future Incorporation of the ECHR in the Republic of Ireland', *Bar Review* 4 (1999), 205.

Hogan, G. and Whyte, G., *The Irish Constitution*, 4th edn (London, 2003).

Hunt, M., 'The horizontal effect' of the Human Rights Act: Moving beyond the public-private distinction', in Jowell, J. and Cooper, J. (eds.), *Understanding Human Rights Principles* (Oxford, 2001), 161.

—, 'The Horizontal Effect of the Human Rights Act', *Public Law* (1998), 423.

—, *Using Human Rights Law in English Courts* (Oxford, 1997).

Jacobs, F.G. and Roberts, S., *The Effect of Treaties in Domestic Law* (London, 1987).

Jowell, J., 'Judicial Deference : Servility, Civility or Institutional Capacity', *Public Law* (2003), 592.

Jowell, J. and Lester, Lord, 'Proportionality: Neither Novel Nor Dangerous', in Jowell, J. and Oliver, D. (eds.), *New Directions in Judicial Review* (London, 1988).

Justice, *Legislating for Human Rights: Developing a Human Rights Approach to Parliamentary Scrutiny* (London, 1999).

Kavanagh, A., 'Statutory Interpretation and Human Rights after Anderson: a more contextual approach', *Public Law* (2004), 537.

—, 'The Elusive Divide between Interpretation and Legislation under the Human Rights Act 1998', *Oxford Journal of Legal Studies* 24 (2004), 259.

Kenna, P., 'Property, Housing and Environment', in Kilkelly, U. (ed.), *ECHR and Irish Law* (Bristol, 2004), 281.

Kilkelly, U., 'Child and Family Law', in Kilkelly, U. (ed.), *ECHR and Irish Law* (Bristol, 2004), 111.

—, 'Introduction', in Kilkelly, U. (ed.), *ECHR and Irish Law* (Bristol, 2004), i.

Kinley, D., *The European Convention on Human Rights: Compliance without Incorporation* (Aldershot, 1993).

Klug, F. and Starmer, K., 'Standing back from the Human Rights Act: How Effective is it Five Years on?', *Public Law* (2005), 716.

Le Sueur, A., 'The Conception of the UK's New Supreme Court', in Le Sueur, A. (ed.), *Building the UK's New Supreme Court, National and Comparative Perspectives* (Oxford, 2004), 3.

Leigh, I., 'Horizontal Rights, The Human Rights Act and Privacy: Lessons from the Commonwealth', *International and Comparative Law Quarterly* 48 (1999), 57.

Lester, Lord, 'The Human Rights Act 1998 – Five Years On', *European Human Rights Law Review* 9 (2004), 258.

—, 'The Art of the Possible: Interpreting Statutes under the Human Rights Act', *European Human Rights Law Review* 3 (1998), 665.

—, 'UK acceptance of the Strasbourg jurisdiction: what really went on in Whitehall in 1965', *Public Law* (1998), 273.

Lester, Lord and Pannick, D., *Human Rights Law and Practice*, 2nd edn (London, 2004).

—, 'The Impact of the Human Rights Act on Private Law: The Knight's Move', *Law Quarterly Review* 116 (2000), 380.

Lord Chancellor's Department, *Study Guide on the Human Rights Act 1998*, 2nd edn (London, 2002).

Loveland, I., 'Incorporating the European Convention on Human Rights into UK law', *Parliamentary Affairs* 112 (1999), 121.

Marshall, G., 'Two kinds of incompatibility: more about Section 3 of the Human Rights Act 1998', *Public Law* (1999), 377.

—, 'Interpreting Interpretation in the Human Rights Bill', *Public Law* (1996), 170.

Marson, G., 'The United Kingdom's Part in the Preparation of the European Convention on Human Rights', *International and Comparative Law Quarterly* 48 (1993), 796.

Martin, D., *Egalité et non-discrimination dans la jurisprudence communautaire* (Bruxelles, 2006).

McDougall, C., 'The Big Sleep – The Horizontal Debate Simplified', *Judicial Review* (2003), 98.

Mullan, G., 'Discrimination Law', in Kilkelly, U. (eds.), *ECHR and Irish Law* (Bristol, 2004), 217.

Nicol, D., 'Statutory Interpretation and Human Rights After Anderson', *Public Law* (2004), 274.

O'Connell, D., 'The ECHR Act 2003: A Critical Perspective', in Kilkelly, U. (eds.), *ECHR and Irish Law* (Bristol, 2004), 1.

—, 'Ireland', in Blackburn, R. and Polakiewicz, J. (eds.), *Fundamental Rights in Europe, The ECHR and its Member States, 1950–2000* (Oxford, 2001), 423.

O'Connell, D., Cummiskey, S. and Meeneghan, E. with O'Connell, P., *ECHR Act 2003, A Preliminary Assessment*, Published by the Law Society of Ireland and the Dublin Solicitors Bar Association (Dublin, 2006) [http://www.lawsociety.ie/documents/committees/hr/ECHR/ECHRreport18oct06.pdf].

O'Donnell, T.E., 'The Constitution, the European Convention on Human Rights Act 2003 and the District Court – A Personal View from a Judicial Perspective', Judicial Studies Institute Journal (2007) 1, 137.

Phelan, D., *Revolt or Revolution: The Constitutional Boundaries of the European Community* (Dublin, 1997).

—, '*Right to Life of the Unborn v. Promotion of Trade in Services: The European Court of Justice and the Normative Shaping of the European Union*', *Modern Law Review* 55 (1992), 55.

Raphael, T., 'The Problem of Horizontal Effect', *European Human Rights Law Review* 4 (1999), 824.

Reed, Lord, and Murdoch, J., *A Guide to Human Rights Law in Scotland* (London, 2001).

Robertson, A.H. and Merrills, J.G., *Human Rights in Europe*, 3rd edn (Manchester, 1993).

Rodger of Earlsferry, Lord, 'The National Perspective in the Protection of Fundamental Rights. Problems of Co-ordination with the European Instruments and Courts: a British Perspective', unpublished manuscript of the conference given at the European Lawyers Conference (Geneva, September 2005).

Rose, D. and Weir, C., 'Interpretation and Incompatibility: Striking the Balance', in Jowell, J. and Cooper, J. (eds.), *Delivering Rights. How the Human Rights Act is Working* (Oxford, 2003), 37.

Ryle, M., 'Pre-legislative Scrutiny: A Prophylactic Approach to Protection of Human Rights', *Public Law* (1994), 192.

Scarman, L., *English Law - The new dimension*. The Hamlyn Lectures, 26th Series (London, 1974).

Simpson, W.B., *Human Rights and the End of Empire - Britain and the Genesis of the European Convention* (Oxford, 2001).

Smith, R., 'Test Case Strategies and the Human Rights Act', *Justice Journal* 1 (2004), 65.

Steyn, Lord, 'The New Legal Landscape', *European Human Rights Law Review* 5 (2000), 549.

—, 'Incorporation and Devolution: Some Reflections on the Changing Scene', *European Human Rights Law Review* 3 (1998), 153.

Young, A., 'Remedial and Substantive Horizontality: *The Common Law and Douglas v. Hello! Ltd*', *Public Law* (2002), 232.

Straw, J., 'Human Rights and Wrongs', *Fabian Review* (2000), 11.

Symmons, C., 'The Incorporation of Customary International Law into Irish Law', in Biehler, G. (ed.), *International Law in Practice: An Irish Perspective* (Dublin, 2005), 111.

Wade, W., 'Horizons of Horizontality', *Law Quarterly Review* 116 (2000), 217.

—, 'Human Rights and the Judiciary', *European Human Rights Law Review* 3 (1998), 520.

Whyte, G., 'The Application of the European Convention on Human Rights Before the Irish Courts', *International and Comparative Law Quarterly* 31 (1982), 856.

3

The Reception Process in France and Germany

Elisabeth Lambert Abdelgawad and Anne Weber

A. Historical Context: Accession and Ratification[1]

1. France

a. France's Accession to the ECHR and its Additional Protocols

Although France was one of the Council of Europe's founding States, signing the text of the Convention on 4 November 1950, it ratified the ECHR only on 3 May 1974,[2] after fifteen European States had already done so, and several prior attempts had failed. The ratification was undertaken to demonstrate faith in the European ideal, rather than to achieve any pressing domestic purpose.[3] As the sixteenth of the then seventeen Council of Europe Members to become party to the Convention (Switzerland being the last), France's accession was quite late.[4] The same can be said of the French position with respect to the two Covenants

---

[1] Abbreviations: AFDI: Annuaire Français du Droit International; AJDA: Actualité Juridique Droit Administratif; Ass.: Assemblée; BGBl: Bundesgesetzblatt (Federal Law Gazette); Bull.: Bulletin; BVerfGE: Entscheidungen des Bundesverfassungsgerichts (Decisions of the Federal Constitutional Court); Cass.: Cour de Cassation; Ch/Chbre: Chambre (Civ.: civile, Crim.: criminelle, Soc.: sociale); CCPR: United Nations Covenant on Civil and Political Rights; CE: Conseil d'Etat; Dall.: Dalloz; CESCR: United Nations Covenant on Economic, Social and Cultural Rights; Doc. Parl.: Document Parlementaire; ECHR: European Convention on Human Rights; ECommHR : European Commission of Human Rights; ECtHR: European Court of Human Rights; EuGRZ: Europäische Grundrechte Zeitschrift; GP: Gazette du Palais; IR: Informations Rapides; JCP: La Semaine Juridique; J.O.: Journal Officiel de la République Française; NJW: Neue Juristiche Wochenschrift; RJF: Revue de Jurisprudence Fiscale; RDP: Revue du Droit Public et de la science politique en France et à l'étranger; RDH: Revue des Droits de l'Homme; RFDA: Revue Française de Droit Administratif; RFDC: Revue Française de Droit Constitutionnel; RIDC: Revue Internationale de Droit Comparé; RTDH: Revue Trimestrielle des Droits de l'Homme; Sect.: Section; ZPO: Zivilprozessordnung (Code of Civil Procedure).

[2] Decree 74-360 dated 3 May 1974 publishing the ECHR, JO, 4 May 1974, 4750.

[3] Lazaud (2006, vol. 1), 21.

[4] Pellet (1974), 1328.

of the United Nations.[5] Obvious distrust[6] (at the very least) characterized the relationship between France and the ECHR during the first 30 years.

Several different reasons contributed to these 30 long years of distrust. In the 50's, France was unable to overcome its internal controversies surrounding secular education. Partisans of secularism feared that Article 2 (Protocol no. 1) would compel the State to finance private denominational schools.[7] Secondary problems included the reluctance of the politically unstable governments of the Fourth Republic to tackle sensitive issues, the existence of special courts as well as the practice of torture and ill treatment of prisoners during the Algerian War, and decolonization. In the 60's, arguments of a more technical nature arose, including: the fear that the state monopoly on radio and television would be challenged; the alleged Anglo-Saxon bias in the Convention's approach to criminal law, and the question of the compatibility of Article 16 of the French Constitution (Presidential emergency powers) with Article 15 ECHR. Perhaps most important, however, was the general hostility to the regime's supranationalism.[8] National officials also routinely asserted that ratification would be superfluous, since national laws provided a sufficient guarantee of the rights of individuals.[9] Further, supporters of ECHR ratification – among members of the university community, the bar, the courts and human rights associations – were not able to unite to form a sufficiently powerful lobbying group.

In addition to being late, the French ratification was also restricted in scope. Although France accepted the compulsory jurisdiction of the Court (former Article 46 ECHR) for a renewable period of three years and on condition of reciprocity in 1974, four months after having denounced the declaration of acceptance of the compulsory jurisdiction of the International Court of Justice, it refused to adopt the declaration under former Article 25 ECHR relative to the competence of the Commission concerning the individual right to petition. Indeed, this position was not limited to the ECHR but characterized the French response to other international treaties on human rights.[10] Once again, France distinguished itself from its closest European partners, which had virtually unanimously accepted the declaration under former Article 25 ECHR at the time of accession. Officials asserted that they needed time to assess the implications of implementing

---

[5] France only acceded to the United Nations Covenants (CESCR and CCPR) on 4 November 1980 and to the CCPR's Optional Protocol on 17 February 1984. See Imbert (1980).

[6] Monnerville, G., J.O., Débats, Sénat, session dated 30 October 1973, 1541.

[7] Errera (1970), 572.

[8] Costa (2004), 6.

[9] Explanatory Report relative to the Bill concerning ratification: The Government "does not believe that this engagement is necessary to secure for its citizens the liberties that our laws guarantee", J.O., Doc. Parl., Sénat, 1° ordinary session, 1973-1974, no. 2.

[10] Cf. the accession to the CCPR and to the 1965 Convention on the Elimination of Racial Discrimination.

the ECHR.[11] In spite of numerous Parliamentary and doctrinal pressures, the individual right to petition was only recognized on 3 October 1981,[12] during the presidency of François Mitterrand, and only for a limited and renewable period of five years (renewed for a period of three years in 1986, for five years in 1989, and again for five years in 1994). Thus, the first judgement against France rendered by the Court only dates from December 1986.[13]

France[14]

Protocol	Signature	Ratification	Entry into force	Declarations/ Reservations
Protocol no. 1	20 March 1952	3 May 1974	3 May 1974	1 Declaration concerning Article 4
Protocol no. 2	2 Oct. 1981	2 Oct. 1981	2 Oct. 1981	–
Protocol no. 3	22 Oct. 1973	3 May 1974	3 May 1974	–
Protocol no. 4	22 Oct. 1973	3 May 1974	3 May 1974	1 Declaration concerning Article 5
Protocol no. 5	22 Oct. 1973	3 May 1974	3 May 1974	–
Protocol no. 6	28 April 1983	17 Feb. 1986	1 March 1986	–
Protocol no. 7	22 Nov. 1984	17 Feb. 1986	1 Nov. 1988	4 Reservations concerning Articles 2-6, 1 Declaration concerning Article 2[15]
Protocol no. 8	19 March 1985	9 Feb. 1989	1 Jan. 1990	–

[11] Cf. the explanatory report relative to the Bill concerning ratification of the ECHR as presented to the Parliament in 1973, J.O., Débats, Sénat, session dated 30 October 1973, 1540.

[12] Decree no. 81–917 dated 9 October 1981.

[13] *Bozano v. France* (appl. no. 9990/82), Judgement (Chamber), 18 December 1986, Series A, Vol. 111.

[14] Source:http://conventions.coe.int/Treaty/Commun/ChercheMembres.asp?CM=3&CL=ENG (all websites in this report were checked at the end of June 2007).

[15] Declaration: "The Government of the French Republic declares that, in accordance with the meaning of Article 2 (1), the review by a higher court may be limited to a control of the application of the law, such as an appeal to the Supreme Court". (1 November 1988 – present). Source: http://conventions.coe.int/Treaty/Commun/ChercheMembres.asp?CM=3&CL=ENG.

Reservation: "The Government of the French Republic declares that only those offences which under French law fall within the jurisdiction of the French criminal courts may be regarded as offences within the meaning of Articles 2 to 4 of this Protocol." (1 November 1988 – present). Source: http://conventions.coe.int/Treaty/Commun/ChercheMembres.asp?CM=3&CL=ENG

Reservation: "The Government of the French Republic declares that Article 5 may not impede the application of the rules of the French legal system concerning the transmission of the patronymic name." (1 November 1988 – present). Source: http://conventions.coe.int/Treaty/Commun/ChercheMembres.asp?CM=3&CL=ENG.

Reservation: "Article 5 may not impede the application of provisions of local law in the territorial collectivity of Mayotte and the territories of New Caledonia and of the Wallis and Futuna Archipelago." (1 November 1988 – present). Source: http://conventions.coe.int/Treaty/Commun/ChercheMembres.asp?CM=3&CL=ENG.

Protocol	Signature	Ratification	Entry into force	Declarations/Reservations
Protocol no. 9	6 Nov. 1990	–	–	–
Protocol no. 10	25 March 1992	–	–	–
Protocol no. 11	11 May 1994	3 April 1996	1 Nov. 1998	–
Protocol no. 12	–	–	–	–
Protocol no. 13	3 May 2002	–	–	–
Protocol no. 14	13 May 2004	7 June 2006	–	–

b. French Reservations and Declarations

Until comparatively recently, France made no effort to adapt its domestic law to the Convention, while citing divergences between the ECHR and national law as an obstacles to ratification. Accession to the ECHR and its various Protocols was thus marked by reservations and declarations, including those pertaining to the question of territorial application. The interpretive declaration concerning Article 10 ECHR was reiterated in 1988. In particular, France attached two reservations in 1974, the first in relation to Articles 5 and 6 ECHR and the law applicable to the armed forces.[16] The second concerned Article 15 ECHR, which gave rise to fears on the part of French authorities that organs of the ECHR could assert control over the acts of the President of the Republic during a state of emergency (Article 16 of the Constitution). France also registered an interpretive declaration in relation to Article 2(1) Protocol no. 7 (concerning the right to appeal in criminal matters).[17] Two reservations were also lodged upon accession to Protocol no. 7, the first concerning Articles 2, 3 and 4, and the second concerning Article 5.

France's reluctant accession to the European system of human rights appears to have been more about duty than choice. Indeed, it was not until 1992 that

---

Reservation: "Protocol no. 7 to the Convention for the Protection of Human Rights and Fundamental Freedoms shall apply to the whole territory of the Republic, due regard being had where the overseas territories and the territorial collectivity of Mayotte are concerned, to the local requirements referred to in Article 63 [Article 56 since the entry into force of Protocol no. 11] of the European Convention on Human Rights and Fundamental Freedoms." (1 November 1988 – present). Source: http://conventions.coe.int/Treaty/Commun/ChercheMembres.asp?CM=3&CL=ENG.

[16] *D. v. France* (appl. no. 10127/82), Decision (Plenary), Commission, 4 July 1984, DR 39, 210. This reservation prevents the Commission from examining the length of proceedings in administrative jurisdictions, and the pertinence of Article 13 to situations covered by Article 5(4) ECHR.

[17] The Court of Cassation thus ruled, in conformity with this declaration, that the ECHR is not in conflict with the fact that the Court of Assize (the criminal court in charge of judging the most serious crimes) takes decisions in the last resort (Cass., Crim., 23 June 1999; Cass., Crim., 22 November 2000). Nonetheless, according to law no.2000-516 dated 15 June 2000, rulings of this Court of Assize may now be appealed before another Court of Assize, which has been appointed by the criminal chamber of the Court of Cassation.

the Bureau of Human Rights was established within the service of European and International Affairs of the Justice Ministry (created in 1991).

2. Germany

a. Germany's Accession to the ECHR and its Additional Protocols

Germany became the fourteenth Member State of the Council of Europe on 13 July 1950, before which it participated as an associated member without vote. Germany signed the ECHR on 4 November 1950, and ratified it on 5 December 1952.[18] It was the fourth State to do so among the initial Parties to the Convention, which entered into force on 3 September 1953.

Germany also rushed to accept the right to individual petition and the compulsory jurisdiction of the Court: it lodged declarations pursuant to former Articles 25 and 46 ECHR on 5 July 1955, for a definite period of five years, which were then renewed periodically until Protocol no. 11 entered into force.

To date, Germany has ratified all additional Protocols to the Convention, with the exception of Protocols nos 7 and 12, which have only been signed. Germany remains cautious concerning Protocol no. 7, which provides a number of additional guarantees regarding the expulsions of aliens, fair trial and equality between spouses, and Protocol no. 12, concerning non-discrimination.

Germany[19]

Protocol	Signature	Ratification	Entry into force	Declarations / Reservations
Protocol no. 1	20 March 1952	13 Feb. 1957	13 Feb. 1957	1 Declaration concerning Article 2
Protocol no. 2	6 May 1963	3 Jan. 1969	21 Sept. 1970	–
Protocol no. 3	6 May 1963	3 Jan. 1969	21 Sept. 1970	–
Protocol no. 4	16 Sept. 1963	1 June 1968	1 June 1968	–
Protocol no. 5	3 March 1966	3 Jan. 1969	20 Dec. 1971	–
Protocol no. 6	28 April 1983	5 July 1989	1 Aug. 1989	1 Declaration
Protocol no. 7	19 March 1985	–	–	1 Declaration
Protocol no. 8	19 March 1985	19 Sept. 1989	1 Jan. 1990	–
Protocol no. 9	22 May 1992	7 July 1994	1 Nov. 1994	–
Protocol no. 10	25 March 1992	7 July 1994	–	–
Protocol no. 11	11 May 1994	2 Oct. 1995	1 Nov. 1998	–

---

[18] Saarland ratified the ECHR on 14 January 1953 and became an integral part of Germany on 1 January 1957.

[19] Source: http://conventions.coe.int/Treaty/Commun/ChercheMembres.asp?CM=3&CL=ENG

Protocol	Signature	Ratification	Entry into force	Declarations / Reservations
Protocol no. 12	4 Nov. 2000	–	–	–
Protocol no. 13	3 May 2002	11 Oct. 2004	1 Feb. 2005	–
Protocol no. 14	10 Nov. 2004	11 April 2006	–	–

The reasons for the early German ratification are twofold. With the adoption of its Basic Law (*Grundgesetz*) in 1949, Germany possessed its own extensive catalogue of fundamental rights and system of rights protection, thereby facilitating ratification of the Convention. With the introduction of the constitutional complaint (*Verfassungsbeschwerde*) in 1951, the guarantees within the German legal order were even higher than within the European system. German ratification of the ECHR can also be understood as an important political signal to the international community of its commitment to democratization and rights protection.[20] The quick ratification of the ECHR demonstrated German good will to live up to the expectations of the international community, and its wish to reintegrate into the latter and to distance itself from the past. Ratification of the ECHR, and acceptance of the right of individual petition, were first important steps toward the country's international rehabilitation.

During the ratification process, the Committee on Legal Affairs (*Rechtsausschuss*) of the German Parliament (*Bundestag*) stressed that the catalogue of fundamental rights contained in the Basic Law was compatible with provisions of the ECHR. Germany therefore made only few reservations and interpretative declarations.

b. German Reservations and Declarations

aa. Declarations in force. Upon ratification, Germany lodged a reservation to Article 7 ECHR, stipulating that it would only apply the provisions of Article 7(2) ECHR within the limits of Article 103, para. 2, of the Basic Law (prohibiting retroactive punishment). This reservation was withdrawn on 5 October 2001. Shortly beforehand, the ECtHR had dealt with cases involving Germany in which the Court found no violation of either Article 7(1) or Article 14 ECHR taken together with Article 7 ECHR.[21] Because the decision to withdraw the

---

[20] See Gusy (2005), 134.
[21] *Streletz, Kessler and Krenz v. Germany* (appl. nos 34044/96, 35532/97 and 44801/98), Judgement (Grand Chamber), 22 March 2001, Reports 2001-II, 409 et seq. and *K.-H. W. v. Germany* (appl. no. 37201/97), Judgement (Grand Chamber), 22 March 2001, Reports 2001-II, 495 et seq.

reservation had been taken prior to these judgements, the withdrawal does not seem, however, to have been a direct consequence of the latter.

Three declarations, which do not seem to modify the substance of Germany's obligations, remain in force today, including one with respect to Article 2 Protocol no. 1.[22] Germany submitted a declaration upon ratifying Protocol no. 6 concerning the abolition of the death penalty, stating that "the obligations deriving from Protocol no. 6 are confined to the abolition of the death penalty within the Protocol's area of application[23] in the respective State, that national non-criminal legislation is not affected,"[24] and that "the Federal Republic of Germany has already met its obligations under the Protocol by means of Article 102 of the Basic Law",[25] which contains a general prohibition on capital punishment. A third declaration concerns Articles 2, 3 and 4 of Protocol no. 7.[26]

bb. Impact of the German reunification. From 1953 to 1990, Germany included a general declaration in every instrument of ratification, stating that "the territory

---

[22] Declaration: "The second sentence of Article 2 of the (First) Protocol entails no obligation on the part of the State to finance schools of a religious or philosophical nature, or to assist in financing such schools, since this question, as confirmed by the concurring declaration of the Legal Committee of the Consultative Assembly and the Secretary General of the Council of Europe, lies outside the scope of the Convention for the Protection of Human Rights and Fundamental Freedoms and of its Protocol." (13 February 1957 – present). Source: http://conventions.coe.int/Treaty/Commun/ChercheMembres.asp?CM=3&CL=ENG

[23] According to the Federal Government, the Protocol did not cover measures such as deportation or extradition to a country where the person may face capital punishment. In the meantime however, a general prohibition to extradite or deport a person to a country where she/he runs the risk of being executed has been introduced into German law.

[24] Source: http://conventions.coe.int/Treaty/Commun/ChercheMembres.asp?CM=3&CL=ENG

[25] Ibid.

[26] Declaration: "1. By 'criminal offence' and 'offence' under Articles 2 to 4 of the present Protocol, the Federal Republic of Germany understands only such acts as are criminal offences under its law. 2. The Federal Republic of Germany applies Article 2.1 to convictions or sentences in the first instance only, it being possible to restrict review to errors in law and to hold such reviews in camera; in addition, it understands that the application of Article 2.1 is not dependent on the written judgement of the previous instance being translated into a language other than the language used in court. 3. The Federal Republic of Germany understands the words 'according to the law or the practice of the State concerned' to mean that Article 3 refers only to the retrial provided for in sections 359 et seq. of the Code of Criminal Procedure (cf. *Strafprozessordnung*)" (19 March 1985 – present). Source: http://conventions.coe.int/Treaty/Commun/ChercheMembres.asp?CM=3&CL=ENG

to which the Convention shall apply extends also to Western Berlin."[27] Following the reunification of Germany in 1990, this declaration was no longer needed.

German reunification meant accession of the German Democratic Republic to the Federal Republic of Germany,[28] in line with the then Article 23 of the Basic Law.[29] In a letter dated 3 October 1990, the Permanent Representative of the Federal Republic of Germany informed the Secretary-General of the Council of Europe that, "through the accession of the German Democratic Republic to the Federal Republic of Germany with effect from 3 October 1990, the two German States have united to form one sovereign State."[30] The application of the ECHR was thus extended to the five new *Länder* as of 3 October 1990.[31]

3. Comparison and Conclusion

The distrust of France *vis-à-vis* the ECHR delayed its ratification of the Convention for more than twenty years. On the other hand, the distrust of the international community, *vis-à-vis* Germany, helps to explain the quick German

---

[27] Ibid.

[28] The other possibility would have been to apply Article 146 of the Basic Law, which provides for entry into force of a new constitution adopted by the free decision of the German people, and to create a new State resulting from the merger of the two States.

[29] At that time, Article 23 read: "For the time being, this Basic Law shall apply in the territory of the *Länder* of Baden, Bavaria, Bremen, Greater Berlin, Hamburg, Hesse, Lower Saxony, North Rhine Westphalia, the Rhineland Palatinate, Schleswig-Holstein, Württemberg-Baden, and Württemberg-Hohenzollern. In other parts of Germany it shall be put into force on their accession." This was the procedure followed in 1956 for accession of Saarland.

[30] This letter was accompanied by a verbal note (dated 3 October 1990) informing the Secretary-General that "with regard to the continued application of treaties of the Federal Republic of Germany and the treatment of treaties of the German Democratic Republic following its accession to the Federal Republic of Germany with effect from 3 October 1990, the Treaty of 31 August 1990 between the Federal Republic of Germany and the German Democratic Republic on the establishment of German unity (Unification Treaty) contains the following relevant provisions: *Article 11 – Treaties of the Federal Republic of Germany* The contracting parties proceed on the understanding that international treaties and agreements to which the Federal Republic of Germany is a contracting party (…) shall retain their validity and that the rights and obligations arising there from (…) shall also relate to the territory specified in Article 3 of this Treaty (Länder of Brandenburg, Mecklenburg-Western Pomerania, Saxe, Saxe-Anhalt and Thuringia as well as the sector of the Land of Berlin where the Basic Law of the Federal Republic of Germany was not applicable)." Source: http://conventions.coe.int/Treaty/Commun/ChercheMembres.asp?CM=3&CL=ENG.

[31] In a number of cases brought before it related to German reunification, the European Court has referred to the exceptional context of reunification and the enormous task faced by the German legislature in dealing with the transition from a communist regime to a democratic market-economy system. For an example of issue that arose after the reunification of Germany (within the context of the *Bodenreform* – compensation for those whose property was expropriated either between 1945 and 1949 in the Soviet Occupied Zone of Germany or after 1949 in the German Democratic Republic), see *Maltzan and Others v. Germany* (appl. nos 71916/01, 71917/01 and 10260/02), Decision on the admissibility (Grand Chamber), 2 March 2005 (not reported): under Article 1 of Protocol no. 1, the Court concluded that the applicants had not shown that their claims were sufficiently established to be enforceable; the Court therefore declared the applications inadmissible. See also, *Jahn and Others v. Germany* (appl. nos 46720/99, 72203/01 and 72552/01), Judgement (Grand Chamber), 30 June 2005, Reports 2005-VI, 55.

ratification. German officials did not have the liberty to adopt the positions the French took in the days and decades following World War II. The French argument to the effect that its domestic legal order was well adapted to the protection of individual fundamental rights, could have been put forward by Germany. But Germany could not afford to postpone ratification of the Convention, given its desire to rejoin Europe as a sovereign equal.

Germany also ratified the Protocols before France, with the exception of Protocol no. 6, which France ratified three years before Germany, which lodged a declaration. The gap between ratification of a given instrument has, however, decreased over the years: there was a difference of 22 years between the two ratifications of the ECHR itself, and even more with regard to the acceptance of the right of individual petition under former Article 25 ECHR; a difference of seventeen years for Protocol no. 1, of twelve years for Protocol no. 2 and of five years only for Protocol no. 3. Since 1989, ratifications took place almost at the same time, in 1989 for Protocol no. 8, in 1995 (Germany) and 1996 (France) for Protocol no. 11, and in 2006 for Protocol no. 14. The quicker pace of these ratifications may be accounted for by the fact that they relate to Protocols reforming the ECHR rather than setting out new substantive rights, and because by then France had already decided to ratify the core instruments.

Remnants of the difference still persist, however. While Germany no longer has any reservations in force today, France still maintains several reservations, including two reservations concerning the ECHR itself.

B. Status of the ECHR in National Law

1. France

a. Relationship between Domestic and International Law
Article 55 of the Constitution determines the relationship between domestic and international law: "Treaties or accords duly ratified or approved have, from the moment of their publication, an authority superior to those of laws, on condition, for each accord or treaty, of application on the part of the other party."[32] France is formally monist – international treaties are automatically integrated into the internal system by the simple formality of their publication in the official gazette. In terms of rank in the hierarchy of norms, treaty law possesses supra-legislative, but infra-constitutional, status.

The monist features of the system, however, have clashed with the separation of powers, specifically, the prohibition of judicial review of statute. The Supreme Court (*Cour de Cassation*), prior to the 1975 *Sté Café Jacques Vabre* judgement,[33]

---

[32] Translated by the authors.
[33] Cass., Ch. Mixte, 24 May 1975, *Sté Café Jacques Vabre.*

and the Council of State (*Conseil d'Etat*), prior to the 1989 *Nicolo*[34] judgement, refused to review the legality of French law with respect to the ECHR, on separation of powers grounds. Today, the Constitutional Council alone reviews the constitutionality of laws, while the civil and administrative judges control the compliance of laws with the Convention. Given these two distinct systems of rights protection, it may be misleading to characterize the French legal order as monist.[35] In any case, the French Constitution contains no clause stipulating that international law be taken into account to interpret domestic law, although the courts have developed such doctrines.

b. Status of the ECHR in the National Legal Order

Like all international treaties which are duly ratified and published, the Convention is automatically integrated into the national legal order. The recognition of its direct application did not raise any problems with either the administrative or the civil judges.[36] In addition, the legal doctrine unanimously considers that the reciprocity rule does not apply to human rights treaties.[37]

According to the Constitution, the ECHR is superior to national law. With regard to the relationship between the ECHR and French constitutional law, however, the Council of State, in its judgement (plenary composition) dated 30 October 1998, *Sarran, Levacher et autres*, unequivocally affirmed that "the superiority conferred upon international agreements by Article 55 of the French Constitution does not, in the internal legal order, apply to provisions of a constitutional nature."[38] The position of the Court of Cassation is the same.[39] This infra-constitutional rank, which one finds in many countries, produces a French particularity. Because the Constitutional Council only has the authority to review the constitutionality of laws before they enter into force, and because the other high courts do not possess this authority post-promulgation, the review of conventionality by the latter operates as a functional substitute for rights protection under the Constitution. In the *Zielinski and Pradal*[40] case of 28 October 1999, the ECtHR handed down a judgement of violation concerning a law that had been judged to be in conformity with the Constitution by the Constitutional Council.[41]

---

[34]   CE, ass., 20 October 1989, *Nicolo.*

[35]   Cf. more generally, Bailleul, (2003), 876.

[36]   Cohen-Jonathan (1994), 2–3; Dupré (2001), 318. For the judicial order, cf. the ruling of the first civil chamber of the Court of Cassation dated 18 May 1989, Bull. no.198. For the administrative judge, cf. CE, 27 October 1978, *Debout.*

[37]   Cohen-Jonathan (1989), 248–250; Sudre (2006*a*), para. 62.

[38]   CE, ass., 30 October 1998.

[39]   Cass., Ass. Plén., 2 June 2000, *Fraisse*, Bull. 2000, no. 4, 7.

[40]   *Zielinski and Pradal* and *Gonzalez and Others v. France* (appl. nos 24846/94; 34165/96; 34173/96), Judgement (Grand Chamber), 28 October 1999, Reports 1999-VII, 95.

[41]   Cf. also Alland (1998), 1094, who considers that "one must be neither surprised nor upset by such a conclusion."

c. Court System and Scope of the Judicial Review

There are three supreme courts in the French system: the Constitutional Council, the Court of Cassation and the Council of State.

In 1975, the Constitutional Council held,[42] if only implicitly, that ordinary judges were empowered to override contradicting laws, even those posterior to an international convention. Civil courts likewise began to exercise the prerogative that same year[43] and finally, in 1989, administrative courts did so.[44] Today, in France, the Constitutional Council reviews statutes in the abstract, that is, facially, prior to their entry into force. The Council of State and the Court of Cassation may review legislation and its application for their conformity with the ECHR. It may happen that a law, compatible with international provisions at the time of its elaboration, will later be judged incompatible due to changes in matters of law or of fact, which it is then the judge's responsibility to ascertain.[45] If need be, the judge will refuse to enforce (disapply) the application of the law in question,[46] a power historically denied to courts. As we will emphasize throughout this report, European human rights law has contributed to the emancipation of the French judge from separation of powers dogmas. They have become rights-protecting courts, through their power to control conventionality.[47]

The organization of the courts and the prohibition of judicial review of statute in the French legal system are fundamental to an understanding of the importance, first, of French resistance to the ECHR and, second, the ECHR's accelerating impact on the legal system today.[48]

2. Germany

a. Relationship between Domestic and International Law

A dualist conception[49] of the relations between the domestic legal order and international obligations prevails in Germany. According to the Federal Constitutional Court, "[t]he Basic Law is clearly based on the classic idea that the relationship of public international law and domestic law is [one] between two different legal spheres [whose nature] can only be determined from the viewpoint of domestic

---

[42] Ruling 74-54 DC dated 15 January 1975, *Interruption Volontaire de Grossesse*.

[43] Cass. Ch. Mixte, 24 May 1975, *Sté Café Jacques Vabre* (for Community law); Cass. Crim., 27 November 1996, *Commandos anti-IVG* (for the ECHR).

[44] CE, ass., 20 October 1989, *Nicolo*, for Community law ; CE, 21 December 1990, *Confédération nationale des associations familiales catholiques et autres* (for the ECHR).

[45] CE, Section, 2 June 1999, *Meyet*.

[46] Cass., Crim., 4 September 2001, no. 00-85329, *Amaury* ; CE, ass., 30 November 2001, *Ministre de la Défense et ministre de l'économie, des finances et de l'industrie c/ M. Diop*, no. 212179.

[47] Sudre (2004), 224; De Gouttes (2003), 4, for whom the ECHR is a "source of legal evasion for the judge" (translated by the authors).

[48] Fromont (2005), 965.

[49] The German version is a "moderate dualism", according to Hans-Jürgen Papier, President of the German Federal Constitutional Court (Papier (2006), 60).

law (…) itself."[50] In order to produce legal effects, and to be directly applicable, in the German legal order, a treaty must be incorporated into the German legal system in the proper form and in conformity with substantive constitutional law, that is by means of a federal law adopted by the Parliament. Pursuant to Article 59 para. 2 of the Basic Law,[51] treaty law has the rank of an ordinary law within the German legal order.

b. Status of the ECHR in the National Legal Order

The ECHR was introduced into the German legal order by a federal law of approval (*Zustimmungsgesetz*), adopted by the German Parliament (*Bundestag*) on 7 August 1952.[52] As with other international law treaties, the ECHR and its Protocols enjoy the status and rank of an ordinary federal law within the German legal system, once they enter into force.[53]

As a federal law, the Convention overrides all laws enacted by the *Länder* (*Landesrecht*). But, despite some proposals in that sense,[54] the Convention does not enjoy the rank of constitutional law within the German legal order: "[T]he guarantees of the European Convention on Human Rights and its Protocols, by reason of this status in the hierarchy of norms, are not a direct constitutional standard of review in the German legal system."[55] As a consequence, until a 2004 ruling (*Görgülü*)[56] by the Federal Constitutional Court, violations of the Convention by judges and other public authorities could not serve as a basis for an individual constitutional complaint before the Federal Constitutional Court. Individuals were restricted to pleading the fundamental rights enshrined in the Basic Law.

In that context, a new federal law could potentially contradict the Convention by virtue of the principle *lex posterior derogat legi priori*, which would normally govern a conflict between treaty law and statute. While this was not a problem early on, the *lex posterior* rule became an issue as time passed. One way to avoid its unfortunate consequences was to consider the Convention as containing specific rights, a body of *lex specialis* that prevails over subsequently enacted statutes including more general provisions (*lex specialis derogat legi generali*). This may,

---

[50] BVerfGE 111, 307 (para. 34). This decision is known as the "*Görgülü* case" (see *infra* Section D). All quotations are taken from the English translation of this decision available in the *Human Rights Law Journal* 25 (2004), 99–107.

[51] Article 59, para. 2, of the Basic Law stipulates: "Treaties which regulate the political relations of the Federation or relate to matters of federal legislation shall require the approval or participation, in the form of a federal law, of the appropriate legislative body" (translated by the authors).

[52] Act on the Convention for the Protection of Human Rights and Fundamental Freedoms (*Gesetz über die Konvention zum Schutze der Menschenrechte und Grundfreiheiten*), BGBl. 1952 II, 685.

[53] This was reiterated by the Federal Constitutional Court in 2004 (BVerfGE 111, 307).

[54] See Langenfeld (2002).

[55] BVerfGE 111, 307 (para. 32).

[56] Discussed *infra*.

however, be an exceptional circumstance.[57] Other means have thus been developed to resolve conflicts of norms.

German judges can read the ECHR as enshrining rules of general, or at least regional, public international law, which have priority over ordinary statute law, according to Article 25 of the Basic Law.[58] Yet, only some provisions of the ECHR, like the prohibition of torture, have been recognized as non-derogable rules of customary international law. They can also read German law in light of treaty law. In 1987 the Federal Constitutional Court provided a means of circumventing the *lex posterior* rule by asserting that treaty law even inform the interpretation of German fundamental rights.[59] The Constitutional Court took the view that German laws "are to be interpreted and applied in harmony with the Federal Republic of Germany's commitments under international law, even when such laws were enacted posterior to an applicable international treaty; it cannot be assumed that the legislature, insofar as it has not clearly declared otherwise, wishes to deviate from the Federal Republic of Germany's international treaty commitments or to facilitate violation of such commitments."[60]

Today, the ECHR serves as an interpretative tool of German norms of a constitutional nature. As stated by the Federal Constitutional Court in 1987 and again in 2004 (*Görgülü*): "The guarantees of the Convention influence the interpretation of the fundamental rights and constitutional principles of the Basic Law. The text of the Convention and the case-law of the European Court of Human Rights serve, on the level of constitutional law, as guides to interpretation in determining the content and scope of fundamental rights and constitutional principles of the Basic Law, provided that this does not lead to a restriction or reduction of protection of the individual's fundamental rights under the Basic Law."[61]

The Basic Law has thus become more open towards the ECHR over time, as reaffirmed by the Federal Constitutional Court in *Görgülü*: the Basic Law is to be interpreted in such a way that no conflict arises between domestic law and the international commitments of Germany. At the same time, the Constitutional Court made some controversial statements concerning sovereignty: when undertaking international commitments, Germany does not waive its sovereignty; for this reason, the legislature may exceptionally deviate from the requirements of

---

[57] G. Ress assumed that this principle had been applied in 1978 by several German courts to give priority to Article 6(3) ECHR over national provisions on costs, after the Commission's decision in the *Luedicke, Belkacem and Koç* cases. *Luedicke v. Federal Republic of Germany* (appl. no. 6210/73), Decision (Plenary), Commission, 11 March 1976, DR 4, 200; *Belkacem v. Federal Republic of Germany* (appl. no. 6877/75), Decision (Plenary), Commission, 4 October 1976, DR 6, 77; *Koç v. Federal Republic of Germany* (appl. no. 7132/75), Decision (Plenary), Commission, 4 October 1976, DR 6, 135. See Ress (1993), 835.

[58] Article 25 reads: "The general rules of public international law are an integral part of Federal Law. They shall take precedence over the laws and shall directly create rights and duties for the inhabitants of the federal territory." (Zimmermann (2001), 338).

[59] Decision of 26 March 1987, BVerfGE 74, 358 (370).

[60] BVerfGE 74, 358 (370).

[61] BVerfGE 111, 307.

treaty law if it is the only way to avoid a violation of the fundamental principles contained in the Constitution.[62]

c. Court System and Scope of the Judicial Review

Germany is a Federal State consisting of 16 federal States (*Bundesländer*). The superior federal courts are the Federal Constitutional Court (*Bundesverfassungsgericht*), the Federal Court of Justice (*Bundesgerichtshof*), and the Federal Administrative Court (*Bundesverwaltungsgericht*).[63] The Federal Court of Justice and the Federal Administrative Court examine appeals on points of law.

The jurisdiction of the Federal Constitutional Court is threefold: it controls the compatibility of laws with the Basic Law ("norm control" proceedings), it is the arbiter of disputes between organs of the Basic Law, the Federation and the *Länder*, and it receives individual complaints alleging the unconstitutionality of court decisions and statutes. Under Article 93 of the Basic Law, a complaint may be lodged with the Federal Constitutional Court by anyone claiming that public authorities have infringed his/her fundamental rights (Articles 1–19 of the Basic Law). The Federal Constitutional Court is the final authoritative interpreter of the Basic Law, and it is the only court authorized to invalidate unconstitutional norms at the federal level.

As applicable federal statute law, the Convention has binding effect on all executive bodies and on all courts, by virtue of Article 20, para. 3, of the Basic Law. According to the Federal Constitutional Court, all German authorities and courts are obliged – under certain conditions – to observe and to apply the ECHR.[64] Thus, the Federal Constitutional Court has "rejected all proposals seeking to minimize the effects of the Convention, for example by declaring that it binds only the State internationally and not its organs internally."[65]

3. Comparison and Conclusion

The relationship between domestic and international law has been conceptualized by France and Germany in opposite ways, subject to rapid doctrinal evolution in recent years. Formally, France is monist and Germany is dualist. The Convention occupies a supra-legislative rank in France, while being on par with Federal statutes in Germany. In France, despite its monist posture, the courts applied the *lex posteriori* rule on separation of powers grounds, before finally abandoning the principle. In Germany, the courts, especially the Federal Constitutional Court,

---

[62] "There is, therefore, no contradiction with the aim of commitment to international law if the legislature, exceptionally, does not comply with the law of international agreements, provided this is the only way in which the violation of fundamental principles of the constitution can be averted." (BVerfGE 111, 307 (para. 35).

[63] The other federal courts are the Federal Labour Court, the Federal Social Court and the Federal Finance Court.

[64] BVerfGE 111, 307 (para. 46).

[65] Hartwig (2005), 874.

developed techniques that have led, in practice, to a circumvention of the *lex posteriori* rule, and to a kind of *de facto* monism with respect to the ECHR.

Neither legal order considers the ECHR as part of the *bloc de constitutionnalité*, that is, the Convention can not be pleaded directly as part of the Constitution, for purposes of constitutional review of laws and acts. At present, in France, the Constitutional Court exercises *ex ante* constitutional review of statutes, while the ordinary courts exercise *ex post* control of the conventionality of laws as applied. In Germany, the Constitutional Court requires all other courts to interpret the Basic Law in light of the ECHR and the judgements of the ECtHR, so long as doing so does not infringe the fundamental rights enshrined in the Basic Law.

Given these developments, it is no longer clear whether the ECHR is more respected and applied in one State or the other. Undoubtedly, the primacy of the ECHR is fully respected with regard to the infra-legislative norms and the statutes elaborated by the *Länder* in Germany. And, post-*Nicolo* in France, both high courts had positioned themselves to enforce the Convention. Nevertheless, in neither country is the conformity of all national statutes with the ECHR absolutely guaranteed, nor does the ECHR override constitutional norms.

C. Overview of the Activity of the European Court of Human Rights

1. France

a. Development of the Jurisdiction of the Court

Although France acceded very late to the European system, the number of French cases increased very quickly in the first years. Between 1981 and 1992, France accounted for the biggest share of the case load before the Strasbourg organs. Its total of 1,827 registered applications ranked it ahead of the United Kingdom, Germany and Italy. While the number of registered cases totalled 93 in 1982 rising to 353 in 1992, by 1998 the total number had reached 643.[66] In 2006, 83 decisions were handed down, comprising 36 inadmissible decisions (43.37%), 30 struck out of the list (36.14%) and seventeen deemed admissible (20.48%). It is also important to emphasize the fact that very few cases against France are subject to a successful friendly settlement (which is somewhat uncommon in the French legal system).[67]

Concerning the judgements on the merits, 146 judgements against France were handed down by the Court since the first one on 18 December 1986 (*Bozano*)[68] to 31 December 1988. Up to 31 December 2006, the total number of judgements handed down by the Court totalled 663.

While in the 90's there were only about ten judgements per year rendered

---

[66] For pre-1999 statistics, cf. Vailhé (2001), 21.
[67] Belliard (2007), 37.
[68] *Bozano v. France* (*supra* note 13).

against France, figures began to rise after the entry into force of Protocol no. 11, which entered into force in November 1998. That year, France was the second largest provider of cases (with 12% of total registered cases, closely following Italy with 16%). The peak was reached in 2006 with a total of 92 judgements on the merits. The increase in the number of petitions brought to Strasbourg also shows a tendency to decline (the number of petitions increased from 7 in 1981 to 600 in 1996 then to 1,032 in 2000, 1,737 in 2004, 1,827 in 2005 and 1,832 in 2006). This tendency will need to be confirmed in the future.

b. The Court's Case Law in Substance

Of the 111 admissibility decisions issued from 2006–2007, Article 6 ECHR is by far most prominently invoked (involving nearly 80% of the cases), followed by a group of Articles (Articles 3, 5, 8, 10, 13, 14, and 1 of Protocol no. 1) that make up 10–20% of cases. Other Articles (Articles 2, 4, 7, 9, 11, 12, etc.) are only rarely invoked (in less than 5% of cases). Out of the twenty decisions declared admissible since 1 January 2006, Article 6 was involved in thirteen cases, Articles 3 and 8 in five, and Article 5 in four.

Article 6(1) ECHR accounts for 70.42% of the legal grounds invoked (of which 21.35% concerned the question of a fair trial and 49.06% the reasonable length of proceedings) and for 74.03% of cases of violation. Article 8 (with 6.56% of legal grounds invoked and 5.7% of violations) comes in third place. Of a total of 1,021 cases (all judgements on the merits brought before the ECtHR and the ECommHR considered together), the ECtHR found Convention violations in 561 cases, while the ECommHR found a violation in 240 (78.45% of cases). In addition, the majority of friendly settlements involving France also concerned Article 6(1). The number of cases related to this issue may decrease in the near future, given certain positive changes in this field recently enacted in the domestic legal order.

Nearly two thirds of the judgements are related to a violation of Article 6(1). The rest of the violations concern, for the most part, Articles 2 and 3, Article 10, Article 1 (Protocol no. 1) and Articles 5(1) and (4). The large majority of cases concerning Article 6(1) ECHR claim inequity in the procedures before the Criminal Division of the Court of Cassation (due to the failure to communicate the report of the reporting judge to the claimant or his counsel before the hearing of that judge and to the participation of the Advocate-General in the deliberations)[69] and before the Council of State (due to the presence of the *Commissaire du gouvernement* at the deliberations)[70] as well as the non-respect of

---

[69] For example, *André v. France* (appl. no. 63313/00), Judgement (Second Section), 28 February 2006 (not yet reported); *De Luca v. France* (appl. no. 8112/02), Judgement (Second Section), 2 May 2006 (not yet reported); *Bertin v. France* (appl. no. 55917/00), Judgement (First Section), 24 May 2006 (not yet reported).

[70] For example, among many others, *Kress v. France* (appl. no. 39594/98), Judgement (Grand Chamber), 7 June 2001, Reports 2001-VI, 1 seq.; *Farange v. France* (appl. no. 77575/01), Judge-

the reasonable time criterion before the administrative courts.[71] Since 2003, the number of cases brought before the Court for violation of the reasonable time criterion has declined sharply, while the number of those brought for fair trial violations has steadily increased. Beginning in 2005, the figures for this latter complaint overtook those concerning the reasonable time criterion, and is now the most common.

Apart from the concentration of cases concerning Article 6(1), most French cases brought to Strasbourg concern Articles 2, 3, 5, 8, 10, and 1 (Protocol no. 1). Article 8 was the object of many judgements (especially cases concerning the right of deported foreigners to a family life). Article 10, treating freedom of expression, has also given rise to important cases.

2. Germany

a. Development of the Jurisdiction of the Court

Germany ratified the ECHR in 1952, but the Court did not render its first judgement against it until 1968,[72] sixteen years after ratification and thirteen years after acceptance of the jurisdiction of the Court. The first finding of violation was issued ten years later, in 1978.[73] Germany has neither submitted a complaint against another State Party nor has been the object of such a complaint.

Until 2006, there have been only 104 Court judgements concerning Germany, and Germany was found to be in violation of the ECHR in 69 cases. Until 1998, the Committee of Ministers had dealt with 24 applications concerning Germany. With 100 judgements[74] over a period of 39 years (1968–2006) and an average of 2.6 judgements per year, Germany ranks among the lower case-count States, especially considered on a *per capita* basis. The peak was reached in 2001, with sixteen judgements against Germany. The average number of judgements per year since 2001 is now nine.

In parallel, the number of applications registered against Germany increased

ment (Third Section), 13 July 2006 (not yet reported); *Malquarti v. France* (appl. no. 39269/02), Judgement (Second Section), 20 June 2006 (not yet reported).

[71] For example, among many others, *Le Bechennec v. France* (appl. no. 28738/02), Judgement (Second Section), 28 March 2006 (not yet reported); *Aiouaz v. France* (appl. no. 23101/03), Judgement (Third Section), 28 June 2007 (not yet reported).

[72] *Wemhoff v. Germany* (appl. no. 2122/64), Judgement (Chamber), 27 June 1968, Series A, Vol. 7. The Court concluded that there had been no breach of Article 5(3) and Article 6(1) ECHR. In 1967, the Committee of Ministers issued a first finding that no violation of the ECHR was found (*Grandrath v. Germany* (appl. no. 2299/64), 29 June 1967, Committee of Ministers Resolution (Res-32) DH(67)1).

[73] *König v. Germany* (appl. no. 6232/73), Judgement (Plenary), 28 June 1978, Series A, Vol. 27 (violation of Article 6(1) as regards the duration of various proceedings). The same year, the Court issued the *Klass* judgement (*Klass and Others v. Germany* (appl. no. 5029/71), Judgement (Plenary), 6 September 1978, Series A, Vol. 28) often presented as an important and symbolic case with regard to the confrontation of the German legal order and the ECHR, even if the Court did not found any violation of the Convention (Gusy (2005), 142–143).

[74] Friendly settlements excluded.

only recently. From 1955 to 1995, there had been a relatively constant number, with an average of 143 applications per year. From 1995, this figure began to grow: there has been a significant progression between 1995 and 2000 (167%) and again between 2000 and 2005 (166%). During the last three years, this number seems to have stagnated (1,527 in 2004, 1,582 in 2005, 1,587 in 2006). As for other countries, this progression can be explained by a better knowledge of the ECHR and its system at the domestic level. The German reunification might be another reason, the population having increased.

b. The Court's Case Law in Substance

The vast majority of applications lodged against Germany concerns procedural rights, especially Article 6 ECHR (lengthy proceedings). Judgements relating to Article 6(1) ECHR also frequently deal with the right to fair hearing.

In all, 76 cases concern Article 6(1) ECHR (right to a fair trial) – and among them 54 cases deal with problems of length of procedure. Other bases of judgements include: 25 cases concerning Article 8 ECHR (right to respect for private and family life), partly in the context of criminal proceedings; fifteen cases Article 14 ECHR (prohibition of discrimination), including one case concerning Article 4 (prohibition of slavery and forced labour) in conjunction with Article 14;[75] ten cases Article 6(3) ECHR (right to defence); eight cases Article 5(1) ECHR (right to liberty and security); eight cases Article 5(3) ECHR (review of lawfulness of detention); seven cases concern Article 10 ECHR (freedom of expression); six cases Article 5(4) ECHR (unlawful detention); five cases Article 6(2) ECHR (presumption of innocence); five cases Article 1 of Protocol no. 1 (protection of property); four cases Article 3 ECHR (prohibition of torture or inhuman or degrading treatment or punishment); three cases Article 13 ECHR (right to an effective remedy); two cases Article 7 ECHR (no punishment without law); one case Article 5(5) ECHR (right to compensation), one case Article 9 ECHR (freedom of thought, conscience and religion); one case Article 11 ECHR (freedom of assembly and association)[76]; and one case Article 12 (right to marry). There are no cases concerning Article 2 ECHR (right to life) and Article 5(2) ECHR (right to prompt information).

When it comes to findings of violation, Article 6 stands out, with grounds of lengthy proceedings accounting for more than 40 such findings. Article 8 and Article 14 ECHR follow. The Court found a violation of Article 8 in conjunction

---

[75] *Karlheinz Schmidt v. Germany* (appl. no. 13580/88), Judgement (Chamber), 18 July 1994, Series A, Vol. 291-B (the Court found that the duty to pay a fire service levy under an Act of the Land of Baden-Württemberg (which made it compulsory for men, but not women, to serve in the fire brigade or pay a financial contribution in lieu of such service) amounted to a violation of Article 4(3)(d) read in conjunction with Article 14 ECHR).

[76] In the well-known *Vogt* case (*Vogt v. Germany* (appl. no. 17851/91), Judgement (Grand Chamber), 26 September 1995, Series A, Vol. 323): the Court held that the dismissal of a teacher from public service, on the ground that she was a member of the German Communist Party, was in breach of Article 11, as well as Article 10, of the Convention.

with Article 14 ECHR seven times (e.g. treating fathers of children born outside marriage differently from fathers of children born within marriage).[77]

The Court has rarely dealt with any serious human rights violations involving Germany. There have been no cases concerning Article 2 and the Court concluded for the first time in 2006 to a violation of Article 3:[78] The Grand Chamber of the Court held by ten votes to seven that there had been a violation of Article 3 ECHR with regard to the forcible administration of emetics to a drug-trafficker in order to recover a plastic bag he had swallowed containing drugs. According to the Court, this administration amounted to an inhuman and degrading treatment, contrary to Article 3.

3. Comparison and Conclusion

The comparison between France and Germany reveals once more a completely diverse overall picture. While Germany ratified the ECHR and accepted the jurisdiction of the ECtHR long before France, the number of judgements against Germany rendered is far lower than against France (104 judgements through 2006 against Germany, compared with 663 against France; the maximum figure per year being sixteen cases in 2001 for Germany, 92 for France in 2006). If the number of applications lodged during the last six years is taken into account, this difference may slightly decrease. The explanation of such a difference is certainly the existence of the individual constitutional complaint in Germany, as distinct from the situation in France. As a result, many cases have been settled by the German Federal Constitutional Court.

Judgements rendered against both States mostly deal with procedural guarantees (Article 6 ECHR). They account for 60% of the cases regarding Germany, and more than 70% of the cases regarding France. The other Articles which are regularly at stake include, for both states, Articles 1, 5, 8, 13, 10, and 14 of Protocol no. 1. Unlike Germany (with the exception of one judgement concluding to a violation of Article 3), France has been found to have violated certain core rights (Articles 2, 3, 4) in several judgements handed down against it, particularly in the past decade.

---

[77] See, for example, *Sahin v. Germany* (appl. no. 30943/96) Judgement (Grand Chamber), 8 July 2003, Reports 2003-VIII, 99 et seq.; *Sommerfeld v. Germany* (appl. no. 31871/96), Judgement (Grand Chamber), 8 July 2003, Reports 2003-VIII, 163 et seq.

[78] *Jalloh v. Germany* (appl. no. 54810/00), Judgement (Grand Chamber), 11 July 2006 (not yet reported).

D. The European Court's Case Law and its Effects in the National Legal Order

1. France

a. Preliminary remarks

French authorities have long distinguished themselves by a tradition of restrictively interpreting their obligations following an ECtHR finding of violation. Indeed, France considers that paying the damages established by the Court is the only formal obligation flowing from a finding of violation. Arguably, other parts of the Court's rulings have only a declaratory effect, and the state thus found in violation of the ECHR has the choice of the means by which to conform to the judgement. In this view, the judgments of the Court would never "call into question the legality of judicial proceedings, and still less, of course, the validity of the administrative decisions which were the object of those proceedings".[79] According to the Criminal Division of the Court of Cassation, an adverse ECtHR judgement, while it allows the appellant to demand compensation, is without incidence on the validity of the procedures governed by domestic law,[80] and generally, has "no direct incidence in domestic law on the decisions of national jurisdictions".[81] While the *res iudicata* authority is interpreted strictly, the authority deriving from interpretation (*res interpretata* authority) is almost totally rejected. More generally, as the current French President of the ECtHR wrote, "the higher courts in France have a tendency to feel that the principle of subsidiarity, on which the European system is based, should lead the Court to show 'self-restraint' when merely procedural matters are at issue".[82]

b. Effects on the Legislator and the Statutory Power

The references to the interpretive authority of the ECtHR are sporadic and implicit rather than systematic and deliberate in Parliamentary oral and written reports.[83] Rarely has a legislative reform occurred after a judgement of violation against another state; an exception is the case of *Burghartz v. Switzerland*,[84] after which the law of 4 March 2002 established equalitarian rules regarding the attribution of the family name. In France, the authority of European jurisprudence remains negligible, whether due to the absence of a firm and binding basis for European interpretation (in the text of the Convention), or because Members of

---

[79] Conclusions in *Arrighi de Casanova*, under CE, opinion, 31 March 1995, *Meric*, *RJF*, 5/95, 330 (translated by the authors).

[80] Cass., Crim., 3 February 1993, *Kemmache*.

[81] Cass., Crim., 4 May 1994, *Saïdi*.

[82] Costa (2004), 17-18.

[83] Marguénaud (2004),168.

[84] *Burghartz v. Switzerland* (appl. no. 16213/90), Judgement (Chamber), 22 February 1994, Series A, Vol. 280-B.

Parliament expect a reversal or weakening of the Strasbourg Court's position as a result of its interactions with national judges.

The case is different when a statute is challenged directly or indirectly in a ECtHR judgement against France. On the basis of the obligation of non-repetition of illicit acts, the state 'convicted' in Strasbourg may be obliged to adopt some general measures to avoid the repetition of the violation.[85] Parliament has modified different aspects of domestic law, such as the Act relating to aliens or civil law. Procedural law in particular was modified very recently: the Act no. 2007-291 of 5 March 2007 reinforces the adversarial principle in the preliminary phase of the judgement in criminal matters, notably by allowing the litigants as much time as the State Prosecutor before the close of the preparatory inquiry. This Act also seeks to speed up proceedings by limiting the growing number of complaints by plaintiffs (claiming damages) that are either unjustified or simply tactics to delay proceedings.[86] At the level of administrative procedure, the decree of 19 December 2005 establishes an assessment of the administrative courts in an attempt to compensate for excessive slowness.

The clearer the violation found by the Court, the more effective such reforms are likely to be. The most representative examples are that of the *Kruslin*[87] and *Huvig*[88] cases in which the Strasbourg Court specified quite clearly why the legislative provisions with regard to phone-tapping were incompatible with the Convention. Less than one year after the judgement, law no. 91.646 of 10 July 1991 reformed practices to take the Court's objections into account.[89] Modifications are more difficult if they undermine deeply-rooted traditions and practices (secularity, the determination of rights and obligations in the civil law, criminal charges, indictments, sanctions, and so on).[90] For a long time, a real or simulated attachment to the specificities of French administrative law explained the Council of State's active resistance to the application of the requirements of Article 6 to disciplinary litigation.[91] The most spectacular example is that of the role of the *Commissaire du gouvernement* in the administrative procedure. After many condemnations of France since the judgements of *Kress*[92] in 2001 and *Martinie*[93] before the Grand Chamber in 2006, France first adopted minimal changes, then finally moved to more substantial reform. The decree of 1 August 2006 excluded

---

[85]   Lambert Abdelgawad (1999), 624.

[86]   Matsopoulou (2007), 5.

[87]   *Kruslin v. France* (appl. no. 11801/85), Judgement (Chamber), 24 April 1990, Series A, Vol. 176-A.

[88]   *Huvig v. France* (appl. no. 11105/84), Judgement (Chamber), 24 April 1990, Series A, Vol.-76-B.

[89]   Following the *Huvig* and *Kruslin* judgements, the explanatory report on the law clearly states that its origin is European jurisprudence. Errera (2003), 851.

[90]   Potvin-Solis (1999), 265.

[91]   Andriantsimbazovina (1998), 290.

[92]   *Kress v. France* (*supra* note 70).

[93]   *Martinie v. France* (appl. no. 58675/00), Judgement (Grand Chamber), 12 April 2006 (not yet reported).

the *Commissaire du gouvernement* from the deliberations in all cases, except in the Council of State unless a party expresses the wish for him not to be present; a new decree is apparently in preparation in order to change the name of the function.[94]

c. Effects on National Judges

Jurists, lawyers, and judges long assumed that the ECHR would have but little impact on French law, as the latter was largely in conformity with the Convention. Under this view, explicit reference to the Convention was unnecessary.[95] Judges tended to base their decisions on domestic law, at most giving the Convention only a subsidiary role; they frequently invoked Article 9 of the Civil Code, for example, instead of Article 8 ECHR. In the post-Protocol no. 11 Europe, which has seen an exponential increase of adverse judgements in Strasbourg, this view is no longer viable. Important changes are taking place, if only gradually. It is also important to stress that, until recently, most lawyers and magistrates were profoundly ignorant of the ECHR system. Today, they would mostly refer to the two best known Articles, Articles 5 and 6 of the ECHR.[96] Knowledge and acceptance of the Court's case law have also come about gradually, and more rapidly in the civil order compared with the administrative order. Two reasons for the different postures of the courts have already been given; but the impact of certain members of the high courts also deserves mention.[97]

The most important factor driving change has been the explosion of repetitive violations found in Strasbourg. The desire to reduce exposure to more condemnations is changing the very basis of France's relationship with the Convention.[98] In this context, the French judges become agents of the ECHR framework in order to avoid the cost of negative rulings (an "avoidance of punishment" argument or hypothesis). More surprisingly, the Council of State agreed to adopt the position of the ECtHR regarding the verification of the proportionality of the measures for the expulsion of foreigners following the argument of the *Commissaire du gouvernement* that, in the absence of such agreement, the Council of State would be stripped of its prerogatives and the subsidiary competence of the ECtHR would govern.[99] In such a case, the compliance with the ECHR, as interpreted by

---

[94] Lambert (2007), 778. Cf. also the commentary and the propositions of Guinchard (2004), 937. See also the most recent national case law on that matter: CE, 25 May 2007, *Courty*, finding that the right of a party to exclude the *Commissaire du gouvernement* from the deliberations constitutes a better protection of the procedural rights contained in Art.6 ECHR, as interpreted by the Strasbourg Court.

[95] Cf. the study by Vailhé (2001), 97.

[96] Vailhé (2001), 97.

[97] Costa (2007), 8, who also alleges the "long-standing" tradition and the "liberalism" of the administrative French courts (translated by the authors).

[98] Cf. the conclusions of *Frydman* under CE, ass., 17 February 1995, *Marie and Hardouin*.

[99] Cf. the conclusions of R. Abraham under CE, ass., *Belgacem and Babas*, 19 April 1991, *RFDA* (1991) 497, specifically 502. Cf. Andriantsimbazovina (1998), 437.

the Court, is ensured in order to increase the power of the judiciary within the national legal order, *vis-à-vis* the legislative and executive authorities (a "judicial empowerment" argument or hypothesis). It is also necessary to emphasize that lawyers and magistrates have a better knowledge of the European jurisprudence than before, though efforts to align the terms of French law with European jurisprudence are often undertaken without enthusiasm.[100]

Be that as it may, the use of the Convention – conceived as part of the native judicial landscape – is becoming more commonplace. The Convention is now rapidly becoming the basic framework for many judicial decisions, especially when the protection of the right of a foreigner to private and family life is at stake.[101] Almost 50% of the decisions of the Council of State now mention the ECHR in their full text.[102] From ratification to 1 January 1997, only 1,738 decisions of the Council of State referred to the ECHR, compared to 15,337 decisions since; and since 1 January 2000, the figure has risen to 12,989 (76% of total references to the ECHR). Thus, we find that awareness of the implications of the Convention is quite recent, but rapidly improving. At the level of the administrative courts of appeal, only 13.8% of the judgements referred to the Convention, although this has accelerated somewhat in later years (almost 43% of the decisions referring to the ECHR were handed down after 1 January 2006).[103] At the level of the Court of Cassation, fewer than 5% of the decisions mention the Convention, but almost 60% of such references concern decisions after 1 January 2000.[104]

It is necessary to deal with the Constitutional Council separately. Since it refuses any control of the compatibility of French law with the ECHR, it seems not to be influenced by the norms of the ECHR and European jurisprudence, even when it acts as the electoral judge. Its conception of the general interest seems also much broader than what is nowadays accepted at the European level. This is probably the reason why some conflict with the ECHR could emerge in the near future; for instance, the functioning of the Constitutional Council could give rise to some conclusions of incompatibility before the ECtHR (regarding Article 6(1) ECHR). More subtly, it may be that the Council, without admitting as much, takes the Convention into account when it elucidates "objectives of constitutional value" or constitutional principles. These include democratic requirements of media pluralism, broader interpretation of individual freedom, the characteristics required of the legislative norm, and the enrichment of procedural

---

[100] Marguénaud (2004), 168.

[101] Sudre (2006), para. 344.

[102] 17,075 decisions out of the 34,955 in the Juripro database (checked on 31 May 2007).

[103] 7,841 decisions out of the 56,604 in the Juripro database (checked on 31 May 2007). After 1.1.2006, the figure rises to 3,361.

[104] 17,321 decisions out of the 360,569 in the Juripro database (checked on 31 May 2007). From 1 January 2000, the figure stands at 10,149. In the Courts of Appeal, only 54 of the 1,671 decisions recorded in this database refer to the ECHR (of which 53 are decisions made after 1 January 2000).

guarantees, notably the rights of the defence and the notion of the presumption of innocence.[105]

French courts do not use Article 6 ECHR as a preferred field of application of the Convention. In the administrative court, Article 8 ECHR is by far the most frequently applied. From 1 January 2000 to 20 September 2005, there are 5,461 decisions of the Council of State which refer to Article 8; 2,293 refer to Article 3, and only 447 to Article 6(1) ECHR.[106] In accordance with the *Bendenoun* jurisprudence, the Council of State admitted that certain fiscal penalties had the character of sanctions under Article 6(1) ECHR.[107] The same court also proceeded to a reversal of its jurisprudence to apply Article 6(1) to all disciplinary instances, in particular to the Bar Association.[108] In the matters of law relating to aliens, the Council of State ensures, since the *Fidan* judgement[109] referring to Protocol no. 6, that the person extradited does not incur the death penalty and that, if such a penalty is pronounced, that the person will not be executed. The Court of Cassation has accepted the extension of fair trial guarantees to proceedings before the regulatory authorities.[110] Major changes such as these have been introduced through the courts, in the absence of any intervention or authorization of the legislator.[111]

The literature on the impact of the ECHR on the French legal system agrees that French judges have tended to accept more easily the substantive rights jurisprudence of the Court than they have that Court's case law on procedural rights.[112] The logic of the Court of Cassation, which favours maintaining the national model, remains in opposition to the ECtHR's reasoning in favour of a harmonization of the diverse models in Europe.[113] On that matter, the most representative example would be, for the civil courts, the *Reinhardt* and *Slimane-Kaïd* cases in which the ECtHR concluded to a double violation of Article 6(1),[114] and for the administrative courts, the *Kress* judgement.[115] Moreover, the French judges seem to be more sensitive to public goods when balancing individual

---

[105] Saillant (2004), 1527. Cf. also the reference in that domain: Szymczak (2007), 849.
[106] CE, Public Report 2006, *Sécurité juridique et complexité du droit*, Etudes et Documents no. 57 (Paris, 2006), 243.
[107] CE, sect., 31 March 1995, *Ministre du budget c/SARL « Auto Industrie Meric »*, 154.
[108] CE, ass., 14 February 1996, *Maubleu*, p.1186, conclusions Sanson.
[109] CE, sect., 27 February 1987, *Fidan, D*, 1987, p.305, conclusions Bonichot.
[110] Cass. Ass. Plénière, 5 February 1999, *COB c/Oury*.
[111] Flauss (2006), 16.
[112] Costa (2007), 10.
[113] De Gouttes (2007), 28.
[114] *Reinhardt and Slimane-Kaïd v. France* (appl. nos 23043/93; 22921/93), Judgement (Grand Chamber), 31 March 1998, Reports 1998-II, 640. The first violation concerned the imbalance created by failure to disclose the whole report of the reporting judge to the applicants' advisers, while doing so to the Advocate-General. The second violation was due to the failure to communicate the Advocate-General's submissions to the applicants.
[115] *Kress v. France* (*supra* note 70).

rights against the "general interest," whereas the ECtHR would likely give more weight to victims.[116]

2. Germany

In a landmark decision of 14 October 2004 in the *Görgülü* case,[117] the Federal Constitutional Court for the first time directly addressed the question of the effects of a judgement of the Strasbourg Court in the German legal order.

The case concerned proceedings relating to the applicant's custody of, and access to, his child, who was born out of wedlock in 1999 and living with a foster-family. Following the refusal of the Higher Regional Court to grant him custody and access, the applicant lodged a complaint with the ECtHR. In a judgement of 26 February 2004,[118] the ECtHR found the German court's position to be a violation of Article 8 ECHR. The Court, moreover, underlined Germany's legal obligation to adopt "general and/or, if appropriate, individual measures to be adopted in [its] domestic legal order to put an end to the violation found by the Court and to redress so far as possible the effects."[119] Although "the respondent State remains free to choose the means by which it will discharge its legal obligation under Article 46 ECHR, provided that such means are compatible with the conclusions set out in the Court's judgement",[120] the Court considered that "in the case at hand this means making it possible for the applicant to at least have access to his child."[121] In subsequent proceedings in which the applicant renewed his request for custody and asked for interim measures, the local court, referring to the ECtHR judgement, decided to grant him visitation rights. These decisions were quashed by the Higher Regional Court issuing an order not to give the applicant access to his child. That court indicated that it did not consider itself bound by the judgement of the ECtHR, reasoning that only the German State, as a Party to the Convention, can be bound. The applicant therefore filed a constitutional complaint before the Federal Constitutional Court,[122] which quashed the decision of the Higher Regional Court on the grounds that it had not properly taken into account the judgement of the ECtHR in this matter.

To reach that conclusion, the Federal Constitutional Court developed a new

---

[116] De Gouttes (2007), 28. This author adds another difference in the reasoning defended by the European and the national Courts: the "reality" logic of the Court of Cassation opposing the 'appearance' reasoning of the ECtHR.

[117] BVerfGE 111, 307. This decision has been largely commented in German (see, *inter alia*, Cremer (2004); Meyer-Ladewig/Petzold (2005); Frowein (2005); Sauer (2005)), in English (Hartwig (2005); Hoffmeister (2006)) as well as in French (Gerkrath (2006)).

[118] *Görgülü v. Germany* (appl. no. 74969/01), Judgement (Third Section), 26 February 2004 (not reported).

[119] Ibid., para. 64.

[120] Ibid., para. 64.

[121] Ibid., para. 64.

[122] The Federal Constitutional Court has issued four decisions regarding the *Görgülü* case, but we refer only to the first decision of 14 October 2004, which is the most important.

doctrine on the scope of application of the ECHR by German courts and the binding force of the ECtHR's judgements. The Federal Constitutional Court first underlined the particular importance of the decisions of the ECtHR: "they reflect the current state of development of the Convention and its protocols."[123] The said Court then held that "the judgements of the Strasbourg Court are binding on the parties to the proceedings and thus have limited substantive *res judicata*."[124] In that context, the finding of a violation entails three main obligations for the State concerned. The first consequence is that the State Party may no longer hold the view that it acts were in compliance with the Convention. Second, the State Party has the obligation to restore, if possible, the state of affairs with regard to the matter in dispute to what it was prior to the declared violation of the Convention (*restitutio in integrum*). Finally, in case of an ongoing violation, the State Party is under an obligation to end this state.

As a consequence, the Federal Constitutional Court explicitly formulated, for the first time, the obligation of German courts "to take into account" (*Berücksichtigungspflicht*) the guarantees of the Convention and the case law of the Strasbourg Court when interpreting fundamental rights and constitutional guarantees.[125] According to the German Constitutional Court, judgements of the ECtHR should not be enforced "in an automatic way",[126] because the German state bodies enjoy a "latitude" in this regard. This obligation "to take into account" exists only within the confines of the Basic Law. This means that the German courts or the authorities responsible must "discernibly consider the decision and, if necessary, justify in an understandable manner why they nevertheless do not follow the international-law interpretation of the law."[127] When taking into account a judgement of the ECtHR, attention must, therefore, be paid to various elements, particularly in cases in which national courts have to rule on situations involving several conflicting fundamental rights, if the decision relates to national partial systems of law shaped by a complex system of case law,[128] or if there is a change in circumstances. The Federal Constitutional Court explained these limits by the difference of jurisdiction between the two systems: while the Strasbourg Court has to decide specific individual cases in the two-party relationship between the complainant and the State Party, another person may be involved in the national

---

[123] BVerfGE 111, 307 (para. 38).

[124] BVerfGE 111, 307 (para. 38). The Constitutional Court added that "the decision of the European Court in proceedings against other States parties merely give the States that are not involved an occasion to examine their domestic legal systems and, if appears that an amendment may be necessary, to adapt themselves to the relevant case law of the European Court" (para. 39).

[125] BVerfGE 111, 307 (paras 46–48).

[126] BVerfGE 111, 307 (para. 47).

[127] BVerfGE 111, 307 (para. 50).

[128] BVerfGE 111, 307 (para. 58). The Federal Constitutional Court notes that, in the German legal system, this may happen in particular in family law, law concerning aliens, and law on the protection of personality.

proceedings. While the outcome of the *Görgülü* decision[129] is a positive one, the limitation of the obligation "to take into account" may send a negative message to the other, particularly new, Member States.[130] The position of the German Federal Constitutional Court has thus been described as ambivalent,[131] fluctuating between openness towards international law and an odd reference to German constitutional sovereignty.

Notwithstanding these statements of the Constitutional Court, the case law of the organs of the ECHR has in general influenced the German legal order, in particular after a conclusion of violation.[132] The Court's case law triggered for instance several amendments of the Code of Criminal Procedure (*Strafprozessordnung*),[133] sometimes even before the Court rendered its judgement.

Following the Court's judgement in the *Öztürk* case,[134] Parliament amended the Court Costs Act and the Code of Criminal Procedure, with the Act of 15 June 1989 (entering into force on 1 July 1989). These reforms provide that, in criminal proceedings or in court proceedings under the Regulatory Offences Act, interpretation and translation costs shall be payable by an accused, or other person concerned who does not understand German, only if these costs are imposed on him by the court on the grounds that he incurred them unnecessarily as a result of his own default or in another culpable manner.

According to Section 147, para. 1, of the Code of Criminal Procedure, defence counsel is entitled to consult the files which have been presented to the trial court, or which would have to be presented to the trial court in case of an indictment, and to inspect the exhibits. But in several cases, the Public Prosecutor had denied the requested access to the file documents on the basis of Section 147, para. 2, of the same Code. Given the importance in the courts' reasoning of the contents of the investigation file, the ECtHR found that the procedure before the said courts, which reviewed the lawfulness of the applicant's detention on remand, did not comply with the guarantees afforded by Article 5(4) ECHR and that this provision had therefore been violated.[135] Even before the Court

---

[129] Ibid.

[130] Meyer-Ladewig (forthcoming).

[131] Ruffert (2007), 246.

[132] See Council of Europe, *General measures adopted to prevent new violations of the European Convention on Human Rights*, Doc. H/EXEC (2006)1, May 2006.

[133] See Odersky (2000), 1039–1047.

[134] *Öztürk v. Germany* (appl. no. 8544/79), Judgement (Plenary), 21 February 1984, Series A, Vol. 73. In this case, the Court held that there had been a breach of Article 6 (3e) of the Convention because the applicant was ordered to bear the interpreter's fees. Following the *Luedicke, Belkacem and Koç* cases, in 1980 German authorities took legislatives measures to provide a free interpreter, but only for criminal cases (*Luedicke, Belkacem and Koç v. Germany* (appl. nos 6210/73, 6877/75, 7132/75), Judgement (Chamber), 28 November 1978, Series A, Vol. 29).

[135] *Garcia Alva v. Germany* (appl. no. 23541/94), Judgement (First Section), 13 February 2001 (not reported); *Lietzow v. Germany* (appl. no. 24479/94), Judgement (First Section), 13 February 2001, Reports 2001-I, 353 et seq.; *Schöps v. Germany* (appl. no. 25116/94), Judgement (First Section), 13 February 2001, Reports 2001-I, 391 et seq., in which applicants complained under Article

concluded to the violation of the ECHR in these cases, Section 147, para. 5, sentence 2, of the Code of Criminal Procedure had been amended,[136] as from 1 November 2000, to the effect, *inter alia*, that an accused in detention be entitled to ask for judicial review of the decision of the Public Prosecutor's Office that denied access to the file.

The German Civil Code (*Bürgerliches Gesetzbuch*) has been modified as well. The statutory provisions governing custody of and access to children have been changed several times, an important instance of which came through the Law on Family Matters (*Reform zum Kindschaftsrecht*) of 16 December 1997,[137] which came into force on 1 July 1998. The previous legislation on Family Matters has been condemned by the ECtHR in the *Elsholz* case[138] and similar cases. Now, according to Article 1626 (1) of the Civil Code, "the father and the mother have the right and the duty to exercise parental authority (*elterliche Sorge*) over a minor child. Parental authority includes the custody (*Personensorge*) and the administration of the child's property (*Vermögenssorge*)." Pursuant to Article 1626 (a)(1), as amended, the parents of a minor child born out of wedlock jointly exercise custody if they make a declaration to that effect or if they marry. According to Article 1684, as amended, a child is entitled to have access to both parents: each parent is obliged to have contact with, and entitled to have access to, the child. Family courts can determine the scope of the right of access and prescribe more specific rules for its exercise, also with regard to third parties; and they may order the parties to fulfil their obligations towards the child. Family courts can, however, restrict or suspend that right if such a measure is necessary for the child's welfare. A decision restricting or suspending that right for a lengthy period or permanently may only be taken if the child's well-being would be endangered in the absence of such measures. The family courts may order that the right of access be exercised in the presence of a third party, such a Youth Office authority or an association.

In the judgements *Niedzwiecki v. Germany*[139] and *Okpisz v. Germany*,[140] the ECtHR found a violation of Article 14 combined with Article 8 ECHR, as, under the reformed Child Benefits Act in force from January 1994, only foreigners with a stable residence permit were entitled to such benefits, whereas the applicants

---

5(4) ECHR that they had been denied access to the investigation file in connection with the judicial review of their detention on remand.

[136] Strafverfahrensänderungsgesetz 1999, BGBl. 2000, Part I, 1253.

[137] Reform zum Kindschaftsrecht 1997, BGBl. 1997, 2942.

[138] *Elsholz v. Germany* (appl. no. 25735/94), Judgement (Grand Chamber), 13 July 2000, Reports 2000-VIII, 345 et seq. (the Court concluded that German court decisions dismissing the applicant's request for access to his son, a child born out of wedlock, amounted to a breach of Article 8 of the Convention).

[139] *Niedzwiecki v. Germany* (appl. no. 58453/00), Judgements (Fourth Section), 25 October 2005 (not yet reported).

[140] *Okpisz v. Germany* (appl. no. 59140/00), Judgement (Fourth Section), 25 October 2005 (not yet reported).

only had provisional residence permits at the material time. On 6 July 2004, i.e. before the judgement of the Strasbourg Court, the Federal Constitutional Court, in a ruling on pilot cases, held that Section 1(3) of the Child Benefits Act, as effective from January 1994 until December 1995, was incompatible with the right to equal treatment under Article 3 of the German Basic Law. Accordingly, the legislator was ordered to amend the Child Benefits Act by 1 January 2006. The Constitutional Court found, in particular, that a difference in treatment between parents on the basis of whether or not they were in possession of a stable residence permit lacked sufficient justification. As the granting of child benefit related to the protection of family life under Article 6(1) of the Basic Law, very weighty reasons would have been required to justify unequal treatment and such reasons had not been given. Parliament enacted the Law in question in December 2006.[141]

Last but not least, following the judgement of the Court in the case *Karlheinz Schmidt*,[142] the authorities of the *Land* Baden-Württemberg and of the two other *Länder* which had similar regulations (Bayern and Sachsen) stopped requesting the payment of outstanding fire service levies (*Feuerwehrabgabe*) and stopped imposing new obligations to pay these levies. Subsequently, the Federal Constitutional Court held, in a judgement of 24 January 1995 concerning the regulations in two of the three *Länder* (Baden-Württemberg and Bayern – the situation in Sachsen was not before the Court in this case), that the impugned provisions, which imposed on men only the duty of doing fire service and of paying fire service levy, amounted to discrimination based on sex contrary to Article 3, para. 3, of the Basic Law. The Federal Constitutional Court also held that this kind of levy was contrary to the general principles applicable to special levies of a tax character (*die Grundsätze über die finanzverfassungsrechtliche Zulässigkeit parafiskalischer Sonderabgaben*). It finally held that the unconstitutionality of the impugned provisions rendered these null and void (*Nichtigerklärung*).

Other changes aimed at an acceleration of proceedings, notably proceedings before the Federal Constitutional Court. In the *Pammel* and *Probstmeier* cases,[143] which concerned the length of the proceedings in the Federal Constitutional Court relating to an objective review of the constitutionality of legislation carried out in connection with an application for a preliminary ruling, the Court held that the proceedings had exceeded the reasonable time referred to in Article 6(1) ECHR.[144] Following these judgements, the number of legal staff assigned to the

---

[141] On 3 May 2006, the Bill was sent to Parliament with comments of the Federal Council (*Bundesrat*) and the Government. It was adopted on 13 December 2006 (*BGBl.* I S. 2915).

[142] *Karlheinz Schmidt v. Germany* (appl. no. 13580/88), Judgement (Chamber), 18 July 1994, Series A, Vol. 291-B.

[143] *Pammel v. Germany* (appl. no. 17820/91), Judgement (Chamber), 1 July 1997, Reports 1997-IV, 1096 et seq.; *Probstmeier v. Germany* (appl. no. 20950/92), Judgement (Chamber), 1 July 1997, Reports 1997-IV, 1123 et seq.

[144] Delays reached, respectively, five years and three months in the *Pammel* case, and seven years and four months in the *Probstmeier* case. See *contra Süssmann v. Germany* (appl. no. 20024/92),

Federal Constitutional Court increased. The Federal Ministry of Justice sent letters to the Federal Constitutional Court informing it about these judgements and the Government was of the opinion that the Federal Constitutional Court should adapt its practice of joining similar cases so as to avoid unjustified delays. The Government noted moreover that the workload of the Federal Constitutional Court has substantially improved over the last years, as the backlog caused by the constitutional problems posed by German unification had been resolved.

Germany sometimes amended its legislation in order to take into account judgements issued with regard to other States Parties. For example, amendments aimed at giving the accused more rights to be heard (in 1964) or granting persons who had been kept in custody without later being sentenced the right to compensation (in 1971) were introduced in the German legislation in order to satisfy the requirements of the Convention.[145] More recently,[146] the German Government indicated that the creation of a new remedy in respect of lengthy proceedings was felt to be necessary in the light of the ECtHR's judgement in *Kudla v. Poland*.[147]

The effects of the ECHR on German judges are less obvious: German courts rarely explicitly take into account the ECtHR's case law. Among the reasons put forward to explain this attitude is the fact that judgements of the Strasbourg Court were not easily available and not always translated into German; as a consequence, the knowledge about the Court's case law was not very significant. Above all, the existence of directly applicable and judicially enforceable domestic guarantees, with which judges are familiar, plays an important role here. While the first argument is no longer valid today, the second one still explains some of the resistance *vis-à-vis* the ECHR.

The idea that rights protection under the national system is better, compared with the ECHR, is widespread, the view being that the substantive guarantees of the Basic Law are in general wider in scope and more effectively monitored than the rights enshrined in the ECHR.[148] Accordingly, there is no need to refer to an

---

Judgement (Grand Chamber), 16 September 1996, Reports 1996-IV, 1158 et seq.: while the European Court concluded that Article 6 (1) of the Convention was applicable to the proceedings at issue before the Federal Constitutional Court (an individual complaint of unconstitutionality), it found no violation of this provision because of "the unique political context of German reunification and the serious social implications of the disputes which concerned termination of employment contracts," to which the Federal Constitutional Court was entitled to decide that it should give priority.

[145] See Zimmermann (2001), 344 et seq., who notes that "an in-depth study was already being undertaken to determine whether both the German Criminal Code and the Code on Criminal Procedure could be considered compatible with the Convention," at the time the Convention was submitted for Parliamentary approval.

[146] *Sürmeli v. Germany* (appl. no. 75529/01), Judgement (Grand Chamber), 8 June 2006 (not yet reported), para. 138.

[147] *Kudla v. Poland* (appl. no. 30210/96), Judgement (Grand Chamber), 26 October 2000, Reports 2000-XI, 197 et seq.

[148] N. Weiss noted that "Germany's own elaborate system of basic rights protection was the main reason why, in the formative years of the Convention, [Convention rights] did not hold the important position they do today." Weiss (2003), 53.

outside, supranational system. These beliefs began to change slightly in the 80's, when Germany was found to be in breach of the ECHR on several occasions,[149] in particular concerning fair trial and *habeas corpus* rights. Both rights were more detailed in the ECHR than in the German Basic Law.

3. Comparison and Conclusion

The case law of the ECtHR has had some substantial effects on both national legal orders. Some major legislative changes have occurred in procedural matters, when it became clear that reforms were necessary to avoid new violations of the ECHR. Judges in both countries seem increasingly sensitive to the 'avoidance of punishment' logic. In France, the 'judicial empowerment' argument may also have force, given traditional separation of powers doctrines and the prohibition of judicial review of statute.

In Germany, a certain tension, if not a conflict, appears to exist between the German judges, in particular the Federal Constitutional Court, and the ECtHR. The statements of the Constitutional Court in its *Görgülü* decision[150] can be seen as a reaction to the judgement of the ECtHR in the case of *Von Hannover v. Germany*,[151] in which the Strasbourg Court condemned the reasoning of the Constitutional Court. The Constitutional Court thus showed its willingness to remain the arbiter of the impact of the ECHR on German law in concrete cases, and more generally to control the effects of the ECtHR's judgements within the German legal order.[152]

The rather open resistance in Germany is to be compared to a more hidden, less explicit and less direct resistance in France today.[153] Although both countries have assumed that standards of domestic rights protection are in complete conformity with the ECHR, a wide range of French authorities have expressed profound irritation at the ECtHR's tendency towards harmonization, and they strongly defend the French model of human rights protection. The same is true of Germany, but these irritations are expressed through the Federal Constitutional Court.

[149] For instance in the *Pakelli* case: *Pakelli v. Germany* (appl. no. 8398/78), Judgement (Chamber), 25 April 1983, Series A, Vol. 63 (violation of Article 6(3)(c) ECHR because of the refusal of the Federal Court, in proceedings concerning an appeal on points of law, to appoint an official defence counsel for the hearings).

[150] BVerfGE 111, 307.

[151] *Von Hannover v. Germany* (appl. no. 59320/00), Judgement (Third Section), 24 June 2004, Reports 2004-VI, 41.

[152] Ruffert (2007), 253.

[153] Costa (2004), 20.

E. Mechanisms of Coordination

1. France

a. Courts

Three stages of reception must be distinguished in France. First, there was the re-fusal and/or indifference regarding the application of the Convention itself. Until 1989 for the administrative court (jurisprudence *Nicolo*),[154] and up to 1975 for the civil court (jurisprudence *Sté Café Jacques Vabre*),[155] the national judge refused as a matter of principle to set aside legislative norms which conflicted with, and were posterior, to the Convention (and to all international or European norms). The same situation applies to all infra-legislative norms established in application of a law (theory of the *'Loi-écran'*). This fourteen-year time-lag between the two orders of jurisdictions still has repercussions today: if, as early as 1995, the Court of Cassation has automatically put forward the grounds relative to the violation of the Convention,[156] the Council of State has not followed this path, the more so as "the Convention formulates rights and obligations which already exist in French law".[157]

The second stage (which began in the mid 80's for the civil courts[158] and in the mid-90's for the administrative courts[159]) was that of an autonomous application of the Convention, as judges were firmly opposed to taking European interpreta-tions into account. The French Council of State used to consider, as one of its commissioners affirmed, that the interpretation of the ECHR has to reconcile, "as far as it is possible, two concerns: on the one hand, avoid any position which would clearly infringe the case law of the Court; on the other hand, also avoid any solution which, on one question, would be in breach with national law".[160] This posture is linked to the absence of a binding legal authority according to the

---

[154] CE, ass., 20 October 1989, *Nicolo*.

[155] Cass., 24 May 1975, *G.P.* (1975) 2470, conclusions *Touffait*, which refers to Community law. Cf. the *Respino* judgement of 3 June 1975 (Cass, crim.) regarding the ECHR.

[156] Cass., com., 19 December 1995, *Mme Garcia-Heller*, Lexi-laser cassation.

[157] CE, *SA Morgane*, 11 January 1991. Costa (1997), 397.

[158] Cass., 1ère civ., 10 January 1984, *Bull. civ.*, 1, no. 8, 6. See also the four judgements of the Court of Cassation, 1 June 1994, based on Article 5 (Protocol no. 7) interpreting the principle of equality of civil rights and liability between spouses in order to refuse effects in France of a repudia-tion pronounced in a foreign country.

[159] CE, sect., 29 July 1994, *Département de l'Indre* ; CE, ass., 17 February 1995, *Marie and Hardouin* (conclusions *Frydman*). In these judgements, under the direct influence of European jurisprudence (Judgements in *Engel and Others v. the Netherlands* (appl. nos 5100/71, 5101/71, 5102/71, 5354/72 and 5370/22), Judgement (Plenary), 8 June 1976, A 22, and *Campbell and Fell v. the United Kingdom* (appl. nos 7819/77 and 7878/77), Judgement (Chamber), 28 June 1984, A 80), the Council of State, while nonetheless maintaining the independence of its reasoning, admitted the claim against abuse of authority concerning the sanctions imposed on members of the armed forces and on prisoners, previously classified as measures of internal order not liable to judicial review, in order to avoid an adverse judgement by the ECtHR. The literature agrees on the fact that the judge-ment in the *Maubleu* case (CE 14 February 1996) was a turning point (Genevois (2007), 13).

[160] Conclusions of Labetoulle in CE, section, 27 October 1978, *Debout*.

text of the Convention and to the absence of a preliminary reference procedure to another court for a ruling, in contrast with what exists at Community level.[161] It is also linked to the legitimacy of the European judge and to the principle of legal certainty that makes it necessary to await confirmation of the new interpretation of the Convention before any new European jurisprudence is taken into account. The existence of a jurisprudence established by the Strasbourg Court (and therefore the strongly improbable character of a reversal on its part) is fundamental to the French courts changing their case law. In the Council of State's *Gisti* judgement, for example, the *Commissaire du gouvernement* R. Abraham invoked the ECtHR's jurisprudence to persuade the judges to reverse case law dating from 1823, according to which the judge was not competent to interpret international treaties and had to refer back to the Ministry of Foreign Affairs for guidance.[162] Concerning the question of the removal of convicted foreigners, the Council of State refused to align its jurisprudence with that of Strasbourg, provoking in return a softening of the more moderate European position. More generally, it is the force of persuasion (through the coherence and legibility of European judgements) that counts. Since the administrative judge does not consider himself legally bound by European jurisprudence, the force of persuasion of the latter depends above all on the quality arguments issuing from Strasbourg. The same is true for rulings of the Constitutional Council, the European Court of Justice of the European Union, and the ECtHR.[163] It also seems quite evident today that the reception of Community law by French courts facilitated acceptance of the ECHR and of the Strasbourg case law,[164] including the *Nicolo* case.[165]

The third stage, which dates back to the beginning of the 21st century, relates to the more systematic practice of referring to the Articles of the Convention as specified by the jurisprudence of Strasbourg, a step facilitated when the final conclusion is to declare French law in compatibility with the ECHR. If references to the European source are rarely present in the introduction and the text of the decisions, especially those of the administrative judge, this influence is nevertheless clearly evident in the conclusions of the *Commissaires du gouvernement*. According to certain authors, even "the supreme administrative judge is close to the pure and simple acceptance of the *res interpretata*".[166] The supreme courts (the Council of State, on one hand, and the Court of Cassation on the other) have, in general, taken longer over this step than the judges of first and second

---

[161] Costa (1997), 397. Cf. Article 234 ECT.
[162] CE, ass., 29 June 1990, *Gisti*. See also the reversal before the judiciary judge on the same point: Cass., 1° civ., 19 December 1995, *Banque africaine de développement*.
[163] Andriantsimbazovina (1998), 195.
[164] S. Braconnier (1997), 115 ; Dupré (2001), 332. Waline (2004), 1708.
[165] Cf. the preface by Abraham (1999),VII.
[166] Andriantsimbazovina/Sermet (2004), 992, citing the conclusions Guyomar under CE, 30 December 2003, *Beausoleil and Mme Richard*, deliberately using the expression "authority deriving from interpretation" in relation to the judgements of the Strasbourg Court.

degree, especially when it is a question of sanctioning French law.[167] Beyond an interpretation in conformity,[168] F. Sudre considers that French courts have now gone one step further, reaching for constructive interpretation of the ECHR. In this mode, the judge interprets Convention rights on his/her own, even going beyond European requirements, in the absence of European jurisprudence,[169] thus stimulating a dialogue with the ECtHR.

b. Legislative and Executive Authorities

There is no specific mechanism to ensure the compatibility of proposed laws with the Convention. The Council of State, as the Government's legal advisor, provides consultative opinion on the conventionality (which includes compatibility with the text of the ECHR) and constitutionality of those texts put forward by the Government (and not those proposed by Members of Parliament), but this procedure does not always constitute a reliable filter. Since 1984, another mechanism has been developed. By virtue of the revised constituent decree of 1984, the National Consultative Commission for Human Rights (NCCHR) "can, of its own initiative, call the attention of the authorities to measures that appear to be of a nature to favour the protection and the promotion of human rights, notably regarding (…) the adjustment of national law to such instruments (…)". Concerning projects initiated by the Government (that represent 90%–95% of the texts submitted to Parliamentary scrutiny), the Prime Minister, in a circular of 22 October 1999, demanded the General Secretary of the Government to ensure that the Commission be consulted on all projects entering its field of competence. This procedure is very important, in practice, as it allows the NCCHR to give its opinion on the project before transmission to the Council of State and, *a fortiori*, before Parliamentary debate.[170] It is important to point out that, in a

---

[167] For example, TGI, Périgueux, 13 December 1988, affirms that the *Verdeille* law of 10 July 1964 setting up approved communal hunting associations was in conflict with Article 11 ECHR; Tribunal de police d'Argentan, 2 October 1991, which quashed a procedure on the basis of Article 6(1) ECHR, in which a defendant who had chosen to defend himself without assistance had not been able to obtain a copy of the file from the court recorder. In both cases, these rulings were annulled by the supreme judge, before obtaining a verdict of violation in Strasbourg (respectively, with the cases *Chassagnou et autres v. France* (appl. nos 25088/94, 28331/95 and 28443/95), Judgement (Grand Chamber), 29 April 1999, Reports 1999-III, 123; *Foucher v. France* (appl. no. 22209/93), Judgement (Chamber), 18 March 1997, Reports 1997-II, 452).

[168] CE, 27 October 2000, *Mme Vignon*, appropriating the interpretation of the ECtHR in the case of *Chassagnou et autres v. France* (appl. no. 25088/94, 28331/95 and 28443/95), Judgement (Grand Chamber), 29 April 1999, Reports 1999-III, 123, concerning the *Verdeille* law. Cass., Crim., 16 January 2001 following *Du Roy et Malaurie v. France* (appl. no.34000/96), Judgement (Third Section), 3 October 2000, Reports 2000-X, 185. Cass., 3° chambre civile, 2 July 2003, following *Yvon v. France* (appl. no. 44962/98), Judgement (Third Section), 24 April 2003, Reports 2003-V, 29.

[169] Cf. Sudre (2004), 218 and the examples cited, which includes the application of European jurisprudence to procedures in which the State was not a party. An example of innovative jurisprudence can be found in the judgement of *Ville d'Annecy* of 29 January 2003 (Council of State), where legal entities were given the right to invoke the provisions of the ECHR.

[170] CDDH(2006)008 Addendum III Bil, *Information submitted by Member States with regard to*

judgement of the Assembly on 8 February 2007, the Council of State found that the violation of a European or an international norm enacted by the Parliament is likely to engage the responsibility of the State. Even if the judge does not refer to the regime of liability for fault, it is nevertheless a major development; in fact, what was at stake was an act contrary to Article 6 ECHR, in so far as the financial interest that justified it was not a defensible general interest. [171]

2. Germany

a. Courts

As Germany has a detailed catalogue of fundamental rights, only few cases decided by national courts refer directly to the ECHR.[172] In most cases, in so far as the standards laid down in the ECHR are the same as those contained in the Basic Law, German courts have expressed a clear preference for domestic provisions and therefore referred to the Basic Law. This attitude, coupled with the fact that the ECHR has the rank of ordinary federal statute, explains the limited interest shown by national courts *vis-à-vis* the ECHR. Compared to the total number of judgements issued each year by the supreme courts, the number of explicit references to the ECHR is quite low.

The Federal Constitutional Court began quoting the ECHR shortly after its entry into force. In a 1957 decision,[173] the Constitutional Court concluded that the German legislation on homosexuality was not contrary to Articles 2, 8, 13 and 14 ECHR. It referred later on to various provisions of the Convention and, sometimes, to judgements issued by the ECtHR.[174] This practice was confirmed by the decision of the Federal Constitutional Court in 1987, which underlined that the ECHR serves as an aid to interpretation in determining the content and scope of fundamental rights enshrined in the Basic Law.

The Federal Constitutional Court most often relies on Article 6 ECHR, as the rights laid down in this Article are broader in scope than the equivalent provisions of the Basic Law.[175] For instance, the Federal Constitutional Court invoked Article 6(2) ECHR, which guarantees the presumption of innocence, not specifically dealt with in the Basic Law.[176]

In order to adjust the German legal order to the requirements of the ECtHR's

---

the implementation of the five recommendations mentioned in the Declaration adopted by the Committee of Ministers at its 114th session (12 May 2004), 7 April 2006.

[171] CE, ass., 8 February 2007, *Guardedieu*, (report Derepas in *RFDA*, 2007, 361): cf. Gautier/ Melleray (2007), 9; Rouault (2007), 53.

[172] According to G. Ress (Ress (1993), 836), "it may be said that references to Strasbourg case-law by German courts is less frequent than in Switzerland or Austria." See also Frowein (2002), 29–33.

[173] BVerfGE 6, 389.

[174] See Szymczak (2007), 170 et seq.

[175] However, pursuant to German constitutional law, the principle of legality, enshrined in Article 20 of the Basic Law, is considered to cover those rights.

[176] BVerfGE 74, 358; BVerfGE 82, 106.

case law, the Federal Constitutional Court can strike down laws but only if they are found to be unconstitutional. Thus, the Court will declare a law null and void on the sole basis that it violates fundamental rights laid down in the Basic Law, even if that law violates at the same time the ECHR. For instance, after the judgement of the ECtHR in the case *Karlheinz Schmidt*,[177] the Federal Constitutional Court nullified the laws which were found to be contrary to Article 4 read in conjunction with Article 14 ECHR, but referred in its decision to the existence of discrimination based on sex contrary to Article 3, paragraph 3, of the Basic Law. By the same token, the Federal Constitutional Court can nullify a decision which violates fundamental rights and, in case of a final court judgement, may send the case back for a retrial.

While the ECHR is regularly cited by the Federal Constitutional Court, the Convention has, thus far, not been decisive in the conclusion reached by this court. The Federal Constitutional Court refers to the ECHR only to support its own interpretation and to confirm its findings under the Basic Law. References to the ECHR and the ECtHR's case law by the Federal Constitutional Court appear to be weak both in quality and quantity.[178] This situation seems, however, to have improved since the *Görgülü* judgement.[179]

The same observation is also true for the other courts concerned: references to the ECHR are in general not significant. In the course of criminal proceedings, the Federal Court of Justice (*Bundesgerichtshof*) most often refers to the procedural rights laid down in the ECHR, and sometimes to the related European case law. For example, in a decision of 18 November 1999, the Federal Court of Justice analyzed in detail the ECtHR's judgement in the case of *Teixeira de Castro v. Portugal*[180] in order to determine how to deal with the admissibility of evidence resulting from undercover agents' activities. The Federal Administrative Court (*Bundesverwaltungsgericht*) sometimes mentions Article 8 ECHR, in decisions which deal with the status of aliens, or Article 3, when deciding whether or not a foreigner should be deported.

More worrying is the approach of local or regional courts which tend to deny any influence to the ECHR or the Strasbourg Court's case law in decision-making. As shown by the *Görgülü* case,[181] in the opinion of the regional court, only the German State, as a party to the Convention, can be bound by judgements of

---

[177] *Karlheinz Schmidt v. Germany* (appl. no. 13580/88), Judgement (Chamber), 18 July 1994, Series A, Vol. 291-B.

[178] Szymczak (2007), 176 and Schlette (1996), 760.

[179] See, for example, the decision of the Federal Constitutional Court of 13 December 2006 (BVerfG, 1 BvR 2084/05, para. 39), where the Federal Constitutional Court went in detail into the question of whether the administrative courts have respected the *Chassagnou* judgement of the European Court issued against France. *Chassagnou et autres v. France* (appl. nos 25088/94, 28331/95 and 28443/95), Judgement (Grand Chamber), 29 April 1999, Reports 1999-III, 123.

[180] *Teixeira de Castro v. Portugal* (appl. no. 25829/94), Judgement (Chamber), 9 June 1998, Reports 1998-IV, 145.

[181] BVerfGE 111, 307.

the ECtHR. The case had to be referred several times to higher courts before the judgement of the Strasbourg Court was finally considered.

b. Legislative and Executive Authorities

While there is no special procedure in Germany to control the conformity of draft legislation with the ECHR, the Convention is taken into account as a standard of scrutiny. As the content of draft legislation is first examined in the light of the Basic Law, there is an indirect control of the compatibility with the ECHR since the Basic Law's fundamental rights encompass largely the rights guaranteed by the ECHR. Second, there is an examination of the draft legislation's compatibility with federal legislation, including the ECHR which has the rank of a federal statute.

This conformity will be examined before the entry into force of the legislation by at least four institutions: the Ministry with the overall responsibility for the particular draft; other Ministries which must approve it; the Federal Ministry of Justice, to which every draft Bill has to be submitted; the Legal Affairs Committee of the Federal Parliament (*Bundestag*); and the Legal Affairs Committee of the Federal Council (*Bundesrat*).[182]

Moreover, the Convention is regularly cited as a reason for adapting the legislation and references to the ECHR were sometimes included in German legislation. The Law on residence (*Aufenthaltsgesetz*), for example, refers to the ECHR and provides that a foreigner cannot be deported when the deportation appears to contradict the ECHR.[183]

3. Comparison and Conclusion

References by French courts to the ECHR have increased and there are more and more decisions taken on the basis of the ECHR and the ECtHR's case law, even if some resistance persists in some cases. In Germany, these references remain limited and some courts resist applying judgements of the Strasbourg Court.

This difference can be explained by two main factors. The first one is the existence, in Germany, of a developed catalogue of rights, which cover almost all the rights included in the ECHR. As a consequence, domestic courts will above all refer to domestic provisions, i.e. to the Basic Law. This is particularly true for the Federal Constitutional Court, which controls the conformity of court decisions and statutes with the German Constitution (Basic Law) and not with the Convention. Furthermore, the ECHR cannot serve as a direct basis for an individual constitutional complaint before the Federal Constitutional Court.

The second factor lies in the fact that, in France, neither of the two supreme

---

[182] CDDH(2006)008 Addendum III Bil (*supra* note 170).

[183] Para. 60(5) (*Verbot der Abschiebung*), *Gesetz über den Aufenthalt, die Erwerbstätigkeit und die Integration von Ausländern im Bundesgebiet (Aufenthaltsgesetz – AufenthG)*, 30 July 2004, *BGBl.* I S. 1950.

courts (Court of Cassation and Council of State) are competent to control the conformity of domestic legislation with the Constitution; they, therefore, sought a secondary way of protecting fundamental rights, developing a control of "conventionality". In Germany, the ECHR serves principally as a guideline for the interpretation of the fundamental rights and principles enshrined in the Basic Law.

Concerning the legislative process, no specific scrutiny procedure exists in either country. For this reason, the compatibility of draft legislation with the ECHR may not be fully guaranteed.

F. Remedies and Proportionality Test

1. France

a. Remedies

aa. Remedies in general. As we have emphasized, the French system of rights protection is incomplete, in that a statute once promulgated is not subject to judicial review by the ordinary courts. As is well known, the founders of the 1958 Constitution designed the Constitutional Council as a means of securing executive dominance of Parliament, not to protect fundamental rights.[184] In any case, the Constitutional Council exercises only abstract review of statutes prior to their entry into force, and it has refused to examine the conformity of such laws with the Convention.[185] In so far as the Constitutional Council acts in its capacity as ordinary judge of electoral litigation, Convention norms may come into play and be enforced.[186] The European influence on the decisions of the Constitutional Council and the interpretation of fundamental rights has remained limited, even if a certain dialogue and a mutual influence between French high courts seems to be taking place.[187] Under French law, the protection of Convention rights falls within the purview of the civil and administrative courts. Today, there is common consensus among doctrinal authorities that protection provided at the European level is complementary to that given internally, helping to close gaps.[188]

The individual is far more likely to plead the Convention than the Constitution before the courts precisely because judges can directly enforce the former. As a consequence, the control of conventionality substitutes for the control of con-

---

[184] Stone 1992; Fatin-Rouge Stéfanini/Gay (2004), 215.
[185] Decision 74-54 DC of 15 January 1975, *IVG*. Cf. the repetition of this absolute provision in the decision 93-335 DC of 21 January 1994, *Loi portant diverses dispositions en matière d'urbanisme et de construction.*
[186] Decision of 21 October1988, *Elections du Val d'Oise*, Rec., 183, on the compatibility of the July 11th 1986 Bill on the two-round election process with Article 3 (Protocol no. 1) of ECHR.
[187] Grewe (1998), 220.
[188] Saillant (2004), 1537.

stitutionality, when it comes to rights protection. Individuals have many fruitful ways of invoking ECHR violations: they can plead the "illegality exception" before an administrative or civil judge at any given time, triggering analysis of the conformity of the relevant act with the Convention. Applications for *ultra vires* (*Recours en excès de pouvoir*) can also be lodged with an administrative judge (the procedure does not recognize the primacy of constitutional rules, but can lead to the enforcement of the ECHR). These points made, French judges, especially in the administrative order, tend to resort to a "neutralising" interpretation of the law in order to mitigate tensions or conflicts with the ECHR. At the same time, they seek to construct the internal law to bring it in line with European law.[189]

In the field of administrative litigation, the Act of 30th June 2000 establishes the so-called 'freedom injunction order in chambers', which aims to prevent manifestly serious violations of fundamental liberties by the administration,[190] as provided in Article L. 521-2 of the Administrative Justice Code. During these proceedings breaches to the rights mentioned by the Convention were invoked,[191] but explicit references to the ECtHR remain rare.[192]

bb. Special remedies. Reopening of judicial proceedings. As a consequence of the *Hakkar* (1994) case,[193] in which the plaintiff had been condemned to life imprisonment as a result of a trial later found to be in violation of Article 6 ECHR, the French legislator enacted provisions for the eventual reopening of the internal criminal proceedings at the request of the Minister of Justice, the Advocate-General of the Court of Cassation, or by the person convicted. According to Articles 626-1 to 626-7 of the Procedural Criminal Code, as amended after enactment of the Act of 15 June 2000, the reopening of a case is only possible for a finding of guilt rendered by a court dealing with the substance of the case or by the Court of Cassation.[194] The finding of a violation of the Convention, the existence of a cause and effect relationship between this violation and the finding of guilt at the domestic level,[195] as well as the existence of consequences damaging to the accused with regard to the nature and seriousness of the violation are conditions for the reopening of a case. Article 626–1 of the Code of Criminal Procedure explicitly states that just satisfaction does necessarily

---

[189] Bonichot (2002), 242.

[190] Wachsmann (2007).

[191] Cf. the examples mentionned by D'Ambra (2006), 164-165.

[192] CE, ordonnance référé, 12 November 2005, *Association SOS Racisme – Touche pas à mon pote*, rec. 496. CE, ordonnance référé, 20 December 2005, *Meyet*, recueil 586, which is the first mention of a judgement of the ECtHR in its visa, (*Boyle and Rice v. the United Kingdom* (appl. nos 9659/82 and 9658/82), Judgement (Plenary) 27 April 1988, Series A, Vol.131.

[193] *Hakkar v. France*, (appl. no. 19033/91), Decision (Second Chamber), Commission, 31 August 1994.

[194] Cass., Commission réexamen (of review), 15 February 2001, *Voisine, Dall.* (2001, *IR*) 983. The review does not cover the litigations under the jurisdiction of the Tribunal de police.

[195] Cass., Commission réexamen, 8 November 2001, bull. crim., no. 231.

close matters for the accused.[196] However, the French Court of Cassation seems to adopt a rather lenient interpretation in practice. Its argumentation is based almost solely on a material approach, taking into account the type of violation in question; thus, a violation of the right to a fair trial, as recognized by the Court, seems automatically to allow for a new trial,[197] under the condition that the violation of procedural guarantees causally determined the result of the trial. According to the French Court of Cassation, the relationship between the violation and the condemnation must stem from the European decision.[198] Moreover the Court of Cassation does not seem particularly sensitive to the ECtHR's granting of just satisfaction.

It is not yet possible to reopen a case in civil and administrative matters. In a ruling of 30 September 2005, the social chamber of the Court of Cassation invoked the *res iudicata* principle (with a reference to Article 1351 of the civil code) and the argument that the "decision of the Committee of Ministers of the Council of Europe or a ruling of the Court (…) does not entitle the re-opening of a case".[199] Similarly, the Council of State, in a judgement of 11 February 2004, asserted that "it does not follow from any provision of the ECHR, notably from Article 46, nor from any internal provision, that the ruling from 13 February 2003 by which France was condemned by the ECtHR, may have as a consequence the reopening of the jurisdictional procedure (…) terminated by the Council of State on 9 April 1999".[200] This position constitutes a major hindrance to ensuring the effectiveness of Convention guarantees, an obstacle that only legislative intervention might remove.

Length of proceedings. Given the high number of French cases in Strasbourg relating to the excessive length of procedures, it is important to consider the internal appeal possibilities in such cases. As there is a sufficiently well established internal jurisprudence condemning the State for denial of justice in case of excessively lengthy proceedings, the ECtHR now considers, after many rulings to the contrary,[201] that the action for defective judiciary administration (*recours en responsabilité pour fonctionnement défectueux de la justice*) contained in Article L. 781-1 of the judiciary organization Code (the liability scheme for gross fault) is a valid mode of recourse under Article 13 ECHR. In the case of a non-specific appeal, the new interpretation by the Court of Cassation (for the needs of the

---

[196] Cass., Commission réexamen, 15 February 2001, *Voisine, Dall.* (2001, I.R.) 983.

[197] Cass., Commission réexamen, 6 December 2001, *Remli,* no. 01-00002. Cass., Commission réexamen, 30 November 2000, *Hakkar, JCP* (2000, II) 10642, *Gaz. Pal.* (2001, no. 84-86) 8. Cass., Commission de réexamen, 14 March 2002, no. 01-99007.

[198] Cass., Commission réexamen, 8 November 2001, *Dall.* (2002) 373. More generally, cf. Lambert Abdelgawad (2006), 197.

[199] Cass., Soc., 30 September 2005, 04-47.130 (no. 1938 FS-P), *Dall.* (10 November 2005, no.40) 2800.

[200] CE, 11 February 2004, *Mme Chevrol.*

[201] *Vernillo v. France* (appl. no. 11889/85), Judgement (Plenary), 20 February 1991, Series A, Vol.198.

European disputes), which defined gross negligence as "any systematic deficiency characterized by a fact or a series of facts exhibiting the incapacity of the public judiciary service to fulfil its mission",[202] has led to a reversal of the case law by the Strasbourg Court.[203]

In the administrative legal order, the Council of State has accepted State liability only in the case of gross judicial negligence.[204] The interpretation has gradually become more flexible: the administrative judges now compensate for simple fault the prejudice resulting from unreasonable lengths of proceedings. Based on Articles 6 and 13 of the ECHR and on the general principles governing the administration of justice, it is considered that the infringement of the "right to a reasonable delay in judicial proceedings" is a "miscarriage of justice" entitling its victims to compensation.[205] This appeal is deemed effective, in conformity with Article 13 of the ECHR, as of 1 January 2003, a date after which knowledge of this jurisprudence was presumed to be common.[206] Further, the Act of 19 December 2005 (complementary to that of 28 July 2005) acknowledged that the jurisdiction of the Council of State is the sole forum (at first and last instance) for opening "liability proceedings against the State for excessive duration of administrative procedures" (Article R. 311-1 of the Administrative Justice Code). France thus joins other European States that have evolved specific appeal processes enabling compensation for the prejudice resulting from the excessive duration of certain trials.[207]

b. Proportionality test

The ECtHR's proportionality test, employed whenever a given case involves the use of a state's margin of appreciation, was relatively easily transposed into French law, as a standard for dealing with *ultra vires* claims (*recours en excès de pouvoir*). Nonetheless, due to requirements laid down by the ECHR, the proportionality test now covers fields where previously only limited control existed, including with regard to statutes. Such was the case, for example, in matters relating to the

---

[202] Cass., Ass. Plénière, 23 February 2001, *Cts Bolle-Laroche c/Agent judiciaire du trésor.*

[203] *Giummarra and Others v. France* (appl. no. 61166/00), Decision (Third Section), 12 June 2001 (not reported); *Nouhaud et autres v. France* (appl. no.33424/96), Judgement (Second Section), 9 July 2002 (not reported).

[204] CE, ass., 29 December 1978, *Darmont*, ruling questioned by *Lutz v. France* (appl. no. 48215/99), Judgement (Second Section), 26 March 2002 (not reported).

[205] CE, ass., 28 June 2002, *Ministre de la justice c/M. Magiera.* See also recently, CE, 22 January 2007, *M. Forzy*, extending the *Magiera* precedent to the financial and budgetary disciplinary court (condemning the state to a fine of 4000 euros).

[206] *Broca et Texier-Micault v. France* (appl. nos 27928/02 and 31694/02), Judgement (Second Section), 21 October 2003 (not reported). On this matter, and focusing on the effects of the Strasbourg case law on national Courts, see Errera (2006) 282.

[207] Cf. Sudre (2006), 286. The first application of this Bill was the *SARL Potchou et autres* case, in which the Council of State deemed itself competent to rule on the rule on the prejudice and damage claims resulting from excessive duration of proceedings then pending before the Marseille Administrative Court of Appeal (CE, 25 January 2006, *SARL Potchou et autres*).

control of public trials of foreigners and minors. In cases pertaining to the right to private and family life of foreigners facing expulsion, the Council of State reversed its case law in the 1991 *Belgacem* and *Babas* rulings,[208] thereby introducing the proportionality test. In previous case law, the means derived from a violation of Article 8 ECHR were considered to be inapplicable. The proportionality test, which was extended to rulings on entry and residence,[209] as well as to the *référé-liberté* jurisdictions cases,[210] has served as a direct inspiration for both the French executive and legislative authorities in this field.[211]

The introduction of the proportionality test has had a double effect. First, it enhanced the ordinary judge's authority and control over State acts, including Parliamentary statute and measures adopted by the administration. The powers of domestic judges, thus "Europeanized," have been enriched, and their role and function in the French state made more complex.[212] In the specific case of public trial control by the Minister of Interior, the administrative judge now exercises increased power in considering whether the Minister's decision was proportional; at a minimum, the judge now requires the Minister to give better reasons for decisions, which the judge then assesses in light of proportionality requirements.[213]

Second, although the issue has yet to be the subject of systematic research, there has been a steady reinforcement of the status and protecting of individual rights when they come up against the "general interest." The Council of State, for example, now extends the application of the right to private and family life to a homosexual alien living in a stable partnership.[214] In matters relating to freedom of expression, the proportionality test has also led to a strengthening of individual liberties. The social chamber of the Court of Cassation has introduced the proportionality test when adjudicating the employee's freedom of expression, "to which only restrictions justified by the nature of the task and proportional to the expected goal may be applied".[215] Necessity analysis is also applied to publication bans, thus restricting ministerial discretion.[216]

---

[208] CE, ass., 19 April 1991, *Belgacem et Babas*.

[209] CE, 10 April 1992, *Akyan* ; CE, 10 April 1992, *Marzini*. CE, sect., 17 July 2003, *Bouhsane*.

[210] CE, 30 October 2001, *Mme Tliba*.

[211] Cf. the two examples cited by Sudre (2006a), 478. The Home Secretary's memorandum dated 25 October 1991 relative to the deportation of aliens; and the Ministry of Justice's memorandum on criminal policy dated 17 November 1999 relative to the statement and to the increase of denial of entry verdicts which insist on the respect of the proportionality principle and on the taking into account of the provisions of Article 8. See also Act no. 98-349 dated 11 May 1998 relative to the entry and stay of aliens in France which is consistent with the 1945 order establishing the right to the respect of a family and private life.

[212] Cass., 1ère civ., 7 February 2006, *FS P B, F. c/L., épouse S. et a.* ; Cass., 1ère civ., 7 March 2006, no.05-16.059, *F. c/Société Hachette Filipacchi associés*.

[213] Péchillon (2006), 303.

[214] CE, 28 April 2000, *Préfet des Alpes maritimes c/M. Maroussitch* ; CE, 29 June 2001, *Préfet de la Haute-Garonne c/M. Zahri*.

[215] Cass. Soc., 22 June 2004.

[216] Péchillon (2006), 298.

While the proportionality test is applied both by the national judge and the ECtHR in their legal reasoning, the question of balancing the divergent public and private interests at stake has, of course, been answered in different ways. Such was the case with regard to foreign nationals who opposed expulsion under Article 8 ECHR. French judges tend to apply a stricter standard than the Strasbourg Court does,[217] giving more weight to the illicit behaviour.[218]

The differing approach to interpreting proportionality taken by the Court and the domestic judges has also influenced reversals of jurisprudence and legislative reforms. The question of the ban on opinion polls in the week preceding elections is a spectacular illustration of this. Following the diverse positions adopted by the administrative and civil courts, concluding either to the compatibility or to the incompatibility with Article 10 ECHR, the legislator decided to amend the law.[219] Likewise, the Act of 6 May 1939 on foreign publications was amended by a decree on the 4th of October 2004, in conformity with Article 10 ECHR, at the behest of the Council of State[220] following the ECtHR ruling in the case of *Association Ekin v. France*.[221]

2. Germany

a. Remedies

aa. Remedies in General. The judicial control of domestic acts for conformity with the ECHR primarily falls within the ambit of the ordinary courts, given the Convention's rank as an ordinary federal statute. The Convention is directly applicable in German law and can be invoked before, and enforced by, German courts. The organs of Strasbourg decided early on that procedures before the Federal Constitutional Court, to which individuals have direct access under domestic law, constitutes a remedy to be exhausted before a complaint may be filed with the ECtHR.[222]

bb. Special remedies. Reopening of Judicial Proceedings. Applicants may apply for the reopening of criminal proceedings under Article 359 (6) of the Code of Criminal Procedure, as amended in 1998, once the ECtHR has determined that a criminal conviction by a German court violates the ECHR and if the decision is based on this violation. In other words, only criminal cases which were brought

---

[217] Cf. Sudre (2006), 473.
[218] CE, 18 May 2005, *Sahel*. For an overall study, Labayle (2007), 101.
[219] CE, 2 June 1999, *Meyet*, (concluding to compatibility); TGI, Paris, 15 December 1998, 5 judgements concluding to incompatibility. The 1977 Act was amended by the Act of 19 February 2002.
[220] CE, 7 February 2003, *GISTI*.
[221] *Association Ekin v. France* (appl. no. 39288/98), Judgement (Third Section), 17 July 2001, Reports 2001-VIII.
[222] *X. v. Germany* (appl. no. 8499/79), Decision, 7 October 1980, DR 21, 176.

before the ECtHR, and are in violation of the ECHR, may lead to the review of the decision by an ordinary court.[223] A law adopted on 22 December 2006 introduced the same possibility into the Code of Civil Procedure (*Zivilprozess-ordnung*) for civil proceedings.[224] As far as administrative proceedings are concerned, the Code of Administrative Court Procedure (para. 153 *Verwaltungsgerichtsordnung*) refers to the Code of Civil Procedure. Therefore, the introduction of the possibility of reopening in the Code of Civil Procedure (para. 580 *ZPO*) automatically leads to a similar possibility before the administrative courts.[225] There is, moreover, a possibility of re-examination in the field of administrative law.[226]

Length of proceedings. Section 75 of the Code of Administrative Court Pro-cedure (*Verwaltungsgerichtsordnung*) provides for a claim to the Administrative Court if the administrative authorities fail to decide within a reasonable time limit (generally three months) without giving sufficient justification for the de-lay.[227]

In the *Sürmeli* case,[228] the Strasbourg Court addressed the question of rem-edies available in the German legal system, complaining of the length of pend-ing civil proceedings. Considering that a constitutional complaint is not capable of affording redress for the excessive length of pending civil proceedings,[229] the Court found that Germany was in violation of Article 13 ECHR because the applicant did not have an effective remedy, given that proceedings had exceeded the "reasonable time" prescribed by Article 6(1). Under Article 46 ECHR, the Court took the view that its findings "suggest that the remedies available in the German legal system do not afford litigants an effective means of complaining

---

[223] The case *Stambuk* (*Stambuk v. Germany* (appl. no. 37928/97), Judgement (Third Section), 17 October 2002 (not reported)) provides an example of a reopening of disciplinary proceedings, following the conviction of the applicant (the fine was found to be in violation of Article 10 ECHR by the European Court).

[224] Para. 580 No. 8 *ZPO*: "Die Restitutionsklage findet statt (…) wenn der Europäische Gerich-tshof für Menschenrechte eine Verletzung der Europäischen Konvention zum Schutz der Menschen-rechte und Grundfreiheiten oder ihrer Protokolle festgestellt hat und das Urteil auf dieser Verletzung beruht" (Zweites Gesetz zur Modernisierung der Justiz, BGBl. I S. 3416). Notice was taken of the Recommendation No. R(2000)2 on the re-examination or reopening of certain cases at domestic level following judgements of the European Court of Human Rights, adopted by the Committee of Ministers of the Council of Europe.

[225] There is in fact a possibility of reopening proceedings pursuant to a violation of the ECHR found by the Strasbourg Court in all court proceedings, given that para. 580 *ZPO* applies to the Code of Procedure of Social Courts (para. 179 Sozialgerichtsgesetz), Labour Courts (para. 79 Arbe-itsgerichtsgesetz) and Financial Courts (para. 134 Finanzgerichtsordnung).

[226] CDDH(2006)008 Addendum III Bil (*supra* note 170170), which cites the case of *Saldiray Yilmaz*: following the judgement of the European Court, the regional immigration office issued a new decision, limiting the effect of the expulsion order.

[227] See *Stork v. Germany* (appl. no. 38033/02), Judgement (Fifth Section), 13 July 2006 (not yet reported), para. 20.

[228] *Sürmeli v. Germany* (appl. no. 75529/01), Judgement (Grand Chamber), 8 June 2006 (not yet reported).

[229] Ibid., para. 108.

of the length of pending civil proceedings and therefore do not comply with the Convention"[230] and reiterated that "a finding of a violation imposes on the respondent State a legal obligation (…) to select (…) the general and/or, if appropriate, individual measures to be adopted in their domestic legal order to put an end to the violation found by the Court and to redress so far as possible the effects."[231] The ECtHR noted that a Bill to introduce into the German written law a new remedy in respect of inaction was tabled before the Parliament in September 2005.[232]

A new remedy. Although a constitutional complaint may not be based on a breach of the Convention as such, in its *Görgülü* decision of 2004[233] the Federal Constitutional Court announced that it would accept complaints challenging, indirectly, a violation of the Convention before it. A complainant may now invoke a violation of the ECHR by way of asserting a violation of the principle of rule of law pursuant to Article 20, para. 3, of the Basic Law in conjunction with the fundamental right relevant in a particular case, in any case in which a German court or other authority had not taken into account a judgement of the Strasbourg Court. In this respect, the Federal Constitutional Court underlined that "it must in any case be possible, on the basis of the relevant fundamental right, to raise the objection in proceedings before the Federal Constitutional Court that state bodies disregarded or failed to take into account a decision of the European Court of Human Rights."[234] To justify this new mechanism, the Federal Court referred to its competence "to prevent and remove, if possible, violations of public international law that arise from the incorrect application or non-observance by German courts of international law obligations".[235] The Federal Constitutional Court reiterated the position that it is "indirectly in the service of enforcing international law, [in order to] reduce the risk of failing to comply with international law."[236]

b. Proportionality test

The proportionality test is native to the German legal order, as developed by the Federal Constitutional Court since the 50's. Its application, however, may lead

---

[230] Ibid., para. 136.

[231] Ibid., para. 137.

[232] Ibid, para. 138. The Bill was submitted on 22 August 2005: *Gesetzentwurf der Bundesregierung, Entwurf eines Gesetzes über die Rechtsbehelfe bei Verletzung des Rechts auf ein zügiges gerichtliches Verfahren (Untätigkeitsbeschwerdengesetz).*

[233] BVerfGE 111, 307. Before this decision, it had been suggested that a constitutional complaint could be based on a violation of Article 2, para. 1, of the Basic Law in cases in which the European Convention was arbitrarily misapplied or non-applied. See Ress (1993), 834.

[234] BVerfGE 111, 307 (para. 63). That is true also for the complaint that a State body has not respected a provision of the European Convention (Decision of the Federal Constitutional Court of 13 December 2006, *BVerfG*, 1 BvR 2084/05, para. 37).

[235] BVerfGE 111, 307 (para. 61).

[236] BVerfGE 111, 307 (para. 61).

to opposite conclusions, as shown by the case *Von Hannover v. Germany.*[237] In that case, the two Courts balance the protection of private life against freedom of expression differently. While the Federal Constitutional Court attached decisive weight to the freedom of the press, the ECtHR stressed the importance of the protection of private life. The applicant, the Princess Caroline of Monaco, lodged a complaint with the German Federal Constitutional Court, submitting that there had been an infringement of her right to the protection of her personality rights (Article 2(1) read in conjunction with Article 1(1) of the Basic Law), due to the publication in Germany of various photos showing her in scenes from her daily life. In a judgement of 15 December 1999, the Federal Constitutional Court held that the publication of some photos featuring the applicant with her children had infringed her right to the protection of her personality rights guaranteed by Articles 2(1) and 1(1) of the Basic Law, reinforced by her right to family protection under Article 6 of the Basic Law, but dismissed her appeal regarding the other photos. Caroline von Hannover therefore brought her case to Strasbourg. In its judgement of 24 June 2004, the Strasbourg Court found that Germany had violated Article 8 ECHR: the Court considered that, despite the margin of appreciation afforded to the State in this area, "the German courts did not strike a fair balance between the competing interests."[238]

In its *Görgülü* decision,[239] the Federal Constitutional Court held that, if "there are decisions of the European Court of Human Rights that are relevant to the assessment of a set of facts, then in principle the aspects taken into account by the European Court of Human Rights when it considered the case must also be taken into account when the matter is considered from the point of view of constitutional law, in particular when proportionality is examined, and there must be a consideration of the findings made by the European Court of Human Rights after weighing the rights of the parties."[240]

3. Comparison and Conclusion

In both countries, the ordinary courts are competent to control the conformity of national norms with the ECHR; the ECtHR even considers the individual complaint before the German Constitutional Court as a national remedy to be exhausted before bringing a case to Strasbourg. In France as well as in Germany, the responsibility to apply the ECHR lies primarily in the hands of ordinary courts, that is of judges in the civil, criminal, and administrative orders. Since 2004, individuals may apply to the German Constitutional Court if the ordinary

---

[237] *Von Hannover v. Germany* (appl. no. 59320/00), Judgement (Third Section), 24 June 2004, Reports 2004-VI, 41 et seq., known in Germany as the "Caroline Judgement" (*Caroline-Urteil*).

[238] Ibid., para. 79. Concerning the just satisfaction, a friendly settlement had been concluded by the Parties. Accordingly, the European Court decided to strike the case out of the list on 28 July 2005.

[239] BVerfGE 111, 307.

[240] Ibid., para. 49.

courts fail to implement properly a pertinent judgement of the European Court of Human Rights.

Comparison also reveals interesting lessons regarding the possibility of reopening a national judicial procedure once the ECtHR has found a violation in a case. This possibility was specifically provided for by a special statute (in 1998 in Germany, in 2000 in France) for criminal procedures. Unlike France, Germany recognizes the same possibility in civil matters.

Although the proportionality test was already known in Germany and France, its application with regard to the ECHR by the Strasbourg Court and the national courts may lead to different conclusions, judges being sensitive to different criteria. In France, the spread of the proportionality test in national court practice has meant a strong reinforcement of judicial control, relative to Parliament and the executive. As a consequence, French judges are, in general, better positioned to protect fundamental rights. Proportionality has also been the source of changes in law, apparent in the drafting of new statutes and also in the case law. However, given that proportionality balancing will always lead to some meaningful differences between national courts and the ECtHR, a dialogue between judges is also to be expected.

G. Knowledge and Practice

1. France

a. Dissemination of the European Court's judgements

Today, the ECtHR's rulings are widely distributed among the relevant bodies. The adoption of Recommendation Rec(2002)13 "on the Publication and dissemination in the member states of the text of the European Convention on Human Rights and of the case law of the European Court of Human Rights" has also increased awareness of the need to better apply the Convention in the national order. The Ministry of Justice's Department of European and International Affairs issues the ECtHR's major rulings. The legal service of the Foreign Office also communicates them via internal memoranda to the relevant administrations and ministries. Rulings which are relevant for the Home Secretary (legislation relating to aliens, civil liberties, police) are distributed to the Minister's Office and to the relevant administrations (Foreigners Division, National Police Headquarters), along with a commentary on their practical consequences. An annual review of the state of the Court's jurisprudence is also edited and distributed.[241] Through various channels, the legal research service of documentation centre at the Council of State distributes the information pertaining to the new ECtHR cases to all of the administrative jurisdictional staff. However, this information is mostly limited to rulings involving France. The European Law Observatory, a

---

[241] CDDH(2006)008 Addendum III Bil (*supra* note 170).

recently instituted cell within the Court of Cassation, also monitors the activities of the Strasbourg Court.

b. Lawyering
There are no NGO or lawyers' associations working solely on the application of the ECHR. A few law firms, mainly located in Paris and Strasbourg, bring cases to the Strasbourg Court. Arguably, this is due to the high rate of inadmissibility decisions of the Strasbourg Court and to the fact that the law firms can be held accountable. Most of the lawyers deal with human rights litigation in general. The lawyers of the Paris Bar Institute of Human Rights, to be sure, are among the ones most receptive towards those disputes, but this does not mean that they are necessarily the ones bringing the majority of the cases to the ECtHR. Some lawyers have extended their original specialization by incorporating a Convention specific perspective (property law, social law, legislation relating to aliens, procedural law, etc). The bar has no specialists in human rights as such; rather, its lawyers are oriented toward the wider domain of public liberties and individual freedoms. The bars do not offer any training on human rights or on the Convention. There are 150 bars in France, and fewer than a dozen of which have a human rights institute. According to a 2006 study, out of 96 cases involving France before the ECtHR, lawyers only appeared in 56 of them, 23 of them from Paris; only one involved an association.[242] Thus, the field is not monopolized by a few lawyers.

c. Teaching
Most universities and political science institutes teaching law have introduced specific courses on human rights law, and on the ECHR (in the 3rd year of the Bachelor of Law or in the 1st year of the Master's degree). Moreover, classes in criminal, civil and administrative law may mention the effect of the ECHR on French law, if only in passing. A few professional and research Master's degrees are specifically focused on European Human Rights law (e.g. at Paris II, Paris X, Caen, Strasbourg III).

Continuing education, of magistrates and lawyers, is organized by law schools and by those schools and institutes officially accredited by the National Bar Council, and has recently become mandatory (20 hours a year or 40 over a period which cannot exceed two years). In that context, there are seminars dealing with the rulings of the ECtHR.[243]

d. Scholarship
Thus far, no new journal has been created to deal with the study of the Convention, with exception of *L'Europe des Libertés* (founded in 1999). A few legal re-

---

[242] Puechavy (2007), 32.
[243] CDDH(2006)008 Addendum III Bil (*supra* note 170).

views have devoted more space to doctrinal commentary, legal theory, and other articles dedicated to the analysis of Strasbourg case law. A comprehensive study of the following journals *Actualité Juridique Droit administratif, La Semaine Juridique (édition générale), Recueil Dalloz, Revue Trimestrielle de Droit civil*, reveals the almost universal absence (with one exception) of papers dedicated to the ECHR prior to 1990. That year is a turning point for these journals,[244] showing a spectacular increase in the coverage given to the ECHR,[245] a situation that has stabilized since 2000. The columns dealing with important ECtHR rulings handed down against France in the mid-90's[246] make up the hard core of the doctrine found today in those periodicals. It must also be underlined that many books have been written on the ECHR and its application in France, the most important of which have been referred to in the bibliography.

2. Germany

a. Dissemination of the European Court's Judgements
Since 2004, the Federal Ministry of Justice (*Bundesministerium der Justiz*) has published an annual report on the case law of the European Court of Human Rights, focusing on cases against Germany. All judgements of the ECtHR against Germany are publicly available via the website of the Federal Ministry of Justice[247] which provides a direct link to the ECtHR's website for judgements in German.[248] Furthermore, a German website[249] provides references to all judgements and decisions of the ECtHR that have been translated into German.

The German translations of the more important judgements concerning Germany, as well as judgements concerning other countries, are also published in the *Europäische Grundrechte Zeitschrift* (*EuGRZ*) and/or the *Neue Juristische Wochenschrift* (*NJW*).[250] These judgements are distributed to all authorities directly concerned, in order to inform them of the Court's conclusions and to avoid similar violations of the Convention in the future.

The newspapers tend to deal only with important decisions of the Court concerning matters of public interest, such as the so-called *Bodenreform* judgements or the *Caroline Judgement*,[251] which were heavily criticized by a large part of German media.

---

[244] Five for the *AJDA*, 7 for *La Semaine Juridique*, one for the *RTDciv.* in 1990.
[245] For instance, 92 entries headed "*Droits et libertés fondamentaux*" (almost exclusively the ECHR) in the 2000 *Dalloz* collection.
[246] In 1992 for the *AJDA*, in 1998 for *La Semaine Juridique*.
[247] Themen: Menschenrechte, EGMR , available at: www.bmj.de.
[248] Council of Europe, European Court of Human Rights, www.coe.int/T/D/Menschenrechtsgerichtshof/Dokumente_auf_Deutsch.
[249] Urteile und Entscheidungen des EGMR in deutscher Sprache, www.egmr.org.
[250] Other judgements in German are also published in various other journals.
[251] For example: "Europas Richter hebeln die Pressefreiheit aus", *Frankfurter Allgemeine Zeitung*, 24 June 2004; "Es trifft die Pressefunktion in ihrem Kern", *Frankfurter Allgemeine Zeitung*, 13 July

b. Lawyering

There exists no stable network of German lawyers active in the field of human rights protection. There are some associations which organize seminars on human rights issues, but these are not only attended by lawyers. There are a few small law firms and individual lawyers who specialized in human rights questions. NGOs normally do not play a significant role in bringing cases against Germany to the Strasbourg Court. At least 80% of the cases brought against Germany before the Court are, in fact, brought by individuals who apply without representation.

c. Teaching

The ECHR as a system, and Convention rights, are generally taught as part of a course on international human rights law. There is no specific diploma devoted to human rights in Germany, but students can choose to specialize in human rights law by attending specific courses (*Schwerpunktfächer*) while preparing their Master of Laws (LL.M.). Since 1999, the European University Viadrina Frankfurt (Oder) has organized a Summer Course on the European system of human rights protection. The Universities of Bochum and Hamburg both participate in the European Master's Degree in Human Rights and Democratization (E.Ma). Further, the *Deutsche Richterakademie*, responsible for the continuing education of judges from all courts and of public prosecutors, regularly runs seminars on issues related to the ECHR and the case law of the ECtHR; and the German Barristers Institute (*Deutsches Anwaltsinstitut*) organizes a course on the application of the ECHR.

There exist few research centres specialized in human rights in Germany. The Human Rights Centre of the University of Potsdam (MRZ, *MenschenRechtsZentrum*), established in 1994,[252] is the only university centre dedicated to human rights in Germany. Moreover, the Nuremberg Human Rights Centre (*Nürnberger Menschenrechtszentrum*), an NGO, promotes public awareness of human rights issues. Finally, the Max Planck Institute for Comparative Public Law and International Law, based in Heidelberg, focuses partially on international protection of human rights.

In March 2001, the German Institute for Human Rights (DIMR) was established as the first national independent human rights institution. The Institute provides information about the state of human rights within and outside Germany, seeks to prevent human rights violations, and contributes to the promotion and protection of human rights.[253] It also publishes information on ECHR procedures and jurisprudence. Last, there are several German-language textbooks on the ECHR.[254]

2004; "Keine Rechtsmittel gegen 'Caroline-Urteil'", *Frankfurter Allgemeine Zeitung*, 1 September 2004.

[252] The directors are Prof. Dr. iur. Eckart Klein and Prof. Dr. phil. Christoph Menke.

[253] German Institute for Human Rights, www.institut-fuer-menschenrechte.de.

[254] Grabenwarter (2005); Peters (2003); Meyer-Ladewig (2003); Villiger (1999); Frowein/Peuk-

d. Scholarship

Doctrinal scholarship in Germany on the ECHR is quite developed. Specialized journals devoted to European human rights law have appeared, in particular the *Europäische Grundrechte Zeitschrift*, created in 1968, and the *MenschenRechts-Magazin*, published by the University of Potsdam since 1996.

The first journal dealing with the Convention and the Strasbourg Court is the *Zeitschrift für ausländisches öffentliches Recht und Völkerrecht (ZaöRV)*, also known as Heidelberg Journal of International Law (HJIL), which has been published since 1929 by the Max Planck Institute for Comparative Public Law and International Law. From 1960 on, this journal has regularly published articles on the activities of the Strasbourg Court.[255] Other major law journals, such as the *Neue Juristische Wochenschrift*, the *Zeitschrift für Rechtspolitik (ZRP)* or the *Neue Zeitschrift für Verwaltungsrecht (NVwZ)*, only began to deal with the ECHR, in a limited way, in the 90's.

3. Comparison and Conclusion

The fact that the judgements of the ECtHR are mainly published in French, one of the Court's official languages, might have led one to believe that the dissemination of these judgements would be wider in France than Germany. This is, however, not the case, as many judgements are translated and published in German, and not only judgements involving Germany as a respondent. In both States, judgements are transmitted to the ministries and authorities concerned, and disseminated to the legal community through specialized journals.

In neither country did we find a network of law firms or NGOs specialising in litigating Convention rights. This may be due to the duality of jurisdiction: cases brought before the Strasbourg Court are dealt with by the various courts at the national level. It may also be due to the fact that the costs of going to Strasbourg outweigh the potential benefits for lawyers, at least at the application stage.

The Convention is now part of the universities' curricula in both countries and is included in the continuing education of barristers. It thus seems to have entered the daily life of jurists in both France and Germany.

H. Comparison and Assessment

Since the 90's, the influence of the ECHR on the French legal system has been profound. Prior to that decade, French distrust of the ECHR's supranationalism, and an over-confidence concerning the compatibility of the national norms with the standards of the ECHR, meant that French authorities did more to hinder

---

ert (1996).

[255] Including a commentary of the first judgement of the European Court: see Matthies, H., "Das Erste Urteil des Europäischen Gerichtshofs für Menschenrechte: Verfahrensfragen in der Sache Lawless", *Zeitschrift für ausländisches öffentliches Recht und Völkerrecht* 21(1961), 249–258.

than to facilitate reception. In the 90's, the rising tide of violations found by the ECtHR made officials anxious about the reputation of France, the country of the *Déclaration des droits de l'homme et du citoyen*. National authorities began to work harder to reconcile French law and the ECHR, through various interpretive techniques, and they sometimes succeeded in doing so. The courts were at the heart of this evolution, despite the fact that they were ill-prepared to confront this challenge. More recently, the major impact of ECHR on the French legal system has been the broad expansion in judicial power. The principle of separation of powers and its corollaries (the *loi écran*, and the prohibition of judicial review) have been weakened, and the judiciary has asserted its authority to control the conventionality of all norms and acts, including statute.

Germany, starting from the standpoint of its own comprehensive system of rights protection, provides a very different picture. On the one hand, the trend is to take the ECHR and the Court's case law more into account (in legislation, teaching etc). On the other hand, a more restrictive attitude persists, based on a particular conception of German sovereignty. Thus, German judges sometimes resist the Strasbourg Court's authority, and insist on necessity, at times, to limit or adapt judgements of the ECtHR to national peculiarities.

The relation between the German Federal Constitutional Court and the ECtHR has its conflictual and competitive aspects. The judges of the Constitutional Court, whose role and authority in the German legal order is paramount, has not backed away from "confronting"[256] their Strasbourg counterparts. In the *Görgülü* decision,[257] the German Constitutional Court not only criticized previous findings of the ECtHR, but also warned it not to overstep its competence under Article 46 ECHR. The fact that the Strasbourg Court, in its *Görgülü* judgement,[258] had explicitly urged the German authorities to reverse its positions on crucial issues,[259] is certainly not irrelevant to the Federal Constitutional Court's response. The situation may worsen in the near future if the ECtHR continues to move in the direction, under Article 46 of the ECHR, of ordering States to adopt specific measures within a specified time period.[260] Future confrontation between judges in France and Strasbourg is also possible, for similar reasons.

---

[256] Hartwig (2005), 868.

[257] BVerfGE 111, 307.

[258] *Görgülü v. Germany* (appl. no. 74969/01), Judgement (Third Section), 26 February 2004 (not reported).

[259] Ibid., para. 64.

[260] For a recent example, see *L. v. Lithuania* (appl. no. 27527/03), Judgement (Second Section), 11 September 2007 (not yet reported), point 5: "Holds, by 5 votes to 2, that the respondent State, in order to meet the applicant's claim for pecuniary damage, is to adopt the required subsidiary legislation to Article 2.27 of its Civil Code on the gender-reassignment of transsexuals, within three months of the present judgment becoming final, in accordance with Article 44§2 of the Convention"; point 6: "Holds, by 6 votes to 1, alternatively, that should those legislative measures prove impossible to adopt within 3 months of the present judgment becoming final, in accordance with Article 44 (2) of the Convention, the respondent State is to pay the applicant 40.000 euros in respect of pecuniary damage."

Notwithstanding the first three decades of the Convention's life, the ECHR has had more impact in France. There have been much more judgements against France than against Germany, and these judgements have forced major structural change in France. Moreover, because France does not have a complete system of constitutional rights protection, the ECHR provides both rights and standards of review, filling the gap. Comparatively, Germany has a developed catalogue of judicially enforceable fundamental rights and the ECHR thus remains supplementary to German constitutional rights.

Both States have been active supporters of human rights, and have been close partners in the construction of Europe, of which the European system of human rights is an important part. Their courts were, nonetheless, reluctant to refer directly and explicitly to the ECHR. The reception of the ECHR can be characterized as "forced" adaptation, rather than a voluntary process: often, authorities had no choice but to adjust the national legal order to the requirements of the ECHR. In both countries, the relationship between the national courts and the European Court of Human Rights has not always been harmonious, and some tensions remain.

Bibliography

Abraham, R., Préface, in Potvin-Solis, L. (ed.), *L'effet des jurisprudences européennes sur la jurisprudence du Conseil d'Etat français* (Paris, 1999), VI.

Alland, D., 'Consécration d'un paradoxe: primauté du droit interne sur le droit international', *RFDA* 6 (1998), 1094.

Andriantsimbazovina, J., *L'autorité des décisions de justice constitutionnelles et européennes sur le juge administratif français, Conseil Constitutionnel, CJCE et Cour européenne des droits de l'homme* (Paris, 1998), 290.

Andriantsimbazovina, A./Sermet, L., 'Jurisprudence administrative et Convention européenne des droits de l'homme', *RFDA* 5 (2004), 991.

Bailleul, D., 'Le juge administratif et la conventionnalité de la loi, Vers une remise en question de la jurisprudence *Nicolo*', *RFDA* 5 (2003), 876.

Belliard, E., 'La défense de la France devant la Cour européenne des droits de l'homme', *GP* (10–12 June 2007), 36.

Bonichot, J.-C., 'Le Conseil d'Etat et la Convention européenne des droits de l'homme', in Teitgen-Colly, C. (ed.), *Cinquantième anniversaire de la Convention européenne des droits de l'homme* (Brussels, 2002), 239.

Braconnier, S., *Jurisprudence de la Cour européenne des droits de l'homme et Droit administratif français* (Brussels, 1997).

Cohen-Jonathan, G., 'La place de la Convention européenne des droits de l'homme dans l'ordre juridique français', in F. Sudre (ed.), *Le droit français et la CEDH 1974–1992, Actes du colloque de Montpellier* (Kehl, 1994), 1.

—, *La Convention européenne des droits de l'homme* (Paris, 1989).

Cohen-Jonathan, G./Flauss, J.-F./Lambert Abdelgawad, E. (eds.), *De l'effectivité des recours internes dans l'application de la Convention européenne des droits de l'homme* (Brussels, 2006).

Costa, J.-P., 'L'application par le Conseil d'Etat français de la Convention européenne des droits de l'homme', *RTDH* 8 (1997), 395.

—, 'The influence of the ECHR on domestic legal systems – the French experience', Conference delivered at the third Brian Walsh Memorial, Dublin, 12 November 2004, paper.

—, 'L'apport de 45 ans de jurisprudence de la Cour européenne des droits de l'homme', *GP* (10–12 June 2007), 7.

Cremer, H.-J., 'Zur Bindungswirkung von EGMR-Urteilen: Anmerkung zum Görgülü-Beschluss des BVerfG vom 14.10.2004', *EuGRZ* 31 (2004), 683.

D'Ambra, D., 'Les mesures conservatoires et d'urgence susceptibles d'être adoptées par le juge national aux fins de prévenir une violation de la Convention', in Cohen-Jonathan, G., Flauss, J.-F. and Lambert Abdelgawad, E. (eds.), *De l'effectivité des recours internes dans l'application de la Convention européenne des droits de l'homme* (Brussels, 2006), 161.

De Gouttes, R., 'Le juge, la loi et la convention', *Les Annonces de la Seine* 8 (2003), 4.

De Gouttes, R., 'L'influence de la Convention européenne des droits de l'homme sur la Cour de Cassation', *GP* (10–12 June 2007), 19.

Dupré, C., 'France', in Blackburn R. & Polakiewicz, J. (eds.), *Fundamental Rights in Europe, The ECHR and its member States, 1950–2000* (Oxford, 2001), 312.

Errera, R., 'La Convention européenne des droits de l'homme et les problèmes de la laïcité et de l'enseignement', *RDH* 4 (1970), 572.

—, 'Les origines de la loi française du 10 juillet 1991 sur les écoutes téléphoniques', *RTDH* 55 (2003), 851.

—, 'Le contrôle externe institutionnalisé: de la responsabilité des magistrats et du service public de la justice', in Andenas, M./Fairgrieve, D., *Independence, Accountability and the Judiciary* (London, 2006), 282.

Fatin-Rouge Stéfanini, M./Gay, L., 'France', Table ronde: Justice constitutionnelle, Justice ordinaire, Justice supranationale: à qui revient la protection des droits fondamentaux en Europe?, Aix en Provence, 17–18 September 2004, *Annuaire International de justice constitutionnelle* XX (2004), 213.

Flauss, J.-F., Préface, in Lazaud, F. (ed.), *L'exécution par la France des arrêts de la CourEDH*, Volumes 1–2 (Marseille, 2006).

Fromont, M., 'Le juge français et la Cour européenne des droits de l'homme', in *Internationale Gemeinschaft und Menschenrechte, Festshrift für Georg Ress*, (Köln, 2005), 965.

Frowein, J., 'Der europäische Grundrechtsschutz und die deutsche Rechtsprechung', *Neue Zeitschrift für Verwaltungsrecht* (2002), 29.

—, 'Die traurigen Missverständnisse: Bundesverfassungsgericht und Europäischer Gerichtshof für Menschenrechte', in Dicke, K. et al. (eds.), *Weltinnenrecht: Liber amicorum Jost Delbrück* (Berlin, 2005), 279.

Frowein, J. and Peukert, W., *Europäische Menschenrechtskonvention: EMRK-Kommentar, Unter Berücksichtigung des 11. Zusatzprotokolls zur Gründung eines ständigen Gerichtshofs* (Strasbourg/Kehl/Arlington, 1996).

Gautier, M. et Melleray, F., 'Le Conseil d'Etat et l'Europe: fin de cycle ou nouvelle ère?', *Droit administratif* (May 2007), 9.

Gerkrath, J., 'L'effet contraignant des arrêts de la Cour européenne des droits de l'homme vu à travers le prisme de la Cour constitutionnelle allemande', *RTDH* 67 (2006), 713.

Genevois, B., 'Le Conseil d'Etat et la Convention européenne des droits de l'homme', *GP* (10–12 June 2007), 13.

Grabenwarter, C., *Europäische Menschenrechtskonvention. Ein Studienbuch* (Munich/Vienna, 2005).

Grewe, C., 'Le juge constitutionnel et l'interprétation européenne', in Sudre, F., (ed.), *L'interprétation de la Convention européenne des droits de l'homme*, (Brussels, 1998), 199.

Guinchard, S., 'O Kress où est ta victoire ? Ou la difficile réception, en France, d'une (demie) leçon de démocratie procédurale', Condorelli, L./Flauss, J.-F./Leben, C./Weckel,P. (eds), *Libertés, Justice, Tolérance, Mélanges en hommage au Doyen Gérard Cohen-Jonathan* (Brussels, 2004), 937.

Gusy, C., 'Die Rezeption der EMRK in Deutschland', in Grewe, C./Gusy, C. (eds.), *Menschenrechte in der Bewährung. Die Rezeption der Europäischen Menschenrechtskonvention in Frankreich und Deutschland im Vergleich* (Baden-Baden, 2005), 129.

Hartwig, M., 'Much Ado About Human Rights: The Federal Constitutional Court confronts the European Court of Human Rights', *German Law Journal* 6 (2005), 868.

Hedigan, J., 'The Princess, the Press and Privacy, Observations on Caroline von Hannover v. Germany', in *Liber amicorum Luzius Wildhaber, Human Rights – Strasbourg Views* (Strasbourg, 2007), 193.

Hoffmeister, F., 'Germany: Status of European Convention on Human Rights in Domestic Law', *International Journal of Constitutional Law* 4 (2006), 722.

Imbert, P.-H., 'La France et les traités relatifs aux droits de l'homme', *AFDI* (1980), 31.

Labayle, H., 'Le droit des étrangers au regroupement familial, regards croisés du droit interne et du droit européen', *RFDA* 1 (2007), 101.

Lambert, F., 'Faut-il maintenir le commissaire du gouvernement?', *AJDA* 15 (16 April 2007), 778.

Lambert Abdelgawad, E., *Les effets des arrêts de la Cour européenne des droits de l'homme, contribution à une approche pluraliste du droit européen des droits de l'homme* (Brussels, 1999).

—, 'Les procédures de réouverture devant le juge national en cas de "condamnation" par la Cour européenne', in Cohen-Jonathan, G., Flauss, J.-F., Lambert Abdelgawad, E., *De l'effectivité des recours internes dans l'application de la Convention européenne des droits de l'homme* (Brussels, 2006), 197.

—, *L'exécution des arrêts de la Cour européenne des droits de l'homme*, Dossiers sur les droits de l'homme no.19, 2nd ed. (Strasbourg, 2008).

—, *The execution of judgements of the European Court of Human Rights*, Human rights files no. 19, 2nd ed. (Strasbourg, 2008).

Langenfeld, C., Die Stellung der EMRK im Verfassungsrecht der Bundesrepublik Deutschland', in Bröhmer, J. (ed.), *Der Grundrechtsschutz in Europa* (Baden-Baden, 2002), 95.

Lazaud, F., *L'exécution par la France des arrêts de la CourEDH*, Volumes 1–2 (Marseille, 2006).

Marguénaud, J.-P., 'La Convention européenne des droits de l'homme et le droit français: approches par le droit privé', Andriantsimbazovina, J. et al. (eds.), *Etudes en l'honneur de J. C. Gautron, Les dynamiques du droit européen en début de siècle* (Paris, 2004), 155.

Matsopoulou, H., 'Renforcement du caractère contradictoire, célérité de la procédure pénale et justice des mineurs', *Droit pénal* (May 2007), 5.

Meyer-Ladewig, J., *Konvention zum Schutz der Menschenrechte und Grundfreiheiten: Handkommentar* (Baden-Baden, 2003).

—, 'The German Federal Constitutional Court and the binding force of judgements of the European Court of Human Rights under Art. 46 ECHR', in *Trente ans de droit européen des droits de l'homme, Recueil à la mémoire de Wolfgang Strasser*, forthcoming.

Meyer-Ladewig, J./Petzold, H., "Die Bindung deutscher Gerichte an Urteile des EGMR – Neues aus Strassburg und Karlsruhe", *Neue juristische Wochenschrift* 58 (2005), 15.

Odersky, W., 'Zum Einfluss der Menschenrechtskonvention und der Rechtsprechung des EGMR auf das deutsche Strasfverfahrensrecht', in *Protection des droits de l'homme: la perspective européenne, Mélanges à la mémoire de Rolv Ryssdal* (Köln, 2000), 1039.

Papier, H.-J., 'Execution and effects of the judgments of the European Court of Human Rights in the German judicial system', in Council of Europe, *Dialogue between judges* (Strasbourg, 2006), 57.

Péchillon, E., 'Les interdictions de publication sous le contrôle du juge, retour sur la loi du 16 juillet 1949 instaurant une police administrative spéciale', AJDA (13 February 2006), 298.

Pellet, A. 'La ratification par la France de la Convention européenne des droits de l'homme', *RDP* 5 (1974), 1328.

Peters, A., *Einführung in die Europäische Menschenrechtskonvention* (Munich, 2003).

Potvin-Solis, L., *L'effet des jurisprudences européennes sur la jurisprudence du Conseil d'Etat français* (Paris, 1999).

Puechavy, M., 'L'avocat devant la Cour européenne des droits de l'homme', *GP* 161–163 (10–12 June 2007), 32.

Ress, G., 'The Effects of Judgments and Decisions in Domestic Law', in Macdonald, R. St. J., Matscher, F. and Petzold, H. (eds.), *The European Protection of Human Rights* (Dordrecht, 1993), 801.

Rouault, M. C., 'L' Etat doit réparer les préjudices dus à l'application d'une loi contraire à la CEDH', *JCP* (14 March 2007) 53.

Ruffert, M., 'Die Europäische Menschenrechtskonvention und innerstaatliches Recht', *EuGRZ* 34 (2007), 245.

Saillant, E., 'Conseil constitutionnel, Cour européenne des droits de l'homme et protection des droits et libertés: sur la prétendue rivalité de systèmes complémentaires', *RDP* 6 (2004), 1497.

Sauer, H., 'Die neue Schlagkraft der gemeineuropäischen Grundrechtsjudikatur: Zur Bindung deutscher Gerichte an die Entscheidungen des Europäischen Gerichtshofs für Menschenrechte', *Zeitschrift für ausländisches öffentliches Recht und Völkerrecht* 65 (2005), 35.

Schlette, V., 'Les interactions entre la jurisprudence de la Cour européenne des droits de l'homme et la Cour constitutionnelle fédérale allemande', *RFDC* (1996), 747.

Stone, A., *The Birth of Judicial Politics in France: The Constitutional Council in Comparative Perspective* (Oxford, 1992), chapters 2–3.

Sudre, F., 'Le "contentieux français" à Strasbourg, bilan de 11 ans de recours individuel', in Sudre, F. (ed.), *Le droit français et la CEDH 1974–1992, Actes du colloque de Montpellier* (Kehl, 1994), 61.

—, 'A propos du "dialogue des juges" et du contrôle de conventionnalité', Andriantsimbazovina, J. et al (eds.), *Etudes en l'honneur de J.-C. Gautron, Les dynamiques du droit européen en début de siècle* (Paris, 2004), 207.

—, *Droit européen et international des droits de l'homme*, 8th ed. (Paris, 2006a).

—, "Conseil d'Etat et Cour européenne des droits de l'homme, Vers la normalisation des relations entre le Conseil d'Etat et la CourEDH", *RFDA* 2 (March–April 2006b), 286.

Szymczak, D., *La Convention européenne des droits de l'homme et le juge constitutionnel national* (Brussels, 2007).

Vailhé, J., *La France face aux exigences de la Convention européenne des droits de l'homme, Analyse du contentieux judiciaire français devant les instances de Strasbourg* (Paris, 2001).

Villiger, M., *Handbuch der Europäischen Menschenrechtskonvention (EMRK): unter besonderer Berücksichtigung der Schweizerischen Rechtslage* (Zürich, 1999).

Wachsmann, P., 'L'atteinte grave à une liberté fondamentale', *RFDA* 1 (Jan.–Febr. 2007), 58.

Waline, J., 'L'influence des décisions de la Cour européenne des droits de l'homme sur le droit positif français', in Condorelli, L./Flauss, J.-F./Leben, C./Weckel, P. (eds), *Libertés, justice, tolérance, Mélanges en hommage au Doyen Gérard Cohen-Jonathan* (Brussels, 2004), 1707.

Weiss, N., 'The Impact of the European Convention on Human Rights on German Jurisprudence', in Örücü, E. (ed.), *Judicial Comparativism in Human Rights Cases* (London, 2003), 49.

Zimmermann, A., 'Germany', in Blackburn, R. and Polakiewicz, J. (eds.), *Fundamental Rights in Europe, The ECHR and its member States, 1950–2000* (Oxford, 2001), 335.

4

The Reception Process in Sweden and Norway

Ola Wiklund

I. Introduction[1]

In the context of European geography, Sweden and Norway are relatively small countries. There is no notable difference in size between Sweden and Norway that might affect mechanisms of reception of the ECHR. The cultural, religious and political homogeneity of the population in both countries is fairly strong. Both are Protestant countries lacking significant overseas colonies. They have been constitutional States for many years. Norway's constitution was adopted in 1814, whilst the first modern Swedish constitution came into force in 1809. Both countries adhere to the principle of dualism, where international legal norms are only regarded as valid and as effective in domestic law once they have been incorporated into national legislation. There are strong connections between academics, practising lawyers and judges within both countries. The links between the countries have historically been upheld by quite elaborate projects of legislative and academic cooperation.[2]

---

[1] Abbreviations:

As regards the references to the Swedish Statute book, (In Sw: *Svensk författningssamling*) it is cited by year and followed by the relevant number. In the references to the Swedish Instrument of Government (In Sw: *Regeringsformen*), the Swedish abbreviation, RF, is sued and followed by the chapter and section number (e.g. RF 11:14). Cases from the Supreme Courts in Norway and Sweden are cited from the semi-official series, Nytt Juridiskt Arkiv (NJA), as regards the practice of the Swedish Supreme Court (In Sw: *Högsta domstolen*) and *Norsk Retstidende* as regards the practice of the Norwegian Supreme Court (In Nor: *Høyesterett*). The Swedish Supreme Admininstrative Court (In Sw: *Regeringsrätten*) official series (In Sw: *Regeringsrättens årsbok*) is referred to as RÅ. References to *travaux préparatoires* are either to the number of the Commission for Investigating the Law, i.e. *Statens Offentliga Utredningar* (SOU), for Sweden, or *Norges offentlige utredninger* (NOU) for Norway, and the year of its report, or the draft Bill put before the Parliament together with its accompanying documentation (In Sw: *Proposition* (prop.) and In Nor: *Proposisjoner* (prop.)). References to Supreme Court cases and *travaux préparatoires* are made to the page number *(sida. s.)*. *Juridisk Tidskrift* (JT) is the law review of the Faculty of Law at Stockholm University. *Svensk jurist-tidning* (SvJT) is a Swedish law review.

[2] See for example, the reports from Nordic law meetings (In Sw: *Nordiska juristmötena*). This

This report will demonstrate that the true Europeanization of the legal systems of the two countries was initiated in the mid-90's. This legal transformation coincided with changes of an economic nature brought about by the process of globalization. From a legal point of view, globalization was brought about by the integration of two important regimes of law into the domestic system: the ECHR and the law of the European Union (EU).

In two advisory referendums in 1972 and 1994 the Norwegian people rejected proposals to join the EU. Norway opted for membership in the European Economic Area (EEA), which does not entail a formal transfer of sovereign rights to a supra-national entity. The EEA is also substantively limited with regard to political coordination. Most importantly, membership required Norway to incorporate the vast majority of EU directives and regulations of the internal market.

Hence, by virtue of Sweden's EU membership in 1995 and Norway's EEA membership in 1994, both countries implemented and transposed large amounts of EU law. As a result, the specific national or European origins of their substantive legal provisions are difficult to ascertain. Large parts of private law presently have their origins in either EU law or in treaties of public international law. Given that national authorities are bound by EU fundamental rights, including ECHR rights, when they apply and enforce EU law, EU law has been a steady and increasing means of reception of ECHR rights in the domestic legal orders of all EU Member States. This mechanism has been of great importance for dualist States like Sweden and Norway. The legal consequences of the political choice to take part in the process of European integration have been significant for both countries, regardless of the formally different modes of incorporation of EU law. The two countries eventually became accustomed to viewing international law as directly effective domestically. However, space precludes identifying and analyzing the specifically European dimension of national substantive legal norms in the present report.

II. Overview of the Swedish and Norwegian Systems: History, Constitutional Traditions, Political Practices and Legal Theory

A. Introduction

In order to fully understand and appreciate the reception of the ECHR regime in the Swedish and Norwegian legal systems, it is necessary to map out some

---

institution has hosted conferences and reports for more than hundred years and served as the main forum for Scandinavian legal integration through the twentieth century. The significance of the institutionalized Nordic legislative cooperation deteriorated as Denmark, Finland and Sweden gradually joined the EU. Most of the legal integration in for example civil law now takes place within the framework of the EU institutions. The main areas of legislative cooperation have been civil and family law.

historical, political, theoretical and normative constitutional characteristics. This broad historical narrative is crucial for the understanding of the reception of international legal norms, since the ideology of the legal machinery (courts, public bodies and universities) was closely connected to the history of ideas of the twentieth century.

The effectiveness and extent of the reception is the result of an acceptance of the separation of powers principles, the role of courts and administration in the tailoring of the Scandinavian welfare State and the general legitimacy of State power. A historical perspective has, therefore, to embrace politics and philosophy as well as doctrinal developments of the law itself.

B. Constitutional Traditions of Sweden and Norway

1. Sweden

Sweden's modern constitutional history begins with the 1809 Instrument of Government (In Sw: *1809 års regeringsform*). While this Instrument of Government was based on the principle of a separation of powers, the legislative powers were divided between the King and the Parliament. The King's Ministers were not politically responsible before the Parliament. Thus, it was not a question of Parliamentarianism in its modern meaning. To a large extent, the 1809 Instrument of Government did not contain provisions about rights and freedoms, apart from a provision stating that citizens should enjoy equality before the law and a ban on *ad hoc* courts.[3]

A different form of Government gradually evolved independently and alongside the 1809 Instrument of Government, and it was not until 1917 that the Government became wholly dependent on the number of votes it could command in the Parliament. The Parliamentary system was thereby established in practice before it was codified in fundamental law. It is noteworthy that this development was slower in Sweden than in both Denmark and Norway.

The 1974 Instrument of Government (In Sw: *Regeringsformen*, the RF) did not originally provide any safeguards for fundamental rights and freedoms. It was not until 1979 that the RF came to include provisions on rights and fundamental freedoms, a change that was partly motivated by the notion that other countries' Constitutions contained a Bill of Rights and, therefore, Sweden ought to have one as well. However, the discussion of constitutional protection for human rights and fundamental freedoms did not stop there, and in 1994 the Parliament adopted the proposal on the incorporation of the ECHR into Swedish law. Following an advisory referendum in 1994, Sweden became a member of the EU on 1 January 1995.[4]

---

[3] Holmberg and Stjernquist (1995), 13.
[4] See also Sveriges Riksdag (2000).

At this stage, it may be pointed out that Swedish court practice of the last two decades shows that it is the ECHR rather than the RF's Bill of Rights that is invoked by the parties and adjudicated by the courts. This may partly be explained by the fact that Swedish courts seldom review whether or not rules contained in the fundamental laws are observed in ordinary law or statutes. The constitutional review is limited to extreme cases by the requisite of manifest fault stated in RF 11:14. Thus, since it is rarely interpreted, the status of the Bill of Rights in the RF has declined. Another explanation is of course that the ECHR contains rights and freedoms that are not explicitly mentioned in the RF's Bill of Rights, such as, for example, Articles 6 and 8.[5] The Swedish court practice concerning constitutional issues is rather dominated by technical questions stemming from the provisions on the division and delegation of legislative powers in chapter 8 of the RF.[6]

While the Norwegian Constitution is a symbol of the State and has a part in Norwegian identity, the same cannot be said of Sweden's RF. Traditionally, Sweden's public attitude towards constitutional rights and constitutional review has been somewhat negative and questions on rights and fundamental freedoms (apart from the freedom of expression and freedom of the press) have played a limited role in the public discourse and in the consciousness of most Swedes. This is also true for the RF's role in the case law of the Swedish judiciary. However, as a consequence of the EU membership and the debate in connection to the plans on ratifying the EU constitutional charter, an increased constitutional attention was noticeable between both the judicial and political spheres, since an EU membership demanded a revision of the RF and also, due to constitutional treaty of EU, would necessitate an increased judicial review.[7]

2. Norway

In January 1814, following the Napoleonic wars, Denmark handed over Norway to Sweden. However, the agreement between Denmark and its opponents (i.e. Napoleon's opposition) firmly established that Norway, despite the union with Sweden, was to take its place among the independent States. A Norwegian assembly formally adopted a Constitution on 17 May 1814 making it the oldest written Constitution in Europe still in force.[8] The main principles of the constitution were founded, for the most part, on the same ideals expressed in the Con-

---

[5] See the report from a conference organized by the sitting Swedish Constitutional Committee, Fri-och rättigheter i grundlagen – behöver regleringen förändras?, 19 October 2006, http://www.grundlagsutredningen.se/upload/Konferensdokumentation%202006.pdf, 103 et seq. (Unless indicated otherwise, all websites were visited last at the end of August 2007).

[6] Nergelius (1996), 673; Nergelius (2000), 128

[7] See SOU 1993:14.

[8] To this day, May 17th is celebrated as the Norwegian National Day. This historical event has a firm place in the conscience of the majority of Norwegians. The link between the Constitution and independence is a foundation upon which the Norwegian identity rests.

stitutions of the United States (1776) and the French Republic (1791–1795), namely the sovereignty of the people, the separation of powers and human rights (inspired by the Declaration of the Rights of Man and of the Citizen from the French Revolution of 1789).

The Constitution stipulates that the people elect representatives to a national assembly (In Nor: *Stortinget*), which is entrusted with, among other things, enacting the laws held to be in force in Norway. Furthermore, the Constitution also establishes that legislative, executive and judicial powers shall be divided between the Parliament, the King (i.e. the Government) and the courts. As regards the principle of human rights, the Constitution gradually came to safeguard the fundamental and inalienable rights of the people, and established freedom of speech, worship, assembly and the rule of law. The Constitution does not contain any modern Bill of Rights, but, motivated by Norway's international obligations in the field of human rights, it has been revized a few times. [9]

In 1884, its success laid the foundation for the first Scandinavian establishment of the principle of Parliamentarianism. The rise of Parliamentarianism led to abandonment of the principle of separation of powers as adopted in its original form, and the King was no longer free to choose his advisers. Cabinet Ministers were now politicians in reality. In comparison, the breakthrough of this principle in Sweden is usually dated to 1917.[10] The Norwegian Parliament has been reluctant to make any major revisions or alterations to the Constitution, and modifications are normally made in the Constitution's original language (which is Danish). The reason for this is, naturally, the Constitution's great symbolic value.[11]

C. Politics and Philosophy – the Significance of the Jurisprudential Heritage of Social Democracy and Scandinavian Legal Realism

1. Preliminary Remarks

The dissolution of the union between Sweden and Norway marks the starting point of the development of two modern States into the characteristic Scandinavian social democracy. The mutual contact and influence were strong, and the similarities between the two States were striking. There were, however, also dissimilarities rooted in the differences in historical inheritance. The industrialization was of a larger scale in Sweden, whereas democratization came earlier and was more far-reaching in Norway.[12] The following chapter examines how these historical similarities and differences interplayed with ideology and philosophy during the early years of the twentieth century. A central question to examine is

---

[9] Andenæs and Fliflet (2006), 375 et seq.
[10] Sterzel (1981), 23; Sterzel (1988), 676 et seq.
[11] Andenæs and Fliflet (2006), 69 et seq.
[12] Sejersted (2005), 5 et seq.

whether the historical, ideological and philosophical aspects of the reception of international law, such as the ECHR, have been integrated in the late process of globalization (and Europeanization) of politics, law and economy.

Sweden and Norway were two of the first countries in the world to codify constitutional rights. Both countries have been dominated by a constitutional ideology placing great emphasis on the political democracy of the welfare State and the primacy of the democratic legislative process. In both legal and political quarters, constitutional rights have been viewed with a high degree of scepticism and suspicion.[13] An explanation for this may be found in the political and philosophical history of Sweden and Norway.

The Social Democratic parties in both countries played a pivotal role in the transformation of Sweden and Norway from relatively poor agrarian societies to modern industrial States. Social Democracy became the vehicle through which traditional rural societies and industrial labour together entered the urban age.[14] Furthermore, the politics of Social Democracy became decisive for the constitutional culture of Sweden and Norway.

The political ideas merged with legal philosophy and formed a heritage that conceptualized constitutional rights as a vehicle for the political centre and right wing parties to create an obstacle to the majoritarian realm of the long-lasting regime of the Social Democratic Parties in Sweden and Norway.[15]

2. The Politics of Social Democracy

In Sweden, all Governments since 1932, save for the periods of 1976–1982, 1991–1994 and 2006–present, have been Social Democratic. Between 1945 and 1968, we saw five Norwegian Governments, three of them Social Democratic.[16]

The Scandinavian welfare States that evolved after 1945 had their origins in the two social pacts of the former decade, namely the one between employees and employers, and the one between labour and farming. The social services and other public provisions promoted universal social rights, equalized incomes, and flat-rate benefits paid from steeply progressive taxation.[17] The Scandinavian welfare system stood in strong contrast to the typical continental European version in which the State transferred or returned income to families and individuals, enabling them to pay for largely subsidized private services like insurance and medicine.[18]

Scandinavian Social Democracy was born out of a modernistic dream and a fascination with social engineering. Beside adjusting incomes, expenditures,

[13] Nergelius (2000), 13 et seq.; Sundberg (1978), 191 et seq.; Sundberg and Sundberg (1992), 211 et seq.
[14] Tingsten (1967), 125 et seq.
[15] Ibid.
[16] Ibid.
[17] Tingsten (1967), 382 et seq.
[18] Judt (2005), 364 et seq.

employment and various social benefits, the authorities also implemented a policy of the so-called "racial hygiene". Between 1934 and 1976, sterilization programmes were pursued in Norway, Sweden and Denmark with the knowledge of Social Democratic Governments. In these years, some 6,000 Danes, 40,000 Norwegians and 60,000 Swedes (90 per cent of them women) were sterilized for "hygienic" purposes, allegedly to improve the population.[19]

The policies of eugenics were pursued concurrently as both Sweden and Norway were obliged to live up to the obligations of the ECHR. With hindsight, it is surprising that neither the courts nor the Administration (nor the Ombudsman) took any notice of the procedural and substantive constraints of the ECHR when implementing these policies. This fact is one indication of the limited effect of the treaty obligations in Sweden and Norway many years after the ratification. The legal machinery was deeply influenced by the prevailing political ideology wherein the State was an almighty provider of good and could do no wrong. In such an effective and generous welfare State, the talk of individual constitutional rights was substantively regarded as superfluous and philosophically perceived as an outcry of metaphysical thinking.[20]

The legitimacy of the State in post-war Scandinavia was unquestioned; authority and initiative were granted to the State by a citizenry that rarely had the conviction or courage to raise criticism. The Governments were, therefore, relatively free to act with remarkably little oversight in what they took to be the common interest. It does not seem to have ever occurred to an Ombudsman to investigate abuse of those who stood outside the rights-bearing community of tax-paying citizens. The line separating progressive taxation and paternity leave from forcible interference in the reproductive capacities of "defective" citizens seems not to have been altogether clear to some post-war Governments in Social Democratic Scandinavia.[21]

3. *The Jurisprudence of Scandinavian Legal Realism*

The history of individual constitutional rights is closely connected to the ideology of the post-war political regimes in both Sweden and Norway. This ideology was underpinned by strong philosophical ideas, originating in the early twentieth century, and shaped into a more or less comprehensive school of thought by Scandinavian philosophers and lawyers: Scandinavian Legal Realism (SLR). The legal culture of the Scandinavian countries was deeply influenced by the legal theories of SLR and ideas of their major proponents Axel Hägerström,[22] Anders Wilhelm Lundstedt, Karl Olivecrona and Alf Ross. It also had an impact on adju-

---

[19] Ibid.
[20] One of the most persistent antagonists of Social Democracy and the SLR-theories was Professor Jacob Sundberg, his critique is compiled in Sundberg and Sundberg (1992).
[21] Judt (2005), 368 et seq.
[22] See Hägerström (1961).

dication and lawyering, since all actors of the legal system had been academically trained in an environment of catch phrases, such as "the talk of individual rights is tantamount to the gibbering of a parrot".[23]

If the American Realists were preoccupied with adjudication and predictions of what judges did with the law, the SLR focused on the legal system and its components. The normative meaning content of a legal norm was generally perceived as an imperative of the Sovereign. Judicial discretion was limited to the unfolding of the will of the political democracy. In interpreting this will, the *travaux préparatoires* became very important. To entrust powers to the judiciary to strike down statutory law as unconstitutional was an alien idea of the SLR-lawyers. These thoughts accompanied the tailoring of a theory of legal reasoning as an exercise of logic and empiricism. The ruling motto was that conceptualizations and theoretical determinations could never serve as valid arguments in legal arguments aiming to solve a practical legal problem.[24]

The SLR influence was not limited to teaching and legal scholarship. It was spread throughout the legal system to judges and other officials entrusted with adjudicative tasks. SLR ideas were transformed into policies through Lundstedt, who, besides being a Professor of Law in Uppsala, was an active politician in the Swedish Parliament (In Sw: *Riksdagen*). Lundstedt was the leading ideologue of the ruling Social Democratic Party and as such he turned the ideas of SLR into practical application in Swedish society. The ideas of SLR became the theoretical underpinnings of the Swedish welfare State and its social engineers.[25]

For Lundstedt, jurisprudence was a normative discipline aimed at offering guidance to the civil authorities. Legal science was perceived as normative science, both in the sense that it described legal prescripts and in the sense that it offered guidance for maintaining the legal order.[26] In addition to regarding law as a fact, the school of SLR considered that it was anti-metaphysical and realistic. Their legal theory was dissociated from doctrines of natural law and other ramifications of the idealistic philosophy of law prevalent on the continent.[27]

The primacy of SLR ideas effectively prevented constitutional rights theories winning ground in the Scandinavian legal culture. The theory and ideology of SLR was detrimental to the legitimacy of constitutionally grounded rights arguments and principles in the legislative process as well as in the day to day adjudication of the Swedish judiciary. Rights theories founded on natural law were practically banned from the public discourse of law and politics in Sweden and Norway for many years.

In the post-war decades, the Supreme Courts of Sweden and Norway never stood in the way of the social-democratic consensual "New Deal"-politics. The

---

[23] Lundstedt (1928).
[24] Hellner (1996–97), 540. Hellner (1992), 67.
[25] Bjarup (1982), 174 et seq.
[26] Ibid.
[27] Ross (1974), Preface o. IX. See also Bjarup (2003).

political reform programmes, aiming at rebuilding the countries into a new social mould and at establishing a welfare State, were achieved without the Supreme Courts putting obstacles in the way of the political powers. On several occasions during this period, the Supreme Courts were criticized for not being the guardians of property rights.[28]

D. Comparison and Conclusion

The politics of the Swedish and Norwegian welfare States were underpinned by a legal and political philosophy that facilitated far-reaching political reforms. In the post-war years of the twentieth century, politicians never regarded constitutionally protected fundamental rights as serious obstacles to political reform programmes.

Most civil servants and judges were philosophically educated to regard legal norms as being deprived of any objective normative content. Legal norms were regarded as imperative propositions by the legislator that should be applied with strict adherence to the legislative purpose expressed in the *travaux préparatoires*. The primacy of politics came to be the ruling principle of the Swedish and Norwegian societies.

The reception of foreign norms was subject to a set of ideas and practises of judges who shared this view of law and its relation to politics. This conviction could be characterized as a sensibility that involved broader aspects of political faith, image of self or society, as well as the epistemological and structural constraints within which judges live and work.[29] This sensibility is still one of the most important factors that influence judges making normative choices in cases of conflict between the ECHR and domestic law.

III. Rights and Judicial Review

A. Codification of Fundamental Rights

1. Sweden

The jurisprudential ideology of SLR was particularly strong in the early years following the ratification of the ECHR (1950) and was one of the reasons why it lasted many years, until Sweden introduced constitutional rights into instruments of law. The first codification of a fully-fledged traditional Bill of Constitutional Rights took place 1974 and constitutional review by the judiciary was formally introduced in 1979. Sweden's present constitutional documents,

[28] Broch (2003), 243.
[29] Koskenniemi (2002), 2.

consisting of individual rights and freedoms conceptually comparable to ECHR-rights, are fairly young.

There are three Swedish constitutional laws dealing with civil rights and freedoms, namely the Freedom of the Press Act (In Sw: *Tryckfrihetsförordningen*), originally in 1766, the RF from 1974, and the Freedom of Expression Act (In Sw: *Yttrandefrihetsgrundlag*) from 1991.

The RF provide protection of certain civil rights and freedoms, whilst the Freedom of the Press Act and the Freedom of Expression Act deal, respectively, with the printed and electronic media and provide prohibition against censorship and lay down the right to communicate official information, even secret information, to the press for publication, subject to certain exceptions. In Chapter 2 of the RF the fundamental rights and freedoms of the people of Sweden are set out in a rights catalogue.

Chapter 2 has been subject to major amendments on three occasions, namely in 1976, 1979 and 1994. The first change introduced new relative rights and general substantive conditions that have to be satisfied before relative rights can be restricted and also provided that aliens present in Sweden were to enjoy equality of protection with Swedish citizens. The second amendment in 1979 saw the introduction of a form of entrenchment: the qualified legislative procedure. This provides that a statute restricting certain relative rights can (subject to minor exceptions) be delayed by a minority of the Members of Parliament for a period of one year; the idea being that during this year opposition both within and without Parliament can be mobilized. The last important amendments to Chapter 2 were made in 1994, which added certain new rights, amended and improved the protection of the right to property so as to correspond in some ways to its formulation in the ECHR, and provided for a quasi-constitutional status for the ECHR.[30]

The normative hierarchy of legal norms set out by the Constitution follows the principles of the liberal *Rechtstaat* based on the Rule of Law. The constitutional laws take precedence over all other laws, meaning that the content of other Swedish laws may never conflict with the provisions set out in the constitutional laws. For an amendment to be enacted, the Swedish Parliament must adopt two identical decisions and these must be separated by a general election.

2. Norway

The Constitution of 1814 includes clauses on basic human rights.[31] However, human rights are certainly more developed in international human rights conventions, such as the ECHR and the two 1966 UN Conventions.[32]

---

[30] Cameron (2001), 835 et seq.; see also section C.1.b.

[31] I.e., the human rights provision in Section 110 c whereby it is incumbent on the State to respect and ensure human rights (In Nor: *Menneskerettighederne*).

[32] International Covenant on Civil and Political Rights, 999 U.N.T.S. 171, entered into force 23

In the late 90's, the Norwegian Government presented an action plan for human rights based on the provision introduced in the Constitution (Section 110 c) in 1994, which stipulates that it is incumbent on the State to respect and secure human rights. Pursuant to this provision, ensuring that the rights of Norway's inhabitants are fulfilled is a cornerstone in the Government's political platform.[33] This also applies to Norway's international efforts to promote human rights.

Following the amendment of the Constitution and the adoption of the action plan for the promotion of human rights, the Norwegian legislator has made during the last few years amendments to both the Criminal Procedure Act and the Civil Procedure Act, through which a monistic human rights regime was established. As of 1 January 2004, it is, therefore, possible under the latter Act to require that a case be reopened when the petition is based on a breach of Norway's international obligations. Unlike earlier, when it was a condition that the breach of international law be established by an international court, opinions issued by the UN Human Rights Committee may serve as a ground for reopening the case. Furthermore, the new Civil Procedure Act authorizes petitions to reopen a case if, in an appeal against Norway in the same litigation, it has been established that these proceedings have violated a Convention that, pursuant to the Human Rights Act, applies in the same way as Norwegian law.[34]

The new Civil Procedure Act is intended to ensure that civil justice is administered in accordance with the requirements that follow from the various human rights instruments, and calls for the judge to play an active part in directing cases. Also, the Act on Free Legal Aid has been amended, highlighting the possibility of obtaining free legal aid in cases that are heard by the Court and where the applicant does not receive sufficient free legal aid from the Court itself.[35]

In 2004, a new Article 100 was introduced into the Constitution. This Article regulates the classical freedom of expression, freedom of information, the right to remain silent and the principle of public access to information. The object of this amendment was to strengthen the protection of political expressions and to reduce the legal safeguards against defamation in accordance with the Court's practice.[36]

March 1976; International Covenant on Economic, Social and Cultural Rights, 993 U.N.T.S. 3, entered into force 3 January 1976.

[33] Stortingsmelding no. 21, 1998–1999.
[34] Mose (2001), 625 et seq.
[35] Ibid.
[36] Andenæs and Fliflet (2006), 384.

B. Constitutional Review

1. Sweden

The RF was amended in 1979, introducing a codification of a power of constitutional review of courts and administrative agencies (RF 11:14). This amendment was the formal recognition of the possibility for both courts and administrative agencies to review the constitutionality of statutes and subordinate legislation. The power of constitutional review was subject to a major limitation; it stipulates that a law (In Sw: *lag*) passed by Parliament or an ordinance (In Sw: *förordning*) passed by the Government must be manifestly in breach of a constitutional provision before a court or administrative agency can refuse to apply it in the case before it (RF 11:14). No such limitation applies to subordinate legislation, issued by administrative agencies on delegation by the Government, that conflicts with higher norms. The final change made in 1979 was the reinstatement of the requirement to submit a legislative proposal involving human rights to pre-legislative scrutiny before the Law Council (In Sw: *Lagrådet*).[37]

Sweden lacks a Constitutional Court with designated powers of judicial review. Instead, Sweden adopted a truly decentralized system of judicial review where all courts and administrative agencies are obliged to refuse to apply a norm that conflicts with the ECHR. Since the scope of power is limited by the criterion of manifest error, lower courts and administrative agencies refuse to make use of judicial review. The highest courts will only very rarely refuse to apply a statute or ordinance on the basis that it breaches the ECHR. It is worthwhile to point out that a declaration of unconstitutionality will only have effect *inter partes*. The legal act struck down remains formally valid.[38]

The will of the Swedish political democracy expressed in the *travaux préparatoires* to the RF Amendment was that constitutional review giving rise to the setting aside of a statutory provision should not to be viewed as a common feature in the day-to-day adjudication of Swedish courts. Striking down the will of the democratically elected Parliament was viewed as an emergency measure. It should also be noted that almost all of the political parties in Parliament at that time (1970–80) firmly rejected the idea of introducing a Constitutional Court responsible for constitutional review.[39]

With regard to the above, it must be stated that Sweden has a weak tradition of constitutional review by the courts. Thus, questions of fundamental rights and freedoms are quite rare in Swedish jurisprudence, even if they are often invoked by the parties.

As mentioned above, legislative review is also carried out to a limited extent. The Law Council, consisting of Supreme Court judges, is assigned to review

---

[37] Nergelius (1996), 670 et seq.; Cameron (2001), 850 et seq.
[38] Ibid.; Cameron (1999), 25 et seq.
[39] Nergelius (1996), 584 et seq.

national law proposals in relation to the ECHR. A brief survey made of the minutes of Law Council meetings during 1998 disclosed several proposals in which the Law Council drew the attention of the Government to possible difficulties relating to the ECHR. In each case, the Law Council contented itself with references to the ECHR itself rather than the Court's case law.[40] It should be noted here that the Law Council has no legal assistants and its membership changes every, two years. The competence of the Law Council in the field of the ECHR thus depends wholly upon the knowledge the individual members have of it. ECHR issues can also be raised in the Parliamentary Committee that scrutinizes the Bill. Proposals relating to the Constitution are sent to the Committee of the Constitution (In Sw: *Konstitutionsutskottet*). Other Committees can also refer a proposal to it for commentary. This Committee has some legal staff capable of making independent investigations.[41]

In 2005, the former (Social Democratic) Government appointed a Working Committee on Constitutional Reform (In Sw: *Grundlagsutredningen*) to conduct a concerted review of the RF. One of the primary tasks of the Working Committee was to review the need for a Constitutional Court; the other tasks concerned the role of the courts.[42] Under both the ECHR and the EU regimes, the courts (The ECtHR and the ECJ, respectively) are the primary guardians and interpreters of the EU law and the ECHR. Courts have not had that role in Sweden, and this will no doubt change. As the powers of the National Parliaments diminish, the national courts will further have to actively safeguard fundamental rights and freedoms.

2. Norway

Norwegian judges have a fairly long tradition of carrying out judicial review regarding the constitutionality of legislation passed by Parliament. Despite the fact that the Constitution itself has no clause relating to judicial review, the practice of judicial review can be traced back to the first years of the Constitution. The right of the courts to review legislation evolved in different, but interrelated stages. The initial stage consisted of courts adopting the Constitution as an instrument of true legal norms, not merely political guidelines, but rules that could be applied in court decisions as supplementing ordinary statutes and other norms of law.[43]

One explanation in this regard was the positive status enjoyed by the Constitution in the years following its adoption in 1814. It was seen as a symbol of the country's new-found independence from Sweden. Against this background, it was not a long step from regarding the relationship between the Constitution and statutory law as a relationship between a superior legal norm and a subordinate

---

[40] Nergelius (2000), 84, 148 et seq.
[41] Nergelius (1996), 619 et seq.; Cameron (2001), 849 et seq.
[42] See http://www.grundlagsutredningen.se for more information.
[43] Nergelius (1996), 182; Broch (2003), 242; Andenæs and Fliflet (2006), 345 et seq.

one. In a number of cases, the Supreme Court affirmed that in as much as the courts of law cannot be required to judge according to both the Constitution and statute law simultaneously, they must necessarily give priority to the Constitution.[44] In the last part of the nineteenth century, the practice of setting aside statutes infringing upon the Constitution was well established. In the 100 years that followed, generations of jurists have been brought up with judicial review of legislation as part of their basic understanding of the legal system.[45]

Norwegian courts may review the constitutionality of statutory provisions, and the interpretation of the Constitution as well as of unwritten constitutional principles may be influenced by international law. Norwegian courts also have competence to review the interpretation and application of administrative law. However, the competence to control the free discretion of the administration is somewhat limited. A decision may be declared invalid only if it is manifestly unreasonable or is based on discrimination. The ECHR is a part of the Human Rights Act and this has priority over other provisions. To sum up, the Norwegian courts may use international law and the ECHR as guides *vis-à-vis* the interpretation of national legislation. It is noteworthy that the Norwegian Supreme Court has stated that when Norwegian courts balance different interests and the principles laid down by the ECHR and the Norwegian legislator they will be able to engage in an interplay with the Court's case law. Therefore, it is necessary for them to act carefully in relation to the Court's jurisprudence and interpretation of the ECHR in order not to interfere with the Norwegian legislator's powers. Norwegian courts should not be too dynamic in their interpretation of the ECHR.[46]

The Norwegian tradition of constitutional review of statutory law (Parliamentary acts) exhibits a less sceptical approach than the Swedish tradition. Starting off in the 70's, constitutional review in Norway had a renaissance. Between 1970 and 1994, the Norwegian Supreme Court played a much more pivotal constitutional role in the society than the Swedish Supreme Courts. This could be explained by the strong position taken by the Norwegian Supreme Court in the *Klofta* judgement of 1976.[47] The power to review the constitutionality of statutes was derived from "established constitutional customary law".[48] According to Norwegian academics this judgement put the judges of the Norwegian Supreme Court on a more politicized course and resulted in a situation where they came to review legislation with far greater intensity than their other Scandinavian brethren.[49]

One of the main causes of the Norwegian development was that the Supreme Court gained more constitutional self-confidence in the 70's. The intensity of

---

[44] Rt. 1966 p. 476. See also Rt. 1961 p. 1350, 1983 p. 1004.
[45] Ibid.; Broch (2003), 243.
[46] See *Norsk Retstidende* (2000), 996. See also Mose (2001), 626 et seq.
[47] Rt 1976 p. 1.
[48] Ibid.
[49] See Smith (1993), 24.

the review was triggered through activist lawyers invoking the Constitution and the ECHR in the Supreme Court. However, one could also discern a greater willingness in the Court to raise constitutional issues. Some commentators have also pointed out that the renaissance stemmed from a stronger influence of the European human rights ideology.[50]

C. Comparison and Conclusion

Even if there are some indications that Norway has a somewhat stronger tradition of constitutional judicial review than Sweden, one should not overestimate the differences. The subjective approach to statutory interpretation, characterized by an ambition to discern and incorporate the will of the legislator into the normative meaning content of a national provision, is the dominating judicial philosophy that governs judicial interpretation in Sweden and Norway. This interpretative approach has its roots in a political conviction and an attitude towards governance that promotes self-restraint.

The Law Schools' legal philosophy curricula lean towards positivism and formalism, and the legal cultures of both countries discourage creativity and emphasise allegiance to the political democracy. With regard to the effects of the ECHR, this results in a reluctance to strike down national statutory legislation when it requires a creative interpretation of the ECHR provisions. If they find a discrepancy between the ECHR and national law, judges are more likely to engage in interpretation that conforms to the treaty.

This approach could be changing slowly as a consequence of the Europeanization of the legal systems, partly as a result of the increasing number of sensitive political issues (e.g. national gambling and alcohol monopolies challenged by EU law) that have ended up in courts. This is especially noticeable in the EU cases where national courts have to engage in more or less fully fledged proportionality tests of national restrictions on sales and marketing of alcohol[51] and gambling services[52] of the Treaty Articles on free movement.

In these cases, national judges have limited or no recourse to the traditional and easily accessible *travaux préparatoires*, and they have to give legal meaning to a voluminous corpus of European case law from the European Court of Justice in Luxembourg. These kinds of cases are presently[53] pending before the Swedish and Norwegian courts. The nature of this kind of policy-drained cases will probably have an impact on the legal interpretation and judicial discretion of Swedish and Norwegian judges over time.

In this context, it is important to point out that many judges in the highest instances in Norway and Sweden have gained an important part of their work-

---

[50] Smith (2003), 284 et seq.
[51] Judgement of the Swedish Market Court (In Sw: *Marknadsdomstolen*) in *Gourmet*, 2003:5.
[52] Judgement of Borgarting Lagmannsrett, 26 August 2005, in case 05-005287ASI-BORG/01.
[53] January 2007.

ing experience in the legal departments of various Ministries and other parts of the State Administration. In both countries, the common feature of a judge's career is to serve as a legal advisor in the Government's Ministries. When judges are appointed to the Supreme Court, civil service in the Ministry of Justice is sometimes regarded higher upon than work as a judge in a District Court. This is notably true for the Swedish Administrative Supreme Court. It is not unusual for a judge, acting as a legal advisor in the drafting of a statute in the Ministry, to later be given the task of reviewing the constitutionality of the same statute.[54] A comparison of the Swedish Supreme Court with the Norwegian Supreme Court leads to the conclusion that previous work experience in Ministries and other parts of the State Administration is less prominent in the latter. The Norwegian Supreme Court has a greater representation of academic as well as practising lawyers. This more heterogeneous composition may perhaps in part explain why the Norwegian Supreme Court has been historically more active in constitutional review than its Swedish counterpart.[55]

In Sweden and Norway, statutes are drafted in a general way, often leaving the courts wide margins of discretion. Still, there is no strong tradition of constitutional review or constitution-conform interpretation to lean on. Constitutional interpretation tends to be top down rather than bottom up, i.e. the higher, more abstract, norm is constructed so as to fit in with the lower, more concrete, norm. The subjective approach to statutory interpretation, whereby the legitimate role of the courts is confined to discerning the intent of Parliament, is strong in Sweden and Norway. Judicial philosophy and training discourages creativity and emphases obedience to the will of the legislator as expressed in the *travaux préparatoires*. This is slowly changing, partly as a result of the influence of EU membership, the

---

[54] Taube (2003), 132.

[55] Some figures may be mentioned to illustrate the previous working experience of the Swedish judges in the highest instances as of September 1997. Putting together the number of years of previous working experience, the total number of working years of Supreme Court judges amounted to 202 years, out of which the years of working experience within the Ministries amounted to 141 (approximately 70%), the years as a judge to 31 (15%), the years as a practising lawyer to twenty (10%) and the years as a university professor to ten (5%). In the Supreme Administrative Court, the total number of working years of these judges was 193 years. The years of working experience within the Ministries amounted to 166 (86%), the years as a judge to 25 (13%), as a practising lawyer to 2 (1%) and as a Professor of law to 0. Importantly, there have been changes to these somewhat out-of-date figures. Perhaps the most interesting change concerns the subsequent appointment of three University Professors to the position of judge, one in the Supreme Court and two in the Supreme Administrative Court. As far as Norway is concerned, some indications based on figures from March 1998 on the previous working experience of those appointed to the position of judge of the Supreme Court may be presented (based on a case of constitutional relevance where seventeen judges participated). The judges who acquired work experience in Ministries and other functions within the State Administration amounted to approximately 53.5%, those with experience from university to 19.5%, experience as a judge 11.6%, and as practising lawyers 15.4%. In the late 90's, these figures changed slightly and there seemed to be a somewhat greater representation of University Professors and of practising lawyers, at the expense of persons who have worked in Ministries and other parts of the State Administration. See also Taube (2003), 132–133.

scarcity of *travaux préparatoires* and the fact that important parts of EU law are heavily case-law based tends to increase judicial discretion.[56]

The ECHR contains rights without remedies. Also, neither the Swedish nor the Norwegian incorporation statutes make any mention of damages or injunctions, or any other remedies. In some instances, it will nonetheless be possible to grant the plaintiff the remedy he or she wishes, e.g., when the issue concerns access to a court and the obvious remedy is to grant standing or a criminal trial has not occurred within a reasonable time and the plaintiff can be given a reduction of sentence. However, in many other cases there are no given national legal consequences following upon a finding of a breach. Both Swedish and Norwegian judges can thus be left with a large degree of discretion, which could be unpleasant for them. They are really being asked to complete a right, not simply to interpret it. Swedish and Norwegian judges are rather unfamiliar with this.[57]

Table 1

	Norway	Sweden
Religion	Protestant	Protestant
Written Constitution	Yes	Yes
Judicial Review	Yes	Yes
Legal Realism/Positivism	Yes	Yes
Constitutional court	No	No
Natural rights	No	No
Relation to international law	Dualist	Dualist
EU Membership	EEA Member since 1994	Since 1995
ECHR Signatories	1952	1952
Entry into force of the ECHR	1953-09-03	1953-09-03
Inception of the right of individual application	1955-12-10	1955-07-05
ECHR incorporated in national law	1994	1995
Population (2005)	4 606 400	9 011 400
Applications lodged in % of the population	0,00158475	0,006514

[56] Cameron (1999), 20–56; Cameron (2001), 843 et seq.
[57] Ibid.

IV. Reception of the ECHR

A. Accession and Ratification

1. Sweden

Sweden signed the ECHR in November 1950 and ratified it in 1952, but it was not until 1 January 1995 that the ECHR was incorporated into Swedish law, and even then as an ordinary statute and not as a constitutional provision. This development coincided with Sweden's accession to the European Union. The incorporation of the ECHR would avoid the situation where Swedish courts and administrative agencies were obliged to take a glance at the ECHR when applying EU law, or national law connected to EU law, but not when applying national law. The Swedish Act (SFS 1994:1219) on the ECHR (In Sw: *Lag om den europeiska konventionen angående skydd för de mänskliga rättigheterna och grundläggande friheterna*) provides that the ECHR and Protocols nos 1 to 8 shall, in their authentic texts, apply as Swedish law.[58]

Table 2

Protocol[59]	Signature	Ratification	Entry into force	Declarations/Reservations
Protocol no. 1	20 March 1952	22 June 1953	18 May 1954	–
Protocol no. 2	6 May 1963	13 June 1964	21 Sept. 1970	–
Protocol no. 3	6 May 1963	13 June 1964	21 Sept. 1970	–
Protocol no. 4	16 Sept. 1963	13 June 1964	2 May 1968	–
Protocol no. 5	20 Jan. 1966	27 Sept. 1966	20 Dec. 1971	–
Protocol no. 6	28 April 1983	9 Feb. 1984	1 March 1985	–
Protocol no. 7	22 Nov. 1984	8 Nov. 1985	1 Nov. 1988	1 declaration concerning Article 1[60]
Protocol no. 8	19 March 1985	10 Jan. 1986	1 Jan. 1990	–
Protocol no. 9	6 Nov. 1990	21 April 1995	1 Aug. 1995	–
Protocol no. 10	9 April 1992	19 Oct. 1992	–	–
Protocol no. 11	11 May 1994	21 April 1995	1 Nov. 1998	–

[58] Amendments made in 1995 and 1998 stipulate that also Protocol no. 9 and Protocol no. 11 are part of Swedish law.

[59] Source:http://conventions.coe.int/Treaty/Commun/ChercheMembres.asp?CM=3&CL=ENG.

[60] Declaration: "The Government of Sweden declares that an alien who is entitled to appeal against an expulsion order may, pursuant to Section 70 of the Swedish Aliens Act (1980:376), make a statement (termed a declaration of acceptance) in which he renounces his right of appeal against the decision. A declaration of acceptance may not be revoked. If the alien has appealed against the order before making a declaration of acceptance, his appeal shall be deemed withdrawn by reason of the declaration." (1 November 1988–present).

Protocol[59]	Signature	Ratification	Entry into force	Declarations/Reservations
Protocol no. 12	–	–	–	–
Protocol no. 13	3 May 2002	22 April 2003	1 Aug. 2003	–
Protocol no. 14	3 Sept. 2004	17 Nov. 2005	–	–

It should be noted that the ECHR and the RF overlap in a number of cases, but there are also notable differences. These differences, briefly outlined below, have also been the subject of a number of judgements, both from the Court and the Supreme Civil and Administrative Courts of Sweden.

RF's Chapter 2 contains neither a general provision relating to access to a court and to the conditions of a fair trial (Article 6) nor a protection of the right to privacy or to family life (Article 8). These two areas have been scrutinized by both the Court and Swedish courts. Furthermore, there is no general requirement in Chapter 2 to provide an effective remedy for the violation of a right (Article 13), a right that, it is now established, can be breached independently of a violation of a substantive right. It should also be noted that there are differences between the system of protection for citizens and aliens in the ECHR and the RF as well as between the provisions against racial and sexual discrimination and Article 14 ECHR. In some areas, Swedish protection, as interpreted until now, seems to go further than the ECHR. Thus, the RF provides for less restrictions to the right of assembly than Article 11 and no alleged offence can be tried by a Court constituted after its alleged commission.[61]

In spring 2006, the Swedish Government adopted a national action plan for the promotion of human rights in Sweden. The communication entitled "A National Action Plan for Human Rights, *2006–2009* (Government Communication 2005/06:95)" sets out a coherent approach to human rights issues in Sweden. It contains a number of measures aimed at promoting respect for human rights during the period 2006 to 2009. In connection with the presentation of the action plan in March 2006, the Government established the Delegation on Human Rights in Sweden entrusted with the responsibility to supervize the compliance with the ECHR and other human rights regimes.[62]

2. Norway

Norway signed the ECHR in 1950 and ratified it in 1952, but it was not until 1994 that human rights were given an explicit protection in the Constitution.

As previously mentioned, since Norwegian law was, and still is, presumed to be in accordance with international law, the lack of implementation of the ECHR was not seen as a problem. Besides, it was clear, through doctrine and

---

[61] Cameron (2001), 850 et seq.; Cameron (1999), 34 et seq.
[62] For more information, see http://www.manskligarattigheter.gov.se.

jurisprudence, that the human rights conventions, especially the ECHR, enjoyed a strong legal status. Leading Norwegian scholars claimed that Norwegian courts should apply the ECHR independently of Norwegian law and that it should be given precedence in case of a conflict between domestic law and the ECHR. Thus, even if the ECHR had yet to be implemented, there was a common understanding that it had a major bearing on national law.[63]

Since 1994, however, Article 110 c of the Constitution states that it is incumbent on the Authorities of the State to respect and to ensure that human rights and further arrangements concerning the implementation of treaties are laid down by statute. In 1999, the Parliament adopted the Act on the Strengthening of the Status of Human rights in Norwegian Law (the Human Rights Act; in Nor: *Lov 1999-05-21 nr 30. Lov om styrking av menneskerettigheternes stilling i norsk rett (menneskerettsloven)*), according to which the ECHR and the two UN Covenants of 1966 on Civil and Political rights (ICCPR) and on Economical, Social and Cultural Rights (ICESCR)[64] became part of Norwegian law. Subsequently, in the Proposition no. 45 (2002-2003) to the *Odelsting*, the Government proposed that the United Nations Convention on the Rights of the Child[65] and its optional protocols be incorporated into Norwegian law through an amendment of the Human Rights Act.

The purpose of the Human Rights Act is to strengthen the position of human rights in Norway. Section 3 of the Human Rights Act stipulates, *inter alia*, that provisions concerning rights and fundamental freedoms shall, in case of conflict, take precedence over other provisions. Thus, the ECHR is protected through the reference in the Constitution to human rights and through the Human Rights Act. Since a change of the Constitution requires the Parliament to adopt two identical decisions separated by a general election, the constitutional protection must be considered to be rather strong.[66]

These legislative amendments may, on the one hand, be seen as a major reform establishing a fundamental protection of human rights within the Norwegian legal system. On the other hand, since human rights conventions were indirect sources of law even before the implementation, the practical differences may have been rather small. However, the symbolic value of having a Bill of Rights clearly stated in national law should not be underestimated. Since its incorporation in 1999, there have been an increasing number of cases before the Norwegian courts concerning violations of the Bill of Rights.[67]

---

[63]　Mose (2001), 633 et seq.

[64]　International Covenant on Civil and Political Rights (*supra* note 32); International Covenant on Economic, Social and Cultural Rights (*supra* note 32).

[65]　Convention on the Rights of the Child, 1577 U.N.T.S. 3, entered into force 2 September 1990.

[66]　Andenæs and Fliflet (2006), 69, 379 et seq.

[67]　Ibid., 380 et seq.

Table 3

Protocol[68]	Signature	Ratification	Entry into force	Declarations/ Reservations
Protocol no. 1	20 March 1952	18 Dec. 1952	18 May 1954	–
Protocol no. 2	6 May 1963	12 June 1964	21 Sept. 1970	–
Protocol no. 3	6 May 1963	12 June 1964	21 Sept. 1970	–
Protocol no. 4	16 Sept. 1963	12 June 1964	2 May 1968	–
Protocol no. 5	20 Jan. 1966	20 Jan. 1966	20 Dec. 1971	–
Protocol no. 6	28 April 1983	25 Oct. 1988	1 Nov. 1988	–
Protocol no. 7	22 Nov. 1984	25 Oct. 1988	1 Jan. 1989	–
Protocol no. 8	19 March 1985	25 Oct. 1988	1 Jan. 1990	–
Protocol no. 9	10 Dec. 1990	15 Jan. 1992	1 Oct. 1994	–
Protocol no. 10	25 March 1992	25 March 1992	–	–
Protocol no. 11	11 May 1994	24 July 1995	1 Nov. 1998	–
Protocol no. 12	15 Jan. 2003	–	–	–
Protocol no. 13	3 May 2002	16 Aug. 2005	1 Dec. 2005	–
Protocol no. 14	13 May 2004	10 Nov. 2004	–	–

3. Comparison and Conclusion

Sweden and Norway were among the first States to sign the ECHR, and they both incorporated the Convention in the 90's. Historically, it is fair to say that constitutional rights have been viewed with scepticism because of the political and the philosophical backgrounds of both countries. This heritage of thought has had detrimental effects on the implementation of ECHR obligations in Norway and Sweden. However, the prevailing legal philosophy of the welfare State and of the Scandinavian Legal Realism (SLR) seems to have had a greater impact on the society as a whole in Sweden than in Norway.

In the case of both Norway and Sweden, the prevailing attitude was that the domestic legal system conformed well to the ECHR. The presumption of compliance could be one factor that explains the lack of pro-active legislative projects aiming to adhere to the obligations stemming from the ECHR.

For Norway, the lack of implementation could be, on the one hand, due to the important symbolic status of the Norwegian Constitution. On the other hand, there was a common understanding in the doctrine and the jurisprudence prior to the implementation of the Convention that international human rights con-

[68] Source: http://conventions.coe.int/Treaty/Commun/ChercheMembres.asp?CM=3&CL=ENG.

ventions enjoyed a strong legal status in Norway. Norwegian law was considered to be in accordance with all international law obligations.

In the case of Sweden, the incorporation of the Convention occurred almost simultaneously with the country's accession to the European Union. A possible explanation for the late incorporation could be the fact that it was not until 1974 and 1979 that provisions on fundamental rights and freedoms (chapter 2 RF) and on judicial review (11:14 RF) were included in the Swedish Instrument of Government (*Regeringsformen*: RF). Fundamental rights questions did not play an important role in Sweden. In fact, the Swedish attitude towards constitutional rights has been negative for a long time due to the strong heritage of Scandinavian Legal Realism.

The slightly more positive attitude towards the ECHR in Norway could be traced back to the stronger status of the Constitution and a more active Supreme Court. The constitutional review performed by the Norwegian Supreme Court was more intense than the review performed by the two Swedish highest courts. The Norwegian Court has also historically shown a stronger independence towards the political branches than the Swedish courts.

B. The Status of International Law in the Swedish and Norwegian Domestic Legal: Formal Doctrinal Elements

1. Preliminary Remarks

The traditional theories that govern the status of international law of the two countries are rather similar. When a treaty is ratified it becomes part of Swedish and Norwegian law either by incorporation (the drafting of a domestic provision which refers to the treaty) or by transformation (the formulation of national provisions corresponding to the international treaty). According to the traditional dualistic view expressed in legal doctrine, domestic law and international law are separate, independent legal systems. International law is, therefore, not part of domestic law and does not create rights or duties for individuals.

However, the technique of ascertaining legislative harmony is frequently used. In this context, a comparative study of the international requirements and existing national provisions may lead to the conclusion that no legislative amendments are necessary or, in case of a conflict, either the national provision is amended or a reservation is submitted when the treaty is ratified. When this method has been used, those engaged in applying the law will in principle interpret the national provisions, which have been found to be in conformity with the treaty.[69]

Still, according to the dualistic view, domestic law is presumed to be in conformity with international law (the presumption principle). If national provisions can be interpreted in several ways, but only one interpretation is in conformity

---

[69] See Mose (2001), 627 et seq.; Cameron (2001), 840 et seq.

with international law, then that interpretation shall be chosen. According to the traditional view, the presumption principle only applies in relation to general (unwritten) international law, whereas treaties must be transformed by way of a specific decision in order to be a relevant source of law in the domestic legal order (the principle of transformation). However, there is currently a general agreement that treaties may also be used as an aid in the interpretation of domestic provisions (the principle of interpretation). Consequently, international law, including treaties, will also be a relevant source of law according to the dualistic doctrine. If, however, there is a clear conflict between the international and the national norm, the latter will prevail (the principle of precedence in case of a conflict).[70]

This theory of public international law has been widely criticized by legal scholars. The term "principle of presumption" should be replaced by the more active expression "principle of the effectiveness of legally binding instruments". According to this view, international law can be regarded as being part of Norwegian law. A special measure of transformation is not necessary to apply international law, but it would ensure that the international norm is given the rank of the national norm that transformed it into Norwegian law. The same method of transformation is applied in Sweden. Conflicts between international and national provisions would have to be solved according to generally recognized domestic principles (*lex superior, lex posterior,* and *lex specialis*).[71]

2. The Status of the ECHR in Sweden

The ECHR has the status of an ordinary statute under Swedish law. An amendment has been made in the RF stipulating that a law or other regulation which is in conflict with Sweden's obligations under the ECHR shall not be issued. Thus, the RF does not endow the ECHR with constitutional status. It should be borne in mind that the RF also states that a court or an administrative agency can refuse to apply a statute only if it is in a manifest breach of a constitutional provision. This means that the courts and the administrative agencies must refuse to apply legislation or subordinate legislation that conflicts with the ECHR. However, when a statute or a Government ordinance allegedly breaches the ECHR, the conflict must be manifest. Accordingly, statutes or ordinances that do conflict with the ECHR, but not manifestly, should consequently be applied.[72]

The legislator has encouraged the courts and administrative agencies to solve the problem of possible conflicts with other Swedish norms by the application of the principle of treaty-conform construction. Consequently, even though the ECHR statute is constitutionally superior to an ordinance, the latter statute must prevail as long as the ordinance does not manifestly breach the ECHR statute.

---

[70] Ibid.
[71] For Norway, see Andenæs and Fliflet (2006), 28 et seq.; Smith (1962), 182–204; Smith (1964), 356–374. For Sweden, see Sundberg and Sundberg (1992), 63 et seq.
[72] Prop. 1993/94:117.

This follows from the somewhat peculiar constitutional provisions regulating judicial review (see RF 11:14), which give statutes and ordinances equal standing with regard to the application of the criterion of manifest breach.

3. The Status of the ECHR in Norway

In Norway, the legal status of the ECHR and the UN conventions, including the Convention of the Rights of the Child (since 2003), is laid down in the 1999 Act incorporating the four conventions into Norwegian law at the statutory level.[73] In practice, the incorporation entails a definite extension of judicial review of legislation in strengthening a jurisprudence already well developed before 1999.

According to Article 3 of the 1999 Act, the incorporated rights are reinforced through a clause whereby they are to take precedence in the event of a conflict with other parts of national legislation. For this reason, it might be said that the Conventions assume a sort of semi-constitutional status: They do not occupy the same rank as the Constitution, but they supersede ordinary legislation. It should be underlined that this is a factual statement, as the incorporating Act has the rank of ordinary law and it can be changed or departed from by statute law. However, the likelihood of such a change or departure is of course in practice very small.

C. Overview of the Activity of the European Court

1. Sweden

After the ECHR was ratified and the right of individual application was introduced, very few Swedish applications were registered at the Court. Statistics show that on average only two to three applications a year were registered during the fifteen years that followed the 1995 inception of the right of individual application. During this period, there are no data on how many applications were lodged with the Court.

It was not until the beginning of the 80's that the number of registered applications increased. In the beginning of the 80's, the registered applications doubled from year to year. In 1989, 84 applications were registered. The rise in number of lodged and registered cases is most likely the consequence of the *Sporrong and Lönnroth* case.[74] The judgements in these cases were rendered in 1982 and 1984. The cases concerned the right to peaceful enjoyment of their possessions as stated in Articles 1 of Protocol no. 1. Due to these cases, many applications were lodged and registered and most of them concerned the right to property.

---

[73] The Act on the Strengthening of the Status of Human rights in Norwegian Law (the Human Rights Act; in Nor: Lov 1999-05-21 nr 30. Lov om styrking av menneskerettigheternes stillning i norsk rett (menneskerettsloven)).

[74] *Sporrong and Lönnroth v. Sweden* (appl. nos 7151/75; 7152/75), Judgement (Plenary), 23 September 1982, Series A, Vol. 52.

In 1994, there were an unusually large number of lodged and registered cases. This rise in cases coincided with the incorporation of the ECHR and Sweden's formal membership in the EEA and then in the EU in 1995, as a full member. Since then, applications lodged and registered have been, with some small exceptions, steadily increasing. With regard to the population figures available at *Eurostat*, the percentage of applications lodged with reference to population (per capita) amounts to 0.006514.

The data available show that the registered applications mainly concern the rights listed in Articles 6, 8 and 13 ECHR, where Article 6 is the most evoked right. As of December 2006, the Court has delivered 75 judgements concerning Sweden. Violations of the ECHR have been found in 37 of these cases.[75]

2. Norway

The ECHR came into force in Norway in late 1953 and the right of individual application was introduced in December 1955. As in Sweden, very few applications were registered in the first twenty years of the inception of the right of individual complaint.

In the 80's, the number of registered applications was still well below ten cases registered per year. More cases were registered in 1990, and in the years just before the ECHR was incorporated into Norwegian law, a few more cases were lodged and registered per year. The number of registered applications reached 50 only in the 21st century. At the time of writing, the most applications were registered in 2004.[76]

Contrary to the Swedish tendency marked by an increasing number of lodged and registered applications (at certain times), the Norwegian applications seem to be in a constant state of ebb and flow. Consequently, there are no incidents that have motivated the citizens to lodge applications; even the Norwegian accession to the EEA in 1994 has not had any impact on this tendency. With regard to the population data available from Eurostat, the percentage of applications lodged with reference to population (per capita) amounts to 0.00158475. As of December 2006, the Court has delivered fifteen judgements concerning Norway. In a total of eleven cases, the Court held that Norway violated the ECHR. Five of these cases concerned Article 6 ECHR, four cases concerned Article 10. Finally, Articles 5 and 8 ECHR were each the subject of one case.

[75] For an overview of the Court's judgements regarding Sweden (including summaries) and an overall overview of the status of human rights in Sweden, see http://www.manskligarattigheter.gov.se and http://www.manskligarattigheter.gov.se/extra/faq/?module_instance=3&action=category_show&id=33.
[76] End of December 2006.

D. The European Courts Case Law and its Effects in The National Legal Orders

1. Sweden

a. The Impact on Swedish Law before Incorporation

The most common complaints against Sweden can be divided into five broad areas: judicial review of administrative decisions, violations of property rights, taking of children into custody, procedural safeguards in civil and criminal trials and matters concerning aliens. Before incorporation, some 50 cases had been referred to the Court and around 50 judgements had been delivered (four cases referred to the Court concerning Protocol no. 9 were not accepted). In half of these cases, at least one violation was found. In sixteen cases, no violation was found. Ten cases were struck off the list.

The Court's judgements in most of the cases did not require any changes or amendments in domestic law for the purpose of harmonization. It is more interesting to point out those cases, where Sweden did not violate any ECHR provisions, but which led to more changes in Swedish law than the remaining ones.[77] The most significant change was brought about by the Court's judgements concerning the lack of an effective remedy for breaches of the ECHR that jeopardized and infringed individual rights.[78]

The lack of remedy issue was first raised in the landmark judgement of the Court in *Sporrong and Lönnroth*.[79] When the Swedish Government bluntly refused to comply with the judgement, the Court took on a number of cases that resulted in judgements affirming the Swedish violations.[80]

In order to comply with these judgements, the Swedish Parliament enacted legislation whereby a general remedy of judicial review was introduced in 1988. Access to the remedy was conditioned by harsh admissibility criteria. The remedy provided for a review of the legality of certain administrative decisions rendered by an administrative agency or the Government as a final instance of appeal. The

---

[77] The opinion of the dissenting minority in the case *Leander v. Sweden* (appl. no. 9248/81), Judgement (Chamber), 8 July 1987, Series A, Vol. 116 concerning the inadequacies of safeguards on vetting checks by the security police was one of the factors behind the reform of the law made eventually in 1996. See e.g. *Cruz Varas and others v. Sweden* (appl. no. 15576/89), Judgement (Plenary), 20 March 1991, Series A, Vol. 201.

[78] Cameron (2001), 855 et seq.

[79] *Sporrong and Lönnroth v.Sweden* (*supra* note 74).

[80] See *Pudas v. Sweden* (appl. no. 10426/83), Judgement (Chamber), 27 October 1987, Series A, Vol. 125-A; *Boden v. Sweden* (appl. no. 10930/84), Judgement (Chamber), 27 October 1987, Series A, Vol. 125-B; *Tre Traktörer AB v. Sweden* (appl. no. 10873/84), Judgement (Chamber), 7 July 1989, Series A, Vol. 159; *Allan Jacobsson v. Sweden* (appl. no. 10842/84), Judgement (Chamber), 25 October 1989, Series A, Vol. 163; *Mats Jacobsson v. Sweden* (appl. no. 11309/84), Judgement (Chamber), 28 June 1990, Series A, Vol. 180-A; *Skärby v. Sweden* (appl. no. 12258/86), Judgement (Chamber), 28 June 1990, Series A, Vol. 180; *Zander v. Sweden* (appl. no. 14282/88), Judgement (Chamber), 25 November 1993, Series A, Vol. 279-B.

law was initially passed for a trial period of three years. It was eventually made permanent (1996). The law applies only to cases in which there are no other judicial remedy available and in which the administrative decisions (including decisions rendered by the Government itself) impose a burden on an individual.[81]

The purpose of this mode of judicial review was to cover the category of civil rights and obligations, and it referred to the Swedish constitutional concepts of RF 8:2 and 8:3. These provisions provide that delegation of legislative power in certain areas – particularly those imposing burdens on the individual – should be enacted through statutory law. This entails, for instance, that decisions to refuse permission to engage in a particular business activity are subject to review, whereas decisions to withhold a benefit, a social security payment or admission to a higher educational course, are not. It has been pointed out that the exclusion of decisions involving benefits from review is not without difficulties, notably in view of a number of the Court's judgements in the mid-eighties.[82]

In addition to this general restriction, the decisions of certain quasi-judicial tribunals and decisions concerning policy issues where the margin of appreciation is wide are excluded from judicial review, notwithstanding the fact that they could have a direct impact on civil rights and obligations.[83] Also worth mentioning are amendments made to the rules on pre-trial detention (*McGoff*) on oral hearings in appeal courts (*Ekbatani*), and to the disqualification of judges in special courts (*Langborger*).[84]

Another Swedish dilemma was the Court's case law on the institutional requirements of judicial bodies entrusted with powers of adjudication. As a result of the ECtHR's finding of violation of the right to trial by an impartial tribunal in the *Holm* case,[85] it was considered that an amendment to the Freedom of the Press Act may be needed. However, the Government and, later, the Parliament considered that the marginal cases in which the composition of the jury constituted a problem could be dealt with by the courts applying the principles from the *Holm* case in conjunction with the general clause in Chapter 4, section 13 of

---

[81] Danelius (2007), 157 et seq.

[82] *Deumeland v. Germany* (appl. no. 9384/81), Judgement (Plenary), 29 May 1986, Series A, Vol. 100; *Feldbrugge v. the Netherlands* (appl. no. 8562/79), Judgement (Plenary), 29 May 1986, Series A, Vol. 99. See further, the dispute between the Supreme Court and the Supreme Administrative Court, analyzed *infra* note 93. It is not by any means clear that all of these tribunals would satisfy the requirements of Article 6 ECHR. Certainly, not all of them are considered to be "courts" in Swedish constitutional law.

[83] Cameron (1999), 40 et seq.

[84] *McGoff v. Sweden* (appl. no. 9017/80), Judgement (Chamber), 26 October 1984, Series A, Vol. 83; *Ekbatani v. Sweden* (appl. no. 10563/83), Judgement (Plenary), 26 May 1988, Series A, Vol. 160; *Langborger v. Sweden* (appl. no. 11179/84), Judgement (Plenary), 22 June 1989, Series A, Vol. 155. For more details on the legislative changes occasioned by these and other cases see Cameron (2001), 833 et seq.

[85] *Holm v. Sweden* (appl. no. 14191/88), Judgement (Chamber), 25 November 1993, Series A, Vol. 279-A.

the Code of Judicial Procedure that provides for disqualification of judges and jury.[86]

b. The Impact on Swedish Law after Incorporation

Generally, it is fair to say that the impact of the ECHR on Swedish law has been more intense since 1995, when the ECHR was incorporated into Swedish domestic law. It should, however, be pointed out that in a large number of these judgements, the ECHR was only of secondary importance and it was not analyzed in detail. In many cases, the ECHR is invoked by the parties, in most cases by the complainant. However, the Swedish courts tend to base their judgements on Swedish law. This is especially the case in administrative courts when it comes to the right to an oral hearing. In Swedish administrative procedural law, there is a Section that gives a party a right to an oral hearing under certain circumstances, such as when it is necessary for the protection of the complainant's interests. Consequently, the administrative courts have a wide discretion to grant the complainant the right to an oral hearing. It is, however, evident that the tendency to grant the complainant an oral hearing has increased since the ECHR was incorporated.

Article 6 ECHR is the main Article invoked in Swedish courts. As Sweden has a tradition of specialized courts, Article 6 has caused some problems. The Swedish Housing Court (In Sw: *Bostadsdomstolen*) was abolished partly as a consequence of the Court's ruling in *Langborger v. Sweden*.[87] Similar arguments have been raised by complainants both regarding the Swedish Labour Court (In Sw: *Arbetsdomstolen*) and certain lay judge panels. In criminal law, issues have included anonymous or absent witnesses, extradition of suspects on the basis of foreign judgements and exceptional powers to investigate tax crimes.

In administrative law, questions have arisen concerning deportation, compulsory detention of mental patients, and access to a court to challenge administrative decisions. Furthermore, in civil procedural law issues concerning capacity to sue and disqualification of judges have arisen.[88] The vast majority of these cases have been politically uncontroversial, even if the courts have found violations of the ECHR.

There have, however, been a few cases dealing with the negative freedom of association and the right to an effective remedy that have had more political implications. For instance, it was decided that claims for damages could be based on ECHR violations and that decisions on tax surcharges were similar to charges on criminal offences.[89] In the latter, the courts were long reluctant to apply the ECHR. It was only when the ECtHR found that surcharges constitute a civil

---

[86] Cameron (1999), 56 et seq.

[87] *Langborger v. Sweden* (*supra* note 84).

[88] Södergren (2002), 659 et seq.

[89] For more details, see Södergren (2002), 659 et seq.; Södergren (2003), 706 et seq.; Södergren (2007), 23 et seq.; Södergren (2005), 662 et seq.

right[90] that the Swedish courts seemed to constantly apply the ECHR where a surcharge was appealed.

One of the most important cases with regard to financial and political implications for the Swedish balance of power on the labour market is the *Evaldsson* case, concerning the legality of provisions of a collective agreement providing for a deduction of wage monitoring fees for workers outside the trade union.[91] The Swedish labour court first settled the *Evaldsson* case in 2001 (AD 20/2001), where the application of the industries organization for an invalidation of the provisions of the agreement was dismissed.[92] The case was brought before the Strasbourg Court, which found that there was a violation of Article 1 of Protocol no. 1. The judgement raises a number of important issues regarding the possibility for private individuals to obtain compensation in national courts for the illegality committed concurrently by the Government, the trade union and to a certain extent, the industries organization.

aa. The Supreme Court. In NJA 2002 s. 288[93], the Supreme Court had to address the question whether the so-called Press Subsidies Council (PSC, In Sw: *Presstödsnämnden*) could be considered to be a court in the meaning of Article 6 ECHR. The PSC is a Governmental organization whose task it is to safeguard the diversity of the daily newspaper market. It carries out its function by distributing the State's subsidies to the daily press. In 1990, the PSC approved of a subsidy to the newspaper Dalslänningen.

In 1997, the subsidy was recalled and the PSC demanded that Dalslänningen should reimburse the PSC. Dalslänningen took legal action against the State demanding that the given subsidies should be distributed. The Supreme Court found that the distribution of the subsidy concerned a civil right in accordance with Article 6 ECHR. Thus, the claimant was entitled to a trial. As to the question whether or not the PSC was a court in the meaning of Article 6 ECHR, the Supreme Court, referring, *inter alia*, to the Court's ruling in *Campbell and Fell v. the United Kingdom*,[94] held that the PSC fulfilled the requirements of independence. However, the PSC was not impartial in the circumstances of the case.

In NJA 2003 s. 414,[95] the Supreme Court addressed the issue of the right to

---

[90] *Västberga Taxi AB and Vulic v. Sweden* (appl. no. 36985/97), Judgement (First Section), 23 July 2002 (not reported); *Janosevic v. Sweden* (appl. no. 34619/97), Judgement (First Section), 23 July 2002, Reports 2002-VII, 1 et seq.

[91] *Evaldsson and others v. Sweden* (appl. no. 75252/01), Judgement (Second Section), 13 February 2007 (not yet reported).

[92] Swedish Labour Court, Judgement 7 March 2001 in Case no. A-150-1999 (referred to as AD 20/2001)

[93] Swedish Supreme Court, Judgement 30 May 2002 in Case no. Ö 062-00 (referred to as NJA 2002 s. 288).

[94] *Campbell and Fell v. the United Kingdom* (appl. nos 7819/77; 7878/77), Judgement (Chamber), 28 June 1984, Series A, Vol. 80.

[95] Swedish Supreme Court, Judgement 14 October 2003 in Case no. B 2100-02 (referred to as NJA 2003 s. 414).

a fair trial within reasonable time and the right to an effective remedy. The case concerned a man, C.R., who in 1994 was served notice that he was suspected of a crime. Legal action against him was taken in 2001 and the final judgement of the Supreme Court was delivered in 2003. The Supreme Court held that there had been a violation of Article 6 ECHR and the right to a fair trial within a reasonable time, since C.R. had to wait almost nine years before receiving a final verdict. In the judgement, the Supreme Court specifically referred to the Court's ruling in *Kudła v. Poland*[96] stating that a State's failure to provide a right of access to court in order to complain about undue delays and to speed up the process, or its failure to provide adequate compensation for this, is a violation of Article 13 ECHR. Since C.R. had to wait for almost nine years for a final ruling, the Supreme Court held that an adequate compensation in accordance with Article 13 ECHR would be to reduce the punitive sanction, in this case by allowing time to be drawn off from a prison sentence.[97] The Supreme Court also referred to the Court's ruling in *Beck v. Norway*,[98] clearly acknowledging the ECHR violation.

In NJA 2003 s. 217,[99] the Supreme Court held that a complaint, based on an issue which the complainant considered to constitute an undue delay, was admissible. B.H. was the subject of an additional taxation process beginning in 1991 and final judgement was not delivered by the administrative courts until 1998. Consequently, B.H. sued the Swedish State. The claim was based on the fact that the additional taxation process had not been put to trial within a reasonable time in accordance with Article 6(1) ECHR. Both the District Court and the Court of Appeals held the claim to be inadmissible. The reason for this, the lower courts argued, was on the one hand that B.H.'s complaint was rather vague but also, on the other hand, that the Swedish Tort Liability Act (In Sw: *Skadeståndslagen*) prohibits bringing claims against the State for the enactment of, or failure to enact, a statute or an ordinance.

However, the Supreme Court found that in accordance with Article 13 ECHR, B.H. had the right to an effective remedy. Thus, B.H.'s complaint should not have been deemed inadmissible by the lower courts. The Supreme Court thereby further established that damages claims for losses caused by ECHR violations do not have to be based on the Tort Liability Act. It is also possible in such cases to bring a claim for damages directly on the basis of Article 13 ECHR. However, it is noteworthy that in its ruling, the Supreme Court did not mention

---

[96] *Kudła v. Poland* (appl. no. 30210/96), Judgement (Grand Chamber), 26 October 2000, Reports 2000-XI, 197 et seq. See Krzyżanowska-Mierzewska, this volume, Sections F.1.b and F.3.

[97] See also Swedish Supreme Court, Judgement 31 January 2001 in Case no. B 4882-98 (referred to as NJA 2001 s. 35) where the Supreme Court held that the delay was not caused by circumstances pertaining to the State, but rather to the complainant wherefore no adequate compensation was deemed necessary.

[98] *Beck v. Norway* (appl. no. 26390/95), Judgement (Third Section), 26 June 2001 (not reported).

[99] Swedish Supreme Court, Judgement 6 June 2003 in Case no. Ö 1092-02 (referred to as NJA 2003 s. 217).

the Court's standpoint in *T.P. and K.M. v. the United Kingdom*.[100] In this case, the Court stated that where there has been an "arguable breach of one or more right under the ECHR, there should be available to the victim a mechanism for establishing any liability of State officials or bodies for that breach. Furthermore, in appropriate cases, compensation for the pecuniary or non-pecuniary damage flowing from the breach should in principle be available as part of the range of the redress".[101]

It was not until NJA 2005 s. 462[102] that the Supreme Court accepted claims for damages solely based on ECHR violations. In this case, the Supreme Court found that Article 6 ECHR had been infringed since it took seven years for the Public Prosecution Authority to bring the case to court. Consequently, the handling of the case was in breach of the right to a fair trial within reasonable time. The Supreme Court then had to decide what consequences should follow an infringement of the ECHR. It was found that the complainant had a right to compensation for income loss during the time of the delay. In accordance with Swedish law, there is no possibility to grant non-pecuniary damages. However, the Supreme Court glanced at the case law of the ECtHR and granted the complainant a relatively large amount of non-pecuniary damages. The case is of great importance to Swedish tort law.[103]

One of the implicit requirements of the right to a fair trial is the principle of equality of arms between the parties. As the systems of evidence differ considerably from State to State, the Court has been rather careful regarding, for example, evidence from non-present or anonymous witnesses, undercover agents and so called surplus information. The principles established by the Court have been carefully monitored and followed by the Swedish courts. In NJA 2003 s. 323,[104] the Supreme Court held that it was permissible to use surplus information gathered during secret phone tapping as evidence and specifically referred to the Court's rulings in *Schenk v. Switzerland* and *Khan v. the United Kingdom*.[105] Consequently, illegally obtained evidence does not in general mean that a criminal trial is unfair.

NJA 2004 s. 393 is of interest to the Swedish legal system. In order to provide the background to the peculiarity of the Swedish legal system, it must be men-

---

[100] *T.P. and K.M. v. the United Kingdom* (appl. no. 28945/95), Judgement (Grand Chamber), 10 May 2001, Reports 2001-V, 119 et seq.

[101] Ibid., para. 107.

[102] Swedish Supreme Court, Judgement 9 June 2005 in Case no. T 72-04 (referred to as NJA 2005 s. 462).

[103] See comments by Åhman, JT 2005–2006, 424 et seq; Lambertz, JT 2004–2005, 3 et seq.; Södergren, JT 2004–05, 762 et seq.

[104] Swedish Supreme Court, Judgement 1 September 2003 in Case no. B 2076-03 (referred to as NJA 2003 s. 323)

[105] *Schenk v. Switzerland* (appl. no. 10862/82), Judgement (Plenary), 12 July 1988, Series A, Vol. 140; *Khan v. the United Kingdom* (appl. no. 35394/97), Judgement (Third Section), 12 May 2000, Reports 2000-V, 279 et seq.

tioned that certain appeals rely on the Superior Court's order of granting leave to appeal. The criteria for granting leave are laid down in the Swedish legislation. In the case at hand, the Court of Appeal had not granted leave to appeal. The plaintiff appealed against the decision and the Supreme Court found that the Court of Appeal should have granted leave. The Supreme Court explicitly stated that courts shall take account of Article 6 ECHR when deciding on granting leave. The result is that the possibilities to grant leave are interpreted in an extensive way, which probably results in further appeals being granted leave to appeal.

The case NJA 2005 s. 805 led to a substantial amount of publicity in Sweden. The case concerns the borderline between liberty of speech, freedom of religion and criminal offences, such as the incitement to hatred in a criminal case. In this case, a preacher had made several disparaging statements about homosexuals during mass. The Supreme Court found that the statements were not recitals of religious scriptures and constituted offensive and diminishing statements and consequently incitement to racial hatred, as it is laid down in the Swedish Criminal Act. However, due to the ECHR, the Swedish Criminal Act should be interpreted in a restrictive way and since the statements were not found to be "hate speech" as laid down in the case law of the Court, the preacher was not convicted for incitement to hatred. The Supreme Court held that the application of the Criminal Act (In Sw: *Brottsbalken*) was in conformity with the RF and the Act on Freedom of Expression, but not in conformity with the ECHR.

bb. The Supreme Administrative Court. Issues concerning deportation, access to a court to challenge decisions and the right to an oral hearing have arisen in administrative law. In Sweden, the procedure before administrative courts is primarily written and oral hearings are rare. The opposite applies to civil courts, even if civil courts are also restrictive with regard to oral hearings when these are deemed to provide little or no new information. However, the Court found in *Ekbatani v. Sweden*[106] that Ekbatani had not received a public hearing in the meaning of Article 6 ECHR because the Court of Appeal had refused him an oral hearing and his testimony concerned important case matters.[107]

In RÅ 1999 ref 27,[108] the Supreme Administrative Court interpreted the definition of a party extensively on the basis of the ECHR. In the Code of Legal Review (In Sw: *Lagen om rättsprövning*), it is stated that a person appealing a decision must have been a party in the case. The Supreme Administrative Court found, however, that when applying Article 6 ECHR, everyone who has the right of access to justice must also be regarded as a party under the Code of Legal Review.

---

[106] *Ekbatani v. Sweden* (*supra* note 84).

[107] The right to an oral hearing also applies in civil proceedings; see *Helmers v. Sweden* (appl. no. 11826/85), Judgement (Plenary), 29 October 1991, Series A, Vol. 212-A.

[108] Swedish Administrative Court, Judgement 16 June 1999 in Case no. 7201-1997 (referred to as RÅ 1999 ref 27).

In a number of cases in late 2000 and early 2001, the Supreme Administrative Court considered whether tax surcharges were in violation of Article 6 ECHR. The most extensive surcharges were reviewed in RÅ 2000 ref 66 I and II. The Supreme Administrative Court found that Article 6 is applicable, as tax surcharges imposed on an individual involve the determination of a criminal charge. This is mainly because a tax surcharge is a severe sanction that can amount to a very high sum of money. Also, its purpose is to persuade the tax payers to comply with the tax rules by imposing a considerable economic sanction on them.

The Supreme Administrative Court found, however, that the rules on tax surcharges comply with Article 6 after comparing them with the principles contained in this provision. First of all, the tax surcharges were not considered to be disproportionate, as the amount of the surcharge is always calculated with respect to the tax amount that would not have been levied.

Furthermore, the Supreme Administrative Court found that the fact that the tax surcharge is imposed and can be executed by the Tax Authority before it has been tried in a court did not constitute a violation of the ECHR. The reason for this was that the taxpayer always has a right to have his case tried before a court and that, generally, the taxpayer in such a case would be allowed respite for payment until the judgement. It should be noted that, despite the Supreme Administrative Court's conclusion, the law was amended in 2003, giving the taxpayer an unconditional right to respite from payment until the tax surcharge has been tried before a court.

The fact that tax surcharges are imposed solely on objective grounds was also found to comply with the ECHR, since the tax surcharge can be remitted if the failure to submit correct information in the tax form is considered to be excusable as a result of the tax payer's subjective situation. The rules on remittance also give the possibility to the courts to protect individuals on grounds of length of proceedings. In conclusion, the Court found that, as long as the rules on remittance are applied in a less rigid and less restrictive manner, the tax surcharge does not violate Article 6 ECHR.

As the jurisprudential development shows, the ECHR has been applied more often and has come to play a more extensive role in the Swedish legal system. It is not uncommon nowadays for Swedish courts to look for guidance in the ECHR or in the case law of the Court when interpreting rules. Courts have examined, *inter alia*, the interpretation of consent in criminal cases (sexual acts)[109] and the interpretation of exercise of official authority in administrative cases. [110]

---

[109] Swedish Supreme Court, Judgement 4 May 2004 in Case no. B 4646/03 (referred to as NJA 2004 s. 231).

[110] Swedish Supreme Administrative Court, Judgement 17 March 2005 in Case no. 3429-01 (referred to as RÅ 2005 ref 22).

2. Norway

a. The Impact on Norwegian Law before Incorporation

In the 70's, the ECHR was applied in one case (Rt 1974 p. 935) concerning a claim for compensation in a situation where procedural security measures had been imposed. The plaintiff argued without success that the court, which had handed down that decision, had committed procedural errors in breach of Article 6 ECHR: The number of cases relating to the Convention then rose sharply to seventeen in the 80's. The increase continued: While the number of annual cases in *Norsk Retstidende* ranged between seven and eleven from 1990 to 1995, the average number in year 2000 and subsequent years was between twenty to 30 cases, that is after the incorporation of the Human Rights Act. These figures relate only to judgements and decisions handed down by the Supreme Court and its Appeals Selection Committee, which have been published in the *Norsk Retstidende*. They do not include, for instance, decisions where that Committee refused to grant leave to appeal to the Supreme Court in cases where the ECHR has played a significant role in the proceedings at the first or second instance.[111]

During the 80's, the Supreme Court made some historical decisions further establishing the ECHR as a fundamental part of Norwegian law and also taking into account the principles of judicial review. First, in the so-called *Alta* case,[112] the Supreme Court stated that Norwegian courts are competent to decide whether or not assessments made by administrative agencies are in conformity with Norway's international obligations, in this case the rights of the minority Sami people. Second, in Rt 1984 s 1175,[113] a mentally ill person had been sentenced by the courts to security measures in pursuance of the Criminal Code. This judicial authorization included the possibility of placing him in a mental hospital. When the administrative authorities decided to do so, the question was the extent of judicial review available to him. The question was whether he could make use of Chapter 33 of the Civil Procedure Act, which allows the courts to review all aspects of administrative decisions, including matters of pure expediency, when a person is committed to a mental hospital. The Supreme Court first observed that neither the wording of the Mental Health Act nor its drafting history gave any direct indication as to how the problem should be solved. The Court then stated that "[t]he decision to be taken must accordingly take into account all relevant circumstances, in particular the consideration that domestic law must be interpreted, as far as possible, in accordance with those treaties under international law which Norway has ratified, in this instance the European Convention on Human Rights".[114]

---

[111] Ibid.
[112] Norwegian Supreme Court Judgement, see *Norsk Retstidende* 1982, 241.
[113] Norwegian Supreme Court Judgement, see *Norsk Retstidende* 1984, 1175.
[114] Ibid., 1192.

Taking the right to effective legal protection of the individual into account, the Supreme Court concluded that the extended judicial review available under Chapter 33 of the Civil Procedure Act was applicable.[115] This solution would also be in conformity with the Strasbourg case law. The Court carried out a comprehensive survey of the ECtHR's judgements.[116]

At this time, the ECHR had become part of the Supreme Court's everyday life in the field of criminal procedure. This development is due to several reasons. Articles 5 and 6 ECHR are relatively determinate, and section 4 of the Criminal Procedure Act has been regarded as an incorporation clause. Moreover, the attention of lawyers to the potential of the ECHR has been drawn in this field by Articles on specific items in legal journals and by the increasing number of decisions handed down the Supreme Court.[117]

In the beginning of the 90's, the Supreme Court rendered two important judgements. In the first case (Rt 1990 p. 312), the lower court had convicted a person of reckless driving causing death. One witness who had been summoned to the main hearing did not appear, and the police report containing his statement was read out. The second case (Rt 1990 p. 319) dealt with the statement of an allegedly sexually abused girl under six years old. It had been recorded by the investigating judge during the police investigation. The defence counsel's request to postpone the main hearing in order to obtain a new statement from her instead of reading her former statement was rejected by the lower court, and the accused was convicted. In both cases the relevant statutory provisions were interpreted in light of Articles 6(1) and (3)(d) ECHR and of the case law of the Court. The Supreme Court acknowledged that the use of the written reports was acceptable. These cases were followed by a large number of Supreme Court decisions, and some of the proceedings of the lower courts were quashed and referred back to the lower court because the reading out of statements was not considered to be in conformity with the statutory provisions and the ECHR.[118]

Article 5(3) ECHR concerning the right of everyone detained to be brought promptly before a judge does not normally cause difficulties in Norwegian law. Under the Criminal Procedural Act, a person charged must be brought before the court as soon as possible and whenever possible on the day after the arrest. However, holiday periods may raise issues in relation to the ECHR. In Rt 1991 p. 777, the accused had been arrested the day before the National Day, followed by a Saturday and Pentecost holidays. Consequently, six days passed from the arrest until he was brought before a judge. The Supreme Court found that the statutory provision must be interpreted so as to avoid any conflict with Article 5(3) ECHR, and that deprivation of liberty for a such an amount of time is dif-

---

[115] Despite the Supreme Courts efforts, this question once again arose in the case *E. v. Norway* (appl. no. 11701/85), Judgement (Chamber), 29 August 1990, Series A, Vol. 101-A.

[116] Mose (2001), 626 et seq.

[117] Ibid.

[118] Ibid.

ficult to reconcile with the requirements of the Criminal Procedure Act and the ECHR.[119]

The Supreme Court also addressed the requirement that arrested persons are entitled to trial within a reasonable time. In Rt 1993 p. 112, the issue was whether a person in custody, charged with drug offences, should be subjected to further detention. The total time in custody before the main hearing would then amount to nine months. The Supreme Court concluded that deprivation of liberty during this period of time was not in itself a violation of Article 5(3) ECHR. However, in spite of the fact that this provision had been invoked before the Court of Appeals, it had not explicitly considered or discussed the relevant criteria from the Strasbourg case law. Consequently, the decision of the Court of Appeals was quashed. When the Court of Appeals tried the case, it solicited further information about the reasons for the delay and then maintained its original decision. This was met with the approval of the Supreme Court (Rt 1993 p. 224), which noted that it had been difficult to find a period of time during which all counsel could be present at the main hearing. The delay was, therefore, attributable to the way in which the accused had exercised their rights to defend themselves through legal assistance of their own choosing. These decisions were followed by a very large number of cases and, in several of them, the lower courts' decisions have been quashed. Eventually, in Rt 1998 p. 1076, the Supreme Court stressed that courts have the duty to discuss the implications of Article 5(3) ECHR when it is applicable, even if the parties have not invoked it.[120]

An interesting statement of principle was made by the Supreme Court in Rt 1994 p. 610. During investigations concerning alleged illegal price-fixing, several persons gave statements to the administrative authorities. In the subsequent criminal case, the prosecuting authorities requested that the reports containing their statements be admitted as documentary evidence. The Supreme Court rejected this application, but allowed the reading out of the reports within the limits laid down by the general provisions of the Criminal Procedure Act. When considering the relevant human rights provisions, the Supreme Court stated: "(...) that Norwegian courts have to apply the procedural provisions in the field of criminal law in such a way that the proceedings are compatible with our treaty obligations, and that the question may arise to set aside the Norwegian provisions in case of a conflict (...) [I]f a Norwegian court shall have the basis to deviate from the solution following from national procedural provisions, the deviating rule based on sources of international law must appear as sufficiently clear and precise to be given such effect. (...) this must in particular be the case if it is a question of changing a legal situation based on clear and well established Norwegian legislation or practice. In determining whether a decision made by an international court shall be given such effect in national law, it is also of importance whether

---

[119]   Ibid.
[120]   Ibid.

the decision is based on a situation which is factually and legally comparable with the situation to be determined by the Norwegian courts."[121]

The accused invoked in vain the principle of presumption of innocence contained in Article 6(2) ECHR, and the general principle of equality of arms. The main issue was whether the use of statements would be a violation of the prohibition against self-incrimination and the right to a fair hearing in Article 6 ECHR and Article 14(3)(g) ICCPR. The Supreme Court considered the implications of the *Funke v. France* judgement.[122] The *Funke* judgement did not address the problem in the present case, where persons had given statements when they were not charged. The Supreme Court concluded that the ECtHR's decision did not give any reason to conclude that it would be a violation of the fair hearing principle to use the summary of the previous statement as evidence in the present criminal case.[123]

The Supreme Court's statement of principle seems to imply that it is important to distinguish between the question of precedence of international or national law, on the one hand, and the requirement that international norms and the corresponding case-law be sufficiently clear in order to supersede other legislation, on the other. There is a connection between them: if a high level of clarity is required, there will be fewer cases in which international norms will be given precedence. However, in principle, it is important to maintain that these are two separate issues, and that the Supreme Court is prepared to give priority to the international norm.[124]

Furthermore, in Rt 1994 p. 721, the Supreme Court assessed the implications of the judgement in *Sekanina v. Austria*.[125] In the domestic case, a person acquitted after 191 days in custody was given compensation under Section 445, but not under Section 444, of the Criminal Procedure Act. The Supreme Court found that Article 6(2) ECHR may be violated if the reasoning of the domestic court contains doubts as to whether the acquittal was legal, or if it includes tampering with the prosecutor's burden of proof by way of presumptions regarding individual guilt under criminal law. However, section 444 was not as such in breach of the Convention.[126]

An important group of cases dealt with freedom of expression. For instance, in Rt 1990 p. 257, a newspaper was acquitted in a defamation case brought by a politician. The Supreme Court found that the following statement was not compliant with Article 100 of the Constitution (freedom of expression): "With

---

[121] Ibid., 626.
[122] See *Funke v. France* (appl. no. 10828/84), Judgement (Chamber), 25 February 1993, Series A, Vol. 256-A.
[123] Mose (2001), 647 et seq.
[124] Ibid. See also Andenaes and Fiflet (2006), 378 et seq.
[125] *Sekanina v. Austria* (appl. no. 13126/87), Judgement (Chamber), 25 August 1993, Series A, Vol. 266-A.
[126] Mose (2001), 648.

disgust they have followed the campaign of the Progress Party and [the politician] to strengthen the xenophobia amongst Norwegians."[127] The statement related to the political arena and dealt with the plaintiff's behaviour as a politician. Referring to the case *Lingens v. Austria*,[128] the Supreme Court found that in this field the freedom of expression must weigh heavily when balanced against the right to honour and reputation. Several cases have dealt with the relationship between freedom of expression and the prohibition against racial discrimination. In the most recent decision, Rt 1997 p. 1821, the leader of a political party against immigration was convicted because of utterances of a discriminatory nature.[129]

In 1996, the Supreme Court handled three cases[130] concerning the question whether the Norwegian authorities' decisions to deport persons violated Article 8 ECHR. All cases concerned persons without permanent residence permits who, after serving time for serious criminal offences, had been deported from Norway, despite having family there. Referring to the Court's judgement in *Beljoudi v. France*,[131] the Supreme Court held that the deportations would not constitute violations of Article 8 ECHR, despite the deportees having established family connections in Norway. The crimes committed by the persons concerned were of such a serious nature that the decisions to deport them were considered to be in accordance with Article 8 ECHR.

The Rt 1997 s 580[132] case dealing with the bound oil platform workers' right to strike was a weak point in the Supreme Court's case law. In order to settle the conflict between the workers and the employer, the Norwegian Government, taking notice of the conflict's implications on the national economy, had ordered the arbitration of the dispute. This practice had previously been criticized by the ILO. The Supreme Court, however, argued that Norwegian law was not in conflict with any international obligations and that, if such conflict had been found, then national law would prevail. Without making any closer analysis of the case, a fair assumption would be that the national economy's wellbeing may be of such importance that, in times of conflict with international law, national law takes precedence. While this case may not be representative of the Supreme Court's view on how conflicts between international and domestic law should

[127] Text inserted by the author.
[128] *Lingens v. Austria* (appl. no. 9815/82), Judgement (Plenary), 8 July 1986, Series A, Vol. 103. Article 10 has also been applied in Rt 1985 p. 1421 (newspaper convicted of defamation because it had called Greenpeace "the terrorists of environmental protection") and Rt 1993 p. 537 (five of seven defamatory statements relating to a Professor's personal integrity and honesty declared null and void).
[129] See also Rt 1977 p. 114 (teacher denying the fact that Jews were exterminated; conviction), Rt 1978 p. 1072 (statement in a newspaper; acquittal) and Rt 1981 p. 1305 (leaflets against immigration; acquittal).
[130] Norwegian Supreme Court Judgement, see *Norsk Retstidende* 1996, 551, 561 and 568, Judgements 29 April 1996 in Sak nr 38/1996, 39/1996 and 40/1996.
[131] *Beljoudi v. France* (appl. no. 12083/86), Judgement (Chamber), 26 March 1992, Series A, Vol. 234-A.
[132] Norwegian Supreme Court Judgement, see *Norsk Retstidende* 1997, 580.

be resolved, it may serve as a reminder of the political influence on the national legal system.

In conclusion, the Supreme Court has played a leading role in the interpretation and application of human rights conventions in Norway. Its analysis of the treaty texts and the Court's case law has influenced both the attitude of lower courts when confronted with such arguments and the viewpoints held by leading parliamentarians. The Supreme Court has been the authoritative force in lawmaking processes where pleading lawyers, Parliamentarians, lower courts and legal scholars offer views both on the interpretation of the law and its impact in the domestic legal system. On several occasions, a Strasbourg solution has had a direct impact on the outcome of a Norwegian case. As a consequence of the Supreme Court's interpretation of national law and the ECHR, there never was a manifest conflict between these two sets of rules.

This development, also seen in Sweden, is due in part to the domestic courts' increased need to modernise their own viewpoints towards international law. It is also a consequence of the increased interdependence between the different European legal systems as they take tentative steps towards a broadened legal system, where both national and international law have to be taken into account by the legislator and the judiciary.

b. The Impact on Norwegian Law after Incorporation

In Rt 2003 s. 301,[133] the right to a fair trial was at stake. A person, X, had been subject to a child care investigation under the Norwegian law on child protection (In Nor: *Barnevernloven*). X caused a summons against the Norwegian Child Care Agency (In Nor: *Barneverntjensten*) claiming that it was unlawful to investigate X's child care competence and that X's right to respect for private and family life under Article 8 ECHR had been violated. The lower courts dismissed the summons. In the Supreme Court, X argued that her private and family life had not been respected and that she had been denied the right to a fair trial under Article 6 ECHR and the right to an effective remedy under Article 13 ECHR since the summons had been dismissed.

The Supreme Court held that the dismissal of X's summons did not constitute a violation of Article 6 ECHR, since the Norwegian limitations on the right to a trial were within the meaning of the limitations as set forth in Article 6 ECHR. Furthermore, regarding the right to an effective remedy, this presupposes that there is an arguable claim that a right under the ECHR has been violated. After investigating whether or not the child care investigation could constitute a breach of Article 8 ECHR, the Supreme Court concluded that the investigation was justified and did not constitute an unjust invasion of X's privacy. Article 8 ECHR

---

[133] Norwegian Supreme Court Judgement, see Norsk Retstidende 2003, 301, Judgement 4 March 2003 in Sak nr 2002/1046.

had not been violated. Article 13 ECHR had not been violated either, since X did not have an arguable claim. This case is now pending before the Court.

In Rt 2003 s. 375,[134] the Supreme Court held that a decision on the deportation of a person to Ghana did not violate Article 3 of the ECHR. After claiming he was from Uganda, X had been granted a working permit in Norway in 1987. Due to the serious crimes committed by X, the Norwegian authorities, tried to deport him to Uganda in 1993. This proved to be unsuccessful when X suddenly claimed that he was from Ghana. Since X's nationality could not be determined, the deportation was postponed for several years. Before the Supreme Court, X argued that the postponement of his deportation for many years, from 1994 and onwards, constituted a breach of Article 3 ECHR and that he, therefore, should be granted a permanent residence permit in Norway.

X argued that the postponed decision to deport him had made him a *persona non grata* in Norwegian society. He had not been able to look for work, get married or have a normal life. The Supreme Court stated that the ECHR does not give a person an explicit right to stay in a foreign country, even if in exceptional cases a deportation in itself may constitute a breach of Article 3 ECHR. Furthermore, X's experience of being an outcast in Norwegian society could not constitute an inhuman or degrading treatment in the wording of Article 3 ECHR. Also, X had not been helpful in giving the authorities necessary information regarding his background, in spite of the fact that, all in all, X had not been treated in breach of Article 3 ECHR.

In Rt 2003 s. 1671[135] the Supreme Court had to address the issue whether a decision of a lower court ordering X to reimburse the plaintiff, when X was considered to be not guilty, constituted a violation of the presumption of innocence in Article 6(2) ECHR. X argued that the Court's judgements in *Ringvold v. Norway* and *Y v. Norway*[136] did not provide an answer to the question whether the Norwegian practice of obliging the accused to reimburse the plaintiffs, even if the accused was considered to be not guilty, was in conformity with the presumption of innocence. The Supreme Court considered that the lower court's finding that X must reimburse the plaintiff breached Article 6(2) ECHR.

This conclusion was based on an extensive comparison between the Norwegian legislation and the wording contained in the Court's judgements in *Ringvold v. Norway* and *Y v. Norway*, especially in paragraphs 42 to 46 of the latter judgement, where the Court stated, *inter alia*, that "if the national decision on compensation contains a statement imputing the criminal liability of the respondent

---

[134] Norwegian Supreme Court Judgement, see *Norsk Retstidende* 2003, 375, Judgement 21 March 2003 in Sak nr 2002/0854.

[135] Norwegian Supreme Court Judgement, See *Norsk Retstidende* 2003, 1671, Judgement 27 November 2003 in Sak nr 2003/0227.

[136] *Ringvold v. Norway* (appl. no. 34964/97), Judgement (Third Section), 11 February 2003, Reports 2003-II, 117 et seq.; *Y. v. Norway* (appl. no. 56568/00), Judgement (Third Section), 11 February 2003, Reports 2003-II, 161 et seq.

party, this could raise an issue falling within the ambit of Article 6 § 2 of the Convention".[137] Thus, the Supreme Court held that, if a decision on compensation imputes criminal liability, then this might violate Article 6(2) ECHR and since the lower court's wording in this particular case contained such a statement, then Article 6(2) ECHR had been violated. However, it was possible to mend the violation – through the competence of the Norwegian courts – in so far as X had an effective remedy under Article 13 ECHR.

The Rt 2004 s. 583[138] case concerned the right to liberty and freedom under Article 5(4) ECHR. Article 5(4) stipulates that everyone who is deprived of his liberty and freedom by arrest or detention shall be entitled to take proceedings by which the lawfulness of his detention shall be decided speedily by a court and his release ordered if his detention is not lawful. A person, X, had been subject to compulsory institutional care. In 2002, X asked to be released from the institutional care. X's petition was denied by the Control Commission for compulsory institutional care (In Nor: *Kontrollkommisjonen for psykisk helsevern*). X then appealed to the District Court claiming that the findings of the Commission should be declared void and that X should no longer be subject to compulsory care.

The District Court dismissed X's claim after X appealed to the Supreme Court, arguing that the handling of the case violated Article 5(4) ECHR in that the question of X's detention had not been decided with enough speed. X's first appeal had been brought to the Commission seventeen months before the case was brought in front of the Supreme Court. Referring to The Court's jurisprudence in *Van der Leer v. the Netherlands, Navarra v. France* and *Weeks v. the United Kingdom*,[139] the Supreme Court found that the claimant could be considered responsible for three out of the seventeen months. The Supreme Court, acknowledging the Court's verdict in *E. v. Norway*,[140] held that the Norwegian court's slow handling of the case constituted a breach of Article 5(4) ECHR. However, this breach did not entitle X to a release from compulsory care.

In the Rt 2004 s. 1737[141] case, a Norwegian broadcasting company, TV Vest, had been ordered to pay a charge for violating the prohibition on political commercials in Norwegian television. TV Vest argued that this prohibition was in violation of Article 10 ECHR (freedom of expression). In its judgement, the

---

[137] *Y. v. Norway,* ibid., para. 42.

[138] Norwegian Supreme Court Judgement, see *Norsk Retstidende* 2004, 583, Judgement 1 April 2004 in Sak nr 2004/0056 HR-2004-00655-A.

[139] *Van der Leer v. the Netherlands* (appl. no. 11509/85), Judgement (Second Section), 21 February 1990, Series A, Vol. 170-A; *Navarra v. France* (appl. no. 13190/87), Judgement (Chamber), 23 November 1993, A, Vol. 273-B; *Weeks v. the United Kingdom* (appl. no. 9787/82), Judgement (Plenary), 2 March 1987, Series A, Vol. 114.

[140] *E. v. Norway* (*supra* note 115).

[141] Norwegian Supreme Court Judgement, see Norsk Retstidende 2004, 1737, Judgement 12 November 2004 in HR 2004-01889-A.

Supreme Court referred extensively to the Court's rulings in *Tierfabriken v. Switzerland*[142] and *Murphy v. Ireland*.[143]

In the former case, the Court said that it "cannot exclude the prohibition of 'political advertising' may be compatible with the requirements of Article 10 of the ECHR in certain situations. Nevertheless, the reasons must be 'relevant' and 'sufficient' in respect of the particular interference with the rights under Article 10".[144] In the latter case, the Court held that the prohibition on religious commercials in Ireland was compatible with Article 10 ECHR, since the motives behind the prohibition were the religious sensitivities in the Irish society.

The Supreme Court held that the prohibition on political commercials in Norway was not so much an issue of freedom of expression, but more a question of how to best promote the democratic process. Therefore, the prohibition was not in violation of Article 10 ECHR and also within the Norwegian State's margin of appreciation. Consequently, there were sufficient and relevant reasons for the prohibition.

In a plenary judgement of 9 November 2006[145], the Supreme Court addressed the right not to be tried or punished twice. A person, A, had been subject to a tax revision by the tax authorities and had been ordered to pay tax surcharges. A had also been convicted of tax fraud and appealed the conviction claiming that the prosecution should have been dismissed in parts, since A was being punished twice. Invoking and referring in detail to the Court's rulings in *Franz Fischer v. Austria*[146] and *Janosevic v. Sweden*,[147] the Supreme Court, also referring to the motives behind the domestic laws, argued that tax surcharge and tax fraud could not be seen as punishment for the same criminal offence, due to the fact that tax surcharges were decided independently of intent, whilst the criminal offence tax fraud presupposed a criminal intent.

The Supreme Court's judgement of 27 November 2006[148], in which it had to address, *inter alia*, the question whether Norwegian law complies with Article 4 of Protocol no. 7, is also of interest. A Spanish fishing company (the Company)

---

[142] *Tierfabriken v. Switzerland* (appl. no. 24699/94), Judgement (Second Section), 28 June 2001, Reports 2001-VI, 243 et seq.

[143] *Murphy v. Ireland* (appl. no. 44179/98), Judgement (Third Section), 10 July 2003, Reports 2003-IX, 1 et seq.

[144] *Tierfabriken v. Switzerland* (*supra* note 142), para. 75.

[145] Norwegian Supreme Court Judgement 9 November 2006, HR-2006-01893 –P. It should be noted that one of the judges, namely judge Skogøy came to a dissenting conclusion in so far as A in part was punished twice, since the Norwegian legislation on tax surcharge not only served the purpose of encouraging the tax payers of presenting correct information, but also served a penal purpose. Thus, in the opinion of Judge Skogøy, the laws on tax surcharge and tax fraud was in violation of Article 4 of Protocol no. 7.

[146] *Franz Fischer v. Austria* (appl. no. 37950/97), Judgement (Third Section), 29 May 2001 (not reported).

[147] *Janosevic v. Sweden* (*supra* note 90).

[148] Norwegian Supreme Court Judgement 27 November 2006 in HR-2006-01997-1 in Sak nr 2006/871.

overdrew its fishing quotas in the Norwegian economic zone and was subject to an injunction. The company did not abide by the injunction and was consequently penalized and ordered to pay a fine. Furthermore, the Company's fishing permit in the Norwegian economic zone was withdrawn. Besides invoking various international treaties regarding economic zones and Svalbard, the Company held that the injunction and the withdrawal of the permission to fish in the Norwegian economic zone were in violation of the right not to be punished twice.

The Supreme Court held that the purpose of Article 4 of Protocol no. 7 was to prohibit the repetition of criminal proceedings that had been concluded by a final decision and that the principle of *ne bis in idem* applies to situations where the offences have the same essential elements. The Supreme Court held that the injunction and the withdrawal of the permit were not in conflict with the ECHR. However, just as in Sweden, the Norwegian Supreme Court noted that the Court's practice is rather unclear and that several interpretations are possible regarding the cases under Article 4 in Protocol no. 7.

3. Comparison and Conclusions

The legal theories of SLR fuelled with thoughts regarding the legal and political sovereignty of the Nation State formed the prerequisites for Swedish and Norwegian theories on the relationship of international and domestic law. The prevailing theory of dualism in both countries created for many years an obstacle for national judges to give direct effect to Treaty obligations in domestic courts. The dualism came to soften up in both countries especially when judges found recourse to the principle of treaty-conform interpretation.

In the 70's, Swedish courts adhered to the opinion that the ECHR and the judgements of the Court were not formally binding on Swedish courts. However, these resistant attitudes began to change in the 80's, especially after the Court's judgement in the case *Sporrong and Lönnroth v. Sweden*.[149] Now, the Supreme Court began to openly refer to the ECHR and the Court's practice. After the Court's judgement in *Ekbatani v. Sweden*,[150] the Supreme Court and Supreme Administrative Court allowed appeals based on the fact that a party in a case in a lower court had been refused an oral hearing. The ECHR thus came to be used actively. Swedish laws were being interpreted as far as possible in the light of the ECHR. The practice of treaty-conform interpretation became the method of giving effect to the ECHR in national law.[151]

Overall, the ECHR has influenced all areas of Swedish law, but perhaps most significantly administrative law, criminal (procedural) law and civil procedural law and civil rights.[152] Through the case law of the Supreme Court and the Su-

---

[149] *Sporrong and Lönnroth v. Sweden (supra* note 74).
[150] *Ekbatani v. Sweden (supra* note 84).
[151] Danelius, (2007), 33 et seq.
[152] Ibid., 134 et seq.

preme Administrative Court, it became apparent in the 90's that Swedish courts ought to interpret national law in conformity with the ECHR, despite the existence of contrary views expressed in the legislative history of the national statutes in question. The academic criticism of the widespread reference to preparatory works by the Swedish judiciary, which was highlighted in conjunction with the obligation to implement EU law loyally, also influenced the attitude of the Swedish courts when trying to construe national law in accordance with the ECHR.[153] It is fair to say that the Swedish accession to the European Union influenced the national judges' overall attitudes to the ECHR.

It is legitimate to assume that during the first twenty years after the ratification the ECHR had little impact on the Norwegian courts or on the legislative process. This has gradually changed. The big change occurred in the last few years, since the adoption of the Human Rights Act. In the 90's, Norway was found guilty of violating the ECHR on several occasions. The three most well known cases concerned the balance between free speech, especially through the media, and the protection of an individual's reputation. In all these cases, the Court found that Norwegian law gave too much protection to the individual and not enough to the press (cf. Article 10 of the ECHR). Lately, another important area of possible conflict between the ECHR and national legislation has been the question whether certain tax penalties under Norwegian law trigger the rights afforded to an individual facing a criminal charge (Article 6(1) of the ECHR).

It is worth noting that out of the Supreme Court's six plenary sittings, which took place in the last few years, four cases concerned judicial review based on the ECHR and one case related to the rights of indigenous people. In addition, there were a large number of ordinary Supreme Court cases in which the ECHR was decisive for the outcome and many more where the ECHR was invoked during the proceedings.

The ECHR has influenced most areas of Norwegian law, but perhaps especially (criminal) procedural law. Other issues which have arisen are the right not to be punished twice, the freedom of speech and the freedom of religion and religious education in schools. Between 1994 and 2006, the ECHR has been invoked 67 times before the Supreme Court. In approximately two thirds of these cases, questions regarding the ECHR have been of central importance. However, in order to understand the development of the last few years, it is necessary to briefly examine the practices of the Supreme Court during the second half of the twentieth century.

---

[153] Case 14/83, *Von Colson och Kamann*, [1984] ECR 1891; Case 222/84, *Johnston*, [1986] ECR 1651; Case C-106/89, *Marleasing*, [1990] ECR I-4135; Case C-271/91, *Marshall*, [1993] ECR I-4367; Case C-66/95, *Sutton*, [1997] ECR I-2165; Case C-180/95, *Draehmpaehl*, [1997] ECR I-2195, Case C-185/97, *Coote*, [1998] ECR I-5199; Case C-412/97, *Ed Srl.*, [1999] ECR I-3845; and Case C-228/98, *Dounias* [2000] ECR I-577.

E. Mechanisms of Coordination

1. Sweden

The primary responsibility for ensuring compliance with the Convention was initially entrusted with the legislator. The legislative processes of both Sweden and Norway are normally initiated through directive to a Committee consisting of either Members of Parliament or civil servants. Their task is to investigate the need to introduce new legislation. External experts (e.g. academic lawyers or judges) often have taken part in these Legislative Committees. After the Committee has submitted its opinion, an opportunity is usually given for a cross-section of interest groups (often including the Law Faculties) to comment upon the merits of proposals before these are laid before Parliament. The Government then decides whether to propose new legislation.

The Ministry in charge then drafts a proposal. About 50% of all proposals are sent to the Law Council, which is constituted of a group of judges from the highest courts. The Law Council reviews the proposal from a technical and constitutional point of view. One of the major tasks is to engage in abstract judicial review by checking the compliance with high ranking legislation, such as the Constitution, EU Treaties and the ECHR. The opinion of the Law Council is not binding on the Government.

The proposal is then submitted as a Bill to Parliament and considered by the relevant Parliamentary Standing Committee. This Committee then submits a report to Parliament. The composition of this Standing Committee reflects the composition of Parliament as a whole. Hence, the vote in Parliament very rarely goes against the proposal of the Committee.

Consequently, there are several points at which the issue of the proposal's compatibility with the ECHR can be raised. Initially, questions of ECHR compatibility may arise at the investigative stage, where the standard directions to a Committee are scrutinized. Further, it is possible to question whether proposed legislative amendments are compatible with the ECHR. This criticism must come from the Government or the Committee itself. Independent criticism can be heard when the proposal is sent out to be reviewed by external institutions and groups. The scrutiny of the Law Faculties is normally regarded as being authoritative.

A further safeguard is the Law Council. A brief survey of the minutes of Law Council meetings, conducted by the author during 1998, disclosed several proposals in which the Law Council drew the attention of the Government to possible difficulties relating to the Convention. In each case, the Law Council contented itself with references to the Convention rather than to the ECtHR case law. It should be noted here that the Law Council has no legal assistants and its composition changes every two years. The competence of the Law Council in the field of the ECHR thus depends wholly upon the level of knowledge of the individual members.[154]

2. *Norway*

As in Sweden, the primary responsibility for ensuring compliance with the Convention is initially entrusted with the legislator. In the process of passing legislation, the Norwegian Parliament (In Nor: *Stortinget*), is divided into two chambers, the *Odelsting* and the *Lagting*. One quarter of the *Storting* serves as members in the *Lagting*. A Bill is introduced by the Government in the form of a proposition to the *Odelsting*. As in Sweden, this proposition is the product of an extensive preparatory procedure in which organizations, other Government bodies and institutions are consulted. Once the proposition has been submitted to the *Odelsting*, the *Odelsting* refers it to the appropriate Committee, which considers the Bill and returns it to the *Odelsting* in the form of a recommendation. Thereafter, the *Odelsting* passes the Bill, in the form of a resolution, to the *Lagting*. The *Odelsting* resolution is deliberated in the *Lagting* and, if approved there, is sent to the King in Council. When the King has sanctioned and signed the Bill, it becomes valid law. Naturally, the role performed by the King has become symbolic. Should the *Lagting* not approve of the resolution, it is sent back to the *Odelsting* with comments. If the *Odelsting* accepts the comments, the Bill is passed. In case the *Odelsting* does not approve of the comments, the resolution is sent back to the *Lagting* for consideration. If the *Odelsting* and the *Lagting* cannot agree on the Bill, it is submitted to the plenary *Storting*. To pass the plenary session, a two-thirds majority is required. Thus, the primary function of the *Lagting* is to act as a safeguard when legislations are passed.[155] Furthermore, the Norwegian constitution expressly states that the *Storting* may obtain the opinion of the Supreme Court on points of law.[156] The opinion of the Supreme Court is not formally binding on the *Storting*.

Hence, as in Sweden, there are several points at which the issue of the proposal's compatibility with the ECHR can be raised. Questions relating to ECHR compatibility may arise at the investigative stage where the standard directions to a Committee are scrutinized. Further, it is possible to question whether proposed legislative amendments are compatible with the ECHR. This criticism must come from the Government or the Committee itself. Independent critique can be heard when the proposal is sent out to be reviewed by external institutions and groups.

---

[154] Cameron (1999), 35 et seq.

[155] For more information, see http://www.stortinget.no.

[156] Article 83 of the Constitution, the *Storting* may obtain the opinion of the Supreme Court on points of law.

F. Remedies and Proportionality Test

1. Sweden

The Swedish Tort Liability Act provides for damages for physical injury to persons or damage to property and consequential financial losses. Purely economic loss may also lead to damages, but only when this loss arises out of a crime. Public authorities are liable to pay damages for physical injury to persons or damage to property and consequential financial losses caused by negligent acts in the exercise of public power. Also, public authorities are liable to pay damages for the non-pecuniary harm of suffering, but only when this has resulted from a crime against freedom, personal integrity or reputation. Purely economic loss may result in damages when it is a result of the public authority negligently giving inaccurate information or advice.[157]

Under the ECHR, the Strasbourg Court can, in accordance with Article 41, award just satisfaction to an applicant whose rights under the ECHR have been breached. Furthermore, according to Article 13 ECHR, national courts are obliged to provide a remedy in damages for violations of ECHR rights. In view of the above and in light of the Court's practice,[158] it was clear after the incorporation of the ECHR in Sweden that there was a tension between the Swedish Tort Liability Act and the possibilities of awarding damages under the ECHR. This is due to the fact that Swedish legislation did not provide a remedy in damages when there was no crime or serious negligence on the part of a public authority, while the Court's new practice demanded that such remedies be available.[159] Hence, the Swedish system of non-pecuniary damages was not harmonized with the Court's practice.

Since Articles 13 and 41 ECHR had, through the incorporation of the ECHR, become parts of Swedish law, the question arose whether these could be used as a statutory basis for awarding damages. Swedish courts were initially reluctant to use the ECHR Articles as a foundation for awarding damages, even after the Court's judgement in *Kudła v. Poland*.[160] Representatives of the Swedish Government argued that Article 41 ECHR did not provide a basis for a damages claim, as according to the Swedish State only the Court can award just satisfaction. Also, the Court was to be considered as a so-called "special court" under the Code of

---

[157] For a further description of the Swedish statutes on torts, see Bengtsson (2000), 300 et seq.

[158] For example, *Klass and Others v. Germany* (appl. no. 5029/71), Judgement (Plenary), 6 September 1978, Series A, Vol. 28;, *Valsamis v. Greece* (appl. no. 21787/93), Judgement (Chamber), 18 December 1996, Reports 1996-VI, 2312 et seq.

[159] *T.P. and K.M. v. the United Kingdom* (*supra* note 100); *Z. and Others v. the United Kingdom* (appl. no. 29392/95), Judgement (Grand Chamber), 10 May 2001, Reports 2001-V, 1 et seq.; *Calvelli and Ciglio v. Italy* (appl. no. 32967/96), Judgement (Grand Chamber), 17 January 2002, Reports 2002-I, 25 et seq.

[160] *Kudła v. Poland* (*supra* note 96).

Judicial Procedure (*In Swe: Rättegångsbalken*) and consequently, only the special court, not ordinary courts, could handle claims for damages.[161]

However, in a number of judgements, the Swedish Supreme Court gradually adjusted this stance. First of all, in NJA 2003 s. 217,[162] the Swedish Supreme Court held that a complaint based on what the complainant considered to be an undue delay, violating his right to trial within a reasonable time, was admissible. B.H., who was subjected to an additional taxation process beginning in 1991 and ending in 1998, sued the Swedish State claiming that his right to a fair trial within a reasonable time had been violated. Both the District Court and the Court of Appeals held the claim to be inadmissible. The reason for this, the lower courts argued, was on the one hand that B.H.'s complaint was rather vague and, on the other hand, that the Swedish Tort Liability Act (In Sw: *Skadeståndslagen*) prohibited bringing claims against the State for the enactment of, or failure to enact, a statute or an ordinance.

Nonetheless, the Swedish Supreme Court found that in accordance with Article 13 ECHR, B.H. had a right to an effective remedy. Thus, B.H.'s complaint should not have been deemed impermissible by the lower courts. This was the first tentative step in making it possible to bring claims for damages for losses caused by ECHR violations and not to base them on the Tort Liability Act. It is noteworthy, however, that in its ruling the Swedish Supreme Court did not mention the ECtHR's standpoint in *T.P and K.M. v. the United Kingdom*,[163] where the Strasbourg Court stated that where there has been an "arguable breach of one or more right under the Convention, there should be available to the victim a mechanism for establishing any liability of State officials or bodies for that breach. Furthermore, in appropriate cases, compensation for the pecuniary or non-pecuniary damage flowing from the breach should in principle be available as part of the range of the redress".[164]

The second, and latest step, was NJA 2005 s. 462,[165] where the Swedish Supreme Court accepted a claim for damages based solely on ECHR violations. A person, X, had been informed in January 1992 that he was suspected of a crime; he was formally charged in 1995 and the trial began in 1998. In December 1998, X was acquitted. X took the case to court, applying for both economic and non-pecuniary damages claiming, *inter alia*, that his rights under Article 6 ECHR (the right to a fair trial within a reasonable time) had been violated. The Supreme Court found that Article 6 ECHR had been infringed, since it took seven years for the Public Prosecution Authority to bring the case to court: there had been a

---

[161] See Government Committee Memo, Ds 2007:10.

[162] Swedish Supreme Court, Judgement 6 June 2003 in Case no. Ö 1092-02 (referred to as NJA 2003 s. 217).

[163] *T.P. and K.M. v. the United Kingdom* (*supra* note 100).

[164] Ibid., para. 107.

[165] Swedish Supreme Court, Judgement 9 June 2005 in Case no. T 72-04 (referred to as NJA 2005 s. 462).

violation of the right to a fair trial within reasonable time. The Swedish Supreme Court then had to decide what consequences would ensue from the infringement of the Convention. The Supreme Court found that the complainant had a right to compensation for income loss during the time of the delay. In accordance with Swedish law, there is no possibility to consider non-pecuniary damages. The Swedish Supreme Court glanced, however, at the case law of the ECtHR and granted the complainant a relatively large amount of non-pecuniary damages.

It is noteworthy that the legislator was reluctant to ensure that legislative remedies comply with the ECtHR's practice. This task has been left up to the Swedish courts to fulfil, which normally means that until there is some practice from the higher courts, the lower courts will be rather reluctant to apply the principles emanating from the Court's practice. However, it should also be noted that the lower courts are catching up and awarding damages even in minor cases.[166] The gradual Europeanization of the Swedish legal system and the Swedish courts will probably result in an increased judicial independence when it comes to assessing potential violations of Sweden's obligations under international law.

A special problem arises from the relationship between the requirement of manifest fault (RF 11:14) to set aside an ordinance or a statute and the right to compensation for breaches of the ECHR. If the Swedish Government violates the Convention by way of the enactment and enforcement of a statute, the question is whether the right to compensation requires a manifest breach of the Convention or if the general criteria for compensation should apply. It seems obvious that a strict application of the requirement of manifest fault in damages cases violates the ECHR obligation, since it creates a protection for the Government that stems from national constitutional law and jeopardizes the principle of uniform interpretation and application of the Convention.

Criteria applicable in normative conflicts of a constitutional nature should also conceptually be treated separately from concepts of tort law. This is due to the fact that the question whether the State has committed a clear breach triggering damages should be settled with regard to the actual boundaries of legislative discretion granted to the State. This assessment should, for example, be separated from an assessment of the often-invoked democratic criteria in situations of judicial review, which imply that a manifest fault could never be committed as

---

[166] For example, see the Stockholm District Court (In Sw: *Stockholms tingsrätt*) Judgement of 29 September 2006 in case FT 5790-06, where the claimant was awarded damages caused by an infringement of Article 8 ECHR. The claimant had been suspected of a narcotic related crime (for which he was acquitted) and had to leave a urine sample. The National Board of Forensic Medicine's (In Sw: *Rättsmedicinalverket*) analyzes of the claimant's urine sample went beyond what was necessary and, therefore, constituted a violation of Article 8 ECHR.

[166a] In addition to the remedies covered in this section, there is a general extraordinary remedy which allows to reopen civil and criminal proceedings in Swedish Law. These proceedings must have given rise to "a manifestly incorrect application of law" (58 Chapter 1-2 §§ Code of Judicial Procedure).

long as the Parliamentary Institutions (The Law Council and the Constitutional Committee) have endorsed the constitutionality of the statute.[166a]

2. Norway

The enactment of the Human Rights Act (In Nor: *mennskerettsloven*) in 1999, which clarified the effects of the incorporation of the ECHR and the UN human rights conventions, settled also the issue of ECHR supremacy *vis-à-vis* national law. The question whether the national constitutional criteria of a clear and manifest breach still applies in conflicts between statutes and the ECHR still remains unresolved.

The Norwegian Tort Liability Act (In Nor: *Lov om skadeserstatning*) also provides for damages for physical injury to persons or damage to property and consequential financial losses. Furthermore, the Norwegian Tort Liability Act also explicitly prescribes damages for violations of the right to private and family life as well as for defamation. Non-pecuniary damages may also be awarded under certain circumstances. Thus, it is possible to award damages for a violation of the ECHR under Norwegian law.

As indicated above, in the late 90's the Norwegian Government presented an action plan for human rights based on the premise, that it is incumbent on the State to respect and to ensure that the rights of Norway's inhabitants are fulfilled. This applies also to Norway's international efforts to promote human rights.

In conclusion, a remedy to seek damages can be derived from both the ECHR, either as incorporated or taken as an instrument of public international law, and the inherent references to the national tort regimes. In order to clear the tensions between the different legal orders, it would be preferable to codify a damage clause (in the respective incorporation act) that would create a right to just or adequate compensation in cases of ECHR violations.[167]

The right to compensation is likely to arise after the European Court's judgement on 29 June 2007 in *Folgero*. In the *Folgero v. Norway*,[168] the ECtHR found that the religious education in Norwegian schools was in violation of Article 2 of Protocol no. 1.

With the help of the Norwegian Humanist Association, three sets of parents had taken the Norwegian Government before the Court, claiming that the KRL subject (Christianity, religion and life stance education) introduced in public schools in 1993 was not objective, critical or pluralistic. Subsequently, the refusal to fully exempt children from the subject was found to be a violation of the parents' rights: "the State shall respect the rights of parents to ensure such education and teaching in conformity with their own religious and philosophical

---

[167] See the discussion between Södergren (2007) and Cameron (SvJT 2006, 553 et seq.) concerning the conditions for damages for ECHR violations.
[168] *Folgero v. Norway* (appl. no. 15472/02), Judgement (Grand Chamber), 29 June 2007 (not yet reported).

convictions".[169] In the verdict, the Court stated: "The State (...) must take care that information or knowledge included in the curriculum is conveyed in an objective, critical and pluralistic manner. The State is forbidden to pursue an aim of indoctrination that might be considered as not respecting parents' religious and philosophical convictions."[170]

The ECtHR concluded that "notwithstanding the many laudable legislative purposes stated in connection with the introduction of the KRL subject in the ordinary primary and lower secondary schools, it does not appear that the respondent State took sufficient care that information and knowledge included in the curriculum be conveyed in an objective, critical and pluralistic manner for the purposes of Article 2 of Protocol No. 1".[171] Thus, the Court found "that the refusal to grant the applicant parents full exemption from the KRL subject for their children gave rise to a violation of Article 2 of Protocol No. 1".[172] In the evaluation of damages, the Court stated that a "finding of a violation will have effects extending beyond the confines of this particular case, since the violation found stems directly from the contested legal framework and not from its manner of implementation".[173] The case is of great importance and it will probably put stress on the Norwegian courts to come up with an effective remedy for compensation for purely economic loss.[169a]

3. Comparison and Conclusion

The influence of the Convention in the field of remedies has been different in Sweden and Norway. In Sweden, there has been for many years a tension between the Swedish Tort Liability Act and the damages available under the ECHR, since Swedish Law provided remedies for non-pecuniary damages only when the losses resulted from a crime. This national system had to be harmonized with the ECtHR's practice. Following an initial reluctance, which could be seen also in other fields of Sweden's attitude towards international law before incorporation, the Swedish Supreme Court gradually came to accept claims for damages based solely on ECHR violations. However, it was not before 2005 that the Supreme Court finally provided sufficient remedies. The Government is presently considering an amendment to the Swedish Tort Liability Act in order to comply with the ECtHR's case law.[174] In Norway, it is possible to award damages for a viola-

---

[169] IArticle 2 of Protcol no.1.

[169a] In addition to the remedies covered in this section, it is possible – pursuant to 391 § of the Norwegian Judicial Code of Procedure – to reopen a case if the national decision infringes a rule enshrined in an ECtHR decision or judgement.

[170] *Folgero v. Norway* (*supra* note 168), para. 84.

[171] Ibid., para. 102.

[172] Ibid.

[173] Ibid., para. 109.

[174] See Government Committee Memo, Ds 2007:10.

tion of the ECHR under the Norwegian Tort Liability Act. A remedy for damages can be derived from both the ECHR and the national tort law.

It is fair to say that today national courts in both countries try to live up to ECHR obligations in terms of the sufficiency of remedies provided. If national law does not provide a remedy, courts – especially the Swedish ones – glance at the ECHR to fill the gap in national provisions.

G. Knowledge and Practice

1. Students and Academics

Students leaving University today know more about human rights than they would have known 30 years ago. For instance, since 1992 basic knowledge in international human rights law has formed part of the obligatory curriculum at the Law Faculty of Oslo University. In addition, for several years students have been able to choose human rights as an optional course at all Law Faculties, or to write a dissertation in that field.

Human rights issues are also increasingly addressed in other disciplines of law, such as constitutional law and criminal procedure. It may be added that, following a Swedish initiative, representatives from Law Faculties in the Nordic countries plead every year a moot case, concerning the ECHR, as part of the *Sporrong-Lönnroth* Competition founded by Professor Jacob Sundberg from the Faculty of Law at Stockholm University. This competition has been very significant for the standing of the subject and the dissemination of knowledge on a Pan-Scandinavian level. It has served as a forum for social, cultural and legal integration between the judiciary and the academia on a Nordic cross-border basis.[175]

The study of the ECHR is presently obligatory for Swedish and Norwegian law students. This was not the case before the incorporation. Then, the study of the ECHR was often part of the general international law course, which incorporated a number of international legal regimes. It is also fair to say that international law has been rather neglected in both Sweden and Norway.

However, the ECHR is currently part of the national constitutional law regime, and law students study this instrument in the constitutional or public law courses as well as in public international law courses. The students also touch upon the subject in the EU law course, where the ECHR is studied as an integral part of Community Law. Hence, the judiciary in Sweden and Norway has a general awareness of the ECHR. In addition, for several years students have been able to choose human rights as a specialized subject at Law Faculties in both Sweden and Norway.

---

[175] This competition was founded by Professor Jacob Sundberg in 1984 and is still an important event for students, academics and judges in the Nordic countries.

Post-incorporation of the ECHR the scholarly interest of the ECHR has increased in both countries. During the last ten years there is a notable raise in research grants awarded both by private and public funds.[176]

2. Nordic Cooperation in European Matters

Human rights law, and notably the ECHR, has been on the agenda at the meetings and conferences of the Scandinavian academia, judiciary and Administration for the last 30 years. One can discern traces of the ECHR in the reports from Nordic Law Meetings (In Sw: *Nordiska juristmötena*). This Institution has hosted conferences and reports for more than a hundred years and served as the main forum for Scandinavian legal integration through the twentieth century. The significance of the institutionalized Nordic legislative cooperation has deteriorated as Denmark, Finland and Sweden gradually achieved EU membership. Most of the legal integration (for instance, in civil law) now takes place within the framework of Pan-European conferences hosted by international research institutes, universities and the EU institutions.

3. The Judiciary

For more than twenty years, Swedish and Norwegian judges have gone for annual study visits to Strasbourg. The National Courts Administration Board (*Sveriges Domstolar*) has set up a procedure for monitoring case law developments before the Strasbourg Court. The Board also disseminates judgements to Swedish courts. It appears that the majority of judges serving in both countries since incorporation have studied the ECHR in law school, either as an independent course or as part of the curriculum of international law studies. The majority of them have also attended at least one vocational training programme concerning the ECHR.

It is fair to say that the level of awareness and willingness to apply and interpret the ECHR depends, on the one hand, on the judges' education and level of knowledge of the ECHR and the ECtHR's case law. On the other hand, there are reasons to believe that it is the political and philosophical conviction of the individual judge that finally determines whether the ECHR will have effect in a specific situation. The reason for this is that the hard-core judicial review of national legislation or the intense treaty-conform interpretation are likely to trigger the judges' fundamental views on legal and political theory as well as the reigning opinion on the proper balance between judges and politicians in the process of governing a Nation State.

---

[176] Vetenskapsrådet, Report 2005.

4. Lawyering

In the early days of the ECHR, which had the status of an instrument of public international law between 1950 and 1980, national courts in both countries were reluctant to engage in judicial review. Courts often avoided a proper assessment of the arguments submitted by the litigants and they rarely set aside a national statute. This early standing of the ECHR as well the deferential judicial attitude influenced litigation strategies. Litigants and their lawyers were discouraged from raising sustained legal arguments of normative conflicts between national law and the ECHR.

Moreover, prior to incorporation of the ECHR in both countries, the roads to Strasbourg were filled with procedural and substantive obstacles. The foreseeability of success was diluted by the indeterminate ECtHR case law. In addition, the considerable legal costs of the advice on the pursuing an ECHR-based claim through the domestic system all the way up to Strasbourg constituted an important consideration for the potential complainants.

A global assessment of these factors often resulted in the advice to abstain from legal action. At this time, there were also very few legal claims raised by private companies, who could both live with the indeterminacy of the outcome and bear considerable legal costs. The non-commercial nature and the indeterminacy of judicial outcomes kept the lawyers at the major business law firms who specialized in European law out of the ECHR trade. Business lawyers would rarely represent private individuals, would charge higher fees, and would apply a harsher commercial yardstick on their assignments.

Most cases prior to incorporation were initiated by private individuals represented by lawyers from small law firms that mainly dealt with criminal law and other human rights law areas, such as immigration and family law. There were practically no law firms profiled as human rights law firms until the early 90's. The incorporation of the ECHR and membership in the EU (Sweden) and the EEA (Norway) has strengthened the standing of European Law as an area of practice. The ECHR has become an additional field of expertise for EU and EEA lawyers. All major business law firms in Sweden and Norway presently offer legal advice in ECHR matters.

However, even if the area has increased in importance from a political and constitutional point of view, the commercial significance of the ECHR legal practice is still negligible. This may be explained by the legal character of this area of law; since most violations of the ECHR concern procedural guarantees, effective legal protection and political rights for private individuals, they rarely trigger significant damage claims.

In domestic courts, the possibility of remuneration is also still subject to a fairly restrictive national law on torts. Even if the legal ground (the remedy) could be derived from either the ECHR itself or from domestic law of torts, the domestic legal regimes still apply rather harsh criteria with regard to the conditions for compensation.[177] Both Swedish and Norwegian constitutional law feature the criteria of serious breach or manifest fault.

The success of the European Community or European Union legal integration is based on the cooperation between the European Court of Justice in Luxemburg (the ECJ) and national courts under the system of preliminary rulings. The entire process of transforming public international law treaties into a common constitutional charter with absolute supremacy over national law and a well-developed system of effective legal protection for enforcing EU law rights is brought about by the system of preliminary ruling.

This highly effective vehicle of legal integration is dependant on the questions of interpretation put to the ECJ by the national courts. There is no doubt that the litigants and their lawyers play a key role in formulating these questions. In fact, the majority of references originating from national courts are initiated by the litigants. Hence, lawyers and their clients have a pivotal role in the integration process. The clients are often small, mid-size or large European corporations seeking to nullify national restrictions on trade, which are detrimental to their businesses. Their commercial incentives to go to court are often strong. The ECJ's judgements in cases concerning the legality of national alcohol and gaming monopolies have had big effects on the State purse and have brought about major changes in the traditional domestic policies.

The ECHR system lacks most of these essential prerequisites for legal integration. Most importantly, the ECHR does not trigger major commercial interests and has no effective remedy for legal integration through uniform interpretation that is comparable to the system of preliminary ruling in the EU. The ECHR-system does not create the conditions for an active and creative legal practice where litigants and their lawyers can mould and process commercial interests into legal rules and principles and put them into a legal framework with effective remedies.

5. Comparison and Conclusion

In both countries, the influence of the Convention has changed over time. While there was reluctance and scepticism regarding the ECHR until the 80's, the influence of the Convention became much stronger following the incorporation in the mid-90's in both Sweden and Norway. The study of the ECHR is currently obligatory for Swedish and Norwegian law students, which was not the case before incorporation. Over the last 30 years, human rights law has played an increasingly important role in the meetings and conferences of the academia, judiciary and administration in both countries. Furthermore, the Scandinavian *Sporrong-Lönnroth* moot court competition, founded by Professor Sundberg at Stockholm University, has brought together the Swedish and Norwegian univer-

---

[177] See *supra* Section F.

sities and judiciary. It has had a great importance for the dissemination of knowledge and practice concerning the ECHR for more than twenty years.

In addition, all major business law firms offer legal advice in ECHR matters. There is, however, a tendency in major business law firms to give a higher priority to the more commercially profitable EU law cases. This is also due to the fact that EU remedies are more develeoped both at the supra-national level and at the domestic level.

In general, the incorporation of the ECHR as well as the membership in the EU and the EEA have strengthened the standing of European Law in both countries. There is, however, no evidence that the Swedish membership in the EU has paved the way for a more active and intense implementation of ECHR obligations than in Norway, an EEA Member State. This is probably due to the fact that judges in both countries are reluctant to fully embrace the well-developed EU remedies system (right to damages, interim relief, restitution, etc.). When faced with a treaty violation (EU or ECHR), judges predominantly adhere to the national tort and procedural regimes.

K. General Conclusions

Today, it is quite obvious that the ECHR has influenced legislation and judicial decision making in Sweden and Norway. One can also discern an increasing willingness on the part of the administrative authorities to take the ECHR into account when they fulfil adjudicative tasks. It is also noteworthy that the Ombudsmen in both Sweden and Norway often invoke the ECHR in the course of their supervisory tasks. It should, however, be noted that the Norwegian Ombudsman has an explicit human rights monitoring function.[178]

When faced with a case in which the judge is compelled to take the ECHR into account there exist two principal courses of action; either the judge finds that the national law is in conflict with the ECHR and sets it aside by way of judicial review or the judge tries to overcome the discrepancies through interpretation.

The Supreme Court of Norway applies the ECHR according to a principle of presumption. It was not until 1994, however, that the Supreme Court first applied the clause on sector monism in a judgement.[179] At the same time, the Court introduced the limitative principle of clarity and non-ambiguity as a prerequisite for application of a treaty provision.

Moreover, Norwegian courts must apply criminal procedural law so that the court proceedings comply with treaty obligations. Norwegian law may be set aside if it is incompatible with the ECHR according to Section 4 of the Criminal Procedure Act. If, however, a Norwegian court is to depart from the national legal procedure, this should only be done when the provision stemming from

---

[178] See the Annual Report of the Ombudsmann, 1990, p. 23.
[179] Supreme Court Reports, Rt. 1994, p. 610.

international sources is sufficiently clear and unambiguous. This is especially the case when the question arises in relation to the review of law on a point that is founded on a clear and established principle of Norwegian legislation or case law. When deciding whether the ECtHR judgement shall have this effect in national law, it is also important to consider whether it is based on factual and legal circumstances that are comparable to the particular circumstances of the case to be determined by the Norwegian court.

The question whether there is a conflict between a Convention rule incorporated into Norwegian law and other Norwegian law (entailing that the Convention rule must take priority) cannot be resolved by a general rule, but must depend on a more detailed interpretation of the legal rules in question. Harmonization through interpretation can resolve an apparent conflict.

It follows from the precedence rule in Section 3 of the Human Rights Act that if the result of the interpretation of an ECHR provision appears to be reasonably clear, the Norwegian courts are obliged to apply the Convention rule, even when this would set aside established principles of Norwegian legislation or legal practice.

In many cases, however, there can be justifiable doubt as to how the ECHR is to be interpreted. This may be due to the fact that many of the ECHR provisions are vague, and the interpretation of the Convention requires a balancing of different interests or values on the basis of a common European interpretation of the law or practice. The doubt can also be due to the fact that the aim of the ECtHR is not only to clarify the content of the Convention; in many previous cases, the ECtHR has aslo interpreted the ECHR provisions dynamically, as a law-maker would.

Although the Norwegian courts apply the same principles of interpretation as the ECtHR when applying the ECHR, the task of developing the Convention lies first and foremost with the Strasbourg Court. The Norwegian courts must respect the wording and the objectives of the Convention and the decisions of the Convention organs. If there is any doubt as to the scope of the ECtHR's judgements and decisions, it will be relevant whether they are based on factual and legal circumstances that are comparable to the particular circumstances to be determined by the Norwegian court. Where different interests or values are to be weighed against each other, the Norwegian Courts must be entitled – within the scope of the method applied by the Strasbourg Court – to apply traditional Norwegian value priorities. This applies, in particular, when the Norwegian legislator has already assessed the relationship between domestic legislation and the ECHR and has concluded that there is no conflict.

Moreover, the frequency of the use of treaty-conform interpretation by the Swedish and Norwegian judiciary depends on a number of factors. If the litigants do not raise the ECHR legal issue by themselves, the courts very rarely raise it on their own. However, if the litigant invokes the ECHR, the intensity and scope of treaty-conform interpretation depends on the general awareness and knowledge of the ECHR.

Most judges are also aware of the fact that all ECtHR judgements should be regarded as authoritative interpretations of the ECHR. Swedish and Norwegian judges are fully acquainted with ECHR or EU judgements. They are generally obliged to follow the case law of the Luxemburg courts (the ECJ and the EFTA court) rather closely. Their reluctance to ground the legal reasoning of a national judgement on more or less indeterminate legal norms enshrined in the Court's judgements is rather justified by reference to their lack of clarity and coherence than to the origin of the legal norms. Swedish and Norwegian judges are just not used to applying a method of principled rights jurisprudence.

The ECHR is now a familiar part of the Swedish and Norwegian legal systems and is invoked more often than domestic constitutional provisions by the parties and courts. Lower courts are less hesitant in applying the ECHR on their own. The courts have benefited from the availability of the Court's recent case law on the internet. On the other hand, the changes in the Swedish legal system during the last ten years have been immense. The majority of the judges, who were educated under and accustomed to a national legal system, are now faced with the task of keeping up to date with new principles of law as well as with the relevant case law originating from both the Strasbourg Court and the European Court of Justice.

Possible conflicts of norms between the incorporated ECHR and other Swedish norms have been avoided, mainly by applying the principle of treaty-conform construction. There have been indications of increasing Europeanization of judicial attitudes, but there is still a great reluctance to engage in constitutional review. There may be some scope for constitutional review as regards the issue of access to a court (Article 6 ECHR). It is unlikely that in the future there will be any constitutional review on the basis of what could be called the "civil liberties" part of the ECHR. This is because the Swedish courts, in general, consider that the courts lack legitimacy to reach a different conclusion than that of Parliament as to whether a particular restriction to a right is "necessary in a democratic society".

The difference between Sweden and Norway with regard to the number of complaints brought before the Court is also of interest. In 2006, the Court received 82 applications from Norway and 472 from Sweden.[180] The number of complaints is increasing in all Scandinavian countries. Until December 2006, the Court has decided in fifteen cases concerning Norway. In eleven of these cases, the Court concluded that the ECHR had been violated.

During the same period, the Court has decided 75 cases concerning Sweden

---

[180] European Court of Human Rights, Survey of Activities 2006, Registry of the European Court of Human Rights, Strasbourg, 2007, p. 40, http://www.echr.coe.int/NR/rdonlyres/69564084-9825-430B-9150-A9137DD22737/0/Survey_2006.pdf.

and found 37 violations of the ECHR in them. In addition, in a number of cases concerning Sweden brought before the Court, Sweden has chosen to settle the dispute before trial. The area in which Sweden has had the most difficulties concerned Article 6 ECHR and the principles of procedural guarantees and effective legal protection for private parties.

Norway, on the other hand, has had problems concerning the freedom of expression, the equality of arms and the right to a fair trial and the presumption of innocence. The cases in which Norway has been found to have violated the ECHR have all been criticized by Norwegian lawyers and judges. The critics argued that the Court had been too harsh or had misunderstood the Norwegian legal system. However, it is noteworthy that Norwegian (as well as Swedish) courts monitor closely the Court's practice and that legal reforms have taken place in order to bring national law in accordance with the Court's recent case law, even when it concerned other States.

It is also relevant that before Swedish courts, it is the ECHR rather than the RF's Bill of Rights that is invoked by the parties. There are several explanations for this. The ECHR does contain rights which have no equivalent in the RF's Bill of Rights. Neither the right to a fair trial in Article 6 ECHR nor the right to privacy in Article 8 ECHR have Swedish counterparts. Furthermore, it has been suggested that the Bill of Rights in Sweden serves more as a reminder to the lawmaker than as a legal basis on which the individual can rely before national courts. One could also argue that the transparency of the law-making process decreases the need for judicial review. Furthermore, the Government is obliged, in principle, to refer major items of draft legislation to the Law Council, which serves to ensure the conformity with the legal system and internal consistency within the laws. All this, combined with what may be called a pragmatic approach to law making, results in a tendency not to use the RF's Bill of Rights, even when the RF should be directly applicable.

Regarding the Swedish discussion concerning the need for a Constitutional Court, the following can be said. Constitutional issues seldom arise before the Supreme Court and the Supreme Administrative Court. Less that one per cent of the total number of judgements delivered by both Supreme Courts during the last 25 years concern constitutional questions. One could perhaps argue that these low figures in themselves indicate that the need for constitutional review is somewhat limited. On the other hand, as critics have pointed out, the limited number of cases concerning constitutional issues indicates that Sweden is still unprepared for the gradual Europeanization of law and the increased need for constitutional review.

Considering that the Strasbourg Court is burdened by approximately 89 900 pending cases, the need for a more active constitutional approach on the part of the national courts becomes apparent.[181] Most probably, national courts will

---

[181]   Ibid, p. 39.

have to consider cases concerning fundamental rights and freedoms where there is no clear practice from the Court. In those cases, it will be up to the national courts to safeguard these rights under the Convention and in those cases, it will be necessary for them not just to abide by the ECHR but also to interpret and to use the Bill of Rights, as stipulated in the national legislation. Thus, the need for an increased constitutional and judicial review is apparent. In Chapter 11, Section 14 of the RF states that a court (or other public body) may disregard a provision if it is in a manifest breach of fundamental law or another superior statute. The condition that a breach must be manifest diminishes the possibility for the national courts to find that a law is in conflict with, for example, the ECHR. Of course, if the requirement of a manifest breach was abolished, the courts' influence over the legislation would increase, thereby disadvantaging the National Parliament.

Nevertheless, the significance of the incorporation of the ECHR in Sweden and Norway could easily be overestimated. The incorporation only provides for a minimum system of protection. The post-incorporation public discourse in both countries, notably in Sweden, has mainly concerned the issue of access to remedies for the determination of civil rights and obligations. The ECHR aspect has often been merged with a general discussion on the principle of effective protection of individual rights in EU law, which in the Swedish context is centred on the access to judicial remedies.

As part of the legislative process in both countries, there are institutional guarantees to ensure that the legislator takes the ECHR sufficiently into account. For the judiciary in both countries, it is fair to say that the courts are essentially trying to live up to the obligations of the ECHR, making use of the principles of interpretation and of the national remedies. There are no obvious signs of judicial rebellion against the ECHR in either Sweden or Norway. After incorporation, there are some indications of what could be characterized as an increased independence in interpretation of the ECHR. The main vehicle for giving effect to the ECHR is the application of the principle of treaty-conform interpretation rather than constitutional review. This is due to the great respect and legitimacy which Swedes and Norwegians attribute to their Parliament.

In order to understand the relationship between political institutions and the judiciary in Sweden and Norway, court practice in cases involving conflicts between international treaty norms and ordinary domestic legislation must be taken into account (in addition to ordinary constitutional and administrative practice). Over the last few years of both Supreme Courts' practice, cases concerning the application of (mainly) EU law (through EU membership and EEA mechanisms) and the ECHR have constituted an even greater concern than the cases in which the statute-constitution relationship was at stake. However, neither the EU nor the ECHR law have been introduced at the constitutional level into domestic law. Moreover, the historical and (probably) ideological approaches to the two sets of competing norms are not the same.

Judicial review has been a part of the Swedish and Norwegian constitutional systems for many years. Nevertheless, the idea that the courts are undemocratic when reviewing ordinary legislation seems to be rather predominant in the legal thinking of both countries. Similar opinions have been expressed by many political scientists as well as by sections of the media and politics. In other words, such a review entails that that the courts and their constitutional activity are seen, at least to some extent, as a threat to democracy. It is difficult to determine how deeply this idea is entrenched in the political systems of both countries. It has been a long time since courts have given politicians reasons to believe that their relationship with the Supreme Court in the constitutional domain is important.

The process of reception of the Convention depends on the judge's constitutional ideology when engaging in judicial review. It appears that the processes of Europeanization and globalization of the legal systems and polities of Sweden and Norway are likely to change ideologies and attitudes towards judicial review and the ECHR. This transformative process of Europeanization can also be portrayed as an example of the so-called "juridification of politics". It has taken place simultaneously with a deeper transformation of the theory and the practice in Sweden and Norway. The familiar catch phrase is "Europeanization of national law".[182] Internationally, one can also speak of the "judicialization of politics" and "governing by judges".[183] The core of this transformative process is that an increasing number of issues, which were previously decided by political institutions, now end up before judges. At the same time, the law is becoming politicized, in that the courts armed with unclear rules are faced with cases of great economic and socio-political significance. The great discretion afforded to the courts and the urgent social significance of the cases make it difficult for lawyers, politicians and laymen to distinguish law from politics.

The concept of Europeanization has been used in legal and political science literature in order to characterize the transformation of Swedish and Norwegian law in connection with the ECHR incorporation and the EU/EEA membership. This entails a general upgrading of the role of law and lawyers in society, an increased court control through judicial review of political decisions, and a generally more prominent role for the courts *vis-à-vis* political power. The great transformative force has been the incorporation of EU law and its well-developed system of judicial review and legal protection. The most important vehicle has been the dialogue between national courts and the ECJ under the system of preliminary rulings. The implementation of the requirements resulting from EU

[182] Wiklund (2004), 713.
[183] Stone Sweet (2000); Stone Sweet (1999); Stone Sweet and Brunell (1998); Weiler (1991); Burley and Mattli (1993); Levitsky (1994); Slaughter, Stone Sweet and Weiler (1998); Maduro (1998).

membership has paved the way for the implementation of other international legal regimes, such as the ECHR system.

The Europeanization of national law, which brings with it radical changes in the legal culture, has been a dominant factor in this context. The time-honoured and homespun legal and interpretation principles in both countries have been challenged by the European Union legal system of legal protection. The principles of legal interpretation have also been affected, and this has given greater scope to the application of legal principles. What is more, the study of the sources of law (the hierarchy, the principles and the methods of interpretation of the rules of law) and the traditional systematization of law have also been influenced.

The process of Europeanization creates a formidable challenge to legal theory, legal practice (i.e. application of the law and legal consultancy work) and legal training. Europeanization and globalization have contributed to the uncovering of legal theory problems that have long been latent. These problems were previously concealed by the widespread acceptance of the fact that the boundaries of the Nation State coincide with the validity and legitimacy of the legal system. Europeanization and globalization have been created, and are still governed, by a similar logic. Europeanization can be said to be part of the more comprehensive globalization, and both processes lead to different degrees of eradication of demarcation lines between the national and international levels, as well as politics and law.

Bibliography

Åhman, K., *Rapport 2003: Kartläggning av i vilka fall svenska domstolar tillämpat bestämmelserna i 2 kap. regeringsformen och i Europakonventionen* (Uppsala, 2003).

—, 'Skadestånd på grund av konventionsbrott – eller har HD blivit naturrättare?', *Juridisk Tidskrift* (2005–2006), 424.

Andenæs, J. and Fliflet, A., *Statsforfatningen i Norge* (Oslo, 2006).

Bengtsson, B., 'Torts and Insurance', in Bogdan, M. (ed.), *Swedish Law in the New Millenium* (Stockholm, 2000), 300.

Bjarup, J., *Reason, Emotion and the Law. Studies in the Philosophy of Axel Hägerström* (Aarhus, 1982).

—, *The Philosophy of Scandinavian Legal Realism*, Workshop Paper, IVR, 2003.

Broch, O., 'Strict or Liberal Interpretation?', in Smith, E. (ed.), *The Constitution as an Instrument of Change* (Stockholm, 2003), 242.

Burley, A. M. and Mattli, W., 'Europe Before the Court: A Political Theory of Legal Integration', *International Organisation* 47 (1993), 41–76.

Cameron, I., 'The ECHR in Sweden Since Incorporation', *International and Comparative Law Quarterly* 48 (1999), 20.

—, 'Sweden', in Blackburn, R. and Polakiewicz, J. (eds.), *Fundamental Rights in Europe: The European Convention on Human Rights and its Member States, 1950–2000* (Oxford, 2001), 833.

—, Skadestånd och Europakonventionen för de mänskliga rättigheterna, SvJT 2006, 553.

Danelius, H., *Mänskliga rättigheter i europeisk praxis* (Stockholm, 2007).

Hägerström, A., 'Är gällande rätt ett uttryck för vilja?', in Olivecrona, K. (ed.), *Rätten och viljan: Två. uppsatser av Axel Hägerström* (Lund, 1961).

Hellner, J., *Rättsteori* (Stockholm, 1992).

—, 'Rättsteori och rättsvetenskap', *Juridisk Tidskrift* 2 (1996–97), 535.

Holmberg, E. and Stjernquist, N., *Vår författning* (Stockholm, 1995).

Høstmælingen, N., *Internasjonale menneskerettigheter* (Oslo, 2003).

Judt, T., *Postwar, A History of Europe since 1945* (New York, 2005).

Knoph, R., *Knophs oversikt over Norges rett* (Oslo, 2004).

Koskenniemi, M., *The Gentle Civilizer of Nations, The Rise and Fall of International Law1870–1960* (Cambridge, 2002).

Lambertz, G., 'Det allmännas skadeståndsansvar i framtiden – trender och utvecklingsmöjligheter', *JT* (2004–2005), 1.

Levitsky, J. E., 'The Europeanisation of the British Style', *American Journal of Comparative Law* 42 (1994), 347.

Lundstedt, A., Editorial article, *Socialdemokraten 10 September 1928*.

Maduro, M. P., *We, the Court: the European Court of Justice and the European Economic Constitution* (Oxford, UK, 1998).

Møse, E., 'Norway', in Blackburn, R. and Polakiewicz, J. (eds.), *Fundamental Rights in Europe: The European Convention on Human Rights and its Member States, 1950–2000* (Oxford, 2001), 625.

—, *Menneskerettigheter* (Oslo 2002).

Nergelius, J., *Förvaltningsprocess, normprövning och europarätt* (Stockholm, 2000).

—, *Konstitutionellt rättsskydd* (Stockholm, 1996).

Ross, A., *On Law and Justice* (London, 1974).

Sterzel F., *Parlamentarismen i författningen* (Uppsala, 1981).

Sejersted, F., *Socialdemokratiets tidsalder, Norge og Sverige i det 20 århundre* (Oslo, 2005).

Slaughter, A. M., Stone Sweet, A. and Weiler, J. H. H., *The European Court and the National Courts – Doctrine and Jurisprudence: Legal Change in its Social Context* (Oxford, 1998)

Smith, C., 'Den internasjonale rettens innvirkning på den nasjonale retten', *Tidsskrift for Rettsvitenskap* (1962), 182.

Smith, E., *Højesteret og folkestyret* (Oslo, 1993).

Södergren, J, 'Axplock II, ur svensk konventionstillämpning', *Europarättslig tidskrift* 4 (2002), 659 et seq.

—, 'Axplock III, ur svensk konventionstillämpning', *Europarättslig tidskrift* 4 (2003), 620 et seq.

—, Rätt till skadestånd i Sverige direkt grundval av Europakonventionen, JT 2004–2005, 782.

—, 'Axplock V, ur svensk konventionstillämpning', *Europarättslig tidskrift* 4 (2005), 662.

—, 'Axplock VI, ur svensk konventionstillämpning', *Europarättslig tidskrift* 1 (2007), 13.

Stone Sweet, A., *Governing with Judges* (Oxford, 2000).

—, 'Judicialization and the Construction of Governance', *Comparative Political Studies* 32 (1999), 147.

Stone Sweet, A. and Brunell, T. L., 'Constructing a Supranational Constitution: Dispute Resolution and Governance in the European Community', *American Political Science Review* 92 (1998), 63.

Stone Sweet, A. and Weiler, H. H. J., *The European Court and the National Courts, Doctrine and Jurisprudence: Legal Change in its Social Context* (Oxford, 1998).

Sundberg, J., *Från Eddan till Ekelöf, Repetitorium om rättskällor i Norden* (Malmö, 1978).

Sundberg, J. and Sundberg, F., *Lagen och Europakonventionen* (Stockholm, 1992).

Sveriges Riksdag (ed.), *The Constitution of Sweden – The Fundamental Laws and the Riksdag Act* (Stockholm, 2000).

Taube, C., 'The Role of Constitutional Justice: Court Models and Procedures', in Smith, E. (ed.), *The Constitution as an Instrument of Change* (Stockholm, 2003), 132.

Tingsten, H., *Den svenska Socialdemokratins idéutveckling* (Stockholm, 1967).

Warnling-Nerep, W., *Rättsprövning och rätten till domstolsprövning* (Stockholm, 2002).

Weiler, J. H. H., 'The Transformation of Europe', *Yale Law Journal* 100 (1991), 2403.

Wiklund, O., 'Europeiseringstendenser och domstolskritik i svensk rätt – Regeringsrättens domar I spelmålen', *Europarättslig tidskrift* 5 (2004), 713.

5

The Reception Process in the Netherlands and Belgium

*Erika de Wet**

A. Historical Context: Accession and Ratification[1]

1. *The Netherlands*

On 31 August 1954 the Kingdom of the Netherlands, currently consisting of the Netherlands, the Netherlands Antilles and Aruba,[2] became a party to the European Convention on Human Rights (ECHR) as well as its Protocol no. 1.[3] However, it took another six years for the Kingdom to recognize the right of individuals to lodge complaints with the European Commission of Human Rights (ECommHR) under former Article 25 (now Article 34) ECHR.[4] The individual complaints procedure was finally recognised on 28 June 1960. Since 1979, the individual complaints procedure has also been in force for the Netherlands Antilles and Aruba.[5]

---

* This Article also constitutes a part of the project, Interactions between International Law and National Law, undertaken at the Amsterdam Center for International Law and funded by the Netherlands Organization for Scientific Research.

[1] Where feasible, paper sources, sources of case law and legislative materials are indicated. Otherwise reference is made to official internet websites. When translating terminology into English, the author essentially relies on the terminology commonly used by Dutch and Belgian authors when describing their legal systems in English. Where the author relies on English translations of the Dutch and Belgian constitutions, these documents are cited in the footnotes.

[2] The relationship between the Netherlands and its overseas territories is regulated in the Charter of the Netherlands of 1954, which together with the Dutch Constitution of 1983 forms the constitutional basis of the Kingdom. At the time of writing, negotiations were under way regarding a new constitutional structure for the five islands constituting the Netherlands Antilles. Although all five islands are to remain within the Kingdom, only the two bigger ones are likely to remain an autonomous territory, while the smaller ones will come under direct administration of the Netherlands. The subsequent passages will deal exclusively with the reception of the ECHR in the Netherlands.

[3] Surinam also constituted part of the Kingdom until its independence in 1975. Zwaak (2002), 597. See also Alkema (1976), 85 et seq.

[4] Zwaak (2002), 597; Engering and Liborang (1999), 29.

[5] Barkhuysen, Van Emmerik and Loof (2000), 336.

The Kingdom of the Netherlands has subsequently ratified all Protocols to the ECHR, with the exception of Protocol no. 7. This Protocol has, however, been signed since 1984. The reluctance of the Netherlands to ratify Protocol no. 7 is based on a concern that the right to an appeal in criminal matters (in Article 2 of Protocol no. 7) would overburden the Dutch court system. According to the letter of the (then) Minister of Justice to Parliament in 2004, the exception provided for in Article 2(2) of Protocol no. 7 concerning offences of a minor nature, is too limited to ensure that the court system will not be overburdened – especially in light of the dynamic interpretation that the European Court of Human Rights (ECtHR) has applied to ECHR obligations.[6] This sentiment is also reflected by the unilateral declaration that the Netherlands submitted on the signing of the Protocol no. 7.

The only ratified Protocols subjected to reservations or declarations at the time of ratification were Protocols nos 1 and 4. In accordance with the reservation to Protocol no. 1, Article 6(3) of Protocol no. 1 (which concerns free legal assistance in criminal matters) did not apply to the Netherlands Antilles. This reservation was ultimately withdrawn in 1980 when it became known that such a system had in any case been in place for the Netherlands Antilles for twenty years.[7]

The ratification of Protocol no. 4 was delayed for almost twenty years, due to differences of opinion between the Netherlands and the Netherlands Antilles pertaining to the potential implications of Articles 2 and 3 of Protocol no. 4 in case of independence of the Netherlands Antilles. These two Articles respectively guarantee the right to choose one's residence freely and a prohibition on expulsion from the territory of the State of which one is a national. On ratification, the Kingdom of the Netherlands attached a declaration according to which the Netherlands and the Netherlands Antilles would be regarded as two separate entities for the application of Articles 2 and 3 of Protocol no. 4.[8] As a result, the inhabitants of the Netherlands Antilles would not have the choice of relocation to the Netherlands in case of independence.[9]

---

[6] See letter dated 12 October 2004, *Kamerstukken II*, 2004/05, 29 800 VI, no. 9, http://www.tweedekamer.nl/kamerstukken/index.jspt (Unless indicated otherwise, all websites were visited on 2 May 2007).

[7] *Tractatenblad* 1981, 13; Barkhuysen, Van Emmerik and Loof (2002), 336.

[8] Barkhuysen, Van Emmerik and Loof (2002), 336–337.

[9] Ibid., 369.

Table 1

Protocol[10]	Signature	Ratification	Entry into force	Declarations/Reservations
Protocol no. 1	20 March 1952	31 Aug. 1954	31 Aug. 1954	3 declarations concerning Articles 2, 4
Protocol no. 2	6 May 1963	11 Oct. 1966	21 Sept. 1970	2 declarations
Protocol no. 3	6 May 1963	11 Oct. 1966	21 Sept. 1970	2 declarations
Protocol no. 4	15 Nov. 1963	23 June 1982	23 June 1982	3 declarations concerning Articles 3, 5[11]
Protocol no. 5	16 June 1970	19 May 1971	20 Dec. 1971	2 declarations
Protocol no. 6	28 April 1983	25 April 1986	1 May 1986	2 declarations concerning Article 2
Protocol no. 7	22 Nov. 1984			1 declaration concerning Article 2[12]
Protocol no. 8	20 March 1985	11 Dec. 1986	1 Jan. 1990	1 declaration
Protocol no. 9	11 May 1992	23 Nov. 1992	1 Oct. 1994	1 declaration
Protocol no. 10	25 March 1992	23 Nov. 1992		1 declaration
Protocol no. 11	11 May 1994	21 Jan. 1997	1 Nov. 1998	1 declaration
Protocol no. 12	4 Nov. 2000	28 July 2004	1 April 2005	1 declaration concerning Article 2
Protocol no. 13	3 May 2002	10 Feb. 2006	1 June 2006	1 declaration
Protocol no. 14	13 May 2004	2 Feb. 2006		1 declaration

[10] Source: http://conventions.coe.int/Treaty/Commun/ChercheMembres.asp?CM=3&CL=ENG. The large majority of declarations submitted by the Netherlands concern the extension of the ECHR and its Protocols to the Netherlands' overseas territories. These declarations are not reproduced here.

[11] Declaration: "Since, following ratification by the Kingdom of the Netherlands, Protocol no. 4 to the Convention on Human Rights and Fundamental Freedoms, securing certain rights and freedoms other than those already specified in the Convention and Protocol no. 1, applies to the Netherlands and to the Netherlands Antilles, the Netherlands and the Netherlands Antilles are regarded as separate territories for the application of Articles 2 and 3 of the Protocol, in accordance with Article 5, paragraph 4 of the Protocol. Under Article 3, no one may be expelled from or deprived of the right to enter the territory of the State of which he is a national. There is, however, only one nationality (Netherlands) for the whole of the Kingdom. Accordingly, nationality cannot be used as a criterion in making a distinction between the 'citizens' of the Netherlands and those of the Netherlands Antilles, a distinction which is unavoidable since Article 3 of the Protocol applies separately to each of the parts of the Kingdom. This being so, the Netherlands reserve the right to make a distinction in law, for purpose of the application of Article 3 of the Protocol, between Netherlands nationals residing in the Netherlands and Netherlands nationals residing in the Netherlands Antilles." (23 June 1982 to the present).

[12] Declaration: "The Netherlands Government interprets paragraph 1 of Article 2 thus that the right conferred to everyone convicted of a criminal offence to have conviction or sentence reviewed by a higher tribunal relates only to convictions or sentences given in the first instance by tribunals which, according to Netherlands law, are in charge of jurisdiction in criminal matters." (Deposited on 22 November 1984).

2. Belgium[13]

The Kingdom of Belgium came into being as an independent State in 1830 when the Southern provinces of the (then) United Kingdom of the Netherlands seceded after a short uprising.[14] It is a federal democracy with a hereditary monarchy. In its current form, the main federal structures include three regions (*gewesten*), three linguistic communities (*gemeenschappen*) and four linguistic regions (*taalgebieden*).[15] The regions consist of the Brussels region, the Flemish region and the Walloon region.[16] The three linguistic communities are the Flemish community, the French community and the German community.[17] The four linguistic regions consist of the Dutch-speaking region comprising Dutch-speaking provinces; the French-speaking region that comprises the French-speaking provinces; the German-speaking region comprising part of the province of Liege; and the bilingual region of Brussels Capital.[18]

From the perspective of public international law, this internal distinction is relevant, as the regions and communities share the power to conclude international treaties with the federal Government in accordance with the division of competencies provided for in the federal Constitution.[19] However, since the Kingdom of Belgium constitutes a single subject of international law, the regions and communities act as organs of the Belgian State when concluding treaties or representing Belgium in international organizations.[20]

Belgium signed the ECHR on the day of its adoption, 11 November 1950, and finally ratified it on 14 June 1955. This passage of time was not due to any particular political or legal delay, but rather to the traditionally slow pace with which the Belgian Parliament(s) approves international treaties.[21] Belgium also accepted the individual complaints procedure a few weeks after ratification, on

---

[13] In referring to the Belgian State structure (including State organs and courts), the author refers to an official English translation of the Belgian federal constitution available on the website of the federal Parliament, at http://www.fed-parl.be/constitution_uk.html.

[14] Craenen (2004), 3.

[15] See Articles 1–4 of the Belgian Constitution.

[16] Ibid., Article 3.

[17] Ibid., Article 2. The term linguistic community is not precisely defined by law. It is, nonetheless, used to indicate a segment of the population that belongs to a particular language and linguistic territory. Craenen (2004), 5.

[18] See Article 4 of the Belgian Constitution. A linguistic region is a region in which the public authorities may only use the language prescribed by law. In a bilingual region the Flemish and French language have to be treated equally by the public authorities. There is no complete overlap between the regions and the linguistic regions. Moreover, there are also 27 linguistically mixed communes, whose inhabitants have the right to request the use of a language other than that of the region where their communes were located in their dealings with the public authorities. See Craenen (2004), 3–4.

[19] See Article 167 of the Belgian Constitution.

[20] Craenen (2004), 6, 9.

[21] Act of 13 May 1955, Belgian Official Gazette *(Belgisch Staatsblad/Moniteur Belge)* of 19 August 1955, available at http://www.ejustice.just.fgov.be/cgi/welcome.pl. See also Marcus-Helmons and Marcus-Helmons (2002), 167.

5 July 1955. It has subsequently ratified all Protocols to the ECHR, with the exception of Protocol no. 12, although it has been signed since 4 November 2000. The most recent ratification concerns Protocol no. 7.[22] The reluctance to ratify the Protocol no. 12 may relate to a concern that the right to equality guaranteed by this Protocol may fuel the tensions between the French and Flemish speaking regions and communities within the country.

Belgium did not attach any reservations to any of the Protocols, but did attach declarations to Protocols nos 7 and 14, respectively. In relation to Protocol no. 7, the declaration pertains to Article 1, which concerns the procedural safeguards relating to the expulsion of aliens. Belgium declared that it understood the terms "resident" and "lawfully" mentioned in this Article in the sense that is given to them in paragraph 9 of the Explanatory Report of the Council of Europe. As a result, Belgium would exclude from its application any alien who has arrived at a port or other point of entry, but has not yet passed through the immigration control, or who has been admitted to the territory for the purpose only of transit, or for a limited period for a non-residential purpose. This period also covers the period pending a decision on a request for a residence permit. Furthermore, the word "lawfully" refers to the domestic law of the State concerned. It is therefore for domestic law to determine the conditions which must be fulfilled for a person's presence in the territory to be considered lawful.[23] By attaching such a declaration, Belgium indicated to the ECtHR that it expected the Court to follow (and not to deviate from) Belgium's interpretation of these terms. However, since the declaration amounts to a mere unilateral statement, the ECtHR is not bound by it.

In relation to the Protocol no. 14, Belgium's declaration related to the admissibility requirement of the future Article 35 ECHR (as amended by Article 12 of this Protocol), in accordance with which applications would be inadmissible where the applicant has not suffered a significant disadvantage. Belgium's declaration, once again referring to the Explanatory Report of the Council of Europe, was intended to prevent single judges or committees of three judges from developing criteria for interpreting this admissibility requirement on their own accord. Instead, these criteria must be developed by the Chambers and Grand Chamber in an objective manner that prevents the rejection of cases warranting an examination on the merits.[24]

---

[22] After adoption by the first Chamber of the federal Parliament on 18 January 2007, the King signed the law on 2 March 2007. At the time of writing, it had not yet been published in the Belgian Official Gazette. http://www.senate.be/www/?MIval=/dossier&LEG=3&NR=1760&LANG=nl.

[23] http://conventions.coe.int/Treaty/en/Reports/Html/117.htm.

[24] http://conventions.coe.int/Treaty/en/Reports/Html/194.htm.

Table 2

Protocol[25]	Signature	Ratification	Entry into force	Declarations/Reservations
Protocol no. 1	20 March 1952	14 June 1955	14 June 1955	
Protocol no. 2	5 June 1963	21 Sept. 1970	21 Sept. 1970	
Protocol no. 3	5 June 1963	21 Sept. 1970	21 Sept. 1970	
Protocol no. 4	16 Sept. 1963	21 Sept. 1970	21 Sept. 1970	
Protocol no. 5	20 Jan. 1966	21 Sept. 1970	20 Dec. 1971	
Protocol no. 6	28 April 1983	10 Dec 1998	1 Jan. 1999	
Protocol no. 7	11 May 2005	2 March 2007	2 March 2007	1 declaration concerning Article 1[26]
Protocol no. 8	19 March 1985	8 Nov. 1985	1 Jan. 1990	
Protocol no. 9	8 Nov. 1990	1 Aug. 1995	1 Dec. 1995	
Protocol no. 10	25 March 1992	21 Dec. 1992		
Protocol no. 11	11 May 1994	10 Jan. 1997	1 Nov. 1998	
Protocol no. 12	4 Nov. 2000			
Protocol no. 13	3 May 2002	23 June 2003	1 Oct. 2003	
Protocol no. 14	20 April 2005	14 Sept. 2006		1 declaration concerning Article 12[27]

3. Comparison and Conclusion

Both countries ratified the ECHR within five years of its adoption and thereafter also ratified almost all of its additional Protocols. In neither instance had there been any extensive reservations or declarations. In the case of the Netherlands, the reservations to Protocols and delays in ratification that did exist, resulted from its relationship with its overseas territories. Belgian ratification was not affected by the issue of overseas territories (which it does not possess), and with the exception of Protocol no. 12, its federal structure did not seem to pose a severe

---

[25] Source: http://conventions.coe.int/Treaty/Commun/ChercheMembres.asp?CM=3&CL=ENG.

[26] Declaration: "Belgium understands the words 'resident' and 'lawfully' mentioned in Article 1 of this Protocol in the sense that is given to them in paragraph 9 of its Explanatory Report." (Deposited on 11 May 2005).

[27] Declaration: "Concerning Article 12 of the amending Protocol modifying Article 35 of the Convention for the Protection of Human Rights and Fundamental Freedoms, Belgium declares that it understands this provision within the meaning specified in particular in paragraphs 79, 80, 83 and 84 of the Explanatory Report, from which it results that: - the Court shall apply the new admissibility criterion by establishing a case-law allowing to define the legal terms which State this criterion on the basis of an interpretation establishing objective critera of definition (paragraphs 79 and 80); - the new criteron is designed to avoid rejection of cases warranting an examination on the merits (paragraph 83); - the single-judge formations and committees will not be able to apply the new critera in the absence of a clear and well established case-law of the Court's Chambers and Grand Chamber (paragraph 84)." (Deposited on 20 April 2005).

obstacle in the ratification of the ECHR or the Protocols. Both countries revealed some hesitation in relation to the ratification of Protocol no. 7 and it is very likely that the reluctance to grant (any additional) procedural safeguards to asylum seekers contributes to the Netherlands' hesitation to ratify this Protocol. It is interesting that Belgium, which is suffering severe problems in bringing persons to trial without unreasonable delay,[28] has nonetheless ratified Protocol no. 7, despite the additional burdens that this would imply for the (criminal) justice system.

B. Status of the ECHR in National Law: Formal (Doctrinal) Elements

1. *The Netherlands*

a. Relationship between Domestic and International Law

The relationship between domestic and international law in the Netherlands is characterized by its monist character[29] and the supreme position of international treaty law in the Dutch constitutional order.[30] The monist legal tradition was recognized by the Dutch Supreme Court in 1919 and subsequently explicitly introduced in the Dutch legal order in Article 93 of the Constitution of 1953.[31] Article 93 of the present Constitution of 1983 provides that: "Provisions of treaties and of resolutions by international institutions, which may be binding on all persons by virtue of their contents shall become binding after they have been published."[32] The words "by virtue of their contents" indicate that Dutch courts can directly enforce international treaties under certain conditions.

The first is that the parties to the treaty intended to create enforceable rights for individuals – a condition fulfilled in the case of the ECHR and its Protocols.[33] The second and frequently most decisive condition is whether the nature and content of the relevant treaty provision is such that it is capable of judicial enforcement in the absence of any further measures for implementation (i.e. self-executing).[34] The fact that a treaty provision is not self-executing does not,

---

[28] See *infra* Sections D.2.a. and D.3.

[29] Article 93 of the Dutch Constitution; See English text at official website of the Ministry of Interior and Kingdom Relations at http://www.minbzk.nl/contents/pages/6156/grondwet_UK_6-02.pdf.

[30] Article 94 of the Dutch Constitution.

[31] Dutch Supreme Court, Judgement, H.R. 3 March 1919, NJ 1919, 371; Nollkaemper (2005), 435; Hartkamp (2000), 24. Note that all decisions of the Dutch Supreme Court are also available at: http://www.rechtspraak.nl.

[32] Available at http://www.minbzk.nl/contents/pages/6156/grondwet_UK_6-02.pdf.

[33] This implies that courts will usually not consider for direct application (in proceedings between the State and an individual or between two individuals) those treaty provisions that are only directed at the State. For example, in a case concerning the NATO bombardments of Serbia in 1999, the Supreme Court determined that the prohibition of the use of force in Article 2(4) of the United Nations Charter was addressed to States and could therefore not be relied upon by individuals in court proceedings. See HR 29 November 2002, NJ 2003, 35; Nollkaemper (2005), 453–454.

[34] Dutch Supreme Court, Judgement, HR 30 May 1986, NJ 1986, 688; more recently see also

however, imply that it has no internal force in the Netherlands. All treaty provisions are binding as such upon all branches of the central and local legislative and executive authorities, which also have to enforce the resulting obligations within the scope of their powers.[35] In principle, the monist legal tradition also extends to customary international law. However, due to the relatively vague and undefined character of customary international law, its impact in the Dutch legal order remains very limited.[36]

In relation to the ECHR, all substantive rights have now acquired self-executing status in the Dutch legal order, although the extent of the self-executing nature will depend on the circumstances of the case. The most problematic of all the rights in this regard was Article 13 ECHR, whose self-executing nature has only been acknowledged since 1994. For many years, the Supreme Court was quite categorical in determining that Article 13 ECHR did not have self-executing effect, but merely obliged the legislature to provide an effective remedy.[37] However, in 1994 the Administrative Litigation Division of the Council of State confirmed the self-executing character of Article 13 ECHR. Without motivating its decision or its deviation from earlier jurisprudence, it declared Article 16 of the Law on the Intelligence and Security Services non-applicable, on the basis that it violated Article 13 ECHR (in combination with Article 8 ECHR).[38] The Supreme Court subsequently emphasized that the self-executing character of Article 13 ECHR could nonetheless be limited by the circumstances of the case, as it could not be relied upon to attribute to the court system more powers than had been granted by national legislation.[39]

The supremacy of international treaties in the Dutch legal order was also first explicitly introduced in the Constitution of 1953 and is currently regulated in Article 94 of the Constitution of 1983.[40] In accordance with this Article, "statutory regulations in force within the Kingdom shall not be applicable if such application is in conflict with provisions of treaties that are binding on all persons or of resolutions by international institutions".[41] This means that whenever the application of a domestic regulation in a specific case will result in a conflict with a self-executing provision of a (human rights) treaty or international organiza-

Dutch Council of State, Judgement, ABBRvS 15 September 2004, LJN AR 2181; Nollkaemper (2005), 451; Zwaak (2002), 598.

[35] Zwaak (2002), 598; Hartkamp (2000), 24.
[36] Nollkaemper (2005), 436.
[37] Dutch Supreme Court, Judgement, HR 24 February 1960, NJ 1960, 483; Dutch Supreme Court, Judgement, HR 18 February 1986, NJ 1987, 62; Barkhuysen, Van Emmerik and Loof (2000), no. 18, 331.
[38] Dutch Council of State, Judgement, AB 1995, 238 (16 June 1994); Barkhuysen, Van Emmerik and Loof (2000), no. 18, 331.
[39] Dutch Supreme Court, HR 19 April 1996, NJ 1996, 474; In 1986 the Supreme Court made a similar determination in a judgement pertaining to Article 6 ECHR in HR 18 February 1986, NJ 1987, 62; see also Barkhuysen, Van Emmerik and Loof (2000), no. 18, 331.
[40] Swart (1999), 40.
[41] See http://www.minbzk.nl/contents/pages/6156/grondwet_UK_6-02.pdf.

tion, the national court is obliged not to apply the regulation in that case.[42] The supremacy rule is not, however, applicable to customary international law. During the Parliamentary debates leading up to the constitutional revision of 1983, customary international law was described as too vague and uncertain for acquiring supremacy above national law. In addition, it was feared that such supremacy would unduly limit the democratic prerogatives of Parliament.[43]

The status of judgements of international courts and tribunals in the domestic legal order is determined by the so-called incorporation theory, developed by the Supreme Court in jurisprudence pertaining to the ECtHR.[44] In accordance with this theory, the authoritative interpretations of the ECtHR are integrated into the particular treaty provisions to which they apply.[45] This means that the treaty provision in question has to be interpreted in the light of all the relevant ECtHR judgements when applied in the national legal order. The practical consequence is that Dutch State organs are also obliged to apply ECtHR judgements rendered against other States through their application and interpretation of the relevant ECHR Article.[46]

b. The Court System and Scope of Judicial Review

aa. The Court System The Dutch judicial system is currently regulated in the Judicial Organization Act of 1927. In principle, justice is administered in three instances. At the first and second instance, the judges decide questions both of fact and of law, whilst the final instance (appeal in cassation) is restricted to questions of law.[47]

The courts that make up the judiciary are the District Courts, the Courts of Appeal and the Supreme Court with its seat in The Hague.[48] The District Courts are divided into a civil, an administrative, a criminal and a local division;[49] and the Courts of Appeal into a civil, a criminal and a fiscal division; whereas the

---

[42] Zwaak (2002), 598; Swart (1999), 40.

[43] See Parliamentary debates in the Second Chamber, *Kamerstukken II* 1977/78, 15 049, available at http://www.tweedekamer.nl/kamerstukken/index.jspt; see also the preceding judgement of the Dutch Supreme Court, HR 6 March 1962, NJ 1962, 2; Nollkaemper (2005), 440.

[44] Practice regarding the status of decisions of other courts and tribunals in the Dutch legal order are hardly available, although it can be assumed that the incorporation theory would apply in a similar fashion. See Nollkaemper (2005), 436.

[45] Dutch Supreme Court, Judgement, HR 10 November 1989, NJ 1990, 628; Dutch Supreme Court, Judgement, HR 10 May 1996, NJCM-Bulletin 21 (1996), 683–695; Barkhuysen and Van Emmerik (1999), 9.

[46] In accordance with a more restrictive theory supported by some authors, judgements of international tribunals are comparable to the decisions of international organizations, as understood by Articles 93 and 94 of the Constitution. As a result, decisions rendered against other States would not be binding on the Dutch State organs. See Barkhuysen, Van Emmerik and Loof (2000), 331.

[47] Ijzermans (2004), 61.

[48] Ibid, 63–64.

[49] Here a single judge hears small civil claims and all claims including labour and rent law. In criminal cases, their jurisdiction is restricted to minor offences such as traffic offences, poaching,

Supreme Court is divided in a civil, criminal and a fiscal division, with an additional division for complaints about judges.[50]

The administrative judiciary, which is currently regulated by the General Administrative Law Act of 1994 (GALA),[51] has a slightly different organization than the civil and criminal judiciary. Complaints against an administrative decision are first reconsidered by the body that issued the decision in question (administrative revision). Thereafter, review is possible at the administrative division of the District Court. Both parties can subsequently appeal to the Administrative Litigation Division of the Council of State. In principle, no further appeal to the Supreme Court is possible. For disputes pertaining to social security law and the law of civil servants, the Central Appeals Board constitutes the (final) Court of Appeal. For certain specialized areas of law, specialized tribunals are the first and only instance of appeal, such as the Regulatory Industrial Organization Appeals Tribunal that adjudicates disputes concerning economic law.[52]

It is important to note that until the introduction of the GALA in 1994, there was no uniform administrative judiciary. Special administrative courts were established as the need arose and it was also possible to entrust the adjudication of administrative disputes to the Administrative Litigation Division of the Council of State.[53] In addition, there was the controversial system of Appeal to the Crown, according to which one had to launch an appeal against an administrative decision (e.g. the refusal or revoking of a licence) with the Queen and relevant Cabinet Minister, who then decided on the matter by means of Royal Decree.[54] This procedure was abolished after the ECtHR decision in *Benthem v. the Netherlands*,[55] as it did not fulfil the conditions of an independent and impartial tribunal set by Article 6(1) ECHR.

According to the ECtHR, the system of Appeal to the Crown implied that administrative disputes were decided by an administrative organ as opposed to an independent an impartial tribunal. A Royal Decree formally constituted an administrative act that emanated from a Cabinet Minister who was responsible to Parliament. In addition, he or she was the hierarchical superior of the local or regional body against which the appeal was launched. As the Royal Decree itself was further not susceptible to judicial review,[56] the requirements of Article 6(1)

---

public drunkenness etc. See Article 382 of the Code of Criminal Procedure and Article 93 of the Civil Code; see also Ijzermans (2004), 62 et seq.

[50] Ijzermans (2004), 61–62.

[51] Ibid., 66.

[52] Brenninkmeijer (1999), *Dutch Law*, 56.

[53] Ibid.

[54] Engering and Liborang (1999), 42.

[55] *Benthem v. the Netherlands* (appl. no. 8848/80), Judgement (Plenary), 23 October 1985, Series A, Vol. 97.

[56] Although the Administrative Litigation Division of the Council of State advised the relevant Cabinet Minister on the matter, the latter was not bound to the advice. See Brenninkmeijer (1999), *Dutch Law*, 56.

ECHR had not been met.[57] The impact of the *Benthem* case went far beyond the abolition of the Appeal to the Crown, as it effectively triggered a reorganization of the Dutch administrative court system that resulted in the GALA in 1994.[58]

Despite the abolition of the Appeal to the Crown and other reforms introduced by the GALA, certain questions pertaining to the compatibility of the administrative court system with Article 6(1) ECHR remained. These mainly concerned the dual role of the Council of State as an advisory body during the legislative process and as a judicial body during (administrative) litigation.[59] In the *Procola v. Luxembourg* case,[60] the ECtHR held that a combination of these two roles raised doubts about the structural impartiality of the Luxembourg Council of State, whose role was very similar to that of the Dutch Council of State.[61] The Dutch Government nonetheless maintained the position that certain practical adjustments to the *modus operandi* of the Council of State were sufficient to give effect to the *Procola* judgement in the Netherlands. In essence, this implied an arrangement of the composition of the chambers of the Administrative Litigation Division in a manner that takes into account whether any particular chamber member had, during the legislative process, given advice on the subject matter before the chamber.[62]

Whether these measures sufficed to prevent an inherent structural bias by the Council of State remained in dispute. In the *Kleyn v. the Netherlands* case,[63] the ECtHR determined that in the particular circumstances of the case the Administrative Litigation Division met the required objective standard of independence and impartiality required by Article 6(1) ECHR. The ECtHR found nothing in the manner and conditions of appointment of the members of the Council of State, or their terms of office to substantiate the applicants' concerns regarding the body's independence; nor was there any indication of personal bias on the part of any member of the bench that had heard the applicant's appeal.[64] The ECtHR left open the broader, more controversial question of whether the internal structure of the Council of State was capable of ensuring the impartiality and independence of the Administrative Litigation Division in relation to all judicial proceedings. Finally, in February 2007 the Dutch Government agreed to

---

[57] Engering and Liborang (1999), 42.

[58] In the interim period leading up to the adoption of the GALA, the former system of Appeal to the Crown was attributed to the Administrative Litigation Division of the Council of State. See Zwaak (2002), 621; Brenninkmeijer (1999), *Execution*, 193.

[59] See also *infra* Section E.1.b.

[60] *Procola v. Luxembourg* (appl. no. 14570/89), Judgement (Chamber), 28 September 1995, Series A, Vol. 326.

[61] Zwaak (2002), 621.

[62] Letter of the Ministers of Justice and Internal Affairs of 12 November 1998, *Kamerstukken II* 1997/98 25 425, no. 3, available at http://www.tweedekamer.nl/kamerstukken/index.jsp; Barkhuysen, Van Emmerik and Loof (2000), 392.

[63] *Kleyn and Others v. the Netherlands* (appl. nos 39343/98; 39651/98; 43147/98; 46664/99), Judgement (Grand Chamber), 6 May 2003, Reports 2003-VI, 61 et seq.

[64] See also Barkhuysen and Van Emmerik (2005), 16.

a legislative amendment that would in future limit the possibility of simultaneous membership of both divisions.[65] This concession resulted from pressure of Parliament which feared for the structural impartiality of the two divisions, along the lines of the ECtHR jurisprudence.[66]

bb. The Scope of Judicial Review Judicial review in the Netherlands is distinguished by the fact that Dutch courts may review primary legislation against international (human rights) treaties with direct effect but not against (human rights in) the Constitution.[67] The Dutch courts have also developed the practice of reviewing legal relationships between third parties (indirectly) against international human rights treaties.

The introduction of the supremacy of international treaty law in the Constitution of 1953 and currently contained in Article 94 of the Constitution of 1983, simultaneously introduced an explicit power of judicial review in the Dutch constitutional order. This marked the beginning of a significant change in the relationship between the courts and the legislature, as henceforth the courts and not Parliament had the final say in matters touching upon (in particular) human rights.[68] Although the Dutch Constitution has contained a number of provisions on fundamental rights since the beginning of the nineteenth century, the Constitution has consistently forbidden the courts to review acts of Parliament against constitutional provisions pertaining to individual rights. During the constitutional revision of 1983, which included a revision and expansion of the constitutional Bill of Rights, this system was preserved in Article 120 of the Constitution which provides that: "The constitutionality of Acts of Parliament and treaties shall not be reviewed by courts."[69]

The practical consequence is that in relation to domestic legislation, the courts are allowed to review secondary legislation (adopted by lower public bodies) against fundamental rights in the Constitution,[70] but are prevented from reviewing primary legislation adopted by Parliament against those same provisions. At the same time, the court can review an act of Parliament against a directly applicable international human rights treaty provision, which is comparable or even identical to a provision in the Constitution.[71] If a domestic legislative provision is

---

[65] NRC Handelsblad, Thursday 1 February 2007, 3.

[66] When the Government submitted the draft legislation on reforming the Council of State, it initially intended to leave intact that the possibility of simultaneous membership of both divisions. For the Parliamentary debates see *Kamerstukken II* 2005/06, 30 585 no. 2–4 and the third proposal for amendment (*derde nota van wijziging*) of 14 February 2007, available at http://www.tweedekamer.nl/kamerstukken/index.jsp.

[67] Article 120 of the 1983 Constitution.

[68] Swart (1999), 40–41.

[69] See http://www.minbzk.nl/contents/pages/6156/grondwet_UK_6-02.pdf.

[70] For example, courts have reviewed whether limitations imposed by local authorities on freedom of speech are permissible under the Constitution. See Dutch Supreme Court, Judgement, HR 16 May 1986, NJ 1987, 251; Swart (1999), 40.

[71] Zwaak (2002), 598; Hartkamp (2000), 23.

not in conformity with an international human rights treaty, the court is obliged not to apply that regulation in that case. The court may not, however, nullify, repeal or amend the provision in question. It formally remains in force until amended or retracted by Parliament, even though it is not applied.[72]

The courts have generally been rather cautious when reviewing domestic law against the ECHR and will not easily determine that the former is in violation of the latter. Instead, they would interpret the ECHR provisions in a manner that brings them into conformity with domestic law or practice, unless ECtHR case law clearly points in the opposite direction. Sometimes the ECHR provisions are given a restrictive scope and regarded as inapplicable to the case before the court.[73] In those instances in which courts do declare domestic legislation non-applicable, the conflict between the domestic and international norm has to be obvious. In addition, the lacuna that is created by the non-applicability has to be of such a nature that it can be easily filled by the court itself – without encroaching on the policy prerogatives of Parliament.[74] The more detailed the activity required to fill the legislative lacuna, the more hesitant the courts will be in declaring the domestic law non-applicable.[75]

Most problematic are situations where the conflict between the domestic and international norm is clear, but the solution to the conflict is unclear, since there are several ways in which it could be resolved. In such an instance, a court is likely to find that the resolution of the conflict should be left to Parliament.[76] In one instance, the Supreme Court refused to declare non-applicable certain discriminatory tax obligations that were in violation of Article 14 ECHR in combination with Article 1 of Protocol no. 1, in light of the range of different possibilities available for removing the discriminatory measure.[77] It nonetheless urged Parliament to introduce the necessary legislative reforms within a reasonable period of time, as its failure to do so would prompt the Supreme Court to reconsider its decision.[78]

---

[72] Zwaak (2002), 599.

[73] Ibid., 600–601; Swart (1999), 41.

[74] Dutch Supreme Court, Judgement, HR 4 June 1982, NJ 1983, no. 32. No. 32; Hartkamp (2000), 31; Zwaak (2002), 603.

[75] Exceptions can occur where the solution to the conflict between the domestic and international norm is obvious. See Dutch Supreme Court, Judgement, HR 21 March 1986, NJ 1986, 585; Hartkamp (2000), 32.

[76] Hartkamp (2000), 32.

[77] Dutch Supreme Court, Judgement, HR 15 July 1998, BNB 1998, 293; Hartkamp (2000), 33; Feteris (2000), 483.

[78] The Supreme Court's restraint was also influenced by the fact that Parliament was already in the process of preparing new legislation, relevant to the case at hand. See also Dutch Supreme Court, Judgement, HR 12 May 1999, NJ 2000, 170. According to Hartkamp (2000), 33, the Supreme Court has in practice introduced an exception to Article 94 of the Constitution: The conflicting domestic norm remains applicable where its non-applicability would result in a violation of the constitutional principle that important policy issues should be decided by the democratically elected legislature. Only where the legislature fails to exercise this function, can the dispute be resolved by the courts.

Authors have criticized this practice, which effectively leaves the plaintiffs empty handed, arguing that a mere determination of a violation of the ECHR without attaching any material consequences, would not be in keeping with the spirit of Articles 1 and 13 ECHR. In addition, it would not give sufficient weight to the superior nature of the ECHR in the Dutch legal order in accordance with Articles 93 and 94 of the Constitution.[79] This argument has thus far not found resonance with the ECtHR. In *Auerbach v. the Netherlands*, the Court determined that a judgement according to which there is a violation of an ECHR provision can under certain circumstances be regarded as adequate redress in itself.[80] Judicial restraint on the part of domestic courts in refusing to provide a (concrete) legal remedy itself would therefore not necessarily constitute a violation of Article 13 ECHR.[81]

Finally, it is worth noting that during the constitutional revision of 1983 the Government took the position that constitutional and treaty based individual rights could have third party applicability (*Drittwirkung*).[82] It was, however, left to the courts to develop the manner in which the third party applicability took shape, as well as the conditions attached thereto.[83] In accordance with court practice, the third party applicability of the rights in the ECHR depends on whether the right in question is self-executing, as well as whether it is capable of imposing an obligation on private persons in addition to public authorities.[84] The courts generally prefer to avoid direct applicability of these rights between third parties (*direkte Drittwirkung*), as this would lead to a high percentage of direct conflicts between such rights and enhance the possibility of the creation of a hierarchy of rights.[85] Instead, they prefer to apply a milder form of third party applicability (*indirekte Drittwirkung*), according to which general principles of civil law such as reasonableness and proportionality are interpreted in the light of the ECHR.[86]

2. Belgium

a. Relation between Domestic and International Law

The Belgian legal system is characterized by its relatively recent acceptance of the monist legal tradition, as well as some ambivalence as to the exact status of international law in the domestic constitutional order. Although it is accepted that

---

[79] Barkhuysen and Van Emmerik, (2006), 62; see also Feteris (2000), 484.

[80] *Auerbach v. the Netherlands* (appl. no. 45600/99), Judgement, 29 January 2002 (not reported), Beslissingen in Belastingzaken, Nederlandse Belastingsrechtspraak, BNB 2002–126, 1104–1107.

[81] See also Nollkaemper (2005), 462.

[82] Alkema (1994), 11.

[83] Hartkamp (2000), 26.

[84] Alkema (1994), 10.

[85] Hartkamp (2000), 28.

[86] Alkema (1994), 10; Hartkamp (2000), 30. However, the line between direct and indirect third party applicability is not always easy to draw. For examples in relation to Article 8 ECHR, see Dutch Supreme Court, Judgement, HR 9 January 1987, NJ 1987, 928; Dutch Supreme Court, Judgement, HR 15 April 1994, NJ 1994, 608; Dutch Supreme Court, HR 1 July 1988, NJ 1988, 1000.

directly applicable international law enjoys supremacy over primary and secondary legislation, it remains disputed as to whether it also enjoys supremacy over the constitution.

Despite the fact that there have been several calls to this effect through the years, the Belgian Constitution does not contain any explicit clause pertaining to the relationship between international and national law.[87] Until 1971 it was generally accepted that Belgium was a dualistic country in relation to international treaties. As a result, a treaty such as the ECHR could only be invoked by means of a reference to the Belgian law which enshrined the relevant treaty clause in the national legislation.[88]

However, in 1971 the Supreme Court of Appeal, under the influence of European law, introduced the monistic theory in Belgium concerning treaties that were validly adopted and of a directly applicable nature.[89] In relation to the first criteria Article 167 of the Belgian Constitution determines that treaties require the consent of either the federal Parliament, or the legislatures of the regions and linguistic communities, in accordance with the division of competencies between them. Where such consent has not been given, the treaty has no effect in the domestic legal order and cannot be applied by the courts.[90] Strictly speaking, treaties also have to be published in the official gazette before they can be binding on third parties.[91] However, such publication tends to take place in a rather haphazard fashion. Some authors claim that only a third of all Belgian treaties are published and frequently in an inaccurate and incomplete fashion.[92]

In order for a treaty norm to qualify as directly applicable, it has to define complete and precise rights and obligations which can be enforced in an immediate fashion that does not require the intervention of the legislature. Whether this is the case will depend on the specific context of the case in question, as well as

---

[87] Alen (2000), 40. During the constitutional reform of 1993, only the Chamber of Representatives was willing to include a clause that determined the non-applicability of statutes and decrees that violated international law with direct application. This proposal was ultimately rejected.

[88] Alen (2000), 40.

[89] Belgian Supreme Court of Appeal, Judgement, Cass., 27 May 1971, Arr. Cass. 1971, 959, 460; Alen (2000), 40. Although the *Franco Suisse Le Ski* case concerned European Community Law, the reasoning was subsequently appplied to the ECHR. In Belgium, the ECHR is closely associated with European Community Law, due to the fact that it represents general principles of Community law, resembling the constitutional traditions common to the Contracting States. See document of the Belgian Senate 2-575/./2002/2001, http://www.senate.be.

[90] Belgian Supreme Court of Appeal, Judgement, Cass. 12 March 2001, Arr. Cass. 2001, 395. Note that executive agreements which are adopted to give effect to another treaty (which has been adopted in accordance with the correct procedure), do not require the separate consent of Parliament or, where applicable, the regions or communities. See Belgian Supreme Court of Appeal, Judgement, Cass., 2 May 2002, no. RC-2521, CASES 557; See also Wouters and Van Eeckhoutte (2006), 152, 155.

[91] See Belgian Supreme Court of Appeal, Judgement, Cass., 19 March 1981, Arr. Cass., 1980–81, 808; Wouters and Van Eeckhoutte (2006), 157.

[92] Ibid.

the nature and scope of the right or obligation that is to be directly applied.[93] In addition to this self-executing nature of the treaty norm (an objective criterion),[94] the Supreme Court of Appeal also examines whether the Contracting Parties had the intention to create directly applicable rights and obligations (subjective criterion).[95] The Supreme Administrative Court, however, seems to focus increasingly on the objective test while distancing itself from the (original) intent of the Contracting Parties.[96]

The monist theory introduced by the *Franco Suisse Le Ski* decision also extends to complete and precise binding decisions of international organizations. Such decisions do not require separate consent by the relevant legislature, but must be published in the official gazette in order to be binding on third parties.[97] As far as customary international law is concerned, the Supreme Court of Appeal already in 1906 confirmed that customary law is part of the law of the land.[98] In addition, it does not require any separate consent by the legislature, or publication in the official gazette. Although the Supreme Court of Appeal has in the past been reluctant to acknowledge the direct effect of customary international law,[99] it has recently taken a more favourable position, notably in relation to the customary law of immunities.[100]

As far as the ECHR is concerned, the question of the direct applicability intensified in the wake of the *Marckx* decision of the ECtHR,[101] according to which the Belgian law of succession discriminated against illegitimate children. Subsequently several lower courts relied directly on Article 8(1) ECHR when refusing to apply discriminatory clauses of Belgian law pertaining to adoption and succession and substituted it with the legislation pertaining to legitimate children.[102] However, the Supreme Court of Appeal thereafter determined that only the negative obligations flowing from Article 8(1) ECHR (such as the prohibition to interfere with family life) could be sufficiently complete and precise to justify their direct applicability. The positive obligations flowing from this

---

[93] Wouters and Van Eeckhoutte (2006), 218.

[94] See Bossuyt (2006), 115 who prefers the term "self-sufficient".

[95] Belgian Supreme Court of Appeal, Judgement, Cass, 21 April 1983; R.J.C.B., 1985, 22; Alen (2000), 42.

[96] Alen (2000), 42; Wouters and Van Eeckhoutte (2006), 214.

[97] Wouters and Van Eeckhoutte (2006), 163.

[98] Belgian Supreme Court of Appeal, Judgement, Cass., 25 January 1906, Pas., 1906, I, 109, CASES, 426; Wouters and Van Eeckhoutte (2006), 159.

[99] Belgian Supreme Court of Appeal, Judgement, Cass., 26 May 1966, Pas. 1966, I, 1211; Wouters and Van Eeckhoutte (2006), 228.

[100] For example, the Supreme Court of Appeal has determined that the then Israeli Prime Minister Sharon can rely on the customary international rule of immunity applicable to a Head of State before a domestic court. See Belgian Supreme Court of Appeal, Judgement, Cass., 12 February 2003, available at http://www.juridat.be. See also Wouters and Van Eeckhoutte (2006), 219.

[101] *Marckx v. Belgium* (appl. no. 6833/74), Judgement (Plenary), 13 June 1979, Series A, Vol. 31.

[102] See for example, Court of First Instance in Gent, Judgement, Rb. Gent., 16 April 1984, R.W. 1984–85, 354; Alen (2000), 521.

Article would not qualify as such, as they left the legislature with several options for ensuring a normal family life for legitimate and illegitimate children alike.[103] The Supreme Court of Appeal therefore concluded that a legislative amendment was required to bring the adoption and succession law in line with the *Marckx* decision.

Although legislation to this effect was introduced in 1987,[104] the issue of unequal treatment of illegitimate children in matters pertaining to succession lingered on with respect to the inter-phase between the *Marckx* decision and the (non-retroactive) 1987 legislation. Both the Constitutional Court[105] and the ECtHR[106] took a different view from the one earlier expressed by the Supreme Court of Appeal and concluded that the positive obligations in question were sufficiently precise and complete for the purpose of having direct effect in Belgian law. As a result, courts had to apply the principle of equal treatment to legitimate and illegitimate children in relation to all questions of succession that arose during the inter-phase. The Supreme Court of Appeal subsequently also adopted this position.[107] This evolution of the direct applicability of the obligations flowing from Article 8(1) ECHR reflects that the objective (contextual) criterion has become decisive in determining whether a particular right or obligation under the ECHR is directly enforceable. Over time, most rights in the ECHR and its Protocols have been accepted as such, with Article 13 ECHR being the most prominent exception.[108]

Before the *Franco Suisse le Ski* decision,[109] treaties had the same status in domestic law as statutory law. As a result and in accordance with the principle of *lex posterior derogat priori*, treaties had overriding power over prior legislation, but not over subsequent, contradictory legislation.[110] However, since the *Franco Suisse le Ski* decision, directly applicable treaties that have been validly adopted have overriding effect over prior as well as subsequent statutory law. The supremacy of treaty law thus only applies when the conditions of validity and direct effect are met.[111]

---

[103] Belgian Supreme Court of Appeal, Judgement, Cass., 3 October 1983, Arr. Cass., 1983–84.
[104] See the Act of 27 April 1987, Belgian Official Gazette, 27 May 1987, available at http://www.ejustice.just.fgov.be/cgi/welcome.pl.
[105] See Belgian Constitutional Court, Judgement, CA no. 18/91, 4 July 1991 and Belgian Constitutional Court, Judgement, CA no. 83/93, 1 December 1993, available at http://www.arbitrage.be.
[106] *Vermeire v. Belgium* (appl. no. 12849/87), Judgement (Chamber), 29 November 1991, Series A, Vol. 214-C.
[107] Belgian Supreme Court of Appeal, Judgement, Cass., 15 May 1992, R.W. 1992–1993, 235; Belgian Supreme Court of Appeal, Judgement, Cass., 21 October 1993, Larcier Cass., 1993, No. 1003; Alen (2000), 522; Marcus-Helmons and Marcus-Helmons (2002), 171.
[108] Alen (2000), 43; Wouters and Van Eeckhoutte (2006), 215; Marcus-Helmons and Marcus-Helmons (2002), 169.
[109] Belgian Supreme Court of Appeal, Judgement, Cass., 27 May 1971, Arr. Cass. 1971, 959, 460.
[110] Alen (2000), 41; Wouters and Van Eeckhoutte (2006), 223.
[111] Ibid.

Although the *Franco-Suisse Le Ski* decision did not concern a conflict between a treaty and the Belgian Constitution, the decision leads many authors to believe that a validly adopted treaty with direct effect would also have supremacy above the Belgian Constitution.[112] However, the position of the Belgian constitutional court is more ambivalent in this regard. This court inter alia has the power to review the legality of legislative acts that amount to consent to be bound by an international treaty.[113] When exercising this power the Constitutional Court also reviews the substantive treaty provisions against the Constitution, including whether the treaty provisions respect the Belgian federal structure and whether they conform to the fundamental rights guaranteed in the Constitution.[114] It is, therefore, theoretically possible that the Constitutional Court may determine that an international treaty infringes the Constitution and therefore cannot be applied in the domestic legal order.

The line of argument of the Constitutional Court is based on the logic that the legislature may not do indirectly what is prohibited directly, namely the adoption of legislative acts that violate of the Constitution.[115] This position deviates from the public international law principle that a State cannot escape international responsibility for binding treaty obligations by relying on provisions of domestic law. Authors have also criticized the Constitutional Court's position for being potentially harmful to Belgium's international relations. In this context one has to keep in mind that the preliminary ruling procedure by means of which lower courts request the Constitutional Court to rule on the constitutionality of certain legislation is still possible years after a treaty has entered into force in Belgium.[116] However, given that the Constitutional Court has, thus far, never concluded that the adoption of an international treaty violated the Constitution, this particular problem for the time being remains theoretical.

In addition, the Act of 9 March 2003 that expanded the judicial review power of the Constitutional Court[117] explicitly excludes any future constitutional review of constitutive acts of the European Union, as well as the ECHR and its Protocols by means of the preliminary ruling procedure. The legislature therefore clearly wished to secure the superior position of primary community law and the ECHR in the Belgian legal order.[118] It is further interesting to note that in 2004 the

---

[112] Alen (2000), 43.

[113] See *infra* Section B.2.b.ii.

[114] Belgian Constitutional Court, Judgement, CA no. 26/91, 16 October 1991 and Belgian Constitutional Court, Judgement, CA no. 12/94, 3 February 1994, available at http://www.arbitrage.be; Alen (2000), 43; Vanden Heede en Goedertier (2006), 280 et seq.

[115] Alen (2000), 43; Vanden Heede and Goedertier (2006), 282.

[116] For example, as late as 1994 the Belgian Supreme Administrative Court presented the Belgian Constitutional Court with the question whether the act consenting to the ratification of the ECHR is compatible with the equality principle in the Belgian Constitution. See Belgian Constitutional Court, Judgement, CA no. 33/94, 26 April 1994; Vanden Heede and Goedertier (2006), 282; see also Alen (2000), 43.

[117] See, more extensively, below in Section B.2.b.ii.

[118] See extensively Vanden Heede and Goedertier (2006), 282 et seq.

Supreme Court of Appeal took an explicit stand in the *Vlaams Blok* decision, by declaring that a directly applicable treaty such as the ECHR prevailed over the Constitution.[119] As will be illustrated below, the motivation for taking a position that deviates from that of the Constitutional Court is closely related to growing tensions between the two courts regarding their respective roles in applying international treaties such as the ECHR.

In relation to customary international law, recent practice confirms that directly applicable customary law can have precedence over conflicting domestic statutory law.[120] However, it remains unclear if and to what extent customary international law would also override the Constitution in case of conflict. As far as the status of judgements of international courts and tribunals in domestic law are concerned, the Supreme Court of Appeal follows the incorporation theory.[121] Consequently, one can base an alleged violation of an ECHR obligation on the interpretation of the relevant obligation by the ECtHR – regardless of whether the interpretation resulted from a decision against Belgium or another Contracting Party.[122]

b. The Court System and Scope of Judicial Review

aa. The Court System The Belgian court system can essentially be divided in the regular courts, the disciplinary councils and a diffuse system of administrative review bodies.[123] The regular court system includes civil courts, criminal courts, labour courts, commercial courts and – in war time – the military courts.[124] The organization of the regular court system is rather complex. At the first level, there are justices of the peace in civil and commercial matters and police judges in criminal matters. An appeal against these judgements can be launched at the Court of First Instance or the Commercial Court.[125] From the Court of First Instance and the Commercial Court an appeal is possible to the Court of Appeal, while an appeal against the Labour Court is lodged with the Labour Court of Appeal. From these courts one can appeal to the Supreme Court of Appeal on points of law. The latter has jurisdiction over the whole of Belgium, in order to guarantee the unity of jurisprudence within the federal structure.[126]

---

[119] Belgian Supreme Court of Appeal, Judgement, Cass., 9 November 2004, available at http://www.juridat.be; Brems (2006), 710.

[120] Wouters and Van Eeckhoutte (2006), 229.

[121] See also *supra* Section B.1.a.

[122] E.g. Belgian Supreme Court of Appeal, Judgement, Cass., 10 May 1989, J.T., 1989 330; Alen (2000), 71; Wouters and Van Eeckhoutte (2006), 171–172.

[123] See also Article 16 of the Belgian Constitution.

[124] See Article 147, Article 150, Article 151, Article 156 and Article 157 of the Belgian Constitution; see also Alen (2000), 345.

[125] In some cases the Court of First Instance, the Commercial Court or the Labour Court directly serves as the court of first instance.

[126] Article 147 of the Belgian Constitution; Alen (2000), 347.

The disciplinary councils were created in accordance with public law for the purpose of supervising professional organizations such as the Bar Association or Medical Council.[127] They consist of a three layered system, within which the respective professional council serves as a first instance. Appeal is possible to an Appeals Board and eventually to the Supreme Court of Appeal. In the wake of the *Le Compte, Van Leuven and De Meyere* case,[128] the Supreme Court of appeal affirmed that the procedures before these bodies concern civil rights and obligations, as a result of which the conditions of Article 6(1) ECHR are applicable.[129]

No unified system of administrative courts exists in Belgium. Instead, legislation provides for a variety of different avenues for appeal against decisions pertaining to administrative disputes. Frequently, the Supreme Administrative Court (the Belgian equivalent of the Council of State) serves as a final instance of appeal.[130] The Supreme Administrative Court was created by the law of 23 December 1946[131] and is divided into an Administration Section and a Legislative Section. Whereas the former serves as the highest administrative judicial body in relation to a range of administrative disputes, the latter exercises *ex ante* review of primary legislation, i.e. the acts of the federal Parliament as well as the decrees of the regions and linguistic communities.[132] Once appointed, members of the Supreme Administrative Court are allocated either to the Administration Section or the Legislative Section and there is no possibility of dual membership.[133] Due to this clear, formal separation between the two sections, it is unlikely that the Belgian Administrative Supreme Court would encounter the kind of structural problems in relation to impartiality and dependence as was the case with the Luxembourg Council of State in the *Procola* decision.[134]

bb. The Scope of Judicial Review The competence to review *a posteriori* whether a fundamental constitutional or treaty right has been violated has not been given to one single court of law. The competence for review partly depends on the nature of the act that is to be reviewed (executive versus legislative) and partly on

---

[127] See also Article 146 of the Belgian Constitution.

[128] *Le Compte, Van Leuven and De Meyere v. Belgium* (appl. nos 6878/75; 7238/75), Judgement (Chamber), 23 June 1981, Series A, Vol. 43; Marcus-Helmons and Marcus-Helmons (2002), 181.

[129] E.g. Belgian Supreme Court of Appeal, Judgement, Cass, 2 June 1983, Arr. Cass. 1982–83, 1217; Alen (2000), 352.

[130] However, due to the diffuse system appeals in administrative proceedings can sometimes also be launched with the Supreme Court of Appeal. See Van Damme (2001), 72.

[131] Since 1993 the Belgian Supreme Administrative Court also enjoys constitutional recognition in Article 160 of the Constiution. See also http://www.raadvst-consetat.be; Van Damme (2001), 71.

[132] Van Damme (2001), 75.

[133] When this happens, the work is organized in such a manner that members who have advised on a certain legislative text cannot be involved in appeals lodged with the Administrative Section against the same text.

[134] Van Damme (2001), 85. *Procola v. Luxembourg* (appl. no. 14570/89), Judgement (Chamber), 28 September 1995, Series A, Vol. 326.

the formal source of the right (constitutional rights versus treaty rights). Only in relation to *executive* acts do all courts have the power to exercise review against the constitution and directly applicable treaties such as the ECHR. In fact, all courts are obliged to refrain from applying general or individual executive acts that are contrary to fundamental rights in the Constitution, the ECHR or other directly applicable treaties.[135] Such acts may also be annulled or suspended by the Supreme Administrative Court.[136]

As far as *legislative acts* are concerned, the competence to review federal and regional legislation against the rights in Title II of the Constitution was introduced (progressively) by constitutional amendment in 1988 and remains reserved for the Constitutional Court. The competence to review federal and regional legislation directly against the ECHR (and other directly applicable treaties) was introduced through the *Franco Suisse Le Ski* decision in 1971 and remains reserved for the ordinary courts and the Supreme Administrative Court.

The creation of a Constitutional Court with the power to review (and subsequently annul contradicting) legislation of the federal and regional Parliaments is a relatively recent phenomenon, as the Court was only created in 1983.[137] Moreover, between 1983 and 1988 the Constitutional Court's competence to review federal and regional legislation was limited to reviewing whether such legislation respected the constitutional division of competencies between the federal Parliament, the regions and the linguistic communities.[138] In accordance with the federal reforms that were introduced in 1980, the regions and linguistic communities could – in relation to certain subject matters – adopted legislation with the same hierarchical standing as Parliamentary statutes. The notion of a Constitutional Court exercising constitutional review was, therefore, introduced as a mechanism for protecting Belgium's federal structure. It also marked the end of the doctrine of the "inviolability of the law", according to which courts were obliged to apply statutory law even if it clearly contradicted the Constitution.[139]

---

[135] Article 159 of the Belgian Constitution; Theunis (2005), par. I. 3.6.

[136] Van Damme (2001), 80; Craenen (2004), 20; Alen (2000), 397, 414. Administrative acts declared non-applicable by the ordinary courts merely have *inter partes* effect and the norm as such remains in force. However, once the Belgian Supreme Administrative Court has nullified an administrative act, this applies *ex tunc* and *erga omnes*.

[137] Van Damme (2001), 82. The Court was recently renamed from Court of Arbitration to Constitutional Court. See Act of 7 May 2007, Belgian Official Gazette, 8 May 2007, available at http://www.ejustice.just.fgov.be/cgi.welcome.pl. The Administrative Section of the Belgian Supreme Administrative Court is authorized solely to annul or suspend administrative acts or decision by lower administrative courts. The power to annul or suspend primary legislation in the form acts or decrees belongs exclusively to the Constitutional Court.

[138] See Article 142 of the Belgian Constitution; Alen (2000), 45; see also Vanden Heede and Goedertier (2006), 240 et seq.

[139] In 1950 the Supreme Court of Appeal watered down this doctrine by introducing the notion of the presumption of constitutionality. In cases where it is doubtful whether a law violated the Constitution, one had to depart from presumption that the legislature did not intend to do so. This presumption offered the courts some leeway to prevent a conflict with the Constitution by interpreting statutes in accordance with the Constitution. However, where this was not possible and

The Constitutional Court's power to review legislation against the fundamental rights in Title II of the Constitution was first introduced during the constitutional reform of 1988 as an extension of this federalist policy. During the 1988 reform, the power to regulate education was transferred to the linguistic communities, resulting in the need for a mechanism that ensured the equal treatment of Belgium's linguistic communities.[140] Consequently, the Constitutional Court was also invested with the power to review legislation against the right to equality before the law laid down in Articles 10 and 11 of the Constitution, as well as the freedom of education as guaranteed in Article 24 of the Constitution.

In the course of time the review of legislation against the equality clauses gained momentum and in practice became the primary task of the Constitutional Court.[141] The Court interpreted its power to review legislation against Articles 10 and 11 of the Constitution in a broad fashion in order to prohibit all kinds of discrimination. Since all legal questions put to the Court could be reformulated (albeit sometimes artificially) in a manner that concerned the equality clauses, the Constitutional Court also increasingly reviewed legislation against the other rights in Title II of the Constitution.[142] When exercising its power of review the Constitutional Court further interpret the rights in Title II of the Constitution in accordance with relevant binding treaty provisions that are similar in scope. For example, the Constitutional Court has followed ECtHR jurisprudence in determining that a higher level of scrutiny is required when reviewing the compatibility of "questionable" limitation criteria such as gender,[143] nationality[144] or birth with the equality principle in Articles 10 and 11 of the Constitution.[145] In this manner, the constitutional and treaty rights form an inseparable whole.[146]

Since 2003, the Constitutional Court has the explicit power to review such legislation against all the rights guaranteed in Title II of the Constitution and it is therefore no longer necessary to link the question posed to the Court to an (artificial construction of) the equality clauses in the Constitution.[147] However,

---

statutory provisions clearly violated the Constitution, the courts remained obliged to apply them. See Belgian Supreme Court of Appeal, Judgement, Cass., 20 April 1950, Pas. 1950, I. 560; Alen (2000), 44.

[140]   Article 127 and Article 130 of the Belgian Constitution.

[141]   Alen (2000), 47; see also Theunis (2005), par. 9.

[142]   Alen (2000), 47; see also Theunis (2005), par. 9; Vanden Heeden and Goedertier (2006), 242.

[143]   Belgian Constitutional Court, Judgement, CA no. 166/2003, available at http://www.arbitrage.be.

[144]   Belgian Constitutional Court, Judgement, CA, no. 166/2003, http://www.arbitrage.be.

[145]   Belgian Constitutional Court, Judgement, CA no. 140/2004, available at http://www.arbitrage.be; see also Theunis (2005), par. 10.

[146]   Such international law friendly interpretation also extends to treaty provisions that do not have direct effect in the domestic legal order. See Belgian Constitutional Court, Judgement, CA no. 106/2003 of 22 July 2003; Belgian Constitutional Court, Judgement, CA, no. 136/2004, available at http://www.arbitrage.be; Theunis (2005), par. 2.4.; Van den Heede and Goedertier (2006), 247–248; Wouters and Van Eeckhoutte (2006), 227; Theunis (2005), par. 6.

[147]   See Act of 9 March 2003; Vanden Heede and Goedertier (2006), 242 et seq.

it still does not have the power to review federal or regional legislation directly against the ECHR, as this competence is reserved for the ordinary courts and the Supreme Administrative Court.[148] In accordance with the *Franco Suisse Le Ski* decision, they have the competence to review such legislation against directly applicable treaty provisions and are obliged to refrain from enforcing any law that is contrary to such treaty provisions.[149] The ordinary courts for their part do not have the right to review federal or regional statutes against the Constitution. If one of the parties in a dispute before an ordinary court claims that a legislative act infringes the Constitution, the court in question must refer the matter to Constitutional Court for a preliminary ruling.[150]

This parallel system of control with ordinary jurisdictions (directly) reviewing the conformity with treaty provisions and the Constitutional Court reviewing the conformity with constitutional provisions can result in practical complications. Since there is a considerable overlap between directly applicable treaty provisions (of the ECHR) and constitutional provisions, parties invoking a violation of human rights habitually rely on both constitutional provisions and treaty provisions.[151] This has lead to a growing tension between the Supreme Court of Appeal and the Constitutional Court in relation to their respective roles in interpreting international treaty rights. This was prominently illustrated by the *Vlaams Blok* decision,[152] in which the applicants invoked Articles 10 and 11 ECHR, as well as Articles 19, 26 and 27 of the Belgian Constitution and subsequently requested a referral to the Constitutional Court for a preliminary ruling. The Supreme Court of Appeal rejected this request, arguing that in light of the ECHR's primacy over the Constitution the latter could not restrict the freedoms of expression, assembly and association any further than the ECHR. As the interpretation and application of the ECHR belongs in the first place to the ordinary judge and the Constitution did not in the present case offer more protection than the ECHR, there was no reason to request a preliminary ruling. In essence, therefore, the Supreme Court of Appeal used the argument of the primacy of the ECHR over the Constitution to strengthen its own position *vis-à-vis* that of the Constitutional Court, which has lead to increased tensions between the two courts.[153]

When reviewing legislative or executive acts against the obligations under the

---

[148] Alen (2000), 43; Brems (2006), 710; Marcus-Helmons and Marcus-Helmons (2002), 178. An attempt to extend the powers of the Constitutional Court to facilitate the reviewing of legislation directly against the ECHR failed in 2000. Such expansion would have encroached upon the powers of the ordinary courts and was therefore politically and legally problematic. See document of the Belgian Senate, 2-575/./, 2000/2001, http://www.senate.be.

[149] Alen (2000), 44; Theunis (2005), par. 6; Alen (2000), 41; Wouters and Van Eeckhoutte (2006), 223.

[150] Brems (2006), 709; Theunis (2005), par. 7; Craenen (2004), 51–52.

[151] Brems (2006), 710; Vanden Heede and Goedertier (2006), 280 et seq.

[152] Belgian Supreme Court of Appeal, Judgement, Cass., 9 November 2004, available at http://www.juridat.be; see also Brems (2006), 710.

[153] See also Brems (2006), 709–710. The Belgian Parliament is currently considering a legislative amendment that would oblige the ordinary courts (subject to some exceptions) to first refer the

ECHR, Belgian courts will not easily conclude that the domestic law or practice violates the ECHR. Instead, they would first attempt to interpret domestic law in accordance with international obligations such as the ECHR, in accordance with the premise that the legislature does not have the intention to violate obligations under international law.[154] Where the violation of an international treaty obligation is clear, non-applicability of the domestic law would result if the lacuna that is created by it can be easily filled by the court itself. The more detailed the activity required to fill the legislative or executive lacuna, the more hesitant the courts will become in declaring the domestic law non-applicable. The controversies surrounding the direct enforceability of positive obligations flowing from Article 8(1) ECHR in the wake of the *Marckx* decision,[155] illustrates the hesitance of the courts to encroach upon the policy prerogatives of the legislature.

At first sight one may be tempted to think that the introduction of constitutional review of the fundamental rights in the constitution in 1988 and the recent expansion of the Constitutional Court's competence in this regard, may have reduced the need for directly invoking international treaty rights before ordinary courts. Given the large overlap between the constitutional and treaty rights and the fact that the Constitutional Court interprets the constitutional rights in light of corresponding international provisions, it is theoretically possible that individuals may be more inclined to invoke their constitutional rights before the ordinary courts and request a referral to the Constitutional Court for a preliminary ruling. However, in practice it seems that individuals rather invoke constitutional as well as treaty rights before the ordinary courts and eventually attempt to obtain a referral to the constitutional court. In this way, they explore all avenues for obtaining a maximum of human rights protection.

Although the Belgian Constitution is silent on the third party applicability of fundamental rights, Belgian practice confirms that constitutional as well as treaty rights can have third party application in the Belgian legal order.[156] Most legal authors recognize that when applying fundamental (treaty) rights between private individuals, the interests at stake are not entirely comparable to those involved when individuals invoke fundamental rights *vis-à-vis* the State.[157] As a result, Belgian doctrine strongly favours indirect *Drittwirkung* (the interpretation of general principles of private law in accordance with fundamental (treaty) rights) to direct *Drittwirkung* (direct invocation of fundamental (treaty) rights between private individuals). Even so, court practice reflects that the Belgian

---

matter to the Constitutional Court, where a party relies on rights covered both in the Constitution an the ECHR. See document of Belgian Senate, 4-12/./, 2007, http://www.senate.be.

[154] Wouters and Van Eeckhoutte (2006), 210–211.

[155] *Marckx v. Belgium* (appl. no. 6833/74), Judgement (Plenary), 13 June 1979, Series A, Vol. 31.

[156] Van Leuven (2006), 171; Alen (2000), 52.

[157] Van Leuven (2006), 175–176; Alen (2000), 53.

courts recognize both direct and indirect *Drittwirkung* and that the distinction between the two concepts is a matter of degree.[158]

3. Comparison and Conclusion

The above analysis reveals remarkable similarities between the Netherlands and Belgium in relation to the status of the ECHR in the two countries, despite marked differences between their constitutional orders. As far as the differences are concerned, the Dutch Constitution on the one hand explicitly accepts the superiority of international treaty law, also in relation to the Constitution. The Belgian Constitution on the other hand does not regulate the status of international law in the domestic order. In addition, there seems to be a difference of opinion between the Belgian Constitutional Court and the Supreme Court of Appeal, as to whether international treaty law would also prevail over the Constitution. In addition, the Netherlands has a centralist form of Government whereas Belgium is a federalist State. The monist legal tradition in relation to treaty law is also much older in the Netherlands than in Belgium. The Netherlands do not have a system for reviewing primary legislation against the fundamental rights in the Constitution, whereas Belgium has introduced such a mechanism progressively since 1988. Finally, Dutch courts do not have the power to nullify administrative or legislative acts (in violation of the ECHR), whereas in Belgium the Supreme Administrative Court and the Constitutional Court respectively have such power.

These differences have not significantly affected the standing of the ECHR in domestic law in the two countries. The practice by means of which the Belgian Constitutional Court interprets the Constitution and the ECHR as an inseparable whole supports the argument that at least in as far as the ECHR is concerned, international law does not rank below the Constitution in either of the two countries. Even though the Belgian Constitutional Court has not yet explicitly acknowledged the superior status of the ECHR in relation to the Belgian Constitution, its treatment of the ECHR when interpreting the Constitution implies that that the ECHR would at least be equal in rank to the Constitution. This position is also supported by the fact that since 2003 legislation prevents Belgian courts from questioning the constitutionality of the ECHR and its Protocols by means of the preliminary ruling procedure.

Moreover, the ordinary courts in both countries have now in principle accepted that direct applicability of the obligations under the ECHR. In both countries, the extent of the direct applicability of a particular ECHR obligation will depend on whether, in the context of the particular case, it is sufficiently complete and

---

[158] Van Leuven (2006), 179. For examples pertaining to Article 8 ECHR, see Court of First Instance, Brussels, 21 November 1990, J.L.M.B. 1991, 24; Court of First Instance, Brussels, 30 June 1997, JT 1997, 710; Judge of the Peace, Vred. Roeselare, 24 June 1998, T. Vred., 1998, 319; see also Court of First Instance, Brussels, 23 November 1967, JT 1967, 741.

precise. The Dutch Supreme Court has not unreservedly accepted the direct applicability of Article 13 ECHR, while the Belgian Supreme Court of Appeal still has to recognise the direct applicability of Article 13 ECHR. The ordinary courts in both countries remain hesitant to find domestic legislation in violation of the ECHR. They would be more inclined to interpret (or reinterpret) legislation in a manner that facilitates compatibility with ECHR. Moreover, even where they do draw a conclusion of incompatibility, courts remain reticent to encroach on the policy prerogatives of parliament. As a result, they will not easily declare an act or practice inadmissible. Courts in both countries acknowledge the third party applicability of ECHR obligations (notably those flowing from Article 8 ECHR), without maintaining a rigid division between direct and indirect third party applicability.

These similarities most likely result from the fact that in both countries the ordinary courts have the power to review primary legislation and executive acts against directly applicable treaties. In both countries this was initially the only avenue for securing review of primary legislation against fundamental human rights norms. Constitutional review was only introduced in Belgium in 1988, while in the Netherlands it is still not possible for courts to review primary legislation against the constitutional rights in the Dutch constitution.

The introduction of constitutional review in Belgium has enhanced the status of the country's constitutional rights. This seems to have been an unintended side-effect of the federal reforms in the 80's, as the constitutional review was initially only intended to secure the constitutional division of powers between the federal Parliament, the regions and linguistic communities. This is not the case in the Netherlands, were the notion of the "inviolability of the law" is still quite strong and the introduction of constitutional review of primary legislation unlikely in the near future. Similarly, the practical relevance of the constitutional rights in the Dutch Constitution remains limited.

C. Overview of the Activity of the European Court

1. *The Netherlands*

Since the availability of statistical data in 1983 and until 2006, a total of 6323 applications have been lodged against the Netherlands in Strasbourg. Of these applications 123 resulted in a decision on the merits, including 65 determinations of violations by the ECtHR and 27 by the ECommHR. Most of these findings of violations concerned the deprivation of liberty in Article 5 ECHR, often in combination with the right to a fair trial in Article 6(1) ECHR. This is confirmed by a closer look at the statistics made available by the Council of Europe.[159]

Of the violations, twelve pertained to Article 5(1) ECHR (right to liberty

---

[159] See Annual Surveys of Activity at http://www.echr.coe.int.

and security of the person) of which eight by the ECtHR and four by the ECommHR; one decision only (by the ECtHR) pertained to Article 5(2) ECHR (promptly charged); four decisions (all by the ECtHR) pertained to Article 5(3) ECHR (promptly brought before judge); nine pertained to Article 5(4) ECHR (lawfulness of detention) of which six by the ECtHR and 3 by the ECommHR; none to Article 5(5) ECHR (compensation for unlawful detention); seventeen decisions pertained to the right to a fair trial in Article 6(1) ECHR (twelve by the ECtHR and five by the ECommHR); 22 decisions pertained to the reasonable time element in Article 6(1) ECHR (seven by the ECtHR and fifteen by the ECommHR); three decisions pertained to Article 6(2) ECHR (presumption of innocence) of which two by the ECtHR and one by the ECommHR; and eleven decisions pertained to Article 6(3) ECHR (minimum rights of the accused) of which six by the ECtHR and five by the ECommHR.

Thus far, there has only been one negative decision (by the ECtHR) in relation to Article 2 ECHR (right to life) and seven negative decisions (all by the ECtHR) in relation to Article 3 ECHR (prohibition of torture, inhuman or degrading treatment). There have been no negative decisions regarding Article 4 ECHR (prohibition of slavery and forced labor); Article 7 ECHR (no punishment without law); Article 9 ECHR (freedom of though, conscience and religion); Article 11 (freedom of assembly and association) and Article 12 (right to marry). Article 8 ECHR (respect for private and family life) has resulted in fifteen negative decisions (fourteen by the ECtHR and one by the ECommHR); there have been three negative decisions all by the ECtHR) pertaining to Article 10 ECHR (freedom of expression); one (by the ECtHR) pertaining to Article 13 ECHR (effective remedy); and three (all by the ECtHR) concerning Article 14 ECHR (non-discrimination).

2. Belgium

As far as Belgium is concerned, 4995 complaints were filed between 1983 and 2006. These complaints resulted in 112 decisions on the merits, including eighteen findings of violations by the ECommHR and 75 by the ECtHR.[160] The bulk of the negative decisions pertained to Articles 5 and 6 ECHR.

In relation to Article 5 ECHR, four negative decisions (by the ECtHR) pertained to Article 5(1) ECHR (right to liberty and security of the person); two decisions (both by the ECtHR) pertained to Article 5(3) ECHR (promptly brought before judge); and nine to Article 5(4) ECHR (lawfulness of detention) of which six were decided by the ECtHR and three by the ECommHR. Article 5(2) ECHR (promptly charged) and Article 5(5) ECHR (compensation for unlawful detention) have thus far not resulted in any findings of violations.

The right to a fair trial in Article 6(1) ECHR has yielded a total of 35 nega-

---

[160] Annual Surveys of Activity at http://www.echr.coe.int.

tive judgements, of which 27 by the ECtHR and eight by the ECommHR. The reasonable time requirement in Article 6(1) ECHR has resulted in 39 findings of violations of which 34 by the ECtHR and five by the ECommHR. Two of them (by the ECtHR) concerned Article 6(2) ECHR (presumption of innocence); whereas six (all by the ECtHR) related to Article 6(3) ECHR (minimum rights of the accused).

Until 2006 there has been no negative decisions in relation to Article 2 ECHR (right to life); Article 4 ECHR (prohibition of slavery and forced labor); Article 7 ECHR (no punishment without law), Article 9 ECHR (freedom of thought, conscience and religion), Article 11 ECHR (freedom of assembly and association); or Article 12 ECHR (the right to marry). Article 3 ECHR (prohibition of torture, inhuman or degrading treatment) have thus far resulted in two negative judgements by the ECtHR.

Article 8 ECHR (respect for private and family life) has resulted in six findings of violations, all by the ECtHR. There have been two negative decisions (both by the ECtHR) pertaining to Article 10 ECHR (freedom of expression); four pertaining to Article 13 ECHR (effective remedy) of which two by the ECtHR and two by the ECommHR; and four (all by the ECtHR) concerning Article 14 ECHR (non-discrimination). Three judgements concern Article 1 of Protocol no. 1 (two by the ECommHR and one by the ECtHR) and one only by the ECtHR concerning Article four of Protocol no. 4.

3. Comparison and Conclusion

At first sight, the number of complaints filed against Belgium and the Netherlands between 1983 and 2006 are very similar. Belgium has totalled 93 findings of violations against, whereas the Netherlands faced 92 negative judgements over the same period. In both countries, the bulk of the violations concerned Articles 5 and 6 ECHR with Article 8 ECHR taking second place.

However, if one takes into account that the Belgian population is about two thirds (circa ten million) of the size of the Dutch population (circa sixteen million), the number of successful complaints against Belgium is significantly higher. Moreover, whereas in the case of the Netherlands, the judgements pertaining to Article 6(1) ECHR peaked during the late 90's, the Belgian statistics reveal an intensification in the findings of violations pertaining to Article 6(1) ECHR since 1995. Since the late 90's there has been a steady stream of violations concerning the right to a fair trial and since 2000 a relative explosion in as far as the reasonable time criterion is concerned. In fact, the violations pertaining to Article 6(1) ECHR constitutes two thirds of the judgements. This reveals a significant structural problem to organize the criminal justice in an efficient way, which will be explored in more depth in subsequent sections.[161]

---

[161] See *infra* Section D.3.

D. The ECtHR's Case Law and its Effects in the National Legal Order

1. *The Netherlands*

a. Violations pertaining to Articles 5 and 6 ECHR

The violations concerning Article 5 and 6 ECHR have concerned all types of proceedings (administrative, civil, criminal and military) and frequently resulted from a lack of independence, even-handedness and/or lack of swiftness of the proceedings in question in one form or another.[162] On occasion, the ECtHR also had to determine whether the dispute in question fell within the scope of "civil rights and obligations" as defined in Article 6(1) ECHR.

The lack of independence and impartiality featured inter alia in the case of the conscientious objectors *De Jong, Baljet and Van den Brink v. the Netherlands*.[163] The ECtHR found a breach of Articles 5(3) ECHR, since the applicants were brought before a military judge-advocate who could not be considered a "judge or other officer authorized by law to exercise judicial power".[164] In *Winterwerp v. the Netherlands*[165] the claimant was confined to a mental hospital by means of administrative proceedings. This confinement was subsequently extended on several occasions by bodies which did not live up to the standards foreseen in Article 5(4) ECHR. By the time the relevant law was amended in the Netherlands, the ECtHR had found two more similar violations in *Van der Leer v. the Netherlands*[166] and *Wassink v. the Netherlands*.[167]

In *Benthem v. the Netherlands*[168] the proceedings granting a (permanent) license to maintain a gas station were not independent in the sense of Article 6(1) ECHR, since the decision of the highest judicial body dealing with the case (Administrative Litigation Division of the Council of State) could be overruled by the Crown in the form of the relevant cabinet Minister.[169] This was also the case in *Van der Hurk v. the Netherlands*,[170] where the discretion of the Crown (cabinet Minister) not to implement a judicial decision by a specialized

---

[162] Engering and Liborang (1999), 34.

[163] *De Jong, Baljet and Van den Brink v. the Netherlands* (appl. nos 8805/79; 8806/79; 9242/81), Judgement (Chamber), 22 May 1984, Series A, Vol. 77.

[164] See also *Van der Sluis, Zuiderveld and Klappe v. the Netherlands* (appl. nos 9362/81; 9363/81; 9387/81), Judgement (Chamber), 22 May 1984, Series A, Vol. 78; *Duinhof and Duijf v. the Netherlands* (appl. nos 9626/81; 9736/82), Judgement (Chamber), 22 May 1984, Series A, Vol. 79.

[165] *Winterwerp v. the Netherlands* (appl. no. 6301/73), Judgement (Chamber), 24 October 1979, Series A, Vol. 33.

[166] *Van der Leer v. the Netherlands* (appl. no. 11509/85), Judgement (Chamber), 21 February 1990, Series A, Vol. 170-A.

[167] *Wassink v. the Netherlands* (appl. no. 12535/86), Judgement (Chamber), 27 September 1990, Series A, Vol. 185 A.

[168] *Benthem v. the Netherlands* (appl. no. 8848/80), Judgement (Plenary), 23 October 1985, Series A, Vol. 97.

[169] *Van der Hurk v. the Netherlands* (appl. no. 16034/90), Judgement (Chamber), 19 April 1994, Series A, Vol. 288.

[170] *Van der Hurk v. the Netherlands* (*supra* note 169).

professional tribunal (the Regulatory Industrial Organization Appeals Tribunal/ RIOAT), constituted a violation of Article 6(1) ECHR.[171]

A prominent example of lack of even-handedness in criminal proceedings was the *Kostovski v. the Netherlands* case.[172] The ECtHR found a violation of Article 6(1) ECHR, as the applicant was convicted on the basis of evidence of anonymous witnesses. This was also the case in *Van Mechelen v. the Netherlands*,[173] whereas in *Doorson v. the Netherlands*[174] the ECtHR determined that the conviction was not solely or decisively based on anonymous statements. Violations of Article 6(1) ECHR also resulted from convictions *in absentia* in the *Lala and Pelladoah v. the Netherlands*.[175] Particularly problematic was the fact that the defendants' lawyers were not given an opportunity to present their defenses, although they were present during the trial.[176]

There are also several examples of lack of even-handedness in administrative and civil proceedings. In *Feldbrugge v. the Netherlands*[177] the domestic proceedings leading to the withdrawal of the applicant's sickness benefit violated Article 6(1) ECHR, as they did not grant her access to the medical evidence that formed the basis of the withdrawal.[178] In *Dombo Beheer v. the Netherlands*[179] the proceedings in question violated Article 6(1) ECHR as the managing director of *Dombo Beheer* (a limited liability company) was not allowed to be heard as witness during civil proceedings against the *Nederlandsche Middenstandsbank/NMB* (a Dutch bank), whilst the manager of the branch office of the *NMB* was allowed to testify.[180]

---

[171] See also *De Haan v. the Netherlands* (appl. no. 22839/93), Judgement (Chamber), 26 August 1997, Reports 1997-IV, 1379 et seq., para. 44; *Oerlemans v. the Netherlands* (appl. no. 12565/86), Judgement (Chamber), 27 November 1991, Series A, Vol. 219; *British American Tobacco Company Ltd. v. the Netherlands* (appl. no. 19589/92), Judgement (Chamber), 20 November 1995, Series A, Vol. 331.

[172] *Kostovski v. the Netherlands* (appl. no. 11454/85), Judgement (Plenary), 20 November 1989, Series A, Vol. 166.

[173] *Van Mechelen and Others v. the Netherlands* (appl. nos 21363/93, 21364/93, 21427/93; 22056/93), Judgement (Chamber), 23 April 1997, Reports 1997-III, 691 et seq., para. 36.

[174] *Doorson v. the Netherlands* (appl. no. 20524/92), Judgement (Chamber), 26 March 1996, Reports 1996-II, 446 et seq., para. 6.

[175] *Lala v. the Netherlands* (appl. no. 14861/89), Judgement (Chamber), 22 September 1994, Series A, Vol. 297-A and *Pelladoah v. the Netherlands* (appl. no. 16737/90), Judgement (Chamber), 22 September 1994, Series A, Vol. 297-B.

[176] See also Zwaak (2002), 615.

[177] *Feldbrugge v. the Netherlands* (appl. no. 8562/79), Judgement (Plenary), 29 May 1986, Series A, Vol. 99.

[178] Engering and Liborang (1999), 39; see also *Terra Woningen BV v. the Netherlands* (appl. no. 20641/92), Judgement (Chamber), 17 December 1996, Reports 1996-VI, 2105 et seq., para. 25.

[179] *Dombo Beheer v. the Netherlands* (appl. no. 14448/88), Judgement (Chamber), 27 October 1993, Series A, Vol. 274.

[180] According to the Dutch Code of Civil Procedure at the time, parties to civil proceedings were not allowed to serve as witnesses during such proceedings. This was particularly problematic in disputes between natural and legal persons. For example, a natural party to the proceedings (such as the managing director of *Dombo Beheer*) was not allowed to give testimony, whereas the manager of the branch office of *NMB*, a mere employee of the legal person *(NMB)* and not an official party to the proceedings himself, was allowed to testify. See also Engering and Liborang (1999), 37.

The *JJ and KDS v. the Netherlands* case[181] concerned tax proceedings before the Supreme Court, during which the applicants were unable to reply to the advisory opinion of the Advocate-General. According to the ECtHR, this infringed their right to adversarial proceedings as protected by Article 6(1) ECHR.[182]

The length of judicial proceedings remains an ongoing challenge to the Dutch judiciary. This matter already arose in the first case against the Netherlands, namely that of *Engel and Others*.[183] According to the ECtHR the military disciplinary proceedings according to which the applicants (five conscripts) were detained, violated Article 5(1) ECHR as they had been detained for two days without having been brought before a competent legal authority.[184] Another well-known example concerned *Koendjbiharie v. the Netherlands*,[185] where the applicant was institutionalised for mental treatment following criminal proceedings. The ECtHR determined that a delay of four months in granting a request for extension of his treatment (institutionalisation) constituted a violation of the requirement of a speedy decision laid down in Article 5(4) ECHR.[186] Other prominent findings of violations for "lack of swiftness" in accordance with Article 5 and/or 6 ECHR include *Abdoella v. the Netherlands*;[187] *Bunkate v. the Netherlands*;[188] the *Van Schouten and Meldrum* case;[189] and *Koster v. the Netherlands*.[190]

The question of whether a "civil right or obligation" in terms of Article 6(1) ECHR was at stake also arose in the *Benthem* case.[191] The ECtHR determined that this was the case, as the authorities initially allowed Mr. Benthem to erect the installations for a gas station and then subsequently revoked this permission.[192] The ECtHR also confirmed that rent determination proceedings[193] and

[181] *J.J. v. the Netherlands* (appl. no. 21351/93), Judgement (Chamber), 27 March 1998, Reports 1998-II, 604 et seq. and *K.D.B. v. the Netherlands* (appl. no. 21981/93), Judgement (Chamber), 27 March 1998, Reports 1998-II, 621 et seq.

[182] See also Zwaak (2002), 616.

[183] *Engel and Others v. the Netherlands* (appl. nos 5100/71; 5101/71; 5102/71; 5354/72; 5370/72), Judgement (Plenary), 8 June 1976, Series A, Vol. 22.

[184] See also *De Jong, Baljet and Van den Brink v. the Netherlands* (appl. nos 8805/79; 8806/79; 9242/81), Judgement (Chamber), 22 May 1984, Series A, Vol. 77; Engering and Liborang (1999), 34.

[185] *Koendjbiharie v. the Netherlands* (appl. no. 11487/85), Judgement (Chamber), 25 October 1990, Series A, Vol. 185-B.

[186] See also *Keus v. the Netherlands* (appl. no. 12228/86), Judgement (Chamber), 25 October 1990, Series A, Vol. 185-C; Engering and Liborang (1999), 16, 33.

[187] *Abdoella v. the Netherlands* (appl. no. 12728/87), Judgement (Chamber), 25 November 1992, Series A, Vol. 248-A.

[188] *Bunkate v. the Netherlands* (appl. no. 13645/88), Judgement (Chamber), 26 May 1993, Series A, Vol. 248-B.

[189] *Van Schouten and Meldrum v. the Netherlands* (appl. nos 19005/91; 19006/91), Judgement (Chamber), 9 December 1994, Series A, Vol. 304.

[190] *Koster v. the Netherlands* (appl. no. 12843/87), Judgement (Chamber), 28 November 1991, Series A, Vol. 221.

[191] *Koster v. the Netherlands* (*supra* note 190).

[192] See also Zwaak (2002), 607–608.

[193] *Terra Woningen BV v. the Netherlands* (appl. no. 20641/92), Judgement (Chamber), 17 December 1996, Reports 1996-VI, 2105 et seq., para. 25.

proceedings pertaining to social security contributions[194] amounted to proceedings concerning "civil rights and obligations".

b. Violations pertaining to Article 8 ECHR

Findings of violations concerning Article 8(1) ECHR have concerned both the right to privacy and the right to family life. In the *X and Y v. the Netherlands* case[195] a mentally disabled minor fell victim to sexual assault. However, as the Dutch criminal law at the time did not facilitate the institution of criminal proceedings by the next of kin, the ECtHR determined a violation of the positive obligations flowing from the right to privacy in Article 8(1) ECHR.[196]

The *Berrehab* case[197] concerned the expulsion of a Moroccan national who divorced his Dutch wife just before their daughter was born and consequently lost his right of residence in the Netherlands. The ECtHR determined a violation of Article 8 ECHR, as the deportation constituted an unreasonable intervention in the rights of the father and child to a family life.[198] However, subsequently in *Ahmut v. the Netherlands*,[199] the ECtHR underscored that Article 8(1) ECHR does not guarantee the right to choose the most suitable place for developing a family life.[200] The *Kroon v. the Netherlands* case[201] affirmed that family life could exist between two persons even if one of them was married to someone else. In this case Dutch law did not allow a male partner to recognise as his own a child with a woman who was legally married to someone else, which resulted in a violation of the positive obligations flowing from Article 8(1) ECHR.[202]

c. Other Violations

Other prominent comdemnations against the Netherlands concerned Articles 2, 3, 10 and 14 ECHR. The only negative decision so far in relation to Article 2 ECHR concerns that of *Ramsahai v. the Netherlands*,[203] in which Mr. Ramsahai was killed by the police when stealing a scooter. The ECtHR determined that the proceedings for investigating the victim's death fell short of required standards

---

[194] *Van Schouten and Meldrum v. the Netherlands* (appl. nos 19005/91; 19006/91), Judgement (Chamber), 9 December 1994, Series A, Vol. 304.

[195] *X. and Y. v. the Netherlands* (appl. no. 8978/80), Judgement (Chamber), 26 March 1985, Series A, Vol. 91.

[196] Engering and Liborang (1999), 52; Zwaak (2002), 621.

[197] *Berrehab v. the Netherlands* (appl. no. 10730/84), Judgement (Chamber), 21 June 1988, Series A, Vol. 138; Zwaak (2002), 616.

[198] Steenbergen (2000), 53.

[199] *Ahmut v. the Netherlands* (appl. no. 21702/93), Judgement (Chamber), 28 November 1996, Reports 1996-VI, 2017 et seq., para. 24; see also *Nsona v. the Netherlands* (appl. no. 23366/94), Judgement (Chamber), 28 November 1996, Reports 1996-V, 1979 et seq., para. 23.

[200] See also Zwaak (2002), 616–617.

[201] *Kroon v. the Netherlands* (appl. no. 18535/91), Judgement (Chamber), 27 October 1994, Series A, Vol. 297-C.

[202] Engering and Liborang (1999), 53; Zwaak (2002), 618.

[203] *Ramsahai and Others v. the Netherlands* (appl. no. 52391/99), Judgement (Grand Chamber), 15 May 2007 (not yet reported).

in Article 2(1) ECHR, as part of the investigation was left to the police force to which the officers involved in the shootout belonged.

The Netherlands was first found to be in violation of Article 3 ECHR in 2003, which coincided with the harshening political climate in the country, especially in the areas of criminal law and immigration law. In the *Van der Ven and Lorsé v. the Netherlands* cases,[204] the circumstances of the claimants' maximum security detention (which, *inter alia*, included routine anal searches), constituted inhuman and degrading treatment.[205] In *Said v. the Netherlands*[206] the pending deportation of a former member of the Eritrean army would result in *refoulement* in terms of Article 3 ECHR. Similarly in *Salah Sheekh v. the Netherlands*,[207] the ECtHR determined that the pending expulsion of a Somali citizen, who was a member of a persecuted minority, violated Article 3 ECHR.

Determinations of violations of Article 10 ECHR have been rare, but nonetheless occurred in *Vereniging Weekblad (Bluf) v. the Netherlands*,[208] where the Dutch authorities obtained a court order to withdraw from circulation the publication of a highly sensitive report of the Internal Security Service. The non-discrimination principle featured in relation to Article 1 of Protocol no. 1, in the well-known *Van Raalte v. the Netherlands* case.[209] The ECtHR determined that a clause in the General Child Benefit Act that obliged single, childless men over the age of 45 to pay social welfare contributions – while exempting single, childless women over the age of 45 from any similar obligation – violated Article 14 ECHR in combination with Article 1 of Protocol no. 1.[210]

---

[204] *Van der Ven and Lorsé v. the Netherlands* (appl. no. 50901/99), Judgement (First Section), 4 February 2003, Reports 2003-II, 1 et seq.

[205] Davids (2004), 303–304. See also *A.B. v. the Netherlands* (appl. no. 37328/97), Judgement (Second Section), 29 January 2002 (not reported). Although the ECtHR was not requested to rule on 3 ECHR, it referred extensively to a report of the European Committee for the Prevention of Torture and Inhuman Treatment, according to which the prison conditions in Curacao qualified as inhuman and degrading treatment. See also *Mathew v. the Netherlands* (appl. no. 24919/03), Judgement (Third Section), 29 September 2005 (not yet reported), concerning detention conditions on Aruba.

[206] *Said v. the Netherlands* (appl. no. 2345/02), Judgement (Second Section), 5 July 2005, Reports 2005-VI, 275.

[207] *Salah Sheekh v. the Netherlands* (appl. no. 1948/04), Judgement (Third Section), 11 January 2007 (not yet reported).

[208] *Weekblad (Bluf) v. the Netherlands* (appl. no. 16616/90), Judgement (Chamber), 9 February 1995, Series A, Vol. 306-A; see also Engering and Liborang (1999), 55.

[209] *Van Raalte v. the Netherlands* (appl. no. 20060/92), Judgement (Chamber), 21 February 1997, Reports 1997-I, 173 et seq., para. 29. See also *Gasus Dosier- und Fördertechniek GmbH v. the Netherlands* (appl. no. 15375/89), Judgement (Chamber), 23 February 1995, Series A, Vol. 306-B.

[210] Engering and Liborang (1999), 55.

2. Belgium

a. Violations pertaining to Articles 5 and 6 ECHR

Lack of (access to) independent and even-handed proceedings regularly featured as the basis for violations of Article 5 and 6 ECHR in disputes of an administrative, civil or criminal nature. In some instances the prison conditions did not meet the standards required by the purpose of the imprisonment. The inability to guarantee a fair trial within a reasonable time has become one of the most pressing problems over the years.

In 1971 the ECtHR ruled that the (review of) detention of vagrants in accordance with the Belgian Vagrancy Act dating from 1891 did not meet the judicial guarantees required by Article 5(4) ECHR.[211] In *Deweer v. Belgium*[212] the ECtHR determined that an agreement to a financial settlement in order to avoid criminal prosecuting resulting from an infringement of price regulations, violated the applicants' right to access to a court as required by Article 6(1) ECHR.[213]

In *Van Droogenbroek v. Belgium*[214] the extension of detention of habitual defenders under the Social Defence Act was overseen by the relevant Minister and not by an independent court of law, resulting in a violation of Article 5(4) ECHR.[215] In *De Cubber v. Belgium*[216] the ECtHR determined a violation of Article 6(1) ECHR, since one of the three magistrates in a criminal case had also acted as the investigative judge.[217] In the *Piersack* case,[218] the ECtHR constituted a violation of the notion of impartiality in Article 6(1) ECHR as one of the judges in the court passing sentence on the merits had previously served as deputy public prosecutor. In the *Pauwels* case,[219] the Belgian law allowing a military official to act both as investigative judge and prosecutor violated the notion of impartiality in Article 5(3) ECHR. In *Borgers v. Belgium* the ECtHR concluded that the participation of the public prosecutor in the deliberations of the Supreme Court of Appeal violated Article 6(1) ECHR.[220] After condemning

---

[211] *De Wilde, Ooms and Versyp v. Belgium* (appl. nos 2832/66; 2835/66; 2899/66), Judgement (Plenary), 18 June 1971, Series A, Vol. 12.

[212] *Deweer v. Belgium* (appl. no. 6903/75), Judgement (Chamber), 27 February 1980, Series A, Vol. 35.

[213] See also Lemmens (1988–89), 793–394; Berbuto and Jacobs (2000), 58.

[214] *Van Droogenbroek v. Belgium* (appl. no. 7906/77), Judgement (Plenary), 24 June 1982, Series A, Vol. 50.

[215] Marcus-Helmons and Marcus-Helmons (2002), 182.

[216] *De Cubber v. Belgium* (appl. no. 9186/80), Judgement (Chamber), 26 October 1984, Series A, Vol. 86.

[217] Marcus-Helmons and Marcus-Helmons (2002), 182; Berbuto and Jacobs (2000), 63.

[218] *Piersack v. Belgium* (appl. no. 8692/79), Judgement (Chamber), 1 October 1982, Series A, Vol. 53.

[219] *Pauwels v. Belgium* (appl. no. 10208/82), Judgement (Chamber), 26 May 1988, Series A, Vol. 135.

[220] *Borgers v. Belgium* (appl. no. 12005/86), Judgement (Plenary), 30 October 1991, Series A, Vol. 214-B. This constituted a deviation from *Delcourt v. Belgium* (appl. no. 2689/65), Judgement (Chamber), 17 January 1970, Series A, Vol. 11. In this instance the ECtHR regarded the involve-

this practice in criminal proceedings in the *Borgers* case the ECtHR also condemned it in relation to civil[221] and disciplinary[222] disputes.

Examples of lack of even-handedness include *Lamy v. Belgium*,[223] where the applicant's lawyers were not allowed to inspect the police file against him when the applicant appeared in court for a determination on pre-trial detention, resulting in a violation of Article 5(4) ECHR.[224] In the *Vidal* case,[225] the lack of opportunity of the applicant to call defense witnesses resulted in a violation of Article 6(1) and 6(3) ECHR. In the *Bouamar* case,[226] the ECtHR found the successive temporary terms of imprisonment which the applicant had suffered in accordance with the Belgian Youth Protection Act to be in breach of Article 5(4) ECHR, as the applicant (who was very young at the time) was not represented by council. The imprisonment of a juvenile in the *Bouamar* case also constituted a breach of Article 5(1) ECHR, as the applicant was kept in a prison that did not meet the educational purposes for which this imprisonment of juveniles were intended.[227] Similarly, in *Aerts v. Belgium*[228] the ECtHR determined a violation of Article 5(1) ECHR, as the conditions of the respective psychiatric prison were such that the necessary medical or therapeutic treatment could not be guaranteed.[229] In *Van Geyseghem v. Belgium*,[230] the ECtHR found the situation to be similar to the *Lala and Pelladoah* case.[231] It determined that the Brussels Court of Appeal had violated Article 6(1) ECHR by not allowing the council of the defendant to appear on her behalf, on the instruction of the defendant who did not wish to appear before the court herself.

ment of the Public Prosecutor's department in the deliberations of the Supreme Court of Appeal as anomalous, but not in breach of Article 6(1) ECHR. The *Piersack* decision was subsequently reaffirmed in *Vermeulen v. Belgium* (appl. no. 19075/91), Judgement (Grand Chamber), 20 February 1996, Reports 1996-I, 224 et seq.; Berbuto and Jacobs (2000), 69–70.

[221] *Vermeulen v. Belgium* (*supra* note 220).
[222] *Van Orshoven v. Belgium* (appl. no. 20122/92), Judgement (Chamber), 25 June 1997, Reports 1997-III, 1039 et seq., para. 39.
[223] *Lamy v. Belgium* (appl. no. 10444/83), Judgement (Chamber), 30 March 1989, Series A, Vol. 151. See generally also Tulkens and Lotarski (2004), 731.
[224] Marcus-Helmons and Marcus-Helmons (2002), 182.
[225] *Vidal v. Belgium* (appl. no. 12351/86), Judgement (Chamber), 22 April 1992, Series A, Vol. 235; *De Moor v. Belgium* (appl. no. 16997/90), Judgement (Chamber), 23 June 1994, Series A, Vol. 292-A.
[226] *Bouamar v. Belgium* (appl. no. 9106/80), Judgement (Chamber), 29 February 1988, Series A, Vol. 129.
[227] *Bouamar v. Belgium* (*supra* note 226).
[228] *Aerts v. Belgium* (appl. no. 25357/94), Judgement (Chamber) 30 July 1998, Reports 1998-V, 1939 et seq., para. 83; see also Berbuto and Jacobs (2000), 59.
[229] The refusal in this case of legal aid by the Legal Aid Board, on the ground that the appeal did not at that time appear to be well-founded, also violated Article 6(1) ECHR. It effectively denied the applicant the right by making an assessment which should have been made by the court itself.
[230] *Van Geyseghem v. Belgium* (appl. no. 26103/95), Judgement (Grand Chamber), 21 January 1999, Reports 1999-I, 157 et seq.; see also Berbuto and Jacobs (2000), 83.
[231] *Lala v. the Netherlands* (appl. no. 14861/89), Judgement (Chamber), 22 September 1994, Series A, Vol. 297-A; *Pelladoah v. the Netherlands* (appl. no. 16737/90), Judgement (Chamber), 22 September 1994, Series A, Vol. 297-B.

The lack of swiftness of the proceedings in one form or another has been an increasing problem within the Belgian judicial system. For example, in *Clooth v. Belgium*[232] the State violated Article 5(3) ECHR, due to the excessive length of the provisional detention of the applicant. Cases pertaining to Article 6(1) ECHR include decisions ranging from the period in remand custody,[233] to the length of the proceedings as such.[234] The problem has aggravated during the last decade which saw a steady stream of decisions condemning Belgium for violation of the reasonable time criterion in Article 6(1) ECHR.[235] As illustrated by the decision of *Landsheer v. Belgium*,[236] the Belgian legislature has persistently failed to organize its judicial system in a manner that provides everyone the possibility with receiving a fair trial within a reasonable time, in particular in the densely populated, bilingual region of Brussels.

The question as to whether Article 6(1) ECHR was applicable to the disciplinary proceedings instituted by Professional Councils was affirmed in the *Le Compte, Van Leuven and De Meyere* case[237] and in the *Albert and Le Compte* case.[238] Belgium was also found to violate Article 6(1) ECHR for adopting retroactive legislation intended to affect the outcome of a pending court dispute.[239]

b. Violations pertaining to Article 8 ECHR

In *Marckx v. Belgium*[240] the ECtHR determined that the distinction between legitimate and illegitimate children in the Belgian law of succession constituted a violation of the right to family life in Article 8(1) ECHR. Since the legislature

---

[232] *Clooth v. Belgium* (appl. no. 12718/87), Judgement (Chamber), 12 December 1991, Series A, Vol. 225.

[233] *Kolompar v. Belgium* (appl. no. 11613/85), Judgement (Chamber), 24 September 1992, Series A, Vol. 235.

[234] *Boddaert v. Belgium* (appl. no. 12919/87), Judgement (Chamber), 12 October 1992, Reports 1996-III, 915 et seq.

[235] See for example, *Enterprises Robert Delbrassine v. Belgium* (appl. no. 49204/99), Judgement (First Section), 1 July 2004 (not reported); *Dumont v. Belgium* (appl. no. 49525/99), Judgement (First Section), 28 April 2005 (not yet reported); *Boca v. Belgium* (appl. no. 50615/99), Judgement (First Section), 15 July 2002, Reports 2002-IX, 255 et seq.; *Affaire Stratégies et Communications et Dumoulin v. Belgique* (appl. no. 37370/97), Judgement (Third Section), 15 July 2002 (not reported); *Sablon v. Belgium* (appl. no. 36445/97), Judgement (Third Section), 10 April 2001 (not reported); *Roobaert v. Belgium* (appl. no. 52231/99), Judgement (First Section), 29 July 2004 (not reported); *Willekens v Belgium* (appl. no. 50859/99), Judgement (First Section), 24 April 2003 (not reported).

[236] *De Landsheer v. Belgium* (appl. no. 50575/99), Judgement (First Section), 15 July 2005 (not yet reported).

[237] *Le Compte, Van Leuven and De Meyere v. Belgium* (appl. nos 6878/75; 7238/75), Judgement (Chamber), 23 June 1981, Series A, Vol. 43; Marcus-Helmons and Marcus-Helmons (2002), 181.

[238] *Albert and Le Compte v. Belgium* (appl. nos 7299/75; 7496/76), Judgement (Plenary), 10 February 1983, Series A, Vol. 58; see also *H. v. Belgium* (appl. no. 8950/80), Judgement (Plenary), 30 November 1987, Series A, Vol. 127-B; Berbuto and Jacobs (2000), 64.

[239] *Stran Greek Refineries and Stratis Andreadis v. Greece* (appl. no. 13427/87), Judgement (Chamber), 9 December 1994, Series A, Vol. 301-B.

[240] *Marckx v. Belgium* (appl. no. 6833/74), Judgement (Plenary), 13 June 1979, Series A, Vol. 31.

subsequently did not remove the unequal treatment of illegitimate children in relation to the inter-phase between the *Marckx* decision and the introduction of the new legislation, Belgium was once again found in violation of Article 8(1) ECHR combined with Article 14 ECHR in the *Vermeire* case in 1991.[241] This inadequacy in relation to the implementation measures resulted in a very high order for compensation against Belgian on the basis of Article 50 ECHR.[242]

In the *Moustaquim* case[243] Belgium was found to violate the right to family life by expelling a Moroccan national with close family ties in Belgium, for having committed several offences in Belgium as an adolescent. However, subsequently in 1996 the ECtHR determined that the expulsion of a Moroccan citizen who was involved in large scale drug trafficking was reasonable and necessary in the circumstances. [244]

c. Other Violations

Other well-known decisions against Belgium concerned Article 10 ECHR, Article 1 of Protocol no. 1 (in combination with Article 13 ECHR) and Article 2 of Protocol no. 1 (in combination with Article 14 ECHR) and Article 4 of Protocol no. 4 (in combination with Article 13 ECHR).

The *De Becker v. Belgium* case[245] constituted an example of the potential pre-emptive effect Article 10(1) ECHR. According to the Belgian Criminal Code at the time the applicant was prohibited from exercising the profession of journalism, due to his collaboration with the enemy during World War II. As there was recognition within the Government that this clearly violated the applicant's right to freedom of expression in accordance with Article 10(1) ECHR, the law was changed before the ECtHR reached a decision and the case was struck from the role.[246] Belgium was, however, found to be in violated of Article 10(1) ECHR in the *De Haes and Gijsels* case.[247] In this instance two journalists were ordered to pay compensation in accordance with the Civil Code for damages caused by their criticism of members of the judicial branch.

In the *Pressos Compania Naviera* case[248] the ECtHR determined that retroactive

---

[241] *Vermeire v. Belgium* (appl. no. 12849/87), Judgement (Chamber), 29 November 1991, Series A, Vol. 214-C.

[242] *Vermeire v. Belgium* (Article 50 ECHR) (appl. no. 12849/87), Judgement (Chamber), 4 October 1993, Series A, Vol. 270; Marcus-Helmons and Marcus-Helmons (2002), 183.

[243] *Moustaquim v. Belgium* (appl. no. 12313/86), Judgement (Chamber), 18 February 1991, Series A, Vol. 193.

[244] See *C. v. Belgium* (appl. no. 21794/93), Judgement (Chamber), 7 August 1996, Reports 1996-III, 915 et seq.

[245] *De Becker v. Belgium* (appl. no. 214/56), Judgement (Chamber), 27 March 1962, Series A, Vol. 127.

[246] Marcus-Helmons and Marcus-Helmons (2002), 180.

[247] *De Haes and Gijsels v. Belgium* (appl. no. 19983/92), Judgement (Chamber), 24 February 1994, Reports 1997-I, 198 et seq., para. 30.

[248] *Pressos Compania Naviera v. Belgium* (appl. no. 17849/91), Judgement (Chamber), 20 November 1995, Series A, Vol. 332.

legislation which effectively cancelled large credits of the applicants against the State without providing for compensation, constituted a violation of Article 1 of Protocol no. 1. The ECtHR subsequently awarded a very high sum of compensation in accordance with Article 50 ECHR, in a second judgement in the same case.[249] In addition, the Belgian law providing for the absolute immunity of (the property of) public authorities against the execution of judgements was found to violate Article 1 of Protocol no. 1 in conjunction with Article 13 ECHR.[250]

In the *Use of Languages in Education* case[251] the right of children to receive education in a particular language (in this instance French) depended on the place of residence of their parents. Since this deprived children living on the periphery of Brussels from attending French-speaking schools, the ECtHR found a violation of Article 2 of Protocol no. 1 in conjunction with Article 14 ECHR. In *Conka v. Belgium*,[252] the ECtHR condemned Belgium for a violation of Article 4 of Protocol no. 4 to the ECHR, in determining that the forced repatriation of a group of Roma to Slovakia amounted to a case of collective expulsion of aliens. This resulted from a variety of factors, including the lack of consideration of the personal circumstances of the individuals in question.

3. Comparison and Conclusion

The large number of findings of violations against both countries in relation to Articles 5 and 6 ECHR reflects the lack of adversarial culture in both domestic systems, which was not conducive to the protection of the procedural rights of parties to a legal dispute.[253] Here, it would suffice to say that due to the influence of the ECHR, which has effectively become the substitute for a system of domestic constitutional review in both countries (at least until 1988 when Belgium introduced constitutional review), both systems have become more adversarial over the years.

The problems Belgium is facing with undue delays of hearings are, at least in part, a reflection of the country's complex federal structure and its attempts at balancing the rights of its linguistic communities. As reflected by the *Landsheer* decision,[254] the backlog in relation to criminal as well as civil proceedings

---

[249] *Pressos Compania Naviera v. Belgium* (appl. no. 17849/91), Judgement (Chamber), 20 November 1995, Series A, Vol. 332; see also Marcus-Helmons and Marcus-Helmons (2002), 183–184.

[250] *Dierckx and Others v. Belgium* (appl. no. 11966/86), Report (Plenary), Commission, 6 March 1990 (not reported). See also Belgian Supreme Court of Appeal, Judgement, Cass., 30 September 1993, R.W. 1993–1994, 954. The Belgian law was subsequently amended by Act of 30 June 1994; Alen (2000), 423.

[251] Case *"Relating to certain Aspects of the Laws on the Use of Languages in Education in Belgium" v. Belgium* (appl. nos 1474/62; 1677/62; 1691/62; 1769/63; 1994/63; 2126/64), Judgement (Plenary), 23 July 1968, Series A, Vol. 6.

[252] *Conka v. Belgium* (appl. no. 51564/99), Judgement (Third Section), 2 February 2002, Reports 2002-I, 934 et seq.

[253] See *infra* Section E.3.

[254] *De Landsheer v. Belgium* (appl. no. 50575/99), Judgement (First Section), 15 July 2005 (not yet reported).

is particularly severe at the court of first instance and court of appeal in the bilingual region of Brussels. A primary cause at the court of first instance relates to the legislative requirements pertaining to the language skills of members of the judiciary. First, magistrates at the court of first instance may only hear a case in the language in which they have received their law degree,[255] as a result of which bilingual Flemish judges may not hear cases which were introduced before the court in the French language. Second, two thirds of the magistrates of the court of first instance in Brussels have to be bilingual in Flemish and French – a requirement which the Francophone judges often find difficult to meet.[256] The combination of these factors have resulted in a huge shortage of Francophone magistrates who can hear the large number of cases introduced at court in the French language. At the level of the Court of Appeal the delays seem to result mainly from the large number of cases, their complicated nature; inefficient organization of hearings and budgetary constraints.[257]

While it is clear to all concerned that legislative amendments are urgently required to remedy the situation, the linguistic communities have so far not been able to reach consensus on the way forward. As will be elaborated below, this impasse has recently resulted in the first determination ever by the Supreme Court of Appeal of State liability for a wrongful act attributable to the legislature.[258]

In addition to struggling with the reasonable time criterion in Article 6(1) ECHR, Belgium is facing challenges regarding the conditions of detention in certain prison prisons, especially where vulnerable groups such as juveniles and psychiatric patients are concerned. In the Netherlands the problem of prison conditions in general is more indirect, in the sense that it has thus far only arisen before the ECtHR in relation to its overseas territories. However, the Netherlands has recently faced several findings of violations of Article 3 ECHR since 2003, of which one related to the detention conditions in a maximum security prison. This judgement as well as the negative judgements for *refoulement*, reflect the harshening political climate in the Netherlands since 2002. The *Salah Seekh* decision[259] in particular illustrated the insufficient scrutiny exercised by the Council of State over a number of years in relation to the merits of expulsion orders. Instead of verifying for itself the factual situation in the country to which

---

[255] Act of 11 July 1994, Belgian Official Gazette, 19 July 1994, available at http://www.ejustice. just.fgov.be/cgi/welcome.pl.

[256] Act of 15 June 1935, Belgian Official Gazette, 22 June 1935, available at http://www.ejustice. just.fgov.be/cgi/welcome.pl.

[257] See also Belgian Supreme Court of Appeal, Judgement, Cass., 28 September 2006, available at http://www.juridat.be.

[258] Belgian Supreme Court of Appeal, Judgement, Cass. ,28 September 2006, available at http://www.juridat.be. See also *infra* Section F.2.a.iv.

[259] *Salah Sheekh v. the Netherlands* (appl. no. 1948/04), Judgement (Third Section), 11 January 2007 (not yet reported).

someone is to be reported, the Council of State relied almost exclusively on the country reports of the Ministry of Foreign Affairs for this purpose.[260]

In each of the cases where the State was condemned of an ECHR violation, the respective Government attempted to give effect to the decision by amending the relevant law or policy. However, some of the legislative measures were taken only after several years of delay. In the case of Belgium this has sometimes resulted in high compensation in accordance with Article 50 ECHR.

E. Mechanism of Coordination

1. *The Netherlands*

a. Coordination through Jurisprudence

This section focuses on the manner in which the highest courts (Supreme Court, Council of State and the Central Appeals Board) in the Netherlands applied the ECHR in their jurisprudence and in this manner coordinated the domestic legal system with the ECHR. The analysis does not attempt to be exhaustive, but rather focuses on those decisions in which the influence of the ECHR has had significant consequences for the area of law affected, or still remains a bone of contention. It includes decisions affecting different areas of law ranging from administrative law, to civil rights, criminal (procedure) law, family law, immigration law and tax law.[261]

In relation to administrative law, the *Benthem* case[262] illustrated the impact of Article 6(1) ECHR on the independence of the administrative justice system. In addition, the concept of a "criminal charge" in Article 6(1) ECHR had consequences for the system of administrative (fiscal) fines.[263] Following the decision of *Özturk v. Germany*,[264] the Dutch Supreme Court first confirmed that heavier

---

[260] NRC Handelsblad, 12.01.2007, 3.

[261] Swart (1999), 39.

[262] *Benthem v. the Netherlands* (appl. no. 8848/80), Judgement (Plenary), 23 October 1985, Series A, Vol. 97.

[263] As far as the concept of "civil rights and obligations" in Article 6(1) ECHR is concerned, most administrative disputes in Dutch law are now covered by the protection guaranteed under this Article. Disputes still excluded from the scope of Article 6(1) ECHR include those pertaining to civil servants who exercise traditional public functions such as policing; to political rights such as the right to vote; to immigration procedures including admission and deportation of immigrants; and to fiscal (tax) procedures not resulting in the imposition of a administrative (fiscal) fine. See *Pellegrin v. France* (appl. no. 28541/95), Judgement (Grand Chamber), 8 December 1999, Reports 1999-VIII, 207 et seq., (civil servants); *Van Schouten and Meldrum v. Netherlands* (appl. nos 19005/91; 19006/91), Judgement (Chamber), 9 December 1994, Series A, Vol. 304, (fiscal procedures); Barkhuysen, Van Emmerik and Loof (2000), 384.

[264] *Özturk v. Germany* (appl. no. 8544/79), Judgement (Plenary), 21 February 1984, Series A, Vol. 73.

fines[265] under Dutch tax law qualified as a "criminal charge" in terms of Article 6(1) ECHR, and subsequently also that lower fines qualifies as such.[266]

As far as civil rights jurisprudence is concerned, Article 10(1) ECHR as well as Articles 2 of Protocol no. 1 deserves attention.[267] Article 10(1) ECHR has been particularly influential in relation to the strengthening of the freedom of expression of journalists.[268] Under influence of *Lingens v. Austria*[269] and *Oberschlick v. Austria II*[270], the Supreme Court determined that tortuous liability for a negative opinion expressed by a journalist could under circumstances constitute a violation of Article 10(1) ECHR.[271] The decision of *Goodwin v. the United Kingdom*[272] was also of significance for the protection of journalistic sources in the Netherlands. Until the *Goodwin* decision, Dutch law did not recognize any general right to the protection of confidential journalistic sources.[273] However, a few months after the *Goodwin* decision, the Supreme Court acknowledged such a right in civil proceedings in accordance with Article 10(1) ECHR. In addition, it confirmed that the burden of evidence for justifying a limitation of this right in accordance with Article 10(2) ECHR lies with those claiming that the conditions for such limitation are present.[274] In 2003 the Supreme Court further confirmed the right to the protection of journalistic sources in criminal proceedings (including instances where the source itself was a suspect) and that the burden of proof for justifying the limitation of the right in accordance with Article 10(2) ECHR, lies with the State.[275]

---

[265] Dutch Supreme Court, Judgement, HR 19 June 1985, NJ 1986, 104; Feteris (2000), 463.

[266] Dutch Supreme Court, Judgement, HR 24 January 1990, BNB 1990, 287; see also Feteris (2000), 467; Barkhuysen, Van Emmerik and Loof (2000), 401.

[267] For a discussion of the (limited) role that Article 9 ECHR has played in Dutch jurisprudence, see Barkhuysen, Van Emmerik and Loof (2000), 348.

[268] For a confirmation that the right to demonstrate, as well as commercial speech was covered by the protection guaranteed in Article 10 ECHR, see Dutch Supreme Court, Judgement, HR 7 November 1967, NJ 1968, 775; and Dutch Council of State, Judgement, ARRS 10 November 1991, AB 1993, 88, respectively.

[269] *Lingens v. Austria* (appl. no. 9815/82), Judgement (Plenary), 8 July 1986, Series A, Vol. 130.

[270] *Oberschlick v. Austria (No. 2)* (appl. no. 20834/92), Judgement (Chamber), 1 July 1997, Reports 1997-IV, 1266 et seq., para. 42.

[271] Dutch Supreme Court, Judgement, HR 13 June 1997, NJ 1998, 361; Barkhuysen, Van Emmerik and Loof (2000) 353. See also the Court of Appeal in Leeuwaarden, which restricted the possibility of the criminal prosecution of a journalist for opinions expressed to him by another, Gh Leeuwarden, 26 January 1995, Mediaforum 1995-3. In this instance the court followed *Jersild v. Denmark,* (appl. no. 15890/89), Judgement (Grand Chamber), 23 September 1994, Series A, Vol. 298. See also Barkhuysen, Van Emmerik and Loof, no. 18, 354.

[272] *Goodwin v. the United Kingdom* (appl. no. 17488/90), Judgement (Grand Chamber), 27 March 1996, Reports 1996-II, 483 et seq., para. 7.

[273] Dutch Supreme Court, Judgement, HR 11 November 1977, NJ 1978, 399. See also Prakken (2004), *waarheidsvinding,* 620.

[274] Dutch Supreme Court, Judgement, HR 10 May 1996, NJ 1996, 578.

[275] See Dutch Supreme Court, Judgement, HR 8 April 2003, LJN AE8771. See also Dutch Supreme Court, Judgement, HR 2 September 2005, NJ 2006, 291, in which the Supreme Court considered *Roemen and Schmitt v. Luxembourg* (appl. no. 51772/99), Judgement (Fourth Section), 25 February 2005, Reports 2003-IV, 87 et seq. In this instance the violation of Article 10(1) ECHR

In the area of criminal (procedure law), complaints against protracted proceedings in violation of Article 6(1) ECHR constitute the highest number of all cases raised in Dutch courtrooms.[276] In less serious cases, courts will normally provide compensation for a breach of Article 6 ECHR by reducing the sentence imposed. In more serious ones they will dismiss the case altogether.[277] Another problematic area concerns trials *in absentia*, which is permitted by law and frequently occur in practice.[278] Under the influence of *Colozza v. Italy*[279] that required States parties to exercise sufficient diligence when trying to serve a summons on the accused, Dutch courts have increasingly required public prosecutors to make greater efforts to reach the accused which have reduced the number of trials *in absentia*.[280] Moreover, in line with the decision of *Lala and Pelladoah v. the Netherlands*,[281] the practice whereby lawyers were not permitted to defend their absent clients – even where the latter had given their consent – was adjusted in order to allow representation by council.[282]

Until the decision of *Unterpertinger v. Austria*,[283] criminal trials in the Netherlands were characterized by the total absence of witnesses who were mainly interviewed during pre-trial investigations by the police and/or an investigating judge. As these out of court statements could be used as evidence virtually without limitation, it was almost superfluous for public prosecutors to summon witnesses in court. However, in *Unterpertinger v. Austria*, the ECtHR affirmed the right of the accused to question witnesses and that evidence could generally not be used where an opportunity for questioning did not exist. Subsequently, the right of the accused to summon and question witnesses became one of the

---

related to the fact that the State authorized the searching of the premises of the journalist in question and the seizing of materials, in order to identify the journalistic source. See also Prakken (2004), *waarheidsvinding*, 622–23.

[276] Swart (1999), 48; Engering and Liborang (1999), 44–45.

[277] Swart (1999), 48.

[278] Although the accused can appeal to the Court of Appeal that will conduct a new trial, any further possibility of a *de novo* trial will be forfeited if he or she once again fails to appear. Swart (1999), 45.

[279] *Colozza v. Italy* (appl. no. 9024/80), Judgement (Chamber), 12 February 1985, Series A, Vol. 89.

[280] Swart (1999), 45.

[281] *Lala v. the Netherlands* (appl. no. 14861/89), Judgement (Chamber), 22 September 1994, Series A, Vol. 297-A; *Pelladoah v. the Netherlands* (appl. no. 16737/90), Judgement (Chamber), 22 September 1994, Series A, Vol. 297-B; Swart (1999), 45; Engering and Liborang (1999), 48.

[282] Note, however, that Article 279 of the Code of Criminal Procedure has subsequently also added the requirement that the representing council has to confirm that her or she is acting on the explicit authority of the defendant. In such a case, the defendant will be regarded as having received sufficient opportunity to refute any evidence against him, and the judgement becomes definite after merely two weeks. This has resulted in a reticence by lawyers to represent clients who have disappeared without any trace, with the net result that they remain unrepresented during criminal trials.

[283] *Unterpertinger v. Austria* (appl. no. 9120/80), Judgement (Chamber), 24 November 1986, Series A, Vol. 110.

most disputed issues in Dutch courts and in time the appearance of witnesses in open court become a frequent and normal occurrence.[284]

The Supreme Court nonetheless still admitted hearsay evidence, where it concerned the out of court statements of vulnerable witnesses. It further allowed for the anonymity of such witnesses, in cases where they feared for their life or physical integrity when speaking out in court. In some instances these anonymous statements even formed the sole basis of the subsequent conviction.[285] The ECtHR ultimately struck a blow against this practice in *Kostovski v. the Netherlands*,[286] ruling that a conviction essentially based on the statements of two anonymous witnesses violated the notion of even-handedness guaranteed by Article 6(1) ECHR. Although the Code of Criminal Procedure was amended in 1993 in order to restrict the use of anonymous witnesses,[287] situations still occurred in which the anonymous statements constituted the sole basis of the conviction. This lead to findings of violations by the ECtHR in *Van Mechelen and others v. the Netherlands*[288] and *Visser v. the Netherlands*.[289]

It is also worth noting that the suspects in Dutch criminal proceedings enjoy no general right to be advised by council before or during a police interrogation – a fact that causes ongoing controversy amongst Dutch criminal lawyers.[290] The Supreme Court has held that such a right cannot be derived from Article 6 ECHR and that the ECtHR's decision in *Murray v. the United Kingdom*[291] did not have any particular consequences for police interrogations in the Netherlands.[292] The Supreme Court's restrictive interpretation of the *Murray* decision is also reflected by its conclusion that courts may draw negative inferences from the silence of the accused during a trial; and that they are not under an obligation to warn the accused of the potential negative consequences of such silence.[293]

The area of family law was significantly influenced by the ECtHR's interpretation of Articles 8 and 14 ECHR *Marckx v. Belgium*.[294] The Supreme Court thereafter determined that legislation pertaining to custody over infants, although originally intended to apply to legitimate children only, had to be interpreted

---

[284] Swart (1999), 45, 47.

[285] Swart (1999), 47.

[286] *Kostovski v. the Netherlands* (appl. no. 11454/85), Judgement (Plenary), 20 November 1989, Series A, Vol. 166.

[287] Zwaak (2002) 621; Engering and Liborang (1999), 49–50.

[288] *Van Mechelen and Others v. the Netherlands* (appl. nos 21363/93, 21364/93, 21427/93; 22056/93), Judgement (Chamber), 23 April 1997, Reports 1997-III, 691 et seq., para. 30.

[289] *Visser v. the Netherlands* (appl. no. 26668/95), Judgement (Third Section), 14 February 2002 (not reported); see also Swart (1999), 47; Zwaak (2002), 615; Engering and Liborang (1999), 51.

[290] Dutch Supreme Court, Judgement, HR 22 November 1983, NJ 1984, 805; Dutch Supreme Court, Judgement, HR 13 May 1997, NJ 1998, 152.

[291] *Murray v. the United Kingdom* (appl. no. 18731/91), Judgement (Grand Chamber), 8 February 1996, Reports 1996-I, 30 et seq., para. 1.

[292] Dutch Supreme Court, Judgement, HR 13 May 1997, NJ 1998, 152.

[293] Dutch Supreme Court, Judgement, HR 3 June 1997, NJ 1997, 584.

[294] *Marckx v. Belgium* (appl. no. 6833/74), Judgement (Plenary), 13 June 1979, Series A, Vol. 31.

as applying equally to illegitimate children.[295] The legislature subsequently also formally equalized the position of legitimate and illegitimate children in the Dutch Civil Code in 1982. During the same year, the Supreme Court declared non-applicable the provision of the Dutch Civil Code granting parents an absolute veto against the marriage of a minor child, on the basis that it violated the right to marry in Article 12 ECHR.[296] The Supreme Court further declared non-applicable a clause in the Dutch Civil Code which effectively terminated parental authority in the case of divorce. It found the clause to be in violation of the right of parents to respect for their family life as laid down in Article 8 ECHR and set conditions under which parents could continue to exercise parental authority, despite the dissolution of their marriage.[297]

In the wake of the *Berrehab v. the Netherlands* case,[298] the Supreme Court deviated from its prior position in accordance with which family life in terms of Article 8 ECHR necessarily existed between a biological father and child. Instead, additional factors pertaining to the nature of the relationship between the father and child had to be considered in order to determine whether such family life was indeed present.[299] In 1994 the Supreme Court also acknowledged in domestic law a "general personality right" which had thereto been unknown in Dutch law. Prompted by the decision of *Gaskin v. the United Kingdom*,[300] the Supreme Court described this right as forming the basis of the right to privacy, as protected in Article 8 ECHR.[301] On the basis of the "general personality right", the plaintiff (an illegitimate childe) had the right to know the identity of her biological father.[302]

In the area of immigration law, Article 8 ECHR has influenced the domestic jurisprudence in relation to the termination of residence permits of foreigners legally residing in the Netherlands; as well as the initial granting of residence permits to foreign family members. In accordance with the *Berrehab* decision,[303] the termination of a residence permit (and subsequent deportation) of a Moroccan father could result in a violation of Article 8 ECHR, where it unduly limited the right of a parent and child to maintain a family life. In as far as the initial admission to the Netherlands of foreign family members is concerned, the Council of

---

[295] Dutch Supreme Court, Judgement, HR 18 January 1980, NJ 1980, No. 463; Zwaak (2002), 602.

[296] Dutch Supreme Court, Judgement, HR 4 June 1982, NJ 1983, no. 32.

[297] Dutch Supreme Court, Judgement, HR 4 May 1984, NJ 1985, n. 510; Zwaak (2002), 603.

[298] *Berrehab v. the Netherlands* (appl. no. 10730/84), Judgement (Chamber), 21 June 1988, Series A, Vol. 138.

[299] Dutch Supreme Court, Judgement, HR 10 September 1989, 628; Zwaak (2002), 603.

[300] *Gaskin v. the United Kingdom* (appl. no. 10454/83), Judgement (Plenary), 7 July 1987, Series A, Vol. 160.

[301] Dutch Supreme Court, Judgement, HR 15 April 1994, NJ 1994, 608; Hartkamp (2000), 34.

[302] Dutch Supreme Court, Judgement, HR 15 April 1994, NJ 1994, 608; Hartkamp (2000), 34.

[303] *Berrehab v. the Netherlands* (appl. no. 10730/84), Judgement (Chamber), 21 June 1988, Series A, Vol. 138.

State developed a line of jurisprudence that was based on the decision of *Abdulaziz v. the United Kingdom*.[304] Accordingly, a refusal of admission by the Dutch authorities did not constitute an interference with family life in terms of Article 8 ECHR, as the State was not revoking a title that resulted in the exercising of family life. The Council of State nonetheless acknowledged that there could be a positive obligation to facilitate family life under the circumstances.[305]

It is also noteworthy that Article 3 ECHR has influenced the jurisprudence relating to the expulsion of asylum seekers who do not qualify as refugees under the Convention relating to the Status of Refugees of 1951. Since *Soering v. the United Kingdom*,[306] such individuals can rely on Article 3 ECHR to prevent expulsion from the Netherlands where it would result in *refoulement*. The Dutch courts have nonetheless emphasized that Article 3 ECHR does not contain a right to political asylum and therefore does not constitute a basis for an entitlement to a residence permit as such.[307] It is, therefore, reconcilable with Article 3 ECHR to allow unsuccessful asylum seekers to remain in the Netherlands without any residency title, although this may be undesirable from a public policy point of view.[308]

As far as tax law is concerned, it remained disputed until 1994 whether tax debts[309] qualified as "civil obligations" in terms of Article 6(1) ECHR.[310] The ECtHR's confirmation in *Schouten and Meldrum v. the Netherlands*[311] that a tax debt could under circumstances qualify as such, was of great significance for the jurisprudence of the Central Appeals Board. Until that point the Central Appeals Board had been reluctant to accept that a social security right qualified as a "civil right" in terms of Article 6(1) ECHR.[312] The Supreme Court subsequently also applied the decision of *Van Schouten and Meldrum*[313] to social security contributions without any further explanation.[314] Under the influence of *Darby v.*

---

[304] *Abdulaziz, Cabales, and Balkandali v. the United Kingdom* (appl. nos 9214/80; 9473/81; 9474/81), Judgement (Plenary), 28 May 1985, Series A, Vol. 94. See also Steenbergen (2000), 447.

[305] Steenbergen (2000), 212, 447.

[306] *Soering v. the United Kingdom* (appl. no. 14038/88), Judgement (Plenary), 7 July 1989, Series A, Vol. 161.

[307] District Court The Hague, Judgement, 11 September 1997, RV 1997, 9 and 10.

[308] The threat of a violation of Article 3 ECHR in the country of origin may also be a relevant factor to be taken into account when deciding on the grant of a residence permit and when reviewing that decision. See Van Dijk (1994), 147–148; Steenbergen (2000), 212, 457.

[309] From tax debts one has to distinguish administrative (fiscal) fines that constitute a "criminal charge" in terms of Article 6(1) ECHR.

[310] Initially the ECommHR determined that this was not the case. See the cases against the Netherlands of 23 May 1966, Appl. No. 1904/63, 9 *Yearbook of the European Convention of Human Rights* (1966), 268 and of 13 April 1989, Appl. no. 12347/86, BNB 1989, 323; Feteris (2000), 465.

[311] *Van Schouten and Meldrum v. the Netherlands* (appl. nos 19005/91; 19006/91), Judgement (Chamber), 9 December 1994, Series A, Vol. 304; Feteris (2000), 465.

[312] Heerma van Voss (1996), 205.

[313] *Van Schouten and Meldrum v. the Netherlands* (*supra* note 311).

[314] Dutch Supreme Court, Judgement, HR 18 June 1997, 342; Feteris (2000), 465.

Sweden,[315] according to which the mentioning of taxes in Article 1 of Protocol no. 1 implied the applicability of 14 ECHR to cases concerning discriminatory taxation, the Supreme Court reviewed national tax legislation against Article 14 ECHR.[316] This implied a deviation from the previous position of the Supreme Court that Article 14 ECHR (in combination with Article 1 of Protocol no. 1) was not applicable outside the context of administrative (fiscal) fines.[317]

b. Coordination through Legislation

As far as legislation is concerned, the process of coordination has a general and specific dimension. The general dimension relates to the extent to which the ECHR forms a yardstick during the general legislative process. The specific dimension pertains to the consequences for specific legislation in the Netherlands of ECtHR decisions against the Netherlands or other States. The growth of ECtHR jurisprudence during the 80's was accompanied with increased attention for the ECHR during the legislative process. Since the 90's the members of the ministries drafting legislation on behalf of the Government almost routinely pay attention to the compatibility of new proposals for legislation with the ECHR. Such compatibility is also debated routinely when the proposals are submitted to Parliament.[318] Examples include a wide range of subject matters ranging from the impact of Article 6(1) ECHR on the system of administrative (fiscal) fines[319] to the implications of Article 2 ECHR for legislation regulating euthanasia.[320]

This routine-like reference by the Government to the ECHR when preparing legislation is further prompted by Article 73 of the Constitution, according to which the Council of State shall be consulted on legislative bills and draft general administrative orders, as well as proposals for the approval of treaties by Parliament. Against the background of the increasing body of ECtHR case law, the advice of this organ in relation to new or amended legislation also includes

---

[315] *Darby v. Sweden* (appl. no. 11581/85), Judgement (Chamber), 23 October 1990, Series A, Vol. 187.

[316] Dutch Supreme Court, Judgement, HR 12 November 1997, BNB 1998, 22.

[317] After it changed its position, the Dutch Supreme Court determined three times in eighteen months that fiscal legislation were in violation of Article 14 ECHR in combination with Article 1 of Protocol no. 1. These include Dutch Supreme Court, Judgement, HR 15 July 1998, BNB 1998, 293; Dutch Supreme Court, Judgement, HR 17 August 1998, BNB 1999, 122; Dutch Supreme Court, Judgement, HR 12 May 1999, BNB1999, 271. See also Feteris, (2000), 484.

[318] See Barkhuysen and Van Emmerik (2005), 12.

[319] Feteris (2000), 469. See also the Parliamentary debates in *Kamerstukken II* 2003/2004, 29 702, no. 3; *Kamerstukken II* 2005/2006, 29 702, no. 7, all available at http://www.tweedekamer.nl/kamerstukken/index.jsp. The cases *Saunders v. the United Kingdom* (appl. no. 19187/91), Judgement (Grand Chamber), 17 December 1996, Reports 1996-VI, 2044 et seq., para 24 and *J.B. v. Switzerland* (appl. no. 31827/96), Judgement (Second Section), 3 May 2001, Reports 2001-III, 455 et seq., formed important points of reference during this debate. See Barkhuysen and Van Emmerik (2005), 17.

[320] See Parliamentary debates in *Kamerstukken II*, 1997/1998, 26 000, no. 3; *Kamerstukken II*, 2000/2001, 26 691, no. 137e, all available at http://www.tweedekamer.nl/kamerstukken/index.jsp; Davids (2004), 299.

recommendations as to its compatibility with the ECHR. The Government is not, however, bound by the Council of State's recommendations.[321] Practice has shown that the Government frequently pushes aside the critical remarks of the Council of State in its reaction to the advice, reflecting a minimalist approach to the ECHR.[322]

A prominent case in point concerns highly contentious draft legislation currently tabled before Parliament that pertains to the combating of international terrorism. If adopted in its current form, this bill will, *inter alia*, expand the investigative powers of the police in areas including telephone tapping and observation; and will introduce of pre-trial detention of persons for a period of up to 90 days where there are "reasonable suspicions" of there involvement in terrorist activity.[323] This detention could then be extended for additional periods of up to 90 days, which may in total not exceed two years. During this entire period the investigating authorities can withhold evidence from the detainee and the judge-commissioner (the legal officer who has to decide on the eventual extension of the pre-trial detention) that are not "essential" for deciding the matter of pre-trial detention.[324] Critical questions of the Council of State as to the necessity of these measures in light of already existing legislation; the vagueness in their formulation; and their compatibility with Article 6(1) ECHR were refuted with what amounted to a mere reiteration of the Government's position.[325]

As far as the specific influence of the ECHR on the legislative process in the Netherlands is concerned, the Dutch Government generally amends legislation where this is required by decisions of the ECtHR, whether rendered against the Netherlands or against other Contracting States. A case that is often hailed as the catalyst for this process is *Marckx v. Belgium*,[326] as it prompted the Dutch Government in 1982 to equalise the position of legitimate and illegitimate children in the Dutch law of succession.[327] It is worth noting, however, that it may take

---

[321] Zwaak (2002), 600.

[322] Barkhuysen, Van Emmerik and Loof (2000), 407.

[323] See Parliamentary debates in *Kamerstukken II*, 2004/2005, 30 164, no. 2; *Kamerstukken II*, 2004/2005, 30 164, no. 3, all available at http://www.tweedekamer.nl/kamerstukken/index.jsp.

[324] See Parliamentary debates *Kamerstukken II*, 2004/2005, 30 164, no. 2; See also *Kamerstukken II*, 2004/2005, 30 164, no. 3. All available at http://www.tweedekamer.nl/kamerstukken/index.jsp.

[325] See Parliamentary debate in *Kamerstukken II*, 2004/2005, 30164, no. 5, available at http://www.tweedekamer.nl/kamerstukken/index.jsp. These measures have also been severely criticized by various professional organizations, including the Netherlands Bar Association *(Nederlandse Orde van Advocaten/NOvA)*, on the basis of their incompatibility with Articles 5, 6 and 8 ECHR. See Van Kempen, (2005), 397–398; Prakken (2004), *Strafrecht*, 2340–2343. For comparable criticism concerning recently adopted legislation that provides for the introduction of anonymous evidence of members of the national intelligence services in court, see Parliamentary debate in *Kamerstukken II*, 2003/2004, 29 743, no. 5, available at http://www.tweedekamer.nl/kamerstukken/index.jsp; *Kamerstukken I*, 2004/2005, 29 743, A, C and E, available at http://www.eerstekamer.nl.

[326] *Marckx v. Belgium* (appl. no. 6833/74), Judgement (Plenary), 13 June 1979, Series A, Vol. 31; Barkhuysen and Van Emmerik (1999), 9.

[327] Barkhuysen and Van Emmerik (2005), 11–12; Zwaak (2002), 623; Hartkamp (2000), 31.

several years for legislative amendment to go through the Parliamentary process, during which time the Netherlands could be confronted with several determinations of violations of the ECHR that are all similar to the one prompting the legislative change in the first place. In addition, some of the legislative amendments following decisions of the ECtHR may result in less protection for the individual than before, even though the Government claims to be bringing its laws in line with Strasbourg jurisprudence. An example in point was the *Brogan v. the United Kingdom* case,[328] according to which the word "promptly" in Article 5(3) ECHR leaves very little room for interpretation. As a result, a period of detention of four days and six hours spent in police custody without the intervention of a judge, constituted a violation of Article 5(3) ECHR. In the Netherlands, the legislature reacted to this decision by changing the (controversial) custody period of four and a half days without judicial review, to a period of six days in total, but allowing for judicial review after three and a half days in custody.[329] The net effect of this amendment seems to have strengthened the position of the State, rather than that of the individual.

Therefore, one can conclude that the Dutch Government is in principle committed to bringing its legislation into line with the jurisprudence of the ECtHR. However, closer scrutiny reveals that the commitment of the Government is on occasion tainted by a minimalist interpretation of the rights in the ECHR and several years of delay in implementing the necessary legislation.

2. Belgium

a. Coordination through Jurisprudence

Coordination of the Belgian law with the ECHR by means of the jurisprudence of its highest courts (notably the Supreme Court of Appeal and the Constitutional Court) has occurred in respect to many areas of the law. Areas significantly affected include administrative law, civil rights, criminal (procedure) law, family law, immigration law and tax law.

In the area of administrative law, the decisions of *Le Compte, Van Leuven and De Meyere v. Belgium*[330] and *Albert and Le Compte v. Belgium*[331] prompted the Supreme Court of Appeal to recognise the right to (continue to) exercise a profession that does not constitute a public function as a civil rights in terms of Article 6(1) ECHR. As a result, this Article had to be applied to disciplinary hearings

---

[328] *Brogan and Others v. the United Kingdom* (appl. nos 11209/84; 11234/84; 11266/84; 11386/85), Judgement (Plenary), 29 November 1988, Series A, Vol. 145-B.

[329] Article 59a(1) of the Dutch Code of Criminal Procedure.

[330] *Le Compte, Van Leuven and De Meyere v. Belgium*, (appl. nos 6878/75; 7238/75), Judgement (Chamber), 23 June 1981, Series A, Vol. 43; Marcus-Helmons and Marcus-Helmons (2002), 181.

[331] *Albert and Le Compte v. Belgium* (appl. nos 7299/75; 7496/76), Judgement (Plenary), 10 February 1983, Series A, Vol. 58. See also *H. v. Belgium* (appl. no. 8950/80), Judgement (Plenary), 30 November 1987, Series A, Vol. 86.

before Professional Councils.[332] The ECtHR subsequently qualified its position by noting that where the disciplinary hearing itself does not conform to Article 6(1) ECHR, it is both sufficient and necessary that an appeal on the facts and the law is possible to a judicial body that does conform to these standards.[333] This effectively meant that the Supreme Court of Appeal could not serve as first and final instance of appeal in disciplinary hearings, given that it only has the competence to review questions of law.[334]

It is also worth noting that both the Constitutional Court and the Supreme Court of Appeal have adopted the position that administrative (fiscal) fines can amount to a "criminal charge" in terms of Article 6(1) ECHR.[335] However, it remains disputed whether the court itself should be able to reduce the fine in instances where it finds the amount unreasonable. Whereas the Constitutional Court seems to be of the opinion that the courts would have this competence,[336] the Supreme Court of Appeal denies such a power unless provided explicitly by law.[337] It also remains unclear whether the principle of *ne bis in idem* would apply in situations where there is an accumulation of financial sanctions.[338] The Supreme Court of Appeal was not willing to accept that disciplinary measures against a magistrate who had violated his officially duties by speaking on the radio without permission of his superiors amounted to a criminal charge in terms of Article 6(1) ECHR. The Court noted that the (mild) nature of the sanctions (which included official warning and censuring) did not amount to the sanctions associated with a criminal charge.[339]

In relation to civil rights jurisprudence Articles 8 (right to privacy), 10 (free-

[332] The Supreme Court of Appeal had previously rejected this position. See Belgian Supreme Court of Appeal, Judgement, Cass., 19 April 1979 and 15 June 1979, R.W., 1979–1980, 1699; Belgian Supreme Court of Appeal, Judgement, Cass., 20 September 1979, J.T. 1980, 172. After some initial resisitance, the Belgian Supreme Court of Appeal adopted the position of the ECtHR. See Belgian Supreme Court of Appeal, Judgement, Cass., 21 January 1982, R.W. 1982–83, 549; Belgian Supreme Court of Appeal, Judgement, Cass., 14 April 1983, J.T. 1983, 607. See Alen (2000), 384; Marcus-Helmons and Marcus-Helmons (2002), 181; Berbuto and Jacobs (2000), 63.

[333] *Diennet v. France* (appl. no. 18160/91), Judgement (Chamber), 26 September 1995, Series A, Vol. 325-A; Alen (2000), 385. See also Lambert (1995), 160 et seq.

[334] Note that the Administration Section of the Council of State concluded that disciplinary action which temporarily deprive someone in the civil service of his position (or certain advantages attached thereto), would not constitute an attack on civil rights and obligations within the meaning of Article 6(1) ECHR. Belgian Supreme Administrative Court, Judgement, CS No. 31 567, 12 July 1987, TBP, 1989, 608; see also Marcus-Helmons and Marcus-Helmons (2002), 178.

[335] Belgian Constitutional Court, Judgement, CA no. 128/99, 7 December 1999; Belgian Constitutional Court, Judgement, CA no. 127/2000, 6 December 2000, both available at http://www.arbitrage.be. See also Belgian Supreme Court of Appeal, Judgement, Cass., 5 February 1999, available at http://www.juridat.be.

[336] Belgian Constitutional Court, Judgement, CA no. 127/2000, 6 December 2000, available at http://www.arbitrage.be.

[337] Alen (2000), 496.

[338] Ibid.

[339] Belgian Supreme Court of Appeal, Judgement, Cass., 17 May 1987, Arr. Cass, 1986–87, 1210; Lemmens (1988–89), 794.

dom of expression) and 11 ECHR (freedom of association) have been particularly influential. Under the influence of the *Klass*[340] and *Malone*[341] decisions, the Supreme Court of Appeal determined that the practice whereby a ministerial notice sufficed as legal basis for investigative judges to order the tracing of telephone conversations, violated the right to privacy under Article 8(1) ECHR.[342] The ministerial notice was not "provided by law" as required by Article 8(2) ECHR, as it was not generally accessible and lacked binding normative force in domestic law. The legislature subsequently provided a legal basis for this practice.[343] In 2004 the Constitutional Court determined that the lack of sufficient judicial control over special investigative measures[344] available to the police in accordance with legislation aimed at combating terrorism, violated several Articles of the Constitution in conjunction with Article 8(1) ECHR.[345] Given the intrusive nature of these measures they had to be subjected to the same control that existed for measures which were of a comparably intrusive nature, such as phone tapping and house searches.[346]

Following the *De Haes and Gijsels* case[347] the Belgian Courts now follow the same strict criteria as the ECtHR in determining whether limitations of freedom of expression are necessary in a democratic society. For example, the Constitutional Court recently annulled a provision of the anti-discrimination legislation on the grounds that it failed to specify when and how discriminatory statements exceed the limits permissible in a democratic society for propounding ideas that may shock, disturb or offend.[348] At the same time, the Supreme Court of Appeal concluded in the *Vlaams Blok* decision that the legislation criminalizing membership in and support of a racist organization did not violate Article 10(1) ECHR. The criminalization of incitement to or advocacy of discrimination, segregation, hatred or violence against a person or group on account of race, colour, descent, origin or nationality could not be considered disproportionate, as it neither

---

[340] *Klass and Others v. Germany* (appl. no. 5029/71), Judgement (Plenary), 6 September 1978, Series A, Vol. 28.

[341] *Malone v. the United Kingdom* (appl. no. 8691/79), Judgement (Plenary), 2 August 1984, Series A, Vol. 82.

[342] Belgian Supreme Court of Appeal, Judgement, Cass., 2 May 1990, Arr. Cass. 1989–90, 1132.

[343] Alen (2000), 477.

[344] See Act of 6 January 2003.

[345] Belgian Constitutional Court, Judgement, CA no. 202/2005, 21 December 2004, available at http://www.arbitrage.be.

[346] Ibid. See also Belgian Constitutional Court, Judgement, CA no. 162/2004 and judgement 16/2005, which determined that the extent of the publicity given to disciplinary suspension of certain sports practitioners violated Article 22 of the Constitution read in conjunction of Article 8(1) ECHR.

[347] *De Haes and Gijsels v. Belgium* (appl. no. 19983/92), Judgement (Chamber), 24 February 1994, Reports 1997-I, 198 et seq., para. 30; see also *Barfod v. Denmark* (appl. no. 11508/85), Judgement (Chamber), 22 February 1989, Series A, Vol. 149.

[348] Belgian Constitutional Court, Judgement, CA no. 157/2004, 6 October 2004; available at http://www.arbitrage.be.

aimed at nor resulted in prohibiting a public debate concerning immigration and the social problems related to it.[349]

An order of the Tribunal of First Instance of Brussels in 2002 according to which two journalists were fined 25 Euro for every hour they continued to refuse the disclosure of their sources for an Article published in a Flemish newspaper,[350] ignited the discussion about the protection of the confidentiality of journalistic sources in accordance with Article 10(1) ECHR. In 2005 the legislature adopted legislation explicitly providing for such a right and protecting journalists against home searches, seizures, phone tapping and the like. Exceptions must be approved by a judge and has to be necessary for preventing crimes that represent a serious attack on the physical integrity of one or several individuals.[351]

The question of freedom of association guaranteed in Article 11(1) ECHR arose in relation to the mandatory membership requirements of professional organizations such as the Bar Association and the Medical Association. As these public law bodies also serve the general interest by monitoring the integrity and reputation of the profession in question, the Supreme Court of Appeal did not regard mandatory membership by members of the profession in question as a violation of their right to freedom of association.[352] This position was subsequently affirmed by the ECtHR in *Le Compte, Van Leuven en De Meyere* case.[353] The Constitutional Court further concluded that Article 11(1) ECHR did not guarantee a union or its members the right to be consulted by the State. The selection of negotiation partners for the purpose of ensuring a permanent and efficient social dialogue in the interest of social peace is reconcilable with Article 11 ECHR.[354]

Belgian criminal law has been strongly influenced by Articles 5 and 6 ECHR.[355] As already indicated, Belgium is facing significant problems in living up to the reasonable time requirement. Articles 5 and 6 ECHR have also made their presence felt in relation to the independence and even-handedness of Belgian criminal

---

[349] Belgian Supreme Court of Appeal, Judgement, Cass., 9 November 2004, available at http://www.juridat.be; Brems (2006), 709.

[350] Pres. Court of First Instance Brussels 29 May 2002, unpubl. and Pres. Court of First Instance, Brussels 7 June 2002.

[351] Act of 7 April 2005, published in Belgian Official Gazette, 27 April 2005, No. 133, Edition 1, p. 19522, http://www.ejustice.just.fgov.be/cgi/welcome.pl.

[352] Belgian Supreme Court of Appeal, Judgement, Cass., 3 May 1974, available at http://www.juridat.be.

[353] *Le Compte, Van Leuven and De Meyere v. Belgium* (appl. nos 6878/75; 7238/75), Judgement (Chamber), 23 June 1981, Series A, Vol. 43.

[354] Belgian Constitutional Court, Judgement, CA no. 71/92, 18 November 1992, available at http://www.arbitrage.be. This jurisprudence is in line with *National Union of Belgian Police v. Belgium* (appl. no. 4464/70), Judgement (Plenary), 27 October 1975, Series A, Vol. 19; and *Swedish Syndicate of Train Drivers v. Sweden* (appl. no. 5614/72), Judgement (Chamber), 6 February 1976, Series A, Vol. 19.

[355] See also extensively Berbuto and Jacobs (2000), 56 et seq.

trials. Until the *Piersack*[356] and *De Cubber*[357] cases the Supreme Court of Appeal consistently ruled that the guarantees contained in Article 6 ECHR only applied at the stage where a court decided the merits of a case, but not to the proceedings before an investigating judge (pre-merits phase).[358] The Supreme Court of Appeal justified this position with the argument that investigating authorities were not concerned with the cogency of criminal accusations, but solely with the existence of sufficient evidence to warrant referral to a court.[359] As a result, it was possible for an investigating judge or a magistrate who had referred the case to the criminal courts, to participate subsequently in trying the merits of the case. However, since the *Piersack* and *De Cubber* rulings,[360] such practice is not permitted anymore, as the Supreme Court of Appeal has ruled that the pre-merits stage must reflect the standards if independence and impartiality contained in this Article 6(1) ECHR.[361]

In 2004 the Constitutional Court emphasized the importance of independent judicial review in accordance with Article 6(1) ECHR, when nullifying certain clauses of legislation that authorized special investigative measures for the purpose of combating terrorism and serious organized crime.[362] In determining a violation of several Articles of the Constitution in conjunction with Article 6(1) ECHR, the Constitutional Court noted that the special investigative measures did not allow an independent judge to have insight into confidential information obtained through surveillance and infiltration.[363] Although the legislature has claimed to remedy this deficit with the Act of 27 December 2005, it remains to be seen whether this substitute legislation lives up to the standards of Article 6(1) ECHR. It has (inter alia) been criticized for not being sufficiently adversarial and not specifying the consequences attached to findings that the special investigative measures were used in an illegal manner.[364]

---

[356] *Piersack v. Belgium* (appl. no. 8692/79), Judgement (Chamber), 1 October 1982, Series A, Vol. 53.

[357] *De Cubber v. Belgium* (appl. no. 9186/80), Judgement (Chamber), 26 October 1984, Series A, Vol. 86.

[358] E.g. Belgian Supreme Court of Appeal, Judgement, Cass., 22 December 1982, Arr. Cass., 1982–83, 547; Belgian Supreme Court of Appeal, Judgement, Cass., 4 May 1983, 16 March 1999, J.T. 2000, 124; Alen (2000), 487; Lemmens (1988–89), 795.

[359] Marcus-Helmons and Marcus-Helmons (2002), 172.

[360] See also *Pauwels v. Belgium* (appl. no. 10208/82), Judgement (Chamber), 26 May 1988, Series A, Vol. 135, where the ECtHR determined that the combination of prosecutorial and investigative functions in one person was contrary to Article 5(3) ECHR; Alen (2000), 493–494.

[361] E.g. Belgian Supreme Court of Appeal, Judgement, Cass. 19 December 1984, J.T. 1985, 447; Belgian Supreme Court of Appeal, Cass., 24 October 1997, Arr. Cass., 1997, 1028; Marcus-Helmons and Marcus-Helmons (2002), 173; Alen (2000), 493–494.

[362] Belgian Constitutional Court, Judgement, CA. no. 202/2004, 21 December 2004, available at http://www.arbitrage.be.

[363] Ibid.

[364] See also *supra* Section E.2.a.

The *Borgers* case[365] resulted in more alertness for even-handedness and an abolition of the practice that the public prosecutor could participate in the negotiations of the members of the Supreme Court of Appeal, without the right to vote, in cases where the prosecution did not request the appeal itself. According to the ECtHR this practice violated the principle of the equality of arms in Article 6(1) ECHR be respected, since Belgian law did not award the other party the possibility to refute the public prosecutor's views that were presented during the court's negotiations.[366] In the wake of the *Von Geysegheim* case,[367] the Supreme Court of Appeal confirmed the right of a defendant to be represented by council in their absence, including where the defendant deliberately chose not to appear in person.[368]

The *Marckx* decision[369] had significant consequences for family and succession law, as it obliged Belgium to adopt measures for enabling illegitimate children and their mothers to develop a normal family life. The *Marckx* decision further obliged the Government to bring the position of illegitimate children in line with that of legitimate children in relation to the law of succession. Together with the *Vermeire* decision[370] it also illustrated the potential direct effect of positive obligations under Article 8 ECHR.

In the area of immigration law, the Supreme Administrative Court has ruled that Article 3 ECHR does not guarantee the right of residence or asylum to non-nationals.[371] However, authorities also recognize that Article 3 ECHR does prevent the expulsion of individuals who do not qualify for asylum where this would result in *refoulement*.[372] Under influence of the decision of *D. v. the United Kingdom*,[373] the Supreme Administrative Court has on occasion determined that expulsion of aliens would violate Article 3 ECHR, where these persons or their family members would subsequently be deprived of essential medical treatment which is not available in the country of origin.[374] The Supreme Administrative

---

[365] *Borgers v. Belgium* (appl. no. 12005/86), Judgement (Plenary), 30 October 1991, Series A, Vol. 214-B.

[366] Alen (2000), 351; see also Berbuto and Jacobs (2000), 66 et seq.

[367] *Van Geyseghem v. Belgium* (appl. no. 26103/95), Judgement (Grand Chamber), 21 January 1999, Reports 1999-I, 157 et seq.

[368] Belgian Supreme Court of Appeal, Judgement, Cass., 16 March 1999, Berbuto and Jacobs (2000), 85.

[369] *Marckx v. Belgium* (appl. no. 6833/74), Judgement (Plenary), 13 June 1979, Series A, Vol. 31.

[370] *Vermeire v. Belgium* (appl. no. 12849/87), Judgement (Chamber), 29 November 1991, Series A, Vol. 214-C.

[371] Belgian Supreme Administrative Court, Judgement, CS no. 38 230 of 29 November 1991, RACE, 1991.

[372] See, for example, Belgian Supreme Administrative Court, Judgement, no 99.769, 12 October 2001; Belgian Supreme Administrative Court, Judgement, no.100.001, 22 October 2001, available at http://www.raadvst-consetat.be. See also Vanheule (2006), 572 et seq.

[373] *D. v. the United Kingdom* (appl. no. 30240/96), Judgement (Chamber), 2 May 1997, Reports 1997-III, 777 et seq., para. 37.

[374] See, for example, Belgian Supreme Administrative Court, Judgement, CS no. 46.098, 11

Court has further affirmed that depending on the circumstances of a case, the expulsion of an alien could violate the right to family life under Article 8(1) ECHR.[375] Belgium has on several occasions been condemned for violations of Article 8 ECHR in this manner.[376]

In the field of tax law, the Supreme Court of Appeal has consistently ruled that Article 6(1) ECHR does not apply to tax disputes, with the exception of fiscal (administrative) fines that constituted a "criminal charge" in accordance with this Article.[377] However, the Constitutional Court has applied Article 1 of Protocol no. 1 to tax disputes, ruling that a tax rate of 90% violated the right of the testator to dispose of his property freely.[378]

b. Coordination through Legislation

As far legislation is concerned, one has to distinguish between general and specific coordinating measures. Whereas the general coordinating measures relate to the extent to which the ECHR constitutes a general yardstick for new legislation, the specific measures concerns legislative responses to ECHR related court decisions regarding specific legislation in Belgium.

The ECHR has become a regular point of reference during the legislative procedure, both on the federal and regional level.[379] For example, in 2006 the federal Parliament adopted legislation that facilitates child adoption by same sex couples.[380] During the Parliamentary debates, the question arose as to whether not allowing same sex couples to adopt children constituted a violation of Article 14 ECHR in conjunction with Article 8(1) ECHR.[381] Similarly, Articles 6(1) and 13 ECHR formed a point of reference in the Parliamentary debates on draft

---

February 1994, *T. Vreemd.* 1994, 97; 574. Belgian Supreme Administrative Court, CS no. 85.529, 22 February 2000, available at http://www.raadvst-consetat.be; see also Vanheule (2006), 574.

[375] Belgian Supreme Administrative Court, Judgement, CS no. 58 969, 1 April 1996; Belgian Supreme Administrative Court, Judgement, CA no. 61 972 of 25 September 1996, available at http://www.raadvst-consetat.be/.

[376] See *Moustaquim v. Belgium* (appl. no. 12313/86), Judgement (Chamber), 18 February 1991, Series A, Vol. 193; *Beldjoudi v. France* (appl. no. 12083/86), Judgement (Chamber), 26 March 1992, Series A, Vol. 234-A; *Nasri v. France* (appl. no. 19465/92), Judgement (Chamber), 13 July 1995, Series A, Vol. 320-B; *Mehemi v. France* (appl. no. 25017/94), Judgement (Chamber), 26 September 1997, Reports 1997-VI, 1959 et seq., para. 51.

[377] Belgian Supreme Court of Appeal, Judgement, Cass., 23 January 1992, Larcier cass, 1992, No. 50C

[378] Belgian Constitutional Court, Judgement, CA no. 107/2005, 22 June 2005, available at http://www.arbitrage.be; Theunis (2005), par. 22.

[379] For an example on the regional level, see references to the ECHR in debates in the Flemish Parliament pertaining to the Flemish housing policy, *Stuk* 15 (2004–2005)-Nr. 7 J; available at http://www.vlaamsparlement.be/vp/index.html.

[380] Act of 18 May 2006 (Belgian Official Gazette, 29 December 2006).

[381] See federal Parliamentary debates in Doc. 51, 0664/008, 168, available at http://www.dekamer.be with reference to *Fretté v. France* (appl. no. 36515/97), Judgement (Third Section), 26 February 2002, Reports 2002-I, 345 et seq.

legislation introducing a filtering procedure for the admission of appeals from lower administrative bodies to the Supreme Administrative Court.[382]

These regular references to the ECHR are also prompted by the *ex ante* review of legislation carried out by the Supreme Administrative Court.[383] During the *ex ante review* the Legislative Section of the Supreme Administrative Court reviews whether the legislation has respected the federal allocation of powers, as well as constitutional and directly applicable treaty rights.[384] However, these advisory opinions are not binding and practice reveals that the Government is not always keen to follow the advice of the Supreme Administrative Court, as will be illustrated below. In addition, the Government sometimes limits the potential human rights scrutiny by the Supreme Administrative Court by qualifying the draft legislation as "urgent". As a result, the Supreme Administrative Court is forced to exercise its review within a couple of days. One such example concerns draft legislation amending the procedure for determining paternity in the Civil Code that was adopted in 2006.[385] The Supreme Administrative Court explicitly criticized the fact that it was granted a mere five days for reviewing such a highly complex and sensitive matter that inter alia touched upon Article 8 ECHR.[386]

As far as the specific measures for coordination are concerned, the Belgian Government(s) in principle amends legislation to bring it line with both Strasbourg and domestic jurisprudence pertaining to the ECHR. However, as the *Marckx* decision already indicated,[387] the legislative amendments sometimes take considerable time and do not always give full effect to the relevant court decision. In that instance, the 1987 legislative amendment did not take into account sufficiently the position of illegitimate children in relation to questions of succession that arose in the inter-phase between the ECtHR decision in 1979 and the 1987 legislation. Moreover, measures that at first sight appear to bring the law in line with the ECHR sometimes contain new restrictions that could effectively undermine any improvement that it is introducing.

A very pertinent example concerns the Act of 27 December 2005, which amended the Act of 6 January 2003, pertaining to special investigative measures in the combating of terrorism and serious, organized crime. The 2005 legislation was a response to a decision of the Constitutional Court of 21 December 2004,

---

[382] See Act of 15 September 2006, published in Belgian Official Gazette, 6 October 2006, No. 322, Edition 1, p. 53468; Federal Parliamentary debates in Doc. 51 2479/011, 11, 20, available at http://www.dekamer.be.

[383] Theunis (2005), par. 3.5.

[384] Van Damme (2001), 77.

[385] See Act of 1 July 2006, published in Belgian Official Gazette, 29 December 2006, No. 431, Edition 6, p. 76040.

[386] Belgian Supreme Administrative Court, Advisory Opinion, no. 39.715/2, 20 January 2006; published in document of Belgian Senate, no. 3-1402/1/2005/2006, available at http://www.dekamer.be.

[387] *Marckx v. Belgium* (appl. no. 6833/74), Judgement (Plenary), 13 June 1979, Series A, Vol. 31.

in which it nullified some of the clauses introduced by the 2003 Act.[388] In doing so, the Constitutional Court *inter alia* concluded that the right to a fair trial in the Constitution was violated as the legislation did not provide for independent, judicial review over the exercise of the special investigative measures.[389] It referred extensively to ECtHR jurisprudence pertaining to Article 6(1) ECHR, emphasizing the equality of arms in access to evidence.[390]

Although the 2005 Act did rectify this deficit, it also authorized new restrictive measures such as unannounced police access to non-residential private property (either through physical or technological means) and the placing of technical surveillance equipment on such property. This Act was adopted despite reservations of the Supreme Administrative Court on several points, including its compatibility with Article 8(1) ECHR.[391] This example further illustrates the occasional reluctance of the Government to follow the advice of the Supreme Administrative Court in relation to its (international) human rights obligations. Moreover, the fact that the 2005 Act was categorised as "urgent" and therefore left the Supreme Administrative Court a mere five days to exercise judicial review, could be interpreted as a deliberate strategy to avoid judicial scrutiny of the legislation in question.

The Supreme Administrative Court alluded to this possibility, indicating that it was not convinced that the entire draft legislation could be regarded as urgent.[392] Similarly, the Government reduced the possibility of an extensive Parliamentary debate on the human rights compatibility of the draft legislation, by submitting it to Parliament in October 2005. This was a mere two months before the legislative deadline of 31 December 2005, which was set by the Constitutional Court in its decision of December 2004. It is, therefore, fair to conclude that while the ECHR has become a regular touchstone during the legislative process, the Government does on occasion tend to minimise its importance, either by not paying heed to criticism from authoritative sources or by attempting to limit judicial scrutiny and public debate on the matter.

3. *Comparison and Conclusion*

From the above overview, one can conclude that the courts in both countries follow the ECtHR in a rather prudent fashion. Although they give effect to rel-

---

[388] Belgian Constitutional Court, Judgement, CA no. 202/2004, 21 December 2004, available at http://www.arbitrage.be.

[389] See also federal Parliamentary debates in Doc 51 2055/005, available at http://www.dekamer.be.

[390] It, *inter alia*, referred to *Edwards and Others v. the United Kingdom* (appl. no. 38260/97), 22 July 2003, Friendly settlement (not reported); *Edwards and Lewis v. the United Kingdom* (appl. nos 39647/98; 40461/98), Judgement (Grand Chamber), 27 October 2004, Reports 2004-X, 61 et seq.

[391] Belgian Supreme Administrative Court, Advisory Opinion, no. 39.092/2 available in document of federal parliament, Doc. 51/2055/001, 28 October 2005, 106–107, http://www.dekamer.be.

[392] The Constitutional Court determined that the annulled clauses had to be replaced by 31 December 2005.

evant decisions, whether rendered against themselves or other State Parties, the domestic courts will rarely initiate new developments themselves.[393] Even so, the ECHR has since the 80's become a touchstone in all areas of jurisprudence. In both countries the ECtHR jurisprudence has affected very similar areas of laws, even if not entirely in the same manner. Without doubt, its impact has been most significant in the field of criminal (procedure) law, which has become more adversarial and even-handed.[394] Other areas of law significantly affected by the impact of the ECHR include administrative law, civil rights jurisprudence, family law, immigration law, and tax law.

The impact of the ECHR in the area of criminal (procedure) law in both countries is in part due to the civil (inquisitorial) nature of their criminal systems; the high value attached in both societies to the avoidance of conflict; and the paternalistic attitude of continental European courts towards criminal offenders. The Dutch and Belgian criminal justice systems operate along the lines of the civil law tradition with roots in the Napoleonic codes. It is inquisitorial in nature, based on the belief that the State is best equipped to carry out an objective investigation into the truth, since parties to the proceedings might have an interest in concealing it. This very premise upon which inquisitorial systems are built makes them more vulnerable to criticism from a human rights perspective than adversarial systems, whatever difficulties adversarial systems may encounter in securing a fair trial to the accused.[395] Typical problems that arose related to lack of impartiality of the procedure as a whole, due to the insufficient attention paid to the adversarial process during the pre-merits phase, as well as the accumulation of functions by the same officials during different stages of the trial.[396]

In addition, it has always been a typical characteristic of Dutch and Belgian societies as a whole that they attach high value to avoiding conflicts, reaching compromises, and building consensus. In this tradition, the primary goal of law and politics is to keep society together and to create a measure of harmony between its members. Relatively low value was, therefore, attached to fighting out conflicts at the point of the sword, since this might jeopardize societal peace. The Dutch and Belgian criminal justice systems were further known for its paternalism and, some would say, mildness. Courts tended to see those who had committed criminal offences as members of a family who should be reintegrated rather than punished. However beneficial these features may often have been to the accused, they did not contribute to placing a high value on their individual rights.[397] It is also worth noting that criminal law in the Netherlands and Belgium tends to be much more politicised than (many areas of) civil law. As a result, the

---

[393] See also Swart (1999), 41 who made this comment in relation to the Netherlands.
[394] See also Swart (1999), 39; Berbuto and Jacobs (2000), 91.
[395] Swart (1999), 43.
[396] See also Lemmens (1988–89), 796, 808.
[397] Swart (1999), 43.

criminal judiciary may be reluctant to be too protective of individual rights when reviewing criminal legislation that amounts to important public policy.

The above analysis has further illustrated that not only their criminal justice systems suffered from paternalistic tendencies that result in a lack of even-handedness and impartiality. Other areas of law have also been plagued by these deficits as is reflected, for example, by the high number of complaints pertaining to Articles 5 and 6 ECHR in the area of administrative law. The influence of Articles 5 and 6 ECHR on domestic courts have increased the quality of jurisprudence in general. The strengthening of adversarial elements such as placing witnesses on the stand more often and allowing parties to testify in their own (civil) proceedings are incentives for the courts to assess the available evidence more thoroughly and more carefully before reaching a decision.[398]

At the same time however, the confrontational elements of the adversarial system may have contributed to an erosion of the traditional mildness of the respective criminal justice systems. The prosecutor has become a more one-sided crime fighter as opposed to a paternalistic father figure who is willing to lead the defendant back to the road of virtue. Moreover, in the Netherlands the role of the "objective" investigating judge, supposedly investigating on behalf of the prosecution and the defence at the pre-trial stage, has been marginalized. The latter has become a more passive figure who awaits the initiative of the prosecutor and the defence council. In Belgium, there has been less formal marginalization of the investigating judges, as they still possess a significant amount of initiative. However, due to the large number of cases, investigative judges struggle to maintain control over the investigation and in practice such control is taken over by the police.

In the area of family law, Article 8 ECHR was of great influence in both countries. This could partly be explained by the fact that the traditional Christian notions of family life have (and still to some extent are) very influential in areas such as family law. In relation to civil rights, Article 10(1) ECHR gained particular prominence in relation to the protection of the confidentiality of journalistic sources. Whereas Belgian legislation now formally recognizes this right, the Dutch legislature still has to adopt comparable legislation, although the right is acknowledged by the jurisprudence of the Supreme Court in relation to both civil and criminal proceedings.[399] The Dutch courts seem to have applied the concept of "civil rights and obligations" in Article 6(1) ECHR more liberally than the Belgian courts in the area of tax law. The right to property in Article 1 of Protocol no. 1 has played a more prominent role in Belgium than in the Netherlands.

---

[398] See Swart (1999), 50; Berbuto and Jacobs (2000), 91. They point out that the reinterpretation of the Code of Criminal Procedure in Belgium in accordance with the ECHR has resulted in interpretations that are sometimes very far removed from the actual text of the Code.

[399] Since 2002 there are guidelines in place in the Netherlands directing police behaviour towards the media during events such as public demonstrations. See *Aanwijzing toepassing dwangmiddelen bij journalisten* at http://archief.om.nl/beleid/beleidsregel.php?cid=1.

Both countries strive to bring their legislation in line with Strasbourg jurisprudence (rendered against themselves and other States alike), or domestic jurisprudence pertaining to the ECHR. It is also fair to say that the ECHR has become a routine touchstone during Parliamentary debates on draft legislation in both legal systems. However, the analysis has also revealed that this does not imply that the respective Governments are always keen to give sufficient effect to their ECHR obligations. In both countries the Governmental authorities sometimes give a limited interpretation to these obligations; push aside criticism of bodies such as the Council of State/Supreme Administrative Court with rhetoric that pays lip-service to the ECHR; or even attempt to limit public debate on the human rights implications of controversial topics such as the combating of international terrorism.

F. Remedies and Proportionality Tests

1. For the Netherlands

a. Remedies

As is well known, the decisions of the ECtHR are declaratory in nature in the sense that it is not competent to quash national legislation or decisions that are contrary to the ECHR, nor does the ECtHR have the power to revise the final decisions of domestic courts. In accordance with Article 53 ECHR, the condemned State is at liberty to choose the means by which to comply with the ECtHR judgement. These measures can include *restitutio in integrum* (re-establishment of the situation prior to the violation); awarding of damages and (regulatory) measures to prevent violations in the future.[400] Sometimes the ECtHR may also come to the conclusion that no damages are to be awarded, as the mere finding of a violation of the ECHR constitutes sufficient satisfaction.[401]

Where the ECtHR awards damages against the Netherlands, the Dutch Government usually pays the awarded sum in a timely fashion. The same holds true for settlements which the parties have agreed to before the ECtHR. Where a settlement is reached it may include the payment of a certain sum of money, sometimes also in conjunction with other measures.[402] There are, nonetheless, shortcomings in relation to the domestic remedies available, resulting from the restricted possibilities for revision of the final, domestic decision that triggered the proceedings before the ECtHR. Since the ECtHR decision does not set aside the flawed decision of the domestic court, the revocation of the domestic decision depends on whether the national system of remedies allows for the reopen-

---

[400] Barkhuysen and Van Emmerik (1999), 7.

[401] See *Auerbach v. the Netherlands* (appl. no. 45600/99), Judgement, 29 January 2002 (not reported), Beslissingen in Belastingzaken, Nederlandse Belastingsrechtspraak, BNB 2002-126, 1104–1107.

[402] See also Barkhuysen and Van Emmerik (1999), 9.

ing of the domestic judicial proceedings, following a successful claim before the ECtHR.[403]

In the Netherlands, one has to distinguish between the reopening of judicial proceedings in criminal proceedings on the one hand and civil and administrative proceedings on the other hand. In addition, there is a (limited) possibility to institute tort proceedings against the State on the basis of State liability for a wrongful act in civil, administrative and criminal proceedings. In criminal proceedings, there is also the possibility of inadmissibility of prosecution and sentence reduction.

aa. Reopening of Criminal Proceedings Since September 2002, Article 457 of the Dutch Code of Criminal Procedure explicitly recognizes the possibility of reopening criminal proceedings, following a judgement of the ECtHR in favour of the person who has been convicted at the domestic level.[404] A request for reopening can be filed with the Supreme Court within a period of three months after the ECtHR judgement, either by the victorious Strasbourg applicant or by the Attorney General. The latter can also use this power against the will of the applicant, a feature that has met with substantial criticism. Third parties whose cases were not decided by the ECtHR but in which a (similar) violation of the ECHR has occurred, cannot file a request for reopening.[405]

In 2005, the Supreme Court clarified the substantive scope of the Article 457 of the Dutch Code of Criminal Procedure, confirming that revision is possible in relation to procedural violations (e.g. Article 6 ECHR), as well as violations of substantive rights (in the case in question Article 8 ECHR in the pre-trial phase).[406] The Supreme Court further confirmed that revision is also possible where it has the exclusive aim of adjusting the domestic sanction that was initially imposed, as a method for compensating the ECHR violation.[407]

Before the 2002 legislative amendment revision in criminal law, proceedings were only possible in two situations. The first concerned decisions that were in conflict with each other, whereas the second concerned a *novum* (a new fact) that would have lead to a different decision if it had been known to the court.[408] Neither of these criteria was considered to be fulfilled where the basis for revision was an ECtHR decision determining the violation of an ECHR provision in criminal proceedings.[409]

---

[403] Barkhuysen and Van Emmerik (1999), 9–10.

[404] Netherlands Official Gazette *(Staatsblad)* 2002, 479, available at http://www.overheid.nl/op/index.html.

[405] Barkhuysen and Van Emmerik (2005), 11.

[406] Dutch Supreme Court, Judgement, HR 27 September 2005, LJN-no. AS8858, available at http://www.rechtspraak.nl.

[407] See also Barkhuysen and Van Emmerik (2006), 59.

[408] Former Article 457 of the Code of Criminal Procedure and subsequent Articles; Barkhuysen and Van Emmerik (1999), 12; Brenninkmeijer (1999), *Execution*, 192.

[409] Dutch Supreme Court, Judgement, HR 13 June 1995, available at http://www.rechtspraak.nl,

This unsatisfactory state of affairs is reflected in the *Van Mechelen* case,[410] where the applicant's conviction of a particularly brutal armed robbery constituted a violation of Articles 6(1) and 6(3) ECHR, as it was essentially based on the statements of anonymous witnesses. Following the ECtHR judgements, Mr. Van Mechelen was released from prison and received damages from the Dutch Government, but was unable to alter the criminal conviction against him.[411] Simultaneously, there was considerable dissatisfaction within Dutch society due to the speedy release of someone whose innocence remained seriously in doubt. The possibility of reopening the proceedings at the time would have served the interest of all parties concerned; it would have offered the accused the possibility to clear his name and the State, on the other hand, to establish their guilt beyond reasonable doubt.[412]

As indicated above, the 2002 legislative amendment introduced the possibility of reopening criminal proceedings in relation to the victorious Strasbourg applicant. Third parties who have been finally and irrevocably convicted in criminal proceedings suffering from the same or similar flaws, but who had not submitted a complaint to the ECtHR, cannot file for reopening. Summary proceedings in a civil court are the only way in which they can effect their release.[413] After the ECtHR's decision in *Van Mechelen* a third party (B), who was also convicted on the basis of anonymous testimony, demanded his release from prison in summary proceedings before the District Court in The Hague.[414] According to District Court, the judge in summary proceedings must briefly review the fairness of the criminal proceedings. If there is any doubt as to the fairness of these proceedings, there is a reason for the judge in summary proceedings to intervene in the current detention. However, the threshold for effecting a release in this manner is very high and the summary proceedings judge will only grant a release in the most obvious cases. In the case of B, the District Court concluded that there was no violation of Article 6 ECHR.[415]

concerning a request for revision as a consequence of the ECtHR's decisions *Lala v. the Netherlands* (appl. no. 14861/89), Judgement (Chamber), 22 September 1994, Series A, Vol. 297-A; *Pelladoah v. the Netherlands* (appl. no. 16737/90), Judgement (Chamber), 22 September 1994, Series A, Vol. 297-B. See also Barkhuysen and Van Emmerik (1999), 11; Brenninkmeijer (1999), Execution, 192.

[410] *Van Mechelen and Others v. the Netherlands* (appl. nos 21363/93, 21364/93, 21427/93; 22056/93), Judgement (Chamber), 23 April 1997, Reports 1997-III, 691 et seq., para. 36.

[411] Similar consequences resulted from *Kostovski v. the Netherlands* (appl. no. 11454/85), Judgement (Plenary), 20 November 1989, Series A, Vol. 166. See Barkhuysen and Van Emmerik (1999), 10.

[412] Barkhuysen and Van Emmerik (1999), 5, 6; Brenninkmeijer (1999), *Execution*, 198.

[413] Spronken (1999), 263.

[414] Court of First Instance of The Hague, 1 Augustus 1997, Nieuwsbrief Strafrecht 1997, 3; Myjer (1999), 263.

[415] A few years earlier, in *Kostovski v. the Netherlands* (appl. no. 11454/85), Judgement (Plenary), 20 November 1989, Series A, Vol. 166, two accomplices of Mr. Kostovski who did not file a complaint in Strasbourg indeed effected their release during summary proceedings. In this instance, the District Court ordered their release, as it was almost certain that a complaint before the ECtHR

bb. Inadmissibility of Prosecution and Sentence Reduction In most instances where the Netherlands are condemned for violating the reasonable time criterion in Article 6(1) ECHR in relation to criminal proceedings, the courts declare the charges by the public prosecutor inadmissible.[416] In 1981 the Supreme Court expressly indicated that the lower courts should follow this line.[417] It held that where a trial is not held without unreasonable delay, the prosecution must be deemed to have been conducted in violation of fundamental principles of a fair trial, as a result of which the prosecutor loses the right to continue the prosecution and the charge becomes inadmissible.[418] However, subsequently the Supreme Court ruled that exceeding the reasonable time limit does not necessarily have to result in the inadmissibility of the prosecution, but may instead be compensated by sentence reduction.[419]

cc. Revision of Civil and Administrative Proceedings For the time being, no comparable legislative regulation to Article 457 of the Code of Criminal Procedure exists in the fields of civil and administrative law. Where the ECtHR determines that such proceedings violated the ECHR, revision is not yet possible.[420] In relation to civil law Article 382 of the Civil Procedure Code limits the scope of revision to an exhaustive list of grounds all pertaining to the fraudulent behaviour of the other party during the original proceedings.[421] A decision of the ECtHR does not fall within these grounds. As far as administrative law is concerned, Article 8:88 of the GALA allows revision in case of a *novum* (new fact), that would have lead to a different decision if it had been known to the Court.[422] However, case law has yet to recognise a judgement of the ECtHR as a *novum*. The only remedy available where the ECtHR determines that civil and administrative proceedings are in violation of the ECHR is the wrongful act procedure against the State discussed below.

Legal writers have frequently called for the introduction of a revision procedure in relation to civil and administrative proceedings conducted in violation

would have been decided in the same manner as that of Mr. Kostovski. See Zwaak (2002), 604 ; Spronken (1999), 263.

[416] Zwaak (2002), 603.

[417] Dutch Supreme Court, Judgement, HR 23 September, 1981, NJ 1981, 116.

[418] Dutch Supreme Court, Judgement, HR 23 September, 1981, NJ 1981, 116.

[419] In accordance with Article 359a of the Code of Criminal Procedure, sentence reduction is also possible in case of irregularities during the investigation leading up to the trial. This would include, for example, where evidence was obtained in violation of Article 8(1) EHCR of the accused. See Dutch Supreme Court, Judgement, HR 20 March 2004, NJ 2004, 376; see also Zwaak (2002), 604.

[420] Revision should be distinguished from a new decision, which could be requested in relation to administrative orders that were given in violation of the ECHR and that do not affect the rights of third parties. A typical example would be an administrative decision concerning the granting or extension of a residence permit. See Barkhuysen and Van Emmerik (2006), 55.

[421] Brenninkmeijer (1999), *Execution*, 192.

[422] Barkhuysen and Van Emmerik (2005), 5; Brenninkmeijer (1999), *Execution*, 192.

of the ECHR, especially in the wake of the *Dombo Beheer v. the Netherlands* case.[423] Following this ECtHR decision, the District Court in The Hague stayed its decision on State liability for a wrongful act, in order to investigate whether the legal system permitted in any way the reopening of the procedure between *Dombo Beheer* and the *NMB* bank.[424] According to the District Court, it was not unreasonable to expect any party to the proceedings to be confronted with the reopening of the proceedings, given the fundamental nature of the principles of procedural law at stake. In addition, these principles have been hotly debated at all domestic levels and it was clear that one of the parties would file a claim before the ECtHR.[425] However, this attempt of the District Court failed as the applicant in this case died soon after the interlocutory judgement and no request for revision was lodged.[426]

dd. State Liability for a Wrongful Act A successful application before the ECtHR can result in tort proceedings against the State for a wrongful act (tort) by a State organ pursuant to Article 6:162 of the Civil Code. In fact, this may sometimes be the only remedy available in situations where revision of the court proceedings is not possible.[427] In the Netherlands, the claim arising out of a wrongful act committed by the State is only directed at the State and does not directly alter the legal position of any party involved in the original proceedings.[428] In most instances, the ECHR violations are attributable to the (highest) domestic court as an organ of State which, in accordance with Articles 93 and 94 of the Constitution, is in a position to either prevent or remedy the ECHR violation through reviewing a particular provision or practice against the ECHR. Tort proceedings arising out of wrongful legislation may in some cases also be possible.[429]

In order to be successful, tort proceedings for a wrongful act by the State has to meet with a high threshold, as non-liability is the main rule and liability the exception. This also holds true for liability claims arising from an ECtHR decision.[430] According to the Supreme Court, a broader notion of liability would not be in keeping with the closed system of remedies known to Dutch law. The legislator is deemed to have thoroughly evaluated whether legal remedies should be granted or not. Allowing tort proceedings against the State would in fact re-subject a closed case to (new) judicial appraisal.[431] Liability can, therefore, only arise in exceptional circumstances, when in the preparation of a judicial decision

---

[423] *Dombo Beheer v. the Netherlands* (appl. no. 14448/88), Judgement (Chamber), 27 October 1993, Series A, Vol. 274.
[424] Court of First Instance of The Hague, 18 September 1996, JOR 1996; 106.
[425] Barkhuysen and Van Emmerik (1999), 5.
[426] Ibid., 6.
[427] Barkhuysen and Van Emmerik (2005), 7.
[428] Barkhuysen and Van Emmerik (1999), 18.
[429] Ibid.
[430] Barkhuysen and Van Emmerik (1999), 19.
[431] Dutch Supreme Court, Judgement, HR 3 December 1971, NJ 1972, 137.

such fundamental principles of law have been ignored that it is no longer possible to speak of a fair and impartial treatment of the case, and no legal remedy is or was available for that decision.[432]

In essence, this means that a violation of the criteria articulated in the first sentence of Article 6(1) ECHR must be at stake.[433] Moreover, even within this category the Supreme Court has differentiated. For example, it did not qualify the principle of proper justification in Article 6(1) ECHR as a fundamental principle of law; nor the exceeding of the reasonable time-limit.[434] Recently the Supreme Court did, however, award damages on the basis of State liability for a wrongful act, subsequent to the ECtHR decision in the *Van Mechelen* case.[435] In this instance the criminal conviction was based on the testimony of anonymous witnesses, which violated Article 6(1) in combination with Article 6(3) ECHR.[436]

It remains to be seen whether a letter of 12 August 2005 of the (then) Minister of Justice to the Lower House of Parliament may encourage the Supreme Court to relax its criteria for determining State liability. The Minister indicated that in the interest of better implementation of the ECtHR jurisprudence one should make more use of tort proceedings against the State for wrongful judicial acts, which implies a broadening of the grounds for State liability.[437] It also remains to be seen whether tort proceedings against the State will still be available in those instances where a finding of violation by the ECtHR leads to a reopening of the (criminal) proceedings in terms of Article 457 of the Code of Criminal Procedure.[438]

b. Proportionality Test

The proportionality test incumbent in the limitation clauses of most ECHR obligations has become the most significant substantive criterion applied by the courts and legislature in the context of the limitation of individual rights. It is important to point out that the limitation clauses attached to the fundamental rights in the 1983 Constitution are of a formal nature and do not go beyond determining that the legislature is competent to limit the right in question. They do not contain substantive limitations comparable to those in the ECHR, notably

---

[432] Subsequently confirmed in Dutch Supreme Court, Judgement, HR 17 March 1978, NJ 1979, 204.

[433] Dutch Supreme Court, Judgement, HR 1 February 1991, NJ 1991, 413; Barkhuysen and Van Emmerik (1999), 19.

[434] See Smits (1996), 136 et seq. and case law cited there.

[435] *Van Mechelen and Others v. the Netherlands* (appl. nos 21363/93, 21364/93, 21427/93; 22056/93), Judgement (Chamber), 23 April 1997, Reports 1997-III, 691 et seq., para. 36.

[436] See Dutch Supreme Court, Judgement, HR 18 March 2005, NJ 2005, 201; Barkhuysen and Van Emmerik (2006) no. 60, 57.

[437] Parliamentary debates, *Kamerstukken II* 2004/05, 29 279, no. 28, http://www.tweedekamer.nl/kamerstukken/index.jspt ; Barkhuysen and Van Emmerik (2006), 57.

[438] This possibility was not yet available following *Van Mechelen and Others v. the Netherlands* (appl. no. 21363/93, 21364/93, 21427/93 and 22056/93), Judgement (Chamber), 23 April 1997, Reports 1997-III, 691 et seq., para. 36.

the requirements of the legitimate aim and proportionality of the limitation.[439] During the constitutional revision of 1983, the legislature did not intend to copy the ECHR, but strived for designing a more precise bill of rights that was tailored to the peculiarities of Dutch society. As a result, the rights in the ECHR and its Protocols do not correspond to the fundamental rights in the Bill of Rights in a one to one fashion.[440]

However, the foregoing analysis revealed that the courts apply the proportionality test consistently in determining whether a law or practice is in accordance with the ECHR. This also applies to situations in which ECHR obligations are applied between third parties, although the courts recognise that the types of interests at stake are not identical to those applicable in relationships between individuals and the State. Similarly, the foregoing analysis illustrated that the proportionality principle is an important touchstone during the legislative procedure in as far as it concerns legislation that affects ECHR obligations.

2. Belgium

a. Remedies

In the case of Belgium, the question also arises whether the payment of (sometimes very limited) damages following a negative judgement by the ECtHR or a settlement agreement constitutes sufficient compensation for the applicants, especially where such persons still have a criminal conviction against their name. When examining the system of domestic remedies, one identifies categories similar to those in the Netherlands. These include the reopening of judicial proceedings in criminal proceedings; suspension of prosecution and sentence reduction in criminal proceedings; (the non-availability of) revision in civil and administrative proceedings; and the (limited) possibility to institute tort proceedings against the State on the basis of State liability for a wrongful act in civil, administrative and criminal proceedings.

aa. Reopening of Criminal Proceedings In April 2007, the federal parliament finally adopted legislation facilitating the reopening of criminal proceedings by persons whose conviction was subsequently condemned by the ECtHR.[441] At the time of adoption of this legislation, Belgium was one of only four Contracting States of the Council of Europe which had not yet facilitated such a reopening procedure and was risking a negative judgement by the Committee of Ministers in this regard.[442]

---

[439] However, even if these criteria were included their impact would remain limited due to the absence of constitutional review. Bark huysen, Van Emmerik and Loof (2000), 334.

[440] Barkhuysen, Van Emmerik and Loof (2000), 333.

[441] Act of 1 April 2007, published in Belgian Official Gazette, 9 May 2007, No. 140. Edition 2, p. 25415, http://www.ejustice.just.fgov.be/cgi/welcome.pl.

[442] See also Federal Parliament, Doc. 51 2819/001, available at http://www.dekamer.be.

The legislation amended Book II, Title III of the Code of Criminal Procedure by adding a Chapter II*bis* to II*octis*.[443] In essence, criminal proceedings could then be re-opened where the domestic decision that resulted in a conviction is subsequently contradicted by a decision of the ECtHR; or where the ECtHR finds a violation of the ECHR resulting from procedural errors which are so serious that doubts exist in relation to the accuracy of the outcome of the domestic trial. However, such reopening would only be possible where the convicted person suffers serious consequences, which can only be remedied by the reopening of the proceedings.[444] Moreover, in the interest of legal certainty, the rights of third parties may not be affected by the reopening of the proceedings.[445]

This procedure has to be launched with the Supreme Court of Appeal 6 months since the decision of the ECtHR. It will be available to the Attorney General (on request of the Minister of Justice), as well as to those convicted persons (or their direct relatives) who have subsequently filed a successful complaint before the ECtHR, and other persons who were convicted on the basis of the same facts and evidence.[446] One could, therefore, assume that all persons convicted during the same trial on the same facts would have access to this procedure. It is not yet clear what would constitute sufficiently serious consequences meriting the reopening of criminal proceedings, but one could argue that the mere existence of a potentially unjust criminal conviction would meet this threshold. It also remains unclear whether the remedy of State liability for a wrongful act on the basis of Articles 1382 and 1383 of the Civil Code would still be open to those persons who succeed in reopening criminal proceedings, following a successful complaint before the ECtHR.

In the absence of this new legislation, the only potential avenue for reopening criminal proceedings following a successful claim in Strasbourg was Article 441 of the Code of Criminal Procedure. In accordance with this Article, the Minister of Justice can order the Attorney General to request the Supreme Court of Appeal to revoke laws or judicial decisions that are in violation of the law.[447] In accordance with the jurisprudence of the Supreme Court of Appeal, this remedy could only be relied on where new facts became available to the court that could not have been considered by it at the time of the appeal. However, the Supreme

---

[443] Article 2, Act of 1 April 2007, published in Belgian Official Gazette, 9 May 2007, No. 140. Edition 2, p. 25415, http://www.ejustice.just.fgov.be/cgi/welcome.pl.

[444] Article 4 and Article 7, Act of 1 April 2007, published in Belgian Official Gazette, 9 May 2007, No. 140. Edition 2, p. 25415, http://www.ejustice.just.fgov.be/cgi/welcome.pl.

[445] For example, where the deficient domestic proceedings have resulted in the convicted person paying damages to a third party, this will be refunded by the State if subsequently revealed that such damages were unjust.

[446] Article 5 and Article 6, Act of 1 April 2007, published in Belgian Official Gazette, 9 May 2007, No. 140. Edition 2, p. 25415, http://www.ejustice.just.fgov.be/cgi/welcome.pl.

[447] See the exposé of Lemmens before the federal parliament in Doc. 50 1083/008, 3 May 2002, 12, available at http://www.dekamer.be.

Court of Appeal has generally not been willing to recognize a finding of violation by the ECtHR pertaining to criminal proceedings as a new fact.[448]

The main exception was the *Piersack* case,[449] in which the ECtHR determined a violation of Article 6(1) ECHR, since a member of the domestic court dealing with the merits also served as an investigating judge at the pre-trial stage. During the subsequent request for reopening the proceedings, the Supreme Court of Appeal accepted the Attorney General's argument that two new facts became known to the court since the time of *Piersack's* appeal. These included the function and effective role of the magistrate during the investigation against *Piersack*, which were previously unknown to the court.[450] The *Piersack* case was thereafter reopened before a different court. Subsequently, in the very similar *De Cubber* case,[451] the Supreme Court of Appeal rejected the notion that an ECtHR determination of a violation of the ECHR during domestic criminal proceedings constituted a new fact. This has since become the dominant position in Belgian law.[452]

Finally, it is noteworthy that section 443 of the Code of Criminal Procedure also provides for revision of final convictions in instances of conflicting decisions resulting from the same facts; where a conviction is based on false evidence; and where new facts emerge that would have lead to a different decision if it had been known to the court. However, a determination of the ECtHR that a domestic judge has erred, interpreted the facts incorrectly, or has not taken note of a new trend in jurisprudence, does not qualify as a new fact in this sense.[453]

bb. Inadmissibility of Prosecution and Sentence Reduction The question of inadmissibility of prosecution and sentence reduction is particularly pertinent in relation to violations of the reasonable time criterion, with which Belgium faces ongoing problems. In the absence of legislation indicating the appropriate remedy to be applied, the Supreme Court of Appeal determined that the court deciding the facts of the case can impose a sentence below the statutory minimum punishment and, in exceptional circumstances, impose a guilty verdict without a sentence.[454]

The possibility for declaring the prosecution inadmissible was also affirmed in an earlier decision in 1986. According to the Supreme Court of Appeal, inadmis-

[448] Belgian Supreme Court of Appeal, Judgement, Cass., 1 January 1987, Pas. 1987, I, 616 nr. 308; See also discussion in federal Parliament, Doc. 3-1769/3 2006/2007, 2, 6, available at http://www.dekamer.be.
[449] *Piersack v. Belgium* (appl. no. 8692/79), Judgement (Chamber), 1 October 1982, Series A, Vol. 53.
[450] Belgian Supreme Court of Appeal, Judgement, Cass. 18 May 2003, Arr. Cass. 1982–83, 1148; Lemmens in Doc. 50 1083/008, 3 May 2002, 13, available at http://www.dekamer.be.
[451] *De Cubber v. Belgium* (appl. no. 9186/80), Judgement (Chamber), 26 October 1984, Series A, Vol. 86.
[452] See Lemmens in Doc. 50 1083/008, 3 May 2002, 14, available at http://www.dekamer.be.
[453] Lemmens in Doc. 50 1083/008, 3 May 2002, 16, available at http://www.dekamer.be.
[454] Belgian Supreme Court of Appeal, Judgement, Cass., 9 December 1997, R.W., 1988–00, 14.

sibility of prosecution could result from loss of evidence due to the lapse of time (as a result of which there may be no case to answer), as well as the consequences of the delay for the accused who may have already spent a considerable time in custody.[455] In a later decision, however, the Supreme Court of Appeal was reluctant to declare a prosecution inadmissible due to the loss of evidence resulting from an unreasonable delay in the trial. It noted that in order to appreciate whether the lost evidence was vital to the proceedings, the court should examine all elements of the case. However, this would be impossible when it declared the prosecution inadmissible.[456]

In 2000 the remedies of sentence reduction and guilty verdict without a sentence in instances where the criminal proceedings exceeded the reasonably delay, were concretised in Article 21ter of the Criminal Procedure Code.[457] It is important to note that in all the cases in which the Supreme Court of Appeal opted for these sanctions (including in the period before the introduction of Article 21ter), the criminal responsibility of the accused had been established beyond reasonable doubt. It is, therefore, possible to argue that the inadmissibility of prosecution remains a possibility in those cases where criminal responsibility had not been proved beyond reasonable doubt, because of the loss of evidence due to the unreasonable delay in the proceedings. In 2001 the Supreme Court of Appeal determined that a trial judge could apply Article 21ter of the Criminal Procedure Code, where the unreasonable delay did not have any influence on the evidence or on the rights of the defendant.[458] This could be interpreted as leaving open the possibility to declare the prosecution inadmissible where the delay had indeed affected the evidence or the rights of the defence.

cc. Revision of Civil and Administrative Proceedings   In Belgian law, the review of civil or administrative proceedings following a successful complaint before the ECtHR is not possible. Although the revision of civil proceedings are possible in accordance with Articles 1088 and 1133 of the Civil Procedure Code, the grounds for revision provided by these Articles do not include a finding of violation of civil proceedings by the ECtHR.

Article 1088 of the Civil Procedure Code permits the Minister of Justice to order the Attorney General to request a revision of civil proceedings from the Supreme Court of Appeal, where judges, public prosecutors have acted *ultra vires*. Although this Article at first sight resembles Article 441 of the Code of

---

[455] Belgian Supreme Court of Appeal, Judgement, Cass., 22 October 1986, R.W. 1987–88, 535.
[456] Belgian Supreme Court of Appeal, Judgement, Cass., 1 February 1994, available at http://www.juridat.be.
[457] Article 21(3) of the Code of Criminal Procedure, which was introduced by the Act of 30 June 2000, published in Belgium Official Gazette, 2 December 2000, No. 233, Edition 1, p. 40488.
[458] Belgian Supreme Court of Appeal, Judgement, Cass., 31 October 2001, available at http://www.juridat.be.

Criminal Procedure, it does not have the same purpose and it is not accepted as a suitable avenue for revision of civil proceedings following a negative judgement by the ECtHR.[459] The grounds for revision contained in Article 1133 of the Civil Procedure Code do not constitute a suitable basis either, given that they all imply fraudulent behaviour by one of the parties that subsequently result in an erroneous judgement.[460] Similarly, revision of administrative proceedings is also only possible in instances where the court has erred because evidence has been withheld in a fraudulent manner.[461] Once again, these grounds do not include a situation where the Supreme Administrative Court rejected the appeal of an applicant who was subsequently successful in Strasbourg.

The legislation recently adopted by the federal Parliament only provides for the reopening of criminal proceedings following a finding of violation by the ECtHR and no similar legislation providing for revision of civil or administrative proceedings is likely to be forthcoming soon.

dd. State Liability for a Wrongful Act A successful application before the ECtHR can result in tort proceedings against the State for a wrongful act (tort) by a State organ pursuant to Articles 1382 and 1383 of the Belgian Civil Procedure Code. In most instances, the ECHR violations are attributable to the (highest) domestic courts that can either prevent or remedy the ECHR violation through reviewing a particular provision or practice directly against the ECHR (in the case of the ordinary courts), or indirectly by interpreting the constitution in accordance with the ECHR (in the case of the Constitutional Court). Since September 2006, violations of Articles 1382 and 1383 can also be attributed to the legislature for having acted or failing to act in accordance with EHCR obligations.[462]

In a well-known decision of 1994, the Supreme Court of Appeal confirmed that State liability in accordance with Articles 1382 and 1383 of the Civil Procedure Code could be triggered where a court wrongfully applies a the law – including a directly applicable international norm.[463] In order to guarantee judicial independence, damages can only be claimed from the State as such and not from

---

[459] Lemmens in Doc. 50 1083/008, 3 May 2002, 20, available at http://www.dekamer.be; See also exposé of De Schutter before federal parliament, Doc 50 1083/008 2001/2002. 27, available at http://www.dekamer.be.

[460] Lemmens in Doc. 50 1083/008, 3 May 2002, 18, available at http://www.dekamer.be.

[461] Act of 12 January 1973; see also De Schutter, in Doc 50 1083/008 2001/2002. 31, available at http://www.dekamer.be.

[462] Belgian Supreme Court of Appeal, Judgement, Cass., 28 September 2006, available at http://www.juridat.be. Note that in accordance with Article 27 of the Act of 13 March 1973, compensation is also possible for detentions in violation of Article 5(1) ECHR. This claim is essentially based on Articles 1382 and 1383 of the Civil Procedure Code, but concretized separately and directed at the Minister of Justice as representative of the State.

[463] Belgian Supreme Court of Appeal, Judgement, Cass., 8 December 1994, R.W. 1995–96, 180; See also Belgian Supreme Court of Appeal, Judgement, Cass., 19 December 1991, R.W. 1992–93; See also Bindels (2002), 396.

the judge or member of the prosecution service in question.[464] Moreover, in order to guarantee legal certainty, the threshold for triggering State liability in this manner is very high. The mere fact that that the ECtHR came to a different decision than the (highest) domestic court, would not necessarily imply that the latter has committed a wrongful act in accordance with Articles 1382 and 1383 of the Civil Procedure Code. One would also have to prove damages resulting from the erroneous decision and a causal link between the damages and the decision of the court. In addition, it must be clear that the respective judge did not live up to the reasonable duty of care incumbent on him or her, in the circumstances of the case.[465] This implies that the legal norm incorrectly applied by the court must have been well established at the time of the court proceedings and that the judge ought to have known that a deviation from well settled case law would result in a violation of the ECHR.[466]

The one area in which ECtHR findings of violations have resulted in State liability for a wrongful act concerns the violation of the reasonable time criterion in Article 6(1) ECHR. This should come as no surprise, given severe problems that Belgium is facing in this regard. Since the late 90's the courts have repeatedly awarded damages on the basis of Article 1382 and 1383 of the Civil Procedure Code in cases where the violation of the reasonable time criterion did not result from the behaviour of the parties or their council, but was due exclusively to the workload of the courts.[467]

In a decision of 28 September 2006, the Supreme Court of Appeal also affirmed that undue delay caused by the legislature can result in State liability on the basis of Articles 1382 and 1383 of the Civil Procedure Code.[468] The tort claim resulted from the fact that a claim for medical negligence that was submitted to the court of first instance in Brussels in November 1986 had still not been heard on the merits by June 2004. The Supreme Court of Appeal reaffirmed that Article 6(1) ECHR obliges the Belgian State to organize its judicial system in such a manner that it guarantees everyone the right to have their case heard within a reasonable time. This also implied a variety of legislative measures which the legislature had thus far failed to take – a fact which had lead to several findings of violations by the ECtHR.

The failure of the legislature to fulfil this directly applicable international obligation can result in a wrongful act in terms of Article 1382 and 1383 of the

---

[464] Alen (2000), 387.

[465] Alen (2000), 388. See also Wouters and Van Eeckhoutte (2006), 222; Bindels (2002), 396; Geldhof (2006), 201 et seq.

[466] De Schutter in Doc. 50 1083/008 2001/2002. 32, available at http://www.dekamer.be.

[467] Court of First Instance, Brussels, 21 March 1980, J.D.F., 1980, 289; Court of Appeal, Brussels, 16 December 1999, J.L.M.B., 2000, 578; Court of First Instance, Brussels, T.M.R. 2000, 273; Court of First Instance, Brussels, 6 November 2001, J.T. 2001, 865. See Alen (2000), 502; Bindels (2002), 397 et seq.

[468] Belgian Supreme Court of Appeal, Judgement, Cass., 28 September 2006, available at http://www.juridat.be.

Civil Procedure Code.[469] State liability in this sense can be triggered either by the violation of a domestic norm or a directly applicable international norm and can result from either an act or an omission.[470] The criteria applied to claims for wrongful behaviour by the judiciary is to be applied by analogy. The claimant, therefore, has to prove damages as well as a causal link between such damages and the behaviour of the legislature. Similarly, it has to be certain that legislature did not act in accordance with the duty of care to be expected from the normally prudent and diligent legislature in the same circumstances. In the current circumstances, this burden of proof was met, given the long-standing problems relating the organization of the judiciary in the Brussels region and the inability of the legislature to find a solution.[471]

It remains to be seen to what extent the courts will also be willing to acknowledge State liability for a wrongful act by the legislature in instances where other ECHR obligations than the reasonable delay criterion is at stake. The decision of the Supreme Court of Appeal of 28 September 2006 has certainly opened the door to such liability in the future.

b. Proportionality Test

The proportionality requirements contained in the ECHR have had a significant influence on the development of substantive limitations applicable to the constitutional rights. This influence has occurred by means of judicial interpretation rather than a formal constitutional amendment. The rights currently guaranteed in Title II of the Constitution still stem from the Belgian Constitution of 1831. In accordance with this tradition, the Constitution merely provides for formal limitation criteria, notably that no preventive measures are imposed and that the other restrictions are laid down by, or in accordance with, the law.[472] However, since the Constitutional Court treats the constitutional rights and their corresponding counterparts in the ECHR as an inseparable whole, it also applies the substantive limitation criteria of the ECHR to the relevant constitutional rights when interpreting and applying them.[473]

---

[469] The Advocate General Leclerq made this argument, *inter alia*, with reference to Article 13 ECHR. Also, for the purposes of activating Article 1382 or Article 1383 of the Code of Civil Procedure, it does not matter whether one is applying a directly applicable norm of EU law or a directly applicable obligation of the ECHR.

[470] The mere confirmation of such a violation would not amount to a violation of the separation of powers, as it is still up to the legislature to decide how the violation has to be remedied. However, where there is no obligation to act (but a mere discretion), State liability in terms of Article 1382 and Article 1383 cannot be triggered, as this would usurp the powers of the legislature. See also Advocate General *Leclerq* in the Belgian Supreme Court of Appeal, Judgement, Cass., 28 September 2006, available at http://www.juridat.be.

[471] Belgian Supreme Court of Appeal, Judgement, Cass., 28 September 2006, available at http://www.juridat.be; see also Bindels (2002), 402 et seq.

[472] Theunis (2005), par. 3; Alen (2000), 473.

[473] Belgian Constitutional Court, Judgement, CA, no. 136/2004, 19 October 2004, available at http://www.arbitrage.be; Theunis (2005), par. 2.4.

Similarly, the ordinary courts consistently apply the ECHR proportionality requirements when reviewing legislation or executive acts against ECHR, or when applying ECHR obligations between third parties. The foregoing analysis has further revealed that proportionality requirements constitute a focal point in Parliamentary debates pertaining to measures aimed at the limitation of individual rights, even though the Government(s) may not always be keen to acknowledge the disproportionate impact of its actions.

3. Comparison and Conclusion

The above analysis reveals that the domestic remedies available to a successful applicant in Strasbourg are limited in both the Netherlands and Belgium. In both countries, damages resulting from State liability for a wrongful act seem to be the only remedy possible in relation to criminal, civil and administrative proceedings. However, the threshold is very high and this remedy is by no means a certainty when an applicant has won his or her case before the ECtHR. In Belgium, courts are willing to acknowledge a violation of the reasonable time criterion in Article 6(1) ECHR as a wrongful act that can trigger State responsibility, whereas this is not (yet) the case in the Netherlands.

This difference relates to the severe challenges that Belgium is facing in relation to long delays during court proceedings, especially in the Brussels region. For the same reason, the possibility of State liability for wrongful acts attributable to the legislature (i.e. the inability to organize the judicial system in an efficient manner) is more relevant in Belgium than the Netherlands. However, one may question whether such an attempt to attribute the State liability to a specific branch of State authority is not slightly artificial, given that court backlogs tend to be a structural problem resulting from the behaviour of all three branches of Government and the manner in which they interact.[474]

Sentence reduction seems to be the favoured remedy in both countries when criminal proceedings result in a violation of the reasonable time criterion. Both countries are providing for a limited possibility to reopen criminal proceedings following a successful complaint in Strasbourg. The Belgian law (once adopted) seems to be slightly more progressive than its Dutch counterpart. Whereas the Dutch law only allows for successful applicants in Strasbourg to have their cases reopened, the Belgian law would also permit reopening for persons such as accomplices who were convicted during the same trial and on the same facts, but who did not subsequently pursue the matter in Strasbourg. Both countries remain keen on protecting the interests of third parties during the reopening of such proceedings. It remains unclear in both countries if and to what extent the remedy of State liability for a wrongful act would remain available to those persons who successfully requested the reopening of their criminal proceedings.

---

[474] Bindels (2002), 408.

In both countries, the domestic remedies available in instances where the ECtHR finds that domestic civil or administrative proceedings violated the ECHR remain inadequate. In essence, the remedy of State liability for a wrongful act (which has a very high threshold) seems to be the only remedy available following a successful complaint in Strasbourg. Neither country provides for the revision of civil or administrative proceedings under such circumstances. According to the proponents of such revision, this would imply that victorious plaintiffs are often left without any meaningful redress if the ECtHR either did not award any damages or only a very limited amount.

They also point to awkward situations of unequal treatment that can arise as a result of the inability to reopen civil or administrative proceedings. A pertinent example is the case of disciplinary (administrative) proceedings resulting in a professional suspension for a certain period of time. Since these are not criminal proceedings, revision would not be possible if the ECtHR were subsequently to find that, for example, the proceedings were not in accordance with Article 6(1) ECHR. However, where a professional suspension constitutes part of a criminal sentence which is subsequently found to be flawed by the ECtHR, reopening of the proceedings would in principle be possible.

Although these claims are very legitimate, it has proven very difficult in both countries to balance them in a satisfactory manner with legal certainty (the notion that all proceedings have to come to an end) and third party interests. First, there is the issue whether only the victorious applicants before the ECtHR should have the possibility to reopen proceedings, or whether other individuals in identical or similar situations should also have the opportunity to do so.[475] In addition, there is the question whether one should limit such revision to proceedings to which the national authorities are a party, in order to protect third party interests.[476] Can one expect civil opponents to re-subject themselves to legal proceedings years after the proceedings had acquired *res judicata* status on the domestic level – while it was in fact the State who was responsible for the violation of the ECHR during the domestic proceedings?[477] In addition, one has to consider that the other civil party did not have the opportunity to argue his or her case before the ECtHR.[478]

Moreover, in situations where the State is party to the proceedings, questions of legal certainty and even-handedness can arise. This would notably be the case in administrative proceedings that affect the rights and interests of third parties,

---

[475] Myjer (1999), 251.

[476] Barkhuysen and Van Emmerik (1999), 15.

[477] Barkhuysen and Van Emmerik (1999), 15; Lemmens in Doc. 50 1083/008, 3 May 2002, 17, available at http://www.dekamer.be.

[478] This was actually a point of critique against the interlocutory judgement of the District Court of the Hague in the *Dombo Beheer v. the Netherlands* (appl. no. 14448/88), Judgement (Chamber), 27 October 1993, Series A, Vol. 274. See Barkhuysen and Van Emmerik (1999), 16; Brenninkmeijer (1999), *Execution*, 118, 199; De Schutter in Doc. 50 1083/008 2001/2002. 32, available at http://www.dekamer.be.

for example where the authorities refused to issue an individual licence for a factory or gas station.[479] The question arises whether it would be acceptable to individuals in the neighborhood who were neither responsible for the flawed domestic proceedings, nor had the opportunity to argue their case before the ECtHR, if many years later they still faced the possibility that a permit may be granted that could affect their interests.[480]

In light of these challenges, it is unlikely that the Dutch or Belgian legislatures will any time soon be introducing the possibility of revision of civil and/or administrative proceedings to victorious applicants before the ECHR. The most likely avenue for the improvement of the domestic remedies available to individuals in such circumstances would be State liability for a wrongful act. This would, however, imply that the threshold for determining wrongful behaviour by the courts and legislatures would need to be lowered.

As far as the proportionality test is concerned, it is very present during the judicial process in both countries. Given the absence of substantive limitations in their constitutions, the proportionality requirements contained in the ECHR are a vital element for determining whether Governmental acts or practices are succeeding in finding a balance between the rights of the individual and society as a whole. However, as illuminated above, the visible presence of the proportionality requirements in the judicial debate does not necessarily imply that the courts or legislatures will apply these requirements in a manner that favours the individual. Courts would not easily come to the conclusion that measures limiting individual rights are disproportionate, while Governments are equally reluctant to acknowledge that their acts may have such an effect. This was poignantly illustrated by the debates in both countries on measures aimed at the combating of international terrorism. In such instances Governments may even be keen to avoid a debate on the proportionality of their measures altogether.

G. Knowledge and Practice

1. *The Netherlands*

The growth of jurisprudence of the ECtHR since the 80's was accompanied by increased attention for the ECHR amongst practising lawyers and academics. The nine law faculties in the Netherlands all pay extensive attention to the ECHR in their mandatory undergraduate courses pertaining to constitutional law. They also offer specialized courses, which are offered on the undergraduate as well as postgraduate level. Since 1986, the Ministry of Justice subsidizes ECHR training courses organized by the Training and Study Centre for the Judiciary (*Studiecentrum voor de Rechterlijke Organisatie/SSR*), an independent body functioning

---

[479] *Benthem v. the Netherlands* (appl. no. 8848/80), Judgement (Plenary), 23 October 1985, Series A, Vol. 97.

[480] Barkhuysen and Van Emmerik (1999), 16.

under the authority of the Council for the Judiciary and the Board of Attorneys General.[481] These courses are mandatory for trainee judges and optional for all judges and prosecutors, as well as supportive personnel working in the secretariats of the courts.

Due to the familiarity of all practising lawyers and law students as well as civil servants in the Netherlands with the English language, there is no need to translate systematically all decisions of the ECtHR into Dutch, especially since they are all available in English in the website of the ECtHR. However, there are, in particular, three journals that contribute to dissemination of ECtHR decisions in the legal community. For 31 years the *NJCM-Bulletin* (*Nederlands Tijdschrift voor de Mensenrechten*) is providing a chronicle on the most important ECtHR jurisprudence.[482] This Government subsidized journal, which is a publication of the Dutch section of the International Commission of Jurists, is published in the Dutch language on a monthly basis. Every three months it gives an overview of the most important ECtHR decisions against the Netherlands (including those declared inadmissible), as well influential decisions against other Contracting States. Since 1925 the NJB (*Nederlands Juristenblad*) is the leading, weekly commercial publication for practitioners in the Dutch language and also contains a chronicle pertaining to ECtHR jurisprudence.[483] Similarly, the scholarly journal *European Human Rights Cases*, which has since 2000 been published by the University of Maastricht on a monthly basis, contains annotated ECtHR jurisprudence in Dutch.

2. Belgium

In Belgium, the interest in and knowledge of the ECHR amongst practising lawyers and scholars have also steadily grown over the last twenty years. The eleven law faculties in the country (five Dutch speaking and six Francophone) all devote considerable attention to the ECHR in mandatory courses on constitutional law on the undergraduate level. Similarly, specialized optional courses on the ECHR are offered on the undergraduate and postgraduate level.

Since 1999, training courses pertaining to the ECHR are organized for members of the judiciary by the High Council of Justice.[484] This independent organ directly resulted from the *Dutroux* scandal which gripped Belgium in 1996 and exposed certain overhauled and dysfunctional elements of the Belgian judicial system. In order to reinstate the faith of the public in the justice system, Parliament amended, *inter alia*, Article 151 of the Belgian Constitution in order to provide for a High Council of Justice. It was created on 1 March 1999 and consists of directly elected members of the prosecution service, as well as lawyers

---

[481] See http://www.ssr.nl/index_en.php.
[482] See http://www.njcm.nl/.
[483] See http://www.njb.nl/NJB2006/default.html.
[484] See http://www.hrj.be.

and judges who are appointed by the Belgian Senate. It further consists of a Dutch speaking and Francophone unit, respectively. It is essentially responsible for supervising the selection and training of members of the judiciary; advising Parliament on issues that affects the functioning of the judiciary; and supervising the functioning of the judicial system. In the course of exercising these functions, the High Council of Justice also organizes optional training courses pertaining to the ECHR for magistrates and trainee judges.

Given that French is one of the official languages in Belgium and that all Dutch speaking lawyers, law students as well as civil servants have at least a passive knowledge of French and/or English, ECHR decisions are not systematically translated into Dutch. Articles and case annotations pertaining to the ECHR are regularly integrated into the main journals for practitioners. In the Dutch speaking community, this includes the weekly *Rechtskundig Weekblad*, which was created in 1931[485] and the *Nieuw Juridisch Weekblad*[486] which has been in existence since 2005. Two prominent weekly journals in the Francophone region include the *Journal des Tribunaux*,[487] which was founded in 1881 and the *Revue de Jurisprudence de Liège, Mons et Bruxelles*,[488] which was created in 1997. The main Belgian based journal focusing exclusively on human rights is the Francophone *Revue trimesterielle des droits de l'homme*. Which was created in 1990.[489] This journal has a broader human rights focus than the ECHR and a broader geographical scope than Belgium.

3. Comparison and Conclusion

In both countries there is, by now, a solid knowledge of the ECHR amongst lawyers, scholars and practitioners. It seems that systematically organized ECHR training for members of the judiciary is better established in the Netherlands than Belgium, where this was given new momentum since 1999 with the creation of the High Council of Justice. However, the attention paid to the ECHR in leading Belgian journals and at universities demonstrates that at least since the 90's practitioners and scholars are quite familiar with the importance of the ECHR for the domestic legal system.

H. Final Remarks

When the Netherlands ratified the ECHR in 1954, the general expectation was that its impact on Dutch law and Dutch legal culture would be negligible.[490]

---

485 See http://www.rwe.be.
486 See http://www.e-njw.be/njw/.
487 See http://jt.larcier.be/welcome.php.
488 See http://jlmbi.larcier.be./welcome.php.
489 See http://www.revtrdrh.be.
490 Swart (1999), 38.

During the Parliamentary debates leading up to the ratification, the Government aptly summarized the prevailing opinion of the time by stating that the complex system of Dutch law already offered sufficient safeguards to ensure that the principles of the ECHR would be respected by the Netherlands.[491] The view that the ECHR added little or nothing to Dutch law remained predominant well into the 60's and part of the 70's. For instance, in 1968 an Advocate General of the Dutch Supreme Court remarked that Article 6 ECHR was meant to protect the accused in systems of criminal justice that, unlike the Dutch system, did not pay sufficient respect to basic rights.[492] Moreover, invoking the ECHR before national courts was at the time regarded as a sign of weakness in the legal reasoning and was only adhered to when no other reasonable argument was available, as the ECommHR and ECtHR still lacked prestige and legitimacy at the time.[493]

A similar sense of complacency seemed to have been present in Belgium.[494] Some authors claim that influence of the wealthy Belgian bourgeoisie had already resulted in significant guarantees for fundamental freedoms in the early nineteenth century. The Belgian Constitution of 1831 was very liberal for its time and many believed that the ECHR had little to add in terms of human rights protection.[495] It therefore did not come as a surprise when the *De Becker* case[496] in the early 60's provoked strong reactions in Belgium. At that stage, the ECtHR had only decided the *Lawless* case and in some circles in Belgium it was considered an insult for a democratic State to defend itself before the ECtHR.[497] The first actual finding of violation in Strasbourg, which concerned the delicate issue of linguistic rights of the two main language communities,[498] also provoked criticism within different communities. In the Flemish community, some were indignant that an international court should condemn Belgian legislation which was the fruit of lengthy negotiations and a strong majority vote in Parliament. The Francophone community on the other hand found the ECtHR decision too limited, as it ultimately only found one clause of the relevant legislation in contravention of the ECtHR.[499]

---

[491] Swart (1999), 38.
[492] Dutch Supreme Court, Judgement, HR 16 January 1968, NJ 1968, 378; Swart (1999), 38.
[493] Zwaak (2002), 595, 601.
[494] Marcus-Helmons and Marcus-Helmons (2002), 188.
[495] Ibid.
[496] *De Becker v. Belgium* (appl. no. 214/56), Judgement (Chamber), 27 March 1962, Series A, Vol. 127.
[497] Marcus-Helmons and Marcus-Helmons (2002), 185; As far as the three *Lawless* judgements are concerned, see *Lawless v. Ireland (No. 1)* (appl. no. 332/57), Judgement (Chamber), 14 November 1960, Series A, Vol. 1; *Lawless v. Ireland (No. 2)* (appl. no. 332/57), Judgement (Chamber), 7 April 1961, Series A, Vol. 2; *Lawless v. Ireland (No. 3)* (appl. no. 332/57), Judgement (Chamber), 1 July 1961, Series A, Vol. 3.
[498] Case *"Relating to certain Aspects of the Laws on the Use of Languages in Education in Belgium" v. Belgium,* (appl. nos 1474/62; 1677/62; 1691/62; 1769/63; 1994/63; 2126/64), Judgement (Plenary), 23 July 1968, Series A, Vol. 6.
[499] Marcus-Helmons and Marcus-Helmons (2002), 186.

Since the 80's both countries have become accustomed to negative judgements on a regular basis.[500] It has also become clear that judgements of the ECtHR in cases against other States may have major implications for Dutch and Belgian law. In fact, some 60 years after ratification of the ECHR by the Netherlands and Belgium, it is easy to be amazed and amused by the self-complacency that reigned in the first decades after ratification. Apparently, at the time nobody was able to foresee the profound influence the ECHR would exert on the administration of justice in either country. This could partly be explained by the fact that the growth of the case law of the EcommHR and ECtHR since the late 70's increased the standing of these bodies, as well as the awareness of the relevance of the ECHR for the Dutch and Belgian legal system.[501]

Another important factor concerns the deep societal changes that have taken place since ratification of the ECHR. At the time of ratification, the Netherlands and Belgium were relatively closed societies with a strong social cohesion and a low criminal rate. Since then, these characteristics have slowly been disappearing in an era of economic growth, industrialization, internationalization, immigration and a rising crime rate. The ratification of the ECHR, therefore, coincided with the beginning of a deep social transformation during which the ECHR (and other human rights treaties) increasingly became a substitute for the loss of traditional values and identity.[502]

However, it remains to be seen whether the influence will remain as strong in the years to come. In the Netherlands and Belgium, the values personified by the ECHR have recently come under pressure due to the challenges posed by, inter alia, international terrorism and human migration. In the wake of the sometimes reactionary responses by Governments and their resulting inroads in the civil liberties of individuals, it becomes clear that the rights and obligations guaranteed by the ECHR remain vulnerable, despite the progress made over the last 60 years.

---

[500] Swart (1999), 39.
[501] See also Alkema (1994), 3.
[502] Swart (1999), 44.

Bibliography

Alen, A., *Compendium van het Belgisch Staatsrecht* (Antwerpen, 2000).

Alkema, E. A., 'Europese Conventie voor de rechten van de mens en de Nederlandse rechtsorde', *Mededelingen van de Nederlandse Vereniging voor Internationaal Recht* (The Hague, 1976).

—, 'The Effects of the European Convention on Human Rights and Other Human Rights Instruments on the Netherlands Legal Order', in Lawson, R. A. (ed.), *The Dynamics of the Protection of Human Rights in Europe Vol. III* (Dordrecht, 1994).

Barkhuysen, T. and Van Emmerik, M. L., 'Improving the implementation of Strasbourg and Geneva decisions in the Dutch legal order: reopening of closed cases or claims of damages against the state', in Barkhuysen, T. (ed.), *The Execution of Strasbourg and Geneva Human Rights Decisions in the National Legal Order* (The Hague, 1999).

—, 'A Comparative View of the Execution of Judgements of the European Court of Human Rights', in Christou, T. and Raymond, J. P., (eds.), *European Court of Human Rights Remedies and Execution of Judgements* (London, 2005).

—, 'Rechtsherstel bij schending van het EVRM in Nederland en Straatsburg', *NJCM-Bulletin* 31 (2006), 62.

Barkhuysen, T., Van Emmerik, M. L. and Loof, P.J., '50 jaar EVRM en het Nederlandse staats- en bestuursrecht – ontwikkelingen en vooruitzichten', *NJCM-Bulletin* 25 (2000), 336.

Berbuto, S. and Jacobs, A., 'Influence de l'Article 6 de la Convention Européene des droits de l'homme sur la procédure pénale Belge', *Revue de droit international et de droit comparé* 77 (2000), 56.

Bindels, R., 'L'influence du droit d'être jugé dans un délai raisonnable prévu par l'Article 6, § 1er, de la Convention européenne des droits de l'homme sur l'administration de la justice civile belge', *Annales de droit de Louvain* 62 (2002), 396.

Brems, E., 'Belgium: The Vlaams Blok political party convicted indirectly of racism', *International Journal of Constitutional Law* 4 (2006), 709.

Brenninkmeijer, A.F.M., 'Judicial Organisation', in Chorus, J. (eds.), *Introduction to Dutch Law* (The Hague 1999).

—, 'Implementation of the decisions of the supervisory bodies of the ECHR by revision of judgements of national courts in the Netherlands', in Tom Barkhuysen, T. (eds.), *The Execution of Strasbourg and Geneva Human Rights Decisions in the National Legal Order* (The Hague, 1999).

Craenen, G. J. E. M., 'Het Koninkrijk België', *Het Staatsrecht van de Landen van de Europese Unie* (2004), 1.

Davids W. J. M., ' De Europeanisering van het strafrecht (invloed van het EVRM), in Haak, W.E. (ed.), *Europeanisering van het Nederlandse Recht* (Deventer, 2004).

Engering, C. and Liborang, N., 'Judgements of the European Court of Human Rights against the Netherlands and their effects: an overview 1960–1997', in Barkhuysen, T (ed.), *The Execution of Strasbourg and Geneva Human Rights Decisions in the National Legal Order* (Leiden, 1999).

Feteris, M., '50 Jaar EVRM en het belastingrecht', *NJCM-Bulletin* 25 (2000), 483.

Geldhof W., 'Een Rol voor het Aansprakelijkheidsrecht inzake doorwerking van internationale rechtsregels?', in Wouters, J. and Van Eeckhoutte, D. (eds.), *Doorwerking van internationale recht in de Belgische rechtsorde* (Antwerpen, 2006).

Hartkamp, A. S., 'Europese mensenrechten en nationaal dwingend recht – De nederlandse rechter en het EVRM', *NJCM-Bulletin* 25 (2000), 24.

Heerma van Voss, G. J. J., 'De Lange, Kronkelige Weg naar Toepassing van het EVRM in het Sociale-Zekerheidsrecht', *NJCM-Bulletin* 21 (1996), 205.

Ijzermans, M., 'Dutch Ways of Doing Justice', in Taekema, H. S. (eds.), *Understanding Dutch Law* (The Hague, 2004).

Jensma, F. and Stokmans, D., 'Nederland in strafbank door Somalische vluchteling', *NRC Handelsblad*, 12.01.2007, 3.

Lambert, P., 'Les droits relatifs à l'administration de la justice disciplinaire dans la jurisprudence des organes de la Convention européenne', *Revue trimestrielle des droits de l'homme* 6 (1995), 160.

Lemmens, P., 'De invloed van het Europees Verdrag over de Rechten van de Mens op bepaalde aspecten van de strafprocedure in België', *Rechtskundig Weekblad* (1988–89), 793.

Marcus-Helmons, S. and Marcus-Helmons, P.,'Belgium' in Blackburn, R. and Polakiewicz, J. (eds.), *Fundamental Rights In Europe* (Oxford, 2002).

Myjer, E., 'To be revised? Revision of res judicata sentences in Dutch criminal cases', in Barkhuysen, T. (ed.), *The Execution of Strasbourg and Geneva Human Rights Decisions in the National Legal Order* (Leiden, 1999).

Nollkaemper, A., *Kern van het internationaal publiekrecht* (The Hague, 2005).

Prakken, E., 'Justitiële versus journalisitieke waarheidsvinding', *Nederlands Juristenblad* 79 (2004), 620.

—, 'Naar een cyclopisch (straf)recht', *Nederlands Juristenblad* 79 (2004), 2340.

Smits, P., *Artikel 6 EVRM en de civiele procedure. Over de betekenis van Art. 6 EVRM voor het Nederlands burgerlijk procesrecht* (Rotterdam, 1996).

Spronken, T., 'Sitting on the ruins of justice, redress for the plaintiff after Strasbourg: reconsideration instead of review', in Barkhuysen, T., Van Emmerik, M.L. and Van Kempen, P.H.P.H.M.C. (eds.), *The Execution of Strasbourg and Geneva Human Rights Decisions in the National Legal Order* (The Hague, 1999).

Steenbergen, H., '50 Jaar EVRM en Nederlandse Immigratierecht', *NJCM-Bulletin* 25 (2000), 447.

Swart, B., 'The European Convention as an Invigorator of Domestic Law in the Netherlands', *Journal of Law and Society* 26 (1999), 38.

Theunis, J., 'The Influence of the ECHR on National Constitutional Jurisprudence: The Example of the Belgian ', European Commission for Democracy through Law (Venice Commission), CCS 2005/09.

Van Damme. M., 'The Council of State: Institution on the Junction of Three Traditional Powers of The State', in Van De Lanotte, J. (ed.), *The Principle of Equality: a South African and Belgian Perspective*, (Antwerpen, Apeldoorn, Maklu, 2001).

Van Dijk, P., 'Article 3 ECHR and Asylum Law and Policy in the Netherlands', in Lawson, R. and De Blois, M. (eds.), *The Dynamics of the Protection of Human Rights in Europe Vol. III* (The Hague, 1994).

Van den Heede, P. and Goedertier, G., 'De Doorwerking van het internationale recht in de rechtspraak van het arbitragehof', in Wouters, J. and Van Eeckhoutte, D. (eds.), *Doorwerking van internationale recht in de Belgische rechtsorde* (Antwerpen, 2006).

Van Kempen, P. H. P. H. M. C., 'Terrorismebestrijding door marginalisering strafvorderlijke waarborgen', *Nederlands Juristenblad* 80 (2005), 397.

Van Leuven, N., 'Derdenwerking van Mensenrechten in de Belgische Rechtsorde', in Wouters, J. and Van Eeckhoutte, D. (eds.), *Doorwerking van internationaal recht in de Belgische rechtsorde* (Antwerpen, 2006).

Vanheule, D., Doorwerking van international recht in het vreemdelingenrecht', in Wouters, J. and Van Eeckhoutte, D., *Doorwerking van internationaal recht in de Belgische Rechtsorde* (Antwerpen, 2006).

Wouters, J. and Van Eeckhoutte, D., 'Doorwerking van Internationaal Recht voor de Belgische Hoven Rechtbanken', *Mededelingen van de Nederlandse Vereniging voor Internationaal Recht* 131 (2006), 152.

Zwaak, L. F., 'The Netherlands', in Blackburn, R. and Polakiewicz, J. (eds.), *Fundamental Rights In European* (Oxford, 2002).

6

The Reception Process in
Austria and Switzerland

Daniela Thurnherr

A. Historical Context: Accession and Ratification[1]

1. *Austria*

a. Austria's Accession to the ECHR and its Additional Protocols

Following seven years of Nazi dictatorship and ten years of military occupation, Austria obtained its full independence and sovereignty only in 1955, when the

---

[1] Abbreviations:

Austria: BGBl = Bundesgesetzblatt (federal law gazette); BlgNR = Beilage(-n) zu den Stenographischen Protokollen des Nationalrates (enclosure(s) to the stenographic protocols of the National Council); B-VG = Bundes-Verfassungsgesetz in der Fassung von 1929 (Federal Constitutional Statute of 1929, BGBl 1/1930); GP = Gesetzgebungsperiode (period of legislation); OGH = Oberster Gerichtshof (Supreme Court of Justice); StProt = Stenographische Protokolle (stenographic protocols); VfGH = Verfassungsgerichtshof (Constitutional Court); VfSlg = Sammlung der Erkenntnisse und Beschlüsse des Verfassungsgerichtshofes (collection of the decisions and resolutions of the Constitutional Court); VwGG = Verwaltungsgerichtshofgesetz (Statute on the Administrative Court); VwGH = Verwaltungsgerichtshof (Administrative Court); VwSlg = Sammlung der Erkenntnisse und Beschlüsse des Verwaltungsgerichtshofes (collection of the decisions and resolutions of the Administrative Court).

Switzerland: AJP = Aktuelle Juristische Praxis; Amtl. Bull. = Amtliches Bulletin der Sessionen von National- und Ständerat (protocols of the sessions of the National Council and the Council of States); AS = Amtliche Sammlung des Bundesrechts (official collection of federal law); BBl = Bundesblatt (Federal Gazette); BGE = Entscheidungen des Schweizerischen Bundesgerichts, Amtliche Sammlung (decisions of the Swiss Federal Supreme Court, official collection); BGG = Bundesgesetz vom 17 Juni 2005 über das Bundesgericht (Federal Statute on the Federal Supreme Court, SR 173.110); BStP = Bundesgesetz vom 15. Juni 1924 über die Bundesstrafrechtspflege (Federal Statute on criminal procedure, SR 312.0); E. = Erwägung (consideration); NR = Nationalrat (National Council); OG = Bundesgesetz vom 16. Dezember 1943 über die Organisation der Bundesrechtspflege (Federal Statute on the organization of the Federal Administration of Justice, rescinded by 1 January 2007 and replaced by the BGG); SR = Systematische Sammlung des Bundesrechts (systematic collection of the federal legislation); StR = Ständerat (Council of States); SZIER/ RSDIE = Schweizerische Zeitschrift für internationales und europäisches Recht/Revue suisse de droit international et de droit européen; VPB = Verwaltungspraxis der Bundesbehörden (case law and other documents of the federal authorities); ZBl = Schweizerisches Zentralblatt für Staats- und

foreign ministers of the four victorious Allied Powers signed the State Treaty for the Restoration of an Independent and Democratic Austria. In the same year, Austria's National Council *(Nationalrat)* adopted the Federal Constitutional Statute on Perpetual Neutrality[2], the (political) *conditio sine qua non* for the Soviet Union's approval of the treaty. By 1956, Austria had already joined the Council of Europe[3] and two years later, it ratified the ECHR[4], becoming the thirteenth Contracting State. When Austria ratified the Convention it also recognized the competence of the European Commission of Human Rights to deal with individual complaints as well as the Court's jurisdiction. This declaration was limited to three years and was always renewed for the same period.[5]

Before Austria ratified the ECHR, fundamental rights were primarily guaranteed by the Basic Law of 1867 on the General Rights of Nationals *(Staatsgrundgesetz über die allgemeinen Rechte der Staatsbürger 1867)*, which was set in force again after the collapse of the Third Reich. The rights assured in the Basic Law symbolize the legal achievements of the Austrian bourgeoisie *vis-à-vis* the police State of the nineteenth century.[6] As the Federal Constitutional Statute of 1929 *(Bundes-Verfassungsgesetz 1929)* does not contain a comprehensive catalogue of fundamental rights[7], it is the ECHR that fills this gap in Austria.

The Austrian Government was of the opinion that the ECHR would have only minor effects on the national legal order. It was convinced that the rights protected by the ECHR and Protocol no. 1 were already guaranteed in the Austrian legal system.[8] Nevertheless, in a speech given in October 1957 the Austrian Foreign Minister held that various instances had requested no less than 19 reservations to the Convention. However, ratifying the ECHR with one or two reservations would have cast a damning light on Austria and have had worse effects than no ratification at all.[9] Thus, the Austrian legislature was not very concerned about whether it would have to adapt or modify statutes before ratification. There was widespread conviction that it was politically essential that Austria ratify the ECHR in order to contribute to solidarity and unity in Western Europe. The attitude towards the Convention was generally positive; some members of the National Council even spoke of the new rights the Convention would bring.[10]

Verwaltungsrecht (until 1988: Schweizerisches Zentralblatt für Staats- und Gemeindeverwaltung). All translations of Austrian and Swiss terms are of the author's making.

[2] Bundesverfassungsgesetz vom 26. Oktober 1955 über die Neutralität Österreichs, BGBl 211/1955.

[3] BGBl 121/1956.

[4] BGBl 210/1958.

[5] BGBl 210/1958, 225/1961, 331/1970, 508/1973, 526/1976, 19/1980, 380/1982, 384/1985, 556/1988, 608/1991, 820/1993, 167/1997.

[6] For the history of fundamental rights in Austria, see Brauneder (1991), 189 et seq.

[7] The main political parties could not reach a consensus on a Bill of Rights. See Tretter (2002), 104.

[8] 459 BlgNR 8.GP; see also Matscher (2003), 8.

[9] Quoted in Weh (1988), 439.

[10] 454 BlgNR 8.GP.

The years ahead showed that the impact of the ECHR on the Austrian legal system was far more significant than expected.[11]

Austria has ratified all additional Protocols except no. 12 concerning non-discrimination:[12]

Table 1

Protocol	Signature	Ratification	Entry into force	Declarations/Reservations
Protocol no. 1	13 Dec. 1957	3 Sept. 1958	3 Sept. 1958	1 reservation concerning Article 1[13]
Protocol no. 2	6 May 1963	29 May 1967	21 Sept. 1970	–
Protocol no. 3	6 May 1963	29 May 1967	21 Sept. 1970	–
Protocol no. 4	16 Sept. 1963	18 Sept. 1969	18 Sept. 1969	1 reservation concerning Article 3[14]
Protocol no. 5	25 Jan. 1966	9 Oct. 1969	20 Dec. 1971	–
Protocol no. 6	28 April 1983	5 Jan. 1984	1 March 1985	–
Protocol no. 7	19 March 1985	14 May 1986	1 Nov. 1988	2 declarations concerning Articles 2, 3, 4[15]
Protocol no. 8	19 March 1985	17 April 1986	1 Nov. 1990	–
Protocol no. 9	6 Nov. 1990	27 April 1992	1 Oct. 1994	–
Protocol no. 10	7 May 1992	1 June 1993	–	–
Protocol no. 11	11 May 1994	3 Aug. 1995	1 Nov. 1998	–
Protocol no. 12	4 Nov. 2000	–	–	–
Protocol no. 13	3 May 2002	12 Jan. 2004	1 May 2004	–
Protocol no. 14	10 Nov. 2004	23 Jan. 2006	–	–

[11] The fact that Austria did not pay enough attention to the question of whether its legal order was in accordance with the ECHR has been criticized in legal literature, see Rill (1989), 17: "Recht schlecht gerüstet trat also Österreich in den Kreis der Konventionsstaaten."

[12] Source: http://conventions.coe.int/Treaty/Commun/ListeTraites.asp?CM=8&CL=ENG (all websites were most recently checked at the end of December 2006).

[13] "Being desirous of avoiding any uncertainty concerning the application of Article 1 of the Protocol in connection with the State Treaty of 15 May 1955 for the Restoration of an Independent and Democratic Austria, (the Federal President) declares the Protocol ratified with the reservations that there shall be no interference with the provisions of Part IV 'Claims arising out of the War ' and Part V 'Property, Rights and Interests ' of the above-mentioned State Treaty." (3 September 1958 – present).

[14] "Protocol no. 4 is signed with the reservation that Article 3 shall not apply to the provisions of the Law of 3 April 1999, StGBl. No. 209 concerning the banishment of the House of Habsbourg-Lorraine and the confiscation of their property as set out in the Act of 30 October 1919, StGBl. No. 501, in the Constitutional Law of 30 July 1925, BGBl No. 292, in the Federal Constitutional Law of 26 January 1928, BGBl No. 30, and taking account of the Federal Constitutional Law of 4 July 1963, BGBl No. 172." (18 September 1969 to present).

[15] "The Republic of Austria declares: 1. Higher Tribunals in the sense of Article 2, paragraph 1, include the Administrative Court and the Constitutional Court. 2. Articles 3 and 4 exclusively relate to criminal proceedings in the sense of the Austrian code of criminal procedure." (1 November

b. Austrian Reservations and Declarations

At the time of ratification, Austria submitted two reservations concerning Articles 5 and 6 of the Convention in order to protect traditional aspects of the national legal order, both of which are still in force. First, the provisions of Article 5 "shall be so applied that there shall be no interference with the measures for the deprivation of liberty prescribed in the laws of administrative procedure (...), subject to review by the Administrative Court or the Constitutional Court as provided for in the Austrian Federal Constitution". Second, "Article 6 shall be so applied that there shall be no prejudice to the principles governing public court hearings laid down in Article 90 of the 1929 version of the Federal Constitutional law." The two reservations to Protocols nos 1 and 4 concern particular aspects of Austrian history, namely the above-mentioned State Treaty for the Restoration of an Independent and Democratic Austria and the so-called Habsburg-law. Under the latter, all sovereign rights and other privileges (titles) of the House of Habsburg-Lorraine were annulled and the court assets, other than private assets of the Habsburg family, were confiscated. Austria was on the one hand concerned with bringing the obligations arising under the Protocols in line with its own history. On the other hand, the reservations to the Convention itself and the two interpretative declarations to Protocol no. 7 show that from the very beginning it was mainly procedural issues that were in conflict with the Conventional guarantees.

The ECtHR in *Chorherr v. Austria* held that Austria's reservation in respect of Article 5 ECHR was compatible with Article 64 of the Convention.[16] Due to broad interpretation by both the Austrian Constitutional Court and the Strasbourg organs, this reservation also forecloses the application of Article 6 in the proceedings concerned.[17] The Strasbourg organs, however, denied the applicability of the reservation in several cases and thereby limited its normative effects.[18] The reservation was originally even applied to criminal proceedings in financial

---

1988 – present). Unlike a reservation, an interpretative declaration shall (only) define the understanding of a guarantee under the ECHR, without constricting it, see Article 53 ECHR; Frowein and Peukert (1996), Article 60.

[16] *Chorherr v. Austria* (appl. no. 13308/87), Judgement (Chamber), 25 August 1993, Series A, Vol. 266-B.

[17] See e.g., Austrian Constitutional Court, Judgement, 25 February 1983, VfSlg. 9613/1983; Austrian Constitutional Court, 14 June 1982, VfSlg. 9409/1982; Austrian Constitutional Court, 24 June 1981, VfSlg. 9158/1981; *Verband der Besatzungsgeschädigten v. Austria* (appl. no. 473/59), Report by the Commission on Human Rights, 29 August 1959, YB 2 (1958/1959), 400, 406; *X. v. Austria* (appl. no. 1452/62), Report (Plenary), Commission, 18 December 1963, YB 6 (1963), 268, 276; *X. v. Austria* (appl. no. 7529/76), Report (Plenary), Commission, 4 October 1976, DR 7, 159. The extensive interpretation of the reservation to Article 5 ECHR has been embraced by Rill (1989), 19. Critical Kopetzki (1982), 29 et seq., 41 et seq.; Herbst (1997), 679.

[18] See e.g., *Schmautzer v. Austria* (appl. no. 15523/85), Judgement (Chamber), 23 October 1995, Series A, Vol. 328-A; *Pfarrmeier v. Austria* (appl. no. 16841/90), Judgement (Chamber), 23 October 1995, Series A, Vol. 329-C.

matters *(Finanzstrafverfahren)*.[19] This practice was later abandoned and the re-spective provisions of the Code of Financial Offences *(Finanzstrafgesetz)* were declared unconstitutional by the Austrian Constitutional Court.[20] After the new Federal Constitutional Statute on the Protection of Personal Liberty *(Bundesver-fassungsgesetz zum Schutz der persönlichen Freiheit)* was enacted[21] and Independ-ent Administrative Senates *(Unabhängige Verwaltungssenate)* were established[22], the reservation concerning Article 5 became less important, but it has not been withdrawn.[23] Also, the reservation to Article 1 of Protocol no. 1 concerning Parts IV and V of the State Treaty for the Restoration of an Independent and Demo-cratic Austria is interpreted broadly and extends to Article 6(1) ECHR.[24]

In the *Ettl and Others* case, the Court considered the Austrian reservation in respect of Article 6 valid and applicable to proceedings before land reform boards.[25] However, in this case the Court did not examine whether the reserva-tion complied with the criteria laid down in Article 57 ECHR. Thirteen years later, in view of the new case law concerning public hearings, the reservation to Article 6 was considered invalid due to the lack of a brief statement of the law which is said not to conform to Article 6.[26]

The interpretative declaration to Protocol no. 7, stating that Articles 3 and 4 exclusively relate to criminal proceedings in the sense of the Austrian Code of Criminal Procedure, was the subject matter of the *Gradinger* case.[27] The Court referred to *Belilos v. Switzerland*[28] and considered that the declaration was to be regarded as a reservation within the meaning of Article 57 ECHR[29]. As there was no brief statement of the law that was said not to conform to Articles 3 and 4 of Protocol no. 7, the interpretative declaration was also found invalid.

---

[19] Critical Schantl and Welan (1970), 623 et seq.

[20] Austrian Constitutional Court, Judgement, 3 December 1984, VfSlg 10291/1984.

[21] Bundesverfassungsgesetz vom 29. November 1988 über den Schutz der persönlichen Freiheit, BGBl 684/1988.

[22] See the Sixth Main Part of the Constitution *(Sechstes Hauptstück des Bundes-Verfassungsgesetzes)* and *infra* Section D.1.

[23] Jann (1994), 2.

[24] *Verband der Besatzungsgeschädigten v. Austria* (app. no. 473/59), Report of the Commission on Human Rights, 29 August 1959, YB 2 (1958/1959).

[25] *Ettl and Others v. Austria* (appl. no. 9273/81), Judgement (Chamber), 23 April 1987, Series A, Vol. 117, para. 42.

[26] *Eisenstecken v. Austria* (appl. no. 29477/95), Judgement (Third Section), 3 October 2000, Reports 2000-X, 157 et seq., para. 29 et seq.; see Adamovich, Funk and Holzinger (2003), 42.128; Haller (2006), 647.

[27] *Gradinger v. Austria* (appl. no. 15963/90), Judgement (Chamber), 23 October 1995, Series A, Vol. 328-C. See also, Grabenwarter (1997), 577 et seq.

[28] See *infra* Section A.2.b.

[29] Article 64 then in force.

c. Procedures of Ratification

According to Austrian constitutional law, the Federal President *(Bundespräsident)* is in charge of concluding international treaties.[30] Treaties that alter or amend constitutional or statutory law have to be approved by the National Council *(Nationalrat)* and, if competences of the provinces are affected, also by the Federal Council *(Bundesrat)*.[31] In general, the procedure of ratification follows the same rules as law-making on the statutory level, with the exception that treaties can be accepted or rejected but not modified. The People are only entitled to vote on complete alterations of the Constitution.[32]

The ECHR and Protocol no. 1 were treated as conventions that altered the Constitution. The National Council accepted them unanimously on 10 July 1957.[33] Both treaties became part of the national legal order by general transformation (or adoption).[34] As the ECHR cannot be considered a complete alteration of the Constitution, it was not submitted to the popular vote.

2. Switzerland[35]

a. Switzerland's Accession to the ECHR and its Additional Protocols

Switzerland joined the Council of Europe in 1963, only after it became clear that it would not become a military or political alliance.[36] In 1974 – sixteen years after Austria acceded to the ECHR – Switzerland finally brought itself to ratify the Convention. This considerable delay was on the one hand caused by concerns of maintaining neutrality, which were already a major obstacle to joining the Council of Europe. On the other hand, incompatibilities between the national legal order and the Convention kept Switzerland from ratifying the latter for many years. In the late 1960's, the Federal Council *(Bundesrat)* proposed to join the ECHR and Protocol no. 1 with five reservations.[37] However, as the Council

---

[30] Article 65(1) B-VG.

[31] Article 50(1) B-VG. The National Council is the first chamber of the Austrian Parliament, elected by the Austrian People. Together with the Federal Council as the second chamber and representative of the provinces, it constitutes the legislative branch.

[32] Article 44(3) B-VG.

[33] StProt Nr 8. G, 2931 et seq.

[34] Jann (1994), 3.

[35] Keller (2005), the pilot study for the research project on the reception of the ECHR, served as starting point and basis for the analysis of the reception process in Switzerland.

[36] Report of the Federal Council to the Parliament concerning the relationship of Switzerland to the Council of Europe, 26 October 1962, BBl 1962 II 1085, 1097.

[37] Report of the Federal Council to the Parliament concerning the ECHR, 9 December 1968. The reservations concerned (1) the extraordinary religious Articles (Prohibition of Jesuits, Article 51 of the Constitution then in force, and prohibition to found new cloisters, Article 52 Constitution then in force, abrogated in the popular vote of 20 May 1973. For the wording of these Articles, see the message by the Federal Council, 23 December 1971, BBl 1972 I 105, for the Federal decree, see AS 1973 1455), (2) the lack of female suffrage, (3) some exceptions to the principle of open public hearing and pronouncement of judgements, (4) the factual inequalities for boys and girls in the school system and (5) the laws in different Cantons concerning commitment to an institution (in several Cantons it was possible to deprive someone of his liberty for medical reasons without

of States *(Ständerat)* voted against it, this attempt failed. Considering the broad scope of the intended reservations, which concerned not only minor aspects, but fundamental values as expressed by the Convention, in retrospect that decision has to be viewed as wise. That is to say, it urged Switzerland to bring its national legal order into accordance with the ECHR before taking further steps. After all, it was questionable whether the above-mentioned reservations were in accordance with the object and purpose of the Convention.[38]

The goal of becoming a Contracting Party of the ECHR was still a priority, but Switzerland first focused on eliminating obstacles in the national legal order. Several important constitutional amendments were drafted within the following months. After female suffrage had been adopted by popular vote in 1971, the Federal Council proposed in a report to the Federal Parliament that Switzerland would first sign the Convention, but not yet Protocols nos 1 and 4. The ratification should be carried out only after the various extraordinary religious Articles had been abrogated in a popular vote.[39] The ECHR also had its effects in respect of administrative and criminal law,[40] international judicial assistance, the Federal Statute on Narcotics and the Federal Statute on Military Criminal Law.[41] There were also consequences in various Cantons, mainly with respect to the laws concerning commitment to an institution, which clearly were not in conformity with the standards of the ECHR. Various rules in the Cantons' Codes of Criminal Procedure were amended as well. However, most of the incompatibilities could be eliminated by an interpretation of the existing rules in the light of the Convention.[42]

Switzerland thus signed the ECHR on 21 December 1972. After the repeal of the extraordinary religious Articles in 1973, the Federal Council proposed the ratification of the Convention, the formulation of various reservations and the simultaneous acceptance of the right of individual petition and the jurisdiction of the Court.[43] In spite of this cautious approach, some Members of Parliament were of the opinion that it was highly unlikely that Switzerland would be con-

---

any judicial control). In addition to these reservations, Switzerland should have formulated an interpretative declaration in respect of Article 6(3)(c) and (e) ECHR, declaring that the costs for legal assistance and interpretation could be imposed on the condemned person.

[38] Keller (2005), 288 et seq.

[39] Additional report by the Federal Council to the Parliament concerning the ECHR, 23 March 1972, BBl 1972 I 989.

[40] See the message by the Federal Council on a draft Federal Statute on administrative criminal law, 21 March 1972, BBl 1971 I 993, p. 997 et seq. The Federal Council postulated the abolition of joint liability in cases of offence in business operations because joint liability was not in conformity with Article 6(1) ECHR.

[41] For the effects of the ECHR on Swiss law at that time, see the additional report by the Federal Council to the Parliament concerning the ECHR, 23 March 1972, BBl 1972 I 989, 997.

[42] Keller (2005), 289.

[43] Message by the Federal Council on the ECHR, 4 March 1974, BBl 1974 I 1035.

demned.[44] The two chambers of Parliament agreed in the same year[45] and Switzerland ratified the ECHR – already amended by Protocols nos 2, 3, and 5 – on 28 November 1974. At the same time, it also recognized the right of individual petition and the Court's jurisdiction. The former declaration was limited to three years and was always renewed for the same period.

At the time of writing, all Protocols except no. 1, no. 4 and no. 12 have been ratified.[46] Protocol no. 1 was signed on 19 May 1976 but the Federal Council did not submit it to the Parliament after the Cantons showed disapproval.

Table 2

Protocol	Signature	Ratification	Entry into force	Reservations/Declarations
Protocol no. 1	19 May 1976	–	–	–
Protocol no. 2	21 Dec. 1972	28 Nov. 1974	28 Nov. 1974	–
Protocol no. 3	21 Dec. 1972	28 Nov. 1974	28 Nov. 1974	–
Protocol no. 4	–	–	–	–
Protocol no. 5	21 Dec. 1972	28 Nov. 1974	28 Nov. 1974	–
Protocol no. 6	28 Apr. 1983	13 Oct. 1987	11 Nov. 1987	–
Protocol no. 7	28 Feb. 1986	24 Feb. 1988	1 Nov. 1988	2 reservations concerning Articles 1 and 5[47]
Protocol no. 8	19 March 1985	21 May 1987	1 Jan. 1990	–
Protocol no. 9	6 Nov. 1990	11 Apr. 1995	1 Aug. 1995	–
Protocol no. 10	25 March 1992	11 Apr. 1995	–	–
Protocol no. 11	11 May 1994	13 July 1995	1 Nov. 1998	–
Protocol no. 12	–	–	–	–
Protocol no. 13	2 May 2002	3 May 2002	1 July 2003	–
Protocol no. 14	13 May 2004	25 April 2006	–	–

[44] Keller (2003), 300, cited the statement of the Federal Council Mr. Graber of 3 October 1972 before the National Council (Amtl. Bull. 1972, NR, 1708).

[45] Federal Decree on the acceptance of the ratification of the ECHR, 3 October 1974, AS 1974 2148, BBl 1974 I 1068.

[46] Source: http://conventions.coe.int/Treaty/Commun/ListeTraites.asp?CM=8&CL=ENG.

[47] "When expulsion takes place in pursuance of a decision of the Federal Council taken in accordance with Article 70 of the Constitution on the grounds of a threat to the internal or external security of Switzerland, the person concerned does not enjoy the rights listed in paragraph 1 even after the execution of the expulsion." (1 November 1988 – present). "Following the entry into force of the revised Swiss Civil Code of 1984, the provisions of Article 5 of the Additional Protocol no. 7 shall apply subject, on the one hand, to the provisions of Federal law concerning the family name (Article 160 CC and 8a final section, CC) and, on the other hand, to the provisions concerning the acquisition of the right of citizenship (Article 161, 134, paragraph 1, 149, paragraph 1, CC and 8b final section, CC). Furthermore, the present reservation also concerns certain provisions of transitional law on marriage settlement (Article 9, 9a, 9c, 9d, 9e, 10 and 10a final section, CC)." (11 November 1988 – present).

b. Swiss Reservations and Declarations

Switzerland made two reservations to the Convention in respect of the laws in different Cantons concerning commitment to an institution and some exceptions of the principle of open public hearing and pronouncement of judgements. Furthermore, two interpretative declarations stating that access to a court in the sense of Article 6(1) was sufficiently guaranteed when a review by a judicial instance of ultimate resort was possible[48] and that the exemption from costs for legal assistance and interpretation (Article 6(3)(c) and (e) ECHR) should not be final were submitted. From the beginning, the reservations were seen as a temporary solution and a mandate to the Swiss legislator to amend the national legal order so that it would be in conformity with the Convention.[49] Today, none of the Swiss reservations and interpretative declarations in respect of the ECHR are in force. In 1982, after the Federal Civil Code had been amended by the new Articles 397f et seq. on deprivation of personal freedom for medical reasons[50], the Swiss Government withdrew the reservation in respect of Article 5 ECHR, relating to the laws in various Cantons concerning commitment to an institution.[51]

However, not all reservations have been voluntarily withdrawn.[52] For the first time ever an international court came to the conclusion that a reservation of a State in respect of an international treaty was not valid, with the consequence that the State was fully bound by the treaty. In its judgement in the case *Belilos v. Switzerland*,[53] the Court stated that the interpretative declaration in respect of Article 6(1) ECHR had the quality of a reservation, because Switzerland meant to exclude certain categories of proceedings from the ambit of that provision. Thus, the Court examined whether the declaration satisfied the requirements of Article 57 ECHR.[54] It came to the conclusion that the words "ultimate control by the judiciary" could be interpreted in different ways. Therefore, the declaration fell "foul of the rule that reservations must not be of a general character".[55] By not drawing up a list of the cantonal and federal laws that were not in accordance with Article 6(1) ECHR, Switzerland had disregarded a clear condition, such as

---

[48] The wording of the clause did not make clear that a review by the Swiss Federal Supreme Court, not having full cognition, should be possible. This would have made it obvious that this clause was actually a reservation. See Keller (2005), 290.

[49] Statement of the National Council Mr. Tenchio, in: Amtl. Bull. 1969, NR, 333: "Die Vorbehalte sind kein Ruhekissen, sondern ein Stimulus, ein Ansporn zur Aktion, zur Tat, um Ordnung in unserem Haus zu machen."

[50] Swiss Civil Code of 10 December 1907, SR 210; Article 397f et seq. inserted by Federal Statute, 6 October 1978, in force since 1 January 1981, AS 1980 31.

[51] Federal Decree, 13 June 1978 AS 1982 928.

[52] For the following, see also Keller (2005), 291 et seq.

[53] *Belilos v. Switzerland* (appl. no. 10328/83), Judgement (Plenary), 29 April 1988, Series A, Vol. 132. Mrs. Belilos had been fined by the cantonal police of Vaud and was not entitled to apply to a court with full jurisdiction.

[54] Article 64 then in force.

[55] *Belilos v. Switzerland* (*supra* note 53), para. 55.

the requirement of a brief statement of the law concerned.[56] Practical difficulties could not justify that omission. For these reasons, the declaration was invalid and consequently Switzerland was bound by the original terms of Article 6(1) ECHR.[57]

In the aftermath of the *Belilos* judgement the Canton of Vaud, whose law was challenged before the Court, adapted it to the requirements of Article 6(1) ECHR. The new act instituted an appeal procedure to the Police Court against any decision announced by a municipality. The judgement and its consequences also gave rise to heated discussions in the Federal Parliament, which indicate the enormous effect of the Strasbourg case law in Switzerland and the difficulties the political establishment had in coming to terms with it.[58] A denunciation of the ECHR and an immediate re-accession was even proposed, making a new reservation in respect of Article 6(1) ECHR.[59] The Federal Council decided to accept the part of the judgement concerning criminal law, but assumed the civil and administrative part of the declaration to be unaffected by the judgement. Thus, the Federal Council submitted a clarification of the interpretative declaration concerning civil proceedings to the Secretary_General of the Council of Europe on 16 May 1988.[60] Seven months later a list of the affected federal and cantonal laws was submitted to the Council of Europe.[61] The belated re-formulation of the interpretative declaration was uniformly qualified as illegitimate by both Swiss and foreign experts.[62] In 1992 the Federal Supreme Court stated that the judgement of the Court in the *Belilos* case not only affected that part of the Swiss declaration to do with criminal matters, but also showed the invalidity of the civil section for the same reasons.[63]

The reservation in respect of Article 6(1) ECHR, concerning some exceptions to the principle of open public hearing and pronouncements of judgements, has been ineffective since the judgement in the case *Weber v. Switzerland*[64] two years after *Belilos*. The Court decided that the reservation was invalid because it did not contain a brief statement of the law concerned, as prescribed by Article 57 ECHR.[65]

The judgements of the Court concerning *Belilos*[66] and *Weber*[67] finally led to

---

[56] Ibid., paras 56, 59.
[57] Ibid., para. 60.
[58] Keller (2005), 293 et seq.
[59] Amtl. Bull. 1988, StR, 554. It is interesting to note that this postulate was only dismissed by a close vote of 16:15, see Amtl. Bull. 1988, StR, 561.
[60] AS 1988 1264.
[61] AS 1989 276.
[62] For the references, see Wildhaber (1993), 333 et seq., notes 41 and 42.
[63] Swiss Federal Supreme Court, Judgement, 17 December 1992, BGE 118 Ia 473.
[64] *Weber v. Switzerland* (appl. no. 11034/84), Judgement (Chamber), 22 May 1990, Series A, Vol. 177.
[65] Article 64 then in force.
[66] *Belilos v. Switzerland* (*supra* note 53).
[67] *Weber v. Switzerland* (*supra* note 64).

an important constitutional amendment providing for a general guarantee of judicial review (*Rechtsweggarantie*) in cases of legal disputes. This constitutional right establishes a rule on the national level that is in accordance with Article 6(1) ECHR.[68] Its ambit is even broader, as it includes not only proceedings concerning civil rights and obligations or criminal charges, but also proceedings based on public law. After the sovereign (i.e. the People and the Cantons) had accepted this amendment on 12 March 2000, it entered into force on 1 January 2007.[69] The new system of remedies that became effective the same day implements the requirements of the guarantee of judicial review on the national level.[70]

In the report of the *Temeltasch* Commission, the interpretative declaration concerning Article 6(3)(a) and (e) ECHR was declared valid,[71] even though Switzerland had failed to deliver a brief statement of the law concerned as prescribed by Article 57 ECHR.[72] However, the Swiss Federal Supreme Court doubted the validity of the declaration in view of the judgement in the *Belilos* case.[73] The two reservations concerning the principles of open public hearing and pronouncement of judgements were finally withdrawn on 23 August 2002 after the acceptance of the Constitution of 1999 and the reform of justice.[74]

Our survey of the Swiss reservations reveals tension mainly between national procedural law and the Convention. All other material incompatibilities between national law and the ECHR had already been eliminated before ratification. Currently, there remain only two reservations concerning Protocol no. 7. However, after the decision of the ECtHR in *Burghartz*[75] and the judgement of the Federal Supreme Court in *Haliti*,[76] they have to be considered at least *de facto* obsolete.

---

[68] Kley (2000), Rz. 2.

[69] Article 29a Constitution, AS 2002 3148 et seq., adopted in the popular vote of 12 March 2000 by the people and the Cantons. For the report by the Federal Council, 20 November 1996, see BBl 1997 I 1.

[70] As to the remedies also see *infra* Section F.2.a.

[71] *Temeltasch v. Switzerland* (appl. no. 9116/80), Report (Plenary), Commission, 5 May 1982, DR 31, 120 et seq.; VPB 48 IV 1984, No. 104. The *Temeltasch* Report is important because the Commission considered the Strasbourg organs to be competent to examine whether reservations of Member States satisfied the requirements of the Convention. The Court took on this argumentation in *Belilos* and *Weber* and also decided on the legal consequences of an invalid reservation, giving itself the *Kompetenz-Kompetenz*.

[72] Article 57 then in force.

[73] Swiss Federal Supreme Court, Judgement, 17 December 1992, BGE 118 Ia 473, 480 et seq. E. 6.

[74] AS 2002 1143, in accordance with the Federal Decree, 8 March 2000, AS 2002 1142; see Swiss Federal Supreme Court, Judgement, 25 April 2001, BGE 127 I 141, 144 E. 3c; Aemisegger (2007b), 380.

[75] *Burghartz v. Switzerland* (appl. no. 16213/90), Judgement (Chamber), 22 February 1994, Series A, Vol. 280-B.

[76] Swiss Federal Supreme Court, Judgement, 21 February 2003 (not published); also see *Haliti v. Switzerland* (appl. no. 14015/02), Decision (Fourth Section), 1 March 2005 (not reported).

c. Procedures of Ratification

According to Swiss constitutional law, the Federal Council *(Bundesrat)* signs international treaties or authorizes a delegation to sign. The signature is under reserve of acceptance by the Parliament *(Bundesversammlung)*.[77] The latter is a prerequisite for ratification, although it is only an authorization, not a binding order to ratify. The Federal Council may still decide not to ratify a particular treaty.

Accession to the ECHR was not submitted to the popular vote. Swiss constitutional law provides an optional – and for some far-reaching treaties even a mandatory – referendum for the accession to some international treaties.[78] At the time the Constitution did not require an optional referendum for treaties that could be denounced.[79] The fact that the ECHR was not submitted to popular vote can be seen as an indicator that at the time the power of the Convention and the Court was underestimated. Given the fact that the extraordinary development of the Strasbourg case law could not have been anticipated in the 70's, however, this is not surprising.[80] When the new Constitution of 1999 was enacted, several guarantees of the ECHR that so far had not been explicitly mentioned in the Constitution became part of it.[81] Thus, to a certain extent, the new Constitution led to a late legitimation of the ECHR.

After Article 89(4) of the Constitution then in force had been revised, the Government submitted the accession to Protocols nos 6[82] and 7[83] to the optional referendum. No vote was demanded. Protocols nos 8, 9, 10, and 11 only affected matters of procedure and, therefore, did not entail a multilateral unification of law in the sense of Article 89(3)(c) of the Constitution of 1874,[84] and an optional referendum was, therefore, not necessary. Because the death penalty was already prohibited by Article 10(1) of the Constitution and the Second Optional Protocol to the International Covenant on Civil and Political Rights[85] Protocol no. 13, concerning the abolition of the death penalty in all circumstances, did not affect the Swiss legal system and was not submitted to the optional referendum. Protocol no. 14 was submitted to the optional referendum because it contains

---

[77] Articles 166(2) and 184(2) Constitution of 1999; also see Tschannen (2004), § 47 Rz. 10 et seq.

[78] Articles 140 and 141 Constitution of 1999; also see Tschannen (2004), § 47 Rz. 20 et seq.; Wildhaber, Scheidegger and Schinzel (2005), 653 et seq.

[79] Article 89 (4) then in force. As to the development of the treaty referendum see Wildhaber, Scheidegger and Schinzel (2005), 653 et seq.

[80] Keller (2005), 291.

[81] See e.g., Article 10(3), Article 31, Article 32 ECHR; de Vries Reilingh (2000), 16.

[82] Parliamentary decision, AS 1987 1806.

[83] Parliamentary decision, AS 1988 1598.

[84] Article 141 (1) lit. d Constitution of 1999.

[85] Second Optional Protocol to the International Covenant on Civil and Political Rights, aiming at the abolition of the death penalty, entered into force 11 July 1991, for Switzerland 16 September 1994, SR 0.103.22.

important provisions in the sense of Article 141(1)(d)(3) of the Constitution,[86] but no vote was demanded.

3. Comparison and Conclusion

A starting point for a comparison between Austria and Switzerland is the fact that both countries are by definition neutral. The questions whether neutrality had an impact on the accession process is thus of particular interest. In Switzerland, neutrality and above all a strong resistance to the decisions of foreign judges play an almost mythical role in the country's history. Although the Swiss concept of neutrality served as a role model for Austria, neutrality in Austria, unlike in Switzerland, has not been an obstacle to joining the Council of Europe and ratifying the ECHR. Austria's neutral status did not have a long tradition but was imposed by the victorious Allied powers and thus did not hinder a political involvement on the supranational level. Whereas Switzerland was reluctant to participate in international politics, in 1955 Austria had already joined the UN. Accession to the ECHR, therefore, undoubtedly meant a smaller step for Austria than for Switzerland. Austria had a further incentive for joining the Council of Europe as it could thereby distinguish itself from the neighbouring Eastern-bloc States. In Switzerland, accession to the ECHR was a step towards European integration in a major sense. Pressure in respect of the external image of the country certainly had an impact. Switzerland was furthermore bound by its long humanitarian tradition; its absence from the Convention would have caused confusion domestically and abroad.[87]

Compared to Austria, the Swiss approach to the ECHR can be described as very cautious and reluctant. This, however, did not indicate a fundamental rejection of the Convention or a deep distrust of the Strasbourg organs, but primarily an understanding that some national rules were not yet in accordance with the Convention.[88] The Swiss Government tried to ensure that there would be no inconformity of national law with the Convention by means of traditional international law, such as reservations and interpretative declarations. Before ratification, Switzerland had to take several steps in order to match the national legal order with fundamental requirements of the Convention. The amendments on the national level, such as female suffrage and an extension of religious freedom, concerned core values of the Constitution. The changes on the statutory level were basically related to procedural issues. Compared to Switzerland, Austria had a much more enthusiastic attitude towards the ECHR and did not attach as much importance to the question of whether the national legal order was

---

[86] Message of the Federal Council on the Acceptance of Protocol no. 14 of 13 May 2004 to the European Convention for the Protection of Human Rights and Fundamental Freedoms, 4 March 2005, BBl 2005, 2119, 2139.

[87] Keller (2005), 347.

[88] Keller (2005), 290.

fully compatible with the ECHR. As a consequence, the Austrian legal order did not undergo any changes with regard to ratification. This leads to the assumption that Austria faced more problems with the Convention's requirements after ratification than did Switzerland. The following analysis will reveal whether this turned out to be the case.

B. Status of the ECHR in National Law: Formal (Doctrinal) Elements

1. Austria

a. Relation between Domestic and International Law

The Austrian Constitutional system is characterized by a moderate position with regard to both the question of monism/dualism and the status of international law in the national legal order. In principle, international law is treated as an independent legal order that does not take priority over national law but that must be implemented and applied in an appropriate way.[89]

The generally acknowledged rules of international law (i.e. some rules of customary international law and the general principles of law recognized by civilized nations[90]) are considered part of national law.[91] According to the – not uncontested – case law of the Constitutional Court (*Verfassungsgerichtshof, VfGH*), they have legislative status.[92] The Constitutional Court furthermore denies their direct applicability and treats them as non-self-executing.[93]

Treaties that alter or amend the Constitution have constitutional status, with the consequence that there are quora with regard to presence and approval.[94] Treaties that alter or amend statutes have legislative status and those that neither alter nor amend the Constitution or statutes have the status of regulations.[95] Treaties (or treaty provisions) that have constitutional status must be explicitly indicated as such.[96] The National Council has the power to determine that a treaty that alters or amends constitutional or statutory law can only be fulfilled by national (constitutional) statutes (so-called *Erfüllungsvorbehalt*).[97] As a consequence, the treaty becomes non-self-executing and cannot be directly applied by courts or

---

[89] Adamovich, Funk and Holzinger (1997), 16.008; Ermacora and Hummer, n. 565.

[90] Adamovich, Funk and Holzinger (1997), 10.013.

[91] Article 9(1) B-VG: "Die allgemein anerkannten Regeln des Völkerrechtes gelten als Bestandteile des Bundesrechtes." International treaty law does not fall under this provision.

[92] See Austrian Constitutional Court, Judgement, 24 June 1954, VfSlg 2680/1954; critical Adamovich, Funk and Holzinger (1997), 16.014 et seq.

[93] Austrian Constitutional Court, Judgement, 27 May 1961, VfSlg 3950/1961; Austrian Constitutional Court, Judgement, 14 December 1974, VfSlg 7448/1974; critical Adamovich, Funk and Holzinger (1997), 16.015.

[94] See Article 44 B-VG.

[95] Adamovich, Funk and Holzinger (1997), 16.029 et seq.

[96] Article 50(3) B-VG.

[97] Article 50(2) B-VG.

administrative authorities.[98] The effect of an international treaty on the national legal order, therefore, lies to a considerable extent in the National Council's hands. Treaties without *Erfüllungsvorbehalt* are not necessarily self-executing; it depends on their content whether they are directly applicable or not.[99] While the former need a so-called special transformation to become applicable in national law, the latter only have to undergo a general transformation or an adoption.[100]

b. Status of the ECHR in the National Legal Order

After its ratification, the Convention was officially published in the Austrian Federal Law Gazette without any comment on its legal status. The question of status initially led to dissension between the National Council and the Constitutional Court. From the very beginning, the National Council as well as the vast majority of legal scholarship[101] was of the opinion that the ECHR altered the Constitution and thus did have constitutional status. Due to the lack of a constitutional provision at that time it was not necessary to explicitly declare that the ECHR and Protocol no. 1 were altering the Constitution.[102] The Constitutional Court, however, tried to confine the ECHR and denied both its constitutional status and self-executing character.[103] The Administrative Court (*Verwaltungsgerichtshof, VwGH*) and the Supreme Court of Justice (*Oberster Gerichtshof*) adopted this approach.[104] As a consequence, in the first years after ratification the ECHR had little impact on the national legal order. In 1964, the dispute about the status of the ECHR was solved: it was retroactively (ex tunc) awarded explicit constitutional status.[105] Austria was the first State to fully incorporate the Convention in its constitutional legal order. The same status has also been attached to Protocols nos 2, 4, 6, 7, and 9.[106]

Nowadays, it is undisputed that the ECHR as well as the additional Protocols[107] have constitutional status from which they derive their direct applicability.

---

[98] See Öhlinger (1973), 110 et seq.; Adamovich, Funk and Holzinger (1997), 16.031 et seq. The National Council for example decided that the Treaty Against all Forms of Racial Discrimination was not self-executing; see BGBl 377/1972.

[99] Austrian Constitutional Court, Judgement, 27 June 1960, VfSlg 12281/1990.

[100] Adamovich, Funk and Holzinger (1997), 16.033; Ermacora and Hummer, n. 587 et seq.

[101] See, *inter alia*, Ermacora (1959), 396.

[102] That has since changed; see Article 50(3) B-VG now in force and *supra* Section a.

[103] The first decision was Austrian Constitutional Court, Judgement, 27 June 1960, VfSlg 3767/1960. See Ermacora (1959), 396: "Damit gelang es ihm für sechs Jahre, sich die MRK samt ihren Problemen vom Leibe zu halten"; Nowak (1983), 48; Schantl and Welan (1970), 617.

[104] Austrian Administrative Court, Judgement, VwSlg 2558 (F)/61; Austrian Supreme Court, Judgement, 29 January 1963, 8 Ob 15/63; Austrian Supreme Court, Judgement, 16 January 1963, 7 Ob 354/62.

[105] Bundesverfassungsgesetz vom 4. März 1964, mit dem Bestimmungen des Bundesverfassungsgesetzes in der Fassung von 1929 über Staatsverträge abgeändert und ergänzt werden, BGBl 59/1964; see von Grünigen (1965), 76.

[106] For Protocol no. 2 see BGBl 329/1970; for Protocol no. 4 BGBl 434/1969; for Protocol no. 6 BGBl 138/1985; for Protocol no. 7 BGBl 628/1988 and for Protocol no. 9 BGBl 593/1994.

[107] Except Protocol no. 8 that does not have a material content.

As a consequence, the legislator has to give effect to the rights and freedoms of the Convention and all courts and administrative authorities have to interpret the law in a manner that does not infringe the rights of the Convention.[108] In case of a conflict between a norm of the Constitution and the ECHR, the *lex posterior derogat legi priori* rule applies: When the Austrian constitutional legislator enacts a law that contradicts the ECHR, the latter must step back as the Court considers itself bound by later constitutional law.[109]

It is well worth noting that the ECHR has a different status in Austria than other international human rights agreements, such as the International Covenant on Economic, Social and Cultural Rights, the International Covenant on Civil and Political Rights or the European Social Charter. Unlike the ECHR, the latter neither have constitutional status nor are they self-executing[110], showing the tremendous importance of the ECHR compared to other treaties in the Austrian legal system.

c. Court System and Scope of Judicial Review

There are three supreme courts in Austria that basically differ in the fields of law they apply. A special Constitutional Court (*Verfassungsgerichtshof, VfGH*) is in charge of reviewing the constitutionality of legislative and executive acts.[111] Its main function is to protect the Constitution. Statutes, regulations and international treaties as well as decisions of administrative authorities (the so-called *Bescheide*) can be challenged before the Constitutional Court.[112] However, there is no possibility to appeal against decisions of other courts before the Constitutional Court.[113] The Constitutional Court is the only court entitled to rescind norms and thus has a monopoly on constitutional matters. It is also responsible in the sphere of competence of the Provinces (*Bundesländer*).

Separation of power doctrines do not prohibit the judicial review of the validity of legislative and executive acts with reference to higher norms. The Constitutional Court is under different circumstances entitled to dispense justice on compliance with the rights and freedoms guaranteed by the Constitution. As the ECHR and its Additional Protocols are part of the body of Austrian constitutional law,[114] the Constitutional Court also has the competence to review whether

---

[108] Tretter (2002), 105. See also Ermacora and Hummer (2004), n. 594.

[109] Austrian Constitutional Court, Judgement, 1987 October14, VfSlg 11500/1987.

[110] Besides the ECHR for example the Convention on the Political Rights of Women (BGBl 256/1969) and Articles 1, 2 and 14 of the Convention on the Elimination of All Forms of Racial Discrimination (BGBl 337/1972) have constitutional status.

[111] The Constitutional Court and its competences are governed by the Sixth Main Part of the Constitutional Statute of 1929 (*VI. Hauptstück des B-VG*) as well as other constitutional provisions.

[112] Articles 139, 140, 140a and 144 B-VG.

[113] Adamovich, Funk and Holzinger (1998), 39.037. Decisions by judicial authorities can only be reviewed by the Supreme Court. See *infra* Section F.1.a.

[114] See *supra* Section B.1.b.

certain acts violate Strasbourg law. On the one hand, the Constitutional Court is entitled to examine whether final decisions of administrative authorities including such of Independent Administrative Panels[115] violate fundamental rights, and to overturn them as the case may be.[116] On the other hand, the Constitutional Court may under different circumstances review the constitutionality of norms. First, there is the so-called preventive control of norms, where the Constitutional Court decides whether a certain act of State lies within the sphere of competence of the Federal Government or the Provinces.[117] Second, the Federal Government can make a claim that a provincial statute or a regulation violates the Constitution and *vice versa*. Third, the Constitutional Court can review the constitutionality of a norm on the occasion of a concrete case. The Constitutional Court itself has the obligation to examine a legal provision *ex officio* when it has to apply this provision in a given case. The entitlement to request the Constitutional Court to annul a norm is limited to the Administrative Court (*Verwaltungsgerichtshof, VwGH*), the Supreme Court of Justice (*Oberster Gerichtshof, OGH*) as well as courts of second instance: They are obliged to file a complaint with the Constitutional Court when they are of the opinion that a legal provision or an ordinance is not in conformity with the Convention. As decisions of these and other courts may not be appealed to the Constitutional Court, the parties to such proceedings may not force the courts to make such a request for annulment. Fourth, every person can make a claim that he or she is harmed by a norm violating the Constitution.[118] If the underlying norm infringes upon a constitutional guarantee, the Constitutional Court rescinds both the norm and the decision; if the application is not in accordance with constitutional law, only the decision as such is invalidated.[119] Invalidation does not mean nullity; however, it creates a legal duty for the competent authorities to rescind the invalid norm.[120]

It is interesting to note that at the beginning of its existence the Austrian Constitutional Court was very reluctant to use fundamental rights in order to set boundaries on the legislators.[121] It was mainly due to the ECHR and the case law of the Court that the Austrian Constitutional Court increasingly based its decisions on material fundamental rights, for example in cases concerning the

[115] The Independent Administrative Panels (*Unabhängige Verwaltungssenate*) are dealt with *infra* Section D.1.
[116] Article 144 B-VG.
[117] Article 138(2) B-VG.
[118] See Oberndorfer (1988), 193 et seq.
[119] Article 144 B-VG; also see the cases cited in Jann (1994), 8 et seq.
[120] See Article 139(5), Article 140(5), 140a(2) B-VG.
[121] This judicial self-restraint is influenced by the epistemological skepticism of Hans Kelsen who considered that general, value-laded constitutional norms are not justiciable. It was given up in 1949 (VfSlg 1908/1949 and 1843/1949). See Oberndorfer (1988), 198.

legislation on aliens.[122] The ECHR thus shaped the role of the Austrian Constitutional Court in an important way.

Besides the Constitutional Court there are two other highest courts, the Administrative Court and the Supreme Court of Justice. Whereas the former is dealing with administrative law[123], the latter is in charge of judging criminal and civil matters[124]. While they may not invalidate norms, they apply the ECHR in concrete cases and are obliged to interpret the law in a manner consistent with the Constitution.[125] However, as has already been mentioned, they (as well as other courts that decide as second instances) can request the Constitutional Court to rescind statutes or provisions thereof. The Constitutional Court is, in no cases, entitled to review decisions of other courts.[126] It is quite possible that the three different supreme courts may take varying doctrinal positions with regard to the ECHR. This does not seem to have ever been a problem thus far.

d. Influence of the Federal System

Austria is a federal State consisting of nine Provinces (*Bundesländer*).[127] They are independent (but not sovereign) entities and are entitled to legislate in their sphere of competence. They furthermore have their own administrative authorities. Compared to Switzerland, Austria has a much stronger tendency towards centralism. Although several steps have been taken in order to strengthen federalism, the polarity between federalism and centralism has not been overcome. The autonomy of the Provinces in constitutional matters is limited, and legislation in important matters is basically in the hands of the federation.

Of particular interest for the study at hand is an organizational monopoly over the whole court system on the federal level, a highly unusual feature in federal States.[128] In civil and criminal matters there exist 140 District Courts (*Bezirksgerichte*), 20 Provincial Courts (*Landesgerichte*), 4 Higher Provincial Courts (*Oberlandesgerichte*)[129] and one Supreme Court (*Oberster Gerichtshof*), all

---

[122] See e.g., Austrian Constitutional Court, Judgement, 12 December 1985, VfSlg 10737/1985 = EuGRZ 1986, 190.

[123] Article 129–136 B-VG.

[124] Article 92(1) B-VG.

[125] After the Statute on the Protection of Personal Freedom had been enacted, a new Fundamental Rights Appeal (*Grundrechtsbeschwerde*) to the Supreme Court was introduced for cases where there was no effective legal protection (*Bundesgesetz über die Beschwerde an den Obersten Gerichtshof wegen Verletzung des Grundrechts auf persönliche Freiheit [Grundrechtsbeschwerde-Gesetz]*, BGBl 864/1992). Its main field of application is the examination of the length of detention and the necessity of detention in general. See Adamovich, Funk and Holzinger (2003), 43.011.

[126] Article 144(1) B-VG *e contrario*.

[127] Article 2(1) B-VG. The nine States are: Burgenland, Carinthia, Lower Austria, Upper Austria, Salzburg, Styria, Tyrol, Vorarlberg and Vienna.

[128] Adamovich, Funk and Holzinger (1997), 13.010.

[129] The four Higher Provincial Courts (*Oberlandesgerichte*) have their seats in Vienna (responsible for Vienna, Lower Austria and Burgenland), Graz (responsible for Styria and Carinthia), Linz (responsible for Upper Austria and Salzburg) and Innsbruck (responsible for Tyrol and Vorarlberg).

of which are federal. The Provinces themselves are only in charge of organizing the Independent Administrative Panels (*Unabhängige Verwaltungssenate*)[130].

In spite of the fact that there is a territorial distribution of powers and competences, Austria's federal nature did not affect the process of reception in a significant way. Basically two factors are responsible for this outcome: On the one hand, the judicial power lies entirely with the federation. On the other hand, the most important legislative decisions are in the sphere of competence of the federal State. Unlike in Switzerland, procedural issues, which proved to be most difficult to harmonize with the ECHR, are not governed by provincial law.

2. Switzerland

a. Relation between Domestic and International Law

It is largely undisputed that Switzerland follows a monistic system.[131] International norms, therefore, become part of the Swiss legal system as soon as they enter into force for Switzerland. If they are formulated clearly and unconditionally enough to have a direct bearing and to be applied in a specific case, all State organs must respect and apply them.[132] The direct applicability of the ECHR was surprisingly undisputed in Switzerland. In 1977, the Federal Supreme Court had already stated without further reasoning that the substantial guarantees of the ECHR (with the exception of Article 13), had become directly applicable by entering into force for Switzerland.[133]

However, the fact that Switzerland follows a monistic system does not answer the question of priority in cases of conflict between domestic and international law. Neither can the solution be found in the wording of the Federal Constitution of the Swiss Confederation. When Parliament was drafting the new Constitution in the late 90's, no consensus on a clear statement in favour of the international rule of law could be reached, apart from the fact that total and partial revisions of the Constitution must comply with *ius cogens*[134] and that popular initiatives shall

---

[130] As to the Independent Administrative Panels see *infra* Section D.1.

[131] See joint comment by the Federal Office of Justice and the Directorate of International Law, 26 April 1989, VPB 53 (1989) No. 54, 403 et seq. with references; Steinmann (2006), 631; Wildhaber, Scheidegger and Schinzel (2005), 658 et seq. with further references.

[132] Swiss Federal Supreme Court, Judgement, 2 September 1986, BGE 112 Ib 183, 184 et seq. E. 2a; Third Report by the Federal Council on Switzerland and the Conventions of the Council of Europe, 22 February 1984, BBl 1984 I 791.

[133] Swiss Federal Supreme Court, Judgement, 19 December 1977, BGE 103 V 190, 192 E. 2a. Nowadays the Swiss Federal Supreme Court also considers Article 13 ECHR directly applicable; see e.g., Swiss Federal Supreme Court, 20 August 1997; BGE 123 II 402, 413 E. 4b/aa. See also Hangartner (2002b), 142 with further reference; for the question of direct applicability during preparatory discussion of the ECHR, see Sciotti-Lam (2004), 377 et seq. and in respect of Article 13 ECHR, 462.

[134] Article 193(4) and Article 194(2) Constitution.

be declared invalid by the Federal Assembly if they do not respect the peremptory norms of international law[135].

Furthermore, several provisions of the Constitution deal with international law: According to Article 5(4) the Federation and the Cantons shall respect international law. Of special importance is Article 190, which, by stating that the "Federal Supreme Court and the other authorities applying the law shall follow the federal statutes and international law", considers Federal Statutes and international law as equally binding to all instances. As cases of conflicts between these two sources of law are not addressed, the hierarchical ranking of international law in general and the ECHR in particular is, therefore, not fully clarified. Hence, it is basically up to the courts to decide in cases of conflicts whether a particular provision of national law or of an international treaty prevails.

b. Status of the ECHR in the National Legal Order

To begin with, the question of whether a Federal Statute or a provision of the ECHR shall prevail very rarely arises. On the one hand, the Federal legislator is generally cautious not to violate the conventional guarantees. On the other hand, it is in most cases possible to synchronize the two rules by interpreting the former in light of the latter, i.e. by giving the Federal Statute a meaning which does not infringe upon the ECHR. Of course this option only exists when the wording of the Federal Statute is open to an interpretation in accordance with international law.

In academic writings some authors hold that the ECHR has the rank of a Federal Statute, some argue for a constitutional rank and some for a rank even higher than the Constitution.[136] According to Article 26 of the Vienna Convention on the Law of Treaties,[137] the principle of *pacta sunt servanda*, it is clear that international obligations must be complied with. The predominance of international law over national law was accepted early on as a basic principle by the Swiss Federal Supreme Court.[138]

In its earlier jurisprudence, the Swiss Federal Supreme Court followed a case-by-case strategy when meeting a conflict between international law and Federal Statutes. In a large number of cases it declared the predominance of international law as a basic principle. In other cases, however, the solution was seen in the *lex posterior* rule. In the famous *Schubert* case[139] the Federal Supreme Court decided that a Federal Statute could derogate an earlier treaty. It followed the

---

[135] Article 193(3) Constitution.

[136] For the references, see Aubert (1995), 1113 et seq., Rz. 1777 and Villiger (1999), 45 et seq., Rz. 59.

[137] Vienna Convention on the Law of Treaties of 23 May 1969, entered into force 27 January 1980, for Switzerland 6 June 1990, SR 0.111.

[138] Swiss Federal Supreme Court, Judgement, 3 December 1881, 7 774, 783 et seq.; Swiss Federal Supreme Court, Judgement, 17 June 1892, BGE 18 189, 193; Swiss Federal Supreme Court, Judgement, 10 February 1893, BGE 19 134, 137.

[139] Swiss Federal Supreme Court, Judgement, 2 March 1973, BGE 99 Ib 39.

clear statement rule and made clear that the Court did not have the competence to disregard a Federal Statute when the Parliament had enacted this Statute in full awareness of its incompatibility with an international obligation. This rule, however, has since been very rarely applied and was generally only repeated in an *obiter dictum*.[140]

In its more recent case law, however, the Federal Supreme Court stresses the predominance of international law even over more recent federal law, particularly when human rights are concerned.[141] The effect was that the national rule could not be applied in particular cases. The Federal Supreme Court did not decide whether in other cases a different solution, in the sense of the *Schubert* rule, could be taken into consideration. Unfortunately, not all Chambers of the Federal Supreme Court have adopted this international law-friendly approach.[142] The clear statement rule was also quite recently adhered to in a decision of the Federal Personnel Appeals Commission.[143]

The approach of the Swiss Federal Supreme Court to award the ECHR supra-legislative status deserves approval. On the one hand, it is required by the general principle of *pacta sunt servanda* which is also expressed by Article 5(4) of the Swiss Constitution. On the other hand, the Statute on the Swiss Federal Supreme Court[144] allows for an extraordinary revision in case of a judgement of the ECtHR finding a violation of the Convention or the Protocols thereto, and if reparation can only be awarded by a rehearing proceeding.[145] The legislator in this provision clearly expresses that, in cases of conflict the ECHR takes priority over national statues. A further indication of the supra-legislative statutes of the Convention can be seen in the fact that the Statute of the Swiss Federal Supreme Court on several occasions only speaks of constitutional law but implicitly includes the

---

[140] See e.g., Swiss Federal Supreme Court, Judgement, 7 June 1991, BGE 117 IV 124, 128 E. 2b; Swiss Federal Supreme Court, Judgement, 14 June 1990, BGE 116 IV 262, 268 E. 3b/cc; Swiss Federal Supreme Court, Judgement, 23 October 1985, BGE 111 V 201, 203 E. 2b. For one of the rare exceptions, see Swiss Federal Supreme Court, Judgement, 9 March 1986, BGE 112 II 1, 13 E. 8. The Federal Supreme Court affirmed the *Schubert* rule and stated that it was not necessary to investigate whether an international obligation was violated, since the Swiss legislator had been aware of a possible violation of international law when enacting the statute.

[141] Swiss Federal Supreme Court, Judgement, 26 July 1999, BGE 125 II 417, 424 et seq. E. 4d; Swiss Federal Supreme Court, Judgement, 1 November 1996, BGE 122 II 485, 487 E. 3a. In Swiss Federal Supreme Court, Judgement, 12 February 2003, BGE 129 II 193, however, this practice seems to be questioned. The Federal Supreme Court did not decide the question of whether its jurisdiction was established by Article 13, but rejected the appeal based on considerations on the merits. The Federal Supreme Court stated that it could not diverge from the rule established by a Federal Statute – Article 100(1) lit. b no. 1 and 4 OG – which could not be interpreted in a manner making it compliant with Article 13 ECHR (E. 4.2.4). For a review of this judgement, see Hangartner (2003), 1112 et seq.

[142] Keller (2003), 615.

[143] Decision by the Federal Personnel Appeals Commission (Eidgenössische Personalrekurskommission), VPB 68 (2004) No. 91, 1211 et seq.

[144] Bundesgesetz vom 17. Juni 2005 über das Bundesgericht (Federal Statute on the Federal Supreme Court, BGG, SR 173.110).

[145] Article 122 lit. b BGG. See *infra* Section F.2.a.

guarantees of the ECHR.[146] It thereby implicitly awards the ECHR – at least in the procedural context – the same status as constitutional guarantees.[147]

c. Court System and Scope of Judicial Review

Unlike in Austria, there is no special Constitutional Court in Switzerland. The Swiss Federal Supreme Court is not only in charge of reviewing whether certain acts and norms are in accordance with constitutional or international law but it also controls whether criminal, civil and federal administrative law has been applied correctly.

However, the position of the Federal Supreme Court is rather weak. As the Swiss constitutional system has always been dominated by the democratic principle, the system of constitutional review is marked by a deep distrust of the judiciary. Due to Article 190 of the Constitution, the Federal Supreme Court – like any court in Switzerland – is bound by federal statues and must apply them even if they are found incompatible with the Constitution.[148] As a consequence, federal law only allows an abstract control of cantonal legal norms (*abstrakte Normenkontrolle*) by the Federal Supreme Court but not in respect of Federal Statutes. Within 30 days following its official publication, each cantonal statute, ordinance or directive may be subject to an appeal in public law matters (*Beschwerde in öffentlich-rechtichen Angelegenheiten*) for a violation, among others, of the Convention, to the Federal Supreme Court.[149] The latter, in the affirmative, is empowered to quash the legislation. In some Cantons, similar cantonal remedies exist. When a Federal Statute is concerned, Swiss law only provides for an examination of an alleged violation of the ECHR or other international law in a specific case. Thus, the Federal Supreme Court usually has to answer the question of whether in a concrete case the application of federal law by federal or cantonal authorities has led to a violation of the ECHR. In this procedure, however, a preliminary question can be asked as to whether the applied rules themselves are in conformity with the ECHR (*konkrete/akzessorische Normenkontrolle*).

Article 190 of the Constitution is, nowadays, interpreted as a commandment of application that gives the Federal Supreme Court the possibility to review the compatibility of a Federal Statute with constitutional or international law. Thus, although it must apply the Federal Statute, the Federal Supreme Court can state that the statute is incompatible with international law and that it is the legislator's

---

[146] See Article 98 BGG concerning precautionary measures and Article 116 concerning the subsidiary constitutional complaint. Other provisions, however, juxtapose international and domestic law; see Article 95 BGG.

[147] Also see *infra* Section E.2.a.

[148] This aspect of the constitutional system of 1848 was maintained on the occasion of the total revision of the Constitution in 1999. The new Constitution was only seen as an update of the already existing written and unwritten rules. There were to be no substantial reformations that might have endangered the whole project. See Kälin (2001), § 74 Rz. 7.

[149] Article 82 et seq. Bundesgesetz vom 17. Juni 2005 über das Bundesgericht (Federal Statute on the Federal Supreme Court, BGG, SR 173.110).

responsibility to bring the Swiss law into conformity with it. In fact, this option must be considered an obligation, following the obligation of interpreting the Federal Statutes in the light of the ECHR. This development helped the strengthening of fundamental rights *vis-à-vis* to the Federal Parliament.[150]

The superimposition of the national judicial system by a strongly legitimated international judiciary body constitutes a tremendous challenge for the Federal Supreme Court. In 1996, the Federal Council mentioned that the Swiss legal order had led to the paradoxical situation that the ECtHR had a larger competence to examine a case, consequently relegating the latter to a mere instance to walk through (*simple instance intermédiaire*).[151] However, the suggestion of the Federal Council to introduce a general constitutional review that included Federal Statutes was dismissed by the Parliament. The existence of a judicial instance on the international level to which individuals can apply forced the Federal Supreme Court to come to terms with these circumstances and to define a general strategy for cases where it is not possible to harmonize the Federal Statute with the ECHR by interpretation. According to the principle of judicial self-restraint, the Federal Supreme Court does not seem to have the will to introduce a constitutional review through the back door. However, in the field of the ECHR it is almost forced to do so.[152]

In its earlier case law the Federal Supreme Court did not dare to tamper with the prohibition of examination under Article 113(3) Constitution of 1874. It declared that the ECHR had not changed anything in the national assignment of competences and that the Convention did not create any powers of audit of the Federal Supreme Court that had not already existed by virtue of national law.[153] In two areas – both politically indisputable and very clear – the Federal Council helped the Federal Supreme Court to overcome the barrier of separation of powers. In an *échange de lettre* motivated by certain judgements of the Court[154] the Federal Department of Justice and Police and the Federal Supreme Court agreed on the incompatibility of two statutes with the ECHR in 1976/77 and 1984. Thus, it was decided that the Federal Supreme Court should not apply the rules

---

[150] See Kälin (2001), Rz. 26 et seq.

[151] Message of the Federal Council on a new Federal Constitution, 20 November 1996, BBl 1997 I1, 50 et seq./FF 1997 I 1, 516.

[152] Keller (2005), 321.

[153] See e.g., Swiss Federal Supreme Court, Judgement, 14 June 1983, not published, see SJIR 1984, 203 et seq.; Swiss Federal Supreme Court, Judgement, 18 October 1984, not published, see SJIR 1985, 250 et seq.

[154] The case of *Lynas v. Switzerland* (appl. no. 7317/75), published in VPB 47 (1983) no. 93, 433 et seq. revealed some faults of the Swiss extradition law in respect of Article 5(4) ECHR, in spite of the fact that the Court declared the appeal inadmissible. The second *échange de lettre* was triggered by the Judgements of the Court concerning *Klass and Others v. Germany* (appl. no. 5029/71), Judgement (Plenary), 6 September 1978, Series A, Vol. 28 and *Malone v. the United Kingdom* (appl. no. 8691/79), Judgement (Plenary), 2 August 1984, Series A, Vol. 81.

contrary to the ECHR until the respective legislative amendments entered into force.[155]

In its more recent case law, the Federal Supreme Court seems to have accepted the necessity of an effective guarantee of the predominance of the ECHR over Federal Statutes. The Federal Supreme Court gave a first hint in that direction in 1991. It stated that the interpretation of national rules in the light of international obligations also affected Article 114bis(3) of the Constitution then in force[156] and that it was also part of the responsibility of the courts to ensure the harmonization of national law and international rules. Therefore, the theoretical possibility existed that the Federal Supreme Court would not apply a Federal Statute that was contrary to the ECHR. In the specific case, however, the Federal Supreme Court did not consider it to be necessary, because it was of the opinion that the Federal Statute could be brought into conformity with the ECHR by interpretation.[157] A time of change and uncertainty began. The opinion expressed in this judgement was not fully established in later judgements or in academic writings.

As explained in connection with the question of status,[158] in 1999 the Federal Supreme Court decided that in cases of conflict, as a matter of principle, international law prevailed over national law, particularly when the protection of human rights was concerned.[159] Also, in 1999 the second civil division of the Federal Supreme Court, which had generally shown a more reserved attitude towards international law in its judgements,[160] declared that this could be the approach of the Federal Supreme Court to solve future conflicts.[161] The Court in *Linnekogel*[162] finally made clear that Switzerland, due to Article 6(1) ECHR, was obliged to guarantee for an effective access to national courts even in cases where a national statute does not allow for an appeal.

The Federal Supreme Court has recognized that the established system of the Convention, with the right of individual petition to an international court, is not an ordinary international treaty and that it has led to an indirect constitutional review. After the judgement in the case of *Linnekogel*, uncertainty has further diminished, as it is now clear for all divisions that the obligation to take an ap-

---

[155] Jacot-Guillarmod (1989), 255 et seq.

[156] Article 190 of the Constitution of 1999 (after the entry into force of Article 29a Constitution [AS 2002 3148]).

[157] Swiss Federal Supreme Court, Judgement, 15 November 1991, BGE 117 Ib 367, 373 E. 2f.

[158] See *supra* Section B.2.b.

[159] Swiss Federal Supreme Court, Judgement, 23 March 1999, BGE 125 II 417, 424 et seq. E.4c.

[160] See e.g., BGE 120 II 384, 387 E. 5a, where the Federal Supreme Court refused to examine some rules of the Civil Code on their compliance with the ECHR.

[161] BGE 125 III 209, 218 E. 6d.

[162] *Linnekogel v. Switzerland* (appl. no. 42874/98), Judgement (Fourth Section), 1 March 2005 (not yet reported).

peal at hand in cases where the ECHR so requires precedes contrary provisions in national statutes.

c. Influence of the Federal System

Compared to Austria, Switzerland's federal structures are much more pronounced.[163] According to Articles 3 and 42 of the Swiss Federal Constitution, the Cantons exercise all rights which are not transferred to the Confederation.[164] It thus takes an amendment to the Constitution, ratified by a majority of the People voting and a majority of the Cantons, to bestow new powers on the Confederation. The Cantons are awarded organizational autonomy to structure their territories and to constitute legislative, executive and judiciary bodies. From the point of view of the reception process, it is particularly noteworthy that the Cantons are still in charge of legislating in the fields of criminal, civil and administrative procedure law.[165]

Although the focus naturally lies in the highest national court, it must be stressed that as the ECHR is directly applicable in Switzerland it can be invoked before all courts, both on the federal and the cantonal level. In all Cantons, two or three levels of criminal courts and administrative tribunals exist. The task to implement the guarantees of the ECHR is, therefore, not primarily that of the Federal Supreme Court, but of the cantonal judiciary bodies. Although Switzerland acceded to the ECHR in 1974, a recent study comes to the conclusion that the reception process in the Cantons only started around 1980 and was not fully effective before the 90's.[166] It shows that in a country such as Switzerland, with strong federal tendencies, the reception process works with a legal lag of 10 to 20 years. According to this study, the change might have occurred some years earlier in the Francophone part of the country due to its more cosmopolitan attitude, and perhaps also to the fact that no language barrier existed. However, it must be noted that from a very early stage some Cantons already made efforts to fully implement the requirements of the ECHR. Information about these efforts is not easily accessible, though, as the Cantons generally chose informal ways to strengthen the position of the ECHR. Presumably, to a considerable extent the effectiveness of the ECHR also depended on the effort of lawyers to invoke the Conventional guarantees before cantonal courts. Nowadays, it can generally be stated that the cantonal courts apply the ECHR without significant trouble.[167]

---

[163] See Steinmann (2006), 629; Wildhaber, Scheidegger and Schinzel (2005), 627.

[164] For example, important functions such as health care, the school system as well as significant parts of police law and planning law are governed by cantonal law.

[165] It is planned that federal codes of criminal and civil procedure will replace the respective statutes in the Cantons by 2010.

[166] Keller (2005), 310.

[167] Keller (2005), 310; see also, Haefliger and Schürmann (1999), 440 with examples.

3. Comparison and Conclusion

Austria is the first country where the ECHR was possessed of a viable supra-legislative status that judges could directly enforce. In spite of this promising starting position, in the first years after ratification, the ECHR was not a quarter as effective as one would expect. This was mainly due to the fact that effectiveness not only depends on the formal status of international law in the national legal order, but first and foremost on the willingness of the national organs to attach adequate value to it. At the beginning, the Austrian Constitutional Court as well as the Administrative Court and the Supreme Court of Justice were very reluctant to leverage the Convention. Nowadays, these obstacles have been overcome and the ECHR attracts the necessary interest by the courts.

Unlike in Austria, in Switzerland there is no specific statement defining the exact position of the ECHR in the hierarchy of legal norms. The uncertainties are, therefore, considerable. It is basically up to the Federal Supreme Court to deal with the difficult task of harmonising the constitutional system with the Court. Moreover, the strong democratic tradition in Switzerland has proved an obstacle to the unreserved recognition of the primacy of international law. However, the moderate monistic system in Switzerland provides advantageous conditions for the reception of international rules. The Swiss example furthermore shows that in a country following a monistic system, with a weakly positioned yet sufficiently independent judiciary, the ECHR can help to strengthen the position of the courts.[168]

After the initial obstacles were overcome, in both countries we can speak of a constitutionalization or constitutional entrenchment of the ECHR. Whereas the Convention has formal supra-legislative status in Austria, it was the Swiss Federal Supreme Court who in the course of time treated the ECHR as supra-legislative.

From a comparative perspective, it is of interest that although both countries are federal States, the nature of that federalism had a different impact on the effectiveness of the ECHR. In Switzerland, federalism is far more pronounced than in Austria. While the Federal Supreme Court quickly and effectively took the ECHR into account, at least some of the lower courts needed more time. In these courts the reception process followed with a considerable delay of 10 to 20 years. The sphere of competence of the Austrian Provinces is smaller; their legislative competences concern minor matters and, most notably, they have no judicial competences at all. As a consequence, it is basically in the federal State's responsibility to implement the Convention. The territorial distribution of powers and competences thus hardly had an effect on the effectiveness of the ECHR in Austria.

---

[168] Keller (2005), 313.

C. Overview of the Activity of the European Court of Human Rights

1. Austria

The first judgement concerning Austria dates from 1968, i.e. from 10 years after ratification.[169] Up until the end of 2006, 261 cases against Austria have been decided on the merits by the Court and the Committee of Ministers.[170] In addition, there were 22 friendly settlements in cases before the Court and 3 in cases before the Committee of Ministers.

The number of judgements per year against Austria has clearly increased over time. Between 1968 and 1985, there were hardly ever more than one or two cases dealing with Austria each year. It is interesting to note that between 1975 and 1981 there were actually only two cases against Austria decided by the Committee of Ministers in total and none at all by the ECtHR. An initial increase can be noted between 1987 and 1994.[171] Starting in 1995, the number of decisions – except from 1998 and 1999 – goes far beyond that of previous years: it mounts to around 20 per year.[172]

Over time, not only the number of decisions but also the number of applications has increased. Whereas in the first 40 years after Austria's accession to the ECHR we count 3095 applications registered, in the short time span of eight years between 1998 and 2006 there were already 2486. Up to the end of 2006, a total of 5581 applications against Austria have been registered.[173]

Article 6(1) ECHR (fair trial/excessive length of procedure) stands out in the statistics. Of a total of 372 invocations, 216 – and thus more than half of them – concern Article 6(1). Excessive length of procedure has been invoked slightly more often (114 cases) than violations of fair trial (102 cases). Thirty-nine cases concern Article 10 ECHR (freedom of expression), 33 cases concern Article 6(3) ECHR (right to defence), seventeen cases concern Article 14 ECHR (prohibition of discrimination), fourteen cases concern Article 13 ECHR (lack of effective remedy), eleven cases concern Article 8 ECHR (private and family life), eleven cases concern Article 6(2) ECHR (*in dubio pro reo*/presumption of innocence), ten cases concern Article 1 of Protocol no. 1 to the ECHR (protection of property), nine cases concern Article 4 of Protocol no. 7 to the ECHR (*ne bis in idem*/ right not to be punished or tried twice), eight cases concern Article 5(3) ECHR

---

[169] *Neumeister v. Austria* (appl. no. 1936/63), Judgement (Chamber), 27 June 1968, Series A, Vol. 8.

[170] 181 by the European Court of Human Rights and 80 by the Committee of Ministers.

[171] Six decisions in 1987, one in 1988, three in 1989, four in 1990, six in 1991, four in 1992, eleven in 1993 and eleven in 1994 (decisions of the Committee of Ministers included).

[172] Twenty decisions in 1995, seventeen in 1996, 34 in 1997, six in 1998, six in 1999, sixteen in 2000, fourteen in 2001, fifteen in 2002, seventeen in 2003, fourteen in 2004, twenty in 2005 and 21 in 2006 (decisions of the Committee of Ministers included).

[173] The number of applications lodged is far higher: From 1983 to 2006 we count 6805 applications lodged (for the years 1958–1982 data about the applications lodged is not available).

(unlawful detention), six cases concern Article 5(4) ECHR (review of lawfulness of detention), four cases concern Article 3 ECHR (prohibition of torture or inhuman or degrading treatment), three cases concern 5(1) ECHR (right to liberty and security) and one case concerns Article 11 freedom of assembly and association). There are no cases concerning Article 2 ECHR (right to life), Article 4 (prohibition of slavery or forced labour), Article 5(2) ECHR (right to prompt information), Article 5(5) ECHR (right to compensation), Article 7 ECHR (no punishment without law), Article 9 ECHR (freedom of thought, conscience and religion) and Article 12 (right to marry).[174]

If we compare the judgements declaring a violation to judgements in which the Court has found no violation, Article 6(1) ECHR still stands out.[175] The fact that there are so many violations of Article 6(1) ECHR is presumably the result of an underlying systematic problem both with regard to procedural fairness and the length of procedure. Until 1990, there was no possible way to complain about excessive length of proceedings in civil and criminal matters on the national level. Then, the Statute on the Organization of the Courts (*Gerichtsorganisationsgesetz*) was amended by § 91, allowing the parties to a case to request the superior court to fix a time-limit for certain acts of the court.[176] The European Court of Human Rights has recognized that, with this provision, the Austrian legal system provides for an effective remedy to expedite proceedings before courts of law.[177] The same holds true of administrative proceedings (except for administrative criminal cases). In addition, section 73 of the General Administrative Procedure Act (*Allgemeines Verwaltungsverfahrensgesetz*) in conjunction with Article 132 of the Federal Constitution provides that if an authority fails to take a decision within six months, a party may request a transfer of jurisdiction to the compe-

---

[174] All these numbers also include the decisions of the Committee of Ministers as well as friendly settlements. If we exclude these decisions and friendly settlements we get the following numbers: Of a total number of 181 judgements concerning Austria (until the end of 2006), 120 cases concern Article 6(1) ECHR (68 cases fair trial and 52 cases length of procedure), i.e. more than half of all cases. Thirty-two cases concern Article 10 ECHR (freedom of expression), ten cases Article 6(2) ECHR (*in dubio pro reo*/presumption of innocence), eighteen cases Article 6(3) ECHR (right to defence), fifteen cases Article 14 (prohibition of discrimination), eight cases Article 8 ECHR (private and family life), seven cases Article 5(3) ECHR (unlawful detention) and Article 13 ECHR (lack of effective remedy) each, six cases Article 1 of Protocol no. 1 to the ECHR (protection of property), five cases Article 5(4) ECHR (review of lawfulness of detention), four cases Article 4 of Protocol no. 7 to the ECHR (*ne bis idem*/right not to be punished or tried twice) two cases Article 3 ECHR (prohibition of torture or inhuman or degrading treatment) and Article 5(1) ECHR (right to liberty and security) each and one case Article 11 (freedom of assembly and association).

[175] Forty-seven findings of violations and 26 findings of no violation of the ECHR concerning fair trial and 90 findings of violation and one finding of no violation of the ECHR concerning length of procedure, i.e. 137 findings of violation and 27 findings of no violations of Article 6(1) in total.

[176] Bundesgesetz vom 29. Juni 1989, mit dem Beträge und Wertgrenzen sowie damit zusammenhängende Regelungen des Zivilrechts und des Verfahrensrechts geändert wurden (Erweiterte Wertgrenzen-Novelle), BGBl 343/1989.

[177] *Holzinger v. Austria (No. 1)* (appl. no. 23459/94), Judgement (Third Section), 30 January 2001, Reports 2001-I, 137 et seq., para. 25.

tent superior order or the Administrative Court.[178] While fixing the sentence in administrative criminal proceedings, attention must be paid to the reasonable length of the proceeding with regard to Article 6(1) ECHR. If the authority fails to comply with this duty, the party may address the Constitutional Court after all other domestic remedies have been exhausted.[179]

With a Bill adopted by Parliament in March 2004, new provisions concerning the length of criminal proceedings have been introduced into the Code of Criminal Procedure.[180] The accused person is granted a right to the termination of the proceedings within a reasonable time. If this right is not respected, remedies are available that may lead to the closing of the proceedings: According to paragraph 108 of the Code of Criminal Procedure the court has – at the request of the accused person – to close the proceedings if the existing suspicion in respect of urgency and importance as well as of the previous length and the scope of the preliminary proceedings do not justify continuation. Additionally, it is required that an intensification of the suspicion cannot be expected through a further clarification of the facts.[181]

A still unresolved problem is the constantly heavy caseload of the Administrative Court, which causes many of the cases concerning excessive length of proceedings.[182] Very often, the reason for the excessive length of proceedings is the fact that in administrative proceedings, the only tribunal that fulfils the requirements of Article 6 ECHR is the Administrative Court. In order to overcome this structural shortcoming, a proposal has been tabled that would, if adopted, introduce a new system of administrative courts at first instance that would be in full compliance with Article 6(1) ECHR to alleviate a good part of the burden of the Administrative Court.

Article 10 ECHR also was violated on various occasions by Austrian authorities although not as often by far as Article 6(1) ECHR. This provision has been invoked several times in order to combat the Austrian broadcasting monopoly.[183] Furthermore, the cases concerning Article 10 in which the Court found a viola-

---

[178] See *Basic v. Austria* (appl. no. 29800/96), Judgement (Third Section), 30 January 2001 (not reported); *Pallanich v. Austria* (appl. no. 30160/96), Judgement (Third Section), 30 January 2001 (not reported).

[179] See Information submitted by Contracting States with regard to the implementation of the five recommendations mentioned in the Declaration adopted by the Committee of Ministers at ist 114th session (12 May 2004), CDDH(2006)0008 Addendum III Bil.

[180] Bundesgesetz, mit dem die Strafprozessordnung 1975 neu gestaltet wird (Strafprozessreformgesetz, Statute concerning the reform of criminal procedural law), BGBl I 19/2004.

[181] These measures will come into force on 1 January 2008. As they are considered the biggest reform of the last decades, some time is needed to train the people involved.

[182] See the Acitivity Report of the Administrative Court for the Year 2005 (Tätigkeitsbericht des Verwaltungsgerichtshofs für das Jahr 2005; http://www.vwgh.gv.at/Content.Node/de/presse/taetigkeitsbericht/taetigkeitsbericht2005.pdf), which refers to the structural and notorious capacity overload of the Administrative Court. According to this report, the number of cases where the length of proceeding is in tension to the requirements of Article 6(1) ECHR stagnates on a high level, without much chance of an improvement of the situation.

[183] See *infra* Section D.1.

tion of the right to freedom of expression reveal a tension between the high level of protection of the personality in the Austrian Criminal Code[184] as well as the media legislation on the one hand and the requirements of the Convention on the other hand.[185]

2. Switzerland

The first judgements concerning Switzerland were decided five years after ratification.[186] Until the end of 2006, 91 cases against Switzerland have been decided on the merits by the Court and the Committee of Ministers.[187] The number of friendly settlements before the Court is 3; there were none in cases before the Committee of Ministers.[188]

Up to now, the annual number of decisions against Switzerland has generally been rather small. Until 1992, there have never been more than five decisions.[189] Starting in 1993, where we count seven judgements, a slight increase can be noticed. The peak years were 2000 and 2006, with nine decisions in total.[190]

The number of applications registered has steadily increased in the course of time. Whereas there were about 40 *per annum* in the first years after ratification, we count more than 200 in the last couple of years. As of the end of 2006, 3474 applications against Switzerland have been registered.[191]

Article 6(1) ECHR has been invoked 41 times (26 cases fair trial and 15 cases length of procedure). Thus, more than one third of all invocations concerned Article 6(1) ECHR. Twelve cases concern Article 8 ECHR (private and family life), eleven cases Article 5(4) (review of lawfulness of detention) and Article 10 ECHR (freedom of expression) each, nine cases Article 5(3) ECHR (unlawful detention), six cases Article 6(3) ECHR (right to defence), five cases Article 3 ECHR (prohibition of torture or inhuman or degrading treatment) and Article 6(2) ECHR (*in dubio pro reo*/presumption of innocence) each, four cases Article 5(1) ECHR (right to liberty and security) three cases Article 2 ECHR (right to life), Article 13 ECHR (lack of effective remedy) and Article 14 ECHR (prohi-

---

[184] See Article 111 and 112 of the Austrian Criminal Code.

[185] See, *inter alia*, *Lingens v. Austria* (appl. no. 9815/82), Judgement (Plenary), 8 July 1986, Series A, Vol. 103.

[186] The first judgement was *Schiesser v. Switzerland* (appl. no. 7710/76), Judgement (Chamber), 4 December 1979, Series A, Vol. 34.

[187] 66 by the European Court of Human Rights and 25 by the Committee of Ministers.

[188] In addition, there were eight in cases before the Commission.

[189] Two decisions in 1979, one in 1980, one in 1981, none in 1982, five in 1983, one in 1984, none in 1985, four in 1986, one in 1987, four in 1988, four in 1989, four in 1990, two in 1991 and two in 1992 (decisions of the Committee of Ministers included).

[190] Seven decisions in 1993, one in 1994, 3 in 1995, six in 1996, six in 1997, five in 1998, one in 1999, nine in 2000, seven in 2001, four in 2002, one in 2003, none in 2004, five in 2005 and nine in 2006 (decisions of the Committee of Ministers included).

[191] Like for Austria, the number of applications lodged for Switzerland is also much higher: From 1983 to 2006, 5491 applications have been lodged (for the years 1958–1982 data about the applications lodged is not available).

bition of discrimination) each. Finally, one judgement deals with Article 5(2) ECHR (right to prompt information), Article 5(5) ECHR (enforceable right to compensation), Article 12 (right to marry) and Article 4 of Protocol no. 7 each. There are no cases concerning Article 4 ECHR (prohibition of slavery and forced labour)[192], Article 7 ECHR (no punishment without law), Article 9 (freedom of thought, conscience and religion) and Article 11 ECHR (freedom of assembly and association).[193]

Besides the procedural rights of Articles 5 and 6 ECHR, in the statistics concerning Switzerland Article 8 ECHR also stands out. However, we should bear in mind that appeals to Article 8 ECHR quite often also occurred in the context of criminal prosecution. A number of cases concerned questions about such issues as the legal bases of telephone tapping by public authorities in the cantonal Codes of Criminal Procedure.[194] Thus, the decisive point in these cases was whether interference by a public authority had been justified in accordance with Article 8(2) ECHR. Other cases concerned the right to family life, which is often affected in the context of a residence permit, the right to family reunion or the right not to be evicted.[195] The number of judgements concerning Article 10 ECHR is quite astonishing. It appears even more significant when we consider that the first judgement concerning Switzerland in respect of the right to freedom of expression was only pronounced in 1988. In parts, this number of cases has its cause in the definition of the ambit of freedom of expression. In Swiss practice, the prevailing case law said that an opinion could be protected only if it was ideational. The Court, however, declared that the fact that the applicant's activities were commercial could not deprive him of the protection of Article 10 ECHR.[196] Advertising is also included within the scope of the guarantees under Article 10

---

[192] There is now a case pending concerning the conformity of non-admission to the military service and the duty to pay a surrogate tax with Article 4(3)(b) and Article 14 ECHR.

[193] All these numbers also include the decisions of the Committee of Ministers as well as friendly settlements. If we exclude these decisions we get the following numbers (friendly settlements not included): Of a total of 66 judgements concerning Switzerland (until the end of 2006), 27 cases concern Article 6(1) ECHR (21 cases fair trial and 6 cases length of procedure), i.e., 40% of all cases. eleven cases Article 10 ECHR (freedom of expression), nine cases concern Article 8 ECHR (private and family life), seven cases Article 5(4) ECHR (unlawful detention), five cases Article 6(3) ECHR (right to defence), four cases Article 5(3) ECHR (review of lawfulness of detention), 4 cases Article 6(2) ECHR (*in dubio pro reo*/presumption of innocence), three cases Article 13 ECHR (lack of effective remedy), 3 cases Article 14 ECHR (prohibition of discrimination), two cases Article 2 ECHR (right to life), two cases Article 5(1) ECHR (right to liberty and security), one case Article 3 ECHR (prohibition of torture), one case Article 5(2) ECHR (right to information of the reasons for detention) and one case Article 12 ECHR (right to marry).

[194] *Kopp v. Switzerland* (appl. no. 23224/94), Judgement (Chamber), 25 March 1998, Reports 1998-II, 524 et seq. (violation of Article 8 ECHR); *Lüdi v. Switzerland* (appl. no. 12433/86), Judgement (Chamber), 15 June 1992, Series A, Vol. 238 (no violation of Article 8 ECHR).

[195] *Boultif v. Switzerland* (appl. no. 54273/00), Judgement (Second Section), 2 August 2001, Reports 2001-IX, 119 et seq.

[196] *Autronic AG v. Switzerland* (appl. no. 12726/87), Judgement (Plenary), 22 Mai 1990 Series A, Vol.178.

ECHR.[197] In addition, Article 10 has an impact on criminal law[198] and can also be of importance in cases subject to private law[199]. It is, furthermore, interesting to note that it took 32 years until the first judgement concerning Article 2 ECHR was decided.[200]

If we take a look at the proportion of judgements declaring a violation to judgements in which the Court and the Committee of Ministers have found no violation of the Convention, the cases of Article 6(1) become less important,[201] whereas those concerning Articles 8 ECHR[202] and 5(4) ECHR[203] predominate.[204] We have to bear in mind, however, that because of the small number of judgements in relation to the length of time, it is difficult to make a further analysis of the statistics. The differences between the various Articles may be of a nearly accidental nature and it takes only a few new judgements to invert the ratio between violations and non-violations.

3. Comparison and Conclusion

The comparison between Austria and Switzerland reveals first of all that in the case of Austria, the number of judgements is almost three times higher, the number of convictions almost four times. Considering that Austria's population is only about half a million people more than Switzerland's,[205] at first sight this seems rather astonishing. However, it can be explained by the circumstances of Austria's ratification: Compared to Switzerland, where a number of statutes were modified in order to comply with the Convention, Austria was much less concerned about the incompatibilities between its legal order and the Convention and, thus, had to adapt its legal order after ratification and at the instigation of the Strasbourg organs. In addition, Austria joined the ECHR 16 years before Switzerland. As a

---

[197] *Casado Coca v. Spain* (appl. no. 15450/89), Judgement (Chamber), 22 February 1994, Series A, Vol. 285-A. This judgement also shows how the ambit of freedom of expression was developed by the case law of the Court, see para. 35.

[198] *Dammann v. Switzerland* (appl. no. 77551/01), Judgement (Fourth Section), 25 April 2006 (not yet reported); *Stoll v. Switzerland* (appl. no. 69698/01), Judgement (Fourth Section), 25 April 2006 (not yet reported).

[199] *Hertel v. Switzerland* (appl. no. 25181/94), Judgement (Chamber), 25 August 1998, Reports 1998-VI, Vol. 87, 2298 et seq; *VgT (Verein gegen Tierfabriken) v. Switzerland* (appl. no. 24699/94), Judgement (Second Section), 28 June 2001, Reports 2001-VI, 243 et seq.

[200] *Scavuzzo-Hager and Others v. Switzerland* (appl. no. 41773/98), Judgement (Fourth Section), 7 February 2006 (not yet reported).

[201] Twenty six declarations of violation and fifteen declarations of no violation of the ECHR.

[202] Eight declarations of violation and four declarations of no violation of the ECHR.

[203] Six declarations of violation and four declarations of no violation of the ECHR. However, two declarations of no violation of the ECHR originate from 1979.

[204] If we exclude the decisions of the Committee of Ministers: Article 6(1) ECHR: Nineteen declarations of violation and eight declarations of no violation of the ECHR; Article 8 ECHR: Seven declarations of violation and two declarations of no violation of the ECHR; Article 5(4) ECHR: Five declarations of violation and two declaration of no violation of the ECHR.

[205] Austria has about 8.30 million inhabitants; Switzerland about 7.55 million (as of 1 January 2007).

consequence, Austrian lawyers have more experience with the Convention than their Swiss colleagues. Due to the explicit constitutional status, Austrian lawyers routinely refer to the Convention and it does not, therefore, take much additional effort to go to Strasbourg. Moreover, Austrian scholars began publishing on the subject earlier and already at an early stage pointed to incompatibilities between the Austrian legal order and the Convention. In recent years, there has been a certain equalization with regard to the number of applications lodged *per capita*. However, there are still about twice as many decisions on the merits in the case of Austria.

The rather low number of cases concerning Switzerland is proof of a functioning system of legal remedies. In contrast, the high number of convictions in cases concerning Article 6(1) ECHR (fair trial and length of procedure) indicates that Austria has an underlying systematic problem in this respect.[206] Although some measures have been taken[207], Austria is still in need of effective solutions for this shortcoming. For the rest, neither Austria nor Switzerland face serious problems. Yet, the statistical data clearly disprove a frequently made assumption: the higher the human rights standards at the national level, the smaller the number of cases going to Strasbourg. The case law for both countries – and especially for Austria – shows that even after a consolidation of the ECHR on the national level the number of cases going to Strasbourg increased over the years. This may be due to the fact that lawyers in both countries became more familiar with the Convention over the years and, as a consequence, more often convinced their clients to go to Strasbourg. Legal scholarship has probably supported this process as it kept on stressing the importance of the conventional rights in fields such as criminal proceeding or alien law.[208] A highly developed national system of remedies generally has a positive impact on the conformity with the ECHR. However, it also simplifies the way for the applicant to take a further step to Strasbourg, which is an additional factor leading to an increase of applications. Another, more general factor for the increase might be that citizens are less and less willing to accept what authorities and courts decide, a phenomenon that is also responsible for the ever-growing case-load of national courts.

It may come as a surprise that in both countries there are more violations in recent years than immediately after accession. The main reason is the increasing number of applications that has already been pointed out above. In addition, in the course of time the Strasbourg case law – mainly with regard to the scope of Article 6 – has become more dynamic than could ever have been foreseen, which has also increased the incompatibilities between the Austrian and the Swiss legal

---

[206] According to Matscher (2003), 11, an additional reason for the high number of cases is that judges often lack the knowledge required to adequately deal with white collar-crime cases.

[207] See *supra* Section C.1.

[208] As to the importance of legal scholarship for the reception of the ECHR in Austria and Switzerland see *infra* Section G.

order and the practice of their courts and authorities on the one hand and the ECHR on the other.

D. The European Court's Case Law and its Effects in the NLO

1. Austria

The Convention itself and the case law of the Strasbourg organs influenced the Austrian legal order in various ways: Existing laws were amended or new laws set into force in reaction to adverse judgements of the Court or due to decisions which, while affecting other countries, raised objections under the Convention against Austrian laws. Other judgements were of interest in the single case but did not affect the Austrian legal order as such. The ECHR also influenced the decision-making of Austrian courts and administrative agencies.[209] In addition, there are other effects that cannot be measured easily, such as the human rights-friendly climate and the awareness of the importance of human rights that the Strasbourg case law created in Austria. Finally, there is a soft normative effect that leads to acts of legislation and jurisdiction that are not legally required but that have been triggered at least partly by the ECHR.[210] As the cases that led to modifications and amendments in the Austrian legal system cannot be listed exhaustively, the following examples shall be indicative of the manifold effects of the Strasbourg case law on the national legal order. The focus will be on those effects that led to changes in the Austrian legislation, whereas the impact of the Strasbourg law on the jurisdictional level will only be addressed briefly.[211]

The case law of the ECHR undoubtedly had its greatest effect in the field of criminal procedural law.[212] In *Pataki v. Austria*[213] and *Dunshirn v. Austria*[214] the plaintiffs claimed that the proceedings before the Higher Provincial Courts *(Oberlandesgerichte)* violated the right to a fair trial, because the accused did not have the right to be represented by an attorney while the public prosecutor was present. According to the Commission, the so-called equality of arms is an imminent part of a fair trial and procedures that are not in accordance with that imperative violate Article 6 ECHR. As a consequence, the Austrian legislator modified the respective provisions of the Code of Criminal Procedure.[215]

---

[209] Concerning the impact of the proportionality principle on the Austrian legal order see *infra* Section F.1.b.

[210] See Grabenwarter (2001), 321.

[211] As to the coordination between national Courts and the ECtHR see *infra* Section E.1.a. For an overview, also see Tretter (2002), 108 et seq.

[212] For a detailed overview of the impact of the ECHR on Austrian criminal procedural law see Okresek (1997), 619 et seq.

[213] *Pataki v. Austria* (appl. no. 596/59), Report (Plenary), Commission, 28 March 1963, YB 6, 718.

[214] *Dunshirn v. Austria* (appl. no. 789/60), Report, Commission, 28 March 1963, YB 6, 718.

[215] Bundesgesetz vom 18. Juli 1962, mit dem die Strafprozessordnung 1960 geändert und er-

The cases of *Neumeister*[216], *Stögmüller*[217], *Matznetter*[218], and later also *Ringeisen*[219] concerned the duration of procedure and remand. *Stögmüller* was 24 months on remand, *Neumeister* and *Matznetter* 26 months and *Ringeisen* 29 months. The ECtHR made clear that the Convention does not have any absolute period of time in mind when speaking of "reasonable time". What reasonable time in a single case means rather depends upon the complexity of the case. However, the duration of remand should be as short as possible and the person affected should be given reasons for the duration. In order to adapt the national legal order to the ECHR and the case law of the Court, the Austrian legislature again revised the Code of Criminal Procedure.[220] The duration of remand should be as short as possible and remand because of danger of collusion should last not longer than two months, remand for other reasons not longer than 6 months.

In the *Simon-Herold* case[221] a person on remand had to be examined by a medical doctor. He was sent to the locked ward of the psychiatric department of a public hospital even though he was not in need of psychiatric treatment. This action was taken because it was cheaper and easier to watch him at the facility. Before the Commission, he argued that he was treated inhumanely. The case ended in an out-of-court settlement. As a consequence, the Ministry of Justice determined that detainees who are not mentally ill may not be sent to locked wards when they need medical treatment.[222]

In a case concerning Article 4 ECHR,[223] the Austrian attorney *Gussenbauer* claimed before the Commission that he was urged to accept mandates as an unpaid defence lawyer for clients without means. According to him, this amounted to forced labour. After negotiations for an out-of-court settlement had been taken

---

gänzt wird (Strafprozessnovelle 1962), BGBl 229/1962; Bundesgesetz vom 27. März 1963 über die Erneuerung von Berufungsverfahren in Strafsachen, BGBl 66/1963.

[216] *Neumeister v. Austria* (appl. no. 1936/63), Judgement (Chamber), 27 June 1968, Series A, Vol. 8.

[217] *Stögmüller v. Austria* (appl. no. 1602/62), Judgement (Chamber), 10 November 1969, Series A, Vol. 9.

[218] *Matznetter v. Austria* (appl. no. 2178/64), Judgement (Chamber), 10 November 1969, Series A, Vol. 10

[219] *Ringeisen v. Austria* (appl. no. 2614/65), Judgement (Chamber), 16 July 1971, Series A, Vol. 13.

[220] Bundesgesetz vom 26. März 1969 über die Einführung eines Strafvollzugsgesetzes (Einführungsgesetz zum Strafvollzugsgesetz), BGBl 145/1969.

[221] *Simon-Herold v. Austria* (appl. no. 4340/69), Report (Plenary), Commission, 19 December 1972.

[222] The decree is printed in Annex I of the Commission report mentioned in footnote 221.

[223] *Gussenbauer v. Austria* (appl. no. 4897/71; 5219/71), Decision (Plenary), Commission, 14 July 1972, YB 15, 448.

up, the Code of Criminal Procedure[224] and the Attorney Statute[225] were revised. They now provide for the defendant's right to Counsel free of charge where this is in the interest of law as well as the right to have an adequate defence.

As a reaction to several complaints[226], the Code of Criminal Procedure Adaptation Act 1974[227] was amended to ensure that the parties to criminal proceedings were given the opportunity to hear witnesses.

In the aftermath of a friendly settlement in the case of *X. v. Austria*[228] a provision was included in the Criminal Code Amendment Act 1983[229] to allow a detained defendant to attend a hearing before the court of appeals if he so requests or where this is in the interest of justice.

Due to the *Can* case[230], Article 45(3) of the Austrian Code of Criminal Procedure was changed so that supervision of consultations between a suspect in detention on remand and his lawyer is respected to exceptional cases and, as a rule, the investigating judge is only permitted to be present at meetings between an accused and his defence counsel during the first two weeks of detention.[231]

The case of *K.*[232] led to the adoption of an amendment to the Code of Criminal Procedure, which provided that persons who run the risk of giving self-incriminating evidence should be exempted from the obligation to testify. In 1996, another amendment ensured that statements by the Public Prosecutor must in any case be transmitted to the accused.[233]

The Court's case law concerning Article 6 also had an impact on Austrian administrative law[234]. Decisions of administrative authorities of a judicial character consisting of administrative officers and judges *(Kollegialbehörden mit richterlichem*

---

[224] Bundesgesetz vom 8. November 1973, mit dem das Einführungsgesetz zur Zivilprozessordnung, die Zivilprozessordnung, die Strafprozessordnung, das Jugendgerichtsgesetz, das Verwaltungsgerichtshofgesetz und das Allgemeine Verwaltungsverfahrensgesetz zur Regelung der Verfahrenshilfe geändert werden (Verfahrenshilfegesetz), BGBl 569/1973.

[225] Bundesgesetz vom 8. November 1973, mit dem die Rechtsanwaltsordnung geändert wird, BGBl 570/1973.

[226] *X., Y. and Z. v. Austria* (appl. no. 5049/71), Decision (Plenary), Commission, 5 February 1973, Collection 43, 3.

[227] Bundesgesetz vom 11. Juli 1974, mit dem die Strafprozessordnung 1960 an das Strafgesetzbuch angepasst wird (Strafprozessanpassungsgesetz), BGBl 423/1974.

[228] *X. v. Austria* (appl. no. 8289/78), Decision (Plenary), Commission, 5 March 1980, DR 18, 160.

[229] Bundesgesetz vom 2. März 1983, mit dem die Strafprozessordnung und das Heeresdisziplinargesetz geändert wurden (Strafverfahrensänderungsgesetz 1983), BGBl 168/1983.

[230] *Can v. Austria* (appl. no. 9300/81), Judgement (Chamber), 30 September 1985, Series A, Vol. 96.

[231] Bundesgesetz vom 25. November 1987, mit dem (inter alia) die Strafprozessordnung geändert wurde (Strafrechtsänderungsgesetz 1987), BGBl 605/1987.

[232] *K. v. Austria* (appl. no. 16002/90), Judgement (Chamber), 2 June 1993, Series A, Vol. 255-B.

[233] BGBl 762/1996. This amendment was triggered by the judgement in the *Bulut* case. See *Bulut v. Austria* (appl. no. 17358/90), Judgement (Chamber), 22 February 1996, Reports 1996-II, Vol. 5, 346 et seq.

[234] Concerning the impact of Article 6 ECHR on Austrian administrative procedural law see Grabenwarter (1997), 355 et seq.; for a detailed overview, see also Herbst (1997), 661 et seq.

Einschlag) are final as they cannot be appealed to the Supreme Administrative Court.[235] After the *Ringeisen* case[236] it became clear that these authorities would in principle be able to fulfil the requirements of Article 6 ECHR concerning the independence and impartiality of tribunals. However, the Federal Constitutional Statute had to be amended by Article 20(2) stating that their members are not bound by instructions.[237]

In the 80's, the Constitutional Court itself raised the question of whether the Austrian system of judicial review in administrative matters was compatible with Article 6.[238] The legislator reacted by making the most profound changes in the Sixth Main Part of the Constitutional Statute[239] since its entry into force: A constitutional amendment establishing Independent Administrative Panels *(Unabhängige Verwaltungssenate)* in the Provinces, organized as independent and impartial tribunals within the meaning of Article 6 ECHR, was enacted in 1988 and entered into force in 1991.[240] By establishing these panels the legislator reacted to the case-law of the Court according to which the terms "civil rights and obligations" and "criminal charge" must be understood in a broad sence to include administrative criminal offences and other traditional administrative matters.[241] The competences of the Independent Administrative Panels can be extended by statutory law, which allows an easy adaptation of Austrian law to further requirements of the ECHR, especially in civil matters.[242] In 1990, a comprehensive amendment of the Code of Administrative Procedure was adopted in order to organize proceedings before the Panels in conformity with Articles 5 and 6.[243] The latter were thereby, among other things, awarded full cognition with

[235] Article 133(4) B-VG.
[236] *Ringeisen v. Austria* (appl. no. 2614/65), Judgement (Chamber), 16 July 1971, Series A, Vol.13.
[237] See Grabenwarter (1999), Art 20/2 B-VG n 3 et seq.; Grabenwarter (1999), Art 133, n 4, 36 et seq.; Pernthaler (1977), 82 et seq.
[238] Austrian Constitutional Court, Judgement, 14 October 1987, VfSlg 11500/1987 = EuGRZ 1988, 166 et seq.
[239] Sechstes Hauptstück des Bundes-Verfassungsgesetzes.
[240] Bundesverfassungsgesetz vom 29. November 1988, mit dem das Bundes-Verfassungsgesetz in der Fassung von 1929 geändert wird (Bundes-Verfassungsgesetz-Novelle 1988), BGBl 685/1988.
[241] See above all *Ringeisen v. Austria* (appl. no. 2614/65), Judgement (Chamber), 16 July 1971, Series A, Vol. 13; *König v. Germany* (appl. no. 6232/73), Judgement (Plenary), 28 June 1978, Series A, Vol. 27; *Benthem v. the Netherlands* (appl. no. 8848/80), Judgement (Plenary), 23 October 1985, Series A, Vol. 97. As to the question of whether an offence qualifies as criminal for the purposes of the Convention, see *Pramstaller v. Austria* (appl. no. 16713/90), Judgement (Chamber), 23 October 1995, Series A, Vol. 329-A; *Palaoro v. Austria* (appl. no. 16718/90), Judgement (Chamber), 23 October 1995, Series A, Vol. 329-B; *Gradinger v. Austria* (appl. no 15963/90), Judgement (Chamber), 23 October 1995, Series A, Vol.328-C.
[242] Adamovich, Funk and Holzinger (1998), 37.0004.
[243] Bundesgesetz vom 6. Juni 1990, mit dem das Einführungsgesetz zu den Verwaltungsverfahrensgesetzen geändert wird, BGBl 356/1990; Bundesgesetz vom 6. Juni 1990, mit dem das Allgemeine Verwaltungsverfahrensgesetz, das Auskunftspflichtgesetz und das Zustellgesetz geändert werden, BGBl 357/1990; Bundesgesetz vom 6. Juni 1990, mit dem das Verwaltungsstrafgesetz geändert wird, BGBl 358/1990.

regard to questions of fact and law. The Court in *Baischer v. Austria*[244] found that Independent Administrative Panels have to be regarded as tribunals within the meaning of Article 6(1) ECHR.

According to the Austrian law then in force, a hearing before the Administrative Court was not necessary when a further clarification of the matter was unlikely. This, however, was not covered by the reservation to Article 6(1).[245] As a consequence § 39(2) Ziff. 6 of the Statute on the Administrative Court (*Verwaltungsgerichtshofgesetz, VwGG*)[246] now states that the Administrative Court can only abstain from a hearing where it is in accordance with Article 6(1) ECHR.

Several amendments aimed at an acceleration of proceedings. In 1984, a constitutional amendment to reduce the burden on the Constitutional and Administrative Court was adopted. Courts of public law were enabled to refuse to deal with an appeal if it had no prospect of success or did not relate to a fundamental question.[247] Due to the cases of *Erkner and Hofauer*[248] as well as *Poiss*[249] the Agricultural Proceedings Act, the Federal Agricultural Authorities Act and the Federal Agricultural Land Planning (General Principles) Act have been amended in order to simplify and speed up proceedings in land consolidation cases and to provide for adequate compensation rules. As a reaction to the case of *B.*[250], a new Article 91 of the Act on the Organization of the Courts was enacted. According to this provision, where a court delays in taking procedural steps such as drawing up a judgement, the parties may request the higher court to prescribe a timelimit for the taking of such procedural steps. The fact, however, that Austria still faces considerable problems with regard to the length of proceedings[251] shows that these measures are apparently only of a limited effect. This is mainly rooted in the fact that Article 91 may only be applied to courts but not to administrative authorities that are responsible for many of the delays.[252]

Moreover, Article 8 ECHR and the respective Strasbourg case law had important impacts on the Austrian legal order: In 1978 the Data Protection Act

---

[244] *Baischer v. Austria* (appl. no. 32381/96), Judgement (First Section), 20 December 2001 (not reported).

[245] *Stallinger and Kuso v. Austria* (appl. nos 14696/89; 1467/89), Judgement (Chamber), 23 April 1997, Reports 1997-II, Vol. 35, 666 et seq.

[246] Bundesgesetz, mit dem das Verfassungsgerichtshofgesetz 1953, das Verwaltungsgerichtshofgesetz 1985 und das Gebührengesetz 1957 geändert werden, BGBl I 88/1997.

[247] Tretter (2002), 109 et seq.

[248] *Erkner and Hofauer v. Austria* (appl. no. 9616/81), Judgement (Chamber), 23 April 1987, Series A, Vol. 117.

[249] *Poiss v. Austria* (appl. no. 9816/82), Judgement (Chamber), 23 April 1987, Series A, Vol. 117.

[250] *B. v. Austria* (appl. no. 11968/86), Judgement (Chamber), 28 March 1990, Series A, Vol. 175.

[251] See *supra* Section C.1.

[252] See *Jancikova v. Austria* (appl. no. 56483/00), Judgement (First Section), 7 April 2005 (not yet reported); *Hauser-Sporn v. Austria* (appl. no. 37301/03), Judgement (First Section), 7 December 2006 (not yet reported).

(*Datenschutzgesetz*)[253] was enacted in order to carry forward the principles contained in Article 8 ECHR. Article 1(2) explicitly states that restrictions of the right to data protection are only allowed in order to protect the valid interests of others or on the basis of laws which are necessary to achieve the aims listed in Article 8(2) ECHR. Also the Chemical Substances Act (*Chemikaliengesetz*)[254] of 1996, which obliges enterprises to inform the authorities on the production, storage, and transport of dangerous chemicals, refers to Article 8 ECHR in § 55 (1) concerning data confidentiality.

The case law of the Strasbourg organs furthermore thoroughly influenced the Austrian broadcast legislation. Austria was one of the last members of the Council of Europe where public broadcasting was fully monopolized. In reaction to the application and the report of the Commission in the case of *Informationsverein Lentia 2000 and others*[255], shortly before the judgement of the Court was delivered, the Austrian Parliament abolished the broadcasting monopoly of the Austrian Broadcasting Corporation (*Österreichischer Rundfunk, ORF*) which the Court held to be a violation of Article 10. Parliament passed the Private Radio Act (*Privatradiogesetz*)[255a] which provided for a small number of broadcasting licences, but only for radio and on a regional level. Later, the Private Television Act (*Privatfernsehgesetz*)[256] and the Exclusive Television Rights Act (*Fernseh-Exklusivrechte Gesetz*)[257] concerning private television licences were passed. If not for the pressure by the Court, this development would certainly have taken longer.

With a view toward Article 5 ECHR and the aim of withdrawing the reservation to this provision, the Federal Constitutional Law on the Protection of Personal Liberty (*Bundesverfassungsgesetz zum Schutz der persönlichen Freiheit*) was enacted in 1988,[258] although the reservation has not yet been withdrawn. As a consequence of the *Engel* case[259], in 1985 the former Federal Army Disciplinary Act (*Heeresdisziplinargesetz*) was amended in order to fulfil the requirements following from the fact that restrictions of personal liberty based on disciplinary law

---

[253] Bundesgesetz über den Schutz personenbezogener Daten (Datenschutzgesetz), BGBl 565/1978.

[254] Bundesgesetz über den Schutz des Menschen und der Umwelt vor Chemikalien (Chemikaliengesetz 1996), BGBl 59/1997.

[255] *Case of Informationsverein Lentia 2000 and Others v. Austria* (appl. nos 13914/88; 15041/89; 15717/89; 1577/89; 17207/90), Judgement (Chamber), 24 November 1993, Series A, Vol. 276.

[255a] Bundesgesetz, mit dem Bestimmungen über privates Hörfunk erlassen wurden (Privatradiogesetz), BGBl I 21/200.

[256] Bundesgesetz, mit dem Bestimmungen über privates Fernsehen erlassen wurden (Privatfernsehgesetz), BGBl I 84/2001.

[257] Bundesgesetz über die Ausübung exklusiver Fernsehübertragungsrechte (Fernseh-Exklusivrechtegesetz), BGBl I 85/2001.

[258] Bundesverfassungsgesetz vom 29. November 1988 über den Schutz der persönlichen Freiheit, BGBl 684/1988. See *supra* Section A.1.b. As to the relation between this statute and Article 5 ECHR see Kopetzki (1997), 270.

[259] *Engel and Others v. the Netherlands* (appl. nos 5100/71; 5101/71; 5102/71; 5354/72; 5370/72), Judgement (Plenary), 8 June 1976, Series A, Vol. 22.

fall within the scope of Article 5. The ECHR furthermore had an impact on the Austrian system of appeals. In order to enable the Supreme Court of Justice to review criminal decisions according to Article 5, the Law on Fundamental Rights Applications (*Grundrechtsbeschwerdegesetz*) was set in force in 1992.[260]

The case law established in respect to Article 3 has been implemented in the Aliens Act (*Fremdengesetz*)[261], prohibiting the deportation of foreigners to countries where they risk being subjected to inhuman or degrading treatment, punishment, or the death penalty.[262] The Aliens Act is furthermore influenced by Article 8 ECHR, especially in connection with the right of legal aliens or new immigrants staying in Austria to have their families reunited.

Finally, in 1987 in the case of *Inze*[263], the Court found a violation of the discrimination ban in connection with the right to respect for property (Article 14 ECHR and Article 1 Protocol no. 1) in a case of unequal treatment of legitimate and illegitimate children under the farm inheritance law in Carinthia. As a consequence, the Carinthian Hereditary Farms Act of 1903 was replaced in 1990.

However, the Austrian legislator did not always manage to comply with its obligations resulting from judgements of the ECtHR. The following example shows that a functioning national system of checks and balances and the willingness of the courts to follow the Strasbourg case law may help to overcome such shortcomings. In the case of *Gaygusuz*[264], the Austrian authorities refused to grant emergency assistance to the applicant who had exhausted entitlement to unemployment benefits on the ground that he did not have Austrian nationality. The Court stated that the difference in treatment between Austrian nationals and foreigners had not been based on any objective and reasonable justification so that the refusal to grant emergency assistance constituted a violation of Article 14 ECHR. Before a political consensus could be found on the required amendments, three further complaints claiming a violation of the Convention were lodged before the Constitutional Court, which changed its former case law and followed the opinion of the Strasbourg court.[265] After this judgement, it became necessary to amend the Unemployment Insurance Act. Although the draft no longer explicitly required Austrian nationality, the conditions for receiving emergency assistance would in practice primarily be fulfilled by Austrian citizens. Only one

---

[260] Bundesgesetz über die Beschwerde an den Obersten Gerichtshof wegen Verletzung des Grundrechts auf persönliche Freiheit (Grundrechtsbeschwerde-Gesetz), BGBl 864/1992.

[261] Bundesgesetz über die Einreise, den Aufenthalt und die Ausreise vom Fremden (Fremdengesetz 1997), BGBl I 75/1997. This statute has since been replaced by a new statute; see Fremdenrechtspaket 2005, BGBl I 100/2005.

[262] A reference to Articles 2 and 3 in conjunction with Protocol no. 6 is found in the Explanatory Report thereto. See Tretter (2002), 108.

[263] *Inze v. Austria* (appl. no. 8695/79), Judgement (Chamber), 28 October 1987, Series A, Vol. 126.

[264] *Gaygusuz v. Austria* (appl. no. 17371/90), Judgement (Chamber), 16 September 1996, Reports 1996-IV, Vol. 14, 1129 et seq.

[265] Austrian Constitutional Court, Judgement, 11 March 1998, VfSlg 15129/1998.

year later, the case was again brought before the Austrian Constitutional Court, which quashed the relevant provision as constituting a breach of Protocol no. 1 in conjunction with Article 14 ECHR.[266]

2. Switzerland

The procedural guarantees of Articles 5 and 6 ECHR also had the greatest bearing on the Swiss legal system.[267] As these provisions are very much influenced by the Anglo-Saxon system of procedure; judicial control of exertion of power plays an important role. It is, therefore, not surprising that the interpretation of "other officer authorized by law to exercise judicial power"[268] has led to various discussions and amendments in the cantonal Codes of Criminal Procedure.[269]

Not long after the ECHR entered into force for Switzerland, a decision of the Commission[270] triggered an amendment to the Federal Statute on military criminal procedure (*Militärstrafgesetz*),[271] as there had been no judicial instance that decided on a close arrest (*scharfer Arrest*) in the military disciplinary procedure. Quite a few judgements of the Strasbourg organs concerned detention on remand and triggered various amendments in cantonal Codes of Criminal Procedure.[272]

The Strasbourg practice may have had its greatest effect on criminal procedure in the Cantons through two judgements concerning Belgium, *De Cubber*[273] and *Piersack*[274]. Following these judgements in 1986 the Federal Supreme Court de-

---

[266] Austrian Constitutional Court, Judgement, 9 June 1999, VfSlg 15506/1999.

[267] As the ECHR and the Strasbourg case law had and still has multifaceted impacts on the Swiss legal order, the following section is not exhaustive but rather puts a focus on the most important cases. It is partly based on Keller (2005), 339 et seq.

[268] Article 5(3) ECHR.

[269] See Trechsel (1988), 686 et seq. with examples; furthermore Schürmann (2006), 270 et seq.

[270] *Eggs v. Switzerland* (appl. no 7431/76), Decision, Commission, 4 March 1978, DR 15, 35; *Eggs v. Switzerland*, resolution, Committee of Ministers, 19 October 1979, EuGRZ 7 (1980), 274, the Committee did not follow the decision of the Commission because the Federal Statute had been amended in the meantime; *Santschi v. Switzerland* (appl. nos 7468/76; 7938/77; 8018/77; 8106/77; 8325/78; 8778/79), Decision, 13 October 1981, DR 31, 5.

[271] Bundesgesetz über den Militärstrafprozess vom 23. März 1979 (MStP), entered into force 1 January 1980, AS 1979 1037, 1058.

[272] *Huber v. Switzerland* (appl. no. 12794/87), Judgement (Plenary), 23 October 1990, Series A, Vol. 188. For the practice of the Federal Supreme Court after this judgement of the Court, see Swiss Federal Supreme Court, Judgement, 20 September 1991, BGE 117 Ia 199, 201 E. 4a; Swiss Federal Supreme Court, Judgement, 24 January 1992, BGE 118 Ia 95, 97 E. 3a. For an extreme example, where a duration of 4 years was found to be legal, see *W. v. Switzerland* (appl. no. 14379/88), Judgement (Chamber), 26 January 1993, Series A, Vol. 254-A.

[273] *De Cubber v. Belgium* (appl. no. 9186/80), Judgement (Chamber), 26 October 1984, Series A, Vol. 86.

[274] *Piersack v. Belgium* (appl. no. 8692/79), Judgement (Chamber), 1 October 1982, Series A, Vol. 53.

cided that the union of the examining magistrate and the subject judge (*Sachrichter*) into one person was not compatible with Article 6(1) ECHR.[275]

As a consequence of the requirement of a judicial control of detention (*habeas corpus*, Article 5(4) ECHR), federal criminal procedure had to be reformed,[276] because it had been in the Federal Prosecutor's competence to decide on the maintenance of the detention on remand. An important judgement was *Sanchez-Reisse v. Switzerland*,[277] which was followed by various amendments of cantonal law.[278] The right to judicial control of detention was also inserted into the new Constitution of 1999.[279]

The judgement by the Court in the case of *Minelli*,[280] who had been committed to pay two-thirds of the court costs despite the termination of the criminal prosecution, triggered a change of practice concerning the imposition of court costs. The Swiss Federal Supreme Court adapted the judgement of the Court and concretized the guarantees under Article 6(2) ECHR.[281]

In *Lüdi v. Switzerland*[282], the Court gave an important judgement concerning the right of an accused to examine or have examined witnesses on his behalf as expressed in Article 6(3) ECHR. The Court stated that an anonymous witness on whose evidence the judge bases his decision must, as a matter of principal, be treated in the same manner as an ordinary witness. The Federal Supreme Court approved this rule in later judgements.[283] Switzerland has very recently enacted a new Federal Statute on undercover inquiry that shall satisfy the requirements established by the Court, such as the legal basis for undercover inquiries and the protection of the rights of defence.[284]

---

[275] Swiss Federal Supreme Court, Judgement, 4 June 1986, BGE 112 Ia 290; Swiss Federal Supreme Court, Judgement, 4 June 1986, not published, see EuGRZ 13 (1986), 670.

[276] Article 52(2) BStP, amended by annex (2), Bundesgesetz vom 22. März 1974 über das Verwaltungsstrafrecht (VStrR, SR 313.0), AS 1974 1857, entered into force 1 January 1975.

[277] *Sanchez-Reisse v. Switzerland* (appl. no. 9862/82), Judgement (Chamber), 21 October 1986, Series A, Vol. 107.

[278] See e.g., Swiss Federal Supreme Court, Judgement, 18 January 1989, BGE 115 Ia 56, 60 E. 2b; Swiss Federal Supreme Court, Judgement, 22 March 1989, BGE 115 Ia 293, 299 et seq. E. 4a; Swiss Federal Supreme Court, Judgement, 14 March 1990, BGE 116 Ia 60, 63 et seq. E. 2; Swiss Federal Supreme Court, Judgement, 28 March 1995, BGE 121 II 53, 55 et seq. E. 2.

[279] Article 31(4) Constitution of 1999. For the recent practice, see Swiss Federal Supreme Court, Judgement, 29 February 2000, BGE 126 I 172.

[280] *Minelli v. Switzerland* (appl. no. 8660/78), Judgement (Chamber), 25 March 1983, Series A, Vol. 62.

[281] Swiss Federal Supreme Court, Judgement, 21 September 1983, BGE 109 Ia 160, 163 et seq. E. 4; Swiss Federal Supreme Court, Judgement, 19 June 1988, BGE 114 Ia 299, 302 E. 2b and c; Swiss Federal Supreme Court, Judgement, 27 June 1990, BGE 116 Ia 162, 165 et seq E. 2a.

[282] *Lüdi v. Switzerland* (appl. no. 12433/86), Judgement (Chamber), 15 June 1992, Series A, Vol. 238.

[283] Swiss Federal Supreme Court, Judgement, 14 August 1992, BGE 118 Ia 457; Swiss Federal Supreme Court, Judgement, 2 December 1998, BGE 125 I 127.

[284] Bundesgesetz vom 20. Juni 2003 über die verdeckte Ermittlung (BVE, SR 312.8), entered into force 1 January 2005. For the message by the Federal Council, 1 July 1998, see BBl 1998 IV 4241, referring to the *Lüdi* judgement (*supra* note 282) on page 4249, the requirements for the protection of the rights of the defence on page 4300 and for the legal basis on page 4303.

Comparable to the situation in Austria, the autonomous interpretation of the term "determination of (...) civil rights and obligations" and "criminal charge" had a profound impact on the Swiss legal order. As shown above, the ECtHR increasingly qualified matters of public law – according to national criteria – as "civil rights and obligations".[285] In the aftermath of the *Schuler-Zgraggen* case[286], the Federal Supreme Court stated that disputes over benefits on all branches of social insurance under federal law were disputes about civil rights and obligations and that there was a demand for the hearing to be public.[287] This development also had a considerable effect on the Cantonal and federal procedure of expropriation. Only after the Federal Supreme Court declared invalid the renewed interpretative declaration in respect of Article 6(1) ECHR in 1992[288] was access to court with full jurisdiction as granted by Article 6(1) ECHR fully accepted in Switzerland. The legal protection demanded by the Strasbourg practice in matters of land use planning made some additional amendments necessary in Switzerland. Land use plans (*Nutzungspläne*) that can cause a material or formal expropriation fall under the guarantee of Article 6(1) ECHR.[289] The subsumption of such cases under the term "civil right and obligations" was difficult, because such decisions were often in the competence of political bodies, sometimes even of an assembly at the municipal level. The judiciary was not seen as competent to give judgement on such decisions.

Swiss criminal tax law was another sector that was highly influenced by Article 6 ECHR and the case law of the Strasbourg organs with regard to the term "criminal charge". The Federal Supreme Court clearly stated only that proceedings of criminal tax law fell under Article 6 ECHR in 1993.[290] As a consequence of this practice, the prohibition of self-incrimination in the proceedings of tax evasion followed.[291]

In its *Zimmermann and Steiner* ruling[292], the Court considered the length of proceedings before the Federal Supreme Court to be excessive (approximately three and a half years). The delay was caused mainly by structural problems,

---

[285] See *supra* Section D.1.

[286] *Schuler-Zgraggen v. Switzerland* (appl. no. 14518/89), Judgement (Chamber), 24 June 1983, Series A, Vol. 263.

[287] Swiss Federal Supreme Court, Judgement, 20 December 20 December 1993, BGE 119 V 375.

[288] Swiss Federal Supreme Court, Judgement, 17 December 1992, BGE 118 Ia 473, 480 et seq. E. 6. For the precedent confusion related to the *Belilos* judgement, see *supra* note 53.

[289] Swiss Federal Supreme Court, Judment, 24 March 1994, BGE 120 Ia 19.

[290] Swiss Federal Supreme Court, Judgement, 11 October 1993, BGE 119 Ib 311, 314 et seq. E. 2 with indications to older, inconsistent case law of the Federal Supreme Court and the decision of the Commission in the case of *Sydow v. Sweden* (appl. no. 11464/85), Decision (Plenary), Commission, 12 May 1987, DR 53, 85.

[291] *J.B. v. Switzerland* (appl. no. 32827/96), Judgement (Second Section), 3 May 2001, Reports 2001-III, 435 et seq.

[292] *Zimmermann and Steiner v. Switzerland* (appl. no. 8737/79), Judgement (Chamber), 13 July 1983, Series A, Vol. 66.

354   *The Reception Process in Austria and Switzerland*

placing the court under too heavy a workload. In the aftermath of this decision, the Swiss Government carried out a reform of the Federal Statute on the organization of the federal administration of Justice (OG)[293] then in force. The changes affected conditions of access to the Federal Supreme Court, the ability of lower courts to try federal administrative cases, simplification of the decision-making procedure and staffing. After undergoing a number of amendments following an initial rejection by popular vote in 1989, the revised version entered into force on 15 February 1992. A thorough overhaul of the organization of the federal judiciary aiming at further lightening the workload of the Federal Supreme Court and protecting its operational capacity entered into force 1 January 2007.

As the procedural guarantees of Articles 5 and 6 ECHR provide for better protection than Article 13 ECHR, the latter usually cannot be invoked in addition to Articles 5 and 6 ECHR.[294] There has only been one important judgement of the Court concerning Switzerland in respect of the right to an effective remedy. However, the judgement of *Camenzind v. Switzerland*[295] reveals a weak point in the Swiss order of remedies *vis-à-vis* Article 13 ECHR. The requirement of a present interest in invoking the protection of courts[296] can deprive an applicant of an effective national remedy. In the actual case the applicant was no longer affected by the measure of a search of residential premises. Thus the national court stated that he was not entitled to lodge an appeal against the search. Although the Swiss system of remedies is generally in accordance with the requirements of the ECHR, recent cases show that there is still need for further improvement in certain constellations.[297]

The conditions of detentions in Switzerland have been examined by the Strasbourg organs on several occasions. However, in most of the decisions they found no violation of Article 3 ECHR. The cases concerned arrest by the police, detention on remand and the enforcement of sentences. The Commission declared a violation of Article 3 ECHR in the case of *Hurtado v. Switzerland*. The applicant had suffered a broken rib on the occasion of his arrest, but was not visited by a doctor until eight days after the injury occurred.[298]

---

[293] BBl 1985 II, 737 et seq.; also see Borghi (2002), 874.

[294] As to the relation between Article 6 and Article 13 ECHR, see Vospernik (2001), 361 et seq. However, in 2000, the ECtHR modified its prior case law and established the rule that there was no absorption of Article 13 by Article 6 in cases concerning length of procedure. See *Kudla v. Poland* (appl. no. 30210/96), Judgement (Grand Chamber), 26 October 2000, Reports 2000-XI, 197 et seq.

[295] *Camenzind v. Switzerland* (appl. no. 21353/93), Judgement (Chamber), 16 December 1997, Reports 1997-VIII, 2880 et seq.

[296] For the requirement of a present interest for the appeal in matters of public law, see Häfelin, Haller and Keller (2006), Rz. 2001.

[297] See *Scavuzzo-Hager and Others v. Switzerland* (appl. no. 41773/98), Judgement (Fourth Section), 7 February 2006 (not yet reported); *Bianchi v. Switzerland* (appl. no. 7548/04), Judgement (Fifth Section), 22 June 2006 (not yet reported); *Jäggi v. Switzerland* (appl. no. 58757/00), Judgement (Third Section), 13 July 2006 (not yet reported).

[298] *Hurtado v. Switzerland* (appl. no. 17549/90), Report (Plenary), Commission, 8 July 1993, see

In 1982, the Commission had to decide in a very serious case.[299] Two suspected terrorists were held in detention on remand under a very strict regime. They were isolated from other detainees and were video-supervized around the clock. By a close vote of 8:5 the Commission decided that the level of cruelty necessary to declare a violation of Article 3 ECHR had not been reached. It seemed that the carefully formulated judgement of the Federal Supreme Court could have turned the balance. It stated that even under the given circumstances the measures just missed exceeding the allowed limit.[300] The Commission examined additional Swiss applications, but did not find a violation of Article 3 ECHR.[301]

Article 8 ECHR is another guarantee invoked very frequently. The main areas of conflict lie above all in alien law, but also in the protection of free communication. Although the Convention does not recognize a right to asylum, the protection of family life under Article 8 ECHR can be violated by an extradition, eviction or denial of family reunion. In 1981, the Federal Supreme Court developed an important and highly disputed practice *(Reneja-Praxis)* based on Article 8 ECHR.[302] The Federal Supreme Court declared that foreigners could deduce a right to residence from the right to respect for private and family life if the consideration of interests under Article 8(2) ECHR showed a predominance of the private interests of the applicant *vis-à-vis* the public interest. Thus, the Federal Supreme Court declared admissible an administrative-law appeal in spite of the rule that this remedy was not available in an immigration-control case if it concerned the issue or refusal of permits to which federal legislation conferred no entitlement.[303] Several applications have been lodged with the Court, but the large margin of appreciation, the generally attentive reception of the Strasbourg case law and the well-balanced consideration of values by the Federal Supreme

VPB 1994, no. 86 B. It did not come to a judgement of the Court since a friendly settlement could be obtained; see VPB 1994, no.86 A.

[299] *Kröcher and Möller v. Switzerland* (appl. no. 8463/78), Decision, 9 July 1981, DR 26, 40.

[300] Swiss Federal Supreme Court, Judgement, 7 June 1978, not published; see Villiger (1999), Rz. 283 et seq.

[301] See *Bonzi v. Switzerland* (appl. no. 7854/77), Decision (Plenary), Commission, 12 July 1978, DR 12, 185; *X. v. Switzerland* (appl. no. 7754/77), Decision (Plenary), Commission, 9 May 1977, DR 11, 216; *J.-A. v. Switzerland* (app. no. 19959/92), Decision (Plenary), Commission, 23 May 1996, VPB 1996, no. 98; *G.K. v. Switzerland* (appl. no. 21084/92), Decision (Second Chamber), Commission, 5 April 1995, VPB 1995, no. 115.

[302] Swiss Federal Supreme Court, Judgement, 12 September 1983, BGE 109 Ib 183 *(Reneja-Dittli I)* and Swiss Federal Supreme Court, Judgement, 7 December 1984, BGE 110 Ib 201 *(Reneja-Dittli II)*. The Federal Supreme Court referred to a decision of the Commission concerning *X, Y and Z. v. the United Kingdom*, 6 July 1982, EuGRZ 10 (1983), 423 no. 54. In later judgements, the Federal Supreme Court rendered more precisely this practice and confined its application. The question of whether the practice was compliant with the Convention was rather disputed after the judgement of the Court concerning *Gül v. Switzerland* (appl. no. 23218/94), Judgement (Chamber), 19 February 1996, Reports 1996-I, 159 et seq.

[303] See Article 100 lit. b no. 3 OG then in force (corresponds to Article 83 lit. c BGG) and Article 4 Bundesgesetz vom 26. März 1931 über Aufenthalt und Niederlassung der Ausländer (ANAG, SR 142.20).

Court led to a few judgements of the Court finding a violation of the Convention. However, in 2001 the Court found a violation of Article 8 ECHR, stating that the national courts had placed too much weight on the grave crime that the applicant had committed.[304]

Various cases before the Court concerned telephone tapping by public authorities. As such surveillance constitutes a grave interference with the right to respect for private life the Court requires high standards for its legal base. Thus, the Court found a violation of Article 8 ECHR in two cases because of an insufficient legal base in Swiss law.[305] Switzerland enacted a Federal Statute that has solved these insufficiencies.[306]

The free communication of a detainee with his lawyer also caused quite a broad discussion in Switzerland. Two Swiss cases concerned the non-forwarding of letters from or to a detainee by the prosecutor's office.[307] As in both cases, the Court declared a breach of the Convention because the measure was not proportional, there was no need to alter national rules that were essentially compatible with Article 8 ECHR.

The Court's case law concerning Article 10 ECHR treats above all the proportionality of graveness and purpose of interference. As the freedom of expression is a base for the exercise of all fundamental rights under Article 10(2) ECHR there is little scope for restrictions on debate on questions of public interest.[308] According to the Court, there is only a narrow margin of appreciation afforded to the national organs. Above all, the judgements concerning *VgT (Verein gegen Tierfabriken)*, *Hertel* and *Autronic* are worth mentioning. In *VgT v. Switzerland*[309] the Court followed an earlier judgement[310] declaring that advertising falls under the protection of Article 10 ECHR. The judgement concerning *Hertel*[311] revealed

---

[304] *Boultif v. Switzerland* (appl. no. 54273/00), Judgement (Second Section), 2 August 2001, Reports 2001-IX, 199 et seq.

[305] *Kopp v. Switzerland* (appl. no. 23224/94), Judgement (Chamber), 25 March 1998, Reports 1998-II, 524 et seq.; *Amann v. Switzerland* (appl. no. 27798/95), Judgement (Grand Chamber), 16 February 2000, Reports 2000-II, 245 et seq.

[306] Bundesgesetz vom 6. Oktober 2000 betreffend die Überwachung des Post- und Fernmeldeverkehrs (BÜPF, SR 780.1), entered into force 1 January 2002. For the report by the Federal Council, 1998.07.01, see BBl 1998 IV, 4241, referring to the *Kopp* judgement (*supra* note 305) on page 4266 and to the judgements of the Court conerning *Klass* (*supra* note 154) and *Malone* (*Malone v. the United Kingdom* (appl. no. 8691/79), Judgement (Plenary), 2 August 1984, Series A, Vol. 82) and their reception in Swiss Federal Supreme Court, Judgement, 1983.11.09, BGE 109 Ib 273.

[307] *Schönenberger and Durmaz v. Switzerland* (appl. no. 11368/85), Judgement (Chamber), 20 June 1988, Series A, Vol. 137; *Stürm v. Switzerland* (appl. no. 22686/93), Report (Second Chamber), Commission, head notes published in VPB 1998, no. 117.

[308] See *Scharsach and News Verlagsgesellschaft v. Austria* (appl. no. 39394/98), Judgement (First Section), 13 November 2003 (not reported), para. 45.

[309] *VgT (Verein gegen Tierfabriken) v. Switzerland* (appl. no. 24699/94), Judgement (Second Section), 28 June 2001, Reports 2001-VI, 243 et seq.

[310] *Casado Coca v. Spain* (appl. no. 15450/89), Judgement (Chamber), 22 February 1994, Series A, Vol.285.

[311] *Hertel v. Switzerland* (appl. no. 25181/94), Judgement (Chamber), 25 August 1998, Reports 1998-VI, 2298 et seq.

some difficult questions concerning the relationship of the protection of competition and the protection of freedom of expression[312]. In *Autronic AG v. Switzerland*[313] the Court made clear that not only ideational opinions fell under the protection of Article 10 ECHR. The judgement, declaring a breach of the right to receive information, also triggered an amendment of national law.[314]

Another development in national law was caused by the famous judgement of the Court concerning *Goodwin v. the United Kingdom*.[315] The Court affirmed the protection of journalistic sources. This judgement triggered the introduction of the protection of journalistic sources as a principle in the Swiss Criminal Code[316] and the Constitution of 1999[317]. As two cases decided by the Court in 2006 show, Switzerland still faces problems with regard to freedom of the press.[318] Stoll, a journalist, received a copy of a strategic document classified as confidential that was drawn up by the then Swiss ambassador to the US in the course of negotiations between, among others, the World Jewish Congress and Swiss banks concerning compensation due to Holocaust victims for unclaimed assets deposited in Swiss banks. Stoll was later sentenced for publishing "official confidential deliberations" within the meaning of Article 293 of the Swiss Criminal Code. The central question before the Court was to determine whether the restriction of the applicant's right to freedom of expression had been necessary in a democratic society. A close majority of the Court found that the confidentiality of diplomatic relations was justified in principle, but could not be protected at any price. Moreover, the role of the media as critic and watchdog also applied to matters of foreign policy. The Court considered that the conviction had, therefore, not been reasonably proportionate to the pursuit of the legitimate aim in question, having regard to the interest of a democratic society in ensuring and maintaining the freedom of the press. When in 2006 Switzerland for the first time ever appealed a judgement of the ECHR to the Grand Chamber in the case of *Stoll*, it clearly expressed that it was not willing to accept the high level of protection of the freedom of the press as acknowledged by the Court. Still, Switzerland is

---

[312] For an overview of the various academic comments concerning the *Hertel* judgement, see Furrer and Krummenacher (2004), 173 et seq.

[313] *Autronic AG v. Switzerland* (*supra* note 196).

[314] Bundesgesetz vom 21. Juni 1991 über Radio und Fernsehen (RTVG, SR 784.40), entered into force 1 April 1992. Article 52 states that "chacun est libre de recevoir tout programme suisse ou étranger qui s'adresse au public en général".

[315] *Goodwin v. the United Kingdom* (appl. no. 17488/90), Judgement (Grand Chamber), 27 March 1996, Reports 1996-II, 438 et seq.

[316] Article 27bis (1) Schweizerisches Strafgesetzbuch vom 21. Dezember 1937 (StGB, SR 311), inserted by Federal Statute of 10 October 1997, entered into force 1 April 1998, AS 1998 852, 856. For the message by the Federal Council, 17 June 1996, see BBl 1996 525, referring to the *Goodwin* judgement on p. 572.

[317] Article 17(3), Constitution of 1999.

[318] *Dammann v. Switzerland* (appl. no. 77551/01), Judgement (Fourth Section), 25 April 2006 (not yet reported); *Stoll v. Switzerland* (appl. no. 69698/01), Judgement (Fourth Section), 25 April 2006. See Breitenmoser (2007), 138 et seq.; and, concerning the *Stoll* case, see Schürmann (2007), 763 et seq.

constantly adapting to new requirements resulting from the activist case law of the ECtHR: In the aftermath of the *Dammann* and *Stoll* cases, the Office of the Federal Prosecutor has enacted new internal guidelines in order to contribute to a better protection of journalists' fundamental rights.

Also well worth mentioning is the only judgement of the Court concerning Switzerland in respect of the right to marry under Article 12. The case of *F. v. Switzerland*[319] is a leading example of a conflict between a Federal Statute and the Convention. Article 113(3) Constitution of 1874 did not allow the national courts to diverge from a Federal Statute that was not compliant with the ECHR.[320] It was, therefore, not always possible for the courts to solve the conflict in accordance with international law. At the time[321], Swiss law provided the possibility for the courts to fix a period of not less than one and not more than two years during which the party at fault should not be entitled to remarry. Where a divorce was granted on the ground of adultery, this period could be extended to three years. The Federal Supreme Court had declared the question whether a rule of the Civil Code was compliant with the Convention to lie outside of its jurisdiction because of the commandment of application of Federal Statutes stated in Article 113(3) Constitution of 1874. Not being bound by any national restriction, the Court found a violation of Article 12 ECHR. It held that this measure affected the very essence of the right to marry and was disproportionate to the aim pursued. As a reaction to this judgement the Federal Department of Justice and Police called on the cantonal courts and the Federal Supreme Court to no longer apply the blamed rule of federal law.[322]

In *Burghartz v. Switzerland*[323], the ECtHR came to the conclusion that Article 14 combined with Article 8 ECHR was violated because the husband was not allowed to have his wife's patronymic preceded by his own. As a reaction, the Decree concerning civil status[324] was modified.

3. Comparison and Conclusion

While the reformations of national statutes triggered by the ECHR or Strasbourg case law were of some significance, they did not lead to a fundamental, much less to a revolutionary change in the Austrian and Swiss legal orders.

---

[319] *F. v. Switzerland* (appl. no. 11329/85), Judgement (Plenary), 18 December 1987, Series A, Vol.128.

[320] Commandment of application, see *supra* Section B.2.b and c.

[321] Article 150 Schweizerisches Zivilgesetzbuch von 1907 (ZGB, SR 210). The Article remained formally in force until the new law on divorce entered into force on 1 January 2000, see AS 1999 1118, 1144. For the message of the Federal Council, 15 November 1995, see BBl 1196 I 1, referring to the judgement of the Court concerning *F. v. Switzerland* on p. 12 and 67.

[322] See VPB 1989, no. 64 B.

[323] *Burghartz v. Switzerland* (appl. no. 16213/90), Judgement (Chamber), 22 February 1994, Series A., Vol. 280-B.

[324] Zivilstandverordnung vom 1. Juni 1953, replaced by the Zivilstandsverordnung vom 28. April 2004 (SR 211.112.2).

Articles 5 and 6 ECHR had the biggest impact in both Austria and Switzerland. Above all, the concept of equality of arms concretizes the fair trial in the sense of Article 6 ECHR. As the procedural guarantees of Articles 5 and 6 are very much influenced by the Anglo-Saxon system of procedure, it was not an easy task to convert the requirements of Articles 5 and 6 into the continental system of criminal procedural law. A special challenge for both countries was to satisfy the requirements of the procedural guarantees in the field of administrative law, which, according to the Strasbourg case law, at least partly falls under the term "civil rights and obligations". The main consequence was a heightened level of legal protection in administrative matters that shaped the role of both administrative authorities and courts in an important way.

Over time, the nature of the effects on the national legal order has changed. In the first period, Austria and Switzerland had to adapt or modify statutes following the ECtHR's judgements and decisions. A comparison between Austria and Switzerland reveals that Austria was more often obliged to adapt its legislation to the Strasbourg standards than was Switzerland. This is a corollary of the fact that Austria did not make these modifications before ratification and that it was less well-prepared than Switzerland by the time of ratification. Currently, the violations of the Convention in Austria and in Switzerland are mainly caused by the way national law – which is not in tension with the ECHR – is applied in a concrete case. A considerable percentage of the judgements of the Court finding a violation of the Convention consider the cause of the breach to lie in the lack of proportionality of a measure. This shows that conventional standards are in general – apart from the problems Austria faces in connection with Article 6(1) ECHR – very well integrated into the Austrian and Swiss legal order.

E. Mechanisms of Coordination

1. Austria

a. Courts

Although the Austrian legislator has awarded constitutional status to the ECHR, the three highest courts (the Constitutional Court, the Administrative Court, and the Supreme Court of Justice) initially limited its effect. As has already been mentioned, they at first denied the constitutional status and the direct applicability of the Convention.[325] By doing so, they deprived the ECHR of all impact on the national level.[326] In 1964, after the legislator had explicitly stated that the ECHR had constitutional status, the problems were not immediately solved. The three supreme courts were still reluctant to ascribe adequate importance to the

---

[325] See *supra* Section B.1.b.
[326] Ermacora (1963), 5.

Convention and important guarantees were still denied direct applicability.[327] From the very beginning, the Constitutional Court considered the Convention as foreign law.[328] This perception and the broad interpretation of the reservation concerning Article 5[329] were the reason that the ECHR at first had only minor effects in Austria. Now that these problems have been overcome the Constitutional Court plays an important role as an intermediary who implements the guarantees of the ECHR while at the same time protecting the established institutions of the Austrian legal order.[330]

During the first stage, the Constitutional Court held that parallel rights in the Austrian legal order and the Convention were identical with regard to their content. As a consequence, more beneficial provisions of the ECHR were equated with national fundamental rights. At least, the courts embraced the guarantees that were not yet protected in national law. This leads to the conclusion that new rights were more easily accepted than old rights that were not entirely congruent with those protected in the Austrian Constitution. Later on, the court adopted a more differentiated view and now examines which right is more beneficial for the person affected.

If a guarantee under both the ECHR and under national law is allegedly violated, the guarantee offering the more effective protection to the individual must be applied.[331] This leads to a double standard: Any interference with fundamental rights has to be examined according to the requirements of both national law and the ECHR.[332] The Constitutional Court has developed a rich jurisdiction regarding the rights and freedoms of the Convention and has quashed a considerable number of administrative decisions[333] and laws which infringed rights granted by the ECHR. An indicator of the growing importance of the ECHR in Austrian law is that over time the Constitutional Court increasingly cited Strasbourg case law in its decisions. By giving the rights and freedoms of the Convention greater standing within national law, the Constitutional Court assumes a central role in promoting the effectiveness of the ECHR.

In general, the Constitutional Court is willing to accept the case law of the Court even if the interpretation of a conventional guarantee of the Court differs

---

[327] See Schantl and Welan (1970), 647 et seq.; Ermacora, Nowak and Tretter (1983), 67 et seq., 87 et seq.

[328] Tretter (2002), 67 et seq. In 1970, Schantl and Welan (1970), 617, stated: "Der VfGH. hat sich in seiner 10jährigen Rechtsprechung zur MRK. nicht gerade als deren Freund erwiesen. Die Haltung des VfGH., die sich in der Mehrzahl der Erkenntnisse widerspiegelt, ist von einer Abneigung gegen die MRK. als etwas Neues und Störendes gekennzeichnet."

[329] See *supra* Section A.1.b.

[330] For an overview of the key human rights cases that have been decided by the Constitutional Court see Tretter (2002), 117 et seq.

[331] Principle of benignity, Artile 53 ECHR.

[332] To the approach of the Austrian Constitutional Court when dealing with the right to personal liberty see Kopetzki (1997), 271.

[333] It has already been mentioned above that the Constitutional Court is not entitled to review decisions by judicial authorities; see *supra* Section B.1.c.

from its own. For example, contrary to its original opinion, the Constitutional Court joined the Court's jurisdiction concerning Article 6(1) ECHR in the *Ringeisen* case.[334] Until 1971, the Strasbourg organs interpreted the term of "civil rights and obligations" in a way that did not affect the Austrian constitutional system. In the *Ringeisen* case the Court came to the conclusion that the term "civil rights" had to be interpreted autonomously and not with regard to the national legal order. It held that Article 6(1) not only applies when both parties to a dispute are private persons but that it is applicable in all proceedings that have an impact on civil rights and obligations.[335] The Court later specified that the impact has to be immediate.[336]

However, as the *Miltner* case of 14 October 1987[337] shows, the Austrian Constitutional Court does not follow the ECtHR's case law without restrictions. In dispute was the question of whether the objections of the neighbours in a construction process fell under Article 6 ECHR. According to the case law of the ECtHR, every legal dispute with an immediate impact on civil rights has to be decided by a tribunal according to Article 6 ECHR.[338] The Constitutional Court held that the Austrian administrative law system was based on the classic distinction between private and public law, which dates back to ancient Roman law. Following the case law of the Strasbourg court would require a modification of the Constitution. According to the Constitutional Court, it was beyond any reasonable doubt that the Austrian President, the Government and the legislative organs believed that Article 6 ECHR was fulfilled due to the competence of courts in civil and criminal matters. Otherwise, Austria would either have made an additional reservation or have changed the Constitution. In the Constitutional Court's view, the ECHR had developed in a way that led to new obligations for the State Parties that they have never been willing to accept. It distinguished

---

[334] Austrian Constitutional Court, Judgement, 29 Septmeber 1970, VfSlg 6239/1970; Austrian Constitutional Court, Judgement, 13 October 1970, VfSlg 6275/1970; Austrian Constitutioanl Court, Judgement, 29 June 1973, VfSlg 7099/1973; Austrian Constitutional Court, Judgement, 19 March 1974, VfSlg 7284/1973; Austrian Constitutional Court, Judgement, 24 June 1974, VfSlg 7333/1974.

[335] *Ringeisen v. Austria* (appl. no. 2614/65), Judgement (Chamber), 16 July 1971, Series A, Vol. 13; see Thürer (1986), 249 et seq.

[336] *Le Compte, Van Leuven and De Meyere v. Belgium* (appl. nos 6878/75; 7238/75), Judgement (Chamber), 23 June 1981, Series A, Vol. 43. Also see *König v. Germany* (appl. no. 6232/73), Judgement (Plenary), 28 June 1978, Series A, Vol. 27; *H. v. Belgium* (appl. no. 8950/80), Judgement (Plenary), 30 November 1987, Series A, Vol. 127-B; *Sporrong and Lönnroth v. Sweden* (appl. nos 7151/75; 7152/75), Judgement (Plenary), 23 September 1982, Series A, Vol. 52; *Allan Jacobsson v. Sweden* (appl. no. 10842/84), Judgement (Chamber), 25 October 1989, Series A, Vol. 163; *Benthem v. the Netherlands* (appl. no. 8848/80), Judgement (Plenary), 23 October 1985, Series A, Vol. 97; *Pudas v. Sweden* (appl. no. 10426/83), Judgement (Chamber), 27 October 1987, Series A, Vol.-25-A; *Feldbrugge v. the Netherlands* (appl. no. 8562/79), Judgement (Plenary), 29 May 1986, Series A, Vol. 99.

[337] Austrian Constitutional Court, Judgement, 14 October 1987, VfSlg 11500/1987 = EuGRZ 1988, 166 et seq.

[338] See *supra* note 336.

between cases which concerned the core of civil rights and matters that only have an impact on civil rights. The first group of cases has to be decided by a tribunal according to Article 6 ECHR; in the second group of cases, which according to Austrian law form part of public law, administrative agencies are entitled to decide. In a second line of arguments, the Constitutional Court stated that the dispute at hand only affected civil rights but did not emerge because of such rights. It did not deny that generally the Constitutional Court had the duty to give the ECHR the content attached to it by the Strasbourg organs. However, the Constitutional Court made clear that under the given circumstances it was not possible for Austria to respect the Court's case law. Although it would generally try to harmonize both legal orders, if there was no margin for harmonization it considered itself bound by the basic principles of national constitutional law.

The different approaches of the Austrian Constitutional Court and the ECtHR with regard to civil matters have an impact, *inter alia*, on cases concerning revocation of concessions. According to the Constitutional Court, such revocations do not concern the core of civil rights and, as a consequence, an administrative authority is entitled to deal with this question[339] whereas the ECHR requires tribunals to decide such cases as they concern civil rights.[340] From the Constitutional Court's point of view, the following matters belong to the core of civil rights and require a decision by a tribunal: disputes about reparation for damage by hunt and game[341], reparations for the payment of fees in hospital law[342], treaties governed by private law between parties covered by social security and medical doctors[343], compensation for expropriation[344]. Decisions about construction permits[345], or deprivations of a concession for a drugstore[346] only have an effect on civil matters and may, therefore, be decided by administrative authorities. The Austrian Constitutional Court thus decides on a case-by-case basis whether the requirements of Article 6 ECHR have to be fulfilled in a particular case. This approach is certainly dissatisfying as it increases the risk of a violation of the Convention and leads to legal uncertainty. At least, its practical consequences are limited because the Administrative Court as the appellate instance in such matters constitutes a tribunal according to Article 6 ECHR. Still, the question of whether a public hearing must be held depends on the qualification of the dispute as involving civil rights or not.

Apart from the situation concerning Article 6 ECHR, the Constitutional Court also interprets Article 1 of Protocol no. 1 differently from the ECtHR.

---

[339] Austrian Constitutional Court, Judgement, 13 December 1988, VfSlg 11937/1988.
[340] *Pudas v. Sweden* (appl. no. 10426/83), Judgement (Chamber), 27 October 1987, Series A, Vol. 125.
[341] Austrian Constitutional Court, Judgement, 13 December 1988, VfSlg 11646/1988.
[342] Austrian Constitutional Court, Judgement, 28 September 1990, VfSlg 12470/1990.
[343] Austrian Constitutional Court, Judgement, 29 November 1994, VfSlg 13946/1994.
[344] Austrian Constitutional Court, Judgement, 14 December 1994, VfSlg 13979/1994.
[345] Austrian Constitutional Court, Judgement, 14 October 1987, VfSlg 11500/1987.
[346] Austrian Constitutional Court, Judgement, 13 December 1988, VfSlg 11937/1988.

It only considers property values as property in the sense of Article 1 of Protocol no. 1.[347] As a consequence, compensation for deprivations is not covered by this provision. In contrast, according to the European Court of Human Rights, Article 1 of the First Additional Protocol also protects some public-law entitlements, i.e. the duty to pay compensation for deprivation.[348]

b. Legislative and Executive Authorities

The legislator regularly refers to the Convention either in the statute itself or in Parliamentary explanatory reports. Convention rights and restrictive clauses have occasionally been quoted partly or wholly in legal provisions, mainly in order to oblige the authorities enforcing the law to include provisions of the Convention in their decisions.[349]

Even though the Federal Constitution does not provide for a compulsory review procedure, there are as a rule regular reviews being carried out in respect of both laws and ordinances. Most importantly, Division V of the Federal Chancellery (the so-called Constitutional Service *[Verfassungsdienst]*) examines draft Bills by all Ministries and Provinces as well as ministerial decrees in respect of their conformity with the Austrian Constitution. Since the ECHR is part of the Constitution, this includes the examination of drafts with a view to their conformity with the Convention as part of a routine procedure.[350] The fact that Division V of the Federal Chancellery is responsible for this duty reflects the importance of the ECHR in the Austrian legal system. In addition, political instances as well as interested groups are invited to comment on the draft.[351] The results of these controls are published on the website of the Austrian Parliament and have considerable weight in the discussion of new statutes. In the case of drafts where the Federal Government suggests that a so-called interference-related federal act be amended, the Constitutional Court and the Administrative Court are regularly requested to give their opinion. A further important instrument to prevent federal legislation from being inconsistent with the ECHR is the Constitutional Committee of the Austrian National Assembly, which discusses all drafts concerning individual constitutional provisions as well as drafts concerning interference-related laws.

---

[347] Austrian Constitutional Court, Judgement, 15 December 1964, VfSlg 4879/1964; Austrian Constitutional Court, Judgement, 25 February 1976, VfSlg 6648/1972; Austrian Constitutional Court, Judgement, 7 June 1972, VfSlg 6733/1972; Austrian Constitutional Court, Judgement, 12 December 1986, VfSlg 11198/1986.

[348] See *Tre Traktörer Aktiebolag v. Sweden* (appl. no. 10873/84), Judgement (Chamber), 7 July 1989, Series A, Vol.159; *James and Others v. the United Kingdom* (appl. no. 8793/79), Judgement (Plenary), 21 February 1986, Series A, Vol. 98; *Lithgow and Others v. the United Kingdom* (appl. nos 9006/80; 9262/81; 9265/81; 9266/81; 9313/81; 9405/81), Judgement (Plenary), 8 July 1986, Series A, Vol.102; see Riedel (1988), 333.

[349] Tretter (2002), 107.

[350] For example, in 2005, the new Asylum Law *(Asyl- und Fremdengesetz)* was heavily criticized by Division V of the Federal Chancellery as some provisions were in tension with the requirements of Article 2 and 8 ECHR.

[351] Haller (2006), 647.

2. Switzerland

a. Federal Supreme Court

The jurisdiction of the Federal Supreme Court is strongly influenced by the Convention and the ECtHR's case law.[352] The Federal Supreme Court referred to the ECHR even before it was ratified: In 1971, it adhered Article 4(a) ECHR[353] and in a judgement one year later it stated that even though Switzerland was not bound by the Convention, the principle expressed in Article 6(3) ECHR corresponded to the national legal order and had to be respected by the administration of justice[354].

In its first judgement concerning the ECHR after its entry into force in Switzerland,[355] the Federal Supreme Court took an important step to facilitate the reception process.[356] At that time, the cantonal remedies were not required to be exhausted by the applicant when he lodged a public-law appeal claiming an infringement of an international treaty.[357] The Federal Supreme Court stated that the applicant could invoke the same rights under the Constitution and the ECHR. As a consequence, an appeal claiming an infringement of the ECHR should be treated procedurally like a constitutional appeal. This had several positive consequences: First, by putting the Convention on the same level as the Constitution in the procedural context, the importance of the ECHR had been stressed. Second, as it was required that the cantonal remedies be exhausted, it was made clear that it was primarily the Cantons' obligation to implement the guarantees of the ECHR. Undoubtedly, another reason for this judgement had been the concern about an increase in workload.[358] This requirement was later codified in 1991.[359]

The fact that the field of application of Article 6(1) ECHR extends to areas which traditionally fell within public law also posed a special challenge for the Federal Supreme Court. Unlike the Austrian Constitutional Court, which showed some reluctance to accept the Strasbourg case law in this respect[360], the Federal Supreme Court took on the broad interpretation of the Strasbourg organs and applied Article 6(1) ECHR to all administrative decisions taken by an

---

[352] Steinmann (2006), 638.

[353] Swiss Federal Supreme Court, Judgement, 17 February 1971, BGE 97 I 45, 51 E. 4.

[354] Swiss Federal Supreme Court, Judgement, 2 February 1972, BGE 98 Ia 226, 235 E. 5c.

[355] Swiss Federal Supreme Court, Judgement, 12 February 1975, BGE 101 Ia 67, 69 E. 2c.

[356] See Keller (2005), 304 et seq.

[357] Article 86 OG, then in force, *Bereinigte Sammlung der Bundesgesetze und Verordnungen 1848–1947* (BS) 2 531, 555. With the entry into force of the new system of legal remedies on the national level on 1 January 2007, the public law appeal has been replaced by the appeal in matters of public law *(Beschwerde in öffentlich-rechtlichen Angelegenheiten)* and the subsidiary constitutional appeal *(subsidiäre Verfassungsbeschwerde)*. See *infra* Section F.2.a.

[358] Swiss Federal Supreme Court, Judgement, 12 February 1975, BGE 101 Ia 67, 69.

[359] Federal Statute of 16 December 1943 on the Organization of the Federal Administration of Justice, for the amendments of 4 October 1991, see AS 1992 288.

[360] See *supra* Section E.1.

authority in the exercise of its public functions, where such decisions had an effect on private rights.[361] The aspect of Article 6(1) ECHR that used to cause the most problems to the Federal Supreme Court was the right of reply. The ECtHR follows a rather strict approach, as it requires that consultations and submissions by opposing parties and public authorities be sent to all endorsing parties so that they may comment on it.[362] In criminal law proceedings before the Federal Supreme Court, the accused always has the final say. In other cases, the consultations and submissions are generally sent to the parties without calling upon them to answer in order to avoid an excessive length of the proceedings. The parties do have the possibility to make a request and such requests are taken into account if handed in timely. Most tensions between Strasbourg law and the Federal Supreme Court occured due to the practice of the former Federal Insurance Tribunal (which is now part of the Federal Supreme Court) to handle the right of reply in a very restrictive way.[363] However, as a recent judgement demonstrates, the Federal Supreme Court currently follows the ECtHR case law and no longer imposes such restrictions.[363a]

A close look at the case law of the Swiss Federal Supreme Court reveals that, in the course of time, Strasbourg law plays an increasing role in the decisions of the Federal Supreme Court: During the first phase, both the Federal Government and the Federal Supreme Court constantly communicated that the rights guaranteed by the ECHR did not affect the Swiss legal order in a vital manner, as they did not reach the level of protection of those guaranteed in the Swiss Constitution.[364] As a consequence, there was no need to additionally examine a case with a view to the rights and freedoms guaranteed under the Convention.[365] However, it seems that the Federal Supreme Court did indeed raise the level of protection by stating to apply Swiss constitutional law, but referring for its interpretation and

---

[361] See e.g., Swiss Federal Supreme Court, Judgement, 9 October 1992, 118 Ia 355, 356 E. 2a; Swiss Federal Supreme Court, Judgement, 1 June 1992, BGE 118 Ia 227, 231 E. 1c; Swiss Federal Supreme Court, Judgement, 30 October 1991, BGE 117 Ia 527, 528 E. 3c/aa; Swiss Federal Supreme Court, Judgement, 20 January 1988, BGE 114 Ia 18, 19 E. 2c. See also Schindler (2006), 41 et seq.

[362] See *Göç v. Turkey* (appl. no. 36590/97), Judgement (Grand Chamber), 11 July 2002 (not reported); *Milatová and Others v. the Czech Republic* (appl. no. 61811/00), Judgement (Second Section), 21 June 2005 (not yet reported).

[363] See *Spang v. Switzerland* (appl. no. 45228/99), Judgement (Fourth Section), 11 October 2005 (not yet reported); *Contardi v. Switzerland* (appl. no. 7020/02), Judgement (Fourth Section), 12 July 2005 (not yet reported); *Ressegatti v. Switzerland* (appl. no. 17671/02), Judgement (Third Section), 13 July 2006 (not yet reported).

[363a] See e.g., Swiss Federal Supreme Court, Judgement, 11 January 2007, BGE 133 I 100, 102 E.4.3–4.6 where the case law of the ECtHR concerning the right of reply was thoroughly analyzed.

[364] See e.g., Swiss Federal Supreme Court, Judgement, 16 July 1976, BGE 102 Ia 196, 200 E. 3; Swiss Federal Supreme Court, Judgement, 19 December 1977, BGE 103 V 190, 193 E. 2b; Swiss Federal Supreme Court, Judgement, 16 February 1978, BGE 104 Ia 17, 18 E. 2; Hottelier (2005), 17.

[365] Keller (2005), 305.

development to the ECHR and the case law of the Strasbourg organs.[366] The case law concerning Article 8 ECHR is illustrative of the Federal Supreme Court's silent reception of the European standards: Although the Federal Supreme Court constantly declared that the protection of free communication under Article 8 ECHR did not grant more than Article 16(4) Constitution of 1874, its case law was clearly influenced by the judgement of the ECtHR concerning *Klass*.[367] This approach is quite widespread in judgements of the Federal Supreme Court concerning the right of personal freedom under the Swiss Constitution.[368] The Federal Supreme Court thus promoted the reception of the ECHR in its case law without overtly stating it was doing so. The demands of the Convention and the case law of the Court could be adopted spontaneously without provoking any political perplexity or reflection on national sovereignty.[369] The Swiss Federal Supreme Court achieved an optimal reception result and could avoid an open clash. However, it also showed a certain lack of frankness and openness towards a new and dynamic legal order.[370]

Starting in the second half of the 80's, after the first convictions of Switzerland, the Federal Supreme Court increasingly based its decisions on the ECHR.[371] It often[372] used the same rhetoric, saying that if an applicant simultaneously invoked a constitutional right and a provision of the ECHR for the same complaint, the Federal Supreme Court would initially investigate if the challenged adjudication infringed upon the Constitution. It would, however, take into account the concretization of certain principles of law by the Strasbourg organs. Above all, the Federal Supreme Court was intellectually geared to the Convention when it had to define the substantial content of the written – and particularly the non-written – constitutional rights and freedoms. This practice of the Federal Supreme Court was partially caused by the fact that before the entry into force of the new Constitution three levels of written fundamental rights existed in Switzerland: On the federal level, the Constitution of 1874 contained a fragmentary fundamental rights catalogue. There were also such catalogues – with varying degrees of detail – in the constitutions of the Cantons and, finally, the guarantees of the ECHR. The fundamental rights catalogue of the Swiss Federal Consti-

---

[366] Thürer (1988), 390.

[367] *Klass and Others v. Germany* (appl. no. 5029/71), Judgement (Plenary), 6 September 1978, Series A, Vol. 28. For an example of the respective case law of the Swiss Federal Supreme Court, see Swiss Federal Supreme Court, Judgement, 9 November 1983, BGE 109 Ia 273.

[368] Unwritten constitutional right under Article 4 Constitution of 1874, Article 10 Constitution of 1999; see Haller (1996), Rz. 10 and Swiss Federal Supreme Court, Judgement, 31 January 1979, BGE 105 Ia 26, 29 et seq.

[369] Wildhaber (1996), 160.

[370] Keller (2005), 306.

[371] See e.g., Swiss Federal Supreme Court, Judgement, 27 November 1985, BGE 111 Ia 239; Swiss Federal Supreme Court, Judgement, 27 November 1990, BGE 116 Ia 359.

[372] See e.g., Swiss Federal Supreme Court, Judgement, 3 March 1993, BGE 119 II 264, 267 E. 4; Swiss Federal Supreme Court, Judgement, 5 February 1986, BGE 112 Ia 97, 99 E. 3; Swiss Federal Supreme Court, Judgement, 19 June 1985, BGE 111 Ia 81, 82 E. 2b.

tution was supplemented step by step by the case law of the Federal Supreme Court concerning the unwritten fundamental rights and the voluminous case law concerning the equal protection clause[373]. Not only the fundamental rights of the Cantons but also ECHR thereby were an important source of inspiration.[374]

Since the 90's, the Federal Supreme Court has thoroughly investigated the two standards.[375] In some cases, the Federal Supreme Court even privileges the conventional guarantees by exclusively applying them or even by explaining that the national Constitution does not guarantee for a better protection.[376] The Federal Supreme Court thus seems to have considered that the criticism of the apodictic statement does not outreach the guarantees of the Constitution[377] to be at least not unfounded. Moreover, the Federal Supreme Court is increasingly willing to explicitly emphasize the importance of the ECHR and its interpretation by the Strasbourg organs.[378] Thus, nowadays it is part of the Federal Supreme Court's routine to check the Convention autonomously and to consider the case law of the Court when a provision of the ECHR is invoked, making no differentiation whether a judgement of the Court concerns Switzerland or any other country.[379] On that score, the Federal Supreme Court plays a leading role in Europe.[380] Nevertheless, it does not hesitate to criticize the ECtHR if it considers its case law to be inconsistent.[381]

By accepting the general predominance of the ECHR over national law, by the equalization of the ECHR with the Constitution, at least on the procedural level, and by taking into account the conventional guarantees for the concretization of constitutional rights, the Federal Supreme Court has very much helped the

---

[373] Article 4, Constitution of 1874.

[374] Keller (2005), 305; also see Aemisegger (2007a), 7 et seq.

[375] E.g., Swiss Federal Supreme Court, 21 February 2003, BGE 129 II 193, 211 et seq. E. 5.3; Swiss Federal Supreme Court, 15 November 2002, 129 I 113, 122 E. 3.2; Swiss Federal Supreme Court, 23 August 2002, BGE 128 I 288, 290 et seq. E. 2.2 et seq.; Swiss Federal Supreme Court, 25 August 2000, BGE 126 II 425; Swiss Federal Supreme Court, 26 July 1997, BGE 125 II 417, 420 et seq. E. 4a and b. Concerning BGE 128 I 288 see Aemisegger (2007b), 386 et seq.

[376] See e.g., Swiss Federal Supreme Court, Judgement, 6 November 2002, BGE 129 I 151, 153 et seq. E. 3.1; Swiss Federal Supreme Court, Judgement, 27 November 2002, BGE 129 I 139, 141 et seq. E. 2; Swiss Federal Supreme Court, Judgement, 7 September 2001, BGE 127 I 213, 215 et seq. E. 3.

[377] Aubert (1995), 115 Rz. 1777bis; Hottelier (1985), 41 et seq.

[378] Swiss Federal Supreme Court, Judgement, 19 December 2003, BGE 130 II 113, 123 E. 6.4 : "En particulier, la Suisse, qui a ratifié en 1974 la Convention européenne de sauvegarde des droits de l'homme et des libertés fondamentales, appliqué depuis lors directement la jurisprudence de la Cour européenne des droits de l'homme."

[379] See e.g., Swiss Federal Supreme Court, Judgement, 15 July 2004, BGE 130 II 377; Swiss Federal Supreme Court, Judgement, 27 November 2002, BGE 129 I 139; Swiss Federal Supreme Court, Judgement, 14 February 2000, BGE 126 I 33; Swiss Federal Supreme Court, Judgement, 1996.11.28, BGE 122 I 360.

[380] Eissen (1990), Annex II, 190 et seq. See also Ackermann, Caroni and Vetterli (2007), 1071 et seq., who criticise the case law of the Swiss Federal Supreme Court concerning anonymous witnesses.

[381] See e.g., Swiss Federal Supreme Court, Judgement, 25 April 2006, BGE 132 I 127 concerning the admissibility of anonymous witnesses.

ECHR to become an essential element of the Swiss legal order. This is particularly noteworthy, as according to the Constitution the Federal Supreme Court's position is rather weak. In return, the ECHR has offered the possibility for the Federal Supreme Court to circumvent Article 190 Constitution.[382]

b. Legislative and executive authorities

The ECHR is well known by all bodies engaged in the legislative process, and the conformity of draft statutes with the obligations under international law is routinely checked: A special Section on Human Rights and the Council of Europe that forms part of the International Affairs Division to the Federal Office of Justice is in charge of examining draft statutes for their compatibility with international instruments for the protection of human rights, such as the ECHR and the ICCPR. Apart from that, every federal draft statute is submitted to those Federal Offices that are interested in, and affected by, the draft statute before its discussion in the Federal Parliament so that they can comment on it from their points of view.[383] The Federal Office of Justice comments on every draft statute. In a second step, the revised draft statute is submitted to the Departments, which can comment on the statute as well.[384] The draft is then forwarded for consultation to interest groups outside of the federal administration, such as the Cantons, political parties, NGOs and important private economic bodies. This part of the legislation process can also have its effects on the conformity of the draft statute with international human rights standards.[385]

The Parliament discusses the draft statute on the basis of a message from the Federal Council. As part of the minimal content of this message, a comment on the legal basis of the statute, its effects on human rights, its compliance with law of a higher ranking, and its relationship with European law is prescribed.[386] The comments in the message by the Federal Council on the compatibility of the draft statute with international law are of a high standard.[387]

Generally, the ECHR is seen as a framework binding Switzerland's legislation. Nevertheless, in 2004, after the acceptance of the popular initiative on the lifelong internment of untreatable, extremely dangerous sexual offenders and

---

[382] See *supra* Section B.2.

[383] In the Cantons, there are similar systems for the control of draft statutes; see Müller (1999), Rz. 148 et seq. with more references.

[384] Id., Rz. 149.

[385] Keller (2005), 310 et seq.

[386] Article 141(2) lit. a Bundesgesetz vom 13. Dezember 2002 über die Bundesversammlung (ParlG, SR 171.10).

[387] E.g., message by the Federal Council on the modification of the Civil Code and the withdrawal of the reservation in respect of Article 5 ECHR, 17 August 1977, BBl 1977 III 1; message by the Federal Council on a Federal Statute on asylum, 31 August 1977, BBl 1977 III 105; message by the Federal Council on a Federal Statute on the protection of trademarks and declarations of origins, 21 November 1990, BBl 1991 I 1; message of the Federal Council on the popular initiative "Equal rights for disabled people" and on the draft Federal Statute on the elimination of disadvantages of disabled persons", 11 December 2001, BBl 2001 1715, 1809 et seq.

violent criminals,[388] the Minister of Justice stated that it was possible to envision a scenario of denunciation and reaccession to the ECHR, making a reservation in order to fulfil the initiators' will. At least, the law commission of the National Council stressed the importance of the ECHR and thus rejected the draft statute for the implementation of this popular initiative[389] due to unbridgeable tensions between the request of the initiators and the conventional guarantees.

The difficulties that arouse in connection with the above-mentioned popular initiative are mainly rooted in the conflict between the rule of law and the democratic principle in Switzerland: Article 139(3) Constitution allows the Parliament to declare a popular initiative invalid only if it does not respect *ius cogens*, i.e. mandatory rules of international law. However, this term must probably be interpreted in a broader sense, meaning some kind of constitutional core of the international system.[390] The question of whether the ECHR is a part of the European constitutional core in that sense of an ordre public is highly disputed. However, it seems likely that the trend is towards such an interpretation.[391]

3. Comparison and Conclusion

The examples of both Austria and of Switzerland show that the ECHR and its dynamic development by the Court constitute an enormous challenge for the courts whose duty it is to determine the ambit of the national and the European guarantees and to decide which of the two provides for a higher level of human rights standard. The principle of benignity (Article 53 ECHR) appears to offer an easy-to-handle rule in a case of conflict, but only at first sight. Doing the splits between the dynamic international system and the more inelastic national legal order often extends beyond a simple control of a minimal standard. The Austrian and Swiss experience leads to the following assumption: The more differentiated and incisive the case law of the Court, the greater the challenges for national courts.

Compared to the Swiss Federal Supreme Court, the Austrian Constitutional Court has narrower competences, as in civil and criminal matters the Supreme Court of Justice (*Oberster Gerichtshof*) is the last judicial authority on the national level.[392] The Supreme Court of Justice, however, has a different self-conception than constitutional courts as it does not consider its primary function to be the

---

[388] See Bundesbeschluss über die Volksinitiative "Lebenslange Verwahrung für nicht therapierbare, extrem gefährliche Sexual- und Gewaltstraftäter", 20 June 2003, AS 2004 2341.

[389] See Schweizerisches Strafgesetzbuch (Lebenslängliche Verwahrung extrem gefährlicher Straftäter) (Entwurf), BBl 2006, 919.

[390] Thürer (1996), Rz. 16.

[391] Hangartner (2002a), Rz. 28, favours a solution recognising the ECHR as a (European) *jus cogens*.

[392] With the exception that the Adinistrative Court, the Supreme Court and other courts of second instance may request the Constitutional Court to rescind statutes or provisions thereof. See *supra* Section B.1.c.

protection of fundamental rights.[393] As a consequence, the ECHR plays a more important role in the protection of human rights in Austria than in countries with a strong constitutional court entitled to leverage the conventional guarantees on the national level.

The Court's interpretation of the term "civil rights and obligations" in Article 6 causes considerable problems for continental European legal systems. While Switzerland dealt with this situation by adapting its legal system to the new requirements[394], Austria first chose the path of an open confrontation in the *Miltner* case. The latter is a clear illustration that those tensions between the national legal order and the Convention that are rooted in the very tradition of a national legal order are the most difficult to handle. The *Miltner* case furthermore shows that Austria, in spite of its enthusiastic attitude when it ratified the ECHR, at first faced more problems with the Strasbourg case law than Switzerland, which was very cautious and adapted and modified various statutes before ratification. Nowadays, the Austrian Constitutional Court does not assume a hostile attitude *vis-à-vis* the ECtHR anymore. From a retrospective point of view, the *Miltner* case should therefore not be overestimated; it is not more and not less than an important example of the punctual difficulties Austria faced in ensuring compliance with the Convention.

In both countries, the analysis of the ECHR and the control of compliance in the legislative process are very much institutionalized. The general commitment to the Convention is politically undisputed, and so abstract instruments such as a control mechanism in the legislative process could be introduced quite efficiently.

F. Remedies and Proportionality Tests

1. Austria

a. Remedies

aa. Remedies in general The international and national systems of human rights protection do not work independently, as it is necessary to exhaust the national remedies before going to Strasbourg. Thus, according to Article 35(1) ECHR the Court may not deal with a matter before all domestic remedies have been exhausted. Only if the national courts constantly deny a certain request are the

---

[393] According to Tretter (2002), 164 et seq., the Convention is, therefore, not sufficiently established within the jurisdiction of the criminal courts. He argues in favour of a mandate for reviewing the judicial power by the Constitutional Court. As the limited jurisdiction of the Constitutional Court has a long tradition in Austria, it seems however rather unlikely that the constitutional legislator would adopt this proposal.
[394] See *supra* Section D.2.

parties entitled to abstain from filing a complaint.[395] The Court itself has declared that the rule of exhaustion of domestic remedies referred to in Article 35(1) ECHR[396] "must be applied with some degree of flexibility and without excessive formalism" and that "it is essential to have regard to the particular circumstances of each case".[397]

An interesting feature of the Austrian system of legal remedies is that decisions of Austrian courts cannot be appealed to the Constitutional Court – not even in cases where other courts base their decisions on constitutional law or apply constitutional law.[398] The review of decisions by judicial authorities is a matter for the Supreme Court of Justice. As shown above, most cases of the ECtHR involving Austria concern questions of fair trial, length of procedure and length of remand that on the national level are in large part decided by the Supreme Court of Justice. In such cases, the parties do not have the possibility to appeal to the Constitutional Court. Only the lower courts and the Independent Administrative Panels as well as the Supreme Court can ask the Constitutional Court to rescind a general provision of law if they believe it to violate the Constitution or the ECHR.[399] Considering that both the Constitutional Court and the ECtHR are the keepers of the conventional guarantees it is surprising that the Constitutional Court's hands are tied and that it is not involved in many cases that later go to Strasbourg. The European Court of Human Rights is, therefore, undoubtedly of particular importance for the protection of fundamental rights in Austria. The fact that the Constitutional Court is to a considerable extent barred from fundamental rights jurisprudence might be one reason for the initial negative attitude *vis-à-vis* the ECtHR. After all, a consequence of the allocation of rights and duties between the Austrian courts is that the ECtHR is much more involved in fundamental rights jurisprudence than the Austrian Constitutional Court.

bb. Reopening of Proceedings. Special legal provisions are required in order to abolish domestic decisions infringing the Convention and to reopen proceedings in order to give full satisfaction to the successful applicants. This has been done in Austria only with regard to criminal law but not to civil and administrative law.[400] In reaction to two judgements of the Court[401], Article 363a of the Code

---

[395] For example, in the Austrian Radio cases concerning the Austrian broadcasting monopoly (Case of *Informationsverein Lentia 2000 and Others v. Austria* (appl. nos 13914/88; 15041/89; 15717/89; 15779/89; 17207/90), Decision, 15 January 1992) the Commission declared that there was no need to file a complaint before the Constitutional Court.

[396] Former Article 26 ECHR.

[397] *Aksoy v. Turkey* (appl. no. 21987/93), Judgement (Chamber), 18 December 1996, Reports 1996-VI, 2260 et seq., para. 53.

[398] Oberndorfer (1988), 206.

[399] Article 139 in conjunction with Article 89(2) B-VG, Article 140 B-VG.

[400] Tretter (2002), 161 et seq.

[401] *Oberschlick v. Austria* (appl. no. 11662/85), Judgement (Plenary), 23 May 1991, Series A, Vol. 204; *Kremzow v. Austria* (appl. no. 12350/86), Judgement (Chamber), 21 September 1993, Series A, Vol. 268-B.

of Criminal Procedure was introduced in 1996, allowing the implementation of judgements of the ECtHR in domestic law. If the Strasbourg Court comes to the conclusion that a decision or order by a domestic criminal court has violated the Convention, the Austrian Supreme Court may *ex parte* reopen the proceedings. The person affected by the decision violating the Convention as well as the Procurator General at the Supreme Court may make a request for reopening and are thereby not bound by a time limit. This possibility of reexamining the case after a judgement of the Court has since proved to be very useful to guarantee full redress after the finding of a violation by the Strasbourg Court.

In Austrian administrative and civil law, there are no general legal provisions comparable to those of the Code of Criminal Procedure, allowing for reopening of cases after a judgement of the European Court of Human Rights. The binding force of court decisions, the interest in legal certainty and the *bona fide* confidence of third parties prevent Austria from introducing mechanisms that permit the reopening of civil proceedings. As a consequence, no reopening can take place to comply with the judgement of the Court in an individual case.[402] Only where a criminal conviction has been abolished that was at the same time the basis for a civil law judgement can a reopening of the latter be instituted. A provision similar to the above-mentioned Article 363a of the Code of Criminal Procedure is lacking in administrative criminal proceedings. In administrative matters, for the time being, only Article 45(1) of the Administrative Court Act 1985[403] provides possibilities to reopen proceedings on a request by one of the parties. Additionally, in cases where no third party interests are involved, for example, concerning residence permits, it is always possible to make a new decision. Given the lack of explicit general legal provisions concerning reopening of proceedings in civil and in administrative matters, it is not surprising that in many cases the applicants have not obtained full redress.[404]

Compared to Austria's readiness to ensure by legal amendments that comparable violations of the Convention are not repeated[405], Austria's will to implement the judgements of the Court concerning specific cases of applicants by taking the appropriate legal measures is limited. A possible explanation for this diagnosis might be that for political reasons Austria first and foremost aims at preventing further convictions by the Court. From a political point of view, the question of whether a specific case is implemented correctly attracts much less attention. This increases the danger that the latter is neglected.

---

[402] The only apparent possibility to reopen proceedings is by considering a finding from the Strasbourg Court a new fact. In light of the Austrian jurisprudence, this seems highly unlikely.

[403] Verwaltungsgerichtshofgesetz, BGBl 10/1985.

[404] Tretter (2002), 162 et seq.

[405] See *supra* Section D.1.

b. Proportionality test

Due to the influence of the ECHR, recourse to principles plays an increasing role in the case law of the Austrian Constitutional Court. Above all, the principle of proportionality, which is inherent in the Convention, exerts a profound impact not only on the jurisdiction of the Constitutional Court but also on the legislature.

The Constitutional Court took on the proportionality principle from the ECHR and the case law of the Court and considers it authoritative with regard to the whole catalogue of fundamental rights.[406] Instead of using the term "proportionality principle" or "proportionality test", the Constitutional Court mainly speaks of the *materielle Gesetzesvorbehalt*, which emphasizes that statutes restricting fundamental rights also have to satisfy requirements as regards content.[407] The proportionality principle nowadays has the status of a general unwritten constitutional principle. It is explicitly stated in some provincial constitutions.[408] Already in 1969 it was addressed in connection with the use of service guns in the Gun Use Act (*Waffengebrauchsgesetz*).[409] On the federal constitutional level, it is furthermore mentioned in Article 1(3) of the Federal Constitutional Statute on the Protection of Personal Liberty[410] and in § 1 (2) of the Data Protection Act of 2000[411]. Moreover, the idea of proportionality is of special importance in the Aliens Act (*Fremdengesetz*)[412].

The proportionality principle narrows the margin of the legislative, executive and judicial powers in their decisions-making processes. Before it became part of the Austrian legal order, it was mainly a principle of police law, stating that State power may not be used in a disproportionate way.[413] Besides that, Austria only knew the *formelle Gesetzesvorbehalt*, which requires a legal basis for

---

[406] See Austrian Constitutional Court, Judgement, 6 September 1975, VfSlg 7539/1975; Austrian Constitutional Court, Judgement, 20 December 1979, VfSlg 8718/1979; Austrian Constitutional Court, Judgement, 8 March 1980, VfSlg 8776/1980; Austrian Constitutional Court, Judgement, 27 February 1981, VfSlg 9014/1981; Austrian Constitutional Court, Judgement, 17 June 1983, VfSlg 9720/1983; Austrian Constitutional Court, Judgement, 14 December 1993, VfSlg 13645/1993 and many more.

[407] See i.a., Austrian Constitutional Court, Judgement, 10 June 1985, VfSlg 10443/1985; Austrian Constitutional Court, Judgement, 28 September 1989, VfSlg 12155/1989; Austrian Constitutional Court, Judgement, 26 Ferbruary 1990, VfSlg 12257/1990.

[408] Article 7 para. 2 of the Constitution of Vorarlberg; Article 7 para. 5 of the Constitution of Tyrol; Article 9 para. 3 of the Constitution of Upper Austria; Article 10 para. 2 of the Constitution of Salzburg; Article 4 para. 6 of the Constitution of Lower Austria.

[409] Bundesgesetz vom 27. März 1969 über den Waffengebrauch von Organen der Bundespolizei, der Bundesgendarmerie und der Gemeindewachkörper (Waffengebrauchsgesetz 1969, Federal Statute on the use of weapons), BGBl 149/1969.

[410] Bundesverfassungsgesetz vom 29 November 1988 über den Schutz der persönlichen Freiheit (Constitutional Statute on the protection of personal liberty), BGBl 684/1988.

[411] Bundesgesetz über den Schutz personenbezogener Daten (Datenschutzgesetz 2000, Data Protection Act), BGBl I 165/1999.

[412] Bundesgesetz über die Einreise, den Aufenthalt und die Niederlassung von Fremden (Fremdengesetz 1997, Aliens Act), BGBl I 75/1997.

[413] See Pesendorfer (1977), 265.

restricting fundamental rights but does not state any requirements concerning the content of the respective norm. Because the idea that fundamental rights only exist according to the content of certain statutes is problematic, the Constitutional Court affirmed the so-called *Wesensgehaltssperre*, i.e. the idea of a minimal guarantee that cannot be limited by the legislator.[414] Until about 1980 the Constitutional Court only decided whether a statute interfered with the core of a fundamental right.[415] Due to the influence of the ECHR, the newer case law of the Constitutional Court is characterized by more differentiated material considerations.[416] The Constitutional Court thus not only examines whether the legislator respected the *Wesensgehalt* or the core of a fundamental right but whether a particular interference with a fundamental right is proportionate and covered by a public interest.[417]

2. Switzerland

a. Remedies

aa. Remedies in general As part of the reform of justice *(Justizreform)*, a new Federal Statute on the Federal Supreme Court *(Bundesgerichtsgesetz)*[418] entered into force on 1 January 2007 that is supposed to contribute to better legal protection and to the efficiency of the Federal Supreme Court.[419] It provides for three types of appeals *(Einheitsbeschwerden)*, one for civil matters, one for criminal matters and one for public law matters[420]. As each of these three appeals is subject to a number of exceptions, the legislator furthermore created the subsidiary con-

---

[414] See Austrian Constitutional Court, Judgement, 10 December 1956, VfSlg 3118/1956; Austrian Constitutional Court, Judgement, 26 March 1962, VfSlg 4163/1962; Austrian Constitutional Court, Judgement, 7 June 1974, VfSlg 7304/1974; Austrian Constitutional Court, Judgement, 6 June 1980, VfSlg 8813/1980; Austrian Constitutional Court, Judgement, 9 October 1981, VfSlg 9233/1981; Austrian Constitutional Court, Judgement, 1 July 1983, VfSlg 9750/1983; Austrian Constitutional Court, Judgement, 16 June 1984, VfSlg 10050/1984.

[415] See Haller (2006), 647.

[416] See Novak (1989), 59 et seq.

[417] See i.a., Austrian Constitutional Court, Judgement, 14 October 1984, VfSlg 10179/1984; Austrian Constitutional Court, Judgement, 27 February 1985, VfSlg 10368/1985; Austrian Constitutional Court, Judgement, 3 December 1985, VfSlg 10718/1985; Austrian Constitutional Court, Judgement, 23 June 1986, VfSlg 10932/1986; Austrian Constitutional Court, Judgement, 14 October 1987, VfSlg 11503/1987; Austrian Constitutional Court, Judgement, 12 December 1987, VfSlg11558/1987.

[418] Bundesgesetz vom 17. Juni 2005 über das Bundesgericht (Federal Statute on the Federal Supreme Court, BGG, SR 173.110).

[419] See Aemisegger (2006), 500 et seq.; Karlen (2006), 8 et seq. Until 2007, basically two remedies existed: the public law appeal *(staatsrechtliche Beschwerde,* Article 84 et seq. OG) and the administrative law appeal *(Verwaltungsgerichtsbeschwerde,* Article 97 et seq.). The distinction between these two remedies became increasingly difficult to draw.

[420] The appeal for civil matters is governed by Article 72 et seq. BGG, the one for criminal matters by Article 78 et seq. BGG and the one for public law matters by Article 82 et seq. BGG.

stitutional appeal[421] *(subsidiäre Verfassungsbeschwerde)*, which deflects decisions of the Cantons from directly being brought before the ECtHR, a solution that also helps to facilitate the work of the ECtHR, which already has an immense workload.[422] A violation of the ECHR may be claimed with all three (ordinary) appeals as well as the subsidiary constitutional appeal.

If, due to the commandment of application of Federal Statutes in Article 190 Constitution[423], the Federal Supreme Court cannot diverge from a Federal Statute that it has found to be contrary to the ECHR and that has led to a decision violating the ECHR, this remedy is not effective and, therefore, may not be invoked before going to Strasbourg.[424] The recent developments of the Federal Supreme Court's case law, however, show that this practice may no longer be necessary. Due to the statement that a Federal Statute must not be applied when it is contrary to an international rule protecting human rights,[425] the three (ordinary) appeals as well as the subsidiary constitutional appeal can be considered as effective remedies in the sense of Article 35(1) ECHR. As the new system of remedies is far less complicated than the one in force until the end of 2006, it should now be easier for the Court and the applicants to decide which remedy must be considered effective and must, therefore, be exhausted before going to Strasbourg.

bb. Reopening of Proceedings. The profound importance of the ECHR in the Swiss legal order is also expressed with the extraordinary revision that since 2001 has provided an extraordinary remedy in case of a judgement of the Court finding a violation of the Convention or the Protocols thereto, and if reparation can only be awarded by a rehearing proceeding.[426] The rules concerning the extraordinary revision look easy to apply, but only at first glance. It is clear that a successful appeal in Strasbourg is not automatically followed by a review: the applicant

---

[421] Article 113 et seq. BGG.

[422] Aemisegger (2007a), 19.

[423] See *supra* Section B.2.

[424] Under the old Federal Statute on the Organization of the Federal Administration of Justice (OG), the Federal Supreme Court has considered that in such a case a civil-law appeal or an appeal in cassation could be sufficient in view of the exhaustion of domestic remedies, since it is possible to obtain the annulment of the questioned decision because of a wrongful application of federal law. For the qualification of a civil-law appeal as an effective domestic remedy, see *Burghartz v. Switzerland* (appl. no. 16213/90), Judgement (Chamber), 22 February 1994, Series A, Vol. 280-B, para. 20. For the qualification of an appeal in cassation as an effective domestic remedy, see *Müller and Others v. Switzerland* (appl. no. 10737/84), Judgement (Chamber), 24 May 1988, Series A, Vol. 133.

[425] Swiss Federal Supreme Court, Judgement, 26 July 1999, BGE 125 II 417. Also, see *supra* Section B.2.

[426] Article 122 BGG. Corresponding rules exist in Article 66(1) *lit. c* VwVG, Article 229(4) and 278bis BStP and Article 200 Bundesgesetz über den Militärstrafprozess vom 23. März 1979 (MStP). See Borghi (2002), 876 et seq.

must demand it. He must lodge the application with the Federal Supreme Court within 90 days after the decision of the Court became definite.[427]

Since the entry-into-force of the new Federal Statute on the Federal Supreme Court, it is no longer possible to ask for compensation in a revision procedure based on a violation of the ECHR; demands for compensation are to be asserted before the Court.[428] Due to this modification, duplications can be avoided. Still, the relationship between national procedural law and Article 41 ECHR gives rise to several problems:[429] According to Article 122 BGG, the Federal Supreme Court is only entitled to revise a judgement if there is no other possibility for reparation. On the other hand, the Court, based on Article 41, affords just satisfaction to the injured party only under the condition that the national law allows not more than partial reparation to be made. Whether the national or the international norm takes priority depends on the circumstances of any given case and is generally answered in a pragmatic way.[430]

Also, the relationship to Article 190 Constitution[431] is not fully clarified. The Federal Supreme Court dealt with this issue in 1998[432] and declared that a judgement of the Court referred only to a specific national judgement. However, if this judgement has been predetermined by a certain statute, the national courts must refrain from applying this statute in order to fulfil the obligations of Articles 50 and 51 ECHR.[433] This should be the case even if the Court did not explicitly comment on the Federal Statute in question.[434] The Federal Supreme Court stated that Article 139a OG[435] was *lex specialis* in respect of a Federal Statute that had been held contrary to the Convention.[436] This reasoning may not be very convincing,[437] but it leads to a logical result that once more allows courts to handle the problems caused by Article 190 Constitution in an efficient way. Thus, Article 122 BGG can be considered an important gate of entry for the implementation of European human rights standards in the Swiss national legal order.

[427] Article 124(1) *lit. c* BGG.
[428] Article 122 *lit. b* BGG. See Karlen (2005), 65.
[429] For the situation under the old Federal Statute on the organization of the federal administration of justice, see Swiss Federal Supreme Court, Judgement, 24 March 1994, BGE 120 V 150, E. 2d; Schürmann (2000), 93 et seq. with further references.
[430] See Swiss Federal Supreme Court, Judgement, 2 March 2001, 2A.232/2000 = EuGRZ 2001, 319 et seq.; Swiss Federal Supreme Court, Judgement, 29 April 2002, 2A.526/2002; Aemisegger (2007a), 9 et seq.
[431] For this provision, see also *supra* Section B.2.
[432] Swiss Federal Supreme Court, Judgement, 24 August 1998, BGE 124 II 480, 486.
[433] Today, Articles 41 and 46 ECHR.
[434] Swiss Federal Supreme Court (*supra* note 432), 486.
[435] Article 122 BGG now in force.
[436] Swiss Federal Supreme Court (*supra* note 432), 487.
[437] Wyss (1999), 3, 96, note 30.

b. Proportionality Test

In 1926, for the first time the Federal Supreme Court applied the proportionality principle as a means to assess whether restrictions of fundamental rights are justified.[438] The first cases concerned the freedom of commerce. The Federal Supreme Court held that measures that are based on a public interest but that could be replaced by less far-reaching measures with the same impact were unconstitutional. In the nineteenth century this principle was already acknowledged in administrative (police) law.[439] The Constitution of 1999 mentions the proportionality principle twice: Article 5(2) refers to it as a general principle of law and Article 36(3) requires that restrictions of fundamental rights need to be proportionate.[440] The proportionality principle thus has a much broader scope in Swiss constitutional law than in the ECHR. Not only do restrictions of fundamental rights have to satisfy this test but all activities of the State need to be proportionate.

As the proportionality test was native to the Swiss legal order long before it became part of the Convention and the case law of the Court, Swiss judges had no reason to resist adopting proportionality tests when dealing with fundamental guarantees. Still, in this respect the ECHR had an impact on Swiss law as it specifies which interests may be taken into account[441]. The Swiss Constitution does not give such clear guidelines, although – according to the doctrine – monetary interests are generally frowned upon and may be used only in rare cases as justification to restrict fundamental rights. In this respect, there certainly was an effect on the substance of judicial decisions. However, it should not be overestimated, as the respective guarantees of the ECHR allow the taking into account of a wide range of different interests.

3. Comparison and Conclusion

An interesting feature of the Austrian legal system is that due to the fact that court decisions may not be appealed to the Constitutional Court, many cases are appealed to Strasbourg without the need for a prior decision of the Constitutional Court. Important constitutional decisions, e.g. concerning procedural guarantees in criminal and civil matters, are, therefore, not taken in Vienna but in Strasbourg. Whereas Austria more or less unhesitatingly amends its statutes in case of convictions, there is still a deficit with respect to extraordinary remedies.

In Switzerland, the uncertainty concerning effective remedies has its roots in

---

[438] Swiss Federal Supreme Court, Judgement, 24 September 1926, BGE 52 I 222.

[439] Zimmerli (1978), 9.

[440] With regard to Article 36(3) of the Swiss Federal Constitution, see Steinmann (2006), 635 with further references to decisions of the Swiss Federal Supreme Court.

[441] See e.g., Article 8(2) ECHR: "There shall be no interference by a public authority with the exercise of this right except such as is in accordance with the law and is necessary in a democratic society in the interests of national security, public safety or the economic well-being of the country, for the prevention of disorder or crime, for the protection of health or morals or for the protection of the rights and freedoms of others." Articles 9, 10 and 11 contain similar specifications of the public interests that may be taken into account.

the complicated system of remedies to the Federal Supreme Court and the fact that judicial control is still geared to control the power of the Cantons. The new system of legal remedies on the federal level, however, will most likely guarantee for more clarity in this respect. Apart from that, much could be gained from an institutionalization of a dialogue between the Court and the relevant national instances.

The system of national remedies can have a notable bearing on the reception process. It is hardly a coincidence that Article 5 and 6 ECHR had the greatest effect in Switzerland. This is linked with the fact that up to the present day cantonal statutes have ruled procedural law.[442] Cantonal statutes have always been exposed to a full control in respect of the ECHR, whereas the Federal Supreme Court's jurisdiction *vis-à-vis* federal authorities is limited. Considering that federal law affects the fundamental rights of individuals to at least the same extent as cantonal law, nowadays this distinction is highly questionable.[443]

While Swiss courts were already familiar with the proportionality principle before the ECHR came into effect, the Austrian Constitutional Court adopted it from the ECHR. The Convention and its application by the Strasbourg organs thus had an effect on the Austrian legal order that outreaches the sphere of human rights. By establishing the proportionality principle, the ECHR also shaped the role of courts and judges in Austria as it offered them a wider scope for judgement evaluation.

G. Knowledge and Practice

1. Austria

a. Dissemination of the Judgements of the ECHR

In the first couple of decades of Austria's accession to the ECHR, judges as well as attorneys and the public lacked any information and knowledge about the ECHR.[444] This has changed since. As the internet has become widespread in Austria, courts and agencies as well as the public have access to the judgements on the Court's website.[445] It might not be possible for everyone to read judgements in French, as knowledge of this language is not prevalent in Austria. However, English is very common and so there exists hardly any language barrier. The

---

[442] The Federal legislator is currently enacting Federal Statutes concerning civil and criminal procedural law which are supposed to replace the respective statutes of the Cantons. Administrative procedural law, however, will remain in the Cantons' sphere of competence.

[443] The unequal treatment of cantonal and federal statutes with respect to judicial review has historical reasons: When the Federal State was created in 1848, cantonal competences not only had a broader scope than today, but they were also much less restricted by federal law. See Keller (2005), 322 et seq.

[444] Ermacora, Nowak and Tretter (1983), 17.

[445] The websites of the Federal Chancellery, the Ministry of Justice, the Constitutional Court and several universities contain a direct link to HUDOC.

most important source of information about the ECHR for the public is daily newspapers. There is media coverage of important decisions, as some Austrian newspapers routinely report about the ECtHR's case law involving Austria.[446]

There are no systematic official translations and publications of the decisions of the Court in Austria. However, summaries of most important judgements against Austria are translated and published in the *Amtsblatt der Österreichischen Justizverwaltung* (Official Gazette of the Austrian Judiciary). Such summaries are also sent to the authorities concerned.

The most important German language forum is the *Europäische GRUND-RECHTE-Zeitschrift (EuGRZ)*, in existence since 1974. It is available in all Austrian law libraries and major public libraries. Up to now, it has published more than 200 Strasbourg judgements in German. Decisions concerning Austria as well as important cases involving other Contracting States have been routinely translated in the *Österreichische Juristenzeitung (ÖJZ)* since 1988. Access to the Court's decisions is thus made relatively easy for Austrian lawyers.

b. Lawyering

There are a number of organizations and institutes dedicated to the protection of human rights in Austria. Especially worth mentioning is the *Ludwig Boltzmann Institut für Menschenrechte*[447] (Ludwig Boltzmann Institute for Human Rights), an independent academic human rights research and service institution, which was founded in 1992 by Felix Ermacora, Manfred Nowak and Hannes Tretter. Its primary focus is on research activities in the field of human rights and it aims to offer a link between academic research and legal practice. There is, furthermore, the Austrian Human Rights Institute[448], which publishes the *Newsletter Menschenrechte* (Newsletter Human Rights), offering precise and timely information on the decisions of the ECtHR and translations in German. It also acts as the national reporter of the Council of Europe for Austria and periodically gives an account of the developments in case law and legislation as well as on publications regarding human rights issues. Lastly, it offers legal advice to individuals, courts and other public authorities.

About 75 per cent of all Austrian applicants are represented by a lawyer, usually the same one who brought the case before the national courts. There are lawyers who specialize in human rights litigation; however, no actual network of activist lawyers has emerged so far.

c. Teaching

Universities are the primary guarantee of continued education in the matter of reception. As a consequence of the constitutional status of the Convention, for

---

[446] E.g., "Die Presse"; "Der Standard".
[447] See http://www.univie.ac.at/bim.
[448] See http://www.menschenrechte.ac.at.

decades constitutional law courses have also dealt with the Strasbourg law and its impact on the Austrian legal order. In addition, there are various courses in European human rights taught at every Austrian law school. The University of Vienna offers a European Master's degree in Human Rights and Democratization. The ECHR thus plays an important part in the curricula of Austria's law schools.

Being part of constitutional law in Austria, the ECHR as well as the most important case-law of the Strasbourg organs are part of every public law textbook. There is one major standard textbook entirely on the ECHR by an Austrian professor which is used in the entire German-speaking part of Europe.[449] In addition, the Ministry of Foreign Affairs has published a manual on human rights education, entitled "Understanding Human Rights".

Human rights and how they can be secured and implemented in legal practice also form an important element of the professional training of judges and public prosecutors. A training programme for judges and public prosecutors is prepared every year by the Federal Ministry of Justice in cooperation with courts and various associations.

d. Scholarship

There is a considerable amount of Austrian scholarship devoted to the ECHR and its influence on the national legal order.[450] Since Austria's accession to the Convention, leading commentators have analyzed the role of the ECHR as well as its impact on Austrian law. Legal scholarship in this field is generally characterized by a critical position *vis-à-vis* the Austrian organs that sometimes did not attach adequate weight to the ECHR and the Strasbourg case law. Scholarship undoubtedly played a decisive role in leveraging the conventional guarantees.

There are no specialized journals devoted to European human rights law in Austria. However, the ECHR and its influence on the national legal order is a common subject in Austrian law journals. A survey of the *Österreichische Juristenzeitung* (*ÖJZ*) reveals that most articles about the impact of the ECHR on the Austrian legal order concern criminal law and criminal procedure law. It is not surprising that criminal matters are in the foreground, as the ECHR had its biggest impact in this field of law. Decisions of the Strasbourg organs are frequently quoted and the number of articles on the impact of the ECHR on the national legal order has increased in the course of time.

---

[449] Grabenwarter (2005).

[450] Mainly four books have systematically addressed the Convention and highlighted its influence on the Austrian legal system: Ermacora, Nowak and Tretter (1983); Machacek, Pahr and Stadler (1991, 1992 and 1997).

2. *Switzerland*

a. Dissemination of the Judgements of the ECHR

Judgements and decisions of the Court are always transmitted to the federal instances that have been involved in the national proceedings and to the Cantons concerned. If at least one violation has been held, such judgements are, if deemed necessary, distributed by the Federal Department of Justice and Police to all Cantons, accompanied by a circular letter explaining the content of the judgement and measures to be taken to avoid similar violations to occur. The International Affairs Division also informs the potentially concerned federal and cantonal instances of cases before the Court concerning other countries that could be of significance for Switzerland.[451] This dissemination practice guarantees that courts and public officials are aware of the Court's activities that are of interest to them. Apart from that, agencies and courts get access to the Court's judgements by the same means practicing lawyers and the informed public do.

Since, in Switzerland, access to the internet belongs to every office and is very common in private households, all judgements of the Court are available to practising lawyers and the informed public on the website of the Court. These judgements of the Court concerning Switzerland are also published in the *Verwaltungspraxis der Bundesbehörden/Jurisprudence des autorités administratives de la Confédération (VPB/JAAC)*[452], which is edited by the Federal Chancellery and is available both in print and on the internet. This publication is limited to the summary and the reference to the Court if the Court's judgement or decision was delivered in English only. French being an official language in Switzerland, judgements in French are translated only in exceptional cases. However, at least the head notes of all judgements are available in French, German and Italian. As both English and French are also very common in the German and Italian-speaking part of the country, there exists little or no language barrier.

Useful information about the Court and the Convention is available on the information platform http://www.humanrights.ch which is edited by the association "humanrights.ch". There is a valuable index of judgements of the Court translated into German on http://www.egmr.org. Furthermore, the Swiss Society for the European Convention on Human Rights (SGEMKO) publishes information about the Strasbourg decisions on its website (http://www.sgemko.ch). The *Europäische GRUNDRECHTE-Zeitschrift (EuGRZ)*, which has already been mentioned in connection with Austria, is also a major source of information in

---

[451] Keller (2005), 333.
[452] The *JAAC*, however, does not contain those judgements that did not end in proceedings in Strasbourg or that are clearly of no interest.

Switzerland. A highly valuable overview on judgements of the Court is edited regularly in the *AJP* (*Aktuelle Juristische Praxis*) in German.[453]

Judgements of the Court are not hot topics in the Swiss media. While the general public knows that there is a judicial instance in Strasbourg, it is not very often aware of its judgements. However, Swiss cases are generally briefly reported in daily newspapers. Important judgements concerning other countries do also come up in the media, mainly in the *Neue Zürcher Zeitung*.

The ECHR holds further interest in Switzerland as an argument for the compatibility or non-compatibility of new national statutes. Before the Swiss people voted on the popular initiative on the lifelong internment of non-treatable, extremely dangerous sexual offenders and violent criminals[454] there were lively discussions in the media whether it was possible to implement the initiators' request in a way consistent with the ECHR. After it had been accepted in the vote of 8 February 2004, the Federal Department of Justice and Police was concerned with implementing it on the statutory level. While the Law Commission of the National Council had initially rejected the draft Statute, a majority now approved the respective amendment of the Swiss Penal Code.[455] The compatibility with the ECHR still draws considerable media attention.

b. Lawyering

No network of activist lawyers specializing in the ECHR exists in Switzerland. There are only few lawyers who – according to the information on their websites – focus on ECHR-oriented human rights litigation.[456] A look at the names of the lawyers representing the plaintiffs in the cases against Switzerland before the ECHR in the past ten years reveals that there are only very few lawyers who submitted more than one case. An explanation for that might be that most plaintiffs going to Strasbourg are represented by the same lawyer, who already represented them in the Swiss Federal Supreme Court. Furthermore, there are not enough cases concerning Switzerland before the Court to make it profitable for lawyers to specialize in this field. Lawyers of course also refer to the ECHR in cases before the Federal Supreme Court. In general, they are not explicitly specialized in ECHR-oriented human rights litigation but in fields of law where the ECHR plays an imminent role such as criminal procedure or alien law.

There are a considerable number of human-rights oriented NGOs and other organized groups in Switzerland.[457] Their primary objective, however, is not the

---

[453] F. Schürmann, Chronik der Rechtsprechung des Europäischen Gerichtshofs für Menschenrechte, in AJP (since 1993).

[454] See *supra* Section E.2.b.

[455] The National Council and the Council of States still have to decide on the draft Statute.

[456] See also Minelli (1994), 85 et seq., where he describes his experience in litigation before the ECtHR.

[457] E.g., humanrights.ch, Amnesty International, International Human Rights Forum Lucerne,

support of individual human rights challenges but rather the provision of information and the promotion of human rights in general.

c. Teaching

The ECHR is the subject of both special and basic courses at universities in Switzerland. Every law student is confronted with the Convention in basic courses, such as constitutional law and criminal procedure. In special courses, such as seminars and additional courses, interested students have the opportunity to specialize in the ECHR to a certain extent.[458] At present, there are no special degrees offered in European or international human rights law. However, since very recently, students are able to obtain Master's degrees in public international law. The Summer University on Human Rights, located in Geneva, is also worth mentioning. Courses in the field of democracy and human rights are taught at the Interdisciplinary Institute of Ethics and Human Rights of the University of Fribourg. This shows that the importance of international and European human rights in the universities' curricula has certainly increased in the last years. Additionally, international training programmes are offered by non-governmental organizations, such as the International Training Centre on Human Rights and Peace Teaching and the International Service for Human Rights, both located in Geneva.

There is one textbook written by Swiss law professors in the field of international and European human rights.[459] Swiss law schools also use German and Austrian textbooks on the subject.[460] Moreover, students give considerable attention to doctrinal scholarship.[461]

Not only law students but also police recruits are trained in human rights issues: There is close cooperation on policing issues with the Association for the Prevention of Torture which was commissioned by the Swiss Police Institute to prepare a training handbook entitled "Police and Human Rights". Recruits are given training in ethics and human rights, which is then tested in the practical professional entrance examination. Moreover, law courses for prison staff lay particular emphasis on the prisoners' constitutional and Convention-based rights and the relevant principles laid down by the Council of Europe.

International Service for Human Rights, Commission for Human Rights of the Council of the Swiss Scientific Academies, Swiss Society for the European Convention on Human Rights, etc.

[458] For example, in the winter term of 2006/2007, students at the University of Zurich had the opportunity to take part in a seminar on the international protection of human rights, taught in English by Professor Villiger, Judge for Liechtenstein at the ECtHR.

[459] See Kälin and Künzli (2005).

[460] E.g., Grabenwarter (2005); Peters (2003).

[461] For a list of published work on the Court by leading commentators, see *infra* note 461.

d. Scholarship

There is a remarkable amount of Swiss scholarship that broaches the issue of the ECHR and its influence on the national legal order.[462] Doctrinal scholarship critically examines the way Swiss organs apply the Convention and the Strasbourg case law and gives important impulses to the legislative, executive and judicial powers. Although there are no specialized journals devoted to European human rights law in Switzerland, the ECHR and its influence on the national legal order is a common subject in Swiss law journals.

As in Austria, most articles concerning the effect of the ECHR on the national legal order in Swiss law journals are published in the field of criminal law and criminal procedure. This is certainly due to the fact that the ECHR had a bigger impact on Swiss criminal procedure law than on any other field. In addition, Convention-based judgements are frequently reported in law journals.

3. Comparison and Conclusion

There are many parallels in Austria and Switzerland with regard to knowledge and practice of the ECHR. This is not surprising, considering that both Austria and Switzerland have a long tradition of democracy and the rule of law and that legal scholarship is characterized by a high standard in both countries. Courts, lawyers and the informed public have easy access to the case law of the Strasbourg organs. There are a considerable number of human-rights oriented NGOs that are mainly concerned with promoting human rights in general, but not with supporting individual human rights challenges. The ECHR plays an increasing role in the universities' curricula in both countries and the possibilities to enjoy education in the field of European human rights law are broad. In Austria as well as in Switzerland, the ECHR is one of the essential instruments a lawyer has to work with, on par with national law. The pressure to look into the subject during university studies as well as later on during one's practical occupation as a lawyer is therefore high. In both countries there is a considerable amount of scholarship devoted to the ECHR and its influence on the national legal order. Scholars have an important function as watchdogs who urge the legislative, executive and judicial powers to observe the Convention as well as the Strasbourg organ's case law. Legal scholarship thus played and still plays an important role in both countries to enhance the effectiveness of the ECHR.

H. Final Remarks

It is of particular interest to compare the reception process in Austria and Switzerland, as both are federal as well as neutral States of a similar population figure, and

---

[462] See e.g., Haefliger (1993); Herzog (1995); Sutter and Zelger (2005); Trechsel (2005); Villiger (1999), Wetzel (1983).

both joined the ECHR at a relatively early stage (although Austria was more than one step ahead when it ratified the ECHR 16 years before Switzerland). Surprisingly, the study shows that this starting position led to different outcomes. The main reason can be seen in the fact that the common denominators of neutrality and federalism in these two countries are actually rather small: As Austria follows a very different concept of neutrality, it did not face any (political) difficulties before and during the ratification process. Switzerland, on the other hand, was very reluctant to join the Council of Europe and careful to avoid any concessions with regard to neutrality. In addition, federalism in Switzerland is much more pronounced than in Austria. Given that the provinces in Austria do not have any judicial competences, there was no time-lag with regard to the application of the Convention by the courts.

The comparison between Austria and Switzerland reveals another interesting point: Austria was the first State to incorporate the ECHR fully into its constitutional legal order, with the consequence that the Convention was granted the same legal status as the Constitution (*Bundes-Verfassungsgesetz*). The difficulties Austria faced in the first years after ratification yet show that the effectiveness of the Convention not only depends on the formal doctrinal status but first and foremost on the willingness of the courts to leverage the Conventional guarantees. In Switzerland, the ECHR does not have formal constitutional status. However, due to the ECHR-friendly case law of the Federal Supreme Court (who could thereby strengthen its own position *vis-à-vis* the legislative power) the Convention after all has *de facto* supra-legislative status. Therefore, one has to take a deeper look at law in action, as law in the books (i.e. in the Constitution) does not necessarily provide an adequate picture.

Whereas Switzerland showed some reluctance at the beginning, Austria was enthusiastic about joining the European human rights protection system and thus lost sight of making the necessary modifications in its national law. Consequently, as the very high number of applications and judgements against Austria shows, it faced more problems after ratification. Austria and Switzerland nevertheless have much in common with regard to the reception process because they both are old Contracting States, both have considerable experience with the ECHR and, in both countries, the Convention enjoys a tremendous esteem.

In Austria as well as in Switzerland, the number of applications has steadily increased over the years. There are no systematic violations of the Convention in Switzerland, while Austria faces considerable problems with respect to Article 6(1) ECHR that are the main cause for the high number of convictions. Apart from that, the problems in both countries nowadays mostly lie in the way a particular piece of legislation is applied. Two phases can be distinguished: At the first stage, laws had to be enacted, modified or amended, whereas at the second stage the focus lies more on the way the laws are applied that on face value do not violate the Convention. The question thus arises of how to react to the particular problems in this second phase. As has been shown above, there are well-established institutionalized mechanisms in both countries that guarantee that new legislation is in accordance with the ECHR. It is certainly more difficult to ensure that public authorities and courts that apply the laws pay adequate regard to the Convention. The question of the function of the ECHR in countries (like Austria and Switzerland) that are governed by the rule of law and have a high standard of human rights protection is linked to this issue. As the recently decided *Stoll* case[463] shows, the high level of protection guaranteed by the Convention and its extensive interpretation by the Strasbourg organs, which understand the ECHR as a living instrument, sometimes courts the Contracting States' resentment. Both the Court and the Contracting States of the Convention have to participate actively in shaping the future role of the ECHR and in finding efficient implementation mechanisms on the national level in order to give full effect to the European human rights protection system.

[463] See *supra* Section D.2.

Bibliography

Ackermann, J.-B., Caroni, M. and Vetterli, L., Anonyme Zeugenaussagen: Bundesgericht contra EGMR, AJP 16 (2007), 1071.

Adamovich, K. L., Funk, B.-C. and Holzinger, G., *Österreichisches Staatsrecht, Band 1: Grundlagen* (Vienna/New York, 1997).

—, *Österreichisches Staatsrecht, Band 2: Staatliche Organisation* (Vienna/New York, 1998).

—, *Österreichisches Staatsrecht, Band 3: Grundrechte* (Vienna/New York, 2003).

Aemisegger, H., 'Zulässigkeitsanforderungen bei Individualbeschwerden nach dem neuen Schweizerischen Bundesgerichtsgesetz', *EuGRZ* 33 (2006), 500.

—, 'Zur Umsetzung von Justizreform 2000 und Bundesgerichtsgesetz im Lichte der EMRK', in: Breitenmoser, S. et al. (eds.), Human Rights, Democracy and the Rule of Law/Menschenrechte, Demokratie und Rechtsstaat/Droits de l'homme, démocratie et Etat de droit, Liber amicorum Luzius Wildhaber, (Zurich/St.Gallen/Baden-Baden, 2007), 3 (cit.: 2007a).

—, 'Öffentlichkeit der Justiz', in Tschannen, P. (ed.), *Neue Bundesrechtspflege. Auswirkungen der Totalrevision auf den kantonalen und eidgenössischen Rechtsschutz* (Bern, 2007), 375 (cit. 2007b).

Aubert, J.-F., *Bundesstaatsrecht der Schweiz, Band II* (Basel, 1995).

Borghi, M., 'Switzerland', in Blackburn, R. and Polakiewicz, J. (eds.), *Fundamental Rights in Europe: The European Convention on Human Rights and its Member States, 1950–2000* (Oxford, 2002), 855.

Brauneder, W., 'Die Gesetzgebungsgeschichte der österreichischen Grundrechte', in Machacek, R., Pahr, W. P. and Stadler, G. (eds.), *Grund- und Menschenrechte in Österreich, Grundlagen, Entwicklungen und internationale Verbindungen* (Kehl am Rhein, etc., 1991), 189.

Breitenmoser, S., 'Subsidiarität und Interessenabwägung im Rahmen der EGMR-Rechtsprechung', in: Breitenmoser, S. et al. (eds.), Human Rights, Democracy and the Rule of Law/Menschenrechte, Demokratie und Rechtsstaat/Droits de l'homme, démocratie et Etat de droit, Liber amicorum Luzius Wildhaber, (Zurich/St.Gallen/Baden-Baden, 2007), 119.

Eissen, M.-A., *L'interaction des jurisprudences constitutionnelles nationales et de la jurisprudence de la Cour européenne des Droits de l'Homme, Droits et libertés en Europe* (Paris, 1990).

Ermacora, F., 'Die Menschenrechtskonvention als Bestandteil der innerstaatlichen Rechtsordnung', *Juristische Blätter* 81 (1959), 396.

—, *Handbuch der Grundfreiheiten und Menschenrechte* (Vienna, 1963).

Ermacora, F. and Hummer, W., 'Völkerrecht, Recht der Europäischen Union und Landesrecht', in Neuhold. H., Hummer, W. and Schreuer, Ch. (eds.), *Österreichisches Handbuch des Völkerrechts, Band 1: Textbuch*, 4th ed. (Vienna, 2004), 111.

Ermacora, F., Nowak, M. and Tretter, H. (eds.), *Die Europäische Menschenrechtskonvention in der Rechtsprechung der österreichischen Höchstgerichte* (Vienna, 1983).

Frowein, J. A. and Peukert, W., *Europäische MenschenRechtsKonvention, EMRK-Kommentar* (Kehl am Rhein, etc., 1996).

Furrer, A. and Krummenacher, P., 'Grundrechtskonflikte im UWG? Was lernen wir aus der Rechtsprechung Hertel?', *Recht* 22 (2004), 169

Grabenwarter, C., 'Entscheidanmerkung zum Fall Gradinger', *Juristische Blätter* 119 (1997), 577.

—, 'Art 20/2 B-VG' and 'Art 133 B-VG', in: Korinek, K. and Holoubek, M. (eds.), *Österreichisches Bundesverfassungsrecht. Textsammlung und Kommentar* (Vienna/New York, 1999).

—, 'Europäisches und nationales Verfassungsrecht, 4. Bericht', in Pernice, I., Huber, P. M., Lübbe-Wolf, G. and Grabenwarter, C. (eds.), *Europäisches und nationales Verfassungsrecht, Veröffentlichungen der Vereinigung der Deutschen Staatsrechtslehrer Heft 60* (Berlin/New York, 2001), 290.

—, *Europäische Menschenrechtskonvention*, 2nd ed. (Munich, etc., 2005).

—, *Verfahrensgarantien in der Verwaltungsgerichtsbarkeit, Eine Studie zu Artikel 6 EMRK auf der Grundlage einer rechtsvergleichenden Untersuchung der Verwaltungsgerichtsbarkeit Frankreichs, Deutschlands und Österreichs* (Vienna/New York, 1997).

von Grünigen, M., 'Die österreichische Verfassungsnovelle über Staatsverträge vom 4. März 1964', *ZaöRV* 25 (1965), 76.

Haefliger, A., *Handbuch der Europäischen Menschenrechtskonvention* (Zurich, 1993).

Haefliger, A. and Schürmann, F., *Die Europäische Menschenrechtskonventon und die Schweiz – die Bedeutung der Konvention für die schweizerische Rechtspraxis*, 2nd ed. (Bern, 1999).

Häfelin, U. and Haller, W., *Schweizerisches Bundesstaatsrecht*, 6th ed. (Zurich, etc., 2005).

Häfelin, U., Haller, W. and Keller, H., *Bundesgericht und Verfassungsgerichtsbarkeit nach der Justizreform* (Zurich, etc., 2006).

Haller, H., 'Kriterien der Einschränkung von Grundrechten in der Praxis der Verfassungsgerichtsbarkeit. Landesbericht Österreich', *EuGRZ* 33 (2006), 644.

Haller, W., 'Persönliche Freiheit', in Aubert, J.-F. et al. (eds.), *Kommentar zur Bundesverfassung der Schweizerischen Eidgenossenschaft vom 29. Mai 1874* (Basel, etc., 1996).

Hangartner, Y., 'Art. 191 BV', in Ehrenzeller, B., Mastronardi, P., Schweizer, R. J. and Vallender, K. A. (eds.), *Die Schweizerische Bundesverfassung, Kommentar* (Zurich, etc., 2002) (cit.: 2002a).

—, 'Recht auf Rechtsschutz', *AJP* 11 (2002), 142 (cit.: 2002b).

—, 'Bemerkungen zu BGE 129 II 193', *AJP* 12 (2003), 1112.

Herbst, C., 'Art. 6 MRK und das österreichische Verwaltungsverfahren', in Machachek, R., Pahr, W. P. and Stadler, G. (eds.), *50 Jahre Allgemeine Erklärung der Menschenrechte, Grund- und Menschenrechte in Österreich, Band II, Wesen und Werte* (Kehl am Rhein, etc., 1997), 661.

Herzog, R., *Artikel 6 EMRK und kantonale Verwaltungsrechtspflege* (Bern, 1995).

Hottelier, M., 'La CEDH et les règles suisses de procédure – aspects historiques et développements récents', *Revue jurassienne de jurisprudence* 15 (2005), 11.

—, *La convention européenne des droits de l'homme dans la jurisprudence du tribunal fédéral – contribution à l'étude des droits fondamentaux* (Lausanne, 1985).

Jacot-Guillarmod, O., 'Problèmes de législation pénale révélés par la jurisprudence de Strasbourg, perspective de droit suisse et de droit comparé', *Schweizerische Zeitschrift für Strafrecht* 106 (1989), 255.

Jann, P., 'Verfassungsrechtlicher und internationaler Schutz der Menschenrechte: Konkurrenz oder Ergänzung?', *EuGRZ* 21 (1994), 1.

Kälin, W., 'Verfassungsgerichtsbarkeit', in Thürer, D., Aubert, J.-F. and Müller, J. P. (eds.), *Verfassungsrecht der Schweiz* (Zürich, 2001).

Kälin, W., Künzli, J., *Universeller Menschenrechtsschutz* (Basel, 2005).

Karlen, P., *Das neue Bundesgerichtsgesetz* (Basel, etc., 2006).

Keller, H., *Rezeption des Völkerrechts. Eine rechtsvergleichende Studie zur Praxis des U.S. Supreme Court, des Gerichtshofes der Europäischen Gemeinschaften und des schweizerischen Bundesgerichts in ausgewählten Bereichen* (Berlin, etc., 2003).

—, 'Reception of the European Convention for the Protection of Human Rights and Fundamental Freedoms (ECHR) in Poland and Switzerland', *ZaöRV* 65 (2005), 283.

Kley, A., 'St. Galler Kommentar zu Art. 29a, Rechtsweggarantie (Justizreform)', in Ehrenzeller, B., Mastronardi, P., Schweizer, R. J. and Vallender K. A. (eds.), *Die Schweizerische Bundesverfassung, Kommentar* (Zurich, etc., 2000).

Kopetzki, C., 'Zur Anwendbarkeit des Art. 6 MRK im (österreichischen) Verwaltungsstrafverfahren', *ZaöRV* 42 (1982), 1.

—, 'Das Recht auf persönliche Freiheit – PersFrG, Art. 5 EMRK', in Machachek, R., Pahr, W. P. and Stadler, G. (eds.), *50 Jahre Allgemeine Erklärung der Menschenrechte, Grund- und Menschenrechte in Österreich, Band III, Wesen und Werte* (Kehl am Rhein, etc., 1997), 261.

Machacek, R., Pahr, W. and Stadler, G., *Grund- und Menschenrechte in Österreich* (Kehl am Rhein, etc., 1991).

Matscher, F., 'Die Rechtsprechung des Europäischen Gerichtshofes für Menschenrechte', in Matscher, F. (ed.), *Erweitertes Grundrechtsverständnis, Internationale Rechtsprechung und nationale Entwicklungen* (Kehl am Rhein, etc., 2003), 5.

Minelli, L. A., 'Die EMRK aus der Sicht des Praktikers', in Thürer, D., Weber, R. H. and Zäch, R. (eds.), *Aktuelle Fragen zur Europäischen Menschenrechtskonvention* (Zurich, 1994), 85.

Müller, G., *Elemente einer Rechtsetzungslehre*, 2nd ed. (Zurich, 2006).

Novak, R., 'Verhältnismässigkeitsgebot und Grundrechtsschutz', in Raschauer, B., *Beiträge zum Verfassungs- und Wirtschaftsrecht, Festschrift für Günther Winkler* (Vienna, etc.,1989), 39.

Nowak, M., 'Allgemeine Bemerkungen zur Europäischen Menschenrechtskonvention aus völkerrechtlicher und innerstaatlicher Sicht', in Ermacora, F., Nowak, M. and Tretter, H. (eds.), *Die Europäische Menschenrechtskonvention in der Rechtsprechung der österreichischen Höchstgerichte* (Vienna, 1983), 37.

Oberndorfer P., 'Die Verfassungsrechtsprechung im Rahmen der staatlichen Funktionen', *EuGRZ* 15 (1988), 193.

Öhlinger, T., *Der völkerrechtliche Vertrag im staatlichen Recht* (Vienna, etc., 1973).

Okresek, W., 'Die EMRK und ihre Auswirkungen auf das österreichische Strafverfahrensrecht', in Machachek, R., Pahr, W. P. and Stadler, G. (eds.), *50 Jahre Allgemeine Erklärung der Menschenrechte, Grund- und Menschenrechte in Österreich, Band III, Wesen und Werte* (Kehl am Rhein, etc., 1997), 619.

Pernthaler, P., *Die Kollegialbehörden mit richterlichem Einschlag (Art. 20 Abs. 2 und 133 Z 4 B-VG). Eine verfassungsrechtliche und verwaltungspolitische Neubestimmung im Lichte des Art. 6 der Europäischen Menschenrechtskonvention und der Bundes-Verfassungsnovelle 1975, BGBl Nr. 302* (Vienna, 1977).

Pesendorfer, W., 'Das Übermassverbot als rechtliches Gestaltungsprinzip der Verwaltung – zugleich ein Beitrag zur Bindung eines "inneren Systems" der Verwaltung', *Österreichische Zeitschrift für öffentliches Recht und Völkerrecht*, 28 (1977), 265.

Peters, A., *Einführung in die Europäische Menschenrechtskonvention, Mit rechtsvergleichenden Bezügen zum deutschen Grundgesetz* (Munich, 2003).

Riedel, E., 'Entschädigung für Eigentumsentzug nach Artikel 1 des 1. ZP zur Europäischen Menschenrechtskonvention', *EuGRZ* 15 (1988), 333.

Rill, P., 'Die Artikel 5 und 6 der Europäischen Menschenrechtskonvention, die Praxis der Strassburger Organe und des Verfassungsgerichtshofes und das österreichische Verfassungssystem', in Raschauer, B. (ed.), *Beiträge zum Verfassungs- und Wirtschaftsrecht. Festschrift für Günther Winkler* (Vienna, etc., 1989), 13.

Schantl, G. and Welan, M., 'Betrachtungen über die Judikatur des Verfassungsgerichtshofes zur Menschenrechtskonvention (Slg. 1968)', *ÖJZ* 25 (1970), 617.

Schindler, B., 'Art. 6(1) ECHR and Judicial Review of Administrative Decision-Making in England and Switzerland – A Comparative Perspective', SZIER/RSDIE (2007), 29.

Schürmann, F., 'Erste Erfahrungen mit Art. 139a OG', in Donatsch, A., Fingerhuth, T., Lieber, V., Rehberg, J. and Walder-Richli, H. U. (eds.), *Festschrift 125 Jahre Kassationsgericht des Kantons Zürich* (Zurich, 2000), 91.

—, 'Der Entwurf für eine Schweizerische Strafprozessordnung und die EMRK', in *Aus der Werkstatt des Rechts, Festschrift zum 65. Geburtstag von Heinrich Koller* (Basel, etc., 2006), 269.

—, 'Bemerkungen zum Urteil des EGMR i.S. *Stoll gegen die Schweiz* vom 25. April 2006', in: Breitenmoser, S. et al. (eds.), Human Rights, Democracy and the Rule of Law/ Menschenrechte, Demokratie und Rechtsstaat / Droits de l'homme, Démocratie et Etat de droit, Liber amicorum Luzius Wildhaber, (Zurich/St.Gallen/Baden-Baden, 2007), 763.

Sciotti-Lam, C., 'L'applicabilité des traités internationaux relatifs aux droits de l'homme en droit interne', *Publications de l'Institut des droits de l'homme* (Brussels, 2004), 377.

Steinmann, G., 'Kriterien der Einschränkung von Grundrechten in der Praxis der Verfassungsgerichtsbarkeit. Landesbericht Schweiz', *EuGRZ* 33 (2006), 629.

Sutter, P., Zelger, U. (eds.), *30 Jahre EMRK-Beitritt der Schweiz: Erfahrungen und Perspektiven* (Bern, 2005).

Thürer, D., 'Europäische Menschenrechtskonvention und schweizerisches Verwaltungsverfahren', *ZBl* 87 (1986), 241.

—, 'Neuere Entwicklungen im Bereich der Europäischen Menschenrechtskonvention', *ZBl* 89 (1988), 390.

—, 'Bundesverfassung und Völkerrecht', in Aubert, J.-F. et al. (eds.), *Kommentar zur Bundesverfassung der Schweizerischen Eidgenossenschaft vom 29 Mai 1984* (Zurich, etc., 1996).

Trechsel, S., 'Der Einfluss der Europäischen Menschenrechtskonvention auf das Strafrecht und Strafverfahrensrecht der Schweiz', *Zeitschrift für die gesamte Strafrechtswissenschaft* 100 (1988), 686.

—, *Human Rights in Criminal Proceedings* (Oxford, 2005).

Tretter, H., 'Austria', in Blackburn, R. and Polakiewicz, J. (eds.), *Fundamental Rights in Europe: The European Convention on Human Rights and its Member States, 1950–2000* (Oxford, 2002), 103.

Tschannen, P., *Staatsrecht der Schweizerischen Eidgenossenschaft* (Bern, 2004).

Villiger, M. E., *Handbuch der Europäischen Menschenrechtskonvention (EMRK) – unter besonderer Berücksichtigung der schweizerischen Rechtslage*, 2nd ed. (Zurich, 1999).

Vospernik, T., 'Das Verhältnis zwischen Art 13 und Art 6 EMRK – Absorption oder "Apfel und Birne"?', *ÖJZ* 56 (2001), 361.

de Vries Reiling, J., 'Les garanties de procédure et en cas de détention: de la CEDH à la Constitution fédérale en un quart de siècle', *ZBl* 101 (2000), 16.

Weh, W. L., 'Der Anwendungsbereich des Art. 6 EMRK – Das Ende des "cautious approach" und seine Auswirkungen in den Konventionsstaaten', *EuGRZ* 15 (1988), 433.

Wetzel, T. A., *Das Recht auf eine wirksame Beschwerde bei einer nationalen Instanz (Artikel 13 EMRK) und seine Ausgestaltung in der Schweiz* (Entlebuch, 1983).

Wildhaber, L., 'Rund um Belilos. Die schweizerischen Vorbehalte und auslegenden Erklärungen zur Europäischen Menschenrechtskonvention im Verlaufe der Zeit und im Lichte der Rechtsprechung', in Riklin A., Wildhaber L. and Wille H. (eds.), *Kleinstaat und Menschenrechte. Festgabe Gerard Baltiner zum 65. Geburtstag* (Basel, 1993), 325.

—, Les résistances nationales en Suisse – à propos des réserves suisses à l'article 6 de la Convention européenne des droits de l'Homme, in Tavernier P. (ed.), *Quelle Europe pour les droits de l'homme?* (Bruxelles, 1996), 159.

Wildhaber, L., Scheidegger, A. and Schinzel, M. D., 'National Treaty Law and Practice: Switzerland', in Hollis, D. B., Blakeslee, M. R. and Ederington, L. B. (eds.), *National Treaty Law and Practice, Dedicated to the Memory of Monroe Leigh* (Leiden/Boston, 2005), 627.

Wyss, M. P., 'EMRK-Verletzung und bundesrechtliche Revision nach Art. 139a OG – Leitlinien für Umsetzung und Vollzug von Urteilen der Strassburger Organe durch die Schweiz anhand der neuesten bundesgerichtlichen Judikatur', *Recht* 17 (1999), 3.

Zemanek, K., 'Das Völkervertragsrecht', in: Neuhold, H., Hummer, W. and Schreuer, Ch. (eds.), *Österreichisches Handbuch des Völkerrechts, Band 1: Textteil*, 4th ed. (Vienna, 2004), 45.

Zimmerli, U., 'Der Grundsatz der Verhältnismässigkeit im öffentlichen Recht', *ZSR* 1978 II, 1.

7

The Reception Process in Spain and Italy

Mercedes Candela Soriano *

I. Introduction[1]

The reception of the European Convention on Human Rights in Spain and Italy differ in significant ways. In both countries, there is a Constitution embodying a comprehensive catalogue of human rights and freedoms, and a judicial system characterized by the existence of more than one High Court at its apex (Supreme Court and Constitutional Court in Spain and Supreme Court of Cassation, Constitutional Court and Council of State in Italy).[2] Nevertheless, they have adopted different approaches to the incorporation of the ECHR into their national legal systems. While reception in Spain is facilitated by its monist character, strong dualism has sometimes hindered the effectiveness of the ECHR in Italy. In Spain, the ECHR possesses supra-legislative status, while in Italy it only holds the position of ordinary law. In Spain, national courts and, particularly, the Spanish Constitutional Court (SCC) apply the ECHR directly against any other infra-constitutional norm. By contrast, the possibility for Italian courts to apply the ECHR, directly, remains contested. The Italian situation is more complicated in that the Italian Constitution, unlike the Spanish Constitution, contains no specific provision concerning the rank and effect of international human rights

* The author would like to express her gratitude to Elena Masetti-Zannini, Virginia Pisasale, Luca Viola, Gloria De Sabbata and Viviana Inguscio for their collaboration in the Italian sections.
[1] Abbreviations: *Spain:* BOE = Boletín Oficial del Estado (Official State Bulletin); FJ = Fundamento Jurídico = Operative part of the judgement; SCC = Spanish Constitutional Court; STC = Sentencia del Tribunal Constitucional (Constitutional Court judgement), LOTC = Ley Orgánica del Tribunal Constitucional (Organic Law of the Constitutional Court). *Italy*: CC = Civil code; Cass. = Court of Cassation; ICC = Italian Constitutional Court; Sez. Pen. = Criminal Section; S.U. = United Sections of the Court of Cassation; CM = Committee of Ministers; CP = Criminal Code; CPP = Criminal procedural Code; PA = Public Administration; DPR. = Decree of the President of the Republic; D.Lgs. = Legislative Decree; DPCM. = Decree of the President of the Council of Ministers; SM = Operative part of the judgement; TU = Unified Text.
[2] In this respect, it is important to emphasize the influence that the Italian Constitution has had on the Spanish Constitution as many Spanish scholars carry out comprehensive studies in Italy.

treaties. Despite these differences, the ECHR has had significant indirect effects on legislative and judicial activity in both countries.

In this chapter, our focus is on the impact of the incorporation of the ECHR on the Spanish and Italian national legal orders. We demonstrate that the application of the ECHR depends not just on the formal constitutional provisions but, even more importantly, on how constitutional courts have enhanced the Convention's effectiveness through their rulings.

II. Overview of the National Constitutional Orders

A. Spain

The Spanish Constitution of 1978 is an effective tool for the protection of citizen's rights and fundamental freedoms.[3] Chapter II of the Constitution establishes a comprehensive catalogue of fundamental rights and freedoms.[4] In addition, Article 10(2) establishes a binding system of interpretation of these rights and freedoms in accordance with applicable international standards: "the norms relative to basic rights and liberties which are recognized by the Constitution shall be interpreted in conformity with the Universal Declaration of Human Rights and the international treaties and agreements on those matters ratified by Spain". Among these international agreements, the ECHR holds a prominent position.[5] The first applications of the Convention by the national courts, in particular by the Spanish Constitutional Court, originated in the need to clarify the scope of constitutional rights. In the early years, Spanish courts lacked an adequate internal framework for interpreting the rights and freedoms embodied in the Spanish Constitution, a gap which the ECHR and the case law of the European Court of human rights helped to fill.

Spain is a constitutional monarchy with a bicameral Parliament[6] with strong regional Government in the form of seventeen Autonomous Communities (*Comunidades Autónomas*).[7] Article 2 of the Spanish Constitution grants the na-

---

[3] Articles 10–55, Title I of the Spanish Constitution of 1978. See Cruz Villalón and Pardo Falcón (2000), 65–154.

[4] Articles 14–29, Title I, Chapter II of the Spanish Constitution of 1978, http://www.constitucion.es/constitucion/lenguas/ingles.html#1 (Unless indicated otherwise, all websites were visited last at end of June 2007).

[5] In practice, Article 10(2) of the Spanish Constitution has been more frequently invoked in relation to the ECHR and to the Strasbourg the case law than to the Universal Declaration of Human Rights.

[6] The two Chambers of the Spanish Parliament are: (i) the Congress of Deputies (*Congreso de los Diputados*) which includes 350 members elected from closed party lists and (ii) the Senate (*Senado*) which comprises 259 members, 208 directly elected and 51 appointed as regional representatives, but with little influence.

[7] Three years after the ratification of the Constitution, the process of setting up the seventeen Autonomous Communities was completed and their Statutes approved. This marked a reversal

tionalities and regions rights to autonomy, though this provision is premised on the unity of the Spanish Nation. The text of the Constitution sets out the powers that the Autonomous Communities may assume and those that are vested solely in the State. The Autonomous Communities have their own Governmental bodies. However, despite the existence of a territorial division, the territorial courts in those regions are part of the Spanish judicial system.

Spanish national courts are classified by territory and by subject matter. For each area of law there are specialized courts,[8] headed by the Supreme Court (*Tribunal Supremo*) with jurisdiction over the whole Spanish territory and over all judicial matters,[9] excepting constitutional (Article 123(1) of the Spanish Constitution). Constitutional questions are dealt with by an *ad hoc* court, the Spanish Constitutional Court (*Tribunal Constitucional*). The Supreme Court and the Spanish Constitutional Court (hereafter, SCC) are the highest courts in the Spanish judicial system.

The SCC exercises *ex post* control over the constitutionality of laws and an *ex ante* and *ex post* control over international treaties. It also has jurisdiction over conflicts of competencies between State bodies, over referrals made to it by the

in the centralist policy of the previous regime. The seventeen Autonomous Communities are: the Basque Country, Catalonia, Galicia, Andalucia, Principality of Asturias, Cantabria, La Rioja, the Region of Murcia, the Community of Valencia, Aragon, Castile-la-Mancha, the Canary Islands, Navarre, Extremadura, the Community of the Balearic Islands, the Community of Madrid and the Community of Castile and Leon.

[8] In addition to the Supreme Court, the Spanish ordinary system comprises a National High Court (*Audiencia Nacional*) which has jurisdiction over criminal and employment cases that cut across regional boundaries and civil cases involving the central State Administration. The Territorial High Courts (*Tribunal Superior de Justicia de las Comunidades Autónomas*) constitute the highest level of jurisdiction within each region (*Comunidad Autonoma*) of Spain. The Provincial Courts (*Audiencia Provincial*) serve as appellate courts in civil matters and as courts of first instance in criminal cases. Labour Courts (*Juzgados de lo Social*) hear all employment and work-related cases. Administrative Courts (*Juzgados de lo Contencioso-Administrativo*), Criminal Courts (*Juzgados de lo Penal*) hear for those crimes where the maximum penalty for the crimes does not exceed 5 years imprisonment. On the lowest level are the Courts of the First Instance (*Juzgados de Primera Instancia*) with jurisdiction over civil cases which are not legally prescribed to be heard by another higher court, the Courts of instruction (*Juzgados de Instrucción*) that investigate and prepare criminal cases to be tried in other courts, (*Provincial Audiences and Criminal Courts*) and justices of the Peace (*Juzgado de Paz*) that hear minor civil cases. To complete this broad picture, it is important to note that the Spanish judicial system includes also: (i) Minor's Courts (*Juzgados de Menores*) with competence to hear cases involving minors under the age of 16. Their jurisdiction may extend several provinces within an Autonomous Community; (ii) Courts of Prison Vigilance (*Juzgados de Vigilancia Penitenciaria*) that look after the legal rights of detainees and (iii) Special Courts established to protect women from violence.

[9] Article 123 of the Spanish Constitution stipulates that: "(1) The Supreme Court, with jurisdiction all over Spain, is the highest jurisdictional organ in all orders, except in matters concerning constitutional guarantees. (2) The President of the Supreme Court shall be appointed by the King at the proposal of the General Council of the judicial branch in the manner determined by law." The *Tribunal Supremo* is composed of nearly 100 judges, organized in five divisions (Civil, Criminal, Social, Military and Administrative), and hears appeals for the annulment or revision, of sentences handed down by the National or Regional High Courts. The Spanish Supreme Court delivers around 15,000 judgements and decisions every year.

judiciary, and over individual complaints through the so-called *amparo* appeal (*recurso de amparo*). The *amparo* is an action that may be lodged by any person who deems that her fundamental rights have been violated.[10] It encompasses all decisions adopted by public authorities, irrespective of rank, as well as by private companies and individuals that are alleged to be in conflict with Article 14 (principle of equal protection of the law and prohibition of any discrimination) and with the rights listed in Articles 15-29 (including the right to life, the right to physical indemnity, the right to privacy, the right to personal freedom, freedom of speech, the right of assembly and to demonstrate, the right to hold office, freedom of religion, the right to strike, etc.). The *amparo* appeal is a remedy of last resort, available only after the exhaustion of all available judicial remedies. The SCC is thus the ultimate guardian of the rights and freedoms guaranteed by the Constitution.

B. Italy

As in Spain, Italy has a Constitution (1947) that contains a human rights catalogue divided in four sections: civil rights (such as personal freedom,[11] confidentiality of correspondence, freedom of movement, freedom of association, freedom of thought, freedom of religion and freedom of the press); social rights (such as right to education and right to wealth); economic rights (professional, economic initiative and private property) and political rights (voting rights, etc.).[12] International human rights instruments and the ECHR, in particular, influenced this catalogue of rights. Italy was one of the original signatory countries of the Convention and participated in the activities carried out by the Council of Europe.

Italy has been a democratic and Parliamentary Republic since 1946.[13] The Parliament is composed of two houses: the Chamber (*Camera*) and the Senate (*Senato*). The Italian judicial system is based on functional division of responsi-

---

[10] Even though the Constitution states explicitly that this appeal may be brought before the Constitutional Court by any citizen, these words must be understood as referring to any person and not only to Spanish citizens.

[11] See Article 13, the Italian Constitution, http://www.servat.unibe.ch/icl/it00000_.html#A013_. This article states: "(1) Personal liberty is inviolable. (2) No one may be detained, inspected, or searched nor otherwise restricted in personal liberty except by order of the judiciary stating a reason and only in such cases and in such manner as provided by law. (3) As an exception, under the conditions of necessity and urgency strictly defined by law, the police may take provisional measures that must be reported within 48 hours to the judiciary and, if they are not ratified within another 48 hours, are considered revoked and remain without effect. (4) Acts of physical and moral violence against persons subjected to restrictions of personal liberty are to be punished. (5) The law establishes the maximum duration of preventive detention".

[12] This catalogue of rights also includes the right to a fair trial within a reasonable time, which was incorporated into the Constitution (Article 111) in 1999.

[13] Italy became a Republic following the referendum of 2 June 1946, after a period of fascist regime and the Second World War (1933– 1945). The Italian Constitution, which sanctioned the Republican form of Government, was adopted on 22 December 1947 and entered into force on 1 January 1948.

bility. Ordinary courts are competent in civil and criminal matters. Specialized courts have been established to deal with administrative, tax and military issues. Other tribunals with specific competences are the Tribunal of Freedoms, which reexamines the provisions or measures restricting human rights, and the Juvenile Court, which receives claims and actions concerning minors. The Supreme Court of Cassation (*Corte Suprema di Cassazione*) is the supreme judicial organ of the State. This Court has the important function of guaranteeing the interpretation and objective adherence to the law. It also deals with conflicts of competence between ordinary judges, or between ordinary and special judges.[14]

There is also a Constitutional Court (ICC), which has both a jurisdictional and a political nature,[15] has competence over questions concerning the constitutional validity of all legal norms. Access to the Italian Constitutional Court is limited to judges or State bodies, and it is not available for individuals.[16] Thus, the Italian judicial system does not include a last resort individual appeal for the protection of constitutional rights similar to the Spanish *amparo* appeal. The existence in Spain of an internal appeal, specifically aimed at protecting human rights and provided as a last instance before lodging an application with the ECtHR, reduces the number of complaints brought against Spain before the ECtHR, an Italy does not possess.

III. The Reception of the ECHR

A. Historical Context: Accession and Ratification

1. Spain

a. Spain's Accession to the ECHR and its Additional Protocols
Newly-democratized Spain, a country that experienced one of the longest dictatorships in Europe (1939-75), prioritized becoming a Member State of the Council of Europe and a Contracting Party to the ECHR. In 1950, when the Convention was drafted in 1950, Spain was under Franco's rule, and any attempt to become a Member was doomed. On 24 November 1977, Spain became the twentieth Member State of the Council of Europe, signing the ECHR on the same day. On 4 October 1979,[17] once the Spanish Constitution of 1978

---

[14] See Onida (2006), 533.

[15] Cerri (2004), 34.

[16] As part of the Italian legal system, individuals cannot directly address the Constitutional Court with questions pertaining to the protection of fundamental rights, but only indirectly, in the course of a trial. In fact, the review of constitutionality is referred to the Constitutional Court by the competent judge either *ex officio* or on the basis of arguments advanced by the parties.

[17] BOE no. 243 of 10 October 1979, 23564. http://www.boe.es/g/es/bases_datos/doc.php?coleccion=iberlex&id=1979/24010&codmap=.

had been approved, it ratified the Convention[18] which entered into force on 10 November 1979. The initial ratification also included three declarations, two reservations, and the ratification of Additional Protocols nos 3, 5, and 11. The right for individuals to lodge an application with the Commission and the EC-tHR was recognized on 1 July 1981.[19]

Spain has signed all Optional Protocols to the Convention, with the exception of Protocols nos 9 and 10. Protocols nos 1, 2, 3, 5, 6, 8, 11, and 14 have been both signed and ratified, whereas Protocols nos 4, 7, 12, and 13 have been signed, but not yet ratified.[20] Spain did not ratify Protocols nos 4, 7, 12, and 13 on the grounds that they contained rights that were not fully provided for in domestic law. A clear example can be found in the area of migrants' rights, a very sensitive issue in which the Spanish Government has moved cautiously.

Upon ratification, Spain submitted two reservations. The first concerned Articles 5 and 6 ECHR in so far as they were incompatible with the provisions contained in Chapter XV of Part II and Chapter XXIV of Part III of the Spanish Code of Military Justice concerning the disciplinary regime of the Armed Forces. The Code of Military Justice was replaced by the Organic Law (*Ley Orgánica*) no. 12/1985 of 27 November 1985, which entered into force on 1 June 1986.[21] The new legislation amended the previous provisions by reducing the duration of deprivation of liberty that can be imposed without judicial intervention. Nonetheless, on 4 September 1986, Spain confirmed its reservations to Articles 5 and 6 ECHR in order to avoid incompatibilities with the provisions contained in Chapter II of Part III and Chapters II, III and IV of Part IV of Organic Law 12/1985 of 27 November.[22] In the *Dacosta Silva v. Spain*[23] case, the ECtHR took the view that the Spanish reservation regarding Articles 5 and 6 ECHR, which concerned the armed forces' disciplinary rules, did not apply to the disciplinary rules of the Civil Guard (*Guardia Civil*).

The second reservation, concerning Article 11 ECHR, aimed at averting conflict with Articles 28 and 127 of the Spanish Constitution. Article 28 of the Constitution recognizes the right of assembly and association, but provides that

---

[18] The most important achievement of the Constitution of 1978 has been its contribution to solving the historic problems of Spanish society. The establishment of a new State of Regional Autonomy (*Estado de las Autonomías*), the regulation of the role of the Crown and the de-establishment of the Church have become essential elements to channel internal conflicts.

[19] See BOE no. 155 of 30 June 1981, 14928, http://www.boe.es/g/es/bases_datos/doc.php?coleccion=iberlex&id=1981/14565 and BOE no. 254 of 23 October 10 1982, 29290, http://www.boe.es/g/es/bases_datos/doc.php?coleccion=iberlex&id=1982/27475&codmap=).

[20] http://conventions.coe.int/Treaty/Commun/ListeTraites.asp?PO=SPA&MA=999&SI=2&DF=&CM=3&CL=ENG

[21] BOE no. 286 of 29 November 1985, 37769.

[22] BOE no. 234 of 30 September 1986, 33400, http://www.boe.es/g/es/bases_datos/doc.php?coleccion=iberlex&id=1986/25799).

[23] *Dacosta Silva v. Spain* (appl. no. 69966/01), Judgement (Fifth Chamber), 2 November 2006 (not yet reported). The ECtHR found that the disciplinary penalty of six days' house arrest imposed on the applicant by his superior's order violated Article 5 (1) ECHR.

legislation may restrict the exercise of this right or subject it to an exception in the case of the armed forces or other corps subject to military discipline. Article 28 also provides that legislation shall regulate the right of assembly and association exercised by civil servants. In addition, Article 127(1) of the Constitution specifies that serving judges, law officers and prosecutors may belong neither to political parties nor trade unions, and provides that legislation shall lay down the system and modalities of association in these groups. Both reservations are still in force. Finally, Spain expressed a reservation in the light of Article 33 of the Spanish Constitution (right to property) with the aim of avoiding any uncertainty as to the application of Article 1 of Protocol no. 1.[24] The Spanish Constitutional Court has recently confirmed the existence of this reservation in its judgement 48/2005 of 3 March 2005.[25]

Finally, at the time of the ratification of the Convention, Spain declared that it would interpret the last sentence of Article 10(1) ECHR as being incompatible with the rules governing the organization of radio and television broadcasting in Spain. At the time, broadcasting constituted a State monopoly. In addition, Spain interpreted Articles 15 and 17 ECHR as allowing the adoption of measures contemplated in Articles 55 and 116 of the Spanish Constitution. These articles provide for the suspension of certain rights[26] when a state of emergency or siege is declared. In addition, Spain recognized, *ipso facto* and without special agreement, the compulsory jurisdiction of the ECtHR for an initial period of three years (as of 14 October 1979), a position renewed by subsequent declarations. With the entry in force of Protocol no. 11, this type of declaration became unnecessary.

---

[24] This reservation stipulates the following: "1. The right to private property and to inheritance is recognised. 2. The social function of these rights shall determine their scope, as provided for by law. 3. No person shall be deprived of their property or their rights except for a cause recognised as being in the public interest or in the interest of society and in exchange for fitting compensation as provided for by law".

[25] See Spanish Constitutional Court, judgement 48/2005 of 3 March 2005, BOE no. 81 of 5 April 2005, 62, http://www.boe.es/boe/dias/2005/04/05/pdfs/T00062-00074.pdf.

[26] These rights are those embodied in Article 17 (personal liberty), Article 18(2) and (3) (honour, privacy, home, secrecy of communications), Article 19 (freedom of movement), Articles 20 (1)(a) and (d) and (5) (specific rights), Article 21 (right of assembly), Article 28(2) (right of workers to strike), and Article 37 (2) (right of workers and employers to adopt measures concerning collective conflict).

Table 1

	Signature	Ratification	Entry into force	Declarations/Reservations
Protocol no. 1	23 Feb. 1978	27 Nov. 1990	27 Nov. 1990	1 reservation concerning Article 1[27]
Protocol no. 2	23 Feb. 1978	6 Apr. 1982	6 Apr. 1982	–
Protocol no. 3	24 Nov. 1977	4 Oct. 1979	4 Oct. 1979	–
Protocol no. 4	23 Feb. 1978			
Protocol no. 5	24 Nov. 1977	4 Oct. 1979	4 Oct. 1979	–
Protocol no. 6	28 April 1983	14 Jan. 1984	1 March 1985	–
Protocol no. 7	22 Nov. 1984			
Protocol no. 8	19 March 1985	23 June 1989	1 Nov. 1990	1 Declaration concerning Article 3[28]
Protocol no. 9	–	–	–	–
Protocol no. 10	–	–	–	–
Protocol no. 11	11 May 1994	11 may 1994	1 Nov. 1998	–
Protocol no. 12	4 Oct. 2005			
Protocol no. 13	3 May 2002			
Protocol no. 14	10 May 2005	15 Mars 2006	–	

b. Ratification Procedures

In Spanish law, the Government concludes international treaties. Under Article 94(1) of the Constitution, the ratification of treaties or agreements that affect fundamental rights and duties contained in Title I of the Spanish Constitution requires authorization of the Parliament,[29] through the majority vote of the Con-

---

[27] The Reservation contained in the instrument of ratification deposited on 27 November 1990 provides that: "In accordance with Article 64 of the Convention for the Protection of Human Rights and Fundamental Freedoms, in order to avoid any uncertainty as to the application of Article 1 of the Protocol, Spain expresses a Reservation in the light of Article 33 of the Spanish Constitution, which stipulates the following: "1. The right to private property and to inheritance is recognized. 2. The social function of these rights shall determine their scope, as provided for by law. 3. No person shall be deprived of their property or their rights except for a cause recognized as being in the public interest or in the interest of society and in exchange for fitting compensation as provided for by law". (Period covered: 27 November 1990–present).

[28] Declaration: "The Council of Ministers of the Kingdom of Spain has, on 7 December 1995, confirmed the signature *ad referendum*, subject to ratification, of Protocol no. 11 to the Convention for the Protection of Human Rights and Fundamental Freedoms, deposited at its time by the Secretary of State Mr Carlos Westendorp y Cabeza", declaration contained in a letter from the Permanent Representative of Spain, dated 6 February 1996, and registered at the Secretariat General on 8 February 1996, http://conventions.coe.int/Treaty/Commun/ListeDeclarations.asp?NT=155& CM=8&DF=1/29/2008&CL=GER&VL=1.

[29] Article 94 of the Spanish Constitution provides that: "(1) The giving of the consent of the State to obligate itself to something by means of treaties or agreements shall require prior authorization of

gress of Deputies and the Senate. The ECHR and its Protocols were subject to this procedure.

2. Italy

a. Italy's Accession to the ECHR and its Additional Protocols

Italy was one of the ten original signatories of the ECHR. It participated in the drafting of the Convention, and was the host State for its final signature. Italy signed the Convention on 4 November 1950 and ratified it on 25 October 1955, without reservation. In 1973, Italy accepted the right of individual petition before the ECHR. Since then, an impressive number of applications have been brought before the Court, mostly concerning procedural and criminal issues.[30]

Italy has ratified all Additional Protocols, with the exception of Protocol no. 12 (concerning non-discrimination) and Protocol no. 13 (regarding the abolition of capital punishment), which have only been signed. The sole declaration lodged by Italy concerned the application of Articles 2, 3 and 4 of Protocol no. 7[31]. Following this declaration, these provisions are to be applied according to the Criminal Procedure Code of 1988, and particularly in light of the "mixed accusatory" system. As part of this system, a criminal action can only be initiated by the Public Prosecutor and the instructing judge cannot both take part in the trial and in the judgement.

Table 2

Protocol	Signature	Ratification	Entry into force	Declarations/ Reservations
Protocol no. 1	20 March 1952	26 Oct. 1955	26 Oct. 1955	–
Protocol no. 2	6 May 1963	3 April 1967	21 Sept. 1970	–
Protocol no. 3	6 May 1963	3 April 1967	21 Sept. 1970	–
Protocol no. 4	16 Sept. 1963	27 May 1982	27 May 1982	–
Protocol no. 5	20 Jan. 1966	25 March 1968	20 Dec. 1971	–
Protocol no. 6	21 Oct. 1983	29 Dec. 1988	1 Jan. 1989	–

the Parliament in the following cases: a) Treaties of a political nature; b) Treaties or agreements of a military nature; c) Treaties or agreements which affect the territorial integrity of the State or the fundamental rights and duties established in Title I; d) Treaties or agreements which imply important obligations for the public treasury; e) Treaties or agreements which involve modification or repeal of some law or require legislative measures for their execution. (2) The House of Representatives and the Senate shall be immediately informed of the conclusion of the treaties or agreements".

[30] See *infra* Section C.2.

[31] The Italian declaration stated the following: "The Italian Republic declares that Articles 2 to 4 of the Protocol apply only to offences, procedures and decisions qualified as criminal by Italian law."

Protocol	Signature	Ratification	Entry into force	Declarations/ Reservations
Protocol no. 7	22 Nov. 1984	7 Nov. 1991	1 Feb. 1992	1 Declaration concerning Articles 2, 3, 4
Protocol no. 8	19 March 1985	29 Dec. 1988	1 Jan. 1990	–
Protocol no. 9	6 Nov. 1990	13 Dec. 1993	1 Oct. 1994	–
Protocol no. 10	25 March 1992	27 Feb. 1995	–	–
Protocol no. 11	21 Dec. 1994	1 Oct. 1997	1 Nov. 1998	–
Protocol no. 12	4 Nov. 2000	–	–	–
Protocol no. 13	3 May 2002	–	–	–
Protocol no. 14	13 May 2004	7 March 2006	–	–

b. Ratification Procedures

According to Italian constitutional law, the President of the Republic has the power to ratify international treaties.[32] In some specific cases governed by Articles 80 and 87 of the Constitution (treaties having a political nature, treaties dealing with modifications of the national territory, treaties having financial implications or implying modifications of laws), the ratification procedure requires Parliamentary authorization. Article 1 of Law no. 848 of 4 August 1955[33] contained the authorization from the Italian Parliament to ratify the ECHR and its Additional Protocols. Article 2 of this Law contained the so-called Implementing Order (*Ordine di Esecuzione*) which was needed to ensure its internal effectiveness.[34] The ECHR and the Additional Protocols entered into force on 26 October 1955.

3. Comparison and Conclusion

Both Spain and Italy joined the Council of Europe and ratified the ECHR after the fall of dictatorial regimes. The accession to the Council of Europe and to the ECHR represented a tremendous step for these two countries, giving them international recognition as democratic States and, by implication, encouraged the consolidation of democracy in their respective territories. Thus, the Italian and Spanish institutions demonstrated their commitment to democratic values.

Unlike Spain, which issued several declarations and reservations to the ECHR and its Protocols, Italy made only one declaration regarding the application of three provisions of Protocol no. 7. This is not surprising, as Italy actively participated in the elaboration of the Convention and fully shared its principles. The

---

[32] Presidential ratification is only a formal act. In order to be valid, it has to be proposed by the Government in accordance with Article 89 of the Italian Constitution.

[33] Gazzetta Ufficiale, 24 September 1955, no. 221.

[34] Article 2 stated: "Full and total compliance is given to the Convention and Protocol subject to their entry into effect."

Spanish declarations and reservations were necessary to avoid contradictions with the Spanish Constitution and existing laws. Spain also sought to avoid possible findings of violation by the Strasbourg bodies and, in particular, by the European Court of Human Rights. The fact that certain Protocols have yet to be ratified is due to the same fear of being brought before the Strasbourg Court for breaching the ECHR.

B. Status of the ECHR in National Law: Formal (Doctrinal) Elements

1. Spain

a. Relation between Domestic and International Law

In Spain, the domestic status of international treaties is established by Article 96(1) of the Constitution, which deals with the question of the general reception of international treaties in Spanish law. According to this provision, a validly concluded international treaty becomes part of national law once it is officially published. The ECHR has thus formed part of the Spanish legal system and has been binding upon the domestic courts since its publication.

Doctrinal authorities consider the Spanish system to be moderately monist. The official publication of treaties does not in itself constitute an act of incorporation but, rather, compliance with constitutional provision requiring the proclamation of legislative acts. This is a regular procedure that needs to be followed for the entry into force of all legislative acts adopted by the Spanish Parliament. As a result, validly concluded and officially published international treaties constitute applicable domestic law and are binding upon national courts and administrative authorities.

b. Status of the ECHR in the National Legal Order

The wording of the Constitution clearly addresses the question of the status of the ECHR within the Spanish legal system. Article 95 of the Spanish Constitution openly states that "the conclusion of any international treaty containing stipulations contrary to the Constitution shall require prior Constitutional amendment". Accordingly, the Spanish Constitution takes precedence over international rules. Treaties, including the ECHR, rank below the Constitution, and may be the subject of review by the SCC. This SCC has always recognized in its judgements the hierarchical superiority of the Constitution,[35] a view defended by most legal scholars.[36]

In contrast, international treaties take precedence over conflicting statutes. Article 96(1) of the Spanish Constitution provides that international treaties can only be repealed, amended or suspended in "the manner provided for in the

---

[35] See its declaration of 1 July 1992, points 2 and 4.
[36] Ruiz Miguel (1997), 110–112.

treaties themselves or in accordance with the general rules of international law".
This means that domestic laws cannot modify and suspend all or part of an international convention. The precedence of international treaties over statute also
follows from the so-called passive force of international treaties, which entails
that they cannot be modified by a national law. In any event, the Spanish Constitution clearly stipulates that posterior domestic laws can not derogate from
international treaties, a position confirmed by the SCC and doctrine.[37]

Although the ECHR does not possess constitutional status, and ranks below
the Constitution, it rapidly became an important source of reference in the interpretation of the rights and freedoms recognized by the Constitution. Article 10(2) of the Constitution provides that international human rights treaties
(naturally, including the ECHR and its Additional Protocols) constitute valid
sources of reference in the interpretation of constitutional rights.[38] Moreover,
the Constitutional Court recognized the binding interpretative effect of Article
10(2) of the Constitution and the direct effect of the ECHR. As a result, national
courts and all other national authorities are obliged to follow the case law of the
European Court of Human Rights. Gradually, references to the ECHR became a
regular component of judgements pertaining to human rights issues.

2. Italy

a. Relation between Domestic and International Law
Italy adopted a dualistic approach with regard to the status of international treaties in domestic law. International agreements cannot be applied domestically
until they are introduced into domestic law by means of a specific act of Parliament authorizing the ratification of the treaty and containing an order of execution of its provisions. The rank of international treaties in the Italian legal system
corresponds to the position occupied by the legal act containing the order of
execution.[39] International treaties that have been incorporated within the Italian national system can be submitted to constitutional control. In the event of a
violation of constitutional norms and values, this control may give rise to an annulment. Following an amendment in 2001, Article 117 of the Italian Constitution obliges the legislative authorities of the State and the regions to exercise their
powers in compliance with international law, including international treaties.[40]

---

[37] Mangas Martín (1994), 9–38.

[38] Ripol Carulla (2007), 143.

[39] Law no. 848 of 4 August 1955 provided for the ratification and enforcement of the ECHR.
The ECHR has thus acquired the rank of an ordinary law.

[40] Article 117 of the Constitution was amended by Article 3 of the Constitutional Law no. 3 of
18 October 2001. See Ivaldi (2003), 122–123.

b. Status of the ECHR in the National Legal Order

The ECHR, an international treaty, possesses the same rank as the instrument containing the execution order, namely the rank of ordinary law. Some legal scholars have argued that the ECHR has, or should have, constitutional status.[41] However, both the ICC and the Court of Cassation have firmly affirmed the non-constitutional value of its provisions.

As the ECHR does not have *per se* priority over ordinary law, the question then arises whether or not the Convention can be derogated from by a posterior conflicting legislation. Until very recently in Italy, there was no provision similar to Article 96 of the Spanish Constitution, establishing the primacy of international treaties over subsequent national legislation. After some hesitation, the ICC and the Court of Cassation have expressly affirmed that the ECHR's provisions cannot be derogated from, or repealed, by means of posterior national legislation. According to the Court of Cassation's ruling in the *Medrano* case,[42] the ECHR benefits from a particular "force of resistance" due to its particular nature of general principles of the legal system. This nature can be deduced in particular from the case law of the European Court of Justice requiring domestic courts to apply the ECHR's provisions as part of European Union law. Italian scholars defended the view that the Convention should be considered a *lex specialis* and thus cannot be derogated from by posterior conflicting legislation (*lex posterior generalis non derogat priori specialis*). However, since 2001 there is an obligation to fully and effectively implement the ECHR that derives from the new wording of Article 117(1) of the Italian Constitution.

For a long time, Italian courts refused to apply the Convention immediately, considering its provisions to be merely programmatic, not compulsory.[43] Both the Constitutional Court and the Court of Cassation developed incoherent bodies of case law on this issue. In some judgements, these courts maintained that the ECHR had a compulsory character, while in others they attributed only a programmatic value.[44] In recent judgements, the Court of Cassation stressed the binding nature and the direct applicability of the Convention.[45] In doing so, the Court declared that treaty norms are to be considered to be directly applicable where they establish complete, precise rights and obligations that can be enforced without further legislative acts on the part of the State. Determining direct effect

---

[41] See Randazzo (2006), 319.

[42] Court of Cassation, Criminal Section I, no. 2194, 10 July 1993, *Rivista di diritto internazionale* 77 (1994), 530, http://www.iuritalia.com.

[43] See Cass., sez. IV, *Biadene*, 11 October 1968.

[44] See, for example, Court of Cassation, Criminal Section, 12 February 1982, *D'Alessio e Fazio*, in Court of Cassation, Criminal Section, 1983, no. 1350; Giust. pen. 1983, III, no. 44; Riv. pen. 1983, no. 46 and Court of Cassation, Criminal Section I, 23 March 1983, *Fignanani*, in Cass. pen. 1984, no. 1453; Giust. pen. 1984, III, no. 226; Giur. it. 1984, II, no. 222.

[45] This has been particularly the case in the context of the application of the *Pinto* law. See especially Court of Cassation 26 January 2004 nos 1338, 1339, 1340, also in Giust. civ. Mass. 2004, 1, http://www.iuritalia.com.

depends on the specific context of the case in question, as well as on the nature and the scope of the right or obligation that is to be directly applied. Nonetheless, while the ECHR should certainly be regarded as a directly applicable treaty, this has not always been the case in practice.

On 24 October 2007, the Constitutional Court handed down two judgements which will further stimulate scholarly debate.[46] Based on Article 117(1) of the Italian Constitution, the ICC declared for the first time the unconstitutionality of a national law (the Italian legislation on the refund for unlawful expropriation) on grounds that it contravened Article 1 of the Protocol no. 1 (right to private property). As noted above, Article 117(1) of the Constitution states that national law shall comply with international law. As a consequence, national laws that are incompatible with international treaties, such as the ECHR, violate Article 117 of the Constitution. According to the ICC, this constitutional provision also imposes an obligation upon judges to interpret domestic rules in accordance with international provisions. When this is not possible, national judges must bring the issue before the ICC Court in order to obtain a declaration of unconstitutionality of the relevant provision, as was the case here.[47]

In these two judgements of 24 October 2007, the Italian Constitutional Court chose to address the question of ECHR's status in the national legal order. After presenting a clear summary of the history of legislative and judicial treatment of the Convention, the Constitutional Court confirmed once again its infra-constitutional character.[48] In the Court's view, neither Article 10 nor Article 11 of the Italian Constitution grants constitutional status to international treaties. Nonetheless, the Constitutional Court distinguished the directly applicable of EU obligations from obligations originating from Italy's membership in the Council of Europe, which cannot be directly applied.[49] The direct applicability of the Convention is still a sensitive issue in Italy[50], and the two judgements of 24 October 2007 will undoubtedly be a subject of debate among legal scholars.

---

[46] Constitutional Court, 24 October 2007, no. 348, published in Gazzetta Ufficiale, 31 October 2007; Constitutional Court, 24 October 2007, no. 349, published in Gazzetta Ufficiale, 31 October 2007, http://www.cortecostituzionale.it.

[47] The Constitutional Court found that Article 5-*bis* comma 7-*bis*, Law Decree no. 333/1992, as applied by Law no. 359/1992, was unconstitutional.

[48] In relation to this issue, the Constitutional Court cited its judgements nos 388/99 and 188/1980 as well as its ordinance no. 464/2005, Constitutional Court judgement, 22 October 1999, no. 388, published in Gazzetta Ufficiale 27 October 1999, http://www.cortecostituzionale.it; Corriere Giuridico, 1999, 12, 1553. Constitutional Court sentence 22 October 1980 no. 188, published in Gazzetta Ufficiale 31 December 1980, no. 357, http://www.cortecostituzionale.it; Giurisprudenza Italiana, 1981, I, 639. Constitutional Court ordinance 23 December 2005, no. 464, published in Gazzetta Ufficiale 28 December 2005, http://www.cortecostituzionale.it.

[49] According to judgements nos 348 and 349, the ECHR is not directly applicable, unlike EU law. The Constitutional Court only established an obligation for domestic judges to interpret Italian law in conformity with the Convention, if there is room for such an interpretation. Otherwise, they should raise the constitutionality issue before the Constitutional Court, which remains the interpretative authority of Article 117 of the Constitution.

[50] For a detailed analysis of this question, see the Bin, Brunelli, Pugiotto and Veronesi (2007).

Finally, it is important to note that, as in Spain, courts use the Convention as a guide for interpreting constitutional rights. The dynamic interpretation of the ECHR by the Court had a significant impact on Italian criminal law, as illustrated below.[51] In the Italian Constitution there is, however, no provision analogous to Article 10(2) of the Spanish Constitution, leading the ICC to approach the Convention as it would any other international treaty.

3. Comparison and Conclusion

The above analysis reveals significant differences between Spain and Italy. These countries have chosen different incorporation models, and have attributed to the ECHR a different legal rank and status. In Spain, the ECHR ranks between the Constitution and ordinary legislation. In Italy, the Convention occupies a lower position than in Spain, ranking on par with ordinary domestic law. Neither country accepts the superiority of the Convention in relation to the Constitution. The incorporation of the ECHR in Spain, however, seems to be less controversial than in Italy for several reasons. First, Article 96(1) of the Spanish Constitution of 1978 expressly grants primacy to international treaties over national laws (once they are published in the State Official Journal). Until recently Italy did not have a similar provision. The recent revision of Article 117 of the Constitution coupled with the Constitutional Court's judgements of 24 October 2007 invites new perspectives for improving the reception of the Convention's provisions in Italian law.

Second, the SCC has clearly stressed the direct applicability of the Convention and the ECtHR's case law in Spain. In contrast, Italy has shown a reticence to recognize the direct binding effect of the Convention. Hopefully, the recent case law of the ICC will help to solve this problem, as that Court has clearly confirmed the constitutional duty of the Italian legislator and national courts to comply with international norms when adopting and interpreting statutes.

Third, the constitutional obligation to interpret constitutional human rights in the light of the international conventions exists in Spain, but not Italy. References to the ECHR by Spanish national courts, including the ConstitutionalCourt, appeared to be logical and even necessary. As there was no legal tradition to protect fundamental rights during Franco's regime, the ECtHR's case law became a source of interpretation of constitutional rights, which is itself a mechanism of reception.

Although the Convention is typically portrayed as representing minimum common denominator standards of rights protection, in both countries the Convention plays an important role in the interpretation of the protection of fundamental rights. The common view is that domestic standards should prevail, provided that they are higher than the ECHR's standards. The Spanish legal lit-

---

[51] See *infra* Section C.2.b.

erature unanimously admits that the interpretation clause contained in Article 10(2) of the Spanish Constitution prohibits reducing standards of protection provided by the Spanish Constitution. Italian scholars have also accepted the primacy of higher domestic standards over the ECHR's provisions.

C. Overview of the Activity of the European Court of Human Rights

1. *Spain*

a. General Observations

The ECtHR issued its first finding of violation against Spain in 1988, ten years after ratification of the Convention. Through 31 December 2006, the Court has decided 56 cases against Spain on the merits,[52] and there have been two friendly settlements.[53] Until then, the number of applications lodged amounted to 7,978. Furthermore, the Court found violations on 35 occasions. Most claims against Spain are based on alleged violations of rights under Articles 6 (fair trial/excessive length of procedures), 8 (right to private and family life) and 10 ECHR (right of freedom of expression). Up to now, the number of decisions against Spain has been rather low. This situation can be firstly explained by the high level of protection granted to fundamental rights in the Spanish Constitution of 1978, which is bolstered by the existence of the *amparo* appeal. Individuals can only seize the European Court after the exhaustion of all internal legal remedies and, in Spain, this exhaustion normally requires the lodging of an *amparo* before the SCC. It represents an additional opportunity to redress human rights violations before a petitioner can go to Strasbourg. In practice, most situations concerning human rights violations are redressed by the SCC. The *amparo* appeal has thus turned out to be a very effective tool for protecting human rights and for ensuring the application of the ECHR.[54]

b. Selected Examples

Although the number of Spanish cases brought before the European Court is relatively low, compared to Italy, condemnations regarding Spain revealed the

---

[52] For more information see,
   http://www.echr.coe.int/ECHR/EN/Header/Reports+and+Statistics/Statistics/Statistical+information+by+year.

[53] See *Trome S.A. v. Spain* (appl. no. 27781/95), Judgement (Fourth Section), 1 April 1999, Reports 1999-III, 1; *Díaz Ruano v. Spain* (appl. no. 16988/90), Judgement (Chamber), 26 April 1994, Series A, Vol. 285-B.

[54] As noted above, the Constitutional Court affirmed the direct applicability of the Convention in the Spanish legal order. The Court often relies on the Strasbourg Court's case law for interpreting the scope of Spanish constitutional rights. See STC 303/1993, 25 October 1993, FJ 8. By contrast, the Spanish Constitutional Court has expressly refused to follow the Human Rights Committee's interpretation of the rights embodied in the International Covenant of Civil and Political Rights, as this Committee lacks judicial powers (see STC 296/2005, 21 November 2005, FJ 3).

obsolete character of certain laws, the lack of sufficient procedural guaranties before domestic courts, and the unreasonable length of legal proceedings. Other cases underlined internal tensions (independence movements and terrorism) and the need to refer to a supra-national jurisdiction to interpret the scope of certain freedoms, such as the freedom of expression. More recently, the Strasbourg Court has handed down landmark decisions in Spanish cases concerning environmental issues. This report concentrates on cases that had the most important impact on Spanish law and society, namely those based on Articles 3, 5, 6, 8 and 10 ECHR.

aa. Articles 3 and 5 ECHR Case Law. In the *Martinez Sala and Others v. Spain* case,[55] the European Court was not satisfied that the inquiries carried out by the investigating judge had been sufficiently thorough in light of the requirements of Article 3 ECHR.[56] The applicants, who were suspected of being sympathizers of a Catalan independence movement, were arrested by the Civil Guard in connection with an investigation into terrorist activities. They complained that they were ill-treated while in custody. The Strasbourg Court noted that, although members of the security forces were involved, the investigating judge failed to take statements from the arresting officers and custody officers. The Court concluded that the judicial authorities had dismissed all the applicants' requests for evidence to be obtained, thereby denying them a reasonable opportunity to participate and respond to findings.

In *Scott v. Spain*,[57] the Strasbourg Court held that the four year term of pre-trial detention imposed on the applicant was contrary to Article 5(3) ECHR in that it could not be justified by the alleged crime or the public interest. In its view, the extradition proceedings in question should have been conducted more diligently and expeditiously. This judgement underlines the problem of the excessive work load of the Spanish courts.

bb. Article 6 ECHR Case Law. In *Barberà, Messegue and Jabardo v. Spain*,[58] the Strasbourg Court considered that the national court had conducted proceedings in a way that did not satisfy the requirements of a fair and public hearing. The ECtHR identified various irregularities (there was an unexpected change in the composition of the Court, the defendants were tried after a sleepless night, etc.) which affected the right to a fair and public trial. In another famous ruling, *Ruiz*

---

[55] *Martínez Salas and Others v. Spain* (appl. no. 41893/98), Judgement (Second Section), 26 July 2001 (not reported).

[56] Ibid., para. 28.

[57] *Scott v. Spain* (appl. no. 21335/93), Judgement (Chamber), 18 December 1996, Reports 1996-VI, 27 et seq.

[58] *Barberà, Messegue and Jabardo v. Spain* (appl. nos 10588/83; 10589/83; 10590/83), Judgement (Plenary), 6 December 1988, Series A, Vol. 146.

Mateos v. Spain,[59] the Court noted that the principle of equality of arms as required by Article 6(1) ECHR had been violated in the proceedings before the Spanish Constitutional Court. This case concerned an expropriation in the public interest of all the shares of a large holding of companies. Alleging that the expropriation was unlawful, the applicants instituted civil proceedings in order to obtain a restitution of the shares. They subsequently asked the Court of First Instance to submit to the Constitutional Court the question whether the relevant law was in conformity with the various provisions of the Spanish Constitution. The SCC answered in the affirmative. In its ruling, however, the Strasbourg Court pointed out that the Counsel for the State had lodged observations before the SCC to which the applicants had not been given the opportunity to reply. In *Hiro Balani v. Spain*,[60] the European Court reiterated that Article 6(1) ECHR imposed an obligation upon domestic courts to give reasoned judgements, but did not require giving a detailed answer to every argument. Following the Court's judgement, the extent of this duty will vary according to the nature of the decision and the circumstances of each case.

The Strasbourg Court has also addressed the right to be judged within a reasonable time on several occasions.[61] The first violation was found in the *Unión Alimentaria Sanders S.A. v. Spain* case (1989)[62] where the Court criticized the domestic courts' late response to the applicant's claim. In *Ruiz Mateos v. Spain*,[63] the Court underlined that the proceedings had lasted seven years and nine months. Even the proceedings before the SCC – which should be the highest guarantor of the right in question – took two years. It is, therefore, not surprising that the Strasbourg Court concluded that Article 6(1) ECHR had been violated. In *González Doria Durán de Quiroga v. Spain*,[64] the Court noted that the national proceedings against the appellants had lasted for more than fourteen years. Even accepting that there had been complex features in these cases, the Court held that there was a breach of the reasonable time requirement laid down in Article 6(1) ECHR. The excessive length of proceedings was also invoked in *Alberto Sanchez v. Spain*.[65] In this case, the Spanish administrative system was the direct object of the Court's finding of violation. The Court noted that recruitment proceed-

---

[59] *Ruiz Mateos v. Spain* (appl. no. 12952/87), Judgement (Plenary), 23 June 1993, Series A, Vol. 262.

[60] *Hiro Balani v. Spain* (appl. no. 18064/91), Judgement (Chamber), 9 December 1994, Series A, Vol. 303-B.

[61] Ripol Carulla (2007), 161–165.

[62] *Unión Alimentaria Sanders S.A. v. Spain* (appl. no. 11681/85), Judgement (Chamber), 7 July 1989, Series A, Vol. 157.

[63] *Ruiz Mateos v. Spain* (*supra* note 59).

[64] *González Doria Durán de Quiroga v. Spain* (appl. no. 59072/00), Judgement (Fourth Section), 28 October 2003 (not reported).

[65] *Alberto Sanchez v. Spain* (appl. no. 72773/01), Judgement (Fourth Section), 16 November 2004 (not reported).

ings which lasted more than five years did not comply with the reasonable time requirement of Article 6 (1) ECHR.

In *Castillo Algar v. Spain*,[66] the Strasbourg Court pointed to the lack of impartiality of a military court in which two judges had previously upheld on appeal the decision whereby the applicant had been found guilty and sentenced to imprisonment. The Court considered that, in the circumstances of the case, the impartiality of the Trial Court could be open to genuine doubt and that the applicant's concerns about the lack of an impartial judgement could be considered objectively justified. Accordingly, it concluded that there had been a violation of Article 6(1) ECHR. The right to an impartial judge was again invoked before the Court in the *Perote Pellón* case.[67] In its judgement, the Court noted that two of the judges of the trial court in question (the President and judge *rapporteur*) had played a role in the investigation that gave rise to the applicant's conviction and seven-years sentence of imprisonment. In *Pescador Valero v. Spain*,[68] the Court observed that the national judge had regular and close professional connections with the applicant's opponents in the proceedings, and found objectively justified the applicant's doubts regarding the impartiality of the Spanish judge.

cc. Article 8 ECHR Case Law. In a set of landmark ECtHR judgements concerning environmental issues, the Court found a way of ensuring the protection of the environment on the basis of the right to respect for private and family life, as guaranteed by Article 8 ECHR. *López Ostra v. Spain*[69] concerned the problem of water contamination caused by a waste-treatment plant located near the applicant's home. In this case, the Spanish Court accepted that the nuisances at issue impaired the quality of life of those living in the plant's vicinity, but concluded that the impairment did not amount to an infringement of the fundamental rights recognized by the Constitution. Surprisingly, the Strasbourg Court quashed this ruling by referring to Article 8 ECHR. The Court stated that severe environmental pollution might affect individuals' well-being and prevent them from enjoying their homes in such a way as to affect their private and family life without, however, seriously endangering their health. The Court underlined the need for finding a fair balance between the competing interests of the individual and

---

[66] *Castillo Algar v. Spain* (appl. no. 28194/95), Judgement (Chamber), 28 October 1998, Reports 1998-VIII (no. 95), 3103.

[67] *Perote Pellón v. Spain* (appl. no. 45238/99), Judgement (Fourth Section), 25 July 2002 (not reported).

[68] *Pescador Valero v. Spain* (appl. no. 62435/00), Judgement (Fourth Section), 17 June 2003, Reports 2003-VII, 117. In this case, the applicant worked as the head of administrative staff on the campus of Albacete University. After eleven years of service, he was removed from his post. The applicant complained that the judge in charge of the case was a Visiting Professor at the University of Castilla-La Mancha and hence had professional and financial links with the University. The Court held unanimously that there had been a violation of Article 6 (1) ECHR.

[69] *López Ostra v. Spain* (appl. no. 16798/90), Judgement (Chamber), 9 December 1994, Series A, Vol. 303-C.

the interests of the community as a whole. In the present case, the Court found that the municipal authorities had failed to strike a fair balance between the interest of the town's economic well-being (that of having a waste-treatment plant) and the applicant's effective enjoyment of her right to private and family life. Consequently, the Court ruled that there was a violation of Article 8 ECHR, an unusual interpretation of Article 8 ECHR that has attracted the attention of scholars.[70]

The *Moreno Gómez v. Spain* judgement[71] followed. In this case, the Court dealt again with an environmental issue (a noise problem) and the national authorities' violation of the applicant's right to respect for her home and her private life. Its progressive interpretation of the notion of respect for home and privacy led the ECtHR to consider noise pollution through the prism of Article 8 ECHR. In this case, the applicant complained of noise from nightclubs situated near her home. She alleged that the Spanish authorities were responsible to control the nuisance[72], and that the resulting "noise pollution" constituted a violation of her right to respect for her home. The Spanish Constitutional Court dismissed the *amparo* appeal, holding that the applicant had neither proven the existence of a direct link between the noise and the alleged damage, nor the existence of a nuisance in her home amounting to a violation of a constitutional right. The Strasbourg Court noted, however, that the applicant lived in an area that was indisputably subject to night-time disturbances, which clearly unsettled her daily life. Thus, it held that there was no need to require a person from an acoustically saturated zone to adduce evidence of a fact which was officially known by the local authorities.[73] In view of the volume of the noise and the fact that it had lasted for years, the Court found a violation of the applicant's right to respect for her home and her private life under Article 8 ECHR. This was the first time that excessive noise was found to be the cause of a violation of Article 8 ECHR.

In the *Valenzuela Contreras v. Spain* judgement,[74] the Court dealt with the question of the monitoring of telephone lines ordered by an investigating judge in connection with criminal proceedings against the appellant. The Court held that the tapping of Mr. Valenzuela Contreras' line constituted interference by a

---

[70] See Carrillo Donaire and Galán Vioque (1995), 271.

[71] *Moreno Gómez v. Spain* (appl. no. 4143/02), Judgement (Fourth Section), 16 November 2004, Reports 2004-X, 327.

[72] It should be noted that in 1996 the City Council designated the area where the applicant lived as an acoustically saturated zone. Thereby, it imposed a ban on new activities that led to acoustic saturation, such as the opening of new bars. Despite the ban, the City Council granted a licence a month later for a discotheque to be opened in the building in which the applicant lived.

[73] An independent police report to the City Council indicated that the local residents' complaints were well founded and that nightclubs and discotheques in the sector did not systematically close on time. In addition, an independent report commissioned by the City Council showed that the noise levels were unacceptable and exceeded permitted levels.

[74] *Valenzuela Contreras v. Spain* (appl. no. 27671/95), Judgement (Chamber), 30 July 1998, Reports 1998-V (no. 83), 1909.

public authority within the meaning of Article 8(2) ECHR.[75] The Court noted that there was a legal basis in Spanish law for such a measure, and that the law was accessible to the applicant.[76] The text of the Spanish law was not, however, sufficiently clear to give citizens an adequate indication as to the circumstances in, and the conditions under which, public authorities were empowered to use this prerogative. Consequently, the applicant did not enjoy the minimum degree of legal protection to which citizens are entitled under the rule of law in a democratic society. The *Prado Bugallo v. Spain* case[77] revealed that the deficiencies of the Spanish laws regarding telephone-tapping measures persist.[78]

dd. Article 10 ECHR Case Law. In *Castells v. Spain,*[79] the Court considered that the penalties imposed on a senator of the Basque separatist group, for writing a newspaper article criticizing the Government's anti-terrorist policy, constituted a violation of his freedom of expression. The Court also recalled that freedom of expression constituted one of the essential foundations of a democratic society and one of the basic conditions for its progress. It also underlined the particular importance of this right when it concerns elected representatives of the people. The ECtHR observed, however, that the competent State authorities could adopt measures, even of a criminal nature, to react appropriately and without excess to expression devoid of factual foundation or formulated in bad faith. In this particular case, the Court took the view that many of the assertions contained in the article had been an attempt to establish their truth. The interference had, therefore, not been necessary in a democratic society. There had been accordingly a violation of Article 10 ECHR.

It is worth noting that at the time of writing there are two pending cases before the ECtHR concerning the compatibility of national decisions declaring

[75] In its judgements *Kruslin v. France* (appl. no. 11801/85), Judgement (Chamber), 24 April 1990, Series A, Vol. 176-A and *Huvig v. France* (appl. no. 11105/84), Judgement (Chamber) 24 April 1990, Series A, Vol. 176-B, the European Court listed the minimum safeguards that national laws must include in order to avoid abuses of power: (i) a definition of the categories of people liable to have their telephones tapped by judicial order; (ii) the nature of the offences which may give rise to such an order; (iii) a limit on the duration of telephone tapping; (iv) a procedure for drawing up the summary reports containing intercepted conversations; (v) the precautions to be taken in order to communicate the recordings intact and in their entirety for possible inspection by the judge and by the defence and (vi) the circumstances in which recordings may or must be erased or the tapes destroyed, in particular where an accused has been discharged by an investigating judge or acquitted by a court.

[76] Article 18(3) of the Constitution, upon which the investigating judge mainly based the order for the applicant's telephone line to be monitored, provides that "communications, particularly postal, telegraphic and telephone communications, should be confidential unless the court decides otherwise".

[77] *Prado Bugallo v. Spain* (appl. no. 58496/00), Judgement (Fourth Section), 18 February 2003 (not reported). See Catalá i Bas (2003), 173.

[78] For a study of the relevant Spanish laws in the *Valenzuela Contreras* and *Prado Bugallo* cases, see Martín-Retortillo Baquer (2003), 377–406.

[79] *Castells v. Spain* (appl. no. 11798/85), Judgement (Chamber), 23 April 1992, Series A, Vol. 236.

the dissolution of political parties and Article 10 ECHR. Both illustrate important tensions in Spain between the fight against terrorism and the protection of fundamental rights and freedoms. In these pending cases, two political parties, *Batasuna* and *Herri Batasuna*, have challenged the judgement of the Spanish Supreme Court, which was later upheld by the SCC, declaring their illegality (based on the links they had with the terrorist separatist group *ETA* and their failure to dissociate themselves from *ETA*'s terrorist activities). As a consequence, the Supreme Court also ordered the liquidation of their assets. The applicants lodged *amparo* appeals before the Constitutional Court, which were dismissed on 16 January 2004.

2. Italy

a. General Observations
Up to 31 December 2006, 38,304 applications were lodged with the ECtHR against Italy, the peak being 2000 with 7,339 applications. During this period, the Court found that Italy had violated the ECHR on 1,358 occasions. Two violations concerned Article 3 ECHR, nine violations concerned to Article 5(1) ECHR; five violations related to Articles 5(3) to 5(5) ECHR; 1,220 violations concerned Article 6(1) ECHR; twenty violations regarded Article 6(3) ECHR; 63 violations concerned Article 8 ECHR; one violation related to Article 10 ECHR; three violations related to Article 11 ECHR; 37 violations related Article 13 ECHR; 254 violations concerned Article 1 of Protocol no. 1; twelve violations concerned Article 3 of Protocol no. 1; and fourteen violations concerned Article 2 of Protocol no. 4. The greatest annual number of violations handed down by the Court was 360 in 2001.

b. Selected Examples
The subjects addressed in the Italian cases before the ECtHR are very diverse. They range from situations regarding the right to life,[80] compensation for damage caused by unfair detention, preventive custody, the impartiality and independence of judges, the assistance of an interpreter in the proceedings, the principle of equality of arms, telephone-tapping, the right of assembly and association, the excessive length of both civil and criminal proceedings, civil rights of prisoners and the protection of private property. The majority of Italian cases concern Article 6 ECHR (right to a fair trial and length of proceedings) and, most recently, Article 1 of the Protocol no. 1 (right to property). Landmark decisions were handed down by the ECtHR, in particular, on trials conducted *in absentia*.

---

[80] *Calvelli and Ciglio v. Italy* (appl. no. 32967/96), Judgement (Grand Chamber), 17 January 2002, Reports 2002-I, 25.

aa. Article 6 ECHR Case Law. The question of conviction *in absentia* was addressed for the first time by the ECtHR in *Colozza v. Italy.*[81] In this emblematic case, the Court stressed that a person charged with a criminal offence is entitled to take part in the hearings on the basis of his right to a fair trial and his right to a defence included in Articles 6(1) and 6(3) ECHR. The ECtHR stated that the Italian system lacked an instrument allowing the accused to have a fresh trial once he became aware of the proceedings against him, if he had not previously renounced his right to defence. As a result, the Court concluded that Italy did not display the diligence expected to ensure the protection of the requirements contained in Article 6 ECHR. In *F.C.B. v. Italy,*[82] again, the Court emphasized that the appellant was absent from the hearing and had not expressly renounced his rights. More recently, in *Somogyi v. Italy,*[83] the appellant, sentenced *in absentia,* claimed not to have received any notice of the trial. The ECtHR decided that the domestic jurisdiction had failed to verify if the accused had any way of knowing about the charges brought against him. In the *Sejdovic v. Italy* case,[84] the ECtHR similarly found a violation of Article 6 ECHR, as the applicant was convicted *in absentia* without having been informed of the trial against him. The Court noted that the applicant, who had neither sought to escape trial nor waived his right to appear, had no means of obtaining a new ruling by the domestic Court on the charges. The ECtHR stressed that there was a shortcoming in Italian domestic law that could lead to new violations in the future. Consequently, Italy should take the appropriate measures for ensuring respect of the rights guaranteed by Article 6 ECHR (a so-called "pilot ruling").

The excessive length of proceedings is one of the most serious problems that the Italian judicial system faces, and it has given rise to a steady stream of violations of the reasonable time criterion enshrined in Article 6(1) ECHR.[85] In the *Foti* and *Corigliano* cases,[86] the ECtHR ruled that, with a view to measuring the length of proceedings, the clock shall begin from the moment when official intervention starts to have serious repercussions for the individual. Italy was found to have breached Article 6 ECHR on several occasions due to the excessive delays in

---

[81] *Colozza v. Italy* (appl. no. 9024/80), Judgement (Chamber), 12 February 1985, Series A, Vol. 89.

[82] *F.C.B. v. Italy* (appl. no. 12151/86), Judgement (Chamber), 28 August 1991, Series A, Vol. 208-B.

[83] *Somogyi v. Italy* (appl. no. 67972/01), Judgement (Second Section), 18 May 2004, Reports 2004-IV, 103.

[84] *Sejdovic v. Italy* (appl. no. 56581/00), Judgement (First Section), 10 November 2004 (not reported); *Sejdovic v. Italy* (appl. no. 56581/00), Judgement (Grand Chamber), 1 March 2006 (not yet reported).

[85] See, for example, *Foti v. Italy* (appl. no. 7604/76), Judgement (Chamber), 10 December 1982, Series A, Vol. 56; *Corigliano v. Italia* (appl. no. 8304/78), Judgement (Chamber), 10 December 1982, Series A, Vol. 57; *Capuano v. Italia* (appl. no 9381/81), Judgement (Chamber), 25 June 1987, Series A, Vol. 119; and *Salesi v. Italia* (appl. no. 13023/87), Judgement (Chamber), 26 February 1993, Series A, Vol. 257-E.

[86] *Foti v. Italy,* ibid; *Corigliano v. Italy,* ibid.

the administration of justice. As illustrated in *Di Mauro v. Italy*,[87] this situation constitutes an important concern for the respect of the rule of law and an unacceptable practice under the Convention.

bb. Article 8 ECHR Case Law. Findings of violations have been handed down against Italy in cases where the right to private and family life was invoked in relation to environmental issues. In *Guerra v. Italy*,[88] the Court condemned Italy for not having informed inhabitants of the health risks posed by their proximity of a chemical factory releasing toxic substances. The ECtHR considered that Italy's omissions interfered with the private and family life of the applicants. In *Giacomelli v. Italy*,[89] The Court found a violation of Article 8 ECHR in respect to the harmful emissions of a plant for storage and treatment of waste, located 30 meters from the applicant's house. The Court condemned Italy for not having carried out an environmental-impact assessment of the plant, as required by the national legislation.

Article 8 ECHR has also been invoked before the Strasbourg Court for the restrictions imposed on prisoners' correspondence by the Prison Administration Act of 1975.[90] Under this law, Italian judges could order the censorship of all prisoners' correspondence for public order and security considerations. Although the law required the judicial decision imposing the restriction to be reasoned, it failed to specify the circumstances under which such an order could take place.

cc. Article 1 of Protocol no. 1 Case Law. The lawfulness and the conformity of the so-called "constructive expropriation" (*occupazione acquisitiva* or *accessione invertita*) with the ECHR has been the question of hundreds of applications. This procedure permitted the Italian Public Administration to take possession of lands without following the formal expropriation procedure. The majority of these petitions concerned the issue of land expropriation and the insufficient compensation awarded to individuals for the deprivation of their property. As a result, the Court focused on the issue of proportionality, in other words, on checking the existence of a fair balance between the State's interests and the protection of the

---

[87] *Di Mauro v. Italy* (appl. no. 34256/96), Judgement (Grand Chamber), 28 July 1999, Reports 1999-V, 31. See also *Bottazzi v. Italia* (appl. no. 34884/97), Judgement (Grand Chamber), 28 July 1999, Reports 1999-V, 1; *Ferrari v. Italia* (appl. no. 33440/96), Judgement (Grand Chamber), 28 July 1999 (not reported). See *infra* Section D.2.b. regarding the *Pinto* law as a general remedy.

[88] *Guerra and Others v. Italy* (appl. no. 14967/89), Judgement (Grand Chamber), Reports 1998-I (no. 64), 210.

[89] *Giacomelli v. Italy* (appl. no. 59909/00), Judgement (Third Section), 2 November 2006 (not yet reported).

[90] Law no. 354 of 26 July 1975, Gazzetta Ufficiale, Supplemento Ordinario, 9 August 1975, no. 212. See *Calogero Diana v. Italy* (appl. no. 15211/89), Judgement (Chamber), 15 November 1996, Reports 1996-V, 1774–1777, paras 26–41 and *Domenichini v. Italy*, (appl. no. 15943/90), Judgement (Chamber), 15 November 1996, Reports 1996-V, 1798–1802, paras 26–42.

individual's right to property.[91] In *Belvedere Alberghiera v. Italy*,[92] *Carbonara and Ventura v. Italy*[93] and *Scordino v. Italy*,[94] the Court criticized the discrepancies between Italian courts in the interpretation of the rule on constructive expropriations resulting in arbitrary outcomes that deprived litigants of effective protection of their rights.[95] In *Prenna v. Italy*,[96] the ECtHR held that the occupation of private land in order to carry out construction work without an expropriation order and without compensation infringed Article 1 of the Protocol no. 1.[97]

In contrast to the initial judgements in which it focused on the issue of adequate compensation, the ECtHR's more recent case law analyzes the legality of expropriation itself. As a result, two situations may be distinguished: First, the situation of lawful expropriation that is not followed by adequate compensation (the *Stornaiuolo v. Italy*[98] and the *Scordino v. Italy (No. 1)*[99] judgements) and second, the situation of illegal expropriation resulting from a constructive expropriation (the *Scordino (No. 3)* judgement[100] of 17 May 2005). In both situations, the ECtHR found a violation of Article 1 of the Protocol no. 1 and applied Article 46 ECHR requesting the Italian authorities to adopt specific implementation measures.[101]

3. Comparison and Conclusion

While Spain is among the States that generate the lowest number of cases brought before the Strasbourg Court, Italy is among those that generate the highest number of such cases. The difference is partly explained by the structural factors already discussed: the clear recognition of the ECHR's primacy over national law

---

[91] See *Zubani v. Italy* (appl. no. 14025/88), Judgement (Chamber), 7 August 1996, Reports 1996-IV (no. 14), 1067.

[92] *Belvedere Alberghiera s.r.l. v. Italy* (appl. no. 31524/1996), Judgement (Second Section), 30 May 2000, Reports 2000-VI, 135.

[93] *Carbonara and Ventura v. Italy* (appl. no. 24638/1994), Judgement (Second Section), 30 May 2000, Reports 2000-VI, 91.

[94] *Scordino v. Italy (No. 1)* (appl. no. 36813/97), Judgement (First Section), 29 July 2004, (not reported); *Scordino v. Italy (No. 3)* (appl. no. 43662/98), Judgement (Fourth Section), 17 May 2005 (not yet reported); *Scordino v. Italy (No. 3)* (appl. no. 43662/98), Judgement (Fourth Section), 6 March 2007 (not yet reported).

[95] For examples of judgements of the Court of Cassation that did not follow the ECtHR's guidance, and where it was found that the acquisitive occupation (*occupazione acquisitiva*) was fully legal and compatible with the ECHR, see Court of Cassation, United Sections, no. 5902/2003 in Giust. civ. Mass. 2003, 4 and Cassation United Sections 6853/2003 in Giust. civ. Mass. 2003, 5, http://www.iuritalia.com.

[96] *Prenna and Others v. Italy* (appl. no. 69907/01), Judgement (Third Section), 9 February 2006 (not yet reported), paras 60–70. See also *Genovese and Others v. Italy* (appl. no. 9119/2003), Judgement (Third Section), 2 February 2006 (not yet reported), paras 58–77.

[97] See Conti (2006), 225.

[98] See *Stornaiuolo v. Italy* (appl. no. 52980/1999), Judgement (Fourth Section), 8 August 2006 (not yet reported).

[99] See *Scordino v. Italy (No. 1)* (*supra* note 94).

[100] See *Scordino v. Italy (No. 3)* (*supra* note 94).

[101] See *Belvedere Alberghiera s.r.l. v. Italy* (*supra* note 92).

in Spain, but not Italy; the direct applicability of the Convention is more contro-versial in Italian than in Spanish law; and the filtering function of *amparo* review in Spain, which does not exist in Italy.

In both countries, the bulk of the violations concerned Article 6(1) ECHR, particularly the right to a fair trial and the right to be judged in a reasonable period of time. This reflects the problem of the workload of the courts in both domestic systems, and the need to organize the judiciary in a more efficient way. In Italy, a problematic area concerns trials *in absentia*, which are permitted by law and occur frequently. In Spain, the lack of access to independent courts has been a more serious problem. In both countries, breaches of Article 8(1) ECHR related to both the right to privacy and the right to family life. Nonetheless, more violations of Article 10(1) ECHR (freedom of expression) have been found in Spanish cases than in Italian cases.

With regard to Italy it is important to underline that an important number of recent cases decided against this country and still pending before the ECtHR concern the violation of the right to property (Article 1 of the Protocol no. 1). In all these Italian cases, one finds the problem of sufficient compensation in situations of public expropriation, and the lack of coherent actions on part the administrative and judicial bodies. This reveals a significant problem of legal cer-tainty and good governance.

In the future, both Italy and Spain will face similar challenges as part of the fight against international terrorism. As a consequence of the terrorist attacks of 11 September 2001 in New York and 11 March 2004 in Madrid, both countries have introduced new amendments to their respective Criminal Codes. Spain, for example, is facing challenges with regard to the conditions of detention of al-leged national or international terrorists. The Spanish Criminal Procedure Code contains severe restrictions to the right to defence, which will be explored in more depth in subsequent sections.[102] Italy has also modified its Criminal Code[103] on several occasions and adopted new measures concerning the expulsion of in-dividuals presumed to be involved in terrorist organizations and/or activities.[104] Under the new law, individuals can be expelled from Italy after having been acquitted, following a fair trial, of international terrorist activities under Article 270bis of the Criminal Code[105] The ECtHR has recently adopted interim meas-ures to prevent the expulsion of two Moroccans who had already been tried in

---

[102] See *infra* Section D.1.b on the remedial action taken by the Spanish judiciary.

[103] See Law of 15 December 2001 no. 438 (*Urgent provisions for combating international ter-rorism*), which inserted a second paragraph in Article 270 *bis* of the Criminal Code and added an Article 270*ter*.

[104] See also Law of 31 July 2005 no. 155, Article 3, in Gazzetta Ufficiale No. 177, 1 August 2005, which provides for the immediate expulsion of individuals against whom there is reasonable suspicion that their continued presence would in any way facilitate terrorist activity on the national and international levels.

[105] See Ordinance of 29 and 31 May 2007 no. 20640, no. 21867 and no. 20659; regarding two Moroccan citizens, El Kaflaoui e Zergout, acquitted of the crime of terrorism in Italy and requested

Italy, and who faced the risk of being subjected to an unfair trial and torture in the country demanding their extradition. It is, therefore, very likely that in the near future the ECtHR will be faced with Italian and Spanish cases concerning the treatment of terrorist suspects and the issue of expulsion.

D. The European Court's Case Law and its Effects in the National Legal Orders

1. Spain

Under Article 46(1) of the ECHR, Contracting States must abide by the Court's judgements in cases to which they are party.[106] Undoubtedly, the remedies to be implemented by the respondent States vary from case to case. Legislative amendments, the adoption of new laws, and the modifications of the national courts' case law are the most relevant forms of remedies for the purpose of the present study[107] as they constitute direct examples of the effects of the Court's case law on the national legal orders. This section will first provide examples of the main legislative amendments, which took place in Spain as a result of the compliance with the Strasbourg decisions. It will then briefly outline the impact of the ECtHR's rulings on the case law of the Spanish Constitutional Court.[108]

a. Remedial Action Taken by the Spanish Legislature

In seven judgements, the European Court found that the relevant Spanish legislation was contrary to the Convention,[109] leading to amendment. Moreover, judgements of the Strasbourg Court in cases involving other States, such as *De Cubber v. Belgium*,[110] have also provoked amendments of Spanish law. The most important legislative changes are described below.

aa. Right to a Fair and Public Hearing. During the proceedings in *Barberà, Messegué and Jabardo v. Spain*,[111] the Organic Law no. 6/1985 of 1 July 1985 was

---

by the Moroccan authorities. See also Guarino (2007), 9. Please ensure that citations of domestic law are uniform everywhere in the report.

[106] See Leuprecht (1993), 792.

[107] The obligation to abide by the Court's judgements also comprizes a duty to prevent new violations of the same kind from occurring.

[108] See also Ripol Carulla (2007), 143.

[109] These cases are *Barberà, Messegue and Jabardo v. Spain* (*supra* note 58); *Unión Alimentaria Sanders S.A. v. Spain* (appl. no. 11681/85), Judgement (Chamber), 7 July 1989, Series A, Vol. 157; *Ruiz Mateos v. Spain* (*supra* note 59); *Pérez de Rada Cavanilles v. Spain* (appl. no. 28090/95), Judgement (Chamber), 28 October 1998, Reports 1998-VIII (no. 96), 3242; *Valenzuela Contreras v. Spain* (*supra* note 74); *Perote Pellón v. Spain* (*supra* note 67) and *Miragall Escolano and Others v. Spain* (appl. nos 38366/97; 38688/97; 40777/98; 40843/98; 41015/98; 41400/98; 41446/98; 41484/98; 41487/98; 41509/98), Judgement (Fourth Section), 25 January 2000, Reports 2000-I, 297.

[110] *De Cubber v. Belgium* (appl. no. 9186/80), Judgement (Chamber), 26 October 1984, Series A, Vol. 86.

[111] *Barberà, Messegue and Jabardo v. Spain* (*supra* note 58).

adopted, which modified the functioning of the judicial system.[112] This new law introduced the possibility to request the annulment of judicial decisions that violate the principle of a fair hearing, the right to be assisted by counsel, or the right to defence. As this law did not fully remedy the breach of Article 6(1) ECHR found by the Court, two more Organic Laws (Organic Laws nos 3/1988 and 4/1988 of 25 May 1988) were adopted to amend the Spanish Criminal Code and the Code of Criminal Procedure.[113] As a result of the new amendments, judges were no longer authorized to extend the time of arrest by seven days but only by 48 hours. New amendments were also introduced to comply with the *De Cubber v. Belgium*[114] and the *Piersack v. Belgium*[115] judgements. For the first time, the Organic Law no. 7/1988 introduced a clear separation between the judicial function of investigation and the judicial function of handing down judgements.[116]

bb. The Right to Be Judged Within a Reasonable Time. The reasonable time guarantee provided by Article 6 ECHR to protect parties against excessive procedural delays has been improved in Spanish law after the *Unión Alimentaria Sanders S.A. v. Spain*[117] and *Ruiz Mateos v. Spain*[118] cases. *Ruiz Mateos v. Spain* led to the adoption of a constitutional amendment through the Organic Law no. 6/1988 of 9 June 1988.[119] Under this new law, the Constitutional Court can reject inadmissible *amparo* appeals by means of a summary procedure. In December 1988, a new law on the territorial organization of the judicial system was adopted.[120] This law reorganized judicial districts and redefined the territorial jurisdiction of the courts. In the aftermath of the *Unión Alimentaria Sanders S.A. v. Spain* decision,[121] the Spanish Government adopted three important regulations increasing the number of courts. The Royal Decree (*Real Decreto*) of 25 May 1989 created the creation of single-judge courts, labour courts and juvenile courts. The Royal Decree of 21 July 1989 established criminal courts of first instance. Finally, the Royal Decree of 17 November 1989 provided for the creation of civil courts of first instance and investigation courts. The objective of the above measures was to reduce the work load of domestic courts and to speed up pending proceedings.

cc. The Right to an Impartial Judge. Several ECtHR judgements handed down against Spain raised the question of the independence and impartiality of the

---

[112] See BOE no. 157 of 2 July 1985, 20632.
[113] See BOE no. 126 of 26 Mai 1988, 16159.
[114] *De Cubber v. Belgium* (*supra* note 110).
[115] *Piersack v. Belgium* (appl. no. 8692/79), Judgement (Chamber), 26 October 1984, Series A, Vol. 85-B.
[116] BOE no. 313 of 30 December 1988, 36573.
[117] *Unión Alimentaria Sanders S.A. v. Spain* (*supra* note 109).
[118] *Ruiz Mateos v. Spain* (*supra* note note 59).
[119] BOE no. 140 of 11 June 1988, 18314.
[120] Organic Law no. 7/1988 (*supra* note 116).
[121] For a comment on this judgement, see Tejera Victory (1991), 89.

military judiciary.[122] Following the *Perote Pellón v. Spain* judgement,[123] a new Law no. 9/2003 of 15 July 2003 was adopted on the competence and organization of military courts. This law amended the previous Law no. 4/1987 to introduce additional guarantees concerning the composition of military courts and the procedural rules applied by military judges sitting on such courts. One of these guarantees was the reduction of the number of judges sitting on appeals (from five to three) with a view to avoiding the situation that appeared in *Perote Pellón v. Spain* in which the same judge heard the case at first instance and on appeal.

dd. Right to Privacy. Following the *Valenzuela Contreras v. Spain* case[124] concerning the issue of telephone tapping, the law in force at the time was amended by Implementing Act no. 4/1988 of 25 May 1988. In addition, the new version of Article 579 of the Code of Criminal Procedure, as amended by the 1988 Act, was to be applied and interpreted by domestic courts in accordance with the meaning of judgements of the European Court of Human Rights.[125]

b. Remedial Action Taken by the Spanish Judiciary
The extensive impact of the ECHR on the Spanish judiciary can be explained by the need for Spanish courts and, in particular, the Constitutional Court to clarify the scope of certain constitutional rights. During the first years of democracy, the ECHR and the case law of the ECtHR became a highly helpful source of reference for interpreting constitutional rights.[126] This Section will focus on the impact of the ECHR in the case law of the SCC, the guarantor of the constitutional rights in Spain. In a number of important cases, the Tribunal has referred expressly to the Strasbourg Court's case law.

aa. Right to Life. On several occasions, the SCC declared the unconstitutionality of all or part of the statutes on the ground that there was a violation of the Convention.[127] One of the first significant judgements of the SCC was the judgement 53/1985[128] which concerned the draft Organic law partially decriminalizing abortion (*Proyecto de Ley Orgánica de reforma del art. 417 bis del Código Penal*). In

---

[122] See Ripol Carulla (2007), 165–168.
[123] *Perote Pellón v. Spain* (*supra* note 67).
[124] *Valenzuela Contreras v. Spain* (*supra* note 74).
[125] See the Supreme Court's judgement of 18 June 1992.
[126] The growing number of references to the ECHR as a source of interpretation can be explained by the existence of Article 10(2) of the Spanish Constitution. This provision stipulates that "the norms relative to basic rights and liberties which are recognized by the Constitution shall be interpreted in conformity with the Universal Declaration of Human Rights and the international treaties and agreements on those matters ratified by Spain". Between these international agreements, the ECHR detains a prominent position.
[127] See Ripol Carulla (2007), 143–181.
[128] STC 53/1985 of 11 April 1985, BOE no. 119 of 18 Mai 1985, 10, http://www.boe.es/g/es/bases_datos_tc/doc.php?coleccion=tc&id=SENTENCIA-1985-0053.

its judgement 53/1985 of 11 April 1985,[129] the SCC referred to the ECtHR's decision of 13 May 1980 which interprets Article 2 ECHR as referring to persons already born, and not to those yet to be born, for the purpose of determining the scope of this right.[130]

bb. Right to Personal Liberty. Pursuant to the ECtHR's case law under Article 5 ECHR, the SCC developed a doctrine of criminal process providing for the protection of the rights of the defendant who is presumed to be innocent until proven guilty.[131] The constitutional doctrine follows the Strasbourg case law on the procedural guarantees relating to pre-trial detention. These guarantees require that individuals be informed of the reasons for their detention and be brought promptly before a judge.[132] In order to determine whether someone has been deprived of his liberty, the SCC followed the *Riera Blume and Others v. Spain* judgement[133] of the Strasbourg Court in its judgement 82/2003 of 5 May 2003.[134] In this context, "[i]n order to determine whether someone has been deprived of his liberty within the meaning of Article 5, the starting-point must be his concrete situation, and account must be taken of a whole range of criteria such as the type, duration, and manner of implementation of the measure in question (...)".[135] In relying on this reasoning, the Constitutional Court gave a new orientation to the domestic legal principles that had been followed by ordinary courts.

cc. Rights of the Defence. The SCC has also considered Article 6 ECHR in numerous judgements. In its ruling of 27 September 1989, the SCC enjoined on domestic courts and national authorities to strictly observe the rights of the accused and the rights to defence in line with the Strasbourg case law.[136] Following

---

[129] See Olmos Giupponi and Díaz Barrado (2003), 35.

[130] D 8416/1979, of 13 Mai 1980, DR, 19, 244, points 9 and 17.

[131] See STC 114/1984 of 29 November 1984.

[132] See STC 224/1998, of 24 November 1998. Currently, Spanish law still contains several restrictions on the rights of persons arrested under suspicion of membership in an armed or terrorist group in terms of both the length and the conditions of detention. This situation has been criticized by the Special Rapporteur, Theo van Boven, in his Report on the question of torture on his visit to Spain, issued in February 2004, 11–13, http://www.unhchr.ch/huridocda/huridoca.nsf/2848af408 d01ec0ac1256609004e770b/c590bcf72e791fa6c1256e5b006bfa70/$FILE/G0410716.pdf).

[133] *Riera Blume and Others v. Spain* (appl. no. 37680/97), Judgement (Fourth Section), 14 October 1999, Reports 1999-VII, 1. In this case the applicants, who were thought to be members of a cult, complained of the unlawfulness of their deprivation of liberty by the Catalan authorities. The ECtHR noted that even though the applicants' families had had the immediate responsibility for the supervision of the applicants during their deprivation of liberty (they were kept under supervision in a hotel), this breach of their liberty could not have taken place without the active cooperation of the domestic authorities. Accordingly, the Strasbourg Court held that there had been a violation of Article 5(1) ECHR.

[134] STC 82/2003 of 5 Mai 2003, BOE no. 118 of 17 Mai 1983, 70, http://www.boe.es/boe/dias/2003/05/17/pdfs/T00070-00075.pdf).

[135] See *Riera Blume and Others v. Spain,* (*supra* note 133), para. 28.

[136] This duty has been confirmed by the Constitutional Court in its judgement of 21 December

the *Campbell and Fell v. United Kindgom* judgement[137] of the Strasbourg Court, the SCC quickly accepted that the expression "all persons" contained in Article 6 ECHR also included aliens.[138] Further, by referring to *Pammel v. Germany*,[139] *Estima Jorge v. Portugal*,[140] *Pailot v. France*[141] and *Mavronichis v. Cyprus*[142] in its case law, the Constitutional Court required that the question of the reasonable length of proceedings be assessed in the light of the complexity of the case as well as the conduct of the applicant and the competent authorities. The right to be assisted by a lawyer, chosen by the accused, and the right to free legal aid have been interpreted by the SCC[143] in the light of the Strasbourg Court's holdings in *Airey v. Ireland*,[144] *Artico v. Italy*[145] and *Pakelli v. Federal Republic of Germany*[146]. Regarding the right to be tried by an independent and impartial tribunal established by law, there is also a consolidated national jurisprudence based on the *De*

1989 and of 14 October 1990. The Supreme Court has also affirmed this duty in its judgements of 11 March and 19 July 1988.

[137] *Campbell and Fell v. United Kindgom* (appl. nos 7819/77; 7878/77), Judgement (Chamber), 28 June 1984, Series A, Vol. 80.

[138] See STC 99/1985 of 30 September 1985.

[139] *Pammel v. Germany* (appl. no. 17820/91), Judgement (Chamber), 1 July 1997, Reports 1997-IV, 1096 et seq. This case concerned the issue of the length of proceedings that involved a preliminary ruling before the Constitutional Court to review the constitutionality of a legislation that was relevant to the case.

[140] *Estima Jorge v. Portugal* (appl. no. 24550/94), Judgement (Chamber), 21 April 1998, Reports 1998-II (no. 69), 762. The case concerned proceedings which had lasted for thirteen years. The ECtHR noted that the competent authorities were responsible for a number of delays and held that there had been a violation of Article 6(1) ECHR.

[141] *Pailot v. France* (appl. no. 32217/96), Judgement (Chamber), 22 April 1998, Reports 1998-II (no. 69), 787. This case concerned the length of compensation proceedings brought by a haemophiliac infected with the AIDS virus following blood transfusions. The ECtHR held that even if the case was complex, the French Court had the information it needed to determine the State's responsibility. According to the ECtHR, the personal situation of the applicant (the disease he was suffering from) called for an exceptional diligence of the competent authorities.

[142] *Mavronichis v. Cyprus* (appl. no. 28054/95), Judgement (Chamber), 24 April 1998, Reports 1998-II (no. 71), 944.

[143] See STC 105/1999 of 14 June 1999.

[144] *Airey v. Ireland* (appl. no. 6289/73), Judgement (Chamber), 9 October 1979, Series A, Vol. 32. In this case, the European Court noted that the applicant did not enjoy an effective right of access to the Irish High Court and accordingly it held that there had been a violation of Article 6 (1) ECHR.

[145] *Artico v. Italy* (appl. no. 6694/74), Judgement (Chamber), 13 May 1980, Series A, Vol. 37. In this case, the appellant – who was sentenced, *inter alia,* to imprisonment for fraud – complained before the European Court that the proceedings before the Italian court had taken place in his absence. The Strasbourg Court confirmed that the object and purpose of Article 6 ECHR is to ensure that individuals charged with a criminal offence are entitled to take part in the proceedings.

[146] *Pakelli v. Federal Republic of Germany* (appl. no. 8398/78), Judgement (Chamber), 25 April 1983, Series A, Vol. 64. In this case, Article 6(3) ECHR was violated since the applicant was refused legal aid in order to be represented in the Federal Court, which was going to hold an oral hearing. The Strasbourg Court considered that "the personal presence of the applicant could not compensate for the lack of a legal practitioner to examine the legal issues arising".

Cubber v. Belgium case[147] that insists on the need to separate the functions between the investigating and the instructing judges.

As far as the right to call and examine witnesses is concerned, the SCC referred to the *Delta v. France* judgement[148] of the ECtHR to indicate the requirements that needed to be respected with regard to indirect witness evidence.[149] The Tribunal applied the Strasbourg case law under which the accused should be given an adequate and proper opportunity to challenge and question a witness against him, either at the time when the witness makes his statement or at some later stage in the proceedings.

dd. Right to Privacy. With regard to the right to private and family life, the SCC quickly adopted the broad interpretation of this right, as given by the European Court. The SCC echoed the *Lopez Ostra v. Spain* case[150] in which the appellant sued the City Council of Valencia for the disturbances caused to her private life and health by the noise of the bars located near her home. In its judgement 119/2001 of 24 May 2001, the SCC analyzed the question of the protection of individuals against noise from the perspective of Article 15 ECHR (physical and moral integrity) and Article 18 (privacy) of the Spanish Constitution. Following the ECtHR's case law, it held that "a constant exposure to preventable and unbearable noises deserves the protection given to the fundamental right to the personal and family privacy at home".[151]

Regarding the confidentiality of communications, the SCC referred in its judgement 114/1984 of 29 November 1984[152] to the ECtHR's ruling in *Malone v. the United Kingdom*.[153] In particular, it recalled that the use of information relating to the date and the length of telephone conversations or to the numbers dialled can give rise to a breach of Article 8 ECHR. In its judgement 49/1996 of 26 March 1996, the SCC referred to *Klass and Others v. Germany*,[154] *Malone v. the United Kingdom*,[155] *Kruslin v. France* and *Huvig v. France*[156] to introduce the

---

[147] *De Cubber v. Belgium* (*supra* note 110).

[148] *Delta v. France* (appl. no. 11444/85), Judgement (Chamber), 19 December 1990, Series A, Vol. 191-A.

[149] STC 35/1995 of 6 February 1995; STC 146/2003 of 14 July 2003.

[150] *López Ostra v. Spain* (appl. no. 16798/90), Judgement (Chamber), 9 December 1994, Series A, Vol. 303-C.

[151] See STC 119/2001 of 24 Mai 2001, BOE no. 137 of 8 June 2001, 56, http://www.boe.es/boe/dias/2001/06/08/pdfs/T00056-00066.pdf).

[152] See para. 7.

[153] *Malone v. the United Kingdom* (appl. no. 8691/79), Judgement (Plenary), 2 August 1984, Series A, Vol. 82, para. 84.

[154] *Klass and Others v. Federal Republic of Germany* (appl. no. 5029/71), Judgement (Plenary), 6 September 1978, Series A, Vol. 28.

[155] *Malone v. the United Kingdom* (*supra* note 153).

[156] *Kruslin v. France* (appl. no. 11801/85), Judgement (Chamber), 24 April 1990, Series A, Vol. 176-A and *Huvig v. France* (appl. no. 11105/84), Judgement (Chamber), 24 April 1990, Series A, Vol. 176-B. These cases concerned the issue of telephone tapping carried out by senior police officers under a warrant issued by an investigating judge. The ECtHR considered that French law,

requirements of proportionality with regard to the legitimate aim that warrants be issued for ordering telephone interventions.[157] In its judgement 184/2003, of 23 October 2003, the Constitutional Court applied without reluctance the *Prado Bugallo v. Spain* judgement.[158]

ee. Protection of Freedom of Expression. The Constitutional Court cited *Handyside v. the United Kingdom*[159] and *Nilsen and Johnsen v. Norway*[160] to stress the importance of the freedom of expression for the functioning and development of the democratic process. It also noted that limitations imposed on this right must be proportionate to the legitimate aim pursued.[161] With regard to the interpretation of the right to freedom of expression in the armed forces, the Constitutional Court followed *Engel and Others v. the Netherlands*[162] to justify the particular aspects of the freedom of expression of the military.[163]

2. Italy

The ECtHR's case law has strongly influenced the Italian legal system both at the legislative and judicial levels.[164] Nonetheless, a large number of ECtHR judgements have not yet been fully implemented, due to delays in the adoption of remedial legislation. The Committee of Ministers has made a good number of declarations indicating that some measures still need to be adopted by Italy in order to comply with the Convention's obligations.[165]

---

written and unwritten, did not indicate with reasonable clarity the scope and manner of the exercise of intercepting communications. As a result, the defendants had not enjoyed the minimum degree of protection to which citizens were entitled under the rule of law in a democratic society. Accordingly, the European Court held that there had been a violation of Article 8 ECHR.

[157] See para. 3.

[158] *Prado Bugallo v. Spain* (*supra* note 77).

[159] *Handyside v. the United Kingdom* (appl. no. 5493/72), Judgement (Plenary), 7 December 1976, Series A, Vol. 24.

[160] *Nilsen and Johnsen v. Norway* (appl. no. 23118/93), Judgement (Grand Chamber), 25 November 1999, Reports 1999-VIII, 57.

[161] See STC 171/90 and STC 62/1982.

[162] *Engel and Others v. the Netherlands* (appl. nos 5100/71; 5101/71; 5102/71; 5354/72; 5370/72), Judgement (Plenary), 23 November 1976, Series A, Vol. 22-B. In this case, the applicants were soldiers serving in the Netherlands Armed Forces. Before the ECtHR, they complained of the penalties that had been imposed on them by their respective commanding officers for their offences against the military discipline.

[163] STC 371/1993 of 13 December 1993.

[164] See Randazzo (2006), 319 and Nascimbene (2006), 645.

[165] See Resolution CM/ResDH (2007) 83: Execution of the decisions of the Committee of Ministers. Case of Dorigo against Italy; Resolution CM/ResDH (2007) 84: Execution of the Judgements of the European Court of Human Rights. Non-Execution of court orders to evict tenants Immobiliare Saffi and 156 other cases against Italy.

a. Remedial Action Taken by the Italian Legislature

aa. Fair Trial and Trials in Absentia. Given the many occasions in which the ECtHR has found violations of Article 6 ECHR, the Italian legislator has acted to comply with the ECtHR's decisions. One of the most significant legislative improvements was the adoption of a new Criminal Code in 1989. An important number of provisions contained in this Code have implemented the judicial guarantees provided by Article 6 ECHR (fair trial, reasonable length of proceedings and right to be present in the proceedings, etc.), as interpreted by the Strasbourg Court. Furthermore, a new Article 111 of the Constitution, implementing the right to a fair trial as required by the Convention, was enacted. The preparatory work for the modification of Article 111 of the Constitution, and particularly the Report of the Parliamentary Commission of Constitutional Affairs, underlined the need to incorporate the ECHR into the Italian Constitution as the only way of ensuring that the ECHR had a full effect in the Italian legal system. To not do so, it was argued, domestic courts would not feel bound to apply the Convention.

Following the ECtHR's judgements in *F.C.B. v. Italy,*[166] *Somogyi v. Italy,*[167] and *Sejdovic v. Italy,*[168] the Criminal Procedural Code was modified in order to implement the right to a new trial for individuals condemned *in absentia.* Italian law limits this right to individuals who were not unequivocally aware of the trial against them, and who had not explicitly waived their right to defence.

bb. Length of Proceedings . Italy has been found to have breached the Convention on a regular basis due to the excessive length of domestic proceedings.[169] The Committee of Ministers recognized the inadequacy of the Italian situation and the risk that it implied for a democratic State based on the rule of law. As a consequence, different measures were adopted to alleviate this problem, among them the so-called *Pinto* law. Issued by the Italian Parliament in 2001,[170] this law introduces a legal remedy before the competent national court which allows individuals to obtain compensation when their right to have the case heard within a reasonable time had been breached.[171] It lays down the criteria that must be followed by judges to verify the reasonable length of the trial, consider the impact of such

---

[166] *F.C.B. v. Italy* (appl. no. 12151/86), Judgement (Chamber), 28. August 1991, Series A, Vol. 208-B.

[167] *Somogyi v. Italy* (*supra* note 83).

[168] *Sejdovic v. Italy* (appl. no. 56581/00), Judgement (Grand Chamber), 1 March 2006 (not yet reported).

[169] See, for example, *Foti v. Italy* (*supra* note 85); *Corigliano v. Italia* (*supra* note 85); *Capuano v. Italia* (*supra* note 85); *Salesi v. Italia* (*supra* note 85); *Di Mauro v. Italy* (*supra* note 87); *Bottazzi v. Italia* (*supra* note 87) and *Procaccini v. Italy* (appl. no. 31631/96), Judgement (Fourth Section), 30 March 2000, (not reported).

[170] Law no. 89 of 24 March 2001, in Gazzetta Ufficiale, 3 April 2001, no. 78.

[171] For a comment of this Law, see Cittarello (2003), 145 and Lana (2004), 9.

length on the case, and to quantify the damage (patrimonial and moral). The Court of Cassation[172] clearly underlined that one of the problematic aspects of the application of the *Pinto* law concerned the definition of the reasonable length of proceedings and the quantification of patrimonial and moral damages.

The first judgements handed down following the entry into force of the *Pinto* law revealed significant differences in its interpretation by the national judges and the Strasbourg judges.[173] Italian judges have long refused to consider the right to be tried within a reasonable period of time as a fundamental human right, in contradiction with the Strasbourg case law wherein damages are automatically awarded according to the gravity of the violation of the reasonable length of proceedings.[174] The domestic interpretation of Article 6(1) ECHR brought new complaints before the ECtHR.[175] It is now clear that the *Pinto* law has proven incapable of resolving the problems for which it was adopted.

Practice, however, has shown that even if this legal remedy has somewhat reduced the number of applications before the ECtHR, it has also created an extra burden on domestic courts in terms of litigation. As a result, in March 2007, the legislative authorities adopted a law to reduce the length of domestic civil proceedings.[176] The new law concerning the provisions for the rationalization and the acceleration of civil trials provides more powers for judges with regard to the management of hearings. Article 52 of the Law establishes the maximum duration of the trial proceedings: two years for first instance trials and two years for appeal trials. Unfortunately, the Law also incorporates an exception to the above time limits in cases of particularly complicated trials.

cc. Secrecy of Correspondence. Following the ECtHR's findings that restrictions imposed on prisoners' correspondence violated Article 8 ECHR, the Italian Parliament adopted in 2004 a new provision (Article 18*ter*) establishing more clearly the conditions required to monitor prisoners' correspondence, and forbidding any form of censorship with respect to the correspondence between the detainees and their lawyers or international human rights organizations.

dd. Protection of Private Property. A new Article 43 was added to the existing law regarding expropriation,[177] to prevent future findings of violation of Article 1 of Protocol no. 2. However, the Strasbourg Court has already noted in two recent

---

[172] Court of Cassation, Section I, 9 September 2005, no. 17999, http://www.iuritalia.com.

[173] For a study of the impact of the *Pinto* law in administrative courts, see Mirate (2006), 425.

[174] See Court of Cassation, Judgement of 3 November 2005 no. 21318, http://www.cortedicassazione.it. See also the journal *Giurisprudenza Italiana* 3 (2007) 617.

[175] Recent judgements of the Court of Cassation applied the compensation criteria proposed by the ECtHR. See Court of Cassation, judgment of 26 January 2004, no. 1340, in *Rivista di diritto internazionale* 87 (2004), 534.

[176] The so-called *Disegno di legge Mastella*, 23 March 2007, http://www.giustizia.it.

[177] Legislative decree of 6 June 2001 no. 327 in force since 30 June 2003, in Gazzetta Ufficiale, 16 August 2001, no. 189, Supplemento Ordinario no. 211.

cases (*Sciarrotta*[178] and *De Sciscio*[179]) that the amendment does not fully comply with its case law.

b. Remedial Action Taken by the Italian Judiciary

The application of the ECHR by the Italian judiciary has been neither immediate nor unanimous. As noted above, this is mainly due to the fact that the Italian Constitution neither provides for the automatic reception of international treaties nor accords them a supra-legislative status once ratified. The reluctance on the part of the courts to apply the Convention's provisions may also be explained by the fact that they overlap to a great extent with the human rights provisions embodied in the Italian Constitution. Domestic courts seem to be more inclined to refer to the Italian constitutional norms rather than to the European standards. This is particularly the case with administrative courts, which normally refer to the ECHR or to the Strasbourg case law only in order to reinforce argumentation based on domestic law. They do not treat the ECHR or the ECtHR's case law as an autonomous source of law in their decisions. This situation may create difficulties in the application of the Convention.[180] Occasionally, Italian courts have faced the choice of either applying the case law of the Constitutional Court which has been found to contravene the Convention by the Strasbourg Court, or applying the ECHR with the risk of their judgement being overruled by a higher court.

Nevertheless, remedial action has been taken by domestic courts and in particular by the Constitutional Court and the Court of Cassation, in response to ECtHR's adverse judgments.[181] There are some interesting cases concerning the right to private property. For example, in the cases concerning expropriation and fair compensation, Italian judges are still confronted with the dilemma of applying Italian law, which has been found by the ICC to be compliant with the Italian Constitution,[182] while nonetheless considered to be in breach of Article 1 of Protocol no. 1 by the ECtHR. Some Italian courts have been drawn to the ECtHR's case law, trying to find possible ways of interpreting the existing domestic law in the light of the Convention's principles.[183] The Court of Cassation

---

[178] *Sciarrotta and Others v. Italy* (appl. no. 14793/02), Judgement (Third Section), 12 January 2006 (not yet reported), para. 69.

[179] *De Sciscio v. Italy* (appl. no. 176/04), Judgement (First Section), 20 April 2006 (not yet reported), para 74.

[180] See, for instance, a decision of the Council of State that excluded the application of Article 6 ECHR, invoked by the applicant, in relation to the guarantee of legal assistance of his own choice during an administrative proceeding imposing disciplinary sanctions, Cons. Stato, Sez. IV, 10 March 2004, no. 1115, http://www.giustizia-amministrativa.it.

[181] As a result of the Strasbourg Court's judgement in the *Somogyi v. Italy* (*supra* note 83), the Court of Cassation ordered the reopening of the proceedings conducted *in absentia*. See judgement of 12 July 2006, no. 32678, http://www.cortedicassazione. it. See also Conti (2007), 680.

[182] Constitutional Court, Judgement 148/1999, http://www.cortecostituzionale.it, published in Gazzetta Ufficiale, 7 June 2000.

[183] The Court of Appeal of Florence adopted a judgement in the *Squadrelli v. National Street Au-*

finally brought before the Constitutional Court the issue of incompatibility of domestic law on expropriation (especially the question of equitable compensation) with the Italian Constitution.[184] In recent cases, the Constitutional Court decided that the law on expropriation was unconstitutional on the basis of Article 117 of the Italian Constitution, which gives priority to international law (in this case Article 1 of the Protocol no. 1) over contradictory national law,[185] thus ratifying the Strasbourg Court's position.

Of course, the influence of the Strasbourg case law varies according to the matter at hand. With regard to the right to a fair trial, and in particular to the principle of the reasonable duration of trial proceedings, the Court of Cassation held that the *Pinto* law must be interpreted in the light of Strasbourg case law. The judgements of the ECtHR, in this regard, have a binding effect.[186] In addition, several domestic judgements concerning the right to a new trial (*Catberro*,[187] *Somogyi*[188] and *Dorigo*[189] cases) have been based on the ECtHR's case law and have underlined the need for Italy to adopt new legislation. For instance, in the *Dorigo* case, the Court of Cassation called upon the judge to request that all final judgements which violate the due process guarantees contained in Article 6 ECHR not be enforced. The Court of Cassation recognized the urgent need for legislative intervention in order to set up the right to a new trial not only in the case of trials *in absentia*, but also in all cases where violations of the right of defence have been identified.

3. Comparison and Conclusion

Remedial action at the legislative level in Italy appears to have been less effective than in Spain, not least, because the amendments took considerable time and did not always give full effect to the relevant ECtHR decision. The high number of applications brought annually before the Court against Italy regarding the issue of trials *in absentia* provides a good illustration of this statement.

thority case, Civil Section I, sentence 27 February 2005, no. 570, granting a total refund of damages to unlawfully dispossessed landowners, corresponding to a real *restitutio in integrum*.

[184] See Court of Cassation, ordinance nos 401/2006; 11887/2006; 402/2006; 22357/2006; 681/2006, http://www.cortedicassazione.it.

[185] See Constitutional Court, judgement of 24 October 2007, no. 349, http://www.corte-costituzionale.it. See also *supra* section B.2.b. Gazetta Ufficiale, 24 October 2007.

[186] See Court of Cassation, judgement of 26 January 2004, no. 1340, http://www.cortedicas-sazione.it.

[187] See Court of Cassation, Criminal Section I, judgement 22 September–3 October 2005, no. 35616. See also Court of Cassation, Section V, judgement 15 November 2006–2 February 2007, http://www.cortedicassazione.it. See Conti (2007), 680.

[188] In the *Somogyi* case, Court of Cassation, judgement of 3 October 2006, no. 32678, the Court of Cassation found for the first time that the right to a new trial takes priority over the principle of *res judicata*. See for a doctrinal analysis, Bartoloni (2007), 29.

[189] See Court of Cassation, Criminal Section I, judgement of 1 December 2006 – 25 January 2007, no. 2800. For a detailed analysis of the *Catberro*, *Dorigo* and *Somogyi* cases, see Bin, Brunelli, Pugiotto and Veronesi, (2007).

As regards the issue of remedial judicial actions, Spanish courts – in particular the SCC and the Supreme Court – have relied on the ECtHR's case law for interpreting national human rights standards. As discussed above, the SCC's case law has been greatly inspired by the Strasbourg jurisprudence, and it requires the strict observance on the part of the courts when they consider cases regarding fundamental rights. In contrast, Italian courts have at times demonstrated a fierce sense of independence *vis-à-vis* the ECtHR's case law. Domestic courts do not always accept that they are bound by the Strasbourg decisions, especially if they are in conflict with the Italian Constitutional Court's case law. The situation has, however, improved as a result of two judgements (24 October 2007) recently handed down by the ICC.[190] As mentioned, the ICC found for the first time that an Italian law was unconstitutional because it contradicted one of the ECHR's provisions. This has been possible thanks to the new wording of Article 117 of the Constitution, which in practice gives priority to international law over contradictory domestic legislation. In its judgement, the ICC calls upon domestic courts to interpret national law consistently with international rules, which include the ECHR and its Additional Protocols.

E. Mechanisms of Coordination

1. Spain

Since the ratification of the ECHR, Spanish legislation regularly refers to the Convention, either in the statute itself or in the Explanatory Reports. Members of the Ministries involved in drafting new legislative proposals routinely check their conformity with the obligations under the ECHR on behalf of the Government. Such conformity is also debated when the proposals are submitted to Parliament. The scrutiny takes place indirectly within the Constitutional Affairs Committee (*Comité de Asuntos Constitucionales*), which analyzes the compatibility of the draft legislation with the fundamental rights listed in the Spanish Constitution. As a consequence, compliance with the ECHR takes place under the umbrella of mechanisms of constitutional compliance.

Spain could improve its mechanisms of coordination by setting up a truly specific system of Parliamentary monitoring coordinated by a human rights committee. In practice, the lack of a formal procedure for monitoring the compliance of legislative activity with the ECHR or the ECtHR's case law does not prevent Spain from meeting its obligations under the ECHR. As noted above, Spain has amended its laws on several occasions in order to bring them into conformity with the Strasbourg case law. A recent example can be found in the Organic Law no. 6/2007 of 24 May 2007 amending the powers and competences of the

[190] Constitutional Court (*supra* note 46).

Constitutional Court.[191]. In the preamble of the new legislation, the Spanish legislator expressly refers to the *Ruiz Mateos v. Spain* judgement[192] of the ECtHR to justify the introduction of several reforms based on the protection of the equality of arms principle. Despite the specific characteristics of constitutional proceedings, the new legislation – which arrived more than ten years after the ECtHR's judgement – allows applicants to comment on the observations filed before the Constitutional Court. It also allows applicants to appear physically before the SCC in proceedings dealing with questions of constitutionality.

As a result, it can be concluded that the Spanish Government is, in principle, committed to bringing its legislation into line with the jurisprudence of the Strasbourg Court. However, this does not mean that the Government is always keen to give sufficient effect to its ECHR obligations. It may take several years before the Government decides to modify legislation to ensure that it conforms to the Strasbourg case law. Moreover, controversy is still present with regard to the compatibility of Spanish counter-terrorism measures with the ECHR. These measures, spelled out in the Code of Criminal Procedure, were developed in the context of the struggle against *ETA*. Since the 11 March 2004 bombing, however, they are also applicable to the fight against international terrorism. The counter-terrorism measures contain several restrictions pertaining to the length and the conditions of detention of persons arrested under suspicion of membership in an armed or terrorist group. For example, the maximum three-day limit in police custody may be extended by 48 hours. The extension must be requested within the first 48 hours of detention and authorized by the competent judge within the following 24 hours.[193] This judge may authorize that individuals be held *incommunicado* in police detention.[194] While detainees have three important guarantees during this period (right to be examined by a doctor every six hours, the right to file a writ of *habeas corpus*, and the right to refer any ill-treatment to the legal aid attorney assigned to the case), *incommunicado* detainees are not given access to a lawyer or to a doctor of their choice. Furthermore, these detainees do not have the right to a private consultation with their lawyer.[195] Compliance with the ECHR is also ensured by the Spanish Ombudsman.[196] In its annual reports, the Obudsman reviews the compatibility of certain Spanish laws with the Strasbourg decisions. The Ombudsman's monitoring activities have proven to be a very useful tool to encourage legislative amendments or changes in the behaviour

---

[191] Organic Law no. 6/2007 of 24 Mai 2007 amending the powers and competences of the Constitutional Court, BOE no. 125 of 25 May 2007, 22541, http://www.boe.es/g/es/bases_datos/doc.php?coleccion=iberlex&id=2007/10483.

[192] *Ruiz Mateos v. Spain* (*supra* note 59).

[193] See Article 520*bis* (1) of the Code of Criminal Procedure.

[194] See Article 520*bis* (2) of the Code of Criminal Procedure.

[195] See Article 527(a) and (c) of the Code of Criminal Procedure.

[196] Reif, (2000).

of the administrative authorities.[197] As a national human rights institution, the Ombudsman has a positive effect on the application of the ECHR in Spain.

As regards the judiciary, it should first be pointed out that the application of the Convention by Spanish courts, in particular by the SCC, serves the need to clarify the scope of human rights more generally. In this context, the ECHR and the ECtHR's case law have been an immensely helpful source of reference.[198] In addition, in its judgement 114/1984 of 29 November 1984, the SCC found that Spanish courts (including itself) needed to follow the ECtHR's case law when interpreting the fundamental rights protected by the Constitution. As a consequence, courts are expected to follow the ECtHR's decisions concerning not only Spain but also the other Contracting States.

As noted above, the jurisprudence of the ECtHR influences the case law of the courts. The SCC and the Supreme Court incorporate this case law into their rulings, and the case law is directly applied by the rest of the domestic courts. In addition, Article 87(1) of the Organic Law of the Constitutional Court[199] establishes an obligation for *all* public authorities to comply with the judgements and decisions of the SCC, which comprize hundreds of cases giving full domestic effect to the Convention. As a consequence, compliance with the SCC's judgements is an indirect mechanism of enforcing the Convention. As a result, the ECHR has a notable impact – although indirect – on national authorities.

2. Italy

Although the Convention does not a have constitutional status in domestic law, and domestic courts have been reluctant to apply its provisions directly, the Italian legislator is presently showing a greater commitment to ensure compliance with the Convention guarantees. Under the pressure of the Strasbourg bodies and, in particular, the Committee of Ministers the Italian Government was forced to react. This has given rise to two major legal developments, namely the creation of the Permanent Observatory of the ECtHR's case law, and the enactment of the *Azzolini* law.

In 2005, a Permanent Observatory of the ECtHR's case law (*Osservatorio Permanente delle sentenze della Corte Europea dei Diritti dell'Uomo*) was set up in the Lower Chamber of the Italian Parliament (*Camera dei Deputati*). This organ collects and systematically lists the ECtHR's judgements in order to provide legal

---

[197] A good example is the absence of the guarantee to legal assistance to migrants in investigation proceedings. In the 2001 Annual Report, the Ombudsman reported that there was no reliable evidence of the presence of a lawyer during return proceedings that took place in Ceuta. The Ombudsman observed that legal assistance is an essential element of the right of defence, which always needs to be guaranteed.

[198] The growing reference to the ECHR as a source of interpretation is due to the existence of Article 10(2) of the Spanish Constitution.

[199] Ley Orgánica no. 2/1979, de 3 de octubre, del Tribunal Constitucional, BOE no. 239 of 5 October 1979, 23186, http://www.boe.es/g/es/bases_datos/doc.php?coleccion=iberlex&id=1979/23709.

advice to both the Italian Delegation at the Parliamentary Assembly of the Council of Europe and the relevant Working Groups in the Chamber. The Permanent Observatory plays an important role in the follow-up and the dissemination of the ECtHR's case law. It also provides significant support and advice in the process of elaboration or modification of national laws in order to harmonize them with the ECHR standards.

In January 2006, a new law was adopted containing important regulations on the enforcement of the ECtHR's judgements.[200] This law, also known as the *Azzolini* law, specifies the Prime Minister's powers and duties relating to the enforcement of the ECtHR's judgements against Italy. These duties include the notifying in a timely manner the Parliament of ECtHR judgements and the drafting of an annual report to it on the implementation of these judgements. Under this law, the Legislature is now promptly informed of the Strasbourg decisions against Italy.

3. Comparison and Conclusion

Although the above analysis illustrates that coordination mechanisms have been developed at both the legislative and judicial levels, Italy and Spain still need to improve them. In Spain, *ex ante* legislative compliance may take place at the level of the Constitutional Affairs Committee of the Parliament. This means, of course, that the control takes place as part of a mechanism of constitutional compliance. One could argue that there is still room for the creation within the Parliament of a specific human rights committee that would monitor the implementation of and the compliance with the Convention's provisions at the legislative level. Italy has recently created two specific mechanisms of legislative and executive compliance, namely the Permanent Observatory and the *Azzolini* law. It still remains to be seen how these two mechanisms will work in practice.

As regards judicial coordination, Spain has developed a better system than Italy; in Spain, there is a constitutional obligation to interpret constitutional rights in light of the international human rights instruments. Thus, there is a duty to take into account the principles laid down in the ECtHR's case law even when it does not concern Spain. In Italy, domestic courts are not legally bound by the ECtHR's case law in their interpretation and application of constitutional rights.[201] The fact that Italian courts often distance themselves from the Strasbourg Court's case law arguably accounts, to a certain extent, for the high number of applications lodged against Italy.

---

[200] Law 9 January 2006 no. 12, "*Disposizioni in materia di esecuzione delle pronunce della Corte Europea dei Diritti dell'Uomo*", Gazzetta Ufficiale 19 January 2006, no. 15. See also D.P.C.M., 1 February 2007 – Measures for the execution of Law 12/2006, http://www.parlamento.it.

[201] Surprisingly, the judgements handed down by the Grand Chamber of the Court of Cassation (the *Sezioni Unite*) are not binding on the chambers (*Sezioni*).

F. Remedies and Proportionality Tests

1. *Spain*

a. Remedies

The question of remedies will be considered from two distinct perspectives, namely the remedies provided to individuals by domestic law to enforce Convention rights and the remedies provided to appellants by domestic law following a successful claim before the ECtHR.

As regards the first type of remedies, the effectiveness of the ECHR clearly depends on the adequacy of the remedies provided by the Contracting States. Article 13 ECHR lays down an obligation to provide individuals with an effective remedy before a national authority against a violation of their rights and freedoms as set forth in the Convention. In other words, Contracting States must provide mechanisms within their respective legal systems for the effective redress of violations of the Convention rights. The European system of human rights protection thus operates under the principle of subsidiarity. Decisions have to be taken at the most efficient level. The primary responsibility for ensuring that human rights are respected lies with the Contracting States, and particularly with the domestic courts. National courts must, whenever possible, interpret and apply domestic law in accordance with the Convention.[202]

In this respect, the Spanish Constitution contains an express provision – Article 10(2) – which provides that the ECHR is a source of interpretation of the constitutional provisions on fundamental rights. Pursuant to Articles 10(2) of the Constitution and 32 ECHR, Spanish courts are required to take into account the Convention and the ECtHR's case law when considering cases pertaining to the fundamental rights guaranteed by the Constitution, and how they do so can be appealed to the SCC through the *amparo* procedure.[203]

In some cases, the SCC has based its decisions solely on the rules established in the Strasbourg jurisprudence. Articles 53 to 58 of the Organic Law on the Constitutional Court, as modified by the new law no. 6/2007 of 23 May 2007[204], regulate the *amparo*. In the event of a violation of a fundamental right, the first effect of a successful *amparo* appeal is the recognition of the violation of the right. The second effect is the declaration of nullity of the judicial or administrative resolution that infringed the fundamental right. The third effect is the adoption of remedies designed to restore the applicant's rights. Thus, the *amparo* appeal constitutes an important domestic mechanism for redressing human rights violations, since it appears just before lodging a claim with ECtHR. This is a key

---

[202] See *Scordino v. Italy (No. 1)* (appl. no. 36813/97), Decision (First Section), 27 March 2003, Reports 2003-IV, 14.

[203] For a detailed analysis of the *amparo* appeal, see Borrajo Iniesta, Díez-Picazo and Fernández Farreres (1995) and Lucas Murillo de la Cueva in Ruiz-Rico Ruiz (1997), 141.

[204] Organic Law no. 6/2007 of 24 May 2007, BOE no. 125 of 25 May 2007, 22541.

factor in explaining the relatively low number of cases brought annually before the Strasbourg Court compared to other Contracting States, such as Italy, which lack a similar mechanism.

Spanish legislation contains certain important shortcomings with regard to remedies following a successful claim before the ECtHR. Similarly to Italian law, Spanish law does not provide for the reopening of domestic judicial proceedings. In Spain, the question of the remedies has been limited to the reparation of rights through the payment of damages. However, the award of pecuniary damages following a finding of violation by the ECtHR or a settlement agreement may not always constitute an adequate compensation for the applicants, especially if they have a criminal conviction. As a consequence, Spain lacks domestic procedures that would fully redress the damage resulting from a violation of the ECHR.

Following the *Barberà, Messegué and Jabard v. Spain*[205] case, in which the ECtHR found that the proceedings did not satisfy the requirements of a fair and public hearing set forth in Article 6(1) ECHR, the SCC ordered the reopening of the proceedings on the grounds that the enforcement of a judgment that violates the Convention must be considered contrary to the Spanish constitutional system. The reexamination of the case following the ECtHR's ruling has proven to be useful. In the new proceedings, the applicants serving prison sentences between fifteen and 30 years were ultimately acquitted. This trend in constitutional case law has created great expectations. However, soon after, in its judgement of 11 March 1999, the SCC overruled its previous case law and stated that the reopening of proceedings was (and still is) not allowed under Spanish law.

Spanish legal scholars have heavily criticized this situation[206] for creating a barrier for individuals seeking to enforce a Strasbourg ruling in domestic law. Aware of the problems that may be caused by this situation, the Spanish Government notified the Committee of Ministers that it was considering possible amendments to the Spanish procedural legislation.[207] These amendments would take into account the Committee of Ministers' Recommendation (2000) on the reexamination or reopening of certain cases at the domestic level following judgements of the European Court of Human Rights.[208] To date, however, the Government has not taken any major steps in this direction. In June 2002, the Federal Parliamentary Group of the United Left (*Izquierda Unida*) proposed, unsuccessfully, a draft regulation concerning the question of enforcement of ECtHR judgements,

---

[205] *Barberà, Messegue and Jabardo v. Spain (supra* note 58).

[206] Ripol Carulla, (2007), 187.

[207] See the latest version (April 2006) of the document issued by the Committee of Ministers concerning the specific measures adopted by the Contracting States to enforce the ECtHR's judgements and decisions as well as to prevent new violations of the Convention from occurring: http://www.coe.int/t/e/human_rights/execution/02_documents/1MI_index.asp#TopOfPage.

[208] Recommendation no. R (2000) 2 on the reexamination or reopening of certain cases at domestic level following judgments of the European Court of Human Rights, Committee of Ministers, 694th meeting of the Ministers' Deputies, 19 January 2000, http://www.coe.int/t/e/human_rights/execution/02_Documents/Rec2000_2.asp.

and the need to develop a mechanism facilitating the *restitutio in integrum*.[209] In its judgement 197/2006 of 3 July 2006, the Constitutional Court called upon legislators to resolve this problem by adopting a new regulation.[210] In his annual rapport of 2006, the Spanish Ombudsman has also underlined the need to remedy this procedural *lacuna*.[211] Unfortunately, Spain is one of the only three Contracting States that has not yet adopted legislation facilitating the reopening of proceedings by persons who have been successful in bringing a case before the ECtHR. As a result, individuals may be discouraged from lodging applications before the ECtHR if they do not have the guarantee that they will get a sufficient compensation for violations of their rights. This may also explain the fact that there are only a few applications filed against Spain before the Strasbourg Court.

b. Proportionality Test

The SCC borrowed the proportionality test from the case law of the German Constitutional Court, although it appears that it has sometimes been more radical in the application of this principle than its German counterpart. This radical position can be explained by the fact that, following a long period of dictatorship, limitations of civil rights and freedoms became very controversial issues. As a consequence, priority has normally been given to the protection of rights and freedoms over State measures restricting them.[212]

In addition, the Spanish Constitutional Court relies on the proportionality-based case law of the ECtHR to determine the scope of the constitutional fundamental rights.[213] The principle of proportionality has been of particular importance with regard to the interpretation to the right to personal privacy and data protection.[214] National courts also apply necessity analysis when assessing the compatibility of public authorities' acts or practices with the ECHR. The ECtHR's case law pertaining to the application of the proportionality test[215] has not only influenced the domestic courts in their interpretation of certain rights but also the Spanish Parliament. The proportionality test is indeed mentioned in Parliamentary debates when the adoption of a new legislation entails certain restrictions on fundamental rights. Embracing the proportionality test does not mean that domestic courts apply this test in a manner that always favours the

---

[209] See Boletín Oficial de las Cortes Generales – Congreso de los Diputados, VII Legislatura, Serie D, General no. 365 of 7 June 2002, 26–28,
http://www.senado.es/legis7/publicaciones/html/maestro/index_D0365.html.

[210] STC 197/2006, BOE of 4 August 2006.

[211] Informe anual del Defensor del Pueblo de 2006, Section 1.14.1, 286.

[212] For an analytical study of the application of the proportionality test by the Spanish Constitutional Court since its origins, see the book of González Beilfuss (2003).

[213] See Bernal Pulido (2005), 381 410.

[214] See *infra* the text accompanying notes 218 and 219.

[215] For a study of the proportionality test under the ECHR system, see the book of Van Drooghenbroeck (2001).

individual. Indeed, several cases brought before the Strasbourg Court against Spain raised the issue of proportionality of the restrictions imposed by the public authorities on ECHR rights. In these cases, the interference often pursued a legitimate aim, but the Court criticized the balance struck between the means employed and the ends sought.

After the Court's decisions in *Valenzuela Contreras v. Spain*[216] and *Prado Bugallo v. Spain*,[217] it became clear for all Spanish courts that minimum safeguards needed to be established under national law with regard to the privacy of telephone communications. The proportionality test has had an important role to play, particularly in determining whether the duration of a measure allowing tapping complies with existing legislation. In 1995 and 1996, the SCC applied the proportionality test in two judgements[218] dealing with limitations imposed on the right to privacy of telecommunications. The Tribunal also referred to the well-established case law of the European Court. With *Castells v. Spain*,[219] Spanish courts familiarized themselves with how the ECtHR applies the principle of proportionality to the freedom of expression. The ECtHR has always underlined the importance of freedom of expression in the development of a democratic society, as has the SCC. The seriousness of the interests at stake is, therefore, very important in the eyes of the Court, and this seriousness now inspires the Spanish courts. Such cases concerning Spain do not give rise to legislative amendments. Instead, since it is how Spanish courts have interpreted the right to privacy and the right to freedom of expression that gave rise to the breach of the Convention. Adjusting how the proportionality test is used, in order to comply with the Convention, becomes the essential task of the Spanish courts.[220]

2. Italy

a. Remedies

In the ECHR system, national legal systems are charged with protecting human rights in the first instance. In Italy, extensive remedies have been provided in the event of an infringement of constitutional rights. The Italian judicial system envisages the possibility of three instances of litigation (*gradi di giudizio*). In the first two instances, courts are empowered to consider evidence and to rule on both the merits and the law, while in the third instance (Court of Cassation), review is limited to questions of law. The observance of civil and political rights is ensured, in addition, by the Constitutional Court. Unlike in Spain, individuals cannot directly address the ICC, but only incidentally, in the course of a trial (*incidenter tantum*). It follows that the ICC's role in the protection of the ECHR's provision

---

[216] *Valenzuela Contreras v. Spain* (*supra* note 74).
[217] *Prado Bugallo v. Spain* (*supra* note 77).
[218] See STC 86/1995 of 6 June 1995 and STC 49/1996 of 26 March 1996.
[219] *Castells v. Spain* (*supra* note 79).
[220] Bernal Pulido (2005).

is usually limited to cases referred to it by ordinary courts in matters specifically falling within the scope of the rights guaranteed by the Italian Constitution. Remedies are thus provided for violation of constitutional rights rather than for violation of the ECHR.

There is nonetheless a specific remedy directly related to the right to a fair trial within a reasonable time, as guaranteed in Article 6 ECHR. As noted earlier, the *Pinto* law introduced a compensative remedy providing the possibility for individuals to bring proceedings before the competent national courts – specifically the Court of Appeal (*Corte d'Appello*) – in order to obtain compensation in the event of excessively lengthy proceedings.

With regard to the issue of remedies provided to appellants by domestic law following a successful claim before the ECtHR, Italian law – like Spanish law – has significant shortcomings. The most important one relates to the fact that it is impossible to review a final domestic decision giving rise to the ECtHR proceedings. This unsatisfactory state of affairs is reflected in cases pending before the ECtHR. Legal scholars have frequently called for the introduction of a revision procedure, especially in relation to criminal proceedings conducted in violation of the ECHR. It is apparent that the reopening of proceedings in situations where there has been a violation of one of the procedural guarantees provided in Article 6 ECHR (such as in situations of trials *in absentia*) could adequately redress this violation. The Italian Constitutional Court now has the possibility to address this issue in the *Dorigo* case[221], recently brought before it by the Court of Appeal of Bologna.[222]

In addition, Italian law does not allow for the review of civil or administrative proceedings following a successful complaint before the ECtHR. This situation is further aggravated by the fact that Italy has often been found to be in breach of property rights under expropriation proceedings. The ECtHR is regularly confronted with cases in which the landowner has *de facto* lost use of land for which he has not been sufficiently compensated. In certain cases,[223] the Strasbourg Court decided to grant *restitutio in integrum*. If there is no adequate domestic procedure to enforce the ECtHR's judgements and decisions, the reception process of the ECHR will undoubtedly be affected.

b. Proportionality test

The Italian legal system inherited the principle of proportionality from European Union law and the European Court of Justice's case law. Pursuant to the principle of proportionality, as enforced by the Luxembourg Court, limitations of rights

---

[221] Court of Cassation (*supra* note 189).

[222] See Court of Appeal of Bologna, Ordinance 22 March 2006, no. 337, http://www.unife.it/amicuscuriae.

[223] See, for instance, *Belvedere Alberghiera s.r.l. v. Italy* (*supra* note 92); *Carbonara and Ventura v. Italy* (*supra* note 93); *Scordino v. Italy (No. 1)* (*supra* note 94) and *Genovese and Others v. Italy* (*supra* note 96).

are only allowed if they are pursued with a legitimate aim and if they constitute the least restrictive option. The Strasbourg Court's case law also played a significant role in determining how the proportionality test should be applied by domestic courts in situations where interferences by the State undermined certain human rights, such as the right to private property (Article 1 of Protocol no. 1), the right of access to court (Article 6 ECHR) and the right to respect for private and family life (Article 8 ECHR).

In *Scordino v. Italy (No. 1),*[224] *Ambruosi v. Italy,*[225] and *Sorrentino Prota v. Italy,*[226] the ECtHR held that an interference with the right to peaceful enjoyment of possessions must strike a "fair balance" between the demands of the community's general interest and the protection of the individual's fundamental rights. In other words, there must be a reasonable relationship of proportionality between the means employed and the aim sought by any measure applied by the State, including measures depriving a person of his possessions. In determining whether this requirement is met, the Court recognized that "the State enjoys a wide margin of appreciation with regard both to choosing the means of enforcement and to ascertaining whether the consequences of enforcement are justified in the general interest for the purpose of achieving the object of the law in question".[227] In these cases, the ECtHR had to determine whether the required balance was maintained in a manner consistent with the applicants' right to the peaceful enjoyment of their possessions within the meaning of the first sentence of Article 1 of Protocol no. 1.

In *Markovic and Others v. Italy,*[228] the ECtHR held that the right to access to a

---

[224] *Scordino v. Italy (No. 1)* (appl. no. 36813/97), Judgement (Grand Chamber), 29 March 2006 (not yet reported), paras 93–98.

[225] *Ambruosi v. Italy* (appl. no. 31227/96), Judgement (Second Section), 19 October 2000 (not reported), paras 31–34. In this case the interference consisted in depriving the applicant of the possibility of seeking the payment of her legal costs and fees directly from the State rather than from her clients, who were of poor means and had passed an agreement with her that, in case of success, they would not have to bear any legal costs. The applicant had obtained a number of rulings in her favour which she could not enforce; further, she was not awarded legal costs in other pending proceedings, despite the fact that she had a legitimate expectation that the magistrate would discharge them directly to her. As a result, the applicant would have seen herself forced to disregard the agreement she passed with her clients and seek the payment of her fees from them. Furthermore, the recovery of the fees from individuals of poor means would likely be more difficult and lengthy than it would have been from the State. The Court found that the applicant's choice not to seek the payment of her fees from her clients was neither unreasonable nor arbitrary. It considered that paragraph 3 of Section 1 of Law Decree No. 166/1996 imposed an excessive burden on the applicant and accordingly upset, to her detriment, the balance that must be struck between the protection of the right to the peaceful enjoyment of one's possessions and the requirements of the public interest. Accordingly, the ECtHR found a breach of Article 1 of Protocol no. 1.

[226] *Sorrentino Prota v. Italy* (appl. no. 40465/98), Judgement (First Section), 29 January 2004 (not reported), para. 56.

[227] See also *Immobiliare Saffi v. Italy* (appl. no. 22774/93), Judgement (Grand Chamber), 28 July 1999, Reports 1999-V, 73, para. 49, and the recent judgment in *Ormanni v. Italy* (appl. no. 30278/04), Judgement (Second Section), 17 July 2007 (not yet reported), para. 55.

[228] *Markovic and Others v. Italy* (appl. no. 1398/03), Judgement (Grand Chamber), 14 December 2006 (not yet reported).

court was not absolute and could be subjected to legitimate restrictions, such as statutory limitation periods, security for costs orders as well as regulations concerning minors and persons of unsound mind.[229] Where the individual's access to a court is limited either by law or in fact, the reviewing judge must examine whether this restriction impairs the essence of Article 6(1) ECHR, pursues a legitimate purpose, and a relationship of proportionality between the means employed and the purpose exists.[230] The ECtHR concluded that the restriction was compatible with these principles and that there was no violation of Article 6 ECHR.

With regard to Article 8 ECHR, two cases are particularly relevant, namely *Giacomelli v. Italy*[231] and *E.P. v. Italy*[232]. In *Giacomelli v. Italy*,[233] the ECtHR noted that the margin of appreciation was exceeded by the respondent Government. As a result, Italy did not succeed in maintaining a fair balance between the interest of the community (having a plant for the treatment of toxic industrial waste) and the applicant's effective enjoyment of her right to respect for her home and her private and family life. In *E.P. v. Italy*,[234] the ECtHR recalled that taking a child from the mother and suspending her parental responsibility should normally be regarded as a temporary measure, to be discontinued as soon as circumstances permitted, and any measure of implementation should be consistent with the ultimate aim of reuniting the natural parent with his or her child. In this case, the Italian authorities established a total ban on contact between the applicant and her daughter. As a result, the Court concluded that Italy failed to take all the necessary steps to give the applicant and her daughter a chance to reestablish their relationship. Hence, the authorities did not strike a fair balance between the best interests of the child and the applicant's rights under Article 8 ECHR.

The ECtHR takes pains to demonstrate to domestic courts how to apply the proportionality test in their judgments when assessing the State's justifications for restricting ECHR rights. In addition, under the margin of appreciation doctrine, the ECtHR grants national courts a certain measure of autonomy when reviewing legislation or executive acts against the ECHR. In any case, allowing a margin of appreciation does not prevent a subsequent control of its application by the Strasbourg Court. Italian scholars have underlined, however, that the judiciary is not yet used to dealing with its interpretation, particularly in administrative

---

[229] In this regard, the ECtHR referred to *Stubbings and Others v. the United Kingdom* (appl. nos 22083/93; 22095/93), Judgment (Chamber), 22 October 1996, Reports 1996-IV (no. 18), 1487, paras 51–52 and to *Tolstoy Miloslavsky v. the United Kingdom* (appl. no. 18139/91), Judgment (Chamber), 13 July 1995, Series A, Vol. 316-B, paras 62–67.

[230] See *Markovic and Others v. Italy* (*supra* note 228).

[231] *Giacomelli v. Italy* (*supra* note 89).

[232] *E.P. v. Italy* (appl. no. 31127/1996), Judgement (Second Section), 16 November 1999 (not yet reported).

[233] *Giacomelli v. Italy* (*supra* note 89), para. 97.

[234] *E.P. v. Italy* (*supra* note 232), para. 69.

cases.[235] Unfortunately, references to the proportionality test seldom appear in the context of limitations of individual rights by public authorities, indeed, proportionality is yet to become a relevant criterion in this context.

3. *Comparison and Conclusion*

This Section shows again the importance of the Spanish *amparo*, allowing the SCC to redress violations of ECHR provisions prior to a claim being lodged with the Strasbourg Court. Given that Italy lacks a similar remedy, it appears comparatively more often before the ECtHR. This Section also reveals that the domestic remedies available to a successful applicant in Strasbourg are insufficient in both countries. The Committee of Ministers has addressed recommendations to Spain and resolutions to Italy urging them to improve the present situation. While in Spain there has been a legislative initiative explicitly aimed at the enforcement of ECtHR judgements, there have not been any significant steps in this direction in Italy.

Both States' Constitutional Courts could play a more significant role by issuing decisions which offer successful applicants the possibility of reopening proceedings before the competent domestic courts. This was the case in Spain for a very limited period of time. Nonetheless, the SCC abandoned this progressive case law in light of the principle of *res judicata*. In Italy, the *Dorigo* case[236] – at the time of writing still pending before the Italian Constitutional Court – may give an answer to the question whether the absence of a national provision permitting the reopening of proceedings following an ECtHR judgment is contrary to the Constitution.

One may suggest here a possible way of improving the Spanish situation. There is a new Article 241 in the Organic Law of the Judicial Power (*Ley Orgánica del Poder Judicial*) which allows parties that have a legitimate interest in bringing a case before the Supreme Court to seek the annulment of a previous judgement that violates one of the fundamental constitutional rights. This new appeal was introduced in the Organic Law of the Judicial Power after the entry into force of the new Organic Law of the Constitutional Court of 24 May 2007.[237] This new appeal could also be used to nullify a domestic judgement which was found to violate the Convention by the ECtHR. If the nullity of a domestic judgement is declared, then the proceedings can resume. This remedy can open new possibilities for the improvement of the Convention's reception in Spain.

As regards the proportionality test, it is important to note that public authorities are often confronted with its application, when they attempt to strike a balance between the State's interests and individual rights. The ECtHR case

---

[235] See Mirate (2006).

[236] Court of Cassation (*supra* note 189).

[237] This appeal is known as the *incidente de nulidad de las actuaciones*, see BOE no. 125 of 25 May 2007.

law and EU law have influenced the definition and application of the principle of proportionality in Spanish and Italian public law. National courts have been given some indications as to the application of this principle and as to the importance of the balancing of interests. Interestingly, this principle has improved the judicial protection of individual rights by attributing a new role to domestic courts, a role which still needs to be better played by them.

G. Knowledge and Practice

1. Spain

In Spain, the knowledge and practice of the ECHR amongst scholars and lawyers have steadily increased over the last fifteen years. The Departments of International Public Law and of Constitutional Law teach and conduct research activities regarding the ECHR. Certain Law Faculties have established research centres or Institutes devoted to the study of human rights, and offer specialized programmes at postgraduate level.[238] There are a considerable number of Spanish scholars devoted to the study of the ECHR and its influence on the national legal order. In December 2006, a first meeting on research and university teaching took place in Valencia and 30 groups working on human rights issues took part in it. This meeting led to the establishment of a Network of Research and University Teaching on Human Rights (*Red de Investigación y Docencia Universitaria sobre Derechos Humanos (RIDUDH)*).[239] Universities, public organizations or private institutions also organize conferences, and these constitute excellent *fora* for discussion. Some of these institutions also offer scholarships, internships and visits to the ECtHR. In addition, training courses are held by public or private human rights institutes, such as the Human Rights Institute of Catalonia (IDHC). These courses are addressed to students, civil servants, security forces and lawyers.

Due to the lack of familiarity of Spanish practising lawyers, scholars, civil servants and civil servants with the French or English languages, all decisions of the ECtHR are translated into Spanish. The Press Service of the Congress of Deputies publishes a translation of the ECtHR's judgements in the *Boletín de Jurisprudencia Constitucional*. In addition, both the Spanish Ministry of Justice and the Home Affairs Ministry publish an information bulletin (the *Boletín de información del Ministerio de Justicia e Interior*) where the case law of the European Court is translated into Spanish in the section entitled "Case law of the

---

[238] This is, for example, the case of the Universidad Carlos III (Madrid) which hosts the *Instituto de Derechos Humanos "Bartolomé de las Casas"* and the University of Deusto (Bilbao) which hosts the *Instituto de derechos Humanos Pedro Arrupe*. These Institutes offer advanced Masters on human rights. The Universities of Deusto (Bilbao) and Seville take part in the European Master's Degree in Human Rights and Democratization organized in Venice. Other universities have developed international research networks in the area of the protection of fundamental rights.

[239] Network of Research and University Teaching on Human Rights, Universidad Carlos III (Madrid), http://turan.uc3m.es/uc3m/inst/BC/red.htm.

ECHR's bodies" (*Jurisprudencia de los órganos del Convenio Europeo de Derechos Humanos*). The SCC publishes an annual report addressed to the public, which includes in its Annex IV a section on the ECtHR's activity regarding Spain. This report is available on the website of the Constitutional Court.[240]

Highly regarded scholars regularly publish books on the European system of human rights protection and on the relationship between Strasbourg law and Spanish law. Some of these scholars were either judges of the Strasbourg Court or judges of the Spanish Constitutional Court. Articles and case annotations pertaining to the ECHR are regularly integrated into the main journals for practitioners, namely in the Spanish Review of Constitutional Law (*Revista Espanola de Derecho Constitucional*), the Spanish Review of Administrative Law (*Revista Espanola de Derecho Administrativo*) and the Spanish Review of International Law (*Revista Espanola de Derecho Internacional*). Moreover, since 2003, there is a specialized law review devoted to European human rights in Spain, the European Review of Fundamental Rights (*Revista Europea de Derechos Fundamentales*). This journal focuses on the ECHR and publishes a number of important articles on the impact of the ECHR on the Spanish legal order.

2. Italy

In Italy, the interest in and knowledge of the ECHR amongst scholars and lawyers have also steadily growing for the last fifteen years. All major Italian Universities offer courses on international human rights law and the ECHR,[241] and a few also provide postgraduate specialization courses.[242] Other educational institutions organize specialized courses on the Convention. Legal scholarship in this field is generally characterized by a critical position *vis-à-vis* the Italian authorities (legislative, executive and judicial), on grounds that the latter do not attach sufficient weight to the ECtHR's case law on a regular basis. Italy hosts a Section of the International Commission of Jurists (ICJ), known as *Jura Hominis*[243], which organizes conferences designed to raise awareness of the Convention's principles and of the ECtHR's case law. In addition, a network of Italian lawyers has been very active in the field of human rights, and plays an important role in the dissemination of the ECtHR's case law.[244] This network publishes a journal, entitled Human Rights: Reports and Battles (*Diritti dell'Uomo: Cronache e battaglie*),

[240] See http://www.tribunalconstitucional.es/memorias/memorias.html.

[241] This is, for example, the case of the Università Cattolica del Sacro Cuore in Milan, the Università La Sapienza in Rome, the Università degli Studi in Florence and the "Università degli Studi di Napoli Federico II" in Naples.

[242] See, for example, the Master of Arts in Human Rights and Conflict Management offered by the Scuola Superiore Sant'Anna in Pisa. Human rights courses are held in the context of the Master's Degrees offered by Roma Tre University and by the SIOI (*Società italiana per l'organizzazione internazionale*, the Italian Society for International Organization, located in Rome). Other courses are offered at the Universities of Siena and Padua as well as at the International Institute of Trieste.

[243] The activities of this organization are described on its website: http://www.jurahominis.it.

[244] The activities of this network are described on its website: http://www.dirittiuomo.it.

which includes selected ECtHR cases, commentaries and articles written by reputable scholars on the most important ECtHR cases.

Until 2003, the International Journal of Human Rights (*Rivista internazionale dei diritti dell'uomo*) published articles and commentaries on the ECtHR's case law. It also translated into Italian the most important judgements of the Strasbourg Court. Apart from the journal entitled Human Rights: Reports and Battles, there were no other publications exclusively focused on the activities of the ECtHR until 2007. In that year, a new legal review appeared, the Human Rights and International Law (*Diritti umani e diritto internazionale*), which deals with international human rights treaties and with the ECHR. In addition, the Juridical Journal (*Il Corriere Giuridico*) hosts a bi-monthly column specifically devoted to the Strasbourg case law. Italian doctrine is also very receptive to the ECHR, and two significant volumes have recently been published containing the English translations of the main ECtHR judgements.[245] Finally, it is important to note that the ECtHR's rulings are rarely presented by the Italian broadcast media. The most interesting cases, however, are generally reported in the main newspapers.

3. Comparison and Conclusion

There are numerous parallels between the Spanish and Italian situations with regard to the level of knowledge of the ECHR. In both countries, domestic courts and lawyers appear informed on the case law of the ECtHR. However, further knowledge and dissemination of the ECtHR's judgements concerning other Contracting States is needed, particularly for judges. At present, human rights courses for judges are frequently organized, but they are not part of their mandatory training.

The ECHR plays an increasingly important role in the Universities' curricula in both countries. The activity of national legal scholars in the field of European human rights law is substantial, although concentrated in specific areas, such as international law or domestic law (mainly, constitutional law, criminal law or administrative law) issues. Nonetheless, the existing literature rarely addresses the impact of the ECtHR's case law on legislative, executive and judicial authorities.

H. Final Remarks

This study demonstrates the importance of formal, structural features of the two legal systems in determining how the Convention has been received. First, in Spain monism has facilitated reception and incorporation, whereas Italian dualism has been an awkward hindrance. Second, in Spain, the ECHR possesses supra-legislative status, while in Italy it occupies the rank of an ordinary domestic statute. Despite its infra-constitutional character, the Convention benefits in

[245] De Salvia and Zagrebelsky (2006).

Spain from a considerable and substantial force. Unfortunately, this has not been the case in Italy. This difference particularly accounts for divergences in the application of the Convention in these two countries. Third, the jurisdictions of the respective constitutional courts, and the positions they have taken, have been hugely important factors. In the hands of the SCC, the *amparo* has become a significant mechanism for enhancing the status of the ECHR in the Spanish legal system, whereas the ICC has no jurisdiction over individual complaints.

The effectiveness of the Convention in these two States depends heavily on how the ECHR is treated, with respect to constitutional rights, by the Constitutional Courts. In Spain, the posture of the Spanish Constitutional Court has been decisive. The SCC has recognized the Convention as a source of interpretation of the rights embodied in the Spanish Constitution and, it has established the direct applicability of the provisions of the ECHR in the legal order, as the ECtHR's interprets those provisions. Moreover, the SCC expressly uses the Convention as a benchmark in the constitutionality review of domestic regulation, while obliging domestic courts to consider the Strasbourg case law when interpreting the scope of the domestic constitutional rights. As a result, one can say that the Convention has acquired in practice a "quasi-constitutional" character. Moreover, given that the SCC's case law is binding upon domestic courts, the Convention finds a domestic constitutional underpinning for its enforcement. Of course, the obligation of compliance and cooperation will be stronger when a domestic legal provision specifically provides for it. In Spain, this duty of compliance and cooperation is laid down in Article 87(1) of the Organic Law on the SCC. Article 87 (1) goes even further by providing an obligation for courts and public authorities to comply with the judgements and decisions of the Constitutional Court. As hundreds of judgements of the SCC refer to the Strasbourg case law, this duty of compliance largely ensures the effectiveness of the Convention in domestic law.

In contrast, Italy has not yet found a way to fully compensate for the lack of the ECHR's constitutional status in its domestic law. The role played by the Italian Constitutional Court has been minor compared to the role played by its Spanish counterpart. However, the Italian situation may soon improve pursuant to the recent ICC's rulings invalidating a national law on grounds that it violated the ECHR. If the ICC consistently follows this progressive case law, the Convention could also gain a quasi-constitutional status in Italy, and its reception within the Italian legal system would be improved.

Statistics show that few cases are brought annually against Spain before the European Court of Human Rights. This study indicates why this is so. With regard to internal legal remedies, Spain, unlike Italy, has a specific legal remedy before the Constitutional Court, the *amparo*, aimed at ensuring the respect of constitutional rights, which are interpreted in the light of the ECHR. The Spanish Constitutional Court acts here as a judge of the ECHR. Nonetheless, if the applicant finds that the judgement of the Constitutional Court is contrary to the

Strasbourg case law, she can then bring the case before the ECtHR. Italy has one of the worst records before the ECtHR, and its legal system has been, compared with Spain, quite resistant to the positive reception of the Convention.

As regards the impact of the ECtHR's judgements, the study shows that general and specific measures have been adopted in the two countries to solve the problems that caused human rights violations. In Spain, new legislation or amendments have been adopted to improve the rights of defence, to shorten the length of the proceedings (including those before the Constitutional Court) and to ensure better compliance with the right to privacy of telecommunications. In addition, there are regular references to the ECHR in Spanish statutes and in the Explanatory Reports. The Convention is generally well known by all bodies engaged in the legislative process. It is certainly more difficult to ensure that all public authorities and domestic courts apply the Convention adequately. In Italy, new legislation has been adopted to avoid further violations and to repair their harmful consequences. However, neither Spanish nor Italian law allows successful applicants before the ECtHR to reopen proceedings at the domestic level to enforce a Strasbourg judgement. This situation creates a severe barrier to the reception process of the ECHR in these two countries.

The Spanish and Italian experiences also show how important the interactions between national court systems and the ECHR are becoming. High Courts can perform the role of oversight bodies, supervising the work of legislative, administrative, and judicial authority, in light of the requirements of the ECHR. The ECtHR then becomes the guardian of the application of the ECHR by the Constitutional and Supreme Courts. Domestic courts are always on the front line, as they are the first ones to receive the applicants' complaints concerning breaches of fundamental rights. Thus, the system needs them to become judges of European human rights law, which would mean actively taking into account the ECHR, and referring to it when interpreting national human rights law. In this context, one can portray the Strasbourg Court as situated at the top of a pyramidal system, controlling compliance with the system's basic norms. In this view, the system also needs to count on the possibility of reopening domestic proceedings when a violation of the Convention has been acknowledged by the ECtHR. Ultimately, only if these elements work together will the full effectiveness of the ECHR in national legal orders be realized.

Bibliography

Agudo Zamora, M. A., 'Eficacia interna y ejecutoriedad de las sentencias del Tribunal Europeo de Derechos Humanos', in [no editor], *Estudios de Derecho Público. Homenaje a Juan José Ruiz-Rico* (Madrid, 1997).

Bandrés Sánchez-Cruzat, J. M., *Derecho Administrativo y Tribunal Europeo de Derechos Humanos (Comentario a la última jurisprudencia administrativa del Tribunal de Estrasburgo)* (Madrid, 1996).

Bartole, S., Conforti, B., and Raimondi, G., *Commentario alla Convenzione Europea per la tutela dei diritti dell'Uomo e delle libertà fondamentali* (Padua, 2001).

Bartoloni, M. E., *L'efficacia interna delle sentenze della Corte Europea dei diritti dell'uomo per il giudice italiano: in margine alle sentenze della Cassazione Somogyi e Dorigo* in Bin, R., Brunelli, G., Pugiotto, A. and Veronesi, P. (eds.), *All'incrocio tra Costituzione e CEDU. Il rango delle norme della Convenzione e l'efficacia interna delle sentenze di Strasburgo*, Atti del Seminario di Ferrara del 9 marzo 2007 (Turin, 2007).

Bernal Pulido, C., 'El principio de proporcionalidad y los derechos fundamentales: el principio de proporcionalidad como criterio para determinar el contenido de los derechos fundamentales vinculante para el legislador', *Revista Española de Derecho Constitucional* 73 (2005), 381.

Bin, R., Brunelli, G., Pugiotto, A. and Veronesi, P. (eds.), *All'incrocio tra Costituzione e CEDU. Il rango delle norme della Convenzione e l'efficacia interna delle sentenze di Strasburgo*, Atti del Seminario di Ferrara del 9 marzo 2007 (Turin, 2007).

Borrajo Iniesta, I., Díez-Picazo, I. and Fernández Farreres, G., *El derecho a la tutela judicial y el recurso de amparo* (Madrid, 1995).

Cannizzaro, E., *Il principio della proporzionalità nell'ordinamento internazionale* (Milan, 2000).

Caringella, F., *Manuale di Diritto Civile – Le Obbligazioni* (Milan, 2006).

Carrasco Durán, M., 'El concepto constitucional de recurso de amparo', *Revista Española de Derecho Constitucional* 63 (2001), 105.

Carrillo Donaire, J. A. and Galan Vioque, R., '¿Hacia un derecho fundamental a un medio ambiente adecuado? ', *Revista Espanola de Derecho Administrativo* 86 (1995), 271.

Cartabia, M., 'La CEDU e l'ordinamento italiano: rapporti tra le fonti, rapporti tra le giurisdizioni' (Ferrara, 2007).

Cassese, A., *Commento agli artt. 10 e 11*, in Branca, G. (ed.), *Commentario alla Costituzione* (Bologna, 1975).

Castellaneta, M., 'Consiglio d'Europa: un monito all'Italia per la reale attuazione delle sentenze', *Guida al diritto* 6 (2006), 12.

Catalá i Bas, A., 'Sentencia del Tribunal Europeo de Derechos Humanos Prado Bugalló c. España de 18 de febrero de 2003', *Revista Europea de Derechos Fundamentales* 1 (2003) 127.

Cavagna, E. and Monteiro, E., 'Iberian Peninsula: Spain and Portugal' in Delmas-Marty, M. (ed.), *The European Convention for the Protection of Human Rights. International Protection Versus National Restrictions* (Dordrecht, 1992).

Cerri, A., *Corso di giustizia costituzionale* (Milan, 2004).

Colella, A., 'Verso un diritto comune delle libertà in Europa. Riflessioni sul tema dell'integrazione della CEDU nell'ordinamento italiano', http://www.forumcostituzionale.it

Conforti, B., *Diritto internazionale* (Naples, 2007).

Conti, R., 'Ancora dissidi fra Cassazione, Consiglio di Stato e Corte dei diritti umani sull'occupazione illegittima', *Corriere Giuridico* 2 (2006), 225.

—, 'Corte Europea dei diritti dell'Uomo e occupazione illegittima, atto secondo: il risarcimento del danno in forma specifica', *Corriere Giuridico* 6 (2004), 731.

—, 'La Cassazione ritorna su occupazione appropriativa e rispetto della CEDU', *Corriere Giuridico* 11 (2004), 1467.

—, 'La Corte dei diritti dell'uomo e la Convenzione europea prevalgono sul giudicato – e sul diritto –nazionale', *Corriere giuridico* 5 (2007), 689.

Cruz Villalón, P. and Pardo Falcón, J.: 'Los Derechos Fundamentals en la Constitución Española de 1978', *Boletín Mexicano de Derecho Comparado* 97 (2000), 65.

Cour européenne des droits de l'homme, *Aperçus, quarante années d'activité, 1959–1998* (Strasbourg, 1999).

De la Oliva Santos, A. and Díez-Picazo Jiménez, I., *Tribunal Constitucional, Jurisdicción ordinaria y derechos fundamentales* (Madrid, 1996).

De Salvia, M., *La Convenzione europea dei diritti dell'uomo* (Naples, 2001).

De Salvia, M. and Zagrebelsky, V., *Diritti dell'uomo e libertà fondamentali. La giurisprudenza della Corte europea dei diritti dell'uomo e della Corte di Giustizia delle Comunità europee* (Milan, 2006).

Drzemczewski, A., *European Human Rights Convention in Domestic Law: A Comparative Study* (Oxford, 1983).

Escobar Roca, G., '*Spain*' in Blackburn, R. and Polakiewicz, J. (eds.), *Fundamental Rights in Europe: The European Convention on Human Rights and its Member States, 1950–2000* (Oxford, 2002).

Fiaren Guillén, V., *Proceso equitativo, plazo razonable y Tribunal Europeo de Derechos Humanos. Variaciones sobre la sentencia de 23 de junio de 1993, Asunto Ruiz-Mateos v. España* (Granada, 1996).

Fernández de Casadevante Romaní, C., *La aplicación del Convenio Europeo de Derechos Humanos en España: análisis de la jurisprudencia constitucional 1980–1988* (Madrid, 1988).

Fernández de Casadevante Romaní, C. and Jiménez García, F., *El Derecho Internacional de los derechos humanos en la Constitución Española: 25 años de jurisprudencia constitucional* (Navarra, 2006).

Garberí LLobregat, J. and Morenilla Allard, P., *Convenio Europeo de Derechos Humanos y jurisprudencia del Tribunal Europeo relativa a España. Textos, Protocolos, Nuevo Reglamento del Tribunal, Normas Complementarias y Formulario de Demanda* (Barcelona, 1999).

García Roca, J. and Santolaya, P. (eds.), *La Europa de los Derechos. El Convenio Europeo de Derechos Humanos*, Centro de Estudios Políticos y Constitucionales (Madrid, 2005).

Gardner, J. P., *Aspects of Incorporation of the European Convention of Human Rights into Domestic Law* (London, 1993).

González Beilfuss, M., *El principio de proporcionalidad en la jurisprudencia del Tribunal Constitucional* (Navarra, 2003).

Ivaldi, P., 'L'adattamento del diritto interno al diritto internazionale', in Carbone, S., Luzzatto, R., and Santa Maria, A. (eds.), *Istituzioni di diritto internazionale* (Turin, 2003).

Jimena Quesada, L., 'De nuevo sobre la problemática ejecución de sentencias del TEDH: en particular, la satisfacción equitativa o indemnización como parte del derecho a un proceso justo', *Revista General de Derecho* 630 (1997), 2017.

Lana, A. G., 'I tempi del processo e l'equa riparazione a tre anni dall'entrata in vigore della cd. Legge Pinto', *I diritti dell'uomo – cronache e battaglie* 1 (2004), 9.

Leuprecht, P., 'The Execution of judgements and decisions' in Macdonald, R., Matscher, F. and H. Petzold, H. (eds.), *The European System for the Protection of Human Rights* (Dordrecht, 1993).

Lucas Murillo de la Cueva, P., 'El amparo judicial de los derechos fundamentales', in Ruiz-Rico Ruiz, G. (ed.), *La aplicación jurisdiccional de la Constitución* (Valencia, 1997).

Lujosa Vadell, L., *Las sentencias del Tribunal Europeo de Derechos Humanos y el ordenamiento español* (Madrid, 1997).

Martín-Retortillo Baquer, L., 'La calidad de la ley según la jurisprudencia del Tribunal Europeo de Derechos Humanos (Especial referencia a los casos «Valenzuela Contreras» y «Prado Bugallo», ambos contra España)', *Derecho Privado y Constitución* 17 (2003), 377.

Mirate, S., *Giustizia amministrativa e convenzione europea dei diritti dell'uomo: L' "altro" diritto europeo in Italia, Francia e Inghilterra* (Naples, 2006).

Montanari L., 'Giudici comuni e Corti sovranazionali: rapporti tra sistemi', in Falzea, P., Spadaio, A. and Ventura, L. (eds.), *La Corte costituzionale e le Corti d'Europa* (Turin, 2003).

Morte Gómez, C., *El procedimiento ante el Tribunal Europeo de Derechos Humanos y los requisitos de admisibilidad de la demanda* (Valencia, 2004).

Nascimbene, B., 'Violazione "strutturale", violazione "grave" ed esigenze interpretative della Convenzione europea dei diritti dell'uomo', *Rivista di diritto internazionale privato e processuale* 3 (2006), 645.

Olmos Giupponi, M.B. and Díaz Barrado, C.M., 'Algunas consideraciones sobre el contenido del derecho a la vida en el sistema del Convenio Europeo de Derechos Humanos y Libertades fundamentales', *Revista Europea de Derechos Fundamentales* 2 (2003), 35.

Onida, V., 'Una nuova frontiera per la Corte costituzionale: istituzione "di confine" fra diritto nazionale e sovranazionale, in Zanon, N. (ed.), *Le Corti dell'integrazione europea e la Corte costituzionale italiana: avvicinamenti, dialoghi, dissonanze* (Naples, 2006).

Pastor Ridruejo, J. A., 'La tutela judicial efectiva en la jurisprudencia del Tribunal Europeo de Derechos Humanos: Temas escogidos', in Mariño Menéndez, F. (ed.), *El Derecho internacional en los albores del siglo XXI. Homenaje al profesor Juan Manuel Castro-Rial Canosa* (Madrid, 2002).

Perassi, T., *Lezioni di diritto internazionale* (Padua, 1962).

Pérez Tremps, P., 'Las garantías constitucionales y la jurisdicción internacional en la protección de los derechos fundamentales', *Anuario de la Facultad de Derecho de la Universidad de Extremadura* 10 (1992), 73.

Pirrone, P., *L'obbligo di conformarsi alle sentenze della Corte Europea dei diritti umani* (Milan, 2004).

Randazzo, B., 'Le pronunce della Corte europea dei diritti dell'uomo: effetti ed esecuzione nell'ordinamento italiano', in Zanon, N. (ed.), *Le Corti dell'integrazione europea e la Corte costituzionale italiana: avvicinamenti, dialoghi, dissonanze* (Naples, 2006).

Reif, L., 'Building Democratic Institutions: The Role of National Human Rights Institutions in Good Governance and Human Rights Protection', *Harvard Human Rights Journal* 13 (2000), 1.

Requejo Pagés, J. L., 'La articulación de las jurisdicciones internacional, constitucional y ordinaria en la defensa de los derechos fundamentales. A propósito de la STC 245/91, caso Bultó', *Revista Española de Derecho Constitucional* 35 (1992), 179.

Ripol Carulla, S., *El sistema europeo de protección de los derechos humanos y el Derecho Español. La incidencia de las sentencias del Tribunal Europeo de Derechos Humanos en el ordenamiento jurídico español* (Barcelona, 2007).

Rodríguez, A., *Integración Europea y derechos fundamentales* (Madrid, 2001).

Ruiz Miguel, C., *El derecho a la proteccion de la vida privada en la jurisprudencia del Tribunal Europo de Derechos Humanos* (Madrid, 1994).

—, *La ejecución de las sentencias del Tribunal Europeo de Derechos Humanos: Un estudio sobre la relación entre el Derecho nacional y el internacional* (Madrid, 1997).

Saiz Arnaiz, A., *La apertura constitucional al derecho internacional y europeo de los derechos humanos: el artículo 10.2 de la Constitución Española*, Consejo General del Poder Judicial (Madrid, 1999).

Sarmiento, D., Mieres Mieres, L. and Presno Linera, M., *Las sentencias básicas del Tribunal Europeo de Derechos Humanos* (Pamplona, 2007).

Selvaggi, E., 'I dispositivi della Corte europea possono travolgere il giudicato', *Guida al diritto* 43 (2005), 86.

Van Drooghenbroeck, S., *La proportionnalité dans le droit de la Convention européenne des droits de l'Homme : Prendre l'idée simple au sérieux* (Brussels, 2001).

Zanghi, C., *La protezione internazionale dei diritti dell'uomo* (Turin, 2006).

Zanon, N. (ed.), *Le Corti dell'integrazione europea e la Corte costituzionale italiana: avvicinamenti, dialoghi, dissonanze* (Naples, 2006).

8

The Reception Process in Greece and Turkey

İbrahim Özden Kaboğlu and Stylianos-Ioannis G. Koutnatzis*

A. Historical Context: Accession and Ratification[1]

1. Greece

a. First Ratification

Soon after becoming the eleventh Council of Europe (CoE) Member State in August 1949, Greece signed the ECHR on 28 November 1950 and incorporated

---

* İbrahim Özden Kaboğlu has co-authored the Turkish sections, Stylianos-Ioannis G. Koutnatzis has authored the Greek and comparative sections and co-authored the Turkish sections of this report.

[1] *A. Abbreviations*

Greece: DiDik = Διοικητική Δίκη (Administrative Trial [journal]); DtA = Δικαιώματα του Ανθρώπου (Human Rights [journal]); EDDD = Επιθεώρησις Δημοσίου και Διοικητικού Δικαίου (Public and Administrative Law Review); EEEurD = Ελληνική Επιθεώρηση Ευρωπαϊκού Δικαίου (Hellenic European Law Journal); EfDimDik = Εφημερίδα Διοικητικού Δικαίου (Administrative Law Journal); FEK A/B = Φύλλο Εφημερίδας της Κυβερνήσεως, Τεύχος A/B (Issue of the Government Gazette, Part A/B); CG = Σύνταγμα της Ελλάδας (The Constitution of Greece) of 11 June 1975, as revised by parliamentary resolution of 6 April 2001 of the VIIth Revisionary Parliament, FEK A 85, 18 April 2001; HellDni = Ελληνική Δικαιοσύνη (Hellenic Justice [journal]); JMGS = Journal of Modern Greek Studies; KPD = Κώδικας Ποινικής Δικονομίας (Code of Criminal Procedure); KPolD = Κώδικας Πολιτικής Δικονομίας (Code of Civil Procedure); NCHR = Εθνική Επιτροπή για τα Δικαιώματα του Ανθρώπου (National Commission for Human Rights); NoB = Νομικό Βήμα (Law Tribune [journal]); PLog = Ποινικός Λόγος (Penal Word [journal]); PoinChron = Ποινικά Χρονικά (Penal Chronicles [journal]); PoinDik = Ποινική Δικαιοσύνη (Penal Justice [journal]); RHDI = Revue hellénique de droit international; S.Eur.Soc.Pol. = South European Society & Politics [journal]; ToS = Το Σύνταγμα (The Constitution [journal]); Yper = Υπεράσπιση (Defence [journal]).

Turkey: AYMKD = Anayasa Mahkemesi Kararları Dergisi (Journal of the Constitutional Court's Decisions); CRT = Türkiye Cumhuriyeti Anayasası (The Constitution of the Republic of Turkey) of 7 November 1982, as revised by the Grand National Assembly of Turkey on 31 May 2007 (Act no. 5678, R.G. no. 26554, 16 June 2007) (XIVth Revision, approved by referendum on 21 October 2007]; DD = Danıştay Dergisi (Council of State Journal); E. = Esas (case); İHDK/HRAB = İnsan Hakları Danışma Kurulu (Human Rights Advisory Board); İHİD = İdare Hukuku ve İlimleri Dergisi (Journal of Administrative Law and Sciences); İHMD = İnsan Hakları Merkezi Dergisi (Journal of the Centre for Human Rights); İHY = İnsan Hakları Yıllığı (Yearbook of Human Rights); K. = Karar (decision); R.G. = Resmi Gazete (Official Gazette); TBB-İHAUM = Türkiye Barolar Birliği – İnsan Hakları Araştırma ve Uygulama Merkezi (Turkish Bar Association-The Centre of Research and

it into the domestic legal order with a 1953 statute.[2] During the 50's and 60's, the status of the ECHR in Greece corresponded to the limited effectiveness of the rights guarantees under its 1952 Constitution. Soon after the end of a disastrous civil war between the Government and the Communist forces, the reality of, or the perception of, the Communist threat undermined the enforcement of rights' guarantees and perpetuated a yawning gap between the "law in the books" and the "law in action." Soon after the 1952 Constitution took effect, the Parliament enacted a resolution providing that "constitutional acts" (συντακτικές πράξεις) and "decrees" (ψηφίσματα) adopted during the civil war would continue to be valid as exceptional legislation, even if they were inconsistent with the new Constitution.[3] Against this background, the Greek authorities neither examined nor understood the obvious inconsistency of a considerable part of domestic legislation with the ECHR as an obstacle to its incorporation. Further, Greek courts adopted a deferential approach to the political branches of Government.[4]

A military coup on 21 April 1967 overthrew Greece's constitutional Government, with the coup leaders citing the Communist danger to justify it. A dictatorship was established, and suspended most rights guarantees under the 1952 Constitution. The military regime prepared two pseudo-constitutions without the participation of a representative body. These documents were ostensibly approved in largely bogus referendums by the overwhelming majority of the electorate. Nonetheless, their most important elements, including their rights guarantees, were never put into effect. The military regime invoked the derogation clause of Article 15 ECHR, asserting that the country faced a "public emergency threatening the life of the nation."

In September 1967, Denmark, Sweden and Norway filed interstate applications against Greece,[5] joined one week later by the Netherlands,[6] alleging

Practice for Human Rights); TBMM = Türkiye Büyük Millet Meclisi (Grand National Assembly of Turkey); TYHR = Turkish Yearbook of Human Rights; YD = Yargıtay Dergisi (Court of Cassation Journal); YKD = Yargıtay Kararları Dergisi (Journal of the Court of Cassation's Decisions).
B. *Translations*
   - English translation of the Greek Constitution by Xenophon Paparrigopoulos/Stavroula Vasilouni, available at: http://www.parliament.gr.
   - English translation of the Turkish Constitution by the Directorate General of Press and Information of the Republic of Turkey, available at: http://www.byegm.gov.tr/mevzuat/anayasa/anayasa-ing.htm.
   - Other translations of Greek and Turkish terms are of the authors' own making, unless otherwise indicated.
C. *Websites*
   Unless otherwise indicated, all websites were last visited at the end of September 2007.

   [2] Act 2329/1953, FEK A 68, 18/21 March 1953.
   [3] See, in general, Alivizatos (1979), 415 et seq.; Pantélis (1979), 45 et seq.
   [4] See, e.g., Dagtoglou (1964), 394 et seq.; Alivizatos (1979), 163 et seq., 462 et seq.; Pollis (1987), 602 et seq.
   [5] *Denmark v. Greece* (appl. no. 3321/67); *Norway v. Greece* (appl. no. 3322/67); *Sweden v. Greece* (appl. no. 3323/67).
   [6] *The Netherlands v. Greece* (appl. no. 3344/67).

violations of several ECHR guarantees as a result of administrative and legislative measures that led to mass internment, torture, trials before extraordinary courts martial and media censorship. The European Commission of Human Rights (ECommHR) found the applications to be admissible[7] and established a Sub-Commission charged with administering evidence. After considering the Sub-Commission's findings, in November 1969, the ECommHR approved an extensive Report.[8] The ECommHR rejected the Greek Government's assertion of an emergency. On the basis of a comprehensive assessment of the evidence it decided that there was no imminent threat of political instability and disorder in Greece[9] and found that the Greek Government had violated ten ECHR rights.[10] The ECommHR devoted more than 400 pages of its Report to allegations of Article 3 ECHR violations, finding a practice of torture and ill-treatment of political detainees as well as unacceptable conditions of detention.[11]

In an attempt to pre-empt its looming expulsion from the CoE due to human rights abuses, in December 1969, the Greek military regime denounced both the CoE's Statute and the ECHR (and Protocol no. 1).[12] Nonetheless, since according to then Article 65(1) ECHR the denunciation came into effect only six months later, the CoE's Committee of Ministers in April 1970[13] was not precluded from endorsing the ECommHR's Report and authorizing its publication.[14] No domestic legislative act followed the denunciation of the ECHR. Thus, the 1953 statute incorporating the ECHR into the Greek legal order remained formally in force.

b. Second Ratification

Following the collapse of Greece's military dictatorship in 1974, a National Unity Government was formed that included eminent politicians of the pre-dictatorship period. Among its first acts was the reapproval of the ECHR[15] and the CoE's Statute.[16] Once again, the approval of the ECHR was not a matter of political debate; the Government considered it an obvious step, demonstrating the end of

---

[7] *Denmark v. Greece; Norway v. Greece; Sweden v. Greece; the Netherlands v. Greece* (appl. nos 3321/67; 3322/67; 3323/67; 3344/67), Decision (Plenary), Commission, 24 January 1968, Yearbook of the European Convention on Human Rights 11 (1968), 690; 31 May 1968, Yearbook of the European Convention on Human Rights 11 (1968), 730.

[8] *The Greek Case* (Denmark, Norway, Sweden and the Netherlands v. Greece), ECommHR Report, 5 November 1969, Yearbook of the European Convention on Human Rights 12 (1969), 11.

[9] Ibid., 29 et seq.

[10] In particular, the Commission found violations of Articles 3, 5, 6, 8, 10, 11, 13; Article 14 read together with Articles 9, 10; and Article 3 of Protocol no. 1. See *The Greek Case* (*supra* note 8), 120 et seq.

[11] *The Greek Case* (*supra* note 8), 186 et seq.

[12] Denunciation, Yearbook of the European Convention on Human Rights 12 (1969), 78 et seq.

[13] Resolution DH (70)1, Yearbook of the European Convention on Human Rights 12 (1969), *The Greek Case*, 511.

[14] See, in detail, Kiss/Vegleris (1971); Valticos (2002); Perrakis (1997).

[15] Legislative Degree no. 53/1974, FEK A 256, 20 September 1974.

[16] Legislative Degree no. 196/1974, FEK A 356, 28 November 1974.

political instability. Similarly, the ECHR and its status in the Greek legal order were largely absent from the polarized debate on the new Constitution.[17] After a considerable delay, Greece recognized the compulsory jurisdiction of the ECtHR on 30 January 1979, and the individual petition right on 20 November 1985, for all allegations of ECHR violations after that date except for the freedoms guaranteed by ECHR Protocol no. 7.

Greece approved by statute and ratified Protocols nos 1,[18] 2, 3 and 5,[19] as well as Protocols nos 6,[20] 7,[21] 8,[22] 11,[23] 13,[24] and 14[25] to the ECHR. None of these ratifications stirred up political controversy. As of 2007, Greece has not signed Protocol no. 4; it has signed, but not (yet) ratified Protocols nos 9, 10 and 12.

c. Reservations and Declarations

The 1953 ratification of the ECHR by Greece included a reservation on the right of parents to ensure education and teaching in conformity with their religious and philosophical convictions (Article 2 *alinea* 2 of Protocol no. 1), providing that the word "philosophical" will conform to the relevant provisions of domestic law. Greece's 1974 ratification included a different reservation with respect to the same right, accepting it only in so far as it is compatible with the provision of efficient instruction and training and with no unreasonable public expenditure. In 1979, Greece withdrew the latter reservation, confirming, however, the former one on the application of the word "philosophical." This reservation was withdrawn in 1985 so that no internationally valid[26] reservation remains in effect today. Similarly, the only declaration accompanying the post-dictatorship ratification of the ECHR in Greece was of limited importance.

---

[17] On the major points of contention, see, e.g., Koutnatzis (2007), 159 et seq. with further references.

[18] Legislative Degree no. 53/1974 (*supra* note 15).

[19] Legislative Decree no. 215/1974, FEK A 365, 7 December 1974.

[20] Act no. 2610/1998, FEK A 110, 22/25 May 1998.

[21] Act no. 1705/1987, FEK A 89, 12 June 1987.

[22] Act no. 1841/1989, FEK A 94, 14 April 1989.

[23] Act no. 2400/1996, FEK A 96, 4 June 1996.

[24] Act no. 3289/2004, FEK A 227, 25/26 November 2004.

[25] Act no. 3344/2005, FEK A 133, 6 June 2005.

[26] The approval statute of Protocol no. 7 in Greece provided that Article 2 (1) (right of appeal in criminal matters) does not affect the validity of Article 489 KPD, which recognizes the right of appeal only when the penalty exceeds certain minimum limits. This provision was not a valid reservation because it did not accompany the internationally valid text of the treaty. However, Greek courts have not consistently made this distinction. On this issue, see e.g., Ioannou (2001), 359.

Table 1

Protocol[27]	Signature	Ratification	Entry into force	Declarations/Reservations
Protocol no. 1	20 March 1952	28 Nov. 1974	28 Nov. 1974	–
Protocol no. 2	28 Nov. 1974	8 Jan. 1975	28 Nov. 1974	1 declaration[28]
Protocol no. 3	30 Nov. 1965	8 Jan. 1975	28 Nov. 1974	1 declaration[29]
Protocol no. 4	–	–	–	–
Protocol no. 5	28 Nov. 1974	8 Jan. 1975	28 Nov. 1974	1 declaration[30]
Protocol no. 6	2 May 1983	8 Sept. 1998	1 Oct. 1998	–
Protocol no. 7	22 Nov. 1984	29 Oct. 1987	1 Nov. 1988	
Protocol no. 8	19 March 1985	6 Sept. 1989	1 Jan. 1990	–
Protocol no. 9	6 Nov. 1990	–	–	–
Protocol no. 10	29 April 1992	–	–	–
Protocol no. 11	11 May 1994	9 Jan. 1997	1 Nov. 1998	–

2. Turkey

a. Ratification

After becoming the thirteenth CoE Member State in August 1949, Turkey participated in drafting the ECHR, signing it at its adoption on 4 November 1950. The Turkish Grand National Assembly approved the ECHR with a 1954 Act[31] under the 1924 Constitution. While Turkey's early adoption of the ECHR signalled its openness to supra-nationalism, this openness did not have an immediate effect on national law. On the contrary, in the second half of the 50's, the National Assembly passed a series of statutes that were incompatible with both the Constitution and the ECHR, and were used to provide a certain degree of legitimacy to the military junta that took power on 27 May 1960. In the aftermath of the coup, a new Constitution was adopted in 1961,[32] which essentially

---

[27] Source: http://conventions.coe.int/Treaty/Commun/ChercheMembres.asp?CM=3&CL=ENG.
[28] Declaration: "In depositing this instrument of ratification, the Permanent Representative stated that Protocols nos 2, 3 and 5 shall enter into force in respect of Greece with effect from 28 November 1974, date of the deposit of the instrument of ratification of the Convention of 4 November 1950 and of the Protocol of 20 March 1952. He recalled the declaration made by the Minister for Foreign Affairs of Greece on 28 November 1974, at the time of deposit of the instrument of ratification of the Convention and the said Protocol and at the occasion of signature of Protocol no. 5 of 20 January 1966, according to which Greece should complete with a minimum of delay the whole set of instruments relating to the Convention with effect from 28 November 1974." (8 January 1975 – present).
[29] See *supra* note 28.
[30] Ibid.
[31] Act no. 6366, 10 March 1954, R.G. no. 8662, 19 March 1954, 8690 et seq.
[32] For more on the 1961 Constitution, see Marcou (1996), 44 et seq.; Kubali (1965), 855 et seq.

founded a democratic regime, relying on the separation of powers and proclaiming that the Republic of Turkey would be governed by the rule of law based on human rights (Article 2). It included an extensive rights catalogue and established a Constitutional Court charged with the judicial review of legislation. While this Constitution reflected the influence of Western European post-World War II constitutionalism, its implementation caused many problems. Under the pressure from the military generals, the 1961 Constitution was revised in 1971 in a radical way, aiming primarily at restricting fundamental rights.

After a 1974 coup d'état led by Greek Cypriot officers, Turkey's military intervention and the continuing division of Cyprus, the Cyprus Government filed four interstate applications against Turkey. Concerning the first two applications,[33] the ECommHR found serious violations of several ECHR rights and forwarded its (never officially published) report to the CoE Committee of Ministers, since neither Turkey nor Cyprus had accepted the ECtHR's jurisdiction. However, the CoE Committee of Ministers limited itself to strongly urging the parties to resume intercommunal talks under the auspices of the United Nations in order to reestablish peace and confidence between the communities.[34] Regarding the third application,[35] the ECommHR found violations of Article 5 ECHR (right to liberty and security) because an indefinite number of missing Greek Cypriots remained in Turkish custody, Article 8 ECHR (right to respect for private and family life) due to the displacement of more than 170,000 Greek Cypriot refugees and the separation of families and Article 1 of Protocol no. 1 (property rights) due to the deprivation of possessions belonging to the displaced Greek Cypriots.[36] After several years, the CoE Committee of Ministers decided to make public the ECommHR report, viewing this decision as completing the consideration of the case.[37] Finally, concerning the fourth application,[38] the ECtHR found violations of several ECHR provisions, relating to the failure of the Turkish authorities to effectively investigate the fate of Greek Cypriot missing persons and their relatives,[39] the rights of displaced persons to respect for their home and property,[40] the rights of the enclaved Greek Cypriots[41] as well as of the Turkish

---

[33] *Cyprus v. Turkey* (appl. nos 6780/74 and 6950/75).
[34] Council of Europe, Committee of Ministers, Resolution, 20 January 1979, DH(79)1, Yearbook of the European Convention on Human Rights 22 (1979), 440.
[35] *Cyprus v. Turkey* (appl. no. 8007/77).
[36] *Cyprus v. Turkey* (appl. no. 8007/77), ECommHR Report, 4 October 1983, European Human Rights Reports 15 (1993), 509.
[37] Council of Europe, Committee of Ministers, Resolution, 2 April 1992, DH(92)12.
[38] *Cyprus v. Turkey* (appl. no. 25781/94).
[39] *Cyprus v. Turkey* (appl. no. 25781/94). Judgement (Grand Chamber), 10 May 2001, Reports 2001-IV, 1 et seq., paras 132–136, 148–150, 157–158 (Articles 2, 3 and 5 ECHR).
[40] Ibid., paras 171–175, 184–189, 193–194 (Articles 8 and 13 ECHR and 1 of Protocol no. 1).
[41] Ibid., paras 245–246, 252–254, 269–270, 277–280, 292–296, 307–311, 324 (Articles 3, 8, 9, 10 and 13 ECHR and Articles 1 and 2 of Protocol no. 1).

Cypriots living in northern Cyprus.[42] The full execution of this ECtHR judgement is still pending.[43]

After another coup d'état in Turkey in 1980, a "Consultative Assembly" controlled by the military drafted the 1982 Constitution. Its framers took pains to formally ensure compliance with the ECHR. Nevertheless, the 1982 Constitution, which relied on a strong executive branch and recognized a limited form of judicial independence, reflected a semi-democracy; in effect, the military still held most of the power. Resting on the implicit understanding that Turkey was in a constant state of emergency, the 1982 Constitution signified a break with the protective tradition of the 1961 Constitution.[44] Since 1987, the 1982 Constitution has been successively amended in the direction of restoring the rule of law and strengthening human rights. Aiming at decreasing the military's role, the 2001 constitutional amendments ensured a civilian majority in the National Security Council and explicitly provided its merely advisory character (Article 118 CRT). Nevertheless, the Turkish military maintains a substantial influence over Turkish politics that is unique in comparison with other European democracies.

The militarization of the Turkish political system and its persistent human rights violations affected the relations between Turkey and the CoE. In June 1982, France, Norway, Denmark, Sweden and the Netherlands filed interstate applications against Turkey[45] alleging violations of Articles 3 (prohibition of torture), 5 (right to liberty and security), 6 (right to a fair trial), 9 (freedom of thought, conscience and religion), 10 (freedom of expression) 11 (freedom of assembly and association) and 15(3) ECHR (derogation clause). The ECommHR found the applications to be admissible.[46] However, the parties eventually reached a friendly settlement that required, *inter alia*, that the Turkish authorities provide continued information to the ECommHR on human rights issues including the conditions of detention, that they progressively lift martial law and facilitate amnesty or similar measures. While the friendly settlement could not guarantee implementation, the Commission's 1985 Report found that the settlement "was secured on the basis of respect for Human Rights" in the sense of then Article 28(b) ECHR.[47]

On 28 January 1987, Turkey recognized the individual petition right, and was

[42] Ibid., paras 358–359 (Article 6 ECHR – trial of civilians by military courts).

[43] See Council of Europe, Committee of Ministers, Interim Resolution, 4 April 2007, ResDH(2007)25.

[44] For a criticism of the 1982 Constitution, see Tanör (1986), 95 et seq.; Sencer (1985–1986), 15 et seq.

[45] *France v. Turkey (*appl. no. 9940/82); *Norway v. Turkey* (appl. no. 9941/82); *Denmark v. Turkey* (appl. no. 9942/82,); *Sweden v. Turkey* (appl. no. 9943/82); *the Netherlands v. Turkey* (appl. no. 9944/82).

[46] *France v. Turkey; Norway v. Turkey; Denmark v. Turkey ; Sweden v. Turkey; the Netherlands v. Turkey* (appl. nos 9940/82; 9941/82; 9942/82; 9943/82; 9944/82), Decision, 6 December 1983, Yearbook of the European Convention on Human Rights 26 (1983), Eur. Comm. Case-Law 1.

[47] *France v. Turkey; Norway v. Turkey; Denmark v. Turkey; Sweden v. Turkey; the Netherlands v. Turkey* (appl. nos 9940/82; 9941/82; 9942/82; 9943/82; 9944/82), ECommHR Report, 7 December

one of the last then CoE Member States to do so; it was also the last Member State to recognize the ECtHR's compulsory jurisdiction on 22 January 1990. Nevertheless, apart from the temporary restriction of the individual petition right, the Turkish Government promulgated far-reaching "conditions" that provided, *inter alia*, that the right of petition extends only to allegations concerning public authorities' acts or omissions performed within the territory to which the Turkish Constitution is applicable – a restriction aimed at precluding individual petitions relating to northern Cyprus; that the conditions of derogation under Article 15 ECHR and the notion of a "democratic society" under Articles 8–11(2) ECHR must be understood based on the Turkish Constitution; that the power of the ECommHR shall not comprise matters regarding the legal status of military personnel and the system of discipline in the armed forces; and that the provisions of the Turkish Constitution on freedom of association, activities of labour unions and public professional organizations must be understood as being in conformity with Articles 10 and 11 ECHR. In addition, Turkey's recognition of the ECtHR's compulsory jurisdiction was territorially limited to the Republic of Turkey's national territory. However, after examining these conditions, the ECtHR found no legal basis for restricting Turkey's declarations under then Articles 25 and 46 ECHR on substantive or territorial grounds.[48] As the ECtHR emphasized, a different approach would seriously weaken the role of ECommHR and ECtHR in the discharge of their functions and diminish the effectiveness of the ECHR as a constitutional instrument of European public order.[49] Given Turkey's main intention to be bound under then Articles 25 and 46 ECHR, the ECtHR found that Turkey's invalid conditions did not render the declarations null and void as a whole because Turkey had disregarded the CoE Member States' consistent practice of accepting the ECommHR and ECtHR's competence unconditionally, the ECommHR and ECtHR's position to that effect in other proceedings and the reaction of other Member States to the Turkish declarations themselves; thus, according to the ECtHR, Turkey knowingly risked to be bound by an unlimited declaration.[50]

As of 2007, Turkey has approved and ratified ECHR Protocols nos 1,[51] 2,[52]

1985, Yearbook of the European Convention on Human Rights 28 (1985), 150, 158. See generally Özdek (2004), 118 et seq.

[48] *Loizidou v. Turkey* (appl. no. 15318/89), Judgement (Preliminary Objections) (Grand Chamber), 23 March 1995, A 310, paras 70–89.

[49] Ibid., para. 75.

[50] Ibid., paras 93–98.

[51] See *supra* note 31.

[52] Approved by Act no. 900, 13 July 1967, R.G. no. 12655, 24 July 1967.

3,[53] 5,[54] 6,[55] 8,[56] 11,[57] 13[58] and 14.[59] It has approved by statute Protocol no. 4,[60] but has not yet deposited the instrument of ratification with the CoE Secretary General. Further, Turkey has signed, but not yet ratified Protocols nos 7 and 12, nor has it signed Protocol no. 10.

b. Reservations and Declarations

Turkey's ratification of the ECHR included a reservation on the right to education, providing that Article 2 of Protocol no. 1 shall not affect the validity of a 1924 domestic statute[61] prohibiting the establishment of private religious schools. Further, citing terrorist threats and invoking Article 15 ECHR, in the early 90's, Turkey submitted several declarations that empowered the executive branch to take sweeping measures in derogation of ECHR guarantees such as banning publications, shutting down printing presses, ordering persons to settle in a place outside a state of emergency region, suspending or requiring permission for strikes and lockouts, ordering the evacuation of villages or residential areas and transferring public officials to other posts. After limiting the scope of its notice of derogation with respect to Article 5 ECHR (right to liberty and security) in 1993, Turkey withdrew these declarations in January 2002.

---

[53] Approved by Act no. 901, 13 July 1967, R.G. no. 12655, 24 July 1967.
[54] Approved by Decree no. 7/3211, 29 September 1966, R.G. no. 14028, 30 November 1971.
[55] Approved by Act no. 4913, 26 June 2003, R.G. no. 24155, 1 July 2003.
[56] Approved by Act no. 3526, 12 April 1989, R.G. no. 20145, 20 April 1989.
[57] Approved by Act no. 4255, 14 May 1997, R.G. no. 22996, 22 May 1997.
[58] Approved by Act no. 5409, 6 October 2005, R.G. no. 25964, 12 October 2005.
[59] Approved by Act no. 5512, 1 June 2006, R.G. no. 26190, 6 June 2006.
[60] Approved by Act no. 3975, 23 February 1994, R.G. no. 21861, 26 February 1994.
[61] Tevhid-i Tedrisat Kanunu [Law Relating to the Unification of Education] Act no. 430, 3 March 1924, R.G. no. 63, 6 March 1924.

Table 2

Protocol[62]	Signature	Ratification	Entry into force	Declarations/Reservations
Protocol no. 1	20 March 1952	18 May 1954	18 May 1954	1 reservation concerning Article 2[63]
Protocol no. 2	6 May 1963	25 March 1968	21 Sept. 1970	–
Protocol no. 3	6 May 1963	25 March 1968	21 Sept. 1970	–
Protocol no. 4	19 Oct. 1992	–	–	–
Protocol no. 5	14 May 1971	20 Dec. 1971	20 Dec. 1971	–
Protocol no. 6	15 Jan. 2003	12 Nov. 2003	1 Dec. 2003	–
Protocol no. 7	14 March 1985	–	–	–
Protocol no. 8	4 Feb. 1986	19 Sept. 1989	1 Jan. 1990	–
Protocol no. 9	6 Nov. 1990	–	–	–
Protocol no. 10	–	–	–	–
Protocol no. 11	11 May 1994	11 July 1997	1 Nov. 1998	–
Protocol no. 12	18 April 2001	–	–	–
Protocol no. 13	9 Jan. 2004	20 Feb. 2006	1 June 2006	–
Protocol no. 14	6 Oct. 2004	2 Oct. 2006	–	–

3. Comparison and Conclusion

There are great similarities between Greece and Turkey concerning the accession and ratification of the ECHR. The two countries acceded to the CoE and ratified the ECHR almost simultaneously in the early 50's. Neither country substantively examined domestic legislation as to its consistency with the ECHR. Rather, the two countries' accession to the CoE and the ECHR was aimed at concealing rule of law deficits and securing their participation in the Western alliance. In both countries, the ECHR remained at a theoretical level and it was not put into practice for a considerable time after ratification. Similarly, to a significant extent, the rights guarantees included both in the 1952 Greek and the 1961 Turkish constitutions were not implemented. In both countries, military dictatorships hindered democratic development and forcefully undermined any concept of rights protection. Other CoE Member States filed interstate complaints against Greece and Turkey, alleging violations of several ECHR guarantees. While the Greek military dictatorship denounced the ECHR to prevent its expulsion from

---

[62] Source: http://conventions.coe.int/Treaty/Commun/ChercheMembres.asp?CM=3&CL=ENG.

[63] Reservation: "Having seen and examined the Convention and the Protocol (First), we have approved the same with the reservation set out in respect of Article 2 of the Protocol by reason of the provisions of Law no. 6366 voted by the National Grand Assembly of Turkey dated 10 March 1954. Article 3 of the said Law no. 6366 reads: Article 2 of the Protocol shall not affect the provisions of Law no. 430 of 3 March 1924 relating to the unification of education." (18 May 1954 – present).

the CoE, the interstate applications against Turkey were either concluded with a friendly settlement or led to findings of violation that remain unaddressed. Nonetheless, both the Greek and the Turkish case tested the ECHR's effectiveness in dealing with regimes whose disregard for human rights reflected a strategic choice. Greece and Turkey were among the last CoE Members to recognize the right of individual petition; further, both nations delayed the recognition of the ECtHR's compulsory jurisdiction. Finally, in compliance with the standard practice not to examine *ex ante* inconsistencies of national legislation with the ECHR, both countries used reservations sparingly.

Nevertheless, after the restoration of democracy in Greece in 1975, the two countries diverged considerably. The 1975 Greek Constitution reflects a break with the country's long-standing political divisions. In contrast, military interventions persisted in Turkey. The country's 1982 Constitution maintained a strong authoritarian hold over society, although successive constitutional amendments since 1987 have brought about some progress towards democracy and human rights. Consistently with this development, Greece recognized the compulsory jurisdiction of the ECtHR in 1979 and the right of individual petition in 1985, eleven years and fourteen months, respectively, before Turkey. Further, after the restoration of democracy in 1975, Greece steadily acted more quickly in ratifying the ECHR Protocols. On the other hand, Turkey attached far-reaching conditions to its recognition of the right to individual petition and the compulsory jurisdiction of the ECtHR, conditions that were deemed invalid by the Strasbourg organs. Moreover, in the 90's Turkey invoked the need to protect itself against terrorism in justifying its derogation from several ECHR guarantees under Article 15 ECHR. It remains to be seen how these differences between the two countries play out in practice and whether they are differences in time, style or substance.

B. Status of the ECHR in National Law: Formal (Doctrinal) Elements

1. Greece

a. Relationship between International and Domestic Law

The 1952 Constitution did not include provisions on the status of international law in the Greek legal system. Nevertheless, Greek courts have recognized, since the nineteenth century, that customary international law is valid as the law of the land. International scholars have also applied this conclusion to the international treaties that Greece had sanctioned by law. Accordingly, in case of a conflict between an international treaty and a Greek statute, the *lex posterior derogat priori* rule applied.[64] Nevertheless, courts sometimes operated on the assumption that

---

[64] See, e.g., Valticos (1958), 223 et seq.

the legislature did not intend to violate an international treaty, unless a statute explicitly required its application despite its inconsistency with a treaty.[65]

Reflecting the Greek populace's intellectual reaction against totalitarianism, the drafters of the present 1975 Constitution[66] relied on international rules and principles[67] as the democratic rules *par excellence*.[68] The Constitution includes several manifestations of this.[69] Article 28 CG is of particular importance; while its second and third paragraphs lay the foundation for Greece's participation in the European integration,[70] Article 28 (1) concerns the position of international law in the Greek legal order. It stipulates that "[t]he generally recognised rules of international law, as well as international conventions as of the time they are ratified by statute and become operative according to their respective conditions, shall be an integral part of domestic Greek law." Against this backdrop, most scholars describe the Greek Constitution as monist with respect to customary international law. While scholars have formed no consensus on whether the statutory approval of international treaties "transforms" them into domestic legislation,[71] the application of international treaties in Greece follows a qualified dualist model.[72]

The Greek Constitution explicitly provides for the supra-legislative status of international law, stipulating that both customary and treaty law "shall prevail over any contrary provision of the law" (Article 28 (1)), even over subsequently enacted norms. Nevertheless, in the case of conflict between an international treaty such as the ECHR and the Greek Constitution, the latter should take precedence from the constitutional perspective. Some scholars construe Article 28 (1) CG as placing international law on an equal footing with Greek constitutional norms.[73] Others argue that international human rights treaties are binding on the Greek Parliament as an organ charged with carrying out constitutional amendments.[74] However, while in the constitutional amendment process drafters

---

[65] See, e.g., Evrigenis (1965), 355 et seq.

[66] Neither the 1986 nor the 2001 amendments affected the status of international law in the Greek legal order. On the 2001 amendments, see, in general, Alivizatos/Eleftheriadis (2002); Venizelos (2003).

[67] See, in general, Fatouros (1976); Roucounas (1976); Roucounas (1996).

[68] Ioannou (2001), 357.

[69] See, e.g., Article 2 (2) CG ("Greece, adhering to the generally recognized rules of international law, pursues the strengthening of peace and of justice, and the fostering of friendly relations among peoples and States"); Article 5 (2) CG (guaranteeing to "[a]ll persons living in the Greek territory [...] full protection of their life, honour and liberty regardless of nationality, race or language and of religious or political beliefs," with exceptions permitted "only in cases provided by international law").

[70] On the doctrinal interrelationship between Article 28 (2) and (3), see generally Iliopoulos-Strangas (2008), 83 et seq. with further references.

[71] Cf., e.g., Fatouros (1976), 498 with Ioannou (2001), 358.

[72] See, e.g., Ioannou (2001), 358.

[73] See Vlachos (1979), 99.

[74] See Pararas (2001), 552.

take international obligations into account, this does not mean that international treaties have a constitutional or supra-constitutional status.

Further, because Article 6 (2) of the European Union Treaty (ex-Art. F 2) – both in the Maastricht and in the Amsterdam versions – refers to the ECHR in connection with the common constitutional traditions of Member States, two Council of State panel decisions in the 90's recognized the ECHR's supra-constitutional status as a component of EU law.[75] Nevertheless, the Court *en banc*[76] avoided any pronouncement on the hierarchical status of the ECHR as part of EU law. In fact, the mere reference to the ECHR in the EU Treaty can scarcely constitute an adequate authority to modify the ECHR's status in national constitutional systems.[77]

The conflict potential between the Greek Constitution and the ECHR is limited[78] because the Constitution includes an extensive bill of rights (Articles 4–25) that in most respects[79] go beyond the ECHR's.[80] Although most of the potential conflicts between the Greek Constitution and the ECHR can be resolved,[81] it is indeed difficult to harmonize in some instances. For example, the Greek Constitution contains a general prohibition against religious proselytizing (Article 13 (2) *alinea* 2 CG), which raises concerns as to whether this prohibition could pass muster under the proportionality standard enunciated in Article 9(2) ECHR.[82] In addition, among the detailed provisions on Parliamentary incompatibilities,[83] Greece's 2001 constitutional amendments made it unconstitutional for a Member of Parliament to exercise any profession during his/her tenure (Article 57 (1) CG), which carried the penalty of forfeiture from Parliamentary office. While

---

[75] See Greek Council of State, Judgement, 1994.11.22, no. 3502/1994, ToS 1995, 891, 895; Greek Council of State, Judgement, 1997.01.28, no. 249/1997, DiDik 1997, 361, 363.

[76] Greek Council of State, Judgement, 1998.11.27, no. 4674/1998, ToS 1999, 106 et seq.

[77] See Iliopoulos-Strangas (2008), 97–98; see also Greek Council of State, Judgement, 1997.05.15, no. 1863/1997, DiDik 1997, 1172, 1174–1175.

[78] See also Chryssogonos (2001), 180; Iliopoulos-Strangas (2008), 98.

[79] Some exceptions include the freedoms of assembly and association that are guaranteed constitutionally only for Greek citizens (Articles 11 (1); 12 (1) CG); the protection of property (Article 17 CG), which Greek courts traditionally limited to rights *in rem*; and the right to a fair trial in light of the narrow way in which Greek courts typically construe Article 20 (1) CG.

[80] See, e.g., Iliopoulos-Strangas (2006), 33 et seq.

[81] For instance, the Parliamentary immunity provision (Article 62 CG) requires a Parliamentary leave for the prosecution of Members of Parliament, which the Parliament has granted only exceptionally. While this practice has led in 2006 to an ECtHR finding of violation of Article 6 ECHR for a refusal to allow criminal proceedings for a complaint that allegedly occurred before election to the Parliament (*Tsalkitzis v. Greece* [appl. no. 11801/04], Judgement [First Section], 16 November 2006 [not yet reported], paras 48–51), it is this Parliamentary practice rather than the constitutional provision that contravenes the ECHR.

[82] See, e.g., Iliopoulos-Strangas (2008), 100.

[83] Article 56 (3) CG provides, *inter alia*, that persons who have held certain posts in public office may not stand for election nor be elected to Parliament notwithstanding their prior resignation. Contrary to the ECommHR, the ECtHR has concluded that this system was neither inconsistent nor arbitrary. *Gitonas and Others v. Greece* (appl. nos 18747/91; 19376/92; 19379/92; 28208/95; 27755/95), Judgement, 1 July 1997, Reports 1997-IV, 1217. See also *infra* note 223 and accompanying text.

pointing out in a 2006 ruling that a general incompatibility is rare among European States, the ECtHR did not clarify whether this incompatibility is consistent with Article 3 of ECHR Protocol no. 1 (right to free elections). It did, however, emphasize that the immediate validity of Article 57 (1) CG that was not sufficiently known before the last elections violated the ECHR right to free elections.[84]

Finally, Article 28 (1) *alinea* 2 CG subjects the application of international law to aliens to the reciprocity requirement. However, this condition does not apply to human rights treaties.[85] International mechanisms, in the case of the ECHR, especially the scrutiny by the ECtHR, serve as a sufficient substitute for reciprocity.

b. Judicial Review

aa. Judicial Organization. The Greek legal system is divided into functionally differentiated sub-systems, each having its own high court.[86] The Areios Pagos (*Άρειος Πάγος*) sits at the apex of civil and criminal courts; the Council of State (*Συμβούλιο της Επικρατείας*), modelled on the French *Conseil d' Etat*, functions primarily as the Supreme Administrative Court (Article 95 CG). The Constitution also provides for a third high court, the Court of Audit (*Ελεγκτικό Συνέδριο*), to which no lower courts correspond, and which has comparatively limited responsibilities.[87] In addition, the Constitution establishes a Supreme Special Court (*Ανώτατο Ειδικό Δικαστήριο*) that is primarily charged with settling controversies when conflicting judgements have been issued among the three high courts of the different jurisdictions.[88] Nevertheless the Supreme Special Court has virtually no power in terms of the interpretation of the ECHR.[89]

bb. Control of Legislative and Executive Acts. The separation of powers doctrine is a fundamental constitutional principle.[90] It is not considered as a general barrier to the judicial review of legislative acts concerning constitutional or other "higher" norms. Nevertheless, Greek courts have been, up to the early 90's, especially cautious in exercising judicial review, reflecting separation of powers con-

---

[84] *Lykourezos v. Greece* (appl. no. 33554/03), Judgement (First Section), 15 June 2006 (not yet reported).

[85] See, e.g., Vegleris (1977), 126–127; Briolas (1993), 91; Dagtoglou (2005), 45.

[86] While justice is administered by three hierarchies of courts (administrative, civil and criminal), the same judges regularly alternate between civil and criminal courts. See, e.g., Kerameus (2008), 342 et seq. On the Greek high courts, see, in general, Klamaris (1997), 289 et seq.

[87] Being primarily an institution charged with auditing Government expenditures, the judicial function of the Court of Audit is limited to disputes concerning pensions and the liability of civil or military servants (Article 98 CG).

[88] See Article 100 CG.

[89] See *infra* in the text.

[90] See Article 26 CG.

cerns. In addition, the political branches of Government repeatedly assert such considerations urging the courts to retain a deferential approach when reviewing the constitutionality of legislation.

Since the late nineteenth century, Greek courts have had a diffuse and incidental system of judicial review that remains in place, in its essentials, up to the present day[91] and resembles the American model of judicial review.[92] Accordingly, all courts are charged with the control of constitutionality and conventionality of statutes, while no possibility of either an abstract review or an individual complaint is provided. Initially resting on the supremacy of the Constitution, judicial review of legislation in Greece was based on constitutional custom until the 1975 Constitution added explicit provisions on judicial review of legislation pertaining to constitutional norms.[93] Although there is no similar provision on the control of conventionality of statutes, the supra-legislative status of international treaties is a sufficient basis for Greek courts to control conventionality. The ECHR is the quintessential example of a self-executing treaty,[94] although scholars disagree on whether the control of conventionality can occur *ex officio*[95] or only after a corresponding claim of a litigant.[96] Provided that Greek courts have found that a statutory provision is inconsistent with the Constitution or international law, this provision cannot be applied in the specific case before the court. However, unconstitutional or unconventional legislation remains in effect and thus can be applied in the future.

Despite the general convergence between the control of constitutionality and conventionality of statutes, some differences remain. First, providing that high courts of different jurisdictions have issued conflicting judgements on the constitutionality of a statute the Constitution provides a conflict-resolving mechanism. In this context, the aforementioned Supreme Special Court is charged with definitely settling the controversy (Article 100 (1) *alinea* e CG)[97] and has the authority to declare unconstitutional statutory provisions to be invalid *erga omnes* (i.e., not only inapplicable) (Article 100 (4) CG). In contrast, there is no such option when the country's high courts reach conflicting judgements on the com-

---

[91] See, in general, Spiliotopoulos (1983); Skouris (1988); Dagtoglou (1989).

[92] In recent months, the Government proposed the establishment of a distinct Constitutional Court. Although the proposal essentially maintains the diffuse judicial review system, it does not seem to garner the necessary bipartisan support for a constitutional amendment. On the constitutional amendment process, see Article 110 CG.

[93] See Article 87 (2) CG ("in no case whatsoever shall [judges] be obliged to comply with provisions enacted in violation of the Constitution"); Article 93 (4) CG ("[t]he courts shall be bound not to apply a statute whose content is contrary to the Constitution").

[94] See, e.g., Vegleris (1980), 303; Briolas (1993), 87, 90; Perrakis (1996), 175.

[95] Papadimitriou (1996), 571; Chryssogonos (2001), 225.

[96] See, e.g., Briolas (1993), 94.

[97] This Court is composed of the presidents of the three high courts, four members of the Council of State, and four members of the Areios Pagos, chosen by lot for two-year terms and – on this occasion – two law professors chosen also by lot (Article 100 (2) CG).

patibility of a statute with the ECHR.[98] Although the Supreme Special Court is also charged with settling controversies on statutory interpretation (Article 100 (1) *alinea* e CG), this jurisdiction does not extend to the ECHR as a matter of principle. Consequently, different supreme courts may take varying doctrinal positions on the interpretation of the ECHR.

Second, with the enactment of the 2001 constitutional amendments, when high court panels find a statutory provision unconstitutional, they are generally bound to refer the question to the respective plenum (Article 100 (5) CG). However, the obligatory reference to the respective plenum does not apply to cases of statutes found to be inconsistent with the ECHR.[99] In fact, some scholars predict that in the future the control of conventionality will outweigh the control of constitutionality, thereby permitting high court panels to evade the obligatory reference procedure.[100]

In terms of the judicial review of executive acts concerning "higher" norms, administrative courts directly review the constitutionality and the legality of administrative acts and regulations,[101] including their consistency with the ECHR. While judicial review of legislative acts results principally in the non-applicability of unconstitutional or unconventional statutes, the Greek Constitution provides for the annulment of executive acts as a penalty in cases of "excess of power or violation of the law" (Article 95 (1) *alinea* a CG).

c. Influence of the Unitary Nature of Greece

Greece is a unitary state with a strong centralist tradition. The vertical separation of powers has always played a very limited role despite recent efforts to relax this centralism. The Constitution (Article 102 (1)) establishes a presumption of power in favour of the local Government agencies for the administration of local affairs,[102] while providing, since the 2001 amendments, that a statute may also enable local Government agencies to exercise central State responsibilities. Local Government agencies do not possess autonomous law-making powers, although a statute can delegate to them the regulation of local interest issues (Article 43 (2) *alinea* 2 CG). Further, local authorities are devoid of judicial responsibilities.

---

[98] Cf. Greek Supreme Special Court, Judgement, 1999.12.13, no. 29/1999, HellDni 2000, 1565 (no jurisdiction in the case of conflicting judgements on the compatibility of a Greek statute with community law).

[99] Cf. Greek Council of State, Judgement, 2005.02.15, no. 372/2005, DtA 2005, 1329, 1341.

[100] See Arnaoutoglou (2007), 184 et seq.

[101] See, in general, Spiliotopoulos (2001).

[102] While theoretically giving the legislature discretion in construing the "local affairs" concept (see, e.g., Greek Council of State, Judgement [Full Bench], 2001.10.05, no. 3415/2001, ToS 2002, 151, 152–153), the Council of State has held that local Government agencies cannot exercise responsibilities on issues such as education (see Greek Council of State, Judgement, 2001.25.06, no. 2237/2001, ToS 2002, 470, 472) and spatial planning (cf. Greek Council of State, Judgement [Full Bench], 2005.11.04, no. 3661/2005, ToS 2006, 119).

Hence, the territorial distribution of powers does not have any meaningful effect on the status of the ECHR.

2. Turkey

a. Relationship between International and Domestic Law

Turkey's 1924 Constitution, which was in force at the time of ratification of the ECHR, contained no explicit references to the status of international agreements in Turkish law, and provided only that "the Grand National Assembly alone exercises such functions as [...] concluding conventions and treaties and making peace with foreign states" (Article 26).

The 1961 and 1982 Constitutions stipulated (in Articles 65 and 90 respectively) that the ratification of treaties with other states and international organizations is subject to the approval of the Grand National Assembly through the enactment of a statute. Upon ratification and promulgation by the President of the Republic, international treaties were incorporated into domestic law and became directly enforceable by domestic courts.[103] According to most scholars, both the 1961 and the 1982 Constitutions established a monist relationship between international and national law.

The 1961 and 1982 Constitutions provided that international treaties that were duly put into effect have the force of law and that no appeal to the Constitutional Court can be made on the grounds that these treaties are unconstitutional. Due to these ambiguous formulations, there was no consensus among Turkish scholars on the rank of international treaties in national law until the 2004 constitutional amendments.[104] Some scholars argued that international treaties have the force of an ordinary statute;[105] others maintained that international treaties have a supra-legislative status,[106] either an intermediate rank between ordinary statutes and the Constitution, or a constitutional or even supra-constitutional status.[107] Despite this debate, most scholars distinguished between human rights treaties and other international treaties on the basis of the constitutional provisions concerning the suspension or limitations of constitutional rights that require compliance with international law (Articles 15, 16, 42 CRT).[108] The former, among them the ECHR, had a privileged, constitutional or even supra-constitutional status.[109]

In a similar vein, the Turkish high courts also adopted different views on the status of international law in the domestic legal order. While the Court of Cassation accorded to international treaties principally the force of statute,[110] the

---

[103] See, in detail, Karacaoğlu and Özdek (2001), 882 et seq.
[104] See, in detail, Kaboğlu (2002), 228 et seq.; see also Özdek (2004), 84 et seq.
[105] See, e.g., Pazarcı (1985), 31.
[106] Çelik (1988), 57; Yüzbaşıoğlu (1993), 57 et seq.
[107] See Karacaoğlu and Özdek (2001), 883.
[108] Akıllıoğlu (1992), 41 et seq.; Karacaoğlu and Özdek (2001), 883 et seq.
[109] See also Çelik (1988), 51 et seq.; Gözübüyük (1987), 8.
[110] Gözübüyük (1991), 8 et seq.

Constitutional Court did not follow a consistent line. In theory, it assigned international treaties a supra-legislative status[111] and sporadically qualified them even as supra-constitutional.[112] Nevertheless, in practice, the Constitutional Court maintained on several occasions that international treaties only have the force of an ordinary statute,[113] more recently, however, recognizing the constitutional status of the ECHR.[114] On the other hand, the Council of State accorded supra-constitutional status to the ECHR so that it could strike down exceptional measures taken by Turkey's military regime on the basis of constitutional provisions.[115] In the course of this, the Council of State emphasized that an international treaty did not cease to apply in Turkey, even if it contained an unconstitutional provision.[116] Finally, the Supreme Military Administrative Court, while ruling against a supra-constitutional rank, avoided any clear pronouncement on the position of the ECHR in Turkish law.[117]

Against this background, a 2004 constitutional amendment to Article 90 CRT on the status of international law provided that "[i]n the case of a conflict between international agreements in the area of fundamental rights and freedoms duly put into effect and the domestic laws due to differences in provisions on the same matter, the provisions of international agreements shall prevail," thus explicitly differentiating human rights treaties from all other treaties. This effectively ended most of the debate. Scholars and the courts now generally recognize that international human rights instruments such as the ECHR have a superior status to common legislation, but inferior to the Constitution.[118]

b. Judicial Review

aa. Judicial Organization. The Turkish legal system establishes a two-tiered judicial system comprising both ordinary and administrative courts. The Court of Cassation (*Yargıtay*) is the supreme civil and criminal court (Article 154 (1) CRT) and the Council of State (*Danıştay*) is the supreme administrative court (Article 155 (1) CRT). In addition, the Constitution establishes the Military Court of Cassation (*Askeri Yargıtay*) and the Supreme Military Administrative Court (*Askeri Yüksek İdare Mahkemesi*). The former is the final court to review the

---

[111] See, in detail, Gönül/Cansel/Aliefendioğlu (1990), 166 et seq.

[112] Turkish Constitutional Court, Judgement, 1991.02.28, E. 1990/15, K. 1991/5, AYMKD, no. 27 Vol. I, 48 et seq. (61).

[113] See, e.g., Turkish Constitutional Court, Judgement, 1994.06.16, E. 1993/3, K. 1994/2, R.G. no. 21976, 30 June 1994, 5 et seq. (90).

[114] See, Turkish Constitutional Court, Judgement, 1997.05.22, E. 1996/3, K. 1997/3, AYMKD, no. 36 Vol. II, 978 et seq. (1026 –1027), R.G. no. 13–53, 2 June 2000.

[115] Turkish Council of State, Judgement, 1989.07.12, E. 1988/6, K. 1989/4, R.G. no. 20428, 9 February 1990, DD Nr. 78–79, 50 et seq.

[116] Turkish Council of State, Judgement, 1991.05.22, E. 86/1723, K. 91/933.

[117] Turkish Supreme Military Administrative Court, Judgement, 1998.12.15, E. 98/1041, K. 98/1059.

[118] See, in detail, TBB-İHAUM (2004b); see also Başlar and İshakoğlu (2006), 201.

decisions of military courts (Article 156 (1) CRT); the latter is the first and final court to review administrative actions involving military personnel or relating to military service, even if such actions have been carried out by civilian authorities (Article 157 (1) CRT). The separate status of military jurisdiction is controversial among scholars, for being inconsistent with the rule of law.

bb. Control of Legislative and Executive Acts. In Turkey, like in Greece, the separation of powers principle[119] does not prohibit judicial review of legislation pertaining to "higher" norms. According to Article 138 (1) CRT, judges hand down judgements on the basis of "the Constitution, law, and their personal conviction conforming with the law". Further, under Article 148 (1) CRT, the Constitutional Court "shall examine the constitutionality, in respect of both form and substance, of laws, decrees having the force of law, and the Rules of Procedure of the Turkish Grand National Assembly." Nevertheless, the Turkish judiciary has traditionally conceived Parliamentary statutes as principal norms for decision-making, thus adopting a deferential approach to legislative actions.

Since its 1961 Constitution, Turkey has followed the European model of a separate Constitutional Court (*Anayasa Mahkemesi*), although the framers of the 1982 Constitution tried to diminish the Court's role in the constitutional system. The Constitutional Court can intervene only *a posteriori*, i.e., after the promulgation of a statute or decree. The Court has two basic modes of control: First, abstract control asserted after an application submitted by the President of the Republic, Parliamentary groups of the party in power, the main opposition party, or a minimum of one-fifth of National Assembly members (Article 150 CRT) within a sixty-day time limit after publication of the contested act in Turkey's Official Gazette (Article 151 CRT); second, concrete control when a court hearing a case refers a statute or a decree having the force of statute to the Constitutional Court, provided that the former finds the statute or decree to be unconstitutional or is convinced that the unconstitutionality claim submitted by one of the parties is serious (Article 152 (1) CRT).

Turkish law does not recognize the right to individual constitutional complaint. Scholars propose the establishment of an individual complaint procedure before the Constitutional Court in case of violation of the ECHR.[120] The recognition of such a procedure could enhance interaction between the Turkish Constitutional Court and the ECtHR and improve rights protection in accordance with the subsidiary character of the ECHR. Nevertheless, this proposal is controversial among the judges of the Court of Cassation and the Council of State, as they are concerned that an individual complaint could create a hierarchy among supreme courts.

The Constitutional Court can annul unconstitutional statutes or decrees that

---

[119] See Preamble, para. IV, Articles 7–9 CRT.
[120] See, e.g., Erözden, İnceoğlu, Sağlam, Tahmazoğlu (Üzeltürk) and Uygun (2003), 8.

have the force of statutes, so that they cease to have effect *erga omnes*. Only positive actions are subject to judicial review, while the control of constitutional amendments is limited to their formal requirements. In exercising judicial review of legislation, the Constitutional Court has generally relied on the Turkish Constitution, mentioning the ECHR only in passing.

The Turkish Constitution explicitly does not allow judicial review of two sets of State actions. No action can be brought "alleging unconstitutionality as to the form or substance of decrees having the force of law issued during a state of emergency, martial law or in time of war" (Article 148 (1) CRT).[121] Further, concerning concrete control, no allegation of unconstitutionality can be made "with regard to the same legal provision until ten years elapse after publication in the Official Gazette of the [Constitutional Court decision] dismissing the application on its merits" (Article 152 (4) CRT).

In terms of executive acts, although, in principle, the "[r]ecourse to judicial review shall be available against all actions and acts of administration" (Article 125 (1) CRT), the acts of the President of the Republic on his or her own power, the decisions of the Supreme Military Council (Article 125 (2) CRT) and the Supreme Council of Judges and Public Prosecutors (Article 145 (2) CRT) fall beyond the scope of judicial review. These far-reaching limitations of judicial review undermine the rule of law and are very controversial in Turkey. Indeed, it is very difficult to reconcile these limitations with Articles 6 and 13 ECHR (rights to a fair trial and to an effective remedy) or with the fair trial guarantee contained in the Turkish Constitution (Article 36).

c. Influence of the Unitary Nature of Turkey

Turkey is a centralized unitary State with no vertical separation of powers. Therefore, local Government agencies hold no meaningful power nor do they play a significant role in the reception of the ECHR. However, the protection of State unity is a central concern as reflected in the Constitutional Court's case law. The Court has repeatedly banned political parties that refer to the Kurdish people or to Kurdish self-determination in their political programme. It has construed such references as being threatening to the territorial integrity and unity of the nation.[122] In contrast, the ECtHR has rebutted this case law, and has found on several occasions violations of the freedom of association (Article 11 ECHR).[123]

---

[121] Further, in its original version, the 1982 Constitution barred claims of unconstitutionality against statutes or decrees that were enacted during the exceptional military regime, i.e., from September 1980 to December 1983 (Provisional Article 15 (3)); this exception was abolished in the 2001 amendments.

[122] See, e.g., Turkish Constitutional Court, Judgement, 1992.07.10, E. 1991/2, K. 1992/1, AYMKD, no. 28 Vol. II, 816 et seq. (Socialist Party).

[123] See, e.g., *Socialist Party and Others v. Turkey* (appl. no. 21237/93), Judgement (Grand Chamber), 25 May 1998, Reports 1998-III, 1233, para. 47 (pointing out that the Socialist Party's aim to democratically establish a federal system might be incompatible with the current structure of the Turkish state, not however with democracy).

In addition, several ECtHR findings of violation that concern other ECHR provisions reflect the Turkish authorities' similar preoccupation with the need to protect unity and the territorial integrity of the Turkish State against separatist threats, among them the activity of the Kurdistan Workers' Party (PKK), which is on the European Union's list of terrorist organizations.[124]

3. Comparison and Conclusion

Contrary to the Greek and Turkish Constitutions that were in force at the (initial) ratification of the ECHR, the Constitutions now in force in both countries include explicit provisions on the status of international treaties in the national legal order. Most Greek scholars find that the Greek Constitution has a moderately dualist approach, while their Turkish counterparts maintain that the Turkish Constitution follows the monist system. Despite this apparent divergence, a comparison between Greece and Turkey indicates that the monism v. dualism dichotomy inadequately describes the nuanced constitutional structures that encompass elements of both traditions. In fact, the procedure that both countries follow to implement an international treaty is quite similar. Nevertheless, while an explicit constitutional provision on the status of international treaties was introduced in Turkey in 1961, fourteen years earlier than in Greece, the rank of international treaties in Turkey remained contentious until recently for legal scholars and courts. In contrast, the corresponding provision of the 1975 Greek Constitution resulted in a broad consensus on the supra-legislative rank of international law in the national legal order. Turkey's 2004 constitutional amendments on the relationship between international and domestic law allow a similar conclusion. However, these amendments are limited to conflicts between international treaties and national statutes concerning fundamental rights and it may be too early to draw definitive conclusions about their application.

With respect to judicial organization, the legal system in both Greece and Turkey is principally divided in two functionally differentiated sub-systems, one for civil and criminal cases, and the other for administrative cases, each having its own supreme court. While the Greek Constitution establishes a Supreme Special Court charged with ensuring a certain consistency among jurisdictions, in terms of the implementation of the ECHR, its power is virtually non-existent. As a result, different high courts may adopt divergent approaches. A fundamental

---

[124] Council Decision 2007/868/EC of 20 December 2007 implementing Article 2 (3) of Regulation (EC) No. 2580/2001 on specific restrictive measures directed against certain persons and entities with a view to combating terrorism, O.J. L 340/100, 22 December 2007, Article 1, Annex, under 2 no. 17. After in January 2007 the European Court of Justice overturned a Court of First Instance decision to deny an appeal by the PKK, a case challenging PKK's inclusion in the EU's "terrorist" list is currently pending before the Court of First Instance. See European Court of Justice, Judgement (First Chamber), 18 January 2007, C-229/05, *Osman Ocalan and Serif Vanly v. Council of the European Union*, O.J. C 56/5, 10 March 2007. The ECtHR as well has qualified the PKK as "a terrorist organisation". See *Zana v. Turkey* (appl. no. 18954/91), Judgement (Grand Chamber), 25 November 1997, Reports 1997-VII, 2533, para. 58.

difference between the two countries relates to military jurisdiction. In Turkey, military supreme courts are not subject to control by any civilian authority; in contrast, Greek military courts are subject to control by civilian courts.

Despite separation-of-powers doctrines and a tradition of deference, judicial review of legislation is recognized in both countries, although the applicable model differs in many respects. Traditionally, Greece follows the American model, empowering all courts with the judicial review of legislation, while the jurisdiction of the Supreme Special Court mitigates the results of this approach. In contrast, Turkey has a distinct European-style constitutional jurisdiction. The consequences of an unconstitutional statute are similarly different: In Greece, as a general rule, the statute is non-applicable; in Turkey, the offending statute is null and void. In neither country is there a possibility of an individual constitutional complaint. Further, in Turkey, despite reforms in the last decade, judicial review of State action is subject to significant limitations. The control of conventionality, as a distinct avenue compared with the control of constitutionality, is more developed in Greece. Indeed, with regard to the ECHR, Greek high court panels occasionally circumvent a 2001 constitutional amendment that reduced their judicial review power. On the other hand, while the Turkish Constitutional Court usually relies on the Turkish Constitution, referring to the ECHR only in passing, the Turkish Council of State is more willing to enforce ECHR guarantees.

Both Greece and Turkey are not only unitary States, but they are also extraordinarily centralized in terms of State organization. Therefore, a vertical separation of powers among State authorities does not play any meaningful role in the effectiveness of the ECHR. Further, the maintenance of State unity has been a key factor in the doctrine of the Turkish Constitutional Court, and has resulted in numerous ECtHR findings of violation. Despite the central State's considerable distrust of local authorities, there is no similar preoccupation with State unity in Greece.

In sum, doctrinal aspects concerning the status of the ECHR and the system of judicial review prompted Greece to effectively receive the ECHR about a quarter century before Turkey. While since 2001 constitutional amendments in Turkey, both on matters relating to international law and on the scope of judicial review, have remedied some deficits, they have done so neither clearly nor absolutely. Further, the powerful military remains partially beyond judicial scrutiny. However, doctrinal considerations shed minimal light on the actual effectiveness of the ECHR in the two countries. Thus, additional substantive elements of the reception process will allow to draw more accurate conclusions about the status of the ECHR in Greece and Turkey.

C. Overview of the Activity of the European Court

1. Greece

The number of applications lodged against Greece with the ECtHR reached a three-digit figure for the first time since the 1987 recognition of the individual petition in 1994, steadily exceeding 200 from 2000 and 400 from 2003. While the number of violations per year has constantly increased since the first finding of violation in 1991, it remained for most of the 90's in the single digits. After fifteen or sixteen findings of violations per year from 2000 to 2002, this figure started to increase more drastically. It reached a peak of 101 violations in 2005 and fell to 53 violations in 2006 (Greece's second highest violation rate). Most ECtHR findings of violation against Greece[125] have focused on Article 6(1) ECHR, both in respect of the length of proceedings (190 violations) and the fair trial guarantee (62 violations), and Article 13 ECHR (52 violations) mostly because of the lack of an effective remedy in length of proceedings cases. While religious freedom cases are not comparable in numbers (seven violations), they include fundamental premises of the ECtHR jurisprudence in this area. The property rights cases are also significant both quantitatively (44 violations) and qualitatively. Several findings of violation fall within a distinct category of breaches of the separation of powers. Furthermore, recent years have seen a wider thematic diffusion of the ECtHR case law, including violations of the right to life (Article 2 ECHR), the prohibition of inhuman or degrading treatment or punishment (Article 3 ECHR) and the freedoms of expression (Article 10 ECHR) and association (Article 11 ECHR).

a. Procedural Guarantees

With respect to procedural safeguards, Greece has been repeatedly found to deprive litigants of access to justice in violation of Article 6(1) ECHR. Some examples include entrusting the assertion of individual civil rights to third entities, such as the Technical Chamber of Greece,[126] dismissing applications for judicial protection for formalist reasons, such as a technical error for which the applicant could not be held liable,[127] or declaring a criminal appeal inadmissible because the applicant had not surrendered to custody.[128] One reason for these ECtHR findings is the discrepancy between Greek courts and the ECtHR in applying the procedural guarantees of the Greek Constitution and the ECHR. While the Greek Constitution guarantees the right to judicial protection in Article 20 (1),

---

[125] See, in general, Lambert (2003).

[126] *Philis v. Greece* (appl. nos 12750/87; 13780/88; 14003/88), Judgement, 27 August 1991, Series A 209.

[127] *Sotiris and Nikos Koutras Attee v. Greece* (appl. no. 39442/98), Judgement (Second Section), 16 November 2000, Reports 2000-XII, 51.

[128] See, e.g., *Skondrianos v. Greece* (appl. nos 63000/00, 74291/01, 74292/01), Judgement (First Section), 18 December 2003 (not reported).

Greek courts usually read this provision narrowly when compared with the ECtHR regarding Article 6 ECHR. In addition, Greek courts construe domestic procedural legislation in a rather formalistic way, typically overlooking the possibility of a broader interpretation that would satisfy ECHR requirements.[129]

Moreover, the excessive length of proceedings before Greek courts has resulted in numerous findings of violation of Article 6(1) ECHR.[130] Some scholars attribute this problem to the courts' chronic understaffing and the lack of necessary technical resources.[131] The disproportionate numbers of lawyers in Greece,[132] their tendency to request adjournments on shaky grounds and the courts' often unjustified willingness to grant them, several long-standing lawyers' strikes over the last decades as well as the administrative authorities' typical tardiness in proceedings before administrative courts have exacerbated the problem. Further, Greek courts typically do not award significant court expenses against the losing party. As a result, a complaint is often filed for dubious claims.

Other ECtHR findings of violation of procedural guarantees are rooted in the traditional tendency of Greek courts to insulate several areas of State activity from judicial scrutiny and to limit their judgements' adverse effects on the State. For instance, the ECtHR has repeatedly condemned Greece for not providing a hearing on matters of compensation[133] to individuals unlawfully detained on remand.[134] In another notable case, the ECtHR found that Greece had violated the procedural equality of arms between the State and its private adversaries.[135]

Greece's breaches of the ECHR's procedural guarantees are not limited to Article 6(1) ECHR. The ECtHR has also found violations of Article 6(1) ECHR in conjunction with Article 6(3) ECHR on the rights of the accused,[136] the presumption of innocence (Article 6(2) ECHR),[137] and Article 5(4) ECHR concern-

---

[129]   See also Stavros (1999), 7.

[130]   Up to the year 2000, the ECtHR reached one or two findings of violation due to length of proceedings per year (occasionally rising to five in 1997); there were ten such cases in 2000, 22 in 2004 and 34 (the all-time high) in 2006.

[131]   Stavros (1999), 5.

[132]   In 2006, 36,000 lawyers were registered with the Greek bar associations, that is, almost one lawyer per 309 persons, compared with one lawyer per 1388, 594 and 1298 persons in France, Germany and Turkey respectively. Cf. Council of Bars and Law Societies of Europe (CCBE), Number of lawyers in CCBE Member Bars, available at: http://www.ccbe.org/doc/En/table_number_lawyers_2006_en.pdf.

[133]   For many years, Greek courts typically granted no compensation based on a statutory provision stipulating that the State had no obligation to compensate a person who had been detained on remand if the individual, intentionally or by gross negligence, was responsible for his/her own detention. See, e.g., Zimianitis (2001), 315 et seq. with further references.

[134]   See, e.g., *Georgiadis v. Greece* (appl. no. 21522/93), Judgement, 29 May 1997, Reports 1997-III, 949.

[135]   *Platakou v. Greece* (appl. no. 38460/97), Judgement (Second Section), 11 January 2001, Reports 2001-I, 21, paras 47–48.

[136]   See, e.g., *Twalib v. Greece* (appl. no. 24294/94), Judgement, 9 June 1998, Reports 1998-IV, 1415, paras 51–57 (no grant of legal aid in cassation proceedings).

[137]   *Diamantides v. Greece (No. 2)* (appl. no. 71563/01), Judgement (First Section), 19 May 2005, (not yet reported), paras 45–53.

ing judicial review of detention.[138] Lastly, the lack of an effective remedy in length of proceedings cases,[139] and also in other instances, such as a school suspension[140] or an eviction order,[141] has resulted in numerous findings of violation of Article 13 ECHR.

b. Religious Freedom

In a second set of cases involving Greece, the ECtHR found a violation of the religious freedom guarantee. In this respect, the Greek Constitution raises concerns as to its consistency with the ECHR;[142] however, the ECtHR findings of violation of Article 9 ECHR stem from statutory provisions and their construction. Specifically, several laws regulating religious practice have been enacted as early as during the pre-World War II Metaxas dictatorship. For example, the statutory prohibition of proselytizing applies only to the use of improper means when anyone is attempting to change someone's religious beliefs; it provides, however, only a non-exhaustive enumeration of such means. The Greek courts had convicted a Jehovah's Witness for proselytism, reciting merely the statutory definition of proselytism, without specifying what improper means he had used. As a result, the ECtHR concluded in 1993, in the much-discussed *Kokkinakis* case, that Greece had breached Article 9 ECHR.[143] Further, if a group wanted to start a non-Orthodox place of worship, a decree enacted during the Metaxas dictatorship required authorisation from the Government that acted in consultation with the local Orthodox bishop. In *Manoussakis*, the ECtHR found the authorization requirement to be consistent with the ECHR only in so far as it allowed the verification of formal conditions.[144] Because the applicants had requested the authorization and never received a substantive response, the ECtHR found that their conviction for not complying with the authorization requirement violated Article 9 ECHR.[145] Moreover, in a recent case, the ECtHR found that Greek authorities had violated the religious freedom's negative aspect in requiring a law-

---

[138] See, e.g., *Kampanis v. Greece* (appl. no. 17977/91), Judgement, 13 July 1995, Series A 318, 29.

[139] See, e.g., *Konti-Arvaniti v. Greece* (appl. no. 53401/99), Judgement (First Section), 10 April 2003 (not reported), paras 29–30.

[140] *Valsamis v. Greece* (appl. no. 21787/93), Judgement, 18 December 1996, Reports 1996-VI, 2312, paras 47–49 (violation of Article 13 ECHR taken together with Article 2 of Protocol no. 1 and Article 9 ECHR).

[141] *Iatridis v. Greece* (appl. no. 31107/96), Judgement (Grand Chamber); 25 March 1999, Reports 1999-II, 75, paras 65–66.

[142] See *supra* note 82 and accompanying text.

[143] *Kokkinakis v. Greece* (appl. no. 14307/88), Judgement, 25 May 1993, Series A, Vol. 260, 1, paras 48–50.

[144] *Manoussakis and Others v. Greece* (appl. no. 18748/91), Judgement, 26 September 1996, Reports 1996-IV, 1346, para. 47.

[145] Ibid., paras 49–53.

yer to declare that he was not an Orthodox Christian in order to make a solemn declaration instead of taking a religious oath of office.[146]

While other ECtHR rulings found breaches of other ECHR guarantees,[147] the substantive violations concerned the status of religious minorities in Greece. Both sets of cases – those referring explicitly to Article 9 ECHR and those raising objections in light of other ECHR guarantees – point in the following direction: In several instances, Greek authorities have construed domestic legislation on religious practice in a way that is inconsistent with the ECHR. While not necessarily creating a conflict between the Greek Constitution and the ECHR, in designating the Greek Orthodox Church as the "prevailing religion in Greece" (Article 3 (1) CG) the former encourages Greek authorities to take a friendly approach to the interests of the Greek Orthodox Church rather than to adopt a neutral approach to all religious denominations.

c. Property Rights

A third set of issues that triggered substantial ECtHR rulings against Greece refers to the property rights under Article 1 of ECHR Protocol no. 1. The relevant ECtHR findings of violation typically concern expropriation proceedings, either *de facto*[148] or lawfully pronounced[149] expropriations without payment of (adequate) compensation.[150] Such cases often intertwine closely with the disproportionate length of proceedings before domestic courts in order to settle controversies regarding land ownership disputes and compensation.[151] Further, Greek law had established a statutory presumption that a road improvement plan benefits the owners of properties fronting the road and that this benefit amounts to sufficient compensation for the partial expropriation of their properties. The ECtHR has repeatedly held that this presumption violates Article 1 of Protocol

---

[146] *Alexandridis v. Greece* (appl. no. 19516/06), Judgement, 21 February 2008 (not yet reported), paras 36–41.

[147] See, e.g., *Tsirlis and Kouloumpas v. Greece* (appl. nos 19233/91; 19234/91), Judgement, 29 May 1997, Reports 1997-III, 909, paras 57–63 (Article 5 ECHR); *Canea Catholic Church v. Greece* (appl. no. 25528/94), Judgement, 16 December 1997, Reports 1997-VII, 2843, paras 39–42 (Article 6(1) ECHR), para. 47 (Article 14 taken together with Article 6(1) ECHR); *Thlimmenos v. Greece* (appl. no. 34369/97), Judgement (Grand Chamber), 6 April 2000, Reports 2000-IV, 263, paras 42–47 (Article 14 taken together with Article 9 ECHR); *Valsamis v. Greece* (*supra* note 140).

[148] *Papamichalopoulos v. Greece* (appl. no. 14556/89), Judgement, 24 June 1993, Series A, Vol. 260, 55. See also *Holy Monasteries v. Greece* (appl. nos 13092/87, 13984/88), Judgement, 9 December 1994, Series A, Vol. 301, 1, paras 74–75.

[149] *Yagtzilar and Others v. Greece* (appl. no. 41727/98), Judgement (Second Section), 6 December 2001, Reports 2001-XII, 19, paras 41–42.

[150] See also *Ouzounoglou v. Greece* (appl. no. 32730/03), Judgement (First Section), 24 November 2005 (not yet reported), paras 30–32 (refusal to award compensation for the depreciation of unexpropriated land).

[151] See, e.g., *Papastavrou and Others v. Greece* (appl. no. 46372/99), Judgement (First Section), 10 April 2003, Reports 2003-IV, 257.

no. 1[152] Both the reluctance of Greek courts to incorporate constitutional and international law considerations into statutory interpretation and their attempt to protect the State's financial interests result in these findings of violations. The number of property rights breaches has increased considerably in recent years, arguably because both the Greek legislature and courts tend to disregard property ownership as a human right.[153]

d. Separation of Powers

Several ECtHR judgements fall within a distinct category of breaches of the separation of powers principle. They are typically directed against the Greek judiciary. While the ECHR does not explicitly guarantee this principle, its substantive rights partially protect against intrusions into the sphere of activity of the other branches of Government. On several occasions, the Greek Parliament had passed statutes while litigation had been pending before domestic courts, in order to influence or determine the outcomes and to avoid or limit the State Treasury's burden. On other occasions, administrative authorities failed to comply with domestic court decisions that ruled in favour of individuals involved in disputes with the state. In both sets of cases, the ECtHR found that Greece had violated the right to a fair trial, and less often, the applicants' property rights as well.[154] An entrenched legal culture that aims to protect the State from the adverse consequences of its actions has also played a considerable role in this respect.

e. Right to Life, Prohibition of Inhuman or Degrading Treatment or Punishment

The increasing awareness of European human rights law among Greek lawyers and the public at large has prompted a wider diffusion of ECtHR findings of violation over the past several years. The ECtHR findings based on a violation of Article 3 ECHR, due to conditions of detention that amount to degrading treatment, are of crucial importance. The ECtHR has denounced the serious overcrowding of Greek prisons and detention centres and has chastized Greek authorities for failing to take steps to improve detention conditions.[155] As the CoE's Parliamentary Assembly noted in 2006, these ECtHR judgements high-

---

[152] See, e.g., *Katikaridis v. Greece* (appl. no. 19385/92), Judgement, 15 November 1996, Reports 1996-V, 1673, paras 49–51.

[153] Voyatzis (2004), 494.

[154] On statutory changes pending litigation, see, e.g., *Stran Greek Refineries and Stratis Andreadis v. Greece* (appl. no. 13427/87), ECHR, Judgement, 9 December 1994, Series A, Vol. 301, 61, paras 72–75. On non-compliance with domestic court decisions, see, e.g., *Hornsby v. Greece* (appl. no. 18357/91), Judgement, 19 March 1997, Reports 1997-II, 495, paras 40–45.

[155] *Dougoz v. Greece* (appl. no. 40907/98), Judgement (Third Section), 6 March 2001, Reports 2001-II, 255, paras 45–49; *Peers v. Greece* (appl. no. 28524/95), Judgement (Second Section), 19 April 2001, Reports 2001-III, 275, paras 69–75; *Kaja v. Greece* (appl. no. 32927/03), Judgement (First Section), 27 July 2006 (not yet reported), paras 47–50; see also *Serifis v. Greece* (appl. no. 27695/03), Judgement (First Section), 2 November 2006 (not yet reported), paras 34–36 (absence of appropriate medical assistance during detention).

light Greece's systemic problem of poor detention conditions resulting in inhuman treatment of detainees.[156]

Recent ECtHR judgements have also revealed another significant problem with respect to the conduct of police authorities. In four rulings, the ECtHR held that Greece violated Article 3 ECHR for not providing a credible explanation about the origins of individuals' injuries while under the control of police officers,[157] and/or for failing to effectively investigate arguable claims of ill-treatment.[158] In addition, in three cases, the ECtHR found that Greece violated both substantive and/or procedural aspects of Article 2 ECHR (right to life) in connection with police actions that failed to ensure that risk to life was kept to a minimum, although the State was not charged with wrongful death.[159] Greece's substantial delay in putting into place a modern regulatory framework with respect to police weapons use, which was essentially governed until 2003 by 1943 legislation, contributed to these findings of violation. While the ECtHR has been generally reluctant to attribute a racial motive to Greek authorities,[160] the disproportional number of immigrants or persons of Roma origin among violation victims under Articles 2 and 3 ECHR is disquieting. Arguably, this demonstrates Greece's substantial difficulties in integrating its increasingly diverse population.[161]

f. Freedom of Expression and Association

In a growing number of recent cases that reflect the wider diffusion of ECtHR activity, the ECtHR has found that Greece has violated Article 10 ECHR (freedom of expression) because of Greek courts' failure to meet proportionality require-

---

[156] Parliamentary Assembly of the Council of Europe, Committee on Legal Affairs and Human Rights, Implementation of Judgments of the European Court of Human Rights, Report, 18 September 2006, no. 11.3.

[157] *Bekos and Koutropoulos v. Greece* (appl. no. 15250/02), Judgement (Fourth Section), 13 December 2005 (not yet reported), paras 47–52; *Alsayed Allaham v. Greece* (appl. no. 25771/03), Judgement (First Section), 18 January 2007 (not yet reported), paras 26–34; see also *Zelilof v. Greece* (appl. no. 17060/03), Judgement (First Section), 24 May 2007 (not yet reported), paras 46–52.

[158] *Bekos and Koutropoulos v. Greece* (*supra* note 157), paras 53–55; *Zelilof v. Greece* (*supra* note 157), paras 57–63; *Petropoulou-Tsakiris v. Greece* (appl. no. 44803/04), Judgement (First Section), 6 December 2007 (not yet reported), paras 47–54.

[159] *Makaratzis v. Greece* (appl. no. 50385/99), Judgement (Grand Chamber), 20 December 2004, Reports 2004-XI, 195, paras 62–72, 75–79; *Karagiannopoulos v. Greece* (appl. no. 27850/03), Judgement (First Section), 21 June 2007 (not yet reported), paras 58–64, 67–71; *Celniku v. Greece* (appl. no. 21449/04), Judgement (First Section), 5 July 2007 (not yet reported), paras 55–59, 64–70

[160] But see *Bekos and Koutropoulos v. Greece* (*supra* note 157), paras 71–75; *Petropoulou-Tsakiris v. Greece* (*supra* note 158), paras 63–66 (finding a violation of Article 14 ECHR taken together with Article 3 ECHR in its procedural limb because of Greek authorities' failure to investigate a possible causal link between alleged racist attitudes and ill-treatment by the police).

[161] Since the 90's, an unprecedented influx of immigrants, mainly from Albania, the surrounding Balkan States and the former USSR, has dissolved Greece's traditional ethnic homogeneity. At the end of 2004, Greece had an estimated 1.15 million immigrants, comprising 10.3% of the country's population compared with an estimated total of 270,000 immigrants in 1991. Mediterranean Migration Observatory, Statistical Data on Immigrants in Greece, available at: http://www.mmo.gr/pdf/general/IMEPO_Exec_Summary_English.pdf.

ments in restricting freedom of expression to protect public figures' reputations.[162] These cases demonstrate Greek courts' partly persisting historical reluctance to effectively implement constitutional and international rights guarantees, coupled with a more general uneasiness in striking the appropriate balance between competing rights and interests related to freedom of expression.

Moreover, the ECtHR held that Greece violated Article 11 ECHR (freedom of association) because of the Greek courts' non-registration of associations due to suspicion that the founders' motives endangered Greece's territorial integrity[163] or promoted the idea that a Turkish ethnic minority exists in Western Thrace province in northern Greece.[164] These findings of violation can be explained by a dominant mindset among Greece's political branches, courts and the general population that recognizes only a religious (Muslim) minority on the basis of the 1923 Lausanne Treaty and firmly rejects the existence of ethnic minorities in the country.

2. Turkey

The number of applications lodged against Turkey reached a three-digit figure for the first time as early as in 1987, the year of Turkey's recognition of the individual petition right. After exceeding 200 applications for the first time in 1996, the number increased dramatically over the coming years, exploding to almost 400 applications in 2002 and 2004. While the number of applications dropped considerably in both 2005 and 2006, it is still too early to tell whether this drop will last.

The ECtHR issued its first finding of violation against Turkey in 1995 when 660 applications had been registered against the country. The number of violations reached double-digit figures for the first time in 1998. After increasing to 168 findings of violation in 2001, it fell again for a couple of years to double-digit figures before exceeding 100 per year since 2004. The peak of violations, 320, was reached in 2006, the last year for which data are available, followed by 266 findings of violation in 2005. All in all, the ECtHR has found 357 violations of property rights, 336 violations of the fair trial guarantee, 184 violations of the right to liberty and security, 155 violations of the effective remedy clause, 127 violations because of excessive length of proceedings, 121 violations of the right to life, 120 violations of the freedom of expression and 109 violations of the prohibition of torture and inhuman or degrading treatment or punishment.

---

[162] See, e.g., *Lionarakis v. Greece* (appl. no. 1131/05), Judgement (First Section), 5 July 2007 (not yet reported), paras 47–54.

[163] *Sidiropoulos and Others v. Greece* (appl. no. 26695/95), Judgement, 10 July 1998, Reports 1998-IV, 1594, paras 44–47 ("Home of Macedonian Civilization").

[164] *Bekir-Ousta and Others v. Greece* (appl. no. 35151/05), Judgement (First Section), 11 October 2007 (not yet reported), paras 40–46 ("Evros Prefecture Minority Youth Association").

a. Right to Life, Prohibition of Torture and Inhuman or Degrading Treatment or Punishment

A significant number of Articles 2 and 3 ECHR breaches concern cases related to the armed clashes between Turkey's security forces and PKK members in Turkey's south-east provinces. Most findings of violation of Article 2 ECHR (right to life) fall into three categories.[165] First, the State authorities' lethal use of force that is not necessary to defend themselves against violence or to effect an arrest as required by Article 2(2) ECHR;[166] second, failure to take reasonable protective measures to prevent an immediate risk to life;[167] third, failure to carry out an effective investigation capable of leading to the identification and punishment of those responsible for death.[168]

In terms of Article 3 ECHR, Turkish security forces have used a wide variety of particularly cruel interrogation methods that are capable of causing severe pain and suffering and, according to the ECtHR, qualify as torture in the sense of Article 3 ECHR.[169] Other ECtHR findings of violation of Article 3 included somewhat less severe instances of inhuman and degrading treatment[170] and the Turkish authorities' failure to effectively investigate arguable claims of ill-treatment while in police custody.[171]

As the CoE's Committee of Ministers has pointed out, most violations of Articles 2 and 3 ECHR in Turkey are due to a number of structural problems, among them the mentality and practices of security forces, their flawed training system, the legal framework governing their activities, the serious shortcomings in the Government's system of administrative, civil and criminal responsibility and lack of sanctions in cases of abuse.[172]

---

[165] See also *Öneryildiz v. Turkey* (appl. no. 48939/99), Judgement (Grand Chamber), 30 November 2004, Reports 2004-XII, 79, paras 109–110, 116–118 (failure to protect individuals living in the vicinity of methane accident site).

[166] See, e.g., *Oğur v. Turkey* (appl. no. 21594/93), Judgement (Grand Chamber), 20 May 1999, Reports 1999-III, 519, paras 76–84.

[167] See, e.g., *Kılıç v. Turkey* (appl. no. 22492/93), Judgement (First Section), 28 March 2000, Reports 2000-III, 75, paras 62–77 (journalist working for a newspaper that reflected Turkish Kurdish opinion).

[168] See, e.g., *Kaya v. Turkey* (appl. no. 22729/93), Judgement, 19 February 1998, Reports 1998-I, 297, paras 86–92; *H.Y. and Hü.Y. v. Turkey* (appl. no. 40262/98), Judgement (First Section), 6 October 2005 (not yet reported), paras 120–129.

[169] See, e.g., *Aksoy v. Turkey* (appl. no. 21987/93), Judgement, 18 December 1996, Reports 1996-IV, 2260, para. 64; *Aydin v. Turkey* (appl. no. 23178/94), Judgement (Grand Chamber), 25 September 1997, Reports 1997-VI, 1866, paras 83–87; *Bati and Others v. Turkey* (appl. no. 33097/96 and 57834/00), Judgement (First Section), 3 June 2004 Reports 2004-IV, 249, paras 117–124.

[170] *Elci and Others v. Turkey* (appl. nos 23145/93 and 25091/94), Judgement (Fourth Section), 13 November 2003 (not reported), para. 647.

[171] See, e.g., *Dikme v. Turkey* (appl. no. 20869/92), Judgement (First Section), 11 July 2000, Reports 2000-VIII, 223, paras 102–104.

[172] Council of Europe, Committee of Ministers, Interim Resolution, 7 June 2005, Actions of the security forces in Turkey. Progress achieved and outstanding problems, ResDH(2005)43. See

b. Freedom of Expression, Association and Assembly

The cases concerning freedom of expression[173] are also representative of the persisting human rights deficits in Turkey, most notably in connection with utterances that are deemed to further a Kurdish separatist agenda. The ECtHR's findings of violation against Turkey concern, for instance, interferences with the applicants' freedom of expression on account of their conviction by the (former) State Security Courts, for example, conviction of a party official for disseminating a leaflet that criticized discrimination against citizens of Kurdish origin;[174] a failure to protect a newspaper's freedom of expression against a long list of attacks on journalists, prosecutions and convictions;[175] a seizure of publications for allegedly disseminating separatist propaganda;[176] and a ban on the publication and distribution of a journal in provinces in which a state of emergency had been declared.[177] According to the ECtHR, in most of these cases, the State targeted publications that made a political statement, rather than incited violence. Therefore, the ECtHR repeatedly found that the Turkish authorities' measures were unnecessary in a democratic society.[178] Both statutory provisions that criminalize certain opinions objected to by the State and the Turkish authorities' restrictive implementation of these provisions are difficult to reconcile with the ECHR.

The Turkish cases on Article 11 ECHR (freedom of assembly and association) are also illuminating because they reflect a divergence between the Turkish Constitutional Court and the ECtHR on the applicable standards of review.[179] On several occasions, the Turkish Constitutional Court ordered the dissolution of political parties soon after their creation based solely on their political programme or declarations made by their leaders. Among the Constitutional Court's reasons for dissolving a political party was the threat to the territorial integrity and the unity of the nation, the use of the term "communist" and the apparent goal to abolish the State's secular character.[180] Rebutting this case law, the ECtHR has

---

also Council of Europe, Committee of Ministers, Interim Resolution, 9 June 1999, Action of the security forces in Turkey: Measures of a general character, ResDH(99)434.

[173] For an analysis of early ECtHR case law, see Kaboğlu (1999), 263–274; on Turkish practice and the implementation failures of recent reforms, see Kaboğlu (2006a).

[174] *Incal v. Turkey* (appl. no. 22678/93), Judgement (Grand Chamber), 9 June 1998, Reports 1998-IV, 1547, para. 59.

[175] *Özgür Gündem v. Turkey* (appl. no. 23144/93), Judgement (Fourth Section), 16 March 2000, Reports 2000-III, 1, para. 71.

[176] *Ayşe Oztürk v. Turkey* (appl. no. 24914/94), Judgement (Second Section), 15 October 2002 (not reported), para. 86.

[177] *Çetin and Others v. Turkey* (appl. nos 40153/98, 40160/98), Judgement (Second Section), 13 February 2003, Reports 2003-III, 145, para. 66.

[178] But see *Zana v. Turkey* (*supra* note 124), para. 62 (finding that proportionality requirements were met).

[179] Kaboğlu (1999), 273 et seq.

[180] See, e.g., Turkish Constitutional Court, Judgement, 1991.07.16, E. 1990/1, K. 1991/1, R.G. no. 21125, 28 January 1992 (United Communist Party of Turkey).

found on several occasions a violation of Article 11 ECHR.[181] Yet, the ECtHR has tended to uphold the reasoning of the Turkish Constitutional Court when the preservation of the Turkish concept of secularism was at stake.[182] In addition, in recent years, an increasing number of Article 11 ECHR violations concern trade union rights[183] and the freedom of assembly.[184]

c. Procedural Guarantees

In terms of procedural guarantees, among the numerous findings of violation concerning the fair trial clause of Article 6 ECHR[185] several types of cases can be cited here. First, on several occasions, the ECtHR has dealt with Turkish State Security Courts, which until 2004 had been established under the Turkish Constitution to punish offences against Turkey's territorial integrity and national unity. Until 1999, one of the judges sitting on a three-judge bench of a State Security Court was required to be a military judge. Finding that because of this there was a legitimate fear of compromising the independence and impartiality of the State Security Courts, the ECtHR held that they did not qualify as independent and impartial tribunals under Article 6 ECHR.[186] Second, in a case concerning criminal defence rights, the defendant, a PKK leader, was not allowed to retain a lawyer during questioning in custody, was unable to communicate with his lawyers confidentially or to access the case file in due time. The ECtHR found a violation of Article 6(1) combined with Articles 6(3)(b) and (c) ECHR (rights of the accused).[187] Other violations of Article 6 ECHR concern the Turkish national authorities' failure to comply in practice and within a reasonable time frame with domestic court decisions,[188] the excessive length of proceedings[189] and the

---

[181] See, e.g., *United Communist Party of Turkey and Others v. Turkey* (appl. no. 19392/92), Judgement (Grand Chamber), 30 January 1998, Reports 1998-I, 1, paras 24–25.

[182] See *infra* notes 205–206 and accompanying text.

[183] *Demir and Baykara v. Turkey* (appl. no. 34503/97), Judgement (Second Section), 21 November 2006 (not yet reported) (pending before the Grand Chamber), paras 29, 36–46 (refusal to accord legal entity status to a trade union and cancellation of a collective bargaining agreement entered into by the union); *Karaçay v. Turkey* (appl. no. 6615/03), Judgement (Second Section), 27 March 2007 (not yet reported), paras 37–39 (disciplinary reprimand of a civil servant for taking part in a trade union demonstration).

[184] *Oya Ataman v. Turkey* (appl. no. 74552/01), Judgement (Second Section), 5 December 2006 (not yet reported) (forceful dispersal of a demonstration held without prior notice).

[185] See, in detail, İnceoğlu (2005).

[186] See, e.g., *Incal v. Turkey* (*supra* note 174), paras 71–73; *Çıraklar v. Turkey* (appl. no. 19601/92), Judgement, 28 October 1998, Reports 1998-VII, paras 39–41.

[187] *Öcalan v. Turkey* (appl. no. 46221/99), Judgement (Grand Chamber), 12 May 2005, Reports 2005-IV, 131, paras 130–148.

[188] See, e.g., *Taşkın and Others v. Turkey* (appl. no. 46117/99), Judgement (Third Section), 10 November 2004, Reports 2004-X, 179, paras 135–137.

[189] While up to the year 2000, findings of violation due to excessive length of proceedings did not exceed two per year, 26 such violations were found in 2001 and, after decreasing to a single-digit figure from 2002 to 2004, 31 in 2005 and 46 in 2006.

dismissal of an application for judicial protection because of non-payment of court fees.[190]

Similarly, in terms of the right to liberty and security, most violations result from the armed clashes between Turkey's security forces and PKK members. Representative findings of violations include unacknowledged detentions by the security forces in the complete absence of ECHR safeguards,[191] a 30-day detention without appearance before a judge[192] and an excessive detention pending trial virtually without justification.[193]

Against the same background, in the case of alleged grave violations of ECHR rights, the effective remedy notion (Article 13 ECHR) entails in addition to other remedies, a thorough investigation capable of leading to the punishment of those responsible. Such findings of violation concern for instance the Turkish authorities' failure to effectively investigate arguable claims of unlawful killing by security forces,[194] torture,[195] disappearance at the hands of the authorities[196] or deliberate destruction by State agents of the homes and possessions of individuals.[197]

d. Property Rights

In terms of property rights, the ECtHR's findings of violation can be summarized on the basis of the following representative cases. Again, in the context of armed clashes between security forces and PKK members, the ECtHR found that the displacement and denial of access to possessions[198] as well as the deliberate burning of homes and their contents by the Turkish security forces constituted an unjustified interference with the peaceful enjoyment of possessions (and with the right to respect for private and family life).[199] Further, in cases concerning proper-

---

[190] *Bakan v. Turkey* (appl. no. 50939/99), Judgement (former Second Section), 12 June 2007 (not yet reported), paras 69–79.

[191] See, e.g., *Çakıcı v. Turkey* (appl. no. 23657/94), Judgement (Grand Chamber), 8 July 1999, Reports 1999-IV, 583, paras 104–107.

[192] *Taş v. Turkey* (appl. no. 24396/94), Judgement (First Section), 14 November 2000 (not reported), para. 86.

[193] *Mansur v. Turkey* (appl. no. 16026/90), Judgement, 8 June 1995, Series A 319-B, 37, paras 55–57.

[194] See, e.g., *Kaya v. Turkey* (*supra* note 168), paras 107–108. See also *Güngör v. Turkey* (appl. no. 28290/95), Judgement (Second Section), 22 March 2005 (not yet reported), paras 99–101 (violation of Article 13 taken together with Article 2 ECHR because Parliamentary immunity prevented prosecutions for ordinary criminal offences).

[195] See, e.g., *Aksoy v. Turkey* (*supra* note 169), paras 98–100; *Bati and Others v. Turkey* (*supra* note 169), paras 142–149; *Abdulsamet Yaman v. Turkey* (appl. 32446/96), Judgement (Second Section), 2 November 2004 (not reported), paras 56–61.

[196] *Kurt v. Turkey* (appl. no. 24276/94), Judgement, 25 May 1998, Reports 1998-III, 1152, paras 140–142.

[197] See, e.g., *Menteş and Others v. Turkey* (appl. no. 23186/94), Judgement (Grand Chamber), 28 November 1997, Reports 1997-VIII, 2689, paras 89–92.

[198] See, e.g., *Doğan and Others v. Turkey* (appl. no. 8803–8811/02, 8813/02 and 8815–8819/02), Judgement (Third Section), 29 June 2004, Reports 2004-VI, 81, paras 153–156, 159–160.

[199] *Akdivar and Others v. Turkey* (appl. no. 21893/93), Judgement (Grand Chamber), 16 September 1996, Reports 1996-IV, 1192, para. 88.

484 *The Reception Process in Greece and Turkey*

ties in northern Cyprus, the ECtHR found that the Turkish troops' negation of property rights violated Article 1 of ECHR Protocol no. 1.[200] In a case concerning the Greek Orthodox minority, Turkish authorities had confiscated a religious minority foundation's property titles after almost four decades of property use due to a change in the interpretation of domestic law. The ECtHR found a violation of Article 1 of Protocol no. 1.[201] Expropriation issues have also resulted in several ECHR violations. Two examples are *de facto* expropriations by Turkish authorities without compensation payment[202] and delays in the payment of expropriation compensation in light of soaring inflation rates.[203]

e. Turkey as a Secular State and Religious Education

A pair of ECtHR judgements relates to the compatibility of the Turkish concept of secularism with the ECHR. While generally dismissive of Turkish Constitutional Court case law on the dissolution of political parties,[204] the ECtHR found that the dissolution of a party that favoured a plurality of legal systems on the basis of religious affiliation and a sharia-based regime met the proportionality standard under Article 11(2) ECHR (freedom of association).[205] Further, the ECtHR upheld Turkish regulations prohibiting the wearing of the Islamic headscarf in institutions of higher education, finding the interference with both religious freedom (Article 9 ECHR) and the right to education (Article 2 of the ECHR Protocol no. 1) to be proportionate to the aim pursued.[206] In both these cases, the national constitutional doctrine inspired the development of the ECtHR case law. However, in a 2007 ruling, the ECtHR found the compulsory "instruction in religious culture and moral education" in primary and secondary schools (Article 24 (4) CRT) that focused on the teaching of Islam to violate Article 2 of Protocol no. 1 (right to education) because of the lack of sufficient exemption procedures.[207]

---

[200] See, e.g., *Loizidou v. Turkey* (appl. no. 15318/89), Judgement (Grand Chamber), 18 December 1996, Reports 1996-VI, 2216, paras 62–64. See also *infra* notes 393–394 and accompanying text.

[201] *Fener Rum Erkek Lisesi Vakfı v. Turkey* (appl. no. 34478/97), Judgement (former Second Section), 9 January 2007 (not yet reported), paras 56–60. A similar case concerning property rights of the Orthodox Ecumenical Patriarchate is now pending before the ECtHR.

[202] *N. A. and Others v. Turkey* (appl. no. 37451/97), Judgement (Second Section), 11 October 2005 (not yet reported), paras 38–43.

[203] See, e.g., *Akkuş v. Turkey* (appl. no. 19263/92), Judgement, 9 July 1997, Reports 1997-IV, 1300, paras 29–31.

[204] See, e.g., *United Communist Party of Turkey and Others v. Turkey* (*supra* note 181); *Socialist Party and Others v. Turkey* (*supra* note 123).

[205] *Refah Partisi (The Welfare Party) and Others v. Turkey* (appl. no. 41340/98, 41342/98, 41343/98 and 41344/98), Judgement (Grand Chamber), 13 February 2003, Reports 2003-II, 267, paras 132–135.

[206] *Leyla Şahin v. Turkey* (appl. no. 44774/98), Judgement (Grand Chamber), 10 November 2005 (not yet reported), paras 118–122 and paras 159–161.

[207] *Hasan and Eylem Zengin v. Turkey* (appl. no. 1448/04), Judgement (former Second Section), 9 October 2007 (not yet reported), paras 58–77.

f. Right to Free Elections

Finally, the ECtHR has repeatedly dealt with complaints of violations of Article 3 of ECHR Protocol no. 1 (right to free elections). In a case currently pending before the Grand Chamber, a ECtHR section upheld a ten per cent national threshold needed for political parties to gain Parliamentary representation.[208] It emphasized that Contracting States enjoy in this respect a wide margin of appreciation, while pointing out that the ten per cent threshold applied in Turkey is the highest in comparison with other European States.[209] On the other hand, in a ruling involving dissolution of political parties, the ECtHR found the proportionality standard violated in a case of the automatic forfeiture of Parliamentary office of all Parliamentarians elected from a banned party regardless of personal activities[210] and a five-year ban on the political activity of party officials.[211]

3. Comparison and Conclusion

A comparison between Greece and Turkey must consider the sheer population differences between the two countries. While Turkey, with a population of 70.6 million, has more than six times the population of Greece, which has 11.1 million people, the total number of ECtHR applications lodged against Turkey is almost five times that of Greece. Further, the ECtHR findings of violation against Turkey total slightly more than three times the corresponding findings against Greece. Thus, adjusted for population, total figures of both applications and findings of violation are comparatively higher in Greece.[212] However, although both countries considerably delayed the reception of the ECHR, plausibly, Greece's legal academy, the legal profession and the public at large became acquainted with the European legal remedy for human rights violations earlier than that of Turkey. Thus, in the last five years (2002–2006), applications against Turkey have exploded to more than seven times the corresponding number for Greece. While findings of violation against Turkey also increased, they remained at a comparatively lower figure, almost four times the corresponding figure for Greece.[213] In light of this, it seems that the reception of the ECHR, as an ongoing process,

---

[208] *Yumak and Sadak v. Turkey* (appl. no. 10226/03), Judgement (Second Section), 30 January 2007 (not yet reported), paras 71–79.

[209] Ibid., paras 76–78.

[210] *Selim Sadak and Others v. Turkey* (appl. no. 25144/94, 26149/95 to 26154/95, 27100/95 and 27101/95), Judgement (Fourth Section), 11 June 2002, Reports 2002-IV, 293, paras 37–40.

[211] See, e.g., *Kavakçı v. Turkey* (appl. no. 71907/01), Judgement (Third Section), 5 April 2007 (not yet reported), paras 44–47.

[212] Up to February 2007, 4,021 ECtHR applications were lodged against Greece compared with 21,570 applications against Turkey, and the ECtHR found 288 violations against Greece compared with 1,091 against Turkey. Greece recognized the right of individual petition 14 months before Turkey.

[213] From 2002 to 2006, 2,119 applications were lodged against Greece, and the ECtHR found 223 violations compared with 15,277 applications and 858 findings of violation against Turkey.

started later in Turkey, and, accordingly, currently has a considerably longer way to go.

Concerning concrete findings of violation, the differences in the two countries' records outweigh their similarities. Both Greece and Turkey have exhibited excessive formalism in the interpretation of domestic law, have protected State financial interests at the expense of individual rights, and have disregarded property as a fundamental right, all of which have been the basis of ECHR violations. Nevertheless, violations of right to life, personal liberty and security, the prohibition of torture and inhuman or degrading treatment or punishment, freedom of expression, freedom of association and assembly are widespread in Turkey, yet comparatively rare in Greece, despite a wider thematic diffusion of the ECtHR case law against Greece in recent years. While the fair trial guarantee and property rights have resulted in numerous findings of violations for both countries, the specific reasons for the violations often differ. Problems such as the flagrant breaches of property rights in south-east Turkey and northern Cyprus or, earlier, the independence and impartiality of Turkey's State Security Courts have not been found in Greece. On the other hand, while religious freedom of non-Orthodox Greek denominations has been a major problem in Greece, the ECtHR has generally upheld the Turkish concept of secularism. A fundamental assumption underlies most of the ECHR violations by Turkish authorities who find the unity and identity of the Turkish State to be incompatible with unqualified ECHR reception, in particular against the backdrop of the Turkish security forces' long-term, deep-rooted conflict with PKK members. Albeit to a much more limited extent, a similar assumption underlies some of the ECHR violations by Greece, concerning religious freedom and freedom of association of minority groups.

D. The European Court's Case Law and Its Effects in the National Legal Order

1. Greece

a. Measures of Compliance
In the *Greek* case, discussed earlier,[214] compliance with the ECommHR findings would have undermined the Greek military dictatorship's *raison d'être*. Following the Greek regime's withdrawal from the CoE and the ECHR in late 1969, the publication of the ECommHR's Report, while politically crucial, was ineffective in terms of ensuring compliance with the ECHR. After Greece's recognition of the right to individual petition in 1985, Greek authorities generally adopted a different approach to the ECtHR rulings. Initially, however, following the *Stran*

---

[214] *The Greek Case (supra* notes 5–14 and accompanying text).

Greek Refineries and Stratis Andreadis judgement,[215] Greece delayed the payment of the just satisfaction award because it would both significantly deplete the nation's treasury and pinpoint the Greek Government's lapses in handling the case. About fourteen months after the deadline for payment, the CoE's Committee of Ministers issued an Interim Resolution "strongly urging" the Greek Government to make the payment.[216] This case sparked a scholarly debate on whether the ECtHR just satisfaction judgements constitute an enforceable instrument in Greece. Some scholars have argued that a statutory provision on the execution of foreign judgements[217] applies by analogy in the case of ECtHR judgements that award just satisfaction.[218] Others have countered that ECtHR judgements are not directly enforceable under international law, nor can the provisions on the execution of foreign judgements be applied in the case of ECtHR rulings.[219] Greece finally paid the award ordered by the ECtHR to Andreadis's heirs about two years after the judgement[220] without recourse to enforcement proceedings.

In future cases, Greece complied more promptly with the ECtHR's just satisfaction rulings. Nevertheless, although Greek authorities have invested considerable effort in bringing Greece's legal order in line with the ECHR requirements, they have not always chosen the most direct means for the ECHR reception. Further, it is not easy to trace with certainty to what extent this new approach stemmed from the Greek authorities' effort to comply with the ECHR standards, or rather from a broader effort to modernize domestic legislation and practice. Indeed, both Greece's executive and legislative branches do not typically invoke obligations under the ECHR – contrary to obligations under EU law – to justify steps aimed at increasing the ECHR's effectiveness.[221]

aa. Constitutional Amendments. Greece's 2001 constitutional amendments included several provisions that may be seen as responding to ECtHR rulings. For instance, against the background of findings of violation due to non-compliance with domestic court decisions,[222] the new Article 94 (4) *alinea* 3 CG provides that judicial decisions against State institutions are subject to compulsory enforcement. Further, the new Article 95 (5) CG explicitly stipulates that the public administration is bound to comply with judicial decisions, and that administra-

---

[215] *Stran Greek Refineries and Stratis Andreadis v. Greece* (*supra* note 154).
[216] Council of Europe, Committee of Ministers, Interim Resolution, 15 May 1996, DH (96)251.
[217] Article 905 KPolD.
[218] See, e.g., Mitsopoulos (1996), 109; Beys (1997), 59 et seq. See also Chryssogonos (2001), 361 et seq. (arguing that the ECHR, after entry into force of Protocol no. 11, requires the compulsory enforcement of ECtHR judgements awarding just satisfaction).
[219] Iliopoulos-Strangas (1996), 58 et seq.
[220] See Council of Europe, Committee of Ministers, Final Resolution, 20 March 1997, DH (97)184.
[221] Stavros (1999), 16.
[222] See, e.g., *Hornsby v. Greece* (*supra* note 154).

tive organs are legally responsible in case of non-compliance. Moreover, the 2001 amendments considerably relaxed the disqualification provisions for persons who have held certain public posts and wish to run for seats in Parliament, provisions that had been challenged in Strasbourg.[223] Among the Government's current amendment proposals is the relaxation of the constitutional norm whereby representatives of Parliament are not allowed to exercise their profession during tenure, which gave rise to the *Lykourezos* judgement of the ECtHR.[224]

bb. Statutory Modifications. A more common response from Greek authorities to an ECtHR violation finding is a statutory modification.[225] Most such breaches of the ECHR do not stem inevitably from the letter of the domestic law. Rather, they result from the Greek courts' narrow construction of domestic legislation. Nevertheless, after an ECtHR finding of violation, the Greek Parliament typically enacts clearer statutory provisions that take into account the Strasbourg case law. For example, Greece made several changes in criminal law. In light of Greek courts' long-standing practice[226] of refusing to grant compensation to persons unlawfully convicted or detained on remand without proper hearings, the Code of Criminal Procedure was amended in 2001[227] to no longer exclude the possibility of compensation in detention cases due to the detainee's gross negligence.[228] In another example, the dismissal of an appeal on points of law due to the fact that an applicant had not surrendered to custody was remedied with the repeal of the relevant Code of Criminal Procedure Article.[229] Moreover, a 2003 statute[230] strictly regulated the use of firearms by police officers, thus revising the obsolete legal framework that resulted in the following years in ECtHR findings of violation.[231]

Second, against the background of numerous violations of Article 6(1) ECHR due to excessive length of proceedings, several recent reforms of Greek procedural

---

[223] *Gitonas and Others v. Greece* (*supra* note 83).

[224] *Lykourezos v. Greece* (*supra* note 84).

[225] In other cases, the implementation of the ECtHR case law rested on regulatory acts issued by the executive by virtue of a statutory delegation (cf. Article 43 CG).

[226] See *supra* note 134.

[227] Act no. 2915/2001, Επιτάχυνση της τακτικής διαδικασίας ενώπιον των πολιτικών δικαστηρίων και λοιπές δικονομικές και συναφείς ρυθμίσεις [Acceleration of Ordinary Proceedings in Civil Courts and Other Procedural and Related Regulations], FEK A 109, 29 May 2001, Article 26.

[228] However, Greek courts have not always applied this provision consistently, resulting in new findings of violation. Cf. *Papa v. Greece* (appl. no. 21091/04), Judgement (First Section), 6 July 2006 (not yet reported).

[229] Act no. 3346/2005, Επιτάχυνση της διαδικασίας ενώπιον των πολιτικών και ποινικών δικαστηρίων και άλλες διατάξεις [Acceleration of Proceedings in Civil and Criminal Courts and Other Provisions], FEK A 140, 16/17 June 2005, Article 18 (3).

[230] Act no. 3169/2003, Οπλοφορία, χρήση πυροβόλων όπλων από αστυνομικούς, εκπαίδευσή τους σε αυτά και άλλες διατάξεις [Carrying and Use of Firearms by Police Officers, Training of Police Officers in the Use of Firearms and Other Provisions], FEK A 189, 24 July 2003.

[231] *Makaratzis v. Greece* (*supra* note 159); *Karagiannopoulos v. Greece* (*supra* note 159); *Celniku v. Greece* (*supra* note 159).

law have aimed to accelerate proceedings in civil,[232] criminal[233] and administrative[234] litigation. This set of measures, coupled with an increase in the number of judges' posts and infrastructural improvements, has brought about some results. According to Greek Government estimates, in 2005, first-instance civil proceedings that, in the past, lasted up to four years were concluded within 1½ years.[235] Nevertheless, the length of proceedings remains a huge problem in Greece most pronouncedly with regard to administrative litigation. Notably, at the end of 2006, almost 30,000 cases were pending before the Council of State.[236] Finally, a 2002 statute implemented the new constitutional provisions on administrative compliance with domestic judicial decisions. It charged a three-member judicial panel within each high court with ensuring executive compliance with decisions within its jurisdiction,[237] establishing a three-month deadline for compliance,[238] and determining a financial amount to be paid in case of non-compliance within the time limit.[239]

cc. Changing the Implementation of Domestic Legislation. On other occasions, the executive authorities have adapted the interpretation of domestic legislation during the process of implementation in order to comply with the ECHR. Most

---

[232] See, e.g., Act no. 2915/2001 (*supra* note 227) (imposing on the parties stricter time limits at the preparatory stage of the proceedings; limiting the possibility of an adjournment; and providing that evidence should be examined at a single hearing); Act no. 3327/2005, Μέτρα ενίσχυσης του εσωτερικού ελέγχου και της διαφάνειας στη Δικαιοσύνη [Measures to Reinforce Internal Control and Transparency in Justice], FEK A 70, 11 March 2005, Article 3 (requiring that judicial decisions are delivered within eight months from hearing); Act no. 3346/2005 (*supra* note 229), Article 1 (prescribing time limits regarding the setting of hearings).

[233] See, e.g., Act no. 3160/2003, Επιτάχυνση της ποινικής διαδικασίας και άλλες διατάξεις [Acceleration of Criminal Proceedings and Other Provisions], FEK A 165, 30 June 2003, and Act no. 3346/2005 (*supra* note 229) (limiting trial adjournments; extending the categories of offences for which the physical presence of the accused at trial is not required; and providing the prescription and termination of prosecution for several minor offences).

[234] See Article 95 (3) CG and Act no. 2944/2001, Τροποποίηση της νομοθεσίας του Συμβουλίου της Επικρατείας και των διοικητικών δικαστηρίων [Modification of the Law Concerning the Council of State and the Administrative Courts], FEK A 222, 8 October 2001, Article 1 (redistributing the jurisdiction between the Council of State and the lower courts in order to alleviate the burden of the former).

[235] Council of Europe, Committee of Ministers, Resolution, 18 July 2005, ResDH(2005)64.

[236] Athens News Agency, Interview with the Council of State President Panagiotopoulos (8 January 2008), available at http://www.ana-mpa.gr. A new draft bill that aims to accelerate administrative litigation provides a fast-track procedure for the adjudication of issues that affect a large number of pending cases. See the interview with the Minister of Justice Papaligouras in the newspaper *Apogevmatini* (23 April 2007), available at: http://www.ministryofjustice.gr (in Greek).

[237] Act no. 3068/2002, Συμμόρφωση της Διοίκησης προς τις δικαστικές αποφάσεις, προαγωγή των δικαστών των τακτικών διοικητικών δικαστηρίων στο βαθμό του συμβούλου Επικρατείας και άλλες διατάξεις [Compliance of the Administration with Judicial Decisions, Promotion of Ordinary Administrative Courts' Judges to the Grade of Councillor of State and Other Provisions], FEK A 274, 12/14 November 2002, Article 2.

[238] Act no. 3068/2002 (*supra* note 237), Article 3 (1) (providing, however, that the time limit applies only to an "unjustified" failure to comply with a judicial decision).

[239] Act no. 3068/2002 (*supra* note 237), Article 3 (3).

notably, Greek authorities have chosen this modest model of reception with respect to religious freedom. For instance, both the constitutional and the statutory provisions on the prohibition of proselytism remain in effect today. However, after the Minister of Justice communicated the 1993 *Kokkinakis* judgement of the ECtHR[240] to all prosecutors, arrests and prosecutions for proselytism virtually stopped.[241] Similarly, while the authorization requirement for operating non-Greek Orthodox places of worship remains generally in effect,[242] Greek executive authorities have granted this authorization much more easily after the *Manoussakis* judgement.[243] While this approach has brought about some results, more direct ways of reception, such as a statutory modification, would guarantee more fully the implementation of ECtHR rulings.

In other instances, Greek courts have changed the interpretation of domestic law following ECHR violations, an approach that subsequent statutory modifications have often confirmed. Cases with adverse consequences to the State treasury are particularly common here. For instance, the domestic courts accepted that the statutory presumption providing that the benefit derived from road improvements amounted to sufficient compensation was no longer absolute.[244] After the ECtHR deemed this change insufficient,[245] the Greek courts accepted that the issues of compensation and rebuttal of the presumption should be considered in the same judicial procedure.[246] In addition, contrary to their previous case law, in recent years, the Greek courts have struck down, albeit not consistently, retroactive statutes that suspended pending litigation against the State.[247] Further, even before the 2001 constitutional amendments, Greek courts had found that a 1952 statute which barred compulsory execution of judicial decisions against the State was incompatible with the Constitution and international law.[248] In addition, contrary to established case law, Greek courts have struck down a statute that sus-

[240] *Kokkinakis v. Greece (supra* note 143).

[241] Cf. Council of Europe, Committee of Ministers, Resolution, 15 December 1997, ResDH (97)576.

[242] See also Areios Pagos, Judgement (Full Bench), 2001.12.06, no. 20/2001, HellDni 2002, 265 (finding the authorization requirement to be consistent with both the Greek Constitution and the ECHR).

[243] *Manoussakis and Others v. Greece (supra* note 144); see also *Pentidis and Others v. Greece* (appl. no. 23238/94), Judgement, 9 June 1997, Reports 1997-III, 983.

[244] Cf., e.g., Areios Pagos, Judgement (Full Bench), 1999.03.11, no. 8/1999, NoB 2000, 442 et seq. (holding that owners who consider themselves to have been damaged can institute a separate set of proceedings).

[245] *Efstathiou and Michailidis & Co. Motel Amerika v. Greece* (appl. no. 55794/00), Judgement (First Section), 10 July 2003, Reports 2003-IX, 79, para. 30.

[246] See, e.g., Areios Pagos, Judgement (Full Bench), 2004.03.18, no. 10/2004, HellDni 2004, 712.

[247] See, e.g., Greek Council of State, Judgement (Full Bench), 1999.02.12, no. 542/1999, ToS 1999, 340 et seq.

[248] See Areios Pagos, Judgement (Full Bench), 2001.12.06, no. 21/2001, HellDni 2002, 83–84 (relying principally on Articles 2 and 14 ICCPR and additionally invoking Articles 6 ECHR and 20 (1) CG).

pended judicial time limits during judicial vacations exclusively in favour of the State,[249] thus complying with the ECtHR's *Platakou* judgement.[250] Finally, after the ECtHR's *Sidiropoulos* judgement,[251] Greek courts initially announced a more stringent standard to justify their refusal to register an association.[252] However, they did not follow this approach consistently,[253] thus resulting in a new ECtHR finding of violation in 2007.[254]

b. Remaining Problems

A systemic problem concerning the implementation of ECtHR judgements pertains to the conditions in the overcrowded Greek detention facilities. In connection with ECtHR case law,[255] since 2001, Greek authorities have announced several remedial measures to address this problem, including the construction of new prisons plus maximum limits for the capacity of detention facilities. Nonetheless, from 2002 to 2005, not a single new prison had been completed despite a continual rise in the prison population, which reached approximately 10,000 individuals in 2005, while existing detention centres could hold only 5,500 persons.[256] In a 2005 Interim Resolution, the CoE's Committee of Ministers called for further remedial measures.[257] Greece's poor conditions of detention led the ECtHR to another finding of violation in 2006.[258] Accordingly, the Committee on Legal Affairs and Human Rights of the CoE's Parliamentary Assembly considered the reasons for Greece's non-compliance and possible solutions. Criticizing its lack of progress, the latter Committee's Report, adopted by the Parliamentary Assembly in a 2006 Resolution, deplored Greece's failure to address the systemic overcrowding of its detention facilities and prisons and urged Greek authorities to give this issue top priority.[259] In 2006–2007, Greece has made some progress: Two new prisons have been completed, and, according to the Government, five more detention facilities are scheduled for construction in 2008. The two new facilities plus the five planned facilities together will hold a total of 2,700 detain-

---

[249] See Areios Pagos, Judgement (Full Bench), 2002.04.18, no. 12/2002, NoB 2003, 659 (relying both on the constitutional equality guarantee and Article 6 (1) ECHR); Greek Council of State, Judgement (Full Bench), 2002.10.04, no. 2807/2002, ToS 2002, 721 (same conclusion but based on the Greek Constitution).

[250] *Platakou v. Greece* (*supra* note 135).

[251] *Sidiropoulos and Others v. Greece* (*supra* note 163).

[252] See Areios Pagos, Judgement, 2002.06.25, no. 1241/2002, NoB 2003, 1018, 1019.

[253] Cf., e.g., Areios Pagos, Judgement, 2006.01.10, no. 58/2006, HellDni 2006, 524 (upholding the non-registration of the "Evros Prefecture Minority Youth Association").

[254] *Bekir-Ousta and Others v. Greece* (*supra* note 164).

[255] *Dougoz v. Greece* (*supra* note 155); *Peers v. Greece* (*supra* note 155).

[256] Report of the Council of Europe's Human Rights Commissioner to Greece, 29 March 2006, CommDH (2006) 13.

[257] Council of Europe, Committee of Ministers, Interim Resolution, 7 April 2005, ResDH(2005)21.

[258] *Kaja v. Greece* (*supra* note 155).

[259] Council of Europe, Parliamentary Assembly, Resolution 1516 (2006), Implementation of Judgments of the European Court of Human Rights, 2 October 2006, nos 11.3, 22.5.

ees.[260] However, it remains to be seen to what extent the additional facilities will bring about an improvement in conditions of detention. While monitoring by independent national bodies could play a significant role in this vein, the Ministry of Justice and the country's Chief Prosecutor practically bar the Ombudsman from monitoring conditions of detention.[261] In addition, despite some efforts to increase human rights awareness among police officials, allegations of police brutality persist. Concerning property rights violations,[262] the CoE's Committee of Ministers encouraged the Greek authorities in a 2006 Interim Resolution to accelerate efforts to complete the national land and forest register to prevent new violations similar to those logged in several ECtHR property rights cases.[263]

A general caveat regarding the status of the ECHR in Greece is that compliance efforts are generally limited to ECtHR findings of violation. Decisions of non-violation remain typically unnoticed even when shortcomings of the Greek legal order do not come before the ECtHR for technical reasons such as non-exhaustion of domestic remedies.[264] While on several issues Greek courts have abandoned their case law found incompatible with the ECHR by the ECtHR,[265] they have not always adopted a consistent approach with respect to similar issues that have not yet given rise to ECtHR findings of violation against Greece.[266] Although legal scholars argue that the ECHR requires Greek courts to follow[267] or at least consider[268] the ECtHR's interpretation of the ECHR, the practical effect of ECtHR judgements against other Contracting States is limited. For instance, the ECtHR concluded that the inadmissibility of an appeal on points of law due to the fact that the applicant had not surrendered to custody is *generally* inconsistent with Article 6 ECHR.[269] In contrast, the Areios Pagos, referring to Article 6 ECHR and Article 20 CG, engaged in a balancing analysis that is based on the importance of the alleged crime.[270] In a rare occasion of clear conflict between

[260] See interview with the Minister of Justice (*supra* note 236).
[261] See also *infra* note 342 and accompanying text.
[262] See *supra* notes 148–153 and accompanying text.
[263] Council of Europe, Committee of Ministers, Interim Resolution, 7 June 2006, ResDH(2006)27.
[264] See, e.g., *Ahmet Sadik v. Greece* (appl. no. 18877/91), Judgement, 15 November 1996, Reports 1996-V, 1638 (conviction for using the term "Turkish" to designate the Muslim minority in Thrace).
[265] See *supra* notes 244–252 and accompanying text.
[266] See, e.g., Greek Council of State, Judgement, 1999.05.04, no. 1522/1999 (State's failure to implement expropriation purpose for 25 years); cf. also Greek Council of State, Judgement, 2007.03.19, no. 802/2007, EDDD 2007, 375, with Areios Pagos, Judgement (Full Bench), 2006.01.12, no. 3/2006, ToS 2006, 553 (conflicting judgements as to permissibility of preferential default interest of State institutions). The issue is pending before the Full Bench of the Council of State.
[267] Papadimitriou (1996), 572–573; Beys (1997), 57–58.
[268] Chryssogonos (2001), 395 et seq. (399).
[269] See, e.g., *Omar v. France* (appl. no. 24767/94), Judgement (Grand Chamber), 29 July 1998, Reports 1998-V, 1841.
[270] See, e.g., Areios Pagos, Judgement (Full Bench [Council]), 2001.07.10, no. 14/2001, HellDni 2002, 262–263.

the ECtHR and a Greek high court, even after this discrepancy led the ECtHR to find a violation against Greece in 2003,[271] an Areios Pagos panel insisted on its own interpretation of Article 6 ECHR,[272] until a 2005 statute unambiguously adopted the ECtHR approach.[273]

2. Turkey

a. Measures of Compliance

In recent years, Turkey's open denial to comply with a ECtHR judgement has resulted in four strongly worded Interim Resolutions of the CoE Committee of Ministers. In connection with the ECtHR *Loizidou* judgement,[274] the Turkish Government declined to pay for damages, costs and expenses as ordered by the ECtHR unless a global settlement is reached that covers all property cases in Cyprus. In a 1999 Interim Resolution, the CoE Committee of Ministers "strongly urge[d]" Turkey to reconsider its position.[275] Further, in a 2000 Resolution, the CoE Committee of Ministers emphasized that the failure on the part of a CoE Member State to comply with a ECtHR judgement is unprecedented and declared that Turkey's position "demonstrates a manifest disregard for its international obligations."[276] In light of Turkey's continuous non-compliance, the CoE Committee of Ministers issued a third Resolution in 2001, stressing that acceptance of the ECHR and the binding nature of the ECtHR judgements has become a requirement for membership in the CoE, and calling upon the Member States to take such action as they deem appropriate to ensure Turkey's compliance.[277] However, not until June 2003 did Turkish authorities declare that they had initiated compliance measures. After a fourth Interim Resolution in November 2003 that "[v]ery deeply deplor[ed] the fact that Turkey did not honour its undertaking",[278] Turkey paid the sums awarded, together with default interest, in December 2003.[279]

In terms of other measures of compliance, Turkish scholars generally agree that an ECtHR finding of violation requires the State to remedy the statutory prob-

---

[271] *Skondrianos v. Greece* (*supra* note 128).

[272] See Margaritis (2007), 192–193 with references to the case law.

[273] Act no. 3346/2005 (*supra* note 229), Article 18 (3).

[274] *Loizidou v. Turkey* (*supra* note 200); see also *Loizidou v. Turkey* (appl. no. 15318/89), Judgement (Just Satisfaction) (Grand Chamber), 28 July 1998, Reports 1998-IV, 1807.

[275] Council of Europe, Committee of Ministers, Interim Resolution, 6 October 1999, ResDH(99)680.

[276] Council of Europe, Committee of Ministers, Interim Resolution, 24 July 2000, DH(2000)105.

[277] Council of Europe, Committee of Ministers, Interim Resolution, 26 June 2001, ResDH(2001)80.

[278] Council of Europe, Committee of Ministers, Interim Resolution, 12 November 2003, ResDH(2003)174.

[279] Council of Europe, Committee of Ministers, Resolution, 2 December 2003, ResDH(2003)190.

lem or Government practice responsible for the violation.[280] However, necessary statutory reforms to comply with the ECtHR case law have not always been implemented.[281]

aa. Constitutional Amendments. A series of constitutional amendments beginning in 1987 repealed to a certain extent, most remarkably in 1995 and 2001, Turkey's constitutional provisions that conflicted with the ECHR and enhanced rights protection and the rule of law. For instance, these amendments lifted some egregious limitations on fundamental rights, such as freedom of expression[282] and association,[283] made the dissolution of political parties somewhat more difficult,[284] banned the death penalty (Article 38 (9)), enshrined the proportionality principle (Article 13), clarified a vague provision on the non-abuse of fundamental rights (Article 14) in light of Article 17 ECHR, redrafted personal liberty and security (Article 19) and privacy (Articles 20–21) rights based on the ECHR, guaranteed the right to a fair trial (Article 36, gender equality (Article 10 (2)) and equality between the spouses (Article 41 (1)), prohibited the imprisonment of an individual merely because he/she is unable to fulfil a contractual obligation (Article 38 (8)), and abolished a constitutional article banning judicial review of statutes and decrees that had been enacted during the military rule of the early 80's. These constitutional modifications remain insufficient; nevertheless, their importance should not be underestimated either, although reforms have virtually stopped since 2005. While the Europeanization of the Turkish legal system has had a considerably positive effect on rights guarantees, institutional and procedural reforms have been rather limited.[285] The maintenance of the *status quo* has been the primary concern of the Turkish establishment in this respect. Further, several constitutional amendments enacted since the late 90's have had a more general reach, as they responded to international standards and pressure to modernize domestic legislation and resulted from the EU accession process.[286] Nevertheless, on other occasions, Turkey's compliance with the ECHR was the direct catalyst for constitutional changes. For instance, in terms of Turkey's State Security Courts, a 1999 constitutional amendment changed their composition

---

[280] Gölcüklü and Gözübüyük (2002), 124 et seq.; Tezcan, Erdem and Sancakdar (2004), 127 et seq.

[281] Tezcan, Erdem and Sancakdar (2004), 125.

[282] See, e.g., Article 26 (3) of the 1982 Constitution (banning the use of languages prohibited by law). On these limitations, see Kaboğlu (1999).

[283] See, e.g., Article 33 (4) of the 1982 Constitution (providing that associations cannot pursue political aims or engage in political activities).

[284] Apart from defining the reasons for party dissolution more concretely and providing an option for lighter penalties (Article 69 CRT), the amendments also require a qualified majority for a Constitutional Court dissolution judgement (Article 149 (1) CRT).

[285] For instance, while both the participation of military officials and the power of the National Security Council have been reduced (Article 118 CRT), similar steps are long overdue with respect to the National Defence Council.

[286] See, in detail, Gönenç (2004), 89 et seq.; Kaboğlu (2004), 9 et seq.

following the ECtHR *Incal* and *Çıraklar* judgements[287] and a 2004 amendment abolished them altogether (Article 143 CRT).

bb. Statutory Modifications. In connection with these constitutional reforms, Turkey enacted a set of eight harmonization reform packages from 2002 to 2004 aimed to align Turkish legislation with the revised Constitution. While these statutes eliminated several repressive provisions that had been enacted by the military regime in the early 80's, Turkish authorities adopted a gradual and incomplete harmonization approach that has not yet addressed all existing deficiencies.[288] A number of legal reforms has had positive consequences on the execution of the ECtHR judgements concerning the actions of security forces in the first half of the 90's.[289] The harmonization statutes have introduced additional safeguards for freedom of association and assembly, freedom of expression,[290] and personal security and freedom. In 2005, the Criminal Code,[291] the Code of Criminal Procedure[292] and the Law on the Enforcement of Sentences[293] were reformed in compliance with the new constitutional standards; in addition, a new statute on the right to information was enacted in 2003.[294]

Also, the new Code of Criminal Procedure aimed to accelerate proceedings in Turkish courts by granting prosecutors greater discretion to drop weak cases and introduced a plea bargaining system to expedite potentially lengthy cases. An increase in the budget of the Ministry of Justice, an information technology project of the judiciary,[295] as well as other statutory reforms aimed at speeding up judicial proceedings.[296] Further, a 2004 statute on compensation for terrorism-

---

[287] *Incal v. Turkey (supra* note 174); *Çıraklar v. Turkey (supra* note 186).

[288] For an overview, see Kaboğlu (2004–2005).

[289] See also European Commission (2007), 12.

[290] Cf. Council of Europe, Committee of Ministers, Interim Resolution, 23 July 2001, ResDH (2001)106 (urging Turkish authorities to initiate, without further delay, ad hoc measures to fully erase the consequences of convictions resulting from public statements contrary to Article 10 ECHR).

[291] Türk Ceza Kanunu, Act no. 5237, 26 September 2004, R.G. no. 25611, 12 October 2004.

[292] Ceza Muhakemeleri Kanunu, Act no. 5271, 4 December 2004, R.G. no. 25673, 17 December 2004.

[293] İnfaz Kanunu, Act. no. 5275, 13 December 2004, R.G. no. 25685, 29 December 2004.

[294] Bilgi Edinme Hakki Kanunu [Right to Information Act], Act no. 4982, 9 October 2003, R.G. no. 25269, 24 October 2003, 1 et seq., entered into effect on 24 April 2004.

[295] "National Judicial Network Project" (UYAP).

[296] Among them, a 2004 statute that limited judicial vacations (Çeşitli Kanunlarda Değişiklik Yapılması Hakkında [Amendment Act of Various Statutes], Act no. 5219, 14 July 2004, R.G. no. 25529, 21 July 2004), and a 2004 statute that established regional Courts of Appeals (Adli Yargı İlk derece Mahkemeleri ile Bölge Adliye Mahkemelerinin Kuruluş, Görev ve Yetkileri Hakkında Kanun [Act on Organization, Duties and Authorities of First Instance Courts and Courts of Appeals], Act no. 5235, 26 September 2004, R.G. no. 25606, 7 October 2004). A shortage of physical infrastructure still prevents these courts from operating, although in May 2007 the locations and areas of jurisdiction were determined for nine regional Courts of Appeals.

related losses[297] reduced the number of damage claims resulting from denial of access to possessions in Turkey's south-east provinces.[298]

cc. Changing the Implementation of Domestic Legislation. In Turkey as well, on numerous occasions, ECtHR case law has prompted executive authorities to change how domestic legislation is implemented. For instance, in early 2006, Turkey's Ministry of Justice issued some 100 new directives, addressed mainly to public prosecutors that provided a clearer framework for the implementation of the new criminal legislation. Intended to eliminate procedural deficits that were revealed in ECtHR rulings on issues such as lawful arrest, custody, and interrogation procedures, these directives aimed at preventing human rights violations, and relied explicitly on the ECHR and ECtHR case law, not only domestic law.

b. Remaining Problems

Despite Turkey's recent progress in implementing the ECHR and ECtHR case law, in 2006 Turkish cases still represented 14.4 per cent of the cases pending before the CoE's Committee of Ministers. Among them, 93 cases related to the control of security forces' actions and effective remedies against abuses, 115 cases related to the freedom of expression in connection with criminal convictions under the old Turkish Criminal Code and 113 cases concerned fairness of proceedings before the former State Security Courts.[299]

The European Commission's 2007 Progress Report on Turkey illustrates both the progress Turkey has made over the years and the remaining issues it needs to address to fully implement ECHR standards and remedy ECHR violations. For instance, in terms of torture and ill-treatment of its detainees and prisoners,[300] a legislative framework that established a "zero tolerance" policy on torture has resulted in a continuous decrease in the number of alleged torture and ill-treatment cases that were reported and has strengthened the system for the medical examination of alleged cases of abuse and the implementation of the Istanbul Protocol, a manual that requires effective investigation and documentation of torture. Nevertheless, cases of torture and ill-treatment are still being reported, especially at the beginning of detention. In addition, concerns remain with regard to the quality and accessibility of medical examinations of persons in custody, the independence of the responsible bodies and the inaccessibility of state-sponsored services for victims of ill-treatment. Although statements made in the absence of lawyers do not constitute admissible court evidence under the new Code of Criminal Procedure, the courts have taken into consideration state-

---

[297] Terör ve Terörle Mücadeleden Doğan Zararların Karşılanması Hakkında Kanun [Compensation Act for Losses Resulting from Terrorism and the Fight against Terrorism] Act no. 5233, 17 July 2004, R.G. no. 25535, 27 July 2004, 10 et seq.

[298] See also European Commission (2006), 21.

[299] European Commission (2006), 11–12.

[300] European Commission (2007), 13–14.

ments obtained in the past, even despite allegations of ill-treatment. Further-more, an impartial investigation into allegations of human rights violations by members of the security forces is generally missing and there is no monitoring of law enforcement establishments by independent national bodies. Concerning access to justice,[301] although detainees' access to a lawyer has improved in recent years, substantial discrepancies persist across the country and according to the type of crime committed. Outstanding problems in prison facilities include, *inter alia*, inadequate health care resources and overcrowding, cases of ill-treatment by prison staff and lack of independent monitoring. Moreover, contrary to ECHR freedom of expression standards, the criminal legislation allows prosecutions and convictions for the expression of certain types of opinions, resulting in a climate of self-censorship.[302] In 2006, the number of persons prosecuted almost doubled compared with 2005 and the number of prosecutions increased further in 2007. Most notably, despite occasional reform proposals, the infamous Article 301 of the Criminal Code continues to penalize individuals for denigrating "Turkishness", the Republic, State organs and institutions. Although this provision stipulates that expression of an opinion for the purpose of criticism does not constitute a crime, Turkey's Court of Cassation has repeatedly used a controversial restrictive interpretation[303] to prosecute utterances expressed by journalists, academics and human rights activists.[304] The legal framework of freedom of assembly is gener-ally consistent with European standards; despite this, contrary to the ECtHR *Oya Ataman* judgement,[305] in some cases security authorities use disproportion-ate force, especially when demonstrations are carried out without Governmental permission.[306] Regarding freedom of association, a revised 2004 statute on the functioning of associations resulted in an increase in the number of associations and their membership. Nonetheless, the requirement to notify authorities when funds are received from abroad constitutes a cumbersome procedure. Some as-sociations face additional difficulties in their work, for instance, the authorities have blocked the bank accounts of Amnesty International Turkey since Janu-ary 2007.[307] Further, political parties are not allowed to use language other than Turkish in their communications.[308] In terms of religious freedom, freedom of worship is generally guaranteed. However, non-Muslim religious communities face problems such as non-recognition of legal entity status and limited property

[301] Ibid., 14.
[302] Ibid., 14–15.
[303] See, e.g., Plenary Assemblies of the Penal Chambers of the Turkish Court of Cassation, Judge-ment, 2004.11.23, E. 2004/8–130, K. 2004/206.
[304] See, in detail, Initiative for Freedom of Expression (2005); Initiative for Freedom of Expres-sion (2006).
[305] *Oya Ataman v. Turkey* (*supra* note 184).
[306] For instance, security forces used excessive force against protestors in a demonstration at the Istanbul Taksim Square on 1 May 2007.
[307] European Commission (2007), 15–16.
[308] Ibid., 16.

rights, while a 2008 statute[309] eased some property rights restrictions concerning minority foundations. In addition, restraints on the training of clergy remain, the Ecumenical Patriarch, the spiritual head of the Orthodox Church, is not free to use the ecclesiastical title Ecumenical, and Turkey's Alevi religious community faces difficulties in opening places of worship.[310] It remains to be seen how Turkish authorities will react to the October 2007 ECtHR ruling concerning the compulsory "instruction in religious culture and moral education" in primary and secondary schools (Article 24 (4) CRT).[311] Concerning cultural rights, while broadcasting in languages other than Turkish is now permitted, time restrictions apply and educational programs teaching the Kurdish language are not allowed. In addition, there are neither opportunities to learn Kurdish in the public or private schooling system nor access to public services for non-speakers of Turkish, while, in a pending case, the Council of State has dismissed a mayor from office for providing multilingual municipal services.[312] Finally, the effect of ECtHR decisions of non-violation against Turkey, along with ECtHR decisions against other Contracting States, is limited.[313]

3. Comparison and Conclusion

In the past, Greece and Turkey's unwillingness to comply with European human rights standards tested the limits of the ECHR supervisory system. In the late 60's, the interstate applications against the Greek military dictatorship resulted in the temporary withdrawal of Greece from the CoE. In the early 80's, similar applications against the Turkish military regime resulted in a friendly settlement that provided no guarantees of ECHR compliance and did not have much concrete effect in terms of improving human rights standards in Turkey. Further, in a case of unprecedented non-compliance with an ECtHR judgement, from 1998 to 2003, Turkey blatantly denied to comply with the ECtHR *Loizidou* judgement concerning property rights in northern Cyprus.[314] While Turkey's long-standing non-compliance reflected the limits of the European human rights protection system, its ultimate concession demonstrates a substantial progress, showing that in the long term non-compliance is no more an option for the CoE Member States.

Both in Greece and Turkey, constitutional amendments, statutory modifications and changes in the interpretation of domestic law have furthered an effective reception of the ECHR. However, it is difficult to assess the extent to which such

---

[309] Vakiflar Kanunu [Statute on Foundations], Act no. 5737, 20 February 2008, R.G. no. 26800, 27 February 2008.

[310] Ibid., 16–18.

[311] *Hasan and Eylem Zengin v. Turkey* (*supra* note 207).

[312] European Commission (2007), 22.

[313] For instance, the directives issued by the Ministry of Justice on the presumption of innocence cite ECtHR case law against France and Austria concerning interrogation procedures.

[314] *Loizidou v. Turkey* (*supra* note 200).

measures have been in direct response to ECtHR rulings. The implementation of EU law in Greece and the EU accession process in Turkey has served as a more direct catalyst for changes in domestic law. Further, both Greece and Turkey's responses to the ECtHR rulings do not always guarantee compliance with the ECHR in the long term. More pronounced on issues that touch upon State and constitutional identity or the perception thereof, both countries have opted for qualified methods of reception. For instance, in complying with the ECtHR religious freedom rulings Greece has successfully altered administrative and judicial practices, rather than effecting a clear-cut statutory modification. Greek courts have initially announced a similar approach concerning freedom of association of minority groups, failing, though, to implement it consistently. On the other hand, for Turkish authorities, the maintenance of State unity and identity against the background of armed clashes with PKK members and the Cyprus problem remains a powerful concern and complicates the effective reception of the ECHR and ECtHR rulings. Thus, despite all the recent progress in human rights, major deficits linger for Turkey in terms of compliance with the ECtHR case law, most notably on issues such as ill-treatment of detainees, freedom of expression and religious freedom; in recent years, persisting allegations of police brutality are made against Greece as well. In addition, systemic problems remain in both countries, most remarkably the deplorable conditions of detention centres and the excessive length of proceedings. Finally, both in Greece and Turkey, compliance efforts are generally limited to findings of ECHR violation. The transformative effect of ECtHR rulings against other Contracting States that could apply to both Greece and Turkey remains to be seen.

E. Mechanisms of Coordination

1. Greece

a. Judiciary

Between 1953 and 1974 no Greek judgement found a legislative or administrative measure to be incompatible with the ECHR. Consistent with the judges' deferential approach to the political branches of Government in national constitutional law, Greek courts referred to the ECHR rarely[315] and without elaboration, highlighting the possibility of limiting rights under Articles 8–11(2) ECHR.[316] In the words of the esteemed scholar *Phaedon Vegleris*, the ECHR remained a useless document, an uninhabited islet in an ocean of laws that were persistently, systematically and permanently inconsistent with its letter and spirit.[317]

---

[315] For example, during this period, the Council of State cited the ECHR only on six occasions. See Chryssanthakis (2001), 118.

[316] See *infra* notes 373–374 and accompanying text.

[317] Vegleris (1977), 54–55; see also Vegleris (1980), 305 et seq.

For a considerable time after restoration of democracy in 1974, Greek courts remained especially wary of applying the ECHR, even after Greece's recognition of the individual petition option in 1985. An increasing number of judgements referred to the ECHR (typically in conjunction with the Greek Constitution).[318] For instance, from 1974 to 1999, the Council of State cited the ECHR on 258 occasions,[319] 224 of them after 1992. Nevertheless, Greek courts typically did not cite Strasbourg case law and rejected claims of ECHR violations virtually without examining the merits of the case.[320] Even when they departed from their deferential approach against the political branches of Government, they generally relied on the Greek Constitution, mentioning the ECHR only in passing.[321] As a Judge at the Council of State put it in the early 90's, the ECHR lived in the shadow of the Constitution.[322]

Since the late 90's, the Greek legal order has shown signs of improvement in implementing the ECHR. Certainly, it is still common for Greek courts either to cite the ECHR, without analyzing its requirements or utilizing ECtHR case law, or to proceed along identical lines of reasoning with respect to both the Greek Constitution and the ECHR.[323] Nevertheless, even when ultimately rejecting a claim of violation, Greek courts have tended to engage with the ECHR provisions in a more detailed way.[324] Further, while insisting on a narrow construction of the Greek Constitution, Greek courts have considered the possibility of a broader interpretation in light of the ECHR. For example, traditionally, Greek courts have opted for a narrow construction of the constitutional property concept. Accordingly, property rights (Article 17 (1) CG) are limited to *rights in rem*. Citing the broad interpretation of the ECtHR's "possessions" concept, the Areios Pagos subsumed, in a seminal 1998 ruling, under the scope of Article 1 of ECHR Protocol no. 1 not only claims, but also all "rights of possessive character"

---

[318] From 1974–1984, Greek legal periodicals published 16 decisions of Greek Courts citing the ECHR, compared with 39 decisions from 1985 to 1994. See Valakou-Theodoroudi (1997), 79.

[319] Among these references, 54% concerned Article 6 ECHR and 21% Article 1 of the First Protocol. Nevertheless, on 124 out of 139 occasions, Article 6 ECHR served only as a secondary norm of reference; on the contrary, in 52 out of 54 references, the Council of State relied on Article 1 Protocol no. 1 as a primary norm. See Chryssanthakis (2001), 115 et seq.

[320] For a case law survey see, e.g., Ioannou (2001), 364 et seq.; Briolas (1993), 94 et seq; Kroustalakis (1993), 117 et seq.

[321] See, e.g., Greek Council of State, Judgement, 1986.05.15, no. 1802/1986, HellDni 1986, 1031 (striking down the authorization requirement for armed forces officers to speak to the press); Greek Council of State, Judgement (Full Bench), 1988.02.19, no. 867/1988, DiDik 1989, 303, 304–305 (striking down the authorization requirement for armed forces officers to get married).

[322] Briolas (1993), 112.

[323] See, e.g., Greek Council of State, Judgement, 1998.18.06, no. 2601/1998, DiDik 1999, 1286 (finding Articles 13 CG and 9 ECHR to require the option of a non-religious invocation instead of a religious oath during university graduation ceremonies).

[324] See, e.g., Areios Pagos, Judgement, 1999.06.28, no. 1196/1999, NoB 1999, 1620 et seq. (upholding the limitation of the right to lodge an appeal against committals for trial for certain crimes in light of Articles 6(1) and (2) ECHR, 2(1) of Protocol no. 7 and 20 (1) CG).

and "acquired economic interests".[325] While initially not reversing the traditional view on the constitutional notion of property, the Areios Pagos has indicated in recent years a willingness to adopt a broader understanding of the Greek Constitution's property concept.[326]

The long-standing non-application of the ECHR in Greece can be attributed to the courts' perception that international law is "foreign" law and thus not relevant. Accordingly, Greek judges have been reluctant to refer to an international instrument out of loyalty to the national Constitution.[327] More to the point, the reserved position of Greek courts against the ECHR and ECtHR case law from the 50's to the 90's correlated with their lack of knowledge and understanding of the ECHR and Strasbourg jurisprudence.[328] As the ECtHR findings of violation against Greece increased, the new generation of jurists became gradually accustomed to European human rights law. Thus, the importance of the ECHR became obvious to jurists and the Greek courts' engagement with Strasbourg case law increased significantly.

Interpretation of domestic law in accordance with the ECHR has enhanced coordination between the ECHR and the Greek legal order. Despite the lack of an explicit constitutional provision to this effect, legal scholars generally acknowledge that the Constitution (as well as statutory law) should be construed in accordance with international human rights treaties.[329] Nevertheless, Greek courts have not always used this approach consistently.

A 1999 set of Areios Pagos rulings provides an example of constitutional interpretation that is consistent with international law: Article 93 (3) CG stipulates that "every court judgement must be specifically and thoroughly reasoned" without differentiating between exonerating and condemning criminal judgements. Consistent with this, earlier case law had applied the same standard of reasoning with respect to both sets of judgements.[330] In contrast, in 1999, the Areios Pagos differentiated the reasoning requirements of criminal judgements based on the presumption of innocence, which, while not mentioned directly in the Greek Constitution, is guaranteed explicitly in Article 6(2) ECHR. Accordingly, the reasoning requirements for an exonerating judgement are lower than for reaching condemning judgements.[331] On the other hand, a case involving expropria-

---

[325] Areios Pagos, Judgement (Full Bench), 1998.12.17, no. 40/1998, ToS 1999, 103 et seq.

[326] See, e.g., Areios Pagos, Judgement (Full Bench), 2007.04.19, no. 6/2007, NoB 2007, 715.

[327] Ioannou (2001), 365.

[328] Perrakis (1996), 187; Roucounas (1996), 302; Iliopoulos-Strangas (2008), 102.

[329] Some scholars rely on Article 25 (1) CG, stipulating that "the rights of the human being as an individual and as a member of the society" are guaranteed by the State and that "all agents of the state shall be obliged to ensure the unhindered and effective exercise thereof." See Chryssogonos (2001), 199 et seq. Others invoke to the same effect Article 2 (2) CG (*supra* note 69). See Iliopoulos-Strangas (2008), 98–99.

[330] See, in general, Areios Pagos, Judgement, 1998.05.06, no. 768/1998, NoB 1998, 1488 et seq.

[331] See, e.g., Areios Pagos, Judgement, 1999.02.16, no. 387/1999, NoB 1999, 1342, 1344–1345 (holding that an exonerating judgement can only be qualified as unreasoned when it does not clarify

tion without compensation of property belonging to the former King of Greece Constantine and his family offers an example of a failed opportunity for Greek courts to consider international law in constitutional interpretation. Relying on Article 1 CG, which defines the form of the Greek regime as a Parliamentary republic, Greek courts held that this provision also implies a definitive ruling on the property issue, legitimating its expropriation without compensation.[332] In doing so, the Greek courts avoided any attempt to harmonize their constitutional interpretation with the ECHR. Finally, contrary to previous case law,[333] in recent years Greek courts have tended to construe unclear statutory provisions in line with the ECHR.[334]

b. Legislative and Executive Authorities

Greece has no specific coordination procedures of its legislative and executive authorities' lawmaking activities with the ECHR and ECtHR case law. However, several institutions that aim to enhance human rights protection, in effect, have substantially contributed to an increased compliance with the ECHR. Beginning in the 90's, the Greek Parliament established by statute a set of independent authorities (ανεξάρτητες αρχές) that were charged with combating poor administration and protecting fundamental rights. With respect to five such authorities, the 2001 constitutional amendments established a general guarantee of their independence,[335] a novelty from a comparative constitutional perspective.[336] Among them, the Greek Ombudsman (Συνήγορος του Πολίτη)[337] who is charged with protecting citizens' rights, combating maladministration and ensuring legality, has a general importance for rights protection.[338] The Ombuds-

why the court was not convinced of the guilt of the accused, without having to explain why the court was convinced of his/her innocence).

[332] See Greek Supreme Special Court, Judgement, 1997.06.25, no. 45/1997, ToS 1997, 756 et seq. Cf. *Former King of Greece and Others v. Greece* (appl. no. 25701/94), Judgement (Grand Chamber), 23 November 2000, Reports 2000-XII, 119.

[333] Cf. *supra* Section C.1.a.

[334] See, e.g., Greek Council of State, Judgement, 2000.03.16, no. 1117/2000, ToS 2001, 600 et seq. (finding on the basis of Article 6(1) ECHR that a public university rector who had initiated disciplinary proceedings could not participate in the decision-making body charged with resolving the disciplinary complaint); Areios Pagos, Judgement (Full Bench), 1999.12.09, no. 2/1999, NoB 2000, 510 (consideration in a criminal trial of testimony given by the accused during preliminary investigation results in procedural invalidity and grounds for appeal in light of Article 6(3) ECHR).

[335] According to Article 101 A CG, members of these authorities "shall enjoy personal and functional independence" (1) and will be selected by a Parliamentary body that seeks a unanimous vote or, if unanimity cannot be achieved, by a qualified majority (2). While this selection mode currently requires bipartisan agreement, the Constitution's wording does not guarantee the decision-making body's composition.

[336] Apart from the Ombudsman, the other constitutionally established independent authorities are the Independent Authority for the Protection of Personal Data; the National Radio and Television Council; the authority ensuring the secrecy of all forms of free correspondence and communication and the authority responsible for the engagement of public servants.

[337] See Article 103 (9) CG.

[338] Act no. 3094/2003, Συνήγορος του Πολίτη και άλλες διατάξεις [The Ombudsman and Other

man, who proceeds to investigate after the submission of complaints and on his/her initiative,[339] communicates a final report to the executive authorities.[340] While the Ombudsman's conclusions are not legally binding, she/he may impose a deadline on the administration, which must inform the Ombudsman of the measures taken. In addition, she/he can initiate criminal or disciplinary proceedings against administrative organs,[341] which are obliged to assist the Ombudsman during the investigation. The Ombudsman's activity extends to a number of issues that concern the Greek executive authorities' reception of the ECHR and the ECtHR case law such as allegations of police brutality, conditions of detention and rights of religious minorities, not hesitating to strongly criticize the executive authorities in cases of non-cooperation, for instance for obstruction of access to detention facilities.[342]

Greece's National Commission for Human Rights (*Εθνική Επιτροπή για τα Δικαιώματα του Ανθρώπου [NCHR]*), the national human rights institution with a consultative status that Greece established under a 1998 statute,[343] also plays a significant role in improving coordination between the Greek legal order and the ECHR. The NCHR is composed of representatives of NGOs, political parties, trade unions, independent authorities, and human rights experts; the Government representatives who sit on this commission do not have voting rights. The commission's composition safeguards its independence, although the State Legal Council, a quasi-judicial organ of the administration, in a 2006 controversy surrounding the election of the commission's new chairperson, considered the Commission to be a public authority hierarchically subordinate to the Prime Minister.[344] The commission's activity record includes, *inter alia*, issuing resolutions on human rights topics, submitting recommendations on issues such as

Provisions], FEK A 10, 22 January 2003, Article 1 as modified by Act no. 3304/2005, Εφαρμογή της αρχής της ίσης μεταχείρισης ανεξαρτήτως φυλετικής ή εθνοτικής καταγωγής, θρησκευτικών ή άλλων πεποιθήσεων, αναπηρίας, ηλικίας ή γενετήσιου προσανατολισμού [Implementation of the Equal Treatment Principle Regardless of Racial or Ethnic Origin, Religious or other Beliefs, Disability, Age or Sexual Orientation], FEK A 16, 26/27 January 2005, Article 20 (1); English translation (without consideration of the 2004 and 2005 amendments) available at: http://www.synigoros.gr.

[339] Act no. 3094/2003 (*supra* note 338), Article 4 (1, 2).

[340] Ibid., Article 4 (6).

[341] Ibid., Article 4 (10–12) as modified by Act no. 3242/2004, Ρυθμίσεις για την οργάνωση και λειτουργία της Κυβέρνησης, τη διοικητική διαδικασία και τους Ο.Τ.Α. [Οργανισμούς Τοπικής Αυτοδιοίκησης] [Regulations on the Organization and Functioning of the Government, the Administrative Procedure and the Local Government Agencies], FEK A 102, 24 May 2004, Article 12 (4).

[342] See, e.g., the 2006 report, available at: http://www.synigoros.gr/annual_2006_gr.htm (in Greek); see also an English summary of the 2005 report at http://www.synigoros.gr/reports/Annual_Report_2005.pdf.

[343] Act no. 2667/1998, Σύσταση Εθνικής Επιτροπής για τα Δικαιώματα του Ανθρώπου και Εθνικής Επιτροπής Βιοηθικής [Establishment of a National Commission for Human Rights and a National Bioethics Commission], FEK A 281, 18 December 1998; English translation available at: http://www.nchr.gr.

[344] Greek State Legal Council, Advisory Opinion, 2006.11.30, no. 540/2006, available at: http://www.nsk.gr/gnompdf/2006/5402006.pdf (in Greek).

Greece's ratification of ECHR Protocols, implementation and dissemination of ECtHR judgements, and publishing an annual report.[345]

In terms of the compatibility of draft legislation with the ECHR, various layers of scrutiny exist in the Greek legal system. The aim of these scrutiny mechanisms is not limited to ensuring compliance with the ECHR; more generally, they strive to ensure the quality of draft legislation and its compatibility with constitutional and international law. Initially, the NCHR examines preliminary draft laws that affect human rights and submits to the Government recommendations that are often detailed and cite ECtHR case law.[346] Nonetheless, the Government does not always submit draft Bills to the NCHR for review. In addition, the Government's Secretariat General (*Γενική Γραμματεία της Κυβέρνησης*), the central commission responsible for drafting legislation (*Κεντρική Νομοπαρασκευαστική Επιτροπή*) and the Parliament's legal service (*Επιστημονικό Συμβούλιο*) act sequentially to ensure that draft legislation is compatible with the Constitution and international law. Finally, concerning presidential decrees, the Constitution requires a review by the Council of State prior to their promulgation (Article 95 (1) *alinea* d) that extends to the decrees' constitutionality and legality. All these bodies review draft legal norms in an advisory capacity. In practice, however, concerning presidential decrees, administrative authorities follow the Council of State's recommendations.

2. Turkey

a. Judiciary

While Turkish Courts started citing the ECHR soon after ratification, they had not used the ECtHR case law as a source of reference until the last decade and remain extremely hesitant to rely on the ECHR as an independent standard of scrutiny. The Turkish Constitutional Court, in operation since 1962, has used the ECHR as a norm of reference since 1963. Nevertheless, the Constitutional Court refers to ECtHR case law only in exceptional circumstances. Despite citing the ECHR in 38 judgements from 1963 to 2003, it has invoked Strasbourg jurisprudence only on five occasions.[347] In fact, the Turkish Constitutional Court started citing ECtHR case law only in 1992 and most references are limited to one or two sentences.[348]

In Turkey's Council of State case law, ECtHR judgements have served as a sup-

---

[345] However, this report reproduces NCHR activities, providing an overview of the human rights situation in Greece only in its relatively brief Foreword. See, e.g., the 2006 report at: http://www.nchr.gr.

[346] Further, both in 2001 and 2007, the NCHR provided detailed comments on constitutional amendment proposals (available at: http://www.nchr.gr), referring to the ECHR and citing ECtHR case law.

[347] For details, see Gerek/Aydin (2004), 83 et seq. (also providing a table of the Constitutional Court judgements citing the ECHR and ECtHR case law).

[348] See, e.g., Turkish Constitutional Court, Judgement, 1999.12.29, E. 1999/33, K. 1999/51.

plementary source of reference for a long period of time.[349] Nevertheless, more references are found in the reporting judges' opinions and the dissents,[350] which are usually written by more junior judges, rather than in the main body of the Council of State case law. An explanation might be that the younger generation of judges is more willing to fully implement the 2004 constitutional amendments on the status of international treaties in national law, and to integrate European norms in constitutional doctrine.

The full bench of the Court of Cassation has cited ECtHR case law on 19 occasions since 1946, most of them since the 90's. Most references pertain to the different facets of Article 6 ECHR (right to a fair trial).[351] While the Court of Cassation has also routinely referred to Article 10 ECHR (freedom of expression),[352] on several occasions it has relied on the limitation clause of Article 10(2), rather than the guarantee of Article 10(1) ECHR. Moreover, some of the most important references made to ECtHR case law are those found in the Court's dissenting opinions.[353] Turkey's Military Court of Cassation relies on Strasbourg jurisprudence in a supplementary fashion. Its references to the ECtHR case law pertain generally to Article 6 ECHR.[354] Finally, according to data compiled by the Ministry of Justice, first-instance courts cited ECtHR case law on 130 occasions during 2004 and 2005. First-instance courts, which are located outside major cities, tend to make use of the ECtHR case law more often.[355] In this respect as well, it is likely that younger judges who serve in these courts are more willing to refer to the ECHR and ECtHR case law than their older counterparts.

b. Legislative and Executive Authorities

Traditionally, Turkey has relied on administrative political structures rather than on independent, expert-based bodies for human rights protection. Since the early 90's, a variety of state-sponsored non-judicial institutions have been established to address human rights abuse.[356] Nevertheless, these institutions are not always

---

[349] See, e.g., Turkish Council of State, Judgement (First Section), 2004.12.20, E. 1992/136, K. 2004/4148.

[350] See, e.g., Turkish Council of State, Judgement (Twelfth Section), 2006.02.22, E. 2005/6353, K. 2006/540; Turkish Council of State, Judgement (Eighth Section), 1999.10.21, E. 1998/1220, K. 1999/5359.

[351] See, e.g., Turkish Court of Cassation, Judgement, 1995.10.24, E. 1995/6–238, K. 1995/305; (reasonable time); Turkish Court of Cassation, Judgement, 2001.12.11, E. 2001/8–248, K. 2001/288 (public hearing); Turkish Court of Cassation, Judgement, 1992.04.20, E. 1992/5–56, K. 1992/107 (defence rights).

[352] See, e.g., Turkish Court of Cassation, Judgement (Criminal Section), 1999.04.20, E. 1999/9–58, K. 1999/69; Turkish Court of Cassation, Judgement, 2006.07.11, E. 2006/9–169, K. 2006/184.

[353] See Turkish Court of Cassation, Judgement (Civil Section), 2000.10.18, E. 2000/18–1186, K. 2000/1300.

[354] See, e.g., Turkish Military Court of Cassation, Judgement, 2003.03.13, E/K 2003/25–23.

[355] See, e.g., Turkish Administrative Tribunal of Kocaeli, Judgement, 2005.02.15, E. 2004/1010, K. 2005/301; Turkish Peace Court of Burdur, Judgement, 2004.03.25, E. 2003/650, K. 2004/107.

[356] Among them, the Human Rights Investigation Commission of the Grand National Assembly

independent. Most have been established via by-laws, which rank at the bottom of the hierarchy of norms. An Ombudsman system has yet to be established.

The Human Rights Advisory Board (HRAB), reporting directly to the Prime Minister, was established in 2001 as Turkey's national human rights institution.[357] Despite facing many difficulties during its work, the HRAB took significant initiatives to increase awareness of human rights. Most importantly, in 2004, the HRAB approved two reports[358] that were embarrassing to the Government: A general detailed report that challenged the Government's human rights policy, and a specific Report on Cultural and Minority Rights, which criticized the Government's policy on the treatment of minorities and communities, highlighted the restrictive interpretation of the 1923 Lausanne Treaty and urged the Government to align its human rights policy with international standards, giving equal rights to non-Muslim groups and recognising cultural rights to citizens of non-Turkish ethnic origin. While the HRAB reports provoked lively debate within Turkey, the Public Prosecutor filed a criminal case against Ibrahim Kaboğlu, chairman of the HRAB and author of its general human rights report (also co-author of the present country report), and Baskin Oran, author of the HRAB report on minority rights, for "inciting hatred and enmity" and "insulting the judiciary". After Kaboğlu and numerous board members resigned in protest, the HRAB has ceased to operate, while the Government formally suspended it in early 2005.[359] In 2007, the Court of Cassation overturned the initial acquittal of Kaboğlu and Oran, invoking a danger to the nation's indivisibility and a threat to social peace.[360] Currently, a retrial is pending, with the two Turkish academics facing a prison sentence of up to three years. Scholars have argued that independent human rights institutions could have been given the responsibility for monitoring the implementation of ECtHR rulings and proposing changes in legislation to better protect human rights in Turkey.[361] However, the State's adversarial stance toward such bodies has prevented them from performing their functions, and from taking on an even greater monitoring role. As a result, political manipulation has undermined the independence and effectiveness of Turkey's human rights institutions. In essence, their power has been limited and their role

of Turkey, a State ministry with responsibility for human rights, the Human Rights Supreme Board, the Human Rights Presidency of the Prime Ministry, and the National Committee of the Decade for Human Rights Education.

[357] Başbakanlık Teşkilatı Hakkında Kanun Hükmünde Kararnamenin Değiştirilerek Kabulü Hakkında Kanunda Değişiklik Yapılmasına Dair Kanun Hükmünde Kararnamenin Değiştirilerek Kabulü ile Genel Kadro ve Usulü Hakkında Kanun Hükmünde Kararnamenin Eki Cetvellerde Değişiklik Yapilmasına İlişkin Kanun [Act Amending the Law on the Organization of the Prime Minister's Office and the By-Law Concerning Government Employees], Act no. 4643, 12 April 2001, R.G. no. 24380, 21 April 2001, 8 et seq.

[358] On these reports, see Kaboğlu and Akkurt (2006), 151 et seq., 287 et seq.

[359] See, in detail, Kaboğlu (2006a); Kaboğlu (2006b); Oran (2007).

[360] Turkish Court of Cassation, Judgement (Eighth Criminal Section), 2007.07.12, E. 2007/5222, K. 2007/5583.

[361] For further elaboration, see Tezcan, Erdem and Sancakdar (2004), 126 et seq.

has devolved to being purely consultative. Consequently, vigorous reconstruction of Turkey's human rights protection machinery is urgently needed to improve the coordination between the national legal order and the ECHR.[362]

3. Comparison and Conclusion

Traditionally, Greece's and Turkey's national judiciaries have had similar practices *vis-à-vis* the ECHR. Although Greece's and Turkey's domestic courts began citing the ECHR soon after the States ratified it, at least until the 90's domestic constitutions were the predominant standards for judicial review of legislation. Greek and Turkish courts invoked the ECHR only in passing to confirm the mostly deferential result of constitutional scrutiny. Consistent with this, the courts in both Greece and Turkey have tended to invoke the ECHR only to highlight that the protected rights are subject to limitations according to Articles 8–11(2) ECHR. In addition, not until the 90's did domestic courts in both countries start citing ECtHR case law more regularly. In light of the divergent notions of property according to the Greek Constitution and the ECHR, a 1998 judgement of the Greek Areios Pagos was a major turning point, because the ECHR became the focal point of supra-legislative property protection. Further, Greek courts have usually, although not consistently, construed domestic law in accordance with the ECHR. In contrast, Turkish courts have not made systematic use of any concrete identifiable mechanism to enhance coordination between the national legal order and the ECHR. In both countries not only the distrust of international law as foreign law, but also the deficient knowledge of the ECHR and ECtHR case law have played a critical role in the considerable delays in Greece's and Turkey's reception of the ECHR.

Both Greece and Turkey have no specific coordination procedures of their legislative and executive authorities' lawmaking activities with the ECHR and ECtHR case law. However, in Greece, several mechanisms are in place to scrutinize the compatibility of draft laws with constitutional and international law. Most importantly, considerable divergence exists between the two countries in terms of the independence and effectiveness of non-judicial human rights bodies. Since its 2001 amendments, the Greek Constitution provides several safeguards for independent authorities such as the Ombudsman, which plays a significant role in rights protection. While the Greek National Commission for Human Rights was established by statute, the Government has had no power to appoint any voting members. On the other hand, in Turkey, despite the plethora of human rights bodies, not all are independent and most face serious obstacles in their day-to-day operations. Most bitterly, the Government suspended the Turkish Human Rights Advisory Board, and two of its members currently face criminal prosecution for pointing out deficits in Turkey's cultural and minority rights. Dif-

---

[362] See, in detail, Kaboğlu (2006a); see also European Commission (2007), 13.

ferences in constitutional and statutory regulations only partly account for this divergence. Most importantly, in Turkey, the lingering perception that human rights protection is not fully consistent with national unity and constitutional identity undermines the efficiency of independent human rights bodies.

F. Remedies and Proportionality Tests

Space precludes any attempt to exhaustively address all remedies available in Greece and Turkey in case of an ECHR violation. Rather, this section focuses on the impact of the ECHR and the ECtHR case law on the system of available remedies and examines to what extent the system of remedies changed in response to the evolution of the ECHR. In addition, special attention is paid to the doctrinal use of proportionality tests.

1. Greece

a. Remedies
Greek law does not deal consistently with the reopening of proceedings in case of an ECtHR finding of violation after a national decision qualifying as *res iudicata*. Since 2000, Greek law provides for the reopening of criminal proceedings in the interest of the convicted person, if an ECtHR judgement found either a procedural or substantive ECHR violation.[363] In application of the general provisions on the reopening of proceedings, the convicted person (as well as his/her close relatives and/or lawyer) and the prosecutor of the court may lodge the relevant application,[364] with no time limits; further, *reformatio in pejus* is explicitly prohibited.[365] In addition, a 2002 statute[366] stipulates that the reopening of proceedings can be requested if the domestic courts did not grant compensation or granted insufficient compensation to persons unlawfully convicted or detained on remand, provided that the ECtHR found that Greece violated the ECHR in this regard. Greek courts have upheld the reopening request on several occasions, declaring the criminal convictions void.[367] However, they have also rejected requests to reopen if the excessive length of proceedings had not had any adverse effect on

---

[363] Act no. 2865/2000, Κύρωση της Συμφωνίας περί συνεργασίας για την πρόληψη και καταπολέμηση του διασυνοριακού εγκλήματος [...] [Approval of the Agreement on Cooperation to Prevent and Combat Trans-Border Crime [...]], FEK B 271, 15/19 December 2000, Article 11 (enacting Article 525 (1) No. 5 KPD).

[364] Article 527 (1) KPD.

[365] Article 530 (2) *in finem* KPD.

[366] Act no. 3060/2002, Ρύθμιση θεμάτων αρμοδιότητος του Υπουργείου Δικαιοσύνης [Regulation of Issues Falling within the Authority of the Ministry of Justice], FEK A 242, 10/11 October 2002, Article 12 (enacting Article 525 A KPD).

[367] See, e.g., Areios Pagos (Council), Judgement, 2005.27.01, no. 159/2005, PoinDik 2005, 839–840.

the criminal court's substantive judgement.[368] Reopening civil or administrative judicial proceedings on application by an individual is not possible. Although scholars propose different avenues to introduce the reopening of proceedings in civil and administrative litigation, their suggestions have little chance of prevailing in practice.

Furthermore, on numerous occasions, the ECtHR has found violations of Article 13 ECHR because Greek law did not provide an effective remedy for length of proceedings cases.[369] After 2003, Greek authorities have repeatedly announced that legislative measures are under way to introduce a specific remedy for such cases.[370] Currently (September 2007), a draft Bill is pending that establishes a claim for damages in cases of unreasonable length of proceedings. Nevertheless, this draft has yet to be enacted into law. Financial concerns overcome the political will to comply with the ECtHR case law. Thus, notwithstanding the efforts made to accelerate judicial proceedings,[371] the lack of an effective remedy in length of proceedings cases continues to result in regular ECHR findings of violation.

Finally, Greek courts in theory recognize the possibility of filing a claim for damages in case of violations of the ECHR by the legislature. However, in practice they are very hesitant to uphold such a claim.[372]

b. The Proportionality Test

Consistent with the deferential approach of Greek judges towards the political branches of the State, the courts did not traditionally use the proportionality test to resolve cases that pit a rights-based claim against a public interest justification for the infringement of that right. During the 50's and 60's, when the Greek courts did exceptionally cite the ECHR, they tended to cite the limitation clauses in Articles 8–11(2) ECHR to assert that legislative or administrative measures were not inconsistent with the ECHR, but they failed to engage in a necessity review of these measures.[373] Further, the Greek Council of State upheld by reference to Article 15 ECHR (derogation clause) the domestic exile, a measure ordered by the executive branch. According to the Council of State, an emer-

---

[368] See Areios Pagos (Council), Judgement, 2002.07.16, no. 1638/2002, PoinChron 2003, 607.

[369] See, e.g., *Konti-Arvaniti v. Greece* (*supra* note 139).

[370] See also Θέσεις-Προτάσεις της ΕΕΔΑ σχετικά με τη βελτίωση εφαρμογής της ΕΣΔΑ στην εσωτερική έννομη τάξη: Πρακτικές αντιμετώπισης του ζητήματος της υπερβολικής διάρκειας των δικών [NCHR Positions-Proposals Concerning Improvement in the Implementation of the ECHR in the National Legal Order: Practices to Address the Issue of the Excessive Length of Proceedings]. NCHR, 31 March 2005, available at: http://www.nchr.gr/media/word/trial_duration_31_03_2005.doc.

[371] See *supra* notes 232–236 and accompanying text.

[372] See, e.g., Ktistaki (2005), 2007–2008 with further references.

[373] See, e.g., Greek Council of State, Judgement (Full Bench), 1967.02.17, no. 607/1967, EDDD 1967, 183–184 (exclusion of citizens from work in public transportation company because of their possible political allegiances); see also Greek Council of State, Judgement (Full Bench), 1966.03.01, no. 575/1966, EDDD 1966, 311–312 (justification of civil mobilisation by reference to Article 4(3)(c) ECHR).

gency threatening the nation existed because no official act had been issued that terminated the 1946–1949 civil war.[374]

During the 70's and 80's, the Greek courts' deferential attitude towards the political branches of Government persisted. For the first time in 1984, the Council of State explicitly recognized the constitutional stature of the proportionality principle, as a corollary of the rule of law principle.[375] Nevertheless, at least up to the late 80's, the Greek courts regularly failed to meaningfully scrutinize the constitutionality of legislative and executive acts on proportionality considerations.[376] Rather, they tended to uphold the constitutionality of State actions by merely invoking the nebulous "public interest" concept.[377]

This situation started to change in the early 90's[378] when the Greek courts developed stricter standards of scrutiny with respect to specific provisions such as Article 24 CG on environmental protection. More generally, since the late 90's, the Greek courts have gradually, but not consistently, subjected legislative and executive actions to a more rigorous scrutiny. In fact, this more demanding scrutiny did not always correspond to a coherent proportionality review. In addition, when the Greek courts did apply a proportionality test, they tended to scrutinize appropriateness and necessity of State action. In contrast, they typically avoided engaging in cost-benefit balancing. Consistent with this, most scholars had considered such balancing equivalent to a scrutiny of the wisdom, rather than the constitutionality of State actions.[379]

The Greek Constitution provides explicitly since its 2001 amendments that "[r]estrictions of any kind which [...] may be imposed upon [the rights of the human being]... should respect the principle of proportionality" (Article 25 (1)). Thus, the Greek Constitution established the proportionality principle as an explicit boundary with which all limitations of rights should comply.[380] Further, in recent years, Greek courts have tended to scrutinize not only the appropriateness and necessity of State measures, but also the proportionality *stricto sensu* between the rights-based claim and the public-interest justification for the infringement of that right,[381] even though the Council of State limits itself to striking down

---

[374] See, e.g., Greek Council of State, Judgement (Full Bench), 1954.04.22, no. 724/1954.

[375] Greek Council of State, Judgement, 1984.05.14, no. 2112/1984, ToS 1985, 63, 64.

[376] See also Gerapetritis (1997), 123–124 (arguing that the proportionality principle is adequately subsumed within Greek administrative law).

[377] See, e.g., Greek Council of State, Judgement (Full Bench), 1986.02.21, no. 400/1986, ToS 1986, 433 et seq. (436–437).

[378] See Koutnatzis (2007), 174 et seq. (providing an overview of the development of the case law).

[379] Cf. Chryssogonos (2006), 90 et seq. with further references.

[380] For a criticism, see e.g., Mitsopoulos (2002), 648 et seq. (arguing that the proportionality principle partially overlaps with traditional teleological interpretation).

[381] See, e.g., Areios Pagos, Judgement (Full Bench), 2005.06.28, no. 43/2005, NoB 2005, 1587 et seq.

State measures that are obviously inappropriate or disproportional.[382] Nevertheless, the application of the proportionality test in Greece did not result from the interaction between the Greek courts and the ECtHR, but rather from the influence of the German fundamental rights doctrine.

2. Turkey

a. Remedies

In Turkey, after a 2001 Interim Resolution of the CoE's Committee of Ministers,[383] a 2002 statute provided, for the first time, for the reopening of proceedings in criminal and civil cases following an ECtHR finding of violation.[384] Nevertheless, reopening of proceedings is subject to strict procedural requirements and time limits. Domestic law allows a case to be reopened in respect of ECtHR judgements that either became final before 4 February 2003, or were handed down in applications lodged with the ECtHR after that date. As a result, the execution of the ECtHR judgements in *Hulki Güneş*[385] and in 113 similar cases, related to fairness of proceedings before the former State Security Courts, remains pending. In addition, a subsequent statute, enacted in 2003, extended the possibility to request the reopening of proceedings to administrative litigation.[386] Although no legislation provides for the reopening of proceedings before the Constitutional Court, the Turkish Constitutional Court accepted a request to reopen proceedings in a 2007 case concerning the dissolution of political parties. In so doing, the Court, for the first time, expressed a willingness to reverse its case law in light of an ECtHR judgement.

Further, breaches of Article 1 of Protocol no. 1 and Article 8 ECHR were a systemic problem in Turkey in connection with denial of access to home and property in Turkey's south-east provinces[387] and in northern Cyprus.[388] Concerning Turkey's south-east provinces, a 2004 statute on compensation for terrorism-

---

[382] See, e.g., Greek Council of State, Judgement (Full Bench), no. 990/2004, DtA 2005, 834, 854 et seq.

[383] Council of Europe, Committee of Ministers, Interim Resolution, 30 April 2002, ResDH(2002)59.

[384] Çeşitli Kanunlarda Değişiklik Yapılmasına İlişkin Kanun [Amendment Act of Various Statutes], Act no. 4771, 3 August 2002, R.G. no. 24841, 9 August 2002, 1 et seq. (enacted as a third set of harmonisation laws).

[385] *Hulki Güneş v. Turkey* (appl. no. 28490/95), Judgement (Third Section), 19 June 2003, Reports 2003-VII; see also Council of Europe, Committee of Ministers, Interim Resolution, 30 November 2005, ResDH(2005)113 (noting that the Turkish authorities have not responded to the Committee's calls to correct this gap in Turkish law).

[386] Çeşitli Kanunlarda Değişiklik Yapılmasına İlişkin Kanun [Amendment Act of Various Statutes], Act no. 4793, 23 January 2003, R.G. no. 25014, 4 February 2003, 1 et seq.

[387] See, e.g., *Doğan and Others v. Turkey* (*supra* note 198); *Akdivar and Others v. Turkey* (*supra* note 199).

[388] See, e.g., *Loizidou v. Turkey* (*supra* note 200).

related losses[389] established compensation commissions that determine damages and make a friendly-settlement offer. In a 2006 ruling, the ECtHR found this remedy to meet the "effectiveness" test established in the ECtHR case law.[390] However, the implementation of the statute has raised several concerns due to in-consistencies in the methods used by the compensation commissions, their large discretionary powers, cumbersome procedures resulting in delays in the payment of the awards and the limited compensation provided.[391] In addition, there has been no progress in establishing a new Governmental body responsible for im-plementing a return programme for internally displaced persons. The absence of basic infrastructure, the lack of capital, limited employment opportunities and the shaky security in Turkey's south-east provinces negatively affect the return of such persons.[392] Concerning northern Cyprus, in *Xenides-Arestis*, decided in 2005, the ECtHR required Turkish authorities to make an effective remedy avail-able with respect to all similar applications within three months and to provide redress three months thereafter.[393] Responding to this ruling, Turkish authorities entrusted a newly established "Immovable Property Commission" with deciding on the restitution, exchange of properties or payment of compensation. In 2006, the ECtHR found that Turkey had, in principle, met the requirements set out in the ECtHR judgement.[394] However, the ECtHR did not have the chance yet to address in detail the effectiveness of the new compensation mechanism.

b. The Proportionality Test

In terms of the limitations of constitutional rights, the original version of the 1982 Turkish Constitution contained a general limitation clause (Article 13). According to this clause, fundamental rights and freedoms could be restricted by law for various purposes such as to maintain the indivisibility of the State, national security and public order. Despite focusing generally on the permis-sible limitations of constitutional rights, Article 13 (2) of the 1982 Constitu-tion held that the restrictions of fundamental rights shall not conflict with the requirements of a democratic society and shall not be imposed for any purpose other than those for which they are prescribed. While not explicitly guarantee-ing the proportionality test, the Constitution's references to the requirements of a democratic society echoed Articles 8–11(2) ECHR. The Constitutional Court occasionally construed the requirements of a democratic society as mandating

---

[389] Compensation Act for Losses Resulting from Terrorism and the Fight against Terrorism (*supra* note 297), Articles 6–7.

[390] *Icyer v. Turkey* (appl. no. 18888/02), Decision (Third Section), 12 January 2006 (not yet reported), para. 82.

[391] European Commission (2006), 22.

[392] Ibid., 23.

[393] *Xenides-Arestis v. Turkey* (appl. no. 46347/99), Judgement (Third Section), 22 December 2005 (not yet reported), paras 38–40.

[394] *Xenides-Arestis v. Turkey* (appl. no. 46347/99), Judgement (Just Satisfaction) (Third Section), 7 December 2006 (not yet reported), para. 37.

the inviolability of the right's essence[395] or followed the three-pronged test of appropriateness, necessity and proportionality *stricto sensu* of State action.[396] On the other hand, Article 14 of the 1982 Constitution on non-abuse of fundamental rights was used in practice to limit fundamental rights, such as freedom of expression, with no consideration of the proportionality issue.[397]

The 2001 amendments reformulated Article 13 CRT as a guarantee, rather than as a limitation clause. Its new version requires that the limitations of fundamental rights do not infringe upon their essence and that they do not contravene the requirements of democratic society, the secular republic and the principle of proportionality. On the basis of this new wording, scholars reasonably expect the Constitutional Court to accord a distinct meaning to each different criterion mentioned in Article 13 CRT. Further, Article 14 CRT on the non-abuse of rights was also modified.[398] Some vague formulations were removed, and the provision now partly corresponds to Article 17 ECHR. As a result, Turkish scholars hope that in the future the non-abuse clause will serve as a guarantee, rather than as a limitation of fundamental rights.

3. Comparison and Conclusion

In both countries, a significant development in the domestic remedies system following the ECtHR findings of violation consisted in the possibility to request the reopening of proceedings when a national decision qualified as *res iudicata*. Currently, Greek law provides reopening of proceedings only in criminal cases. Turkish law, in contrast, explicitly allows the reopening of proceedings not only in criminal, but also in civil and administrative litigation; Turkey's Constitutional Court has also recognized this possibility for constitutional disputes. However, Turkish law subjects the reopening of proceedings to strict procedural prerequisites. While Greek law is very permissive in this regard, Greek courts occasionally require additional conditions for reopening. Therefore, only a case-by-case comparison can determine whether the Greek or the Turkish approach is more favourable to the individual. In addition, against the background of systemic violations of Article 8 ECHR (right to respect for private and family life) and Article 1 of Protocol no. 1 (property rights) in Turkey's south-east provinces and

---

[395] Turkish Constitutional Court, Judgement, 26 November 1986, E. 1985/8, K. 1986/27, AYMKD Vol. 22, 365–366.

[396] See, e.g., Turkish Constitutional Court, Judgement, 23 June 1989, E. 1988/50, K. 1989/27, AYMKD Vol. 25, 312. See also Turkish Constitutional Court (2004), 8–9.

[397] See, in detail, Kaboğlu (2002), 101 et seq.

[398] According to Article 14 CRT, enacted in 2001, constitutional rights shall not be exercised "with the aim of violating the indivisible integrity of the state [...] and endangering the existence of the democratic and secular order of the Turkish Republic based on human rights," neither shall Turkey's Constitution be interpreted "in a manner that enables the state or individuals to destroy the fundamental rights and freedoms embodied in the Constitution or to stage an activity with the aim of restricting them more extensively than stated in the Constitution."

in northern Cyprus, Turkish authorities have introduced new compensation procedures. Nevertheless, the effectiveness of these procedures remains incomplete.

The proportionality principle has a long history in both Greece and Turkey. Until recently, the courts in both countries tended to distort its actual meaning, often relying on proportionality arguments to justify rights limitations. Alternatively, they upheld contested State measures without serious scrutiny, despite professing respect for the proportionality principle, the requirements of a democratic society and the like. Since 2001, the Greek and Turkish Constitutions are among only a handful of national constitutions that explicitly guarantee the proportionality principle as a limit with which all rights limitations should comply. Greek courts as well as the Turkish Constitutional Court now tend to refer to the traditional three-pronged test in implementing the proportionality principle, thus scrutinizing appropriateness, necessity and proportionality *stricto sensu* of State actions. Nevertheless, the application of the proportionality test remains on certain occasions extraordinarily deferential to the political branches of the State.

G. Knowledge and Practice

1. Greece

a. Dissemination of European Court Judgements

All ECtHR judgements against Greece are translated into Greek through the Greek Foreign Affairs Ministry and published on Greece's State Legal Council website (*Νομικό Συμβούλιο του Κράτους*).[399] Further, the translated judgements are forwarded in hardcopy to the implicated judicial and administrative authorities. The dissemination of ECtHR judgements beyond public authorities is a matter of private initiative. Practicing lawyers learn about the ECtHR case law mainly through legal periodicals, which translate and publish the most significant ECtHR judgements that stem from the Greek legal order (of abstracts thereof). Although generally ECtHR rulings against Greece are not covered in the media very extensively, legal scholars and the informed public have gradually become increasingly aware and willing to take advantage of this international remedy for human rights violations. As a scholar has argued, the ECtHR is, for the Greek public opinion, the quintessential example of a court that takes rights seriously.[400] Nevertheless, a great deal of confusion persists as to the exact role of the ECtHR, which the overwhelming majority of the Greek populace would most probably identify as an EU institution.

The ECtHR case law concerning other States is not translated into Greek or systematically made available. A commentary of ECtHR jurisprudence in a

---

[399] State Legal Council, http://www.nsk.gr.
[400] Voyatzis (2004), 487.

casebook-like format partly fills this gap.[401] In addition, in 2006, the Athens Bar Association distributed to its members a compact guide on the protection of human rights in Europe, which provides an overview of ECtHR case law.[402] Finally, cases involving other Contracting States are published to an increasing degree in legal periodicals and referred to in scholarly works.

b. Lawyering

At the time of Greece's recognition of the individual petition right in 1985, virtually no lawyers in Greece were aware of this new international remedy. In contrast, the broader knowledge of the ECHR among Greek lawyers in recent years has enhanced its effectiveness. Due to the limited size of the Greek legal market, there are no law firms which deal exclusively with ECHR-oriented litigation or more generally human rights litigation. Nonetheless, an increasing number of law firms are active in this area.

Furthermore, most Greek NGOs that address human rights issues do not limit their activities to the ECHR. Among them, the Marangopoulos Foundation for Human Rights (*Ίδρυμα Μαραγκοπούλου για τα Δικαιώματα του Ανθρώπου*),[403] founded in 1977, has regularly organized international events on topics of relevance to the ECHR. Further, the Hellenic League for Human Rights (*Ελληνική Ένωση για τα Δικαιώματα του Ανθρώπου*),[404] the oldest human rights NGO in Greece, founded in 1953 and banned by the 1967 dictatorship, has been increasingly active in recent years, focusing on the rights of religious minorities, immigrants and refugees. In addition, in 2001, the League organized a conference on Greece's compliance with the ECtHR case law.[405] While Greek Helsinki Monitor[406] has consistently highlighted Greece's minority rights shortcomings in international bodies, its influence within Greece has been very limited. Finally, the Greek courts' restrictive standing doctrine[407] prevents human rights NGOs from providing much concrete support in adjudicating human rights challenges.

c. Teaching

Up to the 70's, there was very limited interest in constitutional and international law teaching and international human rights were virtually nonexistent in law school curricula. This situation began changing after the restoration of democracy in 1974, with increasing emphasis slowly placed on both constitutional and international rights.

---

[401] Sarmas (2003).
[402] Matthias/Ktistakis/Stavriti/Stefanaki (2006).
[403] Marangopoulos Foundation for Human Rights, http://www.mfhr.gr.
[404] Hellenic League for Human Rights, http://www.hlhr.gr.
[405] See *Το Σύνταγμα/The Constitution*, Vol. 18 (2) (2003), 203 et seq. (publishing the conference papers).
[406] Greek Helsinki Watch, http://cm.greekhelsinki.gr.
[407] See, e.g., Greek Council of State, Judgement, 2001.02.13, no. 575/2001, ToS 2002, 253.

The international protection of human rights is currently an elective course at the undergraduate level in all three of Greece's law schools and in several political science and administrative studies programmes. Compulsory law school courses on constitutional rights and upper-level public law courses (where available) incorporate ECHR law, although the emphasis differs according to the instructor. In addition, the ECHR perspective is playing an increasing role in the syllabi of doctrinal law courses, in particular in procedural law. There is no specialized graduate degree on the ECHR or international human rights in general. Nonetheless, graduate courses on constitutional and international law increasingly focus on the ECHR.[408]

There are no Greek law textbooks devoted exclusively to the ECHR. The general textbooks on constitutional[409] and international[410] human rights most often incorporate the ECHR perspective, although the information provided is not always up to date.

In addition, incoming judges are required to take a course in the National School of Judges (*Εθνική Σχολή Δικαστών*) on rights protection according to the Greek Constitution and the ECHR that focuses extensively on the case law of the ECtHR. Further, in recent years, Greek authorities have tried to increase human rights awareness among police officials on the basis of international law standards. However, these efforts have not been specifically tailored to the ECHR and ECtHR case law.

d. Scholarship

Similar to law teaching, legal scholarship on both constitutional and international rights began developing only in the mid-70's. With entry into force of Greece's 1975 Constitution, several public law book series were launched, with the first volume of one of the most successful, the "Public Law Library" (*Βιβλιοθήκη Δημοσίου Δικαίου*), a seminal work on the ECHR.[411] Further, a specialized constitutional law journal (*The Constitution [Το Σύνταγμα]*), founded in 1975, includes contributions on the ECHR, although rather irregularly, while more often since 2006.[412] The *Human Rights (Δικαιώματα του Ανθρώπου)* law journal, founded in 1999, includes more scholarship on the ECHR.[413] In recent years,

---

[408] See, e.g., University of Athens, Law Faculty, Graduate Program on Public International Law, available at: http://www.law.uoa.gr/diethnon.pdf (mandatory course on "International Human Rights Case Law"); Panteion University, Law Faculty, Graduate Program on "Law and European Integration," Public Law Concentration, available at: http://www.dikee.gr (course on "European Protection of Fundamental Rights").

[409] Dagtoglou (2005); Chryssogonos (2006).

[410] Roucounas (1995), 105.

[411] Vegleris (1977).

[412] An examination of the journal's major contents at five-year intervals showed an average of 0.86 contributions on the ECHR per year, focusing at the beginning on introductory pieces and more recently on comments on ECtHR case law. In addition, in recent years, articles on Greek law have increasingly incorporated the ECHR perspective.

[413] The 2000 and 2005 volumes published four papers per year on the ECHR, including arti-

Public Law Applications (Εφαρμογές Δημοσίου Δικαίου), a student-edited journal of the Athens Law School, has regularly translated and published major ECtHR judgements.[414] It is rather unusual to find scholarship on the ECHR in most administrative[415] and criminal[416] law journals, although there are significant differences both among publications and their respective volumes. Further, in recent years, both general[417] and specialized law[418] journals have published special issues that review ECtHR rulings against Greece.

Moreover, an increasing amount of non-periodical publications focuses on the ECHR and its reception. For instance, in the last two decades, the Marangopoulos Foundation published more than 50 publications of some relevance to the ECHR.[419] In addition, the Center for International and European Economic Law (*Κέντρο Διεθνούς και Ευρωπαϊκού Οικονομικού Δικαίου*) published a practical guide for applicants before the ECtHR[420] and an annotated presentation of all the ECtHR cases against Greece decided between 1991 and 2001.[421] Further, in 2002, the National School of Judges published a volume of scholarly papers on the influence of the ECHR on Greek law.[422] Lastly, the ECHR requirements increasingly penetrate doctrinal scholarship in areas such as criminal law.[423]

---

cles and comments on both the ECtHR and Greek Council of State judgements pertaining to the ECHR.

[414] While the 1990 volume did not include a single piece on the ECHR and the 1995 volume published only one relevant article, the 2000 and the 2005 issues included two and five translated ECtHR judgements, respectively.

[415] An examination of the major contents of the *Public and Administrative Law Review* (EDDD – the oldest administrative law journal in Greece), conducted at five-year intervals, found only one article in 1965 and another one in 1985. In contrast, the *Administrative Trial* (DiDik), published since 1989, includes on average one piece pertaining to the ECHR per year. Further, the *Administrative Law Journal* (EfDimDik) placed in 2006, its first year of publication, special emphasis on the ECHR, including three articles and the translation of six ECtHR judgements, accompanied by scholarly comments.

[416] Based on its contents at five-year intervals, the *Penal Chronicles* (PoinChron), the oldest criminal law journal, virtually ignored the ECHR. In contrast, the *Penal Word* (PLog), published since 2001, placed in its first volume particular emphasis on the ECHR (including translations of 16 ECtHR judgements, comments on three ECtHR judgements, three reports on the ECtHR and the Greek case law, and seven more articles). In contrast, the journal's 2005 volume included only three reports on the ECtHR case law. Similarly, *Penal Justice* (PoinDik), published in the 2000 volume six translated judgements of the ECtHR and two reports on the ECtHR case law. In the 2005 volume, however, only two articles concerning special issues were included. Finally, the journal *Defence* (Yper), published from 1991 to 2000, included an average of two pieces on the ECHR per year.

[417] See *Law Tribune/Νομικό Βήμα*, Vol. 48 (11) (2000), 1721 et seq.

[418] See, e.g., *Εφαρμογές Δημοσίου Δικαίου/Public Law Applications*, Vol. 15 (Special Issue I) (2002); see also *Τὸ Σύνταγμα/The Constitution*, Vol. 17 (2002), (1), 1 et seq.; (2), 195 et seq.; (3), 363 et seq.; (4), 559 et seq.; (5), 673 et seq.; (6), 863 et seq. (including papers presented at a 1998 conference on *Greek Cases in Strasbourg*).

[419] Marangopoulos Foundation for Human Rights, List of publications, available at: http://www.mfhr.gr/dark-red/en/index.htm.

[420] Naskou-Perraki/Sgouridou (2001).

[421] Naskou-Perraki/Ktistakis (2006). A volume on the subsequent years is under preparation.

[422] National School of Judges (2002).

[423] See, e.g., Hellenic Criminal Barristers Association (2004).

2. Turkey

a. Dissemination of European Court Judgements

In Turkey, the ECtHR judgements against Turkey are translated in Turkish, published on the website of the Ministry of Justice[424] and forwarded to judges and prosecutors. Further, in addition to the major cases concerning Turkey that are reproduced in periodical publications of the bar associations and the police, scholars have also published an increasing number of commentaries on the ECtHR case law.[425] Turkey's media are interested in ECtHR judgements concerning Turkey. Nevertheless, there is certainly a need to improve the documentation and publication of ECtHR case law.

b. Lawyering

The proliferation of NGOs called "sivil toplum örgütleri" (civil society organizations) in Turkey corresponds to the restoration process of the rule of law and reflects society's reaction to the authoritarian regime established under the 1982 Constitution. Among these NGOs, the Human Rights Association (*Türkiye İnsan Hakları Derneği*),[426] founded in 1986, is Turkey's oldest and largest human rights organization. With over 10,000 members and activists, it passionately advocates for human rights by organizing campaigns, drafting reports and focusing public attention on rights abuses.[427] Further, the Human Rights Foundation of Turkey (*Türkiye İnsan Hakları Vakfı*),[428] founded in 1990, aims primarily at assisting people subjected to torture and is active in rehabilitation centres that treat victims of torture. In addition, the foundation publishes annual reports on the status of human rights in Turkey.[429]

Apart from human rights NGOs, numerous Turkish associations and foundations are engaged in projects aspiring to increase public awareness of human rights. For instance, in one volunteer project initiated by an association and supported by the EU, after receiving appropriate training, thirty individuals of different professional backgrounds engaged in discussions on human rights and distributed information material in Istanbul cafés. They claim to have reached 9,200 people in a total of 314 *kahvehane*, traditional café houses.

c. Teaching

In Turkey, rights and liberties have been traditionally included in the first-year constitutional law course and studied in law schools' fourth-year general public

---

[424] Ministry of Justice (Adalet Bakanlığı), http://www.edb.adalet.gov.tr/ymb/ymb.htm. See also Anadolu University, http://aihm.anadolu.edu.tr.
[425] See, e.g., Doğru (2004).
[426] Human Rights Association, http://www.ihd.org.tr.
[427] See, e.g., Human Rights Association (2006).
[428] Human Rights Foundation of Turkey, http://www.tihv.org.tr.
[429] See, e.g., Human Rights Foundation (2006).

law course.[430] Nonetheless, the weight accorded to human rights depends on the instructor. Further, in recent years, a separate course on human rights or the "law of freedoms" became compulsory at the Ankara and Istanbul political science departments and at most law schools,[431] while it remains optional at other universities.[432] Only one law school, the University of Bahçeşehir's Faculty of Law, offers an optional course on the application of the ECHR. Most doctrinal law school courses incorporate the human rights perspective, while major universities in Turkey host also research centres on human rights. "Citizenship and Human Rights" is taught as a required course in elementary schools and "Human Rights and Democracy" as an optional course in high schools. Turkish scholars have done some research on eliminating terminology in school textbooks, which contravenes basic human rights concepts.[433]

From 2002 to 2004, the CoE and the European Commission launched in collaboration with the Turkish authorities a joint project, aiming at increasing human rights awareness among judges, other public officials and the public at large and at reviewing draft and existing legislation to ensure its conformity with European standards. Turkey's National Committee for Human Rights Education played an important role in the realization of this project. Further, the Human Rights Advisory Board carried out several initiatives to increase public awareness of human rights. Nonetheless, as discussed in an earlier section, the Government ultimately suspended it.[434] Moreover, the Ministry of Justice and the Justice Academy (*Adalet Akademisi*) recently provided extensive training on the new criminal legislation pertaining to human rights.[435] Yet, much work is needed for the Academy to develop into a strong and independent training centre serving all of Turkey's judiciary.[436]

Finally, several scholarly events on the ECHR, most notably three symposia sponsored by the country's high courts[437] and a major international conference on Turkey's fiftieth anniversary of the ECHR ratification,[438] have helped to increase human rights awareness. Overall, however, the rather tenuous nature of human rights education in Turkey correlates with the political authorities' distrust of independent human rights bodies.

---

[430] See, in detail, Soysal (1981), 172 et seq.
[431] E.g., Başkent, Bilkent, Galatasaray, Bilgi, Marmara, Dicle, and İstanbul.
[432] E.g., Gazi, Kocaeli, Bahçeşehir, and Koç.
[433] See, e.g., Çotuksöken, Erzan and Silier (2003); Bağlı and Eren (2003).
[434] See *supra* note 35 and accompanying text.
[435] See, in detail, Adalet Bakanlığı (2007), 137 et seq.
[436] European Commission (2006), 58.
[437] ECHR and Judicial Power (2003), Court of Cassation, Ankara; ECHR and Administrative Jurisdiction (2003), Council of State, Ankara; ECHR and Constitutional Jurisdiction (2004), Constitutional Court, Ankara. For the proceedings of the first symposium see TBB-İHAUM (2004a).
[438] International Human Rights Congress, European Convention on Human Rights and Turkey, 16–19 May 2004, Istanbul, Fifty Years of the European Convention on Human Rights: Results and Perspectives. See also Institut Luxembourgeois des Droits de L'Homme, Bulletin des Droits de L'Homme, nos 11–12 (2005), 27 et seq.

d. Scholarship

In Turkey, scholarly interest in the ECHR was minimal up to the late 80's. International human rights scholarship focused only marginally on the ECHR and its reception.[439] With the recognition of the individual petition before the ECommHR in 1987 and the ECtHR's compulsory jurisdiction over Turkey beginning in 1990, scholars became more interested in European human rights law.

The *Turkish Yearbook of Human Rights* and its Turkish-language counterpart *İnsan Hakları Yıllığı* (Yearbook of Human Rights),[440] the annual publication of the Constitutional Court (*Anayasa Yargisi/Constitutional Jurisdiction*), the Council of the State's Journal, the Court of Cassation's Journal and the periodical publications of Turkish law faculties contain articles on the ECHR and its reception. The legal periodicals of the bar associations and their affiliates publish ECtHR judgements, while the bar associations and private publishers also publish annotated collections of ECtHR case law.[441] Lastly, several doctoral and post-doctoral theses have focused on the ECHR and the ECtHR case law.[442]

3. Comparison and Conclusion

Greece and Turkey use similar means to disseminate ECtHR case law. While all ECtHR judgements against the two countries are translated into their respective languages and published online, their dissemination beyond public authorities is largely a matter of private initiative. Media coverage of the ECtHR rulings is more extensive in Turkey than in Greece. Arguably, this is partly the case because more ECtHR judgements against Turkey challenge the Turkish State and its constitutional identity; on the other hand, most of the cases against Greece are seen as technical in nature. Further, the reception of the ECHR generates wider media interest in Turkey than in Greece because it is perceived as part and parcel of the EU accession process.

In both countries, human rights NGOs are engaged in activities that further the ECHR's effectiveness. While Greek human rights NGOs have a longer, deeper tradition, their Turkish counterparts are increasing in numbers, activities and commitment in recent years. The depth and breadth of law school courses on the ECHR in both countries depend on the inclinations of the instructors. Gen-

[439] For instance, Türkiye'de İnsan Hakları (*Human Rights in Turkey*), a collective volume, published in 1970 on the commemoration of the Universal Declaration of Human Rights, included only one article on the ECHR; see Balta (1970), 257 et seq. (arguing that Turkey should recognize the right of individual petition before the ECommHR). Further, a special 1978 issue of the *Turkish Yearbook on International Relations* on human rights (volume XVIII), did not include a single contribution on the ECHR.

[440] Between 1949 and 1977, 20 Articles concerning the ECHR were published in IHY. See Aybay and Kartal (1978), 127 et seq.

[441] See, e.g., Doğru (2004); Gemalmaz (2006).

[442] See, e.g., Batum (1993); Batum (1996); Yokuş (1996); Yokuş (2002); Çavuşoğlu (2003); Eren (2004); Üzeltürk (2004); Kılınç (2006).

erally, law schools in Greece and Turkey have neither mandatory undergraduate courses nor specialized graduate degrees on the ECHR or international human rights. While in Turkey constitutional rights that include the ECHR perspective are taught in constitutional and general public law courses, a separate course on human rights is not always compulsory. In contrast, in Greece, students take a separate compulsory course on constitutional rights that incorporates the ECHR perspective. As a result, the average Greek law student can most probably acquire a better knowledge of the ECHR than her/his Turkish counterpart. Furthermore, in both Greece and Turkey, legal scholarship on the ECHR was virtually non-existent for a considerable time after their respective ratification of the ECHR in the 50's. While the development of legal scholarship on the ECHR in Greece began with its 1975 democratic Constitution, the first steps in this vein were very hesitant. In Turkey, a similar process – coinciding with a series of constitutional amendments aimed at restoring the rule of law against the backdrop of the authoritarian 1982 Constitution – began only in the early 90's. While the current status of both legal education and scholarship on the ECHR is the best that it has ever been in both countries, it still depends much on subjective preferences. Thus, substantial discrepancies as to the importance of the ECHR hold sway among different instructors and publications.

H. Concluding Remarks

At first glance, Greece's and Turkey's reception of the ECHR have striking similarities. The two countries ratified the ECHR almost simultaneously in the 50's, without critically and rigorously scrutinizing their domestic laws as to their conformity with the ECHR. In fact, securing participation in the Western alliance against the background of the Cold War era was the dominant motivation for both nations' decision to ratify the ECHR. Military interventions exacerbated the tension between the ECHR and the national legal order in both countries. Interstate applications were filed in Strasbourg against Greece and Turkey, which tested the limits of the ECHR. Further, despite theoretically recognizing judicial review of legislation, both Greek and Turkish courts have traditionally deferred to the other two branches of Government. Consistent with this, for a long period of time, the ECHR served in both countries to perpetuate the discrepancy between law in the "books" and law in "action". While occasionally citing the ECHR, domestic courts in both countries failed to engage with the Strasbourg jurisprudence in any meaningful way; they often construed the ECHR as a mechanism of limitation, rather than as a guarantee of rights.

Nonetheless, in the last three decades, differences in the effectiveness of the ECHR in Greece and in Turkey have become increasingly visible. Following the restoration of democracy in Greece in 1975, the fundamentals of democracy and rule of law soon became commonplace. In contrast, in Turkey, despite the far-reaching reforms from 1999–2004 and some progress in practice, the traditional resistance to reforms in the State bureaucracy, including the Judiciary, the deficient willpower of the Government's political branches for the implementation of the reforms, the rise of nationalism and the role of the military have perpetuated the difficulties for an effective reception of the ECHR. Turkish authorities have cited a resurgence of terrorism as a further obstacle. Specific problems in Turkey, such as those arising from the armed clashes between security forces and PKK members in the country's south-east provinces and the division of Cyprus, are at the core of diverse ECtHR findings of violation. Consistent with this, the implementation problems of ECtHR case law are greater in Turkey than in Greece because they raise, rightly or wrongly, concerns of the Turkish political, judicial and military establishment over the compatibility of international human rights with national unity, and territorial and constitutional identity. Accordingly, the climate in Turkey is not conducive to independent human rights bodies, while judicial review of State action also faces significant limitations. Reception problems persist in Greece as well, both in terms of ECtHR findings of violations and their domestic implementation. However, they reflect deficits that cannot be remedied overnight or, more often, that correlate with a lack of human rights awareness in specific problem areas. Problems of tension with the national or constitutional identity or the perception thereof, such as those concerning the rights of religious and other non-majority groups, arise also, although less often in comparison with Turkey. Such problems are dealt with primarily indirectly and not always effectively. In addition, the overrepresentation of Greece's immigrant population in the violation patterns of fundamental ECHR guarantees is particularly distressing.

Despite all the problems and difficulties, as well as the similarities and differences between the two countries in their reception of the ECHR, neither Greece nor Turkey can continue to ignore the ECHR and the ECtHR case law. Thus, compared with the ratification era from the 50's to the 80's, both countries have made significant progress since then. Nonetheless, much remains to be done, in Turkey and to a considerably lesser extent in Greece, to ensure that the reception of the ECHR is direct rather than indirect, comprehensive rather than selective, and substantive rather than cosmetic. Furthermore, rights adjudication no longer pits an obvious "good" against an equally obvious "evil". Rather, courts and scholars grappling with fundamental rights face competing versions of the "good" that must be balanced against each other. Indeed, this balancing act will be a major challenge for both Greece and Turkey in applying the ECHR and in coordinating national and international rights guarantees in the years ahead.

Bibliography

Alivizatos, N., *Les institutions politiques de la Grèce à travers les crises 1922–1974* (Paris, 1979).

Alivizatos, N. and Eleftheriadis, P., 'The Greek Constitutional Amendments of 2001', *South European Society and Politics* 7 (1) (2002), 63.

Akıllıoğlu, T., 'İnsan Hakları Kurallarının İç Hukuktaki Yeri' [The Position of Norms Related to Human Rights in Domestic Law], İHMD (May–September 1991), 41.

Arnaoutoglou, F., 'Grèce: Le Conseil d'Etat', in Iliopoulos-Strangas, J. (ed.), *Cours suprêmes nationales et cours européennes: concurrence ou collaboration?* (Athens/Brussels, 2007), 179.

Athens Bar Association (Δικηγορικός Σύλλογος Αθηνών), (Matthias, St. (Ματθίας, Στ.), Ktistakis, G. (Κτιστάκις, Γ.), Stavriti, L. (Σταυρίτη, Λ.), Stefanaki, K. (Στεφανάκη Κ.) (eds.), *Η Προστασία των Δικαιωμάτων του Ανθρώπου στην Ευρώπη με Βάση τη Νομολογία του Δικαστηρίου του Στρασβούργου (The Protection of Human Rights in Europe on the Basis of the Case Law of the Strasbourg Court)* (Athens, 2006).

Aybay, R. and Kartal, M. A., 'Human Rights in Turkey', *Milletlerarası Münasebetler Türk Yıllığı* [The Turkish Yearbook of International Relations], *İnsan Hakları Özel Sayısı* [Special Issue: Human Rights], XVIII (1978), 127.

Bağlı, M. T. and Eren, Y. (eds.), *Ders Kitaplarında İnsan Hakları: Tarama Sonuçları* [Human Rights in Schoolbooks: The Results of Observations] (Istanbul, 2003).

Balta, T. B., 'Avrupa İnsan Hakları Sözleşmesi ve Türkiye' [European Convention on Human Rights and Turkey], in Ankara Üniversitesi Hukuk Fakültesi (Ankara University, School of Law) (ed.), *Türkiye'de İnsan Hakları* [Human Rights in Turkey] (Ankara, 1970) 257.

Başlar, K. and İshakoğlu, E, 'National Report of Turkey' in Kellermann, A.E., Czuczai, J., Albi, A., Blockmans, S., Douma, W.Th. (eds.), *The Impact of EU Accession on the Legal Orders of New EU Member States and (Pre) Candidate Countries: Hopes and Fears* (The Hague, 2006), 195.

Batum, S., *Avrupa İnsan Hakları Mahkemesi ve Türkiye* [European Court of Human Rights and Turkey] (Istanbul, 1996).

—, *Avrupa İnsan Hakları Sözleşmesi ve Türk Anayasal Sistemine Etkileri* [European Convention on Human Rights and its Effects in the Turkish Constitutional System] (Istanbul, 1993).

Beys, K., 'Zur Verbindlichkeit der Entscheidungen des Europäischen Gerichtshofs für Menschenrechte', in Schilken, E., Becker-Eberhard, E. and Gerhardt, W. (eds.), *Festschrift für Hans Friedhelm Gaul zum 70. Geburtstag* (Bielefeld, 1997), 53.

Briolas D., 'L'application de la Convention Européenne des Droits de l'Homme dans l'ordre juridique des États contractants: Théorie et pratique helléniques', in Iliopoulos-Strangas, J. (ed.), *Grundrechtsschutz im europäischen Raum/La protection des droits de l'homme dans le cadre européen* (Baden-Baden, 1993), 82.

Çavuşoğlu, N., *İnsan Hakları Avrupa Mahkemesi: Kararların Uygulanması* [European Court of Human Rights: Execution of the Judgements] (Istanbul, 2003).

Çelik, E., 'Avrupa İnsan Hakları Sözleşmesinin Türk Hukukundaki Yeri ve Uygulaması' [The Status and Practice of the European Convention on Human Rights in Turkish Law], İHİD (1988), 47.

Chryssanthakis, Ch. (Χρυσανθάκης, Χ.) (ed.), *Η Ευρωπαϊκή Σύμβαση Δικαιωμάτων του Ανθρώπου στη Νομολογία του Συμβουλίου της Επικρατείας* [The European Convention on Human Rights in the Council of State Case Law] (Athens/Komotini, 2001).

Chryssogonos, K. (Χρυσόγονος, Κ.), *Ατομικά και Κοινωνικά Δικαιώματα* [Individual and Social Rights] (Athens, 2006).

—, *Η ενσωμάτωση της Ευρωπαϊκής Σύμβασης των Δικαιωμάτων του Ανθρώπου στην Ελληνική Έννομη Τάξη* [The Incorporation of the European Convention on Human Rights in the Greek Legal Order] (Athens/Komotini, 2001).

Commission of the European Communities [European Commission], Commission Staff Working Document, *Turkey 2006 Progress Report*, COM(2006) 649 final, available at http://ec.europa.eu/enlargement/pdf/key_documents/2006/nov/tr_sec_1390_en.pdf.

—, Commission Staff Working Document, *Turkey 2007 Progress Report*, COM(2007) 663 final, available at http://ec.europa.eu/enlargement/pdf/key_documents/2007/nov/turkey_progress_reports_en.pdf.

Çotuksöken, B., Erzan, A. and Silier, O. (eds.), *Ders Kitaplarında İnsan Hakları Projesi: İnsan Haklarına Duyarlı Ders Kitapları İçin* [The Human Rights in Schoolbooks Project: For Schoolbooks Sensitive to Human Rights] (Istanbul, 2003).

Dagtoglou, P., 'Die Verfassungsentwicklung in Griechenland von der Einführung der geltenden Verfassung bis zum Tode König Pauls', *Jahrbuch des Öffentlichen Rechts der Gegenwart N.F.* 13 (1964), 381.

—, 'Judicial Review of Constitutionality of Laws', *European Review of Public Law* 1 (1989), 309.

Dagtoglou, P. (Δαγτόγλου, Π.), *Συνταγματικό Δίκαιο – Ατομικά Δικαιώματα* [Constitutional Law – Individual Rights], (Athens/Komotini, 2005).

Doğru, O., İnsan Hakları Avrupa Mahkemesi İçtihatları [The Case Law of the European Court of Human Rights], Volumes 1–2 (Istanbul, 2004).

Eren, A., *Özgürlüklerin Sınırlandırılmasında Demokratik Toplum Düzeninin Gerekleri* [The Requirements of the Democratic Order of Society in Restricting Freedoms] (Istanbul, 2004).

Erözden, O., İnceoğlu, S., Sağlam, F., Tahmazoğlu (Üzeltürk), S. and Uygun, O. in collaboration with Gülmez M., İlkiz F., Kollu A., Öztan E. and Yancı N., National Report – Turkey. Human Rights and Political Structure, International Symposium Organized by the Turkish Bar Association (Ankara, 2003).

Evrigenis, D., 'Les conflits de la loi nationale avec les traites internationaux en droit hellénique', *Revue Héllenique de Droit International* 18 (1965), 353.

Fatouros, A. A., 'International Law in the New Greek Constitution', *American Journal of International Law* 70 (1976), 492.

Gemalmaz, S., *Ulusalüstü İnsan Hakları Usul Hukuku* [The Procedural Law of Supranational Human Rights], Volume 2 (Istanbul, 2006).

Gerapetritis, G., *Proportionality in Administrative Law* (Athens/Komotini, 1997).

Gerek, Ş. and Aydın, A. R., 'Türk Anayasa Yargısında İnsan Hakları Avrupa Sözleşmesinin Yeri' [The Position of the European Convention on Human Rights in the Case Law of the Turkish Constitutional Court], *Amme İdaresi Dergisi* 37 (3) (2004), 83.

Gölcüklü, F. and Gözübüyük, Ş., *Avrupa İnsan Hakları Sözleşmesi ve Uygulaması* [European Convention on Human Rights and its Implementation], (Ankara, 2002).

Gönenç, L., 'The 2001 Amendments to the 1982 Constitution of Turkey', *Ankara Law Review*, 1 (1) (2004), 89.

Gönül, M., Cansel, E. and Aliefendioğlu, Y., 'Turkish Report', in Turkish Constitutional Court (ed.), *The Hierarchy of Constitutional Norms and its Function in the Protection of Human Rights*, VIII. European Constitutional Courts Conference (7–10 May 1990, Ankara), Volume 2 (Ankara, 1996), 141.

Gözübüyük, Ş., "Avrupa İnsan Hakları Sözleşmesi'nin Türk Hukukundaki Yeri" [The Position of the European Convention on Human Rights in Turkish Domestic Law] (Ankara, 1992), 26.

—, 'La Place des traités internationaux dans le droit turc', *Turkish Yearbook of Human Rights* 13 (1991), 3.

Hellenic Criminal Barristers Association (Ενωση Ελλήνων Ποινικολόγων) (ed.), *Η Ευρωπαϊκή Σύμβαση για τα Δικαιώματα του Ανθρώπου. Πενήντα Χρόνια Εφαρμογής* [The European Convention on Human Rights: 50 Years of Implementation] (Athens/Komotini, 2004).

Human Rights Association (İnsan Hakları Derneği) (ed.), *İHD 20 Yaşında – Uzun İnce Bir Yoldayız* [20 Years Human Rights Association – We Are on a Road that Thin and Long] (Ankara, 2006).

Human Rights Foundation of Turkey (Türkiye İnsan Hakları Vakfı) (ed.), *Türkiye İnsan Hakları Raporu 2005* [Human Rights Report – Turkey 2005] (Ankara, 2006).

—, *Türkiye İnsan Hakları Vakfı Tedavi ve Rehabilitasyon Merkezleri Raporu/2005* [Human Rights Foundation 2005 Report on Centers of Treatment and Rehabilitation in Turkey] (Ankara, 2006).

Iliopoulos-Strangas, J., 'Offene Staatlichkeit: Griechenland', in Bogdandy, A.v., Cruz Villalón, P. and Huber, P.M. (eds.), *Handbuch Ius Publicum Europaeum*, Volume II (Heidelberg, 2008), 71.

Iliopoulos-Strangas, J. (Ηλιοπούλου-Στράγγα, Τζ.), *Η εκτέλεση των αποφάσεων του Ευρωπαϊκού Δικαστηρίου Ανθρωπίνων Δικαιωμάτων (The Execution of the Judgements of the European Court of Human Rights)* (Athens/Baden-Baden, 1996).

Iliopoulos-Strangas, J. in collaboration with Koutnatzis, S., 'Impulse aus dem griechischen Verfassungsrecht für den europäischen Grundrechtsschutz', in Tettinger, P. and Stern, K. (eds.), *Kölner Gemeinschaftskommentar zur Europäischen Grundrechte-Charta* (Munich, 2006), 31.

Iliopoulos-Strangas, J. and Leventis, G., 'La protection des droits sociaux fondamentaux dans l' ordre juridique de la Grèce', in Iliopoulos-Strangas, J. (ed.), *La protection des droits sociaux fondamentaux dans les Etats membres de l'Union européenne* (Athens/Brussels/Baden-Baden, 2000), 395.

İnceoğlu, S., *İnsan Hakları Avrupa Mahkemesi Kararlarında Adil Yargılanma Hakkı* [The Right to Fair Trial in the European Court of Human Rights' Case Law] (Istanbul, 2005).

Initiative for Freedom of Expression (Düşünce Suçuna Karşı Girişim) (ed.), *Düşünceye Özgürlük* [Freedom of Thought] (Istanbul, 2006).

Initiative for Freedom of Expression (ed.), *Picture of Freedom of Expression in Turkey* (Istanbul, 2005).

526   *The Reception Process in Greece and Turkey*

Ioannou, K., 'Greece', in Bluckburn, R. and Polakiewicz, J. (eds.), *Fundamental Rights in Europe. The European Convention on Human Rights and its Member States, 1950–2000* (Oxford/New York, 2001), 355.

Kaboğlu, İ. Ö., 'Cinquantenaire de la Convention européenne des droits de l'homme: bilan et perspectives', *Bulletin des droits de l'homme* 11–12 (2004–2005), 46.

—, 'De la réforme constitutionnelle en Turquie, *Les Chroniques de l'OMIJ* 1 (2004), 9.

—, 'Human Rights Education in Turkey', in Marmara University European Community Institute (ed.), *Human Rights Education and Practice in Turkey in the Process of Candidacy to the EU* (Istanbul, 2002), 103.

—, 'La liberté d'expression en Turquie', *Revue Trimestrielle des Droits de l'Homme* 10 (38) (1999), 253.

—, 'Le Conseil des droits de l'homme devant le Tribunal pénal (Cas de Turquie)', *Revue des sciences criminelles* (July–September 2006a), 521.

—, 'Quelques remarques préliminaires à propos d'une institution nationale des droits de l'homme (le cas de la Turquie)', *Revue Trimestrielle des Droits de l'Homme* 17 (68) (2006b), 1057.

—, *Özgürlükler Hukuku* [The Law of Freedoms] (Ankara, 2002)

Kaboğlu, İ. Ö. and Akkurt K. (eds.), *İnsan Hakları Danışma Kurulu Raporları* [Human Rights Advisory Board Reports] (Ankara, 2006).

Kerameus, K. D., 'Judicial Organization and Civil Procedure', in Kerameus, K.D. and Kozyris, Ph.J. (eds.), *Introduction to Greek Law*, (Alphen aan Den Rijn, 2008), 341.

Kılınç, B., *Avrupa İnsan Hakları Mahkemesi Kararlarının İnfazı* [Execution of the Judgements of the European Court of Human Rights] (Ankara, 2006).

Kiss, A. C./Vegleris, Ph., 'L'affaire grecque devant le Conseil de l'Europe et la Commission europeenne des droits de l'homme', *Annuaire Français de Droit International* XVII (1971), 889.

Klamaris, N. K., 'Die Funktion und die Rolle der obersten Gerichtshöfe Griechenlands', in Schilken, E., Becker-Eberhard, E. and Gerhardt, W. (eds.), *Festschrift für Hans Friedhelm Gaul zum 70. Geburtstag* (Bielefeld, 1997), 289.

Koutnatzis, S.-I. G., 'Grundlagen und Grundzüge staatlichen Verfassungsrechts: Griechenland', in Bogdandy, A.v., Cruz Villalón, P. and Huber, P. M. (eds.), *Handbuch Ius Publicum Europaeum*, Volume I (Heidelberg, 2007), 151.

Kroustalakis, E., 'L'application de la Convention Européenne des Droits de l'Homme dans l'ordre juridique des États contractants: Théorie et pratique helléniques', in Iliopoulos-Strangas, J. (ed.), *Grundrechtsschutz im europäischen Raum/La protection des droits de l'homme dans le cadre européen* (Baden-Baden, 1993), 117.

Ktistaki, S. (Κτιστάκη, Στ.), Ἀστικὴ Εὐθύνη του Κράτους στο πλαίσιο της Ευρωπαϊκής Σύμβασης Δικαιωμάτων του Ανθρώπου' [State Civil Responsibility in the Context of the European Convention on Human Rights], *Νομικό Βήμα (Law Tribune)* 53 (2005), 2003.

Kubali, H.N., 'Les traits dominants de la Constitution de la seconde République turque', *Revue internationale de droit comparé* 4 (1965), 855.

Lambert, P., *La Grèce devant la Cour européenne des droits de l'homme* (Brussels, 2003).

Marcou, J., 'L'expérience constitutionnelle Turque', *Revue de Droit Public* 2 (1996), 425.

Margaritis, M., 'Grèce: La Cour de Cassation', in Iliopoulos-Strangas, J. (ed.), *Cours suprêmes nationales et cours européennes: concurrence ou collaboration?* (Athens/Brussels, 2007), 187.

Mitsopoulos, G., 'Rechtskraft und Vollstreckung eines auf Geldleistung gerichteten Urteils des Europäischen Gerichtshofs für Menschenrechte', in Yessiou-Faltsi, P., Jost, F., Kaissis, A. and Apalagaki, Ch. (eds.), *Recht in Europa. Festschrift für Hilmar Fenge zum 65. Geburtstag* (Hamburg, 1996), 97.

Mitsopoulos, G. (Μητσόπουλος, Γ.), '«Τριτενέργεια» και «αναλογικότητα» ως διατάξεις του αναθεωρηθέντος Συντάγματος' ["Drittwirkung" and Proportionality as Provisions of the Amended Constitution], *Δικαιώματα του Ανθρώπου (Human Rights)* 4 (15) (2002), 641.

Naskou-Perraki, P. (Νάσκου-Περράκη, Π.) and Ktistakis, G. (Κτιστάκις, Γ.) (eds.), *Οι Ελληνικές Υποθέσεις στο Στρασβούργο* [The Greek Cases in Strasbourg], Volume A, 1991–2001 (Athens/Komotini, 2006).

Naskou-Perraki, P. (Νάσκου-Περράκη, Π.) and Sgouridou, A. (Σγουρίδου, Α.) (eds.), *Ευρωπαϊκή Σύμβαση για την Προάσπιση των Δικαιωμάτων του Ανθρώπου και των Θεμελιωδών Ελευθεριών. Οδηγός* [The European Convention for the Protection of Human Rights and Fundamental Freedoms. Guide] (Athens/Komotini, 2001).

National School of Judges (Εθνική Σχολή Δικαστών) – Ktistakis, G. (Κτιστάκις, Γ.) (eds.), *Η επίδραση της Ευρωπαϊκής Σύμβασης των Δικαιωμάτων του Ανθρώπου στην Ερμηνεία και Εφαρμογή του Ελληνικού Δικαίου* [The Influence of the European Convention on Human Rights in the Interpretation and Implementation of Greek Law] (Athens/Komotini, 2002).

Oran, B., 'The Minority Report Affair in Turkey', *Regent Journal of International Law* 5 (2007), 2.

Özdek, Y. and Karacaoğlu, E., 'Turkey', in Bluckburn, R. and Polakiewicz, J. (eds.), *Fundamental Rights in Europe. The European Convention on Human Rights and its Member States, 1950–2000* (Oxford/New York, 2001), 879.

Özdek, Y., *Avrupa İnsan Hakları Hukuku ve Türkiye* [European Human Rights Law and Turkey] (Ankara, 2004).

Pantélis, A., *Les grands problèmes de la nouvelle Constitution hellénique* (Paris, 1979).

Papadimitriou, G. (Παπαδημητρίου, Γ.), 'Η διεθνοποίηση και η κοινοτικοποίηση της δικαστικής προστασίας' [The Internationalisation and Communitisation of Judicial Protection], *Νομικό Βήμα (Law Tribune)* 44 (1996), 569.

Pararas, P. (Παραράς, Π.), 'Το κεκτημένο του ευρωπαϊκού συνταγματικού πολιτισμού' (The „Acquis" of the European Constitutional Culture), *Δικαιώματα του Ανθρώπου (Human Rights)* 3 (10) (2001), 543.

Pazarcı, H., *Uluslararası Hukuk Dersleri* [International Law Courses], (Ankara, 1985).

Perrakis, S., 'Le juge grec et la Cour de Strasbourg', in Tavernier, P. (ed.), *Quelle Europe pour les droits de l'homme?* (Brussels, 1996), 171.

Perrakis, S. (Περράκης, Στ.), *Η «Ελληνική Υπόθεση» Ενώπιον των Διεθνών Οργανισμών (1967–1974)* [The «Greek Case» before the International Organizations (1967–1974)] (Athens/Komotini, 1997).

Pollis, A., 'The State, the Law, and Human Rights in Modern Greece', *Human Rights Quarterly* (1987) 587.

Roucounas, E., 'Le droit international dans la Constitution de la Grèce du 9 juin 1975', *Revue Héllenique de Droit International* 29 (1976), 51.

—, 'Grèce', in Eisemann, P.M. (ed.), *L'intégration du droit international et communautaire dans l'ordre juridique national/The Integration of International and European Community Law into the National Legal Order* (The Hague/London/Boston, 1996), 287.

Roucounas, E. (Ρούκουνας, Ε.), Διεθνής Προστασία των Ανθρωπίνων Δικαιωμάτων [International Protection of Human Rights] (Athens, 1995).

Sarmas, I. (Σαρμάς, I.), Κράτος και δικαιοσύνη. Ελευθερία με υπεροχή του δικαίου. Η νομολογία του Ευρωπαϊκού Δικαστηρίου Δικαιωμάτων του Ανθρώπου [State and Justice. Liberty in the Rule of Law. The Case Law of the European Court of Human Rights] (Athens/Komotini, 2003).

Sencer, M., 'From the Constitution of 1961 to the Constitution of 1982', *Turkish Yearbook of Human Rights* 7–8 (1985–1986), 15.

Skouris, W., Constitutional Disputes and Judicial Review in Greece, in Landfried, Ch. (ed.), *Constitutional Review and Legislation* (Baden-Baden, 1988), 177.

Soysal, M., 'Human Rights in the Turkish Context', in *International Colloquy on Human Rights*, Istanbul, 28–30 March 1979 (Ankara, 1981), 166.

Spiliotopoulos, E., 'Judicial Review of Legislative Acts in Greece', *Temple Law Quarterly* 56 (1983), 463.

—, 'The Judicial Review of Administrative Action', in Spiliotopoulos, E. and Makrydemetres, A. (eds.), *Public Administration in Greece* (Athens/Komotini, 2001), 119.

Stavros, St., 'Human Rights in Greece: Twelve Years of Supervision from Strasbourg', *JMGR* 17 (1999), 3.

Tanör, B., *İki Anayasa: 1961–1982* [Two Constitutions: 1961–1982] (Istanbul, 1986).

Taşkın, A. (ed.), *Adalet Bakanlığı Faaliyetleri* [The Activities of the Ministry of Justice] (Ankara, 2007).

Tezcan, D., Erdem, M. R. and Sancakdar, O., *Avrupa İnsan Hakları Sözleşmesi Işığında Türkiye'nin İnsan Hakları Sorunu* [The Human Rights Problematic in Turkey under the European Convention on Human Rights] (Ankara, 2004).

Turkish Bar Association- Centre of Research and Practice for Human Rights (Türkiye Barolar Birliği-İnsan Hakları Araştırma ve Uygulama Merkezi) (TBB-İHAUM) (ed.), *İnsan Hakları Avrupa Sözleşmesi ve Adli Yargı* [The European Convention on Human Rights and the Judicial Power] (Ankara, 2004a).

—, (ed.), *İnsan Hakları Uluslararası Sözleşmelerinin İç Hukukta Doğrudan Uygulanması (Anayasa, md. 90/son)* [The Direct Application of International Human Rights Conventions in Domestic Law (Article 90 CRT)] (Ankara, 2004b).

Turkish Constitutional Court (ed.), *Turkish National Report. XIIIth Conference of the European Constitutional Courts* (May 2005) (Ankara, 2004).

Üzeltürk, S., *1982 Anayasası ve İnsan Hakları Avrupa Sözleşmesine Göre Özel Hayatın Gizliliği Hakkı* [Right to Privacy of Individual Life in the 1982 Constitution and the European Convention on Human Rights], (Istanbul, 2004).

Valakou-Theodoroudi, M. (Βαλάκου-Θεοδωρούδη, M.), Παράμετροι Καταγραφής της Παραπομπής από τον Έλληνα Δικαστή στην Ευρωπαϊκή Σύμβαση Δικαιωμάτων του Ανθρώπου [Citation Parameters of the Greek Judge's Reference to the European Convention on Human Rights], Ελληνική Επιθεώρηση Ευρωπαϊκού Δικαίου (*Hellenic Review of European Law*) 17 (1) (1997), 79.

Valticos, N., 'Droits de l'homme et démocratie: la crise grecque', in Teitgen-Colly, C. (ed.), *Cinquantième anniversaire de la Convention européenne des droits de l'homme* (Brussels, 2002), 97.

—, 'Monisme ou Dualisme? Les rapports des traités et de la loi en Grèce (spécialement à propos des conventions internationales du travail)', *Revue Héllenique de Droit International* 11 (1958), 203.

Vegleris, Ph., 'Statut de la Convention des droits de l'homme dans le droit grec', in *Mélanges dédiés à Robert Pelloux* (Lyon, 1980), 299.

Vegleris, Ph. (Βεγλερής, Φ.), *Η Σύμβαση των Δικαιωμάτων του Ανθρώπου και το Σύνταγμα* [The Convention on Human Rights and the Constitution] (Athens, 1977).

Venizelos, E., 'The 2001 Revision of the Greek Constitution and the Relevance of the Constitutional Phenomenon', *Jahrbuch des Öffentlichen Rechts der Gegenwart N.F.* 51 (2003), 513.

Vlachos, G. (Βλάχος, Γ.), *Το Σύνταγμα της Ελλάδος (The Constitution of Greece)* (Athens, 1979).

Voyatzis, P. (Βογιατζής, Π.), 'Οι Ελληνικές Υποθέσεις στο Δικαστήριο του Στρασβούργου Πριν και Μετά την Αναγνώριση της Ατομικής Προσφυγής' [The Greek Cases in the Strasbourg Court Before and After the Recognition of the Individual Petition], in Tsapogas, M. (Τσαπόγας, M.) and Christopoulos, D. (Χριστόπουλος, Δ.) (eds.), *Τα δικαιώματα στην Ελλάδα 1953–2003* [The Rights in Greece 1953–2003] (Athens, 2004) 487.

Yokuş, S., *Avrupa İnsan Hakları Sözleşmesi'nde ve 1982 Anayasası'nda Hak ve Özgürlüklerin Kötüye Kullanımı* [The Prohibition of the Abuse of Rights in the European Convention on Human Rights and the 1982 Constitution] (Ankara, 2002).

—, *Avrupa İnsan Hakları Sözleşmesi'nin Türkiye'de Olağanüstü Hal Rejimine Etkisi* [The Effect of the European Convention on Human Rights on the State of Emergency Regime in Turkey] (Istanbul, 1996).

Yüzbaşıoğlu, N., *Türk Anayasa Yargısında Anayasallık Bloku* [The Block of Constitutionality in Turkish Constitutional Jurisdiction], (Istanbul, 1993).

Zimianitis, D. (Ζημιανίτης, Δ.), 'Η αποζημίωση των αδίκως καταδικασθέντων ή προσωρινώς κρατηθέντων, υπό το πρίσμα των πρόσφατων αποφάσεων του Ευρωπαϊκού Δικαστηρίου Δικαιωμάτων του Ανθρώπου' [The Compensation of Persons Unlawfully Convicted or Detained in Remand in Light of the Recent Judgements of the European Court of Human Rights], *Ελληνική Επιθεώρηση Ευρωπαϊκού Δικαίου (Hellenic Review of European Law)* 21 (2) (2001), 315.

9

The Reception Process
in Poland and Slovakia

Magda Krzyżanowska-Mierzewska

A. Introduction[1]

The reasons for a comparative study of the Slovak and Polish reception process were manifold, the most important being their similarity, in that they are both referred to as "transition countries" of Central Europe, with a communist past.[2] Further, a significant parallel between these two countries can be drawn from their shared history as young democracies. In Poland, the transition to democracy was sparked by the so-called Round Table talks of 1989, between the democratic opposition and the communist Government. The first partially free elections to the Sejm (lower house of Parliament) and fully free elections to the Senate (upper house of Parliament) were held in June of that year, resulting in a landslide victory for the opposition party. As for Slovakia, in the then Czech and Slovak Federal Republic the democratic process was set in motion by the Velvet Revolution of 1989 and led to the Federal Republic's dissolution into the nations of the Czech Republic and Slovakia on 1 January 1993.

Besides a shared communist past, Poland and Slovakia are similar in further respects: the two countries are predominantly Catholic and have both closely-knit and family-oriented societies. Under the communist regime, both countries underwent a process of massive and rapid industrialization imposed from above. Large segments of the population have peasant roots and middle class traditions are relatively weak. Since the collapse of communism social changes have been profound, but on the whole the construction of legal foundations of the rule of

---

[1] Abbreviations: DU = Dziennik Ustaw (Journal of Laws); OSNCP = Orzecznictwo Sądu Najwyższego – Izba Cywilna i Izba Pracy.

[2] The author is of the view that the term "transition countries" is rather a misnomer. First, it seems to suggest that the "transition" countries are an homogenous group, which is far from being the case. Second, it ignores the fact that many years have passed since communism collapsed in these countries and that profound changes occurred in all of them. However, as it is a widely accepted term, it may facilitate reading.

law seems to have been equally successful in both countries. As for differences, it should be noted that Poland boasts a long history of independence, while Slovakia existed as an independent State only briefly before the Czechoslovak Republic split in 1992. Further, Slovakia was formerly part of a Federal State, while since it regained independence in 1918, Poland has been a unitary country.

Another good reason for a comparative study of Poland and Slovakia in their response to the ECHR is that, using a comparative method, groundwork has been done in respect of Poland,[3] while no such comprehensive work in English in respect of Slovakia has been published thus far. The present text is a modest attempt to fill this lacuna.

B. Accession and Ratification History

1. Poland

On 8 June 1989, immediately after its first semi-free elections had been held,[4] Poland was granted special guest status with the Council of Europe. It signed the ECHR on 26 November 1991, after the first fully free Parliamentary elections of October 1991. Protocols nos 1, 4, 7, 9, and 10 were signed on 14 September 1992.[5] A statute approving the ratification was enacted on 2 October 1992. The ratification instruments were deposited with the Council of Europe on 19 January 1993. Protocols nos 1, 4, 9, and 10 were ratified on 10 October 1994. Protocol no. 6 was ratified with effect from 1 November 2000. Protocol no. 7 came into effect on 1 March 2003.

On 1 March 1993 the Polish Government made a declaration recognizing "the competence of the Commission to receive individual applications from any person, non-governmental organization or group of individuals claiming to be a victim of a violation of the rights recognized in the ECHR through any act, decision or event occurring after 30 April 1993".[6] It is manifest that it was the intention of Poland to exclude responsibility for any events prior to 1 May 1993. In practice, such declarations made in connection with the ratification of the ECHR by new States Parties are quite common and the ECHR organs have so far never challenged the validity of such declarations, which are in any event compatible with Article 28 of the Vienna Convention on the Law of Treaties.

A declaration recognizing the jurisdiction of the ECtHR was also made on 1 March 1993. The text of the ECHR was officially published in July 1993.[7] At the

---

[3] Keller (2005).

[4] Part of the seats were reserved for the parties of the communist regime; the remainder were distributed following the results of electoral vote.

[5] Dziennik Ustaw (Journal of Laws, hereafter referred to as DU) 1992, no. 61, item 427.

[6] See, for example, *Musiał v. Poland* (appl. no. 24557/94), Judgement (Grand Chamber), 25 March 1999, Reports 1999-II, 155, para. 41; *Potocka and Others v. Poland* (appl. no. 33776/96), Judgement (Fourth Section), 4 October 2001, Reports 2001-X, 49, para. 39.

[7] DU 1993, no. 61, item 284.

time of the ratification, "[t]here was a universal feeling that [the Polish accession to the Council of Europe] constitutes a long-awaited return to our European roots; that history has found its logical fulfilment (...) [A]t that time, our entry to the structures of the Council of Europe had a symbolic political meaning perhaps even more significant than the integration with the European Union. It was seen as a reinforcement of a genuine revolution which we had had in our country and a return to the family of democratic European countries (...) But we sometimes forget that what was most important was Poland's entry into the sphere of the standards of human rights guaranteed by the European Convention on the Protection of Human Rights and Fundamental Freedoms and protected by the Strasbourg Court".[8] These words of M. Safjan, who, in 1997, became the President of the Polish Constitutional Court, characterize well the atmosphere of hope and eager anticipation that prevailed in Poland in connection with the ratification of the ECHR in 1992. It is, therefore, not surprising that Poland made no reservations at the time of ratification.

As to Protocol no. 14, Poland belongs to the group of States which were reluctant to ratify it. It was signed on 10 November 2004.[9] Poland notified the Council of Europe of the ratification on 27 October 2006. Neither Protocol no. 12 nor Protocol no. 13 was ratified.

Ratification table[10]

Protocol	Signature	Ratification	Entry into force	Declarations/Reservations
Protocol no. 1	14 Sept. 1992	10 Oct. 1994	10 Oct. 1994	–
Protocol no. 2	26 Nov. 1991	19 Jan. 1993	19 Jan. 1993	–
Protocol no. 3	26 Nov. 1991	19 Jan. 1993	19 Jan. 1993	–
Protocol no. 4	14 Sept. 1992	10 Oct. 1994	10 Oct. 1994	–

---

[8] Safjan (2003), 3 (text inserted by the author).

[9] The signature of the Protocol was accompanied by a rather curious declaration that "[t]he Government of Poland declares that it interprets the amendments introduced by Protocol no. 14 to the ECHR, amending the control system of the Convention, in accordance with the provisions of Article 59, paragraph 3, of the said Convention, following the general principle of non-retroactivity of treaties, contained in Article 28 of the Vienna Convention on the Law of Treaties of 23 May 1969" (deposited on 10 November 2004). The legal meaning of this declaration is puzzling: as Protocol no. 14 is meant to amend the procedures before the ECtHR, it is difficult to imagine how it could be applied retroactively. It has been said that it was dictated by the Government's sensitivity to the embarrassing and politically awkward issue of the absence of any laws concerning compensation entitlements for past expropriations carried out by the communist authorities. See Declaration handed over by the Minister of Foreign Affairs of Poland to the Secretary-General at the time of signature of the instrument, on 10 November 2004. It is available in English at: http:/ conventions.coe.int/Treaty/Commun/ListeDeclarations.asp?NT=194&CM=3&DF=9/11/2007 &CL=ENG&VL=1 (Unless otherwise indicated, all web sites in this report were checked on 31 December 2006).

[10] Source: http://conventions.coe.int/Treaty/Commun/ChercheMembres.asp?CM=3&CL=ENG.

[11] The Polish Declaration (*supra* note 9).

Protocol	Signature	Ratification	Entry into force	Declarations/Reservations
Protocol no. 5	26 Nov. 1991	19 Jan. 1993	19 Jan. 1993	–
Protocol no. 6	18 Nov. 1999	30 Oct. 2000	1 Nov. 2000	–
Protocol no. 7	14 Sept. 1992	4 Dec. 2002	1 March 2003	–
Protocol no. 8	26 Nov. 1991	19 Jan. 1993	19 Jan. 1993	–
Protocol no. 9	14 Sept. 1992	10 Oct. 1994	1 Feb. 1995	–
Protocol no. 10	14 Sept. 1992	10 Oct. 1994	–	–
Protocol no. 11	11 May 1994	20 May 1997	1 Nov. 1998	–
Protocol no. 12	–	–	–	–
Protocol no. 13	3 May 2002	–	–	–
Protocol no. 14	10 Nov. 2004	12 Oct. 2006	–	1 declaration[11]

2. Slovakia

The Czech and Slovak Federal Republic ratified the ECHR together with its Protocols on 18 March 1992. At the same time, it also acknowledged the right of individual petition provided by Article 25 of the Convention. At the time of the ratification, the tumultuous process of a so-called "velvet divorce" was already well under way. On 17 July 1992, the Slovak Parliament (the Slovak National Council), adopted a declaration of sovereignty of the Slovak Republic.

On 1 September 1992, the Constitution of the Slovak Republic was adopted (entry into force on 1 October 1992). Subsequently, on 25 November 1992, the Federal Republic's Parliament (the Federal Assembly) adopted an Act providing that the Federal Republic would cease to exist as an entity as of 1 January 1993. On that date, two new independent States – the Czech Republic and the Slovak Republic – came into existence.[12]

In the face of the disintegration of the Federal State, which was sometimes called an experiment imposed on the Czechs and the Slovaks by Thomas Masaryk, the issue of succession of obligations arising out of the ECHR emerged. On 1 January 1993, the Slovak Government wrote to the Secretary-General of the Council of Europe expressing a wish to become a member of the Council of Europe and declaring that "in accordance with the current rules of international law, the Slovak Republic, as a successor State of the Czech and Slovak Federal Republic, would consider itself bound, from 1 January 1993, by the multilateral international treaties to which the Czech and Slovak Federal Republic was a party at that date, including the reservations and declarations as to their provisions made by the Czech and Slovak Federal Republic".[13] The Government gave notice

---

[12] Constitutional Law no. 542/92 of the Collection of Laws (R.-J.O. Slovak) on the dissolution of the Czech and Slovak Federative Republic, Article 1.
[13] Council of Europe, List of Declarations made by Slovakia, available at:

that "the Slovak Republic felt bound by the ECHR and the declarations under Articles 25 and 46 of the Convention".[14]

On 30 June 1993, the Committee of Ministers of the Council of Europe decided that the Slovak Republic was to be considered as a Party to the ECHR with retroactive effect from the date of ratification of the ECHR by the Federal Republic.[15] Likewise, declarations concerning the right of individual petition and recognition of the jurisdiction of the ECtHR made by the Federal Republic became binding in respect of Slovakia. By the same token, Slovakia became bound by Protocols nos 1, 4, 6, and 7. As a result, Slovakia became party to the ECHR without there having been a specific ratification process. The special character of the process by which Slovakia became bound by its provisions found its reflection in a decision of the European Commission of Human Rights (Eur. Comm. HR) in which it replied positively to the question whether Slovakia was to be regarded as bound by the ECHR retrospectively, from 18 March 1992, the date of the accession of the Federal Republic.[16] At that time, Slovakia made a reservation concerning the application of Articles 5 and 6.[17]

Slovakia signed, but did not ratify, Protocol no. 12. Protocol no. 13 was ratified on 15 September 2005, with effect from 1 December 2005. As to Protocol no. 14, Slovakia notified the Council of Europe of the ratification on 20 June 2005.

Ratification table[18]

Protocol	Signature	Ratification	Entry into force	Declarations/Reservations
Protocol no. 1	21 Feb. 1991	18 March 1992	1 Jan. 1993	–
Protocol no. 2	21 Feb. 1991	18 March 1992	1 June 1993	–
Protocol no. 3	21 Feb. 1991	18 March 1992	1 June 1993	–
Protocol no. 4	21 Feb. 1991	18 March 1992	1 Jan. 1993	–
Protocol no. 5	21 Feb. 1991	18 March 1992	1 June 1993	–

http://conventions.coe.int/Treaty/Commun/ListeDeclarations.asp?PO=SLK&NT=&MA=44&CV=1&NA=&CN=999&VL=1&CM=5&CL=ENG.

[14] Ibid.

[15] Pursuant to Assembly Opinion no. 175 (29 June 1993) and to Committee of Ministers Resolution (93) 33.

[16] *Brežny and Brežny v. Slovakia* (appl. no. 23131/93), Decision (Plenary), Commission, 4 March 1996, DR 85, 65–83.

[17] "The Czech and Slovak Federal Republic in accordance with Article 64 of the Convention for the Protection of Human Rights and Fundamental Freedoms [Article 57 since the entry into force of the Protocol no. 11] makes a reservation in respect of Articles 5 and 6 to the effect that those articles shall not hinder to impose disciplinary penitentiary measures in accordance with Article 17 of the Act no. 76/1959 of Collection of Laws, on Certain Service Conditions of Soldiers.", Council of Europe, List of Declarations made by Slovakia (*supra* note 13) (text inserted by the author).

[18] Source: http://conventions.coe.int/Treaty/Commun/ChercheMembres.asp?CM=3&CL=ENG.

Protocol	Signature	Ratification	Entry into force	Declarations/Reservations
Protocol no. 6	21 Feb. 1991	18 March 1992	1 Jan. 1993	–
Protocol no. 7	21 Feb. 1991	18 March 1992	1 Jan. 1993	–
Protocol no. 8	21 Feb. 1991	18 March 1992	1 Jan. 1993	–
Protocol no. 9	5 Feb. 1992	7 May 1992	1 Oct. 1994	–
Protocol no. 10	7 May 1992	26 June 1992	–	–
Protocol no. 11	11 May 1994	28 Sept. 1994	1 Nov. 1998	–
Protocol no. 12	4 Nov. 2000	–	–	–
Protocol no. 13	24 July 2002	18 Aug. 2005	1 Dec. 2005	–
Protocol no. 14	22 Oct. 2004	16 May 2005	–	–

3. Comparison and Conclusions

The process of ratification of the ECHR in the two nations was markedly different: in Poland, the ratification was one of those measures that the newly democratic State regarded as an obvious and necessary thing to take in order to restore democracy and consolidate its return to the family of truly European States. The ratification was to provide Poland with a certain certificate of legitimacy for a country embarking on the road to the rule of law. A fortunate set of circumstances accounted for the ease of the ratification process: the ratification itself met with no opposition, nor were there any serious objections voiced as to concrete steps to be taken to harmonize the national legal system with the ECHR requirements. The drawback of the enthusiastic welcome that it enjoyed was that there was really no in-depth domestic discussion about the practical consequences that the ratification might entail.

As for Slovakia, the ratification process was initiated by the break-up of the Czech and Slovak Federal Republic,[19] and State succession issues hijacked the debate, so to speak. However, the Slovak ratification process bears comparison to the Polish one in that, in the context of the split, it was likewise taken for granted that the ECHR is a part of the baggage that any democratic State is obliged to accept. Moreover, the new Slovak Republic was anxious to show that despite originating from a break-up of a democratic republic, it had all the necessary credentials to be considered a *bona fide* democracy. There was no doubt that the ECHR formed a part of these credentials. In this sense, the accession in Slovakia was similar to the Polish history. As a result of the special circumstances of the Slovak accession, there was no Parliamentary ratification. Slovakia became a Contracting Party with retrospective effect from 1 January 1993 by virtue of a

---

[19] Flauss (1994), 1–5.

declaration of the Committee of Ministers of the Council of Europe of 30 June 1993.

While no reservations were issued by Poland, Slovakia upheld the validity of the reservations previously made by the Federal Republic concerning the application of Articles 5 and 6 of the ECHR upon recognition of its being bound by the ECHR. Both countries acknowledged the right of individual petition; however, Poland did so with a two-month delay, which was much frowned upon at the time. The delay was ascribed to the Government's fear that the right of individual petition would give rise to many applications challenging expropriations effected by the communist regime. In the absence of any restitution law, this would put the Government in a difficult position. However, despite the fact that no restitution law was ever adopted in Poland, this right was eventually accepted.

C. Status of the ECHR in National Law

Fundamental rights were not an entirely novel concept in Slovakia or Poland. The Constitutions of the communist countries did include these rights, the theory of which had been elaborated as a socialist concept of fundamental rights. It was an important element of this theory that the enjoyment of rights was partly dependent on whether a given individual complied with his or her obligations towards the State. However, despite elaborate provisions on individual rights in the constitutions of Poland and of Slovakia's legal predecessor, the Federal Republic, legal theories made it clear that these provisions could not serve as a source of any individual rights to be vindicated before the courts. It was even more obvious that international law, including its provisions on human rights, was not a part of internal legal systems, this feature being common to rigorously dualist communist legal systems throughout the region.

D. Domestic and International Law: Constitutional Regulations

1. Poland

The Polish Constitution of 1952, still in force when the ECHR was ratified (even though extensively amended in 1989 and 1992), contained an extensive list of political and social and economic rights.[20] It was conspicuously silent on the relationship between domestic and international law. Prior to 1989, this led to a practical exclusion of international law from the legal system. One writer referred to this situation as a conspiracy of silence.[21] Such a critical assessment could hardly be surprising, given that the only reference to international law in the 1952 Constitution was its Article 30, referring to the competence of the then

---

[20] The Constitution of the Polish Popular Republic, Chapter 9, Articles 94–102.
[21] Zajadło (1990), 17.

Council of State (a sort of a collegial head of the State) to ratify international agreements.

By 1972, it was said that it was "improper still to pretend that this problem [did] not exist in Poland".[22] The same legal writer later tried to remedy this short-coming by developing an argument according to which international human rights conventions, by their very nature and purpose, could be applied by the courts *ex proprio vigore*, without there being any need to incorporate them into the internal legal order.[23] It was no accident that his seminal article was published in a leading legal monthly journal in 1981, at the height of the fragile and heady carnival of freedom in the wake of creation of the *Solidarność* Trade Union in 1980. It should be borne in mind that before domestic courts a mere reference to international law was considered by the communist regime as a subversive, anti-State act.

Despite the fact that the months of relative freedom that *Solidarność* meant for many Poles came to an abrupt end in December 1981 when martial law was declared by the Government, this monistic argument had already begun to make a modest mark on judicial practice in the 80's. The 1952 Constitution was exten-sively amended in 1989, following the return to democracy and the formation of the first non-communist Government, and again in 1992.[24] Importantly, the amended Article 1 provided that the Republic of Poland was a democratic State abiding by the rule of law.[25] In its subsequent judicial practice the Constitutional Court interpreted this provision in such a way as to read into it many guarantees and principles essential for the rule of law, which were not at that time to be found in any express form in the constitutional text, respect and applicability of international law being one of them.

Following the 1989 and 1992 amendments, there was a lively and long consti-tutional debate in Poland, culminating in a new Constitution adopted by the Na-tional Assembly on 2 April 1997.[26] It entered into force on 17 October 1997.

In contrast to the previous Constitution, the 1997 Constitution contains ex-plicit regulations on the relationship between international and national law. Its Article 9 provides that the Republic of Poland shall respect international law binding upon it. Under Article 87, ratified international agreements are binding sources of law on a par with the Constitution, statutes, and regulations. Pursuant to Article 88(3), international agreements ratified with prior consent granted by statute shall be promulgated in accordance with the procedures required for stat-utes. International agreements pertaining to human rights require such a prior consent to be given by Parliament, under Article 89(1)(2) of the Constitution. Article 91 further provides that, after promulgation in the Journal of Laws, a

[22] Skubiszewski (1972), 18.
[23] See, in particular, Skubiszewski (1981), 20 (text inserted by the author).
[24] DU 1992, no. 84, item 426.
[25] DU 1989, no. 75, item 444.
[26] DU 1997, no. 78, item. 483.

ratified international agreement shall be part of the domestic legal order and shall be applied directly, unless its application depends on the enactment of a statute. An international agreement ratified upon consent granted by statute has precedence over statutes, if such an agreement cannot be reconciled with the provisions of such statutes. Eventually, under Article 188 of the Constitution, the Constitutional Court has jurisdiction to assess the conformity of statutes and international agreements with the Constitution, the conformity of statutes with ratified international agreements whose ratification required prior consent and the conformity of legal provisions issued by central State organs with the Constitution, ratified international agreements and statutes.

Hence, the legal landscape pertaining to the internal role of the ECHR was radically overhauled in 1997. These provisions aimed at putting in place a comprehensive regulation of the relationship between national and international law and at doing away with the uncertainty that had governed this issue for years. It should be noted that during the constitutional debate, a proposal was made to introduce a provision to the effect that the constitutional provisions on human rights should be interpreted in compliance with international human rights norms, or even more forcefully, in compliance with the Convention, but it failed.[27]

The case law of the Constitutional Court further clarified and strengthened the place of international law in the domestic system. The Court repeatedly stated that the Convention can be directly applied by domestic courts.[28] Further, it took a clear stand as to the status of the Strasbourg Court's judgements in domestic law. It held that "[r]espect for Poland's international obligations and consideration to ensure cohesion of legal order (which is shaped by the national legal order as well as by international covenants and supranational law) require that no discrepancies arise between the laws (legal provisions, principles of law, legal standards) developed by various bodies interpreting and applying laws. A decision of the ECtHR in an individual case (…) in which a finding of a breach of standards provided for by Article 6(1) of the ECHR in respect of the applicant was made, following a Strasbourg supervision procedure, must therefore be taken into account by the Constitutional Court in its assessment of legal provisions".[29] Likewise, the practice of the Supreme Court well before the new Constitution (entered into force in 1997) supported the conclusion that the ECHR was to be regarded as a source of law. As to the substance of rights guaranteed by the

---

[27] Zieliński (2004), 519.

[28] E.g., K 7/01, 5 March 2003; P 6/01, 8 November 2001; K 28/99, 11 July 2000; K 14/98, 14 September 1999; K 11/98, 9 June 1999; K 28/97 9 June 1998 – all of them concerning the right of access to a court, P 4/01, 9 June 2002 – defence rights in criminal proceedings; SK 12/03, 9 June 2003; SK 53/03, 2 March 2004; SK 1/04, 27 October 2004; K 14/96, 8 April 1997; P 12/99, 15 November 2000; K 1/98, 27 January 1999.

[29] The Polish Constitutional Court, Decision, 18 October 2004, P 8/04.

Polish Constitution, the impact of the ECHR has been repeatedly recognized as a source of inspiration for the drafters of the Constitution.

2. Slovakia

It came as no surprise that, in the federal communist Czechoslovakia, international law was subordinate to the domestic law pursuant to the socialist tradition of constitutional law. The traditional radically dualist position, typical for communist countries, was reversed only when the Federal Charter of Fundamental Rights and Freedoms was enacted in January 1991.[30] Section two of this instrument provided that international human rights treaties ratified by the Federal Republic had priority over statutes. The importance of making those rights a living reality was subsequently stressed by a judgement of the Federal Constitutional Court of Czechoslovakia, which held that "each state, especially one which had to suffer violations of fundamental rights and freedoms by totalitarian authorities for over forty years, [was] entitled to introduce democratic order by legal measures which would avert or at least restrict the risk of relapse into totalitarianism".[31]

Later on, this line of reasoning was followed by the Slovak Republic. Its Constitution, adopted on 1 September 1992, provided in Article 11 that the provisions of international human rights treaties took precedence over national laws "insofar as the treaties provided for a stronger protection of human rights and fundamental freedoms".[32] Theoretical and practical consequences of such a constitutional relationship between international and domestic law subsequently became the subject of a heated debate.[33] However, the Constitutional Court adopted an international law-friendly stance, when it held that nothing prevented it from applying the Constitution in the light of international law binding on Slovakia.[34]

Article 11 had to be "understood as a constitutional rule that all public authorities of the Slovak Republic must respect and promote, in their decision-making or other activities, protection of human rights and fundamental freedoms regulated by international treaties and national laws. An application of a (domestic) regulation on a human right or fundamental freedom when conditions of Article 11 of the Constitution (…) are met shall be deemed a breach of the order of the constitutional principle it lays down".[35]

As the Constitution stands today, following extensive amendments made in

---

[30] Constitutional Law no. 23/1991 on the Charter of Fundamental Rights and Freedoms, enacted on 9 January 1991.

[31] The Federal Constitutional Court, PL US 1/92, 26 November 1992 (text inserted by the author).

[32] Repik (1996), 372.

[33] Blaško (2001), 755–779.

[34] Constitutional Court, PL US 5/1993.

[35] Constitutional Court, dec. PL ÚS 14/98, 22 June 1998.

February 2001,[36] its Article 154c(1) provides that "[i]nternational treaties on human rights and fundamental freedoms which the Slovak Republic has ratified and were promulgated in the manner laid down by a law before taking effect of this constitutional act, shall be a part of its legal order and shall have precedence over laws if they provide a greater scope of constitutional rights and freedoms."[37] This provision is also applicable to the ECHR and, consequently, its legal position in the national system has not changed following the 2001 constitutional reform. Additionally, Article 7(5) of the Constitution currently provides that "[i]nternational treaties on human rights and fundamental freedoms and international treaties for whose exercise a law is not necessary, and international treaties which directly confer rights or impose duties on natural persons or legal persons and which were ratified and promulgated in the way laid down by a law shall have precedence over laws."[38] It has been said that one of the objectives of introducing these amendments was to create constitutional mechanisms for complying with Slovakia's international obligations flowing from international instruments, Community law and other sources of the international law.[39] However, it is interesting to note that the status of a human rights treaty, therefore, depends on the date on which it was ratified. As a result, there are two categories of such treaties which have a different status in national law.

Pursuant to Article 86(d) of the Constitution, the ratification of international treaties on human rights and fundamental freedoms as well as treaties which directly confer rights or impose duties on physical or legal persons requires the prior approval of Parliament (National Council). Under Article 144(1) of the Constitution, international treaties shall also be binding on judges.[40]

The Constitution, in its Chapter Two, guarantees individual rights and freedoms similar to these safeguarded by the ECHR, although the scope of some of them is much broader than in the ECHR.[41] It has been said that "[b]ecause the fundamental human rights are directly comparable with the articles of the Constitution, relations between the ECHR and the Constitution [have been simplified], especially in case of their application by the Constitutional Court".[42] This statement seems to be a little overly optimistic, given that it is not the mere substantive similarity between the rights guaranteed by a Constitution of any given country and those guaranteed by the ECHR which is decisive for a relationship between them. Nevertheless, it clearly reflects the idea that the concept

---

[36] Law no. 90/2001 Coll.; the amendments entered into force partly on 1 July 2001 and partly on 1 January 2002.
[37] Article 154c(1) of the Constitution.
[38] Article 7(5) of the Constitution.
[39] Mazak (2001), 7.
[40] Article 144(1) of the Constitution.
[41] Articles 12–32 of the Constitution; see also Blaško (2001), 756.
[42] Čič (2000), 239 (text inserted by the author).

of fundamental rights as entrenched in the Slovak Constitution was regarded by its drafters as based on the ECHR.

3. Comparison and Conclusions

Many a constitution adopted in Central and Easterm Europe after the fall of communism made an express point that the rule of law was to prevail. Neither Slovakia nor Poland was an exception and their constitutions followed this trend. A strictly dualist constitutional practice, reminiscent of the communist period, consisting of drawing a distinct line between international and domestic law, to the point where the former did not penetrate at all into the latter, was replaced in both countries by new constitutions, which expressly provide that international law is a part of the law of the land.

There was, however, a major difference between Poland and Slovakia as to the way in which such clarifications were brought into their respective constitutions. In Poland, from 1989 to 1997, when a new Constitution entered into force, no provisions of a constitutional rank regulated the status of international law in the national legal order, including the ECHR. This lacuna was filled by the case law of the highest domestic courts, which interpreted the principle of the rule of law, stipulated in the Constitution in the early 90's, in such a way as to include international law into the sources of national law. In Slovakia, the Constitution adopted in 1992 already expressly provided that international law was part of the internal legal order, but only in so far as relevant norms guaranteed broader protection than domestic ones. Further clarifications were effected by way of the constitutional revision of 2001, but they did not do away with this distinction between norms affording broader protection and all others. Consequently, the ECHR enjoys precedence over statutes – within the limits dictated by this distinction, which gives rise to some continuing uncertainties – and the same has been the case in Poland since 1997. To provide clear guidance to judges, currently both constitutions expressly provide that international human rights treaties are to be applied by the courts. This should be seen as an attempt on the part of the constitutional legislator to encourage judges to have practical recourse to international law.

In both countries, the substantive content of human rights listed by the Constitutions has been expressly recognized as having largely been influenced by the Convention. It has also been said time and time again in legal writings that the same values underpin the catalogue of human rights in both countries. Another similarity is that the constitutional and ECHR rights are now regarded as a direct source of law that can be relied on before the courts. This was not the case under the communist regime, when such rights were merely a façade.

E. Implementation of International Law by Domestic Courts

1. Poland

Even before the ECHR was ratified in 1993, a number of highest courts' decisions had been adopted, indicating that international law could be applied domestically. However, the practice was erratic and marked by uneven development. As to the latter quality, in 1987 the Supreme Court stated, for example, that in light of the 1952 Constitution there were no grounds on which to hold that the ratification of an international treaty resulted in its automatic transformation into the domestic order, or in a presumption of transformation. Hence, until there was an act of internal law reiterating the norms contained in the treaty, there were no grounds on which such treaty could be regarded as a source of internal law.[43] On the other hand, there were also judgements in which high courts expressed opinions to the contrary.[44]

It is interesting to see that it was not so much the black-letter constitutional situation as the radical political change effected after the first partially free Parliamentary elections held in June 1989 which brought about a significant change in judicial practice concerning the role of international law. Well before the ratification of the ECHR and in the absence of any reference to international law in the Constitution as it stood at that time, some courts stated that it had become universally accepted that international law was to be applied and respected by the courts, or regarded the internal applicability of international human rights as being on a par with respect for constitutional rights.[45] This willingness to refer to international law in the absence of any explicit legal basis in the Constitution for doing so shows how politically charged the issue was and how much the actual role played by international law in judicial practice depended on the political climate. It had been suggested that, by virtue of its being relied upon and quoted by the courts, the law of the ECHR had become a living instrument in Polish law as early as 1996.[46] The somewhat self-congratulatory tone of this statement is perhaps not entirely justified, given that such references are still relatively difficult to find in judgements handed down by the lower judiciary.

Nonetheless, the message coming from the higher courts is clear, and it has remained consistent over time. The Supreme Court started to refer to the ECHR even before its entry into force, and has continued to do so.[47] Later on, in a

---

[43] I PRZ 8/87, 25 August 1997

[44] E.g., Constitutional Court, K 8/91; K 1/92; the Supreme Court, I PZP 9/92.

[45] E.g., the Supreme Administrative Court, NSA II SA 759/90; the Supreme Court, SN III KRN 41/90 ONSA 1991/1/4 ; 1991.01.11 SN III KRN 41/90; ONSA 1992/11/4, the Constitutional Court, U 8/90.

[46] See, for instance, Leszczyński (1996), 19; Hofmański (1998), 107.

[47] See e.g., the Supreme Court decisions: I PZP 9/92, 10 April 1992, OSNCP No 2/1992, item 210; III RN 49/93, 18 November 1993, OSNCP No 9/1994, item 181; III RN 23/94, 12 May 1994, OSNAP No 5/1994, Item 77; III ARN 18/94, 8 April 1994, OSNAP No 4/1994, item 55.

landmark decision of 1995, it expressly stated that the case law of the ECtHR can and must be relied upon by the courts in their interpretation of Polish law.[48] The Supreme Court's position in the *Mandugueqi* case, which was then pending before the ECtHR, provides a good example. The case concerned the threatened extradition of two Chinese citizens to China; at the time, it was also pending before the European Commission of Human Rights.[49] The applicants argued that extradition would expose them to a risk of inhumane treatment contrary to Article 3 of the ECHR. Referring to the ECHR judgement in the *Soering* case,[50] the Supreme Court refused permission to extradite, invoking the obligation of the Contracting Party not to expose persons to such a risk outside its territory. One can hardly imagine a more express and forceful authorization, coming from the highest judicial authority in the country, for the effective use of the ECHR in domestic judicial practice.

Similarly, the Supreme Court referred to the ECHR on many occasions, both before and after the 1997 Constitution entered into force.[51] Likewise, the administrative courts have been known to refer to the Convention both before and after the 2002 reform of those courts.[52]

In spite of this, the practical role played by the ECHR in day-to-day judicial decisions appears to remain rather modest. From many a private talk with both advocates and junior judges, it transpires that they would hesitate before invoking the ECHR in their pleadings or in written grounds for judgements. According to the advocates, a lower court would, at best, overlook or ignore any reference they might make to the Convention; at worst it would feel annoyed by being lectured by an advocate and would react negatively. What judges on the lower steps of the judicial hierarchy tend to report informally is that they would not be interested in referring to the ECHR or its case law in their judgements, for fear of a knee-jerk

---

[48] III ARN 75/94, 11 January 1995, OSNAP No 9/1995, item 106.

[49] *Mandugeqi and Jinge v. Poland* (appl. no. 35218/97), Decision (Plenary), 19 September 1997 (struck off the list).

[50] *Soering v. the United Kingdom* (appl. no. 14038/88), Judgement (Plenary), 7 July 1989, Series A, Vol. 161.

[51] The Supreme Court, Judgement, 8 January 2003, IV KK 418/02; Judgement, 1 July 2003, III KK 343/02; Judgement, 18 December 2002, II KK 298/02; Judgement, 4 December 2002; III KKN 361/00; Judgement, 3 September 2002, III KKN 414/99; Judgement, 28 May 2002, III KK 116/02; Judgement, 11 February 2002; IV KKN, 435/01 (Article 451 of the Code of Criminal Procedure); Decision, 11 January 1995, ARN 75/94; Judgement, 12 July 2002, V CKN 1095/00; Decision, 3 July 2003, II KK 146/03; Decision, 15 October 2002, V KK 140/02; Decision, 29 May 2003, I KZP 15/03 (no obligation to provide motives for a refusal to examine a manifestly ill-founded cassation appeal); Judgement, 9 November 1999, II KKN 295/98 (on anonymous witnesses); Resolution of the Supreme Court of 17 January 2001 (nr III CZP 49/00) – an assessment of provisions of the Code of Civil Procedure on cassation appeal as amended in May 2000.

[52] E.g., SK 1269/04, 30 November 2004 ; GPP 1/04, 25 November 2004 ; II OSK 554/05, 30 June 2005; II OSK 656/05, 31 August 2005; II OSK 964/05, 30 November 2005; II OSK 1148/05, 30 November 2005; II SA 220/99, 10 December 1999 ; II SAWr 291/01, 5 April 2005; OSK 959/04, 22 December 2004; SA Ka 1974/95, 2 October 1995 ; SA L 2722/95, 6 February 1996; V SA 230/ 99, 3 August 1999; V SA 717/97, 25 February 1998; V SA 1068/00, 14 December 2000; V SA 2880/99, 30 June 2000; FPS 1/ 97, 17 June 1997.

reaction on part of their senior colleagues on higher benches: "Who does she/he think she/he is to lecture us on human rights?" Lower courts would of course be more likely to rely on the Convention, if appellate courts were themselves doing so. It points to the responsibility for the judges on higher benches to make the reference to the ECHR a well-entrenched habit among junior judges.

Of course, the reception of the ECHR by the judiciary in any country is a process which needs to be linked to its temporal aspects. Hence, statements made about its current state always reflect the situation at the time of writing. As things stand today, it seems that there are no grounds for an overly enthusiastic assessment of the situation, which must also be regarded in the light of a recent assessment concerning the constitutional thinking of Polish judges as a whole. A former Ombudsman expressed the view that "there is no tradition of judicial reliance on the Constitution. In addition, the interpretation of constitutional provisions is far from being simple since the Constitution uses very broad terms, is formulated in a specific language and based on public law, not necessarily known to the judges of general courts, who are specialists in civil or criminal law".[53]

If there is no tradition of reliance on the Constitution, it is even less likely that the judges will be willing to invoke the ECHR in their judgements. A certain reluctance of the lower judiciary can also be attributed to the historically unclear relationship that existed between domestic and international law.[54] In this respect, the same authority stated that "Polish judges are not too well prepared to resort to international law in their work. Neither are they adequately trained in this respect. Day-to-day case law of the Polish courts testifies to that. Despite the fact that it is now more common for judges to rely in their judgements on international law (and the Constitution) than it used to be the case in the past, it still happens rarely."[55]

This state of affairs is not helped by a controversy between the Supreme and the Constitutional Courts which is relevant, albeit indirectly, for the issue at hand. It has arisen in an attempt to answer the question of what a judge should do if he/she finds that a statutory provision is incompatible with the Constitution in a manner, which cannot be elucidated by any interpretational efforts. Pursuant to Article 193 of the 1997 Constitution, any court may refer a question of law to the Constitutional Tribunal as to the conformity of a normative act with the Constitution, ratified international agreements or statute, if the answer to such a question of law is decisive for the determination of an issue pending before such court.

However, there is disagreement as to whether a judge in such a situation is obliged to have recourse to this procedure, or whether he or she is free to disapply this dubious statutory norm and give a ruling in a case directly on the basis

---

[53] Zielinski (2004), 533.
[54] See remarks on the status of the ECHR in national law in Poland in Section D.1. *supra*.
[55] Zieliński (2004), 522.

of the Constitution and with reference to its Article 8(2), according to which the provisions of the Constitution shall apply directly. The Supreme Court tends to espouse the view that it is for every court to use provisions of constitutional rank in its interpretation of the law and, if necessary, to conclude that it will have to disregard inferior provisions. By contrast, the Constitutional Court emphasizes that any decision on incompatibility with the Constitution is its exclusive domain.

Understandably, this debate does little to encourage judges on lower benches to refer to either the Constitution or the ECHR – even in the much less controversial context of their direct application or the dis-application of a statutory provision. This debate has, unfortunately, been couched in terms of competition between the courts as to which one owns the Constitution. The same issue could well be put in less territorial terms in order to better address the question how the Constitution should be applied and resorted to in the interpretation of various norms of domestic law. It is the task of the courts to ensure that constitutional values – which, importantly, happen also to underpin the ECHR – pervade judicial application of statutes and other legal norms throughout the whole system.

Further, this unhappy controversy must be seen as both a result and manifestation of what has been deplored as a "[s]trong attachment to black-letter law, equal respect for laws (passed by the legislature) and regulations (passed by administrative bodies), the conviction that judges are so bureaucratic in their understanding and application of laws that they do not even ask if a legal act agrees with the Constitution, and limited interest in what can be learned from law in practice – these are all characteristic of the ways East and Central Europeans, including Poles, think about law."[56]

In more practical terms, one can also attempt to explain this judicial reluctance by certain internal dynamics between higher and lower courts. In a recent article, Łętowska stated that "written grounds of judgments serve many purposes: it is a tool by which a court exercises some form of self-supervision; it makes possible a judicial review by a higher instance, performs various explanatory and interpretational functions (including facilitation of the execution of a judicial decision and educating other actors of legal life). It is through written grounds of judicial decisions that these decisions come to be accepted in their individual function and are also legitimized in a more general context (pedagogical function, a voice in a social discourse). All these functions are anchored in the constitutional principles and values, such as – to mention but a few – rule of law, human dignity, right of access to a court".[57] Nonetheless, Łętowska considers that written grounds of judicial decisions in Poland are imperious, not explanatory. Hence, "[i]t is a bench of a higher court to which the court essentially addresses itself; not the parties

---

[56] Łętowska (1997), 78.
[57] Łętowska (2005), 40.

of the case, let alone the general public."[58] As a result, judges of the lower courts often focus primarily on the possible future reaction of a higher court, when it comes to examine an appeal against a judgement.[59] Their essential concern is to have a decision upheld, not least because the ratio of the decisions upheld and quashed by an appellate instance is one of most important factors of a judge's professional assessment. This rather bureaucratic *modus operandi* of the administration of justice results, perhaps inadvertently, in the judges speaking in their judgements essentially to higher courts, in a manner that goes over the heads of the parties and the general public. A concern to convince the parties that the legal and factual grounds for a decision are sound is much lower on their agenda, while a general motivation to provide legitimacy for judicial decisions (also legitimacy grounded in respect for human rights) in the eyes of the general public figures even less prominently.

These interesting insights, confirmed by conversations with many judges, shed some light, first, on the internal workings of the judicial system. They go some way towards supporting a thesis that the judges themselves, despite the fact that institutional and procedural foundations of their independence are well entrenched in the Polish legal system, might be perceiving their position as that of agents of the State bound by strong hierarchical links, rather than as independent and impartial powers.

Further, it is only common sense to accept that judicial independence cannot be seen as independent from the manner in which administrative supervision of judicial work is carried out by judges' administrative superiors. In the historical context of Central and Eastern Europe, the importance of this issue should not be underestimated, given the novelty, and sometimes fragility, of judicial independence throughout the region.[60] Relations between higher and lower courts in the administrative context in which judges operate might also bring about a situation in which the reluctance (or willingness) of judges in a given jurisdiction of appellate or regional courts, sitting as courts of second instance, might depend on how these concrete higher courts like (or do not) the ECHR being referred to in the judgements of lower courts. Hence, the factors shaping the reception of the ECHR are much less of a systemic legal character than simply springing from the local and personal lines of thinking and modes of reasoning of second-instance courts. In countries where higher courts are in favour of applying the Conven-

---

[58] Ibid.

[59] It is relevant to note here that in Polish judicial practice written grounds of judicial decisions contain the court's complete reasoning as to the facts and law, while the operative parts of judgements are normally very succinct.

[60] It is a separate and very interesting question, so far unexplored academically as far as the author is aware, whether and to what extent the internal administrative and management practices in the Polish courts, including the way in which the Ministry of Justice itself treats judges, contribute to the judges' having full conscience of their powers and responsibilities as independent agents of justice or, to the contrary, whether they rather reinforce an unfortunate perception of judges as public officials subject to intrusive interference.

tion, the lower courts will also be willing to do so; in countries where this is not the case, judges will rather try to avoid the reprimand of having their judgement quashed by carefully avoiding any reference to the ECHR.

2. Slovakia

Prior to the 2001 amendments, the domestic courts could directly apply the ECHR by virtue of Article 144(1) of the Constitution. This provision indicates the sources of law to be applied by judges, including the Constitution, constitutional law, law as such and international treaties – within the above-mentioned limits set out by Article 7 of the Constitution. Both prior to and after the 2001 constitutional reform, the Constitutional Court held that it was not only its own duty, as a judicial authority for the protection of constitutionality, to observe during its operation, *inter alia*, the international treaties binding for the Slovak Republic; it emphasized that, as primary defenders of constitutionality, ordinary courts also had this obligation.[61] It further emphasized that "ordinary courts which are obliged to interpret and apply, in civil proceedings, the relevant laws to concrete cases in compliance with the Constitution or international treaties under Article 11 of the Constitution, are also primarily responsible for the observance of the rights and fundamental freedoms guaranteed by the Constitution or by international treaties".[62]

References to the ECHR are very often made in the judgements of the Constitutional Court.[63] It has even been said that "by way of generalisation it is possible to conclude that the Constitutional Court of the Slovak Republic in its decision-making activity effectively applies the decisions of the ECHR [and] the experience [drawn from the case-law] of the Constitutional Court confirms the legal and also moral significance of [references to] the judgements of the ECtHR, especially in the reasoning given for decisions".[64]

The Constitutional Court made it clear that international treaties on human rights and fundamental freedoms take precedence over the laws of the Slovak Republic, but not over the Constitution.[65] It also reiterated that Article 11 of the Constitution should be regarded as a directive of a constitutional character obliging all State authorities to respect and implement protection of those human rights which are subject to international and domestic legal regulation.[66]

The Constitutional Court started referring to the ECHR in its decisions early on. In one early case, a group of Members of Parliament complained that the Act no. 370/1994 concerning privatization of State-owned enterprises was in direct

---

[61] E.g., Constitutional Court, Decision no. III. ÚS 79/02, 21 August 2002.

[62] Constitutional Court, Decision no. I. ÚS 9/00, 22 March 2000.

[63] As demonstrated by the fact that 848 references to the ECHR was found in the judgements and decisions of that Court as of 20 May 2007.

[64] Čič (2000), 243 (text inserted by the author).

[65] Constitutional Court, II ÚS 91/97.

[66] Constitutional Court, Decision PL ÚS 8/96.

conflict with Articles 13(2) and 13(4) of the Constitution and also Article 1 of Protocol no. 1. The Court found conflicts between the impugned act and Article 1 of Protocol no. 1.[67] In another case,[68] it examined whether a conscript's obligation to make a declaration that they wished to avail themselves of the right of conscientious objection to military service prior to being drafted was compatible with the freedom of conscience and religion. The Court found it to be the case. It relied on the concept of *forum internum* in the context of freedom of religion, as developed by the ECtHR. It also made references to Articles 9 and 14 ECHR and to the case law of the European Commission of Human Rights.[69] In another judgement, the Court held that the positive obligation to ensure respect for certain human rights provided for by the ECHR and as interpreted by its organs, was also incorporated in the Constitution of the Slovak Republic. It referred to the ECtHR judgement in the *Pakelli v. Germany* case.[70]

The question of the relationship between the restrictions on the exercise of rights was addressed by the Court in another judgement in which the petitioner complained that his freedom of speech as well as his right to information had been violated by a procedural decision of the Supreme Court not to allow audio recordings of the proceedings. The Constitutional Court considered that the criteria for the restriction of the right to information, as applied by the ECtHR but not provided for in the Constitution, were not deemed to be a source of law in the Slovak Republic. It was of the view that the ECHR was superior to the laws of the Republic only if it provided for a more extensive protection of rights and freedoms than the relevant national legislation.[71]

When called upon to determine the scope of the State's obligation to protect individuals against private acts of aggression, the Court held that the rights and freedoms as guaranteed under the Constitution were also guaranteed in relations between private persons. State authorities were, consequently, obliged to act in such a manner as to protect the rights and freedoms guaranteed by the Constitution. It did not invoke the ECHR or the case law of the ECtHR, but this judgement is clearly in line with the latter's case law regarding the State's positive obligations under Articles 2 and 8.[72]

In a case echoing the principles established by the EtCHR in respect of guarantees of the right to liberty, the Constitutional Court examined the obligations of the authorities when taking into custody a person suspected of having committed a criminal offence. It concluded that it was sufficient to provide grounds for the

[67] Constitutional Court, ÚS 16/95.
[68] Constitutional Court, ÚS 18/95.
[69] *X. v. Austria* (appl. no. 5591/72), Decision, Commission, 2 April 1973, Collection 43, 161; *X. v. Federal Republic of Germany* (appl. no. 7705/76), Decision (Plenary), Commission, 5 July 1977, DR 9, 201.
[70] Constitutional Court, II ÚS 8/96, 4 September 1996.
[71] Constitutional Court, II ÚS 28/96, 12 May 1997.
[72] Constitutional Court, II ÚS 47/97, 27 October 1997.

suspicion that the detainee had committed the offence concerned. It further held that even though Article 5(1)(c) ECHR required a "reasonable suspicion" as a necessary component of the guarantees against arbitrary detention, this requirement was met if there were facts or information that could allow an impartial observer to conclude that the suspicion was justified, echoing the established case law of the ECtHR.[73]

The much-discussed issue of legal certainty, this time in the context of criminal proceedings, was considered by the Constitutional Court in a case in which a petitioner complained that a decision to discontinue prosecution against him had been subsequently overturned. His crucial argument was that the prosecution had requested the Court to do so after the time limit for the submission of such a request had elapsed. The Court referred to the standards adopted by the ECtHR and held that the petitioner's freedom from unlawful detention had been violated.[74]

In a case brought before the Constitutional Court by Greenpeace, the NGO complained that its right to a fair hearing and access to information had been breached. An administrative authority charged with supervision of a nuclear electricity plant had refused to disclose some information on the grounds of commercial secrecy. The Constitutional Court criticized the Supreme Court in so far as it had failed, acting as a court of a single instance, to provide the applicant with an opportunity to comment, before delivering its decision on the lawfulness of the decision of the office. It also criticized the Supreme Court's decision for its arbitrariness in that it had failed to provide cogent reasons therein.[75] There was no express reference to the ECHR in the reasoning of the Constitutional Court, but its content is clearly compatible with the ECHR standards. It should also be noted that after the Constitutional Court became competent to examine complaints against excessive length of judicial proceedings, it started referring to the relevant ECHR standards on a regular basis.

With regard to the use made by the lower courts of the Convention, the Constitutional Court emphasized the decision no. I. ÚS 9/00 of 22 March 2000, that ordinary civil courts are under an obligation to interpret and apply the relevant laws in accordance with the Constitution and with the international treaties. Accordingly, the ordinary courts have the primary responsibility for upholding rights and fundamental freedoms guaranteed by the Constitution or international treaties.

Other domestic courts also increasingly started to apply the European Court's judgements in different cases.[76] Nonetheless, it was stated as late as 2000, that

---

[73] Constitutional Court, II ÚS 112/02, 10 July 2002.
[74] Constitutional Court, II ÚS 4/99, 17 April 1999.
[75] Constitutional Court, I ÚS 59/04, 24 June 2004.
[76] See in particular the Supreme Court's decisions concerning the right to liberty and security, Nos Ntv I – 19/02 and Ntv I – 20/02 of 10 January 2003.

references to the ECHR in judgements given by lower courts were sporadic.[77] It has also been said that "judges were severely overburdened by rapidly changing legislation without adequate training",[78] which might explain why referring to the ECHR was not their priority.

3. Comparison and Conclusions

The Constitutional Courts in both countries are of the same view, namely that the impact of the judgements of the ECtHR extends beyond an individual case and that they can and should be relied on by the judiciary. It has been repeatedly stated in their judgements that such an impact should not only be limited to judgements given in cases against that country, but that judgements against other countries can and should be applied by the courts. While the ECHR and the ECtHR judgements are referred to in the judicial reasoning, they only appear as one of the arguments on which solutions are based and not as the sole legal basis for a given decision. There is no practice of disapplying domestic provisions on the basis of the ECHR or the ECtHR judgements. Despite the existing agreement that judicial interpretation should be ECHR-friendly, the courts prefer an interpretation which does not create overt conflicts between the ECHR and the domestic law.

In spite of this agreement, the lower courts seem to be more circumspect when referring to the Convention. Their attitude depends not only on the letter of the Constitution, but also seems to be rooted in the remnants of the traditional, even though currently obsolete, concept of separation between the domestic and international order. It could also originate from certain deficiencies of judicial training.

F. Domestic Remedies

1. Poland

a. Individual Constitutional Complaint

From the time of the ratification of the ECHR until 1997, under the 1952 Constitution there was no individual constitutional remedy available. It was only the 1997 Constitution which instituted a mechanism of individual constitutional complaint.[79] Everyone whose constitutional freedoms or rights have been infringed, has the right to seek a decision of the Constitutional Court on the conformity with the Constitution of a statute or another normative act on the

---

[77] Blaško (2001), 765.

[78] U.S. State Department, Human Rights Report 2005, http://www.state.gov/g/drl/rls/hrrpt/2005/61674.htm.

[79] The Constitution of the Republic of Poland, DU 1997, no. 78, item 483, Article 79; Constitutional Court Act, DU 1997 no. 102, item 43.

basis of which a court or an administrative authority has issued a final decision in the complainant's case.[80] The time-limit for the submission of such a demand is currently three months from the final decision.

First, there was hope that this new remedy would somewhat stem the number of applications against Poland lodged with the ECHR. However, after 1997 there was no decrease in the number of cases brought to Strasbourg. It may be assumed that the apparition of a constitutional remedy was irrelevant in the face of social factors which were decisive for making the ECHR so popular in Poland. Second, and importantly, the limitations of the constitutional remedy must not be over-looked. The constitutional complaint was conceived by the drafters of the Constitution in order to allow the removal of unconstitutional provisions from the legal system, rather than as an instrument that would help individuals vindicate their rights as guaranteed by the Constitution. It is not open for an individual to challenge a breach of human rights that arises out of a wrongful application of the law, as is the case in Germany, Austria, Spain or Slovakia. In fact, "[t]he Constitutional Court lacks jurisdiction (…) to determine whether interpretation of a given legal act in an individual case was right or wrong. It does not exercise the function of an appellate instance competent to reexamine judicial decisions; it only examines compatibility of legal regulations on the basis of which such decisions were given with the Constitution."[81] Furthermore, even an individual who obtains a judgement of the Constitutional Court in his or her favour does not by the same token obtain a declaration that an individual decision given in his or her case loses its binding force. In order to obtain an individualized result, a successful complainant must institute a further set of proceedings in order to seek a reopening of the case on the merits. This rather tortuous way of obtaining a tangible individual result can only encourage individuals to circumvent the procedure altogether and go directly to Strasbourg.

These shortcomings of the constitutional complaint as an instrument of vindi-cation of individual rights have been subject to the prudent criticism of Garlicki, the current Polish judge of the ECtHR. He wrote that the features of the com-plaint "have made it less attractive for the parties to judicial or administrative proceedings; hence the number of such complaints brought to the Constitu-tional Court in Poland remains much lower than it is the case in, for example, Germany".[82] There have also been much bolder criticisms of the circumspection with which the constitutional legislator chose to model the individual constitu-tional complaint. In any event, the interrelationship between the Polish consti-tutional complaint and the application to Strasbourg remains fraught with many unanswered questions.

Only in 2003, six years after the individual constitutional complaint had been

---

[80] With effect as of 8 October 2000.
[81] The Polish Constitutional Court, Ts 51/03, 17 July 2003, 2.
[82] Garlicki (2002a), 73.

introduced into Polish law, the ECtHR examined whether individual constitutional complaint is a remedy which had to be tried in order to comply with the requirement of exhaustion of domestic remedies. It held, in a rather convoluted language, that it is a remedy to be tried only where "the individual decision, which allegedly violated the Convention, had been adopted in direct application of an unconstitutional provision of national legislation and [when applicable] procedural regulations (...) provide for the re-opening of the case or quashing the final [offending] decision upon the judgement of the Constitutional Court in which unconstitutionality had been found".[83]

This decision was also cited in subsequent cases.[84] As a result, a failure to use the constitutional complaint mechanism provided for by Polish law – which is a problem that seems to be grounded in laws, not in their application – currently entails that a Polish application is likely to fail before the ECtHR. This insistence on the necessity to have recourse to the constitutional complaint is, on the one hand, understandable, given the subsidiary character of the protection system set up under the ECHR and, more pressingly, also the heavy caseload under which the ECtHR labours.

On the other hand, in light of the case law of the Polish Constitutional Court this requirement appears somewhat paradoxical. Under domestic law, this Court cannot examine the compatibility of the individual decisions with the Constitution when dealing with individual constitutional complaints. There is established case law of the Constitutional Court to the effect that within the framework of a constitutional complaint it cannot examine the compatibility of the laws concerned with the ECHR. The Court has consistently held that it lacks jurisdiction to do so, as only the Constitution can be relied on as a measure against which to assess observance of human rights. Hence, it discontinued the proceedings in the part in which the complainants referred to the ECHR as a model with which the contested provisions of domestic law should be compared.[85]

In these circumstances, it is questionable why the failure to file an individual constitutional complaint should be considered as a failure to exhaust the relevant domestic remedies for the purposes of the Strasbourg proceedings. It can be argued that the substance of rights guaranteed by the Polish Constitution is largely similar to those guaranteed by the ECHR. Hence, a reference to the constitutional rights in a complaint would serve the same function as reliance on the ECHR rights. Nevertheless, it is puzzling that a remedy in which one cannot refer to the ECHR expressly is construed by the ECtHR as a remedy to be tried

---

[83] *Szott-Medyńska and Others v. Poland* (appl. no. 47414/99), Decision (Third Section), 9 October 2003 (not reported) (text inserted by the author).

[84] E.g, *Wypych v. Poland* (appl. no. 2428/05), Decision (Fourth Section), 5 October 2005 (not reported); *Pachla v. Poland* (appl. no. 8812/02), Decision (Fourth Section), 8 November 2005 (not reported).

[85] E. g., SK 2/993, 18 April 2000.

first at a domestic level. It remains to be seen how these requirements will be applied by the ECtHR in further cases.

In particular, these decisions may very well limit the actual accessibility of the Strasbourg petition to the Polish applicants. Furthermore, the requirement to have recourse to the constitutional complaint puts prospective applicants to the Strasbourg court in a difficult position for purely practical reasons, which exacerbates further the difficulties described earlier.[86] First, applicants have to establish whether, in so far as the Constitutional Court has passed judgement in the complainant's favour, the "procedural regulations [...] provide for the re-opening of the case or quashing the final decision upon the judgement of the Constitutional Court in which unconstitutionality had been found"[87] as required in the *Szott-Medyńska* decision, referred to above. Another, still more difficult assessment to be made is whether a situation of which the applicant wants to complain has arisen out of a legal provision itself or rather out of its application in his or her case. The difficulty of this assessment must be seen against the judicial practice of the Constitutional Court, which in its decisions often emphasizes that the individual constitutional complaint is a remedy of an extraordinary and subsidiary character.[88] That Court rejects many complaints on the ground that they contest the application and not a provision as such. Sometimes it takes a number of pages containing complicated legal arguments to explain this distinction. Hence, a party that brings a case to the Strasbourg court, having failed to make a constitutional complaint first, runs the risk that the ECtHR will declare the application inadmissible for non-exhaustion if it considers that it concerned the laws and not merely their application.[89]

This alone would be detrimental to the party's interests. However, those are also exposed to another risk, namely that, the Constitutional Court having first rejected the case on the ground that it concerned application of laws, not the laws themselves, the ECtHR may later declare the application inadmissible on the ground of failure to submit it within six months – if the ECtHR considers that this period should not run from the date of the Constitutional Court's decision, but from an earlier decision on the merits of the case. The ECtHR can also hold that the applicant failed to exhaust relevant domestic remedies – as for this requirement to be satisfied, all domestic procedural and substantive requirements must be met before the case is brought. In these complex circumstances, a Polish applicant is hard pressed to know whether he/she should first file a complaint with the Constitutional Court.

This quandary should, for all practical purposes, be assessed against the low number of Polish applicants represented by lawyers before the ECtHR. Only a

[86] For a detailed analysis, see Krzyżanowska-Mierzewska (2005), 3.
[87] *Szott-Medyńska and Others v. Poland* (*supra* note 82).
[88] E.g., Ts 1/97, 5 December 1997.
[89] It effectively happened in *Szott-Medyńska and Others v. Poland* (*supra* note 82).

fraction of them come to Strasbourg assisted by a professional. It cannot but put into question, the famous effectiveness of the protection offered by the Strasbourg system – in the sense that at the end of the day, neither the Constitutional Court nor the ECtHR will be willing to examine a complaint about alleged breach of human rights in the Polish context. While this mutual judicial courtesy can be praized as a part of what is usually termed "a dialogue of courts", it should not be lost from sight that as a result of this laudable judicial restraint no court might ultimately be willing to take up an individual case against Poland.

Decisions given by the ECtHR and relating to the Polish constitutional complaint gave rise to a brief, but intense exchange of views in legal writings. The decision in the *Szott-Medyńska* case has been criticized as a coercive attempt on part of the ECtHR to make it obligatory for the applicants to have recourse to the constitutional remedy and, worse, to impose on the Constitutional Court a function of an appellate court, competent to examine the cases as yet another level of ordinary jurisdiction.[90] This severe assessment should certainly be nuanced considering that, according to the ECtHR's established case law, the ECHR does not guarantee a right of access to a constitutional tribunal competent to examine the constitutionality of laws. Nevertheless, it cannot be denied that this decision and those following do send a clear signal to the domestic system that any legal arrangement to alleviate the burden of the ECtHR – including an obligation to use an individual constitutional complaint – is welcome. These Polish decisions must, therefore, be seen in the context of a tendency on the part of that court to repatriate the complaints before domestic authorities, with all the difficulties that this might engender for individuals.

b. Remedies Against Length of Judicial Proceedings

For many years, the approach of the ECtHR was that under Article 13 it was not necessary to examine the complaint about the lack of effective domestic remedy in cases in which it found a violation of Article 6(1) on the ground of excessively lengthy judicial proceedings.[91] However, in a judgement given on 26 October 2000 it observed, for the first time, that the growing frequency with which violations in this regard had been found led it to note the important danger that exists for the rule of law within national legal orders where excessive delays in the administration of justice occur in respect of which litigants have no domestic remedy. The ECtHR reminded the Contracting Parties thereby that, in accordance with the principle of subsidiarity, it was first and foremost their responsibility to provide a national remedy when an individual suffers a violation of the Convention. This principle has acquired a heightened importance since it became

---

[90] Trzciński (2004), C 3.
[91] *Pizzetti v. Italy* (appl. no. 12444/86), Judgement (Chamber), 26 February 1993, Series A, Vol. 257-C, para. 21.

obvious in recent years that the ECHR system's survival or at least efficacy was threatened by the growing caseload it attracted.[92]

The judgement in the *Kudła v. Poland* case[93] reinforced a trend towards creating specific remedies in case of excessively long judicial proceedings.[94] In Poland itself, it set in motion a legislative process that ultimately led to the entry into force, on 17 September 2004, of the Act on complaints about a breach of the right to a trial within a reasonable time, largely modelled on the Italian *Pinto* law providing for the first European length remedy of a judicial character.[95] The 2004 Law provides for a special action by which a party can seek a declaration that his or her right to have the case heard within a reasonable time has been breached. The court shall take into consideration the same criteria, which were developed over the years by the ECtHR and serve as a yardstick for the examination of the length of proceedings. The complaint can be lodged with the court superior to that before which the proceedings concerned are pending. The complainant can request a financial award (*suma pieniężna*) for the excessive length. Pursuant to the terms of this provision, which do not refer to either compensation for damage (*naprawienie szkody*, a term denoting only pecuniary damage under Polish civil law) or to just satisfaction (*zadośćuczynienie*) for non-pecuniary damage, it appears that this term is of a *sui generis* character and does not fit neatly into the Polish civil law system.

It is also possible to request that an order be given for the court, before which the case is pending, to take some specific procedural measures in order to speed up the proceedings. Hence, the remedy has a compensatory and a remedial character. The court shall give its decision regarding the complaint within two months from the date on which the complaint has been lodged. When a length complaint has been declared well-founded, a complainant may, in separate civil proceedings, claim compensation from the State Treasury for damages arising from the excessive length of proceedings. Also, a party to proceedings that did not lodge a complaint as provided for by the Act can claim such a compensation.

As a result of the adoption of the Act of 17 June 2004, the length complaints have been, so to speak, repatriated before the Polish courts. The ECHR obviously requires national remedies to have been exhausted for a case to be admissible, but

---

[92] This has given rise to endeavours to undertake a far-reaching reform of the system, by way of extensive amendments to the Convention. See, for instance, Steering Committee for Human Rights (CDDH), *Guaranteeing the long-term effectiveness of the European ECtHR of Human Rights, Final report containing proposals of the CDDH*, adopted by the CDDH on 4 April 2003, Committee of Ministers (2003)55 – 8 April 2003; The Council of Europe Steering Committee for Human Rights (CDDH), *Draft Recommendations and Resolution of the Committee of Ministers*, adopted by the CDDH at its 57th Meeting (5–8 April 2004); and, ultimately, Protocol no. 14 to the Convention.

[93] *Kudła v. Poland* (appl. no. 30210/96), Judgement (Grand Chamber), 26 October 2000, Reports 2000-XI, 197, para. 92.

[94] Garlicki (2002b); 11–14; Beernaert (2004), 905–907.

[95] *Brusco v. Italy* (appl. no. 69789/01), Decision (Second Section), 6 December 2001, Reports 2001-IX, 405. See Candela Soriano, this volume, Section D.2.a.bb.

only those that the Strasbourg court finds effective.[96] The ECtHR examined the remedies introduced by that Act and held that they are capable of both preventing the alleged violation of the right to have a case heard within a reasonable time and providing adequate redress, by way of compensation, for any violation of this right which has already occurred.[97] Hence, it was found to satisfy the effectiveness test. The Court further examined whether these remedies introduced by the 2004 Act were effective in respect of proceedings that had come to an end prior to bringing an application to the ECtHR. It found this to be the case in respect of persons who on 17 September 2004, the date of the Act's entry into force, could still lodge a civil action based on a tort with the relevant domestic courts. It concerned cases where less than three years (the statute of limitation for tort claims) had elapsed on that date from the day on which the allegedly lengthy proceedings had come to end.[98] In cases that had come to an end more than three years before 17 September 2004, the remedy provided for by the 2004 Act could not be resorted to and was thus not effective.[99]

Immediately after the *Kudła v. Poland* judgement, it was observed that it might bring a new type of complaints before the ECtHR: the applicants argued that the remedies made available at the national level to comply with Article 13 did not themselves meet the requirements of Article 6.[100] It seems that the importance of this type of objection against the national length remedies should not, at least for the time being, be overestimated. It should rather be said that the national length remedies suffer from certain growing pains in that the domestic courts do not examine the length complaints in a manner that is fully compatible with the Strasbourg criteria. However, the fact that such remedies are available should rather be seen as a positive phenomenon, with the task of harmonizing the relevant case law of domestic courts with the requirements of the ECtHR being left to the dialogue between the latter and the former.

Nevertheless, it should not be lost from sight that the operation of the 2004 Law leaves many questions thus far unanswered. One such difficulty is that it creates in fact more than one remedy: the specific length complaint which can only be lodged in respect of pending cases and, separately, a compensation claim.

---

[96] *Giacometti and 5 Others v. Italy* (appl. no. 34939/97), Decision (First Section), 8 November 2001, Reports 2001-XII, 137; *Giummarra and Others v. France* (appl. no. 61166/00), Decision (Third Section), 12 June 2001 (not reported); *Mifsud v. France* (appl. no. 57220/00), Decision (Grand Chamber), 11 September 2002, Reports 2002-VIII, 389; *Andrasik and Others v. Slovakia* (appl. nos 57984/99; 60237/00; 60242/00; 60679/00; 60680/00; 68563/01; 60226/00), Decision (Fourth Section), 22 October 2002, Reports 2002-IX, 357; *Brusco v. Italy*, ibid. See also Krzyżanowska-Mierzewska, (2002), 123–138.

[97] *Kudła v. Poland* (*supra* note 92) paras 158–159; *Krasuski v. Poland* (appl. no. 61444/00), Judgement (Fourth Section), 14 June 2005, Reports 2005-V, 1, para. 66; *Charzyński v. Poland* (appl. no. 15212/03), Decision (Fourth Section), 1 March 2005 (not reported).

[98] *Krasuski v. Poland*, ibid.

[99] *Ratajczyk v. Poland* (appl. no. 11215/02), Decision (Fourth Section), 31 May 2005 (not reported).

[100] Flauss (2002), 186.

Nevertheless, in light of the case law, as it stands at the time of writing, it seems that the ECtHR currently acts on the assumption that it is enough to lodge a simple length complaint in order to exhaust domestic remedies.

A further issue that has already arisen is the question of the amount of damages awarded by national courts in respect of the length complaints. Repeated criticisms have been voiced that they are too timid and that the amounts they award are often derisory.[101] It is said that the fact that the financial recompense for the length has to be paid from the budget of the court concerned, not from any specifically allocated funds in the State budget, makes judges reluctant to be more generous. Some suggestions have also been advanced that judges prefer to abstain from criticizing their colleagues in the context of length complaints, bearing in mind the overburdening of the judicial system. It is also informally reported by lawyers that they are not willing to bring length complaints on behalf of their clients for fear of putting their good relations with local courts and judges under strain.

Another effectiveness problem is that the courts sometimes find that the proceedings were excessively long, but do not award any money to the complainants. A further question related to the effectiveness of the length remedies concerns the compatibility of the method of examination of length complaints adopted by the 2004 Act with the length criteria consistently applied by the Strasbourg Court. The problem is that the construction of the 2004 Act seems to prevent the courts from examining the length of proceedings in their entirety.

The ECtHR has already considered that it could be useful to send a certain warning signal to the Polish courts in this respect. In one judgement, it criticized the fact that a domestic court had failed to examine the length of proceedings as a whole. It noted that its own approach consisted in examining the overall length of proceedings, covering all stages of the proceedings, which had not been done in this case.[102] It is true that the ECtHR carefully side-stepped the question whether the approach of domestic courts had resulted from an error of interpretation of the 2004 Act in the case under examination or whether it had systemic roots, i.e. in that this Act did not allow for the examination of the length of proceedings as a whole. The ECtHR exercised judicial restraint here, making it clear at the same time to the Polish authorities that cutting the duration of proceedings under examination into convenient pieces, may eventually give rise to serious problems, if the warning is not taken into consideration.

---

[101] E.g., Safjan (2005), 120.

[102] *Majewski v. Poland* (appl. no. 52690/99), Judgement (Fourth Section), 11 October 2005 (not yet reported).

c. Action for Damages Against the State

Both the 1964 Civil Code of and the 1960 Administrative Procedure Code contained provisions that could serve as a legal basis for the State's liability in tort.[103] These procedures were not found to constitute effective remedies to be tried before bringing the case to the ECtHR.[104]

d. Express Reliance on the Convention before Domestic Courts as Exhaustion Requirement

There is a strand of the ECtHR case law according to which, with a view to complying with the requirement of exhaustion of domestic remedies, it is sufficient that the complaints intended to be made subsequently in Strasbourg should have been raised, at least in substance, before the national authorities.[105] As a result, where the Convention forms a part of the national legal system, it is necessary for the applicant to invoke his or her Convention rights, more or less expressly, before national courts.[106] It is interesting to note that there has been so far no Polish case in which a mere failure to rely on the provisions of the Convention domestically would have led to the inadmissibility of the application on the ground of non-exhaustion. This seems to be a good policy, given that it is extremely rare for the parties to the proceedings in Poland to refer to the Convention in the domestic proceedings. It is rather as an afterthought that the Polish complainants lodge their applications with the ECtHR. It is, therefore, *post-hoc* that they formulate their complaints in the language of the ECHR. Had the ECtHR applied the requirement to rely on the Convention very strictly, it would have had to declare inadmissible almost 100 per cent of cases brought to it against Poland.

2. Slovakia

a. Individual Constitutional Complaint

Before the constitutional reform of 2001, there were two parallel kinds of constitutional complaints available. Pursuant to Article 127, the Constitutional Court was competent to review challenges (*ústavná stažnost*) to final decisions made by central Governmental authorities, local Governmental authorities and local self-governmental bodies in cases concerning alleged violations of fundamental rights and freedoms of citizens, unless the protection of such rights fell under

---

[103] Articles 417–418 (the latter derogated in 2001) of the Civil Code; Article 160 of the Administrative Procedure Code.

[104] *Skawińska v. Poland* (appl. no. 42096/98), Decision (Fourth Section), 4 March 2003 (not reported).

[105] *Castells v. Spain* (appl. no. 11798/85), Judgement (Chamber), 23 April 1992, Series A, Vol. 236, 19, para. 27; *Akdivar and Others v. Turkey* (appl. no. 21893/93), Judgement (Grand Chamber), 16 September 1996, Reports 1996-IV, 1192, 1210–1211, paras 65–69.

[106] E.g., *Peree v. the Netherlands* (appl. no. 34328/96), Decision (First Section), 17 November 1998 (not reported); *Klavdianos v. Greece* (appl. no. 38841/97), Decision (Third Section), 21 September 1999 (not reported).

the jurisdiction of another court. Article 130(3) provided that that Court could commence proceedings upon a petition (*podnet*) submitted by legal entities or individuals claiming a violation of their rights. The petition was a relevant remedy in cases in which a party alleged that a breach of fundamental rights had arisen in connection with situations other than issuing a final decision by public powers and where no other legal procedure was available to remedy the alleged violation. It could be directed against "violations of fundamental rights and freedoms caused by actions, by failure to act or by a decision given by the State authority".[107]

The "[a]pplication of the regulations on petition has caused considerable problems of interpretation in the experience of the Constitutional Court."[108] That Court consistently held that, in the context of proceedings under Article 130(3) of the Constitution, it lacked jurisdiction to draw practical consequences from its finding of a violation of a petitioner's constitutional right. It could neither grant damages to the person concerned nor impose a sanction on the public authority liable for the violation found. It considered that it was, therefore, for the authority concerned to provide subsequent redress to the person whose constitutional rights were violated.

This stance of the Constitutional Court caused some difficulties to the applicants bringing their cases to Strasbourg. In many early applications, the applicants first had recourse to the petition. The Commission had then regard to the view expressed by the Constitutional Court that it lacked jurisdiction to review decisions of ordinary courts and to award compensation. Hence, it repeatedly held that the six-month time limit should be counted from a final decision of such a court, not from the day on which the Constitutional Court dealt with the party's complaint. Many applicants found themselves in a situation in which their applications were rejected for such failure to comply with the six-month period.[109]

Later on, the ECtHR also observed that the proceedings instituted under Article 130(3) could not be considered an effective remedy because they were not directly available to the applicant. The proceedings were instituted only if the Constitutional Court decided to admit a petition. The ECtHR noted that even a decision in the petitioner's favour would not fully remedy the state of affairs, because the Constitutional Court lacked jurisdiction to quash the ordinary courts' decisions and to award damages. Finally, it noted that such a decision did not give rise to an automatic right to a retrial.[110] Hence, it was not an effective remedy in the ECHR sense of the term. On the other hand, the procedures instituted

---

[107] Constitutional Court, I US 19/96.

[108] Bröstl (2001), 157.

[109] *Preložnik v. the Slovak Republic* (appl. no. 25289/94), Decision (First Chamber), 15 January 1997 (not reported).

[110] E.g., *Feldek v. the Slovak Republik* (appl. no. 29032/95), Decision (Second Section), 15 June 2000, (not reported).

pursuant to Article 127 were found to be an effective remedy which had to be tried prior to bringing a case before the ECtHR.[111]

The provisions concerning individual constitutional remedies were amended in 2001. As a result, individuals and legal persons can currently complain under Article 127 of the Constitution to the Constitutional Court about a violation of their fundamental rights and freedoms which arose from a final decision or other measures taken by any public authority. The individual constitutional complaint became a principal instrument of protection of fundamental rights in the Slovak legal system.

It is noteworthy that Article 127(1) of the Constitution expressly states that this complaint can also be lodged with respect of alleged breach of human rights and fundamental freedoms enshrined in international treaties ratified by the Slovak Republic. Further, the broad powers of the Constitutional Court to examine an individual complaint should be emphasized: if the Court finds that the complaint is justified, it can give a decision to this effect and quash the impugned decision or measure. It may also order that the authority found to be at fault take the necessary action; or return the case to the authority concerned for further proceedings. In addition, it can request the authority concerned to abstain from violating fundamental rights and freedoms or, where appropriate, order it to restore the situation existing prior to the violation. Adequate financial satisfaction may also be granted to the victim.

Thus, "(…) an effective domestic tool of protection of fundamental rights and freedoms has been created. Its application will obviously be a precondition for submission of complaints at the European Court for Human Rights. Failure to apply it will also influence proceedings at this international authority for the protection of fundamental human rights and freedoms".[112] It has been said that "the objective of the extension of the scope of constitutional protection of natural and [legal] persons in the Slovak Republic was to bring constitutional regulations closer to international norms".[113] It is also noteworthy that the Constitutional Court, in its case law after 2001, gave many decisions in which it made use of its broad powers to remedy human rights breaches occasioned by decisions of lower authorities.[114] On the whole, in the proceedings instituted under Article 127 of the Constitution, the Constitutional Court found a violation of Article 6 of the Convention in 669 cases, violation of Article 5 of the Convention in 36 cases, violation of Article 3 of the Convention in three cases, violation of Article

---

[111] E.g., *Lacko and Others v. Slovakia* (appl. no. 47237/99), Decision (Fourth Section), 2 July 2002 (not reported).

[112] Mazak (2001), Executive Summary, 1.

[113] Bröstl (2001), 158 (text inserted by the author).

[114] E.g.,Constitutional Court, I US 122/03, III US 2002/02, I US 226/03, I US 139/02, III US 186/02, I US 59/03 – with respect to the right to a fair hearing; III US 169/03 – with respect to freedom of expression; I US 59/04 – with respect to freedom of assembly; III US 138/02, IV US 23/05, III US 60/04, II US 31/04 – with respect to the right to the peaceful enjoyment of one's possessions.

10 of the Convention in three cases, violation of Article 8 in three cases and violation of Article 1 of the Protocol no. 1 in one case.[115] The fact that the Slovak applicants currently have at their disposal an effective domestic remedy in respect of both remedial and compensatory character certainly makes the application to the ECtHR less attractive for them.

b. Action for Damages Against the State

In certain circumstances, a claim for compensation against the State was found to be a remedy which had to be exhausted prior to lodging a case with the Strasbourg organs. The Act no. 58/1969 on the liability of the State for damage caused by a State organ's decision or by its erroneous official action provided that the State was liable for damages caused by unlawful decisions delivered by a public authority in the context of, *inter alia*, civil proceedings.[116] However, this remedy could only be used in respect of decisions which had already been declared unlawful by domestic authorities.[117] Further, it did not allow for compensation to be awarded for damage of a non-pecuniary nature, the only exception being compensation for damage to health.[118]

The Act no. 514/2003 on Liability for Damage Caused in the Context of Exercise of Public Authority was adopted on 28 October 2003. It became operative on 1 July 2004 and replaced the State Liability Act of 1969.[119] The explanatory report to this Act provides that its purpose is to make the mechanism of compensation for damage caused by public authorities more effective and, also, to reduce the number of cases in which persons are obliged to seek redress before the ECtHR.[120] Additionally, the Act no. 385/2000 governs the civil and disciplinary liability of judges for unjustified delays in the conduct of judicial proceedings. However, in order to exhaust domestic remedies it is not necessary to have recourse to any procedures under this Act, but to remedies against excessive length, described below.

c. Remedies Against Excessive Length of Judicial Proceedings

In the wake of the *Kudła* judgement, mentioned earlier, the question arose whether the Slovak legal system provided an effective remedy in respect of the length of judicial proceedings. The ECtHR first examined whether the State Liability Act

---

[115] The data from the homepage of Constitutional Court, available at: http://www.concourt.sk.

[116] *Zákon o zodpovednosti za škodu spôsobenú rozhodnutím orgánu štátu alebo jeho nesprávnym úradným postupom,* 28 October 2003, Zbierka zakonov, č. 215/2003, p. 3966.

[117] *D.K. v. Slovakia* (appl. no. 41263/98), Decision (Fourth Section), 14 May 2002 (not reported).

[118] *Pavletić v. Slovakia* (appl. no. 39359/98), Decision (Fourth Section), 22 June 2004 (not reported); *Tám v. Slovakia* (appl. no. 50213/99), Judgement (Fourth Section), 22 June 2004 (not reported); *E.O. and V.P. v. Slovakia* (appl. nos 56193/00; 57581/00), Judgement (Fourth Section), 27 April 2004 (not reported); and *Z.M. and K.P. v. Slovakia* (appl. no. 50232/99), Judgement (Fourth Section), 17 May 2005 (not yet reported).

[119] *Zákon o zodpovednosti za škodu spôsobenú pri výkone verejnej moci a zmene niektorých zákonov.*

[120] *Tám v. Slovakia* (*supra* note 117)

of 1969, referred to above, offered any prospects of success to parties dissatisfied with the lengthy conduct of their cases. It found that a claim for compensation for non-pecuniary damage resulting there from could not be successful.[121] Likewise, a constitutional petition provided for at that time by Article 130 of the Constitution was not an effective remedy, given that the Constitutional Court could neither grant damages nor impose a sanction on the public authority responsible for the violation.[122]

Following the 2001 changes of the Slovak constitutional landscape, the ECtHR was called upon to ponder whether the individual constitutional complaint under Article 127 of the Constitution could be said to be effective. It had regard to the broad powers of the Constitutional Court when dealing with individual complaints.[123] The ECtHR was satisfied that the array of measures which can be taken by the Constitutional Court was effective, as they were of both a preventive and compensatory character.[124]

In compliance with the line of case law adopted following its decision in *Brusco v. Italy*[125], concerning the effectiveness of the Italian length remedy, the ECtHR departed from the principle that exhaustion of domestic remedies should be assessed by reference to the time when the application was lodged with it. It held that this rule was subject to exceptions "which may be justified by the particular circumstances of each case"[126] and found that nothing prevented the Slovak applicants from having recourse first to the new remedy provided for by Article 127 of the Constitution. It should be noted that, curiously, in the light of the now considerable body of case law, the mere fact that the case concerned the length of proceedings seemed to constitute such particular circumstances.

The Slovak length remedy also suffers from some growing pains. The first of them concerns the amounts awarded domestically for a breach of the reasonable time requirement. The applicant's status as a victim before the ECtHR depends, *inter alia*, on whether the redress afforded at the domestic level was adequate and sufficient having regard to just satisfaction as provided for under Article 41 of the ECHR.[127] In a case that set the tone for the examination of similar Slovak cases, the ECtHR noted the modest nature of the compensation granted to the par-

---

[121] *J.K. v. Slovakia* (appl. no. 38794/97), Decision (Second Section), 13 September 2001 (not reported); *Havala v. Slovakia* (appl. no. 47804/99), Decision (Second Section), 13 September 2001 (not reported).

[122] E.g., *Bánošová v. the Slovak Republic* (appl. no. 38798/97), Decision (Second Section), 27 April 2000 (not reported).

[123] Constitutional Court, e.g., no. III US 17/02-35; of 30 May 2002; no. I US 15/02 of 10 July 2002; ÚS 145/02; III ÚS 123/02.

[124] *Andrasik and Others v. Slovakia* (*supra* note 95); *Paška v. Slovakia* (appl. no. 41081/98), Decision (Fourth Section), 3 December 2002 (not reported).

[125] *Brusco v. Italy* (*supra* note 94).

[126] Ibid.

[127] E.g., *Andersen v. Denmark* (appl. no. 12860/87), Decision (Plenary), 3 May 1988 (not reported); *Fredriksen and Others v. Denmark* (appl. no. 12719/87), Decision, Commission, 3 May 1988, DR 56, 237; *Normann v. Denmark* (appl. no. 44704/98), Decision (Second Section), 14 June 2001

ties compared with the sums awarded for comparable delays in the ECHR case law.[128] The Strasbourg Court observed that the question "[w]hether the amount awarded may be regarded as reasonable, however, falls to be assessed in the light of all the circumstances of the case. These include not merely the duration of the proceedings in the specific case but the value of the award judged in the light of the standard of living in the State concerned, and the fact that under the national system compensation will in general be awarded and paid more promptly than would be the case if the matter fell to be decided by the Court (…)".[129] In light of these considerations, including the promptness of the findings and award made by the Constitutional Court, the ECtHR was of the view that the sum granted to the applicant could not be considered as unreasonable.[130] However, there is a possibility that a rather cryptic reference to the standard of living in the State concerned may serve as a loophole and eventually lead the ECtHR to accept as sufficient very low compensations awarded by domestic courts.

In addition to this, more serious problems can – and indeed do – arise when domestic courts find that the proceedings were too lengthy, but refuse, for various reasons, to award any compensation to the aggrieved party. In a case where the Constitutional Court found a breach of the right to have a case heard speedily, but refused to award compensation on the ground that the applicant had contributed to the length of proceedings, the ECtHR was not satisfied that the applicants were no longer victims of a breach of their rights.[131]

Another thorny issue is the compatibility of the criteria used by domestic authorities to gauge the length of proceedings against the criteria used by the ECtHR. As has been said above, the compatibility with these criteria would require that the whole period be taken into consideration. The practice of the Constitutional Court does not appear to be fully coherent. In some judgements, it has entertained constitutional petitions pertaining to the excessive length of proceedings only where the proceedings complained of were pending before the authority liable for the alleged violation at the moment when such petitions or complaints were lodged.[132] In other cases, it examined the length of the proceedings taken as a whole, from the beginning. In that connection, the ECtHR referred to the established principle that "the ECHR is intended to guarantee rights

---

(not reported); and *Jensen and Rasmussen v. Denmark* (appl. no. 52620/99), Decision (First Section), 20 March 2003 (not reported).

[128] *Bako v. Slovakia* (appl. no. 60227/00), Decision (Fourth Section), 15 March 2005 (not reported).

[129] Ibid.

[130] Ibid. See also *Dubjaková v. Slovakia* (appl. no. 67299/01), Decision (Fourth Section), 19 October 2004 (not reported).

[131] *Palgutová v. Slovakia* (appl. no. 9818/02), Judgement (Fourth Section), 17 May 2005 (not yet reported); *Gàbriška v. Slovakia* (appl. no. 3661/04), Judgement (Fourth Section), 13 December 2005 (not yet reported).

[132] E.g., Constitutional Court, I. ÚS 34/99, II. ÚS 55/02, III. ÚS 20/00, I. ÚS 29/02, II. ÚS 55/02, IV. ÚS 96/02, II. ÚS 138/02, ÚS 139/02, I. ÚS 161/02, IV.ÚS 176/03.

that are not theoretical or illusory, but rights that are practical and effective".[133] Transposed to the assessment of the effectiveness of length remedies, this principle entails that the remedy under Article 127 of the Constitution, as in force from 1 January 2002, did not offer the applicant reasonable prospects of success in seeking adequate and sufficient redress in these cases where the duration of domestic proceedings was cut into convenient bits and pieces instead of being seen as a whole.[134] The ECtHR observed that "where courts at different levels of jurisdiction dealt with the same case, applicants should formulate their complaint under Article 127 of the Constitution in a manner giving the Constitutional Court the opportunity to examine the overall length of the proceedings (...) The Court has reached this conclusion despite the fact that, as the applicant in the present case objected, the relevant practice of the Constitutional Court has not been uniform".[135]

It is to be noted that the Constitutional Court adopted consistent case law to the effect that victims of criminal offences, claiming compensation in criminal proceedings against the perpetrator, could not seek compensation for excessive length of such proceedings.[136] Nonetheless, the ECtHR, having regard to its case law,[137] held that the guarantees of Article 6 under its civil head should also apply to such proceedings.[138]

d. Express reliance on the Convention before domestic courts as exhaustion requirement

In cases against Slovakia, the Court has been, similarly to its practice in Polish cases, very circumspect when penalizing the applicants for their failure to rely on the Convention in domestic proceedings.

3. Comparison and Conclusions

In both countries, the legislator made considerable efforts to introduce an individual constitutional complaint remedy for alleged breaches of rights guaranteed by the Constitution. The difference between the countries lies in the time

---

[133] *Airey v. Ireland* (appl. no. 6289/73), Judgement (Chamber), 9 October 1979, Series A, Vol. 32.

[134] E.g., *Jakub v. Slovakia* (appl. no. 2015/02), Judgement (Fourth Section), 28 February 2006 (not yet reported); *Jenčová v. Slovakia* (appl. no. 70798/01), Judgement (Fourth Section), 4 May 2006 (not yet reported); *Malejčík v. Slovakia* (appl. no. 62187/00), Judgement (Fourth Section), 31 January 2006 (not yet reported).

[135] *Orel v. Slovakia* (appl. no. 67035/01), Judgement (Fourth Section), 9 January 2007, para. 72 (not yet reported); see also *Šidlová v. Slovakia* (appl. no. 50224/99), Judgement (Fourth Section), 26 September 2006 (not yet reported), para. 53, with further references.

[136] Constitutional Court, IV ÚS 4/02, IV ÚS 166/03, IV ÚS 92/04, IV. ÚS 52/04.

[137] E.g., *Perez v. France* (appl. no. 47287/99), Judgement (Grand Chamber), 12 February 2004, paras 67–70, Reports 2004-I, 119; *Pfleger v. the Czech Republic* (appl. no. 58116/00), Judgement (Second Section), 27 July 2004, paras 37–41 (not reported).

[138] *Krumpel and Krumpelová v. Slovakia* (appl. no. 56195/00), Judgement (Fourth Section), 5 July 2005, paras 39–41, (not yet reported).

frame during which this remedy was created: in Slovakia, there was an immediate constitutional agreement that such a remedy was needed when the 1992 Constitution of the new country was adopted. In Poland, despite the fact that the Constitutional Court, created in 1986, was already a well-established institution at the time of the ratification of the Convention, the immediate introduction of such a remedy was not considered necessary. It was eventually set up under the Constitution adopted in 1997. The period from 1993 to 1997 should, therefore, have been seen as a window of opportunity for the Polish applicants, who during this time were not obliged to make a constitutional complaint before lodging an application with the ECtHR.

In Slovakia, the ECtHR quickly identified shortcomings of the individual constitutional complaint as a mechanism of vindicating individual rights as it existed before 2001. These shortcomings were remedied by the constitutional revision of 2001, following which the Constitutional Court was vested with broad powers to improve the situation of a successful complainant and the system of individual constitutional remedies was simplified.

It took the ECtHR much longer to examine the effectiveness of the Polish constitutional complaint. Surprisingly enough, it was essentially considered as a remedy to be tried prior to lodging an application under the ECHR. The Strasbourg Court did not mind that this remedy could not result in having an individual decision quashed on account of it being based on provisions found to be unconstitutional, nor was it concerned by the fact that under Polish law separate proceedings had to be launched in order to obtain any individualized result. It did not take into consideration the fact that no compensation could be obtained as a result of successful constitutional proceedings. Hence, the approach of the ECtHR in relation to the national constitutional remedies does not seem to be consistent. It appears to be the same factors that led the Court to conclude that the Slovak remedy prior to 2001 lacked effectiveness, while the Polish remedy introduced in 1997 was effective. It is difficult to justify this difference, especially when the ECtHR weighed identical considerations in respect of both countries. The analysis of these factors led it to different conclusions, creating thereby a discrepancy in its case law is to the detriment of the Polish applicants.

Following the *Kudła v. Poland*[139] judgement in which the ECtHR emphasized the need for specific national remedies against excessive length of judicial proceedings, both countries reacted by promptly adopting these remedies. In Slovakia, the case law of the Constitutional Court made it clear that the constitutional remedy adopted in 2001 could also be used in respect of excessive length complaints and now it has became a routine practice of that Court to examine such complaints. In Poland, a different option was chosen, namely that of a specific length remedy provided by a special statute adopted in 2004. In the light of the case law of the domestic courts, both the Polish and Slovak remedies are tainted

---

[139] *Kudła v. Poland* (*supra* note 92).

by shortcomings, in particular concerning the modest amounts of compensation awarded for the excessive length of proceedings and the fact that in either country the practice of examining the length of proceedings does not always seem to be compatible with the criteria established by the Strasbourg court. For the time being, the ECtHR has been lenient towards the domestic legal systems and limited itself to pointing out certain shortcomings in the practical application of length remedies by the Polish and Slovak authorities, without challenging their effectiveness as a whole.

G. Overview of the Case Law

1. Poland

The high expectations connected to the ECHR becoming binding on Poland were realized when Poland very quickly became a high case-count country.[140] When seen against the number of the population (38,191,000), there were 1.52 Polish applications for 10,000 inhabitants in 2004 and 1.32 in 2005. Only Romania and Croatia had a higher ratio (1.84 and 1.57 respectively), Slovenia having an identical one.[141]

At first sight, it seems that the mere size of the Polish caseload before the ECtHR over the years indicates that in the 90's Poland suffered from serious deficiencies regarding its human rights situation. However, even the briefest overview of the judgements of the ECtHR in cases against Poland refutes such a superficial assumption. There have been virtually no cases which would suggest that Poland was a particularly deficient human rights country throughout this time, as there were, so far, no cases indicating serious breaches of the right to liberty, or any cases that would suggest political oppression.

It is a striking feature of the Polish case law that it has been, so far, largely dominated by two issues: length of proceedings and excessive length of detention on remand. Out of 345 judgements given until the end of 2006, as many as 262 concerned the former issue, while 81 related to the latter. This justified an opinion that Poland is essentially a "length country". It is true that such a prevalence of "length judgements", in which the ECtHR found no violation of the right to a hearing within a reasonable time in only seventeen cases, testifies to a systemic problem. The same can be said about the length of detention on remand cases. They suggest that, while procedural guarantees of the right of liberty were duly

---

[140] In 1992, the year of the ratification, 240 applications were lodged with the Commission, the number of new cases exceeded one thousand in 1995. In subsequent years the numbers were as follows: in 1996 – 1127, 1997 – 1318, in 1998 – 1914, in 1999 – 2895, in 2000 – 3175, in 2001 – 3429, in 2002 – 4521, in 2003 – 5359, in 2004 – 5796. In 2005, there was, for the first time, a slight decrease in numbers with 4744 new applications lodged, and in 2006, there were 4470 new ones.

[141] San Marino's ratio was 1,71 per million, but for obvious reasons it must be seen as a special case.

put in place shortly after the ratification, using detention on remand for long periods once it has been ordered in the context of criminal proceedings does not seem to be problematic for the judges. As to the lawfulness of detention, there has been only a fraction of cases in which detention was found unlawful: out of eighteen judgements concerning such complaints, in sixteen a violation of Article 5(1) of the ECHR was found.

The procedure governing the imposition and maintenance of detention on remand was found problematic in cases concerning mostly the early 90's, when provisions of the Code of Criminal Procedure pre-dating the ratification were still in force. There were sixteen such judgements in which the ECtHR found violations.

The ECtHR has often stated that the right to a fair trial holds a prominent place in a democratic society. This importance of the respect for the tenets of fair hearing is not borne out by the Polish case law, in which a mere 21 judgements concerned fair hearing issues, either in the context of criminal or civil proceedings. This seems to be accounted for by the characteristics of the Polish legal culture in which no excessive attention is paid by the general public to the fairness and transparency of procedures, and procedural as opposed to substantive justice is held in low esteem. There were eighteen violations found in these cases.

Thirty judgements concerned the right to respect for private and family life, home and correspondence. Many of them, however, pertained to the rather mundane issue of the compatibility of monitoring the prisoners' correspondence with the ECtHR, a question that is not very high on the agenda of the applicants, who complained primarily about the outcome of criminal proceedings against them, rather than about the excessive curiosity of the prison authorities. It is interesting to note that only in two cases did the ECtHR find that the applicants' right to lodge a petition had also been breached.[142] The ease with which Poles, including prisoners, complain to Strasbourg seems to show that the freedom of expression is well established in the country. This is also apparent in the small number of cases concerning the freedom of expression: there have been six such judgements so far, with violations found in five of them. Freedom of association issues have thus far been examined in only one case, in which neither the Chamber nor the Grand Chamber found a violation. This is hardly surprising, given that a vibrant third sector was created in Poland during the 90's.

The right to the peaceful enjoyment of one's possessions gave rise to only seven judgements. Despite the fact that violations were found in all of them, this low number could indicate that the public authorities tend to respect guarantees of individual ownership. On the other hand, it may also suggest that the Polish complainants to Strasbourg simply do not know how to argue property cases. In

---

[142] *Drozdowski v. Poland* (appl. no. 20841/02), Judgement (Fourth Section), 6 December 2006 (not yet reported); *Maksym v. Poland* (appl. no. 14450/02), Judgement (Fourth Section), 19 December 2006 (not yet reported).

most cases a finding of a violation of Article 1 of Protocol no. 1 by the ECtHR hinges on the examination whether a fair balance has been struck between the individual and the public interest. It is true that the proportionality principle, in so far as it concerns the permissible scope of restrictions imposed on individual rights, is well known and often relied on in the case law of the Polish Constitutional Court. However, it is obviously difficult for an average Polish applicant, who is usually not legally represented, to make such a balancing argument in his or her case in order to convince the ECtHR.

Contrary to many countries in the region, Poland did not enact any legislation specifically aimed at redressing wrongs committed by the communist regime in the area of property rights: "[t]here is therefore no specific legal framework to mitigate the effects of certain infringements resulting from the deprivations of property. However, persons whose property was expropriated, or their legal successors, may institute administrative proceedings under Article 155 of the Code of Administrative Procedure, in order to claim that the expropriation decisions should be declared null and void as having been in breach of the laws laying down criteria for expropriation, as applicable at the material time. If it is established that the contested decision was contrary to the legislation applicable at the time of the expropriation, the administrative authority shall declare it null and void."[143] There is no specific entitlement to compensation for an unlawful expropriation. As a result, the former owners have no substantive restitution claim under domestic law and the ECtHR considers that the procedural claim to have the old expropriation decision reexamined does not attract the guarantees of Article 1 of Protocol no. 1 to the ECHR.[144]

In a 2003 article, written ten years after the Polish ratification, it was charged that there was "a conspicuous absence" of leading judgements in the voluminous Polish case law as it stood at that time (with the exception of *Kudła*).[145] The authors made an attempt at identifying reasons for this state of affairs. In connection with this, it is interesting to explore how a case becomes leading. Is this classification due to the issue that is brought by the applicant or to the reasoning that the ECtHR applies to the case? It could be argued for the latter, for it is doubtful that it is necessarily the inherent characteristics of a case that make it leading.[146] Further questions formulated in this respect were the following: "Could it be that Poland is perceived to have to be a passive recipient of European human rights law? Rather than being a motor within this law – which it could potentially be,

---

[143] *Potocka and Others v. Poland* (appl. no. 33776/96), Judgement (Fourth Section), 4 October 2001, Reports 2001-X, 49, para. 30.

[144] *J.S. and A.S. v. Poland* (appl. no. 40732/98), Judgement (Fourth Section), 24 May 2005 (not yet reported).

[145] Dembour and Krzyzanowska-Mierzewska (2004b), 517–543.

[146] Benoît-Rohmer has once observed in a footnote that "the Strasbourg judge shows less interest when examining an application from a CEE country" in Benoît-Rohmer (2002), 12, note 31. It is interesting how this bold statement could have been backed by hard evidence.

given the sheer number of Polish cases – is Poland expected to assume the role of good pupil, ready to absorb lessons? Our hypothesis is that the way the Polish case law has been developed is not unrelated to this part of the western-eastern dynamics which we would call the dynamics of condescension."[147]

Leaving aside answers to these interesting questions – which, if pursued, would shed an interesting light on the mechanisms of reception of the ECHR in the so-called "new democracies" in Europe – it should be noted that the situation has significantly changed; not only in respect of Poland, but also in respect of the case law regarding these new democracies. There has been an outburst of ECtHR activity in the last couple of years, characterized by a dramatic increase in the number of judgements and decisions handed down in cases brought against the Central European Countries. As regards Polish cases, there have recently been a number of cases that can be termed as "leading" in the proper sense of the term, i.e. namely cases establishing principles, which in turn can be applied to other cases.[148] Further, the application of a pilot judgement procedure to Polish cases – and Polish cases pioneered in this category[149] – radically changed the assessment of the Polish case law as boring and uninteresting. Moreover, there has been a recent influx of cases raising interesting human rights issues of both an individual and a systemic character, addressing problems that figure high on the agenda of domestic legal and political debates. Hence, the relevance and importance of the ECHR can grow if the ECtHR manages to speed up the examination of these cases.[150]

2. Slovakia

To the extent that statistics can be considered as a reliable indicator of the popularity enjoyed by the ECHR among the general public in any given country – and, indeed, annual statistics of cases newly brought to Strasbourg can be viewed as an accurate indicator of popularity – the Slovak applicants do not seem to be overly interested in invoking the ECtHR.[151] Until the end of 2006, the ECtHR

---

[147] Dembour and Krzyzanowska-Mierzewska (2004b), 542.

[148] *Kudła v. Poland* (*supra* note 92); *Gorzelik and Others v. Poland* (appl. no. 44158/98), Judgement (Grand Chamber), 17 February 2004, Reports 2004-I, 219.

[149] *Broniowski v. Poland* (appl. no. 31443/96), Judgement (Grand Chamber), 22 June 2004, Reports 2004-V, 1; *Hutten-Czapska v. Poland* (appl. no. 35014/97), Judgement (Grand Chamber), 19 June 2006 (not yet reported).

[150] It has already been noted above that many Polish cases become, after they have been pending for years before the ECtHR, of a historical character. Furthermore, there is currently a considerable backlog of Polish cases pending before the ECtHR in which such interesting issues might potentially be involved. If the ECtHR, following internal changes in organization of work and, possibly, also the entry into force of Protocol no. 14, eventually finds a way to tackle these cases soon – it will be then that an application brought to the ECtHR by a Polish applicant will become a fully-fledged instrument of conscious legal advocacy and legal change – alongside continuing to be what it become early on and still remains, an instrument of popular justice.

[151] In 1993, 36 Slovak applications were brought to the attention of the Commission. This figure rose to 100 in 1994. In subsequent years the numbers were as follows: in 1995 – 83 new applica-

gave 112 judgements on the merits in cases brought against Slovakia. In five of these cases it was found that there had been no violation. Following a friendly settlement, seventeen cases were struck out of the list.

In 2005, in 25 out of 28 cases the ECtHR delivered judgements in which it found a violation concerning a breach of the right to have one's case heard within a reasonable time. Such a proportion of length of proceedings cases shows the magnitude of the problem in Slovakia. Numerous academic articles published recently have discussed this issue.[152] It was also noted that in 2005 "ninety percent of complaints [brought to the Office of the Human Rights Ombudsman] concerned delays in court proceedings",[153] despite the fact that the Constitution expressly guarantees a right to have one's case heard without unjustified delay.[154] The ECtHR itself observed that "the information before the Court indicates that the excessive length of proceedings has been a widespread problem in the national legal system, and several hundreds of applications against Slovakia in which the applicants allege a violation of the 'reasonable time' requirement have been filed with the Court".[155]

In two cases concerning the lawfulness of detention, a violation was found in both. Various procedural problems concerning the imposition and the maintenance of detention on remand were examined by the ECtHR in four cases where violations of Article 5(4) of the ECHR were found.

As regards the right to a fair hearing and access to a court, the ECtHR gave fourteen judgements in which it found violations in ten cases. Four judgements concerned the right to respect to private and family life, home and correspondence, with three violations found. The observance of freedom of expression by Slovak public authorities was examined in the context of six cases. The ECtHR established that there were violations in five of them. In cases where the applicants alleged that they had no right to an effective remedy guaranteed by Article 13 of the ECHR, twelve judgements were handed down and in eleven of them violations were found. In cases where the applicants complained that they were discriminated against in the enjoyment of their Convention rights, the State was found to be at fault in one of the three judgements given. Finally, in five cases in which the right to the peaceful enjoyment of possession was at stake, the ECtHR found violations in two of them. There were no judgements concerning Articles 2 (right to life), 3 (prohibition of torture and inhuman or degrading treatment) or of freedom of religion and conscience, peaceful assembly or association.

---

tions, in 1996 – 165, 1997 – 160, in 1998 – 154, in 1999 – 227, in 2000 – 479, in 2001 – 546, in 2002 – 432, in 2003 – 539, in 2004 – 484. In 2005, 478 new cases were submitted to the Court. When seen against a number of population (5,380,0000), there were 0.6 registered applications per 10,000 of inhabitants in 2003 and 0,7 in 2004.

[152] E.g., Urban (2004); Bàlintova (2005); Pirosikova (2005).

[153] U.S. State Department Human Rights Report 2005 (*supra* note 77) (text inserted by the author).

[154] Article 48(2) of the Constitution.

[155] *Andrasik and Others v. Slovakia,* (*supra* note 95).

Slovakia enacted a number of statutes specifically designed by the Federal Republic to redress acts of injustice committed by the communist regime.[156] The grant of various kinds of redress provided for by these statutes was conditional on certain substantive requirements and a number of cases before the ECHR organs concerned decisions and judgements given on the basis of this legislation.[157] The outcome of these cases could rarely be seen as satisfying for the applicants, as they essentially followed its stand that deprivation of property is essentially an instantaneous act which did not give rise to a continuing situation of deprivation of rights.

In the 90's, after the populist Government of Vladimir Meciar acceded to power in 1992, the media sometimes described Slovakia as a country whose human rights performance was watched very closely and on some occasions its record was found to be "uneven. [In 2002,] Roma faced continued violence, discrimination, and police abuse, occasionally with fatal consequences. The State response to discrimination was inadequate, with Roma, gays and lesbians, and domestic violence victims lacking full legal protection. A punitive criminal defamation law impinged on free expression. Reforms were also needed to curb the trade in weapons with human rights abusers",[158] stated the Human Rights Watch Report in 2002. This picture, viewed in light of the ECtHR case law, does not appear to be entirely fair. Admittedly, there are well-defined problematic areas which emerge in any serious analysis of the situation in Slovakia. In its 2005 Human Rights Report, the US Department of State averred that the Government generally respected the human rights of its citizens, but that there were problems in some areas. These can be said to arise in respect of "lengthy pre-trial detention, restrictions on freedom of religion, corruption in the judiciary, local government, and health sector, violence against women and children, trafficking in persons, societal discrimination and violence against Roma".[159]

However, it can be argued that the limelight shone on the human rights situation in Slovakia was, essentially caused by undeniable problems that arose in the areas of the country with substantial Roma populations. In particular, the much-publicized cases of forced sterilization of Roma women in Eastern Slo-

---

[156] The Judicial Rehabilitation Act 1990, *Sbirka Zakonu, 1990-04-23, no. 25, 518–52;* the Land Ownership Act 1991, Act no. 229/1991, *Sbirka Zakonu, 1991-06-24, no. 45, 1062–1071.*

[157] See e.g., *Brežny and Brežny v. Slovakia* (appl. no. 23131/93), Decision (Plenary), Commission, 4 March 1996, DR 85, 65–83.; *Gasparetz v. the Slovak Republic* (appl. no. 24506/94), Decision (Second Chamber), 28 June 1993 (not reported); *Nemanova v. the Slovak Republic* (appl. no. 32683/96), Decision (Second Chamber), Commission, 14 January 1998 (not reported); *Seidlova v. the Slovak Republic* (appl. no. 25461/94), Decision (Second Chamber), Commission, 6 September 1995 (not reported); ECHR, *Kopecký v. Slovakia* (appl. no. 44912/98), Judgement (Grand Chamber), 28 September 2004, Reports 2004-IX, 125; *Bzdusek v. Slovakia* (appl. no. 48817/99), Decision (Fourth Section), 16 November 2004 (not reported); *Csepyová v. Slovakia* (appl. no. 67199/01), Decision (Fourth Section), 8 April 2003 (not reported).

[158] Human Rights Watch, Slovakia, World Report 2002, http://hrw.org/wr2k2/europe17.html (text inserted by the author).

[159] U.S. State Department, Human Rights Report 2005 (*supra* note 77).

vakia generated widespread indignation.[160] While not denying the reality and seriousness of these problems, it can also be said that there are no grounds on which it can be seriously advanced that Slovakia is a particularly deficient human rights country and that it stands out in the Central and Eastern Europe. This is an assumption which has sometimes been too readily made.[161] Furthermore, the populist tenor of many statements made in Slovak internal politics in 1990 made the public opinion more wary of the human rights assessment record of the country. However, it seems that this domestic political atmosphere did not find its more concrete expression in serious human rights breaches warranting findings of ECHR violations by the Strasbourg Court.

3. Comparison and Conclusions

Poland has very quickly become one of the major clients of the ECHR system and the number of Polish cases brought to the ECtHR every year since the ratification remains consistently high. In contrast, and taking into account the difference in the size of population, the popular interest of Slovak would-be applicants in taking a case to Strasbourg has been remarkably lower, as can be inferred from the relevant figures. There has been no rapid increase immediately after the ratification in the interest of the Slovak applicants in bringing cases to Strasbourg, as opposed to the Polish figures, which sharply increased from one year to another. This seems to indicate that the relationship between the general public and the ECHR in these countries is remarkably different. In Poland, it is perceived as a last resort and a more or less regular means of seeking popular justice. In Slovakia, it is viewed as a quirky oddity and not normally considered by dissatisfied users of the legal system as an obvious step to be taken immediately after a disappointing judgement of a domestic court. Poland's somewhat embarrassing rise to ECHR stardom poses many intriguing questions, both as to the human rights situation in the country and as to the way in which those rights are perceived by the general public. The striking fact that Poland became one of the biggest clients of the Convention system is certainly significant.

A question arises with regard to what this tells us about the human rights situation in Poland: "[A] standard assumption is often made that the less developed the standard of human rights in a Member State, the more applications in respect of this country can be expected in Strasbourg."[162] However, it has also been noted by the same author that it would clearly be simplistic to say that the bigger the influx of cases from a given country, the more likely it is that respect for human rights in that country is low. There is a much more complex interplay between

---

[160] See, for example, the home page of the European Roma Rights Center, http://www.errc.org.

[161] It can be argued that the human rights culture in Slovakia is not deeply entrenched, given that it does not seem to provide effective guidance to the official authorities when dealing with Roma, who are considered to be different from the rest of the society (this is covered by the concept of human rights).

[162] Keller (2005), 347.

a situation in any given country and the number and character of cases that are brought from this country to the ECtHR. The fact that the popularity of the ECHR in any given country would fuel further popularity should be taken into consideration; cases brought before the ECtHR and reported in the press undoubtedly generate further cases in the country. The high number of Polish cases is certainly, at least in part, a result of this phenomenon, belonging rather to the sphere of public communication than of law. It therefore seems that neither the large number of the Polish applications nor the low number of the Slovak ones are by themselves sufficient for drawing any easy conclusions as to the respect for human rights in these countries.

This immediate and lasting popularity of the ECHR in Poland has contributed to its organs being flooded with Polish cases, most of them often politely referred to as being of a non-meritorious character. If the influx of Polish cases had "been of a less haphazard and 'popular' character, and had (...) been stemmed at the domestic level by more effective domestic remedies, it arguably would have served better the purpose of the Convention as a system of collective protection of human rights, based on the principle of subsidiarity"[163] and essentially aimed at providing the impulse for legal reform in important human rights issues.

As a result of this haphazard character, the development of the Polish case law before the ECHR institutions has long been characterized by the absence of many issues that raise significant human rights concerns in Poland. There has been, and still is, a certain lack of consistency between these topics, which are hotly disputed domestically, and the applications that eventually make it to the Strasbourg Court. This large area of what can be termed "missing issues" accompanied by thousands of cases that at the end of the day prove to be inadmissible, is an important feature of the Polish presence before the ECtHR.

This Polish popularity is both a negative and a positive phenomenon. It certainly does not arise out of the widespread practice of domestic violations of human rights. For a long time, the decisions and judgements of the ECHR were rather of a fine-tuning nature, applying principles hitherto developed in the older case law to minor issues. On the positive side, the popularity of the ECHR testifies to the fact that human rights have become a yardstick by which citizens measure the acts and legitimacy of the Polish public powers.   Seen in the light of the number of applications brought before the Strasbourg Court, the ECHR has been received much less enthusiastically by the Slovaks, and its popularity did not take off as rapidly as in Poland. The general public does not seem to share the assumption that the ECHR mechanism can be helpful in solving various legal and social problems that can be couched in human rights terms. As a result, the issue of the negative impact of the popularity of the ECHR on the effectiveness of the system does not arise in respect of the Slovak cases.

As regards the substance of the Polish and Slovak cases before the Court, the

---

[163] Dembour and Krzyżanowska-Mierzewska (2004a), 523.

obvious similarity between both countries is that a large part of the judgements concern the difficult issue of the length of judicial proceedings. This seems to reflect accurately certain difficulties shared by both countries in reforming their judicial systems, despite their recent efforts to make the administration of justice quicker and more effective.[164]

However, it can be argued that in both countries, despite the very real problems of efficiency that their judicial systems grapple with, there is a certain over-representation of "length" issues, accompanied by an arguable under-representation of other fair hearing issues. It should be noted that "the procedural rules of the Court favour an over-representation of the length issue in the case law. Neither the Convention nor the Rules of Court determine the order in which the Court examines cases. Length cases, which do not raise difficult legal problems, are likely to be ready for examination within a much shorter time than cases which give rise to more serious difficulties".[165] The large number of length cases cannot serve as a sound basis to assume that there are no fair hearing problems in the proceedings before national courts. However, a certain degree of widespread procedural culture is necessary for these cases to be seen by the public as problematic. It is posited that in neither Poland nor Slovakia is the attachment of the general public to the issues of procedural fairness and transparency sufficient to generate many fair hearing cases before the ECtHR.

One striking difference between the countries is that Poland seems to have a serious problem of excessive length of detention on remand, which does not exist in Slovakia. This might indicate that respect for personal liberty does not figure high on the agenda of the Polish authorities. In view of the fact that both countries have a significant record relative to the excessive length of judicial proceedings, this is all the more surprising, since there is often a correlation between the latter and cases of prolonged detention. One might, therefore, expect that the performance of both countries as regards detention on remand would be the same – which is far from being the case, as length of criminal proceedings does not feature prominently among the Slovak "length" cases, the gist of the problem being manifest in the proceedings before civil courts.

The case law concerning transitional justice issues linked with restitution of property expropriated by the communist regimes in both countries is markedly different in the two nations. This difference originates from radically different stands taken by national legislators. In Slovakia, restitution legislation was adopted, whereas Poland chose not to adopt any restitution laws: "An unfortunate paradox arises. Poland, which has chosen not to do anything on a systemic scale to remedy the wrongs committed by the communist regime as regards property rights, is left without any obligation – either domestic or international. (...) In stark contrast, states which have tried to redress past injustice by creating legal

---

[164] See *infra* Sections H.1.a. and H.1.b.
[165] Dembour and Krzyżanowska-Mierzewska (2004b), 520.

frameworks for restitution and/or compensation are, as it were doubly penalized. First, they are under the admittedly self-imposed but nonetheless onerous domestic law obligation to restore property or to pay compensation. Second, they face the additional burden of running the risk of being found in violation of the Convention if they do not comply in these proceedings with the procedural guarantees of Article 6."[166] Slovakia, which chose a courageous approach and adopted rehabilitation and restitution acts, finds itself in this difficult position.

In the absence – so far – of serious cases concerning political oppression as well as freedoms of religion and conscience, expression, assembly and association, it seems that neither Poland nor Slovakia are countries in which serious human rights problems have arisen.

Furthermore, the limelight in which Slovakia found itself in the 90's, following the ascension to power of a populist Government that sparked criticism on the part of the international community with regard to the human rights situation, is now mirrored in Poland, where a populist Government has been put into place following the 2005 Parliamentary elections. It remains to be seen whether this change of political climate will find its expression in any alarming cases brought to the attention of the Strasbourg Court.

In any event, in both countries the cases that end up before the Strasbourg Court seem to have been lodged somewhat at random. This must be, at least in part, attributed to the fact that very few Slovak and Polish applicants are legally represented when bringing their cases to Strasbourg. In other words, the judgements and decisions given by the Court do not fully reflect human right issues which exist domestically and which could indeed give rise to concern. By and large, what the ECtHR deals with in its judgements does not concur with what is regarded domestically as important human rights problems. There are, therefore, many missing human rights issues in both Poland and Slovakia which could usefully be examined by the Court, but which do not find their way to Strasbourg. For example, it was mentioned above that the case law in respect of both countries has been marked by a relative absence of fair hearing issues. It should also be noted that the subject-matter of cases brought against any given Contracting State of the ECHR is not determined by what human rights specialists see as important or interesting, but what the applicants perceive as such. This is valid for both Slovakia and Poland where the interest in the mechanism of the ECHR is not lawyer-driven.

Finally, the cases which are eventually examined by the ECtHR must first go through the filtering mechanism of the domestic remedies criterion. Slovak applicants, having at their disposal an efficient constitutional complaint mechanism capable of remedying their situation concretely and promptly, are less interested in a far away court than the Poles, whose access to the Constitutional Court was tailored by the legislator in a much less useful manner with regard to indi-

---

[166] Ibid., 530.

vidualized redress. This is perhaps the factor which, after the 2001 constitutional reform of, makes the situation of an individual faced with the public authorities breaching his/her rights in Poland and in Slovakia so different.

H. The ECtHR Case Law and its Effects in the National Legal Systems

1. General measures

a. Poland

In anticipation of problems that might be caused by the failure of certain provisions of Polish criminal procedure to comply with the ECHR standards, important amendments were enacted in the early 90's. They provided in particular for judicial decisions to order detention on remand and for certain time limits for which it could be maintained. These changes "were very much in the spirit of the Convention".[167] Further changes were introduced by the new Code of Criminal Procedure which entered into force on 1 September 1998 (and replaced the previous Code enacted in 1969), in particular to ensure that a person deprived of liberty be brought promptly before a judge.

Following judgements of the ECtHR in cases concerning Poland, various general measures were adopted by the Polish authorities in order to avoid future repetitive violations in similar cases. As a follow-up to the only Polish case where a breach of Article 3 was found (because the imprisoned applicant had been ordered to strip naked in order to be allowed to vote),[168] on 31 October 2003 the Ministry of Justice adopted an Ordinance on safety in prisons. It was designed to provide more clear criteria with regard to the circumstances in which a body search could be ordered in a prison setting.

In the *Belziuk* case,[169] the ECtHR found a violation in that the applicant, in criminal proceedings against him, had been refused leave to attend a hearing held by the second-instance court, which is competent to rule on both the facts and the law. The public prosecutor had been present, while the applicant had been neither present nor represented. The Court found a violation of Articles 6(1) and 6(3)(c) ECHR on account of lack of equality of arms. When in 1997 the new Code of Criminal Procedure was enacted, it was the intention of the drafters to bring the criminal procedure in line with requirements of European law.[170] Article 451 of the new Code provided that an appellate court could order that an

---

[167] Keller (2005), 286.

[168] *Iwańczuk v. Poland* (appl. no. 25196/94), Judgement (Fourth Section), 15 November 2001 (not reported).

[169] *Belziuk v. Poland* (appl. no. 23103/93), Judgement (Chamber), 25 March 1998, Reports 1998-II 558.

[170] Explanatory Report to the Bill: Code of Criminal Procedure - Parliamentary working paper, second mandate, no. 1276. For an acknowledgement of the direct influence of this case on the content of the new provisions, see Commentary to the Code of Criminal Procedure (Warsaw, 2001), at 831.

accused detained on remand be brought to the courtroom to attend a hearing. In 1999, the Supreme Court interpreted the relevant provisions in a manner consistent with the fair hearing standards of Article 6 and in 2000 and 2003 the new Code was further amended.[171] It became mandatory for a criminal court to order that an accused remanded in custody be brought before the court for an appellate hearing, unless the court considered that it was sufficient that the accused was represented by a lawyer.[172] In 2003, this provision was further amended and it became mandatory for a court to inform the accused of his or her right to be present during the hearing before it.

When the ECtHR found a violation of Article 6 arising out of the provisions governing appointment and dismissal of a trustee in bankruptcy, the relevant regulations were introduced to the new Insolvency Act of 38 February 2003. It entered into force on 1 October 2003.[173] The Constitutional Court, in a judgement given following the Strasbourg judgement, expressly acknowledged its impact on the change of legislation.[174]

In a number of cases, the Strasbourg Court found a violation of the right of access to a court on account of excessive court fees.[175] On 28 July 2005 a new Law on Court Fees in civil cases was adopted, endorsing and thus giving practical effect to certain conclusions to be drawn from those judgements.

As a result of cases in which the prison administration was found to be too eager to open the prisoners' correspondence with the ECtHR, relevant provisions of the Code of Enforcement of Criminal Sentences were amended in September 2003 in order to provide better protection of the prisoners' right to respect for their correspondence. In one case where the system of registration of press titles was criticized by the ECtHR[176], an ordinance setting out the criteria for such registration was found to lack clarity and foreseeability. It was subsequently repealed and replaced by a new one.

In a highly publicized Polish case, a pilot judgement procedure was applied for the first time ever. Under the pilot judgement procedure, the Court gives a judgement finding a violation that is systemic and widespread and orders the national Government to provide general measures at the national level to redress the breach found. The case was raised by an applicant whose legal predecessors lost property in formerly Polish territories, which as a result of a redrawing of Polish borders after World War II, fell into the borders of the Ukrainian Republic

---

[171] The Act of 20 July 2000 on amendments to the Code of Criminal Procedure, entered into force on 1 September 2000, DU No, 62, item 717.

[172] Wąsek-Wiaderek and Sakowicz (2002), 205 and 216.

[173] *Werner v. Poland* (appl. no. 26760/95), Judgement (Fourth Section), 15 November 2001 (not reported).

[174] The Polish Constitutional Court, P 8/04, Judgement of 18 October 2004.

[175] *Kreuz v. Poland* (appl. no. 28249/95), Judgement (First Section), 19 June 2001, Reports 2001-VI, 127.

[176] *Gawęda v. Poland* (appl. no. 26229/95), Judgement (First Section), 14 March 2002, Reports 2002-II, 105.

of the Soviet Union. Since the 50's, Polish laws provide for a right to compensation in kind for such properties. However, as a result of some legislative changes and compensation-hostile administrative practices, it became almost impossible to have these claims satisfied.

In the *Broniowski* case, the ECtHR found that a systemic problem underlies a violation of Article 1 of Protocol no. 1.[177] It observed that "one of the relevant factors considered by the Court was the growing threat to the Convention system and to the Court's ability to handle its ever-increasing caseload that resulted from large numbers of repetitive cases deriving from, among other things, the same structural or systemic problem".[178] As a result of this judgement, new legislation was adopted, namely the Act of 8 July 2005 on the recognition of the right to compensation for property situated beyond the present borders of the Polish State. The new Act was aimed at remedying the situation criticized in the judgement. The compensation procedures provided by the Act allow for the settlement at the domestic level of claims from persons in a situation similar to the applicant's. Over 200 similar cases are currently pending before the ECtHR, awaiting the outcome of the new domestic compensation procedures. As soon as these applicants' claims are compensated at the domestic level, the ECtHR will have an opportunity to assess the effectiveness of this mechanism.

The domestic impact of the *Kudła v. Poland* judgement (lack of domestic remedy against excessive length of proceedings) has been presented above. In addition, some structural measures have been adopted to reform the judicial system and to make it more efficient. They include certain procedural simplifications, recruitment of new judges and of qualified non-judicial staff, the introduction of more sophisticated methods of court administration and case management and, also, certain steps to reduce the backlog of particularly overburdened courts.[179]

b. Slovakia

In the first two judgements against Slovakia,[180] a breach was found of the applicants' right of access to a court. It originated from a provision contained in the 1990 Minor Offences Act,[181] preventing the courts from administrative decisions in cases where a fine of less than 2000 Slovak crowns had been imposed. In a judgement published on 23 October 1998, the Slovak Constitutional Court granted a direct effect to these judgements and declared this provision unconstitutional. This provision subsequently became null and void under Article 132

---

[177] *Broniowski v. Poland* (*supra* note 148).

[178] Ibid, para. 35.

[179] For details, see a document of the European Commission for Efficiency of Justice, prepared for the project Evaluation of European Judicial Systems, http://www.coe.int/t/dg1/legalcooperation/2006/Poland.pdf

[180] *Kadubec v. Slovakia* (appl. no. 27061/95), Judgement (Chamber), 2 September 1998, Reports 1998-VI, 2518; *Lauko v. Slovakia* (appl. no. 26138/95), Judgement (Chamber), 2 September 1998, Reports 1998-VI, 2492.

[181] Minor Offences Act no. 372/1990 (*Zákon o priestupkoch*), Official Gazette 1990, vol. 60.

of the Constitution.[182] Currently, administrative decisions concerning minor offences are subject to judicial review regardless of the amount of the fine imposed.

Certain reforms were undertaken after the Strasbourg judgements in which Slovakia was found to be in breach of the right to a hearing within a reasonable time. In May 2004, the National Council adopted an Act which reorganized the structure of the courts. It reduced the number of district courts from 55 to 45, in an effort aimed at, *inter alia*, promoting specialization of judges and increase the efficiency of the overburdened lower courts.

A further reform of the system that attempts to improve judicial efficiency ("the court system optimization") is currently under way. The specialization of judges as well as changes in the system of allocation of cases to judges by way of computerized court management systems are said to enhance judicial efficiency. Some judicial functions have been devolved to the administrative staff of the registries. It was reported that practically all courts have been computerized and that the case management systems have been introduced across the country.[183] In order to alleviate the judges' workload, the position of court clerk was created and certain hitherto judicial tasks were delegated to them.

In pursuit of increased efficiency in judicial proceedings, a new Act amending the Code of Civil Procedure, which entered into force on 1 January 2002, amended the existing rules of civil procedure in order to reduce the courts' workload and to accelerate the judicial proceedings.[184] This Act removed the inquisitorial principle from civil proceedings, already weakened by amendments to that Code adopted in 1995, and replaced it with the adversarial principle. Under the former, common to many civil procedures in the former communist countries, the courts were under an obligation to establish the "substantive truth", if need be, by taking steps themselves to find the evidence. Under the adversarial principle, it is the duty of the parties to submit to the court the evidence to make their case. This Act also confirms the general first-instance jurisdiction of district courts.

2. Individual Measures: Reopening of National Proceedings

a. Poland

With regard to the practical consequences that the ECHR might have in the domestic legal system, provisions were enacted that made it possible to reopen a domestic case after a judgement of the ECtHR. Under Article 540 (3) of the

---

[182] See also *Čanady v. Slovakia* (appl. no. 53371/99), Judgement (Fourth Section), 16 November 2004 (not reported).

[183] For details, see the document of the European Commission for Efficiency of Justice, prepared for the project on the Evaluation of European Judicial Systems, http://www.coe.int/t/dg1/legalcooperation/2006/Slovakia.pdf

[184] The Act amending the Code of Civil Procedure, no. 501/2001 Coll.

Code of Criminal Procedure adopted in 1997, judicial proceedings that were terminated by a final decision can be reopened for the benefit of the convicted person, if such a need arises out of a decision of international body acting on the basis of an international covenant ratified by Poland. No such provision is available in respect of decisions given in civil proceedings. As a result, there is no basis on which domestic proceedings can be reopened in a case where the ECtHR found a violation of the Convention.

Article 399 of the Code of Civil Proceedure provides that a civil case terminated by a final judgement on the merits can be reopened if applicable requirements set out in the Code are met. Article 401 of that Code, after major amendments adopted in 2001, merely provides that a party to civil proceedings terminated by a final judgement on the merits can request that these proceedings be reopened, if the Constitutional Court has found that the legal provision on the basis of which this judgement was given was unconstitutional.

These provisions were the subject of a major controversy that arose between the Supreme and the Constitutional Courts. The former was staunchly of the view that they did not allow for the reopening of any proceedings in which a decision – even a decision on the merits of the case – was given in the form of an interlocutory decision. (Such decisions are given in so-called non-contentious procedure, a huge and important section of civil cases). On the other hand, the Constitutional Court gave two major judgements in which it eventually found that it was manifestly unreasonable to hold that interlocutory decisions based on provisions subsequently declared unconstitutional could be left intact.[185]

This controversy serves here only to highlight the shortcomings of the provisions of the civil procedure in so far as they relate to the possibility of reopening of civil proceedings in which decisions were given on the basis of unconstitutional provisions.[186] One can also argue that, in the absence of a well thought-out framework that would allow the Constitutional Court's judgements to become operational in individual civil procedure cases, it is all the less surprising that there is no provision to that effect for the ECtHR judgements.

This controversy is also significant for the question why judicial reception of the ECHR seems to be rather timid in Poland. To put it simply, the two highest judicial authorities of the country seem to disagree as to scope of the lower courts' discretion in interpreting the law pursuant to the Constitution. Hence, it can hardly be surprising that the lower courts, which look up to the judgements of the Supreme and Constitutional Courts for guidance, prefer to abstain from making too bold ventures into the field, which is rife with controversy between these highest domestic authorities.

---

[185] Constitutional Court, SK 53/03, 2 March 2004; SK 1/04, 27 October 2004.

[186] This controversy itself reached the ECtHR and was briefly analyzed in one admissibility decision. However, the ECtHR, having regard mostly to formal characteristics of the case, declared the application inadmissible: *Międzyzakładowa Spółdzielnia Mieszkaniowa "Warszawscy Budowlani" v. Poland* (appl. no. 13990/04), ECtHR decision, 26 October 2004 (not reported).

The failure of the Code of Civil Procedure to accommodate the Strasbourg rulings has recently found its expression in a 2005 decision of the Supreme Court regarding a request to reopen civil proceedings after a judgement of the ECtHR. In one case in which the applicant was successful before the latter Court,[187] the former subsequently refused to reopen civil proceedings, holding that "a judgment of the ECtHR in the complainant's favour does not constitute a ground for reopening of a case. A civil case can be reopened if the proceedings have been tainted with one of circumstances expressly listed in Article 401 [of the Code of Civil Procedure]. A judgment of the [Strasbourg] Court is not listed in this provision. Hence, as the complainant's request has not been based on a statutory ground [for the reopening], it must be rejected".[188] The practical result of this decision is quite simple: the applicant is back to square one, despite being successful in Strasbourg.[189]

Łętowska criticized this approach of the Supreme Court and saw it as a "proof of agnosticism regarding human rights and, also, of the fact that constitutional values are poorly anchored in judicial minds (...) Once again, it has been shown that tradition regarding interpretation of provisions of positive domestic law (not even the potential content of these provisions) makes the courts overlook both their constitutional obligations and those originating from international legal obligations of Poland".[190] It remains to be seen whether this decision should be regarded as an isolated incident, or whether it will launch an unfortunate trend in the case law of the Supreme Court with regard to the domestic effects of the Strasbourg judgements in civil cases or – and it would be even more alarming – with regard to the relationship between the ECHR and domestic law. As to administrative proceedings, Articles 145, 145a, 146 and 147 of the Code of Administrative Procedure of 1960 specify situations in which an administrative case can be reopened. They do not provide specific grounds for such a reopening following an ECtHR judgement.

b. Slovakia

Article 394 § 4 of the Code of Criminal Procedure, adopted on 24 May 2005,[191] allows for the reopening of proceedings, terminated by a final judicial decision, on the basis of novel facts. An ECtHR judgement containing a finding of an ECHR violation in connection to judicial proceedings terminated by a final deci-

---

[187] *Podbielski and PPU Polpure v. Poland* (appl. no. 39199/98), Judgement (Fourth Section), 26 July 2005 (not yet reported).

[188] Supreme Court, Decision, 19 October 2005, V CO 16/05 (text inserted by the author).

[189] See also the critical opinions about this decision in articles published by various dailies: E. Siedlecka (2006); Semprich (2005); an opposite view was expressed in Gontarski (2006). The case is currently pending for enforcement before the Council of Europe Committee of Ministers. Under Article 46(2) of the Convention, the final judgement of the ECtHR shall be transmitted to the Committee of Ministers which shall supervise its execution.

[190] Łętowska (2006), 48.

[191] It entered into force on 1 January 2006.

sion also constitutes a fact justifying a reopening. It is interesting to note that the judgement of the ECtHR can serve as a basis for reopening, despite the fact that it cannot be considered as an existing yet unknown fact when the case was pending before the domestic court. Usually, an ECtHR judgement would be handed down after the final decision was given in domestic proceedings.

As to the civil procedure, Article 228 § 1 (d) of the Code of Civil Procedure, adopted on 24 June 2005,[192] provides for the possibility of reopening domestic proceedings resulting from an ECtHR judgement. A party to the proceedings is entitled to claim the reopening of a case when significant consequences arising from a violation found by that court have not been duly remedied by the award of just satisfaction under Article 41 of the ECHR. Pursuant to Article 230 § 2 of the Code, such a request can be made regardless of the period which had expired from the final judgement of the domestic court.

There is no separate system of judicial review of administrative decisions in Slovakia. Such decisions fall under the review of administrative divisions of ordinary courts. The provisions on civil procedure are applicable to the proceedings in which such a review is sought. Article 46(2) of the Constitution provides a legal basis for such a review, but only where it is expressly provided for by law. However, the same provision extends considerably the scope of administrative decisions which can fall within the purview of judicial review by civil courts by stating that "the examination of decisions concerning fundamental human rights and freedoms must not be excluded from the jurisdiction of the courts". The Constitutional Court emphasized the importance of access to a court for the purposes of judicial review of administrative decisions, regardless of their subject-matter. It stressed that "where a decision of an administrative authority, regardless of its type or formal characteristics, affects any fundamental rights and freedoms, it must not be excluded from judicial review".[193] Hence, it can be argued with regard to the strength of this reasoning that the same principles as those applicable in civil proceedings can be used in the reopening of administrative proceedings following a judgement of the ECtHR.

3. Comparison and Conclusions

Both Poland and Slovakia seem to be loyal players in the ECHR system. When the ECtHR rules against them, both countries make efforts to introduce the required adjustments into their respective legal systems with the aim of preventing similar violations in the future. Both countries suffered from a certain lack of effectiveness of the judicial system, and a remedy against excessive length of proceedings was put into place. However, while it was an ECtHR judgement against Poland that initiated a trend in the case law requiring the existence of such a remedy, Slovakia's reaction was much faster than Poland's, where the relevant

---

[192] It entered into force on 1 September 2005.
[193] Constitutional Court, II. ÚS 50/01, 8 November 2001.

legislation came into force four years after the *Kudła* judgement. On the whole, both countries show willingness to cooperate with the ECHR system and there were no major problems at the level of enforcement of judgements.

As regards individual measures, there is a certain difference between Poland and Slovakia; the possibility of reopening criminal proceedings was introduced much earlier in the former than in the latter. This is counterbalanced by the total absence of any such possibility in respect of civil cases in Poland, further compounded by the reticence of the Supreme Court to even consider such a possibility, while in Slovakia legislation expressly providing for it has been put into place.

I. Mechanisms of Coordination

1. Poland

When Bills are prepared by the Government or by the MPs, it is the responsibility of the various Ministerial legislative services or of the Parliament itself to ensure that they are compatible with the Constitution and that they are of a good quality. However, there is no normal part of the legislative process that serves as a specific mechanism to assess and ensure the compatibility of Bills and statutes with the ECHR, and none is currently planned. There exists a special advisory body, the Legislative Council (*Rada Legislacyjna*)[194], established long ago and entrusted with the task of ensuring a good quality of legislation. Unfortunately, the practical role it might play in the legislative process, given the expertise of its members and staff, appears to be largely disregarded by Members of Parliament.

It has been observed that "Poland's accession to the European Union (...) required an enormous legislative output in order to bring the national law in conformity with the *acquis communautaire*. The whole legislative process suffered from this tremendous workload. In this context, experts refer to an 'inflation of law'. Examining draft statutes in the context of their conformity with international human rights standards may suffer because of these developments".[195] This does seem to have been the case, given that there are regular co-ordination mechanisms in place to assess the conformity of Bills and ordinances with EU law, in the absence of any such mechanism regarding the ECHR.

Article 122(3) of the Constitution vests the President with the power to refer a Parliamentary Bill, prior to signing it, to the Constitutional Court for a decision whether it is compatible with the Constitution. As to the *ex-post* review, Article 188 of the Constitution empowers the Constitutional Court to examine the conformity of statutes and ordinances with ratified international agreements. Such a review can be carried out at any time and can be initiated by the President

---

[194] The Ordinance of the President of the Council of Ministers of 23 February 1998, Journal of Laws, 27 February 1998, no. 725, Item 134.
[195] Keller (2005), 314.

of the Republic, the Speakers of both Chambers of Parliament, the First President
of the Supreme Court, the President of the Supreme Administrative Court, the
Prosecutor-General, the President of the Supreme Chamber of Audit and by the
Ombudsman.[196] In addition, any court may refer a question of law to the Constitutional Court, requesting it to examine the conformity of a legal act with the
Constitution, ratified international agreements or a statute, if the answer to such
question is relevant for the outcome of a case pending before that court.[197] Thus
far, there have been no cases in which these competencies would have been used
to test specifically the compatibility of laws with the ECHR.

2. Slovakia

In Parliament, in the National Council of the Slovak Republic, submitters of
Bills are responsible for ensuring that explanatory reports elaborate on their
compliance with international treaties, including the Council of Europe treaties.
Pursuant to Section 68 of the Act no. 350/1996 Coll. on Rules of the National
Council,[198] a Parliamentary Bill should contain explanatory reports that must
also include a statement on its compliance with the Constitution, its relation to
other laws and international treaties and on its compliance with EU law. Under
Section 59 of that Act, the Constitutional and Legal Affairs Committee is obliged
to see to it that these requirements are fulfilled.

As an advisory body of the Government, the Legislative Council of the Slovak
Republic, prepares opinions on the compatibility of Bills with international law.
The Institute for Approximation of Law, a Governmental Advisory Body, also
prepares such opinions.

Under Article 125a(1) of the Constitution, as amended in 2001, the Constitutional Court is empowered to carry out a review of the compatibility of a broad
range of domestic legal acts with "negotiated international treaties to which the
assent of the National Council of the Slovak Republic with the Constitution and
constitutional law is necessary".[199] Thus, the Court can decide whether statutes,
Government orders, generally binding legal regulations of Ministries and other
central State administration bodies, and, also, generally binding regulations given
pursuant to Article 68 of the Constitution comply with the international treaties
concluded. As the ECHR was ratified by the National Council, the compliance of
the enumerated domestic instruments with this treaty can be reviewed. Interestingly, other acts of public authorities, such as generally binding legal regulations
of the local bodies of State administration and generally binding regulations of

---

[196] Article 191 of the Constitution.
[197] Article 193 of the Constitution.
[198] Act no. 350/1996 Coll. on Rules of the National Council (*Zàkon Narodnej Rady Slovenskej Republiky o rokovacom poriadku Narodnej Rady Slovenskej Republiky*), Official Gazette 1996, vol. 123.
[199] Article 125a(1) of the Constitution.

the bodies of territorial self-government can also be reviewed for their compatibility with international treaties promulgated in the manner prescribed by law.

In case of a finding of incompatibility handed down by the Constitutional Court – in any of these configurations – the provisions found to be incompatible shall lose effect, in their entirety or in part. The authorities that have issued such regulations or acts are obliged to amend them and ensure their compatibility with the provisions concerned, within six months of the Court's decision.

The Constitutional Court is not empowered to carry out an *ex-ante* review of the compatibility of any draft laws or regulations with any other acts. Motions to have various statutes and legal acts reviewed as to their compatibility with international laws can be lodged with the Court by not less than one fifth of all members of the National Council, the President of the Republic, the Government, any court (in relation to its decision-making) and by the Prosecutor-General.[200]

3. Comparison and Conclusions

In both countries, there are no systemic mechanisms to ensure that compatibility of Parliamentary Bills or other draft laws with the ECHR would be assessed on a regular basis as a normal and necessary part of the legislative process. Such an assessment, if it is carried out, is rather done on an ad hoc basis. It is difficult to find any trends that would explain why some drafts are assessed against the ECHR and others are not; it seems that there is no regular pattern either in Poland or in Slovakia. In both countries the Constitutional Courts have broad powers to review legislation, the difference being that in Slovakia it is impossible to have a draft law reviewed, while in Poland it can be done.

The Slovak Constitutional Court is competent to examine the compatibility of an extremely broad range of legislative and administrative acts with the Constitution and with international law. In comparison to this, the powers of the Polish Constitutional Court are severely limited due to the narrow scope of examination it is allowed to carry out in respect of individual constitutional complaints. The consequences of a finding of incompatibility are the same: in both countries the impugned legal provisions lose their binding force.

J. Knowledge and Practice

1. Poland

a. Ombudsman
Immediately after the ratification, the Ombudsman's Office published a highly popular and regularly updated booklet explaining what can be gained from bring-

---

[200] Act no. 38/1993 Coll. on Organization of the Constitutional Court of the Slovak Republic, Proceedings before it and Status of its Judges, Article 37.

ing a case to the Strasbourg system.[201] Its home page contains guidance notes on how to bring an application to the ECtHR.

b. The ECHR in the Press

From early on, the former Polish Commissioner Marek A. Nowicki made continuous efforts to inform the general public about the Convention, regularly publishing information about the case law of the ECtHR in a leading daily called *Rzeczpospolita*. Both the quality and the persistence of his work are remarkable. He has certainly contributed to raising the profile of the ECHR in Poland. The same daily publishes comments on the judgements against Poland given by the ECtHR. Other dailies only publish information about the most colourful cases, which do not necessarily have the same legal significance. However, it does not stem from any special approach to the ECHR, but rather from the fact that, generally speaking, the Polish press does not seem to be either willing or able to comment on legal issues when they do not have immediate political relevance.

c. The Council of Europe Information Office in Warsaw

The Office was established in 1992.[202] The formal status of the Council of Europe's Office evolved over the years, but its essential task was and remains the dissemination of information about the activities of the Council in Poland. The Office provides information on the programmes and work of the Council, enables access of the general public to the publications of the Council of Europe; publishes the main documents in Polish and organizes presentations and seminars on the Council of Europe for the general public. The Warsaw Office has acquired a reputation of being a lively and creative centre for various activities, and it has either organized or coorganized many high-profile events aimed at highlighting various aspects of the ECHR in the Polish context.

In recent years, a growing number of students from various faculties – i.e. not only prospective lawyers, but also students of political science, sociology and international relations – have used the Office's library and information services for preparing theses on various issues pertaining to ECHR. The Office publishes a Bulletin in which many ECtHR judgements and some decisions concerning Poland are published. Thanks to the Office's regular cooperation with the Ministry of Justice, many of the translations are subsequently distributed to the courts and to the prosecutors' offices *via* information channels organized by the Ministry. Most of the contributions of Polish academia to the growing body of knowledge about the ECHR have also been published in this Bulletin.[203]

The Office has played a particularly important role in the popularization of the ECHR since 1991. It organized the following professional training sessions:

---

[201] The Ombudsman's Office (1993).
[202] Ms H. Machińska Ph.D. is the Director of the Office.
[203] *Biuletyn Biura Informacji Rady Europy.*

an annual seminar on the substantive and procedural issues, seven editions, each containing six meetings (1996, 1997, 1999, 2000/2001, 2003, 2004, 2005) and study trips to Strasbourg (1996, 1998, 2000, 2001, 2004, 2005; 2006; four seminars for judges, prosecutors and advocates concerning human rights; one seminar for judges of the Supreme ECtHR (1997); one seminar for civil servants on the European standards in the legislative process.

d. Idea of Satellite Offices

In December 2005, Lord Woolf's Report of the Working Methods of the ECtHR was made public. Its aim was to conduct an audit of its working methods and suggest new solutions that would allow it to process its caseload more efficiently. The remit of the audit was specifically limited to such measures as would not necessitate any amendments of the Convention, all suggestions to the latter measures being left to the Group of Wise Persons.[204]

Among the concrete ideas designated to achieve this aim, one was that "Satellite Offices of the Registry should be established in key countries that produce high numbers of inadmissible applications. The Satellite Offices would provide applicants with information as to the Court's admissibility criteria, and the availability, locally, of Ombudsmen and other alternative methods of resolving disputes. This could divert a significant number of cases away from the Court. Satellite Offices would also be responsible for the initial processing of applications. They would then send applications, together with short summaries in either French or English, to the relevant division in Strasbourg. This would enable Strasbourg lawyers to prepare draft judgements more quickly."[204a]

In Poland, given that a high number of inadmissible cases against this country are filed with the ECtHR, such an idea has already been launched as a pilot project even prior to the adoption of the Report. In December 2003, a trial scheme was set up, involving the recruitment of a lawyer by the Council of Europe Information Office in Warsaw. The purpose of the scheme was to determine the extent to which the provision of additional information at the national level by the Council of Europe Information Office could have an impact on the influx of applications from a high-count country.

An issue arises whether and to what extent the idea of Satellite Offices could contribute to stemming the influx of new cases at the source. It would be interesting to assess the impact the operation of the ECtHR's caseload. Thus far, there are no signs that the overall popularity of the ECHR in Poland has abated as a result of the project – which is, admittedly, modest in scale. While it is not in doubt that the project serves a useful purpose of disseminating, on a permanent basis,

---

[204] The Right Honourable the Lord Woolf, Review of the Working Methods of the European Court of Human Rights, December 2005, http://www.echr.coe.int/Eng/Press/2005/Dec/LORDWOOLFSREVIEWONWORKINGMETHODS.pdf.
[204a] Ibid., 5.

sound information about the ECHR and the ECtHR to the general public, it is far from certain that, in the face of the many legal and societal factors that made the ECHR so popular in Poland, much can be achieved in stemming the influx of cases from Poland in this way.

Lord Woolf's report suggested that "the Warsaw Information Office concept should be developed and expanded to create 'Satellite Offices of the Registry'. These Satellite Offices would work both as regional versions of Registry, and as information offices, providing information on the ECtHR's admissibility criteria (…)".[205] According to the report, satellite offices would be an obligatory port of call for all applicants from a given country. Applications would be subject to an initial screening at the Satellite Office, with manifestly inadmissible applications being forwarded to Strasbourg with the relevant notice. The report concluded that this arrangement would entail "a significant cut in the number of cases processed by the Strasbourg Registry".[206] It remains to be seen what will happen in due time to the idea of Satellite Offices. The ECtHR's response has until now been cautious. A Working Group on the proposal has been set up, but any decisions in this respect had been stayed, pending the final report of the Wise Persons.

e. Legal Profession

A striking feature of the Polish cases before the ECtHR is that the great majority of applicants are not represented by a lawyer at the outset of the procedure. Legal representation is not mandatory at this early stage. Still, the fact that only five to seven per cent of Polish applicants are represented when they first submit their application is puzzling. Even more surprisingly, this figure does not appear to have increased significantly over the years. It could be reasonably surmized that the more Polish clients of the ECHR system there are – and it has already been said that there are indeed many ECHR users in Poland – the more likely it would be that they will be represented by lawyers as they acquire knowledge of the law of the Convention. It is baffling that this is still not the case, even today.

This paradox can be partly explained by the conclusions of a survey on access to legal aid conducted in 2002 by the Polish Helsinki Foundation of Human Rights as part of the Promoting Access to Justice in Central and Eastern Europe programme.[207] One of the aims of the survey was to identify the factors that explain why parties to judicial proceedings decide to use – or, rather, not to use – the services of a lawyer in Poland. The results found with regard to domestic proceedings can serve to illuminate the dearth of legal representation in cases before the ECtHR.

Fifty-five per cent of those who were not represented (because they had not tried to hire a lawyer) explained that they did not feel they needed legal represen-

---

[205] Ibid., 28.
[206] Ibid., 27.
[207] Bojarski (2003), 37–125.

tation. Forty per cent answered that the high cost was why they had not retained a lawyer. Five per cent did not know how to find a lawyer. Among the non-represented respondents, who were serving prison sentences, 40 per cent said that they did not need legal representation, while 25 per cent invoked too-high legal fees and ten per cent did not know how to find a lawyer. Sixty-five per cent of respondents who were not represented, but had tried to hire a lawyer, cited the high costs of legal representation as the reason for having refrained from seeking a lawyer's services. The results of the survey suggest that Poles tend to perceive legal assistance in domestic proceedings as either redundant or too expensive.

It is only after the respondent Government is notified of the case that the applicants should be legally represented before the ECtHR.[208] When the applicant is unable to find a legal representative, the Registry of the ECtHR requests assistance from the Polish National Bar Council. It should not be too difficult for the Council to find a lawyer well versed in human rights, given that a Commission of Human Rights was set up several years ago at the National Bar Council.[209] The Commission is a self-selected body of advocates interested in human rights issues. It organizes periodic meetings at which the participants are informed about various ECHR developments.

Although these institutional developments are to be warmly welcomed, they have not resulted in many lawyers showing an effective interest in taking up Strasbourg cases in their day-to-day practice. The names of the same twenty or so representatives recur in the applications sent to the ECtHR. This relative lack of interest on part of the profession is puzzling, especially in view of the fact that the popularity of the ECHR indicates that there is no shortage of prospective clients. One would have thought that more lawyers would have been interested in building their reputations – and their incomes – on being recognized nationwide as human rights Strasbourg experts.

The role played by the Council of Europe Information Office in Warsaw in the dissemination of knowledge about the ECHR among lawyers is noteworthy. The Office has been training lawyers in its substantive and procedural aspects since 1996. Its courses, lasting approximately one year, acquired a very good reputation and were attracting lawyers from all over Poland. To date, it has trained well over 160 of them. It should be stressed that a number of lawyers who had followed this training, subsequently represented applicants in various cases brought before the ECtHR. The training sessions for lawyers bore fruit also in that some people trained during the first rounds have subsequently acquired the ECHR experience and became trainers for the following courses.

---

[208] Under Rule 54(2)(b) of the Rules of ECtHR.
[209] It is currently presided by Mr P. Sendecki.

f. Judges and Prosecutors

Following the success of its training sessions for lawyers, the Office started a long-term training project for judges and prosecutors. Annual training sessions have been organized for them since 2001. At the end, the participants travel to Strasbourg for a study visit. Information about the judicial trainings organized by the Office is sent to the appellate and regional courts. It is left to them to either select the judges or just to disseminate the information to all judges in a given jurisdiction. It seems that the decisions to attend these training events is most often left to the individual judges, there being no countrywide practice adopted as to this form of training.

The Polish judges sometimes seem to have a feeling that they are too harshly criticized by the ECtHR, in particular for their conduct in length cases. This has not so far discouraged some 100 judges and prosecutors from participating in the sessions organized by the Office. It should be noted that in the absence of any systematic training on the ECHR specifically designated for judges and prosecutors and organized by the State authorities, the courses organized by the Office for a long time had practically no competition.

The importance of the systematic training of judges for effective reception of the ECHR was stressed in a recommendation of the Committee of Ministers of the Council of Europe in which the States were called upon to "ascertain that adequate university education and professional training concerning the ECHR and the case law of the ECtHR exist at national level and that such education and training are included, in particular (…) as a component of the preparation programmes of national or local examinations for access to the various legal professions and of the initial and continuous training provided to judges, prosecutors and lawyers".[210] Nonetheless, until September 2006 the training of future judges and prosecutors remained at the discretion of the Regional Courts and Regional Prosecutors, which did not follow any nationally set curricula. As a result, the ECHR has for a long time remained outside the training which lawyers undertake to become judges. The ECHR issues were not either a part of a systematic and nationwide ongoing professional training of judges. Consequently, the ECHR training has entirely been at the mercy of local initiatives.

However, after years-long debate, efforts to introduce some kind of centralization in judicial training, along the French model, ultimately resulted in the adoption of a recent statute aiming at achieving some degree of nationwide uniformity in judicial training.[211] In September 2006, a national centre for the training of judges and prosecutors was officially inaugurated. It remains to be seen whether

---

[210] Recommendation Rec(2004)4 of the Committee of Ministers to Member States on the European Convention on Human Rights in university education and professional training, adopted by the Committee of Ministers on 12 May 2004, at its 114th Session.

[211] Act of 1 July 2005 on the National Training Centre for Judges and Prosecutors, DU no. 169, item 1410 and no. 264, item 2204.

the training programme adopted by the centre will include a module on the ECHR in so far as it is relevant for the Polish realities.

Further, the reception of the ECHR by the judiciary cannot but be hindered by insufficient access of national courts to the case law. While the ECtHR judgements are instantly available through the Internet, and the more important admissibility decisions are also available within a few days of their adoption, they exist only in the ECtHR's official languages, namely English and French. As such, they are only available to a restricted section of the Polish judicial profession. To facilitate its task, the Ministry of Justice cooperates with the Council of Europe Information Office, which translates the most directly relevant Strasbourg judgements into Polish.[212] It is noteworthy that they are also available at the Ministry's home page.[213] It has been repeatedly noted in the Resolutions of the Committee of Ministers of the Council of Europe concerning Polish cases that judgements raising issues of practice have been disseminated to the authorities concerned, including judicial authorities. Translated paper versions of these judgements are said to be circulated to the courts, but there are conflicting reports as to their actual availability.

It is also interesting to note that the official translations available on the Ministry's home page are almost exclusively translations of judgements. The almost systematic failure to translate admissibility decisions in Polish cases – both those declaring the cases inadmissible or admissible – is to be deplored. Important lessons can be drawn from both admissible and inadmissible cases. From the former, knowledge that the ECtHR found an issue arising under the ECHR in a given set of circumstances might serve as a warning sign for judges, or, as the case may be, for other public officials, that similar treatment meted out to a party in a case might possibly result in a violation. As to the latter, knowledge of such decisions might at least serve the purpose of informing public officials why the ECtHR considered that a given case does not raise a human rights issue. From a pedagogical point of view, this information could also be valuable. It is noteworthy that the Supreme Court has recently decided to publish analyzes and presentations of the ECHR case law relevant to criminal cases on its home page.[214]

One particularly innovative element in the dissemination of knowledge about the ECHR was put in place in 2001 by the Polish section of the International Commission of Jurists. Under the patronage of the Secretary-General of the Council of Europe, the Presidents of the Supreme and the Constitutional Courts, it organizes a competition for judges in which they can win an honorary title of "European Judge". This prize is awarded to the authors of the best judgements, referring to the provisions of the Constitution, to the ECHR, to the ECtHR's case law or other international instruments for the protection of human rights.

---

[212] See *supra* Section J.1.c.
[213] The Polish Ministry of Justice, http://www.ms.gov.pl/re/re_wyroki.shtml.
[214] See http://www.sn.pl/orzecznictwo/index.html, ed. by M. Wąsek-Wiaderek.

It was also reported that the office of the Agent of the Polish Government for the proceedings before the ECHR, placed in the Ministry of Foreign Affairs, has a project of publishing quarterly *communiqués* about the latest developments in the ECtHR's case law relevant for the Polish practice. Such a regular publication would certainly be welcomed by the judiciary and the legal profession alike. It is apparently planned that the report will be made accessible free of charge on the Internet site of the Ministry of Foreign Affairs.

g. Non-Governmental Organizations

Remarkably enough, interest groups who push for reforms through legal action have for a long time been strikingly missing from the Polish scene, despite the fact that from 1989 on a vibrant third sector was created in Poland.[215] The NGOs have for a long time remained largely uncommitted to the development of strategic litigation where test cases are being brought before domestic and/or international courts in order to bring legislative change. The process by which various group interests would be asserted by having recourse to strategic litigation, with the purpose of launching legal reforms, is still in its fledgling stage. The NGOs have not been an active intermediary between the public and the lawyers, who would be able to put various interests in the language of law and litigation.

There has, however, recently been an important development with regard to strategic litigation, which followed in the steps of the various cases sometimes brought to the attention of the ECtHR by the Warsaw Helsinki Foundation of Human Rights in cooperation with other lawyers.[216] In October 2004, the Foundation set up a Strategic Litigation Programme.[217] Its purpose is to institute and join, if need be, judicial and administrative proceedings in which issues of importance are involved. Also, "[t]hrough its participation in those proceedings, the Helsinki Foundation for Human Rights intends to strive towards obtaining breakthrough verdicts that would change the practice or legal regulations concerning particular legal issues, which give rise to serious doubts from the point of view of human rights protection."[218] The programme has been quite active in the context of the Strasbourg cases: the ECtHR has already granted leave to lodge five *amicus curiae* in pending cases.[219] Moreover, the lawyers working for

---

[215] For an insightful analysis of reasons for this weakness of public interest litigation in countries of Central and Eastern Europe, see Petrova (1996).

[216] *Mandugeqi and Jinge v. Poland* (appl. no. 35218/97), Decision (Plenary), 19 September 1997 (struck off the list).

[217] Run by Mr A. Bodnar, Ph. D.

[218] The Warsaw Helsinki Foundation for Human Rights, http://www.hfhrpol.waw.pl/en/index.html; for the Strategic Litigation Programe, see http://www.hfhrpol.waw.pl/precedens.

[219] See *Reinprecht v. Austria* (appl. no. 67175/01), Judgement, (Fourth Section) 15 November 2005 (not yet reported); *Turek v. Slovakia* (appl. no. 57986/00), Judgement (Fourth Section), 14 February 2006 (not yet reported); *Tysiąc v. Poland* (appl. no. 5410/03), Decision (Fourth Section), 7 February 2006 (not reported); *Staroszczyk v. Poland* and *Siałkowska v. Poland* (appl. no. 59519/00 and 8932/05), Decision (First Section), 15 June 2006 (not reported); *Laskowska v. Poland* (appl. no. 77765/01), Judgement (Fourth Section), 13 March 2007 (not yet reported).

the programme have submitted four cases to the ECtHR, raising legal issues of general significance. It will be interesting to observe the results brought by their activities, both domestically[220] and in Strasbourg.

Regardless of the results that the activities of the programme will bring in the long run, it is a valuable first step for Polish civil society to seek legal change by way of an organized and carefully planned legal action, orchestrated by a non-governmental organization. The Warsaw Helsinki Foundation of Human Rights also has a well-established tradition of organizing Schools of Human Rights. They are designed for people from all walks of life, lawyers being a tiny minority among them. They have been held since 1990 and comprise several months of training on all human rights issues, including a module and moot court exercises on the ECHR. They are intended to educate local leaders of civil society.

2. Slovakia

a. Judges and Prosecutors

The training of judges and prosecutors is organized and supervized by the Ministry of Justice. Moreover, to promote a certain degree of uniformity in judicial training, a Judicial Academy was established in 2004, within the framework of a nationwide reform of the judicial system.[221] It became operative on 1 September 2004 and its task is to adapt the education of judges, prosecutors, court officials as well as candidates to these professions. Interested persons can attend courses on the condition that their superiors agree to their participation. It is likely that this form of centralized training will improve the dissemination of knowledge about the ECHR. Since 2005, the Academy provides training for prosecutors and lawyers on ECHR issues. It also organizes courses on English legal terminology, which can undoubtedly improve the availability of the ECtHR's case law among judges and prosecutors.[222] Previously, the office of the Government's Agent also gave a lecture on the criminal law aspects of the ECtHR's case law.

b. The Role of the Agent of the Slovak Government

In 1994, the Office of the Agent of the Slovak Republic obtained a statute regulating its powers and functions. This statute was amended in 2002 following both

---

[220] The Programme has also been granted leave to act as a *amicus curiae* in a number of cases pending before Polish courts, including in four cases pending before the Constitutional Court. It was for the first time ever that the Constitutional Court had granted such leave to a non-governmental organization and established the official status of *amicus curiae* in proceedings before this Court; see its judgement SK 30/05 of 16 January 2006. Other cases, currently pending, are SK 43/05 – constitutionality of criminal law provisions on defamation; SK 50/06 – procedural aspects of ordering psychiatric observation examination for the purposes of criminal proceedings.

[221] Act no. 548/2003 Coll. on the Judicial Academy, 4 December 2003.

[222] The Slovak Ministry of Justice, Judicial Academy, http://www.justice.gov.sk/wfn.aspx?pg=ld3&uc=ja/ls06.

the constitutional changes and the changes in the ECHR system. In 2005, a new statute was adopted.[223]

The availability on the home page of the Agent of the Slovak Republic of very detailed information about the Slovak cases before the ECtHR should be emphasized.[224] It is meant for any layman (the Frequently Asked Questions part), but can also be used by lawyers (the Manual On the Case law of the ECtHR). To facilitate their task, a translation of Rules of the Court into Slovak has been prepared.

Further, the Agent publishes annual surveys of his or her activities before the ECtHR. These surveys, covering the period from 1999 until the present, are also available on the site. This obligation has been provided for by the statute of the Agent's Office under which the Minister is obliged to inform the Government of the Agent's activities and of the state of proceedings before the ECtHR. Indeed, it seems that the Agent of the Government has assumed a central role in the co-ordination of many national activities linked to the ECHR, both in the judicial sphere (by representing the Government before the ECtHR) as well as in the domain of training and dissemination of relevant information. The Agent is currently assisted by an advisory board composed of representatives of various ministries, charged with helping her in the exercise of the functions. Furthermore, the Agent informs the general public, by way of regularly updated tables, of amounts paid to each of the successful applicants in the proceedings before the ECtHR, both as regards just satisfaction and the claims for costs and expenses.[225] It is also laudable that the Agent informs the general public *via* her home page, on an ongoing basis, at least from September 2005, about the admissibility of decisions given by the ECtHR in cases against Slovakia, presenting short summaries of the facts and the legal aspects of these decisions. The same part of the homepage contains short summaries of the Slovak judgements. Recommendations of the Council of Europe pertinent to the ECtHR's activities are also to be found there, both translated and in English.

The Agent's Office translates the judgements of the ECtHR in Slovak cases. Since 1995, most of these judgements and important admissibility decisions are published in a State-subsidized legal magazine "Justična revue". The same magazine also publishes translations of the ECtHR's rulings in cases against other countries on a regular basis. Since 2003, the revue publishes a separate supplement on the ECtHR's case law. This magazine is officially distributed to all the courts in the country. As apparently a limited number of judges are proficient in either English or French, this publication seems to play an important role.

---

[223] Ordinance no. 543, 13 July 2005.

[224] The Slovak Ministry of Justice, Agent of the Slovak Republic before the ECtHR, http://www.justice.gov.sk/wfn.aspx?pg=l8.

[225] These amounts were as follows: 3 001 741, 20 Sk in 2003, 1 042 972,00 Sk in 2004, 5 359 553,00 Sk in 2005 and 3 687 783,78 Sk in 2006.

Translations of important ECtHR judgements are also sent to other authorities, if they concern the subject matter of their jurisdiction.

Between August 2001 and November 2002, the Agent's Office ran a project entitled "Education of Judges and Candidate Judges on the Case law of the ECtHR". It consisted of seven workshops for judges and one workshop for trainee judges. The participants of the programme became acquainted with the ECtHR's case law concerning those Articles of the Convention that appear to be the most relevant for Slovakia. The workshops were attended by a total of 170 judges and trainee judges. The participants of the workshops were taught how to apply domestic law in compliance with the provisions of the Convention. The discussions conducted during the workshops helped to identify the need to initiate certain legislative changes. The Office of the Agent passed these discoveries on to the responsible legislative sections at the Ministry of Justice.

A collection of lectures was published after the course that was subsequently disseminated to all participants, to the presidents of district and regional courts and to the members of the board of the Slovak Bar Association. When the project came to an end, judges of ordinary courts sent several decisions to the Office of Agent in which direct references to the ECHR were made. Since 2002, the Slovak National Human Rights Centre has organized training courses on the "Assertiveness and Pro-Social Behaviour Enhancing the Protection of Human Rights in the Work of the Regional Public Prosecutor's Offices".[226]

c. The Council of Europe Information Office in Bratislava

The status of the Office, which was created in 1993, is currently governed by the Memorandum of Understanding between the Government of the Slovak Republic and the Council of Europe concerning the statute of the Information Office of the Council of Europe in Bratislava.[227] Its tasks are identical to those of other national Council of Europe Offices: they primarily consist in disseminating information to the public at large about the Council's activities. As regards the ECHR, the Office regularly provides free legal advice about the Convention in various Slovak towns. Information meetings on human rights for high school and university students are also held regularly. In addition, the Office organized a number of nationwide conferences about various aspects of the ECHR. It has put into place a national network of information centres about the activities of the Council of Europe. Annual Human Rights Olympics are held nationwide and the Office contributes to the organization by preparing cases for the moot court exercise.

In 2005, the Office concluded an agreement with the Judicial Academy per-

---

[226] It is interesting to note that the current Slovak Prime Minister, Mr R. Fico, was the first Agent of the Slovak Government after Slovakia became a State Party to the ECHR.

[227] Memorandum of Understanding between the Government of the Slovak Republic and the Council of Europe concerning the statute of the Information Office of the Council of Europe in Bratislava, Official Gazette, no. 118/2000.

taining to cooperation in judicial training. In 2006, special training sessions were organized in order to familiarize the judges with access available to ECtHR case law via the HUDOC database and with documents relevant for the work of the ECtHR translated into Slovak. Slovak translations of certain ECtHR decisions and judgements have been prepared for the judges participating in the training. The Office closely cooperates with the office of the Government Agent before the ECtHR.

d. Education of Police Officers
Students attending the Police Force Academy are taught human rights issues during the courses "Human Rights and the Police Force", "Constitutional law of the Slovak Republic" and "The Theory and Practice of Investigation".

e. Education of Teachers
The ongoing education of teachers is provided and supervized by regional centres of the Ministry of Education, the Methodology Centres. Several projects run by non-governmental organizations featured presentations by representatives of the Office of the Agent before the ECtHR. In addition, the Information Office of the Council of Europe in Bratislava published a handbook entitled "The European Convention on Human Rights – Essential Points for Teachers" and intended for teachers. The centres also organize the "Human Rights Olympics", which is a nationwide contest for high school students.

3. Comparison and Conclusions
The Agents representing the Governments in the proceedings before the ECtHR have, one might say, a vested interest in making the ECHR known to the public authorities, if only in order to minimize the risk of future violations. It can be argued that this is due to the fact that the number of violations found by the ECtHR can be used to assess the quality of the work of the Agent's office. Hence, the role of the agents in shaping the national perception of the ECHR is important. The Agent is also in the best institutional position to know the ECHR developments relevant to a given country. In this respect, the difference between Slovakia and Poland is remarkable. While the office of the Agent has a solid and specific legal basis in both countries, it seems to play a stronger role in Slovakia – if only because it is obliged by law to prepare and to submit to the Government annual reports regarding its activities. There is no corresponding obligation in Poland and, therefore, no general picture of the Polish response to the Convention – and how it evolves in time – is readily available to the executive and to the public. This difference in the approach is puzzling, given that one might rather expect that Poland, having a voluminous caseload before the ECtHR, should be the most interested in such knowledge. Further, in Slovakia it is the Agent's Office that seems to have had a pivotal role in making the ECHR known, while in

Poland the Council of Europe Information Office in Warsaw has rather played this role.

The developments in the field of judicial training have followed a relatively similar course. Judicial training only recently became somewhat centralized through the establishment of training centres aimed at setting certain minimum and uniform standards for all judges in the country. However, the difference between Poland and Slovakia with regard to the ECHR is that in the latter the ECHR is said to have already been included in the judicial training modules, while no such reports exist in respect of Poland. This is, again, paradoxical, for the same reasons as those explained above in relation to the Agents' Offices. The training of legal professionals in both countries followed similar patterns, being largely entrusted to the bar associations on an *ad hoc* basis.

K. Final remarks

The status of the ECHR in both countries is similar, and shows the willingness of the constitutional legislator to make international law, and in particular human rights law, an element of the domestic legal orders. This similarity was not, however, of a decisive significance, because ultimately the reception process in both countries yielded quite different results.

The comparison of Poland and Slovakia demonstrates that, despite the similar historical situation of both countries, the patterns of reception of the ECHR differ considerably. While the circumstances of the ratification were comparable, in that there was a broad consensus that the ratification was necessary, the outcome can be said to be markedly different. In Poland, the ECHR became immensely popular and gained the status of an instrument of popular justice, resorted to by individuals in a spontaneous and unorganized manner. In Slovakia, it plays a similar role in so far as it is used extremely rarely by organized civil society institutions as a legal advocacy instrument. This occurs in spite of the fact that the Slovaks' recourse to the individual petition procedure is much less frequent than in Poland. This immense popularity of the ECHR in Poland calls, by itself, for in-depth analysis.[228] There are certainly country-specific factors that shape the perception of the ECHR in each Contracting State. These factors belong to various spheres and, contrary to what might appear to be an obvious assumption, the legal sphere does not necessarily have the most decisive influence over the reasons of its popularity in any given country.

Despite the ECHR being used by the Polish public quite indiscriminately, there are a number of judgements in which important systemic issues were addressed by the ECtHR by way of pilot judgements. The future effectiveness of this procedure in the ECHR Contracting States remains to be seen, as does the

---

[228] For a detailed presentation of a variety of factors which influence the reception of the ECHR in Poland, see Dembour and Krzyżanowska-Mierzewska (2004a).

question whether these countries will bring lasting results by way of domestic legal reform in Poland. There have been no such judgements given in Slovak cases so far, and it is impossible to predict whether there will be any in the future so as to make European class actions a living and common reality before the Strasbourg Court.[229]

---

[229] But see *Urbárska Obec Trenčanske Biskupice and Jan Kratky v. Slovakia* (appl. no. 74258/01), Decision (Fourth Section), 12 September 2006 (not reported) – there is potential here for a judgement of a great systemic importance.

Bibliography

Bàlintova, M., 'O (ne)účinnosti ústavnej sťažnosti podľa článku 127 ústavy vo vzťahu k prieťahom v konaní' [(On (in) effectiveness of the constitutional complaint according to the article 127 of the Constitution in relation to the delays in judicial proceedings], *Justične revue* 5 (2005), 637.

Beernaert, M.-A., 'De l'épuisement des voies de recours internes en cas de dépassement du délai raisonnable', *Revue trimestrielle des droits de l'homme* 60 (2004), 905.

Benoît-Rohmer, F., 'Le particularisme du contentieux concernant les pays d'Europe centrale et orientale', *L'Europe des Libertés* 9 (2002), 8.

Bojarski, Ł., 'Dostępność nieodpłatnej pomocy prawnej. Raport z monitoringu' .[Availability of Legal Aid. Monitoring Report], Helsinki Foundation of Human Rights (Warsaw, 2003).

Blaško, M., 'Slovakia', in R. Blackburn and J. Polakiewicz (eds.), *Fundamental rights in Europe: the ECHR and its Member States, 1950–2000* (Oxford, 2001), 755.

Bröstl, A., *The Constitutional Court of the Slovak Republic (organization, process, doctrine)* (Košice, 2001), 157.

Čič, M., 'Interaction between the ECHR and the Protection of Human Rights and Fundamental Freedoms in the Legal System of the Slovak Republic', in: Mahoney, P., Matscher, F., Petzold, H., and Wildhaber, L. (eds), *Protection des droits de l'homme: la perspective européenne, mélanges à la mémoire de Rolv Ryssdal, Protecting human rights: the European perspective, studies in memory of Rolv Ryssdal* (Cologne/Berlin/Bonn/Munich, 2000), 237.

Dembour, M.-B. and Krzyżanowska-Mierzewska, M., 'Ten Years On: The Popularity of the European Convention on the Protection of Human Rights and Fundamental Freedoms in Poland', *European Human Rights Law Review* 4 (2004), 400. (cit.: 2004a).

—, 'Ten Years On: The Voluminous and Interesting Polish Case Law', European Human Rights Law Review 5 (2004), 517. (cit.: 2004b)

Flauss, J.-F., 'Convention européenne des droits de l'homme et succession d'Etats aux traités: une curiosité, la décision du Comité des Ministres du Conseil de l'Europe en date du 30 juin 1993 concernant la République tchèque et la Slovaquie', *Revue Universelle des Droits de l'Homme* 6 (1–2) (1994), 1.

—, 'Le droit à un recours effectif au secours de la règle du délai raisonnable: un revirement de jurisprudence historique', *Revue trimestrielle des droits de l'homme* 49 (2002), 179.

Garlicki, L., 'Wolności i prawa jednostki w Konstytucji Rzeczpospolitej Polskiej z 1997 roku'in Jerzmański H. (ed.) [Individual Freedoms and Rights In the 1997 Constitution of the Republic of Poland], in *Pięć lat Konstytucji Rzeczypospolitej Polskiej* [Five Years of the Constitution of the Republic of Poland], (Warsaw, 2002), 60. (cit.: 2002a).

—, 'Interpretacja orzecznictwa ETPC na szczeblu krajowym (problemy przewlekłości postępowania)' [Interpretation of the Case law of the ECHR At A National Level: Problems of Excessive Length of Proceedings], *Biuletyn Biura Informacji Rady Europy*, 2 (2002), 5. (cit.: 2002b).

Gontarski, P., 'Ile władzy sądu, tyle odpowiedzialności' [Judicial Powers: As Much Responsibility As Power], Rzeczpospolita, 29 January 2006, C 3.

Hofmański, P., 'Wpływ standardów w zakresie prawnomiędzynarodowej ochrony praw człowieka na system prawa karnego i praktykę sądow karnych' [Influence of international human rights standards on criminal law and its application by criminal courts], 1998 *Biuletyn Centrum Informacji Rady Europy* 3–4 (1998), 107.

Keller, H., 'Reception of the European Convention for the Protection of Human Rights and Fundamental Freedoms (ECHR) in Poland and Switzerland', *ZaöRV* 65 (2005), 283.

Krzyżanowska-Mierzewska, M., 'Krajowe środki odwoławcze przewidziane przez prawo polskie jako warunek dopuszczalności skargi' [Exhaustion of Domestic Remedies Under Polish Law as Requirement of Admissibility of Individual Applications to the European ECtHR of Human Rights, A Survey of Case Law], in Machińska H (ed.), *Polska w Radzie Europy – 10 lat czlonkostwa* [Poland in the Council of Europe – Ten Years of Membership], (Warsaw, 2002), 203.

—, 'Polska skarga konstytucyjna w kontekście wymogu wykorzystania krajowych środków odwoławczych przed wniesieniem skargi do Europejskiego Trybunalu Praw Człowieka' [The Polish Constitutional Complaint in the Context of The Requirement of Exhaustion of Domestic Remedies before the ECtHR] in Izdebski, H. and Machińska, H. (eds.), *Dostęp obywateli do europejskiego wymiaru sprawiedliwości* [Citizen's Access to the European Justice], (Warsaw, 2005), 27.

Leszczyński, L., 'Application of the European Convention of Human Rights in the Polish Courts: An Impact on the Judicial Argumentation', *Human Rights Review* 2(1) (1996), 19.

Łętowska, E., 'A Constitution of Possibilities', *East European Constitutional Review* 6(2/3) (1997), 76.

—, 'Udział trzeciej władzy w dyskursie społecznym – sądy i trybunały najwyższych instancji', [Judicial Powers In Social Discourse: Highest Courts and Tribunals] in Hauser, R. and Nawacki, L. (eds.) *Państwo w służbie obywateli, Księga jubileuszowa Jerzego Świątkiewicza* (Warsaw, 2005), 38.

—, 'Korzystny dla skarżącego wyrok ETPCz jako podstawa skargi o wznowienie postępowania – glosa do postanowienia SN z 19.10.2005 (V CO 16/05)', [A Judgement of the ECtHR In the Applicant's Favour as A Ground for the Re-opening of Proceedings; A Comment on A Decision of the Supreme Court], *Europejski Przegląd Sądowy* 1(4) (2006), 45.

Màzak, J., 'Further Constitutional Developments (Amendments to the Constitution of the Republic of Slovakia)', 2001, Venice Commission, H.R. 2001.

Nowicki, M. A., *Europejska Konwencja Praw Człowieka. Wybór orzecznictwa* [The European Court of Human Rights. Selection of Case law] (Warsaw, 1999).

—, *Europejski Trybunał Praw Człowieka. Orzecznictwo. Tom 1: Prawo do rzetelnego procesu sądowego* [The European Court of Human Rights. Case law, Vol. 1: The Right to a Fair Hearing] (Cracow, 2001).

—, *Europejski Trybunał Praw Człowieka. Orzecznictwo. Tom 2: Prawo do życia i inne prawa* [The European Court of Human Rights. Case law, Vol. 2: The Right to Life and Other Rights] (Cracow, 2002).

—, *Wokół Konwencji Europejskiej. Krótki komentarz do Europejskiej Konwencji Praw Człowieka* [Around The European Convention. A Brief Commentary to the European Convention on Human Rights], (Cracow, 2003).

The Obudsman's Office, M. A. Nowicki, Obudsman, (ed.), *Zanim napiszesz skargę – przeczytaj* [Read before you write a complaint] (Warsaw, 1993).

Petrova, C., 'Political and Legal Obstacles to the Development of Public Interest Law', *East European Constitutional Law Review* 5(4) (1996), 62.

Pirosikovà, M., 'O výške spravodlivého zadosťučinenia priznávaného na vnútroštátnej úrovni za prieťahy v konaní z pohľadu najnovšej judikatúry Európskeho súdu pre ľudské práva' [About the amount of the fair satisfaction awarded at national level for delays in proceedings in the light of the newest case law of the European Court of Human Rights], *Justične revue* 6–7 (2005), 794.

Repik, B., 'La place de la Convention Européenne des Droits de l'Homme dans l'ordre juridique interne de la Republique Slovaque', in Tavernier, P., *Quelle Europe pour les Droits de l'Homme?*, (Brussels, 1996), 372.

Safjan, M., 'Czy szykuje się nowy podział Europy?' [Is a New Division of Europe Under Way?], Rzeczpospolita, 7 July 2003, 3.

—, 'Meandry systemu ochrony praw podstawowych. O rzeczywistości realnej i wirtual-nej', [Meandering Human Rights Justice: Virtual versus Real Realities] in Izdebski, H. and Machińska, H. (eds.), *Dostęp obywateli do europejskiego wymiaru sprawiedliwości*, [Citizens' Access to the European Justice] (Warsaw, 2005), 120.

Siedlecka, E.,'Strasbourg sobie, a nasz sąd sobie' [Strasburg Goes One Way, Our Court Happily Ignores It], Gazeta Wyborcza, 4 January 2006.

Semprich, Z., 'Wygrał w Strasburgu, stracił w Polsce' [Won In Strasburg, Lost In Poland], Rzeczpospolita, 2 December 2005.

Skubiszewski, K., 'Prawo PRL a traktaty' [Law of the Polish People's Republic and Trea-ties], *Ruch Prawniczy, Ekonomiczny i Socjologiczny* XXXIV 3 (1972), 17.

—,'Prawa jednostki, umowy międzynarodowe i porządek prawny PRL0' [Individual Rights, International Conventions and Legal Order of the Polish Popular Republic], *Państwo i Prawo* 7 (1981), 20.

Trzciński, J., 'Błędna interpretacja polskich przepisów' [An Erroneous Interpretation of Polish Laws], Rzeczpospolita, 31 May 2004, C 3.

Urban, R., 'Právo na prerokovanie veci bez zbytočných prieťahov' [Right to a Hearing without Unreasonable Delays], *Justične revue* 2 (2004), 161.

M. Wąsek-Wiaderek, M. and Sakowicz, A. 'Glosy do uchwały składu 7 sędziów Sądu Najwyższego z 18 października 2001 r., I KZP 25/2001', *Palestra* 9–10 (2002), 205 and 216.

Zajadło, J., 'Some Remarks on the Relation of International Law to Internal Law in the Polish Legal System', in Rosas A. (ed.), *International Human Rights Norms in Domestic Law: Finnish and Polish perspective* (Helsinki, 1990).

Zieliński, A., 'Sędzia a standardy ochrony praw człowieka' [Judge and Human Rights Protection standards], in J. Białocerkiewicz (ed.), *Księga jubileuszowa Profesora Tadeusza Jasudowicza* (Toruń, 2004), 519.

10

The Reception Process in Russia and Ukraine

Angelika Nußberger

A. Historical Context: Accession and Ratification[1]

1. Russia

a. The Accession Process

Russia's accession to the Council of Europe was a difficult and prolonged process.[2] Although the Soviet Union had already been accepted as the first country with a special guest status in 1989[3] and the former President of the Soviet Union, Mikhail Gorbachov, had paved the way with a speech before the Parliamentary Assembly of the Council of Europe[4] in the same year, the accession process lasted from 7 May 1992 up to 28 February 1996, when Russia's application for full membership was finally accepted. The process was suspended in 1995 due to the "indiscriminate and disproportionate use of force by the Russian military, in particular against the civilian population"[5] in the war in Chechnya and resumed only after Russia's reassurance that it intended to settle the conflict in a peaceful manner and to investigate human rights violations.[6]

---

[1] Abbreviations: SZ RF = Sobranie Zakonodatel'stva Rossijskoj Federacii; P.A. = Parliamentary Assembly of the Council of Europe; VVS = Vedomosti Verchovnogo Soveta Rossiyskoy Federastii.

[2] For the historical development see Althauser (1997), 95 et seq.

[3] Together with Russia the guest status was conferred on the delegations of Hungary, Poland, Yugoslavia, and the Soviet Union on 8 June 1989. The category of guest status had been created on 11 May 1989 in order to support the process of democratization in the countries of Central and Eastern Europe; for further details see Althauser (1997), 79.

[4] The speech is published in *Pravda* 7 July 1989, no. 188, p. 2 et seq.; see also Nußberger (2007), *Russland und der Europa Rat*, 1 et seq.

[5] See P.A. Resolution 1055 (1995) 1 on Russia's request for membership in the light of the situation in Chechnya, http://assembly.coe.int/Documents/AdoptedText/ta95/eres1065.htm (Unless indicated otherwise, all websites were visited on 14 March 2007; last access for the website in this footnote: 20 May 2007).

[6] P.A. Resolution 1065 (1995) 1 on procedure for an opinion on Russia's request for membership of the Council of Europe, http://assembly.coe.int/Documents/AdoptedText/ta95/eres1065.htm (last visited 25 May 2007).

However, it was not only the war in Chechnya which was considered "a grave violation of the Council of Europe's most elementary human rights principles".[7] In 1994[8] and in 1996,[9] two expert opinions came to negative conclusions about Russia's ability to fulfil the provisions for membership in the Council of Europe as set forth in Article 3 of the Statute. It was submitted that legislation in such important areas as criminal law and criminal procedural law was still inadequate, the judiciary and the penitentiary system were not functioning properly, the rule of law was not implemented in practice and that there was a big gap between law in the books and law in action, although the adoption of a new Russian Constitution in 1993 saw a burst of legislative activity.

The discussion on the accession of Russia to the Council of Europe was, therefore, full of controversy. On the one hand, it was feared that the standards might not be fulfilled and, as a consequence, become watered down.[10] On the other hand, the Council of Europe was seen as a promising framework for the continuation of the discussion on democracy and human rights in Russia.[11] The compromise found was an invitation for Russia to become a member on the basis of clearly formulated and demanding "commitments and understandings".[11a] Thus, Russia was expected to ratify the ECHR and the Protocols nos 1, 2, 4, 7 and 11 within one year and Protocol no. 6 within three years, and to recognize the right of individual application to the European Commission and the compulsory jurisdiction of the European Court. Furthermore, Russia was required to pass a great number of laws, such as a new criminal code, a new code of criminal procedure, a new civil code and a code of civil procedure, and to put in place a moratorium on executions with effect from the day of accession.[12] The long list of inadequacies and demands indicated that the gap between the legal order existing at the time of accession and a legal order based on the rule of law was enormous. As a consequence, a process of monitoring was institutionalized in order to follow further developments closely and to sanction violations of the obligations resulting from membership.

On the basis of these "considerations and commitments", the Russian Federation became the 39th Member of the Council of Europe on 28 February 1996.

---

[7] See P.A. Resolution 1055 (1995) 1 (*supra* note 5).

[8] P.A., Doc. AS/Bur/Russia (1994) 7 of 28 September 1994, Report on the conformity of the legal order of the Russian Federation with Council of Europe standards, prepared by Rudolf Bernhardt, Stefan Trechsel, Albert Weitzel and Felix Ermacora, printed in HRLJ 1994, Vol. 15, no. 7, 251.

[9] P.A., Doc. 7443 of 2 January 1996, Report of the Political Affairs Committee, Report on Russia's request for membership of the Council of Europe, rapporteur: Ernst Muehlemann, printed in HRLJ 1996, Vol. 17, nos 3–6, 187–194.

[10] See Janis (1997), 4.

[11] For more details see Althauser (1997), 95 et seq.

[11a] Committee of Ministers of the Council of Europe, Resolution (96)2, Doc. 7490 of 14 February 1996, Invitation to the Russian Federation to become a Member of the Council of Europe.

[12] See for the details Opinion no. 193 (1996) 1, adopted by the P.A. on 25 January 1996, http://assembly.coe.int/documents/AdoptedText/ta96/EOPI193.htm (last visited 25 May 2007).

The immediate expectations connected with the invitation to become a member were not fulfilled. Only one year after the accession the Parliamentary Assembly criticized Russia's "flagrant violation of her commitments and obligations", as in the first half of 1996, 53 executions were carried out.[13] Although the reports in 1998,[14] 2002[15] and 2005[16] stated progress in many areas, the overall impression of the human rights record and of the development of the legal system was that they were still inadequate. Many of the conditions made at the time of accession were unfulfilled. More than ten years after accession, not even a quarter of the treaties of the Council of Europe had been ratified.[17]

Currently, tensions between the Council of Europe and Russia are exacerbated by Russia's refusal to abolish finally the death penalty.[18] Furthermore, new legal acts, such as the law on non-governmental organizations,[19] the changes to the electoral laws,[20] regulation of the registration of parties[21] and the changes to the law on extremism[22] are considered a "reason for concern".[23] The Committee for the Prevention of Torture and Inhuman or Degrading Treatment or Punishment accuses Russia of not cooperating and of not improving the situation in Chechnya.[24] Russian commentators consider criticism coming from the Council of Europe as well as resolutions such as the Resolution 1481 (2006), "Need for international condemnation of crimes of totalitarian communist regimes", as counterproductive. Some Russian commentators even claim that Russia should

[13] P.A. Resolution 1111 (1997) 1 on the honouring of the commitment entered into by Russia upon accession to the Council of Europe to put into place a moratorium on executions.

[14] P.A., Honouring of obligations and commitments by the Russian Federation, Doc. 8127 of 2 June 1998, http://assembly.coe.int/main.asp?Link=/documents/workingdocs/doc98/edoc8127.htm.

[15] P.A., Honouring of obligations and commitments by the Russian Federation, Doc. 9396 of 26 March 2002, http://assembly.coe.int/Main.asp?link=/Documents/WorkingDocs/Doc02/EDOC9396.htm

[16] P.A., Honouring of obligations and commitments by the Russian Federation, Doc. 10568 of 3 June 2005, http://assembly.coe.int/Documents/WorkingDocs/Doc05/EDOC10568.htm.

[17] As of 14 March 2007, Russia has ratified 49 out of 200 treaties; http://conventions.coe.int.

[18] See Nußberger and Marenkov (2006), 1 et seq.

[19] Law 18 FZ On Introducing Amendments to Certain Legislative Acts of the Russian Federation; see European Parliament resolution on human rights in Russia P6_TA-PROV(2005)0534 and the new NGO legislation, http://eng.kavkaz.memo.ru/docstext/engdocs/id/904468.html; see Nußberger and Schmidt (2007), 16 et seq.

[20] SZ RF 2006, no. 3, pos. 282.

[21] SZ RF 2004, no. 52, pos. 5272.

[22] SZ RF 2006, no. 31, pos. 3447; see Schmidt (2006), 409 et seq.

[23] See the report (*supra* note 16), para. 42: "The cumulative effect of the package of changes reinforcing the 'vertical of power' of the President of the Russian Federation is therefore a reason for concern. While we fully understand and support President Putin's efforts to succeed in the fight against terrorism and to increase the efficiency of Russia's political and administrative system, such efficiency should not be – and does not have to be – achieved at the expense of democracy. For the latter to function properly, power must not only be vertically reinforced, but also horizontally shared."

[24] European Committee for the Prevention of Torture and Inhuman or Degrading Treatment or Punishment, Public Statement concerning the Chechen Republic of the Russian Federation, made on 13 March 2007, http://cpt.coe.int/documents/rus/2007-17-inf-eng.pdf.

retreat from the "*pustaya govoril'nya*" (empty talking shop) and point to the high costs involved. However, for both sides it is clear that the marriage, even if unhappy, should continue.[25] For Russia, membership in the Council of Europe means "reintegration into the legal and cultural European space";[26] leaving the Council of Europe would be interpreted as a step towards a new isolationism.[27] Furthermore, Russia hopes to influence the solution of European problems, and to promote quicker and more effective reforms.[28] For the Council of Europe, it is of utmost importance to continue the dialogue with Russia in order to justify the Council's role as a decisive political player in the relationship between Eastern and Western Europe.

b. Ratification of the ECHR and the Protocols

In 1997, experts from Russia and the Council of Europe analysed the compatibility of the ECHR and Russian law. They identified major problems and recommended changes in many areas.[29] Despite this result, the Convention, as changed or amended by Protocols nos 2, 3, 5, and 8 together with Protocols nos 1, 4, 7, 9, 10, and 11, was ratified on 5 May 1998 and thus more than a year after the short time frame set in 1996. The respective law on the ratification of the Convention and its Protocols was passed on 30 March 1998 and entered into force upon the official publication of the law on 7 April 1998.[30] It contains explicit provisions on the acceptance of the right to individual petition and the compulsory jurisdiction of the European Court of Human Rights in all questions concerning the interpretation and application of the Convention. Although the provision is unequivocal, there are voices in the literature holding that the Court's decisions only have a recommendatory character and that the Court is a quasi-judicial body.[31]

At the time of ratification, Russia already adhered to the International Covenant on Civil and Political Rights,[32] which entered into force on 23 March 1976. The Soviet Union had signed the Covenant on 18 March 1968, and ratified it on 16 October 1973. It acceded to the Optional Protocol just before the dissolution of the Soviet Union on 1 October 1991. International human rights conventions played a significant role in the beginning of the transformation pro-

---

[25] See e.g. the comment of Elena Ovcharenko, Razvod s Sovetom Evropy – i devich'ya familiya, Izvestiya, 16 February 2006, http://www.izvestia.ru/comment/article3062219.

[26] Vodolagin (2001), 26.

[27] See the interview with Vladimir Ryzhkov, Deputy of the *Duma* and the head of the Committee "Russia in the unified Europe", 23 January 2006, Radio Svoboda, http://www.svobodanews.ru/Transcript/2006/01/23/20060123120607743.html.

[28] Entin (2006), 444.

[29] Kovler (2004), 149 refers to a report under the title "The Compatibility of law of the Russian Federation with the requirements of the European Convention on Human Rights".

[30] Rossiyskaya Gazeta, 7 April 1998, SZ RF 1998, no. 14, pos. 1514.

[31] See Kovler (2004), 5, quoting this opinion in the literature without specifying the authors; see also Bowring (1997), 628.

[32] International Covenant on Civil and Political Rights, 999 U.N.T.S. 171, entered into force on 23 March 1976.

cess in the late 1980's and early 1990's, when the deficiencies in the national legislation had to be filled in with generally acceptable standards.[33] Even before its entry into force in Russia, the ECHR – as well as the International Covenants on human rights – served as models for the human rights section of the Russian Constitution adopted in 1993.[34] Still, the ratification of the ECHR is considered as "revolutionary" as it confronts Russian legal science and practice with legal structures hitherto completely unknown.[35]

Protocol no. 6 on the abolition of the death penalty was signed on 16 April 1997, but never ratified. The Duma (Russian Parliament) rejected a law on the ratification on repeated occasions; it was not even adopted in the first hearing.[36] Protocol no. 13 on the abolition of the death penalty in all circumstances was not even signed. Protocol no. 12 on the general prohibition of discrimination was signed on 4 November 2000 and Protocol no. 14 amending the control system of the Convention was signed on 4 May 2006, just at the beginning of Russia's chairmanship of the Committee of Ministers. At present, Russia is the only country blocking the entry into force of Protocol no. 14, intended to help solve or at least mitigate the problem of the excessive workload of the Court. In the last vote on 20 December 2006 only 27 deputies voted in favour of the ratification, whereas 138 deputies voted against.[37] In January 2007, the President explained that the Duma's decision not to ratify Protocol no. 14 was understandable due to the "politicisation of some of the decisions".[38] On the other hand, the president of the committee on international affairs of the Federation Council, Margelov, clearly stressed the necessity to ratify the Protocol.[39] Officially, the non-ratification is justified on the basis of the following arguments: first, it is stressed that the level of human rights protection would be lowered if decisions could be taken by single judges. Second, Protocol no. 14 is considered to provide only for provisional measures and thus to threaten the stability of the human rights control system as a whole.[40]

Shortly after Russia had joined the Council of Europe, the Russian Consti-

---

[33] On the application of international human rights treaties in the jurisprudence of the Committee on Constitutional Control and the Russian Constitutional Court cf. Rückert (2005), 65 et seq.; Danilenko (1994), 460.

[34] Kovler (2004), 2; Alekseeva (2002), 98–119; Glotov (1999), Attachment no. 1, 512; see also the interview with Evgeniy Prokhorov, summarized in Althauser (1997), 72, footnote 183.

[35] Baranov (2004), 26; Laptev (2001), 46.

[36] Nußberger and Marenkov (2006), 2; Nußberger and Marenkov (2007), *Todesstrafe*, 9 et seq.

[37] Rodin/Samarina, Pouprazhnyalis' v plyuralizme. Duma otkazalas' ratifitsirovat' predstavlenny prezidentom proekt mezhdunarodnogo dogovora, Nezavisimaya Gazeta, 21 December 2006.

[38] Stenographic Report on the Meeting of Members of the Council for Enhancing Institutions of Civil Society and Human Rights and President Putin, http://www.kremlin.ru/text/appears/2007/01/116614.html.

[39] Mikhail Margelov, *Nado li byt' dissidentom v. Sovete Evropy?*, Nezavisimaya Gazeta, 22 December 2006.

[40] See the translation of the resolution of the *Duma* Committee in EuGRZ (2007), 507; the political implications of the non-ratification are discussed by Engel (2007), 241.

tutional Court cited Protocol no. 4 in a case concerning the right of free movement.[41] The purpose of mentioning the Convention was to "enrich and strengthen the argumentation".[42] Between the signature of the Convention in 1996 and its ratification in 1998, the Convention was referred to in three decisions and in one dissenting opinion.[43]

Table 1

Protocol[44]	Signature	Ratification	Entry into force	Declarations/Reservations
Protocol no. 1	28 Feb. 1996	5 May 1998	5 May 1998	–
Protocol no. 2	28 Feb. 1996	5 May 1998	5 May 1998	–
Protocol no. 3	28 Feb. 1996	5 May 1998	5 May 1998	–
Protocol no. 4	28 Feb. 1996	5 May 1998	5 May 1998	–
Protocol no. 5	28 Feb. 1996	5 May 1998	5 May 1998	–
Protocol no. 6	16 April 1997	–	–	–
Protocol no. 7	28 Feb. 1996	5 May 1998	1 Aug. 1998	–
Protocol no. 8	28 Feb. 1996	5 May 1998	5 May 1998	–
Protocol no. 9	28 Feb. 1996	5 May 1998	1 Sept. 1998	–
Protocol no. 10	28 Feb. 1996	5 May 1998	–	–
Protocol no. 11	28 Feb. 1996	5 May 1998	1 Nov. 1998	–
Protocol no. 12	4 Nov. 2000	–	–	–
Protocol no. 13	–	–	–	–
Protocol no. 14	4 May 2006	–	–	3 Declarations concerning Articles 8, 19[45]

c. Reservations and Declarations

At the time of the ratification of the Convention, the Russian Federation declared that the application of Article 5(3) and (4) ECHR did not prevent the applica-

[41] Judgement of the Russian Constitutional Court, 4 April 1996, SZ RF 1996, no. 16, pos. 1909.
[42] Tiunov (2001), *O roli konventsii*, 93.
[43] Burkov (2007), 36.
[44] Source: http://conventions.coe.int/Treaty/Commun/ChercheMembres.asp?CM=3&CL=ENG
[45] Declaration: "The Russian Federation declares that, signing the Protocol under the condition of its subsequent ratification, it proceeds from the following: - the Protocol will be applied in accordance with the understanding contained in the Declaration on "Ensuring the effectiveness of the implementation of the European Convention on Human Rights at national and European levels" adopted by the Committee of Ministers of the Council of Europe at its 114th session on 12 May 2004; - the provisions of the Protocol and their application will be without prejudice to further steps aimed at reaching a full consensus between Member States of the Council of Europe on issues of strengthening the control mechanism of the Convention for the Protection of Human Rights and Fundamental Freedoms and of the European Court of Human Rights, including elaboration of a new additional protocol to the Convention based on the proposals of the "Group of Wise

tion of certain provisions of the Code of Criminal Procedure of 1960[46] and of the Disciplinary Regulations of the Armed Forces of 1993[47] concerning the procedure for the arrest, holding in custody and detention of persons suspected of having committed a criminal offence. The reservations mirrored the transitional provisions on criminal procedural law in the Constitution of 1993,[48] but contradicted the obligations Russia had inherited from the Soviet Union under the International Covenant on Civil and Political Rights.[49] Although the reservations touched upon the core of Articles 5(3) and 5(4) ECHR,[50] the Court found that these Articles could still be applied with respect to the length of the detention on remand[51] and to the lack of an effective review procedure.[52]

The Code of Criminal Procedure was adopted on 18 December 2001.[53] Its entry into force was foreseen as occurring in stages between 1 July 2002 and 1 January 2004. In the new Code of Criminal Procedure, the right of the *prokuratura* and of other investigative bodies to arrest, search, or seize without a court

Persons" established to consider the issue of the long-term effectiveness of the Convention control mechanism; - the application of the Protocol will be without prejudice to the process of improving the modalities of functioning of the European Court of Human Rights, first of all to strengthening the stability of its Rules, not excluding supplementary measures to be adopted by the Committee of Ministers of the Council of Europe aimed at reinforcing the control over the use of financial means allocated to the European Court of Human Rights and at ensuring the quality of staff of its Registry, with the understanding that procedural rules relating to examination of applications by the European Court of Human Rights must be adopted in the form of an international treaty subject to ratification or to another form of expression by a State of its consent to be bound by its provisions." (Deposited on 4 May 2006).

Declaration: "The Russian Federation declares that, signing the Protocol under the condition of its subsequent ratification, it proceeds from the following: the application of Article 28, paragraph 3 of the Convention as amended by Article 8 of the Protocol does not exclude the right of a High Contracting Party concerned, if the judge elected in its respect is not a member of the committee, to request that he or she be given the possibility to take the place of one of the members of the committee." (Deposited on 4 May 2006).

Declaration: "The Russian Federation declares that, signing the Protocol under the condition of its subsequent ratification, it proceeds from the following: no provision of the Protocol will be applied prior to its entry into force in accordance with Article 19." (Deposited on 4 May 2006).

[46] Vedomosti Verkhovnogo Soveta RSFSR", 1960, no. 40, pos. 593.

[47] Collection of Instruments of the President and the Government of the Russian Federation, 1993, no. 51, p. 4931.

[48] See Article 6 of the Second Part of the Russian Constitution: "Until the enforcement of criminal-procedural legislation of the Russian Federation in accordance with the provisions of this Constitution, the prior procedures of the arrest, custody and detention of individuals suspected of committing crimes shall be maintained."

[49] Cf. Article 9(3) of the ICCPR which provides that anyone arrested or detained on a criminal charge "shall be brought promptly before a judge or other officer authorised by the law to exercise judicial power". Due to this contradiction it was argued that the reservations to the ECHR were not effective at all, cf. Bulakova (2003), 44 et seq.

[50] Ferschtman (2001), 741.

[51] See e.g. *Kalashnikov v. Russia* (appl. no. 47095/99), Judgement (Third Section), 15 July 2002, Reports 2002-VI, 93 et seq.

[52] See e.g. *Klyakhin v. Russia* (appl. no. 46082/99), Judgement (Second Section), 30 November 2004 (not reported).

[53] Rossiyskaya Gazeta, 22 December 2001, SZ RF 2001, no. 249, pos. 2861.

order was withdrawn. It also required that everyone arrested be brought before a judge within 48 hours. These amendments were originally scheduled to enter into force on 1 January 2004; however, following a ruling by the Constitutional Court of 14 March 2002,[54] the relevant provisions were applied as of 1 July 2002. Although the reservations of the Russian Federation to the ECHR were thus no longer necessary,[55] they were not yet withdrawn.

2. Ukraine

a. The Accession Process

Ukraine's accession to the Council of Europe was initiated on the basis of the same arguments as those used in Russia. After having declared sovereignty on 16 July 1990 and independence on 24 August 1991, Ukraine went down the road of political changes and applied for membership to the Council of Europe on 14 July 1992, i.e. just a few months after Russia. The process lasted over three years (until 9 November 1995) and although it was not suspended as in Russia, it was very difficult and marked by controversy. Two years after the application, on 13 July 1994, a political dialogue between Ukraine and the Committee of Ministers of the Council of Europe was initiated in order to bring constitutional provisions and general legislation into conformity with the general principles of the Council of Europe.

The Council of Europe required Ukraine to take steps to consolidate the exercise of State power and to solve problems in the bilateral relationship with Russia. Following a constitutional agreement reached on 8 June 1995 between the President and the Parliament on basic principles of the organization and functioning of State power and local self-government, a special status was granted to the Crimean peninsula, and the difference with Russia about the division of the Black Sea fleet and access to the naval facilities in Sevastopol[56] was settled. Ukraine was then deemed ready for Council of Europe membership. Nevertheless, much still remained to be done to bring national legislation in line with European standards. On 9 November 1995, Ukraine became the 38th Contracting State of the Council of Europe,[57] just before Russia in 1996.

Upon accession, Ukraine agreed to comply, within special deadlines, with a number of obligations and commitments listed in Parliamentary Assembly Opinion no. 190 (1995).[58] Thus Ukraine was called upon to adopt a new constitution within one year from accession, and to frame an act on the legal policy for the

---

[54] Rossiyskaya Gazeta, 21 March 2002, SZ RF 2002, no. 50, pos. 2918.

[55] Zorkin (2006), 36.

[56] Agreement of 9 June 1995, Vidomosti Verkhovnoy Rady Ukraiiny 1995, no. 18, pos. 133, http://zakon.rada.gov.ua/cgi-bin/laws/main.cgi?nreg=1%EA%2F95%2D%E2%F0).

[57] See Verkhovna Rada Ukraiiny; Zakon vid 31.10.1995 N° 398/95-WR Pro priyednannya Ukraiiny do Statutu Rady Yevropy//Vidomosti Verkhovnoy Rady Ukraiiny vid 19.09.1995–1995 r., N° 38, stat'ya 287.

[58] P.A. Opinion no. 190 (1995) on the application by Ukraine for membership of the Council

protection of human rights and on legal and judicial reforms. Other require-ments concerned, above all, a new Criminal Code, Criminal Procedure Code, Civil Code, Civil Procedure Code, and new laws on elections and on political parties.

The new constitution was adopted within one year after accession on 28 June 1996.[59] Apart from that, the legislative process was extremely slow. Most of the legal statues promised in the accession process were adopted only after years of delay (Criminal Code 2001, Code of Civil Procedure 2004, Code of Administra-tive Procedure 2005), and a Code of Criminal Procedure has yet to be adopted. The Parliamentary Assembly started a monitoring procedure on 11 December 1995, initially under Order no. 508 (1995)[60] and, subsequently, under resolu-tion 1115 (1997).[61] The monitoring process has not yet been completed. On 27 January 1999, the Parliamentary Assembly of the Council of Europe decided that it would proceed to the annulment of the credentials of the Ukrainian Parliamen-tary Delegation and to recommend to the Committee of Ministers to suspend Ukraine from its right of representation, should substantial progress not be made by 21 June 1999. In June 1999, the procedure aimed at suspending Ukranian rights was started.[62] In April 2001, Ukraine was threatened for the second time with the imposition of sanctions if no substantial progress in honouring the obligations and commitments was made. Since September 2001, however, sub-stantial progress has been made with respect to significant new legislation. The relationship with the Council of Europe was generally improved in the aftermath of the "Orange Revolution" that was welcomed as a "pivotal moment in the nation's history" when the "Ukrainian people stood up in unprecedented mass peaceful protest (...) against the Government's attempt to steal the 2004 presi-dential election, choosing freedom, democracy and the rule of law over corrup-tion and intimidation".[63] Nonetheless, the Committee of Ministers still deems that a wide range of activities need to be carried out in order to strengthen the democratic development and to live up to the obligations of a Contracting State of the Council of Europe.

It is worth mentioning that it is not only the process of bringing legislation

of Europe, http://assembly.coe.int/Documents/AdoptedText/TA95/eopi190.HTM (last visited 25 May 2007).

[59] Vidomosti Verkhovnoy Rady Ukraiiny 1996, no. 30, pos. 141; cf. on the constitutional process in Ukraine Protsyk (2005), 23.

[60] http://assembly.coe.int/Documents/AdoptedText/TA95/EDIR508.htm.

[61] http://assembly.coe.int/Main.asp?link=/Documents/AdoptedText/ta97/ERES1115.htm.

[62] http://assembly.coe.int//main.asp?link=http://assembly.coe.int/documents/adoptedtext/TA99/ERES1194.htm.

[63] P.A., Honouring of obligations and commitments by Ukraine, Doc. 10676 of 19 September 2005, http://assembly.coe.int/Documents/WorkingDocs/Doc05/EDOC10676.htm.

into conformity with European standards that is delayed; at the present time, Ukraine has yet to ratify many treaties of the Council of Europe.[64]h

b. Ratification of the ECHR and the Protocols

The ECHR had to be signed at the moment of accession. Ukraine was given one year to ratify the ECHR, Protocols nos 1, 2, 4, 7 and 11 and a series of other conventions of the Council of Europe.[65] In addition, it was given three years to ratify Protocol no. 6.

The ECHR and several Protocols[66] were thus signed on the day of accession on 9 November 1995. The law on ratification was passed only on 17 July 1997.[67] The ECHR and Protocols nos 1, 2, 3, 4, 5, 8 and 11 were then ratified and entered into force on 11 September 1997. Protocol no. 7 and Protocol no. 11 followed shortly after on 1 December 1997 and 1 November 1998.

The ratification of Protocol no. 6, however, encountered major difficulties. Executions continued beyond accession and on 11 March 1997 a *de facto* moratorium on executions was introduced.[68] The rebound was brought about by the decision of the Ukrainian Constitutional Court on 29 December 1999[69] declaring the death penalty unconstitutional. Protocol no. 6, already signed on 5 May 1997, was ratified on 4 April 2000[70] and came into force on 1 May 2000. On 22 February 2000, the Parliament of Ukraine had already replaced the death penalty in the former Criminal Code (Article 25) with life imprisonment. Protocol no. 13, concerning the abolition of the death penalty in all circumstances, was signed on 3 May 2002, ratified on 11 March 2003, and entered into force on 1 July 2003.[71] Protocol no. 12 was signed on 4 November 2000, but ratified only on 23

---

[64] As of 25 May 2007 Ukraine has ratified 60 out of 200 Treaties, http://conventions.coe.int/Treaty/Commun/ListeTraites.asp?PO=U&MA=999&SI=2&DF=&CM=3&CL=ENG.

[65] European Convention for the Prevention of Torture, Framework Convention for the Protection of National Minorities, European Charter of Local Self-Government, European Charter for Regional or Minority Languages.

[66] Protocols nos 2, 3, 5, 8 and 11; Protocols nos 1, 4 and 7 have been signed on 19 December 1996.

[67] Verkhovna Rada Ukraiiny; Zakon wid 17.07.1997 N° 475/97-WR Pro ratifikatsiyu Konventsiyi pro zakhist prav lyudyny i osnovopolozhnykh svobod 1950 roku, Pershoho protokolu ta protokoliv N 2, 4, 7 ta 11 do Konventsiyi //Vidomosti Verkhovnoyi Rady Ukrayiny vid 14.10.1997–1997 r., N° 40, statt'ya 263.

[68] 212 persons were executed between 9 November 1995 and 11 March 1997, P.A. Resolution 1179 (1999) Honouring of obligations and commitments by Ukraine, http://assembly.coe.int/Main.asp?link=/Documents/AdoptedText/ta99/ERES1179.htm (last visited 25 May 2007).

[69] UKR-2000-1-003.

[70] Verkhovna Rada Ukraiiny; Zakon vid 22.02.2000 N° 1484-III Pro ratifikatsiyu Protokolu Konventsiji pro zakhist prav lyudyny i osnovopolozhnykh svobod, yaky stosuyet'sya skasuvannya smertnoyi kary //Vidomosti Verkhownoyi Rady Ukraiiny vid 31.03.2000–2000 r., N° 13, statt'ya 111.

[71] Verkhovna Rada Ukraiiny; Zakon vid 28.11.2002 N° 318-IV Pro ratifikatsiyu Protokolu N 13 do Konventsiyi pro zakhist prav lyudyny i osnovopolozhnykh svobod, yaky stosuyet'sya skasuvannya smertnoyi kary za bud'yakykh obstavyn //Vidomosti Verkhownoyi Rady Ukraiiny vid 24.01.2003–2003 r., N° 4, statt'ya 36.

March 2006; it has been binding upon Ukraine since 1 July 2006. Protocol no. 14 amending the control system of the ECHR was ratified on 23 March 2006.

Table 2

Protocol[72]	Signature	Ratification	Entry into force	Declarations/ Reservations
Protocol no. 1	19 Dec. 1996	11 Sept. 1997	11 Sept. 1997	–
Protocol no. 2	9 Nov. 1995	11 Sept. 1997	11 Sept. 1997	–
Protocol no. 3	9 Nov. 1995	11 Sept. 1997	11 Sept. 1997	–
Protocol no. 4	19 Dec. 1996	11 Sept. 1997	11 Sept. 1997	–
Protocol no. 5	9 Nov. 1995	11 Sept. 1997	11 Sept. 1997	–
Protocol no. 6	5 May 1997	4 April 2000	1 May 2000	1 Declaration[73]
Protocol no. 7	19 Dec. 1996	11 Sept. 1997	1 Dec. 1997	–
Protocol no. 8	9 Nov. 1995	11 Sept. 1997	11 Sept. 1997	–
Protocol no. 9	–	–	–	–
Protocol no. 10	–	–	–	–
Protocol no. 11	9 Nov. 1995	11 Sept. 1997	1 Nov. 1998	–
Protocol no. 12	4 Nov. 2000	27 March 2006	1 July 2006	–
Protocol no. 13	3 May 2002	11 March 2003	1 July 2003	–
Protocol no. 14	10 Nov. 2004	27 March 2006	27 March 2006	–

c. Reservations and Declarations

Ukraine also made reservations with regard to Article 5(3) ECHR. This provision should be applied only insofar as it did not contradict the Interim Disciplinary Statute of the Armed Forces. It was feared that the possibility of imposing an arrest as a disciplinary sanction might contradict the Convention. The reservation

---

[72] Source: http://conventions.coe.int/Treaty/Commun/ChercheMembres.asp?CM=3&CL=ENG

[73] Declaration: "On 29 December 1999, the Constitutional Court of Ukraine ruled that the provisions of the Criminal Code of Ukraine which provided for death penalty were unconstitutional. According to the Law of Ukraine of 22 February 2000 "On the Introduction of Amendments to the Criminal, Criminal Procedure and Correctional Labour Codes of Ukraine", the Criminal Code of Ukraine has been brought into conformity with the above-mentioned ruling of the Constitutional Court of Ukraine). The death penalty was replaced by life imprisonment (Article 25 of the Criminal Code of Ukraine). The Law of Ukraine On the ratification of Protocol No. 6 to the Convention for the Protection of Human Rights and Fundamental Freedoms concerning the abolition of the Death Penalty, of 1983 envisages retaining of application of the death penalty for offences committed in time of war by means of introduction of appropriate amendments to the legislation in force. Pursuant to Article 2 of the Protocol No. 6 to the Convention for the Protection of Human Rights and Fundamental Freedoms, Ukraine will notify the Secretary-General of the Council of Europe in case of introduction of these amendments." (1 May 2000 – present).

was withdrawn by Law on 3 February 2004.[74] Detention in the guardhouse as a disciplinary punishment of conscripts was abolished.[75] Furthermore, reservations have been made with regard to the provisions of Articles 5(1) and 8 ECHR, concerning the detention of a person and the arrest warrant issued by the public prosecutor. These reservations became ineffective with the expiration of the deadline (28 June 2001).

The second (still existing) reservation concerns the right of suspects to examine witnesses on the basis of Article 6(3)(d) ECHR.[76]

When it ratified Protocol no. 6, Ukraine announced in a letter of 30 June 2000 that it would use the right granted under Article 2 of the Protocol, which allowed it to maintain the death penalty in times of war. With the ratification of Protocol no. 13, this declaration has lost its meaning.

3. Comparison and Conclusion

At the outset, the process of accession to the Council of Europe and ratification of the European Convention on Human Rights together with the Protocols is very similar and differs only in some details. Both Russia and Ukraine inherited the Soviet legislation and the Soviet legal culture. Therefore, the problems caused by the incompatibility of legal regulations with European human rights standards were more or less the same in Russia and Ukraine. Both countries were invited to become members of the Council of Europe for political reasons. In the case of Russia, the obstacles were even more significant because of the war in Chechnya. After accession, the developments in the respective bilateral relationships were comparable as well. To a certain extent, it can be argued that Ukraine demonstrated more goodwill than Russia and was less hesitant to open the door for Europe. Signs of this goodwill were the abolition of the death penalty and the ratification of Protocols nos 12 and 14. In Ukraine, there was a clear shift in the bilateral relationship after the "Orange Revolution", which was warmly welcomed and supported by the Council of Europe. Still, there might be doubts as to the sustainability of the move towards democracy. In Russia isolationist tendencies are obvious,[77] but not uncontested. The impact of the Council of Europe membership on the legal development in both Russia and Ukraine is undeniable.

---

[74] P.A., Honouring of obligations and commitments by Ukraine, Doc. 10676 of 19 September 2005, p. 41 (244).

[75] Ibid.

[76] http://conventions.coe.int/Treaty/Commun/ListeDeclarations.asp?NT=005&CM=8 &DF=8/30/2007&CL=ENG&VL=1.

[77] E.g., it is important to note that Russian President Putin decided not to join the Warsaw summit in 2005, whereas the Ukrainian President Yushchenko gave an important speech there.

B. Status of the ECHR in National Law: Formal (Doctrinal) Elements

1. Russia

a. Domestic and International Law

Whereas the Soviet Union was rather hostile to international law before the Second Word War and did not accept any prevalence of international law over national law, after 1945 this attitude slowly changed.[78] At the beginning of the 1960's, the dominance of international treaty law over national law was enshrined for the first time in the Basic Principles of Civil Law of the Soviet Union and the Republics;[79] other codifications containing similar provisions followed. Still, a dualistic conception prevailed.[80] The Constitution of the Soviet Union (1977) and the Constitution of Russia (1978) both contained a provision on the implementation of international law into the domestic legal order, but did not allow the direct application of international law in the domestic setting.[81] International law was never considered to be a part of the national law. In addition, the Soviet Union found that international law should not be invoked before domestic courts.[82] It was clearly apparent that the "isolationist tendency of Soviet society in general and of the Soviet legal system in particular"[83] still prevailed. This attitude changed in the late *perestroika* period, which witnessed a new openness in the field of international relations. This even led to changes in the Russian Constitution of 1978. In 1992, a provision was inserted allowing for the primacy of "generally accepted principles in the field of human rights" over the laws of the Russian Federation.[84]

Within the framework of this development, it was a significant step forward to insert the following provision in the Russian Constitution of 1993: "The commonly recognised principles and norms of the international law and the international treaties of the Russian Federation shall be a component part of its legal system. If an international treaty of the Russian Federation stipulates other rules than those stipulated by the law, the rules of the international treaty shall apply."[85] This newly introduced Article 15(4) of the Russian Constitution clearly shows that the Russian Constitution adopts a very friendly view on international law.

---

[78]   Khlestov (1994), 52 et seq.

[79]   Basic Principles of Civil Law of the Soviet Union and the Republics, 8 December 1961 (Sovetskoe gosudarstvo i pravo, no. 2 (1961), p. 110–114).

[80]   Khlestov (1994), 55; Danilenko (1995), 458.

[81]   Cf. Article 29 of the Constitution of the Soviet Union (1977): "The USSR's relations with other States are based on observance of the following principles: ...fulfilment in good faith of obligations arising from the generally recognised principles and rules of international law, and from the international treaties signed by the USSR."

[82]   Danilenko (1994), 458.

[83]   Ibid.

[84]   Article 32 of the Constitution after the change of the Constitution on 9 December 1992, VVS RF 1993, no. 2, pos. 55.

[85]   Article 15(4) of the Russian Constitution.

That is also confirmed by other relevant provisions. Article 17(1) of the Russian Constitution stipulates that the basic rights and liberties shall be recognized and guaranteed "in conformity with the commonly recognized principles and norms of the international law". Article 55(1) of the Russian Constitution clarifies that the "listing of the basic rights and liberties in the Constitution of the Russian Federation shall not be interpreted as the denial or belittlement of the other commonly recognized human and citizens' rights and liberties". Thus, it is the international dimension of human rights law that is seen to be of special importance.[86] These constitutional provisions are repeated in various ordinary laws.

It is not surprising that these new provisions of the Constitution have given rise to a thorough debate on the monist or dualistic character of the new legal system. The Soviet international legal theory was based on the dualistic approach.[87] This changed, however, after the adoption of the new Constitution. Although there are some scholars claiming that Russia still adheres to the dualistic approach,[88] the monistic understanding is more widespread.[89] This interpretation of the current legal system is more convincing given that in Russia, as in other monistic systems, a ratified international treaty becomes part of the domestic law and is directly applicable following its promulgation, unless its application depends on the enactment of a statute.[90]

In defining the position of international law in the hierarchy of norms, the Russian Constitution differentiates between international treaty norms and customary law. Whereas the already mentioned amendments to the Russian Constitution of 1978 between 1989 and 1992 had provided for the first time in Russian legal history that "[g]enerally accepted international norms relating to human rights have supremacy over the laws of the Russian Federation and directly give rise to the rights and obligations of citizens of the Russian Federation" the Russian Constitution of 1993 provides only for the primacy of international treaty law. That is criticized as "unfounded from an international legal perspective",[91] but can be explained by the traditional scepticism of Soviet and Russian international lawyers towards customary law.

---

[86] This conception is mirrored in the corresponding provisions in the Federal Law on international treaties (Article 5(1)) and the Federal Constitutional Law on the judicial system in the Russian Federation (Article 3) as well as in special clauses in other laws.

[87] Khlestova (1997), 20 with references to the leading Soviet international lawyers Ametistov, Butkevich, Gaveridovskiy, Mullerson, Urenko, Chernichenko.

[88] See Biryukov (1998), 73, who argues that the term "pravovaya sistema" (legal system) used in Article 15(4) is different from "pravo" (law). Although international law is part of the "pravovaya sistema" it is not part of the "pravo". Therefore, even if international norms are incorporated in the national legal system they differ from national norms.

[89] Khlestov (1994), 55; Khlestov (1995), 55; Kahn (2003), 78; Burkov (2006), *Primenenie*, 16.

[90] Cf. the Article 5(3) of the Law on international treaties: "Provisions of officially published international treaties of the Russian Federation, that do not necessitate the enactment of inner-State acts for their application are directly applied within the Russian Federation." (translation by the author).

[91] Lukashuk (1995), 16.

The primacy of the ECHR in relation to statutory law is generally not called into doubt. The status of the Convention in the hierarchy is, however, controversial, that is whether it ranks on a par with the Constitution or with constitutional laws[92] or whether it occupies an intermediate rank between constitutional laws and statutory laws.[93] The starting point of this discussion is the wording of Article 15(1) of the Constitution: "The Constitution of the Russian Federation shall have supreme legal force and direct effect, and shall be applicable throughout the entire territory of the Russian Federation. Laws and other legal acts adopted by the Russian Federation may not contravene the Constitution of the Russian Federation." On the basis of the interpretation of the expression "other legal acts" as comprising ratified international treaties such as the European Convention on Human Rights, it is argued that the rank of the Convention is lower than that of the Constitution.[94] On the other hand, it is postulated that the Constitution and the Convention have the same rank, as the Convention is an expression of "basic rights and liberties in conformity with the commonly recognized principles and norms of the international law" in the sense of Article 17 of the Russian Constitution.[95] In this context the Convention is characterized as a "constitutional instrument of the European legal order".[96] It is stressed that its place within the Constitutional legal system is "unique in comparison to other international treaties and other norms of international law".[97] Articles 17(1) and 55(1) of the Constitution could even be interpreted as conferring a higher rank to the ECHR in comparison to the Constitution.[98] This idea was called "a very bold proposition, which to date has not found confirmation in judicial practice".[99]

The expansive meaning of Article 15(4) of the Constitution takes the "evolutionary aspect of international law" into account; the interpretation of treaties emanating from the work of international bodies has generally to be taken into account.[100] Therefore, the Russian courts are obliged to follow the jurisprudence of the European Court,[101] as explicitly stated in the law on the ratification of the ECHR.[102] This is also in line with the constitutional jurisprudence. In 1996, the Constitutional Court already provided an interpretation that "established an obligation to give direct domestic effect to decisions of international bodies, including the European Court of Human Rights".[103] Still, the status in the legal system

---

[92] "Constitutional laws" are laws that regulate especially important aspects of the constitutional order in Russia and require special majorities in both chambers of the Federal Assembly.
[93] This view is held by Ferschtman (2002), 737; Danilenko (1994), 466.
[94] Petrukhin (1998), 4.
[95] Vitruk (2006), *O nekotorkch osobennostyakh*, 84; Zorkin (2006), 36.
[96] See Zorkin (2006), 36; Vitruk (2006), *O nekotorykh osobennostyach*, 84.
[97] Zorkin (2005), 2.
[98] Butler (1997), 26.
[99] Danilenko (1999), 64.
[100] Danilenko (1994), 465.
[101] See Zorkin (2006), 36.
[102] See *supra* note 30.
[103] Danilenko (1999), 68.

of the Strasbourg Court's case law remains a matter of controversy.[104] According to Zorkin, "the decisions of the European Court of Human Rights are part of the Russian legal system only in so far as they are an expression of generally recognized principles and norms of international law".[105] That could mean that new jurisprudence going beyond the minimum standards universally accepted are excluded. On the other hand, Zorkin argues that the case law is "obligatory" for the courts.[106] This controversy will be outlined in more detail together with the mechanisms of coordination.[107]

It is worth mentioning that the Russian Constitution contains an explicit provision allowing citizens to apply to international judicial bodies.[108]

b. Implementation of International Law by Domestic Courts

aa. Judicial System. The Russian judicial system[109] is composed of federal courts and courts of the subjects of the Russian Federation. But the latter do not play an important role. Their task is only to settle minor disputes on the lowest level or to safeguard the particularities of the basic law of the relevant subject.[110] On the federal level, the Russian Constitutional Court is responsible for the adjudication of certain disputes enumerated in the Constitution.[111] The system is further subdivided into courts of general jurisdiction and arbitrazh (commercial) courts.

The four-tiered system of the courts of general jurisdiction comprises the Russian Supreme Court, regional courts in the 86 subjects of the Federation,[112] district courts and justices of the peace. The regional courts are divided into civil and criminal chambers. Both the Russian Supreme Court and the regional courts have a Presidium, a body made up of the President and certain other judges, which is empowered under certain circumstances to review decisions of the civil and criminal chambers. The three-tiered system of the military courts is an integral part of the courts of general jurisdiction.[113]

Arbitrazh courts hear cases involving business disputes between legal entities,

---

[104] Baranov (2004), 26.

[105] Zorkin (2005), 3.

[106] Ibid.

[107] See *infra* Section E.

[108] Cf. Article 46(3) of the Russian Constitution: "In conformity with the international treaties of the Russian Federation, everyone shall have the right to turn to interstate organs concerned with the protection of human rights and liberties when all the means of legal protection available within the State have been exhausted."

[109] Law adopted on 31 December 1996, amended on 15 December 2001, 4 July 2003 and 5 April 2005, SZ RF 2005, no. 1, pos. 1.

[110] Thus only the so-called justices of peace as well as the Constitutional Courts of the subjects of the Russian Federation are not federal courts.

[111] Article 125 of the Constitution.

[112] The original number of 89 subjects was changed to 86 subjects.

[113] See Federal Constitutional Law on Military Courts of the Russian Federation, 23 June 1999, SZ RF 1999, no. 26, pos. 3170; on the judicial system see Krug (2006), 6; Butler (2003), 215 et seq.

and between legal entities and the State. The highest instance is the Russian Supreme Arbitrazh Court in Moscow. There are ten federal district arbitrazh courts, Arbitrazh appellate courts and federal Arbitrazh courts of the subjects of the Russian Federation.

Administrative courts are provided for in the Constitution. But as of yet, all attempts to institutionalise administrative jurisdiction have failed due to squabbles over competences.

bb. The ECHR in the Practice of the Constitutional Court. The Constitutional Court refers to the Convention on a regular basis.[114] In the first years after the entry into force of the ECHR, the jurisprudence of the Strasbourg Court was cited in Russia in a relatively small number of cases.[115] However, it should be noted that in the last two years this approach has been changed and the Court's decisions are frequently cited.[116] It is interesting to note that the Russian Constitutional Court not only refers to the jurisprudence concerning Russia, but also to the jurisprudence concerning other States Parties of the Convention. It thus underscores the *erga omnes* effect of the decisions.[117]

Generally speaking, it is questionable whether the mere enumeration of provisions of the Convention without any further explanations as to their contents as well as to their meaning in the context of the decision is helpful.[118] Potential discrepancies between national and international law are only visible on the basis of a detailed analysis; the autonomous interpretation of the provisions of the Convention by the Court must not be neglected. Therefore, as long as quotations do not confer any substantial added value to the decisions, observers rightly criticize them as a "domestication" of international law that may lead to undesirable results.[119]

Opinions are divided as to the real impact of the decisions of the Strasbourg Court on the jurisprudence of the Russian Constitutional Court. The judges of the Constitutional Court themselves argue that "the Constitutional Court refers arguments based on international law not only in order to underscore the cor-

---

[114] Up to the year 2004 the Russian Constitutional Court had referred to the ECHR in 54 out of 215 rulings since 1991 when the Law on the Constitutional Court entered into force or out of 116 since 1998 when the ECHR entered into force for Russia; cf. Burkov (2006), *Primenenie*, 31. A part of the judgements mentioning the ECHR has been published in a documentation volume, Evropeyskiye pravovyye standarty v postanovleniyakh Konstitutsionnogo Suda RF (Moscow, 2003).

[115] Up to 2004 the jurisprudence is referred to in twelve out of 56 cases, cf. Burkov (2006), *Primenenie*, 35.

[116] In 2005 and 2006 the Russian Constitutional Court cited the ECHR in sixteen out of 22 decisions (postanovleniya); in twelve decisions it also referred to the case law of the Court. In 886 procedural decisions (opredeleniya) the ECHR was cited 67 times, whereas the case law was referred to in 22 cases.

[117] It is being discussed controversially in how far decisions of the ECHR that do not concern Russia should have an impact on Russian law; see Bondar (2006), 113 et seq.

[118] For a critical view on this practice see Burkov (2006), *Primenenie*, 39.

[119] Danilenko (1999), 63; Burkov (2006), *Primenenie*, 40; Burkov (2007), 41.

rectness of the legal positions worked out on the basis of the Constitution, but also for explaining the idea and the meaning of the text of the Constitution and for working out the constitutional idea of the legal provision controlled".[120] Other authors are more reluctant to acknowledge a substantial influence.[121]

In fact, there are decisions where the interpretation of the Russian Constitution and Russian law is based on the legal positions of the European Court. One example of this would be the ruling on the compensation of creditors in the bankruptcy procedure. In this case, the Russian Constitutional Court argued that an expropriation without any compensation is not proportional and grounded this assumption on the jurisprudence of the Court.[122] Similarly, in a case on the right of the accused to have access to a lawyer in the pre-trial period, the Russian Constitutional Court built its reasoning on the case law of the ECHR.[123] The right to fair trial as interpreted by the Strasbourg Court plays an important role in the Constitutional Court's decision in a case concerning the failure to execute judgements against Government entities.[124] In other cases, the allusion to the case law of the Court was not an essential element of the argumentation. Thus, in the judgement on the constitutionality of a change in the compensation system for Chernobyl victims, the Constitutional Court cited the *Burdov* case and stressed that courts' decisions must be complied with. This reflection is nothing more than an *obiter dictum*, as it is not related to the judgement on the new compensation system.[125]

Some of the references made by the Russian Constitutional Court to the jurisprudence of the Court are rather cryptic and need further explanations. For example, in the ruling of 23 November 1999 on the freedom of religion, a religious group protested against limitations of their rights. These limitations were based on the fact that the group had been registered for less than fifteen years. The Constitutional Court explained in a general section of the judgement not dealing with the concrete case that the right to religion can be limited, and referred to Article 9(2) ECHR. In this context, it cited two ECHR decisions without explaining their applicability to the solution of the question raised. The reasoning of the Constitutional Court is not based on the admissibility of limitations of the right, but on the specific interpretation of the provisions of Russian law in the light of the Constitution. The main question is whether the new law can be applied to organizations that already existed before this law entered into force. The

---

[120] Zorkin (2006), 34; Tiunov (2001), *O roli konventsii*, 96; Bondar' (2006), 113 et seq.

[121] Burkov (2006), *Primenenie*, 35.

[122] Judgement of the Russian Constitutional Court, 16 May 2000, SZ RF 2000, no. 21, pos. 2258.

[123] Judgement of the Russian Constitutional Court, 27 June 2000, SZ RF 2000, no. 27, pos. 2882.

[124] Judgement of the Russian Constitutional Court, 14 July 2005, SZ RF 2005, no. 30, pos. 319.

[125] Judgement of the Russian Constitutional Court, 19 June 2002, SZ RF 2002, no. 27, pos. 2779.

reference to the jurisprudence of the Court is thus nothing but an illustration of the fact that freedom of religion is not an absolute right but can be limited.[126]

In some cases, the references to the Convention or the jurisprudence of the Court become doubtful. One example might be the ruling on limitations of the freedom of expression in the period preceding elections. The Russian Constitutional Court cited the judgement *Bowman v. the United Kingdom*[127] in order to justify strict limitations on the media.[128] It is true that the Strasbourg Court acknowledged a potential conflict between free elections and freedom of expression: "Nonetheless, in certain circumstances the two rights may come into conflict and it may be considered necessary, in the period preceding or during an election, to place certain restrictions, of a type which would not usually be acceptable, on freedom of expression, in order to secure the free expression of the opinion of the people in the choice of the legislature". In the decision of the European Court, however, such a limitation is applied only to electoral campaigns of individuals, not to the coverage of election campaigns in the media, as was the case in the decision of the Russian Constitutional Court. It would have been necessary to at least compare and evaluate the differences between the two cases.

It is also worth mentioning that the quotations of the case law of the Strasbourg Court are, as a rule, imprecise, and do not allow one to locate the relevant arguments of the Court in the original decisions.[129] Moreover, the arguments of the complainants based on the ECHR are not explicitly taken up in the decisions.[130]

As a rule, the judgements are based only on the Russian Constitution; the provisions of the Convention as well as the jurisprudence of the Strasbourg Court are cited in order to support the argumentation[131] and to stress the harmony between the jurisprudence of the Russian Constitutional Court and European standards. Still, sometimes the Articles of the Convention are cited in the resolutive part of the decision together with the provisions of the Russian Constitution.[132] In one exceptional case the ruling of the Court was based directly on the Convention.[133]

---

[126] Judgement of the Russian Constitutional Court, 23 November 1999, SZ RF 1999, no. 51, pos. 6363.

[127] *Bowman v. the United Kingdom* (appl. no. 24839/94), Judgement (Grand Chamber), 19 February 1998, Reports 1998-I, 175 et seq.; HRLJ 1998, 84, para. 43.

[128] Judgement of the Russian Constitutional Court, 30 October 2003, SZ RF 2003, no. 44, pos. 4358.

[129] Burkov (2007), 42 et seq.

[130] Ibid., 43.

[131] Burkov (2006), *Primenenie*, 37; Danilenko (1999), 62; Zorkin (2005), 1101 explains that the Constitutional Court refers to the ECHR "in search for additional reasons to support its legal position".

[132] See e.g. the Judgement of the Russian Constitutional Court, 11 May 2005, SZ RF 2005, no. 22, pos. 2194; Judgement of the Russian Constitutional Court, 25 January 2001, SZ RF 2001, no. 7, pos. 700; Judgement of the Russian Constitutional Court, 17 July 2002, SZ RF 2001, no. 7, pos. 700.

[133] Judgement of the Russian Constitutional Court, 25 January 2001, SZ RF 2001, no. 7, pos. 700.

The Russian Constitutional Court examined a constitutional complaint against a provision of the Civil Code on the compensation for damage occasioned by the administration of justice. According to this provision, compensation must be awarded where misconduct by the judge was established by a binding court judgement. The Constitutional Court argued on the basis of Articles 6 and 41 ECHR and Article 3 of Protocol no. 7 (compensation for wrongful conviction) that the State must assume liability for the court's error regardless of how the judge's responsibility is confirmed. This rule is also applied in all the cases where judges fail to adhere to reasonable time limits in court proceedings.

Even if the concrete reference practice is not always convincing, the tendency of the Russian Constitutional Court to refer to the ECHR and to the case law of the Court frequently is helpful and can serve as an example to the lower courts.

cc. The ECHR in the Practice of the Supreme Court. In the first years after the ECHR entered into force, the Supreme Court of the Russian Federation dealt with the Convention only rarely. A 2004 survey showed that out of almost 4000 judgements, the Convention was mentioned in only twelve. Eight decisions hinted at the conformity of legal norms with the Convention, four decisions just quoted the arguments put forward by the claimants. The jurisprudence of the Court was not taken into account. Usually only the number of the Article of the Convention was mentioned; only in exceptional cases was the text of the provision quoted.[134] Anton Burkov criticizes that the jurisprudence of these courts – at least up to 2004 – "to a greater or lesser extent resembles to an attempt to demonstrate to the Council of Europe that the Convention is being applied rather than to implement the Convention in fact".[135]

dd. The ECHR in the Practice of the Lower Courts. The practice of the lower courts is difficult to access as the rulings are not usually published. Still, an analysis of the practice has shown that there is a growing number of cases in which they refer to the Convention, especially if the claimants base their arguments on the relevant norms.[136] The jurisprudence of the Strasbourg Court is especially important for the development of the civil defamation law, given that basic concepts such as the differentiation between the statement of facts and value judgements are taken into account.[137]

---

[134] For a detailed analysis of the decisions of the Supreme Court see Burkov (2006), *Primenenie*, 44 et seq.; it is possible that the practice of the Supreme Court has changed since. Within the framework of this analysis the newest jurisprudence of the Supreme Court was not analysed in detail.

[135] Burkov (2006), *Implementation*, 69. These results are preliminary as there is no analysis as to the development of the jurisprudence of the Supreme Court since 2004.

[136] See for more details Burkov (2006), *Primenenie*, 52 et seq.; Burkov (2007), 52.

[137] See the *Karelia* Decision of 12 March 2002. available at http:///www.medialaw.ru/article10/7/2/08.htm, in which the Judgement *Lingens v. Austria* (appl. no. 9815/82), Judgement (Plenary), 8 July 1986, Series A, Vol. 103 is quoted; see for more details on the development of the jurisprudence in civil defamation law Krug (2006), 26 et seq.; see also Shishkin/Bykov, Stat'ya

ee. The ECHR in the Practice of the Arbitrazh Courts. Recent developments in the practice of the arbitrazh courts, especially after the circulation of an "information letter" by the Supreme Arbitrazh Court,[138] show that references to the ECHR and to case law of the Court are quite frequent. The quotations are used to prove general principles of law, such as the prohibition to misuse the law, the demand to offer an effective legal remedy, or the necessity to balance public and private interests.[139] This practice might be seen as filling a lacuna in the Russian legal system where the positivist application of the law does not allow references to general principles.

ff. The ECHR in the Practice of the Constitutional Courts of the Subjects of the Russian Federation. The Russian State is a federation. According to the constitution, powers are divided between the centre and the 86 Federal Subjects. According to the Law on the judicial system in the Federal Subjects, constitutional courts (ustavnye sudy) can be established. They are independent from the Russian Constitutional Court and control the conformity of normative acts of the respective subject with its Constitution (ustav). Currently, there are constitutional courts in only sixteen regions of the Russian Federation. An analysis published in 2006 shows that these courts had not yet referred to the Convention or the jurisprudence of the Court. This did not occur even in cases where the claimants had based their arguments on European law.[140]

c. Domestic Remedies in the View of the European Court on Human Rights

According to Article 35 ECHR, an individual application is only admissible after the exhaustion of all domestic remedies. Thus, there is an intersection between the procedural rules of the Court and the structure of the domestic judicial systems of the Contracting States.

According to the jurisdiction of the European Court, it is not a prerequisite for accession to lodge a complaint with the Russian Constitutional Court.[141] As it does not control potential human rights violations on the basis of the application of the laws, but supervises only the conformity between laws and the Constitution, the two control systems only partially overlap.

Furthermore, it is not necessary to initiate a supervisory procedure[142] before going to Strasbourg. The supervisory review is only an extraordinary remedy that

---

10 Evropeyskoy Konventsii o zashchite prav cheloveka v grazhdanskikh protsessakh o zashchite dobrogo imeni, http://www.medialaw.ru/publications/books/book45/33.html.

[138] See Section E.1.c.aa. *infra.*

[139] See Tereshkova (2007), http://www.demos-center.ru/projects/6B3771E/70688C12/1167160792.html

[140] Burkov (2006), *Primenenie,* 44; see also Burkov (2007), 44.

[141] *Tumilovich v. Russia* (appl. no. 47033/99), Decision (Third Section), 22 June 1999 (not reported); see Zorkin (2006), 37; Laptev (2002), 47.

[142] See Zorkin (2006), 37.

is within the discretionary power of the authorities. Therefore, the Court did not accept a preliminary objection as to the non-exhaustion of domestic remedies in this respect.[143] This jurisprudence is criticized by the Russian judge at the European Court of Human Rights, Kovler, pointing to the fact that 60 per cent of mistakes within the judicial procedure are corrected within the supervisory procedure. One third of the claims lodged by Russian citizens are inadmissible because they are not well informed and await the end of the supervisory procedure.[144] Thus the six months deadline following the final decision elapses.[145]

There is a new initiative to introduce a specific remedy against violations of the ECHR within the Russian legal system and thus to reduce the amount of Russian claims in Strasbourg. According to the proposal of the president of the Russian Constitutional Court, Valeriy Zorkin, the Russian supervisory system has to be reorganized in order to guarantee every citizen a specific legal remedy before bringing a claim to Strasbourg.[146] By the end of the year 2007, the Supreme Court has elaborated a law project entitled "On the compensation of damage inflicted by the violation of the right to trial within reasonable delays and the right to execution of final legally binding judgements within reasonable delays".[146a] On the one hand, such a change of the system might indeed stop the exodus of Russian citizens to the Strasbourg Court. On the other hand there is a well-founded fear that serious human rights violations might not be handled properly on the national level so that the claimants loose time before bringing their cases to Strasbourg. Taking into account the long waiting period for a decision in Strasbourg the whole mechanism might be rendered inefficient.[147]

The jurisprudence of the Court relies on the criterion of the effectiveness of the remedy. This was an important point in the Chechen cases. The Russian Government submitted that, although the courts in Chechnya had ceased to function in 1996, civil remedies were still available to those who moved out of Chechnya. Established practice allowed them to apply to the Supreme Court or to the courts at their new place of residence, which would then consider their applications. In

---

[143] See e.g. *Tumilovich v. Russia* (*supra* note 141); *Berdzenishvili v. Russia* (appl. no. 31697/03), Decision (First Section), 29 January 2004, Reports 2004-II, 317 et seq.

[144] Cf. for critique on the information of the population about the functioning of the ECHR in the first years after its entry into force Bowring (2000), 376.

[145] Kovler (2004), 4.

[146] See Ekaterina Savina, Alisa Ivanitskaya, Valeriy Zor'kin obratilsya v Evrosud, Kommersant', 9 July 2007.

[146a] Cf. on the elaboration of the new law, see the communication in the online newspaper Kommersant.ru, "VS podgotovil al'ternativu Evropeyskomu sudu po pravam cheloveka", http://www.kommersant.ru/doc.aspx?DocsID=832421 (last visited 4 January 2008); for a critical assessment of the new law, see Roman Maranov, Verkhovniy Sud R. F. khochet pomoch' Evropeyskomu sudu, http://news.invictory.org/print.php?id=14421 (last visited 4 January 2008).

[147] For a critical view on the initiative see Yuriy Skuratov, Otdat' pod sud sistemny krizis. Popytka perekhvatit' iski grazhdan protiv svoego gosudarstva ne privedet k kardinal'nomu umen'sheniyu potoka obrashcheniy v Strasburgskiy sud, Nezavisimaya Gazeta, 20 July 2007; see also Grigoriy Nekhoroshev, Zakon obyazhet rossiyan 'ne vynosit' sor iz izby', http://www.dp.ru/msk/news/politics/2007/07/16/228429 (last visited 30 July 2007).

2001, the courts in Chechnya resumed their work and reviewed a large number of civil and criminal cases. Furthermore, the Supreme Court of the Russian Federation could act as a court of first instance in civil cases. The argumentation of the Strasbourg Court in this respect was based on the consideration that the existence of the remedies must be "sufficiently certain, in practice as well as in theory"; no recourse should be had to remedies that are inadequate or ineffective. In the context of the Chechen cases the Court argued that the question of the effectiveness of legal remedies in criminal cases in Chechnya was closely linked with the substance of the cases. Therefore, it did not accept preliminary objections as to the non-exhaustion of domestic remedies.[148]

In other cases, this problem also played a decisive role in the admission procedure. The Court always stressed the need to use a flexible interpretation of the effectiveness requirement. In very serious cases of inhuman treatment and torture, it argued that in view of the delays involved the applicant is not obliged to wait until the formal completion of the official investigation.[149] Given the cases of intimidation and violation of victims of alleged human rights violations in the north Caucasus region who attempted to seek redress through the national judicial system, the Parliamentary Assembly recommended that the Court systematically wave the requirement of exhaustion of internal remedies.[150] So far, the Court has not taken this step.

d. Legislation

There is no special procedure for reviewing the compatibility of Governmental draft legislation with the Convention. In the last years, major new projects were fiercely criticized from abroad on the basis of potential human rights violations. This did not stop the Parliament from enacting the relevant acts. The 2005 report on the "Honouring of obligations and commitments" mentions in this context the new law on non-governmental organizations as well as the new law on political parties.[151]

---

[148] *Isayeva, Yusipova, Bazaeva v. Russia* (appl. nos 57947/00, 57948/00 and 57949/00), Judgement (First Section), 24 February 2005 (not yet reported); *Isayeva v. Russia,* (appl. no. 57950/00), Judgement (First Section), 24 February 2005 (not yet reported).

[149] See e.g., *Mikheyev v. Russia* (appl. no. 77617/01), Judgement (First Section), 26 January 2006 (not yet reported); for a more detailed overview over the problems involved see Nußberger (2005), 88 et seq.

[150] P.A., Member States' duty to cooperate with the European Court of Human Rights, Doc. 11183 of 9 February 2007, http://assembly.coe.int/Documents/WorkingDocs/Doc07/EDOC11183.htm.

[151] Report (*supra* note 16), paras 36–42, 121–124; cf. on the law on non-governmental organizations Nußberger and Schmidt (2007), 16 et seq.

2. Ukraine

a. Domestic and International Law

The starting point for Ukraine as well as for Russia was the Soviet dualistic attitude towards international law. Similarly to Russia, this approach was later abandoned.[152] The provisions on the implementation of international law in the new Ukrainian Constitution of 1996 adopt a monistic approach. According to Article 9 of the Constitution of Ukraine, a ratified international treaty becomes part of domestic law after promulgation.[153] Furthermore, it is stipulated that the conclusion of international treaties that contravene the Constitution of Ukraine is possible only after the introduction of the relevant amendments to the Constitution. The hierarchical position of international law in the Ukrainian legal system can be deduced from the wording of Article 18 of the Constitution: "The foreign political activity of Ukraine is aimed at ensuring its national interests and security by maintaining peaceful and mutually beneficial cooperation with members of the international community, according to generally acknowledged principles of international law." On the basis of this provision, it is possible to argue that the generally acknowledged principles and norms of international law prevail over contradictory domestic law and even over constitutional provisions. The status of international treaties is not, however, regulated by this norm.

Since the ECHR entered into force for Ukraine on 11 September 1997, it has become an integral part of Ukrainian legislation and enjoys a special status. That is clearly stated in the Law on international treaties that entered into force in 2004. According to Article 19(2) of the Law on international treaties, rules contained in international treaties take precedence over domestic legislation.[154] On this basis, the Ukrainian Constitutional Court confirmed that international treaties range in the hierarchy of norms between the Constitution and statutory laws. In connection with a judgement on the Rome Statute of the International Criminal Court, the Ukrainian Constitutional Court explained that:

> International treaties become a part of Ukrainian domestic legislation, after consent to be bound by the treaties which was given by parliament (Verkhovna Rada). In this way, the issue of national sovereignty is reconciled with the fact that the jurisdiction of the international courts of justice covers Ukrainian territory (provided that the provisions of the statutes of the international courts do not contradict the Constitution).[155]

---

[152] Fric'kij (2006), 203 et seq.

[153] Cf. the wording: "International treaties that are in force, agreed to be binding by the Verkhovna Rada of Ukraine, are part of the national legislation of Ukraine." (Translation provided on the homepage of the Ukrainian Parliament http://www.rada.kiev.ua/const/conengl.htm#r1).

[154] Article 19(2) Law On International Treaties of 29 June 2004, Vidomosti Verkhovnoy Radi Ukraiiny 2004, no. 50 Article 540, which replaced the Law "On the Effect of International Treaties on the Territory of Ukraine" of 10 December 1991.

[155] Judgement of the Ukrainian Constitutional Court, 11 July 2001, UKR-2001-2-006.

Thus, the ECHR occupies a lower rank than the Constitution, but higher than laws and by-laws.[156] If it is viewed as enshrining generally acknowledged principles and norms of international law, it could even be considered that it prevails over the Constitution.

The Ukrainian Constitution also contains a provision allowing for complaints before international judicial bodies.[157]

b. Implementation of International Law by Domestic Courts

aa. Judicial System. The judiciary in Ukraine consists of the Constitutional Court of Ukraine, the courts of general jurisdiction and specialized courts.[158] Specialized courts are the Arbitrazh courts, military courts and administrative courts. According to the transitory provisions of the Law on the Judicial System adopted on 7 February 2002,[159] administrative courts had to be created within a three-year period starting on 1 June 2002. However, within this deadline, only the High Administrative Court was established.[160] The Code on Administrative Procedure was only adopted in July 2005 and it came into force on 1 September 2005.[161] Two months later, the first judges for the administrative courts of appeal,[162] and in January 2006 the first judge for a local administrative court in Vinnica[163] were appointed. During a transitional period all cases within the jurisdiction of the administrative courts fell in the competence of the courts of general jurisdiction.

The local courts are subdivided into district courts, urban district courts and town courts. They function as courts of general jurisdiction, military courts, Arbitrazh courts and administrative courts. The appellate courts in each branch form the second level of the court system. There are two Cassation Courts: the High Arbitrazh Court and the High Administrative Court. The Law on the Judiciary also mentioned a High Cassation Court, however this provision was declared

---

[156] Potapenko and Pushkar' (2001), 919.

[157] Cf. Article 55(3) of the Ukrainian Constitution: "After exhausting all domestic legal remedies, everyone has the right to appeal for the protection of his or her rights and freedoms to the relevant international judicial institutions or to the relevant bodies of international organisations of which Ukraine is a member or participant."

[158] Cf. Article 124(3) of the Ukrainian Constitution: "Judicial proceedings are performed by the Constitutional Court of Ukraine and courts of general jurisdiction." Article 125(1): "In Ukraine, the system of courts of general jurisdiction is formed in accordance with the territorial principle and the principle of specialisation."

[159] Vidomosti Verkhovnoyi Rady Ukraiiny 2002, nos 27–28, Article 180.

[160] The first nine judges were appointed in December 2003; on February 2006 42 judges out of required 65 have been appointed, Vidomosti Verchovnoyi Rady Ukraiiny 2004, no. 13, Article 184; 2005, no. 24, Article 330; 2006, no. 1, Articles 26–28, nos 19–20, Article 168, no. 26, Article 227.

[161] Vidomosti Verkhovnoyi Rady Ukraiiny 2005, nos 35–37, Article 446.

[162] Vidomosti Verchovnoyi Rady Ukraiiny 2006, no. 1, Articles 26–28.

[163] Vidomosti Verchovnoyi Rady Ukraiiny 2006, no. 21, Article 176.

unconstitutional by the Constitutional Court of Ukraine.[164] Therefore, the cassation instance for the general and military courts is exercised by the Supreme Court of Ukraine. It comprises four Chambers (respectively one on civil, one on economic, one on criminal and one on administrative cases) and the Military Collegium. According to the new Code on Administrative Court Procedure, administrative claims can be brought to the Supreme Court only under exceptional circumstances.

bb. The ECHR in the Practice of the Constitutional Court. The Constitutional Court of Ukraine refers to the Convention only in a few cases;[165] references to the Court's case law are rare exceptions.[166] Thus the Constitutional Court exhibits a rather reserved attitude towards international human rights. As a rule, the judgements are based only on the Constitution. The ECHR as well as other international treaties are used for justifying the interpretation of the Constitution. One example for this approach is the ruling of the Ukrainian Constitutional Court on the death penalty. Article 27 of the Ukrainian Constitution provides: "No one shall be arbitrarily deprived of life. The duty of the State is to protect human life." While the word "arbitrarily" suggests that the execution of the death penalty is not excluded if provided for by law, the Constitutional Court interpreted this provision within the context of the Constitution and came to the conclusion that the death penalty was unconstitutional. The Constitutional Court backed this judgement with references to the ECHR as well as to the Protocols. As important, in its decision, the Constitutional Court cited the Strasbourg Court's case law to the effect that imposing the death penalty violates Article 3 ECHR.[167] The Court argued that it was competent to interpret the Convention on the basis of statutory law.

The Constitutional Court also emphasized the harmony between Ukrainian and international law, e.g. concerning regulations on the independence of judicial power,[168] the inadmissibility of retroactive laws,[169] the right to judicial

---

[164] Judgement of the Ukrainian Constitutional Court, 11 December 2003, no. 20-rp7, 2003.

[165] The ECHR is mentioned in thirteen cases out of 144 decisions between 1999 and 2005; for the statistical data see cf. http://www.ccu.gov.ua/pls/wccu/indx.

[166] Decisions of the Court are mentioned in five cases. For a reference to case law see for example the Judgement of the Ukrainian Constitutional Court, 10 October 2001, UKR-2000-1-003, no. 11.

[167] Judgement of the Ukrainian Constitutional Court, 29 December 1999, UKR-2000-1-003, no. 11.

[168] Articles 124, 126, 129, 130 Constitution, Article 6(1) ECHR; cf. Dec. no. 6 of 24 June 1999, UKR-1999-2-004.

[169] Article 15 Constitution, Article 7 ECHR, Article 15 ICCPR; cf. Dec. no. 6 of 19 April 2000, UKR-2000-1-008.

protection,[170] the right to property,[171] the freedom of movement,[172] and the right to social protection.[173] Sometimes, the Constitutional Court was satisfied with general statements as to the non-conformity of national laws with international and European standards. Such a statement can be found in a case concerning the lack of provisions regulating the use of confidential data on mental health.[174]

This sort of "cumulative approach" can also be observed in a case concerning the mitigation of punishment for minor offences. The Constitutional Court referred to a number of constitutional provisions,[175] but also to Article 10 of the Declaration on Human Rights, Article 14 ICCPR and Article 6 ECHR.[176] The exclusion of judicial protection in the pre-trial investigation phase is not only considered as a violation of constitutional provisions, but also of Articles 6(1) and 13 ECHR.[177]

c. Domestic Remedies in the View of the European Court on Human Rights

The requirement of exhausting all effective domestic remedies is satisfied with a final decision of the Supreme Court. It is neither necessary to lodge a complaint with the Constitutional Court nor to have recourse to the supervisory system (nadzor).

The constitutional complaint (*constitutsionnoe obrashchenie*) provided for on the basis of the Law on the Constitutional Court of 16 October 1996[178] is restricted to giving an official interpretation of the Constitution of Ukraine and the laws of Ukraine in order "to secure implementation or protecting the constitutional rights and freedoms of the individual and citizen as well as the rights of a legal entity".[179] Although the relevant legal norm can lose its legal force as a result of this procedure, this remedy is not considered as an effective means within the meaning of Article 35 ECHR.

[170] Articles 8, 55, 64 Constitution, Article 8 of the Universal Declaration of Human Rights; cf. Dec. no. 6 of 23 May 2001, UKR-2001-2-003.

[171] Article 41(1) Constitution, Article 1 of Protocol no. 1; cf. Dec. no. 13 of 10 October 2001 (2001-3-007).

[172] Article 3(1) Constitution (freedom of movement), Article 2 of Protocol no. 4, Article 13 Universal Declaration of Human Rights, Article 12 ICCPR; cf. Dec. no. 15 of 14 November 2001, UKR-2001-3-009.

[173] Article 46 Constitution, Article 22 Universal Declaration of Human Rights, International Covenant on Economic, Social and Cultural Rights, European Social Charter; Dec. of 17 March 2005, UKR-2001-1-001.

[174] UKR-1997-3-005.

[175] The following provisions are cumulatively quoted: Article 1 (rule of law), Article 3 (recognition of human being, life and health, honour and dignity, inviolability and security as the highest social value, human rights and freedoms as essence and orientation of the activity of the State), Article 21 (inalienability and inviolability of human rights and freedoms), Article 28 (right to respect of dignity), Article 55 (protection of human rights by court) and Article 129 (equality before the law and the court).

[176] Dec. no. 15 of 2 November 2004, UKR-2004-3-017.

[177] Dec. no. 3 of 30 January 2003, UKR-1.2003.

[178] Vidomosti Verkhovnoyi Rady Ukrainy 1996, no. 49, Article 272.

[179] Article 42 of the Law on the Constitutional Court of 16 October 1996.

The same applies to the supervisory system. In the Court's view, complaints with a superior prosecutor do not offer adequate safeguards for an independent and impartial review of the applicant's complaints as the prosecutors are part of the executive branch of Government and not of the judicial system even if they act as guardians of the public interest.[180]

According to the Court, it is not necessary to bring civil proceedings in order to lodge a complaint before a court in the case of inhuman imprisonment conditions, if it is obvious that such recourse would not bring about any improvement.[181]

d. Legislation

The Government has amended the Rules of Procedure of the Cabinet of Ministers and introduced a mandatory verification of draft legal acts as to their compliance with the ECHR and the Court's case law.[181a] This verification procedure is part of the obligatory State registration of legal acts. There is an effective means to sanction violations: Incompatibility with the ECHR is a ground to refuse State registration, which entails invalidity of the legal act. As this is a very new law, it remains to be seen how it will be implemented in practice. At least it shows the presence of the good will to avoid contradictions between new legislation and the ECHR as well as the Court's case law.

3. Comparison and Conclusion

Not only are the Russian and Ukrainian legal systems both based on the Soviet heritage, they have also developed in a similar manner with respect to certain issues. That is especially true for the definition of the status of international treaty law in national constitutional law. Although the Russian Constitution of 1993 goes even further than the Ukrainian Constitution of 1996 in opening up for the inclusion of international law, both legal systems do provide for the supremacy of the Convention over domestic statutory law. Both Constitutional Courts regularly refer to the Convention and, to a lesser extent, to the case law. The Ukrainian Constitutional Court refers to the Convention and the case law in a comparatively superficial way without going into the details of the interpretation of the Convention. Both Courts use the Convention and the jurisprudence in order to prove the harmony between national and international law as well as to strengthen the argumentation in their decisions.

---

[180] *Merit v. Ukraine* (appl. no. 66561/01), Judgement (Second Section), 30 March 2004 (not reported).
[181] *Khokhlich v. Ukraine* (appl. no. 41707/98), Judgement (Fourth Section), 29 April 2003 (not reported).
[181a] Ministerstvo Iustytsii Ukrainy, Nakaz pro vdoskonalennia poriadku derzhavnoi reiestratsii normatyvno-pravovykh aktiv u Ministerstvi iustystii Ukrainy ta skasuvannia rishennia pro derzhavnu reiestratsiiu normatyvno-pravovykh aktiv vid 12 April 2005, as amended on 2 August 2007, http://zakon.rada.gov.ua/cgi-bin/laws/main.cgi?nreg=z0381-05 (last visited 8 January 2008).

The constitutional complaint or the remedies within the supervisory system are not accepted as preliminary objections to Article 35(1) ECHR in both Russian or Ukrainian cases.

While the Ukrainian system provides for a mechanism to check the conformity of new legislative acts with the Convention, a comparable possibility does not exist in the Russian system.

C. Overview of the Activity of the Court[182]

1. Russia

Four years after the ratification of the ECHR, the first decision on the merits was taken in the famous *Burdov* case.[183] Since then, the number of judgements has increased exponentially from two judgements in 2002 to 82 judgements in 2005. In 2006, 103 judgements were passed. That means that within four years, the judgements on human rights issues in Russia outnumbered the judgements on human rights issues in many other Contracting States that had been rendered in the course of 50 years. Although the great majority of the applications are still being declared inadmissible because of formal reasons (lapse of the six month time limit set in Article 35(1) ECHR) or *ratio temporis*, in 2004 sixteen per cent of the newly lodged applications concerned Russia.[184] This is due to various reasons. First, Russia has the largest population among the Council of Europe's Contracting States (144 millions).[185] Second, the Russian Constitutional Court does not function as a filter, as it has no competence to rectify human rights violations caused by the wrong application of a law. It is limited to controlling the constitutionality of the laws themselves.[186] Third, the European Court has discovered structural human rights problems in Russian jurisprudence in the penitentiary system as well as in the judiciary that affect many people in the same way. As the jurisprudence touches on everyday life and offers relief, the Convention has become very popular. The applications come from all over Russia, not only from the big cities. It is worth mentioning that, out of 206 final judgements, there were no violations of the Convention in very few cases.[187] In two cases, a

---

[182] The overview takes into account decisions up to 31 December 2006.

[183] *Burdov v. Russia* (appl. no. 59498/00), Judgement (First Section), 7 May 2002, Reports 2002-III, 317 et seq.

[184] http://www.echr.coe.int/NR/rdonlyres/F2B964EE-57C5-4C86-8B8F-8B4B6095D89C/0/MicrosoftWordstatistical_charts_2004__internet_.pdf.

[185] According to the statistics given by the Court, 0,4 applications out of 10,000 citizens are lodged at the Court. This figure is significantly higher in other countries (e.g. Poland or Slovenia), see http://www.echr.coe.int/NR/rdonlyres/F2B964EE-57C5-4C86-8B8F-8B4B6095D89C/0/MicrosoftWordstatistical_charts_2004__internet_.pdf.

[186] See Article 125(4) of the Russian Constitution; for a critique see Brunner (2002), 224.

[187] According to the statistical data of the Court, there are only six decisions where the Court has not found any violations. But in fact, there are seven such decisions: *Bordovskiy v. Russia* (appl. no. 49491/99), Judgement (Second Section), 8 February 2005 (not yet reported); *Nikitin v. Russia*

preliminary objection was allowed. In one case, Russia had acknowledged the violation of Article 3 ECHR in substance and had offered appropriate and sufficient redress.[188]

As in the other member countries, the highest percentage of the violations concerns Article 6(1) ECHR. However, it is not only the length of procedure that causes problems (86 cases; violation of Article 6 and eventually also Article 13 ECHR), but also other issues regarding fair trial (71 cases). The majority of them concern the non-execution of judgements against the State or State companies (violation of Article 6(1) ECHR and Article 1 of Protocol no. 1). Furthermore, problems are caused by the unlawful composition of the courts (three cases) and the system of supervisory reviews (eleven cases). Other problems linked to the right to a fair trial (e.g. trial with the accused being absent and incitement to commit an offence) account for eleven cases.

The quantity of violations of Article 3 ECHR (prohibition of torture or inhuman or degrading treatment) as well as of Article 2 ECHR (right to life) is the most disturbing figure (24 respective eleven cases). In most of these cases, not only did the Court find a direct violation of the rights concerned, it also referred to a lack of investigation into the abuses of State power. The seriousness of the cases can be assessed on the basis of the sometimes extremely high amounts of non-pecuniary damage awarded (e.g. 120,000 € in the *Mikheyev* case[189] and 180,000 in the *Ilaşcu* case for pecuniary and non-pecuniary damage[190]).

Thirteen cases concern respectively Article 5(3) and Article 5(1) ECHR (unlawful detention), nine cases Article 5(4) ECHR (review of lawfulness of detention), eight cases Article 8 ECHR (private and family life), three cases Article 10 ECHR (freedom of expression), and two cases Article 11 ECHR (freedom of assembly and association). Although in the report of the Parliamentary Assembly on Russia, forced labour as well as slave labour of soldiers was criticized,[191] there were not yet any cases concerning Article 4 ECHR brought before the European Court. Neither are there cases concerning Article 9 ECHR (freedom of thought,

---

(appl. no. 50178/99), Judgement (Second Section), 20 July 2004, Reports 2004-VIII, 321 et seq.; *Zhigalev v. Russia* (appl. no. 54891/00), Judgement (First Section), 6 July 2006 (not yet reported); *Fadin v. Russia* (appl. no. 58079/00), Judgement (Third Section), 27 July 2006 (not yet reported); *Andandovskiy v. Russia* (appl. no. 24015/02), Judgement (Third Section), 28 September 2006 (not yet reported); *Klimentyev v. Russia* (appl. no. 46503/99), Judgement (Fifth Section), 16 November 2006 (not yet reported); *Zaytsev v. Russia* (appl. no. 22644/02), Judgement (First Section), 16 November 2006 (not yet reported).

[188] *Rytsarev v. Russia* (appl. no. 63332/00), Judgement (First Section), 21 July 2006 (not yet reported); a preliminary objection was also allowed in the case of *Markin v. Russia* (appl. no. 59502/00), Judgement (First Section), 30 March 2006 (not yet reported), because of the non-exhaustion of domestic remedies.

[189] *Mikheyev v. Russia* (appl. no. 77617/01), Judgement (First Section), 26 January 2006 (not yet reported).

[190] *Ilaşcu and Others v. Russia and Moldova* (appl. no. 48787/99), Judgement (Grand Chamber), 8 July 2004, Reports 2004-VII, 179 et seq.

[191] See report (*supra* note 16), paras 311 et seq.

conscience and religion) and Article 12 ECHR (right to marry). Article 14 ECHR (prohibition of discrimination) was violated once in a Chechen case.[192] In addition to the cases concerning the non-execution of judgements, Article 1 of Protocol no. 1 (right to property) was violated in seven cases. As far as other provisions of the Protocols are concerned, Article 2 of Protocol no. 4 (right to free movement) was violated in two cases and Article 2 of Protocol no. 1 (right to education) was violated in one case. In 2006, Article 1 of Protocol no. 7 (expulsion of aliens) was violated for the first time.

In the judgement *Gusinskiy v. Russia*,[193] Article 18 ECHR (Limitation on use of restriction of rights) was considered to be violated. This is the first time that the Court had recourse to this provision in its jurisprudence. Furthermore, a violation of Article 34 ECHR (hindering of an individual application) was found in five cases and a violation of Article 38 ECHR (examination of the case) in four cases. This is especially worrying as it shows the lack of cooperation between the Russian authorities and the Court. The Parliamentary Assembly dedicated a critical report to this subject in spring 2007.[194] It was found that there were major violations of treaty obligations such as interferences with the applicants' communication with the Court, disappearance of mail sent off from Russia, the initiation of unfounded disciplinary proceedings and tax inspections, as well as flagrant acts of intimidation.[195]

The majority of the most serious human rights violations, such as torture and deliberate killing of civilians by the military, are connected to the political instability in Chechnya and Transdniestria. However, serious human rights violations occur in other parts of Russia, not only in unstable regions. Thus, normal conditions in Russian prisons were criticized as "inhuman treatment" in the sense of Article 3 ECHR. The cases brought before the Court, therefore, confirm the sceptical findings of the expert commission before Russia's accession to the Council of Europe.[196]

The problems related to the implementation of Article 6 ECHR mirror the *status quo* of the judicial system in Russia. Although the reforms were already initiated in the last years of the *perestroika* and led to the adoption of new procedural codes in civil and criminal law, the deficiencies of the system have not been fundamentally improved. The lengthiness of the procedures is often caused by the so-called *nadzor*-system, i.e. the possibility for the general procurator or the Court to reopen the procedure even after a final and binding decision in

---

[192] *Timishev v. Russia* (appl. no. 55762/00; 55974/00), Judgement (Second Section), 13 December 2005 (not yet reported).

[193] *Gusinskiy v. Russia* (appl. no. 70276/01), Judgement (First Section), 19 May 2004, Reports 2004-IV, 129 et seq.

[194] P.A., Member States' duty to cooperate with the European Court of Human Rights, Doc. 11183 (rapporteur: Christos Pourgourides) of 9 February 2007, http://assembly.coe.int/Documents/WorkingDocs/Doc07/EDOC11183.htm.

[195] Ibid., para. 20 et seq.

[196] See *supra* note 8 and 9.

favour of the person concerned has been passed. This has been changed in the Code of Criminal Procedure. The Constitutional Court, however, found that the amendment was incompatible with the Constitution and once more allowed a reopening of the case without new evidence within a period of one year.[197]

2. Ukraine

The first judgement concerning Ukraine was passed five years after the ratification of the Convention in 2002.[198] It was the only judgement that year. The process thus started slowly. In 2003 there were six judgements, in 2004 fourteen judgements. In 2005, the number of judgements went up to 119. In 2006, 120 decisions on the merits were passed.[199] There were only two admissible cases, where the Court did not find a breach of the Convention.[200]

The number of applications lodged has been constantly above 2000 per year, with a peak, in 2002, of 2,944 complaints and a record of 3,906 complaints in 2006. Thus, statistically, out of 10,000 citizens, 0.5 complaints were brought to Strasbourg. Approximately two thirds of them were declared inadmissible. With regard to the number of applications lodged, Ukraine is the fourth country after Russia, Poland and Turkey.[201]

The vast majority of judgements concern Article 6(1) ECHR. In 134 out of 260 decisions, the length of the judicial procedure both in criminal and in civil law cases constitutes a violation of the ECHR. Furthermore, the failure to enforce various judgements awarding applicants compensation, such as payment of salary arrears, compensation in relation to detention and search and seizure of property, are very frequent (94 decisions). In these cases, the Court relied on Article 6(1) ECHR, Article 13 ECHR, and Article 1 of Protocol no. 1.

Moreover, final and binding judgements in the applicant's favour were set aside by higher courts' supervisory review proceedings following applications of public prosecutors or courts' deputy chairmen. In these cases, a breach of the principle of legal certainty and of the right of access to court was found.

Article 3 ECHR was violated in fourteen cases, and Article 2 ECHR was violated in two cases. This means that there are serious human rights violations in Ukraine as well. There was only one violation of Article 5(4) ECHR because of

---

[197] Judgement of 8 May 2004; see Angelika Nußberger, Putins neue Menschenrechtsidee, in Frankfurter Allgemeine Zeitung, no. 131 (9 June 2005).

[198] *Sovtransavto Holding v. Ukraine* (appl. no. 48553/99), Judgement (Fourth Section), 25 July 2002, Reports 2002-VII, 133 et seq.

[199] In the statistical survey 178 judgements are enumerated by 10 August 2006. This number is taken as a basic for the following data.

[200] *Svetlana Naumenko v. Ukraine* (appl. no. 41984/98), Judgement (Second Section), 9 November 2004 (not reported); *Sukhovetskyy v. Ukraine* (appl. no. 13716/02), Judgement (Second Section), 28 March 2006 (not yet reported).

[201] See the statistical data provided by the Court http://www.echr.coe.int/NR/rdonlyres/4753F3 E8-3AD0-42C5-B294-0F2A68507FC0/0/2005_SURVEY__COURT_.pdf.

the absence of a possibility to apply for release from psychiatric detention.[202] Breaches of Article 5(1) and Article 5(3) ECHR have also been found in only a few cases.[203] The right to private and family life was violated in ten cases, the right to religious freedom in two cases, and the right of freedom of expression in three cases.

The provisions of the Protocols – except for breaches of Article 1 of Protocol no. 1 – were violated only in exceptional cases: Article 3 of Protocol no. 1 (right to free elections),[204] Article 2 of Protocol no. 4 (freedom of movement,[205] and Article 2 of Protocol no. 7 (right of appeal in criminal matters)[206] were violated only once.

3. Comparison and Conclusion

This short overview shows that human rights violations in Russia and Ukraine are not substantially different. In both countries, it is above all the judicial as well as the penitentiary system that exhibits major deficits. In Ukraine, the highly politicised *Gongadze* case[207] has caused the most trouble, whereas in Russia the most controversial and important issues are linked to the human rights situation in Chechnya and Transdniestria.

D. The Courts Case Law and its Effect in the National Legal Order

1. Soviet Heritage in Russia and Ukraine

The Soviet system was not based on the rule of law. Executive commands that could be adapted to revolutionary aims replaced reliable legal regulations. Courts only played a marginal role in solving societal conflicts. There was no transparency. As a rule, important regulations were not contained in laws, but in administrative acts that were never published. Although there were some lip services to the rights of the individuals, the interests of the State were always considered to be predominant. Therefore, the standards of human rights protection in criminal law and criminal procedure were archaic; freedom of the press and freedom of opinion were not guaranteed at all. The individual was at the mercy of a corrupt

---

[202] *Gorshkov v. Ukraine* (appl. no. 67531/01), Judgement (Second Section), 8 November 2005 (not yet reported).

[203] See e.g. *Salov v. Ukraine* (appl. no. 65518/01), Judgement (Second Section), 6 September 2005 (not yet reported); *Nevmerzhitsky v. Ukraine* (appl. no. 54825/00), Judgement (Second Section), 5 April 2005, Reports 2005-II, 307 et seq.

[204] *Sukhovetskyy v. Ukraine* (appl. no. 13716/02), Judgement (Second Section), 28 March 2006 (not yet reported).

[205] *Antonenkov and Others v. Ukraine* (appl. no. 14183/02), Judgement (Second Section), 21 November 2005 (not yet reported).

[206] *Gurepka v. Ukraine* (appl. no. 61406/00), Judgement (Second Section), 6 September 2005 (not yet reported).

[207] *Gongadze v. Ukraine* (appl. no. 34056/02), Judgement (Second Section), 8 November 2005 (not yet reported).

and powerful State encroaching on the private sphere in a totalitarian way.[208] On the basis of this experience, the Russian judge at the European Court, Kovler, speaks of a "sort of repentance of the Soviet State towards its citizens for the innumerable victims and sufferings in the name of the greatest utopia in history".[209]

The deficiencies of such a system were voiced only at the end of the 1980's during the *perestroika*. The historical turning point was the Declaration on the rights of the individual of 5 September 1991 shortly before the dissolution of the Soviet Union. In Russia a similar declaration was adopted on 22 November 1991.

It was clear that changes must be introduced into all the different aspects of social life. Law was considered as a motor for the reforms. Within fifteen years, the legal system was changed completely. In all the different branches of law new legal regulations were enacted. However, whereas it is – despite all the difficulties involved – possible to change the law within a short period of time, it is impossible to change the legal consciousness and the legal culture from one day to the other.[210] For this reason, many of the new laws, inspired by models from abroad and mirroring modern liberal standards, do not really work in Russia. The constant and considerable gap between law in the books and law in action continued to widen during the period of reform.

2. Russia

The jurisprudence of the Strasbourg Court reveals many of the persistent problems of the practical implementation of human rights standards in Russia. The main areas of conflict are the judicial system, the penitentiary system, the development of a civil society based on diversity, and the protection of individual interests. General problems in the implementation of human rights are aggravated in Chechnya and Transdniestria, so that issues linked to the instability in this region have to be analysed separately.

a. Judicial System

In the famous *Burdov* case,[211] the Court was first confronted with the problem of non-execution of final and binding judgements. This problem is widespread in Eastern Europe, but more or less unknown in the old Member Countries of the Council of Europe. In 1986, the applicant had been called up by the military authorities to take part in emergency operations at the site of the Chernobyl nuclear plant disaster. As he suffered from extensive exposure to radioactive emissions, he was awarded compensation payments in 1991 that by 1997 had not been paid. In the judgement, the Court decided that the right to have any claim brought

---

[208] Schroeder (1992), 1 et seq.; Mommsen and Nußberger (2007), 90 et seq.
[209] Kovler (2004), 1.
[210] On the Russian legal culture cf. Nußberger (2006), 35 et seq., Schomacher (2004), 427 et seq.
[211] *Burdov v. Russia* (*supra* note 183).

before a court "would be illusory if a Contracting State's domestic legal system allowed a final, binding judicial decision to remain inoperative to the detriment of one part. (…) Execution of a judgement given by any court must therefore be regarded as an integral part of the 'trial' for the purposes of Article 6."[212] Furthermore, the Court argued that the non-execution of judgements also constituted a violation of Article 1 of Protocol no. 1. This interpretation of the Convention and Protocol no. 1 opened the way to Strasbourg for thousands of applicants claiming that final decisions ordering welfare payments, pension increases, disability allowance increases and other types of payments had not been complied with. Thus, a serious problem of malfunctioning of the judicial system in Russia was brought to the light. The Strasbourg Court determined that systematic failures to enforce judgements, or unreasonable delays in enforcement, were a result of several factors: unlawful decision of bailiffs, adjournments caused by the intervention of supervisory review authorities; poorly-reasoned judicial rulings; inadequate organization capacities of the State enforcement services and the lack of effective enforcement procedures. Although some special measures have been taken, such as the execution of over 5,000 domestic judgements concerning the indexation of allowances and the allocation of the necessary budgetary means to the local authorities, the problem has yet to be solved. A memorandum prepared by the Secretariat of the Council of Europe[213] suggested several measures[214] that are being discussed by the Russian authorities.

Another break-through decision of the Court was the *Ryabykh* case,[215] where the Court held that setting aside a final and binding judgement in a civil law case in favour of an applicant by the supervisory review constitutes an infringement of the right to a court. Alluding to the rule of law and the principle of legal certainty, the Court argued that "where the courts have finally determined an issue, their ruling should not be called into question".[216] In order to remedy the systemic problem various laws have been modified.[217] However, despite these measures, the existence of the *nadzor*-system still underscores the general priority of community interests over individual interests.

---

[212] Ibid., para. 34.

[213] Memorandum on Non-enforcement of Domestic Judicial Decisions in Russia: General Measures to Comply with the European Court's Judgements and First Comments by the Russian Authorities, prepared by the Department for the Execution of the European Court's Judgements (Application of Article 46 ECHR), CM/Inf/DH(2006)19 revised 6 June 2006, http://www.sutyajnik. ru/rus/echr/res_com_of_min/memo_06_2006_eng.htm.

[214] Improvement of budgetary procedures within the R.F., establishment of a subsidiary mechanism of compulsory enforcement including seizure of State assets, ensuring effective State liability for the enforcement of judgements through judicial remedies, introducing adequate default interest in case of non-enforcement, ensuring effective liability of civil servants for non-enforcement, reconsideration of the bailiffs' role and increasing their efficiency.

[215] *Ryabykh v. Russia* (appl. no. 52854/99), Judgement (First Section), 24 July 2003, Reports 2003-IX, 265, para. 51.

[216] Ibid.

[217] See *infra* Section D.2.a.

The problem of the length of civil and criminal proceedings is as serious in Russia as in many other member countries. The ground-breaking case for Russia in the field of civil law was the *Kormacheva* case,[218] and in the field of criminal law, the *Kalashnikov* case.[219] The remedies existing in Russian law were not considered to be efficient. Among other things, the Russian law provided for disciplinary actions against the judge responsible for delays before the higher judicial or other authorities. The Court explicitly noted that such an approach was not helpful.[220]

Other cases on the right to a fair trial concern the deprivation of an opportunity to attend the hearings.[221] Violations in this regard were exclusively explained as a wrong application of legal norms; the norms themselves were not considered to be contrary to the Convention. In the case of *Vanyan v. Russia*,[222] on the contrary, the discretionary power of the court in deciding on the presence of the accused or his counsel in a supervisory review was deemed to be a violation of the Convention, even if the supervisory review was not detrimental to the accused. In the same case, the Court also found a breach of the principle of equality of arms because the commission of the offence had been procured by undercover Agents of the State in the absence of any element suggesting the applicant's guilt. Problems were also caused by the composition of the courts. In the case of *Posokhov v. Russia*,[223] the Court criticized the lack of a tribunal "prescribed by law" because the participation of lay judges did not correspond to the rules prescribed. The entry into force of the new codes of civil and criminal procedure has brought an end to the participation of lay judges. Another prevailing problem is the lack of effective remedies in national law, leading to manifold violations of Article 13 ECHR (22 cases). This also applies to effective remedies concerning violations of the reasonable length of proceedings.[224]

b. Penitentiary system

In the experts' report before Russia acceded to the Council of Europe, the penitentiary system was already attacked as not being in conformity with common European standards. In the leading case of *Kalashnikov v. Russia*,[225] the Court did not hesitate to equate the conditions in a Russian prison in the high North of

---

[218] *Kormacheva v. Russia* (appl. no. 53084/99), Judgement (First Section), 29 January 2004 (not reported).

[219] *Kalashnikov v. Russia* (*supra* note 51).

[220] *Kormacheva v. Russia* (*supra* note 218).

[221] *Yakovlev v. Russia* (appl. no. 72701/01), Judgement (Fourth Section), 15 March 2005 (not yet reported); *Groshev v. Russia* (appl. no. 69889/01), Judgement (First Section), 20 October 2005 (not yet reported).

[222] *Vanyan v. Russia* (appl. no. 53203/99), Judgement (First Section), 15 December 2005 (not yet reported).

[223] *Posokhov v. Russia* (appl. no. 63486/00), Judgement (Second Section), 4 March 2003, Reports 2003-IV, 137 et seq.

[224] *Kormacheva v. Russia* (*supra* note 218); Demeneva (2005), 66 et seq.

[225] *Kalashnikov v. Russia* (*supra* note 51).

the country to "degrading treatment" due in particular to severe overcrowding and an unsanitary environment with detrimental effects on the health. Similar poor conditions have been found in other detention facilities as well.[226] These cases demonstrated that there is more of an infrastructural than a legal problem involved. According to the Russian authorities, general measures have been taken in order to improve the situation. Among other things, it is planned to continuously increase the budgetary means allocated to the Penitentiary Department of the Ministry of Justice and to construct new detention centres and to reconstruct old ones.

Problems within the penitentiary as well as within the judicial system are also caused by the plain abuse of official powers. In the *Mikheyev* case,[227] torture was inflicted on the applicant while in custody at the police station by several police officers with the aim of extracting a confession. The Court found a double violation of Article 3 ECHR: The infliction of torture and the lack of an effective investigation. According to the Court's findings one of the main problems was the lack of independence of the officials responsible for the investigation from those allegedly involved in the ill-treatment. The ineffectiveness of the inquiry into the death of relatives of the applicants led to findings of violations on the basis of Article 2 ECHR in several cases. The majority of them, but not all[228] were linked to the death or disappearance of people in Chechnya.[229] The Court also found violations of Article 3 ECHR in connection with the lack of medical treatment in a prison[230] as well as with inhumane treatment of a seriously ill prisoner tied to bed in hand cuffs.[231]

To a certain extent, problems in the pre-trial detention facilities are also linked to the legislation. In a considerable number of cases, the length of the pre-trial detention as well as the ineffectiveness of judicial review was interpreted as a violation to Articles 5(3) and 5(4) ECHR.[232] From the view of the Court, the gravity

---

[226] *Labzov v. Russia* (appl. no. 62208/00), Judgement (First Section), 16 June 2005 (not yet reported); *Mayzit v. Russia* (appl. no. 63378/00), Judgement (First Section), 20 January 2005 (not yet reported); *Novoselov v. Russia* (appl. no. 66460/01), Judgement (First Section), 2 June 2005 (not yet reported); *Khudoyorov v. Russia* (appl. no. 6847/02), Judgement (Fourth Section), 8 November 2005 (not yet reported); *Romanov v. Russia* (appl. no. 63993/00), Judgement (Third Section), 20 October 2005 (not yet reported); *Fedotov v. Russia* (appl. no. 5140/02), Judgement (Fourth Section), 25 October 2005 (not yet reported).

[227] *Mikheyev v. Russia* (appl. no. 77617/01), Judgement (First Section), 26 January 2006 (not yet reported); see also *Menesheva v. Russia* (appl. no. 59261/00), Judgement (First Section), 9 March 2006 (not yet reported). A similar case is *Sheydayev v. Russia* (appl. no. 65859/01), Judgement (First Section), 7 December 2006 (not yet reported).

[228] See e.g., the case of *Trubnikov v. Russia* (appl. no. 49790/99), Judgement (Second Section), 5 July 2005 (not yet reported).

[229] See Section D.2.c. *infra*.

[230] *Khudobin v. Russia* (appl. no. 59696/00), Judgement (Third Section), 26 October 2006 (not yet reported).

[231] *Tarariyeva v. Russia* (appl. no. 4353/03), Judgement (Fifth Section), 14 December 2006 (not yet reported).

[232] See e.g. *Kalashnikov v. Russia* (*supra* note 51); *Mayzit v. Russia* (appl. no. 63378/00), Judge-

of the accusation alone without consideration of the facts could not justify the extension of the detention on remand.[233]

Special problems inherited from Soviet times are linked to the enforced internment in a psychiatric hospital. In the case of *Rakevich v. Russia*,[234] the Court found that the internment was not confirmed by a Court order in time and the lawfulness of the internment could not be contested before a Court.

c. Rights of individuals in a free civil society

It is generally acknowledged that the development of a strong civil society is crucial for building up democracy. That presupposes an effective protection of the freedom of expression and freedom of assembly as well as the protection of private and family life and private property.

Although according to the report of the Parliamentary Assembly entitled "Honouring of obligations and commitments of the Russian Federation of 2005", "government pressure on the media resulting in numerous infringements of these rights"[235] persists, as yet there are very few cases concerning freedom of expression, but many more cases are expected.[236] In the case of *Grinberg v. Russia*,[237] the Court found that the Russian courts had not distinguished between "opinion" and "statement" and demanded the proof of the truth of a value judgement. As such a requirement was impossible to fulfil, the Court established that there was an infringement of the freedom of expression.[238] In the case of *Dolgova v. Russia*,[239] the applicant also complained of a violation of the right to freedom of expression. Together with other young people she was involved in a demonstration against President Putin, chanted slogans and distributed leaflets critical of Putin's politics. She was arrested and charged with an attempted violent overthrow of the State power; the charge was later amended to that of participation in

---

ment (First Section), 20 January 2005 (not yet reported); *Panchenko v. Russia* (appl. no. 45100/98), Judgement (Forth Section), 8 February 2005 (not yet reported).

[233] See e.g. *Kalashnikov v. Russia* (*supra* note 51); *Klyakhin v. Russia* (appl. no. 46082/99), Judgement (Second Section), 30 November 2004 (not reported); *Panchenko v. Russia* (*supra* note 232); *Rokhlina v. Russia* (appl. no. 54071/00), Judgement (First Section), 7 April 2005 (not yet reported); *Smirnova v. Russia* (appl. nos 46133/99; 48183/99), Judgement (Third Section), 24 July 2003, Reports 2003-IX, 241 et seq. (extracts); *Nakhmanovich v. Russia* (appl. no. 55669/00), Judgement (First Section), 2 March 2006 (not yet reported).

[234] *Rakevich v. Russia* (appl. no. 58973/00), Judgement (Second Section), 28 October 2003 (not reported).

[235] Report (*supra* note 14), para. 109.

[236] Kovler (2004), 3.

[237] *Grinberg v. Russia* (appl. no. 23472/03), Judgement (First Section), 21 July 2005 (not yet reported).

[238] Similar cases are *Zakharov v. Russia* (appl. no. 14881/03), Judgement (First Section), 5 October 2006 (not yet reported), (criticism of a civil servant for irregular and unlawful behaviour); *Karman v. Russia* (appl. no. 29372/02), Judgement (Fifth Section), 14 December 2006 (not yet reported), (criticism of someone as "neofascist").

[239] *Dolgova v. Russia* (appl. no. 11886/05), Judgement (First Section), 2 March 2006 (not yet reported).

mass disorders. The Court confirmed a violation of Articles 5(1) and 5(3) because of an excessively long detention on remand of almost one year. The complaint on a violation of freedom of expression was rejected for non-exhaustion of domestic remedies.

In this context, it is necessary to mention the case of *Gusinskiy v. Russia*,[240] although it did not concern a violation of the freedom of expression *per se*. Gusinskiy who was the Chairman of the Board and majority shareholder of ZAO Media Most, which included NTV, a popular Russian television channel, was arrested on suspicion of fraud. During his detention, the Acting Minister for Press and Mass Communications offered to drop the criminal charges against the applicant if he would sell Media Most to Gazprom, a State-controlled company holding the natural gas monopoly. The Court held that in this case criminal proceedings and detention on remand were used as part of commercial bargaining strategies and thus not applied for the purpose for which they had been prescribed. Therefore, Russia was held responsible for a violation of Article 18 ECHR. As a consequence of transferring Media Most to Gazprom, the influence of private individuals on media in Russia was significantly diminished.[241]

Two cases concern the non-registration of political parties, which led to their exclusion from participation in elections. In the case of *Presidential Party of Mordovia v. Russia*,[242] the Court found a violation of Article 11 ECHR, whereas in the *People's Democratic Party Vatan* case,[243] it did not analyse the merits of the case, as the applicant was not considered to be a "victim". In the important *Moscow Branch of the Salvation Army* case,[244] the authorities refused the re-registration of the regional branch of the organization without giving any reason that would have been acceptable under the ECHR. According to judge Kovler, these cases show the clear unwillingness of local judicial organs to register religious and political organizations they do not like, even if the central organization has been registered by the Ministry of Justice.[245]

The cases concerning Article 8 ECHR show misuse of official power or a lack of understanding for the concerns of the individual. In the case of *Prokopovich v. Russia*,[246] the applicant was driven out of her partner's apartment after his death. The eviction was effected regardless of procedural safeguards provided for in the Housing Code, and the apartment was reallocated to a police officer. These

---

[240] *Gusinskiy v. Russia* (*supra* note 193).

[241] See Mommsen and Nußberger (2007), 125 et seq.

[242] *Presidential Party of Mordovia v. Russia* (appl. no. 65659/01), Judgement (Second Section), 5 October 2004 (not reported).

[243] *Vatan v. Russia* (appl. no. 47978/99), Judgement (Third Section), 7 October 2004 (not reported).

[244] *Moscow Branch of the Salvation Army v. Russia* (appl. no. 72881/01), Judgement (First Section), 5 October 2006 (not yet reported).

[245] Kovler (2004), 3.

[246] *Prokopovich v. Russia* (appl. no. 58255/00), Judgement (First Section), 18 November 2004, Reports 2004-XI, 1 et seq. (extracts).

clearly illegal actions were upheld by all Russian courts. The Strasbourg Court unanimously found a violation of Article 8 ECHR, as the eviction from the flat was "not in accordance with the law". In the case of *Znamenskaya v. Russia*,[247] a time limit set by law was applied so as to exclude a necessary correction of personal data. In the case of *Smirnova v. Russia*,[248] the confiscation of a passport led to unbearable consequences; the applicant could not register her marriage, could not get medical treatment free of charge and could not be hired.

There were also applications lodged with regard to confiscation measures under Article 1 of Protocol no. 1 in the cases of *Frizen v. Russia*[249] and *Baklanov v. Russia*.[250] In these instances, the Court found that either there were no legal regulations at all or that the legal regulations were not sufficiently precise.

Two environmental issues were raised in the jurisdiction of the Court concerning Russia. In the case of *Fadeyeva v. Russia*,[251] the applicant lived in a sanitary zone established around a steel work where the pollution level was much higher than the maximum permitted according to Russian law. Although the courts confirmed the right to resettlement in a safer area, the authorities did not offer any effective solution, but only placed the applicant on a general waiting list. The pollution was not reduced to a safe level undetrimental to the health of the inhabitants of the region.[252] It is clear that this problem concerned a large number of people. If further measures are not taken, there will be thousands of complaints in Strasbourg.

Numerous other problems faced by Russian citizens on a daily basis are not covered by the Court's case law. These problems concern rights of a social and economic nature, such as the loss of savings because of inflation[253] or the low pensions that make survival difficult.[254]

In the case of *Bolat v. Russia*,[255] the expulsion of an alien, a Turkish national, was deemed for the first time to be a violation of Article 1 of Protocol no. 7. The

---

[247] *Znamenskaya v. Russia* (appl. no. 77785/01), Judgement (First Section), 2 June 2005 (not yet reported).
[248] *Smirnova v. Russia* (appl. nos 46133/99; 48183/99), Judgement (Third Section), 24 July 2003, Reports 2003-IX, 241 et seq. (extracts).
[249] *Frizen v. Russia* (appl. no. 58254/00), Judgement (First Section), 24 March 2005 (not yet reported).
[250] *Baklanov v. Russia* (appl. no. 68443/01), Judgement (First Section), 9 June 2005 (not yet reported).
[251] *Fadeyeva v. Russia* (appl. no. 55723/00), Judgement (First Section), 9 June 2005 (not yet reported).
[252] A similar case was *Ledyayeva, Dobrokhotova, Zolotareva, Romashina v. Russia* (appl. nos 53157/99; 53247/99; 56850/00; 53695/00), Judgement (First Section), 26 October 2006 (not yet reported).
[253] *Appolonov v. Russia* (appl. no. 47578/01), Judgement (First Section), 29 August 2002 (not reported); for a critique on this admissibility decision see Karapetjan (2005), 107 et seq.
[254] *Larioshina v. Russia* (appl. no. 56869/00), Judgement (Second Section), 25 June 1999 (not reported).
[255] *Bolat v. Russia* (appl. no. 14139/03), Judgement (First Section), 5 October 2006 (not yet reported).

Russian authorities had disregarded procedural safeguards and expelled the applicant without any judicial decision. This case might become a leading judgement in relation to the expulsion of Georgian nationals that took place after squabbles between Russia and Georgia in 2006. Until now, none of these cases has been decided on the merits.

d. Human Rights Violations in Chechnya and Transdnjestria

In the reports of the Council of Europe, the human rights situation in Chechnya is still described as "dramatic": "(…) a climate of impunity continued to prevail in the Chechen Republic due to the fact that the Chechen and Federal law enforcement authorities were still either unwilling or unable to hold accountable for their actions the vast majority of perpetrators of serious human rights violations."[256] Against this background, it is not surprising that the Court found violations of Article 2, 3, 14 ECHR and Article 2 of Protocol no. 1 (right to education) and Article 2 of Protocol no. 4 (right to free movement). The leading cases are *Isayeva v. Russia*,[257] *Isayeva, Yusupova and Bazayeva v. Russia*[258] and *Khashiyev and Akayeva v. Russia.*[259] All these cases concerned the death of applicants' relatives during Russian military operations in Chechnya in 1999 and 2000. Either the State was directly responsible for the killings and abductions or it was responsible for the failure to prepare and execute military operations with the requisite care for the lives and property of the civilians. Furthermore, the State was reproached for not having conducted effective investigations and not to provide any effective remedy. The pain of the relatives of those that disappeared was also understood as leading to a violation of Article 3 ECHR.[260]

In addition, the only case regarding discrimination in Russia concerned ethnic Chechens. In the cases of *Gartukayev v. Russia*[261] and *Timishev v. Russia,*[262] the applicants were refused entry into Kabardino-Balkaria on the basis of an unwritten instruction from the Ministry of the Interior. Whereas in the first case the Court only found a violation of Article 2 of Protocol no. 4, in the second case it condemned Russia for "racial discrimination" and it considered that the restric-

---

[256] Report (see *supra* note 16), para. 11.

[257] *Isayeva v. Russia* (appl. no. 57950/00), Judgement (First Section), 24 February 2005 (not yet reported).

[258] *Isayeva, Yusupova and Bazayeva v. Russia* (appl. nos 57947/00; 57948/00; 57949/00), Judgement (First Section), 24 February 2005 (not yet reported).

[259] *Khashiyev and Akayeva v. Russia* (appl. nos 57942/00; 57945/00), Judgement (First Section), 24 February 2005 (not yet reported). Further similar decisions are *Estamirov v. Russia* (appl. no. 60272/00), Judgement (First Section), 12 October 2006 (not yet reported) and *Imakayeva v. Russia* (appl. no. 7615/02), Judgement (First Section), 9 November 2006 (not yet reported).

[260] *Bazorkina v. Russia* (appl. no. 69481/01), Judgement (First Section), 27 July 2006 (not yet reported).

[261] *Gartukayev v. Russia* (appl. no. 71933/01), Judgement (Second Section), 13 December 2005 (not yet reported).

[262] *Timishev v. Russia* (appl. no. 55762/00; 55974/00), Judgement (Second Section), 13 December 2005 (not yet reported).

tions only applied to representatives of one ethnic group and could thus never be justified "in a contemporary democratic society built on the principles of pluralism and respect for different cultures".[263] In the *Timishev* case, the children of the applicant were also refused admission to their school because the applicant could not produce his migrant's card, a local document confirming registration and the status as a forced migrant from Chechnya. This refusal was against Russian law, which did not allow making the children's right to education conditional upon the registration of the parents' residence. The Court therefore found a violation of Article 2 of Protocol no. 1.

Human rights problems in both Chechnya and in Transdniestria are political problems; the solution of individual cases does not change the situation as a whole. The difference between the cases is that Chechnya is part of Russia, whereas Transdniestria is part of Moldova, despite the existence of a *de facto* regime (which is not recognized by any State or international organization). The legal problem in the case of *Ilaşcu, Lesco, Ivantoc, Petrov-Popa v. Russia*[264] was, therefore, if the Convention could be applied on human rights violation in Transdniestria, i.e. if Russia had jurisdiction over Transdniestria in the sense of Article 1 ECHR. With reference to the *Loizidou* case, the Court confirmed the applicability of the Convention because the Russian authorities had contributed both militarily and politically to the creation of the separatist regime and the region remained "under the effective authority, or at the very least under the decisive influence of the Russian Federation".[265] In the opinion of the Court Transdniestria survived "by virtue of the military, economic, financial and political support that Russia gave it".[266] The assumption of territorial jurisdiction on this basis is controversial and it was contested in the dissenting opinion of the Russian judge Kovler. He argued that neither Russia nor Moldova had jurisdiction over the territory; in his opinion there was a "'legal vacuum' or 'lawless area' in Transdniestria to which the Convention provisions are inapplicable *de facto*".[267] He stressed the "objective impossibility" of enforcing the judgement that in its substance condemned both Russia and Moldova for violations of Articles 3 and 5 ECHR.

The Russian authorities have called into question the validity of the judgement and have insisted that, by paying the just satisfaction awarded, they have fully executed the judgement. The execution of the judgement caused a major dispute between the Council of Europe and Russia. The Committee of Ministers has passed four resolutions with regard to this issue and announced its "resolve

---

[263] Ibid.
[264] *Ilaşcu and Others v. Russia and Moldova* (appl. no. 48787/99), Judgement (Grand Chamber), 8 July 2004, Reports 2004-VII, 179 et seq.
[265] Ibid., para. 392.
[266] Ibid.
[267] Dissenting Opinion of Judge Kovler in *Ilaşcu and Others v. Russia and Moldova* (*supra* note 264), 179 et seq.

to ensure, with all means available to the Organization, the compliance by the Russian Federation with its obligations under this judgement".[268]

e. Lack of Cooperation Between the Russian Authorities and the Council of Europe

Major tensions between the Council of Europe and Russia were caused by violations of Articles 34 and 38 ECHR. The Court reproached the Russian authorities for blocking individual applications and for not cooperating in the preparation of the cases. In the cases of *Klyakhin v. Russia*[269] and *Poleshchuk v. Russia*,[270] the Court found that applicants' letters addressed to the Court had been blocked. In the case of *Fedotova v. Russia*,[271] the police initiated an inquiry into tax payments by the applicant's representative and translator. The Court held that to be an arbitrary measure that constituted an interference with the right of individual petition. In the cases of *Shamayev and 12 Others v. Russia, Trubnikov v. Russia*,[272] *Mikheyev v. Russia*,[273] the authorities were accused of withholding the relevant material. The refusal to allow a fact-finding visit in the case of *Shameyev and 12 Others v. Georgia and Russia*[274] was strongly criticized. It was found that "the lack of cooperation of the Russian authorities (…) will inevitably cast serious doubts as to Russia's will to abide in good faith with the commitments entered into upon ratification of the European Convention of Human Rights".[275]

Human rights activists found out in 2005 that in at least five cases the applicants complaining of the death of their relatives had died or disappeared under unclear circumstances.[276] These cases were investigated and the findings were published in a resolution of the Parliamentary Assembly.[277] Many of the applicants have sought asylum and now live abroad.

---

[268] Interim Resolutions ResDH(2005)42 of 22 April 2005, ResDH(2005)84 of 13 July 2005 and ResDH(2006)11 of 1 March 2006, ResDH(2006)11 of 10 May 2006.

[269] *Klyakhin v. Russia* (appl. no. 46082/99), Judgement (Second Section), 30 November 2004 (not reported).

[270] *Poleshchuk v. Russia* (appl. no. 60776/00), Judgement (First Section), 7 October 2004 (not reported).

[271] *Fedotova v. Russia* (appl. no. 73225/01), Judgement (First Section), 13 April 2006 (not yet reported).

[272] *Trubnikov v. Russia* (appl. no. 49790/99), Judgement (Second Section), 5 July 2005 (not yet reported).

[273] *Mikheyev v. Russia* (appl. no. 77617/01), Judgement (First Section), 26 January 2006 (not yet reported).

[274] *Shamayev and 12 Others v. Georgia and Russia* (appl. no. 36378/02), Judgement (Second Section), 12 April 2005, Reports 2005-III, 153 et seq.

[275] P.A., Honouring of obligations and commitments by the Russian Federation, Doc. 10568 of 3 June 2005, para. 258. http://assembly.coe.int/Documents/WorkingDocs/Doc05/EDOC10568.htm.

[276] Peter Finn, Obrashcheniya rossiyan v Evropeyskiy sud po pravam cheloveka oborachivayutsya dlya nikh zapugivaniem i smert'yu (The application of Russians to the European Court of Human Rights turns for the applicants into terror and death), The Washington Post, 4 July 2005.

[277] See *supra* note 194.

3. Ukraine

a. Judicial System

For Ukraine, the first decision, *Sovtransavto v. Ukraine*,[278] already constituted a landmark case. It shed more light on major deficits concerning the judiciary system. In a litigation between a Russian and a Ukrainian company, the lack of independence of the judges and the interferences of the authorities in the judicial decisions were all too obvious. In the case file, a letter was even found from the President advising a judge on how to decide. The Court's comments are abundantly clear: "Lastly, the Court can but note that the Ukrainian authorities acting at the highest level intervened in the proceedings on a number of occasions. Whatever the reasons advanced by the Government to justify such interventions, the Court considers that, in view of their content and the manner in which they were made (…), they were *ipso facto* incompatible with the notion of an 'independent and impartial tribunal' within the meaning of Article 6 § 1 of the Convention."[279] Furthermore, the supervisory system was criticized because of its structural deficits. Quashing a final and binding judgement was considered to be a violation of Article 6(1) ECHR.

The independence of investigation and adjudication was a problem in other cases as well. The failure to conduct an effective and independent investigation into the death of a lieutenant of the Ukrainian Air Force was considered to be a violation of Article 2 ECHR.[280] In the case of *Svetlana Naumenko v. Ukraine*,[281] the Court found that the practice where the protest is lodged by the deputy president of the court with the Presidium of the same court was incompatible with the "subjective impartiality" of a judge hearing a particular case. Another closely related problem was the violation of the presumption of innocence.[282]

Besides these flagrant violations of Article 6 ECHR, the non-execution of judgements as well as the length of the procedure account for a large number of breaches of the Convention. All those cases are almost identical clone cases showing the dysfunction of the judiciary.

The *Gorshkov* case[283] was also linked to the lack of a judicial remedy. The Court found that Article 5(4) ECHR was violated because of the absence of the possibility to apply for release from psychiatric detention.

---

[278] *Sovtransavto Holding v. Ukraine* (*supra* note 198).

[279] Ibid., para. 80.

[280] *Sergey Shevchenko v. Ukraine* (appl. no. 32478/02), Judgement (Second Section), 4 April 2006 (not yet reported).

[281] *Svetlana Naumenko v. Ukraine* (appl. no. 41984/98), Judgement (Second Section), 9 November 2004 (not reported).

[282] *Grabchuk v. Ukraine* (appl. no. 8599/02), Judgement (Fifth Section), 21 September 2006 (not yet reported); *Panteleyenko v. Ukraine* (appl. no. 11901/02), Judgement (Fifth Section), 29 June 2006 (not yet reported).

[283] *Gorshkov v. Ukraine* (appl. no. 67531/01), Judgement (Second Section), 8 November 2005 (not yet reported).

The right to have a conviction or sentence reviewed by a higher tribunal, granted in Article 2 of Protocol no. 7 has been infringed in the *Gurepka* case[284] due to the lack of sufficient remedies against administrative detention for contempt of court.

b. Penitentiary System

In 1997 and 1998, several detainees who had been sentenced to death brought complaints against the detention conditions on death row. In 2003, the Court admitted the complaints and confirmed a violation of Article 3 ECHR because of inhuman conditions in prison and of Article 8 ECHR because of restrictions placed on the prisoners' correspondence, receipt of parcels and family visits.[285]

While these cases are closely linked to the situation on death row, violations of Article 3 ECHR occurred within the penitentiary system as well. The Court confirmed a violation of Article 3 ECHR in eight other cases: A violation of Article 3 in the form of torture (force-feeding of detainee on hunger-strike) and degrading treatment (unacceptable conditions of detention) was found in the *Nevmerzhitsky* case.[286] In the *Afanasyev* case,[287] the violence of police officers during detention was considered as an inhuman and degrading treatment. In the *Melnik* case,[288] the applicant did not receive the necessary treatment and assistance for tuberculosis while serving his sentence. Furthermore the non-satisfactory conditions of hygiene and sanitation amounted to an inhuman treatment.[289] Police brutality, ill-treatment of persons in custody and illegal detention remains a serious problem.[290]

c. The Gongadze case

The most serious human rights violation was found in the case of the famous political journalist and editor-in-chief of the *Ukrainskaya Pravda* Internet journal, Mr. Gongadze.[291] He was actively involved, both nationally and internationally,

---

[284] *Gurepka v. Ukraine* (*supra* note 206).

[285] *Poltoratskiy v. Ukraine* (appl. no. 38812/97), Judgement (Fourth Section), 29 April 2003, Reports 2003-V, 89 et seq.; *Kuznetsov v. Ukraine* (appl. no. 39042/97), Judgement (Fourth Section), 29 April 2003 (not reported); *Nazarenko v. Ukraine* (appl. no. 39483/98), Judgement (Fourth Section), 29 April 2003 (not reported); *Dankevich v. Ukraine* (appl. no. 40679/98), Judgement (Fourth Section), 29 April 2003 (not reported); *Aliev v. Ukraine* (appl. no. 41220/98), Judgement (Fourth Section), 29 April 2003 (not reported); *Khokhlich v. Ukraine* (appl. no. 41707/98), Judgement (Fourth Section), 29 April 2003 (not reported).

[286] *Nevmerzhitsky v. Ukraine* (appl. no. 54825/00), Judgement (Second Section), 5 April 2005, Reports 2005-II, 307 et seq.

[287] *Afanasyev v. Ukraine* (appl. no. 38722/02), Judgement (Second Section), 5 April 2005 (not yet reported).

[288] *Melnik v. Ukraine* (appl. no. 72286/01), Judgement (Second Section), 28 March 2006 (not yet reported).

[289] See also *Dvoynykh v. Ukraine* (appl. no. 72277/01), Judgement (Fifth Section), 12 October 2006 (not yet reported).

[290] P.A. Doc. 10676 of 19 September 2005, p. 40 (233, 240).

[291] *Gongadze v. Ukraine* (*supra* note 207).

in raising awareness about the lack of freedom of speech in Ukraine and reported on corruption among high-level State officials. Mr Gongadze disappeared on 16 September 2000 and a few months later a decapitated body was found. Years later it was proven to be the corpse of the journalist. A tape of a conversation between President Kuchma and the Minister of the Interior on the planned disappearance of the journalist was made public. The investigations into the case were only resumed after the election of President Yushchenko. Five years after the disappearance of Mr. Gongadze the Parliament of Ukraine heard the report of the chairman of its *ad hoc* investigating committee on the murder of Mr Gongadze, which concluded that the kidnapping and the murder of Mr. Gongadze had been organized by the former President Kuchma and Mr Kravchenko, and that the Speaker of Parliament who was still in office as well as another Member of Parliament were involved in the crimes. The report finally noted that the General Procurator's Office had failed to take any action or to react to the conclusions of the *ad hoc* committee.

The application in this case was brought to the Court by the wife of the journalist. The Court found a violation of Article 2 ECHR because the authorities had failed to protect the life of the journalist. Furthermore, Article 3 ECHR was violated, as the Court considered that the numerous contradictory statements about the journalist's fate and the denial of access to the files for the relatives up to 2005 were considered as degrading treatment. Last but not least, Article 13 ECHR was violated, given that there had not been any effective criminal investigation within a period of more than four years.

d. Rights of individuals in a free civil society

Breaches of the freedom of thought, conscience and religion (Article 9 ECHR) are rather rare. In the *Poltoratsykiy* and *Kuznetsov* cases,[292] the Court found that there was a violation of Article 9 ECHR, given that the applicants' right to be visited by a priest while in prison was restricted without any legal basis.

Article 8 ECHR has been the subject of proceedings ten times: In the *Novoseletskiy* case,[293] the unlawful entry into the applicant's apartment was considered to be a violation of Article 8 ECHR. The unlawful disclosure of psychiatric data at a court hearing as well as an unlawful search of the apartment infringed the right to respect private and family life in the *Panteleyenko* case.[294] The case of an interception of correspondence without sufficient clarity as to the scope and the duration showed the misuse of powers granted to the authorities by the criminal

---

[292] *Poltoratskiy v. Ukraine* (appl. no. 38812/97), Judgement (Fourth Section), 29 April 2003, Reports 2003-V, 89 et seq.; *Kuznetsov v. Ukraine* (*supra* note 285).

[293] *Novoseletskiy v. Ukraine* (appl. no. 47148/99), Judgement (Second Section), 22 February 2005, Reports 2005-II, 115 et seq. (extracts).

[294] *Panteleyenko v. Ukraine* (appl. no. 11901/02), Judgement (Fifth Section), 29 June 2006 (not yet reported.

procedural law.[295] In the case of *Hunt v. Ukraine*,[296] the applicant, an American national, was prohibited from entering Ukraine and thus could not defend his interests in a case concerning his parental rights. Here, too, Article 8 ECHR was violated.

In the case of *Ukrainian Media Group v. Ukraine*,[297] the Court considered the application of Article 10 ECHR. Damages were awarded against a newspaper in respect of Articles defaming politicians. The Court found that the sentence with regard to defamation was disproportionate to the aim pursued as no distinction between value judgements and statements of facts had been made. In the *Salov* case,[298] the conviction for disseminating false information about a presidential candidate prior to the election was considered as a violation of Article 10 ECHR. In a third case concerning the freedom of expression, the applicant was a journalist and editor-in-chief of the Ukrainian newspaper *Polityka* who had been charged with intentional defamation in print, with making unfounded accusations of committing serious crime and abusing his position of power.[299] He was sentenced to two (suspended) years in prison and barred from working in media management for two years. The Court pointed to the fact that two of the indiscriminated Articles contained value judgements that were not susceptible of proof. As all four Articles were written on matters of serious public interest and concerned public figures and politicians, the Court qualified the conviction as not proportionate.

In the *Melnychenko* case,[300] the electoral candidate was prevented from registering on the grounds of having given untruthful information, namely his official address although living abroad. In this case a violation of Article 3 of Protocol no. 1 was found. Here, too, interference with human rights was clearly politically motivated. Melnychenko had been responsible for tape recordings of the President's personal conversations relating to the disappearance of the journalist Gongadze.

---

[295] *Volokhy v. Ukraine* (appl. no. 23543/02), Judgement (Fifth Section), 2 November 2006 (not yet reported).

[296] *Hunt v. Ukraine* (appl. no. 31111/04), Judgement (Fifth Section), 7 December 2006 (not yet reported).

[297] *Ukrainian Media Group v. Ukraine* (appl. no. 72713/01), Judgement (Second Section), 29 March 2005 (not yet reported).

[298] *Salov v. Ukraine* (*supra* note 203).

[299] *Lyashko v. Ukraine* (appl. no. 21040/02), Judgement (Fifth Section), 10 August 2006 (not yet reported).

[300] *Melnychenko v. Ukraine* (appl. no. 17707/02), Judgement (Second Section), 19 October 2004, Reports 2004-X, 1 et seq.

e. Lack of Cooperation Between the Ukrainian Authorities and the Council of Europe

Ukraine was condemned by the Court for not complying with its obligations under Article 38 ECHR. In the case of *Nevmerzhitsky v. Ukraine*,[301] the Court found that Ukraine had failed to provide all necessary facilities to enable the Court to establish the facts in the case.

4. Comparison and Conclusion

The case law concerning Russia and Ukraine is marked by common characteristics. Both countries have a human rights record full of serious cases in which high officials are involved. Most of the problems can be explained by the fact that, despite all the progress in the legislation, the mentality of the authorities has not changed. Many of the authorities still act as they used to in Soviet times. Human rights violations are caused by a behaviour that is based on the idea of the uncontrollability of the State and the complete submission of the individual. The judiciary is still in various ways dependent on the executive power. As opinion polls demonstrate, the population does not trust the judges in general. The large number of individual applications before the Court is, therefore, a sign of deeply rooted problems in Russia's and Ukraine's post-soviet societies.

E. Mechanisms of Coordination

1. Russia

a. Preliminary Remarks

Most of the violations of the Convention by Russia are not caused by the laws, but by their non-application or wrongful application. For this reason, the execution of the judgements mainly demands changes in the practical work of the courts as well as changes in the behaviour of the executive towards the citizens. Moreover, in various fields such as in the penitentiary system or the system of environmental protection, it is necessary to implement comprehensive programs in order to prevent further abuses of power and human rights violations.

b. Individual Measures

In a ruling that was adopted right before the Convention entered into force in Russia, the Russian Constitutional Court referred to the International Covenant on Civil and Political Rights and explicitly accepted its dominance over domestic law.[302] Having recourse to Article 46(3) of the Russian Constitution, the Con-

---

[301] *Nevmerzhitsky v. Ukraine* (appl. no. 54825/00), Judgement (Second Section), 5 April 2005, Reports 2005-II, 307 et seq.

[302] Judgement of the Russian Constitutional Court, 2 February 1996, Vestnik Konstitutsionnogo Suda RF 1996, no. 2, pos. 2.

stitutional Court stressed "that decisions of international bodies can lead to the revision (*peresmotr*) of individual cases by the highest courts of the Russian Federation and, therefore, make it possible to confer competences to them in order to change earlier decisions including those of the highest domestic judicial instances".[303] This was understood as opening the door for the taking of individual measures as a follow-up to the decisions of the European Court.

The relevant provisions were inserted within the reform of the procedural codes. Thus, Russian law provides for a reopening of the procedure in the case of a judgement of the Court concerning Russia. This applies to the criminal procedure as well as to the Arbitrazh Courts' procedure. Article 413 of the new Code on Criminal Procedure stipulates that decisions of the European Court are considered as "new circumstances" if they concern the non-conformity of a Russian federal law with the Constitution or other violations of the European Convention on Human Rights. A similar provision is contained in Article 311 of the Code of Arbitrazh procedure.[304] However, the applicant concerned does not have a legal right to a reexamination of the case; the procedure is initiated by the authorities. There is no comparable provision in the Code on Civil Procedure, but the general clause pertaining to the reopening of a case after the discovery of new circumstances (Article 392) might be applied by way of analogy.

For a long time the main enforcement problem was the fact that two of the applicants in the case of *Ilaşcu v. Russia*[305] had been further detained in the Moldovan Republic of Transdniestria even after Ilaşcu had been released. Whereas Russia claimed that it had no influence in Transdniestria, the Parliamentary Assembly argued that this contention could not be taken seriously.[306] The two remaining applicants were released in June 2007 after having served the complete sentence.

c. General Measures

aa. Measures Taken by the Judiciary. In comparison to other legal systems, some courts in the Russian legal system have quasi-legislative competences that are unique. The Plenary Assembly of the Supreme Court and the Plenary Assembly of the Supreme Arbitrazh Court have the power to issue "regulations" (*postanovleniya*) that determine the practice of the lower courts.[307] Although these *postanovleniya* are not regarded as legal acts in the proper sense, they are binding and the lower courts must obey them. The application of the ECHR by the courts is

---

[303] Ibid.

[304] Edidin (2004), 22.

[305] *Ilaşcu and Others v. Russia and Moldova* (*supra* note 264).

[306] See the Report of the Committee on Legal Affairs and Human Rights (Rapporteur Erik Jurgens), Doc. 11020, 18 September 2006, Implementation of judgements of the European Court of Human Rights, para. 11.2.

[307] See Articles 126 and 127 of the Constitution; for more details see Bachrach/Burkov (2004), 11 et seq.; Krug (2006), 11 et seq. (the term used in this Article is "explanations").

determined by several *postanovleniya*. In a *postanovlenie* on the application of the Constitution in the jurisprudence of the ordinary courts, it is stressed that laws contradictory to international treaties that have been implemented on the basis of a Federal law must not be applied.[308] In a *postanovlenie* dating from 18 November 1999, the Court directly referred to Article 6 ECHR and urged the ordinary courts "to decide on criminal as well as on civil cases without any unjustified delays and thus to secure the right to court in an optimal way".[309] The *postanovlenie* entitled "Application of generally accepted principles and norms of international law and international treaties in the Russian Federation",[310] where the application of international law is dealt with in detail, is of fundamental importance. In this context the Supreme Court also provided advice with regard to the consequences ensuing from the jurisprudence of the European Court, which have a bearing for the daily work of ordinary courts in Russia. On the basis of the first cases handed down by the Court concerning Russia, special hints were given with regard to Articles 3, 5, 6, and 13 ECHR; cases concerning other member countries were not considered. The Supreme Court recommended that the judges take the jurisprudence of the Strasbourg Court into account and to direct questions to the Ministry of Justice, if necessary. It also stressed that judgements disregarding applicable international treaty law can be quashed.[311] In another *postanovlenie* of 2003, the Plenary Assembly of the Supreme Court requested the courts not only to quote the rulings of the Constitutional Court, but also the judgements of the European Court.[312] In 2005, the Court passed a *postanovlenie* giving details on the application of provisions on the protection of honour in civil law.[313]

---

[308] Postanovlenie Plenuma Verkhovnogo Suda Rossiyskoy Federatsii N. 8 dating from the 31 October 1995, "O nekotorykh voprosakh primeneniya sudami Konstitutsii Rossiyskoy Federatsii pri osushchestvlenii pravosudiya" (Questions relating to the application of the Constitution of the R.F. by the Courts in rendering judgements), Byulleten' Verkhovnogo Suda RF 1996, no. 2, p. 1.

[309] Postanovlenie Plenuma Verkhovnogo Suda Rossiyskoy Federatsii N. 79 dating from 8 November 1999, "O khode vypolneniya postanovleniya plenuma Verkhovnogo Suda Rossiyskoy Federatsii ot 24 avgusta 1993 no. 7 'O srokakh rassmotreniya ugolovnykh i grazhdanskikh del sudami Rossiyskoy Federatsii" (Execution of the postanovlenie of the Plenary Assembly of the Supreme Court of the R.F. of 24 August 1993, prescribed periods for the decision on criminal and civil cases by the courts of the R.F.), Byulleten' Verkhovnogo Suda RF 1993, no. 12, p. 2.

[310] Postanovlenie Plenuma Verkhovnogo Suda Rossiyskoy Federatsii N. 5 dating from 10 October 2003, "O primenenii sudami obshchej jurisdiktsii obshchepriznannykh principov i norm mezhdunarodnogo prava i mezhdunarodnykh dogovorov Rossiyskoy Federatsii", Byulleten' Verkhovnogo Suda RF 2003, no. 12, p. 3.

[311] Section 9 of the Postanovlenie, ibid. In Section 4 of the Postanovlenie Verkhovnogo Suda N. 23 dating from 19 December 2003 "O rešenii suda" the Supreme Court stresses the necessity of citing the legal acts applied. This also concerns the ECHR and the Judgements of the Court. Byulleten' Verkhovnogo Suda RF 2004, no. 2.

[312] Postanovlenie Plenuma Verkhovnogo Suda Rossiyskoy Federatsii N. 23 dating from the 19 December 2003, "O sudebnom reshenii" (Judicial decisions), Rossiyskaya Gazeta, 6 December 2003, SZ RF 2003, no. 260.

[313] Postanovlenie Plenuma Verkhovnogo Suda Rossiyskoy Federatsii N. 3 dating from the 24 February 2005, "O sudebnoj praktike po delam o zashchite chesti i dostoinstva grazhdan, a takzhe delovoy reputatsii grazhdan i yuridicheskikh lits" (Judicial practice concerning the honour and di-

The Supreme Arbitrazh Court circulated an "information letter" concerning the interpretation of the right to property in conformity with the Convention,[314] where it summarized the jurisprudence of the Court on Article 6 ECHR and Article 1 Protocol no. 1.[315] Although there is no legal basis for such "information letters", they became a widespread means to convey information and they have a important impact on legal practice.[316]

Apart from this way of communicating general reaction patterns to the lower courts, there are special "circular letters" concerning specific questions related to the prevention of further violations of the Convention. The courts are urged to observe strictly the legal time limits set by the Code of Criminal Procedure for investigation and trial in general,[317] as well as for judicial review of the lawfulness of compulsory psychiatric confinement.[318]

Furthermore, the Constitutional Court can give binding interpretations to the existing laws and thus remedy inconsistencies with the Convention.[319] That is deemed to be sufficient even if the legal provision itself is contrary to the European Convention. Thus, the Russian Constitutional Courts declared a constitutional complaint against Article 255 of the Code on Criminal Procedure inadmissible.[320] Although the wording of this provision was clearly contrary to Article 5(3) ECHR, the Constitutional Court argued that the provision had to be interpreted in the light of the Convention. Therefore, it did not see any need to

---

gnity of citizens as well as their reputation of citizens and legal persons), Rossiyskaya Gazeta, 15 March 2005, SZ RF 2005, no. 3719; see for details Krug (2006), 29 et seq.

[314] Informatsionnoe pis'mo Vysshego Arbitrazhnogo Suda RF, dating from 20 December 1999 (N C1-7/CMP-1341), "Ob osnovnykh polozheniyakh, primenyaemykh Evropeyskim sudom po pravam cheloveka pri zashchite imushchestvennykh prav i prava na pravosudiye" (Basic positions of the European Court on Human Rights for the protection of the right to property and the right to court), Vestnik Vysshego Arbitrazhnogo Suda RF 2000, no. 2.

[315] The nine points mentioned are the following: Private character of property rights, balance between public and individual interests, access to court, decision on property rights by independent courts, decision by impartial courts, fairness of the judicial procedure, fair hearing, reasonableness of time limits, public procedure.

[316] Burkov (2006), *Primenenie*, 29; see also Burkov (2007), 31.

[317] Cf. the circular letter of the vice-President of the Supreme Court, 5 September 2002, stressing the precedent value of Kalashnikov judgement and requesting that all courts ensure strict compliance with the time limits set by the Code of Criminal Procedure for investigation and trial and prevent unjustified delays in proceedings.

[318] Cf. the circular letter of the vice-President of the Supreme Court, 31 August 2004, drawing the attention to the strict observance of legal time limits for judicial review of the lawfulness of compulsory psychiatric confinement.

[319] See e.g., the decision of the Russian Constitutional Court, 8 July 2004, Vestnik Konstitutsionnogo Suda RF 2005, no. 1, in which it explains that "confiscation" can mean "a measure ordered by a court following proceedings in relation to a criminal offence resulting in the final deprivation of property" as provided for by Article 86(4) of the Code of Criminal Procedure. Thus there is a legal basis for measures such as the confiscation of money in the *Baklanov* case (*Baklanov v. Russia* (appl. no. 68443/01), Judgement (First Section), 9 June 2005 (not yet reported)). In this judgement, the Court criticized that the confiscation was not "based on law".

[320] Judgement of the Russian Constitutional Court 27 May 2004, Vestnik Konstitutsionnogo Suda RF 2004, no. 6.

judge on the merits of the constitutional complaint. Although these arguments are theoretically correct, in view of the general deficiencies in the judiciary system in Russia, it would be highly recommendable to change the wording of the provision in order to avoid misinterpretations in practice.

The execution of the rulings of the Constitutional Court is regulated in Article 80 of the Law on the Constitutional Court. As Russia has not yet adopted a comprehensive law on the implementation of the Convention, it is argued that the provisions applicable to the Russian Constitutional Court should also be applied to the decisions of the European Court by way of analogy.[321] However, as far as can be seen, this theoretical possibility is not followed in practice.

The reference to case law is generally considered to be a new challenge for Russian courts.[322] The constitutional judge Vitruk argues that the acceptance of case law in the legal system of the Russian Federation "can seriously weaken the legal force of the Constitution, of the statutes and lead to their deformation in the law-applying practice".[323] Therefore, he stresses the discretion of the courts in the selection of legal positions of the European Court: "But in this case the national organs of legislative, executive and judicial power do not lose the famous right of discretion and selection of the legal positions that are contained in the decisions."[324] In the same way, Zimnenko argues that the Contracting States are not bound by the case law of the Court: "The States accepting the Convention were convinced that the Court has been given the competence to apply and interpret the given international treaty, but not to create new legal norms binding the Contracting States of the Convention."[325] Marchenko interprets the notion of "precedent" in the case of the Strasbourg jurisprudence as a "helpful example".[326] These approaches to the implementation of the judgements are much more restrictive than the position expressed by the German Constitutional Court in the famous *Görgülü* decision.[327] Whereas the German Constitutional Court does not accept the "'enforcement' of the decisions in a schematical way", it also stresses that the courts are obliged to take the jurisprudence of the Strasbourg Court into account. Only in exceptional cases can they decide not to follow it. If they do not give convincing reasons for not applying the Convention in the light of the jurisprudence of the Court, they violate the principle of the "Rechtsstaat".[328] There is no free "discretion".

The Russian discussion on the value of "precedents" has to be seen in the

---

[321] Edidin (2004), 23.

[322] Laptev (2004), 46.

[323] Vitruk (2006), *O nekotorykh osobennostyakh*, 83.

[324] Vitruk (2006), *O nekotorykh osobennostyakh*, 83.

[325] Zimnenko (2006), 307.

[326] Marchenko (2006), 19.

[327] *Görgülü v. Germany* (appl. no. 74969/01), Judgement (Third Section), 26 February 2004 (not reported). See Lambert Abdelgawad/Weber, this volume, Section D.2.

[328] Decision of the German Constitutional Court, 14 October 2004, headnote, BVerfG 2005, 111, 307.

context of the general developments of the legal system. Accepting precedents is linked to a specific danger. It is not desirable to make the already existing gap between law and practice still wider by applying case law contrary to the written letter of the law.[329] However, according to Kovler, "the majority of the progressively thinking judges and practitioners already accept the idea of case law being a source of law".[330]

bb. Legislative measures. As many of the provisions criticized date back to Soviet times, the general reform projects provide remedies for quite a lot of the problems. Important new laws in this context are the Code on criminal procedure,[331] the Code on civil procedure[332] and the Law on Psychiatric Treatment[333] that were elaborated or changed after the entry into force of the Convention. Sometimes, the inconsistencies persist due to transitional provisions that still allow for the application of the old norms.[334] Sometimes, the new laws are not even consistent with the standards of the European Convention and show the heritage of past legal concepts.[335] An example of this could be Article 3(1) of the Code of Criminal Procedure stipulating that the Russian legislation on criminal procedure takes into consideration international treaties of the Russian Federation on the execution of judgements and the treatment of the accused "in accordance with the economic and social possibilities of the country and the society". The ECHR does not accept such a reservation.[336] Another example is the *nadzor*-system, which has been changed, but not abolished. By now it contains a limit on those who have the right to lodge a supervisory appeal[337] and it also restricts the time limit to one year after the entry into force of the judgement.[338] But still, quashing a final judgement is not only possible in exceptional circumstances, but for any violation of material or procedural law.[339] Thus, it amounts to an "appeal in

---

[329] Baranov (2004), 26.

[330] Kovler (2004), 5.

[331] Code on criminal procedure (2002) SZ RF 2001, no. 52, pos. 4921; (last modification of eighteen modifications on 27 July 2006).

[332] Code on civil procedure (2002): SZ RF 2002, no. 46, pos. 4532 (last modification of seven modifications on 27 December 2005).

[333] Law on psychiatric help and human rights guarantees (1992), VSNDiVS RF 1992, no. 33, p. 1913; (last modification out of five modifications on 22 August 2004). It is worth mentioning that by now the major deficiency in this law, the lack of a procedure for the detained person to initiate proceedings against the detention, has not been changed; cf. Demeneva (2005), 92.

[334] Thus the new Family Code in force since 1 March 1996 sets no time limit for disclaiming paternity. However, by its Resolution no. 9 of 25 October 1996, the Supreme Court established that the Code of 1969 should continue to be applied in respect of children born before the entry into force of the new Code; therefore, for them there is a time limit.

[335] See Report (*supra* note 16).

[336] Cf. Andrianov (2002), 119.

[337] Article 376(1) Code of Civil Procedure.

[338] Article 376(2) Code of Civil Procedure.

[339] Koroteev, Supervisory Review Procedure in Civil Proceedings: New Reforms Needed, EHRAC

disguise".[340] For this reason, the Committee of Ministers criticized the violations of the requirement of legal certainty.[341] Furthermore, a profound reform of the *prokuratura* system, as demanded in the opinion before Russia's accession to the Council of Europe,[342] was never undertaken. Many claim that the lack of willingness to change the *prokuratura* system renders the efficient reform of the judiciary impossible. The Committee of Ministers criticizes above all the deficient judicial review of pre-trial detention cases, which results in excessively lengthy procedures and overcrowding of detention facilities.[343]

The efforts to repair other deficiencies of the Russian legal system that lead to many clone cases in Strasbourg stop half-way as well. Thus, on the basis of a Government Decree,[344] the responsibility for the execution of judgements was transferred from the bailiff service to the Ministry of Finance. This was declared unconstitutional because it lacked a legislative basis.[345] Although the Constitutional Court clearly set up the principles for establishing an appropriate enforcement procedure, the new law passed by the *Duma* in 2005 did not live up to these requirements.[346] It does not contain any right for claimants to use coercive enforcement mechanisms against the public authorities. That means that monetary judgements against the Government still cannot be effectively enforced. Therefore, the chronic non-enforcement of domestic judicial decisions delivered against the State remains a major concern for the Council of Europe.[347]

Whereas the Parliamentary Assembly greeted the prompt reaction to the first judgements of the Court, it criticized the later developments. In October 2006, it expressed its concern that "the execution process has slowed down in the adoption of further legislative and other reforms to solve important structural problems revealed in Strasbourg".[348]

Bulletin, Summer 2006, Issue 5, p. 10, http://www.ecracmos.memo.ru/bulletin/bulletin-en-5.pdf; Yurin (2006), 75 et seq.

[340] *Ryabykh v. Russia* (*supra* note 215), para. 51.

[341] CM Interim Resolution DH (2006), 1, https://wcd.coe.int/ViewDoc.jsp?id=964289 &BackColorInternet=9999CC&BackColorIntranet=FFBB55&BackColorLogged=FFAC75.

[342] Cf. Bowring (2000), 64 et seq.

[343] CM Interim Resolution DH (2003) 123, https://wcd.coe.int/ViewDoc.jsp?Ref= ResDH(2003)123&Sector=secCM&Language=lanEnglish&Ver=original&BackColorInternet=99 99CC&BackColorIntranet=FFBB55&BackColorLogged=FFAC75.

[344] Decree no. 143 of 22 February 2001 concerning the Rules of enforcement of the judgements on the basis of writs of execution delivered by courts against the entities which receive their funds from the budget, SZ RF 2001, no. 10, pos. 959, followed by the Decree no. 666 of 22 September 2002, (cf. CM/Inf/DH(2006) 19, revised 17 October 2006.

[345] See the Judgement of the Russian Constitutional Court, 14 July 2005, SZ RF 2005, no. 30, pos. 3199.

[346] Law No. 197 of 27 December 2005 amending the Budgetary Code, the Code of Civil Procedure, the Arbitrazh Code and the Federal Law on Enforcement proceedings, SZ RF 2006, no. 1, pos. 8.

[347] See CM/Inf/DH (2006), 19.

[348] Report of the Committee on Legal Affairs and Human Rights (Rapporteur Erik Jurgens), Doc. 11020, 18 September 2006, Implementation of Judgements of the European Court of Human

cc. Executive measures. A lot of short-term and long-term measures are required to prevent further human rights violations by the executive. One of the main points concerns the shortcomings of investigations into abuse of official power, especially in Chechnya. For Chechnya, measures such as the creation of a Prosecutor's Office of the Chechen Republic, the creation of a Military Prosecutor's office, the creation of investigative groups, and the setting-up of a Single Register of kidnapped or disappeared persons have been reported. However, despite these measures both the Parliamentary Assembly and the Committee of Ministers have repeatedly expressed their concern about the persistent violations.

With regard to the situation in police custody, pre-trial detention centres and prison camps, as well as problems caused by environmental pollution, solutions can only be found on the political level. It is necessary to allocate financial means and to strengthen the efforts in order to really change systemic human rights violations. Therefore, the comments of the Committee on Legal Affairs and Human Rights of the Parliamentary Assembly made in October 2006 are very harsh. The Committee noted "with grave concern the continuing existence of major structural deficiencies which cause a large numbers of repetitive findings of violations of the ECHR and represent a serious danger to the rule of law".[349]

2. Ukraine

a. Preliminary Remarks

In Ukraine, a special statutory law regulates the enforcement and the implementation of the practice of the Court. This law was adopted by Parliament on 23 February 2006[350] and came into effect on the day of publication. The draft law had been submitted to Parliament in 1999, but failed to be accepted six times because of the veto imposed by former President of State Kuchma.[351]

The law stipulates strict rules for the publication of judgements of the court, for awarding compensation and other measures to ensure implementation of the judgements of the Court and to prevent future violations of the ECHR. The obligations earmarked in the law are incumbent upon the body that represents Ukraine before the Court and that enforces the Court's judgements (Article 1). According to the final provisions of the law, funds for the enforcement of the Court's judgements have to be disclosed in the State's draft budget.

Judgements of the Court are to be compulsorily enforced (Article 2) at the

---

Rights, para. 55, http://assembly.coe.int/Main.asp?link=/Documents/WorkingDocs/Doc06/EDOC11020.htm (last visited 25 May 2007).

[349] Report of the Committee on Legal Affairs and Human Rights (Rapporteur Erik Jurgens), Doc. 11020, 18 September 2006, Implementation of Judgements of the European Court of Human Rights, para. 10.

[350] Vidomosti Verchovnoy Rady Ukraiiny 2006, no. 30, Article 260.

[351] P.A. Doc. 10676 of 19 September 2005, p. 39 (229), http://assembly.coe.int/main.asp?Link=/documents/workingdocs/doc05/edoc10676.htm (last visited 25 May 2007).

expense of the State budget (Article 3). The relevant law on the enforcement of judgements also contains a reference to the judgements of the Court.[352] According to Article 17, the courts in Ukraine have to implement the Convention and the Court's practice as legal sources.

Also within the three-day period, the representative of Ukraine has to call on the complainant and beneficiary of the Court's judgement to apply for compensation to the enforcement authority and to inform the enforcement authority. The notice has to comprise the Court's judgement and a translation of its operative provisions into Ukrainian (Article 7). Within a short period of time, the enforcement authority has to open the enforcement procedure and inform the treasury. The payment must be made within three months of the Court's judgement. In case of delay, the law recognizes a claim of default interests (Article 8). If the complainant's domicile is unknown, the treasury must deposit the compensation. The claim of the deceased complainant subrogates to the heir (Article 9).

The law does not restrict enforcement to compensation, as it also provides measures of so-called general nature (Article 10). The law distinguishes between measures to restore the legal situation in which the complainant was before the violation of his rights (*restitutio in integrum*) and those measures which the Court's judgements provide as friendly settlement. *Restitutio in integrum* is defined as a new decision regarding the case, and it includes the reopening of proceedings and the taking of a new decision by the relevant administrative body. Here, the new law can refer to the provisions in the procedural codes. Article 235 of the new Code on Administrative Procedure allows for the review of judgements by the Supreme Court in the case of a binding decision of an international judicial body. If the judgement in question infringes international obligations, the Supreme Court has to accede to the complaint and cancel the judgement in whole or in part. According to Article 243(3) Code of Administrative Procedure, the Supreme Court is free to take a decision itself or to transfer the appeal to the court that had rendered the judgement contradicting international law. Similar rules have been included in the new Civil Procedural Code of 18 March 2004[353] and in the Arbitrazh Procedural Code of 6 November 1991 in 2001.[354] Until now, there were no equivalent measures introduced in the Code of Criminal Procedure.[355]

The new law enumerates other general measures, such as (1) amendments to legal acts, (2) modification of the practice of law enforcement, (3) reviewing

---

[352] Vidomosti Verkhovnoy Rady Ukraiiny 1999, no. 24, Article 207; 2003, no. 5, Article 46; 2004, no. 6, Article 37; 2005, no. 33, Article 431, no. 42, Article 464; 2006, no. 35, Article 295, Article 296.

[353] Article 354 Civil Procedure Code, Vidomosti Verkhovnoy Rady Ukraiiny 2004, no. 40–42, Article 492.

[354] Article 111[15] Arbitraz Procedure Code, Vidomosti Verkhovnoy Radi Ukraiiny 2001, no. 36, Article 188.

[355] The Criminal Procedure Code of 28 December 1960 is still in force, but has experienced numerous amendments.

the compatibility of draft legislation with the Convention and (4) education of judges, prosecutors, investigators and of other persons dealing with law enforcement (Article 13).

Furthermore, within a month the representative has to provide the Government with an analysis of the facts that caused the violation of the Convention and recommendations on measures to adopt with regard to legislation, law enforcement and education (Article 14). It is the task of the representative to review the compatibility of the draft legislation, of all the statutory laws and other legal texts in force with the Convention (Article 19), particularly those concerning law enforcement authorities, criminal procedure and imprisonment. Ministries and central State authorities are obliged to supervise the work of administrative authorities.

Only future practice will show if such a comprehensive and all-encompassing approach will work. For the time being, it is necessary to have regard to the specific individual and general measures undertaken to remedy the deficiencies found in the decisions of the Court.

With regard to new legislation dealing with structural problems in the judicial system and procedures, no progress has been made as of yet. In the Committee of Ministers' view, these problems are aggravated by serious interference with judicial independence.[356] In this context, the current discussion of the new laws on the judiciary in the *Verkhovna Rada* (Parliament) is a welcome development.[357]

b. Individual Measures

Most domestic judgements have been enforced after the Court's judgement. Criminal investigations against political authorities as well as police officers have been initiated, but they have not always been completed. In the *Gongadze* case,[358] the investigation was split in two parts. The investigation against the direct perpetrators of the murder (four policemen) was completed and the case sent to court for trial. However, it is still not clear who instigated and ordered the murder. Here, no progress was made. In the *Afanasyev* case,[359] criminal proceedings against police officers were initiated, but discontinued. In the *Sovtransavto Holding* case,[360] the case was reopened and the lower courts' judgements were first confirmed and then quashed. Only two years later the first instance court passed

---

[356] CM Interim Resolution DH (2004), 14, https://wcd.coe.int/ViewDoc.jsp?Ref=ResDH (2004)14&Sector=secCM&Language=lanEnglish&Ver=original&BackColorInternet=9999CC &BackColorIntranet=FFBB55&BackColorLogged=FFAC75 (last visited 25 May 2007).

[357] Cf. Draft laws on the Status of Judges and the Law on the Judiciary that were submitted by the President of the Ukraine to the *Verkhovna Rada* (Parliament) of Ukraine on 27 December 2006; cf. the opinions adopted on these laws by the Venice Commission at its 70th Plenary Session (Venice 16–17 March 2007), Opinion no. 401/2006, CDL-AD(2007)003.

[358] *Gongadze v. Ukraine* (*supra* note 207).

[359] *Afanasyev v. Ukraine* (*supra* note 287).

[360] *Sovtransavto Holding v. Ukraine* (*supra* note 198).

a partly positive judgement in favour of *Sovtransavto Holding*. In the *Salov* case,[361] the sentence given with regard to defamation was cancelled and the legal effects of the conviction were annulled by striking the judgement out of the criminal record.

c. General Measures – Amendments and New Legislation to Meet Judgements of the Court

As part of the general reform process in Ukraine, the special laws enacted are to be understood as answers to the human rights violations brought to light by the jurisdiction of the Court.

Thus, the new Civil Procedure and Administrative Codes provide for the possibility to review a final binding ruling in "exceptional circumstances" (different application of law in cassation court judgements or a decision of an international court) or newly detected circumstances only, which is in line with Article 4 of Protocol no. 7. The supervisory review procedure as such is also absent from the new draft Code of Criminal Procedure, which envisages that a final judgement can only be reviewed when new or exceptional circumstances are discovered.[362] However, the *prokuratura* system, as well as the problem of political influence on the judiciary, persists despite all the reform efforts made.

On 1 December 2005, a law was passed proposing that letters (statements, complaints) of arrested (convicts) addressed to the Court shall not be censored, and should be sent to the addressee within one day.[363] A comparable regulation is already provided for in the case of letters addressed to national ombudspersons and prosecutors. On 23 June 2005, a law was adopted reforming the judgement execution system in order to improve and accelerate the enforcement of judgements. Special divisions are now responsible for the enforcement of judgements against State authorities.[364] Furthermore, the President of Ukraine adopted a National Plan for Ensuring the Proper Enforcement of Judgements.[365] Defamation legislation was amended in 2003 and exemption from defamation liability for value statements was introduced.[366] Remedies against the excessive length of investigation should be provided by a draft law on pre-trial and trial procedures and enforcement of judgements within reasonable time. In order to remedy the deficit found in the case of *Gurepka v. Ukraine*,[367] the Government submitted draft amendments to the Code of Administrative Offences and to the Customs Code providing for appeal procedures in relevant cases.

Inhuman treatment of detainees remains a very serious problem. Thus, it was

---

[361] *Salov v. Ukraine* (*supra* note 203).
[362] P.A. Doc. 10676 of 19 September 2005, p. 44 (264).
[363] P.A. Doc. 10676 of 19 September 2005, p. 39 (231).
[364] P.A. Doc. 10676 of 19 September 2005, p. 45 (267).
[365] Decree no. 587 of 27 June 2006.
[366] P.A. Doc. 10676 of 19 September 2005, p. 50 (304).
[367] *Gurepka v. Ukraine* (*supra* note 206).

planned that investigations of alleged ill-treatment will take place and that medical staff will be obliged to visit cells regularly.

As in the case of Russia, the Parliamentary Assembly generally adopts a critical attitude towards the progress made in coping with structural deficits. Thus, it stated in October 2006 that "notwithstanding comprehensive and thorough reforms initiated by the authorities, the European Court is now confronted with the constantly increasing influx of clone cases in respect of Ukraine, providing clear evidence of systemic problems".[368] The Parliamentary Assembly points particularly to the non-execution or lengthy execution of national court decisions, delays in pre-trial and trial proceedings in violation of reasonable time requirements and conditions of detention amounting to inhuman or degrading treatment or punishment. In answer to this critique, a draft resolution was submitted to the *Verkhovna Rada* that provides for the introduction of Parliamentary control over the execution of the Court's judgements. In March 2007, the Parliament's Committee on the Judiciary created a Sub-Committee on the Execution of Judgements of the Strasbourg Court.

3. Comparison and Conclusion

While in the Russian legal doctrine it is fiercely debated whether the case law on the Convention is a source of law, in Ukraine the new Law on the Implementation of the Convention in Ukraine acknowledges case law explicitly as a legal source.

Both in Russia and in Ukraine, an improvement of the implementation of the ECHR can be achieved only within the general political reform process. As of yet, it is not clear which direction the reform processes in the two countries will take. Whereas in Russia there is a strong tendency to reestablish a more authoritarian rule, in Ukraine the squabble between the different forces within the democratic process creates instability. A comprehensive and demanding law such as the new law on implementation in Ukraine might generally be helpful. It is doubtful, however, if it can be implemented effectively under the political circumstances in Ukraine. In Russia, the main question is the will of the relevant political forces to continue the close cooperation with European institutions that was initiated under the rule of President Yeltsin.[369]

The highly politicized decisions are the most difficult to implement. In the *Gongadze* case,[370] an investigation into the case was only made possible by the change of Government in Ukraine. This investigation has not yet yielded convincing results. Russia did not accept the decision of the Court in the *Ilaşcu*

---

[368] Report of the Committee on Legal Affairs and Human Rights (Rapporteur Erik Jurgens), Doc. 11020, 18 September 2006, Implementation of Judgements of the European Court of Human Rights, para. 84.

[369] Mommsen and Nußberger (2007), 172 et seq.

[370] *Gongadze v. Ukraine* (*supra* note 207).

case.[371] The decision was never implemented, but the problem was solved by the passing of time.

F. Remedies and Proportionality Test

1. Russia

Without providing a detailed analysis of the jurisprudence of the Russian Constitutional Court, some comments can be made on the proportionality test as a standard pattern in the legal argumentation of the Russian Constitutional Court. The words "proportional" (*nesorazmerno*) as well as "not arbitrarily" (*ne proizvol'no*) are commonly used. In controversial human rights issues, however, the Constitutional Court is satisfied to explain that the human rights provided for in the Constitution are not unlimited. In this context, it usually cites Article 55(3) of the Russian Constitution without analysing in detail if each of the limitations set by Russian laws are "necessary in a democratic society". Usually, all the restrictions provided for are taken together without differentiating between various measures.

It is possible to discern different phases in the development of the Court's lines of argumentation.[371a] In the early decisions, the legal argumentation was undifferentiated; the meaning of the constitutional norms was not clarified. In the late 90's, the Constitutional Court started to develop new approaches based on the concept of proportionality and essence of a right (*sushchnost'*).[372] In recent decisions, the Constitutional Court again changed course. For instance, in a recent decision on the constitutionality of the provisions of the law on political parties, the Court ruled that "in the current circumstances, when there are serious challenges on behalf of the separatist, nationalist and terrorist forces, who tend to abuse their constitutional rights and freedoms, and whereas the Russian society did not yet gain lasting experience of democratic life, creation of regional political parties, which aim at defending their regional and local interests, would lead to the destruction of State integrity and unity of the State Governance system as a basis of the federal constitution of Russia".[373] The Court also referred to the "political expediency" as a criterion for the legislature's discretion in determining the minimum number of parties' members and requirements to their territorial spread.[374] In an important decision on a law prohibiting suspected terrorists killed in a terrorist attack to be buried by their relatives[375] the Russian Consti-

---

[371] *Ilaşcu and Others v. Russia and Moldova* (*supra* note 264).

[371a] See, in general, on the development of the case law of the Russian Constitutional Court, Nußberger (2007), *Ende des Rechtstaats*, 10 et seq

[372] Lapaeva (2005), 21.

[373] Judgement of Russian Constitutional Court, 2 January 2005, SZ RF 2005, no. 6, pos. 491.

[374] Ibid.

[375] Judgement of the Russian Constitutional Court, 28 June 2007, SZ RF 2007, no. 27, pos. 3346.

tutional Court also stressed the "under-the-present-conditions-clause", outlined the contents of the principle of proportionality theoretically, but refused to apply it in substance.[375a] Thus the description of vague dangers and consequences of the burial of suspected terrorists was deemed to satisfy the proportionality test. In the view of the dissentinig judge Kononov, the Russian Constitutional Court "mocked" at the applicants seeking constitutional justice.[376]

2. Ukraine

The decisions of the Ukrainian Constitutional Court are not yet as refined as to have resort to the proportionality test. As a rule, a larger number of constitutional provisions are quoted to prove the constitutionality or unconstitutionality without going into the details of the interpretation.

3. Comparison and Conclusion

It appears that the Russian and the Ukrainian constitutional courts have developed different styles of argumentation. The proportionality test, as developed by the European Court on Human Rights, does not yet constitute a continuous pattern that could be observed in the decisions.

G. Knowledge and Practice

1. Russia

The Russian authorities are active in the dissemination of the judgements of the European Court. The *postanovlenie* of the Supreme Court of 10 October 2003[376a] recommended the transfer of the responsibility on the information on the jurisprudence of the Court to the *Sudebny Departament pri Verkhovnom sude R.F.* (Judicial department of the Supreme Court of the Russian Federation) together with the Russian representative at the European Court of Human Rights. There are various websites where information on the Convention, the jurisprudence of the Court and the execution of the judgements can be found.[377]

The Russian Academy of Justice is called upon to prepare the learning process. However, as Burkov convincingly argues: as long as judgements are never quashed for not quoting the ECHR, there is no real motivation to integrate the ECHR into the national jurisdiction.[378] Furthermore, the continuing education of judges in Russia is provided for only at long intervals.

Translations of the judgements are of crucial importance, as only a negligible

---

[375a] Nußberger (2007), *Der "Russische Weg"*, 371.
[376] See the dissenting vote of the judge Kononov, Vestnik Konstitutsionnogo Suda 2007, no. 4, p. 18 et seq.
[376a] Postanovlenie, 10 October 2003 (*supra* note 310).
[377] See http://www.echr.ru; http://sutyajnik.ru.
[378] Burkov (2007), 78 et seq.

part of the judges knows English or French. Therefore, it is commendable that translations are published in the *Rossiyskaya Gazeta*, the official journal of the Russian Government as well as, since 2002, in the journal of the Supreme Court, the *Byulleten' Verkhovnogo Suda*, the journal of the Supreme Arbitrazh Court, the *Vestnik Vysshevo Arbitrazhnogo Suda Rossiyskoy Federatsii* and since 2006 on a regular basis, in the journal *Rossiiyskaya Yustitsiya*.[379] The official bulletin of the European Court has also been edited in Russian since 2002.[380] Translations of the judgements are also provided for by the apparatus of the constitutional Court[381] as well as in various books.[382] Analytical articles on the jurisprudence of the Court, the implementation of the Convention in Russia and the relationship between international and domestic law are published in all the main legal journals.

It is doubtful, however, whether the information on the Strasbourg case law reaches the general public. The reports in the most widespread media can be said to be biased against the Court. The Court is reproached for not being neutral, for trying to condemn Russia whenever possible, and for encroaching upon sovereignty of the State.[382a] The reports on the jurisdiction of the Court convey the impression that the only aim of the claimants is to draw financial advantages from human rights violations. Quite often, the judicial information on the work of the Court and the decisions is imprecise or even incorrect.[383]

The ECHR is still a rather neglected element in the legal education programmes of the Russian universities. Usually, it is not dealt with in comprehensive courses, but only as part of general lectures of human rights.[384] Special seminars are rarely organized within the Law Faculties, but more often within the framework of faculties dealing with international relations.[385] It is worth mentioning, however, that questions on the ECHR are integrated in the State exam on constitutional

---

[379] What is surprising, though, is the selection of the judgements. So far (as of February 2007), in the Rossijskaja Iusticija 29 judgements have been printed, most of them touching upon Article 6 ECHR and Article 1 of Protocol no. 1. Most of the judgements refer to successful, some to inadmissible complaints. In all the judgements the Russian Federation is the defendant; only in the judgement Sliwenko it is Latvia. The really controversial judgements are not taken into account. Probably the selection is meant to illustrate everyday problems of Russian judges (e.g. setting of time limits) in the light of the jurisprudence of the Court.

[380] Nußberger and Marenkov (2007), *Europäischer Gerichtshof*, 2.

[381] Vitruk (2006), *O nekotorykh osobennostyakh*, 86.

[382] See e.g. Rossiyskaya Akademiya Pravosudiya, Sudebnaya Reforma v proshlom i nastojashchem, Moskva 2007, where the most important judgements of the Court are translated into Russian.

[382a] Cf. the interviews with the President of the Russian Constitutional Court, published in Rossiykaja Gazeta, 12 Decemeber 2007, http://www.rg.ru/printable/2007/12/12/zorkin.html (last visited 4 January 2008)

[383] Anna Demeneva, Davayte nauchimsya preodolevat' strasburgskie porogi, Biznes Advokat, no. 19 (91), October 2000, 2.

[384] See e.g. the study plan of the Lomonosov University in Moscow where there are no specialized lectures on human righs (http://www.msu.ru, last visited 24 May 2007).

[385] http://www.usu.ru/inform/?code=win&info=faculty/inter.htm.

law at the University of St. Petersburg[386] as well as in entrance exams used by Law Departments.[387]

2. Ukraine

The new law on the implementation of the European Convention also contains provisions on the dissemination of the judgements. Within three days of notification of a judgement a Ukrainian language abstract of the judgement must be published in the official newspapers *Uryadovy kur'er* and *Golos Ukraiiny* (Article 4). An abstract and a copy of the judgement must be delivered to all parties, State authorities and other persons involved and to the Authorized Representative for Human Rights of the Parliament (Article 5). Later on, the State has to provide the full translation and the publication as well as the adequate supply of courts, *prokuratura*, judicial, security and enforcement authorities (Article 6). The Prosecutor General ordered reactivation of the programme of cooperation with the Council of Europe, which included training aiming to provide Ukrainian prosecutors with a better knowledge of the Convention and the Court's case law.[388]

Information about the Convention and the case law of the Court is available on the website of the Ministry of Justice.[389] The text of the Convention, information about application to the Court and all judgements that concern Ukraine are published in Ukrainian. Human rights protection is a regular rubric of the law journal *Pravo Ukraiiny* published by the Ministry of Justice. A special Ukrainian language journal dedicated to human rights protection and available to the public on the internet[390] comprises case law of the European Court of Human Rights. NGOs also provide information websites, for instance the Kharkiv Human Rights Protection Group.[391]

A Judges' Academy was established in October 2002, and in-service training for judges on the Convention and the Court's case law has been introduced. Seminars and conferences organized since April 2003 serve the same purpose. At the universities, the ECHR forms part of courses on human rights law. Generally, it is a subject that only students specialising in international law are dealing with in more detail.[392]

3. Comparison and Conclusion

Both Russia and Ukraine are active in disseminating information on the Convention and the Court's jurisprudence. It will take some time, however, before all

---

[386] http://jurfak.spb.ru/science/cafedral/2/question/gos_ekz_kprf2006.htm.
[387] Cf. http://jurfak.spb.ru/reception/2004/progr_obsh.htm.
[388] P.A. Doc. 10676 of 19 September 2005, p. 31 (165).
[389] Cf. http://www.minjust.gov.ua/?do=s&sid=about_int_2_1.
[390] Cf. http://www.Eurocourt.org.ua.
[391] Cf. http://www.khpg.org.
[392] Information given in an interview with the lecturers Opeyda Zvenyslava (Donetsk) and Oksana Oleksiv (L'vov).

judges and procurators accept and apply the new rules. In both countries, there are contradictory signs. On the one hand, it seems that the implementation of the decisions will be improved. In this regard, the Constitutional Court's regular references to the Strasbourg Court's case law in Russia and the passing of the new legislation on implementation of the judgements in Ukraine are promising. On the other hand, due to State control of the media in Russia, the critique originating from the Parliamentary Assembly on non-compliance with European standards remains more or less ignored in the official discourse. Voices from outside seem to be important in the political debate in Ukraine. This is a major difference.

H. General conclusions

The starting point for the reception of the ECHR in Russia and Ukraine is very similar. The judicial and penitentiary systems inherited from the past are marked by unintelligibility and striking imbalance in the relationship between the citizens and the State. The Soviet Union was endowed with the ideological mission of building a communist egalitarian society. Therefore, the rights of the individuals had to be subordinated to this specific aim. Legislation in many areas, especially in criminal and criminal procedural law, was built on repressive concepts. There was no separation of powers, no open discussion of political issues and no civil society independent from the State. Changes were initiated only in the late 80's when Gorbachov used the *perestroika* and *glasnost* slogans. After the collapse of the Soviet Empire in 1991, there was for a short period of time an enthusiastic move towards human rights concepts developed in Western Europe. As a result, both Russia and Ukraine applied for membership in the Council of Europe, an organization which was seen as a door to Europe. It was, however, clear that the legal orders in Russia and Ukraine were not compatible with European human rights standards. Thus, the two countries were admitted only on the basis of their "commitments and considerations". Accession was deemed not to be the end, but rather the beginning of a long and difficult process.

While the starting point is the same in Russia and Ukraine, the later developments are marked by numerous divergences. The development in Russia led after a period of instability in the 1990's to the reestablishment of a more authoritarian rule under President Putin. Internally, Russia is struggling with the consequences of the war in Chechnya, but externally it takes a leading role in world politics and, with newly acquired self-confidence, starts to close the doors for criticism from abroad. In Ukraine, on the contrary, the transitory period continues. The country is torn between East and West. The different concepts and ideologies are, however, often blurred by power politics, so that the "Orange Revolution" has not provided the effects expected. Thus, the political background of the implementation of the ECHR is very different in Russia and Ukraine.

While neither the prolonged transitory period in Ukraine nor the Russian move away from democracy creates good preconditions for the implementation of the ECHR, the legal mechanisms for integrating international law in the national legal orders are quite promising. The Russian and the Ukrainian constitutions show a remarkable openness for international law, but the gap between theory and practice is wide. Although in Russia the courts accept more and more often to refer to European and international standards and even to cite cases of the Strasbourg Court, these references are often not more than lip services and do not have an important impact on the outcome of the cases. Ukraine has different problems. The judicial system is not functioning smoothly and references to the ECHR and the ECtHR case law are still rare.

The first judgements of the ECHR demonstrated already the existence of major systemic problems in Russia's and Ukraine's judicial and penitentiary systems hitherto almost unknown in the other Contracting States of the Convention. Thus, the non-execution of judgements or the disregard of final judgements is very widespread. Violations of the right to life and the prohibition of torture and inhuman treatment were found in a considerable number of cases. Although this is very important, it is clear that these deficiencies cannot be cured by the reform of legal acts alone. The reform process that had started in Russia in a promising way has slowed down in the meantime; the relevant reforms to cure the ills evidenced in the case law of the Court often stop half-way. In Ukraine, the reform process was generally much slower and often blocked by a political stalemate.

Contrary to Russia, Ukraine has passed a law providing for a comprehensive system of implementation of the Strasbourg judgements. Time will only show if this law proves to be an efficient mechanism. In Russia, the implementation is guided by incoherent regulations, especially orders and letters of the highest courts addressed to the lower courts. Another marked difference in the reception processes in the two countries is the reaction of the authorities to criticism originating from Strasbourg. Contrary to the Ukrainian authorities, the Russian authorities tend to show their unwillingness to cooperate with Strasbourg more and more openly. The war in Chechnya and the related human rights violations continue to be a matter of concern. The same is true for Russia's refusal to ratify Protocol no. 14 blocking the reform of the Court.

Thus, the process of reception in both States exhibits different nuances. Despite the openness of both constitutional systems with regard to the reception of international norms and the scattered references of the courts to the ECHR and – at least in Russia – to the Strasbourg case law, the Convention has not yet had the desired effect on the legal system. Until now, the case law of the European Court on Human Rights is conceived in both countries to be "chuzhoy". "Chuzhoy" means "strange, coming from outside". As Russian and Ukrainian history shows: What has come from outside, has either been welcomed enthusiastically or deeply condemned.

Bibliography

Afanas'yev, D. V., 'Predvaritel'nye mery, prinimaemye evropeyskim sudom po pravam cheloveka', *Zakonodatel'stvo* 9 (2004), 56.

Althauser, C. D., *Rußlands Weg in den Europarat* (Heidelberg, 1997).

Ametistov, E. M., 'About the Domestic Implementation of the European Convention on Human Rights in the Soviet Union: Prospects and Problems', *All-European Human Rights Yearbook,* Vol. 2 (1992), 1993, 77.

Andrianov, V. I., 'Stat'ya 15', in Karpova, V. A., *Kommentarii k Konstitutsii Rossiyskoy Federatsii* (Moskau, 2002), 114.

Amnesty International, *Denial of Justice – The Russian Federation* (London, 2002).

Arnold, R., 'Evropeyskaya Konventsiya o zashchite prav cheloveka i osnovnykh svobod i yeyo vliyanie na gosudarstva Tsentral'noy i Vostochnoy Evropy', in Avtnomov, A. S., Varlamova, N. V., Vasel'yevna, T. A., Medushevskiy, A. N., Sidorovich, O. B. (eds.), *Rossiya i sovet Evropy: Perspektivy Vzaimodeystviya* (Moskau, 2001).

Arnold, R. and Gerasimtchuk, E., *Der Begriff des Rechtsstaates in der Rechtsprechung des Verfassungsgerichtes der RF* (Regensburg, 2003).

Bakhrakh, D. N. and Burkov, A. L., 'Sudebnye akty kak istochniki administrativnogo prava', *Zhurnal Rossiyskogo Prava* 2 (2004), 11.

Baranov, I. V., 'Dostup k pravosudiyu v grazhdanskom sudoproizvodstve na osnove pret-sedentov Evropeyskogo Suda po pravam cheloveka', *Arbitrazhny i grazhdanskiy process* 3 (2004), 26.

Barcic, I. N., 'Mezhdunarodnoe pravo i pravovaya sistema Rossii', *Zhurnal rossiyskogo prava* 2 (2001), 61.

Beknazar, T., 'Das neue Recht der völkerrechtlichen Verträge in Russland', *ZaöRV* 56 (1996), 406.

Belianskaia, O. V. and O. A. Pugina, 'Implementation of international legal norms in Russian legislation', *Theory and Practice* 1 (2006), 82.

Beyme, K. von, *Russland zwischen Anarchie und Autokratie* (Wiesbaden, 2001).

Bindig, R., 'Opinion on Russia's application for membership of the Council of Europe (Bindig-Report), Parliamentary Assembly of the Council of Europe, Straßbourg, Doc. 7463 – 18 January 1996 – Opinion by the Committee on Legal Affairs and Human Rights', *Human Rights Law Journal* 17 (1996), 218.

Biryukov, P. H., *Mezhdunarodnoe Pravo* (Moskau, 1998).

Bondar', N. S., 'Konventsionnaya yurisdiktsiya Evropeyskogo Suda po pravam cheloveka v sootnoshenii s kompetentsiey Konstitutsionnogo Suda RF', *Zhurnal rossiyskogo prava* 6 (2006), 113.

Bowring, B., 'Russia's Accession to the Council of Europe and Human Rights: Compliance of Cross-Purposes?', *European Human Rights Law Review* 6 (1997), 628.

—, 'Russia's Accession to the Council of Europe and Human Rights: Four Years On', *Helsinki Monitor* (2000), 53.

Brunner, G., 'Die Quellen des Völkerrechts', in Maurach, R., Meissner, B., *Völkerrecht in Ost und West* (Stuttgart, Berlin, 1967).

Bulakova, E. J., 'Lovkost' ruk i nikakogo obmana', in Burkov, A.L. (ed.), *Sudebnaya zashchita prav grazhdan v yeyo naibolee effektivnykh formakh* (Ekaterinburg, 2003), 44, http://www.sutyajnik.ru/rus/library/sborniki/sud_zaschita.pdf.

Burkov, A. L., 'Implementation of the Convention for the Protection of Human Rights and Fundamental Freedoms in Russian Courts', *Russian Law: Theory and Practice* No. 1 (2006), 68, http://www.sutyajnik.ru/rus/library/articles/2006/russian_law_2006.pdf.

—, *Primeneniye Evropeyskoj konventsii o zashchite prav cheloveka v sudakh Rossii* (Ekaterinburg, 2006), http://sutyajnik.ru/rus/library/sborniki/echr6/echr6.pdf.

—, *The Impact of the European Convention on Human Rights on Russian Law. Legislation and Application in 1996–2006* (Stuttgart, 2007).

Butler, W. E., 'Perestroika and International Law', in Butler, W. E. (ed.), *Perestroika and International Law* (Dordrecht, Boston, London, 1990).

—, *The Russian Law of the Treaties* (London, 1997).

—, *Russian Law* (Oxford, 2nd ed., 2003).

Khabrieva, T. J., 'Processual'nye voprosy tolkovanija konstitutsii v deyatel'nosti konstitutsionnogo suda RF', *Gosudarstvo i Pravo* 10 (1996), 15.

Khlestov, O. N., 'Mezhdunarodnoe pravo i Rossiya', *Moskovskiy zhurnal mezhdunarodnogo prava* 4 (1994), 52.

—, 'Rossiya i Mezhdunarodnoe pravo', *Diplomaticheskiy Vestnik MID RF* 9 (1995), 49.

Khlestova, I. O., 'Sootnoshenie mezhdunarodnogo i vnutrigosudarstvennogo prava i Konstitutsijya Rossiyskoy Federatsii', *Zhurnal rossiyskogo prava* 2 (1997), 20.

Chirkin, V. E., 'Organy konstitutsionnogo kontrolya: Rossiya i mezhdunarodnyj opyt, *Zhurnal rossiyskogo prava* 4/5 (1998), 145.

Danilenko, G. M., 'The New Russian Constitution and International Law', *The American Journal of International Law* 88 (1994), 451.

—, 'Primenenie mezhdunarodnogo prava v vnutrenney pravovoy sisteme Rossii: praktika Konstitutsionnogo Suda', *Gosudarstvo i Pravo* 11 (1995), 115.

—, 'Implementation of International Law in CIS States: Theory and Practice', *European Journal of International Law EJIL* 10 (1999), 51.

Demeneva, A. V., 'Problemy ispolneniya resheniy Evropeyskogo Suda v Rossiyskoy Federatsii', in Churkina, L. (ed.), *Obyazatel'stva gosudarstv-uchastnikov Evorpeyskoy konventsii o zashchite prav cheloveka po ispolneniyu postanovleniy Evropeyskogo Suda* (Ekaterinburg, 2005), 92, http://sutyajnik.ru/rus/library/sborniki/echr5/echr5.pdf.

Demicheva, Z. B., 'Evropeyskiy sud po pravam cheloveka i rossiyskoe pravo', *Zakon* 11 (2003), 104.

Di Gregio, A., 'The Evolution of Constitutional Justice in Russia: Normative Imprecision and the Conflicting Positions of Legal Doctrine and Case-Law in the Light of the Constitutional Court Decision of June 16 1998', *Review of Central and East European Law* 5/6 (1998), 387.

Drzemczewski, A. Z., *European Human Rights Convention in Domestic Law, a Comparative Study* (Oxford, 1983).

Edidin, B. A., 'Ispolnenie resheniy Evropeyskogo suda po pravam cheloveka: sovremennye problemy teorii i praktiki', *Arbitrazhny i grazhdanskiy process* 11 (2004), 22.

Engel, N. P., 'Russland setzt Europäischen Gerichtshof für Menschenrechte unter Druck. Ablehnung des EMRK-Protokolls Nr. 14 durch Staatsduma mit offensichtlicher Duldung durch Präsident Wladimir Putin', *EuGRZ* 6–9 (2007), 241.

Entin, M. L., *V poiskakh partnerskikh otnosheniy: Rossiya i Evropeyskiy Soyuz v 2004–2005 godakh* (St. Petersburg, 2006).

Ferschtman, M., *Russia, in Fundamental Rights in Europe. The European Convention on Human Rights and its Member States, 1950–2000* (Oxford, 2001).

Fogelklou, A., 'Constitutional Order in Russia: A New Territory for Constitutionalism?', *Review of Central and East European Law* 3 (2000), 231.

Franz, O., 'Europa und Rußland – Das Europäische Haus', in Franz, O. (eds.), *Europa und Russland – Das Europäische Haus?* (Göttingen, 1993).

Friberg, É., 'Evropejskiy Sud po pravam cheloveka: segodnyashnie zaboty i zavtrashnie reformy', *Rossiyskaja Justitsiya* 12 (2002), 2.

Fric'kij, O. F., *Konstitsuijne pravo Ukraini*, (Kiev, 2006).

Frowein, J. W., 'Der Straßburger Grundrechtsschutz in seinen Auswirkungen auf die nationalen Rechtsordnungen und das Gemeinschaftsrecht', in Hutter, F. J., Speer, H., Tessmer, C. (eds.), *Das gemeinsame Haus Europa. Menschenrechte zwischen Atlantik und Ural* (Baden-Baden, 1998).

Giesecke, B., *Die auswärtige Gewalt in der Russischen Föderation und die Rolle des Völkerrechts in der russländischen Rechtsordnung,* (Frankfurt am Main, 2004).

Glotov, S. A., 'Sovet Evropy i Rossiya: Soyuz sostoyalsya, in Skvortsov, I. P. (eds.), *Pravo Soveta Evropy i Rossiya – sbornik dokumentov i materialov* (Krasnodar, 1996).

—, *Konstitucionno-pravovye problemy sotrudničestva Rossii i Soveta Evropy v oblasti prav čeloveka* (Saratov, 1999).

Gorshkova, S. A., 'Rossiya i yuridicheskie posledstviya resheniy Evropeyskogo suda po pravam chekloveka', Zhurnal rossiyskogo prava 5/6 (2000), 91.

Hausmann, H., 'Ein dorniger Weg zur Rechtsstaatlichkeit. Zwischenbericht des Europarats zur Entwicklung in Russland', *Das Parlament* 28 (3 July 1998).

Hussner, M., *Die Übernahme internationalen Rechts in die russische und deutsche Rechtsordnung* (Stuttgart, 2004).

—, *Die Umsetzung der Standards von Art. 6 Abs. 3 EMRK in der neuen Strafprozessordnung Russlands,* in print.

Yurin, M.V., 'Nadzornaya instantsiya: vzglyad Evropeyskogo suda po pravam cheloveka', *Rossiyskoe pravosudie* 5 (2006), 75.

Yagodkin, A., 'Pochemu Rossiyane idut v sud g. Strasburga? Bolee10 tys. chelovek uzhe obratilis' imeno tuda', *Novaya Gazeta* (3–5 February 2003), 12.

Janis, M., 'Russia and the ‚Legality' of Strasbourg Law', *EJIL* 1 (1997), 95.

Kann, D. (Kahn, J.), 'Ispolneniye Rossiey st. 5 i 6 EKPCH kak pokazatel' soblyudeniya prav cheloveka', *Rossiyskiy Byulleten' po pravam cheloveka* 17 (2003), 73.

Karapetyan, L. M., 'Metamorfozy v resheniyakh Evropeyskogo suda po pravam cheloveka', *Zhurnal rossiyskogo prava* 7 (2005) 107.

Kovler, A. I., 'Evropeyskoe pravo prav cheloveka i Konstitutsia Rosii', *Zhurnal rossiyskogo prava* 1 (2004), 149.

Krug, P., 'The Russian Federation Supreme Court and Constitutional Practice in the Courts of General Jurisdiction: Recent Developments', *Review of Central and East European Law* 2 (2000), 129.

—, 'Internalizing European Court of Human Rights Interpretations: Russia's Courts of General Jurisdiction and New Directions in Civil Defamation Law', *Brooklyn Journal of International Law* 32 (1) (2006), 1.

Kuchin M. V., 'Prava cheloveka i problema primeneniya v Rossiyskoy Federatsii pretsedentnogo prava Soveta Evropy', *Rossiyskij Yuridicheskiy Zhurnal* 4 (1998), 83.

Kurochkina, L. A., 'Principy i normy Soveta Evropy v ugolovnom sudoproizvodstve Rossiyskoy Federatsii', *Zhurnal rossiyskogo prava* 4 (2005), 116.

Lapaeva, V. V., 'Problemy ogranicheniya prav i svobod cheloveka i grazhdanina v Konstitutsii RF (opyt doktrinal'nogo osmysleniya)', *Zhurnal rossiyskogo prava* 7 (2005), 13.

Laptev, P. A., 'Precedent v Evropeyskom Sude po pravam cheloveka', *Gosudarstvo i Pravo* 12 (2001), 12.

—, 'Precedenty Evropeyskogo Suda po pravam cheloveka i rossiyskaya sudebnaya praktika', *Konstitutsionnoe Pravo: Vostochnoeevropeyskoe Obozrenie* 1 (2002), 46.

Lobov, M., 'Pryamoe deystvie postanovleniy Evropeyskogo Suda po pravam cheloveka vo vnutrennem prave: sravnitel'nyj obzor', *Sravnitel'noe Konstitutsionnoe Obozrenie* 1 (2006), 88.

Luchterhandt, O., 'On Issues of Harmonisation of the Legislation of Ukraine with the European Convention for the Protection of Human Rights and Fundamental Freedoms' in *Proceedings of the Scientific-practical Conference of the Institute of Legislation of the Verkhovna Rada of Ukraine* (Kyiv, 1998).

Lukayntsev, G. E., 'O nekotorykh tendentsiyakh razvitiya mezhdunarodnogo sotrudnichestva i mezhdunarodnogo kontrolya v oblasti prav cheloveka', *Jurist-mezhdunarodnik* 3 (2004), 10, http://www.lawmix.ru/comm.php?id=2425.

Lukashuk I. I., 'Russia's Conception of International Law', *Parker School Journal of East European Law* 2 (1995), 1.

—, 'Primenenie norm mezhdunarodnogo prava v svete federal'nogo zakona o mezhdunarodnykh dogovorakh Rossii', *Rossiyskiy Yuridicheskiy zhurnal* 4 (1996), 46.

—, 'Das neue russische Gesetz über internationale Verträge und das Völkerrecht', *Osteuropa-Recht* 2/3 (1997), 182.

Malinin, S. A., 'Operation of Rules of International Law in the Territory of Russia under the 1993 Constitution', in Koskenniemi, M. (ed.), *The Finnish Yearbook of International Law* 10 (The Netherlands, 1999), 336.

Marchenko, M. N., 'Yuridicheskaya priroda i charakter resheniy Evropeyskogo Suda po pravam cheloveka', *Gosudarstvo i Pravo* 2 (2006), 11.

Meleshnikov, A. V., 'Prava cheloveka i mezhdunarodno-pravovaya otvetstvennost' za narushenie', *Sotsialisticheskoe Gosudarstvo i Pravo* 3 (1992), 95.

Mityukov, M. A., 'Konstitutsionnye sudy na postsovetskom prostranstve', *Vostochnoe Obozrenie* 3 (1997), 36.

—, 'Zashchita konstitutsionnykh prav i svobod grazhdan konstitutsionnymi sudami na postsovetskom prostranstve', *Zhurnal rossiyskogo prava* 10/11 (1998), 168.

Mommsen, M. and Nußberger, A., *Das System Putin. Gelenkte Demokratie und politische Justiz* (München, 2007).

Morshchakova, T. G., 'Die Bedeutung von demokratischen Veränderungen im System der Rechtsprechung für die Bewältigung der totalitären Vergangenheit', in Kühnhardt, L. and Tschubajan, A. (eds.), *Rußland und Deutschland auf dem Weg zum antitotalitären Konsens* (Baden-Baden, 1999).

Muehlemann, E., 'Report on Russia's request for membership of the Council of Europe (Muehlemann-Report), Parliamentary Assembly of the council of Europe, Straßbourg, Doc.7443 – 2 January 1996 – Report of the Political Affairs Committee', *Human Rights Law Journal* 17 (1996), 187.

Nußberger, A., *Verfassungskontrolle in der Sowjetunion und in Deutschland – Eine rechtsvergleichende Gegenüberstellung des Komitet Konstitucionnogo Nadzora und des Bundesverfassungsgerichts* (Baden-Baden, 1994).

—, 'Razvitiye pretsedentnogo prava Evropeyskogo suda po pravam cheloveka na osnove resheniy o Rossii' (The Development of the case law of the European Court of Human Rights on the basis of decisions on Russia), *Pravo i Politika* 10 (70) (2005), 88.

—, 'Rechts- und Verfassungskultur in der Russischen Föderation', *Jahrbuch des öffentlichen Rechts der Gegenwart* 54 (2006), 35.

—, 'Russland und der Europarat. Von der ersten Rede Michail Gorbatschows vor der parlamentarischen Versammlung bis zu Russlands Vorsitz im Ministerrat', in Braun, R. and Handke, G. M. (eds.), *Herausforderungen. Michail S. Gorbatschows Leben und Wirken* (Neu-Isenburg, 2007).

—, *Ende des Rechtstaats*, (Cologne, 2007).

—, 'Der "Russische Weg" – Widerstand gegen die Globalisierung des Rechts?', *Osteuropa Recht* 53 (2007), 371.

Nußberger, A. and Marenkov, D., 'Death Penalty in Russia', *Russian Analytical Digest* 21, No. 10 (November 2006), 2.

—, 'Das „Jein" zur Todesstrafe in Russland', *Osteuropa Recht* 53 (2007), 9.

—, 'Russland vor dem Europäischen Gerichtshof für Menschenrechte', *Russlandanalysen* 140 (2007), 1.

Nußberger, A. and Schmidt, C., 'Zensur der Zivilgesellschaft', *EuGRZ* (2007), 16.

Oda, H., 'The Emergence of Pravovoe Gosudarstvo in Russia', *Review of Central and East European Law* 3 (1999), 373.

Petrukhin, I., 'Federal'ny zakon „O ratifikatsii Konventsii o zashchite prav cheloveka i osnovnykh svobod i Protokolov k ney"', *Rossiyskaja Yustitsiya* 7 (1998), 2.

Pickel, G., 'Legitimität von Demokratie und Rechtsstaat in den osteuropäischen Transistionsstaaten 10 Jahre nach dem Umbruch', in Becker, M., Lauth, H. J., Pickel, G. (eds.), *Rechtsstaat und Demokratie. Theoretische und empirische Studien zum Recht in der Demokratie* (Wiesbaden, 2001).

Potapenko, V. and Pushkar, P., 'Ukraine', in *Fundamental Rights in Europe. The European Convention on Human Rights and its Member States, 1950–2000* (Oxford, 2001).

Protsyk, O., 'Constitutional Politics and Presidential Power in Kuchma's Ukraine', *Problems of Post-Communism* 52 (2005), 23.

Rosenfeld, M., 'Rule of Law versus Rechtsstaat', in Häberle, P., Müller, J. P. (eds.), *Menschenrechte und Bürgerrecht in einer vielgestaltigen Welt. Wissenschaftliche Begegnung einiger Freunde von Thomas Fleiner zu Ehren seines 60. Geburtstages* (Basel, Genf, München, 2000).

Schmidt, C., 'Der Journalist – ein potentieller "Extremist"', *Osteuropa-Recht* (2006), 409.

Schomacher, G., 'Geschichte, Mentalität und Recht. Zum Problem der Differenz zwischen respektive des Gegensatzes von ‚westlicher' und russischer Rechtskultur', in Krawietz, W., Spröde, A., *Gewohnheitsrecht – Rechtsprinzipien – Rechtsbewusstsein. Transformationen der Rechtskultur in West- und Osteuropa*, 35. Band, 3/4 (2004), 427.

Schroeder, C. F., *74 Jahre Sowjetrecht* (München, 1992).

Shevchuk, S., *Porivnyal'ne pretsedentne pravo z prav lyudyni*, (Kiev, 2002).

Simon, G., 'Russland – eine Kultur am Rande Europas', in Bundesinstitut für ostwissenschaftliche und internationale Studien, *Russland in Europa? Innere Entwicklungen und internationale Beziehungen* (Köln, Weimar, Wien, 2000).

Tereshkova, V., *Primenenie reseniy Evropeyskogo Suda po pravam cheloveka v deyatel'nosti arbitrazhnykh sudov Rossiyskoy Federatsii (predvaritel'nye resul'taty analiza)*, http://www.demos-center.ru/projects/6B3771E/70688C12/1167160792.

Tikhonov, A. A., 'Sovet Evropy i prava cheloveka: normy, instituty, praktika', *Sotsialisticheskoe Gosudarstvo i Pravo* 6 (1990), 121.

Tyunov, O. I., 'Konstitutsionnyj Sud RF i mezhdunarodnoe pravo', Rossiyskiy ezhegodnik mezhdunarodnogo prava (St-Peterburg, 1996).

—, 'Resheniya Konstitutsionnogo Suda RF i mezhdunarodnoe pravo', *Rossiyskaya Yustitsiya* 10 (2001), 14.

—, 'O roli Konventsii o zashchite prav cheloveka i osnovnykh svobod i resheniy Evropeyskogo suda po pravam cheloveka v praktike Konstitutsionnogo Suda RF', *Konstitutsionnoe Pravo: Vostochnoevropeyskoe Obozrenie* 3 (2001), 92.

Trautmann, L., *Rußland zwischen Diktatur und Demokratie. Die Krise der Reformpolitik seit 1993* (Baden-Baden, 1995).

Usenko, E. T., 'Sootnoshenie i vsaimodeystviye mezhdunarodnogo i natsional'nogo prava i Rossiyskaya Konstitutsiya', *Moskovskiy zhurnal mezhdunarodnogo prava* 2 (1995), 13.

Vashanova, O. V., 'Rol' Evropeyskogo Suda po pravam cheloveka v razvitii printsipa nediskriminatsii', *Jurist-mezhdunarodnik* 2 (2004), 32.

Vereshchetin, V. S., 'New Constitutions and the Old Problem of the Relationship between International Law and National Law', *EJIL* 7 (1996), 29.

Vitruk, N. V., 'O nekotorykh osobennostyakh ispol'zovaniya resheniy Evropeyskogo Suda po pravam cheloveka v praktike Konstitutsionnogo Suda Rossiyskoy Federatsii i inykh sudov', *Sravnitel'noe konsituttsionnoe obozrenie* 1 (2006), 83.

—, 'Praktika Konstitutsionnogo Suda Rossiyskoy Federatsii v kontekste deystviya Konventsii 'O zashchite prav cheloveka i osnovnykh svobod'', *Rossiyskoe pravosudie* 3 (2006), 4.

Vodolagin, S., 'Konventsiya o pravakh cheloveka kak sostavnaya chast' pravovoy sistemy Rossii', *Rossiyskaja Yustitsiya* 8 (2001), 24.

Voskobitova, M. R., 'Obzor resheniy Evropeyskogo Suda o pravakh cheloveka na predmet priemlimosti po zhalobam, podannym protiv RF', *Gosudarstvo i pravo* 8 (2002), 24.

Zimnenko, B. L., 'Mezhdunarodnye dogovory v sudebnoy sisteme Rossiyskoy Federatsii', *Moskovskyj zhurnal mezhdunarodnogo prava* 2 (1999), 104.

Zimnenko, B. L., 'Mezhdunarodnoe pravo v sudebnoy praktike Rossii: grazhdanskoe i administrativnoe sudoproizvodstvo', *Rossyjskaja Yustitsiya* 11 (2003), 4.

—, 'Mezhdunarodnoe pravo v sudebnoy praktike Rossii: konstitutsionnoe pravosudie', *Rossiyskaya Yustitsiya* 9 (2003), 6.

—, *Mezhdunarodnoe pravo in pravovaya sistema Rossiyskoy Federatsii,* (Statut-Moskau, 2006).

Zorkin, V. D., 'Konstitutsionny Sud Rossii v evropeyskom pravovom pole', *Zhurnal rossiyskogo prava* 3 (2005), 3.

—, 'The Constitutional Court of Russia in the European Law Landscape', in Baer, C. M., Bernet, B., Nobel, U., Waldburger, R. (eds.), *Wirtschaftsrecht zu Beginn des 21. Jahrhundert, Festschrift für Peter Nobel* (Bern, 2005), 1095.

—, 'Rol' konstitutsionnogo Suda Rossiyskoy Federatsii v realizacii Konventsii o zashchite prav cheloveka i osnovnykh svobod', *Sravnitel'noye konstitutsionnoye obozreniye* 1 (2006), 34.

PART III
ASSESSMENT

11

Assessing the Impact of the ECHR on National Legal Systems

Helen Keller and Alec Stone Sweet

This book tracks and evaluates the impact of the ECHR on eighteen national legal orders. As the reports demonstrate, national systems are increasingly porous to the influence of the ECHR and the case law of its Court. European States no longer embody insular, autonomous, self-defined legal systems, if ever they did. At the constitutional level, the systems of every country surveyed in this volume have experienced significant structural change. To take two dramatic examples, judges once prohibited from engaging in judicial review of statute now do so routinely, with reference to European rights; and the dualist features of many legal systems have given way to a sophisticated monism, when it comes to the Convention. Further, how the different branches of Government interact with one another has been changed, radically in some States, to the extent that the regime's evolution has served to undermine traditional separation of powers dogmas. This volume also examines the impact of the Strasbourg Court's jurisprudence on legislators, executives, and judges. Thousands of discreet legal and policy outcomes have been altered as a result of the influence of Convention rights. It is also clear that legal education and scholarship are also changing in ways that will help to consolidate the regime's domestic presence and legitimacy.

The impact of the ECHR is organized by a complex social process that we call *reception*.[1] The reports identify a diverse range of *mechanisms* of reception: those stable procedures that national officials construct and use in order to adapt the national legal order to the ECHR, as it develops over time. The reports show that no State can fully insulate itself from the regime's reach and influence. The best States can do is to build and maintain their own system of strong national rights protection, and to develop effective mechanisms of reception. The reports also show that the intensity of the influence of the jurisprudence of the Strasbourg Court on domestic systems varies widely across States; and the Court's impact has increased over time, in some legal domains more than others, within each

---

[1] Reception is defined and discussed at length in chapter 1 of this book, Section B.1.

State. Although we will venture a number of general propositions about reception processes in this chapter, such statements should be carefully considered in light of the cross-national and temporal diversity documented and evaluated in the national reports.

A. Reception as Process

Viewed as a cross-national phenomenon, the reception of the ECHR into domestic law and practice can neither be easily summarized, nor neatly encapsulated in overarching generalizations. Indeed, it would seem to be all but impossible to model the Court's impact on States in any scientifically parsimonious way. The reasons are clear enough. First, although we can identify the most important factors that condition, or impinge upon, the reception process, not all of these factors are present or carry the same weight across all jurisdictions. When they are present, they typically combine in diverse ways to affect States differently. Second, the ECHR regime – considered sociologically as a continuous set of interactions between individual applicants, national political and legal systems, and the Strasbourg Court – does not possess a stable social structure. Convention rights, for example, have evolved in ways that have been virtually impossible to predict, not least by national officials, from any specific *ex ante* moment. States have been put under pressure to adapt national law to the Convention, but the manner in which they have done so has never been fixed or pre-determined. Instead, the relationship between the ECHR and domestic legal orders has been an open-ended product of interactive social processes. In this section, the most important factors that have impinged upon the reception process will be briefly analyzed.

1. Accession and Expansion

Most of the original Contracting States (including the UK, Ireland, Italy, Germany, Belgium, the Netherlands, Austria, Norway and Sweden in this volume) seriously underestimated the degree to which the ECHR would impact on their domestic legal systems. The *travaux préparatoires* provide scant evidence to the contrary. When the ECHR entered into force, none of these States (with the important exception of Ireland) possessed effective systems of rights protection in the contemporary sense. The fact that the Convention system developed during the same period that many national systems of rights protection emerged and matured no doubt facilitated the Court's efforts to build its own political legitimacy. During this formative period, the absence of sceptical States, such as France (which was hostile to supranational authority in general) was a benefit: the Court avoided the kinds of head-on collisions that had paralyzed the EC in the 60's and 70's. Both France and Switzerland (which was concerned with issues of neutrality) ratified relatively late, after several failed tries. For other late-ratifying States (Spain, Slovakia, Poland and the re-ratification of Greece after military rule), the political legitimacy of the Convention and the Court was largely taken for granted. Each of these States were then in the throes of democratization, following long years under repressive, authoritarian rule. Democracy and rights protection were strongly equated. It is testimony to the remarkable success of the ECHR that, for these States, the Convention offered an established, "external", and therefore legitimate, normative standard for the transition to constitutional democracy. Accession would serve, in effect, to certify their membership in the circle of good European countries, otherwise dominated by Western Europe. These States ratified the Convention enthusiastically without lodging important reservations. Russia, Turkey, and Ukraine also took advantage of certification, if perhaps with less commitment to common values.

The use of declarations and reservations also varies across States and time. Some countries (France, Switzerland) once made extensive use of reservations and declarations; others have done so sparingly or not at all (Poland). Some States (Turkey) did not seriously examine the compatibility of national law with the ECHR at the time of ratification. Over time, the use of reservations and declarations has declined, and many States have allowed those they had lodged to elapse. One reason for this is that, as it has evolved, the Convention system has gained the trust and goodwill of its members; consider the ratification of Protocol no. 11, and the broad incorporation of the ECHR into national law. At the same time, most countries have made considerable progress in redressing incompatibilities between the domestic law and the Convention guarantees. Reservations made it possible for many States to join the regime, given quite specific concerns, but these concerns have been relaxed with changing circumstances and socialization into the regime. For its part, the ECtHR interprets reservations narrowly, to ensure that the Contracting Parties do not undermine the Convention's purposes.[2]

The Council of Europe, too, has played an important role in developing Convention rights. It is a well-established practice of international law for States to amend treaties to which they belong through supplementary instruments, like protocols. Since 1952, the Council of Europe has adopted fourteen Protocols to the ECHR. Most importantly, Protocol no. 11 reformed the institutional structure, and made obligatory State acceptance of the individual complaint procedure and of the Court's compulsory jurisdiction. Today, acceptance of Protocol no. 11 is a pre-condition for the ratification of the ECHR.[3] In hindsight, we observe that the ratification of Protocols nos 2, 3, 5 and 8 proved to be relatively unproblematic, and all Contracting States would eventually ratify them. It is important, therefore, to recognize that the Contracting States have themselves fully participated in expanding the Court's competences, as well as the ECHR's rights

---

[2] *Belilos v. Switzerland* (appl. no. 10328/83), Judgement (Plenary), 29 April 1988, Series A, Vol. 132. See *in extenso* Thurnherr, this volume, Section A.2.b.

[3] Protocol no. 9 has been repealed as from 1 November 1998, the date of entry into force of Protocol no. 11. Since then, Protocol no. 10 has lost its purpose.

catalogue, including rights to peaceful enjoyment of property, to education, and to free elections by secret ballot, and the abolition of the death penalty.

These reforms have fundamentally altered the ECHR, compared with the *status quo ex ante* of the 50's. When the ECHR was negotiated, States failed to agree on the inclusion of the right to property. In the end, Article 6(1) ECHR provided for procedural guarantees for "civil rights", which the Court interpreted broadly, but not so broadly as to include property rights *per se*. The right to property in Protocol no. 1,[4] which entered into force in 1954, proved to be tremendously important in the 90's, as statistics on the Court's activities demonstrate. In the post-Protocol no. 11 era, the Court has been flooded with applications claiming violations of the right to property, which have in turn revealed systemic failures (Greece, Italy, and Turkey's administration of Cyprus). Having received literally hundreds of clone applications from Poland, the Court began to experiment with pilot judgments to help States resolve such failures.[5]

On the other hand, Protocol no. 4 generated reluctance, with Greece, Turkey, Italy, Spain, Switzerland and the United Kingdom, among the States covered in this book, withholding ratification. That Protocol established human rights in a politically sensitive domain (*inter alia* prohibiting expulsion of nationals and collective expulsion of aliens); States that ratified it may now regret having done so.[6] In another once sensitive area – the death penalty – the Council of Europe has had more success, banning its use through Protocols no. 6 and no. 13. Russia alone has not ratified these Protocols. Russia is also the only country that blocks the entry into force of Protocol no. 14, which the Court, the Council of Europe, and we see as an essential reform, given the regime's present burdens.[7] Russia's general reluctance to enhance the discretionary authority of the Court should be understood in the context of the conflict-filled relationship it has with both the ECHR and the Council of Europe.[8]

Finally, the fate of Protocol no. 12 (non-discrimination) remains an open question. Among the States covered in our survey, only the Netherlands, Spain,[9] and Ukraine have ratified it. The others resist transitioning from the limited non-discrimination guarantee provided by the Convention (Article 14 ECHR) to a general, stand-alone right on various grounds. Failure to ratify Protocol no. 12 (only 16 of the 46 States have done so[10]) may well be a blessing in disguise for the

---

[4] Among the countries in our survey, Switzerland is now the only country that has not yet ratified. See, this volume, Thurnherr, Section A.2.a.

[5] *Broniowski v. Poland* (appl. no. 31443/96), Judgement (Grand Chamber), 22 June 2004, Reports 2004-V, 1. See Krzyżanowska-Mierzewska, this volume, Section H.1.a.

[6] For the situation in Spain, see Candela Soriano, this volume, Section III.A.1.a.

[7] See also *infra* Section E.3.

[8] See Nußberger, this volume, Section A.1.a.

[9] Spain ratified Protocol no. 12 on 13 February 2008, after this book went into production.

[10] Information on ratification presented by the Council of Europe on its website: http://conventions.coe.int/Treaty/Commun/ChercheSig.asp?NT=177&CM=8&DF=3/2/2008& CL=ENG (Unless indicated otherwise, all websites were visited last at end of March 2008).

system. The Court is already overloaded; and non-discrimination claims would require it to intrude even more deeply into policy areas that are, by their very nature, politically controversial. It may be that some national Governments have reached a saturation point, feeling that the time is not ripe to develop new human rights standards, given the density of problems that have yet to be resolved.

2. European Integration and Reception

European integration – the evolution of the EU's legal system, in particular – has shaped reception in a number of crucial ways. First, the ECJ's commitment to the doctrines of the supremacy and direct effect of Community law provoked processes that, ultimately, transformed national law and practice. Supremacy required national courts to review the legality of statutes with respect to EC law, and to give primacy to EC norms in any conflict with national norms. For judges in many EU States, the reception of supremacy meant overcoming a host of constitutional orthodoxies, including the prohibition of judicial review of statute, the *lex posteriori derogat legi priori*, and separation of powers notions. These same structural issues arose anew under the Convention. Second, as the EU's legal system evolved, national judges were required to develop new remedies, including in the sensitive area of State liability for damages to individuals. Further, as the ECJ embraced the proportionality principle in one area after another (e.g., the four freedoms, sex discrimination, administrative and competition law), it pressured national courts to replace deference postures (under manifest error, reasonableness and *ultra vires* doctrines, for example) with much more intrusive forms of judicial review (requirements of necessity and proper balancing of rights against the public good). Although one can describe these innovations in formal doctrinal language, it is indisputable that these changes served to enhance judicial authority – across the Community – relative to political authority. Further, national courts also learned to interact closely, and to enter into a dialogue with a supranational court, giving to, as well as receiving from, the ECJ. The ECJ's move to embrace rights as general principles of EU law, citing the ECHR and the constitutional traditions of the Member States as sources, is a striking example. Thus, in a myriad ways, European legal integration under the Treaty of Rome helped to prepare national legal systems for the kinds of major challenges that were to come under the ECHR.

With the disintegration of the Soviet bloc, the EU worked to reinforce the authority of the ECHR in a more direct way. In the 90's, the EU (whose Members also belonged to the Council of Europe) made ratifying the ECHR a prerequisite for EU membership,[11] which entailed a great deal of preparatory work in the human rights field for candidate countries in Central Europe.[12] In two States covered in this volume, Poland and Slovakia, the EU demanded specific reforms

---

[11] Pinelli (2004).

[12] In Greece and Turkey, the implementation of EU law and the accession process has served as a

(countering anti-corruption, enhancing judicial independence and efficiency, re-organizing the penitentiary system, etc.) to safeguard the rule of law and the effective guarantee of Convention's rights.

3. Mechanisms of Reception and Coordination

The national reports make it possible to evaluate mechanisms of reception in terms of their relative capacity to enhance the ECHR's status in domestic law. The ECHR can be said to be effective, domestically, to the extent that national officials recognize, enforce, and give full effect to Convention rights and the interpretive authority of the Court, in their decisions. The most important mechanisms operate at the constitutional level and are associated with the monist-dualist distinction and how States incorporate the ECHR. They serve to coordinate the national legal order, as a whole, on an ongoing basis, with the Convention. Other mechanisms operate in discrete institutional settings, including those procedures that require legislative and judicial officials to take account of the ECHR in their decision-making. A third set of practices – related to knowledge and its production – also impinge on the reception process and, arguably, ought to be considered to be informal mechanisms of coordination, in their own right.

a. Doctrinal Factors

A formal, doctrinal understanding of the reception process is an indispensable first step in any attempt to explain the impact of the ECHR on national legal systems. The reports focus on four interrelated questions. First, does a given constitutional order adopt a monist or dualist posture with respect to international treaty law? Second, what rank does the legal system assign to the Convention in the national hierarchy of norms? Third, are the Convention's guarantees directly binding on public authority, can they be pleaded before national courts, and can judges directly enforce them against conflicting national norms, including statute? And, fourth, have the answers to these questions changed over time, and through what procedures? The national reports address these questions, and they trace the impact of these formal elements on the decision-making of national officials.

The domestification of the ECHR constitutes the most important, overarching narrative of this volume. Convention rights are domesticated through their incorporation into national legal orders. As Polakiewicz has emphasized,[13] the ECHR does not require any specific mode of incorporation and, for many decades, some States refused to incorporate it. Until the 80's, for example, the French position was that the Convention had virtually no legal status in the internal order. In that State's view, a High Contracting Party, faced with a violation of the Conven-

---

more direct catalyst for changes in the domestic law than the reception of the ECHR, see Kaboğlu and Koutnatzis, this volume, Section D.3.

[13] Polakiewicz (2001), 31–33.

tion, entirely discharged its responsibilities merely by compensating the affected applicant. It incurred no obligation to change its internal law even when the Court had ruled that law to be in breach of the Convention. Today, every State covered by this book has incorporated the Convention, albeit in different ways, and no States argue in favour of the former French position.

Other things being equal, the ECHR is most effective where Convention rights, *de jure* and *de facto*: (1) bind all national officials in the exercise of public authority; (2) possess at least supra-legislative status (they occupy a rank superior to that of statutory law in the hierarchy of legal norms), and (3) can be pleaded directly by individuals before judges who may directly enforce, while disapplying conflicting norms. In such States, the Convention is not subject to the principle of *lex posteriori derogat legi priori*, but takes precedence over all conflicting infra-constitutional norms. From the point of view of the international lawyer, the status of these systems toward the ECHR can be characterized as strongly monist. Among West European States covered in this book, Austria, Belgium, the Netherlands, Spain, and Switzerland have reached this position, through different routes. Of course, the fact that national officials, including judges, are well positioned to enforce the ECHR does not mean that they will always choose to do so.

b. Incorporation and the Hierarchy of Norms

One of our core comparative findings is that formal distinctions between system-ic monism and systemic dualism *ex ante* do not, in and of themselves, determine the status of the ECHR in national law *ex post*. What ultimately matters is if and how the Convention is incorporated. France, for example, is a monist country, under Article 55 of its Constitution. However, for decades, Article 55 was simply overridden by the prohibition of judicial review of statutes (a corollary of separa-tion of powers).[14] Belgium is formally dualist, but that State's courts – on their own and without constitutional authorization – embraced a sophisticated mon-ism with respect to the ECHR (and EU law).[15] As the national reports show, over the past three decades, the ECHR has had far more impact in Belgium than in France, precisely because Belgian judges chose to confer supra-legislative status on Convention rights and to directly apply them, while French judges declined to do so. The French position began to change only in the late 80's; today, the Convention overrides conflicting law, including statutes adopted later in time. Consequently, complex reception processes are now underway in France, and the gap between the Convention's *de jure* and *de facto* status is bound to narrow.

The Spanish and Dutch Constitutions are both monist but, again, it is the po-sition of the courts that makes the difference. The Spanish Constitutional Court has consistently worked to enforce the ECHR as a quasi-constitutional body of law. The Tribunal will strike down any statutes that violate the Convention as un-

---

[14] For the reasons, see Lambert-Abdelgawad and Weber, this volume, Section B.1.a.
[15] De Wet, this volume, Section B.2.a.

constitutional; it interprets Spanish constitutional rights in light of the ECHR; and it has ordered the ordinary courts to abide by the Strasbourg Court's case law, as a matter of constitutional obligation. If the judiciary ignores the dictates of the Convention, individuals can use the *amparo* procedure to appeal the issue directly to the Constitutional Tribunal. In Spain, then, the capacity of the legal system to guarantee the effectiveness of the ECHR is virtually perfect. Indeed, by every measure, Spain is one of the great success stories of post-authoritarian, rights-based democratization, and the ECHR is an important part of that story. The Netherlands, arguably, is the world's most monist State. The Dutch Constitution provides for the supremacy of treaty law over the Constitution itself, but it does not provide for the judicial review of Statutes. The Supreme Court, however, has chosen to directly enforce the ECHR, in effect, incorporating it as a *de facto* Bill of Rights. In her report, Erika de Wet notes that, generally, the Dutch Court has thus far used its judicial review powers cautiously.[16] However, she also stresses that the relationship between the courts and the legislature is changing as a result, and that the Court is developing some of the features of a constitutional jurisdiction with respect to rights enforcement.

Norway and Sweden are formally dualist States, but each has moved to monist positions with respect to the Convention, embracing the effectiveness criteria listed above, at least formally. Austria blends both dualist and monist features, but it too has moved to a strong monist posture. The Austrian Constitution provides for a Constitutional Court and review, but it contains only a short list of rights in comparison with the Convention. The Constitutional Court's initial position, which the administrative and civil courts followed, was that the ECHR neither possessed supra-legislative status nor was directly enforceable in the domestic legal order. In 1964, the political parties revised the Constitution, to confer upon the Convention constitutional status and direct effect. Today, conflicts between the Austrian Constitution and the ECHR are governed by the *lex posteriori derogat legi priori* rule, an apparently unique situation. Norway and Sweden also possessed, at the time of ratification, a short list of basic rights, and judicial review was known but virtually never used. In the 90's, four decades later, both countries adopted comprehensive Bills of Rights modeled on the Convention. In Norway, the charter is entrenched, requiring two successive votes of Parliament, the second after an intervening election. The Charter overrides conflicting statutes. The Swedish Charter has only the rank of a statute, and Sweden maintains certain dualist orthodoxies, including the application of the *lex posteriori* rule to resolve conflicts between norms of statutory rank. However, the Constitution states that all Swedish laws shall be interpreted and applied in light of international treaties.

A State may be formally monist but nonetheless treat the Convention as alien, foreign law, leaving it without much force in the domestic order. Such has been

---

[16] De Wet, this volume, Section B.1.b.bb.

the case, for different reasons, in pre-Protocol no. 11 France, and – today – in Russia, Slovakia, Turkey (at least until 2004), and the Ukraine. In these latter States, a surface, systemic monism is belied by a lack of commitment to the ECHR among political officials, and by massive structural problems in the functioning of judicial institutions. In Poland, a nominally monist State, the Constitutional Court has worked hard to enhance the status of the Convention before the courts.

Finally, most dualist systems have incorporated the Convention either through statute or the decisions of Constitutional or Supreme Courts, the details and consequences of which vary widely. In the UK, under the 2000 Human Rights Act (HRA) litigants may plead Convention rights against any public authority, and courts may enforce the ECHR against all but conflicting Parliamentary statutes, while certain appellate judges have the authority to declare such statutes incompatible with Convention rights (but not to annul them). As Besson's report emphasizes, the HRA is in the process of transforming the UK's legal system, not least, because it carves out important exceptions to doctrines of Parliamentary sovereignty.[17] For the first time, UK judges have jurisdiction over what is, in effect, a Bill of Rights. In Ireland, which incorporated the ECHR in 2003, Convention rights function only as a supplement to its own highly effective domestic Charter and system of rights protection. Parties may not plead the Convention in Irish courts against judges or the legislature, and the *lex posteriori* rule holds sway, but this situation has yet to expose Ireland to the scrutiny and censure of the Strasbourg Court in any systematic way.

In Germany and Italy, both dualist States with complete systems of domestic rights protection, the incorporation has proceeded through rulings of the constitutional courts. In Germany, the ECHR was initially treated according to dualist orthodoxy: treaty law occupied the same rank as statute (*lex posteriori* taking primacy in case of conflict). Gradually, however, the Federal Constitutional Court began to treat the ECHR as *lex specialis* and, in 2004, it threw its weight behind the ECHR. It now requires the judiciary to enforce Convention rights even against statutes passed later in time, an activity that can be monitored through the individual constitutional complaint. In Italy, the courts' attitude towards the Convention has been marked by longstanding reluctance to recognize the Convention's primacy over statutes. In this context, a 2007 ruling of the Italian Constitutional Court declaring the unconstitutionality of a statute found to contravene Article 1 of Protocol no. 1, may well be a landmark change.[18] It remains to be seen whether this new approach will be followed consistently by the Italian Constitutional Court and other high courts.

In summary, there is no necessary causal linkage between *ex ante* monism or dualism, on the one hand, and the reception of the ECHR on the other.

---

[17] See Besson, this volume, Section III.B.1.b.
[18] See Candela Soriano, this volume, Section III.B.2.b.

Put differently, the manner in which the ECHR is incorporated is an outcome of the reception process which will, in turn, impinge on reception *ex post*. The assumption that dualistic States have, *a priori*, an unfriendly attitude towards international law, and will, therefore, generate a relatively poorer rights record, is untenable. That point accepted, some States – including Ireland, Norway, Italy, Sweden, and the UK – have found it difficult to confer supra-legislative rank on the Convention, precisely because of their dualist natures, though there is a great deal of variation even among this small group.[19] Other dualist States (notably Belgium) have done so relatively quickly and easily. Dualistic countries tend to incorporate through statute, whereas monist States tend to do so through judicial decisions. Clearly, a monistic constitutional structure can provide the judiciary with more leeway in the reception process, as in the Netherlands, helping courts overcome certain obstacles when they are motivated to do so. Finally, in dualistic countries where a powerful Constitutional or Supreme Court defends national human rights, we observe reticence among judges to base their rulings on the Convention as an independent source of rights. This is the case with Germany, Italy, and Ireland. Paradoxically, perhaps, a pre-existing human rights judicial tradition in a particular country can sometimes hamper reception of the Convention or, at least, the jurisprudence of the ECtHR.

c. The Convention as a Shadow Constitution
Today, in Belgium, France, the Netherlands, Switzerland, and the UK, we can say that the ECHR constitutes a kind of surrogate, or shadow, Constitution. These are States that, while not possessing their own judicially enforceable Bills of Rights have incorporated the Convention in ways that make Convention rights directly effective, supra-legislative norms in the domestic system. In the Scandinavian countries in our survey, new Bills of Rights have been modeled on the ECHR, but the latter text tends to be more important than the former. This type of reception is deeply structural and is, or will be, momentous in its significance. In States where Constitutions provide both an entrenched Bill of Rights and an effective system of constitutional justice, the ECHR tends to function as a supplement to the Constitution. We find this situation in Germany, Ireland, Spain and, arguably, in some Central European States.

d. Legislative Coordination Mechanisms
As the ECHR has evolved, national officials have developed procedures designed to provide legislative authorities with information and counsel on the relevance of the ECHR to their agenda. In many States (including Austria, Belgium, France, Italy, the Netherlands, Slovakia, Spain, and Switzerland), one of the tasks of the Government's legal advisor is to provide an opinion on the conformity of pro-

---

[19] With regard to the differences between the UK and Ireland, see Besson, this volume, Recapitulative comparative table.

posed Bills with the Convention, or on reforms that ought to be undertaken in order to bring the national legal order into conformity. The Government is free to disregard this advice. In most States (an important exception is Russia), one or more Parliamentary Committees also routinely examine the conventionality of Bills. In some (including France, Greece, Ireland, and Italy), lawmakers are now advised by independent Human Rights Committees. In Poland and Spain, an Ombudsman may advise executive and legislative bodies, and she or he possesses the power to challenge laws before the Constitutional Court. In Scandinavia, *ex ante* review of a legislative Bill is undertaken by judges, but these decisions (of the Swedish Law Council and the Norwegian Supreme Court) are non-binding. By contrast, in Ukraine, a 2006 reform made *ex ante* Ministerial review of the conventionality of proposed legislation obligatory. If a Bill is found to be contrary to the ECtHR, it will be declared void.

Although the national reports identify and discuss these mechanisms, much more research would be needed to evaluate their effects on policy outcomes. Their impact on the overall reception process, we suspect, depends heavily on the general commitment of political officials to improving rights protection and compliance with the ECHR. Many Russian national officials regularly expressed scorn for the Court's judgements. In Turkey, the Chairman of the Human Rights Advisory Board was prosecuted in 2004 for authoring a report criticising the Government's lack of commitment to rights, and the Board was then dissolved. Some States have no such mechanisms *per se*, but we know that German legislators take very seriously their responsibility to assess the conventionality of Bills before them, both in the Cabinet and the Bundestag, whereas Russian lawmakers do not.

e. Judicial and Other *Ex Post* Mechanisms of Coordination

Judges play a special role in the reception process. Due to the requirement that local remedies be exhausted, it is normally the courts that have the last word on the compatibility of national law with the ECHR, prior to an applicant going to Strasbourg. In addition, the Convention establishes standards that govern the operation of national systems of justice (notably through Articles 5, 6, and 13 ECHR). Of all national officials, judges are the most systematically exposed to the direct supervision of the ECtHR. It is hardly surprising that, in many States, the courts have taken the lead in incorporating the Convention, and in strengthening other quasi-constitutional mechanisms of reception. Today, all national high courts have a powerful interest in closely monitoring the ECtHR's activities, and in staying one step ahead of the latter when it comes to developing standards of rights protection. Such may be easier said than done, of course.

The national reports provide a rich trove of detail on specific interactions between the ECtHR and national courts. At the risk of some over-generalization, three overlapping points deserve emphasis. First, in most States, the incorporation of the ECHR has enhanced the overall authority of the ordinary courts *vis-à-vis* all other non-judicial officials. As judges have consolidated their jurisdiction over the ECHR, they have increased their capacities to control policy outcomes; the move to proportionality review is a strong example.[20] In Europe today, judicial authority includes the competence to review the legal validity of all Government acts under the Convention. Second, the authority of national Constitutional Courts has been weakened: their final word (if not monopoly) on rights interpretation can no longer be presumed. It is to the credit of the constitutional courts on the continent (in Spain, Poland, Slovakia; and, more recently, in Germany and Italy) that they have chosen to require the judiciary – as a matter of constitutional duty – to enforce the ECHR and to follow the Strasbourg Court's jurisprudence. At the same time, all constitutional courts have taken pains to stress that it is the national Constitution that ultimately regulates the relationship between the domestic legal order and the Convention system. Third, rights protection in Europe is characterized by an important jurisdictional pluralism, an "open architecture"[21] whose tensions and contradictions will not be worked out easily, if at all. With the accession of the EU to the Convention, this architecture will become even more complex and its future development even less predictable.

The courts also manage the most important reception mechanisms following a finding of violation by the ECtHR, to the extent that they harmonize the substance of their jurisprudence to relevant judgments of the Court. Courts in most States do so routinely (though Russian, Ukrainian, and Turkish courts are exceptions). The national reports also identify a number of non-judicial *ex post* mechanisms of coordination. The fast-track procedure in the UK is a prominent example[22]; and it will be fascinating to monitor the Ukrainian experiment, just underway, to build a host of innovative mechanisms of reception, in order to improve its future record.[23] Some States have also adopted major legislative reforms in order to deal with failures of a systemic nature identified by the Court. Italian lawmakers, for instance, fashioned the *Azzolini* law with the hope of improving its capacity – notoriously infirm – to implement the Court's rulings.[24]

f. Informal Mechanisms: Knowledge and Practice

The state of knowledge about the ECHR and the Court's jurisprudence in national legal systems conditions the reception process in obvious ways. The more ignorant of the Convention are national officials, the less likely it is that they will be able to perform their duties properly. In all States, teaching and scholarly research about the ECHR and the Court's case law have steadily increased since the entry into force of Protocol no. 11 in 1998, but problems remain. Among

---

[20] See *infra* C.4
[21] Krisch (2008).
[22] See Besson, this volume, Section III.E.1.b.
[23] See Nußberger, this volume, Section E.2.a.
[24] See Candela Soriano, this volume, Section III.E.2.

lawyers and lower court judges in many States, knowledge of the Court's case law and access to translations of judgments involving applications from other States remains poor, a situation that weakens the judiciary's overall capacity to guarantee the ECHR's effectiveness.[25]

One negative finding concerning practice deserves comment. As the importance of the ECHR to domestic law increased, we expected networks of human rights litigators and Non Governmental Organizations (NGOs) to grow at both the national and transnational levels. We also expected that these networks would steadily develop capacity to influence the reception process. While human rights NGOs have at least some relevance in most States, none of the reports shows that they regularly exercise decisive influence on important outcomes.[26] Further, law firms seem to have little incentive to invest in the domain. Compared with litigating EU law in national courts, which typically has a heavy commercial content, the sums at stake in litigating the ECHR are relatively small. If a case does make it through the admissibility stage in Strasbourg, it will be subject to long delay and little hope of a large financial payout. Despite these initial findings, more systematic research on the organization and impact of human rights litigating in Europe is clearly needed.

B. The Court's Docket

In this section, we examine, from the point of view of the reception process, inputs into the ECHR legal system (applications) and the most important outputs (judgements of the Court and other decisions).

1. Applications to the ECtHR

The entry into force of Protocol no. 11 on November 1, 1998 removed any formal obstacle to access to the Court for individuals, beyond the requirement that petitioners exhaust available domestic remedies. In addition, the Court makes applying to it simple and virtually cost-free: the required forms and easy-to-follow instructions are posted online, and applicants do not need legal counsel, at least not initially. The data on Post-Protocol no. 11 applications are, therefore, a fairly direct measure of the social demand for rights protection under the Convention. Table 1 reports these data, broken down by State and per annum.

[25] See also the Committee of Ministers Recommendation Rec (2004)4 on the ECHR in universities and professional training, 12 May 2004.
[26] For a prominent exception concerning the Warsaw Helsinki Foundation of Human Rights, see Krzyżanowska-Mierzewska, this volume, Section J.1.g.

Table 1: Individual Applications to the ECtHR
(November 1, 1998–December 31 2006)

	Received	Per Year	Per Cap.*	Admissible	Per Cap.**	Rank p/c*
Average per state	12,631	1,546	41.29	332.4 (4.7%)	1.64	
Spain	5,367	656.9	15.13	38 (1%)	0.108	2
Ireland	522	63.9	15.21	12 (2%)	0.357	4
Norway	603	73.8	16.04	17 (3%)	0.456	6
Germany	16,005	1,958	23.73	69 (0.4%)	0.101	1
Belgium	2,095	256.4	24.41	89 (4%)	1.038	11
UK	12.072	1,477.6	24.54	303 (3%)	0.616	9
Netherlands	3,641	445.6	27.33	57 (2%)	0.429	5
Greece	2,935	359.2	32.36	295 (10%)	3.252	17
Turkey	20,141	2,465.2	33.81	1,500 (7%)	2.518	15
Russia	48,791	5,972	41.93	353 (0.7%)	0.303	3
Switzerland	2,542	311.1	42.04	31 (1%)	0.513	8
France	23,582	2,886.4	47.39	590 (3%)	1.185	12
Sweden	3,590	439.4	48.82	37 (1%)	0.500	7
Ukraine	18,860	2,308.4	49.53	310 (2%)	0.813	10
Italy	24,141	2,954.8	50.42	1,617 (7%)	3.377	18
Austria	3,427	419.5	51.15	156 (5%)	2.329	14
Slovakia	3,823	467.9	86.64	133 (3%)	3.018	16
Poland	35,225	4,311.5	112.86	377 (1%)	1.206	13

* Calculated as the number of applications per State divided by population.

** Calculated as the number of admissible applications per State divided by population. Rank p/c refers to the ordinal ranking of States, from lowest to highest, on the basis of admissible applications generated, *per capita*.

The source for the raw data on applications is the annual *Survey of Activities*, the European Court of Human Rights, 1998–2006. The source for the population data is Eurostat (2006).

Applicants activate the ECHR's legal system in order to achieve outcomes – justice, a change in national law and practice, and so on – that have been denied to them in the domestic system. Although any given application may be unique in important respects, it is reasonable to assume that the aggregate data can tell us something of general significance about the relationship between the ECHR and national legal orders. Consider, for example, the following simple proposition, in effect, a "pathology hypothesis": the more a State violates the Convention rights of individuals, the more it will generate applications to Strasbourg. In this view of the regime, the ECHR functions to reveal problems in domestic orders which the Court helps States to resolve. The cross-national data will, therefore, chart the relative extent to which rights are protected in national legal orders or, much the same thing, the degree to which States are in non-compliance with the Convention. This view has much to recommend it, but it does not provide a complete picture, as the case studies demonstrate.

A second view, which may partly overlap with the first, emphasizes a different function. The ECHR will be important to the extent that it fills important gaps in national legal orders. In those States that do not possess a comprehensive, entrenched Bill of Rights, for example, the ECHR may be used to perform that role, as a shadow Bill of Rights. If and how it does so depends heavily on how the Convention is incorporated into the national legal order. In addition, a State's constitutional rights provisions may not accord precisely with the Convention, or national judges may give a narrower reading to a right than the Strasbourg Court, situations that will attract applicants to Strasbourg. In this account, the data will reflect, at least in part, gaps between domestic rights protection and the ECHR, as the latter evolves.

In contrast to the "pathology hypothesis", we would not assume, under the "gap-filling hypothesis", that levels of petitions only measure the extent of pathology. The numbers may also chart a healthy social demand for perfecting rights protection in States whose basic commitment to protecting rights is already relatively robust. In many contexts, national law is likely to be more ossified and path dependent than the more malleable Convention. In so far as it is, Strasbourg will attract applicants.

A third logic rests on a still more complex view of how individual applicants, national officials, and the Strasbourg Court interact with one another. This view takes seriously the capacity of the Court's case law to "feedback" on petitioners and national officials. Applications from each country tend to be clustered in specific areas, due to pathology (including systemic failures), national gaps in protection, or for other reasons. Nonetheless, the extent to which applications in these domains increase over time will be partly a function of how the Court constructs its jurisprudence. If the Court responds positively to the demand for the expansion in the scope and application of a specific right, it will tend to attract more applications in that area. A feedback loop is thereby constituted. Theoretically, the inverse might be true. It is possible that applications will decline or stop altogether, in a given domain, if a State successfully adapts its law to the relevant case law. However, such instances may be rare in important areas of litigation in which relatively large or coherent classes of applicants are concerned. Petitions may actually increase even after a State adequately complies with a specific ruling, as individuals seek to extend the scope of a new interpretation of rights.

At the heart of this dynamic lies a tension (which inheres in rights adjudication more generally) between two functions of the Court. The Court constructs Convention rights as general norms, which it treats as having prospective legal consequences for States. At the same time, its powers are largely limited to the rendering of individual (retrospective and particular) justice to victims of specific abuse. The Court may move to recognize a new right, or it may clarify the nature and scope of an existing right in an innovative way, while narrowly tailoring its ruling to the facts of the case. Indeed, this is a standard technique of judicial prudence in rights adjudication. Yet this type of ruling invites future applications, whose purpose will be to extend the coverage of the right even further, given remaining restrictions of national law. In this view, then, numbers of applications will also reflect the Court's own engagement in rights innovation, in the context of the social demand for such innovation (which varies cross-nationally).

Such propositions, and the data presented in Table 1, should be assessed in conjunction with the case studies presented in this volume. In the left-hand column, States are listed, lowest to highest, in terms of the average annual number of applications generated per one million inhabitants. States are ranked ordinally, in the right-hand column, with reference to the annual number of applications that are judged to be admissible by the Court, on a *per capita* basis. These numbers comprise a direct measure of the extent to which each State contributes to establishing the Court's agenda.

Not surprisingly, the States with the largest, most intractable, problems supply the Court with the bulk of its caseload. The average number of applications judged admissible by the Court per year, among our 18 States, is 40.6. Only five States – Russia, Poland, France, Turkey, and Italy, in that order – exceed this average. States that have relatively high levels of admissible applications *per capita*[27] also include Greece and Slovakia which, like France, Italy, Russia and the Ukraine, have not succeeded in rectifying various structural failures, particularly as regards the functioning of the judiciary. In its 2006 Report,[28] the Court presented data on the 89,900 cases pending before it on 1 January 2007. Eight of the regime's forty-seven States generated 70% of all pending cases: Russia (21.5%), Romania (12.1%), Turkey (10%), Ukraine (7.6%), Poland (5.7%), France (4.8%), Germany (3.9%), and Italy (3.8%);[29] and applications from the first five comprise a majority of pending cases. For the foreseeable future, then, the Court will expend the bulk of its time and resources dealing with pathology: massive structural problems in sometimes intransigent States.

The countries that generate the least number of admissible petitions *per capita*[30] are Germany, Ireland, and Spain, States that possess the most effective domestic

---

[27] Austria (14th) is also ranked in the bottom third of admissible applications per year, *per capita*. In Austria, a small State with a legalistic culture, the ECHR possesses directly effective, constitutional status, but its courts remain hesitant to apply the Convention aggressively.

[28] European Court of Human Rights, Annual Report 2006, Registry of the European Court of Human Rights, Strasbourg, 2007.

[29] Ibid., p. 114.

[30] Third on that list is Russia (with by far the largest population). Arguably (see Nußberger's report, this volume, Section D.2.e.), Russia has the worst record of rights protection among ECHR Contracting States (even blocking the mailing of applications to the Court). Petitions from Russia are now flooding the Court.

systems of rights protection in Europe, as well as Norway, which possesses little experience with rights review. Although Belgium, Germany, Norway, Spain, and Switzerland, among other countries, interact with the ECHR less systematically or only sporadically than most of the States covered in this volume, the influence of the ECHR on their respective legal systems should not be underestimated. Considered on their own, each is experiencing significant legal change as a result of membership in the regime. As the respective national reports show, we find some of the dynamics of gap filling and feedback discussed above. The ECHR is an important structural backdrop, and the Court is a powerful agent, for steady progress in the direction of stronger rights protection.

2. Findings of Violations

Cross-national data on rulings of violation against States are relatively direct measures of the pressure that the ECHR regime places on national officials to adapt national legal orders to the Convention. Table 2 reports this information for the 18 States examined in this volume. States are listed, from lowest to highest, with respect to the number of violations declared annually by the Court, since 1 January 1998. States with the best records (under 6 violations found per year) include, in order, Ireland, Norway, Sweden, Spain, the Netherlands, Switzerland, Belgium, and Germany. At the bottom of the table, with more than 50 violations found per year, we find France, Turkey, and Italy. If we control for population – ranking countries with respect to the number of violations per annum and *per capita* – the order changes dramatically. Spain and Germany have far better records than all other States in our survey; whereas Slovakia, Italy, and Greece (in that order) have the worst records.

Table 2: Rulings on the Merits and Friendly Settlements: 1998-2006

	Judgements	/ Per Yr	Violations	/ Per Yr	/ Per Cap*	Non-Viol.	FS**
Average	260.7	29	246.3	27.4	0.926	14.9	40.2
Ireland	11	1.2	7	0.8	0.190 (6)	4	0
Norway	10	1.1	8	0.8	0.173 (4)	2	0
Sweden	21	2.3	14	1.6	0.177 (5)	7	13
Spain	34	3.8	26	2.9	0.066 (1)	8	1
Netherlands	52	5.8	39	4.3	0.263 (7)	13	8
Switzerland	60	6.7	41	4.6	0.621 (11)	29	2
Belgium	57	6.3	51	5.7	0.542 (9)	6	7
Germany	67	7.4	53	5.9	0.071 (2)	14	4
Slovakia	112	12.4	107	11.9	2.203 (16)	5	17
Austria	120	13.3	111	12.3	1.500 (14)	9	17

	Judgements / Per Yr		Violations / Per Yr / Per Cap*			Non-Viol.	FS**
UK	175	19.4	146	16.2	0.269 (8)	29	15
Russia	206	22.9	199	22.1	0.155 (3)	7	0
Ukraine	260	28.9	258	28.7	0.615 (10)	2	0
Greece	271	30.1	265	29.4	2.648 (18)	6	18
Poland	340	37.8	321	35.7	0.934 (13)	19	32
France	500	55.6	447	49.6	0.814 (12)	53	84
Turkey	1111	123.4	1080	120	1.646 (15)	31	182
Italy	1285	142.8	1260	140	2.389 (17)	25	324

* Ordinal rank in parentheses: Ireland is ranked sixth in terms of violations found per annum and per 1 million inhabitants; Spain is ranked first, and Greece last.

** Friendly settlements.

Source: Appendix, this volume.

Although our project was not designed to explain the cross-national variation depicted in Table 2, at least some of that variation is a product of the reception process. Those States with stable, robust systems of national rights protection (Germany, Ireland, Spain) are less vulnerable to censure from Strasbourg, all the more so once constitutional courts decided to require the judiciary to enforce both the Convention and the Court's case law directly and with fidelity, even against Parliamentary statutes. The majority of States in our survey, however, did not possess strong domestic systems of constitutional justice when they began to confront a more expansive ECHR and a more aggressive Court. These States can best reduce their exposure to censure in Strasbourg by developing effective reception mechanisms: stable rules and procedures that serve to coordinate the national legal order and the ECHR, on an ongoing basis. As the national reports demonstrate, developing such mechanisms is rarely an easy, simple, or smooth process, to the extent that it requires significant structural change. Such change will usually be slow and incremental, at least at first. New mechanisms are typically grafted onto older, institutionally embedded, ways of doing things, and some officials may seek to resist change. The evidence presented in this book, however, shows that national officials are being steadily socialized into a Europe whose Convention not only binds the State, as a matter of international law, but also binds domestic officials, as a matter of enforceable national law. Those States for which the Convention now functions as a *de facto* or shadow Constitution (Austria, Belgium, the Netherlands, Switzerland, the UK, and, increasingly, Norway, Sweden, and France) provide significant examples of these dynamics.

In some countries (including Italy, Poland), the commitment to protecting rights (of both Constitutional and Conventional origin) may be relatively high but insufficient, in itself, to counter certain structural deficiencies or specific legal pathologies. In other countries (Austria, France), long-standing judicial resistance to the Court and its case law has undoubtedly exposed the national system to more applications and findings of violations than would have been the case had courts been more open to enforcing the ECHR. Finally, there are States whose commitment to rights has not always been strong, though gradually improving (Greece, Slovakia, and perhaps Ukraine); and there are States whose attitude toward the ECHR and its Court has been generally hostile (Russia, Turkey, and until recently Ukraine). In any event, as the data in Table 1 show,[31] it is applications from States with the poorest records that dominate the Court's docket.

C. The Court's Impact on National Legal Systems

The Court protects Convention rights in multiple, highly differentiated ways. While we recognize that the Court operates under unified jurisdictional rules and procedures, the role it performs, in fact, varies across Convention norms and State contexts. The Court functions (1) as a kind of High Cassation Court when it comes to procedure, (2) as an international watchdog when it comes to grave human rights violations and massive breakdowns in rule of law, and (3) as an oracle of constitutional rights interpretation when it comes to fine-tuning the qualified rights of Articles 8–11 and 14 ECHR.

1. Procedural Law

The Court has played its most prominent role in the field of civil and criminal procedure, for three main reasons. First, simplifying what is in fact a fiercely complex topic, Civil Law States on the continent base their procedural law on the so-called accusatorial model, rather than on the adversarial practices of the Anglo-Saxon Common Law. The Court, in its case law on Articles 5 and 6 ECHR, has pointedly criticized civil law systems (including Austria, Belgium, France, Germany, Italy, the Netherlands, and Switzerland) for their general lack of impartiality, insufficient transparency during the pre-merits phase, and the accumulation of functions by the same officials during different phases of the trial, which are values commonly associated with the adversarial system. As John Jackson has cogently argued, the Court is actively constructing a new "participatory model" that lies between the classic forms.[32] In any event, its case law on procedure has not been easy to digest by many States. Since implementation typically requires fundamental changes in judicial organization,[33] the Court's impact in this domain has transformative potential. Second, as the Convention itself does not protect the right to peaceful enjoyment of property, the Court adopted

[31] See Stone Sweet and Keller, this volume, Section A.2.b.
[32] Jackson (2005).
[33] In particular for France, see Lambert Abdelgawad and Weber, this volume, Section D.1.c.

a broad interpretation of the procedural guarantee in Article 6(1) ECHR, thereby filling the gap. This move, and others like it, gave an extremely wide scope to civil rights that in turn generated strong resistance in countries like Austria, Switzerland and Germany.[34] Third, the Court's emphasis on procedural guarantees for defendants has to be seen as part of a more general trend toward juridification in international law. After a first phase in which substantive human rights have been developed, the international community is now focused on procedural aspects, and on how domestic institutions enforce rights. Since the 70's, scholars and judges have worked to upgrade procedural rights. It is today a mega-trend of international human rights law, and with it comes an associated expansion of judicial authority. Among international courts, the ECtHR has been the most important progenitor of this trend.[35] In response, several countries have made important legislative efforts to reduce the length of proceedings (Austria, France, Germany, Italy, Poland, Slovakia).[36] Nonetheless, it remains an open question whether these reforms will, in fact, give results that meet the high requirements formulated by the Court.[37]

For every State in our survey, the majority of violations of the ECHR found by the Court concern Article 6 ECHR guarantees. Most alarming are broad failures across Europe to ensure trial within a reasonable time period. As the duration of court proceedings before the ECtHR has stretched to indefensible lengths,[38] the Court's demand for timely proceedings in the Contracting States may lose

---

[34] See Thurnherr, this volume, Section E.1.a.

[35] Aromaa and Viljanen (2006).

[36] For the famous *Pinto* law see Candela Soriano, this volume, Section III.D.2.a.bb.

[37] *Scordino v. Italy* (appl. no. 36813/97), Judgment (Grand Chamber), 29 March 2006, (not yet reported), para. 183.

[38] For the time period since the date of allocation for pending Committee and Chamber cases in 2006 (all data were provided by the Court), http://www.echr.coe.int/NR/rdonlyres/C8F656AA-94 C4-4A3F-A69D-0E4C6D510CA8/0/Analysis_of_statistics_2007.pdf.

Time period	Chamber cases	Committee cases
one year or less	8817 or 32%	27107 or 55%
one to two years	5530 or 20%	15717 or 32%
two to three years	4844 or 17%	5029 or 10%
three to four years	4064 or 15%	999 or 2%
tour to five years	2537 or 9%	
more than five years	1917 or 7%	
Total of cases	27709	48852

It is difficult to say what the final average time period per case is. The large figure of 55% of Committee cases are mainly due to inadmissibility decisions on the grounds of Article 35 ECHR. For nearly one third (31%) of the Chamber cases, the average length of proceedings is between three and more than five years.

much of its persuasive and authoritative force.[39] Lord Woolf has formulated it poignantly: "If 'justice delayed is justice denied', then a large proportion of the ECtHR's applicants – even those who are the victims of serous violations – are effectively denied the justice they seek."[40] In view of the notorious human rights records of countries like Russia, Ukraine and Turkey, the assumption that the Court no longer has the necessary capacity to deal with grave human rights situations due to its own excessive caseload and delays cannot be easily dismissed.

2. Articles 2 and 3 ECHR

Violations of the right to life (Article 2 ECHR) and the right to be free from torture, and inhuman and degrading treatment (Article 3 ECHR) are justifiably understood to be the most serious types of violations of the Convention. For every State in our survey, the Court has ruled on at least one claim based on either Article 2 or 3 ECHR. Ireland, Norway, and Slovakia have never been found in violation of either provision. To date, the Court has found a single violation of at least one of these provisions by Austria, German, Italy, Spain, and Switzerland, and it has found only two violations by Belgium, Italy, Poland, and Sweden. Without downplaying the seriousness of any of these cases, it is clear that compliance with Articles 2 and 3 ECHR is not a systemic problem in any of these States. Indeed, one might argue that part of the Court's case law in these areas is a type of fine-tuning (conditions of prisons, food and body searches in detention, and so on). Other countries have had a more difficult time complying with these norms. Greece (5 violations), the Netherlands (8), France (10) make up an intermediate group, followed by Ukraine (16) the UK (21), and Russia (34). Turkey, with 230 findings of violation and 91 friendly settlements, constitutes an unfortunate class by itself.

In its jurisprudence on Article 3 ECHR, the Court has exposed deplorable conditions in detention centres and prisons across Europe, including in France, Greece, Italy, Turkey, Russia, and Ukraine, situations otherwise tolerated by national politicians and judges. In response, the Council of Europe has committed itself to observing these situations closely, and in articulating higher standards for the regime as a whole. Another area of serious concern is the conduct of police authorities. In several countries, including Greece and Italy in our survey, the disproportionate number of immigrants of Roma origin among victims of violations of Articles 2 and 3 ECHR is disquieting.[41] Across Europe, the trend towards an increasingly multicultural composition of society has taken its toll on

---

[39] In a similar vein, see Paraskeva, 189 et seq.

[40] The Right Honourable the Lord Woolf, Review of the Working Methods of the European Court of Human Rights, December 2005, http://www.echr.coe.int/Eng/Press/2005/Dec/LORDWOOLFSREVIEWONWORKINGMETHODS.pdf, 8.

[41] See Kaboğlu and Koutnatzis, this volume, Section C.1.e. The Council of Europe sees discrimination against the Roma population as a general human rights problem in Europe, see http://www.coe.int/t/dg3/romatravellers/.

standards of protection. In this area, too, the Convention (and Protocol no. 4) will continue to play a vital role, backed up by Council of Europe initiatives.

In countries in which the most serious human rights violations are observed, such as Russia and Turkey, the Court confronts delicate political conflicts (as it had before with respect to the UK's problems in Northern Ireland). Turkey faces long-standing problems with the Greek population on Cyprus, with organized Kurdish separatists in the southeast provinces, and the still fragile control of the military by civilian authorities. In Russia, national officials have justified State-sponsored assassination, torture, and measures resulting in massive dislocation and suffering as necessary responses to rebellion in Chechnya. Moreover, Russia, Turkey, and Ukraine have yet to establish firm foundations for the development of stable pluralist democracy and rule of law. Often enough to matter a great deal, officials in these States express hostility to human rights as alien (West European) norms and values that are imposed upon them. Clearly, the Court is not well equipped to deal with deep-rooted problems such as these; indeed, they test the limits of the supervisory system in dramatic fashion. Moreover, these States (to-day the biggest drain on the Court's resources) routinely choose not to comply with the Court's rulings, thus undermining the credibility of the system as a whole. On the other hand, these cases reflect the Court's strong commitment to closing gaps in domestic accountability where officials refuse to investigate or choose to ignore credible claims of serious human violations.[42]

3. Articles 5 and 6 ECHR: Anti-Terrorism

In Western European countries, anti-terrorism measures have generated serious complaints, most prominently against the UK[43] and Spain.[44] The Court's role in this area has been pivotal. Experience has shown that, in many cases, fundamental rights were not sufficiently guaranteed in the absence of supranational control. National courts, being close to the events, proved unable to accord sufficient weight to fundamental rights when balanced against security imperatives. The Court's caseload in relation to Articles 5 and 6 ECHR will undoubtedly become more politically sensitive in the coming years, as new anti-terrorist measures are implemented in these countries and in France and Italy.[45]

4. Article 8–11 and 14: Fine-Tuning and Proportionality

The Strasbourg Court plays an important role as an oracle of rights in Europe to the extent that it helps to define the scope and content of substantive rights, in particular, those provided by Articles 8–11 and 14 ECHR. Because these rights overlap with national rights provisions, or fill a constitutional gap in those States

---

[42] Helfer (2008), 144.
[43] See Besson, this volume, Section III.C.1.b.
[44] See Candela Soriano, this volume, Section III.C.1.b.aa.
[45] See also Wildhaber (2007), 534 et seq.

without Bills of Rights, the Court's jurisprudence tends to take on a transnation-al-constitutional character. Through this jurisprudence, the Convention commands the obedience of national legal systems in the way that national constitutional rights do, without being constitutional in any formal sense. Further, the Court has adopted proportionality as the framework for adjudicating qualified rights under the Convention. Proportionality analysis, it can be argued, is an inherently constitutional mode of adjudication.[46] It is also deeply intrusive in that it gives judges the final word on how non-judicial policy makers have already balanced conflicting interests and values. In the ECHR context, the move to proportionality means that it is often the Strasbourg Court that will have the final say on how all national officials, including judges, balance competing interests.

The Court adopted proportionality as a means of ensuring that States would take qualified rights seriously, notwithstanding the principles of subsidiarity and margin of appreciation. The necessity phase of the procedure – a least restrictive means test – narrows the scope of permissible derogations to Convention rights to those measures that are necessary to achieve some important public interest. The Court's move not only empowered ordinary judges across Convention States by making them *de facto* constitutional judges, it also gave life to Articles 8–11 and 14 ECHR.

Of these provisions, Article 8 ECHR has generated the greatest number of applications and findings of violation. Here we find a combination of the gap-filling and feedback effects discussed above.[47] The Court has used proportionality analysis to fashion an innovative and expansive jurisprudence on privacy and family life in ever-expanding zones of protection. The Court developed the right to family reunification as a core value of Article 8 ECHR, and that guarantee now plays a major role in national immigration law throughout Europe. The Court also invoked Article 8 ECHR to exercise control over telephone tapping, now extended to other forms of private communication. Since national legal regimes lagged behind the technological capacity of the State to eavesdrop on its citizens, a flood of complaints gave the Court the opportunity to define the basic standard of rights protection. Perhaps most spectacularly, the Court used Article 8 ECHR to recognize the rights of transsexuals and homosexuals, furthering *inter alia* the decriminalization of homosexuality in Europe and, in conjunction with Article 14 ECHR, the construction of a general right to non-discrimination on grounds of gender and sexual preference.

The Court's caseload concerning Article 10 ECHR (freedom of expression) is also striking, given that these are not new, or boutique, rights. The older States of the Council of Europe, Austria (28 violations), France (11), the UK (9), and Switzerland (7) have generated the highest number of rulings of violation, with

[46] Stone Sweet (2008).
[47] See *supra* Section B.1.

the exception of Turkey (120). In its balancing of freedom of the press and other media against other values, the Strasbourg Court has tended to downplay rights to personality, personal honor, and other values that national systems may accord more weight. The Court appears anxious to accord a vital role to the press in democratic society, as a watchdog of Government, and therefore interprets the scope of possible restrictions narrowly (through the necessity phase of proportionality). In some States, including Russia, Ukraine and Turkey, the Government openly seeks to control the press and visual media for its own, often illiberal, purposes.[48] Given the Court's conception of Article 10 ECHR, it will confront very serious challenges from these and other States in the years to come.

The Court's role in protecting Articles 8–11 and 14 ECHR deserves to be evaluated in light of its overloaded caseload and in light of the principle of subsidiarity. In post-Protocol no. 11 Europe, the Court can expect to receive a steady stream of applications asking it, in effect, to supervise how national officials have balanced, that is, how they have made and applied law with reference to qualified rights. When the Court reviews how national officials have balanced competing interests under this part of the Convention, it rarely if ever guarantees the core essence of a right; neither does it represent an external control on allegations that a State grossly violates the most basic human rights, such as those under Articles 2 and 3 ECHR. It is instead fine-tuning outcomes that would normally be subject to national decision-making. Proportionality is an instrument *par excellence* of judicial fine-tuning, and of helping policy makers achieve the right balance between competing interests and values. There is, however, no fixed limit to its reach: on the contrary, proportionality fixes the boundaries of the margin of appreciation.

This situation poses a delicate problem for the Court. From the standpoint of reception, the Court often ends up with the last word on how rights are to be defined and applied in general measures, and used in concrete situations. From the point of view of its caseload, the Court's position means that it attracts an ever-increasing number of demands for fine-tuning. It is obvious that the ECtHR cannot abandon proportionality as a general approach to the qualified rights; to do so at this point would undermine the Convention and the national judiciary's capacities to enforce it. The Court could, however, take a more permissive posture with respect to how national judges enforce the proportionality principle. The Court could, for example, reiterate that Article 13 ECHR requires national judges to employ proportionality analysis; and it could announce that it will ensure, as a matter of procedure, that judges in fact have done so. At the same time, it could choose to limit the scope of its substantive review on the merits to how national judges have used proportionality analysis in important or extreme cases.

---

[48] See Nußberger, this volume, Section D.3.c. For the infamous Article 301 of the Turkish Criminal Code, see also Kaboğlu and Koutnatzis, this volume, Section D.2.b.

Such a move would reduce the exposure of the Court, enable it to counter charges of usurping national autonomy and the margin of appreciation, and help to forge a better partnership with national judges. It would also give the Court a tool to manage its docket more flexibly. On the downside, some would accuse the Court of abandoning its true mission, which consists in providing justice in individual cases. Skeptics of proportionality,[49] those who consider the framework to be inherently unprincipled, will renew their attacks, though this cost is already being paid.

D. The ECHR and National Legal Systems

In this Section, we focus on how the evolution of certain structural features of the Convention has complicated the reception process at the domestic level.

1. Exhaustion of Local Remedies

The principle of subsidiarity is a cornerstone, a *ratio conventionis*, of the European system of human rights protection. It is a duty of national officials to protect human rights within their domestic legal systems and to ensure respect for the rights safeguarded by the Convention. For its part, the ECtHR may accept an application only after domestic remedies have been exhausted, and within a period of six months from the date on which the final decision was taken (Article 35 ECHR). At first glance, these elements would seem to comprise a framework under which there would be a simple and smooth transition from the national system to the ECHR. Yet as the reports on Switzerland, Poland, Russia, and Italy, among others, make apparent, determining when national remedies have been exhausted may be a difficult and time-consuming task, introducing a great deal of inter-systemic friction. The three factors that matter most – the organization of the national judiciary, the competences of constitutional and high courts, and the effectiveness of ordinary (and the availability of extraordinary) remedies – vary considerably across Europe. When the Court does not pay close attention to these differences, it produces incoherent case law.[50]

The Court also uses Article 35 ECHR strategically, for its own purposes: a restrictive interpretation of the exhaustion of local remedies rule will tend to close the door to applicants, whereas a broader construction will invite more applications. In practice, the Court seems to choose between progressive and narrow approaches, for different reasons. If an applicant can show that there would be no point in exhausting national remedies, and if the problem at hand seems important, the Court may simply ignore the requirement and dismiss the

---

[49] Bruach (2005) is a good example.

[50] *Sürmeli v. Germany* (appl. no. 75529/01), Judgement (Grand Chamber), 8 June 2006 (not yet reported); *Szott-Medyńska and Others v. Poland* (appl. no. 47414/99), Decision, 9 October 2003 (not reported).

Government's preliminary objections.[51] In doing so, the Court sends a powerful signal about the inadequacy of national rights protection and invites reform. The Court needs to be able to restrict access in order to cope with its overloaded docket, although the result will be denial of justice in some individual cases.

Thus, despite its *prima facie* intelligibility, applying the local remedies rule on the ground is fraught with both factual and political complexity. As this book shows, the Court's decisions on admissibility deserve to be evaluated more closely, both by scholars and States. States should consider translating and distributing such decisions: they are crucial to a proper understanding of the interaction between the national and European systems. In some countries, scholarly commentary on Article 35 ECHR is both abundant and highly technical whereas, in others, the topic is just being noticed. What is clear is that, at the interface of the national legal order and the ECHR, there exists considerable friction, with all the attendant inefficiencies (of time, money, and intellectual effort) that add to the system's burdens.

2. Convention Rights as Minimal Standards

As discussed in the introduction, the traditional view was that the Convention established European standards of rights protection in the form of a floor below which national legal protection may not fall.[52] In this sense, it has always been recognized that the Convention harmonizes rights protection, at least at this minimal level. Moreover, under Article 53 ECHR, the Contracting States may develop higher human rights standards than those entrenched in the Convention. As with Article 35 ECHR, however, this view misses what is arguably most important. The Court treats the Convention as a "living instrument", and understands its role to be an autonomous and authoritative defender of human rights. Further, it has expressly committed itself to raising human rights standards whenever possible, although it typically does so only after asserting that it has identified an emerging consensus among the Contracting States. What this means for laggard States – that is, those national legal systems that are not part of the identification of a new consensus – is that the Convention does not constitute the minimal, but rather the sole, obligatory, higher standard. Thus, one important meta-narrative of reception is that States are always playing catch-up to the Court, if some more than others.

---

[51] See, e.g., *Isayeva, Yusipova, Bazaeva v. Russia* (appl. no. 57947/00; 57948/00; 57949/00), Judgement (First Section), 24 February 2005 (not yet reported); *Isayeva v. Russia*, (appl. no. 57950/00), Judgement (First Section), 24 February 2005, (not yet reported); *Akdivar v. Turkey* (appl. no. 21893/93), Judgement (Grand Chamber), 16 September 1996, Reports 1996-IV (no. 15), 1192, para. 67; *Bosphorus Hava Yollari Turizm Ve Ticares AS v. Ireland* (appl. no. 45036/98), Decision (Fourth Section), 13 September 2001 (not reported); *Selçuk and Asker v. Turkey* (appl. nos 23184/94;23185/94), Judgement (Chamber), 24 April 1998, Reports 1998-II (no. 71), 891, paras 70–71; *McCann and Others v. United Kingdom* (appl. no. 18984/91), 27 September 1995, Series A, Vol. 324, para. 161.

[52] See Stone Sweet and Keller, this volume, Section A.1.

The national reports show clearly that these dynamics have influenced how national judges perform their tasks, and how they justify new, more active, roles in rights protection. Some national courts directly equate national human rights with European standards. Switzerland is a telling example,[53] but one finds variation on this theme wherever the Convention functions as a surrogate Bill of Rights. It is striking that most national courts have learned to follow the Court, and to widen the scope and standards of the rights that they enforce, with few difficulties. There are, arguably, a few notable exceptions. Irish judges, for example, consider the ECHR to state minimal standards in comparison to the higher standards offered under their own Constitution; and German and Italian judges sometimes state, or imply, as much as well. In the UK, where the courts cannot adopt an interpretation of the Convention that goes beyond benchmark standards set by the ECtHR, the Convention constitutes both a minimal and a maximal standard.[54]

This dynamic puts strains on the reception process in obvious ways, not least, since a State in compliance at one moment in time will be put out of compliance at a later point, every time the Court decides to raise levels of protection. In practice, Convention rights do not comprise minimal common-denominator standards, but rather obligatory, relatively free-standing standards above which national judges have an interest in developing, if they are to stay in compliance with the regime.

3. Beyond Individual Justice

To read the Convention literally (Articles 41 and 46 ECHR, for example), one might conclude that the regime's legal system is primarily geared to delivering individual justice. States bear a duty to give just satisfaction to any individual who has been a victim of a violation of the ECHR for which they are responsible. However, as this book emphasizes, the Court is increasingly engaged in delivering what the former President of the Court, Luzius Wildhaber, Stephen Greer, and others characterize as "constitutional justice".[55] Today, the Court often behaves more as a general and prospective lawmaker than as a judge whose reach is primarily particular and retrospective. In the post-Protocol no. 11 world, the Court functions as an authoritative oracle of rights jurisprudence for all of Europe; it supervises State compliance with the ECHR, whose standards are continuously rising; and it seeks general solutions to general problems with which it is confronted. This shift in emphasis has enormous consequences for the reception processes. States are routinely required to reform their internal law and practices in response to findings of violation by the Court, not simply to provide compensation to individual victims. Still more problematic, the Court finds itself in the

---

[53] See Thurnherr, this volume, Sections B.2.b. and B.2.c.
[54] See Besson, this volume, Section III.D.1.b.
[55] Wildhaber (2000); Greer (2006), 173.

role of a socio-political engineer when it seeks to solve systemic failures through pilot judgements and other types of rulings.

4. Reopening of Proceedings

It is now commonplace for States to allow the reopening of national criminal proceedings after a non-favourable judgement from Strasbourg (the only exceptions in our survey are Italy, Spain and Ukraine).[56] This quiet revolution in European procedural law is remarkable for several reasons. Formally, the States enjoy a degree of discretion as to the means by which to comply with a final ECtHR judgement in accordance with Article 46 ECHR, while the Court refers to the well-known principle of *restitutio in integrum* in international law. Thus, whenever the Court concludes that there has been a breach of the Convention, the respondent State is under a legal obligation to put an end to the breach and make reparation for its consequences in such a way as to restore, as far as possible, the situation existing prior to the violation.[57] The idea that proceedings must be reopened after a negative judgement is not required.[58] On the contrary, the idea is clearly borrowed from a hierarchical system with a super-ordinate court structure.

This particular *acquis conventionnel* developed in a domain traditionally reserved to national law. The diversity and complexity of national legal systems concerning procedural requirements (juridical time limits and formal requirements) and jurisdictional competences (e.g., *ratione personae, rationae materiae* and *ratione temporis*) have thus far impeded international harmonization in this area (prominent exceptions like the Lugano Convention[59] and the Brussels Convention[60] only prove the rule). Although national procedural law remains a pretext for national parochialism, the ECHR has provoked a first important

---

[56] The coordination in civil law and administrative law has not substantially evolved. Only some countries provide –under certain conditions – for the reopening in civil or administrative proceedings (such as Germany, United Kingdom, Ireland, Norway, Russia, Sweden, Switzerland, Ukraine, Turkey).

[57] See, for instance, *Carbonara and Ventura v. Italy* (appl. no. 24638/94), Judgement (Second Section), 30 May 2000, Reports 2000-VI, 91; *Scordino v. Italy* (No. 1) (appl. no. 36813/97), Judgement (First Section), 29 July 2004, (not reported).

[58] That said, the Committee of Ministers recognized the very importance of the possibility of reopening national proceedings for the reception of the ECHR and recommended the adoption of national remedies to the Member States. Recommendation Rec. (2000)2 of the Committee of Ministers to member States on the re-examination or reopening of certain cases at domestic level following judgements of the European Court of Human Rights, 19 January 2000.

[59] Lugano Convention of 16 September 1988 on jurisdiction and the enforcement of judgments in civil and commercial matters, 28 I.L.M. 620 (1989) (among EC and EFTA Member States).

[60] Brussels Convention on Jurisdiction and the Enforcement of Judgments in Civil and Commercial Matters, 27 September 1968, 8 I.L.M. 229, reprinted as amended in 29 I.L.M. 1413 (1990), substantially replaced by the Council Regulation (EC) No. 44/2001 of December 22, 2000, on jurisdiction and the recognition and enforcement of judgements in civil and commercial matters, OJ 2011 L 12/1 (among EC Member States).

breakthrough in this sensitive area of national procedure. No other international treaty has triggered the same effect.

5. Inter-Judicial Cooperation and Conflict

The ECHR does not provide a blueprint for an integrated system of human rights protection for Europe, nor does it establish how the Court should interact with its national counterparts. Nonetheless, the Convention, once incorporated into domestic law, has had an enormous impact on the judiciary across Europe. As discussed above, incorporation has enhanced judicial authority *vis-à-vis* the legislative and executive branches in virtually every country in our survey. The book also documents the extent to which the ECtHR's case law has provoked changes in how national courts operate and, in countries such as France, Italy, and the UK, it has been a decisive factor in judicial reorganization.[61]

The absence of formal rules governing inter-judicial interaction in the regime has meant that national courts have had to choose how to define their relationship with Strasbourg, and these choices have evolved over time. Some national courts initially opted for a strong emphasis on national autonomy, leading to a competitive relationship, or even conflict, open or disguised. Examples include the German Constitutional Court, the Austrian Constitutional Court in its early case-law, the Italian Constitutional Court, the Irish and British courts, and the French high courts until the 90's, although judges on each of these courts have laboured to reduce tensions in recent years. Other courts have chosen to defer to the Convention and to its Court, for their own reasons, as the Spanish Constitutional Tribunal did in its early jurisprudence, and as the Dutch and Belgian judges do. One might identify a mid-point, between conflict and deference, wherein courts seek to forge a cooperative relationship with the Strasbourg Court through dialogue and comity. The Swiss Federal Supreme Court, the Polish Constitutional Court, and, more recently, the House of Lords and the French Supreme Court and Council of State are good examples; and this position may well become the norm. Finally, through negligence or ignorance, some courts have failed to negotiate much of a relationship at all (typical for the Greek courts until the 90's, for the Turkish courts at least until 2004 and for the Russian courts until today).

The reports address why national judges made the choices they did, with what consequences for reception, and why they may have changed their attitudes over time. Although more research on these issues needs to be undertaken, it is clear that no single factor, or simple combination of factors, can explain the choices judges have made. In some important cases (notably France and the UK), high courts became more open to the Strasbourg Court's jurisprudence in order to re-

---

[61] See this volume, Lambert Abdelgawad and Weber, Section B.1.c. and D.1.c.; Besson, Section III.D.1.b.; Candela Soriano, Section III.D.2.b.

duce their vulnerability to findings of violation. Non-legal factors also influence judicial attitudes to the ECHR regime. Independently of the formal structure and legal constraints (a system's monist or dualist nature, the formal rank of the Convention within the legal order, the existence and extent of judicial review of Government acts, etc.), those national judges who desired to enforce Convention rights directly, as supra-legislative norms, found ways to do so. The reports also show that judicial reception of the ECHR is conditioned by the judges' expertise, access to the Court's case law, trust in the ECtHR to perform its tasks in good faith, and self-understanding as regulators of Government action and rights protectors. The fact that judges interact with non-judicial national officials (who are often pursuing quite different goals) complicates matters. Indeed, the more national judges seek to increase the effectiveness of Convention rights in the domestic order, the more likely it is that they will face resistance on the part of other government actors.

The ECHR has thus evolved in ways that generate politics – between courts, and between courts and non-judicial officials – that will always be, in our view, significantly open-ended and difficult to model.

E. The Future of the Court

The Court faces two dramatic challenges: an exploding caseload, and a steady stream of applications that raise very serious human rights abuses from a handful of problematic States. Fears that the Court has reached its extreme capacity are both widespread and justified. It is difficult to see how the individual complaint system can survive without fundamental changes in how the Court processes applications. The Court does not possess the necessary power and resources for it to oversee the kinds of deep structural domestic reform required for some countries to bring domestic rights standards up to bare minimal levels. In this Section, we briefly examine, from the perspective adopted in this book, how the ECHR regime might best meet its challenges in the future.[62]

1. Reception and Burden Sharing

One of the general claims of this volume is that the ECHR and domestic legal systems are significantly enmeshed in one another. If the protection of human rights in Europe is carried out at different levels and through various mechanisms, the question is how one can best distribute the overall charge of protecting human rights. In the Council of Europe system, other bodies such as the European Committee for the Prevention of Torture, the European Commission against Racism and Intolerance, the Advisory Committee on the Framework Conven-

---

[62] We do not survey all of the reform proposals here, but see Helfer (2008). Helfer reviews the growing literature on ECHR reform, and develops an interesting approach that emphasizes "embeddedness" and burden sharing.

tion for the Protection of National Minorities and the European Committee on Social Rights, also have rights-based remits.[63] The Council of Europe also maintains Information Offices in some States (including Poland and Slovakia in our survey[64]), providing not only potential applicants with information on admissibility issues, but also giving counsel on existing domestic remedies. These offices save potential applicants from initiating proceedings unnecessarily or prematurely. The functions of such offices could be expanded and strengthened, in particular in Contracting States that have a strong share in the Court's docket.

As this volume shows, national officials have a crucial role to play in monitoring and enforcing Convention rights. Most important, they can incorporate the ECHR in ways that make it directly effective in the legal order, and they can develop and use mechanisms of reception. The book also demonstrates a strong correlation between relatively higher domestic human rights standards and relatively lower numbers of applications to Strasbourg. One obvious way to reduce the ECtHR's caseload is, therefore, to enhance rights protection domestically.

As the data show, a small handful of countries, with massive, systemic problems, generate a large proportion of total applications. Such problems include judicial dysfunction (underpaid judges, poor infrastructure, and lack of impartiality), the failure on the part of politicians to commit themselves to values associated with the rule of law, corruption, and deep-rooted political problems, including the oppression of minorities and secessionist movements. Among the countries covered in this volume, Russia, Turkey and Ukraine fit this description. In these contexts, a judgment of the Court may have little effect beyond the individual applicant. The Court, in pilot rulings, may seek to persuade or cajole such States to take comprehensive measures to correct problems at the root, but it can ill afford to allow dealing with the worst pathologies to preempt its other important roles. Since the advent of Protocol no. 11, the number of applications to the ECtHR has also steadily increased in Contracting States with fairly good human rights records (such as Austria, Ireland, Norway, Poland, Slovakia, Spain, Sweden, and Switzerland). We have to accept that in a Europe of Rights, "going to Strasbourg" will be attractive to those who wish to see new rights recognized, or to raise standards of protection for established rights. It is an important function of the Court to respond to these demands and to participate fully in the progressive development of rights in Europe, in meaningful partnership with national judges and other officials.

---

[63] In addition, it is important to mention the Commissioner for Human Rights established under the auspices of the Council of Europe. See Resolution (99)50 on the Council of Europe Commissioner for Human Rights, adopted by the Committee of Ministers on 7 May 1999 at its 104th Session and Article 13 of Protocol no. 14 amending Article 36(3) ECHR.

[64] See Krzyżanowska-Mierzewska, this volume, Sections J.1.c. and J.2.c.

2. Remedies

Reform of the remedial requirements under the Convention could provide an-other means of burden-sharing between the Strasbourg and the national courts. The Court continuously emphasizes the States' obligation to vest the domestic courts with the necessary competencies and resources to enable them to give full effect to Convention rights.[65] National judges normally constitute the final phase of national remedial systems, and thus act as the gatekeepers between domestic legal orders and the Court. Although Article 13 ECHR was for many years a "dormant effective remedy clause",[66] the Court now stresses the importance of that Article,[67] not least in order to urge a more proactive stance on the part of the national courts. As this volume shows, States will not be able to manage the variegated demands of the ECHR regime without enabling strong judicial enforcement of rights.

Entrusting the determination of "reparation" and "just satisfaction" to the national courts (reform of Article 41 ECHR) has also been proposed,[68] not least since national authorities are normally better acquainted with the relevant criteria for assessing damages. Any delegation of tasks under the ECHR will run the risk of producing too much variation across the States, and the same would be true in the area of compensation. The ECHR makes awards in accordance with its own criteria, autonomously, rather than on the basis of national concepts. Conferring such authority on national courts would entail divergence, and such variation could, if too great, offend the very principles of fairness and justice that the ECHR is designed to protect. There would, therefore, need to be clear safeguards to protect individuals against States that might not live up to expectations, and this control function could only be performed by the Court.

---

[65] See *Kudła v. Poland* (appl. no. 30210/96), Judgement (Grand Chamber), 26 October 2000, Reports 2000-XI, 197, para. 152: "(...) Article 13, giving direct expression to the States' obligation to protect human rights first and foremost within their own legal system, establishes an additional guarantee for an individual in order to ensure that he or she effectively enjoys those rights. The object of Article 13, as emerges from the travaux préparatoires (...), is to provide a means whereby individuals can obtain relief at national level for violations of their Convention rights before having to set in motion the international machinery of complaint before the Court. From this perspective, the right of an individual to trial within a reasonable time will be less effective if there exists no opportunity to submit the Convention claim first to a national authority; and the requirements of Article 13 are to be seen as reinforcing those of Article 6 § 1, rather than being absorbed by the general obligation imposed by that Article not to subject individuals to inordinate delays in legal proceedings."

[66] Malinverni (1998), 647–650.

[67] See, e.g., *Kudła v. Poland* (*supra* note 65), paras 146–160; *Sürmeli v. Germany* (appl. no. 75529/01), Judgement (Grand Chamber), 8 June 2006 (not yet reported), paras 97–117; *Aksoy v. Turkey* (appl. no. 21987/93), Judgement, 18 December 1996, Reports 1996-IV, 2260, paras. 51–57.

[68] Mahoney (2007).

3. Reforming the Regime

Over the past twenty years, the ECHR has been amended by a series of Protocols,[69] ultimately leading to the transformation of the legal system occasioned by Protocol no. 11. This strategy – of building the regime progressively through protocols – may have reached its limits. Most important, with the accession of the Eastern European States, the Council of Europe now comprises a much less homogeneous family of Contracting States. Because each additional Protocol requires ratification by all Contracting States (each State possesses a veto over proposed changes), it may be difficult or impossible to reform the regime through protocols in the future. If so, the ECHR regime may itself become mired in systemic problems for which no systemic solutions will be forthcoming. The Court might be allowed to propose changes to its jurisdiction to the Council of Europe, which would approve them by majority or a qualified majority of States. Yet such a reform would itself require unanimity, which may not be forthcoming.

Protocol no. 14 – which is strongly supported by the Court – illustrates the problem.[70] Protocol no. 14 aims at giving the Court the necessary procedural means and flexibility to process applications within a reasonable time, while enabling it to concentrate on those it finds most important. Under Protocol no. 14, the Court could declare a case inadmissible unless the applicant has not suffered a "significant disadvantage".[71] These and other provisions would reduce the time spent by the Court on manifestly inadmissible and repetitive cases. Although these reforms are no doubt necessary, it is already clear that they would not be sufficient to overcome the Court's overload.[72] Yet, alone among High Contracting Parties, Russia refuses to ratify Protocol no. 14, blocking its adoption.

One possible solution might be to allow the Court to undertake significant systemic reform on its own. The Council of Europe could authorize the Court to use Rule 103 (of the Rules of the Court) to amend its procedures as the Court sees fit, while reserving its own authority (under unanimity) to quash such changes. The Convention (Article 32 ECHR) also confers jurisdiction on the Court over all matters concerning the interpretation and application of the Convention and the Protocols. The Court might use these plenary powers to decide, in an appropriately explicit manner, to delegate some types of cases (of minor importance and without systemic implications) to national judges. As we argued above,[73] the Court could also choose to reduce its level of scrutiny when it comes to how national judges fine-tune the protection of qualified rights through pro-

---

[69] See *supra* Section A.1.

[70] For an overview of Protocol no. 14, see Caflisch and Keller; Greer (2005). For the ECtHR's view on Protocol No. 14 and other proposed reforms, see *Opinion of the Court on the Wise Persons' Report*, adopted by the Plenary Court, 2 April 2007.

[71] Article 12(3)(b) of Protocol no. 14 amending Article 35 ECHR.

[72] For a discussion of a range of reform proposals, see the *Report of the Group of Wise Persons to the Committee of Ministers*, CM(2006)203, 15 November 2006.

[73] See *supra* Section C.4.

portionality balancing. Such changes would enable the Court to concentrate on cases involving more serious human rights violations, and on defining the content and scope of rights, which national judges would then help to fine-tune.

F. A Europe of Rights

In post-Protocol no. 11 Europe, it makes little sense to conceptualize the ECHR as an international regime, external to the Contracting States. The Convention has a significant presence within national legal orders, even where this presence is resisted and opposed. Today, national officials routinely participate in a transnational judicial process whose reach into domestic law and politics is limited only by the ever-widening scope of the Convention itself, as determined by a transnational court. In virtually every State examined in this book, the Convention has provoked some measure of significant structural and procedural innovation, including the development of mechanisms for coordinating national law and the Convention, as the latter evolves. Reception processes have, in turn, provoked deep changes in European Government, through the accumulation of incremental, step-by-step adjustments to the demands of the Strasbourg Court. National officials are, gradually but inexorably, being socialized into a Europe of rights, a unique transnational legal space now seeking to develop its own logic of political and juridical legitimacy. The success of this endeavor will depend partly on the Council of Europe's ability to reform the ECHR legal system, and partly on the extent to which national officials sustain reception processes as means of further incorporating the Convention into national legal orders.

Bibliography[74]

Aromaa, K. and Viljanen, T. (eds.), International Key Issues in Crime Prevention and Criminal Justice (Helsinki, 2006).

Bárd, K., 'The Role of the ECHR in Shaping the European Model of the Criminal Process', in Aromaa, K. and Viljanen, T. (eds.), International Key Issues in Crime Prevention and Criminal Justice (Helsinki, 2006), 34.

Bruach, J.A., 'The Margin of Appreciation and the Jurisprudence of the European Court of Human Rights: Threat to the Rule of Law', *Columbia Journal of European Law* 11 (2005), 113.

Caflisch, L. and Keller, M., 'Le Protocole additionnel no. 15 à la Convention européenne des droits de l'homme', in Caflisch, L., Callewaert, J., Liddell, R., Mahoney, P., and Villiger, M. (eds.), Liber amicorum Luzius Wildhaber: Human Rights - Strasbourg Views/Droits de l'homme - Regards de Strasbourg (Kehl, 2007), 91.

Greer, S., The European Convention on Human Rights: Achievements, Problems and Prospects (Cambridge, 2006).

—, 'Protocol 14 and the Future of the European Court of Human Rights', *Public law* (Spring 2005), 83.

Helfer, L.R., 'Redesigning the European Court of Human Rights: Embeddedness as a Deep Structural Principle of the European Human Rights Regime', *European Journal of International Law* 19 (2008), 125.

Jackson, J.D., 'The Effect of Human Rights on Criminal Evidentiary Processes: Towards Convergence, Divergence or Realignment?', *Modern Law Review* 68/5 (2005), 737.

Krisch, N., 'The Open Architecture of European Human Rights Law', forthcoming in *Modern Law Review* 71 (2008), 183.

Mahoney, P., 'Thinking a Small Unthinkable: Repatriating Reparation from the European Court of Human Rights to the National Legal Order', in Caflisch, L., Callewaert, J., Liddell, R., Mahoney, P., and Villiger, M. (eds.), Liber amicorum Luzius Wildhaber: Human Rights - Strasbourg Views/Droits de l'homme - Regards de Strasbourg (Kehl, 2007), 263.

Malinverni, G., 'Observations –Variations sur un thème encore méconnu: l'article 13 de la Convention européenne des droits de l'homme', *Revue trimestrielle des droits de l'homme* 33/9 (1998), 647.

Paraskeva, C., 'Reforming the European Court of Human Rights. An Ongoing Challenge', *Nordic Journal of International Law* 76/2–3 (2007), 185.

Polakiewicz, J., 'The Status of the Convention in National Law', in Blackburn, R. and Polakiewicz, J. (eds.), Fundamental Rights in Europe (Oxford, 2001), 31.

Pinelli, C., 'Conditionality and Enlargement in Light of EU Constitutional Developments', *European Law Journal*, 10/3 (May 2004), 354.

Stone Sweet, 'Proportionality Balancing and Global Constitutionalism,' *Columbia Journal of Transnational Law* 47 (forthcoming 2008).

---

[74] See also the bibliography of the Introduction.

Wildhaber, L., 'A Constitutional Future for the European Court of Human Rights?', *Human Rights Law Journal* 23 (2000), 161.

—, 'The European Court of Human Rights: The Past, the Present, the Future', *American University International Law Review* 22 (2007), 521.

Overview of the Activity of the European Court of Human Rights

Statistics – Explanatory Note

The appendix includes statistics on decision on the merits and friendly settlements. Decisions on admissibility of applications, and on just satisfaction, are omitted.

Due to its general importance, data on the problem of lengthy trial proceedings under Article 6(1) ECHR are reported separately. All other aspects of Article 6(1) ECHR are reported under the heading, "Art. 6(1) (fair trial)".

Because Article 6(3) ECHR "merely exemplifies the minimum guarantees which must be accorded to the accused in the context of the 'fair trial' referred to in Art. 6(1)",[1] instances in which the Court found a violation of Article 6(3) ECHR appear only under that heading, not under both Article 6(1) and Article 6 (3) ECHR.

Information on findings of violation under Article 14 ECHR in combination with another provision is only given under Article 14, unless the Court examined the complaint separately under both provisions.

For each State covered, Table 1 reports data on the annual number: of applications lodged (provisional files opened: available since 1983); of applications registered; and of decisions rendered on the merits. The latter includes the number of decisions of both the Court and the Committee of Ministers. The fourth column reports data on violations found (V), non-violations (NV), and friendly settlements (FS). The last column – "Articles Concerned" – refers to the provision(s) of the ECHR on which the complaint, decision, or friendly settlement was based.

The statistics presented in this Appendix were collected from the following sources: *HUDOC* (the on-line data base of the ECHR); *European Court of Human Rights Series A: Judgments and Decisions*; *Reports of Judgments and Decisions of the European Court of Human Rights*; *European Commission of Human Rights Decisions and Reports*; *European Court of Human Rights Annual Reports*; *European Court of Human Rights Survey of Activities* (annual); *Yearbook of the European Convention on Human Rights*.

---

[1] *Adolf v. Austria* (appl. no. 8269/78), Report of the Commission (Plenary), 8 October 1980, Series B, Vol. 43, para. 64.

Ireland

1. Applications, Decisions on the Merits, and Friendly Settlements per Year

Year	Applications lodged	Applications registered	Decisions on the merits	Court:			Committee of Ministers:			Articles concerned
				V	NV	FS	V	NV	FS	
1955	not available	1								
1956	not available	1								
1957	not available	3								
1958	not available	1								
1959	not available	3								
1960	not available	3								
1961	not available	2	1		1					Court: Art. 7: 1 NV
1962	not available									
1963	not available	1								
1964	not available									
1965	not available	2								
1966	not available									
1967	not available	2								
1968	not available	1								
1969	not available	4								
1970	not available	1								

Year	Applications lodged	Applications registered	Decisions on the merits	Court:			Committe of Ministers:			Articles concerned
				V	NV	FS	V	NV	FS	
1971	not available	6								
1972	not available	4								
1973	not available	2								
1974	not available	2								
1975	not available	6								
1976	not available	5								
1977	not available	3								
1978	not available	9								
1979	not available	5	1	1						Court: Art. 6 (1) (fair trial): 1 V; Art. 8: 1 V
1980	not available	4								
1981	not available	9								
1982	not available	23								
1983	42	9								
1984	46	8								
1985	40	5								
1986	29	4	1	1						Court: Art. 8: 1 V, 1 NV; Art. 12: 1 NV; Art. 14: 1 NV
1987	40	5								
1988	32	5	1	1						Court: Art. 8: 1 V
1989	28	11								

Year	Applications lodged	Applications registered	Decisions on the merits	Court:			Committe of Ministers:			Articles concerned
				V	NV	FS	V	NV	FS	
1990	21	13								
1991	27	7	1	1						Court: Art. 13: 1 NV; Art. 14: 1 V, 1 NV; Prot. 1 Art. 1: 1 NV
1992	25	9	1	1						Court: Art. 10: 1 V; Art. 14: 1 NV
1993	29	5								
1994	43	18	1	1						Court: Art. 6 (1) (fair trial): 1 V; Art. 8: 1 V
1995	36	20								
1996	50	18								
1997	51	20	1				1			Committee of Ministers: Art. 6 (1) (length): 1 V
1998	41	19								
1999	37	20	1				1			Committee of Ministers: Art. 6 (1) (length): 1 V
2000	59	18	2	2						Court: Art. 5 (4): 1 FS; Art. 6 (1) (fair trial): 2 V; Art. 6 (2): 2 V
2001	56	16	1		1					Court: Art. 6 (1) (fair trial): 1 NV
2002	85	45	1	1						Court: Art. 3: 1 NV; Art. 5 (1): 1 V; Art. 5 (5): 1 V; Art. 8: 1 NV; Art. 14: 1 NV
2003	76	29	2	1	1					Court: Art. 6 (1) (length): 1 V; Art. 10: 1 NV; Art. 13: 1 V
2004	64	32	2	2						Court: Art. 6 (1) (length): 2 V; Art. 13: 1 V

Year	Applications lodged	Applications registered	Decisions on the merits	Court: V	NV	FS	Committe of Ministers: V	NV	FS	Articles concerned
2005	62	45	3	1	2					Court: Art. 6 (1) (length): 1 V; Art. 10: 1 NV; Prot. 1 Art. 1: 1 NV
2006	69	40								
Total	1088	524	20	13	5	0	2	0	0	

V   finding at least one violation
NV   finding no violation
FS   friendly settlement

Entry intro force of the Convention: 9.3.1953
Inception of right of individual application: 6.5.1955

Population in 2006 (Eurostat): 4209019
Applications lodged in % of population: 0,00150881

Ireland

2. Distribution of Decisions by ECHR Provision

	Court			Committee of Ministers			Total
	finding of violation	finding of no violation	FS	finding of violation	finding of no violation	FS	
Art. 3		1					1
Art. 5 (1)	1						1
Art. 5 (4)			1				1
Art. 5 (5)	1						1
Art. 6 (1) fair trial	4	1					5
Art. 6 (1) length	4			2			6
Art. 6 (2)	2						2
Art. 7		1					1
Art. 8	4	2					6
Art. 10	1	2					3
Art. 12		1					1
Art. 13	2	1					3
Art. 14	1	4					5
Prot. 1-1		2					2

Ireland

3. Distribution of Decisions by ECHR Provision per Year

Article	1961	1962	1963	1964	1965	1966	1967	1968	1969	1970	1971	1972	1973	1974	1975	1976	1977	1978	1979	1980	1981	1982	1983	1984	1985	1986	1987
3																											
5 (1)																											
5 (4)																											
5 (5)																											
6 (1) fair trial																			1								
6 (1) length																											
6 (2)																											
7	1																										
8																			1							2	
10																											
12																										1	
13																											
14																										1	
Prot. 1-1																											

Article	1988	1989	1990	1991	1992	1993	1994	1995	1996	1997	1998	1999	2000	2001	2002	2003	2004	2005	2006
3															1				
5 (1)															1				
5 (4)													1						
5 (5)															1				
6 (1) fair trial							1						2						
6 (1) length										1		1		1		1	2	1	
6 (2)													2						
7																			
8	1						1								1				
10					1											1		1	
12																			
13				1												1	1		
14				2											1		1		
Prot. 1-1				1														1	

United Kingdom

1. Applications, Decisions on the Merits, and Friendly Settlements per Year

Year	Applications lodged	Applications registered	Decisions on the merits	Court:			Committe of Ministers:			Articles concerned
				V	NV	FS	V	NV	FS	
1965	not available									
1966	not available	26								
1967	not available	62								
1968	not available	70								
1969	not available	50								
1970	not available	126								
1971	not available	271								
1972	not available	294								
1973	not available	105								
1974	not available	179								
1975	not available	197	1	1						Court: Art. 6 (1) (length): 1 V; Art. 8: 1 V
1976	not available	153	1		1					Court: Art. 10: 1 NV; Art. 14: 1 NV; Prot.1 Art. 1: 1 NV
1977	not available	148								
1978	not available	97	2	2						Court: Art. 3: 2 V; Art. 14: 1 NV

Year	Applications lodged	Applications registered	Decisions on the merits	Court:			Committe of Ministers:			Articles concerned
				V	NV	FS	V	NV	FS	
1979	not available	100	3	1				2		Court: Art. 10: 1 V; Art. 14: 1 NV Committee of Ministers: Art. 5 (1): 1 NV; Art. 8: 1 NV; Art. 9: 1 NV; Art. 10: 2 NV; Art. 14: 2 NV
1980	not available	103								
1981	not available	138	7	3			2	2		Court: Art. 5 (1): 1 NV; Art. 5 (4): 1 V; Art. 8: 1 V; Art. 11: 1 V; Art. 13: 1 NV Committee of Ministers: Art. 5 (4): 1 NV; Art. 6 (1) (fair trial): 1 NV; Art. 12: 2 V; Art. 13: 1 NV
1982	not available	190	2	1			1			Court: Art. 3: 1 NV; Prot.1 Art. 2: 1 V Committee of Ministers: Art. 8: 1 V
1983	785	152	3	1			2			Court: Art. 6 (1) (fair trial): 1 V; Art. 8: 1 V; Art. 13: 1 V Committee of Ministers: Art. 5 (4): 1 V; Art. 6 (1) (length): 1 V
1984	825	128	2	2						Court: Art. 6 (1) (fair trial): 1 V; Art. 6 (3): 2 V; Art. 8: 2 V; Art. 13: 1 V
1985	768	113	4	1	1		2			Court: Art. 5 (1): 1 NV; Art. 5 (4): 1 NV; Art. 6 (1) (fair trial): 1 NV; Art. 13: 1 V; Art. 14: 1 V Committee of Ministers: Art. 5 (1): 1 NV; Art. 5 (4): 2 V

Year	Applications lodged	Applications registered	Decisions on the merits	Court:			Committe of Ministers:			Articles concerned
				V	NV	FS	V	NV	FS	
1986	763	138	10	1	4		5			Court: Art. 6 (1) (fair trial): 3 NV; Art. 8: 1 V, 1 NV; Art. 12: 1 NV; Art. 13: 2 NV; Art. 14: 3 NV; Prot. 1 Art. 1: 3 NV Committee of Ministers: Art. 5 (1): 1 NV; Art. 5 (4): 1 V; Art. 6 (1) (fair trial): 3 V; Art. 8: 3 V; Art. 10: 1 V
1987	781	140	9	6	1		2			Court: Art. 5 (1): 2 NV; Art. 5 (4): 1 V; Art. 6 (1) (fair trial): 3 V, 1 NV; Art. 6 (1) (length): 3 V; Art. 6 (3): 1 NV; Art. 8: 3 V, 1 NV; Art. 14: 2 NV Committee of Ministers: Art. 6 (1) (fair trial): 2 V; Art. 8: 2 V; Art. 13: 1 V
1988	768	145	4	2				2		Court: Art. 5 (1): 1 NV; Art. 5 (3): 1 V; Art. 5 (4): 1 NV; Art. 5 (5): 1 V; Art. 8: 1 V; Art. 13: 1 NV Committee of Ministers: Art. 6 (1) (fair trial): 1 NV; Art. 6 (1) (length): 2 NV; Art. 13: 1 NV; Art. 14: 1 NV; Prot. 1 Art. 1: 1 NV
1989	925	224	7	2	1		2	2		Court: Art. 3: 1 V; Art. 6 (3): 1 NV; Art. 8: 1 V, 1 NV; Art. 10: 1 NV; Art. 13: 1 NV Committee of Ministers: Art. 8: 1 V, 2 NV; Art. 12: 1 NV; Art. 13: 1 V; Prot. 1 Art. 2: 1 V
1990	1067	236	6	4	1		1			Court: Art. 5 (1): 1 V; Art. 5 (2): 1 NV; Art. 5 (4): 1 V; Art. 5 (5): 2 V; Art. 6 (3): 1 V; Art. 8: 1 V; Art. 13: 1 NV Committee of Ministers: Art. 8: 1 V; Art. 13: 1 V

Year	Applications lodged	Applications registered	Decisions on the merits	Court:			Committee of Ministers:			Articles concerned
				V	NV	FS	V	NV	FS	
1991	843	202	3	2	1					Court: Art. 3: 1 NV; Art. 10: 2 V; Art. 13: 3 NV; Art. 14: 2 NV
1992	908	222	3	1	1	1	1			Court: Art. 3: 1 FS; Art. 6 (1) (fair trial): 1 NV; Art. 8: 1 V, 1 FS; Art. 13: 1 FS Committee of Ministers: Art. 10: 1 NV; Art. 13: 1 NV; Art. 14: 1 NV
1993	648	205	4	1	3	2				Court: Art. 3: 1 NV; Art. 5 (5): 1 NV; Art. 6 (1) (length). 1 V; Art. 8: 1 NV, 1 FS; Art. 10: 1 FS; Art. 11: 1 NV, Art. 13: 2 NV, 1 FS; Art. 14: 1 FS
1994	946	236	13	3	3	1	6	1		Court: Art. 5 (1): 1 V; Art. 5 (2): 1 V; Art. 5 (4): 1 NV; Art. 5 (5): 1 V; Art. 6 (1) (fair trial): 2 NV; Art. 6 (3): 2 V; Art. 8: 1 V, 1 FS; Art. 13: 1 V Committee of Ministers: Art. 3: 1 NV; Art. 5 (1) 1 NV; Art. 5 (3): 1 V; Art. 5 (4): 3 V; Art. 5 (5): 2 V; Art. 6 (1) (fair trial): 2 V; Art. 13: 1 NV
1995	1249	413	12	5	3		4			Court: Art. 2: 1 V; Art. 6 (1) (fair trial): 2 V, 2 NV; Art. 7: 1 V, 2 NV; Art. 8: 1 V; Art. 10: 1 V; Art. 14: 2 NV; Prot. 1 Art. 1 1 V Committee of Ministers: Art. 5 (1): 1 V; Art. 5 (2): 1 V; Art. 5 (4): 1 V; Art. 5 (5): 1 V; Art. 8: 1 V, 1 NV; Art. 13: 2 V

Year	Applications lodged	Applications registered	Decisions on the merits	Court:			Committe of Ministers:			Articles concerned
				V	NV	FS	V	NV	FS	
1996	1415	471	14	7	4		3			Court: Art. 3: 1 V; Art. 5 (1): 2 NV; Art. 5 (4): 3 V; Art. 6 (1) (fair trial): 1 V, 3 NV; Art. 6 (2): 1 NV; Art. 8: 2 NV; Art. 10: 1 V, 1 NV; Art. 13: 1 V; Art. 14: 3 NV Committee of Ministers: Art. 5 (1): 1 V; Art. 5 (4): 2 V; Art. 6 (1) (length): 1 V
1997	1209	451	22	6	4		12			Court: Art. 3: 1 V; Art. 5 (1): 1 V; Art. 6 (1) (fair trial): 2 V, 2 NV; Art. 6 (1) (length): 1 V; Art. 8: 1 V, 2 NV; Art. 13: 1 V, 1 NV; Art. 14: 3 NV, Prot. 1 Art. 1: 1 NV Committee of Ministers: Art. 5 (3): 1 V; Art. 5 (4): 2 V; Art. 5 (5): 2 V; Art. 6 (1) (length): 1 V; Art. 6 (2): 2 V; Art. 6 (3): 5 V; Art. 8: 1 V
1998	1092	407	15	6	3		3	3		Court: Art. 2: 1 NV; Art. 3: 1 V; Art. 5 (1): 1 NV; Art. 5 (5): 1 NV; Art. 6 (1) (fair trial): 2 V, 1 NV; Art. 6 (3): 1 NV; Art. 8: 1 V, 3 NV; Art. 10: 2 V, 2 NV; Art. 11: 1 NV; Art. 12: 1 NV; Art. 14: 1 NV, Prot. 1 Art. 3: 1 NV Committee of Ministers: Art. 5 (4): 1 V; Art. 5 (5): 1 V; Art. 6 (1) (fair trial): 2 NV; Art. 6 (1) (length): 1 NV; Art. 6 (2): 2 NV; Art. 6 (3): 1 V, 2 NV; Art. 8: 1 V; Art. 13: 1 V

Year	Applications lodged	Applications registered	Decisions on the merits	Court:			Committee of Ministers:			Articles concerned
				V	NV	FS	V	NV	FS	
1999	1028	431	19	12		2	7			Court: Art. 3: 5 NV; Art. 5 (1): 2 NV; Art. 5 (3): 1 V; Art. 5 (4): 2 V, 1 NV; Art. 5 (5): 1 V; Art. 6 (1) (fair trial): 8 V, 1 FS; Art. 6 (1) (length): 2 NV; Art. 8: 2 V; Art. 10: 1 V; Art. 14: 2 NV, 1 FS; Prot. 1 Art. 1: 1 FS; Prot. 1 Art. 3: 1 V Committee of Ministers: Art. 5 (1): 4 V; Art. 5 (5): 4 V; Art. 6 (1) (fair trial): 7 V; Art. 6 (3): 5 V
2000	1594	625	23	15	3	5	5			Court: Art. 3: 2 NV; Art. 5 (3): 2 V; Art. 5 (4): 2 V; Art. 5 (5): 3 V; Art. 6 (1) (fair trial): 6 V, 6 NV, 2 FS; Art. 6 (1) (length): 1 V, 1 NV; Art. 6 (2): 1 NV; Art. 6 (3): 2 V; Art. 8: 3 V, 1 NV, 2 FS; Art. 9: 1 NV; Art. 13: 1 V; Art. 14:1 NV, 3 FS Committee of Ministers: Art. 6 (1) (fair trial): 2 V
2001	1494	479	28	19	9	1				Court: Art. 2: 4 V, 1 NV; Art. 3: 4 V, 2 NV; Art. 5 (1): 1 NV; Art. 5 (3): 2 V; Art. 5 (4): 1 V; Art. 5 (5): 2 V; Art. 6 (1) (fair trial): 4 V, 13 NV, 1 FS; Art. 6 (2): 1 NV; Art. 6 (3): 1 V, 2 NV; Art. 8: 4 V, 7 NV; Art. 13: 5 V, 7 NV; Art. 14: 10 NV; Prot. 1 Art. 1: 5 NV; Prot. 1 Art. 2: 3 NV
2002	1525	986	34	30	4	6				Court: Art. 2: 3 V, 1 NV; Art. 3: 1 V, 3 NV; Art. 5 (1): 1 V, 1 NV; Art. 5 (3): 1 V; Art. 5 (4): 3 V; Art. 6 (1) (fair trial): 6 V, 6 NV; Art. 6 (1) (length): 5 V; Art. 6 (3): 2 V, 1 NV; Art. 8: 11 V, 3 NV, 1 FS; Art. 9: 1 NV; Art. 11: 1 V; Art. 12: 2 V; Art. 13: 7 V, 3 NV, 1 FS; Art. 14: 1 V, 7 NV, 6 FS; Prot. 1 Art. 1: 1 NV, 2 FS

Year	Applications lodged	Applications registered	Decisions on the merits	Court:			Committe of Ministers:			Articles concerned
				V	NV	FS	V	NV	FS	
2003	1396	685	22	20	2	3				Court: Art. 2: 1 V; Art. 3: 1 V, 1 FS; Art. 5 (1): 1 NV; Art. 5 (4): 4 V; Art. 5 (5): 1 V; Art. 6 (1) (fair trial): 2 V, 1 NV; Art. 6 (1) (length): 4 V; Art. 6 (3): 2 V; Art. 8: 5 V, 1 NV, 1 FS; Art. 10: 1 NV; Art. 11: 1 NV; Art. 13: 5 V, 1 NV, 2 FS; Art. 14: 2 FS; Prot. 1 Art. 1: 1 V
2004	1423	745	19	19		4				Court: Art. 5 (1): 1 V, 2 FS; Art. 5 (3): 1 V; Art. 5 (4): 2 V; Art. 5 (5): 2 V; Art. 6 (1) (fair trial): 8 V, 1 NV, 2 FS; Art. 6 (1) (length): 4 V, 2 FS; Art. 6 (3): 2 V, 2 FS; Art. 8: 3 V, 1 FS; Art. 13: 1 V, 1 NV; Art. 14: 1 V, 1 FS; Prot. 1 Art. 3: 1 V
2005	1652	1007	15	15		2				Court: Art. 2: 2 NV; Art. 5 (1): 2 V, 3 NV, 2 FS; Art. 5 (4): 2 V; Art. 5 (5): 4 V, 1 NV, 1 FS; Art. 6 (1) (fair trial): 3 V, 1 NV, 2 FS; Art. 6 (1) (length): 2 V; Art. 6 (3): 3 V, 2 FS; Art. 8: 1 V; Art. 10: 1 V, 1 NV; Art. 12: 1 V; Art. 13: 1 V, 4 NV; Art. 14: 1 V, 2 NV; Prot. 1 Art. 1: 1 V, 1 NV; Prot. 1 Art. 3: 1 V
2006	1557	844	18	10	8	6				Court: Art. 2: 1 NV; Art. 3: 1 NV; Art. 5 (1): 1 NV; Art. 5 (2): 1 V; Art. 5 (3): 1 NV; Art. 6 (1) (fair trial): 2 V; Art. 6 (1) (length): 1 V; Art. 6 (2): 1 V; Art. 8: 4 V, 2 NV, 1 FS; Art. 12: 1 NV, 1 FS; Art. 13: 2 V, 1 FS; Art. 14: 1 V, 7 NV, 5 FS
Total	26661	11994	325	198	57	33	58	12	0	

V   finding at least one violation
NV   finding no violation
FS   friendly settlement

Entry intro force of the Convention: 9.3.1953
Inception of right of individual application: 7.14.1966

Population in 2006 (Eurostat):   60393100
Applications lodged in % of population: 0,002751751

United Kingdom

2. Distribution of Decisions by ECHR Provision

	Court			Committee of Ministers			Total
	finding of violation	finding of no violation	FS	finding of violation	finding of no violation	FS	
Art. 2	9	6					15
Art. 3	12	16	2		1		31
Art. 5 (1)	7	17	4	6	4		38
Art. 5 (2)	2	1		1			4
Art. 5 (3)	8	1		2			11
Art. 5 (4)	22	4		13	1		40
Art. 5 (5)	17	3	1	10			31
Art. 6 (1) fair trial	51	44	8	16	4		123
Art. 6 (1) length	23	3	2	3	3		34
Art. 6 (2)	1	3		2	2		8
Art. 6 (3)	20	7	4	11	2		44
Art. 7	1	2					3
Art. 8	50	25	9	11	4		99
Art. 9		2			1		3
Art. 10	9	7	1	1	3		21
Art. 11	2	3					5
Art. 12	3	3	1	2	1		10
Art. 13	28	28	6	6	4		72
Art. 14	5	48	19		4		76
Prot. 1-1	3	12	3		1		19
Prot. 1-2	1	3		1			5
Prot. 1-3	3	1					4

United Kingdom

3. Distribution of Decisions by ECHR Provision per Year

	1975	1976	1977	1978	1979	1980	1981	1982	1983	1984	1985	1986	1987	1988	1989	1990
Article																
2																
3				2				1						1		
5 (1)					1		1				2	1	2	1		1
5 (2)																1
5 (3)														1		
5 (4)							2		1		3	1	1	1		1
5 (5)														1		2
6 (1) fair trial							1		1	1	1	6	6	1		
6 (1) length	1								1				3	2		
6 (2)																
6 (3)										2			1		1	1
7																
8	1				1		1	1	1	2		5	6	1	5	2
9					1											
10		1			3							1			1	
11							1									
12							2					1			1	
13							2		1	1	1	2	1	2	2	2
14		1		1	3						1	3	2	1		
Prot. 1-1		1										3		1		
Prot. 1-2								1							1	
Prot. 1-3																

1991	1992	1993	1994	1995	1996	1997	1998	1999	2000	2001	2002	2003	2004	2005	2006
				1			1			5	4	1		2	1
1	1	1	1		1	1	1	5	2	6	4	2			1
			2	1	3	1	1	6		1	2	1	3	7	1
			1	1											1
			1				1		1	2	2	1	1		1
			4	1	5	2	1	3	2	1	3	4	2	2	
		1	3	1		2	2	5	3	2		1	2	6	
	1		4	4	4	4	5	16	16	18	12	3	11	6	2
		1				1	2	1	2	2	5	4	6	2	1
					1	2	2			1	1				1
			2		3	5	4	6	2	3	3	2	4	5	
				3											
	2	2	2	3	2	4	5	2	6	11	15	7	4	1	7
									1		1				
2	1	1		1	2		4	1				1		2	
		1					1				1	1			
							1				2			1	2
3	1	3	2	2	1	2	1		1	12	11	8	2	5	3
2	1	1		2	3	3	1	3	4	10	14	2	2	3	13
				1		1		1		5	3	1		2	
										3					
							1	1					1	1	

France

1. Applications, Decisions on the Merits, and Friendly Settlements per Year

Year	Applications lodged	Applications registered	Decisions on the merits	Court: V	NV	FS	Committe of Ministers: V	NV	FS	Articles concerned
1981	not available	7								
1982	not available	93								
1983	315	45								
1984	253	59								
1985	342	70								
1986	381	86	1	1						Court: Art. 5 (1): 1 V
1987	513	115								
1988	560	139	1		1	1				Court: Art. 5 (3): 1 FS; Art. 5 (4): 1 FS; Art. 6 (1) (fair trial): 1 NV; Art. 6 (1) (length): 1 FS; Art. 6 (2): 1 NV
1989	714	212	1	1		1				Court: Art. 6 (1) (length): 1 V; Art. 6 (3): 1 FS
1990	1017	248	4	3		1	1			Court: Art. 6 (1) (length): 1 FS; Art. 6 (3): 1 V; Art. 8: 1 V; Committe of Ministers: Art. 6 (1) (length): 1 V

Year	Applications lodged	Applications registered	Decisions on the merits	Court:			Committe of Ministers:			Articles concerned
				V	NV	FS	V	NV	FS	
1991	1728	400	7	3	1	1	2	1	1	Court: Art. 3: 1 FS; Art. 5 (3): 2 V; Art. 5 (4): 1 NV; Art. 6 (1) (length): 1 V, 1 NV; Art. 8: 1 FS; Art. 11: 1 V; Committe of Ministers: Art. 6 (1) (fair trial): 1 NV; Art. 6 (1) (length): 2 V
1992	1648	353	9	7	2	1				Court: Art. 3: 1 V; Art. 5 (1): 1 NV; Art. 5 (3): 1 V, 1 FS; Art. 6 (1) (fair trial): 1 V, 3 NV; Art. 6 (1) (length): 4 V; Art. 6 (2): 1 NV; Art. 6 (3): 1 V; Art. 8: 1 V
1993	1383	399	14	7	4		2	1		Court: Art. 5 (4): 1 NV; Art. 6 (1) (fair trial): 1 V, 1 NV; Art. 6 (1) (length): 1 V, 1 NV; Art. 6 (3): 2 V, 1 NV; Art. 8: 4 V; Committe of Ministers: Art. 6 (1) (length): 2 V, 1 NV
1994	1637	439	11	4	2	1	2	3		Court: Art. 5 (1): 1 NV; Art. 6 (1) (fair trial): 1 NV; Art. 6 (1) (length): 4 V, 1 FS; Art. 6 (2):1 NV; Committe of Ministers: Art. 6 (1) (length): 2 V, 3 NV
1995	1620	471	33	8	6	1	16	3		Court: Art. 5 (1): 1 V; Art. 5 (3): 1 NV; Art. 5 (4): 1 NV; Art. 6 (1) (fair trial): 2 V, 1 NV; Art. 6 (1) (length): 1 V, 1 NV, 1 FS; Art. 6 (2):1 V; Art. 7: 1 V, 1 NV; Art. 8: 1 V; Art. 10: 1 V; Prot. 4 Art. 2: 1 NV; Committe of Ministers: Art. 5 (3): 2 V; Art. 5 (4): 1 V; Art. 6 (1) (length): 12 V, 3 NV; Art. 8: 1 V

Year	Applications lodged	Applications registered	Decisions on the merits	Court:			Committe of Ministers:			Articles concerned
				V	NV	FS	V	NV	FS	
1996	2175	600	30	4	7	1	19			Court: Art. 5 (1): 1 V; Art. 6 (1) (fair trial): 2 V, 3 NV, 1 FS; Art. 6 (1) (length): 1 V, 1 NV; Art. 6 (3): 2 V; Art. 7: 1 NV; Art. 8: 2 NV; Prot. 1 Art. 1: 1 NV Committe of Ministers: Art. 5 (3): 3 V; Art. 6 (1) (fair trial): 1 NV; Art. 6 (1) (length): 14 V, 1 NV; Art. 8: 4 V
1997	1968	558	97	5	5		84	3		Court: Art. 3: 1 V; Art. 5 (3): 1 V; Art. 6 (1) (fair trial): 3 V, 1 NV; Art. 6 (1) (length): 10 V, 2 FS; Art. 6 (3): 2 V; Art. 8: 1 V, 1 NV, 1 FS; Art. 10: 1 V; Art. 11: 1 V; Art. 14: 2 V; Prot. 1 Art. 1: 1 V Committe of Ministers: Art. 5 (1): 1 V; Art. 5 (3): 3 V; Art. 5 (4): 4 V; Art. 6 (1) (fair trial): 9 V, 1 NV; Art. 6 (1) (length): 61 V, 1 NV; Art. 6 (3): 3 V; Art. 8: 9 V, 1 NV; Art. 11: 1 NV; Art. 13: 1 V; Art. 14: 2 NV; Prot. 1 Art. 1: 1 V, 2 NV
1998	2198	643	69	20	3		44	2		Court: Art. 3: 1 NV; Art. 5 (3): 1 V; Art. 5 (4): 1 V; Art. 6 (1) (fair trial): 8 V, 2 NV; Art. 6 (1) (length): 11 V, 1 NV; Art. 6 (2): 1 NV; Art. 8: 1 V, 1 NV; Art. 10: 1 V Committe of Ministers: Art. 5 (2): 1 V; Art. 5 (3): 1 V; Art. 5 (4): 4 V; Art. 5 (5): 1 V; Art. 6 (1) (fair trial): 4 V; Art. 6 (1) (length): 32 V, 2 NV; Art. 8: 5 V; Art. 13: 1 V

Year	Applications lodged	Applications registered	Decisions on the merits	Court:			Committe of Ministers:			Articles concerned
				V	NV	FS	V	NV	FS	
1999	2581	870	62	16	2	3	41	3		Court: Art. 3: 1 V; Art. 5 (3): 1 V; Art. 6 (1) (fair trial): 3 V, 1 NV; Art. 6 (1) (length): 10 V, 2 FS; Art. 6 (3): 2 V; Art. 8: 1 V, 1 NV, 1 FS; Art. 10: 1 V; Art. 11: 1 V; Art. 14: 2 V; Prot. 1 Art. 1: 1 V. Committe of Ministers: Art. 5 (3): 1 NV; Art. 6 (1) (fair trial): 6 V, 1 NV; Art. 6 (1) (length): 30 V, 1 NV; Art. 6 (2): 1 V; Art. 8: 5 V; Prot. 1 Art. 1: 1 V
2000	2937	1032	66	48	8	11	10			Court: Art. 3: 1 NV; Art. 5 (3): 1 V; Art. 6 (1) (fair trial): 6 V, 3 NV; Art. 6 (1) (length): 40 V, 5 NV, 10 FS; Art. 6 (3): 1 V; Art. 8: 1 NV, 1 FS; Art. 9: 1 NV; Art. 10: 1 V; Art. 14: 1 V, 1 NV; Prot. 1 Art. 1: 1 V. Committe of Ministers: Art. 6 (1) (fair trial): 2 V; Art. 6 (1) (length): 7 V; Art. 8: 2 V
2001	2829	1117	34	31	3	8				Court: Art. 5 (1): 1 NV; Art. 5 (3): 3 V, 1 NV; Art. 5 (5): 1 NV; Art. 6 (1) (fair trial): 8 V, 2 NV; Art. 6 (1) (length): 21 V, 8 FS; Art. 6 (3): 2 V; Art. 8: 2 V; Art. 10: 1 V; Art. 13: 1 NV; Prot. 4 Art. 2: 1 V; Prot. 7 Art. 2: 1 V
2002	2934	1606	67	61	6	6				Court: Art. 3: 1 V; Art. 5 (1): 1 FS; Art. 5 (4): 4 V; Art. 6 (1) (fair trial): 9 V, 8 NV; Art. 6 (1) (length): 41 V, 2 NV, 5 FS; Art. 6 (3): 1 V, 1 NV; Art. 8: 1 V, 1 FS; Art. 10: 1 V; Art. 11: 1 NV, 1 FS; Art. 13: 1 V; Art. 14: 1 NV; Prot. 1 Art. 1: 3 V; Prot. 7 Art. 2: 1 NV; Prot. 7 Art. 4: 1 NV

Year	Applications lodged	Applications registered	Decisions on the merits	Court:			Committe of Ministers:			Articles concerned
				V	NV	FS	V	NV	FS	
2003	2904	1481	84	76	7	7	1			Court: Art. 3: 1 V; Art. 6 (1) (fair trial): 14 V, 5 NV, 2 FS; Art. 6 (1) (length): 60 V, 4 NV, 5 FS; Art. 6 (3): 1 V; Art. 8: 1 V, 3 NV; Art. 13: 7 V, 1 FS; Art. 14: 2 V, 1 NV; Prot. 1 Art. 1: 1 V; Prot. 7 Art. 2: 1 FS Committe of Ministers: Art. 5 (3): 1 V
2004	3025	1737	70	59	11	4				Court: Art. 2: 1 V, 1 NV: Art. 3: 2 V, 2 NV, 1 FS; Art. 5 (1): 2 V; Art. 5 (3): 1 V; Art. 6 (1) (fair trial): 20 V, 6 NV, 1 FS; Art. 6 (1) (length): 32 V, 1 NV, 3 FS; Art. 6 (2): 1 NV; Art. 6 (3): 2 V, 1 NV; Art. 7: 1 V, 1 NV; Art. 8: 1 V, 1 NV; Art. 10: 1 V, 3 NV; Art. 13: 2 V, 1 NV; Art. 14: 2 V; Prot. 1 Art. 1: 1 NV
2005	2826	1827	57	51	6	1				Court: Art. 3: 1 NV; Art. 4: 1 V; Art. 5 (3): 2 V; Art. 5 (4): 1 V; Art. 6 (1) (fair trial): 25 V, 6 NV, 1 FS; Art. 6 (1) (length): 14 V, 1 NV; Art. 6 (3): 6 V, 1 NV; Art. 8: 3 V, 3 NV; Art. 10: 1 V, 1 NV; Art. 13: 2 V, 2 NV; Art. 14: 1 FS; Prot. 1 Art. 1: 4 V; Prot. 1 Art. 3: 1 NV
2006	2841	1832	92	85	7					Court: Art. 2: 1 V; Art. 3: 2 V, 3 NV; Art. 5 (1): 1 V, 1 NV; Art. 5 (3): 1 V; Art. 5 (4): 5 V; Art. 6 (1) (fair trial): 38 V, 6 NV; Art. 6 (1) (length): 27 V, 1 NV; Art. 6 (3): 9 V, 1 NV; Art. 7: 1 V, 1 NV; Art. 8: 1 V, 1 NV; Art. 10: 3 V; Art. 13: 9 V; Prot. 1 Art. 1: 5 V, 1 NV
Total	41329	16439	809	490	81	92	180	14	0	

V   finding at least one violation
NV   finding no violation
FS   friendly settlement

Entry into force of the Convention: 5.3.1974
Inception of right of individual application: 10.2.1981

Population in 2006 (Eurostat):   62998773
Applications lodged in % of population: 0,004666354

France

2. Distribution of Decisions by ECHR Provision

	Court			Committee of Ministers			Total
	finding of violation	finding of no violation	FS	finding of violation	finding of no violation	FS	
Art. 2	2	1					3
Art. 3	8	9	2				19
Art. 4	1						1
Art. 5 (1)	6	4	2	1			13
Art. 5 (2)				1			1
Art. 5 (3)	14	2	2	10	1		29
Art. 5 (4)	11	3	1	9			24
Art. 5 (5)	1	1		1			3
Art. 6 (1) fair trial	139	49	5	21	4		218
Art. 6 (1) length	270	19	37	163	12		501
Art. 6 (2)	1	5		1			7
Art. 6 (3)	31	6	2	3			42
Art. 7	3	4					7
Art. 8	20	16	4	26	1		67
Art. 9		1					1
Art. 10	11	4					15
Art. 11	2	1	1		1		5
Art. 13	21	4	1	2			28
Art. 14	7	3	1		2		13
Prot. 1 Art. 1	11	2		2	2		17
Prot. 1 Art. 3		1					1
Prot. 4 Art. 2	1	1					2
Prot. 7 Art. 2	1	1	1				3
Prot. 7 Art. 4		1					1

France

3. Distribution of Decisions by ECHR Provision per Year

Article	2006	2005	2004	2003	2002	2001	2000	1999	1998	1997	1996	1995	1994	1993	1992	1991	1990	1989	1988	1987	1986
2	1		2																		
3	5	1	5	1	1				1	1	1	1			1	1			1		
4		1																			
5 (1)	2		2	1	1	1	1	1		2	1	1	1		1						1
5 (2)									1												
5 (3)	1	2	1	1				2	2	4	3	3			3	2					
5 (4)	5	1	1		4	4	1	2	5	4	4	2				1			1		
5 (5)			1			1			1												
6 (1) fair trial	44	32	27	21	17	10	11	11	14	13	7	3	1	2	3	1	2	1	1		
6 (1) length	28	15	36	69	48	29	62	43	46	63	17	18	10	5	4	4	2	1	1		
6 (2)			1					1	1			1	1		1				1		
6 (3)	10	7	3	2	2	2	4	2	7	5	2			3	3	1	1				
7			2								1	2									
8	2	6	2	4	2	2		8		14	6	2		4	1	2	2	1			
9	2						1														
10	3	2	4	4	1	1	1	1	1	1		1				1					

Year	11	13	14	P 1-1	P 1-3	P 4-2	P 7-2	P 7-4
2006		9						
2005		4	4	1				
2004		3	2	1				
2003		8	3	1			1	
2002	2	1	1	3			1	1
2001	1					1	1	
2000			2	1				
1999	1		2	2				
1998		1						
1997	1	1	2	3				
1996			1	1				
1995					1			
1994				1				
1993								
1992								
1991	1							
1990								
1989								
1988								
1987								
1986								

Germany

1. Applications, Decisions on the Merits, and Friendly Settlements per Year

Year	Applications lodged	Applications registered	Decisions on the merits	Court: V	NV	FS	Committe of Ministers: V	NV	FS	Articles concerned
1955	not available	121								
1956	not available	94								
1957	not available	81								
1958	not available	54								
1959	not available	131								
1960	not available	185								
1961	not available	199								
1962	not available	235								
1963	not available	152								
1964	not available	181								
1965	not available	183								
1966	not available	163								
1967	not available	230	1					1		Committe of Ministers: Art. 9: 1 NV; Art. 14: 1 NV
1968	not available	241	2		1			1		Court: Art. 5 (3): 1 NV; Art. 6 (1) (length): 1 NV; Committe of Ministers: Art. 3: 1 NV
1969	not available	235								

Year	Applications lodged	Applications registered	Decisions on the merits	Court: V	Court: NV	Court: FS	Committe of Ministers: V	Committe of Ministers: NV	Committe of Ministers: FS	Articles concerned
1970	not available	142								
1971	not available	164	2					2		Committe of Ministers: Art. 5 (3): 1 NV; Art. 6 (1) (length): 1 NV
1972	not available	156								
1973	not available	174								
1974	not available	141								
1975	not available	113								
1976	not available	142	2					2		Committe of Ministers: Art. 6 (1) (length): 2 NV
1977	not available	95								
1978	not available	115	6	2	1			3		Court: Art. 6 (1) (fair trial): 1 NV; Art. 6 (1) (length): 1 V; Art. 6 (3): 1 V; Art. 8: 1 NV; Art. 13: 1 NV. Committe of Ministers: Art. 5 (1): 2 NV; Art. 5 (3): 1 NV; Art. 5 (5): 1 NV; Art. 6 (1) (length): 1 NV; Art. 6 (3): 1 NV; Art. 8: 1 NV
1979	not available	120							1	Committe of Ministers: Art. 6 (1) (length): 1 FS
1980	not available	106								
1981	not available	109	1		1					Court: Art. 3: 1 NV; Art. 6 (1) (length): 1 NV; Art. 8: 1 NV; Art. 12: 1 NV
1982	not available	98	1	1						Court: Art. 6 (1) (length): 1 V
1983	770	93	2	1	1					Court: Art. 6 (1) (length): 1 NV; Art. 6 (3): 1 V
1984	752	115	1	1						Court: Art. 6 (3): 1 V

Year	Applications lodged	Applications registered	Decisions on the merits	Court:			Committe of Ministers:			Articles concerned
				V	NV	FS	V	NV	FS	
1985	578	106	2	2						Court: Art. 6 (1) (length): 1 V; Art.10: 1 V
1986	539	106	3	1	2					Court: Art. 6 (1) (length): 1 V; Art.10: 2 NV
1987	522	108	3		3					Court: Art. 6 (2): 3 NV
1988	606	113	1		1					Court: Art. 6 (1) (fair trial): 1 NV
1989	717	169	5	1	1		3			Court: Art. 6 (1) (length): 1 V; Art. 10: 1 NV; Committe of Ministers: Art. 6 (1) (length): 1 V; Art. 6 (3): 2 V
1990	618	146	1				1			Committe of Ministers: Art. 6 (1) (length): 1 V
1991	620	139	2		1			1		Court: Art. 5 (1): 1 NV; Art. 6 (1) (fair trial): 1 NV; Committe of Ministers: Art. 6 (3): 1 NV
1992	601	137	5	2	2		1			Court: Art. 5 (4): 1 V; Art. 6 (1) (fair trial): 2 NV; Art. 6 (3): 1 NV; Art. 8: 1 V; Committe of Ministers: Art. 6 (1) (length): 1 V
1993	672	148	3		1		1	1		Court: Art. 3: 1 NV; Committe of Ministers: Art. 6 (1) (fair trial): 1 NV; Art. 6 (1) (length): 1 V; Art. 6 (3): 1 NV
1994	836	188	6	1	1		4			Court: Art. 10: 1 NV; Art. 14: 1 V; Committe of Ministers: Art. 6 (1) (length): 4 V
1995	890	223	1	1						Court: Art. 10: 1 V; Art. 11: 1 V
1996	1080	334	2		1		1			Court: Art. 6 (1) (length): 1 NV; Committe of Ministers: Art. 5 (3): 1 V; Art. 6 (1) (length): 1 V

Year	Applications lodged	Applications registered	Decisions on the merits	Court:			Committe of Ministers:			Articles concerned
				V	NV	FS	V	NV	FS	
1997	1224	383	4	3			1			Court: Art. 5 (1): 1 V; Art. 6 (1) (length): 2 V Committe of Ministers: Art. 6 (1) (length): 1 V
1998	1601	350								
1999	1599	535	2		2					Court: Art. 6 (1) (fair trial): 2 NV
2000	1685	595	3	2	1					Court: Art. 6 (1) (fair trial): 1 V; Art. 6 (1) (length): 1 V, 1 NV; Art. 8: 1 V; Art. 14: 1 NV
2001	1620	718	16	13	3					Court: Art. 5 (3): 1 V; Art. 5 (4): 3 V; Art. 6 (1) (fair trial): 2 V, 1 NV; Art. 6 (1) (length): 5 V; Art. 6 (3): 1 V; Art. 7: 2 NV; Art. 8: 2 V, 2 NV; Art. 14: 3 V, 3 NV; Prot. 1 Art. 1: 1 NV
2002	1781	1019	8	6	2	1				Court: Art. 6 (1) (fair trial): 1 NV; Art. 6 (1) (length): 3 V; Art. 6 (2): 1 V; Art. 8: 1 V, 1 NV, 1 FS; Art. 10: 1 V; Art. 14: 1 NV; Prot. 1 Art. 1: 1 NV
2003	1935	998	11	10	1	1				Court: Art. 5 (1): 1 NV; Art. 5 (4): 1 V, 1 NV; Art. 6 (1) (fair trial): 1 V, 1 NV; Art. 6 (1) (length): 5 V, 1 FS; Art. 8: 2 V, 2 NV; Art. 14: 3 V; Prot. 1 Art. 1: 1 NV
2004	2562	1527	6	6						Court: Art. 5 (3): 1 V; Art. 6 (1) (fair trial): 1 NV; Art. 6 (1) (length): 2 V; Art. 8: 3 V, 1 NV; Prot. 1 Art. 1: 1 V

Year	Applications lodged	Applications registered	Decisions on the merits	Court:			Committe of Ministers:			Articles concerned
				V	NV	FS	V	NV	FS	
2005	2164	1582	13	10	3					Court: Art. 5 (1): 2 V, 1 NV; Art. 5 (3): 1 V; Art. 6 (1) (fair trial): 3 NV; Art. 6 (1) (length): 3 V, 1 NV; Art. 6 (2): 1 NV; Art. 8: 3 V, 2 NV; Art. 14: 2 V; Prot. 1 Art. 1: 1 NV
2006	2151	1587	8	6	2	2				Court: Art. 3: 1 V; Art. 5 (3): 1 NV; Art. 6 (1) (fair trial): 1 V, 1 NV; Art. 6 (1) (length): 5 V, 2 FS; Art. 13: 1 V, 1 FS
Total	28123	15579	123	69	31	4	12	11	1	

V   finding at least one violation
NV   finding no violation
FS   friendly settlement

Entry into force of the Convention: 9.3.1953
Inception of right of individual application: 7.5.1955

Population in 2006 (Eurostat):   82437995
Applications lodged in % of population: 0,002623005

Germany

2. Distribution of Decisions by ECHR Provision

	Court			Committee of Ministers			Total
	finding of violation	finding of no violation	FS	finding of violation	finding of no violation	FS	
Art. 2							0
Art. 3	1	2			1		4
Art. 4							0
Art. 5 (1)	3	3			2		8
Art. 5 (2)							0
Art. 5 (3)	3	2		1	2		8
Art. 5 (4)	5	1					6
Art. 5 (5)					1		1
Art. 6 (1) fair trial	5	16			1		22
Art. 6 (1) length	31	5	3	10	4	1	54
Art. 6 (2)	1	4					5
Art. 6 (3)	4	1		2	3		10
Art. 7		2					2
Art. 8	13	10	1		1		25
Art. 9					1		1
Art. 10	3	4					7
Art. 11	1						1
Art. 12		1					1
Art. 13	1	1	1				3
Art. 14	9	5			1		15
Prot. 1 Art. 1	1	4					5

Germany

3. Distribution of Decisions by ECHR Provision per Year

	1967	1968	1969	1970	1971	1972	1973	1974	1975	1976	1977	1978	1979	1980	1981	1982
Article																
3		1													1	
5 (1)												2				
5 (3)		1			1							1				
5 (4)																
5 (5)												1				
6 (1) fair trial												1				
6 (1) length	1				1					2		2	1		1	1
6 (2)																
6 (3)												2				
7																
8												2			1	
9	1															
10																
11																
12															1	
13												1				
14	1															
P 1-1																

	1983	1984	1985	1986	1987	1988	1989	1990	1991	1992	1993	1994	1995	1996	1997	1998
Article																
3											1					
5 (1)									1						1	
5 (3)														1		
5 (4)										1						
5 (5)																
6 (1) fair trial	1					1			1	2	1					
6 (1) length			1	1			2	1		1	1	4		2	3	
6 (2)					3											
6 (3)	1	1					2		1	1	1					
7																
8											1					
9																
10			1	2			1					1	1			
11													1			
12																
13																
14												1				
P 1-1																

1999	2000	2001	2002	2003	2004	2005	2006
							1
				1		3	
		1			1	1	1
		3		2			
2	1	3	1	2	1	3	2
	2	5	3	6	2	4	7
			1		1		
		1					
		2					
	1	4	3	4	4	5	
			1				
							1
	1	6	1	3		2	
		1	1	1	1	1	

Sweden

1. Applications, Decisions on the Merits, and Friendly Settlements per Year

Year	Applications lodged	Applications registered	Decisions on the merits	Court:			Committe of Ministers:			Articles concerned
				V	NV	FS	V	NV	FS	
1955	not available	2								
1956	not available	1								
1957	not available	1								
1958	not available	1								
1959	not available	2								
1960	not available	4								
1961	not available	2								
1962	not available	3								
1963	not available	3								
1964	not available	2								
1965	not available	2								
1966	not available	1								
1967	not available	3								
1968	not available	7								
1969	not available	9								
1970	not available	5								

Year	Applications lodged	Applications registered	Decisions on the merits	Court: V	Court: NV	Court: FS	Committe of Ministers: V	Committe of Ministers: NV	Committe of Ministers: FS	Articles concerned
1971	not available	4								
1972	not available	8								
1973	not available	3								
1974	not available	7								
1975	not available	9								
1976	not available	2	2		2					Court: Art. 11: 2 NV; Art. 13: 1 NV; Art. 14: 2 NV
1977	not available	9								
1978	not available	4								
1979	not available	9								
1980	not available	11								
1981	not available	8								
1982	not available	18	1	1						Court: Art. 6 (1) (fair trial): 1 V; Art. 14: 1 NV; Prot.1 Art. 1: 1 V
1983	240	46								
1984	192	51	2	1		1	1			Court: Art. 5 (3): 1 V, 1 FS; Art. 5 (4): 1 NV; Committe of Ministers: Art. 6 (1) (fair trial): 1 V
1985	168	64								
1986	180	68								
1987	198	77	3	2	1					Court: Art. 6 (1) (fair trial): 2 V; Art. 8: 1 NV; Art. 10: 1 NV; Art. 13: 1 NV

Year	Applications lodged	Applications registered	Decisions on the merits	Court: V	NV	FS	Committe of Ministers: V	NV	FS	Articles concerned
1988	208	88	2	2						Court: Art. 3: 1 NV; Art. 6 (1) (fair trial): 1 V, 1 NV; Art. 8: 1 V; Art. 13: 1 NV; Art. 14: 1 NV; Prot. 1 Art. 2: 1 NV
1989	223	84	8	4			2	2		Court: Art. 6 (1) (fair trial): 4 V; Art. 6 (1) (length): 1 NV; Art. 8: 1 V, 1 NV; Art. 11: 1 NV; Art. 13: 1 NV Committe of Ministers: Art. 5 (4): 1 NV; Art. 5 (5): 1 NV; Art. 6 (1) (fair trial): 2 V, 2 NV; Art. 13: 1 NV
1990	247	125	7	4		1	3			Court: Art. 3: 1 FS; Art. 6 (1) (fair trial): 3 V; Art. 8: 1 FS; Art. 13: 1 FS; Art. 14: 1 V, 1 NV; Prot. 1 Art. 1: 1 NV Committe of Ministers: Art. 6 (1) (fair trial): 3 V
1991	225	90	7	2	3		2			Court: Art. 3: 1 NV; Art. 6 (1) (fair trial): 2 V, 2 NV; Art. 8: 1 NV; Art. 14: 1 NV; Prot. 1 Art. 1: 1 NV Committe of Ministers: Art. 6 (1) (fair trial): 2 V
1992	233	82	4	1	1		2			Court: Art. 8: 1 V, 1 NV; Art. 13: 1 NV Committe of Ministers: Art. 6 (1) (fair trial): 2 V
1993	242	106	6	4			2			Court: Art. 6 (1) (fair trial): 4 V Committe of Ministers: Art. 6 (1) (fair trial): 1 V; Art. 6 (1) (length): 1 V
1994	360	161	2	1	1					Court: Art. 6 (1) (fair trial): 1 V, 1 NV
1995	334	165	1	1						Court: Art. 6 (1) (fair trial): 1 V; Art. 8: 1 V, 1 NV
1996	374	169	1		1					Court: Art. 6 (1) (fair trial): 1 NV; Art. 11: 1 NV; Art. 13: 1 NV; Prot. 1 Art. 1: 1 NV

Year	Applications lodged	Applications registered	Decisions on the merits	Court:			Committe of Ministers:			Articles concerned
				V	NV	FS	V	NV	FS	
1997	331	146	4		3		1			Court: Art. 6 (1) (fair trial): 3 NV; Art. 8: 1 NV; Art. 13: 2 NV Committe of Ministers: Art. 6 (1) (fair trial): 1 V
1998	323	156	5	1	1		3			Court: Art. 3: 1 FS; Art. 6 (1) (fair trial): 2 NV; Art. 6 (1) (length): 1 V; Art. 8: 1 NV Committe of Ministers: Art. 6 (1) (fair trial): 1 V; Art. 6 (1) (length): 2 V
1999	302	175								
2000	395	233	1			1	1			Court: Art. 6 (2): 1 FS; Art. 8: 1 FS Committe of Ministers: Art. 6 (1) (length): 1 FS
2001	399	246	0			3				Court: Art. 6 (1) (fair trial): 2 FS; Art. 6 (1) (length): 1 FS
2002	371	296	6	4	2	1				Court: Art. 6 (1) (fair trial): 4 V, 2 NV, 1 FS; Art. 6 (1) (length): 2 V, 1 FS; Art. 6 (2): 2 NV; Art. 6 (3): 1 NV
2003	436	257	3	2	1					Court: Art. 6 (1) (fair trial): 2 NV; Art. 6 (3): 1 NV; Art. 13: 1 V; Prot 1 Art. 1: 2 V
2004	524	398	1		1	5				Court: Art. 6 (1) (fair trial): 1 NV, 2 FS; Art. 6 (1) (length): 4 FS; Art. 6 (2): 1 FS
2005	587	448	4	4		2				Court: Art. 2: 1 V; Art. 3: 1 V; Art. 6 (1) (fair trial): 1 V, 3 FS; Art. 6 (1) (length): 1 V, 1 FS; Art. 8: 1 FS; Art. 13: 1 FS

Year	Applications lodged	Applications registered	Decisions on the merits	Court:			Committe of Ministers:			Articles concerned
				V	NV	FS	V	NV	FS	
2006	472	371	5	3	2	1				Court:Art. 6 (1) (fair trial): 1 V; Art. 6 (1) (length): 2 V, 1 FS; Art. 8: 1 V, 2 NV; Art. 10: 1 V; Art. 11: 1 V, Art. 13: 1 V; Prot. 1 Art. 1: 1 V
Total	7564	4242	75	37	19	15	17	2	0	

V   finding at least one violation
NV   finding no violation
FS   friendly settlement

Entry intro force of the Convention: 03.09.1953
Inception of right of individual application: 05.07.1955

Population in 2006 (Eurostat):   9047752
Applications lodged in % of population: 0,006513971

Sweden

2. Distribution of Decisions by ECHR Provision

	Court			Committee of Ministers			Total
	finding of violation	finding of no violation	FS	finding of violation	finding of no violation	FS	
Art. 2	1						1
Art. 3	1	2	2				5
Art. 5 (3)	1		1				2
Art. 5 (4)		1			1		2
Art. 6 (1) fair trial	25	15	8	13	2		63
Art. 6 (1) length	6	1	7	3		2	19
Art. 6 (2)		2	2				4
Art. 6 (3)		2					2
Art. 8	5	9	3				17
Art. 10	1	1					2
Art. 11	1	4					5
Art. 13	2	8	2		1		13
Art. 14	1	6					7
Prot. 1-1	4	3					7
Prot. 1-2		1					1

Sweden

3. Distribution of Decisions by ECHR Provision per Year

	1976	1977	1978	1979	1980	1981	1982	1983	1984	1985	1986	1987	1988	1989	1990	1991
Article																
2																
3													1		1	1
5 (3)									2							
5 (4)									1					1		
5 (5)														1		
6 (1) fair trial							1		1			2	2	8	6	6
6 (1) length														1		
6 (2)																
6 (3)																
8												1	1	2	1	1
10												1				
11		2												1		
13		1										1	1	2	1	
14		2					1						1		2	1
Prot. 1-1							1								1	1
Prot. 1-2													1			

1992	1993	1994	1995	1996	1997	1998	1999	2000	2001	2002	2003	2004	2005	2006
													1	
					1								1	
2	5	2	1	1	4	3			2	7	2	3	4	1
	1					3		1	1	3		4	2	3
								1		2		1		
										1	1			
2			2		1	1		1					1	3
														1
				1										1
1					1	2					1		1	1
				1							2			1

Norway

1. Applications, Decisions on the Merits, and Friendly Settlements per Year

Year	Applications lodged	Applications registered	Decisions on the merits	Court:			Committe of Ministers:			Articles concerned
				V	NV	FS	V	NV	FS	
1958	not available	1								
1959	not available	3								
1960	not available	2								
1961	not available	1								
1962	not available	1								
1963	not available	1								
1964	not available	5								
1965	not available	2								
1966	not available	1								
1967	not available	3								
1968	not available	1								
1969	not available	3								
1970	not available	7								
1971	not available	2								
1972	not available	4								
1973	not available	-								

Year	Applications lodged	Applications registered	Decisions on the merits	Court:			Committe of Ministers:			Articles concerned
				V	NV	FS	V	NV	FS	
1974	not available	1								
1975	not available	5								
1976	not available	1								
1977	not available	2								
1978	not available	2								
1979	not available	1								
1980	not available	1								
1981	not available	3								
1982	not available	2								
1983	14	4								
1984	16	4								
1985	17	3								
1986	12	3								
1987	14	2								
1988	31	4								
1989	30	7								
1990	34	18	1	1						Court: Art. 5 (4): 1 V
1991	27	11								
1992	34	15								
1993	31	18								

Year	Applications lodged	Applications registered	Decisions on the merits	Court: V	NV	FS	Committe of Ministers: V	NV	FS	Articles concerned
1994	34	16								
1995	34	21	1				1			Committe of Ministers: Art. 6 (1) (length): 1 V
1996	57	20	2	2						Court: Art. 6 (1) (fair trial): 1 V; Art. 6 (1) (length): 1 NV; Art. 8: 1 V
1997	41	18	1		1					Court: Art. 5 (1): 1 NV; Art. 5 (3): 1 NV
1998	49	22								
1999	41	20	2	2						Court: Art. 10: 2 V
2000	64	30	1	1						Court: Art. 10: 1 V
2001	61	49	1		1					Court: Art. 6 (1) (length):1 NV
2002	79	48								
2003	74	51	5	4	1					Court: Art. 6 (1) (fair trial): 1 V; Art. 6 (2): 3 V, 1 NV
2004	110	82								
2005	73	57								
2006	82	67	1	1						Court: Art. 6 (1) (fair trial): 1 V; Art. 6 (3): 1 V
Total	1059	645	15	11	3	0	1	0	0	

V finding at least one violation
NV finding no violation
FS friendly settlement

Entry into force of the Convention: 9.3.1953
Inception of right of individual application: 12.10.1955

Population in 2006 (Eurostat): 4640219
Applications lodged in % of population: 0,001584752

Norway

2. Distribution of Decisions by ECHR Provision

	Court			Committee of Ministers			Total
	finding of violation	finding of no violation	FS	finding of violation	finding of no violation	FS	
Art. 5 (1)		1					1
Art. 5 (3)		1					1
Art. 5 (4)	1						1
Art. 6 (1) fair trial	3						3
Art. 6 (1) length		2		1			3
Art. 6 (2)	3	1					4
Art. 6 (3)	1						1
Art. 8	1						1
Art. 10	3						3

Norway

3. Distribution of Decisions by ECHR Provision per Year

Article	1990	1991	1992	1993	1994	1995	1996	1997	1998	1999	2000	2001	2002	2003	2004	2005	2006
5 (1)								1									
5 (3)								1									
5 (4)	1																
6 (1) fair trial							1							1			1
6 (1) length						1	1					1					
6 (2)														4			
6 (3)							1										
8										2							
10											1						1

The Netherlands

1. Applications, Decisions on the Merits, and Friendly Settlements per Year

Year	Applications lodged	Applications registered	Decisions on the merits	Court:			Committe of Ministers:			Articles concerned
				V	NV	FS	V	NV	FS	
1959	not available									
1960	not available	21								
1961	not available	17								
1962	not available	8								
1963	not available	19								
1964	not available	10								
1965	not available	14								
1966	not available	11								
1967	not available	15								
1968	not available	15								
1969	not available	16								
1970	not available	11								
1971	not available	18								
1972	not available	18								
1973	not available	16								
1974	not available	12								

Year	Applications lodged	Applications registered	Decisions on the merits	Court: V	NV	FS	Committe of Ministers: V	NV	FS	Articles concerned
1975	not available	7	1					1		Committee of Ministers: Art. 5 (1): 1 NV
1976	not available	9	1	1						Court: Art. 5 (1): 1 V; Art. 5 (4): 1 NV; Art. 6 (1) (fair trial): 1 V; Art. 6 (2): 1 NV; Art. 6 (3): 3 NV; Art. 10: 1 NV; Art. 11: 1 NV; Art. 14: 1 NV
1977	not available	15	1					1		Committee of Ministers: Art. 10: 1 NV; Art. 14: 1 NV
1978	not available	19								
1979	not available	22	1	1						Court: Art. 5 (1): 1 NV; Art. 5 (4): 1 V; Art. 6 (1) (fair trial): 1 V
1980	not available	24								
1981	not available	21								
1982	not available	24	1					1		Committe of Ministers: Art. 3: 1 NV; Art. 6 (1) (fair trial): 1 NV; Art. 6 (1) (length): 1 NV; Art. 8: 1 NV
1983	98	29								
1984	71	45	3	3						Court: Art. 5 (1): 1 NV; Art. 5 (3): 3 V; Art. 5 (4): 1 V; Art. 14: 1 NV
1985	102	35	3	2			1			Court: Art. 6 (1) (fair trial): 1 V; Art. 8: 1 NV; Committe of Ministers: Art. 6 (1) (length): 1 V
1986	96	48	2	1	1					Court: Art. 6 (1) (fair trial): 1 V; Prot.1 Art. 1: 1 NV
1987	150	53								
1988	164	75	1	1						Court: Art. 3: 1 NV; Art. 8: 1 V
1989	187	107	1	1						Court: Art. 6 (3): 1 V

Year	Applications lodged	Applications registered	Decisions on the merits	Court:			Committe of Ministers:			Articles concerned
				V	NV	FS	V	NV	FS	
1990	178	109	4	3	1					Court: Art. 5 (1): 2 V; Art. 5 (2): 1 V, 1 NV; Art. 5 (4): 2 V, 2 NV; Art. 5 (5): 1 NV
1991	165	98	3	1	1		1			Court: Art. 5 (3): 1 V; Art. 6 (1) (fair trial): 1 NV / Committe of Ministers: Art. 5 (1): 1 V; Art. 5 (4): 1 NV; Art. 5 (5): 1 NV; Art. 6 (1) (length): 1 NV
1992	174	75	2	1				1		Court: Art. 6 (1) (length): 1 V / Committe of Ministers: Art. 6 (1) (fair trial): 1 NV
1993	171	93	6	2	1		2	1		Court: Art. 6 (1) (fair trial): 1 V, 1 NV; Art. 6 (1) (length): 1 V / Committe of Ministers: Art. 6 (1) (length): 2 V, 1 NV; Art. 13: 1 NV
1994	192	104	10	4			5	1		Court: Art. 6 (1) (fair trial): 1 NV; Art. 6 (1) (length): 1 V; Art. 6 (3): 2 V; Art. 8: 1 V / Committe of Ministers: Art. 5 (1): 3 V; Art. 5 (2): 1 NV; Art. 5 (4): 3 V; Art. 6 (1) (fair trial) 1 NV; Art. 6 (1) (length): 1 V
1995	236	126	6	1	2		3			Court: Art. 6 (1) (fair trial): 2 NV; Art. 10: 1 V; Prot. 1 Art. 1: 1 NV / Committe of Ministers: Art. 6 (1) (fair trial): 1 V; Art. 6 (1) (length): 2 V; Art. 8: 1 NV
1996	246	138	9	1	4		3	1		Court: Art. 3: 1 NV; Art. 6 (1) (fair trial): 1 V; Art. 6 (2): 1 NV; Art. 6 (3): 1 NV; Art. 8: 2 NV / Committe of Ministers: Art. 6 (1) (fair trial): 1 NV; Art. 6 (1) (length): 3 V; Art. 6 (3): 1 NV

Year	Applications lodged	Applications registered	Decisions on the merits	Court:			Committe of Ministers:			Articles concerned
				V	NV	FS	V	NV	FS	
1997	274	155	8	3			5			Court: Art. 6 (1) (fair trial): 1 V; Art. 6 (3): 1 V; Art. 14: 1 V; Prot. 1 Art. 1: 1 V Committe of Ministers: Art. 6 (1) (fair trial): 2 V; Art. 6 (1) (length): 3 V; Art. 6 (3): 2 V
1998	273	138	6	3	1		1	1		Court: Art. 5 (1): 1 V; Art. 6 (1) (fair trial): 2 V, 2 NV Committe of Ministers: Art. 6 (1) (fair trial): 1 V; Art. 6 (1) (length): 1 NV; Art. 6 (3): 2 V
1999	278	206	6	3	1	1	5			Court: Art. 2: 1 FS; Art. 3: 1 FS; Art. 5 (1): 1 NV; Art. 5 (4): 1 NV Committe of Ministers: Art. 6 (1) (fair trial): 1 V; Art. 6 (1) (length): 3 V; Art. 6 (2): 1 V; Art. 6 (3): 1 V
2000	310	175	5	3	1	1	1			Court: Art. 6 (1) (fair trial): 1 V; Art. 6 (1) (length): 1 FS, Art. 6 (3): 1 NV; Art. 8: 1 V, 1 NV; Art. 14: 1 V Committee of Ministers: Art. 8: 1 V
2001	333	200	3	2	1	4				Court: Art. 3: 2 FS; Art. 5 (1): 1 NV; Art. 5 (4): 1 V; Art. 6 (1) (length): 1 FS; Art. 6 (3): 1 NV, 1 FS; Art. 8: 1 V; Art. 14: 1 NV
2002	574	317	9	6	3	1				Court: Art. 5 (4): 1 FS; Art. 6 (1) (fair trial): 1 V; Art. 6 (1) (length): 2 V; Art. 6 (3): 1 V; Art. 8: 3 V, 2 NV; Art. 13: 1 V; Art. 14: 1 V; Prot. 4 Art. 2: 2 NV
2003	451	278	7	6	1					Court: Art. 3: 2 V, 1 NV; Art. 6 (1) (fair trial): 1 NV; Art. 6 (1) (length): 1 V; Art. 6 (2): 1 V; Art. 8: 1 V, 2 NV; Art. 10: 1 V; Art. 13: 1 NV

Year	Applications lodged	Applications registered	Decisions on the merits	Court:			Committee of Ministers:			Articles concerned
				V	NV	FS	V	NV	FS	
2004	553	350	9	6	3	1				Court: Art. 3: 2 NV; Art. 5 (1): 2 V; Art. 6 (1) (fair trial): 1 V; Art. 6 (1) (length): 1 V; Art. 6 (2): 1 V; Art. 8: 2 V, 1 NV; Art. 13: 1 NV; Art. 14: 1 NV
2005	511	412	8	7	1					Court: Art. 2: 1 V, 1 NV; Art. 3: 2 V, 1 NV; Art. 5 (1): 2 V; Art. 5 (4): 1 V; Art. 6 (3): 1 V; Art. 8: 1 V, 1 NV
2006	536	397	7	6	1					Court: Art. 3: 3 V; Art. 8: 2 V, 1 NV; Art. 10: 1 V
Total	6323	4125	123	65	23	8	27	8	0	

V   finding at least one violation
NV   finding no violation
FS   friendly settlement

Entry into force of the Convention: 8.31.1954
Inception of right of individual application: 6.28.1960

Population in 2006 (Eurostat): 16334210
Applications lodged in % of population: 0,00313391

The Netherlands

2. Distribution of Decisions by ECHR Provision

	Court			Committee of Ministers			Total
	finding of violation	finding of no violation	FS	finding of violation	finding of no violation	FS	
Art. 2	1	1	1				3
Art. 3	7	6	3		1		17
Art. 4							0
Art. 5 (1)	8	4		4	1		17
Art. 5 (2)	1	1			1		3
Art. 5 (3)	4						4
Art. 5 (4)	6	4	1	3	1		15
Art. 5 (5)		1			1		2
Art. 6 (1) fair trial	12	8		5	4		29
Art. 6 (1) length	7		3	15	4		29
Art. 6 (2)	2	2		1			5
Art. 6 (3)	6	6	1	5	1		19
Art. 8	14	10		1	2		27
Art. 10	3	1			1		5
Art. 11		1					1
Art. 13	1	2			1		4
Art. 14	3	4			1		8
Prot. 1 Art. 1	1	2					3
Prot. 4 Art. 2		2					2

The Netherlands

3. Distribution of Decisions by ECHR Provision per Year

	1975	1976	1977	1978	1979	1980	1981	1982	1983	1984	1985	1986	1987	1988	1989
Article															
2															
3								1						1	
4															
5 (1)	1	1			1					1					
5 (2)															
5 (3)										3					
5 (4)		1			1					1					
5 (5)															
6 (1) fair trial		1			1			1			1	1			
6 (1) length								1			1				
6 (2)		1													
6 (3)		3													1
8								1			1			1	
10		1	1												
11		1													
13															
14		1	1							1					
P 1-1												1			
P 4-2															

1990	1991	1992	1993	1994	1995	1996	1997	1998	1999	2000	2001	2002	2003	2004	2005	2006
									1						2	
						1			1		2		3	2	3	3
2	1		3					1	1		1			2	2	
2			1													
	1															
4	1		3						1		1	1			1	
1	1															
	1	1	2	2	3	2	3	5	1	1		1	1	1		
	1	1	4	2	2	3	3	1	3	1	1	2	1	2		
					1					1		1	1			
			2			2	3	2	1	1	2	1			1	
			1	1	2					3	1	5	3	3	2	3
				1									1			1
		1										1	1	1		
						1				1	1	1		1		
				1		1										
												2				

Belgium

1. Applications, Decisions on the Merits, and Friendly Settlements per Year

Year	Applications lodged	Applications registered	Decisions on the merits	Court:			Committe of Ministers:			Articles concerned
				V	NV	FS	V	NV	FS	
1955	not available	14								
1956	not available	7								
1957	not available	12								
1958	not available	13								
1959	not available	32								
1960	not available	22								
1961	not available	34								
1962	not available	51								
1963	not available	27								
1964	not available	32								
1965	not available	36								
1966	not available	55								
1967	not available	55								
1968	not available	64	1	1						Court: Art. 8: 1 NV; Art.14: 1 V
1969	not available	72								
1970	not available	42	1		1					Court: Art. 6 (1) (fair trial): 1 NV; Art. 13: 1 NV

Year	Applications lodged	Applications registered	Decisions on the merits	Court:			Committe of Ministers:			Articles concerned
				V	NV	FS	V	NV	FS	
1971	not available	60	1	1						Court: Art. 3: 1 NV; Art. 4: 1 NV; Art. 5 (1): 1 NV; Art. 5 (4): 1 V; Art. 8: 1 NV; Art. 13: 1 NV
1972	not available	56	1				1			Committe of Ministers: Art. 5 (4): 1 V
1973	not available	53								
1974	not available	32								
1975	not available	41	2		2					Court: Art. 11: 1 NV; Art.14: 1 NV
1976	not available	28								
1977	not available	21								
1978	not available	13								
1979	not available	32	1	1						Court: Art. 8: 1 V; Art.14: 2 V
1980	not available	26	1	1						Court: Art. 6 (1) (fair trial): 1 V
1981	not available	22	1	1						Court: Art. 6 (1) (fair trial): 1 V; Art. 11: 1 NV
1982	not available	27	3	2			1			Court: Art. 4: 1 NV; Art. 5 (1): 1 NV; Art. 5 (4): 1 V; Art. 6 (1) (fair trial): 1 V; Committe of Ministers: Art. 6 (1) (fair trial): 1 NV; Art. 6 (3): 1 NV
1983	230	18	2	1	1					Court: Art. 3: 1 NV; Art. 4: 1 NV; Art. 6 (1) (fair trial): 1 V; Art. 6 (2): 1 NV; Art. 6 (3): 1 NV; Art. 11: 1 NV; Art. 14: 1 NV; Prot. 1 Art. 1: 1 NV
1984	192	41	1	1						Court: Art. 6 (1) (fair trial): 1 V
1985	166	33								

Year	Applications lodged	Applications registered	Decisions on the merits	Court:			Committe of Ministers:			Articles concerned
				V	NV	FS	V	NV	FS	
1986	181	44								
1987	196	64	4	1	1		2			Court: Art. 6 (1) (fair trial): 1 V; Art. 14: 1 NV; Prot.1 Art. 3: 1 NV Committe of Ministers: Art. 6 (1) (fair trial): 2 V
1988	191	46	3	2				1		Court: Art. 5 (1): 1 V; Art. 5 (3): 1 V; Art. 5 (4): 1 V; Art. 14: 1 NV Committe of Ministers: Art. 3: 1 NV; Art. 5 (1): 1 NV; Art. 5 (4): 1 NV; Art. 7: 1 NV
1989	196	65	2	2						Court: Art. 5 (2): 1 NV; Art. 5 (3): 1 NV; Art. 5 (4): 1 V; Art. 6 (1) (fair trial): 1 V, 1 NV; Art. 6 (3): 1 NV
1990	202	94								
1991	158	67	5	4		1	1			Court: Art. 5 (3): 1 V; Art. 6 (1) (fair trial): 1 V, 1 FS; Art. 8: 1 V; Art. 14: 1 V, 1 NV; Prot. 1 Art. 1: 1 FS Committe of Ministers: Art. 5 (4): 1 V
1992	139	62	3	1	2					Court: Art. 5 (1): 1 NV; Art. 5 (4): 1 NV; Art. 6 (1) (length): 1 NV; Art. 6 (3): 1 V
1993	128	70								
1994	212	78	4	1	1		1			Court: Art. 6 (1) (fair trial): 1 V, 1 NV; Art. 6 (1) (length): 1 V Committe of Ministers: Art. 13: 1 V; Prot. 1 Art. 1: 1 V

Year	Applications lodged	Applications registered	Decisions on the merits	Court:			Committe of Ministers:			Articles concerned
				V	NV	FS	V	NV	FS	
1995	185	62	4	1			3			Court: Prot. 1 Art. 1: 1 V Committe of Ministers: Art. 5 (4): 1 V; Art. 6 (1) (fair trial): 1 V; Art. 13: 1 V; Prot. 1 Art. 1: 1 V
1996	191	54	4	1	1		2			Court: Art. 6 (1) (fair trial): 1 V; Art. 8: 1 NV Committe of Ministers: Art. 6 (1) (length): 2 V
1997	197	58	7	2			4	1		Court: Art. 6 (1) (fair trial): 2 V; Art. 10: 1 V Committe of Ministers: Art. 6 (1) (fair trial): 3 V; Art. 6 (1) (length): 1 V, 2 NV
1998	225	71	4	1			3			Court: Art. 3: 1 NV; Art. 5 (1): 1 V; Art. 5 (4): 1 NV; Art. 6 (1) (fair trial): 1 V Committe of Ministers: Art. 6 (1) (fair trial): 1 V; Art. 6 (1) (length): 2 V
1999	262	136	3	1	1		1			Court: Art. 6 (1) (fair trial): 1 NV; Art. 6 (3): 1 V Committe of Ministers: Art. 6 (1) (fair trial): 1 V
2000	274	74	1	1		1				Court: Art. 6 (1) (fair trial): 2 V, 3 NV; Art. 6 (1) (length): 1 NV, 1 FS; Art. 7: 1 NV
2001	239	108	4	2	2	1				Court: Art. 3: 1 FS; Art. 6 (1) (fair trial): 2 V, 1 NV; Art. 6 (1) (length): 1 NV; Art. 6 (3): 2 V
2002	265	139	13	12	1					Court: Art. 5 (1): 1 V; Art. 5 (2): 1 NV; Art. 5 (3): 1 NV; Art. 5 (4): 1 V; Art. 6 (1) (fair trial): 1 V, 1 NV; Art. 6 (1) (length): 10 V, 1 NV; Art. 13: 2 V, 1 NV; Prot. 4 Art. 4: 1 V

Year	Applications lodged	Applications registered	Decisions on the merits	Court:			Committe of Ministers:			Articles concerned
				V	NV	FS	V	NV	FS	
2003	216	117	7	7		1				Court: Art. 6 (1) (fair trial): 1 NV; Art. 6 (1) (length): 6 V, 1 FS; Art. 8: 1 V; Art. 10: 1 V; Art. 13: 1 NV; Art. 14: 1 NV
2004	247	125	11	11		1				Court: Art. 6 (1) (fair trial): 1 V; Art. 6 (1) (length): 8 V, 1 FS; Art. 6 (3): 1 V; Art. 8: 1 V
2005	283	169	13	12	1	1				Court: Art. 6 (1) (fair trial): 8 V, 3 NV; Art. 6 (1) (length): 7 V, 1 FS; Art. 6 (2): 1 V; 1 NV; Art. 6 (3): 1 V; Art. 7: 1 NV; Art. 8: 1 NV
2006	220	106	5	4	1	2				Court: Art. 3: 2 V; Art. 5 (1): 1 V, 1 NV; Art. 5 (4): 1 V, 1 NV; Art. 6 (1) (fair trial): 1 NV; Art. 6 (1) (length): 2 V, 2 FS; Art. 6 (2): 1 V; Art. 8: 2 V; Art. 10: 1 NV
Total	4995	2880	112	75	15	8	18	3	0	

V   finding at least one violation
NV   finding no violation
FS   friendly settlement

Entry into force of the Convention: 6.14.1955
Inception of right of individual application: 7.5.1955

Population in 2006 (Eurostat):   10511382
Applications lodged in % of population: 0,0027092

Belgium

2. Distribution of Decisions by ECHR Provision

	Court			Committee of Ministers			Total
	finding of violation	finding of no violation	FS	finding of violation	finding of no violation	FS	
Art. 3	2	3	1		1		7
Art. 4		3					3
Art. 5 (1)	4	4			1		9
Art. 5 (2)		2					2
Art. 5 (3)	2	2					4
Art. 5 (4)	6	3		3	1		13
Art. 6 (1) fair trial	27	14	1	8	1		51
Art. 6 (1) length	34	4	6	5	2		51
Art. 6 (2)	2	2					4
Art. 6 (3)	6	2			1		9
Art. 7		2			1		3
Art. 8	6	4	1				11
Art. 10	2	1					3
Art. 11		3					3
Art. 13	2	3		2			7
Art. 14	4	7					11
Prot. 1 Art. 1	1	1	1	2			5
Prot. 1 Art. 3		1					
Prot. 4 Art. 4	1						1

Belgium

3. Distribution of Decisions by ECHR Provision per Year

	1968	1969	1970	1971	1972	1973	1974	1975	1976	1977	1978	1979	1980	1981	1982	1983
Article																
3				1												1
4				1											1	1
5 (1)				1											1	
5 (2)																
5 (3)																
5 (4)				1	1										1	
6 (1) fair trial			1									1	1	1	2	1
6 (1) length																
6 (2)																1
6 (3)															1	1
7																
8	1			1								1				
10																
11								1						1		1
13				1												
14	1							1				2				1
P 1-1																1
P 1-3																
P 4-4																

1984	1985	1986	1987	1988	1989	1990	1991	1992	1993	1994	1995	1996	1997	1998	1999	2000	2001	2002
				1										1			1	
				1				1						1				1
					1													1
				1	1		1											1
				2	1		1	1		1			1					1
1			3		2		2			2	1	1	5	3	2	5	3	2
								1		1		2	3	2		2	1	11
					1			1							1		2	
				1												1		
							1					1					1	
													1					
										1	1							3
		1	1				2					1						
							1			1	2							
			1															
																		1

	2003	2004	2005	2006
Article				
3				2
4				
5 (1)				2
5 (2)				
5 (3)				
5 (4)				2
6 (1) fair trial	1	1	11	1
6 (1) length	7	9	8	4
6 (2)			2	1
6 (3)		1	1	
7			1	
8	1	1	1	2
10	1			1
11				
13	1			
14	1			
P 1-1				
P 1-3				
P 4-4				

Austria

1. Applications, Decisions on the Merits, and Friendly Settlements per Year

Year	Applications lodged	Applications registered	Decisions on the merits	Court:			Committe of Ministers:			Articles concerned
				V	NV	FS	V	NV	FS	
1958	not available	16								
1959	not available	56								
1960	not available	45								
1961	not available	81								
1962	not available	136								
1963	not available	139	1					1		Committe of Ministers: 6 (3): 1 NV
1964	not available	62								
1965	not available	67								
1966	not available	44								
1967	not available	64								
1968	not available	43	1	1						Court: Art. 5 (3): 1 V; Art. 5 (4): 1 NV; Art. 6 (1) (fair trial): 1 NV
1969	not available	46	3	1	1			1		Court: Art. 5 (3): 1 V, 1 NV; Art. 5 (4): 1 NV; Art. 6 (1) (fair trial): 1 NV; Committe of Ministers: Art. 5 (4): 1 NV; Art. 6 (1) (fair trial): 1 NV; Art. 6 (3): 1 NV

Year	Applications lodged	Applications registered	Decisions on the merits	Court:			Committe of Ministers:			Articles concerned
				V	NV	FS	V	NV	FS	
1970	not available	37								
1971	not available	62	2	1				1		Court: Art. 5 (3): 1 V; Art. 6 (1) (length): 1 NV; Committe of Ministers: Art. 6 (1) (fair trial): 1 NV; Art. 13: 1 NV
1972	not available	92								
1973	not available	74								
1974	not available	36								
1975	not available	34								
1976	not available	24	1					1		Committe of Ministers: Art. 14: 1 NV; Prot 1 Art. 1: 1 NV
1977	not available	20								
1978	not available	27								
1979	not available	23	1					1		Committe of Ministers: Art. 6 (1) (fair trial): 1 NV; Art. 6 (1) (length): 1 NV
1980	not available	28								
1981	not available	32								
1982	not available	30	1		1					Court: Art. 6 (1) (fair trial): 1 NV; Art. 6 (2): 1 NV; Art. 6 (3): 1 NV
1983	102	29	1				1			Committe of Ministers: Art. 6 (1) (length): 1 V
1984	125	36	1	1						Court: Art. 6 (1) (fair trial): 1 V

Year	Applications lodged	Applications registered	Decisions on the merits	Court:			Committe of Ministers:			Articles concerned
				V	NV	FS	V	NV	FS	
1985	126	42	1	1		1				Court: Art. 5 (3): 1 FS; Art. 6 (1) (fair trial): 1 V; Art. 6 (3): 1 FS
1986	133	61	2	2						Court: Art. 6 (3): 1 V; Art. 10: 1 V
1987	183	76	6	4	1		1			Court: Art. 6 (1) (fair trial): 1 NV; Art. 6 (1) (length): 3 V; Art. 14: 1 V; Prot.1 Art. 1: 2 V / Committe of Ministers: Art. 6 (1) (length): 1 V
1988	176	61	1		1					Court: Art. 13: 1 NV
1989	214	137	3	1	1		1			Court: Art. 6 (1) (fair trial): 1 V; Art. 6 (2): 1 NV; Art. 6 (3): 1 NV; Art. 14: 1 NV; Prot.1 Art. 1: 1 NV / Committe of Ministers: Art. 6 (1) (length): 1 V
1990	254	159	4	3			1			Court: Art. 5 (3): 1 NV; Art. 6 (1) (length): 2 V; Art. 6 (3): 1 V / Committe of Ministers: Art. 6 (1) (length): 1 V
1991	195	135	6	4	1		1		2	Court: Art. 5 (3): 1 V; Art. 6 (1) (fair trial): 2 V; Art. 6 (1) (length): 1 V; Art. 6 (3): 2 NV; Art. 10: 1 V; Prot.1 Art. 1: 1 NV / Committe of Ministers: Art. 6 (1) (length): 1 V, 2 FS
1992	232	156	4	3	1	1				Court: Art. 3: 1 NV; Art. 5 (1): 1 NV; Art. 5 (3): 1 NV; Art. 5 (4): 1 V; Art. 6 (1) (fair trial): 1 V; Art. 6 (1) (length): 1 FS; Art. 6 (3): 1 NV; Art. 8: 2 V; Art. 10: 2 V

Year	Applications lodged	Applications registered	Decisions on the merits	Court:			Committe of Ministers:			Articles concerned
				V	NV	FS	V	NV	FS	
1993	245	161	11	4	4	1	3			Court: Art. 5 (1): 1 NV, 1 FS; Art. 5 (4): 1 FS; Art. 6 (1) (fair trial): 3 NV, 1 FS; Art. 6 (2): 1 V, 1 NV; Art. 6 (3): 2 NV; Art. 10: 1 V, 1 NV, 1 FS; Art. 14: 1 V Committe of Ministers: Art. 6 (1) (length): 3 V
1994	238	154	11	1	2		7	1		Court: Art. 6 (1) (fair trial): 2 NV; Art. 10: 2 V, 1 NV; Art. 13: 1 V, 1 NV Committe of Ministers: Art. 6 (1) (fair trial): 1 NV; Art. 6 (1) (length): 7 V
1995	235	146	20	8	1	1	8	3		Court: Art. 3: 1 V; Art. 6 (1) (fair trial): 7 V, 1 NV; Art. 8: 1 FS; Art. 10: 1 NV; Art. 13: 1 FS; Prot. 7 Art. 4: 1 V Committe of Ministers: Art. 3: 2 NV; Art. 6 (1) (length): 7 V, 1 NV; Prot. 1 Art. 1: 1 V
1996	333	186	17	2	2		13			Court: Art. 6 (1) (fair trial): 1 V, 3 NV; Art. 13: 1 NV; Art. 14: 1 V; Prot. 1 Art. 1: 1 NV Committe of Ministers: Art. 6 (1) (length): 12 V; Art. 8: 1 V
1997	374	238	34	6	2	1	26			Court: Art. 6 (1) (fair trial): 6 V, 2 NV; Art. 10: 2 V, 1 NV Committe of Ministers: Art. 6 (1) (fair trial): 16 V; Art. 6 (1) (length): 9 V; Art. 6 (3): 1 V
1998	349	210	6		1	1	5			Court: Art. 14: 1 NV; Prot. 7 Art. 4: 1 FS Committe of Ministers: Art. 6 (1) (fair trial): 7 V, 1 NV; Art. 6 (1) (length): 3 V, 1 NV; Art. 10: 1 V

Year	Applications lodged	Applications registered	Decisions on the merits	Court:			Committe of Ministers:			Articles concerned
				V	NV	FS	V	NV	FS	
1999	355	227	6	3			3			Court: Art. 6 (1) (fair trial): 1 V; Art. 6 (1) (length): 2 V Committe of Ministers: Art. 6 (1) (fair trial): 1 V; Art. 6 (1) (length): 2 V; Art. 8: 1 V
2000	403	241	16	13	2	6	1		1	Court: Art. 6 (1) (fair trial): 7 V, 2 NV, 1 FS; Art. 6 (1) (length): 4 V; Art. 6 (2): 1 V, 1 FS; Art. 6 (3): 2 V, 2 NV; Art. 10: 3 V, 2 NV; Art. 13: 4 FS; Prot. 7 Art. 4: 4 FS Committe of Ministers: Art. 6 (1) (fair trial): 1 FS; Art. 6 (1) (length): 1 V
2001	385	229	14	14		1				Court: Art. 6 (1) (fair trial): 2 V, 1 NV, 1 FS; Art. 6 (1) (length): 6 V; Art. 6 (2): 3 V; Art. 8: 1 V; Art. 10: 1 V; Art. 13: 1 FS; Art. 14: 1 FS; Prot. 1 Art. 1: 1 FS; Prot. 7 Art. 4: 1 V
2002	432	309	15	14	1	5				Court: Art. 5 (4): 1 V; Art. 6 (1) (fair trial): 3 V, 1 FS; Art. 6 (1) (length): 3 V, 2 FS; Art. 6 (2): 2 V; Art. 6 (3): 1 V, 1 NV; Art. 8: 1 V; Art. 10: 3 V, 2 FS; Prot. 1 Art. 1: 1 FS; Prot. 7 Art. 4: 2 V
2003	445	324	17	16	1	2				Court: Art. 6 (1) (fair trial): 2 V, 1 NV; Art. 6 (1) (length): 8 V, 2 FS; Art. 8: 2 V; Art. 10: 3 V; Art. 13: 1 NV; Art. 14: 3 V; Prot. 1 Art. 1: 1 NV
2004	421	304	14	13	1	1				Court: Art. 6 (1) (fair trial): 2 V, 1 NV; Art. 6 (1) (length): 10 V, 1 FS; Art. 6 (3): 1 V; Art. 8: 1 V; Art. 14: 1 V

Year	Applications lodged	Applications registered	Decisions on the merits	Court:			Committe of Ministers:			Articles concerned
				V	NV	FS	V	NV	FS	
2005	418	301	20	18	2	1				Court: Art. 5 (4): 1 NV; Art. 6 (1) (fair trial): 4 V, 1 NV; Art. 6 (1) (length): 10 V, 1 FS; Art. 10: 2 V; Art. 13: 1 V; Art. 14: 3 V
2006	432	341	21	20	1					Court: Art. 6 (1) (fair trial): 6 V; Art. 6 (1) (length): 2 V; Art. 6 (3): 2 V; Art. 8: 1 V; Art. 10: 7 V, 1 NV; Art. 11: 1 V; Art. 13: 1 V; Art. 14: 2 V, 1 NV
Total	6805	5581	261	154	27	22	71	9	3	

V   finding at least one violation
NV   finding no violation
FS   friendly settlement

Entry into force of the Convention: 9.3.1958
Inception of right of individual application: 9.3.1958

Population in 2006 (Eurostat):   8265925
Applications lodged in % of population: 0,00509352

Austria

2. Distribution of Decisions by ECHR Provision

	Court			Committee of Ministers			Total
	finding of violation	finding of no violation	FS	finding of violation	finding of no violation	FS	
Art. 3	1	1			2		4
Art. 5 (1)		2	1				3
Art. 5 (3)	4	3	1				8
Art. 5 (4)	2	3	1		1		7
Art. 6 (1) fair trial	47	21	4	8	5	1	86
Art. 6 (1) length	41	1	7	49	4	2	104
Art. 6 (2)	14	6	2				22
Art. 6 (3)	8	10	1	1	1		21
Art. 8	8		1	2			11
Art. 10	28	7	3	1			39
Art. 11	1						1
Art. 13	3	4	6		1		14
Art. 14	12	3	1		1		17
Prot. 1 Art. 1	2	4	2	1	1		10
Prot. 7 Art. 4	4		5				9

Austria

3. Distribution of Decisions by ECHR Provision per Year

	1963	1964	1965	1966	1967	1968	1969	1970	1971	1972	1973	1974	1975	1976	1977	1978
Article																
3																
5 (1)																
5 (3)						1	2		1							
5 (4)						1	2									
5 (5)																
6 (1) fair trial						1	2		1							
6 (1) length							1		1							
6 (2)																
6 (3)	1						1									
8																
10																
11																
13									1							
14														1		
P 1-1														1		
P 7-4																

1979	1980	1981	1982	1983	1984	1985	1986	1987	1988	1989	1990	1991	1992	1993	1994	1995	1996	1997
													1			3		
													1	2				
			1								1	1	1					
													1	1				
1			1		1	1		1		1		2	1	4	3	8	4	24
1		1						4		1	3	4	1	3	7	8	12	9
			1							1				2				
			1		1		1			1	1	2	1	2				1
													2			1	1	
							1					1	2	3	3	1		3
									1						2	1	1	
					1		1							1			1	
					2		1			1						1	1	
																1		

	1997	1998	1999	2000	2001	2002	2003	2004	2005	2006
Article										
3										
5 (1)										
5 (3)										
5 (4)						1		1		
5 (5)										
6 (1) fair trial	24	8	2	11	4	4	3	3	5	6
6 (1) length	9	4	4	5	6	5	10	11	11	2
6 (2)				2	3	2				
6 (3)	1			4		2		1		2
8			1		1	1	2	1		1
10	3	1		5	1	5	3		2	8
11										1
13				4	1		1		1	1
14		1			1		3	1	3	3
P 1-1						1	1	1		
P 7-4			1		4	1	2			

Switzerland

1. Applications, Decisions on the Merits, and Friendly Settlements per Year

Year	Applications lodged	Applications registered	Decisions on the merits	Court:			Committe of Ministers:			Articles concerned
				V	NV	FS	V	NV	FS	
1974	–	–								
1975	not available	30								
1976	not available	30								
1977	not available	40								
1978	not available	31								
1979	not available	32	2		1			1		"Court: Art. 5 (3): 1 NV Committe of Ministers: Art. 5 (1): 1 NV; Art. 5 (4): 1 NV"
1980	not available	44	1					1		Committe of Ministers: Art. 5 (3): 1 NV
1981	not available	31	1					1		"Committe of Ministers: Art. 5 (3): 1 NV; Art. 6 (1) (length): 1 NV"
1983	165	27	5	2			1	2		"Court: Art. 6 (1) (length): 1 V; Art. 6 (2): 1 V Committe of Ministers: Art. 3: 1 NV; Art. 5 (1): 1 V; Art. 6 (3): 1 NV"
1984	149	49	1		1					Court: Art. 6 (1) (fair trial): 1 NV

Year	Applications lodged	Applications registered	Decisions on the merits	Court:			Committee of Ministers:			Articles concerned
				V	NV	FS	V	NV	FS	
1985	100	33								
1986	135	50	4	1			2	1		"Court: Art. 5 (4): 1 NV / Committe of Ministers: Art. 6 (1) (fair trial): 1 V; Art. 6 (1) (length): 1 NV; Art. 6 (2): 1 V"
1987	143	60	1	1						Court: Art. 12: 1 V
1988	166	58	4	2	2					"Court: Art. 6 (1) (fair trial): 1 V, 1 NV; Art. 6 (2): 1 NV; Art. 8: 1 V; Art. 10: 1 NV"
1989	180	104								
1990	187	107	4	3	1					"Court: Art. 5 (3): 1 V; Art. 6 (1) (fair trial): 1 V; Art. 10: 2 V, 1 NV"
1991	227	113	2	2						Court: Art. 6 (3): 2 V
1992	235	115	2	1				1		"Court: Art. 6 (3): 1 V; Art. 8: 1 NV / Committee of Ministers: Art. 6 (1) (length), 1 NV"
1993	181	123	7	1	3			3		"Court: Art. 5 (3): 1 NV; Art. 6 (1) (fair trial): 1 V, 3 NV; Art. 6 (3): 1 NV; Art. 14: 1 V / Committee of Ministers: Art. 3: 1 NV; Art. 6 (1) (fair trial): 1 NV; Art. 6 (1) (length): 1 NV; Art. 8: 1 NV"
1994	229	156	1	1		1				"Court: Art. 3: 1 FS; Art. 14: 1 V "
1996	217	137	6		3		2	1		"Court: Art. 6 (1) (fair trial): 2 NV; Art. 8: 1 NV / Committee of Ministers: Art. 5 (3): 1 V; Art. 5 (4): 1 NV; Art. 5 (5): 1 NV; Art. 6 (1) (fair trial): 1 V, 1 NV; Art. 6 (1) (length): 1 V"

Year	Applications lodged	Applications registered	Decisions on the merits	Court:			Committe of Ministers:			Articles concerned
				V	NV	FS	V	NV	FS	
1997	248	155	6	5			1			"Court: Art. 5 (4): 1 V; Art. 6 (1) (fair trial): 1 V; Art. 6 (2): 2 V; Art. 8: 1 NV; Art. 13: 1 V Committe of Ministers: Art. 5 (3): 1 V"
1998	294	177	5	2	2			1		"Court: Art. 8: 1 V; Art. 10: 1 V, 1 NV; Prot. 7 Art. 4: 1 NV Committe of Ministers: Art. 10: 1 NV"
1999	290	156	1				1			Committe of Ministers: Art. 6 (1) (length): 1 V
2000	318	187	9	5	1	1	3			"Court: Art. 2: 1 FS; Art. 3: 1 FS; Art. 5 (4): 2 V; Art. 6 (1) (fair trial): 1 V, 1 NV; Art. 6 (1) (length): 2 V; Art. 8: 2 V; Art. 13: 1 NV Committe of Ministers: Art. 5 (4): 1 V; Art. 6 (1) (length): 2 V"
2001	327	162	7	6	1	1				"Court: Art. 5 (2): 1 NV; Art. 5 (3): 1 V, 1 FS; Art. 5 (4): 1 V, 1 FS; Art. 6 (1) (fair trial): 2 V; Art. 6 (3): 1 NV; Art. 8: 1 V; Art. 10: 1 V; Art. 13: 1 NV; Art. 14: 1 NV"
2002	281	214	4	2	2					"Court: Art. 5 (1): 1 NV; Art. 6 (1) (fair trial): 1 V; Art. 6 (1) (length): 1 V; Art. 10: 1 NV"
2004	311	203								
2005	296	232	5	5						"Court: Art. 6 (1) (fair trial): 4 V; Art. 6 (1) (length): 1 V"

Year	Applications lodged	Applications registered	Decisions on the merits	Court:			Committe of Ministers:			Articles concerned
				V	NV	FS	V	NV	FS	
2006	334	277	9	9						"Court: Art. 2: 1 V, 1 NV; Art. 3: 1 NV; Art. 5 (4): 1 V; Art. 6 (1) (fair trial): 1 V; Art. 6 (1) (length): 1 V; Art. 8: 2 V; Art. 10: 3 V"
Total	5491	3474	91	48	18	3	12	13	0	

V: finding at least one violation
NV: finding no violation
FS: friendly settlement

Entry into force of the Convention: 28.11.1974
Inception of right of individual application: 28.11.1974

Population in 2006 (Eurostat):   7459128
Applications lodged in % of population: 0,003990079

Switzerland

2. Distribution of Decisions by ECHR Provision

	Court			Committee of Ministers			Total
	finding of violation	finding of no violation	FS	finding of violation	finding of no violation	FS	
Art. 2	1	1	1				3
Art. 3		1	2		2		5
Art. 5 (1)		2		1	1		4
Art. 5 (2)		1					1
Art. 5 (3)	2	2	1	2	2		9
Art. 5 (4)	5	2	1	1	2		11
Art. 5 (5)					1		1
Art. 6 (1) fair trial	13	8		3	2		26
Art. 6 (1) length	6			4	5		15
Art. 6 (2)	3	1		1			5
Art. 6 (3)	3	2			1		6
Art. 8	7	2		1	2		12
Art. 10	7	4					11
Art. 12	1						1
Art. 13	1	2					3
Art. 14	2	1					3
Prot. 7 Art. 4		1					1

Switzerland

3. Distribution of Decisions by ECHR Provision per Year

	1974	1975	1976	1977	1978	1979	1980	1981	1982	1983	1984	1985	1986	1987	1988	1989
Article																
2																
3										1						
5 (1)						1				1						
5 (2)																
5 (3)						1	1	1								
5 (4)						1							1			
5 (5)																
6 (1) fair trial											1		1		2	
6 (1) length								1		1			1			
6 (2)										1			1		1	
6 (3)										1						
8															1	
10															1	
12														1		
13																
14																
P 7-4																

1990	1991	1992	1993	1994	1995	1996	1997	1998	1999	2000	2001	2002	2003	2004	2005	2006
										1						2
		1	1							1						1
												1	1			
										1						
1			1			1	1			2						
						1	1		3	2			1			1
			1													
1			5		1	4	1			2	2	1			4	1
	1		1		1	1			1	4		1			1	1
				2												
	2	1	1								1					
	1	1			1	1	1	1		2	1					2
3								2			1	1				3
					1					1	1					
		1	1								1					
							1									

Spain

1. Applications, Decisions on the Merits, and Friendly Settlements per Year

Year	Applications lodged	Applications registered	Decisions on the merits	Court:			Committe of Ministers:			Articles concerned
				V	NV	FS	V	NV	FS	
1981	not available	4								
1982	not available	12								
1983	66	10								
1984	76	15								
1985	55	19								
1986	63	17								
1987	110	16								
1988	134	34	1	1						Court: Art. 6 (1) (fair trial): 1 V
1989	256	71	1	1						Court: Art. 6 (1) (length): 1 V
1990	216	69								
1991	159	75								
1992	194	78	2	1	1					Court: Art. 5 (1): 1 NV; Art. 10: 1 V
1993	228	90	1	1						Court: Art. 6 (1) (fair trial): 1 V; Art. 6 (1) (length): 1 V
1994	254	138	4	3	1	1				Court: Art. 2: 1 FS; Art. 3: 1 FS; Art. 6 (1) (fair trial): 2 V; Art. 8: 1 V; Art. 10: 1 NV

Year	Applications lodged	Applications registered	Decisions on the merits	Court:			Committee of Ministers:			Articles concerned
				V	NV	FS	V	NV	FS	
1995	249	143	4		2		2			Court: Art. 5 (3): 1 NV; Art. 6 (3): 1 NV Committee of Ministers: Art. 5 (3): 2 V
1996	269	139	2	1	1					Court: Art. 5 (1): 1 NV; Art. 5 (3): 1 V; Art. 6 (3): 1 NV
1997	289	153	2		2					Court: Art. 6 (1) (fair trial): 2 NV
1998	178	72	6	3	1		2			Court: Art. 6 (1) (fair trial): 2 V, 1 NV; Art. 8: 1 V Committee of Ministers: Art. 6 (1) (fair trial): 2 V
1999	315	227	4	1	1	1	1	1		Court: Art. 5 (1): 1 V; Art. 6 (1) (fair trial): 1 NV, 1 FS Committee of Ministers: Art. 6 (1) (fair trial): 1 V; Art. 6 (1) (length): 1 V
2000	546	284	4	3			1			Court: Art. 6 (1) (fair trial): 2 V; Art. 10: 1 V Committee of Ministers: Art. 5 (3): 1 V
2001	1099	807	2	1	1					Court: Art. 6 (1) (fair trial): 1 NV; Art. 6 (1) (length): 1 V
2002	822	798	3	1	2					Court: Art. 6 (1) (fair trial): 1 V, 1 NV; Art. 10: 1 NV
2003	604	455	9	8	1					Court: Art. 5 (1): 1 NV; Art. 6 (1) (fair trial): 2 V; Art. 6 (1) (length): 3 V; Art. 7: 1 V; Art. 8: 2 V
2004	690	423	6	5	1					Court: Art. 3: 1 V, 1 NV; Art. 6 (1) (fair trial): 1 V, 2 NV; Art. 6 (1) (length): 2 V; Art. 8: 1 V
2005	634	493								

Year	Applications lodged	Applications registered	Decisions on the merits	Court:			Committe of Ministers:			Articles concerned
				V	NV	FS	V	NV	FS	
2006	472	371	5	4	1					Court: Art. 3: 1 NV; Art. 5 (1): 1 V, 1 NV; Art. 6 (1) (fair trial): 2 V, 1 NV; Art. 6 (2): 1 V
Total	7978	5013	56	34	15	2	6	1	0	

V   finding at least one violation
NV   finding no violation
FS   friendly settlement

Entry into force of the Convention: 10.4.1979
Inception of right of individual application: 7.1.1981

Population in 2006 (Eurostat):   43758250
Applications lodged in % of population: 0,0014473117

Spain

2. Distribution of Decisions by ECHR Provision

	Court			Committee of Ministers			Total
	finding of violation	finding of no violation	FS	finding of violation	finding of no violation	FS	
Art. 2			1				1
Art. 3	1	3	1				5
Art. 5 (1)	2	4					6
Art. 5 (2)							0
Art. 5 (3)	1	1		3			5
Art. 5 (4)							0
Art. 5 (5)							0
Art. 6 (1) fair trial	14	9	1	2	1		27
Art. 6 (1) length	8			1			9
Art. 6 (2)	1						1
Art. 6 (3)		2					2
Art. 7	1						1
Art. 8	5						5
Art. 9							0
Art. 10	2	2					4
Art. 11							0
Art. 13							0
Art. 14							0

Spain

3. Distribution of Decisions by ECHR Provision per Year

Article	1988	1989	1990	1991	1992	1993	1994	1995	1996	1997	1998	1999	2000	2001	2002	2003	2004	2005	2006
2							1												
3							2												1
5 (1)					1				1			1					2		1
5 (2)																1			
5 (3)								3	1				1						
6 (1) fair trial	1					1	2			2	5	3	2	1	2	2	3		3
6 (1) length		1				1					3	1		1		3	2		
6 (2)								1											
6 (3)								1	1										
7																1			
8							1				1					2	1		
9															1				
10					1		1						1						

Italy

1. Applications, Decisions on the Merits, and Friendly Settlements per Year

Year	Applications lodged	Applications registered	Decisions on the merits	Court: V	NV	FS	Committe of Ministers: V	NV	FS	Articles concerned
1973	not available	7								
1974	not available	15								
1975	not available	15								
1976	not available	18								
1977	not available	12								
1978	not available	14								
1979	not available	21								
1980	not available	31	2	2						Court: Art. 3: 1 NV; Art. 5 (1): 1 V; Art. 6 (1) (fair trial): 1 NV; Art. 6 (3): 1 V; Art. 8: 1 NV; Art. 9: 1 NV
1981	not available	20	2					2		Committe of Ministers: Art. 5 (1): 1 NV; Art. 5 (3): 1 NV; Art.5 (4): 1 NV; Art. 6 (1) (fair trial): 1 NV
1982	not available	15	2	2						Court: Art. 6 (1) (length): 2 V
1983	110	17	2		1			1		Court: Art. 6 (1) (fair trial): 1 NV; Art. 6 (1) (length): 1 NV Committe of Ministers: Art. 3: 1 NV

Year	Applications lodged	Applications registered	Decisions on the merits	Court: V	NV	FS	Committe of Ministers: V	NV	FS	Articles concerned
1984	143	21	2	2						Court: Art. 5 (1): 1 NV; Art. 5 (4): 1 V; Art. 6 (3): 1 V
1985	190	54	1	1		1				Court: Art. 5 (3): 1 FS; Art. 6 (1) (fair trial): 1 V; Art. 6 (1) (length): 1 FS
1986	200	62								
1987	369	110	3	3						Court: Art. 6 (1) (length): 3 V
1988	599	171								
1989	667	142	8	3			4	1		Court: Art. 5 (1): 1 V; Art. 5 (4): 1 V; Art. 5 (5): 1 V; Art. 6 (1) (fair trial): 1 V; Art. 6 (3): 1 V Committe of Ministers: Art. 6 (1) (length): 3 V; Art. 6 (3): 1 V; Prot. 1 Art. 1: 1 NV
1990	353	154	1	1			1			Committe of Ministers: Art. 6 (1) (length): 1 V
1991	463	133	26	22	1		3	1		Court: Art. 6 (1) (length): 21 V; Art. 6 (3): 2 V, 1 NV Committe of Ministers: Art. 6 (1) (length): 3 V
1992	474	196	43	35	6			2		Court: Art. 5 (3): 1 V; Art. 6 (1) (fair trial): 1 V; Art. 6 (1) (length): 33 V, 6 NV Committe of Ministers: Art. 6 (1) (length): 2 NV
1993	3032	142	13	9	1			3		Court: Art. 6 (1) (fair trial): 1 NV; Art. 6 (1) (length): 9 V; Art. 8: 1 V Committe of Ministers: Art. 6 (1) (length): 3 NV

Year	Applications lodged	Applications registered	Decisions on the merits	Court:			Committe of Ministers:			Articles concerned
				V	NV	FS	V	NV	FS	
1994	1858	507	13	3	2		7	1		Court: Art. 6 (1) (length): 1 V, 3 NV; Art. 6 (3): 1 NV; Prot. 1 Art. 1: 2 V, 2 NV; Prot. 4 Art. 2: 1 V Committe of Ministers: Art. 6 (1) (length): 6 V, 1 NV; Art. 6 (3): 1 V
1995	1455	545	313	3	2		307	1		Court: Art. 6 (1) (length): 3 V, 1 NV; Art.14: 1 NV; Prot. 1 Art. 1: 1 V, 1 NV Committe of Ministers: Art. 6 (1) (fair trial): 2 V; Art. 6 (1) (length): 304 V, 1 NV; Art. 6 (3): 1 V; Art. 13: 1 NV
1996	1920	729	486	8			477	1		Court: Art. 6 (1) (fair trial): 1 V; 6 (1) (length): 5 V; Art. 6 (3): 1 V, 1 NV; Art. 8: 2 V; Art.13: 1 V; Prot. 1 Art. 1: 1 V Committe of Ministers: Art. 6 (1) (fair trial): 1 V; Art. 6 (1) (length): 476 V, 1 NV
1997	2066	833	409	5	1		399	4		Court: Art. 5 (1): 1 NV; 6 (1) (length): 5 V Committe of Ministers: Art. 6 (1) (fair trial): 2 V; Art. 6 (1) (length): 394 V, 3 NV; Art. 8: 2 V
1998	3113	1101	276	3	2		268	3		Court: Art. 5 (3): 1 NV; 6 (1) (length): 2 V; Art. 8: 1 V, 1 NV Committe of Ministers: Art. 6 (1) (length): 266 V, 2 NV; Prpt. 1 Art. 1: 3 V, 2 NV

Year	Applications lodged	Applications registered	Decisions on the merits	Court:			Committe of Ministers:			Articles concerned
				V	NV	FS	V	NV	FS	
1999	2645	882	498	44		25	450	4		Court: Art. 6 (1) (fair trial): 4 V; 6 (1) (length): 40 V, 25 FS; Art. 6 (3): 1 V; Art. 8: 1 V, 1 NV; Prot. 1 Art. 1: 1 V; Prot. 7 Art. 5: 1 NV Committe of Ministers: Art. 5 (1): 1 V; Art. 5 (4): 1 V; Art. 6 (1) (fair trial): 3 V; Art. 6 (1) (length): 443 V, 4 NV; Art. 8: 1 V; Art. 13: 1 NV
2000	7339	868	237	232	2	160	2	1		Court: Art. 3: 1 V, 3 NV; Art. 5 (1): 1 V; Art. 5 (3): 2 V; Art. 6 (1) (fair trial): 7 V, 1 FS; 6 (1) (length): 217 V, 158 FS; Art. 6 (3): 2 V, 1 NV; Art. 8: 5 V, 3 NV, 1 FS; Art. 13: 1 V; Art. 14: 1 NV; Prot. 1 Art. 1: 8 V, 1 FS; Prot. 1 Art. 2: 1 NV; Prot. 1 Art. 3: 1 V; Prot. 4 Art. 2: 1 V Committe of Ministers: Art. 6 (1) (length): 2 V, 1 NV; Art. 8: 1 V
2001	3779	587	364	360	4	45				Court: Art. 3: 1 V, 1 NV; Art. 5 (1): 1 V; Art. 5 (5): 1 NV; Art. 6 (1) (fair trial): 3 V, 1 NV, 32 FS; 6 (1) (length): 345 V, 1 NV, 20 FS; Art. 6 (3): 1 V, 1 NV; Art. 8: 2 V, 1 NV; Art. 10: 1 V, 1 NV; Art. 11: 2 V; Art. 13: 3 V; Prot. 1 Art. 1: 5 V, 3 NV, 34 FS
2002	1360	1302	331	325	6	49				Court: Art. 2: 3 NV; Art. 3: 1 FS; Art. 5 (5): 1 NV; Art. 6 (1) (fair trial): 31 V, 3 NV, 42 FS; Art. 6 (1) (length): 288 V, 2 NV, 6 FS; Art. 6 (2): 1 NV; Art. 6 (3): 1 V, 1 NV; Art. 8: 1 V; Art. 13: 1 V, 1 FS; Prot. 1 Art. 1: 30 V, 42 FS; Prot. 4 Art. 4: 1 FS

Year	Applications lodged	Applications registered	Decisions on the merits	Court:			Committe of Ministers:			Articles concerned
				V	NV	FS	V	NV	FS	
2003	1848	1351	108	106	2	29				Court: Art. 5 (1): 2 V; Art. 5 (3): 1 NV; Art. 5 (5): 1 V; Art. 6 (1) (fair trial): 96 V, 29 FS; Art. 6 (1) (length): 3 V; Art. 6 (3): 1 NV; Art. 7: 1 NV; Art. 8: 5 V, 5 NV; Art. 10: 1 NV; Art. 13: 1 V; Prot. 1 Art. 1: 91 V, 1 NV, 29 FS; Prot. 4 Art. 2: 4 V
2004	1867	1480	37	36	1	7				Court: Art. 6 (1) (fair trial): 15 V, 2 NV, 7 FS; Art. 6 (1) (length): 12 V; Art. 6 (3): 2 V; Art. 8: 4 V; Art. 11: 1 V; Art. 13: 1 V, 1 NV; Prot. 1 Art. 1: 15 V, 1 NV, 7 FS; Prot. 1 Art. 3: 1 V; Prot. 4 Art. 2: 3 V
2005	1186	848	70	67	3	7				Court: Art. 3: 2 NV; Art. 5 (1): 2 V, 1 NV; Art. 5 (3): 2 V; Art. 5 (4): 2 V; Art. 5 (5): 2 V; Art. 6 (1) (fair trial): 15 V, 1 NV, 1 FS; Art. 6 (1) (length): 2 V, 3 FS; Art. 6 (3): 3 V, 2 NV; Art. 8: 9 V, 1 NV; Art. 13: 2 V; Prot. 1 Art. 1: 49 V, 7 FS; Prot. 4 Art. 2: 2 V
2006	1268	934	92	87	5	2				Court: Art. 3: 2 NV; Art. 5 (1): 1 V, 2 NV; Art. 5 (4): 1 V; Art. 5 (5): 1 V; 1 NV; Art. 6 (1) (fair trial): 4 V, 5 NV; Art. 6 (1) (length): 20 V, 2 FS; Art. 6 (3): 4 V, 1 NV; Art. 8: 32 V, 3 NV; Art. 13: 26 V; Prot. 1 Art. 1: 51 V, 1 NV, 2 FS; Prot. 1 Art. 3: 10 V; Prot. 4 Art. 2: 3 V, 1 NV; Prot. 7 Art. 4: 1 NV
Total	38304	13337	3339	1358	39	325	1918	24	0	

V   finding at least one violation
NV   finding no violation
FS   friendly settlement

Entry into force of the Convention: 10.26.1955
Inception of right of individual application: 8.1.1973

Population in 2006 (Eurostat):   58751711
Applications lodged in % of population: 0,002028654

Italy

2. Distribution of Decisions by ECHR Provision

	Court			Committee of Ministers			Total
	finding of violation	finding of no violation	FS	finding of violation	finding of no violation	FS	
Art. 2		3					3
Art. 3	2	9	1		1		13
Art. 5 (1)	9	5		1	1		16
Art. 5 (2)							0
Art. 5 (3)	5	2	1		1		9
Art. 5 (4)	5			1	1		7
Art. 5 (5)	5	3					8
Art. 6 (1) fair trial	179	15	111	8	1		314
Art. 6 (1) length	1011	14	215	1898	18		3156
Art. 6 (2)		1					1
Art. 6 (3)	20	10		3			33
Art. 7		1					1
Art. 8	63	16	1	4			84
Art. 9		1					1
Art. 10	1	2					3
Art. 11	3						3
Art. 13	37	1	1		2		41
Art. 14		3					3
Prot. 1 Art. 1	254	9	122	5	7		397
Prot. 1 Art. 2		1					1
Prot. 1 Art. 3	12						12
Prot. 4 Art. 2	14	1					15
Prot. 4 Art. 4			1				1
Prot. 7 Art. 4		1					1
Prot. 7 Art. 5		1					1

Italy

3. Distribution of Decisions by ECHR Provision per Year

Article	1980	1981	1982	1983	1984	1985	1986	1987	1988	1989	1990	1991	1992	1993	1994	1995
2																
3	1			1												
5 (1)	1	1			1					1						
5 (2)																
5 (3)			1			1								1		
5 (4)			1		1					1						
5 (5)										1						
6 (1) fair trial	1	1		1		1				1			1	1		2
6 (1) length			2	1		1		3		3	1	24	41	12	11	309
6 (2)																
6 (3)	1				1					2		3			2	1
7																
8	1													1		
9	1															
10																
11																
13																1
14																1
P 1-1										1					4	2
P 1-2																
P 1-3																
P 4-2															1	
P 4-4																
P 7-4																
P 7-5																

1996	1997	1998	1999	2000	2001	2002	2003	2004	2005	2006
						3				
				4	2	1			2	2
	1		1	1	1		2		3	3
		1		2			1		2	
			1						2	1
					1	1	1		2	2
2	2		7	8	36	76	124	24	17	9
482	402	270	512	378	366	296	3	12	5	22
						1				
2			1	3	2	2	1	2	5	5
							1			
2	2	2	3	10	3	1	10	4	10	35
				2			1			
				2				1		
2			1	1	3	2	1	2	2	26
				1						
1	6	5	1	1	42	72	120	23	56	54
				1						
				1				1		10
				1			4	3	2	4
						1				
										1
		1								

Greece

1. Applications, Decisions on the Merits, and Friendly Settlements per Year

Year	Applications lodged	Applications registered	Decisions on the merits	Court:			Committe of Ministers:			Articles concerned
				V	NV	FS	V	NV	FS	
1981	not available									
1982	not available									
1983	9									
1984	7									
1985	1									
1986	13	1								
1987	39	11								
1988	30	19								
1989	37	17								
1990	51	26								
1991	88	29	1	1						Court: Art. 6 (1) (length): 1 V
1992	78	68	2	1				1		Court: Art. 6 (3): 1 V; Art. 10: 1 NV; Committe of Ministers: Art. 8: 1 NV
1993	73	111	3	2			1			Court: Art.7: 1 NV; Art. 9: 1 V; Prot. 1 Art. 1: 1 V; Committee of Ministers: Art. 6 (1) (length): 1 V

Year	Applications lodged	Applications registered	Decisions on the merits	Court:			Committe of Ministers:			Articles concerned
				V	NV	FS	V	NV	FS	
1994	118	48	2	2						Court: Art. 6 (1) (fair trial): 2 V; Art. 6 (1) (length): 1 NV; Art. 9: 1 NV; Art. 11: 1 NV; Art. 13: 1 NV; Art. 14: 1 NV; Prot. 1 Art. 1: 1 V, 1 NV
1995	155	40	2	2						Court: Art. 5 (4): 1 V; Art. 6 (1) (length): 1 V; Prot. 1 Art. 1: 1 NV
1996	110	43	7	5	1		1			Court: Art. 3: 2 NV; Art. 5 (1): 1 NV; Art. 6 (1) (length): 1 NV; Art. 9: 1 V, 2 NV; Art. 13: 4 V; Prot. 1 Art. 1: 2 V; Prot 1 Art. 2: 2 NV. Committe of Ministers: Art. 6 (1) (length): 1 V
1997	134	56	11	10	1	1				Court: Art. 3: 1 NV; Art. 5 (1): 1 V; Art. 5 (5): 1 V; Art. 6 (1) (fair trial): 3 V; Art. 6 (1) (length): 5 V; Art. 7: 1 NV; Art. 9: 1 FS; Art. 10: 1 V; Art. 14: 1 V; Prot. 1 Art. 3: 1 NV
1998	236	84	10	5			5			Court: Art. 6 (1) (length): 2 V, 1 NV; Art. 6 (3): 1 V, 1 NV; Art. 7: 1 NV; Art. 9: 1 V, 2 NV; Art. 11: 1 V; Art. 14: 1 NV. Committe of Ministers: Art. 6 (1) (fair trial): 1 V; Art. 6 (1) (length): 5 V; Prot. 1 Art. 1: 1 V
1999	184	144	12	5		1	7			Court: Art. 6 (1) (fair trial): 1 V; Art. 6 (1) (length): 1 V, 1 NV; Art. 9: 1 V; Art. 13: 1 V; Prot. 1 Art. 1: 3 V, 2 NV. Committe of Ministers: Art. 6 (1) (fair trial): 2 V; Art. 6 (1) (length): 5 V

Year	Applications lodged	Applications registered	Decisions on the merits	Court: V	NV	FS	Committee of Ministers: V	NV	FS	Articles concerned
2000	265	123	15	15		3				Court: Art. 6 (1) (fair trial): 4 V, 2 FS; Art. 6 (1) (length): 10 V, 1 FS; Art. 6 (3): 1 V; Art. 14: 1 V; Prot. 1 Art. 1: 3 V
2001	274	192	16	15	1	5				Court: Art. 3: 2 V; Art. 5 (1): 1 V; Art. 5 (4): 1 V; Art. 6 (1) (fair trial): 6 V, 2 FS; Art. 6 (1) (length): 6 V, 1 NV, 3 FS; Art. 8: 1 V; Prot. 1 Art. 1: 5 V
2002	379	311	17	16	1	3				Court: Art. 6 (1) (fair trial): 7 V, 1 NV; Art. 6 (1) (length): 6 V, 3 FS; Art. 9: 1 V; Art. 14: 1 NV; Prot. 1 Art. 1: 6 V, 1 NV
2003	480	354	23	23		3				Court: Art. 6 (1) (fair trial): 5 V, 1 FS; Art. 6 (1) (length): 14 V, 2 FS; Art. 6 (3): 1 V; Art. 8: 1 NV; Art. 13: 2 V; Prot. 1 Art. 1: 9 V, 1 FS
2004	405	274	35	32	3					Court: Art. 2: 2 V; Art. 3: 1 NV; Art. 5 (4): 1 V; Art. 6 (1) (fair trial): 5 V, 1 NV; Art. 6 (1) (length): 22 V, 3 NV; Art. 8: 1 V; Art. 9: 1 NV; Art. 10: 1 V; Art. 13: 6 V; Prot. 1 Art. 1: 5 V
2005	425	369	102	101	1	1				Court: Art. 3: 1 V; Art. 6 (1) (fair trial): 19 V; Art. 6 (1) (length): 18 V, 1 NV, 1 FS; Art. 6 (2): 1 V; Art. 11: 1 V; Art. 13: 31 V; Art. 14: 1 V, 1 NV; Prot. 1 Art. 1: 5 V

Year	Applications lodged	Applications registered	Decisions on the merits	Court: V	NV	FS	Committe of Ministers: V	NV	FS	Articles concerned
2006	430	371	53	53		2				Court: Art. 3: 2 V; Art. 5 (1): 1 V; Art. 5 (4): 1 V; Art. 6 (1) (fair trial): 10 V, 1 FS; Art. 6 (1) (length): 34 V; Art. 9: 2 V; Art. 13: 8 V; Prot. 1 Art. 1: 4 V, 1 FS; Prot. 1 Art. 3: 1 V
Total	4021	2691	311	288	8	19	14	1	0	

V finding at least one violation
NV finding no violation
FS friendly settlement

Entry into force of the Convention: 11.28.1974
Inception of right of individual application: 11.20.1985

Population in 2006 (Eurostat): 11125179
Applications lodged in % of population: 0,00838165

Greece

2. Distribution of Decisions by ECHR Provision

	Court			Committee of Ministers			Total
	finding of violation	finding of no violation	FS	finding of violation	finding of no violation	FS	
Art. 2	2						2
Art. 3	5	4					9
Art. 4							0
Art. 5 (1)	3	1					4
Art. 5 (2)							0
Art. 5 (3)							0
Art. 5 (4)	4						4
Art. 5 (5)	1						1
Art. 6 (1) fair trial	62	2	6	3			73
Art. 6 (1) length	190	9	10	12			221
Art. 6 (2)	1	1					2
Art. 6 (3)	4	1					5
Art. 7		3					3
Art. 8	2	1	1		1		5
Art. 9	7	6	2				15
Art. 10	2	1					3
Art. 11	2	1	1				4
Art. 13	52	1					53
Art. 14	3	4	1				8
Prot. 1 Art. 1	44	5	2	1			52
Prot. 1 Art. 2		2					2
Prot. 1 Art. 3	1	1					2

Greece

3. Distribution of Decisions by ECHR Provision per Year

	1991	1992	1993	1994	1995	1996	1997	1998	1999	2000	2001	2002	2003	2004	2005	2006
Article																
2														2		
3						2	1				2			1	1	2
5 (1)						1	1				1					1
5 (4)				1							1			1		1
5 (5)							1									
6 (1) fair trial				2			3	1	3	6	8	8	6	6	19	11
6 (1) length	1		1	1	1	2	5	8	7	11	10	9	16	25	90	34
6 (2)											1			1		
6 (3)		1					2	1					1			
7		1				1	1									
8		1						1			1		1	1		
9			1	1		3	1	3	1			1		1		2
10		1				1								1		
11				1			1	1							1	
13				1		4		1					2	6	31	8
14				1			1	1	1	1		1			2	
P 1-1			1	2	1	2		1	5	3	5	7	10	5	5	5
P 1-2						2										
P 1-3							1									1

Turkey

1. Applications, Decisions on the Merits, and Friendly Settlements per Year

Year	Applications lodged	Applications registered	Decisions on the merits	Court:			Committe of Ministers:			Articles concerned
				V	NV	FS	V	NV	FS	
1964	not available									
1965	not available									
1966	not available									
1967	not available									
1968	not available									
1969	not available									
1970	not available									
1971	not available									
1972	not available									
1973	not available									
1974	not available									
1975	not available									
1976	not available									
1977	not available									
1978	not available									
1979	not available									

Year	Applications lodged	Applications registered	Decisions on the merits	Court:			Committe of Ministers:			Articles concerned
				V	NV	FS	V	NV	FS	
1980	not available									
1981	not available									
1982	not available									
1983	7									
1984	10									
1985	4									
1986	5									
1987	119									
1988	67	10								
1989	118	37								
1990	104	85								
1991	90	33								
1992	126	180								
1993	104	128							1	Committe of Ministers: Art. 3: 1 FS; Art. 5 (1): 1 FS; Art. 5 (3): 1 FS; Art.5 (4): 1 FS
1994	130	187								
1995	193	214		2			1			Court: Art. 5 (3): 2 V; Art. 6 (1) (length): 2 V; Committee of Ministers: Art. 3: 2 NV; Art. 5 (1): 2 NV; Art. 8: 1 V, 1 NV; Art. 13: 2 NV

Year	Applications lodged	Applications registered	Decisions on the merits	Court:			Committe of Ministers:			Articles concerned
				V	NV	FS	V	NV	FS	
1996	271	526		4			1			Court: Art. 3: 1 V; Art. 5 (3): 1 V; Art. 6 (1) (length): 1 V; Art. 8: 1 V, 1 NV; Art. 13: 1 V; Art. 14: 1 NV; Prot. 1 Art. 1: 2 V Committe of Ministers: Art. 3: 1 V
1997	292	356		5	2	1				Court: Art. 2: 1 NV; Art. 3: 1 V, 2 NV, 1 FS; Art. 5 (1): 2 NV; Art. 5 (3): 1 V; Art. 5 (4): 1 V; Art. 5 (5): 1 V; Art. 6 (1) (length): 1 V; Art. 6 (3): 1 V; Art. 8: 1 V, 1 NV; Art. 9: 1 NV; Art. 10: 1 NV; Art. 13: 2 V, 1 NV; Art. 14: 1 NV; Prot. 1 Art. 1: 1 V
1998	491	729	14*	13	1		2	1		Court: Art. 2: 4 V, 4 NV; Art. 3: 3 V, 1 NV; Art. 5 (1): 1 V, 1 NV; Art. 5 (3): 1 V; Art. 6 (1) (fair trial): 2 V; Art. 8: 1 V, 1 NV; Art. 10: 1 V, 1 NV; Art. 11: 2 V; Art. 13: 6 V, 1 NV; Art. 14: 6 NV; Prot. 1 Art. 1: 2 V, 1 NV Committee of Ministers: Art. 5 (3): 1 V; Art. 6 (1) (fair trial): 1 V, 1 NV; Art. 6 (1) (length): 2 V; Art. 8: 1 NV
1999	515	653	18	18			5			Court: Art. 2: 3 V, 1 NV; Art. 3: 1 V, 1 NV; Art. 5 (1): 1 V; Art. 5 (3): 1 V; Art. 5 (4): 1 V; Art. 6 (1) (fair trial): 9 V; Art. 7: 1 V, 2 NV; Art. 10: 12 V, 2 NV; Art. 11: 1 V; Art. 13: 2 V; Art. 14: 2 NV Committee of Ministers: Art. 2: 1 V; Art. 5 (3): 2 V; Art. 5 (4): 2 V; Art. 5 (5): 1 V; Art. 10: 1 V; Art. 13: 1 NV; Art. 14: 1 NV; Prot. 1 Art. 1: 1 V

Year	Applications lodged	Applications registered	Decisions on the merits	Court:			Committee of Ministers:			Articles concerned
				V	NV	FS	V	NV	FS	
2000	1117	735	26	23	3	12	2			Court: Art. 2: 17 V, 3 NV; Art. 3: 13 V, 2 NV, 3 FS; Art. 5 (1): 2 V; Art. 5 (2): 1 NV; Art. 5 (3): 2 V, 1 FS; Art. 5 (4): 1 V; Art. 5 (5): 1 V; Art. 6 (1) (fair trial): 3 V; Art. 6 (1) (length): 1 V, 6 FS; Art. 6 (3): 1 NV; Art. 8: 1 V, 1 NV; Art. 9: 1 FS; Art. 10: 4 V, 1 NV; Art. 13: 11 V, 1 NV; Art. 14: 2 NV; Prot. 1 Art. 1: 2 V, 3 FS Committee of Ministers: Prot. 1 Art. 1: 2 V
2001	2530	1059	170	168	2	57				Court: Art. 2: 7 V, 3 NV, 2 FS; Art. 3: 5 V, 6 NV, 20 FS; Art. 5 (1): 4 V, 3 NV, 11 FS; Art. 5 (3): 2 V, 3 FS; Art. 5 (4): 5 FS; Art. 5 (5): 3 FS; Art. 6 (1) (fair trial): 15 V, 10 FS; Art. 6 (1) (length): 26 V, 1 NV, 2 FS; Art. 6 (3): 3 V, 1 FS; Art. 7: 1 V; Art. 8: 1 V, 7 FS; Art. 10: 1 FS; Art. 11: 1 NV; Art. 13: 13 V, 24 FS; Art. 14: 6 NV, 9 FS; Prot. 1 Art. 1: 130 V, 10 FS
2002	3879	3866	55	53	2	45				Court: Art. 2: 7 V, 4 NV, 10 FS; Art. 3: 3 V, 3 NV, 14 FS; Art. 5 (1): 1 V, 14 FS; Art. 5 (3): 5 V, 5 FS; Art. 5 (4): 4 V, 2 FS; Art. 5 (5): 2 V, 1 FS; Art. 6 (1) (fair trial): 7 V, 3 NV, 7 FS; Art. 6 (1) (length): 9 V, 3 FS; Art. 6 (3): 2 FS; Art. 7: 1 V; Art. 8: 2 V, 2 NV, 3 FS; Art. 10: 6 V, 6 FS; Art. 11: 2 V; Art. 13: 4 V, 2 NV, 6 FS; Art. 14: 1 NV, 6 FS; Prot. 1 Art. 1: 25 V, 1 NV, 16 FS; Prot. 1 Art. 3: 1 V

Year	Applications lodged	Applications registered	Decisions on the merits	Court:			Committe of Ministers:			Articles concerned
				V	NV	FS	V	NV	FS	
2003	2944	3558	76	74	2	44				Court: Art. 2: 2 V, 2 NV, 10 FS; Art. 3: 8 V, 4 NV, 18 FS; Art. 5 (1): 2 V, 2 NV, 6 FS; Art. 5 (3): 5 V, 11 FS; Art. 5 (4): 2 V, 5 FS; Art. 6 (1) (fair trial): 53 V, 1 NV, 8 FS; Art. 6 (1) (length): 3 V, 1 NV, 2 FS; Art. 6 (2): 1 NV; Art. 6 (3): 2 V, 2 FS; Art. 7: 1 NV; Art. 8: 5 V, 2 FS; Art. 10: 6 V, 6 FS; Art. 11: 2 V 1 NV; Art. 13: 4 V, 1 NV, 10 FS; Art. 14: 5 NV, 4 FS; Prot. 1 Art. 1: 5 V, 5 FS
2004	3930	3679	156	152	4	10				Court: Art. 2: 22 V, 17 NV, 3 FS; Art. 3: 18 V, 17 NV, 6 FS; Art. 5 (1): 4 V, 8 NV; Art. 5 (3): 14 V, 1 NV, 4 FS; Art. 5 (4): 5 V; Art. 5 (5): 2 V; Art. 6 (1) (fair trial): 74 V, 2 NV, 7 FS; Art. 6 (1) (length): 7 V, 2 NV; Art. 6 (2): 1 V; Art. 6 (3): 2 NV; Art. 7: 1 NV; Art. 8: 6 V, 4 NV, 3 FS; Art. 9: 2 NV; Art. 10: 19 V, 1 NV, 2 FS; Art. 13: 22 V, 1 NV, 6 FS; Art. 14: 1 V, 13 NV, 3 FS; Prot. 1 Art. 1: 42 V, 2 NV, 3 FS
2005	2244	2489	276	266	10	6				Court: Art. 2: 35 V, 15 NV; Art. 3: 30 V, 29 NV, 1 FS; Art. 5 (1): 6 V, 10 NV; Art. 5 (3): 31 V, 1 NV; Art. 5 (4): 7 V, 1 NV; Art. 5 (5): 4 V; Art. 6 (1) (fair trial): 89 V, 1 NV, 2 FS; Art. 6 (1) (length): 31 V, 8 NV, 1 FS; Art. 6 (2): 1 NV; Art. 6 (3): 3 V, 2 NV; Art. 7: 1 V; Art. 8: 3 V, 7 NV; Art. 9: 2 NV; Art. 10: 40 V, 2 NV, 3 FS; Art. 11: 4 V, 3 NV; Art. 13: 36 V, 6 NV, 2 FS; Art. 14: 12 NV, 1 FS; Prot. 1 Art. 1: 66 V, 3 NV; Prot. 1 Art. 2: 1 NV

Year	Applications lodged	Applications registered	Decisions on the merits	Court:			Committe of Ministers:			Articles concerned
				V	NV	FS	V	NV	FS	
2006	2280	2330	320	313	7	8				Court: Art. 2: 24 V, 14 NV, 2 FS; Art. 3: 26 V, 22 NV, 1 FS; Art. 5 (1): 3 V, 16 NV; Art. 5 (2): 2 NV; Art. 5 (3): 44 V, 1 NV, 2 FS; Art. 5 (4): 16 V, 1 NV, 1 FS; Art. 5 (5): 4 V; Art. 6 (1) (fair trial): 84 V, 6 NV, 2 FS; Art. 6 (1) (length): 46 V, 5 NV; Art. 6 (2): 1 NV; Art. 6 (3): 4 V, 1 NV; Art. 8: 8 V, 7 NV; Art. 9: 1 FS; Art. 10: 32 V, 2 NV, 3 FS; Art. 11: 7 V, 1 NV; Art. 13: 54 V, 3 NV, 1 FS; Art. 14: 11 NV; Prot. 1 Art. 1: 82 V, 6 NV, 1 FS; Prot. 1 Art. 2: 1 V, 1 NV
Total	21570	20854	1097	1091	33	183	11	1	1	

V	finding at least one violation
NV	finding no violation
FS	friendly settlement

Entry into force of the Convention:	5.18.1954
Inception of right of individual application:	1.28.1987

Population in 2006 (Eurostat):	72519974
Applications lodged in % of population:	0,003133597

Turkey

2. Distribution of Decisions by ECHR Provision

	Court			Committee of Ministers			Total
	finding of violation	finding of no violation	FS	finding of violation	finding of no violation	FS	
Art. 2	121	64	27	1			213
Art. 3	109	87	64	1	2	1	264
Art. 5 (1)	24	42	21		2	1	90
Art. 5 (2)		3	3				6
Art. 5 (3)	109	3	61	3		1	177
Art. 5 (4)	37	2	13	2		1	55
Art. 5 (5)	14		4	1			19
Art. 6 (1) fair trial	336	13	36	1	1		387
Art. 6 (1) length	127	17	14	2			160
Art. 6 (2)	1	3					4
Art. 6 (3)	13	6	5				24
Art. 7	4	4					8
Art. 8	29	24	15	1	2		71
Art. 9		5	3				8
Art. 10	120	10	21	1			152
Art. 11	18	6					24
Art. 13	155	16	49		3		223
Art. 14	1	60	23		1		85
Prot. 1 Art. 1	357	13	38	3			411
Prot. 1 Art. 2	1	2					3
Prot. 1 Art. 3	1						1

Turkey

3. Distribution of Decisions by ECHR Provision per Year

	1993	1994	1995	1996	1997	1998	1999	2000	2001	2002	2003	2004	2005	2006
Article														
2					1	8	5	20	12	21	14	42	50	40
3	1		2	2	4	4	2	18	31	20	30	41	60	48
5 (1)	1		2		2	2	1	2	18	5	10	12	16	19
5 (2)							1	3						2
5 (3)	1		2	1	1	2	3	3	40	10	16	19	32	47
5 (4)	1				1		3	1	5	6	7	5	8	18
5 (5)					1		1	1	3	3		2	4	4
6 (1) fair trial					4	9	3		25	17	62	83	92	92
6 (1) length			2	1	1	2		7	29	12	6	9	40	51
6 (2)											1	1	1	1
6 (3)					1			1	4	2	4	2	5	5
7							3		1	1	1	1	1	
8			2	2	2	3		2	8	7	7	13	10	15
9						1		1		1		2	2	1
10					1	2	15	5	1	6	12	22	45	37
11						2	1		1	2	3		7	8
13			2	1	3	7	3	12	37	12	15	29	44	58
14				1	1	6	3	2	15	7	9	17	12	11
P 1-1				2	1	3	1	7	140	42	10	47	69	89
P 1-2													1	2
P 1-3										1				

Poland

1. Applications, Decisions on the Merits, and Friendly Settlements per Year

Year	Applications lodged	Applications registered	Decisions on the merits	Court: V	NV	FS	Committe of Ministers: V	NV	FS	Articles concerned
1992	240	-								
1993	630	39								
1994	979	161								
1995	1113	222								
1996	1127	458								
1997	1318	430	2		1		1			Court: Art. 6 (1) (length of proceedings): 1 V Committee of Ministers: Art. 6 (1) (length): 1 V
1998	1914	491	4	3			1			Court: Art. 6 (1) (fair trial): 1 V; Art. 6 (1) (length): 2 V; Art. 6 (3): 1 V Committee of Ministers: Art. 5 (3): 1 V; Art. 6 (1) (length): 1 NV
1999	2895	691	5	1	2		1	1		Court: Art. 5 (4): 1 V; Art. 6 (1) (length): 1 NV; Art. 10: 1 NV Committee of Ministers: Art. 3: 1 NV; Art. 8: 1 V
2000	3175	775	12	12		2				Court: Art. 3: 1 NV; Art. 5 (1): 2 V, 1 NV; Art. 5 (3): 4 V, 1 FS; Art. 5 (4): 5 V; Art. 6 (1) (length): 8 V, 1 NV, 2 FS; Art. 13: 1 V, 1 FS

Year	Applications lodged	Applications registered	Decisions on the merits	Court:			Committe of Ministers:			Articles concerned
				V	NV	FS	V	NV	FS	
2001	3429	1763	19	17	2	1				Court: Art. 3: 1 V; Art. 5 (1): 1 V; Art. 5 (3): 5 V; Art. 5 (4): 2 V; Art. 6 (1) (fair trial): 2 V, 1 NV; Art. 6 (1) (length): 18 V, 1 NV, 1 FS; Art. 6 (3): 1 V; Art. 11: 1 NV
2002	4521	4032	22	20	2	3				Court: Art. 3: 1 NV, 1 FS; Art. 5 (1): 1 V; Art. 5 (3): 3 V, 1 NV, 1 FS; Art. 5 (4): 2 V, 1 FS; Art. 6 (1) (fair trial): 1 NV; Art. 6 (1) (length): 11 V, 2 NV, 1 FS; Art. 6 (3): 1 V; Art. 8: 4 V; Art. 10: 1 V
2003	5359	3658	43	43		22				Court: Art. 5 (1): 2 V, 1 NV; Art. 5 (3): 4 V; Art. 5 (4): 1 V; Art. 6 (1) (length): 40 V, 1 NV, 22 FS; Art. 8: 6 V, 1 NV; Art. 10: 1 V; Art. 13: 3 V
2004	5796	4321	75	74	1	4				Court: Art. 5 (1): 3 V; Art. 5 (3): 6 V; Art. 5 (4): 3 V; Art. 6 (1) (fair trial): 1 V; Art. 6 (1) (length): 66 V, 1 NV, 4 FS; Art. 8: 1 V; Art. 11: 1 NV; Art. 13: 3 V; Prot. 1 Art. 1: 1 V
2005	4744	4571	48	44	4					Court: Art. 5 (1): 3 V; Art. 5 (3): 11 V; Art. 5 (4): 1 V; Art. 6 (1) (fair trial): 5 V, 1 NV; Art. 6 (1) (length): 20 V, 5 NV; Art. 8: 6 V, 1 NV; Art. 10: 1 V; Art. 13: 3 NV; Prot. 1 Art. 1: 3 V

Year	Applications lodged	Applications registered	Decisions on the merits	Court:			Committe of Ministers:			Articles concerned
				V	NV	FS	V	NV	FS	
2006	4470	3990	115	107	8					Court: Art. 2: 1 V; Art. 5 (1): 4 V; Art. 5 (3): 39 V, 5 NV; Art. 5 (4): 1 V; Art. 5 (5): 1 V; Art. 6 (1) (fair trial): 6 V; Art. 6 (1) (length): 51 V, 4 NV; Art. 8: 11 V, 1 NV; Art. 10: 2 V; Art. 13: 2 V, 1 NV; Prot. 1 Art. 1: 3 V
Total	41710	25602	345	321	20	32	3	1	0	

V   finding at least one violation
NV   finding no violation
FS   friendly settlement

Entry into force of the Convention: 1.19.1993
Inception of right of indiviual application: 5.1.1993

Population in 2006 (Eurostat):   38157055
Applications lodged in % of population: 0,012427372

Poland

2. Distribution of Decisions by ECHR Provision

	Court			Committee of Ministers			Total
	finding of violation	finding of no violation	FS	finding of violation	finding of no violation	FS	
Art. 2	1						1
Art. 3	1	2	1		1		5
Art. 5 (1)	16	2					18
Art. 5 (3)	72	6	2	1			81
Art. 5 (4)	16		1				17
Art. 5 (5)	1						1
Art. 6 (1) fair trial	15	3					18
Art. 6 (1) length	213	17	30	2			262
Art. 6 (3)	3						3
Art. 8	29	3		1			33
Art. 10	5	1					6
Art. 11		2					2
Art. 13	9	4	1				14
Prot. 1 Art. 1	7						7

Poland

3. Distribution of Decisions by ECHR Provision per Year

	1997	1998	1999	2000	2001	2002	2003	2004	2005	2006
Article										
2										1
3			1	1	1	1				
5 (1)				3	1	1	3	3	3	4
5 (3)		1		4	5	4	4	6	11	34
5 (4)			1	5	2	2	1	3	1	1
5 (5)										1
6 (1) fair trial		1			3	1		1	6	6
6 (1) length	2	3	1	9	19	13	41	67	25	55
6 (3)		1			1	1				
8			1	1		4	7	1	7	12
10			1			1	1		1	2
11					1			1		
13				1			3	3	3	3
P 1-1								1	3	3

Slovakia

1. Applications, Decisions on the Merits, and Friendly Settlements per Year

Year	Applications lodged	Applications registered	Decisions on the merits	Court:			Committe of Ministers:			Articles concerned
				V	NV	FS	V	NV	FS	
1992	-	-								
1993	36	4								
1994	100	36								
1995	83	45								
1996	165	80								
1997	160	81								
1998	154	77	3	2			1			Court: 6 (1) (fair trial): 2 V; Committe of Ministers: 6 (1) (length of proceedings): 1 V
1999	227	163	3	1		1	2			Court: Art. 6 (1) (length): 1 V, 1 FS; Art. 8: 1 NV; Committe of Ministers: Art. 5 (3): 1 V; Art. 5 (4): 1 V; Art. 6 (1) (length): 1 V
2000	479	284	3	3						Court: Art. 5 (4): 1 V; Art. 6 (1) (length): 2 V
2001	546	343	5	5	1	3				Court: Art. 6 (1) (accession to a court): 1 FS; Art. 6 (1) (length): 3 V, 1 FS; Art. 10: 2 V; Art. 14: 1 NV; Prot. 1 Art. 1: 1 FS

Year	Applications lodged	Applications registered	Decisions on the merits	Court:			Committee of Ministers:			Articles concerned
				V	NV	FS	V	NV	FS	
2002	432	406	4	4		3				Court: Art. 6 (1) (fair trial): 2 V; Art. 6 (1) (length): 2 V, 3 FS
2003	539	349	19	17	2	8				Court: Art. 5 (1): 1 V; Art. 6 (1) (fair trial): 1 V, 1 NV; Art. 6 (1) (length): 14 V, 8 FS; Art. 10: 1 NV; Art. 13: 1 V; Art. 14: 1 NV; Prot. 1 Art. 1: 1 V, 1 NV
2004	484	403	13	11	2	1				Court: Art. 5 (1): 1 V; Art. 5 (3): 1 V; Art. 5 (4): 3 V; Art. 5 (5): 1 V; Art. 6 (1) (fair trial): 1 V, 3 NV; Art. 6 (1) (length): 5 V, 1 FS; Art. 10: 1 V; Art. 13: 1 V, 1 NV; Prot. 1 Art. 1: 1 V, 2 NV
2005	478	444	28	28		1				Court: Art. 6 (1) (fair trial): 3 V; Art. 6 (1) (length): 25 V, 2 NV, 1 FS; Art. 13: 3 V
2006	537	486	36	36						Court: Art. 6 (1) (fair trial): 2 V; Art. 6 (1) (length): 30 V; Art. 8: 3 V; Art. 10: 3 V; Art. 13: 6 V; Art. 14: 1 V
Total	4420	3201	114	107	5	17	3	0	0	

V   finding at least one violation
NV finding no violation
FS friendly settlement

Entry into force of the Convention:	1.1.1993
Inception of right of individual application:	1.1.1993

Population in 2006 (Eurostat):	5389180
Applications lodged in % of population:	0,008876839

Slovakia

2. Distribution of Decisions by ECHR Provision

	Court			Committee of Ministers			Total
	finding of violation	finding of no violation	FS	finding of violation	finding of no violation	FS	
Art. 5 (1)	2						2
Art. 5 (3)	1			1			2
Art. 5 (4)	4			1			5
Art. 5 (5)	1						1
Art. 6 (1) fair trial	10	4	1				15
Art. 6 (1) length	83	2	17	2			104
Art. 8	3	1					4
Art. 10	5	1					6
Art. 13	11	1					12
Art. 14	1	2					3
Prot. 1 Art. 1	2	3	1				6

Slovakia

3. Distribution of Decisions by ECHR Provision per Year

	1998	1999	2000	2001	2002	2003	2004	2005	2006
Article									
5 (1)						1	1		
5 (3)		1					1		
5 (4)		1	1				3		
5 (5)							1		
6 (1) fair trial	2				2	2	4	3	2
6 (1) length	1	2	2	3	2	14	5	27	30
8									3
10									3
13						1	2	3	6
14				1		1			1
P 1-1				1		2	3		

Russia

1. Applications, Decisions on the Merits, and Friendly Settlements per Year

Year	Applications lodged	Applications registered	Decisions on the merits	Court:			Committe of Ministers:			Articles concerned
				V	NV	FS	V	NV	FS	
1996										
1997	401									
1998	858	113								
1999	1790	971								
2000	2312	1323								
2001	4490	2105								
2002	4716	3989	2	2						Court: Art. 3: 1 V; Art. 5 (3): 1 V; Art. 6 (1) (fair trial): 1 V; Art. 6 (1) (length): 1 V; Prot. 1 Art. 1: 1 V
2003	6062	4738	5	5						Court: Art. 5 (1): 1 V; Art. 5 (3): 1 V; Art. 5 (4): 1 V; Art. 6 (1) (fair trial): 3 V; Art. 6 (1) (length): 1 V; Art. 8: 1 V
2004	7855	5835	14	13	1					Court: Art. 3: 4 V; Art. 5 (1): 5 V; Art. 5 (3): 1 V; Art. 5 (4): 1 V; Art. 6 (1) (fair trial): 3 V; Art. 6 (1) (length): 6 V; Art. 8: 2 V; Art. 11: 1 V; Art. 13: 4 V, 1 NV; Prot. 1 Art. 1: 2 V, 1 NV

Year	Applications lodged	Applications registered	Decisions on the merits	Court:			Committe of Ministers:			Articles concerned
				V	NV	FS	V	NV	FS	
2005	8781	8088	82	81	1					Court: Art. 2: 3 V, 2 NV; Art. 3: 8 V, 2 NV; Art. 5 (1): 2 V, 2 NV; Art. 5 (2): 1 NV; Art. 5 (3): 4 V; Art. 5 (4): 3 V, 2 NV; Art. 5 (5): 1 V; Art. 6 (1) (fair trial): 39 V; Art. 6 (1) (length): 27 V; Art. 6 (3): 3 V, 1 NV; Art. 8: 3 V; Art. 10: 1 V; Art. 13: 5 V; Art. 14: 1 V; Prot. 1 Art. 1: 52 V, 1 NV; Prot. 4 Art. 2: 2 V, 1 NV
2006	10569	10177	103	98	5					Court: Art. 2: 8 V; Art. 3: 10 V, 2 NV; Art. 5 (1): 6 V, 1 NV; Art. 5 (3): 6 V; Art. 5 (4): 4 V; Art. 6 (1) (fair trial): 25 V, 2 NV; Art. 6 (1) (length): 51 V, 2 NV; Art. 6 (2): 1 NV; Art. 6 (3): 3 V, 3 NV; Art. 8: 2 V; Art. 10: 2 V, 2 NV; Art. 11: 1 V; Art. 13: 13 V; Prot. 1 Art. 1: 45 V, 1 NV; Prot. 4 Art. 2: 2 V; Prot. 7 Art. 1: 1 V; Prot. 7 Art. 4: 1 NV
Total	47834	37339	206	199	7	0	0	0	0	

V	finding at least one violation
NV	finding no violation
FS	friendly settlement

Entry into force of the Convention:	5.5.1998
Inception of right of individual application:	5.5.1998

Population in 2006 (estimate by Eurostat):	142753300
Applications lodged in % of population:	0,006120273

Russia

2. Distribution of Decisions by ECHR Provision

	Court			Committee of Ministers			Total
	finding of violation	finding of no violation	FS	finding of violation	finding of no violation	FS	
Art. 2	11	2					13
Art. 3	23	4					27
Art. 4							0
Art. 5 (1)	14	3					17
Art. 5 (2)		1					1
Art. 5 (3)	13						13
Art. 5 (4)	9	2					11
Art. 5 (5)	1						1
Art. 6 (1) fair trial	71	2					73
Art. 6 (1) length	86	2					88
Art. 6 (2)		1					1
Art. 6 (3)	6	4					10
Art. 8	8						8
Art. 9							0
Art. 10	3	2					5
Art. 11	2						2
Art. 13	22	1					23
Art. 14	1		14				15
Prot. 1 Art. 1	101	4					105
Prot. 4 Art. 2	4	1					5
Prot. 7 Art. 1	1						
Prot. 7 Art. 4		1					1

Russia

3. Distribution of Decisions by ECHR Provision per Year

	2002	2003	2004	2005	2006
Article					
2				5	8
3	1		4	10	12
5 (1)		1	5	4	7
5 (2)				1	
5 (3)	1	1	1	4	6
5 (4)		1	1	5	4
5 (5)				1	
6 (1) fair trial	1	3	3	39	27
6 (1) length	1	1	6	27	53
6 (2)					1
6 (3)				4	6
8		1	2	3	2
10				1	4
11			1		1
13			5	5	13
14				1	
P 1-1	1	2	3	53	46
P 4-2				3	2
P 7-1					1
P 7-4					1

Ukraine

1. Applications, Decisions on the Merits, and Friendly Settlements per Year

Year	Applications lodged	Applications registered	Decisions on the merits	Court: V	NV	FS	Committe of Ministers: V	NV	FS	Articles concerned
1995										
1996	238	-								
1997	270	3								
1998	595	212								
1999	764	434								
2000	1520	727								
2001	2108	1057								
2002	2944	2819	1	1						Court: Art. 6 (1) (fair trial): 1 V; Prot. 1 Art. 1: 1 V
2003	2287	1858	6	6						Court: Art. 3: 8 V, 4 NV; Art. 8: 6 V, 5 NV, Art. 9: 2 V; Art. 13: 1 V, 1 NV
2004	2265	1538	14	13	1					Court: Art. 3: 1 NV; Art. 6 (1) (fair trial): 12 V; Art. 6 (1) (length): 3 V; Art. 13: 4 V, 1 NV; Prot. 1 Art. 1: 8 V; Prot. 1 Art. 3: 1 V
2005	2457	1870	119	119						Court: Art. 2: 1 V; Art. 3: 3 V; Art. 5 (1): 1 V; Art. 5 (3): 2 V; Art. 5 (4): 1 V; Art. 6 (1) (fair trial): 60 V; Art. 6 (1): 47 V; Art. 8: 1 V; Art. 10: 2 V; Art. 13: 33 V; Prot. 1 Art. 1: 67 V; Prot. 4 Art. 2: 1 NV; Prot. 7 Art. 2: 1 V

Year	Applications lodged	Applications registered	Decisions on the merits	Court:			Committe of Ministers:			Articles concerned
				V	NV	FS	V	NV	FS	
2006	3906	2482	120	119	1					Court: Art. 2: 1 V; Art. 3: 3 V; Art. 6 (1) (fair trial): 21 V, 1 NV; Art. 6 (1): 84 V 1 NV; Art. 6 (2): 2 V; Art. 8: 3 V; Art. 10: 1 V; Art. 13: 25 V; Prot. 1 Art. 1: 62 V; Prot. 1 Art. 3: 1 NV; Prot. 4 Art. 2: 1 V
Total	19354	13000	260	258	2	0	0	0	0	

V   finding at least one violation
NV   finding no violation
FS   friendly settlement

Entry into force of the Convention: 9.11.1997
Inception of right of individual application: 9.11.1997

Population in 2006 (Eurostat):   46749200
Applications lodged in % of population: 0,005216505

Ukraine

2. Distribution of Decisions by ECHR Provision

	Court			Committee of Ministers			Total
	finding of violation	finding of no violation	FS	finding of violation	finding of no violation	FS	
Art. 2	2						2
Art. 3	14	5					19
Art. 4							0
Art. 5 (1)	1						1
Art. 5 (2)							0
Art. 5 (3)	2						2
Art. 5 (4)	1						1
Art. 5 (5)							0
Art. 6 (1) fair trial	94	1					95
Art. 6 (1) length	134	1					135
Art. 6 (2)	2						2
Art. 6 (3)							0
Art. 8	10	5					15
Art. 9	2						2
Art. 10	3						3
Art. 11							0
Art. 13	63	2					65
Art. 14							0
Prot. 1 Art. 1	138						138
Prot. 1 Art. 3	1	1					2
Prot. 4 Art. 2	1	1					2
Prot. 7 Art. 2	1						1

Ukraine

3. Distribution of Decisions by ECHR Provision per Year

Article	2002	2003	2004	2005	2006
2				1	1
3		12	1	3	3
5 (1)				1	
5 (2)					
5 (3)				2	
5 (4)				1	
6 (1) fair trial	1		12	60	22
6 (1) length			3	47	85
6 (2)					2
6 (3)					
8		11		1	3
9		2			
10				2	1
13		2	5	33	25
P 1-1	1		8	67	62
P 1-3			1		1
P 4-2				1	1
P 7-2				1	

Index

remedies *(cont.)*
extraordinary 213, 331, 375–376,
377–378, 554, 623–624
inadmissibility of prosecution 563
individual constitutional complaint,
see **judicial review**
reopening of administrative and civil proceedings 77, 100, 146, 152, 190–191,
213, 215, 372, 435, 436, 441, 446, 509,
511, 513, 658, 660, 704
reopening of criminal proceedings 77, 100,
145, 152, 213, 215, 288–289, 300–301,
371–372, 375–376, 435, 436, 438, 441,
446, 508, 511, 513, 580, 582, 584, 651,
704–705
revision of civil and administrative proceedings 88–89, 290–291, 296–297,
300–302, 301, 375–376, 438, 581–585,
651
see also **length of proceedings/***nazdor-
system*
reopen proceedings, *see* **remedies**
repetitive cases 11, 13, 128, 642, 646,
656–657, 661, 680, 691; *see also* **length of
proceedings/pilot judgement**
reservation 19, 38–39, 42, 44, 46, 99, 110,
112–113, 115, 230, 233–234, 314–315,
316–317, 319–321, 348, 349, 360–361,
369, 398, 402–403, 454, 459, 461, 533,
534, 537, 608–610, 613–614, 655, 679
res judicata 126, 131, 146, 301, 441, 513;
see also **remedies**
restitutio in integrum 132, 287, 436, 438,
658, 704
review procedure, *see* **remedies**
right of reply 259, 365
**right to an effective remedy (Article 13
ECHR)** 9, 11, 24, 46, 57, 63, 87, 89,
122, 124, 141, 146–147, 183, 190, 192,
194, 203, 205, 211–212, 236, 245, 254,
266, 354, 414, 434, 473, 475, 479, 496,
509, 555, 557, 558–559, 563, 564,
566–567, 571, 583, 623, 624–625, 629,
634, 638, 648, 682, 687, 700, 706, 708;
see also **remedies**
right to asylum 355
right to education (Article 2 Protocol no. 1)
9, 37–38, 208, 214–215, 266, 484,
644–645, 680
right to individual application 3–7, 12–13,
19, 108–109, 111–112, 181, 188–189,
317, 334, 458, 461, 473, 486, 515, 568,
604, 606, 633, 645, 683;
see also **Protocol no. 11**
right to liberty and security (Article 5 ECHR)

compensation for unlawful detention 136,
201, 414, 474, 488, 508
conditions of detention 67, 263, 354–355,
418, 457, 491–492, 577, 638–640, 647,
656, 660–661
lawfulness of the detention 65–66, 70,
81, 122, 124, 133, 191–192, 205, 259,
262–263, 342, 351, 414, 483, 550, 571,
613, 632, 634, 639, 641, 646, 647, 653
period of detention 200, 483, 567, 572,
575, 577
pre-trial detention 191, 409, 422, 577,
656–657
promptly brought before a judge 199–200,
257, 259, 262, 264, 276, 409, 414, 422,
483, 577, 632, 635, 639, 641
promptly charged 422
promptly informed 124
special protection for children and juveniles 57, 190, 263
right to life (Article 2 ECHR) 9, 45, 58, 80,
122–125, 141, 274, 414, 421–422, 473,
478–480, 486, 549, 571, 632, 634, 639,
643, 646, 648, 667, 697–698
right to marry (Article 12 ECHR) 9, 60, 122,
124, 272, 358
**right to respect for private and family life
(Article 8 ECHR)**
in general 9, 57, 60–64, 67, 70, 100,
122–124, 128–129, 134, 183, 203–204,
213, 223, 244–245, 264–265, 272, 282,
286, 341–342, 408, 414, 416, 418, 424,
427, 439, 440, 456, 458, 511, 513, 549,
568–569, 571, 632, 635, 641–642, 647,
648–649, 662–663, 698–701
data protection 348–349, 373, 629,
642–643
deportation 147, 192, 196, 202, 260–261,
265, 272
excessive environmental pollution 411–412,
416, 642, 657
family reunion 131, 260, 272–273, 282,
341, 350, 355, 699
homosexuality 33, 57, 59–60, 62, 66, 70,
141, 699
telephone tapping 57, 127, 275, 278, 341,
356–357, 412–413, 414, 421, 424–425,
437, 446, 699
right to respect of property, *see* **property rights**
Roma, *see* **discrimination/minority rights**
rule of law 13, 47, 55, 87, 169, 174, 369,
384, 413, 416, 426, 456–457, 460,
469–470, 494, 510, 518, 521, 531, 536,
538, 542, 546, 555, 604, 611, 635, 637,
657, 682, 695, 698, 707
Satellite Offices of the Registry 588–589